The Web
Collection

PREMIUM EDITION

ADOBE DREAMWEAVER CS6, FLASH CS6, PHOTOSHOP CS6

Revealed

The Web
Collection

PREMIUM EDITION

ADOBE DREAMWEAVER CS6, FLASH CS6, PHOTOSHOP CS6

Sherry Bishop
Jim Shuman
Elizabeth Eisner Reding

DELMAR
CENGAGE Learning

Australia • Brazil • Japan • Korea • Mexico • Singapore • Spain • United Kingdom • United States

DELMAR
CENGAGE Learning·

The Web Collection CS6, Premium Edition
Sherry Bishop, Jim Shuman, Elizabeth Eisner Reding

Vice President, Career and Professional Editorial: Dave Garza

Director of Learning Solutions: Sandy Clark

Senior Acquisitions Editor: Jim Gish

Managing Editor: Larry Main

Product Managers: Jane Hosie-Bounar, Nicole Calisi

Editorial Assistant: Sarah Timm

Vice President Marketing, Career and Professional: Jennifer Baker

Executive Marketing Manager: Deborah S. Yarnell

Associate Marketing Manager: Erin DeAngelo

Senior Production Director: Wendy Troeger

Production Manager: Andrew Crouth

Content Project Manager: Allyson Bozeth

Developmental Editors: Barbara Clemens, Pam Conrad, Karen Stevens, Barbara Waxer

Technical Editors: John Shanley, Sarah Mosser, Susan Whalen

Director of Design: Bruce Bond

Cover Design: Riezebos Holzbaur/Tim Heraldo

Cover Photo: Riezebos Holzbaur/Andrei Pasternak

Text Designer: Liz Kingslein

Production House: Integra Software Services Pvt. Ltd.

Proofreader: Kim Kosmatka

Indexer: Alexandra Nickerson

Technology Project Manager: Jim Gilbert

Adobe® Premiere Pro®, Adobe® Bridge®, Adobe® After Effects®, Adobe® Audition®, Adobe® Encore®, Adobe® Photoshop®, Adobe® InDesign®, Adobe® Illustrator®, Adobe® Flash®, Adobe® Dreamweaver®, Adobe® Fireworks®, and Adobe® Creative Suite® are trademarks or registered trademarks of Adobe Systems, Inc. in the United States and/or other countries. Third party products, services, company names, logos, design, titles, words, or phrases within these materials may be trademarks of their respective owners.

Adobe product screenshots reprinted with permission from Adobe Systems Incorporated.

Library of Congress Control Number: 2011945476

ISBN-13: 978-1-133-81514-3
ISBN-10: 1-133-81514-6

Delmar
5 Maxwell Drive
Clifton Park, NY 12065-2919
USA

Cengage Learning is a leading provider of customized learning solutions with office locations around the globe, including Singapore, the United Kingdom, Australia, Mexico, Brazil, and Japan. Locate your local office at: **international.cengage.com/region**

Cengage Learning products are represented in Canada by Nelson Education, Ltd.

To learn more about Delmar, visit **www.cengage.com/delmar**

Purchase any of our products at your local college store or At our preferred online store **www.cengagebrain.com**

Printed in China
2 3 4 5 6 7 16 15 14

Revealed Series Vision

The Revealed Series is your guide to today's hottest multimedia applications. For years, the Revealed Series has kept pace with the dynamic demands of the multimedia community, and continues to do so with the publication of 13 new titles covering the latest Adobe Creative Suite products. Each comprehensive book teaches not only the technical skills required for success in today's competitive multimedia market, but the design skills as well. From animation, to web design, to digital image editing and interactive media skills, the Revealed Series has you covered.

We recognize the unique learning environment of the multimedia classroom, and we deliver textbooks that include:

- Comprehensive step-by-step instructions
- In-depth explanations of the "why" behind a skill
- Creative projects for additional practice
- Full-color visuals for a clear explanation of concepts
- Comprehensive online material offering additional instruction and skills practice
- Video tutorials for skills reinforcement as well as the presentation of additional features

- ■ **NEW** icons to highlight features that are new since the previous release of the software

With the Revealed series, we've created books that speak directly to the multimedia and design community—one of the most rapidly growing computer fields today.

—The Revealed Series

New to This Edition

The latest edition of *The Web Collection CS6 Revealed—Premium Edition* includes many exciting new features, some of which are:

- An all new chapter on Adobe Bridge
- In Dreamweaver, new HTML5 file layouts and validation for HTML5 standards
- New coverage of CSS3
- CSS Validation using W3C CSS Validation Service
- In Flash, coverage of how to create and publish AIR for Android and AIR for iOS smartphone applications
- Mobile application testing via USB port
- Coverage of testing mobile applications using the Accelerometer and Mobile Content Simulator
- In Photoshop, coverage of layer filtering

CourseMate

A CourseMate is available to accompany *Adobe Web Collection Premium CS6 Revealed*, which helps you make the grade!

This CourseMate includes:

- An interactive eBook, with highlighting, note-taking, and search capabilities
- Interactive learning tools including:
  - Chapter quizzes
  - Flash cards
  - Instructional video lessons from Total Training, the leading provider of video instruction for Adobe software. These video lessons are tightly integrated with the book, chapter by chapter, and include assessment.
  - And more!

Go to login.cengagebrain.com to access these resources.

AUTHOR'S VISION

This book will introduce you to a fascinating program that will hopefully inspire you to create rich and exciting websites. Although the world of technology is always spinning more quickly than we would sometimes like, we are in a particularly exciting time in the world of web design. With HTML5 and CSS3, we are challenged to learn more efficient, sleek methods for designing sites. I hope you will find this as fascinating as I do. Through the work of many talented and creative individuals, this text was created for you. Our Product Manager, Jane Hosie-Bounar, guided and directed the team from start to finish. She is a talented and tireless individual—the ultimate professional and visionary. She is rock solid—someone I can always count on for sage advice and guidance. Barbara Clemens, my Development Editor, is an example of so many things I value: joy, kindness, patience, and determination. I miss both of these friends and mentors each time we finish a book project.

The copyright content was generously provided by my dear friend Barbara Waxer. Barbara contributed even more for this edition by editing the Bridge chapter and did a wonderful job, as usual.

John Shanley did double duty this time. As the Bridge and Dreamweaver Technical Editor for both Mac and PC, he carefully tested each step to make sure that the end product was error-free. He gave exceptional feedback as he reviewed each chapter. This part of the publishing process is what truly sets Delmar Cengage Learning apart from other publishers.

Suwathiga Velayutham, and Kathy Kucharek, our Content Project Managers, and Nicole Calisi, Delmar Product Manager, worked on the layout and kept the schedule on track. We thank them for keeping up with the many details and deadlines. The work is beautiful.

Kathleen Ryan patiently contacted the websites we used as examples to obtain permission for their inclusion. This component adds much to the content of the book and would not have been possible without her good work. Thank you to each of you that allowed us to use images of your websites.

Harold Johnson quietly worked behind the scenes to ensure that all grammatical and punctuation errors were corrected. He also provided valuable insight in regard to the accuracy of content specifics.

Special thanks go to Jim Gish, Senior Acquisitions Editor, and Sandy Clark, the Director of Learning Solutions. They have embraced the Revealed books with enthusiasm and grace and provided us with excellent resources to produce books that make us all proud. Attending Adobe MAX was beyond expectation and a tremendous boost for my research efforts.

Thanks to the Beach Club in Gulf Shores, Alabama for being such a delightful place to visit. Several photographs of their beautiful property appear in The Striped Umbrella website.

Typically, your family is the last to be thanked. My husband, Don, supports and encourages me every day, as he has for the last forty-two years. Our travels with our children and grandchildren provide happy memories for us and content for the websites. You will see the faces of my precious grandchildren Jacob, Emma, Thomas, and Caroline peeking out from some of the pages.

—Sherry Bishop

Writing a textbook on an application development and animation program is quite challenging. How do you take such a feature-rich program like Adobe Flash Professional CS6 and put it in a context that helps users learn? My goal is to provide a comprehensive, yet manageable, introduction to Adobe Flash Professional CS6—just enough conceptual information to provide the needed context—and then move right into working with the application. My thought is that you'll get so caught up in the hands-on activities and compelling projects that you'll be pleasantly surprised at the level of Flash skills and knowledge you've acquired at the end of each chapter.

What a joy it has been to be a part of such a creative and energetic publishing team. The Revealed Series is a great format for teaching and learning Flash, and the Revealed Series team took the ball and ran with it. I would like to thank Jim Gish, who provided the vision for the project, and Jane Hosie-Bounar for her management expertise, and everyone at Delmar and Cengage Learning for their professional guidance. A special thanks to my Developmental Editor Pam Conrad for her hard work, editorial expertise, and constant encouragement. Jane and Pam made this book possible for me. I also want to give a heartfelt thanks to my wife, Barbara, for her patience, support, and use of her remarkable artwork. This book is dedicated to my two precious granddaughters, Daniela and Mariana, who bring such joy to my life.

—Jim Shuman

To the reader, a book magically appears on the shelf with each software revision, but to those of us "making it happen" it means not only working under ridiculous deadlines (which we're used to), but it also means working with slightly different teams with slightly different ways of doing things. Karen Stevens, Susan Whalen, Jane Hosie-Bounar, and I have all worked together before on this project that has spanned more years than we care to admit. Thanks also to Jim Gish, Sarah Timm, Kathy Kucharek, Glenn Castle, Meaghan Tomaso, and Nicole Calisi. Special thanks to Shanthi Guruswamy, who quickly became part of the team and Ann Fisher, who oversees and compiles the Instructor Resources. Most of us have never met face-to-face, yet once again we managed to work together in a professional manner, while defying the time-space continuum with its many time zones, cultural holidays, and countless vacation plans.

I would also like to thank my husband, Michael, who is used to my disappearing acts when I'm facing deadlines, and to Bix and Jet, who know when it's time to take a break for food, water, and some good old-fashioned head-scratching.

—Elizabeth Eisner Reding

Introduction to The Web Collection, Premium Edition

Welcome to *The Web Collection Premium Edition: Adobe Dreamweaver CS6, Flash CS6, and Photoshop CS6—Revealed*. This book offers creative projects, concise instructions, and coverage of basic Dreamweaver, Flash, Photoshop, and Creative Suite integration skills, helping you to create polished, professional-looking websites, animations, and art work. Use this book both in the classroom and as your own reference guide. It also includes many of the new features of CS6.

This text is organized into 21 chapters. In these chapters, you will learn many skills, including how to move amongst the Creative Suite applications, which provide familiar functionality from one application to the next.

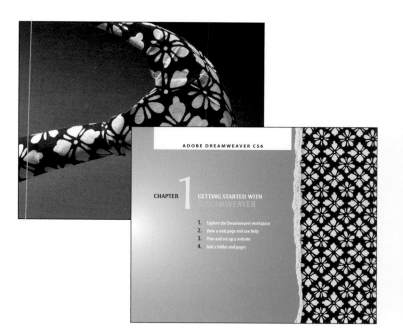

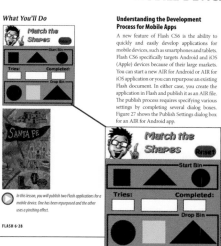

What You'll Do

A What You'll Do figure begins every lesson. This figure gives you an at-a-glance look at what you'll do in the chapter, either by showing you a file from the current project or a tool you'll be using.

Comprehensive Conceptual Lessons

Before jumping into instructions, in-depth conceptual information tells you "why" skills are applied. This book provides the "how" and "why" through the use of professional examples. Also included in the text are tips and sidebars to help you work more efficiently and creatively, or to teach you a bit about the history or design philosophy behind the skill you are using.

Step-by-Step Instructions

This book combines in-depth conceptual information with concise steps to help you learn Adobe Bridge, Adobe Dreamweaver, Adobe Flash, and Adobe Photoshop CS6. Each set of steps guides you through a lesson where you will create, modify, or enhance a Photoshop file. Step references to large colorful images and quick step summaries round out the lessons. The Data Files for the steps are provided on Cengage Brain.

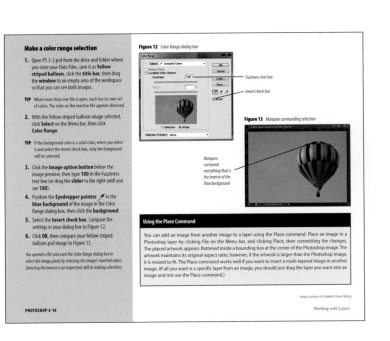

Make a color range selection

1. Open PS 3-2.psd from the drive and folder where you store your Data Files, save it as **Yellow striped balloon**, click the **title bar**, then drag the **window** to an empty area of the workspace so that you can see both images.

   TIP When more than one file is open, each has its own set of rulers. The ruler on the inactive file appears dimmed.

2. With the Yellow striped balloon image selected, click **Select** on the Menu bar, then click **Color Range**.

   TIP If the background color is a solid color, when you select it and select the Invert check box, only the foreground will be selected.

3. Click the **Image option button** below the image preview, then type **100** in the Fuzziness text box (or drag the **slider** to the right until you see **100**).

4. Position the **Eyedropper pointer** in the **blue background** of the image in the Color Range dialog box, then click the **background**.

5. Select the **Invert check box**. Compare the settings in your dialog box to Figure 12.

6. Click **OK**, then compare your Yellow striped balloon.psd image to Figure 13.

   You opened a file and used the Color Range dialog box to select the image pixels by selecting the image's inverted colors. Selecting the inverse is an important skill in making selections.

Figure 12 *Color Range dialog box*

Fuzziness text box
Invert check box

Figure 13 *Marquee surrounding selection*

Marquee surrounds everything that is the inverse of the blue background

Using the Place Command

You can add an image from another image to a layer using the Place command. Place an image in a Photoshop layer by clicking File on the Menu bar, and clicking Place, then committing the changes. The placed artwork appears *flattened* inside a bounding box at the center of the Photoshop image. The artwork maintains its original aspect ratio; however, if the artwork is larger than the Photoshop image, it is resized to fit. The Place command works well if you want to insert a multi-layered image in another image. (If all you want is a specific layer from an image, you should just drag the layer you want into an image and not use the Place command.)

Image courtesy of Elizabeth Eisner Reding

Working with Layers

This project begins with the Striped Umbrella site you created in Dreamweaver Chapter 6.

You have been asked to enhance the Striped Umbrella site by adding a Flash movie and changing a graphic image on the cafe page. Figure 27 shows the completed page for this part of the website. The idea is to replace the static cafe logo image with a Flash animation that plays in the same space on the page.

1. In Photoshop, open the cafe_logo.psd file.
2. Turn the visibility off and on for each layer to see how the image is constructed.
3. In Flash, start a new Flash ActionScript 2.0 document, save it as **crabAn.fla**, and import the cafe_logo.psd file to the Library, specifying that each layer is editable.
4. In Flash, create an animation using the cafe_logo.psd image. You decide on the type of animation, which could be a zoom or fade in; the entire crab moving; the crab claws moving; and so forth. (*Hint*: The crab image is made up of a body, left and right claws, and six legs.) Include a rollover effect or some other form of user interaction. Display the Publish Settings dialog box, deselect the HTML Wrapper option, and publish the document.
5. In Dreamweaver, open the Striped Umbrella site.

6. Open the cafe.html page and save it as **cafeRev.html**.
7. Delete the cafe_logo graphic on the page and insert the crab_Anim.swf file in the cell where the cafe_logo graphic had been.

8. Select the Flash movie placeholder and use the Property inspector to play and stop the animation.
9. Save your work.
10. View the web page in your browser, close your browser, then exit Dreamweaver.

Figure 27 *Sample completed Project Builder 2*

Crab is animated on mouse over

Integrating Adobe CS6 Web Premium

Projects

This book contains a variety of end-of-chapter materials for additional practice and reinforcement. The Skills Review contains hands-on practice exercises that mirror the progressive nature of the lesson material. The chapter concludes with four projects: two Project Builders, one Design Project, and one Portfolio Project. The Project Builders and the Design Project require you to apply the skills you've learned in the chapter. The Portfolio Project encourages students to address and solve challenges based on the content explored in the chapter in order to create portfolio-quality work.

What Instructor Resources Are Available with This Book?

The Instructor Resources are Delmar's way of putting the resources and information needed to teach and learn effectively into your hands. All the resources are available for both Macintosh and Windows operating systems. These resources can be found online at **http://login.cengage.com**. Once you log in or create an account, search for the title under 'My Dashboard' using the ISBN. Then select the instructor companion site resources and click 'Add to my Bookshelf.'

Instructor's Manual

The Instructor's Manual includes chapter overviews and detailed lecture topics for each chapter, with teaching tips.

Sample Syllabus

The Sample Syllabus includes a suggested syllabus for any course that uses this book.

PowerPoint Presentations

Each chapter has a corresponding PowerPoint presentation that you can use in lectures, distribute to your students, or customize to suit your course.

Data Files for Students

To complete most of the chapters in this book, your students will need Data Files, which are available online. Instruct students to use the Data Files List at the end of this book. This list gives instructions on organizing files.

To access the Data Files for this book, take the following steps:

1. Open your browser and go to http://www.cengagebrain.com
2. Type the author, title, or ISBN of this book in the Search window. (The ISBN is listed on the back cover.)
3. Click the book title in the list of search results.
4. When the book's main page is displayed, click the Access button under Free Study Tools.
5. To download Data Files, select a chapter number and then click on the Data Files tab on the left navigation bar to download the files.

Solutions to Exercises

Solution Files are Data Files completed with comprehensive sample answers. Use these files to evaluate your students' work. Or distribute them electronically so students can verify their work. Sample solutions to all lessons and end-of-chapter material are provided, with the exception of some Portfolio Projects.

Bridge Solution Files

The Solution Files for the Bridge chapter are figures of Bridge screen captures. As you complete each set of steps, you can compare your screen to its related figure.

Test Bank and Test Engine

ExamView is a powerful testing software package that allows instructors to create and administer printed and computer (LAN-based) exams. ExamView includes hundreds of questions that correspond to the topics covered in this text, enabling students to generate detailed study guides that include page references for further review. The computer-based and LAN-based/online testing component allows students to take exams using the EV Player, and also saves the instructor time by grading each exam automatically.

BRIDGE

Chapter 1   Using Adobe Bridge to Manage Assets

Lesson 1   Explore the Bridge Workspace   1-4

2   Use Metadata, Ratings, and Labels   1-8

DREAMWEAVER

Chapter 1   Getting Started with Dreamweaver

Lesson 1   Explore the Dreamweaver Workspace   1-4

2   View a Web Page and Use Help   1-12

3   Plan and Set Up a Website   1-18

4   Add a Folder And Pages   1-26

Chapter 2   Developing a Web Page

Lesson 1   Create Head Content and Set Page Properties   2-4

2   Create, Import, and Format Text   2-10

3   Add Links to Web Pages   2-18

4   Use the History Panel and Edit Code   2-24

5   Modify and Test Web Pages   2-30

Chapter 3   Working with Text and Cascading Style Sheets

Lesson 1   Create Unordered and Ordered Lists   3-4

2   Create, Apply, and Edit Cascading Style Sheets   3-10

3   Add Rules and Attach Cascading Style Sheets   3-20

4   Use Coding Tools to View and Edit Rules   3-26

Chapter 4   Adding Images

Lesson 1   Insert and Align Images   4-4

2   Enhance an Image and Use Alternate Text   4-12

3   Insert a Background Image and Perform Site Maintenance   4-18

4   Add Graphic Enhancements   4-24

Chapter 5   Working with Links and Navigation

Lesson 1   Create External and Internal Links   5-4

2   Create Internal Links to Named Anchors   5-10

3   Create, Modify, and Copy a Spry Menu Bar   5-16

4   Create an Image Map   5-26

5   Manage Website Links   5-30

6   Incorporate Web 2.0 Technology   5-34

Chapter 6   Positioning Objects with CSS and Tables

Lesson 1   Create a Page Using CSS Layouts   6-4

2   Add Content to CSS Layout Blocks   6-8

3   Edit and Format CSS Layout Blocks   6-14

4   Create a Table   6-22

5   Resize, Split, and Merge Cells   6-26

6   Insert and Align Images in Table Cells   6-30

7   Insert Text and Format Cell Content   6-34

Chapter 7   Managing a Web Server and Files

Lesson 1   Perform Website Maintenance   7-4

2   Publish a Website and Transfer Files   7-14

3   Check Files Out and In   7-22

4   Cloak Files   7-28

5   Import and Export a Site Definition   7-32

6   Evaluate Web Content For Legal Use   7-36

7   Present a Website to a Client   7-40

FLASH

Chapter 1 **Getting Started with Flash**

Lesson 1 Understand the Flash Workspace 1-4

2 Open a Document and Play a Flash Movie 1-12

3 Create and Save a Flash Movie 1-18

4 Work with the Timeline 1-32

5 Distribute a Flash Movie/Application 1-38

6 Plan an Application 1-42

Chapter 2 **Drawing Objects in Adobe Flash**

Lesson 1 Use the Flash Drawing and Alignment Tools 2-4

2 Select Objects and Apply Colors 2-20

3 Work with Drawn Objects 2-28

4 Work with Text and Text Objects 2-36

5 Work with Layers and Objects 2-46

Chapter 3 **Working with Symbols and Interactivity**

Lesson 1 Create Symbols and Instances 3-4

2 Work with Libraries 3-10

3 Create Buttons 3-16

4 Assign Actions to Frames and Buttons 3-22

5 Import Graphics 3-30

Chapter 4 **Creating Animations**

Lesson 1 Create Motion Tween Animations 4-4

2 Create Classic Tween Animations 4-20

3 Create Frame-by-Frame Animations 4-24

4 Create Shape Tween Animations 4-30

5 Create Movie Clips 4-36

6 Animate Text 4-42

Chapter 5 **Creating Special Effects**

Lesson 1 Create A Mask Effect 5-4

2 Add Sound 5-8

3 Add Video 5-12

4 Create an Animated Navigation Bar 5-18

5 Create Character Animations Using Inverse Kinematics 5-28

6 Create 3D Effects 5-36

7 Use the Deco Tool 5-42

Chapter 6 **Preparing and Publishing Applications**

Lesson 1 Publish Movies Using Different Formats 6-4

2 Reduce File Size to Optimize a Movie 6-10

3 Create a Preloader 6-16

4 Publish AIR Applications 6-22

5 Create and Publish Applications for Mobile Devices 6-28

PHOTOSHOP

Chapter 1 **Getting Started with Adobe Photoshop CS6**

Lesson 1 Start Adobe Photoshop CS6 1-4

2 Learn How to Open and Save an Image 1-8

3 Examine the Photoshop Window 1-16

4 Close a File and Exit Photoshop 1-24

5 Learn About Design Principles and Copyright Rules 1-26

Chapter 2 **Learning Photoshop Basics**

Lesson 1 Use Organizational and Management Features 2-4

2 Use the Layers and History Panels 2-12

3 Learn About Photoshop by Using Help 2-16

4 View and Print an Image 2-22

Chapter 3 **Working with Layers**

Lesson 1 Examine and Convert Layers 3-4

2 Add and Delete Layers 3-8

3 Add a Selection from One Image to Another 3-14

4 Organize Layers with Layer Groups and Colors 3-18

Chapter 4   **Making Selections**

Lesson 1   Make a Selection Using Shapes   4-4

      2   Modify a Marquee   4-14

      3   Select Using Color and Modify a Selection   4-18

      4   Add a Vignette Effect to a Selection   4-24

Chapter 5   **Incorporating Color Techniques**

Lesson 1   Work with Color to Transform an Image   5-4

      2   Use the Color Picker and the Swatches Panel   5-10

      3   Place a Border Around an Image   5-16

      4   Blend Colors Using the Gradient Tool   5-18

      5   Add Color to a Grayscale Image   5-22

      6   Use Filters, Opacity, and Blending Modes   5-26

      7   Match Colors   5-32

Chapter 6   **Placing Type in an Image**

Lesson 1   Learn About Type and How It Is Created   6-4

      2   Change Spacing and Adjust Baseline Shift   6-8

      3   Use the Drop Shadow Style   6-12

      4   Apply Anti-Aliasing to Type   6-16

      5   Modify Type with Bevel and Emboss and 3D Extrusion   6-20

      6   Apply Special Effects to Type Using Filters   6-24

      7   Create Text on a Path   6-28

INTEGRATION

Chapter 1   **Integrating Adobe CS6 Web Premium**

Lesson 1   Insert a Photoshop Image into a Dreamweaver Document   1-4

      2   Create a Photoshop Document and Import It into Flash   1-12

      3   Insert and Edit a Flash Movie in Dreamweaver   1-20

Data Files List   1

Glossary   23

Index   43

CONTENTS

 BRIDGE CHAPTER 1: USING ADOBE BRIDGE TO MANAGE ASSETS

INTRODUCTION 1-2

Accessing Adobe Bridge 1-2

LESSON 1
Explore the Bridge Workspace 1-4

Examining the Adobe Bridge Workspace 1-4
Tasks   Start Adobe Bridge 1-6
          Change modes 1-7

LESSON 2
Use Metadata, Ratings, and Labels 1-8

Tasks   Add and view metadata 1-9
          Filter files with keywords 1-11
          Label and rate files 1-12
          Filter files with labels and ratings 1-13

INTRODUCTION 1-2

Using Dreamweaver Tools 1-2

LESSON 1
Explore the Dreamweaver Workspace 1-4

Examining the Dreamweaver Workspace 1-4
Working with Dreamweaver Views 1-6
Tasks   Start Dreamweaver (Windows) 1-7
          Start Dreamweaver (Macintosh) 1-8
          Change views and view panels 1-9

LESSON 2
View a Web Page and Use Help 1-12

Opening a Web Page 1-12
Viewing Basic Web Page Elements 1-12
Getting Help 1-13
Tasks   Open a web page and view basic page
          elements 1-14
          Use Dreamweaver Help 1-16

LESSON 3
Plan and Set Up a Website 1-18

Understanding the Website Development Process 1-18
Planning a Website 1-18
Planning the Basic Structure 1-19
Creating the Web Pages and Collecting the Page Content 1-20
Testing the Pages 1-21
Modifying the Pages 1-21
Publishing the Site 1-21
Tasks   Select the location for your website 1-22
          Create a local site folder 1-23
          Set up a website 1-24
          Set up web server access 1-25

LESSON 4
Add a Folder And Pages 1-26

Adding a Folder to a Website 1-26
Creating the Home Page 1-27
Adding Pages to a Website 1-27
Tasks   Add a folder to a website (Windows) 1-28
          Add a folder to a website (Macintosh) 1-28
          Set the default images folder 1-29
          Create the home page 1-30
          Save an image file in the assets folder 1-31
          Add pages to a website (Windows) 1-32
          Add pages to a website (Macintosh) 1-33

INTRODUCTION 2-2

Understanding Page Layout 2-2

LESSON 1
Create Head Content and Set Page Properties 2-4

Creating the Head Content 2-4
Setting Web Page Properties 2-4
Choosing Colors to Convey Information 2-5
Tasks Edit a page title 2-6
Enter keywords 2-7
Enter a description 2-8
Set the page background color 2-9

LESSON 2
Create, Import, and Format Text 2-10

Creating and Importing Text 2-10
Formatting Text Two Ways: HTML vs. CSS 2-10
Changing Fonts 2-11
Changing Font Sizes 2-11
Formatting Paragraphs 2-11
Tasks Enter text 2-12
Format text 2-13
Save an image file in the assets folder 2-14
Import text 2-15
Set text properties 2-16
Check spelling 2-17

LESSON 3
Add Links to Web Pages 2-18

Adding Links to Web Pages 2-18
Using Menu Bars 2-18
Following WCAG Accessibility for Navigation 2-19
Tasks Create a menu bar 2-20
Insert a horizontal rule 2-20
Add links to web pages 2-21
Create an email link 2-22
View the email link in the Assets panel 2-23

LESSON 4
Use the History Panel and Edit Code 2-24

Using the History Panel 2-24
Viewing HTML Code in the Code Inspector 2-24
Tasks Use the History panel 2-26
Use the Code Inspector 2-27
Use the Reference panel 2-28
Insert a date object 2-29

LESSON 5
Modify and Test Web Pages 2-30

Testing and Modifying Web Pages 2-30
Testing a Web Page Using Different Browsers and Screen
Sizes 2-30
Using Adobe BrowserLab 2-31
Testing a Web Page as Rendered in a Mobile Device 2-31
Tasks Modify a web page 2-32
Test web pages by viewing them in a browser 2-33

INTRODUCTION 3-2

Using Cascading Style Sheets 3-2
Formatting Text as Lists 3-2

LESSON 1
Create Unordered and Ordered Lists 3-4

Creating Unordered Lists 3-4
Formatting Unordered Lists 3-4
Creating Ordered Lists 3-5
Formatting Ordered Lists 3-5
Creating Definition Lists 3-5
Tasks Create an unordered list 3-6
Create an ordered list 3-8
Format an ordered list heading 3-9

LESSON 2
Create, Apply, and Edit Cascading Style Sheets 3-10

Understanding Cascading Style Sheets 3-10
Using the CSS Styles Panel 3-10
Understanding the Advantages of Using Style Sheets 3-11
Understanding CSS Code 3-11
Tasks Create a Cascading Style Sheet and add a rule 3-12
Apply a rule 3-14
Edit a rule 3-15
View code with the Code Navigator 3-16
Use the Code Navigator to edit a rule 3-17
Add a Tag selector to an existing style sheet 3-18

LESSON 3
Add Rules and Attach Cascading Style Sheets 3-20

Understanding External and Embedded Style Sheets 3-20
Understanding Related Page Files 3-21
Tasks Add a class rule to a Cascading Style Sheet 3-22
Attach a style sheet 3-24
Use the Related Files toolbar to view styles 3-25

LESSON 4
Use Coding Tools to View and Edit Rules 3-26

Coding Tools in Dreamweaver 3-26
Using Coding Tools to Navigate Code 3-27
Using Code Hints to Streamline Coding 3-27
Converting Styles 3-27
Tasks Collapse code 3-28
Expand code 3-29
Move an embedded style to an external CSS 3-30

INTRODUCTION 4-2

Using Images to Enhance Web Pages 4-2
Graphics Versus Images 4-2

LESSON 1
Insert and Align Images 4-4

Understanding Graphic File Formats 4-4
Understanding the Assets Panel 4-4
Inserting Files with Adobe Bridge 4-5
Aligning Images 4-5
Tasks   Insert an image 4-6
            Insert an image placeholder 4-8
            Replace an image placeholder with an image 4-9
            Use Adobe Bridge 4-10
            Align an image 4-11

LESSON 2
Enhance an Image and Use Alternate Text 4-12

Enhancing an Image 4-12
Using Alternate Text 4-13
Tasks   Add a border 4-14
            Add horizontal and vertical space 4-14
            Edit image settings 4-15
            Edit alternate text 4-16
            Set the alternate text accessibility option 4-17

LESSON 3
Insert a Background Image and Perform Site Maintenance 4-18

Inserting a Background Image 4-18
Managing Images 4-18
Creating a Website Color Palette 4-19
Tasks   Insert a background image 4-20
            Remove a background image from a page 4-21
            Delete files from a website 4-22
            Add a color to your design palette 4-23

LESSON 4
Add Graphic Enhancements 4-24

Adding a Link to a Larger Image 4-24
Adding Favicons 4-24
Adding a No Right-Click Script 4-25
Tasks   Use an image to link to another image 4-26
            Insert a favicon on a page 4-27

INTRODUCTION 5-2

Understanding Internal and External Links 5-2

LESSON 1
Create External and Internal Links 5-4

Creating External Links 5-4
Creating Internal Links 5-4
Tasks   Create an external link 5-6
          Create an internal link 5-8
          View links in the Assets panel 5-9

LESSON 2
Create Internal Links to Named Anchors 5-10

Inserting Named Anchors 5-10
Creating Internal Links to Named Anchors 5-10
Tasks   Insert a named anchor 5-12
          Create an internal link to a named anchor 5-14

LESSON 3
Create, Modify, and Copy a Spry Menu Bar 5-16

Creating a Spry Menu Bar 5-16
Copying and Modifying a Menu Bar 5-17
Tasks   Create a Spry menu bar 5-18
          Add items to a menu bar 5-20
          Use CSS to format a menu bar 5-21
          Copy and paste a menu bar 5-25

LESSON 4
Create an Image Map 5-26

Understanding Image Maps 5-26
Tasks   Create an image map 5-28

LESSON 5
Manage Website Links 5-30

Managing Website Links 5-30
Tasks   Manage website links 5-31
          Update a page 5-32

LESSON 6
Incorporate Web 2.0 Technology 5-34

What Exactly Is Web 2.0? 5-34

INTRODUCTION 6-2

Using Div Tags Versus Tables for Page Layout 6-2

LESSON 1
Create a Page Using CSS Layouts 6-4

Understanding Div Tags 6-4
Using CSS Page Layouts 6-4
Viewing CSS Layout Blocks 6-5
Tasks   Create a page with a CSS layout 6-6

LESSON 2
Add Content to CSS Layout Blocks 6-8

Understanding Div Tag Content 6-8
Understanding CSS Code 6-9
Tasks   Add text to a CSS container 6-10
           Add images to a CSS block 6-12

LESSON 3
Edit and Format CSS Layout Blocks 6-14

Editing Content in CSS Layout Blocks 6-14
Tasks   Edit block properties to align content 6-15
           Edit type properties in CSS layout blocks 6-17
           Edit CSS layout block properties 6-18
           Edit page properties 6-20

LESSON 4
Create a Table 6-22

Understanding Table Modes 6-22
Creating a Table 6-22
Using Expanded Tables Mode 6-23
Setting Table Accessibility Preferences 6-23
Tasks   Create a table 6-24
           Set table properties 6-25

LESSON 5
Resize, Split, and Merge Cells 6-26

Understanding Table Tags 6-27
Tasks   Split cells 6-28
           Merge cells 6-29

LESSON 6
Insert and Align Images in Table Cells 6-30

Inserting Images in Table Cells 6-30
Aligning Images in Table Cells 6-30
Tasks   Insert images in table cells 6-32
           Align graphics in table cells 6-33

LESSON 7
Insert Text and Format Cell Content 6-34

Inserting Text in a Table 6-34
Formatting Cell Content 6-34
Formatting Cells 6-34
Tasks   Insert text 6-35
           Format cell content 6-36
           Format cells 6-37
           Modify cell content 6-39
           Check layout 6-40
           Validate HTML5 markup 6-41

INTRODUCTION 7-2

Preparing to Publish a Site 7-2

LESSON 1
Perform Website Maintenance 7-4

Maintaining a Website 7-4
Using the Assets Panel 7-4
Checking Links Sitewide 7-4
Using Site Reports 7-4
Validating Markup 7-5
Testing Pages 7-5
Tasks   Check for broken links 7-6
         Check for orphaned files 7-6
         Check for untitled documents 7-7
         Check for missing alternate text 7-7
         Validate for HTML5 standards 7-8
         Validate CSS 7-9
         Enable Design Notes 7-10
         Associate a Design Note with a file 7-11
         Edit a Design Note 7-12

LESSON 2
Publish a Website and Transfer Files 7-14

Defining a Remote Site 7-14
Viewing a Remote Site 7-15
Transferring Files to and from a Remote Site 7-15
Synchronizing Files 7-16
Tasks   Set up a web server connection on an FTP site 7-17
         Set up a web server connection to a local or
              network folder 7-18
         View a website on a remote server 7-19
         Upload files to a remote server 7-20
         Synchronize files 7-21

LESSON 3
Check Files Out and In 7-22

Managing a Website with a Team 7-22
Checking Out and Checking In Files 7-22
Enabling the Check Out Feature 7-23
Using Subversion Control 7-23
Tasks   Activate the Enable file check-out feature 7-24
         Check out a file 7-25
         Check in a file 7-26
         Edit site preferences 7-27

LESSON 4
Cloak Files 7-28

Understanding Cloaking Files 7-28
Cloaking a Folder 7-28
Cloaking Selected File Types 7-29
Tasks   Cloak and uncloak a folder 7-30
         Cloak selected file types 7-31

LESSON 5
Import and Export a Site Definition 7-32

Exporting a Site Definition 7-32
Importing a Site Definition 7-32
Tasks   Export a site definition 7-33
         Import a site definition 7-34
         View the imported site 7-35

LESSON 6
Evaluate Web Content For Legal Use 7-36

Can I Use Downloaded Media? 7-36
Understanding Intellectual Property 7-36
What Exactly Does the Copyright Owner Own? 7-36
Understanding Fair Use 7-37
How Do I Use Work Properly? 7-37
Understanding Licensing Agreements 7-37
Obtaining Permission or a License 7-38
Posting a Copyright Notice 7-38

LESSON 7
Present a Website to a Client 7-40

Are You Ready to Present Your Work? 7-40
What Is the Best Way to Present Your Work? 7-41

INTRODUCTION 1-2

LESSON 1
Understand the Flash Workspace 1-4

Organizing the Flash Workspace 1-4
Stage 1-4
Timeline (Frames and Layers) 1-5
Panels 1-5
Tasks   Start Adobe Flash and work with panels 1-9
Change the Stage view and display of the
Timeline 1-11

LESSON 2
Open a Document and Play a Flash Movie 1-12

Opening a Movie in Flash 1-12
Previewing a Movie 1-12
Control Menu Commands (and Keyboard Shortcuts) 1-13
Control Buttons 1-13
Testing a Movie 1-13
Documents, Movies, and Applications 1-14
Using the Flash Player 1-14
Tasks   Open and play a movie using the Control menu and
movie control buttons 1-15
Test a movie 1-16
Change the document properties 1-17

LESSON 3
Create and Save a Flash Movie 1-18

Creating a Flash Movie 1-18
Creating an Animation 1-19
The Motion Tween Animation Process 1-19
Motion Presets 1-21
Adding Effects to an Object 1-21
Tasks   Create objects using drawing tools 1-22
Create a motion tween animation 1-23
Reshape the motion path 1-25
Change the transparency of an object 1-27
Resize an object 1-28
Add a filter to an object 1-29
Add a motion preset 1-30

LESSON 4
Work with the Timeline 1-32

Understanding the Timeline 1-32
Using Layers 1-32
Using Frames and Keyframes 1-33
Interpreting the Timeline 1-33
Tasks   Add a layer 1-35
Create a second animation 1-35
Work with layers and view Timeline features 1-36
Modify the frame rate and change the layer
names 1-37

LESSON 5
Distribute a Flash Movie/Application 1-38

Distributing Movies for Viewing on a Website 1-38
Distributing Movies for Viewing on a Computer or Mobile
Device 1-39
Other Distribution Options 1-39
Tasks   Publish a movie for distribution on the web 1-40
Create a backdrop color layer for the Stage 1-41

LESSON 6
Plan an Application 1-42

Planning an Application 1-42
Using Screen Design Guidelines 1-43
Using Interactive Design Guidelines 1-44
Using Storyboards 1-44
Rich Media Content and Accessibility 1-45
The Flash Workflow Process 1-45
Project Management 1-46
Tasks   Use Flash Help 1-47

INTRODUCTION 2-2

LESSON 1
Use the Flash Drawing and Alignment Tools 2-4

Using Flash Drawing and Editing Tools 2-4
Working with Grouped Tools 2-6
Working with Tool Options 2-6
Tools for Creating Vector Graphics 2-6
Positioning Objects on the Stage 2-6
Using the Align Panel 2-7
Tasks   Show gridlines and check settings 2-8
          Use the Rectangle, Oval, and Line tools 2-9
          Use the Pen, Pencil, and Brush tools 2-10
          Modify an object using tool options 2-13
          Use the Spray tool with a symbol 2-14
          Use XY coordinates to position objects on the
              Stage 2-16
          Use the Align options 2-18

LESSON 2
Select Objects and Apply Colors 2-20

Selecting Objects 2-20
Using the Selection Tool 2-20
Using the Lasso Tool 2-20
Drawing Model Modes 2-20
Working with Colors 2-21
Working with Gradients 2-21
Tasks   Select a drawing using the Selection tool 2-22
          Change fill and stroke colors 2-24
          Apply a gradient and make changes to the
              gradient 2-25
          Work with Object Drawing Model mode 2-27

LESSON 3
Work with Drawn Objects 2-28

Copying and Moving Objects 2-28
Transforming Objects 2-28
Resizing an Object 2-28
Rotating and Skewing an Object 2-28
Distorting an Object 2-29
Flipping an Object 2-29
Reshaping a Segment of an Object 2-29
Tasks   Copy and move an object 2-30
          Resize and reshape an object 2-31
          Skew, rotate, and flip an object 2-32
          Use the Zoom, Subselection, and Selection
              tools 2-33
          Use the Rectangle Primitive and Oval tools 2-34

LESSON 4
Work with Text and Text Objects 2-36

Learning About Text 2-36
Entering Text and Changing the Text Block for Classic
    Text 2-36
Changing Text Attributes 2-36
Working with Paragraphs 2-37
Transforming Text 2-37
The Text Layout Framework (TLF) 2-37
Tasks   Enter text and change text attributes 2-38
          Add a Filter effect to text 2-39
          Skew text and align objects 2-40
          Reshape and apply a gradient to text 2-41
          Use the Text Layout Framework 2-42

LESSON 5
Work with Layers and Objects 2-46

Learning About Layers 2-46
Working with Layers 2-47
Tasks   Create and reorder layers 2-48
          Rename and delete layers, expand the Timeline,
              and hide and lock layers 2-49

INTRODUCTION 3-2

LESSON 1
Create Symbols and Instances 3-4

Understanding Symbol Types 3-4
Creating a Graphic Symbol 3-4
Working with Instances 3-5
Tasks Create a symbol 3-6
Create and edit an instance 3-7
Edit a symbol in the edit window 3-8
Break apart an instance 3-9

LESSON 2
Work with Libraries 3-10

Understanding the Library 3-10
Tasks Create folders in the Library panel 3-12
Organize items within Library panel folders 3-13
Rename symbols and delete a symbol 3-14
Use multiple Library panels 3-15

LESSON 3
Create Buttons 3-16

Understanding Buttons 3-16
Tasks Create a button 3-18
Edit a button and specify a hit area 3-19
Test a button 3-20

LESSON 4
Assign Actions to Frames and Buttons 3-22

Understanding Actions 3-22
Analyzing ActionScript 3-22
ActionScript 2.0 and 3.0 3-22
Using Frame Actions 3-24
Understanding the Actions Panel 3-25
Using Frame Labels 3-25
Tasks Assign a stop action to frames 3-26
Assign a play action to a button 3-27
Assign a goto frame action to a button 3-28
Assign a second event to a button 3-29

LESSON 5
Import Graphics 3-30

Understanding Graphic Types 3-30
Importing and Editing Graphics 3-31
Tasks Import graphics 3-32

INTRODUCTION 4-2

How Does Animation Work? 4-2
Flash Animation 4-2

LESSON 1
Create Motion Tween Animations 4-4

Understanding Motion Tween Animations 4-4
Tween Spans 4-5
Motion Path 4-6
Property Keyframes 4-6
Tasks Create a motion tween animation 4-7
Edit a motion path 4-8
Change the ease value of an animation 4-10
Resize and reshape an object 4-11
Create a color effect 4-12
Orient an object to a path 4-13
Copy a motion path 4-14
Rotate an object 4-16
Remove a motion tween 4-17
Work with multiple motion tweens 4-18

LESSON 2
Create Classic Tween Animations 4-20

Understanding Classic Tweens 4-20
Understanding Motion Guides 4-20
Transformation Point and Registration Point 4-21
Tasks Create a classic tween animation 4-22
Add a motion guide and orient the object to the
guide 4-22

LESSON 3
Create Frame-by-Frame Animations 4-24

Understanding Frame-by-Frame Animations 4-24
Creating a Frame-by-Frame Animation 4-25
Using the Onion Skin Feature 4-25
Tasks Create an in-place frame-by-frame animation 4-26
Copy frames and add a moving background 4-27
Create a frame-by-frame animation of a moving
object 4-28

LESSON 4
Create Shape Tween Animations 4-30

Understanding Shape Tweening 4-30
Using Shape Tweening to Create a Morphing Effect 4-30
Properties Panel Options 4-31
Shape Hints 4-31
Tasks Create a shape tween animation 4-32
Create a morphing effect 4-33
Adjust the rate of change in a shape tween
animation 4-34
Use shape hints 4-35

LESSON 5
Create Movie Clips 4-36

Understanding Movie Clip Symbols 4-36
Tasks Break apart a graphic symbol and select parts of the
object to separate from the graphic 4-38
Create and edit a movie clip 4-39
Animate a movie clip 4-40

LESSON 6
Animate Text 4-42

Animating Text 4-42
Tasks Select, copy, and paste frames 4-44
Animate text using a motion preset 4-45
Create rotating text 4-46
Resize and fade in text 4-47
Make a text block into a button 4-48
Add an action to the button 4-49

INTRODUCTION 5-2

LESSON 1
Create A Mask Effect 5-4

Understanding Mask Layers 5-4
Tasks   Create a mask layer 5-6
           Create a masked layer 5-7

LESSON 2
Add Sound 5-8

Incorporating Animation and Sound 5-8
Tasks   Add sound to a movie 5-10
           Add sound to a button 5-11

LESSON 3
Add Video 5-12

Incorporating Video 5-12
Using the Import Video Wizard 5-13
Using the Adobe Media Encoder 5-13
Tasks   Import a video 5-14
           Attach actions to video control buttons 5-16
           Synchronize sound to a video clip 5-17

LESSON 4
Create an Animated Navigation Bar 5-18

Understanding Animated Navigation Bars 5-18
Using Frame Labels 5-19
Understanding Scenes 5-19
Tasks   Position the drop-down buttons 5-20
           Add a mask layer 5-22
           Assign an action to a drop-down button 5-24
           Add a frame label and assign a rollOver action 5-25
           Add an invisible button 5-26

LESSON 5
Create Character Animations Using Inverse Kinematics 5-28

Understanding Inverse Kinematics 5-28
Creating the Bone Structure 5-28
Animating the IK Object 5-29
Creating a Movie Clip with an IK Object 5-30
Runtime Feature 5-30
Tasks   Create the bone structure 5-31
           Animate the character 5-32
           Create a movie clip of the IK object and animate the
               movie clip 5-33
           Apply an ease value 5-34
           Set the play to runtime 5-35

LESSON 6
Create 3D Effects 5-36

Understanding 3D Effects 5-36
The 3D Tools 5-37
Using a Motion Tween with a 3D Effect 5-37
Tasks   Create a 3D animation 5-38

LESSON 7
Use the Deco Tool 5-42

Understanding the Deco Tool 5-42
Basic Types of Deco Effects 5-42
Tasks   Create screen design and animations with the
               Deco tool 5-44

INTRODUCTION 6-2

LESSON 1
Publish Movies Using Different Formats 6-4

Using Publish Settings 6-4
Using Publish Preview 6-5
Tasks   Publish using the default settings 6-6
          Create a GIF animation from a movie 6-7
          Create a JPEG image from a frame of a movie 6-8
          Create an executable file 6-9

LESSON 2
Reduce File Size to Optimize a Movie 6-10

Testing a Movie 6-10
Using the Bandwidth Profiler 6-10
Using the Simulate Download Feature 6-11
Tasks   Test the download time for a movie 6-12
          Use the Bandwidth Profiler 6-14
          Optimize a movie by reducing file size 6-15

LESSON 3
Create a Preloader 6-16

Preloading a Movie 6-16
Tasks   Add layers for a preloader 6-18
          Add actions to the preloader 6-19
          Create the preloader animation 6-20
          Testing the preloader 6-21

LESSON 4
Publish AIR Applications 6-22

Understanding the Development Process for AIR
          Applications 6-22
Settings on the General Tab 6-23
Settings on the Signature Tab 6-24
Settings on the Icons Tab 6-24
Settings on the Advanced Tab 6-24
Tasks   Repurpose a Flash file as an AIR app 6-25

LESSON 5
Create and Publish Applications for Mobile Devices 6-28

Understanding the Development Process for Mobile
          Apps 6-28
Settings on the General tab 6-28
Settings on the Deployment Tab 6-29
Settings on the Icons Tab 6-30
Settings on the Permissions Tab 6-30
Settings on the Languages Tab 6-30
Mobile App Gestures and Events 6-30
Tasks   Repurpose a Flash app for use on mobile
          devices 6-31
          Create a mobile app with events 6-34
          Publish a mobile app 6-36

INTRODUCTION 1-2

Using Photoshop 1-2
Understanding Platform User Interfaces 1-2
Understanding Sources 1-2

LESSON 1
Start Adobe Photoshop CS6 1-4

Defining Image-Editing Software 1-4
Understanding Images 1-4
Using Photoshop Features 1-4
Starting Photoshop and Creating a File 1-5
Task Start Photoshop (Windows) 1-6
Start Photoshop (Mac OS) 1-7

LESSON 2
Learn How to Open and Save an Image 1-8

Opening and Saving Files 1-8
Customizing How You Open Files 1-8
Browsing Through Files 1-9
Understanding the Power of Bridge 1-10
Getting There with Mini Bridge 1-10
Using Save As Versus Save 1-10
Getting images into Photoshop 1-11
Task Open a file using the Menu bar 1-12
Open a file using the Folders panel in Adobe
Bridge 1-12
Open a file using Mini Bridge 1-13
Use the Save As command 1-13
Change from Tabbed to Floating Documents 1-14
Rate and filter with Bridge 1-15

LESSON 3
Examine the Photoshop Window 1-16

Learning About the Workspace 1-16
Finding Tools Everywhere 1-17
Using Tool Shortcut Keys 1-18
Customizing Your Environment 1-18
Task Select a tool 1-19
Select a tool from the Tool Preset picker 1-20
Add a tool to the Tool Preset picker 1-21
Change the default display and theme color 1-21
Show and hide panels 1-22
Create a customized workspace 1-23

LESSON 4
Close a File and Exit Photoshop 1-24

Concluding Your Work Session 1-24
Closing Versus Exiting 1-24
Task Close a file and exit Photoshop 1-25

LESSON 5
Learn About Design Principles and Copyright Rules 1-26

Print Design vs. Web Design 1-26
Composition 101 1-26
Arranging Elements 1-27
Overcoming the Fear of White Space 1-27
Balancing Objects 1-28
Considering Ethical Implications 1-28
Understanding Copyright Terms 1-29
Licensing Your Work with Creative Commons 1-31

INTRODUCTION 2-2

Working Magic with Photoshop 2-2
Using Management Tools 2-2
Learning to Love Layers 2-2
Finding Help when You Need It 2-2
Viewing and Printing 2-2

LESSON 1
Use Organizational and Management Features 2-4

Managing the Creative Suite 2-4
Learning About CS Live 2-4
Signing into Acrobat.com 2-5
Using Acrobat.com 2-6
Reusing Housekeeping Tasks in Bridge and Mini Bridge 2-8
Understanding Metadata 2-8
Assigning Keywords to an Image 2-8
Task   Assigning a keyword 2-10
        Filtering with Bridge 2-11

LESSON 2
Use the Layers and History Panels 2-12

Learning About Layers 2-12
Understanding the Layers Panel 2-12
Filtering layers 2-12
Displaying and Hiding Layers 2-13
Using the History Panel 2-13
Task   Hide and display a layer 2-14
        Move a layer on the Layers panel and delete a state
            on the History panel 2-15

LESSON 3
Learn About Photoshop by Using Help 2-16

Understanding the Power of Help 2-16
Using Help Topics 2-16
Task   Find information in Adobe reference titles 2-18
        Get help and support 2-19
        Find information using Search 2-20
        Learning what's new in Photoshop CS6 2-21

LESSON 4
View and Print an Image 2-22

Getting a Closer Look 2-22
Viewing an Image in Multiple Views 2-22
Printing Your Image 2-23
Understanding Color Handling in Printing 2-23
Choosing a Photoshop Version 2-23
Using the Photoshop File Info Dialog Box 2-24
Task   Use the Zoom tool 2-25
        Modify print settings 2-26
        Create a PDF with Bridge 2-27
        Save a PDF output file 2-28
        Create a Web Gallery with Bridge 2-29

INTRODUCTION 3-2

Layers Are Everything 3-2
Understanding the Importance of Layers 3-2
Using Layers to Modify an Image 3-2

LESSON 1
Examine and Convert Layers 3-4

Learning About the Layers Panel 3-4
Recognizing Layer Types 3-4
Organizing Layers 3-5
Converting Layers 3-6
Task   Convert an image layer into a Background layer 3-7

LESSON 2
Add and Delete Layers 3-8

Adding Layers to an Image 3-8
Naming a Layer 3-10
Deleting Layers from an Image 3-11
Task   Modifying a workspace 3-12
             Add a layer using the Layer menu 3-12
             Delete a layer 3-13
             Add a layer using the Layers panel 3-13

LESSON 3
Add a Selection from One Image to Another 3-14

Understanding Selections 3-14
Making and Moving a Selection 3-14
Understanding Color Range Command 3-15
Defringing Layer Contents 3-15

Task   Make a color range selection 3-16
             Move a selection to another image 3-17
             Defringe the selection 3-17

LESSON 4
Organize Layers with Layer Groups and Colors 3-18

Understanding Layer Groups 3-18
Organizing Layers into Groups 3-18
Adding Color to a Layer 3-19
Flattening an Image 3-19
Understanding Layer Comps 3-20
Using Layer Comps 3-20
Task   Create a layer group 3-21
             Move layers to the layer group 3-21
             Rename a layer and adjust opacity 3-22
             Create layer comps 3-22
             Flatten an image 3-23

INTRODUCTION 4-2

Combining Images 4-2
Understanding Selection Tools 4-2
Understanding Which Selection Tool to Use 4-2
Combining Imagery 4-2

LESSON 1
Make a Selection Using Shapes 4-4

Selecting by Shape 4-4
Creating a Selection 4-4
Using Fastening Points 4-5
Selecting, Deselecting, and Reselecting 4-5
Placing a Selection 4-6
Using Guides 4-7
Task   Create a selection with the Rectangular Marquee
           tool 4-9
           Position a selection with the Move tool 4-10
           Deselect a selection 4-11
           Create a selection with the Magnetic Lasso tool 4-12
           Move a complex selection to an existing image 4-13

LESSON 2
Modify a Marquee 4-14

Changing the Size of a Marquee 4-14
Modifying a Marquee 4-14
Moving a Marquee 4-14
Using the Quick Selection Tool 4-15
Task   Move and enlarge a marquee 4-16
           Use the Quick Selection tool 4-17

LESSON 3
Select Using Color and Modify a Selection 4-18

Selecting with Color 4-18
Using the Magic Wand Tool 4-18
Using the Color Range Command 4-19
Transforming a Selection 4-19
Understanding the Healing Brush Tool 4-19
Using the Healing Brush Tool 4-19
Task   Select using Color Range 4-20
           Select using the Magic Wand and the Quick Selection
           tools 4-21
           Flip a selection 4-22
           Fix imperfections with the Healing Brush tool 4-23

LESSON 4
Add a Vignette Effect to a Selection 4-24

Understanding Vignettes 4-24
Creating a Vignette 4-24
Task   Create a vignette 4-25

INTRODUCTION 5-2

Using Color 5-2
Understanding Color Modes and Color Models 5-2
Displaying and Printing Images 5-2

LESSON 1
Work with Color to Transform an Image 5-4

Learning About Color Models 5-4
Lab Color Mode 5-5
HSB Color Model 5-5
RGB Model 5-5
CMYK Model 5-6
Understanding the Bitmap and Grayscale Modes 5-6
Changing Foreground and Background Colors 5-6
Tasks Set the default foreground and background
colors 5-7
Change the background color using the Color
panel 5-8
Change the background color using the Eyedropper
tool 5-9

LESSON 2
Use the Color Picker and the Swatches Panel 5-10

Making Selections from the Color Picker 5-10
Using the Swatches Panel 5-11
Tasks Select a color using the Color Picker dialog box 5-12
Select a color using the Swatches panel 5-12
Add a new color to the Swatches panel 5-13
Use Kuler from a web browser 5-14
Use Kuler from Photoshop 5-15

LESSON 3
Place a Border Around an Image 5-16

Emphasizing an Image 5-16
Locking Transparent Pixels 5-16
Tasks Create a border 5-17

LESSON 4
Blend Colors Using the Gradient Tool 5-18

Understanding Gradients 5-18
Using the Gradient Tool 5-18
Customizing Gradients 5-19
Tasks Create a gradient from a sample color 5-20
Apply a gradient fill 5-21

LESSON 5
Add Color to a Grayscale Image 5-22

Colorizing Options 5-22
Converting Grayscale and Color Modes 5-22
Tweaking Adjustments 5-22
Colorizing a Grayscale Image 5-23
Tasks Change the color mode 5-24
Colorize a grayscale image 5-25

LESSON 6
Use Filters, Opacity, and Blending Modes 5-26

Manipulating an Image 5-26
Understanding Filters 5-26
Choosing Blending Modes 5-27
Understanding Blending Mode Components 5-27
Softening Filter Effects 5-27
Balancing Colors 5-28
Tasks Adjust brightness and contrast 5-29
Work with a filter, a blending mode, and an opacity
setting 5-30
Adjust color balance 5-31

LESSON 7
Match Colors 5-32

Finding the Right Color 5-32
Using Selections to Match Colors 5-32
Tasks Match a color 5-33

INTRODUCTION 6-2

Learning About Type 6-2
Understanding the Purpose of Type 6-2
Getting the Most Out of Type 6-2

LESSON 1
Learn About Type and How It Is Created 6-4

Introducing Type Types 6-4
Getting to Know Font Families 6-4
Measuring Type Size 6-4
Acquiring Fonts 6-5
Tasks   Create and modify type 6-6
          Change type color using an existing color in the
                image 6-7

LESSON 2
Change Spacing and Adjust Baseline Shift 6-8

Adjusting Spacing 6-8
Understanding Character and Line Spacing 6-8
Using the Character Panel 6-9
Understanding Type Styles 6-9
Adjusting the Baseline Shift 6-9
Tasks   Kern characters 6-10
          Shift the baseline 6-11

LESSON 3
Use the Drop Shadow Style 6-12

Adding Effects to Type 6-12
Applying a Style 6-13
Using the Drop Shadow 6-13
Controlling a Drop Shadow 6-13
Tasks   Add a drop shadow 6-14
          Modify drop shadow settings 6-15

LESSON 4
Apply Anti-Aliasing to Type 6-16

Eliminating the "Jaggies" 6-16
Knowing When to Apply Anti-Aliasing 6-16
Understanding Anti-Aliasing 6-17
Tasks   Apply anti-aliasing 6-18
          Undo anti-aliasing 6-19

LESSON 5
**Modify Type with Bevel and Emboss and 3D
Extrusion 6-20**

Using the Bevel and Emboss Style 6-20
Understanding Bevel and Emboss Settings 6-20
Learning About 3D Extrusion 6-21
Tasks   Add the Bevel and Emboss style with the Layer
                menu 6-22
          Modify Bevel and Emboss settings and apply 3D
                Extrusion 6-23

LESSON 6
Apply Special Effects to Type Using Filters 6-24

Understanding Filters 6-24
Producing Distortions 6-24
Using Relief 6-24
Blurring Imagery 6-24
Tasks   Apply a filter to a type layer 6-26
          Modify filter settings 6-27

LESSON 7
Create Text on a Path 6-28

Understanding Text on a Path 6-28
Creating Text on a Path 6-28
Tasks   Create a path and add type 6-29

INTRODUCTION 1-2

LESSON 1
Insert a Photoshop Image into a
Dreamweaver Document 1-4

Inserting a Photoshop Image into Dreamweaver 1-4
Setting Photoshop as the Primary External Image Editor 1-5
Setting up the Folder Structure for the Files 1-6
Using Design Notes 1-6
Tasks   Designate the primary external image editor 1-7
         Edit a Photoshop document 1-8
         Insert a Photoshop image into a Dreamweaver
            document 1-9
         Edit a Photoshop image from a Dreamweaver
            document 1-10
         Copy and paste a Photoshop image into
            a Dreamweaver document 1-11

LESSON 2
Create a Photoshop Document and Import It into
Flash 1-12

Importing a Photoshop Document into Flash 1-12
Using Photoshop to Edit an Image in Flash 1-13
Tasks   Create a Photoshop image with several layers 1-14
         Import a Photoshop document into Flash 1-15
         Edit a Photoshop image that has been imported
            into Flash 1-17
         Use Photoshop to edit an image in Flash 1-18
         Create an animation using the Photoshop-created
            text 1-19

LESSON 3
Insert and Edit a Flash Movie in Dreamweaver 1-20

Inserting a Flash Movie into a Dreamweaver Document 1-20
Using the Property Inspector with the Movie 1-20
Tasks   Insert a Flash movie into Dreamweaver 1-22
         Play a Flash movie and change settings from
            Dreamweaver 1-23
         Edit a Flash movie from Dreamweaver 1-24

DATA FILES LIST 1

GLOSSARY 23

INDEX 43

Data Files

To complete the lessons in this book, you need the Data Files. To access the Data Files for this book, take the following steps:

1. Open your browser and go to http://www.cengagebrain.com
2. Type the author, title, or ISBN of this book in the Search window. (The ISBN is listed on the back cover.)
3. Click the book title in the list of search results.
4. When the book's main page is displayed, click the Access button under Free Study Tools.
5. To download Data Files, select a chapter number and then click on the Data Files tab on the left navigation bar to download the files.
6. To access additional materials, click the Additional Materials tab under Book Resources to download the files.

Dreamweaver CS6
Intended Audience

This text is designed for the beginner or intermediate user who wants to learn how to use Dreamweaver. The book is designed to provide basic and in-depth material that not only educates, but also encourages you to explore the nuances of this exciting program. Features new to Dreamweaver CS6 and covered in this book are indicated by **NEW** .

Approach

The text allows you to work at your own pace through step-by-step tutorials. A concept is presented and the process is explained, followed by the actual steps. To learn the most from the use of the text, you should adopt the following habits:

- Proceed slowly: Accuracy and comprehension are more important than speed.
- Understand what is happening with each step before you continue to the next step.
- After finishing a skill, ask yourself if you could do it on your own, without referring to the steps. If the answer is no, review the steps.

General

Throughout the initial chapters, students are given precise instructions regarding saving their work. Students should feel that they can save their work at any time, not just when instructed to do so.

Icons, Buttons, and Pointers

Symbols for icons, buttons, and pointers are shown in the step each time they are used. Icons may look different in the files panel depending on the file association settings on your computer.

Skills Reference

As a bonus, a Power User Shortcuts table is included at the end of chapters. This table contains the quickest method of completing tasks covered in the chapter. It is meant for the more experienced user, or for the user who wants to become more experienced.

Fonts

The Data Files contain a variety of commonly used fonts, but there is no guarantee that these fonts will be available on your computer. In a few cases, fonts other than those common to a PC or a Macintosh are used. If any of the fonts in use is not available on your computer, you can make a substitution, realizing that the results may vary from those in the book.

Windows and Macintosh

Adobe Dreamweaver CS6 works virtually the same on Windows and Macintosh operating systems. In those cases where there is a significant difference, the abbreviations (Win) and (Mac) are used.

Your instructor will tell you where to store the files as you work, such as the hard drive, a network server, or a USB drive. The instructions in the lessons will refer to "the drive and folder where you store your Data Files" when referring to the Data Files for the book.

When you copy the Data Files to your computer, you may see lock icons that indicate that the files are read-only when you view them in the Dreamweaver Files panel. To unlock the files, right-click on the locked file name in the Files panel, then click Turn off Read Only.

Images vs. Graphics

Many times these terms seem to be used interchangeably. For the purposes of this book, the term images is used when referring to pictures on a web page. The term graphics is used as a more encompassing term that refers to non-text items on a web page such as photographs, logos, navigation bars, Flash animations, graphs, background images, and drawings. You may define these terms in a slightly different way, depending on your professional background or business environment.

Dreamweaver Preference Settings

All Data and Solution Files in this edition are of the HTML5 document type. To follow the steps correctly, it is easier if you set your Dreamweaver Default Document Type (DTD) setting to HTML5. To do this, use the Edit, Preferences, New Document command, then choose HTML5 for the Default Document Type (DTD).

System Preference Settings

The learning process will be much easier if you can see the file extensions for the files you will use in the lessons. To do this in Windows, open Windows Explorer, click Organize, Folder and Search Options, click the View tab, then uncheck the box Hide Extensions for Known File Types. To do this for a Mac, go to Finder, click the Finder menu, and then click Preferences. Click the Advanced tab, then select the Show all file extensions check box.

In Windows 8, open Windows Explorer, click the View tab, and then select the File name extensions check box in the Show/Hide group.

The figures in the book were taken using the Windows setting of Smaller - 100% (default). If you want to match the figures exactly, change your system to match this setting. It is located in the Control Panel, Appearance and Personalization, Display dialog box.

Creating a Portfolio

The Portfolio Project and Project Builders allow you to use your creativity to come up with original Dreamweaver designs. It is a good idea to create a portfolio in which you can store your original work.

System Requirements

For a Windows operating system:

- Intel Pentium® 4 or AMD Athlon® 64 processor
- Microsoft Windows® XP with Service Pack 2 (Service Pack 3 recommended); Windows Vista® Home Premium, Business, Ultimate, or Enterprise with Service Pack 1; or Windows 7
- 512 MB of RAM
- 1 GB of available hard-disk space for installation; additional free space required during installation (cannot install on removable flash-based storage devices)
- 1280 × 800 display with 16-bit video card
- Java(TM) Runtime Environment 1.6 (included)
- DVD-ROM drive
- QuickTime 7.6.6 software required for HTML5 media playback
- This software will not operate without activation.
- Broadband Internet connection and registration are required for software activation, validation of subscriptions, and access to online services. Phone activation is not available.

For a Macintosh operating system:

- Multicore Intel® processor
- Mac OS X v10.6 or v10.7
- 512 MB of RAM
- 1.8 GB of available hard-disk space for installation; additional free space required during installation (cannot install on a volume that uses a case-sensitive file system or on removable flash storage devices)
- 1280 × 800 display with 16-bit video card
- Java Runtime Environment 1.6
- DVD-ROM drive
- QuickTime 7.6.6 software required for HTML5 media playback
- This software will not operate without activation.
- Broadband Internet connection and registration are required for software activation, validation of subscriptions, and access to online services. Phone activation is not available.

Memory Challenges

If, instead of seeing an image on an open page, you see an image placeholder with a large X across it, your RAM is running low.

Try closing any other applications that are running to free up memory.

Building a Website

You will create and develop several websites named The Striped Umbrella, Blooms & Bulbs, TripSmart, and Carolyne's Creations in the lesson material and end of unit exercises in this book. Because each chapter builds from the previous chapter, it is recommended that you work through the chapters in consecutive order.

Websites Used in Figures

Each time a website is used for illustration purposes in a lesson, where necessary, a statement acknowledging that we obtained permission to use the website is included, along with the URL of the website. Sites whose content is in the public domain, such as federal government websites, are acknowledged as a courtesy.

Flash CS6

Intended Audience

This book is designed for the beginner or intermediate user who wants to learn how to use Adobe Flash CS6. The book is designed to provide basic and in-depth material that not only educates, but encourages you to explore the nuances of this exciting program.

Approach

The book allows you to work at your own pace through step-by-step tutorials. A concept is presented and the process is explained, followed by the actual steps. To learn the most from the use of the text, you should adopt the following habits:

- Proceed slowly: Accuracy and comprehension are more important than speed.
- Understand what is happening with each step before you continue to the next step.
- After finishing a process, ask yourself: Can I do the process on my own? If the answer is no, review the steps.

Icons, Buttons, and Pointers

Symbols for icons, buttons, and pointers are shown each time they are used.

Fonts

Data Files contain a variety of commonly used fonts, but there is no guarantee that these fonts will be available on your computer. Each font is identified in cases where fonts other than Arial or Times New Roman are used.

If any of the fonts in use are not available on your computer, you can make a substitution, realizing that the results may vary from those in the book.

Windows and Macintosh

Adobe Flash CS6 works virtually the same on Windows and Macintosh operating systems. In those cases where there is a difference, the abbreviations (Win) and (Mac) are used.

Windows System Requirements

Adobe Flash CS6 requires the following:

- Intel® Pentium® 4 or AMD Athlon® 64 processor
- Microsoft® Windows® XP with Service Pack 3 or Windows 7
- 2GB of RAM (3GB recommended)
- 3.5GB of available hard-disk space for installation; additional free space required during installation (cannot install on removable flash storage devices)
- 1024x768 display (1280x800 recommended)
- DVD-ROM drive
- QuickTime 7.6.6 software required for multimedia features

Macintosh System Requirements

Adobe Flash CS6 requires the following:

- Multicore Intel processor
- Mac OS X v10.6 or v10.7
- 2GB of RAM (3GB recommended)
- 4GB of available hard-disk space for installation; additional free space required during installation (cannot install on a volume that uses a case-sensitive file system or on removable flash storage devices)
- 1024x768 display (1280x800 recommended)
- DVD-ROM drive
- QuickTime 7.6.6 software required for multimedia features-Java Runtime Environment 1.6

Your instructor will tell you where to store the files as you work, such as the hard drive, a network server, or a USB drive. The instructions in the lessons will refer to "the drive and folder where you store your Data Files" when referring to the Data Files for the book.

Projects

Several projects are presented at the end of each chapter that allow students to apply the skills they have learned in the unit. Two projects, Ultimate Tours and the Portfolio, build from chapter to chapter. You will need to contact your instructor if you plan to work on these without having completed the previous chapter's project.

Creating a Portfolio

The Portfolio Project and Project Builders allow students to use their creativity to come up with original Flash animations, screen designs and applications. Creating a portfolio is an excellent way to store and display original work.

Photoshop CS6
Intended Audience

This text is designed for the beginner or intermediate user who wants to learn how to use Photoshop CS6. The book is designed to provide basic and in-depth material that not only educates, but also encourages you to explore the nuances of this exciting program. Features new to Photoshop and covered in this book are indicated by a New icon.

Approach

The text allows you to work at your own pace through step-by-step tutorials. A concept is presented and the process is explained, followed by the actual steps. To learn the most from the use of the text, you should adopt the following habits:

- Proceed slowly: Accuracy and comprehension are more important than speed.
- Understand what is happening with each step before you continue to the next step.
- After finishing a skill, ask yourself if you could do it on your own, without referring to the steps. If the answer is no, review the steps.

General

Throughout the initial chapters, students are given precise instructions regarding saving their work. Students should feel that they can save their work at any time, not just when instructed to do so.

Students are also given precise instructions regarding magnifying/reducing their work area. Once the student feels more comfortable, he/she should feel free to use the Zoom tool to make their work area more comfortable.

Icons, Buttons, and Pointers

Symbols for icons, buttons, and pointers are shown in the step each time they are used. Once an icon, button, or pointer has been used on a page, the symbol will be shown for subsequent uses on that page *without* showing its name.

Skills Reference

As a bonus, a Power User Shortcuts table is included at the end of the Photoshop chapters. This table contains the quickest method for completing tasks covered in the chapter. It is meant for the more experienced user, or for the user who wants to become more experienced. Tools are shown, not named. Brief directions are given, with no tool or command locations.

Fonts

The Data Files contain a variety of commonly used fonts, but there is no guarantee that these fonts will be available on your computer. In a few cases, fonts other than those common to a PC or a Macintosh are used. If any of the fonts in use is not available on your computer, you can make a substitution, realizing that the results may vary from those in the book.

Windows and Macintosh

Adobe Photoshop CS6 works virtually the same on Windows and Macintosh operating systems. In those cases where there is a significant difference, the abbreviations (Win) and (Mac) are used.

Preference Settings

The learning process will be much easier if you can see the file extensions for the files you will use in the lessons. To do this in Windows, open Windows Explorer, click Organize, Folder and Search Options, click the View tab, and then uncheck the Hide Extensions for Known File Types check box. To do this for a Mac, go to the Finder, click the Finder menu, and then click Preferences. Click the Advanced tab, and then select the Show all file extensions check box.

System Requirements

For a Windows operating system:

- Intel® Pentium® 4 processor or AMD Athlon 64 processor with 64-bit support
- Microsoft® Windows® XP SP3, or Windows 7 with Service Pack 1
- 1GB of RAM (4GB recommended)
- 256MB of video RAM (512MB recommended)
- 1GB of available hard-disk space (additional free space required during installation)
- 1,024 × 768 (1280×800 recommended) monitor resolution with 16-bit or higher Open GL 2.0-capable system video card
- DVD-ROM drive required
- Broadband Internet connection required for activation and/or validation of subscription

For a Macintosh operating system:

- Intel processor with 64-bit support
- Mac OS X v.10.68 or v10.7 or higher
- 1G of RAM
- 256MB of video RAM (512MB recommended)
- 2GB of available hard-disk space (additional free space required during installation)
- 1,024 × 768 monitor resolution (1280×800 recommended) with 16-bit or higher open GL video card
- DVD-ROM drive required
- Broadband Internet connection required for activation and/or validation of subscription.

File Identification

Instead of printing a file, the owner of a Photoshop image can be identified by reading the File Info dialog box.

Use the following instructions to add your name to an image:

1. Click File on the Menu bar, then click File Info.
2. Click the Description, if necessary.
3. Click the Author text box.
4. Type your name, course number, or other identifying information.
5. Click OK.

There are no instructions with this text to use the File Info feature other than when it is introduced in Chapter 1. It is up to each user to use this feature so that his or her work can be identified.

Measurements

When measurements are shown, needed, or discussed, they are given in pixels. Use the following instructions to change the units of measurement to pixels:

1. Click Edit (Win) or Photoshop (Mac) on the Menu bar, point to Preferences, then click Units & Rulers.
2. Click the Rulers list arrow, then click pixels.
3. Click OK.

You can display rulers by clicking View on the Menu bar, and then clicking Rulers, or by pressing [Ctrl][R] (Win) or ⌘ [R] (Mac). A check mark to the left of the Rulers command indicates that the Rulers are displayed. You can hide visible rulers by clicking View on the Menu bar, then clicking Rulers, or by pressing [Ctrl][R] (Win) or ⌘ [R] (Mac).

Menu Commands in Tables

In tables, menu commands are abbreviated using the following format:

Edit ➤ Preferences ➤ Units & Rulers

This command translates as follows: Click Edit on the Menu bar, point to Preferences, and then click Units & Rulers.

Grading Tips

Many students have web-ready accounts where they can post their completed assignments. The instructor can access the student accounts using a browser and view the images online. Using this method, it is not necessary for the student to include his/her name on a type layer, because all of their assignments are in an individual password-protected account.

Creating a Portfolio

One method for students to submit and keep a copy of all of their work is to create a portfolio of their projects that is linked to a simple web page that can be saved on a CD-ROM. If it is necessary for students to print completed projects, work can be printed and mounted at a local copy shop; a student's name can be printed on the back of the image.

USING ADOBE BRIDGE TO
MANAGE ASSETS

Introduction

Adobe Bridge is a media content manager integrated with many of the Adobe products for quick access to project files. Bridge is very easy to use as your "bridge" between your library of assets and your project files you are developing in programs such as Dreamweaver, Photoshop, Fireworks, Flash, Illustrator, and InDesign. In Bridge, you can open and preview any file format that Adobe recognizes such as JPGs, SWFs, PNGs, and PDFs. Although the most common use of Bridge is to organize and view media, it has many powerful features that you will find useful, such as adding metadata and keywords to files. **Metadata** is file information you add to a file with tags (words) that are used to identify and describe the file. **Keywords** are words you add to a file to identify, group, and sort files.

Accessing Adobe Bridge

Adobe Bridge is packaged with the Adobe Creative Suite. There are several ways to access the program: by opening it directly from your Applications or Program Files folder on your computer's hard drive, or within Adobe Illustrator, Photoshop, Fireworks, Flash, or

InDesign by using the Go to Bridge button on the Menu bar (in Windows, this is on the Menu bar next to the Help, on Mac it is on the Application bar), or by choosing File on the Menu bar, and then clicking Browse in Bridge within the program. A streamlined version of Bridge called Mini Bridge is also available in Photoshop, InDesign, and InCopy; it appears as a panel that opens directly within the application work area. You can always use Bridge as your primary tool for viewing, copying, and moving media files similar to the way you use Windows Explorer or Macintosh Finder. You can also configure Bridge to start automatically each time you log in or start your computer or device by choosing Start Bridge At Login on the Advanced tab in the Adobe Bridge Preferences dialog box. You can enable (or disable) a script that enables other applications to communicate with Bridge when you start Bridge by checking the Adobe Bridge CS6 check box on the Startup Scripts tab in the Preferences dialog box. To access the Preferences dialog box, click Edit on the Menu bar, then choose Preferences (Win) or click the Adobe Bridge CS6 menu and then choose Preferences (Mac).

Explore the Bridge WORKSPACE

What You'll Do

In this lesson, you will start Bridge, examine the components that make up the Bridge workspace, and change modes.

Examining the Adobe Bridge Workspace

When you start Bridge, you see the Bridge **Essentials workspace**, the default workspace that includes all of the menus, panels, buttons, and panes that you use to organize your media files. Other workspace choices are the Filmstrip, Metadata, Output, Keywords, Preview, Light Table, and Folders workspaces. You can change workspaces by using the Window menu or by clicking one of the Workspace buttons on the Application bar. You can also arrange the panes and panels to create a custom workspace and then assign it a unique name using the Window > Workspace > New Workspace command. You can work in **Compact mode**, which is a mode with a smaller, simplified workspace window. Press [Ctrl][Enter] (Win) or [[⌘]][return] (Mac) to switch back and forth between your workspace and Compact mode.

The Essentials workspace is divided into three panes, which are arranged in columns and further divided into panels. Each panel can be expanded or collapsed by clicking the panel title bar. You can also hide panels using the Windows > Display or Hide command.

Refer to Figure 1 as you locate the components described below.

QUICK TIP:

You can resize panels by dragging the horizontal divider bar between panels or the vertical divider bar on either side of the Content panel. You can also lighten the Bridge interface by choosing a different color theme on the General tab in the Preferences dialog box. From this point forward, the light gray theme is used for maximum readability.

The left pane includes the Favorites, Folders, Filter, Collections, and Export panels. You can use the **Favorites panel** to quickly access folders that you designate as folders you use frequently. You can use the **Folders panel** to navigate through and select a folder, and review its contents. The **Filter panel** is used for filtering files to view in the Content panel. The **Collections panel** is used to group assets located in different locations into a single collection. The **Export panel** is used to optimize images by saving them as JPEGs for use on the web.

The center pane is the **Content panel**, where thumbnails of the files from the selected drive and folder in the Folders panel appear.

You can change the size of the thumbnails by using the Thumbnail slider at the bottom of the workspace.

The right pane includes the Preview, Metadata, and Keywords panels. The **Preview panel** is where a preview of a selected file appears. The **Metadata panel** lists the metadata for a selected file. You use the Metadata panel to assign new metadata to a file. The **Keywords panel** lists the keywords assigned to a file. You use the Keywords panel to add new keywords to a file.

The **Menu bar** with the program commands is at the top of the Bridge workspace. Below the Menu bar is the **Application bar** that contains navigation buttons, the Workspace buttons, and the Search text box. Under the Application bar is the **Path bar**, where you see the path for the selected folder in the Folders panel that you are currently viewing. The Path bar makes it easy to navigate quickly from folder to folder.

Figure 1 *The Bridge Essentials workspace*

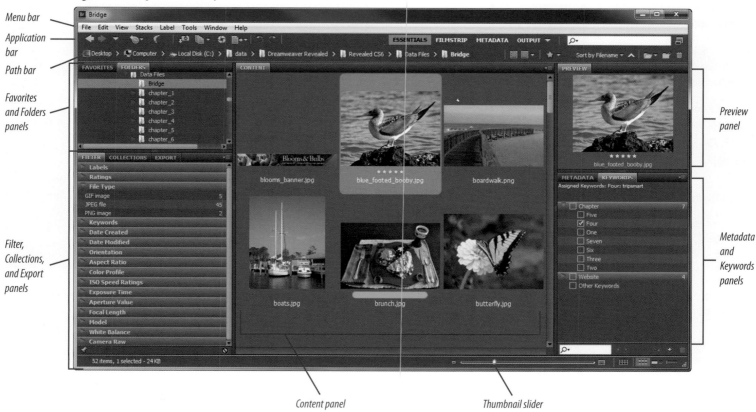

Start Adobe Bridge

To start Adobe Bridge directly using Windows:

1. Click the **Start button** 🔵 on the taskbar.

2. Point to **Programs** (if necessary), then click **Adobe Bridge CS6**, as shown in Figure 2.

To start Adobe Bridge directly using Macintosh:

1. Click **Finder** in the Dock, then click **Applications**.

2. Click the **Adobe Bridge CS6 folder**, then double-click the **Adobe Bridge CS6 application**.

TIP Once Bridge is running, you can add it to the Dock permanently by [control]-clicking the Bridge icon, clicking Options, then clicking Keep in Dock.

To start Adobe Bridge from an Adobe Creative Suite 6 component that is integrated with Bridge:

1. Click **File** on the Menu bar, then click **Browse in Bridge**.

   Or

   Click the **Adobe Bridge button** 📷 on the Menu bar.

   The button you use to start Bridge varies by Adobe application. There is no Browse in Bridge button in Dreamweaver on a Mac.

TIP Photoshop users can also click Mini Bridge in iconic panels.

You started Bridge CS6.

Figure 2 *Starting Adobe Bridge*

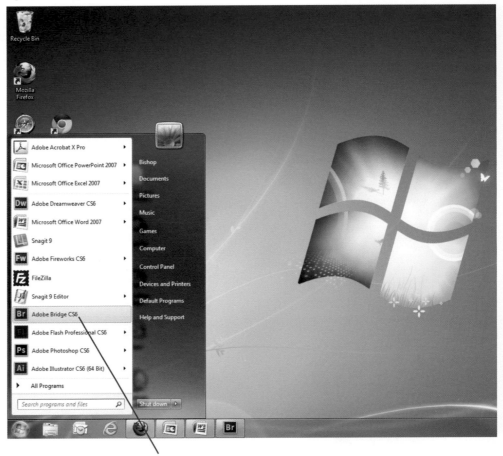

Adobe Bridge CS6

Figure 3 *Viewing the Bridge Data Files folder*

Essentials workspace button

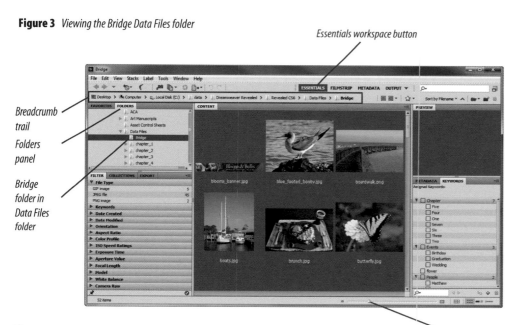

Breadcrumb trail

Folders panel

Bridge folder in Data Files folder

Thumbnail slider

Figure 4 *Using Review Mode and the Loupe tool*

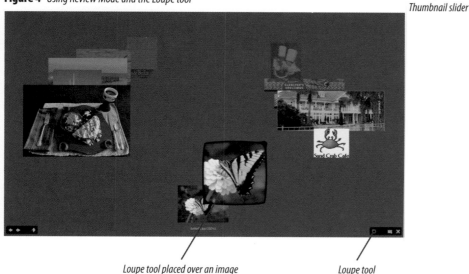

Loupe tool placed over an image

Loupe tool

Change modes

1. Verify that you are in the Essentials workspace.

2. Use the breadcrumb trail across the top of the Bridge window on the Path panel or use the Folders panel to navigate to and select the **Bridge folder** from the drive and folder where you store your Data Files, as shown in Figure 3.

   Thumbnails of each file in the Bridge Data Files folder appear in the Content panel.

3. Use the **Thumbnail slider** on the bottom of the Bridge window to adjust the size of the thumbnails, as shown in Figure 3.

4. Click **View** on the Menu bar, click **Review Mode** to display the contents of the Bridge folder in a carousel arrangement, then use the keyboard arrow keys to shuffle through the images.

TIP You can also press [Ctrl][B] (Win) or ⌘ [B] (Mac) to change to Review Mode.

5. Click the **Loupe tool** in the lower-right corner of the window, then click and drag the **mouse pointer** over the image to magnify a selected area so you can examine the detail more closely, as shown in Figure 4.

TIP You can also activate the Loupe tool by moving the mouse pointer over an image, then clicking the image.

6. Press **[Esc]** (Win) or ⌘ **[W]** (Mac) to exit Review Mode, then click a blank area of the Content panel to deselect the files.

You viewed the Data Files, used the Thumbnail slider to adjust the size of the thumbnails, changed to Review Mode, used the Loupe tool to magnify a selected area in an image, then exited Review Mode.

Use Metadata, Ratings, AND LABELS

What You'll Do

In this lesson, you will add and view metadata, use keywords to filter files, label and rate files, then filter files with labels and ratings.

The Metadata panel is a rich source of information about a file, including the camera settings used (descriptive information that you cannot change) and copyright information (additive data that you can change). You can view and edit the copyright information in the IPTC (International Press Telecommunications Council) Core section of the Metadata panel. Image resolution, author name, and keywords are also examples of metadata you can view in the Metadata panel.

Metadata is saved using the **Extensible Metadata Platform (XMP) standard**. XMP metadata is used by Adobe products, such as Illustrator, InDesign, Flash, and Photoshop, and is usually stored with the file name. If a file contains metadata, XMP allows the metadata to stay with the file when the file is converted to a different file type or placed in a project. You can add metadata using the File > File Info command.

QUICK TIP

You cannot add metadata to .gif files.

You use the Keywords panel to view and add keywords to a file to help group, organize, and sort files. There are two types of keywords: **parent keywords** and **child keywords**. Child keywords are also referred to as **sub keywords**. Child keywords are subcategories of parent keywords. For instance, you could have a parent keyword "food" and a child keyword "desserts." After you have added keywords to files, you can use the Filter panel to sort files by their keywords.

QUICK TIP

In the following steps, you will create keywords for the four websites used in the Dreamweaver lessons. After assigning the keywords, you can sort them by website, copy all of the files for each website, then paste them in the assets folders you will create when you set up the websites. This will save you some time as you work through the lessons, but it is not necessary if you choose not to do so.

You can also identify groups of files by using labels. Labels allow you to assign a file a color or a star rating from zero to five stars. This is an easy way to mark the files you want to keep and others you may want to delete.

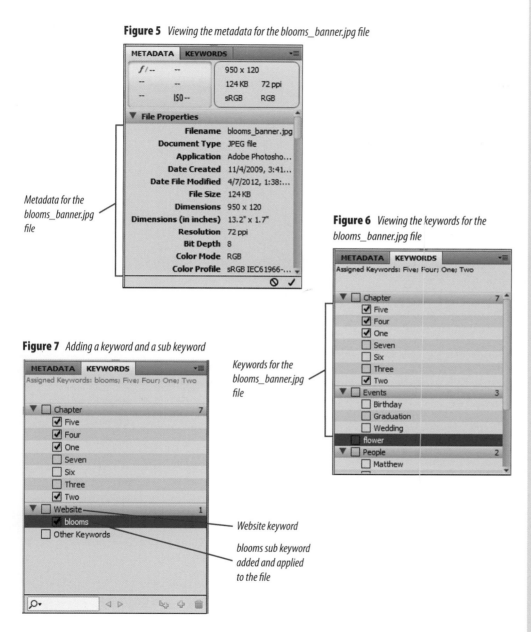

Figure 5 *Viewing the metadata for the blooms_banner.jpg file*

Metadata for the
blooms_banner.jpg
file

Figure 6 *Viewing the keywords for the blooms_banner.jpg file*

Keywords for the
blooms_banner.jpg
file

Figure 7 *Adding a keyword and a sub keyword*

Website keyword

blooms sub keyword
added and applied
to the file

Add and view metadata

1. Open the Metadata panel, click the first file listed, **blooms_banner.jpg**, then click **File Properties** (if necessary) to expand the panel to view the file size, dimensions, and resolution of the selected file, as shown in Figure 5.

2. Click the **Keywords panel**, then view the keywords for the selected file, as shown in Figure 6.

   Each file is assigned one or more chapter numbers that correspond to the chapter or chapters the file is used in. The blooms_banner.jpg file is used in chapters five, four, one, and two. It would also be nice to include a keyword for each file that corresponds to the website the file is used with.

3. Click the **New Keyword button** ⊞ on the lower-right corner of the panel.

4. Type **Website** in the New Keyword text box, then press **[Enter]** (Win) or **[return]** (Mac).

   Keywords let you search for and quickly locate files with common characteristics.

TIP If you want to delete the default keywords and sub keywords, click the keyword you want to delete, then click the Delete Keyword button 🗑. The default keywords have been deleted in Figure 7.

5. With the Website keyword selected, click the **New Sub Keyword button** 🖪, type **blooms** in the Keywords text box, press **[Enter]** (Win) or **[return]** (Mac), then click to place a check mark in the check box next to the new keyword.

   The check mark applies the keyword to the file, as shown in Figure 7.

(continued)

6. Repeat Step 5 to add three more sub keywords under the Website keyword: **striped_umbrella**, **carolynes**, and **tripsmart**, as shown in Figure 8.

7. Using Table 1 as a reference, apply the striped_umbrella sub keyword to each image listed in the table to associate them with The Striped Umbrella website.

   There are four files that will be used in The Striped Umbrella website that you cannot add the striped_umbrella sub keyword to: cafe_logo.gif, spacer_30px.gif, su_logo.gif, and su_banner.gif.

8. Using Table 2 as a reference, repeat Step 7 to add sub keywords for the Blooms & Bulbs website.

   There is one file you cannot add a sub keyword to: gardening_gloves.gif.

Figure 8 *Adding three additional sub keywords*

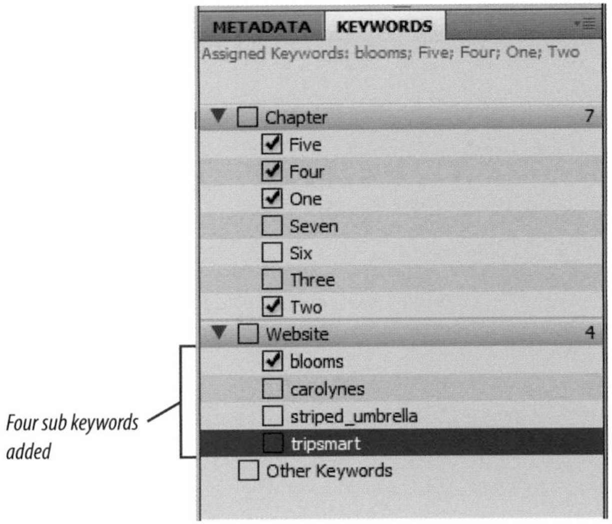

Four sub keywords added

TABLE 1	
Add the striped_umbrella sub keyword to these files:	
boardwalk.png	map_large.jpg
boats.jpg	map_small.jpg
cafe_photo.jpg	pool.jpg
chocolate_cake.jpg	sea_spa_logo.png
club_house.jpg	two_dolphins_small.jpg
family_sunset.jpg	water.jpg
fisherman.jpg	

© Cengage Learning 2013

TABLE 2	
Add the blooms sub keyword to these files:	
blooms_banner.jpg	rose_bloom.jpg
butterfly.jpg	ruby_grass.jpg
chives.jpg	trees.jpg
coleus.jpg	tulips.jpg
fiber_optic_grass.jpg	two_roses_large.jpg
lady_in_red.jpg	two_roses.jpg
plants.jpg	water_lily.jpg
rose_bud.jpg	

© Cengage Learning 2013

Figure 9 *Viewing files with the striped_umbrella sub keyword*

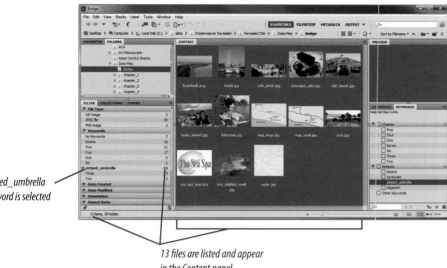

striped_umbrella keyword is selected

13 files are listed and appear in the Content panel

Figure 10 *Viewing files with the blooms sub keyword*

blooms keyword is selected

15 files are listed and appear in the Content panel

Filter files with keywords

1. Click the **Filter panel title bar** to expand the panel if necessary, then click to select **striped_umbrella** under the Keywords criteria.

   13 files appear in the Content panel, as shown in Figure 9.

   TIP If the files are not listed in alphabetical order, click View > Sort > By Filename.

2. Click to select **blooms** under the Keywords criteria, then click to deselect **striped_umbrella**.

   The Content panel now shows 15 files listed for the Blooms & Bulbs website, as shown in Figure 10.

3. Click to deselect **blooms** under the Keywords criteria.

   All 52 files appear in the Content panel.

You used the Filter panel to view the Data files with the keywords striped_umbrella and blooms. You then removed the filter to view all Data files.

GETTING STARTED WITH
DREAMWEAVER

Introduction

Adobe Dreamweaver CS6 is a web development tool that lets you create dynamic web pages containing text, images, hyperlinks, animation, sounds, video, and interactive elements. You can use Dreamweaver to create individual web pages or complex websites consisting of many web pages. A **website** is a group of related web pages that are linked together and share a common interface and design. Dreamweaver lets you create design elements such as text, forms, rollover images, and interactive buttons, or import elements from other software programs. You can also save Dreamweaver files in many different file formats, including XHTML, HTML, JavaScript, CSS, or XML, to name a few. **XHTML** is the acronym for eXtensible HyperText Markup Language, the current standard language used to create web pages. You can still use **HTML** (HyperText Markup Language) in Dreamweaver; however, it is no longer considered the standard language. You use a web browser to view your web pages on the Internet. A **web browser** is a program, such as Microsoft Internet Explorer, Google Chrome, Apple Safari, or Mozilla Firefox, which displays web pages.

Using Dreamweaver Tools

Creating a robust website is a complex task. Fortunately, Dreamweaver has an impressive number of tools that can help. Using Dreamweaver design tools, you can create dynamic and interactive web pages without writing a word of code. However, if you prefer to write code, Dreamweaver makes it easy to enter and edit the code directly and see the visual results of the code instantly. Dreamweaver also contains organizational tools that help you work with a team of people to create a website. You can also use the Dreamweaver management tools to help you manage a website. For instance, you can use the **Files panel** to create folders to organize and store the various files for your website, and to add pages to your website.

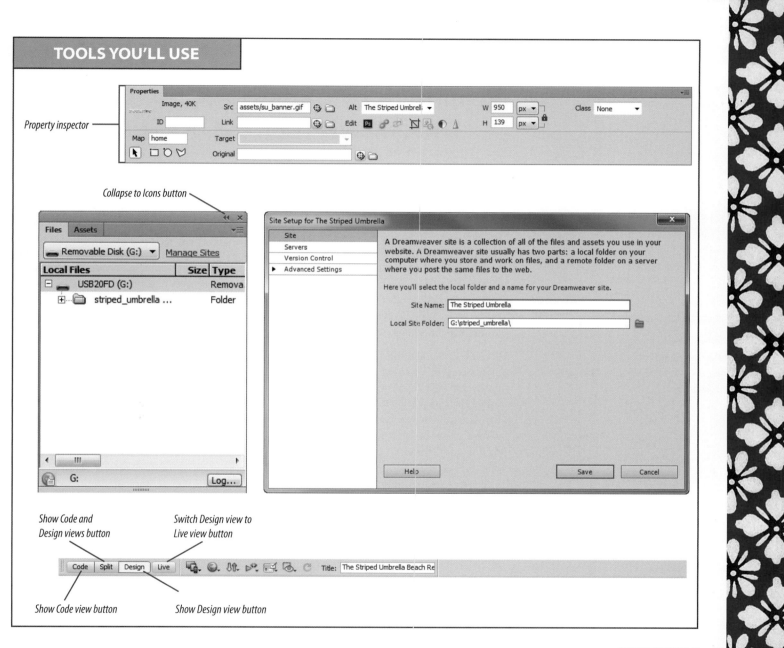

Property inspector

Collapse to Icons button

Show Code and Design views button

Switch Design view to Live view button

Show Code view button

Show Design view button

Explore the
DREAMWEAVER WORKSPACE

What You'll Do

In this lesson, you will start Dreamweaver, examine the components that make up the Dreamweaver workspace, and change views.

Examining the Dreamweaver Workspace

After you start Dreamweaver, you see the **Dreamweaver workspace**, the screen that includes all of the menus, panels, buttons, inspectors, and panes that you use to create and maintain websites. It is designed to give you easy access to all the tools you need to create web pages. Refer to Figure 1 as you locate the components described below.

The **Document window** is the large area in the Dreamweaver program window where you create and edit web pages. The **Menu bar** (also called the **Application bar**), located above the Document window, includes menu names, a Workspace switcher, and other application commands. The Menu bar appears on either one bar or two bars, depending on your screen size and resolution. To choose a menu command, click the menu name to open the menu, then click the menu command. The Insert panel appears at the top of the Dreamweaver workspace on the right side of the screen. The **Insert panel**, sometimes called the Insert bar, includes nine categories of buttons displayed through a drop-down menu: Common, Layout, Forms, Data, Spry, jQuery Mobile, InContext Editing, Text,

and Favorites. Clicking a category in the Insert panel displays the buttons and menus for inserting objects associated with that category. For example, if you click the Layout category, you find buttons for using div tags for creating blocks of content on pages; for inserting Spry interactive page elements such as buttons or drop-down menus; and for inserting and editing tables.

QUICK TIP

Two additional options are available through the Insert panel drop-down menu. To display the icons in color, click Color Icons, or right-click the Insert panel, then click Color Icons. To hide the button labels, click Hide Labels.

The **Document toolbar** contains buttons and drop-down menus you can use to change the current work mode, check browser compatibility, preview web pages, debug web pages, choose visual aids, and view file-management options. One of the buttons on the Document toolbar, the Switch Design view to Live view button, is used to view the current page in Live view.

Live view displays an open document as if you were viewing it in a browser, with interactive elements active and functioning. When you switch to Live view, navigation buttons are added to the Document toolbar.

Two additional toolbars do not appear by default: the Standard toolbar and the Style Rendering toolbar. The **Standard toolbar** contains buttons you can use to execute frequently used commands that are also available on the File and Edit menus. The **Style Rendering toolbar** contains buttons that you can use to display data for different platforms, such as a cell phone or television. To display or hide the Document, Standard, and Style Rendering toolbars, right-click an empty area of an open toolbar, then click the toolbar name you wish to display or hide. You can also use the View > Toolbars menu.

The **Related Files toolbar** is located below an open document's filename tab and displays the names of any related files. **Related files** are files that are linked to a document and are necessary for the document to display and function correctly. An external style sheet, which contains formatting rules that control the appearance of a document, is a good example of a related file. The **Coding toolbar** contains buttons you can use when working directly in

Figure 1 *Dreamweaver CS6 workspace*

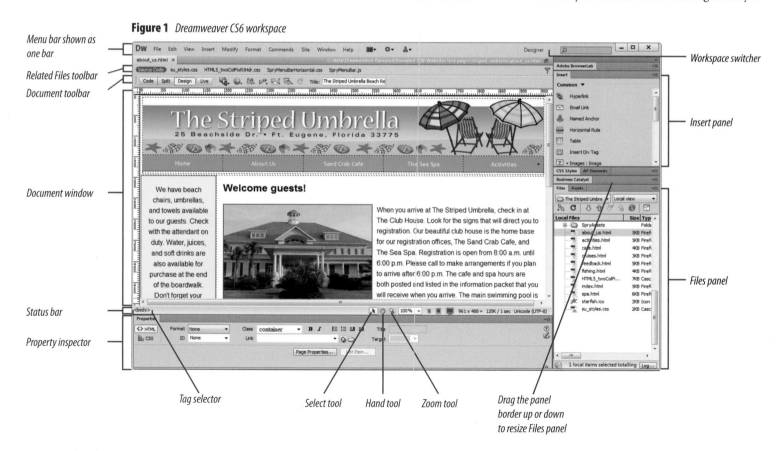

Menu bar shown as one bar

Related Files toolbar

Document toolbar

Document window

Status bar

Property inspector

Tag selector

Select tool

Hand tool

Zoom tool

Drag the panel border up or down to resize Files panel

Workspace switcher

Insert panel

Files panel

the code and is not visible unless you are in Code view. When visible, it appears on the left side of the Document window.

The **Property inspector**, sometimes referred to as the **Properties pane**, located at the bottom of the Dreamweaver window, lets you view and change the properties (characteristics) of a selected object. The Property inspector is context sensitive, which means it changes according to what is selected in the Document window. The **status bar** is located below the Document window. The left side of the status bar displays the **tag selector**, which shows the HTML tags used at the insertion point location. The right side displays the Select tool, used for page editing; the Hand tool, used for panning; the Zoom tool, used for magnifying; and the Set Magnification menu, used to change the percentage of magnification. It also displays the window size and estimated download time for the current page.

A **panel** is a tabbed window that displays information on a particular topic or contains related commands. **Panel groups** are sets of related panels that are grouped together. A collection of panels or panel groups is called a **dock**. To view the contents of a panel in a panel group, click the panel's tab. Panels are docked by default on the right side of the screen. You can undock or "float" them by dragging the panel tab to another screen location. To collapse or expand a panel group, double-click the panel tab, as shown in Figure 2. When you first start Dreamweaver, the Adobe BrowserLab, Insert, CSS Styles, AP Elements, Business Catalyst,

Files, and Assets panels appear by default. You can open panels using the Window menu commands or the corresponding shortcut keys.

QUICK TIP

The Collapse to Icons button ▶▶ above the top panel lets you collapse all open panels to icons to enlarge the workspace.

Working with Dreamweaver Views

A **view** is a particular way of displaying page content. Dreamweaver has three working views. **Design view** shows the page as it would appear in a browser and is primarily used for designing and creating a web page. **Code view** shows the underlying HTML code for the page; use this view to read or edit the underlying code.

QUICK TIP

You can also split Code view to enable you to work on two different sections of code at once. To change to Split Code view, click View on the Menu bar, then click Split Code.

Show Code and Design views is a combination of Code view and Design view. Show Code and Design views is the best view for **debugging** or correcting errors because you can immediately see how code modifications change the appearance of the page. The view buttons are located on the Document toolbar. If you want to switch to the same view for all open documents, hold down the Ctrl key (Win) or Control key (Mac) while you click a view button.

Figure 2 *Panels in panel group*

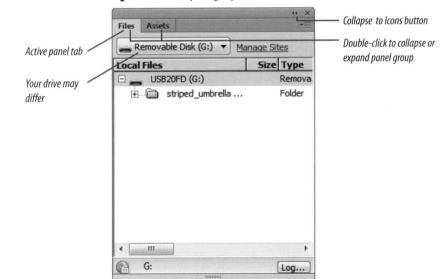

Figure 3 *Starting Dreamweaver CS6 (Windows)*

Click Adobe
Dreamweaver CS6

Start Dreamweaver (Windows)

1. Click the **Start button** 🔵 on the taskbar.
2. Point to **All Programs**, then click **Adobe Dreamweaver CS6**, as shown in Figure 3.
3. If the Default Editor dialog box opens, click **OK**.

You started Dreamweaver CS6 for Windows.

Hiding and Displaying Toolbars

To hide or display the Style Rendering, Document, or Standard toolbars, click View on the Menu bar, point to Toolbars, then click Style Rendering, Document, or Standard. The Coding toolbar is available only in Code view and the Code window in Split view, and appears vertically in the Document window. By default, the Document toolbar appears in the workspace.

Start Dreamweaver (Macintosh)

1. Click **Finder** in the Dock, then click **Applications**.

2. Click the **Adobe Dreamweaver CS6 folder**, then double-click the **Adobe Dreamweaver CS6 application**, as shown in Figure 4.

TIP Once Dreamweaver is running, you can add it to the Dock permanently by [control]-clicking the Dreamweaver icon, clicking Options, then clicking Keep In Dock.

You started Dreamweaver CS6 for Macintosh.

Figure 4 *Starting Dreamweaver CS6 (Macintosh)*

Getting Started with Dreamweaver

Figure 5 *Code view for new document*

Show Code view button

Show Code and Design views button

Show Design view button

Switch Design view to Live view button

Menu bar may be displayed as two bars

Click to collapse all panels to icons

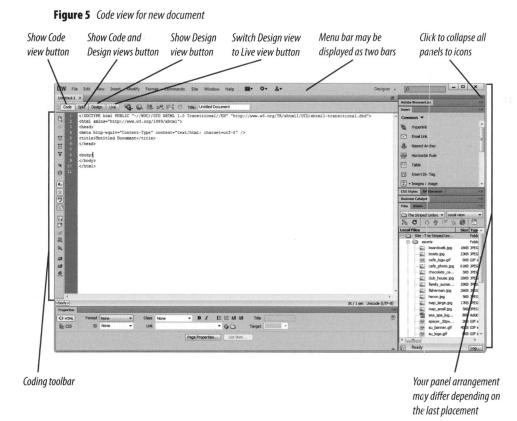

Coding toolbar

Your panel arrangement may differ depending on the last placement

---

Change views and view panels

1. Click **HTML** in the Create New category on the Dreamweaver Welcome Screen.

The Dreamweaver Welcome Screen provides shortcuts for opening files and for creating new files or websites.

TIP If you do not want the Dreamweaver Welcome Screen to appear each time you start Dreamweaver, click the Don't show again check box on the Welcome Screen or remove the check mark next to Show Welcome Screen in the General category in the Preferences dialog box.

2. Click the **Show Code view button** [Code] on the Document toolbar.

The default code for a new document appears in the Document window, as shown in Figure 5.

TIP The Coding toolbar is available only in Code view and in the Code window in Split view.

3. Click the **Show Code and Design views button** [Split] on the Document toolbar.

4. Click the **Show Design view button** [Design] on the Document toolbar.

TIP If your icons appear in black-and-white and you would like to display them in color, click the Insert panel drop-down menu, then click Color Icons.

(continued)

Using Two Monitors for Optimum Workspace Layout

One option you have for workspace layout is Dual Screen layout. **Dual Screen layout** is the layout you would choose when you are using two monitors while working with Dreamweaver. The Document window and Property inspector appear on the first monitor and the panels appear on the second monitor. It is seamless to work between the two monitors and optimizes your workspace by allowing you to have multiple panels open without compromising your Document window space.

Lesson 1   Explore the Dreamweaver Workspace

5. Click the **Assets panel tab**, then compare your screen to Figure 6.

TIP If the Assets panel is not visible, click Window on the Menu bar, then click Assets.

6. Click the **Files panel tab** to display the contents of the Files panel.

7. Double-click **Assets** to collapse the panel group.

8. View the contents of the CSS Styles and AP Elements panels.

9. Click and drag the **blank area** next to the AP Elements tab to the middle of the document window.

   The panel group is now in a floating window.

   (continued)

Figure 6 *Displaying a panel group*

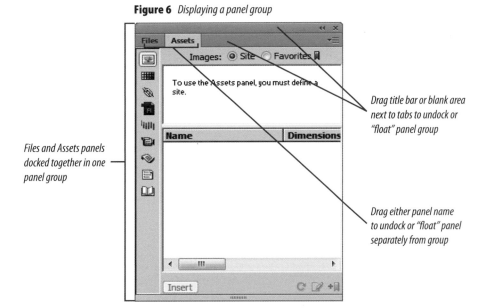

Files and Assets panels docked together in one panel group

Drag title bar or blank area next to tabs to undock or "float" panel group

Drag either panel name to undock or "float" panel separately from group

Choosing a Workspace Layout

The Dreamweaver interface is an integrated workspace, which means that all of the document windows and panels appear in a single application window. Each open document appears as a tab below the document toolbar. (In the Mac OS, documents can either be tabbed together in a single window or displayed in separate windows.) To view a tabbed document, click the tab with the document's filename. The **Workspace switcher**, a drop-down menu in the top right corner on the Menu bar, lets you change the workspace layout. The default layout is the Designer workspace layout, where the panels are docked on the right side of the screen and Split view is the default view. Other workplace layouts include App Developer, App Developer Plus, Business Catalyst, Classic, Coder, Coder Plus, Designer Compact, Dual Screen, Fluid Layout and Mobile Applications. To change the workspace layout, click the Workspace switcher, then click the desired layout. You can also rearrange the workspace using your own choices for panel placement and save the workspace with a unique name using the "New Workspace" and "Manage Workspaces" commands on the Workspace switcher. The Reset 'Current view' option resets the workspace layout to return to the default positions on the screen for the selected view.

Getting Started with Dreamweaver

Figure 7 *Docking a panel group*

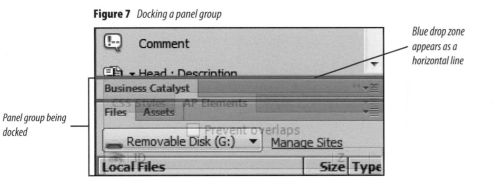

Panel group being docked

Blue drop zone appears as a horizontal line

10. Click and drag the **panel title bar** back to its original position, then drop it to dock the panel group below the Insert panel.

    Release the mouse only when you see the blue drop zone. The **blue drop zone** is a heavy blue line that appears when the panel is in the correct position to be docked. See Figure 7. If the blue drop zone appears as a box, releasing the button adds the panel to the boxed panel group.

TIP If you have rearranged the panels from their original positions and want to reset them back to their default positions, click the Workspace switcher drop-down menu, then click Reset 'Designer'. You will also have to reset the Color Icons, as color icons are not part of the default Designer workspace.

11. Click **File** on the Menu bar, then click **Close** to close the open document.

You viewed a new web page using three views, opened panel groups, viewed their contents, then closed panel groups.

Viewing Your Page in Live View

When you view your web pages in Dreamweaver, the page elements appear similar to the way they will appear on the web, but not exactly. To get a better idea of how it will look, you can use the Switch Design view to Live view button on the Document toolbar. This button causes the open document to appear as it would in a browser, with interactive elements active and functioning. If you are viewing the page in Live view, the Shows the Live view source in code view button will appear to the right of the Switch Design view to Live view button. This button will display the code as read-only; it cannot be modified without exiting "Shows the Live view source in code view." The code is highlighted in yellow and allows you to see the dynamic changes in the code while you interact with the dynamic content on the page. When the Switch Design view to Live view button is active, the Shows the Live view source in code view button can be toggled on or off. If Live view is not active, the Shows the Live view source in code view button will not appear. When you click the Live view button the first time, you may see a message that you need to install the Flash plug-in from the Adobe website, www.adobe.com. Download the plug-in and your page can then be viewed using Live view.

View a Web Page AND USE HELP

What You'll Do

In this lesson, you will open a web page, view several page elements, and access the Help system.

Opening a Web Page

After starting Dreamweaver, you can create a new website, create a new web page, or open an existing website or web page. The first web page that appears when users go to a website is called the **home page**. The home page sets the look and feel of the website and directs users to the rest of the pages in the site.

Viewing Basic Web Page Elements

There are many elements that make up web pages. Web pages can be very simple and designed primarily with text, or they can be media-rich with images, sound, and movies, creating an enhanced interactive web experience. Figure 8 shows a web page with text and graphics that work together to create a simple and attractive page.

Most information on a web page is presented in the form of text. You can type text directly onto a web page in Dreamweaver or import text created in other programs. You can then use the Property inspector to format text so that it is attractive and easy to read. Text should be short and to the point to engage users and prevent them from losing interest and leaving your site.

Hyperlinks, also known as **links**, are images or text elements on a web page that users click to display another location on the page, another web page on the same website, or a web page on a different website.

Images add visual interest to a web page. The saying that "less is more" is certainly true with images, though. Too many images cause the page to load slowly and discourage users from waiting for the page to download. Many pages have **banners**, which are images that appear across the top or down the side of the screen that can incorporate a company's logo, contact information, and links to the other pages in the site.

Menu bars, also called navigation bars, are bars that contain multiple links that are usually organized in rows or columns. Sometimes menu bars are used with an image map. An **image map** is an image that has been divided into sections, each of which serves as a link. The way that menu bars and other internal links are used on your pages is referred to as the **navigation structure** of the site.

Rich media content is a comprehensive term that refers to attractive and engaging images, interactive elements, video, or animations. Some of this content can be created in Dreamweaver, but much of it is created with other programs such as Adobe Flash, Fireworks, Photoshop, or Illustrator.

Getting Help

Dreamweaver has an excellent Help feature that is comprehensive and easy to use. When questions or problems arise, you can use the commands on the Help menu to find the answers you need. Clicking the Dreamweaver Help command opens the Dreamweaver Help page that contains a list of topics and subtopics by category. The Help feature in Dreamweaver CS6 is based on Adobe AIR technology. **Adobe AIR** is an Adobe product used for developing content that can be delivered with a browser or as a desktop application.

The Search text box at the top of the window lets you enter a keyword to search for a specific topic. Context-specific help can be accessed by clicking the Help button on the Property inspector.

Figure 8 *Common web page elements*

National Endowment for the Arts website – www.arts.endow.gov

Open a web page and view basic page elements

1. Click **File** on the Menu bar, then click **Open**.

2. Click the **Look in list arrow** (Win), or **navigation list arrow** (Mac), locate the drive and folder where you store your Data Files, then double-click the **chapter_1 folder** (Win), or click the **chapter_1 folder** (Mac).

3. Click **dw1_1.html**, then click **Open**. You may not see the .html file extension if the option for hiding file extensions for known file types is selected on your operating system.

TIP If you want your screen to match the figures in this book, make sure the Document window is maximized and the Windows display setting is 100% (Win).

4. Click **Window** on the Menu bar, then click **Hide Panels** to temporarily hide the panels.

   Hiding the panels gives you a larger viewing area for your web pages. You can also press [F4] to show or hide the panels.

   Note to Mac users: On the newest Mac OS, the F-keys are assigned to system functions. (F1=monitor brightness and F4=widgets) You can change this in your system preferences. Newer keyboards have an "FN" or "fn" key that can be used in conjunction with the F-keys so that they function "normally."

5. Locate each of the web page elements shown in Figure 9.

TIP Because you are opening a single page that is not in a website with access to the other pages, the links will not work.

(continued)

Figure 9 *Viewing web page elements (Win)*

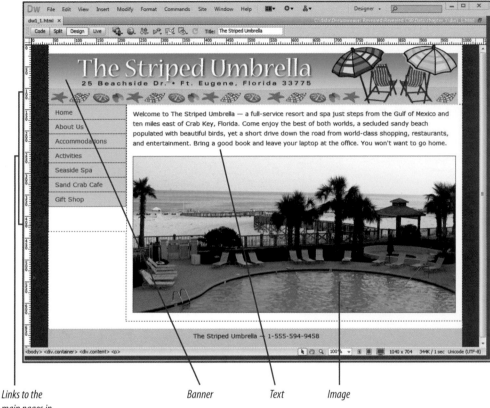

Links to the main pages in the website

Banner   Text   Image

Getting Started with Dreamweaver

Figure 9 *Viewing web page elements (Mac)*

Banner

Links to
the main
pages in the
website

Text

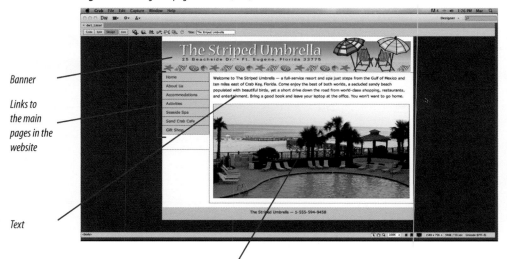

Image

6. Press **[F4]** to show the panels.

7. Click the **Show Code view button** [Code] to view the code for the page.

8. Scroll down to view all the code, if necessary, then click the **Show Design view button** [Design] to return to Design view.

TIP To show and highlight the code for a particular page element, select the page element in Design view, then click the Show Code view button.

9. Click **File** on the Menu bar, then click **Close** to close the open page without saving it.

TIP You can also click the Close button (the X) on the filename tab to close the page.

You opened a web page, located several page elements, viewed the code for the page, then closed the page without saving it.

Use Dreamweaver Help

1. Click **Help** on the Menu bar, then click **Dreamweaver Help**.

   The Dreamweaver Help window opens in your browser window. Since the help feature is online content, you must have Internet access to use it. Also, because help is online, the pages are "live," and subject to change. So your screens may not match the figures in these steps exactly.

2. Click the drop-down menu next to the Adobe Community Help search text box, select **Dreamweaver** if necessary, click to place the insertion point in the Adobe Community Help search text box, then type **"CSS Property inspector"**, as shown in Figure 10.

3. Press [**Enter**] (Win) or [**Return**] (Mac).

   The Search Community Help window opens with results from the search.

4. Click to select the **Only Adobe content** option button, click the **Toggle the product filter menu visibility drop-down menu**, then click **Dreamweaver**, if necessary, as shown in Figure 11.

   The Help topic list changes to display only Dreamweaver help from the Adobe website.

   (continued)

Figure 10 *Dreamweaver Help window*

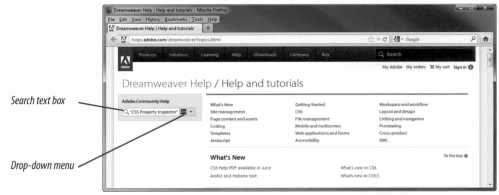

Search text box

Drop-down menu

Figure 11 *Displaying Help content*

Only Adobe content option button

Click a topic to open related content

Toggle the product filter menu visibility drop-down menu

Getting Started with Dreamweaver

Figure 12 *Searching for a topic in Help*

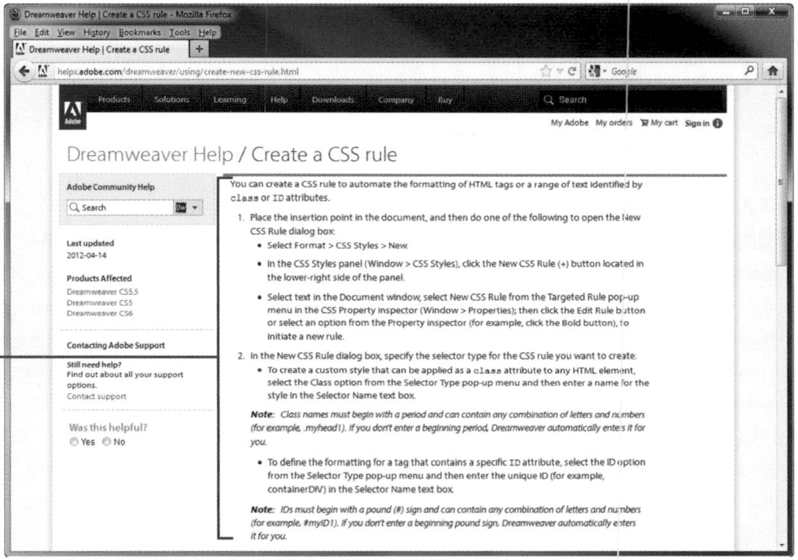

Scroll to read content

5. Scroll down to scan the list of topics, click one of the links to read information about a topic of your choice, then follow several sublinks to learn more.

The content appears on the right side of the window. The left side of the window shows the Dreamweaver versions to which the current topic relates, and a link for other contact support options, as shown in Figure 12.

6. Close the Adobe Community Help window.

You used Adobe Help to read information in the Adobe Dreamweaver CS6 documentation.

Using Adobe Help

When you access the Help feature in Dreamweaver, you have the choice of downloading a PDF for offline help (which is similar to searching in a Dreamweaver manual) or using online help. The online help feature is called Adobe Community Help. Adobe Community Help is a collection of materials such as tutorials, published articles, or blogs, in addition to the regular help content. All content is monitored and approved by the Adobe Community Expert program.

Plan and Set Up
A WEBSITE

What You'll Do

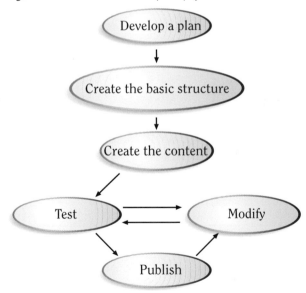

In this lesson, you will review a website plan for The Striped Umbrella, a beach resort and spa. You will also create a local site folder for The Striped Umbrella website, and then set up the website.

Understanding the Website Development Process

Creating a website is a complex process. It can often involve a large team of people working in various roles to ensure that the website contains accurate information, looks good, and works smoothly. Figure 13 illustrates the phases in a website development project.

Planning a Website

Planning is probably the most important part of any successful project. Planning is an essential part of creating a website, and is a continuous process that overlaps the subsequent phases. To start planning your website, you need to create a checklist of questions and answers about the site. For

Figure 13 *Phases of a website development project*

Develop a plan
↓
Create the basic structure
↓
Create the content

Test ⇄ Modify

Publish

Getting Started with Dreamweaver

example, what are your goals for the site? Who is the audience you want to target? Teenagers? Children? Sports enthusiasts? Senior citizens? How can you design the site to appeal to the target audience? What content is appropriate for the target audience? What content is relevant to the purpose of the website? The more questions you can answer about the site, the more prepared you will be when you begin the developmental phase. Because of the public demand for up-to-date information, your plan should include not just how to get the site up and running, but how to keep it current. Table 1 lists some of the basic questions you need to answer during the planning phase for almost any type of website. From your checklist, you should create a statement of purpose and scope, a timeline for all due dates, a budget, a task list with work assignments, and a list of resources needed. You should also include a list of deliverables, such as page prototypes and art for approval. The due dates for each deliverable should be included in the timeline.

Planning the Basic Structure

Once you complete the planning phase, you need to determine the structure of the site by creating a wireframe. A **wireframe**, sometimes referred to as a storyboard, is an illustration that represents every page in a website. Like a flowchart, a wireframe shows the relationship of each page in the site to all the other pages. Wireframes also show how each page element is to be placed on each page. Wireframes are helpful when planning a website, because they allow you to visualize how each page in the site links to others. They are also an important tool to help the client see how the pages will look and work together. Make sure that the client and all other interested stakeholders approve the wireframe before the site construction actually begins. Wireframes range from very simple (known as low-fidelity wireframes) to interactive and multidimensional (known as high-fidelity wireframes). You can create a simple wireframe by using a pencil and paper or by using a graphics program on a computer, such as Adobe Illustrator, Adobe Fireworks, or Microsoft PowerPoint. To create more complex wireframes that simulate the site

TABLE 1: WEBSITE PLANNING CHECKLIST	
Question	**Examples**
1. Who is the target audience?	Seniors, teens, children
2. How can I tailor the site to reach that audience?	Specify an appropriate reading level, decide the optimal amount of media content, use formal or casual language
3. What are the goals for the site?	Sell a product, provide information
4. How will I gather the information?	Recruit other employees, write it myself, use content from in-house documents
5. What are my sources for media content?	Internal production department, outside production company, my own photographs
6. What is my budget?	Very limited, well financed
7. What is the timeline?	Two weeks, one month, six months
8. Who is on my project team?	Just me, a complete staff of designers
9. How often should the site be updated?	Every 10 minutes, once a month
10. Who will update the site?	Me, other team members

© Cengage Learning 2013

navigation and user interaction, use a high-fidelity wireframe program such as OverSite, ProtoShare, Microsoft Visio, or Adobe Proto. The basic wireframe shown in Figure 14 shows all the The Striped Umbrella website pages that you will create in this book. The home page appears at the top of the wireframe, and it has four pages linked to it. The home page is called the **parent page**, because it is at a higher level in the web hierarchy and has pages linked to it. The pages linked below it are called **child pages**. The Activities page, which is a child page to the home page, is also a parent page to the Cruises and Fishing pages. You can refer to this wireframe as you create the actual links in Dreamweaver. More detailed wireframes also include all document names, images, text files, and link information. Use your wireframe as your guide as you develop the site to make sure you follow the planned site structure.

In addition to creating a wireframe for your site, you should also create a folder hierarchy on your computer for all of the files that will be used in the site. Start by creating a folder for the site with a descriptive name, such as the name of the company. This folder, known as the **local site folder**, will store all the pages or HTML files for the site. Traditionally, this folder has been called the **root folder** and many people still use this term; in this book we will call it the local site folder. Then create a subfolder, often called **assets** or **images**, in which you store all of the files that are not pages, such as images and sound files.

QUICK TIP

You should avoid using spaces, special characters, or uppercase characters in your folder names to ensure that all your files can be read and linked successfully on all web servers, whether they are Windows- or UNIX-based.

After you create the local site folder, you are ready to set up your site. When you **set up** a site, you use the Dreamweaver Site Setup dialog box to assign your site a name and specify the local site folder. After you have set up your site, the site name and any folders and files it contains appear in the **Files panel**, the panel you use to manage your website's files and folders. Using the Files panel to manage your files ensures that the site links work correctly when the website is published. You also use the Files panel to add or delete pages.

Creating the Web Pages and Collecting the Page Content

This is the fun part! After you create your wireframe, obtain approvals, and set up your site, you need to gather the files you'll need to create the pages, including text, images, buttons, video, and animations. You will import some of these pages from other software programs, and some you will create in Dreamweaver. For example, you can create text in a word-processing program and import or paste it into Dreamweaver, or you can create and format text in Dreamweaver.

Images, tables, colors, and horizontal rules all contribute to making a page attractive and interesting, but they can increase file size.

Figure 14 *The Striped Umbrella website wireframe*

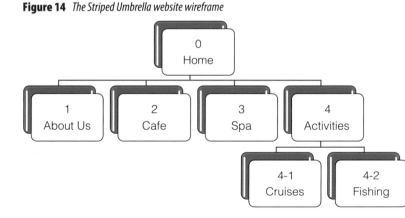

In choosing your page elements, carefully consider the file size of each page. A page with too many graphic elements might take a long time to load, which could cause visitors to leave your site.

Testing the Pages

Once all your pages are completed, you need to test the site to make sure all the links work and that everything looks good. It is important to test your web pages using different browser software. The four most common browsers are Microsoft Internet Explorer, Mozilla Firefox, Google Chrome, and Apple Safari. Test your site using different versions of each browser, because older versions may not support the latest web technology. You should also test your site using a variety of screen sizes. Some users may have small monitors, while others may have large, high-resolution monitors. Also consider connection download time.

Although most people use cable modems or DSL (digital subscriber line), some in rural areas still use slower dial-up modems. Testing is a continuous process, for which you should allocate plenty of time.

Modifying the Pages

After you create a website, you'll probably find that you need to keep making changes to it, especially when information on the site needs to be updated. Each time you make a change, such as adding a new button or image to a page, you should test the site again. Modifying and testing pages in a website is an ongoing process.

Publishing the Site

Publishing a website refers to the process of transferring all the files for the site to a **web server**, a computer that is connected to the Internet with an IP (Internet Protocol) address, so that it is available for viewing on the Internet. A website must be published so that Internet users can view it. There are several options for publishing a website. For instance, many **Internet Service Providers (ISPs)** provide space on their servers for customers to publish websites, and some commercial websites provide limited free space for their users. Although publishing happens at the end of the process, it's a good idea to set up web server access in the planning phase. Use the Files panel to transfer your files using the Dreamweaver FTP capability. **FTP (File Transfer Protocol)** is the process of uploading and downloading files to and from a remote site.

Managing a Project with a Team

When working with a team, it is essential that you define clear goals for the project and a list of objectives to accomplish those goals. Your plan should be finalized after conferring with both the clients and other team members to make sure that the purpose, scope, and objectives are clear to everyone. Establish the **deliverables**, or products that will be provided to the client at the product completion such as new pages or graphic elements created, and a timeline for their delivery. You should present the web pages at strategic times in the development process to your team members and to your clients for feedback and evaluation. Analyze all feedback objectively, incorporating both the positive and the negative comments to help you make improvements to the site and meet the clients' expectations and goals. A common pitfall in team management is **scope creep**. Scope creep means making impromptu changes or additions to a project without corresponding increases in the schedule or budget. Proper project control and communication between team members and clients can minimize scope creep and achieve the successful and timely completion of a project.

Set up a website

1. Click **Site** on the Menu bar, then click **New Site**.

2. Click **Site** in the category list in the Site Setup for Unnamed Site dialog box (if necessary), then type **The Striped Umbrella** in the Site name text box.

TIP You can use uppercase letters and spaces in the site name because it is not the name of a folder or a file.

3. Click the **Browse for folder icon** 📁 next to the Local Site Folder text box, click the **Select list arrow** (Win) or the **navigation list arrow** (Mac) in the Choose Root folder dialog box, navigate to and click the **drive and folder** where your website files will be stored, then click the **striped_umbrella folder**.

4. Click **Open** (Win) or **Choose** (Mac), then click **Select** (Win). See Figure 18.

You created a website and set it up with the name The Striped Umbrella. You then told Dreamweaver the folder name and location to use for the local site folder.

Figure 18 *Site Setup for The Striped Umbrella dialog box*

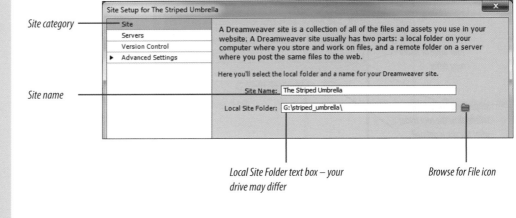

Site category

Site name

Local Site Folder text box – your drive may differ

Browse for File icon

Understanding the Process of Publishing a Website

Before publishing a website so that web users can access it, you should first create a **local site folder**, also called the **local root folder**, to house all the files for your website, as you did on page 1-23. This folder usually resides on your hard drive. Next, you need to gain access to a remote server. A **remote server** is a web server that hosts websites and is not directly connected to the computer housing the local site. Many Internet Service Providers, or ISPs, provide space for publishing websites on their servers. Once you have access to a remote server, you can then use the Servers category in the Site Setup dialog box to enter information such as the FTP host, host directory, login, and password. After entering this information, you can then use the Put File(s) button in the Files panel to transfer the files to the designated remote server. Once the site is published to a remote server, it is called a **remote site**.

Figure 19 *Adding a server for Remote Access for The Striped Umbrella website*

Servers
category

Add new
Server icon

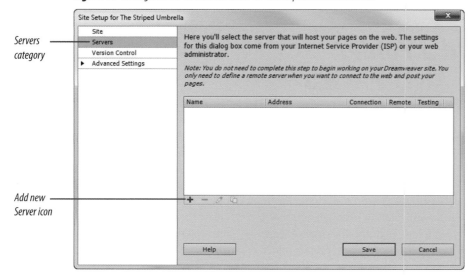

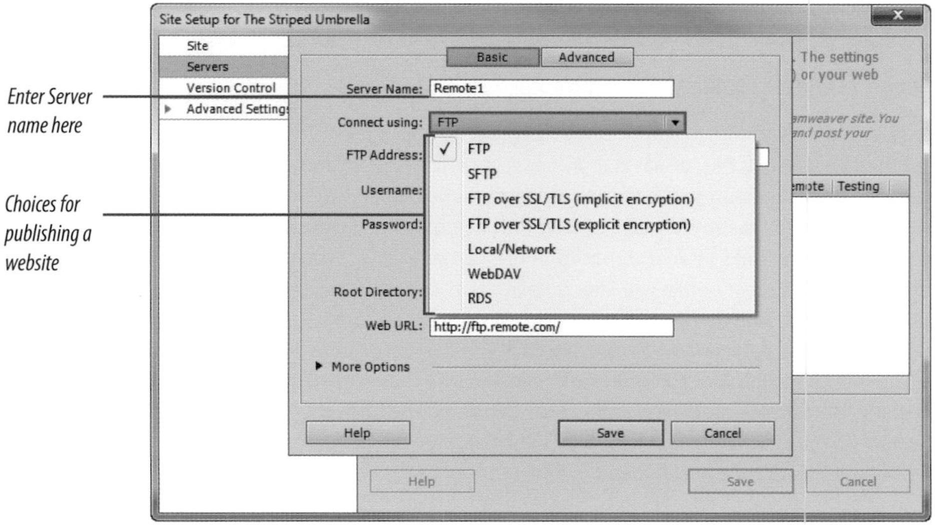

Set up web server access

1. Click **Servers** in the Category list, then click the **Add new Server icon** ➕, as shown in Figure 19.

TIP If you do not have the information to publish your website, skip step 2 and continue to step 3. You can specify this information later.

2. Click the **Connect using: list arrow**, choose the method you will use to publish your website, as shown in Figure 20, enter any necessary information in the Site Setup for The Striped Umbrella dialog box based on the setting you chose, then click **Save**.

TIP Your network administrator or web hosting service will give you the necessary information to publish your website.

3. Click **Save** to close the Site Setup dialog box.

You set up the remote access information to prepare you for publishing your website.

Figure 20 *Entering server information for The Striped Umbrella website*

Enter Server
name here

Choices for
publishing a
website

Add a Folder
AND PAGES

What You'll Do

In this lesson, you will use the Files panel to create a new folder and new pages for the website.

Adding a Folder to a Website

After setting up a website, you need to create folders to organize the files that will make up the site. Creating a folder called **assets** is a good beginning. There is nothing magic about the word "assets," though. You can name your folder anything that makes sense to you, as long as you follow proper folder naming conventions such as avoiding the use of spaces. You can use the assets folder to store all non-HTML files, such as images or sound files. Many designers name this folder "images" and use additional folders to store other types of supporting files. After you create the assets folder, it is a good idea to set it as the default location to store the website images. This saves a step when you import new images into the website.

DESIGNTIP

Creating an Effective Navigation Structure

When you create a website, it's important to consider how your users will navigate from page to page within the site. A menu bar, or navigation bar, is a critical tool for moving around a website, so it's important that all text, buttons, and icons used in a menu bar have a consistent look across all pages. If you use a complex menu bar, such as one that incorporates JavaScript or Flash, it's a good idea to include plain text links in another location on the page for accessibility. Otherwise, users might become confused or lost within the site. A navigation structure can include more links than those included in a menu bar, however. For instance, it can contain other sets of links that relate to the content of a specific page and which are placed at the bottom or sides of a page in a different format. No matter which navigation structure you use, make sure that every page includes a link back to the home page. Don't make users rely on the Back button on the browser toolbar to find their way back to the home page. It's possible that the user's current page might have opened as a result of a search and clicking the Back button will then take the user out of the website.

Creating the Home Page

The **home page** of a website is the first page that users see when they visit your site. Most websites contain many other pages that all connect back to the home page. The home page filename usually has the name index.html (.htm), or default.html (.htm).

Adding Pages to a Website

Websites might be as simple as one page or might contain hundreds of pages. When you create a website, you can add all the pages and specify where they should be placed in the website folder structure in the local site folder. Once you add and name all the pages in the website, you can then add the content, such as text and graphics, to each page. One method is to add as many blank pages as you think you will need in the beginning, rather than adding them one at a time with all the content in place. This enables you to set up the navigation structure of the website at the beginning of the development process and view how each page is linked to others. When you are satisfied with the overall structure, you can then add the content to each page. This is strictly a personal preference, however. You can also choose to add and link pages as you create them, and that will work just fine, too.

You have a choice of several default document types you can generate when you create new HTML pages. The default document type is designated in the Preferences dialog box. XHTML 1.0 Transitional is the default document type when you install Dreamweaver, but you can change it to HTML5 or any other document type. It's important to understand the terminology—the pages are still called HTML pages and the file extension is still HTML, but the document type will be XHTML 1.0 Transitional. We will use HTML5 as our standard document type for the files we create in each lesson.

Using the Files Panel for File Management

You should use the Files panel to add, delete, move, or rename files and folders in a website. It is very important that you perform these file-maintenance tasks in the Files panel rather than in Windows Explorer (Win) or in the Finder (Mac). Working outside of Dreamweaver, such as in Windows Explorer, can cause linking errors. You cannot take advantage of the simple, yet powerful, Dreamweaver site-management features unless you use the Files panel for all file-management activities. You might choose to use Windows Explorer (Win) or the Finder (Mac) only to create the local site folder or to move or copy the local site folder of a website to another location. If you move or copy the local site folder to a new location, you will have to set up the site again in the Files panel, as you did in Lesson 3 of this chapter. Setting up a site is not difficult and will become routine for you after you practice a bit. If you are using Dreamweaver on multiple computers, such as in labs or at home, you will have to set up your sites the first time you change to a different computer.

Add a folder to a website (Windows)

1. Right-click **Site - The Striped Umbrella** in the Files panel, then click **New Folder**.

2. Type **assets** in the folder text box, then press **[Enter]**.

TIP To rename a folder, click the folder name once, pause, click again, then type the new name.

3. Compare your screen to Figure 21.

You used the Files panel to create a new folder in the striped_umbrella folder and named it "assets".

Add a folder to a website (Macintosh)

1. Press and hold **[control]**, click the **striped_umbrella folder**, then click **New Folder**.

2. Type **assets** in the new folder name text box, then press **[return]**.

TIP To rename a folder, click the folder name text box, type the new name, then press **[return]**.

3. Compare your screen to Figure 22.

You used the Files panel to create a new folder in the striped_umbrella folder and named it "assets".

Figure 21 *The Striped Umbrella site in Files panel with assets folder created (Windows)*

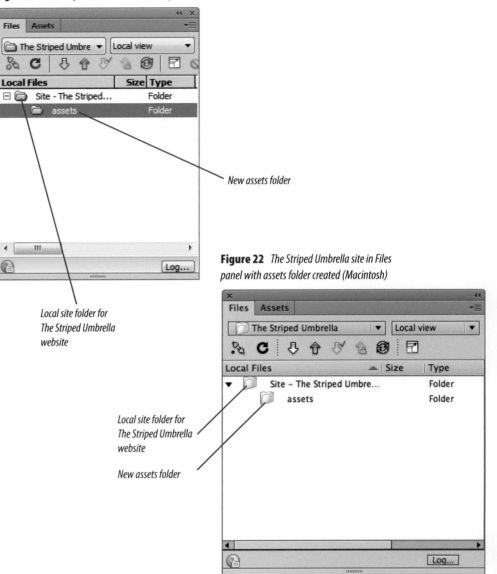

New assets folder

Local site folder for The Striped Umbrella website

Figure 22 *The Striped Umbrella site in Files panel with assets folder created (Macintosh)*

Local site folder for The Striped Umbrella website

New assets folder

Getting Started with Dreamweaver

Figure 23 *Site Setup for The Striped Umbrella dialog box with the assets folder set as the default images folder*

Advanced Settings category

Default Images folder text box

Browse for folder button

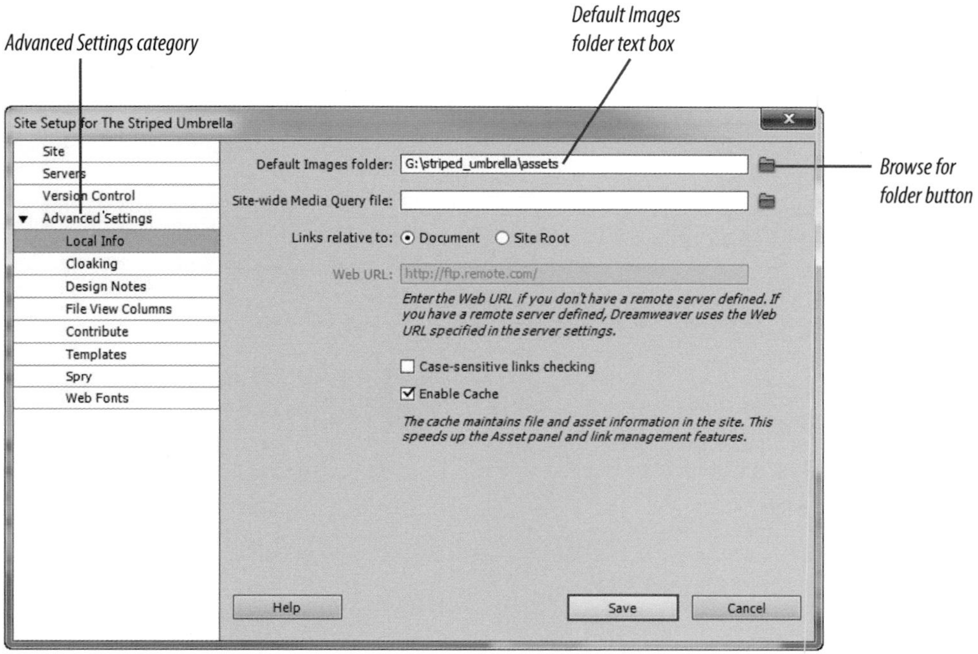

Set the default images folder

1. Click the **Site pop-up menu** in the Files panel, click **Manage Sites**, then click the **Edit the currently selected site button** ✐.

2. Click **Advanced Settings** in the category list in the Site Setup dialog box, then click **Local Info** if necessary.

3. Click the **Browse for folder button** 📁 next to the Default Images folder text box.

4. If necessary, navigate to your striped_umbrella folder, double-click the **assets folder** (Win) or click the **assets folder** (Mac) in the Choose Image Folder dialog box, then click **Select** (Win) or **Choose** (Mac).

   Compare your screen to Figure 23.

5. Click **Save**, then click **Done**.

You set the assets folder as the default images folder so that imported images will be automatically saved in it.

Create the home page

1. Open **dw1_2.html** from the drive and folder where you store your Data Files.

   The file has several elements in it, including a banner image.

2. Click **File** on the Menu bar, click **Save As**, click the **Save in list arrow** (Win) or the **Where list arrow** (Mac), navigate to your striped_umbrella folder, select **dw1_2.html** in the File name text box (Win) or select **dw1_2** in the Save As text box (Mac), then type **index.html**.

   Windows users do not have to type the file extension. It will be added automatically.

3. Click **Save**, then click **No** when asked to update links.

   As shown in Figure 24, the drive where the local site folder is stored, the local site folder name, and the page's filename are displayed to the right of the document tab and in the Address text box in the Browser Navigation toolbar. This information is called the **path**, or location of the open file in relation to other folders in the website.

   The banner image is no longer visible and a gray broken link placeholder appears in its place. This is because although you saved the .html file under a new name in the website's local site folder, you have not yet copied the image file into the website's assets folder. The banner image is still linked to the Data Files folder. You will fix this in the next set of steps.

   You opened a file, then saved it with the filename index.

Figure 24 *index.html saved in the striped_umbrella local site folder*

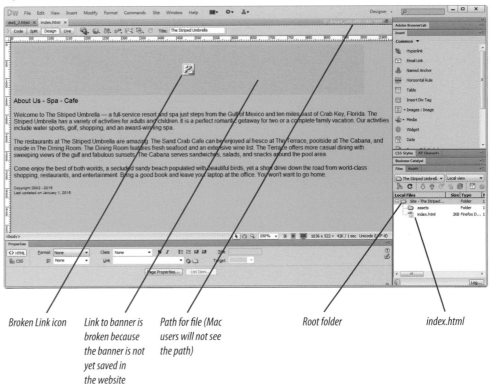

Broken Link icon

Link to banner is broken because the banner is not yet saved in the website

Path for file (Mac users will not see the path)

Root folder

index.html

Figure 25 *Property inspector showing properties of The Striped Umbrella banner*

The Striped
Umbrella banner

Selection handles

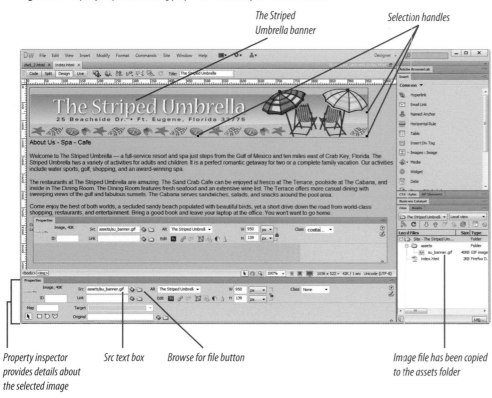

Property inspector
provides details about
the selected image

Src text box

Browse for file button

Image file has been copied
to the assets folder

Save an image file in the assets folder

1. Click the **broken link placeholder** to select it.

   Small, black selection handles appear around the broken link. To correct the broken link, you must copy the image file from the Data Files folder into the assets folder of your website.

2. Click the **Browse for File button** 📁 next to the Src text box in the Property inspector, navigate to the assets folder in your Data Files folder for this chapter, click **su_banner.gif**, click **OK** (Win) or **Open** (Mac), then click on a blank part of the page. (Click the banner placeholder image again if the banner still doesn't appear.)

   The file for The Striped Umbrella banner, su_banner.gif, is automatically copied to the assets folder of The Striped Umbrella website, the folder that you designated as the default images folder. When the image is selected, the Src text box shows the path of the banner to the assets folder in the website, and the banner image is visible on the page.

   TIP If you do not see the su_banner.gif file listed in the Files panel, click the Refresh button 🔄 on the Files panel toolbar.

3. Select the banner to view the banner properties in the Property inspector, then compare your screen to Figure 25.

   TIP Until you copy an image from an outside folder to your website, the image is not part of the website and will appear as a broken link.

You saved The Striped Umbrella banner in the assets folder.

Add pages to a website (Windows)

1. Click the **plus sign** to the left of the assets folder (if necessary) to open the folder and view its contents, su_banner.gif.

TIP If you do not see a file listed in the assets folder, click the Refresh button 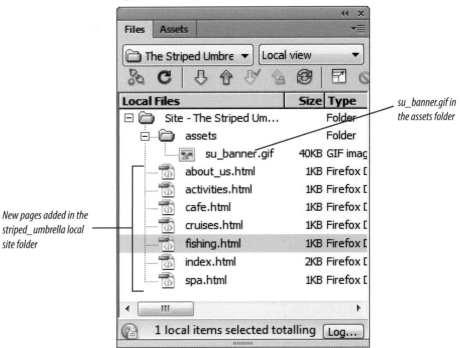 on the Files panel toolbar.

2. Right-click the **striped_umbrella local site folder**, click **New File**, type **about_us** to replace untitled, then press **[Enter]**.

Each new file is a page in the website. This page does not have page content or a page title yet.

TIP If you create a new file in the Files panel, use care to make sure the .html file extension is not deleted or that the file does not end up with a double file extension.

3. Repeat Step 2 to add five more blank pages to The Striped Umbrella website, naming the new files **spa.html**, **cafe.html**, **activities.html**, **cruises.html**, and **fishing.html**.

TIP Make sure to add the new files to the site folder, not the assets folder. If you accidentally add them to the assets folder, just drag them to the site folder.

4. Click the **Refresh button** on the Files panel to list the files alphabetically, then compare your screen to Figure 26.

5. Click **File**, **Save**, to save the index.html file, if necessary, close both open files, click **File** on the Menu bar then click **Exit**.

TIP If you are prompted to save changes to the dw1_1.html file, click No.

You added the following six pages to The Striped Umbrella website: about_us, activities, cafe, cruises, fishing, and spa.

Figure 26 *New pages added to The Striped Umbrella website (Windows)*

su_banner.gif in the assets folder

New pages added in the striped_umbrella local site folder

DESIGNTIP

Adding Page Titles

When you view a web page in a browser, its page title appears in the browser window title bar. (The page title is different from the filename, the name used to save the page on a computer.) The page title reflects the page content and sets the tone for the page. It is especially important to use words in your page title that are likely to match keywords users might enter when using a search engine. Search engines compare the text in page titles to the keywords typed into the search engine. When a title bar displays "Untitled Document," the designer has neglected to give the page a title. This is like giving up free "billboard space" and looks unprofessional.

Getting Started with Dreamweaver

Figure 27 *New pages added to The Striped Umbrella website (Macintosh)*

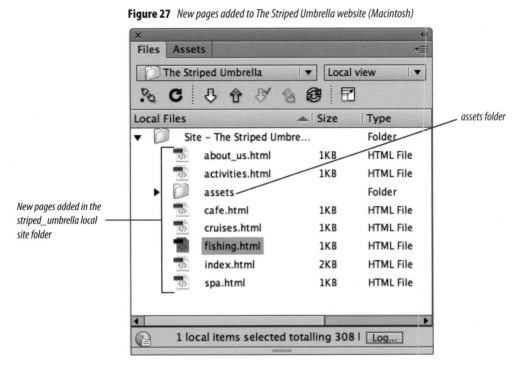

assets folder

New pages added in the striped_umbrella local site folder

POWER USER SHORTCUTS	
To do this:	**Use this shortcut:**
Open a file	[Ctrl][O] (Win) or ⌘ [O] (Mac)
Close a file	[Ctrl][W] (Win) or ⌘ [W] (Mac)
Create a new file	[Ctrl][N] (Win) or ⌘ [N] (Mac)
Save a file	[Ctrl][S] (Win) or ⌘ [S] (Mac)
Get Dreamweaver Help	[F1]
Show/Hide panels	[F4]
Switch between Code view and Design view	[Ctrl][`] (Win) or [control] [`] (Mac)

© Cengage Learning 2013

Add pages to a website (Macintosh)

1. Click the **triangle** to the left of the assets folder to open the folder and view its contents.

   TIP If you do not see a file listed in the assets folder, click the Refresh button ⟳ on the Files panel.

2. [control]-click the **striped_umbrella local site folder**, click **New File**, type **about_us** to replace untitled, then press **[return]**.

   TIP If you create a new file in the Files panel, use care to make sure the .html file extension is not deleted or that the file does not end up with a double file extension.

3. Repeat Step 2 to add five more blank pages to The Striped Umbrella website, naming the new files **spa.html**, **cafe.html**, **activities.html**, **cruises.html**, and **fishing.html**.

   TIP Make sure to add the new files to the site folder, not the assets folder. If you accidentally add them to the assets folder, just drag them to the site folder.

4. Click the **Refresh button** ⟳ to list the files alphabetically, then compare your screen to Figure 27.

5. Click **File**, **Save**, to save the index.html file, then close both open files.

6. Click **Dreamweaver** on the Menu bar, and then click **Quit Dreamweaver**.

   TIP If you are prompted to save changes, click No.

You added six pages to The Striped Umbrella website: about_us, activities, cafe, cruises, fishing, spa.

Explore the Dreamweaver workspace.

1. Start Dreamweaver.
2. Create a new HTML document.
3. Change the view to Code view.
4. Change the view to Code and Design views.
5. Change the view to Design view.
6. Collapse the panels to icons.
7. Expand the panels.
8. Undock the Files panel and float it to the middle of the document window. Dock the Files panel back to its original position.
9. View the Assets panel.
10. Close the page without saving it.

View a web page and use Help.

1. Open the file dw1_3.html from where you store your Data Files.
2. Locate the following page elements: a banner, an image, and text.
3. Change the view to Code view.
4. Change the view to Design view.
5. Use the Dreamweaver Help command to search for information on docking panels.
6. Display and read one of the topics you find.
7. Close the Dreamweaver Help window.
8. Close the page without saving it.

Plan and set up a website.

1. Use the Files panel to select the drive and folder where you store your website files.
2. Create a new local site folder in this folder or drive called **blooms**.
3. Create a new site called **Blooms & Bulbs**.
4. Specify the blooms folder as the local site folder.
5. Use the Servers Info category in the Site Setup for Blooms & Bulbs dialog box to set up web server access. (*Hint*: Skip this step if you do not have the necessary information to set up web server access.)
6. Click Save to close the Site Setup dialog box.

Add a folder and pages.

1. Create a new folder in the blooms local site folder called **assets**.
2. Edit the site to set the assets folder as the default location for the website images.
3. Open the file dw1_4.html from where you store your Data Files, save this file in the blooms local site folder as **index.html**, then click No to updating the links.
4. Select the broken image for the Blooms & Bulbs banner on the page.
5. Use the Property inspector to browse for blooms_ banner.jpg, then select it to automatically save it in the assets folder of the Blooms & Bulbs website.

(Remember to click off of the banner anywhere else on the page to show the banner as it replaces the broken image if necessary.)

6. Create seven new pages in the Files panel, and name them: **plants.html**, **workshops.html**, **newsletter.html**, **annuals.html**, **perennials.html**, **water_plants.html**, and **tips.html**.
7. Refresh the view to list the new files alphabetically, then compare your screen to Figure 28.
8. Close all open pages.

Figure 28 *Completed Skills Review*

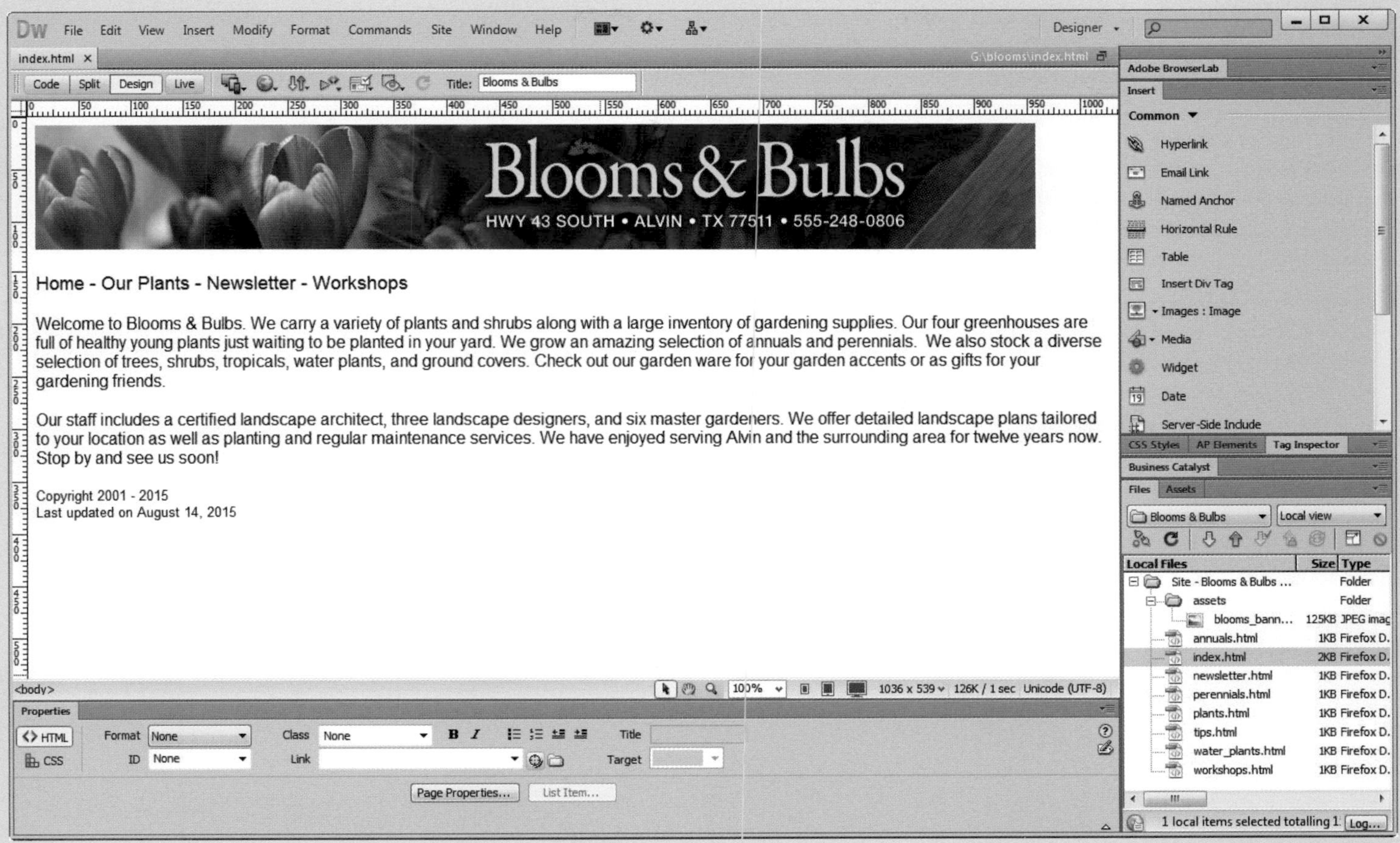

You have been hired to create a website for a travel outfitter called TripSmart. TripSmart specializes in travel products and services. In addition to selling travel products, such as luggage and accessories, they organize trips and offer travel advice. Their clients range from college students to families to vacationing professionals. The owner, Thomas Howard, has requested a dynamic website that conveys the excitement of traveling.

1. Using the information in the preceding paragraph, create a wireframe for this website, using either a pencil and paper or a program such as Microsoft Word. Include the home page with links to four child pages named **catalog.html**, **newsletter.html**, **services.html**, and **tours.html**. Include two child pages under the tours page named **peru.html** and **galapagos.html**.

2. Create a new local site folder named **tripsmart** in the drive and folder where you store your website files.

3. Start Dreamweaver, if necessary, then create a site with the name **TripSmart**. Set the tripsmart folder as the local site folder for the site.

4. Create an assets folder and set it as the default location for images.

5. Open the file dw1_5.html from where you store your Data Files, then save it in the tripsmart local site folder as **index.html**. (Remember not to update links.)

6. Correct the path for the banner by selecting the banner on the page, browsing to the original source in the Data Files folder, then selecting the file to copy it automatically to your TripSmart assets folder.

7. Create six additional pages for the site, and name them as follows: **catalog.html**, **newsletter.html**, **services.html**, **tours.html**, **peru.html**, and **galapagos.html**. Use your wireframe and Figure 29 as a guide.

8. Refresh the Files panel.

9. Close all open pages.

Figure 29 *Completed Project Builder 1*

Getting Started with Dreamweaver

Your company has been selected to design a website for a catering business called Carolyne's Creations. In addition to catering, Carolyne's services include cooking classes and daily specials available as take-out meals. She also has a retail shop that stocks gourmet treats and kitchen items.

1. Create a wireframe for this website that includes a home page and child pages named **shop.html**, **classes.html, catering.html,** and **recipes.html**. Create two more child pages under the classes.html page called **children.html** and **adults.html**.

2. Create a new local site folder for the site in the drive and folder where you save your website files, then name it **cc**.

3. Create a website with the name **Carolyne's Creations**, using the cc folder for the local site folder.

4. Create an assets folder for the site and set the assets folder as the default location for images.

5. Open dw1_6.html from the where you store your Data Files then save it as **index.html** in the cc folder.

6. Reset the source for the banner to automatically save the cc_banner.jpg file in the assets folder.

7. Using Figure 30 and your wireframe as guides, create the additional pages shown for the website.

8. Refresh the Files panel to sort the files alphabetically.

9. Close all open pages.

Figure 30 *Completed Project Builder 2*

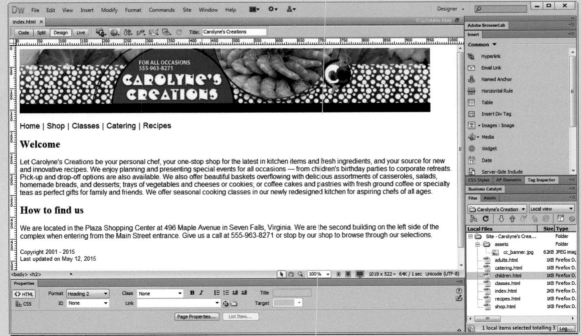

Figure 31 shows the Department of Defense website, a past selection for the Adobe Site of the Day. To visit the current Department of Defense website, connect to the Internet, then go to www.defense.gov. The current page might differ from the figure because dynamic websites are updated frequently to reflect current information. The main navigation structure is under the banner. The page title is The Official Home of the Department of Defense.

Go to the Adobe website at www.adobe.com, click the Customer Showcase link under the Company menu, then choose one of the sites listed to visit. Explore the site and answer the following questions:

1. Do you see page titles for each page you visit?
2. Do the page titles accurately reflect the page content?
3. Is the navigation structure clear?
4. How is the navigation structure organized?
5. Why do you think this site was chosen as a Site of the Day?

Figure 31 *Design Project*
United State Department of Defense website – www.defense.gov

The Portfolio Project will be an ongoing project throughout the book, in which you will plan and create an original website without any Data Files supplied. The focus of the site can be on any topic, organization, sports team, club, or company that you would like. You will build on this site from chapter to chapter, so you must do each Portfolio Project assignment in each chapter to complete your website. When you finish this book, you should have a completed site that would be an excellent addition to a professional portfolio.

1. Decide what type of site you would like to create. It can be a personal site about you, a business site that promotes a fictitious or real company, or an informational site that provides information about a topic, cause, or organization.
2. Write a list of questions and answers about the site you have decided to create.
3. Create a wireframe for your site to include at least four pages. The wireframe should include the home page with at least three child pages under it.
4. Create a local site folder and an assets folder to house the assets, then set up your site using the local site folder as the website local site folder and the assets folder as the default images folder.
5. Create a blank page named **index.html** as a placeholder for the home page.
6. Begin collecting content, such as pictures or text to use in your website. You can use a digital camera to take photos, use a scanner to scan pictures, or create your own graphics using a program such as Adobe Fireworks or Adobe Illustrator. Gather the content in a central location that will be accessible to you as you develop your site.

2

DEVELOPING A
WEB PAGE

Introduction

The process of developing a web page requires a lot of thought and planning. Besides developing the page content, you also need to write descriptive head content. Head content does not appear on the page but in the HTML code; it contains information search engines use to help users find your website. Next, choose the page background and text colors. Then add the page content, format it attractively, and add links to let users navigate between the site pages. Finally, to ensure that all links work correctly and are current, test them regularly.

Understanding Page Layout

Before you add content to a page, consider the following guidelines for laying out pages:

Use white space effectively. A room with too much furniture makes it difficult to appreciate the individual pieces. The same is true of a web page. Too many text blocks, links, animations, and images can be distracting. Consider leaving white space on each page. **White space**, which is not necessarily white, is the area on a page with no content.

Limit media elements. Too many media elements, such as images, video clips, or sounds, can result in a page that takes too long to load. Users might leave your site before the entire page finishes loading. Use media elements only if they serve a purpose.

Keep it simple. Often the simplest websites are the most appealing and are also the easiest to create and maintain. A simple, well-designed site that works well is far superior to a complex one that contains errors.

Use an intuitive navigation structure. Make sure your site's navigation structure is easy to use. Users should always know where they are in the site and be able to easily find their way back to the home page. If users get "lost," they might leave the site rather than struggle to find their way around.

Apply a consistent theme. To help give pages in your website a consistent appearance, consider designing your pages using elements that relate to a common theme. Consistency in the use of color and fonts, the placement of the navigation links, and the overall page design gives a website a unified look and promotes greater ease of use and accessibility. Style sheets and pre-developed page layouts called **templates** can make this easier.

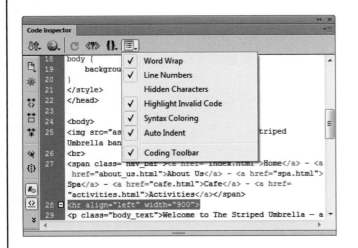

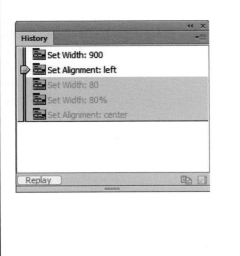

Create Head Content and SET PAGE PROPERTIES

What You'll Do

In this lesson, you will learn how to enter titles, keywords, and descriptions in the head content section of a web page. You will also change the background color for a web page.

Creating the Head Content

A web page is composed of two distinct sections: the head content and the body. The **head content** includes the page title that appears in the title bar of the browser and some important page elements, called meta tags, that are not visible in the browser.

Meta tags are HTML codes that include information about the page, such as keywords and descriptions. Meta tags are read by screen readers for users who have visual impairments. **Keywords** are words that relate to the content of the website. A **description** is a short paragraph that describes the content and features of the website. For instance, the words "beach" and "resort" would be appropriate keywords for The Striped Umbrella website. Search engines find web pages by matching the title, keywords, and description in the head content of web pages with keywords that users enter in search engine text boxes. Therefore, it is important to include concise, useful information in the head content. The **body** is the part of the page that appears in a browser window. It contains all the page content that is visible to users, such as text, images, and links.

QUICK **TIP**

Don't confuse page titles with filenames, the names used to store files on the server.

Setting Web Page Properties

When you create a web page, one of the first design decisions that you should make is to choose properties that control the way the page appears in a browser, such as the **background color**, the color that fills the entire page. The background color should complement the colors used for text, links, and images on the page. Often, backgrounds consist of images for either the entire page or a part of the page, such as a Cascading Style Sheet (CSS) layout block. A **CSS layout block** is a section of a web page that is defined and formatted using a Cascading Style Sheet, a set of formatting characteristics you can apply to text, links, and other page objects. You will learn more about CSS layout blocks in Chapter 6. When you use the Page Properties dialog box to set page properties such as the background color, Dreamweaver automatically creates a style that modifies the body tag to include the properties you added.

A strong contrast between the text color and the background color makes it easier for users to read your text. One of the Web Content Accessibility Guidelines (WCAG), Version 2.0, from the World Wide Web Consortium (W3C) states that contrast will "make it easier for users to see content including separating foreground from background." You can choose a light background color with dark text, or a dark background color with light text. A white background with dark text, though not terribly exciting, provides good contrast and is easiest to read for most users. Another design decision you need to make is whether to change the **default font** and **default link colors**, which are the colors used by the browser to display text, links, and visited links. The default color for **unvisited links**, or links that the user has not clicked yet, is blue. Unvisited links are usually simply called **links**. The default color for **visited links**, or links that have been previously clicked, is purple. You change the background color, text, and link colors using the color picker in the Page Properties dialog box. You can choose colors from one of the five Dreamweaver color palettes, as shown in Figure 1.

Choosing Colors to Convey Information

Before 1994, colors appeared differently on different types of computers. In 1994, Netscape developed the first web-safe color palette, a set of colors that appears consistently in all browsers and on Macintosh, Windows, and UNIX platforms. The evolution of video cards has made this less relevant today, but use of appropriate colors is an important factor

in creating accessible pages. Be sure to use only colors that provide good contrast on your pages. Dreamweaver has two web-safe color palettes, Color Cubes and Continuous Tone, each of which contains 216 web-safe colors. Color Cubes is the default color palette. To choose a different color palette, open the color picker. You can find the color picker on the

CSS Property inspector, in various dialog boxes, and in various panels. Click the color picker list arrow, then click the color palette you want.

Another WCAG guideline states that color should never be the only visual means of conveying information. Never refer to a page object solely by the color, like the "red" box.

Figure 1 *Color picker showing color palettes*

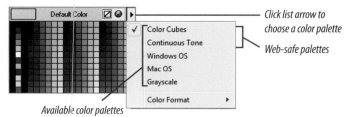

Click list arrow to choose a color palette

Web-safe palettes

Available color palettes

Edit a page title

1. Start Dreamweaver, click the **Site list arrow** on the Files panel, then click **The Striped Umbrella** if necessary.

2. Double-click **index.html** in the Files panel to open The Striped Umbrella home page, click **View** on the Menu bar, then click **Head Content**.

   The Meta icon ⚏, Title icon ⚏, and CSS icon ⚏ are now visible in the head content section. See Figure 2.

3. Click the **Title icon** ⚏ in the head content section.

   The page title The Striped Umbrella appears in the Title text box in the Property inspector.

4. Click after the end of The Striped Umbrella text in the Title text box in the Property inspector, press **[Spacebar]**, type **beach resort and spa, Ft. Eugene, Florida,** press **[Enter]** (Win) or **[return]** (Mac), then click in the title text box.

   Compare your screen with Figure 3. The new title is better, because it incorporates the words "beach resort" and "spa" and the location of the resort—words that potential customers might use as keywords when using a search engine.

TIP You can also change the page title using the Title text box on the Document toolbar. To view hidden text in the Title box, click in the title and scroll using the left and right keyboard arrow keys.

You opened The Striped Umbrella website, opened the home page, viewed the head content section, and changed the page title.

Figure 2 *Viewing the head content*

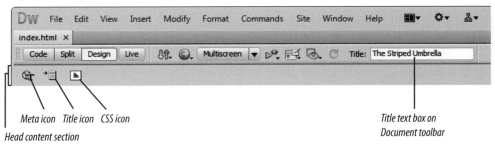

Meta icon   Title icon   CSS icon

Head content section

Title text box on Document toolbar

Figure 3 *Property inspector displaying new page title*

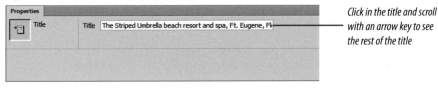

Click in the title and scroll with an arrow key to see the rest of the title

---

DESIGN**TIP**

Designing Appropriate Content for Your Target Audience

When you begin developing the content for your website, you need to decide what content to include and how to arrange each element on each page. You must design the content with the target audience in mind. What is the age group of your audience? What reading level is appropriate? Should you use a formal or informal tone? Should the pages be simple, consisting mostly of text, or rich with images and media files? Evaluate the font sizes, the number and size of images and animations, the reading level, and the amount of technical expertise necessary to navigate your site, and make sure they fit your audience. Usually, the first page that your audience will see when they visit your site is the home page. Design the home page so that users will understand your site's purpose and feel comfortable finding their way around your site's pages.

To ensure that users do not get "lost" in your site, design all the pages with a consistent look and feel. You can use templates and Cascading Style Sheets to maintain a common look for each page. **Templates** are web pages that contain the basic layout for each page in the site, including the location of a company logo or a menu of buttons. You'll learn more about Cascading Style Sheets in Lesson 2 and templates in Chapter 12.

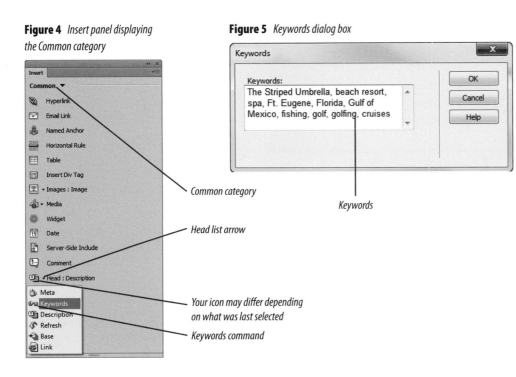

Figure 4 *Insert panel displaying the Common category*

Common category

Head list arrow

Your icon may differ depending on what was last selected

Keywords command

Figure 5 *Keywords dialog box*

Keywords

Enter keywords

1. Click the **Insert panel list arrow**, then on the dropdown menu, click the **Common category** (if it is not already selected).

2. Click the **Head list arrow**, as shown in Figure 4, then click **Keywords**.

TIP Some buttons on the Insert panel include a list arrow indicating that there is a menu of choices available. The button that you selected last will appear on the, Insert panel until you select another.

3. Type **The Striped Umbrella**, **beach resort**, **spa**, **Ft. Eugene**, **Florida**, **Gulf of Mexico**, **fishing**, **golf, golfing, cruises** in the Keywords text box, as shown in Figure 5, then click **OK**

The Keywords icon appears in the head content section, indicating that there are keywords associated with this page. When you click the icon to select it, the keywords appear in the Keywords text box in the Property inspector.

You added keywords relating to the resort to the head content of The Striped Umbrella home page.

DESIGNTIP

Entering Keywords and Descriptions

Search engines use keywords, descriptions, and titles to find pages based on search terms a user enters. Therefore, it is very important to anticipate the search terms your potential customers would use and include these words in the keywords, description, and title. Many search engines display page titles and descriptions in their search results. Some search engines limit the number of keywords that they will index, so make sure you list the most important keywords first. Keep your keywords and descriptions short and concise to ensure that all search engines will include your site. To choose effective keywords, many designers use focus groups to learn which words potential customers or clients might use. A **focus group** is a marketing tool that asks a group of people for feedback about a product, such as the impact of a television ad or the effectiveness of a website design.

Enter a description

1. Click the **Head list arrow** on the Insert panel, then click **Description**.

2. In the Description text box, type **The Striped Umbrella is a full-service resort and spa just steps from the Gulf of Mexico in Ft. Eugene, Florida**.

   Your screen should resemble Figure 6.

3. Click **OK**.

   The description appears in the Description text box in the Property inspector.

4. Click the **Show Code view button** `Code` on the Document toolbar, then click on the page to deselect the text.

   The title, keywords, and description tags appear in the HTML code in the document window, as shown in Figure 7. The order of your lines of code may vary slightly from the figures that show Code view, but this is usually not a problem unless the code is in the wrong section.

   TIP You can enter and edit the title tag and the meta tags directly in the code in Code view.

5. Click the **Show Design view button** `Design` to return to Design view.

   The Description icon 🗐 appears in the head content section, indicating that this page includes a description.

6. Click **View** on the Menu bar, then click **Head Content** to close the head content section.

   You added a description of The Striped Umbrella resort to the head content of the home page. You then viewed the page in Code view and the head content in the HTML code.

Figure 6 *Description dialog box*

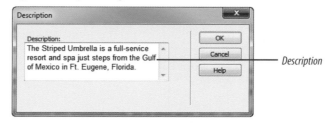

Description

Figure 7 *Head Content displayed in Code view*

Your head content line numbers may differ

Opening Head tag

Title tag

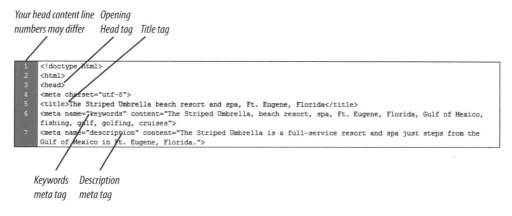

Keywords meta tag

Description meta tag

Using Descriptions for POWDER Authentication

A website description can be stored in an XML file to provide POWDER authentication. **XML** stands for Extensible Markup Language, a type of file that is used to develop customized tags to store information. **POWDER** is the acronym for **Protocol for Web Description Resources**. This is an evaluation system for web pages developed with the World Wide Web Consortium (W3C) that provides summary information about a website. Examples include the date the site was created, the name of the person or company responsible for the content on the site, and a description of the content. It is designed to help users determine if a site would be considered a trustworthy resource of value and interest. It replaces the previous system called PICS, or Platform for Internet Content Selection.

Figure 8 *Page Properties dialog box*

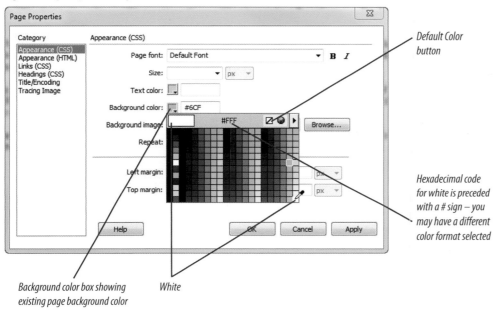

Default Color button

Hexadecimal code for white is preceded with a # sign – you may have a different color format selected

Background color box showing existing page background color

White

Each color is assigned a **hexadecimal RGB value**, a value that represents the amount of red, green, and blue present in the color. For example, white, which is made of equal parts of red, green, and blue, has a hexadecimal value of FFFFFF. This is also called an RGB triplet in hexadecimal format (or a **hex triplet**). Each pair of characters in the hexadecimal value represents the red, green, and blue values. The hexadecimal number system is based on 16, rather than 10 in the decimal number system. Because the hexadecimal number system includes only numbers up to 9, values after 9 use the letters of the alphabet. "A" represents the number 10 in the hexadecimal number system. "F" represents the number 15. The hexadecimal values can be entered in the code using a form of shorthand that shortens the six characters to three characters. For instance: FFFFFF become FFF; 0066CC becomes 06C. The number value for a color is preceded by a pound sign (#) in HTML code.

Set the page background color

1. Click **Modify** on the Menu bar, then click **Page Properties** to open the Page Properties dialog box.

2. Click the **Background color box** ☐ to open the color picker, as shown in Figure 8.

   The background color box in the Page Properties dialog box changes color based on the currently selected color. It is now blue, reflecting the current page background color, rather than the default icon color shown in the step instructions.

3. Click the rightmost color in the bottom row (white), as shown in Figure 8.

4. Click **Apply**, then click **OK**.

   Clicking Apply lets you see the changes you made to the web page without closing the Page Properties dialog box.

TIP If you don't like the color you chose, either click the Default Color button ☐ in the color picker to switch to the default color or click a different color. Not all browsers apply the same default colors for page backgrounds, so if you want your pages to display a specific color for the background, use style sheets to specify which color to use. You can also specify transparent (rather than a color) as a background. Black is generally the default text color used by browsers, but specify that also in your style sheets just to be safe.

   The background color of the web page is now white. The black text against the white background provides a nice contrast and makes the text easy to read.

5. Save your work.

You used the Page Properties dialog box to change the background color to white.

Create, Import, AND FORMAT TEXT

What You'll Do

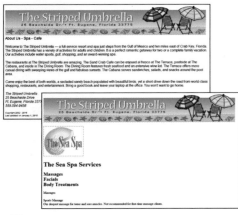

In this lesson, you will create a new page to replace the blank spa page, enter and format text, import text, set text properties, and check the spelling on the Striped Umbrella home page.

Creating and Importing Text

Most information in web pages is presented in the form of text. You can type text directly on a page in Dreamweaver, import, or copy and paste it from another software program. (Macintosh users do not have the option to import text. They must open a text file, copy the text, then paste it into an HTML document.) When using a Windows computer to import text from a Microsoft Word file, it's best to use the Import Word Document command. Not only will the formatting be preserved, but Dreamweaver will generate clean HTML code. **Clean HTML code** is code that does what it is supposed to do without using unnecessary instructions, which take up memory.

When you format text, it is important to keep in mind that your site users must have the same fonts installed on their computers as the fonts you use. Otherwise, the text might appear incorrectly. To avoid font compatibility and accessibly issues, you can use TypeKit, a company acquired by Adobe in 2011, that provides access to web fonts through the Adobe Creative Cloud. TypeKit offers fonts though a subscription-based service that can be read correctly by all browsers and devices. To learn more about TypeKit, go to typekit.com.

QUICK TIP

Some software programs can also convert text into images so that the text retains the same appearance, no matter which fonts are installed. However, text converted into images is no longer editable.

If text does not have a font specified, the default font on the user's computer will be used to display the text. Keep in mind that some fonts might not appear the same on both a Windows and a Macintosh computer. The way fonts are **rendered** (drawn) on the screen differs because Windows and Macintosh computers use different technologies to render them. If you are not using embedded fonts, it is wise to stick to the standard fonts that work well with both systems. Test your pages using both operating systems.

Formatting Text Two Ways: HTML vs. CSS

Because text is more difficult and tiring to read on a computer screen than on a printed page, you should make the text in your website attractive and easy to read. One way to do this is to format text by changing its font, size, and color. Previously web designers used the Property inspector to apply formatting attributes, such as font type, size, color, alignment, and indents. This created HTML tags in the code that directed the way the fonts would appear in a browser. **Tags** are the parts of the code that specify the appearance for all page content when viewed in a browser.

The more accepted method today is to create Cascading Style Sheets (CSS) to format and place web page elements. **Cascading Style Sheets** are sets of formatting attributes that you use to format web pages to provide a consistent presentation for content across the site. Cascading Style Sheets make it easy to separate page content from the page design. The content is placed in the body section on web pages, and the styles are placed in either an external style sheet file or in the page head content. Separating content from design is preferable because editing content and formatting content are two separate tasks. Creating the page content is a separate process from formatting the content. So when you use CSS styles, you can update or change the page content without disturbing the page formatting.

You can apply some formatting without creating styles by using the Bold and Italic HTML tags. You can also use HTML heading tags, which determine the relative size and boldness of text, and which help to show the importance of text relative to the rest of the text on the page.

To apply CSS or HTML formatting, you use the Property inspector, which has a panel for each method: the CSS Property inspector and the HTML Property inspector. You display them by clicking the CSS or the HTML button on the left side of the Property inspector. Some coding options are unique to each one and some coding options are available on both. For instance, HTML heading tags are only available on the HTML Property inspector. Font tags are only available on the CSS Property inspector. The Bold tag is available on both. Regardless of which Property inspector you use, CSS styles will be created when you format page objects.

Because CSS is a lot to learn when you are just beginning, we are going to begin by using HTML tags for formatting. Although they are not the currently preferred formatting method, it's still a good idea to know about HTML tags because you might "inherit" a web page that contains them. Then in Chapter 3, we will use the preferred method, CSS.

> **QUICK TIP**
>
> Even if you use the Property inspector to format text with HTML tags, Dreamweaver automatically creates styles when you apply most formatting attributes.

Changing Fonts

You can format your text with different fonts by choosing a font combination from the Font list in the CSS Property inspector. A **Font-combination** is a set of font choices that specify which fonts a browser should use to display the text on your web page. Font combinations ensure that if one font is not available, the browser will use the next one specified in the font combination. For example, if text is formatted with the font combination Arial, Helvetica, sans serif, the browser will first look on the user's system for Arial. If Arial is not available, then it will look for Helvetica. If Helvetica is not available, then it will look for a sans-serif font to apply to the text. Using fonts within the default settings is wise, because fonts set outside the default settings might not be available on all users' computers.

Changing Font Sizes

There are two ways to change the size of text using the Property inspector. When the CSS option is selected, you can select a numerical value for the size from 9 to 36 pixels (or type a smaller or larger number). Or you can use a size expressed in words from xx-small to larger, which sets the size of selected text relative to other text on the page. On the HTML Property inspector, you do not have font sizes available.

Formatting Paragraphs

The HTML Property inspector displays options to format blocks of text as paragraphs or as different sizes of headings. To format a paragraph as a heading, click anywhere in the paragraph, and then select the heading size you want from the Format list in the HTML Property inspector. The Format list contains six different heading formats. Heading 1 is the largest size, and Heading 6 is the smallest size. Browsers display text formatted as headings in bold, setting them off from paragraphs of text. It is considered good practice to use headings because heading tags give the user an idea of the importance of the heading relative to other text on the page. Text with a level 1 heading would be at a higher importance level than text with a level 2 heading. You can also align paragraphs with the alignment buttons on the CSS Property inspector and indent paragraphs using the Blockquote and Remove Blockquote buttons on the HTML Property inspector.

> **QUICK TIP**
>
> Mixing too many different fonts and formatting attributes on a web page can result in pages that are visually confusing or difficult to read.

Enter text

1. Position the insertion point directly after "want to go home." at the end of the paragraph, press **[Enter]** (Win) or **[return]** (Mac), then type **The Striped Umbrella**.

   Pressing [Enter] (Win) or [return] (Mac) creates a new paragraph.

   TIP If the new text does not assume the formatting attributes as the paragraph above it, click the Show Code and Design views button Split , position the insertion point right after the period after "home", then go back to the page in Design view and insert a new paragraph.

2. Press and hold **[Shift]**, press **[Enter]** (Win) or **[return]** (Mac), then type **25 Beachside Drive**.

   Pressing and holding [Shift] while you press [Enter] (Win) or [return] (Mac) creates a line break. A **line break** places a new line of text on the next line down without creating a new paragraph. Line breaks are useful when you want to add a new line of text directly below the current line of text and keep the same formatting.

3. Add the following text below the 25 Beachside Drive text, using line breaks after each line:

   Ft. Eugene, Florida 33775

   555-594-9458

4. Compare your screen with Figure 9.

   You entered text for the address and telephone number on the home page.

Figure 9 *Entering the address and telephone number on The Striped Umbrella home page*

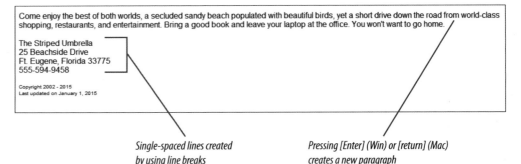

Single-spaced lines created by using line breaks

Pressing [Enter] (Win) or [return] (Mac) creates a new paragraph

TABLE 1: HTML FORMATTING TAGS	
HTML tag	**Represents**
<p> </p>	Opening and closing paragraph tag
 	Line break tag (does not require a closing tag)
<em> </em>	Opening and closing italic (emphasis) tag
<strong> </strong>	Opening and closing bold tag
<u> </u>	Opening and closing underline tag

© Cengage Learning 2013

Using Keyboard Shortcuts

When working with text, the keyboard shortcuts for Cut, Copy, and Paste are very useful. These are [Ctrl][X] (Win) or ⌘ [X] (Mac) for Cut, [Ctrl][C] (Win) or ⌘ [C] (Mac) for Copy, and [Ctrl][V] (Win) or ⌘ [V] (Mac) for Paste. You can view all Dreamweaver keyboard shortcuts using the Keyboard Shortcuts dialog box, which lets you view existing shortcuts for menu commands, tools, or miscellaneous functions, such as copying HTML or inserting an image. You can also create your own shortcuts or assign shortcuts that you are familiar with from using them in other software programs. To view or modify keyboard shortcuts, click the Keyboard Shortcuts command on the Edit menu (Win) or Dreamweaver menu (Mac), then select the shortcut key set you want. Each chapter in this book includes Power User shortcuts, a list of keyboard shortcuts relevant to that chapter.

Figure 10 *Formatting the address on The Striped Umbrella home page*

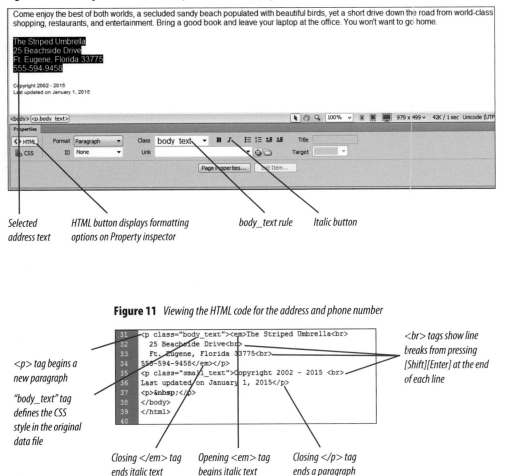

Selected
address text

HTML button displays formatting
options on Property inspector

body_text rule

Italic button

Format text

1. Select the entire address and telephone number, then click the **HTML button** `<> HTML` in the Property inspector (if it is not already selected) to change to the HTML Property inspector, as shown in Figure 10.

2. Click the **Italic button** *I* in the Property inspector to italicize the text, then click after the text to deselect it.

3. Click the **Show Code view button** `Code` to view the HTML code, as shown in Figure 11.

   It is always helpful to learn what the HTML code means. Refer to Table 1 to locate some basic HTML formatting tags. As you edit and format your pages, read the code to see how it appears for each element. The more familiar you are with the code, the more comfortable you will feel with Dreamweaver and web design. A strong knowledge of HTML is a necessary skill for professional web designers.

4. Click the **Show Design view button** `Design` to return to Design view.

5. Save your work, then close the page.

You changed the Property inspector options from CSS to HTML, then formatted the address and phone number for The Striped Umbrella by changing the font style to italic.

Figure 11 *Viewing the HTML code for the address and phone number*

```
31  <p class="body_text"><em>The Striped Umbrella<br>
32     25 Beachside Drive<br>
33     Ft. Eugene, Florida 33775<br>
34  555-594-9458</em></p>
35  <p class="small_text">Copyright 2002 - 2015 <br>
36  Last updated on January 1, 2015</p>
37  <p> </p>
38  </body>
39  </html>
40
```

<p> tag begins a
new paragraph

"body_text" tag
defines the CSS
style in the original
data file

 tags show line
breaks from pressing
[Shift][Enter] at the end
of each line

Closing </em> tag
ends italic text

Opening <em> tag
begins italic text

Closing </p> tag
ends a paragraph

Save an image file in the assets folder

1. Click **File** on the Menu bar, click **New**, click **Blank Page** (if necessary), click **HTML** in the Page Type column, click **<none>** as shown in Figure 12, click the **DocType list arrow**, click **HTML5**, click **Create**, then click the **Show Design view button** Design if necessary.

   A new blank page opens in the Document window.

2. Click **File**, click **Save As**, navigate to your Striped Umbrella site root folder, then save the file as **spa.html**, overwriting the existing (blank) spa.html file.

3. Click the **Insert bar menu**, click **Common**, click the **Images list arrow**, then click **Image**.

   The Select Image Source dialog box opens, as shown in Figure 13.

4. Browse to and open the website assets folder, double-click **su_banner.gif**, type **The Striped Umbrella banner** in the Image Tag Accessibility Attributes dialog box, then click **OK**.

   The banner appears at the top of the new page. You will learn more about the Image Tag Accessiblity Attributes dialog box in Chapter 4.

   TIP You can also drag the banner image from the Files panel onto the page since it is already saved in the website assets folder.

5. Click to the right of the image to deselect it, press **[Shift][Enter]** (Win) or **[Shift][Return]** (Mac), repeat Step 3 to open the Select Image Source dialog box, then navigate to the assets folder in your chapter_2 data files folder.

6. Double-click **sea_spa_logo.png**, type **The Sea Spa logo** in the Image Tag Accessibility Attributes dialog box, then click **OK**.

   (continued)

Figure 12 *Creating a new HTML document with the New Document dialog box*

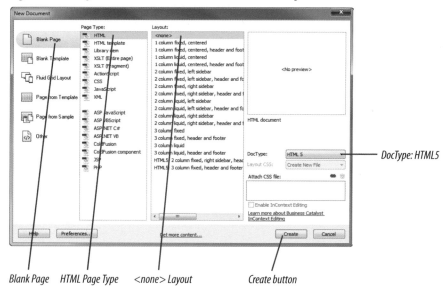

Blank Page   HTML Page Type   <none> Layout   Create button

DocType: HTML5

Figure 13 *Selecting the source file for the banner*

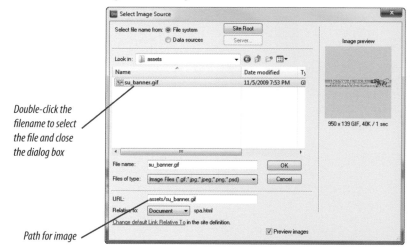

Double-click the filename to select the file and close the dialog box

Path for image

Figure 14 *Image file added to the Striped Umbrella assets folder*

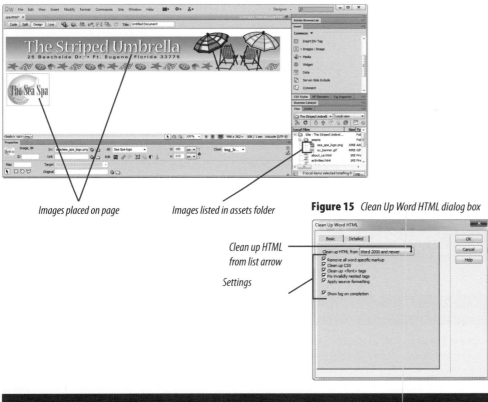

Images placed on page *Images listed in assets folder*

Figure 15 *Clean Up Word HTML dialog box*

Clean up HTML
from list arrow

Settings

Choosing Filenames for Web Pages

When you choose a name for a web page, you should use a short, simple descriptive name that reflects the contents of the page. For example, if the page is about your company's products, you could name it products.html. You should also follow some general rules for naming web pages, such as naming the home page index.html. Most file servers look for the file named index.html or default.html to use as the initial page for a website. Do not use spaces, special characters, or punctuation in filenames for files or folders that you will use in your site. Use underscores rather than spaces for readability; for example: use sea_spa_logo.jpg rather than sea spa logo.jpg. Just to be totally safe for all file servers, use only letters, numbers, or underscores in file or folder names. Many designers also avoid the use of uppercase letters.

---

7. Save your work.

A copy of the sea_spa_logo.png file appears in the assets folder, along with the banner image, as shown in Figure 14.

You created a new file to replace the blank spa file, inserted the website banner image, then inserted the spa logo under the banner image and saved it in the website assets folder.

Import text

1. Click to place the insertion point to the right of the spa graphic on the spa.html page.

2. Click **File** on the Menu bar, point to **Import**, click **Word Document**, navigate to the **chapter_2 folder** from the location where you store your Data Files, then double-click **spa.doc** (Win); or double-click **spa.doc** from where you store your Data Files, select all, copy, close spa.doc, then paste the copied text on the spa page in Dreamweaver (Mac).

3. Click **Commands** on the Menu bar, then click **Clean Up Word HTML**.

TIP If a dialog box appears stating that Dreamweaver was unable to determine the version of Word used to generate this document, click OK, click the Clean up HTML from list arrow, then choose the Word 2000 and newer version of Word if it isn't already selected.

4. Make sure each check box in the Clean Up Word HTML dialog box is checked, as shown in Figure 15, click **OK**, then click **OK** again to close the results window.

You imported a Word document, then used the Clean Up Word HTML command.

Set text properties

1. Select the Common category on the Insert panel if necessary, then scroll up the page and select the text "The Sea Spa Services."

2. Click the **Format list arrow** in the HTML Property inspector, then click **Heading 1**.

   The Heading 1 format is applied to the paragraph. Even a single word is considered a paragraph if there is a paragraph break (also known as a hard return) after it. The HTML code for a Heading 1 tag is <h1>. The tag is then closed with </h1>. For headings, the level of the heading tag follows the h, so the code for a Heading 2 tag is <h2>.

3. Select the text **Massages**, **Facials**, and **Body Treatments**, click the **Format list arrow** in the HTML Property inspector, click **Heading 2**, then click outside the heading to deselect the text.

   The H1 and H2 tags make the text a little large for the page, but it is more in keeping with semantic markup to begin with level 1 headings and work down. **Semantic markup** means coding to emphasize meaning. You can change the size of the text for each heading using style sheets if you want to change the default settings. We will do this in Chapter 3.

4. Click after the word "Treatments", insert a line break, click the **Show Code and Design views button** Split on the Document toolbar, then compare your screen to Figure 16.

   The word "Massages" after the words "Body Treatments" may be in a different position on your screen. Figure 16 was sized down, so your page will be much wider than the figure shows.

   (continued)

Figure 16 *Viewing the heading tags in Show Code and Design views*

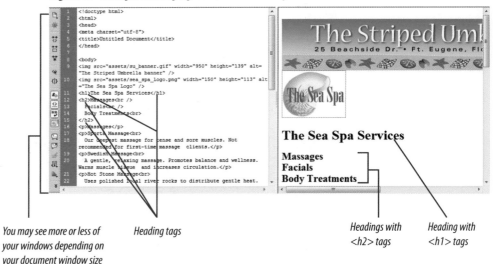

You may see more or less of your windows depending on your document window size

Heading tags

Headings with <h2> tags

Heading with <h1> tags

Importing and Linking Microsoft Office Documents (Windows)

Adobe makes it easy to transfer data between Microsoft Office documents and Dreamweaver web pages. When importing a Word or Excel document, click File on the Menu bar, point to Import, then click either Word Document or Excel Document. Select the file you want to import, then click the Formatting list arrow to choose among importing Text only; Text with structure (paragraphs, lists, and tables); Text, structure, basic formatting (bold, italic); or Text, structure, full formatting (bold, italic, styles) before you click Open. The option you choose depends on the importance of the original structure and formatting. Always use the Clean Up Word HTML command after importing a Word file.

You can also create a link to a Word or Excel document on your web page. To do so, browse to locate the Word or Excel document you want to add as a link, then drag the file name to the location on the page where you would like the link to appear. (If the document is located outside the site, you can browse for it using the Site list arrow on the Files panel, Windows Explorer, or Mac Finder.) Next, select the Create a link option button in the Insert Document dialog box, then save the file in your site root folder so it will be uploaded when you publish your site. If it is not uploaded, the link will be broken.

Figure 17 *Check Spelling dialog box*

Facials

Revitalizing Facial
A light massage with a customized essential oil blend that moisturizes the skin and restores circulation.

Gentlemen's Facial
A cleansing facial that restores a healthy glow. Includes a neck and shoulder massage.

Milk Mask
A soothing mask that softens and moisturizes the face. Leaves your skin looking

Body Treatments

Salt Glow
Imported sea salts are massaged into the skin, exfoliating and cleansing the pores

Herbal Wrap
Organic lavender blooms create a detoxifying and calming treatment to relieve ac

Seaweed Body Wrap
Seaweed is a natural detoxifying agent that also helps improve circulation.

Call The Sea Spa desk for prices and reservations. Any of our services can be p
until 9:00 p.m. Call 555-594-9458, extension 39.

Check Spelling

Word not found in dictionary:
masage.   Add to Personal

Change to: massage.
Suggestions: massage.   Ignore
            manage.
            ma-sage.   Change
            mas-age.
            mas age.   Ignore All
            ma sage.
            sage.   Change All

                              Close   Help

Click "Change" to correct spelling

Checking for Spelling Errors

It is very important to check for spelling and grammatical errors before publishing a page. A page that is published with errors will cause the user to immediately judge the site as unprofessional and carelessly made, and the accuracy of the page content will be in question. If you have text in a word processing file that you plan to import into Dreamweaver, check the spelling in the word processor first. Then check the spelling in the imported text again in Dreamweaver. This allows you to add words such as proper names to the Dreamweaver dictionary so the program will not flag them again. Click the Add to Personal button in the Check Spelling dialog box to add a new word to the dictionary. Even though you might have checked a page using the Check Spelling feature, you still must proofread the content yourself to catch usage errors such as misuse of "to," "too," and "two." Accuracy in both content and delivery is critical.

Tip: If your <h1> tag is before the image tag rather than before "The Sea Spa Services" heading, cut and paste it to match the code in Figure 16.

You applied two heading formats, then viewed the HTML code.

Check spelling

1. Click the **Show Design view button** Design to return to Design view.

2. Place the insertion point in front of the text "The Sea Spa Services".

   It is a good idea to start a spelling check at the top of the document because Dreamweaver searches from the insertion point down. If your insertion point is in the middle of the document, you will receive a message asking if you want to check the rest of the document. Starting from the beginning saves time.

3. Click **Commands** on the Menu bar, then click **Check Spelling**.

   The word "masage" is highlighted on the page as a misspelled word and suggestions are listed to correct it in the Check Spelling dialog box, as shown in Figure 17.

4. Click **massage.** in the Suggestions list if necessary, then click **Change**.

   The word is corrected on the page. If the Check Spelling dialog box highlights "exfoliating" click Ignore.

5. Click **OK** to close the Dreamweaver dialog box stating that the Spelling Check is completed.

6. Save and close the spa page.

You checked the spa page for spelling errors.

Add Links
TO WEB PAGES

What You'll Do

In this lesson, you will open the home page and add links to the menu bar that link to the About Us, Spa, Cafe, and Activities pages. You will then insert an email link at the bottom of the page.

Adding Links to Web Pages

Links, or hyperlinks, provide the real power for web pages. Links make it possible for users to navigate all the pages in a website and to connect to other pages anywhere on the web. Users are more likely to return to websites that have a user-friendly navigation structure. Users also enjoy websites that have interesting links to other web pages or other websites.

To add links to a web page, first select the text or image that you want to serve as a link, and then, in the Link text box in the Property inspector, specify a path to the page to which you want to link.

When you create links on a web page, it is important to avoid **broken links**, or links that cannot find their intended destinations. You can accidentally cause a broken link by typing the incorrect address for the link in the Link text box. Broken links can be caused by companies merging, going out of business, or simply moving their website addresses.

In addition to adding links to your pages, you should provide a **point of contact**, or a place on a web page that provides users with a means of contacting the company. A common point of contact is a **mailto: link**, which is an email address that users with questions or problems can use to contact someone at the company's headquarters.

Using Menu Bars

A **menu bar**, or **navigation bar**, is an area on a web page that contains links to the main pages of a website. Menu bars are usually located at the top or side of each page in a website and can be created with text, images, or a combination of the two. Menu bars are the backbone of a website's navigation structure, which includes all navigation aids for moving around a website. To make navigating a website as easy as possible, you should place menu bars in the same position on each page. The web page in Figure 18 shows a menu bar that contains a set of main links with additional links that appear when a user moves a mouse pointer over (known as a rollover) each main link. You can create a simple menu bar by typing text representing each of your site's pages at the top of your web page, formatting the text, and then adding links to each of the text references. It is always a good idea to provide plain text links like this for accessibility, regardless of the type of navigation structure you choose to use. For example, if you use Flash for your navigation links, it is a good idea to include a duplicate set of text with links to the same pages. Most websites typically have links at the bottom of each page for accessing company contact information, terms of use, copyright, and terms of use statements.

Following WCAG Accessibility for Navigation

The WCAG Guideline 2.4 lists ways to ensure that all users can successfully and easily navigate a website. It states: "Provide ways to help users navigate, find content, and determine where they are." Suggestions include limiting the number of links on a page, using techniques to allow users to quickly access different sections of a page, and making sure that links are readable and easily distinguishable.

Figure 18 *The CIA website*
Central Intelligence Agency website – www.cia.gov

Additional links appear when mouse pointer rolls over a main link

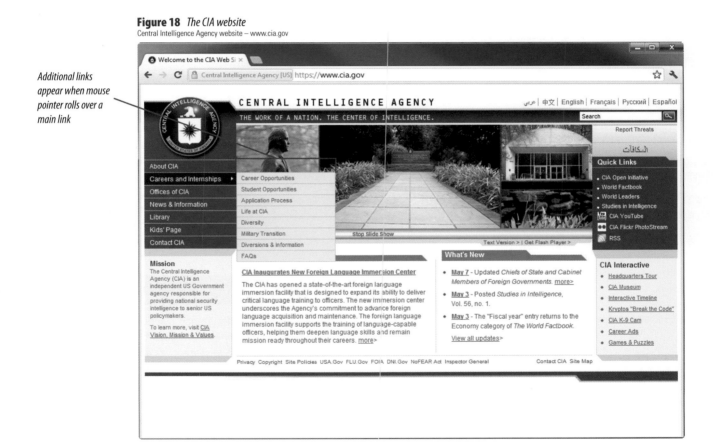

Create a menu bar

1. Open **index.html**.
2. Position the insertion point to the left of "A" in About Us, then drag to select **About Us - Spa - Cafe**.
3. Type **Home - About Us - Spa - Cafe - Activities**, as shown in Figure 19.

   These five text labels will serve as a menu bar. You will add the links later.

You created a new menu bar using text, replacing the original menu bar.

Insert a horizontal rule

1. Click in front of the word "Welcome".
2. Click **Horizontal Rule** in the Common category on the Insert panel to insert a horizontal rule between the menu bar and the first paragraph.

   A horizontal rule is a line used to separate page elements or to organize information on a page.
3. Compare your screen to Figure 20, then save your work.

TIP An asterisk after the filename in the title bar indicates that you have altered the page since you last saved it. After you save your work, the asterisk no longer appears.

You added a horizontal rule to separate the menu bar from the page content.

Figure 19 *Viewing the new menu bar*

Figure 20 *Inserting a horizontal rule*

Asterisk indicates page has not been saved

Horizontal Rule command

Horizontal rule

Properties for horizontal rule

Preventing Data Loss

It is always a good idea to save your files frequently. A good practice is to save a file after you have completed a successful edit, before you attempt a difficult edit, and when you have finished working on an open file. It is also a good idea to close a file when you are not working on it. Having unnecessary files open can be a distraction to your work flow. Do not open files from a different website other than the open site in the Files panel, or you might accidentally save them in the wrong folder!

Developing a Web Page

Figure 21 *Selecting text for the Home link*

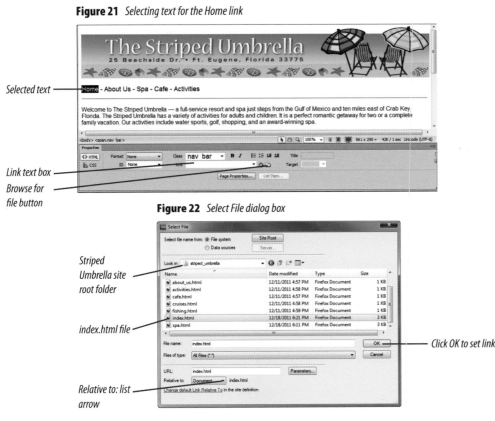

Selected text

Link text box

Browse for
file button

Figure 22 *Select File dialog box*

Striped
Umbrella site
root folder

index.html file

Relative to: list
arrow

Click OK to set link

Figure 23 *Links added to menu bar*

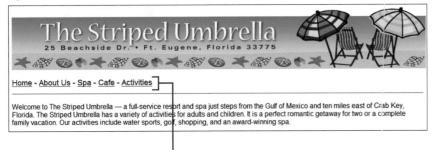

Menu bar with links added

Add links to web pages

1. Double-click **Home** to select it, as shown in Figure 21.

2. Click the **Browse for File button** 📁 next to the Link text box in the HTML Property inspector, then navigate to the striped_umbrella local site folder if necessary.

3. Verify that the link is set Relative to Document in the Relative to: list.

4. Click **index.html** as shown in Figure 22, click **OK** (Win) or **Open** (Mac), then click anywhere on the page to deselect Home.

TIP Your file listing might differ depending on your view settings.

Home now appears in blue with an underline, indicating it is a link. If users click the Home link, a new page will not open, because the link is on the home page. It might seem odd to create a link to the same page on which the link appears, but this will be helpful when you copy the menu bar to other pages in the site. Always provide users a link to the home page.

5. Repeat Steps 1–4 to create links for About Us, Spa, Cafe, and Activities to their corresponding pages in the striped_umbrella site folder.

6. When you finish adding the links that link to the other four pages, deselect all, then compare your screen to Figure 23.

You created a link for each of the five menu bar elements to their respective web pages in The Striped Umbrella website.

Create an email link

1. Place the insertion point after the last digit in the telephone number, then insert a line break.

2. Click **Email Link** in the Common category on the Insert panel to insert an email link.

3. Type **Club Manager** in the Text text box, type **manager@stripedumbrella.com** in the Email text box, as shown in Figure 24, then click **OK** to close the Email Link dialog box.

TIP If the text does not retain the formatting from the previous line use the Edit, Undo command to undo Steps 1–3. Switch to Code view and place the insertion point immediately to the right of the telephone number, then repeat the steps again in Design view.

4. Save your work.

The text "mailto:manager@stripedumbrella.com" appears in the Link text box in the HTML Property inspector. See Figure 25. When a user clicks this link, a blank email message window opens in the user's default email software, where the user can type a message.

TIP You must enter the correct email address in the Email text box for the link to work. However, you can enter any descriptive name, such as customer service or Bob Smith in the Text text box. You can also enter the email address as the text if you want to show the actual email address on the web page.

You inserted an email link to serve as a point of contact for The Striped Umbrella.

Figure 24 *Email Link dialog box*

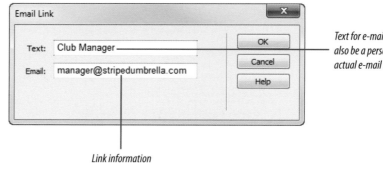

Text for e-mail link on the page (this could also be a person's name or position or the actual e-mail link)

Link information

Figure 25 *mailto: link on the Property inspector*

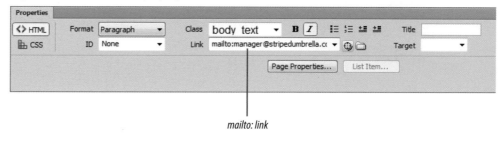

mailto: link

Figure 26 *The Assets panel URL category*

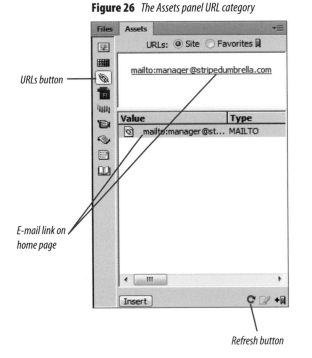

URLs button

E-mail link on home page

Refresh button

View the email link in the Assets panel

1. Click the **Assets panel tab** to view the Assets panel.

2. Click the **URLs button** to display the URLs in the website.

3. Click the **Refresh button** at the bottom of the Assets panel, if necessary, to view the code for the link, then compare your screen to Figure 26.

   URL stands for **Uniform Resource Locator**. The URLs listed in the Assets panel show all of the **external links**, or links pointing outside of the website. An email link is outside the website, so it is an external link. You will learn more about URLs and links in Chapter 5. The links you created to the site pages are internal links (inside the website), and are not listed in the Assets panel.

4. Click the **Files panel tab** to view the Files panel.

You viewed the email link on the home page in the Assets panel.

Use the History
PANEL AND EDIT CODE

What You'll Do

In this lesson, you will use the History panel to undo formatting changes you make to a horizontal rule. You will then use the Code Inspector to view the HTML code for the horizontal rule. You will also insert a date object and then view it using the Code Inspector.

Using the History Panel

Throughout the process of creating a web page, you will make mistakes along the way. Fortunately, you have a tool named the History panel to undo your mistakes. The **History panel** records each editing and formatting task you perform and displays them in a list in the order in which you completed them. Each task listed in the History panel is called a **step**. You can drag the **slider** on the left side of the History panel to undo or redo steps, as shown in Figure 27. You can also click in the bar to the left of a step to undo all steps below it. You click the step to select it. By default, the History panel records 20 steps. You can change the number of steps the History panel records in the

General category of the Preferences dialog box. However, keep in mind that setting this number too high will require additional memory and could affect Dreamweaver's performance.

Viewing HTML Code in the Code Inspector

If you enjoy writing code, you occasionally might want to make changes to web pages by writing the code rather than using the panels and tools in Design view. Often it is actually easier to make editing or formatting corrections in the code. You can view the code in Dreamweaver using Code view, Code and Design views, or the Code Inspector. The **Code Inspector**,

Understanding Other History Panel Features

Dragging the slider up and down in the History panel is a quick way to undo or redo steps. However, the History panel offers much more. It has the capability to "memorize" certain tasks and consolidate them into one command. This is a useful feature for steps that you perform repetitively on web pages. The History panel does not show steps performed in the Files panel or any program-wide changes, such as editing preferences or changing panel arrangements.

shown in Figure 28, is a separate window that displays the current page in Code view. The advantage of using the Code Inspector is that you can see a full-screen view of your page in Design view while viewing the underlying code in a floating window that you can resize and position wherever you want.

You can add advanced features, such as JavaScript functions, to web pages by copying and pasting code from one page to another using the Code Inspector. A **JavaScript** function is a block of code that adds dynamic content such as rollovers or interactive forms to a web page. A **rollover** is a special effect that changes the appearance of an object when the mouse moves over it.

Figure 27 *The History panel*

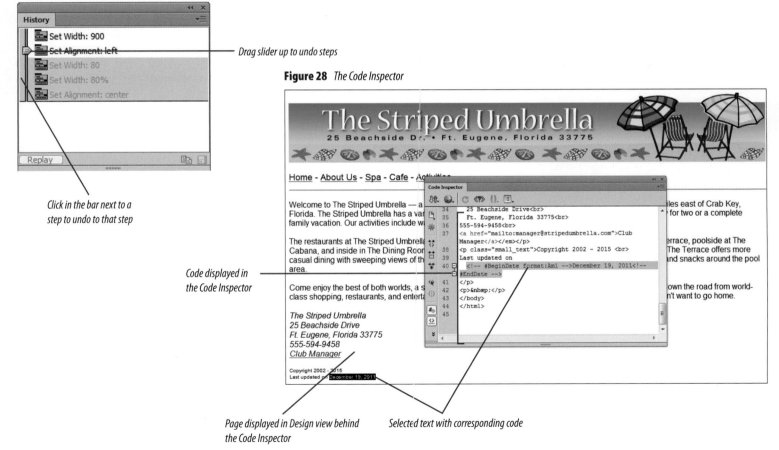

Drag slider up to undo steps

Click in the bar next to a step to undo to that step

Figure 28 *The Code Inspector*

Code displayed in the Code Inspector

Page displayed in Design view behind the Code Inspector

Selected text with corresponding code

Use the History panel

1. Click **Window** on the Menu bar, then click **History**.

   The History panel opens and displays steps you have recently performed.

2. Click the **Panel options button**, ⬛ click **Clear History**, as shown in Figure 29, then click **Yes** to close the warning box.

3. Select the **horizontal rule** on the index page.

   The Property inspector shows the properties of the selected horizontal rule.

4. Click the **W text box** in the Property inspector, type **900**, click the **Align list arrow**, click **Left**, then compare your Property inspector to Figure 30.

   Horizontal rule widths can be set in pixels or as a percent of the width of the window. If the width is expressed in pixels, the code will only show the number, without the word "pixels". Pixels is understood as the default width setting.

5. Using the Property inspector, change the W text box value to **80**, change the measurement unit to **%**, click the **Align list arrow**, then click **Center**.

6. Drag the **slider** on the History panel up to Set Alignment: left, as shown in Figure 31.

   The bottom three steps in the History panel appear gray, indicating that these steps have been undone.

7. Right-click (Win) or Control-click (Mac) the **History panel title bar**, then click **Close** to close the History panel.

   You formatted the horizontal rule, made changes to it, then used the History panel to undo some of the changes.

Figure 29 *Clearing the History panel*

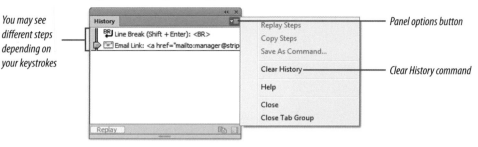

You may see different steps depending on your keystrokes

Panel options button

Clear History command

Figure 30 *Property inspector settings for horizontal rule*

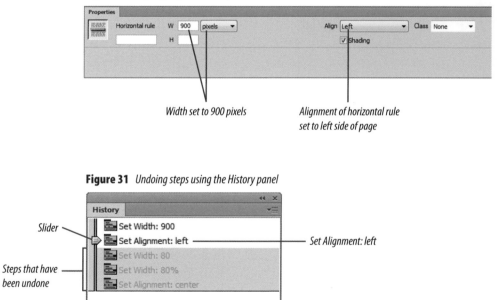

Width set to 900 pixels

Alignment of horizontal rule set to left side of page

Figure 31 *Undoing steps using the History panel*

Slider

Set Alignment: left

Steps that have been undone

Figure 32 *Viewing the View Options menu*

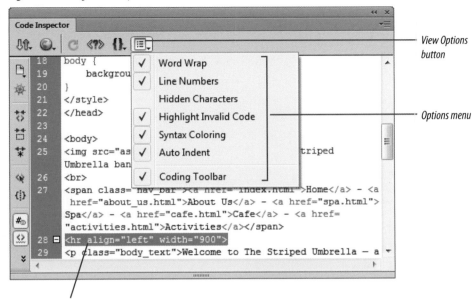

View Options button

Options menu

Code for Horizontal rule

1. Click the **horizontal rule** to select it if necessary, click **Window** on the Menu bar, then click **Code Inspector**.

   Because the horizontal rule on the page is selected, the corresponding code is highlighted in the Code Inspector.

   TIP You can also press [F10](Win) or [fn][option][F10] (Mac) to display the Code Inspector.

2. Click the **View Options button** 🔲. on the Code Inspector toolbar to display the View Options menu, then if **Word Wrap** is unchecked, click it once to activate it.

   The Word Wrap feature forces text to stay within the confines of the Code Inspector window, allowing you to read without scrolling sideways.

3. Repeat Step 2 to activate Line Numbers, Highlight Invalid Code, Syntax Coloring, Auto Indent, and Coding Toolbar as shown in Figure 32.

4. Select **900** in the horizontal rule width code, type **950**, then press **[Tab]**.

You changed the width of the horizontal rule by changing the code in the Code Inspector.

POWER USER SHORTCUTS	
To do this:	**Use this shortcut:**
Select All	[Ctrl][A] (Win) or ⌘ [A] (Mac)
Copy	[Ctrl][C] (Win) or ⌘ [C] (Mac)
Cut	[Ctrl][X] (Win) or ⌘ [X] (Mac)
Paste	[Ctrl][V] (Win) or ⌘ [V] (Mac)
Line Break	[Shift][Enter] (Win) or [Shift][return] (Mac)
Show or hide the Code Inspector	[F10] (Win) or [fn][option][F10] (Mac)
Preview in browser	[F12] (Win) or [fn][option][F12] (Mac)
Check spelling	[Shift][F7] (Win) or [fn][Shift][F7] (Mac)

© Cengage Learning 2013

Use the Reference panel

1. With the horizontal rule still selected, click the **Reference button** on the Code Inspector toolbar, as shown in Figure 33, to open the Results Tab Group below the Property inspector, with the Reference panel visible.

TIP If the horizontal rule is not still selected, you will not see the horizontal rule description in the Reference panel.

2. Read the information about horizontal rules in the Reference panel, as shown in Figure 34, right-click in an empty area of the **Results Tab Group title bar**, then click **Close Tab Group** (Win) or click the **Panel options button** then click **Close Tab Group** (Mac and Win) to close the Results Tab Group.

   The preferred method of formatting and positioning horizontal rules is to use CSS, rather than use the Property inspector. After you learn how to use CSS, you will then use them to format your horizontal rules.

3. Close the Code Inspector.

You read information about horizontal rule settings in the Reference panel.

Figure 33 *Reference button on the Code Inspector toolbar*

Reference button

Figure 34 *Viewing the Reference panel*

Information on <HR>
(horizontal rule tag)

Developing a Web Page

Figure 35 *Insert Date dialog box*

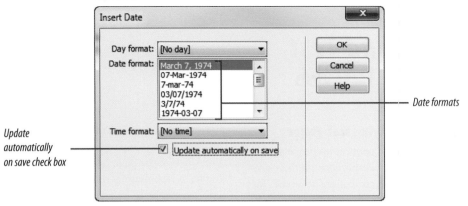

Update automatically on save check box

Date formats

Insert a date object

1. Scroll down the page, if necessary, to select **January 1, 2015**, then press **[Delete]** (Win) or **[delete]** (Mac).

2. Click **Date** in the Common category in the Insert panel, then click **March 7, 1974** if necessary in the Date format list.

3. Check the **Update automatically on save check box**, as shown in Figure 35, click **OK**, then deselect the text.

4. Change to Code and Design views.

   The code has changed to reflect the date object, which is set to today's date, as shown in Figure 36. (Your date will be different.) The new code is highlighted with a light yellow background, indicating that it is a date object, automatically coded by Dreamweaver, rather than a date that has been manually typed on the page by the designer or developer.

5. Return to Design view, then save the page.

You inserted a date object that will be updated automatically when you open and save the home page.

Figure 36 *Viewing the date object code*

Code for date object (if the date object is selected, your code will be highlighted in blue instead of yellow)

```
39   Last updated on
40     <!-- #BeginDate format:Am1 -->December 19, 2011<!--
     #EndDate -->
41   </p>
42   <p> </p>
43   </body>
44   </html>
```

Inserting Comments

It is easy to insert comments into HTML code in Dreamweaver. Comments can provide helpful information describing portions of the code, such as a JavaScript function. You can create comments in any Dreamweaver view, but you must turn on Invisible Elements to see them in Design view. Use the Edit (Win) or Dreamweaver (Mac) > Preferences > Invisible Elements > Comments command to enable viewing of comments; then use the View > Visual Aids > Invisible Elements command to display them on the page. To create a comment, select the Common category on the Insert panel, click Comment, type a comment in the Comment dialog box, and then click OK. Comments are not visible in browser windows.

Modify and Test
WEB PAGES

What You'll Do

In this lesson, you will preview the home page in the browser to check for typographical errors, grammatical errors, broken links, and overall appearance. After previewing, you will make slight formatting adjustments to the page to improve its appearance.

Testing and Modifying Web Pages

Testing web pages is a continuous process. You never really finish a website, because there are always additions and corrections to make. As you add and modify pages, you must test each page as part of the development process. The best way to test a web page is to preview it in Live view or in a browser window to make sure that all text and image elements appear the way you expect them to. You should also test your links to make sure they work properly. You need to proofread your text to make sure it contains all the necessary information for the page with no typographical or grammatical errors. Designers typically view a page in a browser, return to Dreamweaver to make

necessary changes, and then view the page in a browser again. They repeat this process many times before the page is ready for publishing. In fact, it is sometimes difficult to stop making improvements to a page and move on to another project. You need to strike a balance among quality, creativity, and productivity.

Testing a Web Page Using Different Browsers and Screen Sizes

Because users access the Internet using a wide variety of computer systems, it is important to design your pages so that all browsers and screen sizes can display them well. You should test your pages using different browsers and a wide variety of screen sizes to ensure the best

DESIGN**TIP**

Using "Under Construction" or "Come Back Later" Pages

Many people are tempted to insert an unfinished page as a placeholder for a page that they intend to finish later. Rather than have real content, these pages usually contain text or an image that indicates the page is not finished, or "under construction." You should not publish a web page that has a link to an unfinished page. It is frustrating to click a link for a page you want to open only to find an "under construction" note or image displayed. You want to make the best possible impression on your users. If you cannot complete a page before publishing it, at least provide enough information on it to make it "worth the trip."

view of your page by the most people possible. Most web users today use a desktop computer with a screen resolution above 1024 by 768. Very few users use a resolution below this. So design your pages for this higher resolution. However, you'll also need to accommodate users who will view your pages with laptops, tablets, and mobile phones, so make sure your pages look good at these sizes, as well. To view your page using different screen sizes, click the Window Size pop-up menu on the status bar, then choose the setting you want to use.

QUICK TIP NEW

You can also use the Mobile size, Tablet size, and Desktop size buttons (introduced in Dreamweaver version 5.5) on the status bar to view your pages.

To view your pages using several different browsers, click the Preview/Debug in Browser button on the Menu bar, click Edit Browser List, then use the Add icon to add additional browsers installed on your computer to the list. You can also designate which browser to use as the default browser, the browser which opens when users press the F12 key. Remember also to check your pages using Windows and Macintosh platforms. Some page elements such as fonts, colors, table borders, layers, and horizontal rules might not appear consistently in both.

Using Adobe BrowserLab

Adobe BrowserLab is a tool that checks pages by simulating multiple browsers and

platforms. You can use it to test your pages in browsers that are not installed on your computer. For example, if you are using a PC, you can use BrowserLab to test your pages with Apple Safari. BrowserLab is a great way to test your pages with multiple browsers and multiple versions of the same browser, which would be impossible otherwise without using multiple computers. You can access BrowserLab through the Adobe BrowserLab panel or the Preview/Debug in Browser button. To use BrowserLab, you need an Adobe ID. Visit the Adobe website to obtain an Adobe ID.

NEW Testing a Web Page as Rendered in a Mobile Device

Dreamweaver has another preview feature (introduced in Dreamweaver version 5.5) that allows you to see what a page would look like if it were viewed on a mobile hand-held device, such as a phone or tablet. This is a new feature called the **Multiscreen Preview**. The Multiscreen button is located on the Document toolbar. With the Multiscreen Preview, you can view a page in three device sizes in one window, as shown in Figure 37. The Viewport Sizes button is used to change the default size settings to sizes of your choice.

Figure 37 *Using the Multiscreen Preview*

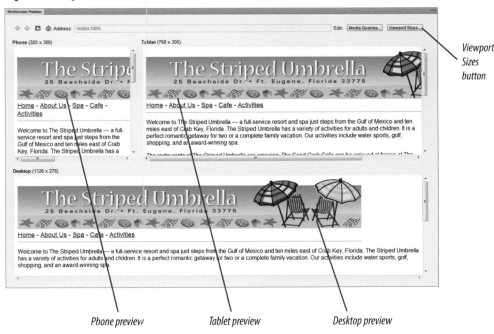

Viewport Sizes button

Phone preview   *Tablet preview*   *Desktop preview*

Modify a web page

1. Click the **Tablet size button** 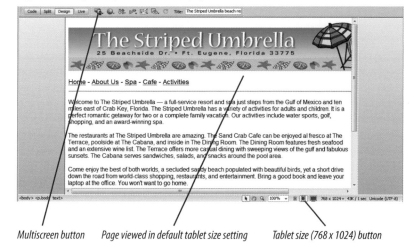 on the status bar to see how the page would appear on a tablet using the default tablet settings, as shown in Figure 38.

   A user viewing this page on a tablet will be forced to use the horizontal scroll bar to view the entire page.

   NEW As you develop your pages with CSS, you can use **Media Queries** (introduced in Dreamweaver version 5.5) to detect which type of device is displaying your pages. By customizing your style sheets for different screen size and orientations, you can control how your pages will look when viewed with different devices. We will learn more about Media Queries in Chapter 8.

2. Replace the period after the last sentence, "You won't want to go home." with an exclamation point.

3. Click the **Multiscreen button** on the Document toolbar, then click **Full Size**.

   The page returns to full Design view.

4. Save your work.

   You viewed the home page using two different window sizes and made a simple edit.

Figure 38 *Using Tablet preview to view the page*

Multiscreen button   Page viewed in default tablet size setting   Tablet size (768 x 1024) button

---

Using Smart Design Principles in Web Page Layout

As you view your pages in the browser, take a critical look at the symmetry of the page. Is it balanced? Are there too many images compared to text, or vice versa? Does everything "heavy" seem to be on the top or bottom of the page, or do the page elements seem to balance with the weight evenly distributed between the top, bottom, and sides? Use design principles to create a site-wide consistency for your pages. Horizontal symmetry means that the elements are balanced across the page. Vertical symmetry means that they are balanced down the page. Diagonal symmetry balances page elements along the invisible diagonal line of the page. Radial symmetry runs from the center of the page outward, like the petals of a flower. These principles all deal with balance; however, too much balance is not good, either. Sometimes it adds interest to place page elements a little off center or to have an asymmetric layout. Color, white space, text, and images should all complement each other and provide a natural flow across and down the page. The **rule of thirds**—dividing a page into nine squares like a tic-tac-toe grid—states that interest is increased when your focus is on one of the intersections in the grid. The most important information should be at the top of the page where it is visible without scrolling, or "above the fold," as they say in the newspaper business.

Figure 39 *Viewing The Striped Umbrella home page in the Firefox browser*

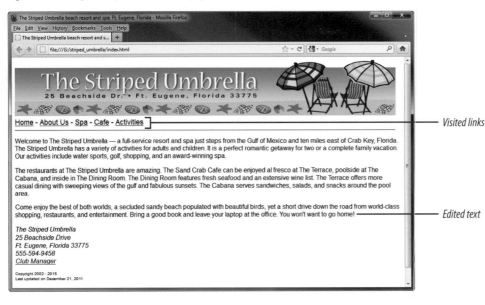

Visited links

Edited text

1. Click the **Preview/Debug in browser button** ⊙ on the Document toolbar, then choose your browser from the menu that opens.

   The Striped Umbrella home page opens in your default browser.

2. Click each link on the menu bar, then after each click, use the Back button on the browser toolbar to return to the home page.

   Pages with no content at this point will appear as blank pages. Compare your screen to Figure 39. The links in Figure 39 have all been clicked, which made them visited links. So they appear in purple rather than blue, the color of unvisited links.

3. Close your browser window, then close all open pages in Dreamweaver.

You viewed The Striped Umbrella home page in your browser and tested each link on the menu bar.

DESIGNTIP

Choosing a Window Size

Today, most users use a screen resolution of 1024 × 768 or higher. Because of this, more content can be displayed at one time on a computer monitor. Some people might use their whole screen to view pages on the Internet. Others might choose to allocate a smaller area of their screen to the browser window. In other words, people tend to use their "screen real estate" in different ways. The ideal web page will not be so small that it tries to spread out over a larger screen size or so large that the user has to use horizontal scroll bars to read the page content. The WCAG guideline 1.4.8 states that " ... Text can be resized without assistive technology up to 200 percent in a way that does not require the user to scroll horizontally to read a line of text on a full-screen window." Achieving the best balance and meeting accessibility guidelines is one of the design decisions that you must make during the planning process.

Create head content and set page properties.

1. Open the Blooms & Bulbs website.
2. Open the index page and view the head content.
3. Edit the page title so it reads **Blooms & Bulbs - Your Complete Garden Center**.
4. Insert the following keywords: **garden, plants, nursery, flowers, landscape, bulbs, Blooms & Bulbs, Alvin, Texas**.
5. Insert the following description: **Blooms & Bulbs is a premier supplier of plants, trees, and shrubs for both professional and home gardeners**.
6. Switch to Code view to view the HTML code for the head content, then switch back to Design view.
7. Open the Page Properties dialog box to view the current page properties.
8. Change the background color to a color of your choice and use the Apply button to view the change.
9. Change the background color to white, then save your work.

Create, import, and format text.

1. Create a new paragraph after the second paragraph of text and type the following text, inserting a line break after each line.
   Blooms & Bulbs
   Highway 43 South
   Alvin, Texas 77511
   555-248-0806
2. Verify that the HTML button is selected in the Property inspector, and select it if it is not.
3. Italicize the name, address and phone number lines.

4. Change to Code view to view the formatting code for the italicized text.
5. Return to Design view, save your work, hide the head content, then close the home page.
6. Create a new blank HTML5 file and save it as **tips.html** in the Blooms & Bulbs website, overwriting the existing file.
7. Insert the blooms & bulbs banner (from your website assets folder) at the top of the page, add appropriate alternate text, then enter a paragraph break after the banner. Insert the file butterfly.jpg from the chapter_2 assets folder where you store your Data Files, then add appropriate alternate text.
8. Place the insertion point to the right of the butterfly image, then insert a paragraph break.
9. Import gardening_tips.doc from where you store your Data Files, using the Import Word Document command (Win) or copy and paste the text (Mac).
10. Use the Clean Up Word HTML command to correct or remove any unnecessary code.
11. Click inside the Seasonal Gardening Checklist heading, then use the Property inspector to apply a Heading 1 format.
12. Click inside the Basic Gardening Tips heading, then use the Property inspector to format the selected text with a Heading 1 format.
13. Place the insertion point at the top of the document, then check the page for spelling errors by using the Check Spelling command, and make any necessary corrections.
14. Save your work and close the tips page.

Add links to web pages.

1. Open the index page, then select the current menu bar and replace it with **Home - Featured Plants - Garden Tips - Workshops - Newsletter**. Use a hyphen with a space on either side to separate the items.
2. Add a horizontal rule between the menu bar and the first paragraph of text.
3. Use the Property inspector to link Home on the menu bar to the index.html page in the Blooms & Bulbs website.
4. Link Featured Plants on the menu bar to the plants.html page.
5. Link Garden Tips on the menu bar to the tips.html page.
6. Link Workshops on the menu bar to the workshops.html page.
7. Link Newsletter on the menu bar to the newsletter.html page.
8. Create a line break after the telephone number and then use the Insert panel to create an email link, with **Customer Service** as the text and **mailbox@bloomsandbulbs.com** as the email address. (*Hint:* If your text does not retain the formatting from the previous line, reapply the settings.)
9. Save your work.
10. View the email link in the Assets panel, refreshing it if necessary, then view the Files panel.

Use the History panel and edit code.

1. Open the History panel, then clear its contents.
2. Select the horizontal rule under the menu bar, then change the width to 900 pixels and the alignment to Left.
3. Change the width to 70% and the alignment to Center.

4. Use the History panel to restore the horizontal rule settings to 900 pixels wide, left aligned.

5. Close the History panel.

6. Open the Code Inspector and verify that Word Wrap is selected.

7. Edit the code in the Code Inspector to change the width of the horizontal rule to 950 pixels.

8. Open the Reference panel and scan the information about horizontal rules.

9. Close the Code Inspector and close the Reference panel tab group.

10. Delete the current date in the Last updated on statement on the home page and replace it with a date using the March 7, 1974 format that will update automatically when the file is saved.

11. Examine the code for the date at the bottom of the page to verify that the code that forces it to update on save is included in the code. (*Hint*: The code should be highlighted with a light yellow background if it is not selected, or a blue background if it is selected.)

12. Return to Design view, then save your work.

Modify and test web pages.

1. View the index page with the Tablet size and Mobile size settings, then return to Desktop size.

2. View the page in your browser.

3. Verify that all links work correctly, then close the browser.

4. On the home page, add the text "We are happy to deliver or ship your purchases." to the end of the first paragraph.

5. Save your work, then view the pages in your browser, comparing your pages to Figure 40 and Figure 41.

6. Close your browser, then close the open page.

Figures 40 & 41 *Completed Skills Review, home page and tips page*

You have been hired to create a website for TripSmart, a travel outfitter. You have created the basic framework for the website and are now ready to format and edit the home page to improve the content and appearance.

1. Open the TripSmart website, then open the home page.
2. Enter the following keywords: **TripSmart, travel, trips, vacations, Fayetteville, Arkansas,** and **tours**.
3. Enter the following description: **TripSmart is a comprehensive travel service. We can help you plan trips, make travel arrangements, and supply you with travel gear**.
4. Change the page title to **TripSmart - Serving all your travel needs**.
5. Replace the existing menu bar with the following text: **Home**, **Catalog**, **Services**, **Tours**, and **Newsletter**. Between each item, use a hyphen with a space on either side to separate the items.
6. Replace the date in the last updated statement with a date that will update automatically on save.
7. Add a paragraph break after the last paragraph, then type the following address, using line breaks after each line:
   TripSmart
   1106 Beechwood
   Fayetteville, AR 72704
   555-848-0807

8. Insert an email link in the line below the telephone number, using **Contact Us** for the text and **mailbox@tripsmart.com** for the email link.
9. Italicize TripSmart, the address, phone number, and email link.
10. Link the menu bar entries to index.html, catalog.html, services.html, tours.html, and newsletter.html.
11. View the HTML code for the page, then return to Design view.

12. Insert a horizontal rule above the address.
13. Change the horizontal rule width to 950 pixels and align it to the left side of the page.
14. Save your work.
15. View the page using two different window sizes, then test the links in your browser window.
16. Compare your page to Figure 42, close the browser, then close all open pages.

Figure 42 *Completed Project Builder 1*

Home - Catalog - Services - Tours - Newsletter

Welcome to TripSmart — the smart choice for the savvy traveler. We're here to help you with all your travel needs. Choose customized trips to any location or one of our Five-Star Tours, recently rated first in customer satisfaction by *Traveler* magazine. We are happy to arrange travel for small groups, large groups, or individuals. Our specialty is custom itineraries for independent travelers who enjoy travel at their own pace and on their own schedule. With over 30 years of experience, we can provide knowledgeable guides, comfortable and convenient hotels, and dining recommendations for every size budget.

Call 555-848-0807 today to speak with one of our friendly staff.

_____

TripSmart
1106 Beechwood
Fayetteville, AR 72704
555-848-0807
Contact Us

Copyright 2002 - 2015
Last updated on December 22, 2011

Your company has been selected to design a website for a catering business named Carolyne's Creations. You are now ready to add content to the home page and apply formatting options to improve the page's appearance, using Figure 43 as a guide.

1. Open the Carolyne's Creations website, then open the home page.

2. Edit the page title to read **Carolyne's Creations: Premier Gourmet Food Shop**.

3. Add the description **Carolyne's Creations is a full-service gourmet food shop. We offer cooking classes, take-out meals, and catering services. We also have a retail shop that stocks gourmet items and kitchen accessories.**

4. Add the keywords **Carolyne's Creations, gourmet, catering, cooking classes, kitchen accessories, take-out, Seven Falls, Virginia**.

5. Place the insertion point in front of the sentence in the second paragraph beginning "Give us a call" and type **We also have a pick-up window on the right side of the building for take-out orders**.

6. Add the following address below the second paragraph using line breaks after each line:
   Carolyne's Creations
   496 Maple Avenue
   Seven Falls, Virginia 52404
   555-963-8271

7. Enter another line break after the telephone number and type **Email**, add a space, then add an email link using **Carolyne Kate** for the text and **carolyne@carolynescreations.com** for the email address.

8. Create links from each menu bar element to its corresponding web page.

9. Replace the date that follows the text "Last updated on" with a date object that will automatically update on save, then save your work.

10. Insert a horizontal rule between the menu bar and the Welcome heading.

11. Set the width of the horizontal rule to 400 pixels, then left-align the horizontal rule.

12. Save your work, view the completed page in your default browser, then test each link.

13. Close your browser.

14. Close all open pages.

Figure 43 *Completed Project Builder 2*

Home | Shop | Classes | Catering | Recipes

Welcome

Let Carolyne's Creations be your personal chef, your one-stop shop for the latest in kitchen items and fresh ingredients, and your source for new and innovative recipes. We enjoy planning and presenting special events for all occasions — from children's birthday parties to corporate retreats. Pick-up and drop-off options are also available. We also offer beautiful baskets overflowing with delicious assortments of casseroles, salads, homemade breads, and desserts; trays of vegetables and cheeses or cookies; or coffee cakes and pastries with fresh ground coffee or specialty teas as perfect gifts for family and friends. We offer seasonal cooking classes in our newly redesigned kitchen for aspiring chefs of all ages.

How to find us

We are located in the Plaza Shopping Center at 496 Maple Avenue in Seven Falls, Virginia. We are the second building on the left side of the complex when entering from the Main Street entrance. We also have a pick-up window on the right side of the building for take-out orders. Give us a call at 555-963-8271 or stop by our shop to browse through our selections.

Carolyne's Creations
496 Maple Avenue
Seven Falls, Virginia 52404
555-963-8271
Email Carolyne Kate

Copyright 2001 - 2015
Last updated on January 2, 2012

Albert Iris is looking for a durable laptop case that he can use for the frequent trips he takes with his laptop. He is searching the Internet looking for one that is attractive, strong, and that provides quick access for removing the laptop for airport security. He knows that websites use keywords and descriptions in order to receive "hits" with search engines. He is curious about how they work. Follow the steps below and write your answers to the questions.

1. Connect to the Internet, then go to **www.sfbags.com** to view the WaterField Designs website's home page, as shown in Figure 44.
2. View the page source by clicking View on the Menu bar, then clicking Source (Internet Explorer) or Tools > Web Developer > Page Source (Mozilla Firefox).
3. Can you locate a description and keywords? If so, what are they?

4. How many keyword terms do you find?
5. Is the description appropriate for the website? Why or why not?
6. Look at the numbers of keyword terms and words in the description. Is there an appropriate number?
7. Use a search engine such as Google at www.google.com, then type the words **laptop bag** in the Search text box.
8. Click a link in the list of results and view the source code for that page. Do you see keywords and a description? Do any of them match the words you used in the search?

Figure 44 *Design Project*
Waterfield Designs website used with permission from Waterfield Designs – www.sfbags.com

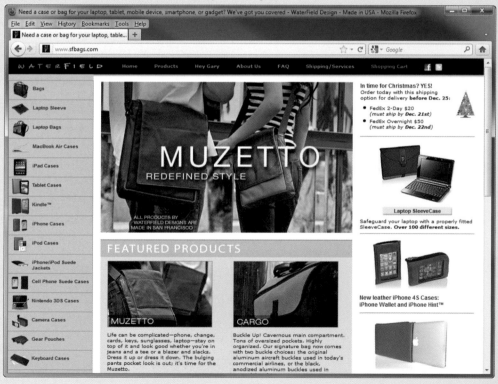

In this assignment, you will continue to work on the website you defined in Chapter 1. In Chapter 1, you created a wireframe for your website with at least four pages. You also created a local site folder for your site and an assets folder to store the site asset files. You set the assets folder as the default storage location for your images. You began to collect information and resources for your site and started working on the home page.

1. Think about the head content for the home page. Add the title, keywords, and a description.
2. Create the main page content for the home page.
3. Add the address and other contact information to the home page, including an email address.
4. Consult your wireframe and design the menu bar.
5. Link the menu bar items to the appropriate pages.
6. Add a last updated on statement to the home page with a date that will automatically update when the page is saved.
7. Edit the page content until you are satisfied with the results. You will format the content after you have learned to use Cascading Style Sheets in the next chapter.
8. Verify that all links, including the email link, work correctly.
9. When you are satisfied with the home page, review the checklist questions shown in Figure 45, then make any necessary changes.
10. Save your work.

Figure 45 *Portfolio Project*

Website Checklist

1. Does the home page have a page title?
2. Does the home page have a description and keywords?
3. Does the home page contain contact information, including an email address?
4. Does the home page have a menu bar that includes a link to itself?
5. Does the home page have a "last updated on" statement that will automatically update when the page is saved?
6. Do all paths for links and images work correctly?
7. Does the home page look good using at least two different browsers and screen resolutions?

CHAPTER 3 WORKING WITH TEXT AND CASCADING STYLE SHEETS

1. Create unordered and ordered lists
2. Create, apply, and edit Cascading Style Sheets
3. Add rules and attach Cascading Style Sheets
4. Use coding tools to view and edit rules

3

WORKING WITH TEXT AND
CASCADING STYLE SHEETS

Introduction

Most web pages depend largely on text to convey information. Dreamweaver provides many tools for working with text that you can use to make your web pages attractive and easy to read. These tools can help you format text quickly and make sure it has a consistent look across all your web pages.

Using Cascading Style Sheets

You can save time and ensure that all your page elements have a consistent appearance by using **Cascading Style Sheets (CSS)**. CSS are sets of formatting instructions, usually stored in a separate file, that control the appearance and position of text and graphics on a web page or throughout a website. CSS are a great way to define consistent formatting attributes for page elements such as paragraph text, lists, and table data. You can then apply the formatting attributes to any element in a single document or to all of the pages in a website.

Formatting Text as Lists

If a web page contains a large amount of text, it can be difficult for viewers to digest it all. You can break up the monotony of large blocks of text by dividing them into smaller paragraphs or by organizing them as lists. You can create three types of lists in Dreamweaver: unordered lists, ordered lists, and definition lists.

Lists are also excellent for creating simple navigation bars. You can format list items to look like buttons by applying styles to assign background colors for each list item. You can even create rollover effects for list items by having the background color change when the user rolls the mouse over them. This technique gives your links a more professional look than plain text links without requiring the use of JavaScript, Spry, or Flash. Cascading Style Sheets are indeed a powerful tool. This chapter will focus on using Cascading Style Sheets to format text.

Create Unordered
AND ORDERED LISTS

What You'll Do

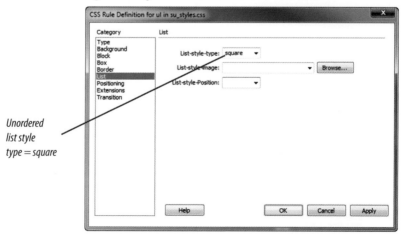

In this lesson, you will create an unordered list of spa services on the spa page. You will also import text with questions and format them as an ordered list.

Creating Unordered Lists

Unordered lists are lists of items that do not need to appear in a specific sequence, such as a grocery list, which often lists items in a random order. Items in unordered lists are usually preceded by a **bullet**, a small dot or similar icon. Unordered lists that contain bullets are sometimes called **bulleted lists**. Although you can use paragraph indentations to create an unordered list, bullets can often make lists easier to read. To create an unordered list, first select the text you want to format as an unordered list, then use the Unordered List button in the HTML Property inspector to insert bullets at the beginning of each paragraph of the selected text.

Formatting Unordered Lists

In Dreamweaver, the default bullet style is a round dot. To change the bullet style to a square, use Cascading Style Sheets. You can create a rule to modify the <ul> tag that will apply to all unordered lists in a website, as shown in Figure 1 or you can create an

Figure 1 *Using CSS to format all unordered lists in a website*

inline rule to only modify one unordered list as shown in Figure 2. You will learn about Cascading Style Sheets in the next lesson.

Creating Ordered Lists

Ordered lists, which are sometimes called **numbered lists**, are lists of items that are presented in a specific sequence and that are preceded by sequential numbers or letters. An ordered list is appropriate for a list in which each item must be executed according to its specified order. A list that provides numbered directions for driving from Point A to Point B or a list that provides instructions for assembling a bicycle are both examples of ordered lists.

Formatting Ordered Lists

You can format an ordered list to show different styles of numbers or letters by using Cascading Style Sheets, as shown in Figure 3. You can apply numbers, Roman numerals, lowercase letters, or uppercase letters to an ordered list.

Creating Definition Lists

Definition lists are similar to unordered lists but have a hanging indent and are not preceded by bullets. They are often used with terms and definitions, such as in a dictionary or glossary. To create a definition list, select the text to use for the list, click Format on the Menu bar, point to List, and then click Definition List.

Figure 2 *Using CSS to format only one unordered list in a website*

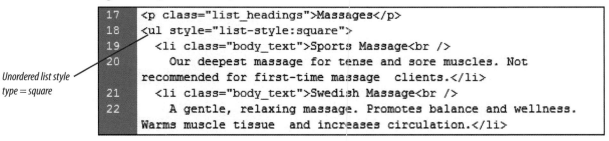

Unordered list style type = square

```
17  <p class="list_headings">Massages</p>
18  <ul style="list-style:square">
19     <li class="body_text">Sports Massage<br />
20     Our deepest massage for tense and sore muscles. Not
    recommended for first-time massage  clients.</li>
21     <li class="body_text">Swedish Massage<br />
22     A gentle, relaxing massage. Promotes balance and wellness.
    Warms muscle tissue  and increases circulation.</li>
```

Figure 3 *Using CSS to format all ordered lists in a website*

Ordered list style type = lower alpha

Create an unordered list

1. Open the spa page in The Striped Umbrella website.

2. Select the three items and their descriptions under the Massages heading.

3. Click the **HTML button** <> HTML in the Property inspector to switch to the HTML Property inspector if necessary, click the **Unordered List button** to format the selected text as an unordered list, click anywhere to deselect the text, then compare your screen to Figure 4.

   Each spa service item and its description are separated by a line break. That is why each description is indented under its corresponding item, rather than formatted as a new list item. You must enter a paragraph break to create a new list item.

4. Repeat Step 3 to create unordered lists with the three items under the Facials and Body Treatments headings, being careful not to include the contact information in the last paragraph on the page as part of your last list.

TIP Pressing [Enter] (Win) or [return] (Mac) once at the end of an unordered list creates another bulleted item. To end an unordered list, press [Enter] (Win) or [return] (Mac) twice.

(continued)

Figure 4 *Creating an unordered list*

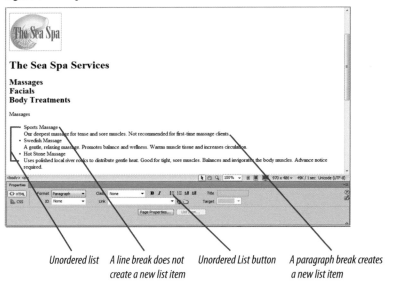

Unordered list   A line break does not create a new list item   Unordered List button   A paragraph break creates a new list item

DESIGN TIP

Coding for the Semantic Web

You may have heard the term "semantic web." The word "semantics" refers to the study of meanings of words or sentences. So the term "semantic web" refers to the way page content can be coded to convey meaning to other computer programs such as search engines. One example is to use the <em> tag which means "emphasis" rather than the <i> tag which means "italic" to show emphasis. Another example would be to use font size attributes such as <small> or <medium> rather than using font size attributes expressed in pixels. Cascading Style Sheets are used to define the appearance of semantic tags. For instance, you can specify the attributes of the <h1> heading tag by choosing the Selector Type: Tag (redefines an HTML element) rules in the New CSS Rules dialog box. CSS and semantic coding work together to enhance the meaning of the page content and provide well-designed pages that are attractive and consistent throughout the site. An ideal website would incorporate semantic coding with external style sheets to format all website content. This approach will enable "Semantic Web" programs to interpret the content presented, make it easier for web designers to write and edit, and enhance the overall experience for site users.

Figure 5 *Viewing the three unordered lists*

Massages

- Sports Massage
  Our deepest massage for tense and sore muscles. Not recommended for first-time massage clients.
- Swedish Massage
  A gentle, relaxing massage. Promotes balance and wellness. Warms muscle tissue and increases circulation.
- Hot Stone Massage
  Uses polished local river rocks to distribute gentle heat. Good for tight, sore muscles. Balances and invigorates the body muscles. Advance notice required.

Facials

- Revitalizing Facial
  A light massage with a customized essential oil blend that moisturizes the skin and restores circulation.
- Gentlemen's Facial
  A cleansing facial that restores a healthy glow. Includes a neck and shoulder massage.
- Milk Mask
  A soothing mask that softens and moisturizes the face. Leaves your skin looking younger.

Body Treatments

- Salt Glow
  Imported sea salts are massaged into the skin, exfoliating and cleansing the pores.
- Herbal Wrap
  Organic lavender blooms create a detoxifying and calming treatment to relieve aches and pains.
- Seaweed Body Wrap
  Seaweed is a natural detoxifying agent that also helps improve circulation.

Figure 6 *HTML tags in Code view for unordered lists*

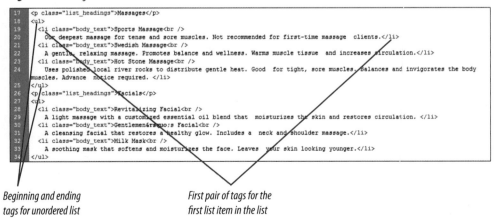

```
17  <p class="list_headings">Massages</p>
18  <ul>
19    <li class="body_text">Sports Massage<br />
20      Our deepest massage for tense and sore muscles. Not recommended for first-time massage  clients.</li>
21    <li class="body_text">Swedish Massage<br />
22      A gentle, relaxing massage. Promotes balance and wellness. Warms muscle tissue  and increases circulation.</li>
23    <li class="body_text">Hot Stone Massage<br />
24      Uses polished local river rocks to distribute gentle heat. Good  for tight, sore muscles. Balances and invigorates the body
    muscles. Advance notice required. </li>
25  </ul>
26  <p class="list_headings">Facials</p>
27  <ul>
28    <li class="body_text">Revitalizing Facial<br />
29      A light massage with a customized essential oil blend that  moisturizes the skin and restores circulation. </li>
30    <li class="body_text">Gentlemen&rsquo;s Facial<br />
31      A cleansing facial that restores a healthy glow. Includes a  neck and shoulder massage.</li>
32    <li class="body_text">Milk Mask<br />
33      A soothing mask that softens and moisturizes the face. Leaves  your skin looking younger.</li>
34  </ul>
```

Beginning and ending tags for unordered list

First pair of tags for the first list item in the list

5. Save your work, then compare your page to Figure 5.

6. Position the insertion point to the left of the first item in the first unordered list, then click the **Show Code view button** `Code` on the Document toolbar to view the code for the unordered list, as shown in Figure 6.

   A pair of HTML tags surrounds each type of element on the page. The first tag in each pair begins the code for a particular element, and the last tag ends the code for the element. For instance, the tag <ul> begins the unordered list, and the </ul> tag ends it. The tags <li> and </li> surround each item in the list.

7. Click the **Show Design view button** `Design` on the Document toolbar.

8. Save your work.

You opened the spa page in Design view and formatted three spa services lists as unordered lists. You then viewed the HTML code for the unordered lists in Code view.

Create an ordered list

1. Place the insertion point at the end of the page, after the words "extension 39."

2. Click the **Word Document** command on the File, Import menu, browse to the location where you store your Data Files, then double-click **questions.doc** (Win) or open **questions.doc** from where you store your Data Files, select all, copy, then paste the copied text on the page (Mac).

   The inserted text appears on the same line as the existing text.

3. Click **Commands** on the menu bar, click **Clean Up Word HTML**, click **OK** to close the Clean Up Word HTML dialog box, click **OK** to close the Dreamweaver dialog box, place the insertion point to the left of the text "Questions you may have," then click **Horizontal Rule** in the Common category on the Insert panel.

   A horizontal rule appears and separates the unordered list from the text you just imported.

4. Select the text beginning with "How do I schedule" and ending with the last sentence on the page.

5. Click the **Ordered List button** ≟≡ in the HTML Property inspector to format the selected text as an ordered list.

6. Deselect the text, then compare your screen to Figure 7.

You imported text on the spa page. You also added a horizontal rule to help organize the page. Finally, you formatted selected text as an ordered list.

Figure 7 *Creating an ordered list*

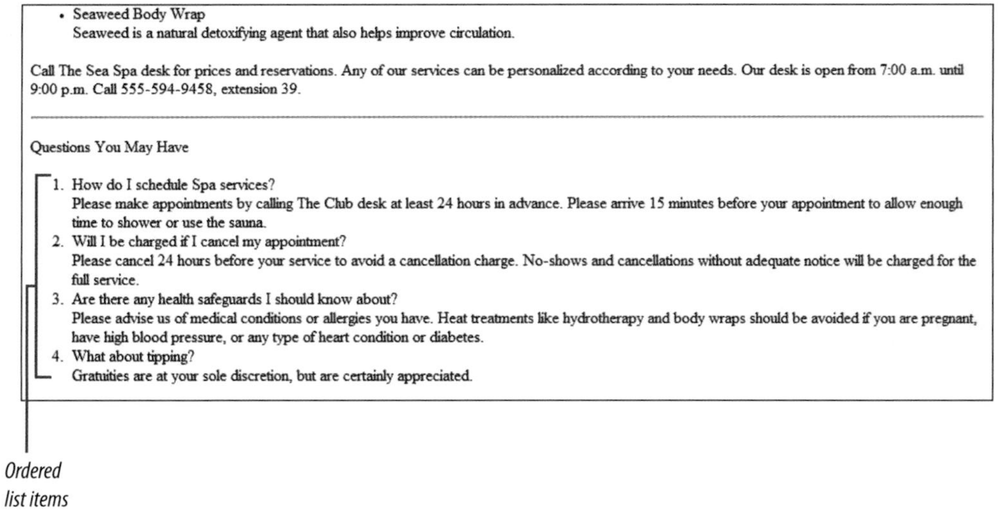

- Seaweed Body Wrap
  Seaweed is a natural detoxifying agent that also helps improve circulation.

Call The Sea Spa desk for prices and reservations. Any of our services can be personalized according to your needs. Our desk is open from 7:00 a.m. until 9:00 p.m. Call 555-594-9458, extension 39.

Questions You May Have

1. How do I schedule Spa services?
   Please make appointments by calling The Club desk at least 24 hours in advance. Please arrive 15 minutes before your appointment to allow enough time to shower or use the sauna.
2. Will I be charged if I cancel my appointment?
   Please cancel 24 hours before your service to avoid a cancellation charge. No-shows and cancellations without adequate notice will be charged for the full service.
3. Are there any health safeguards I should know about?
   Please advise us of medical conditions or allergies you have. Heat treatments like hydrotherapy and body wraps should be avoided if you are pregnant, have high blood pressure, or any type of heart condition or diabetes.
4. What about tipping?
   Gratuities are at your sole discretion, but are certainly appreciated.

Ordered list items

Figure 8 *Formatting a list heading*

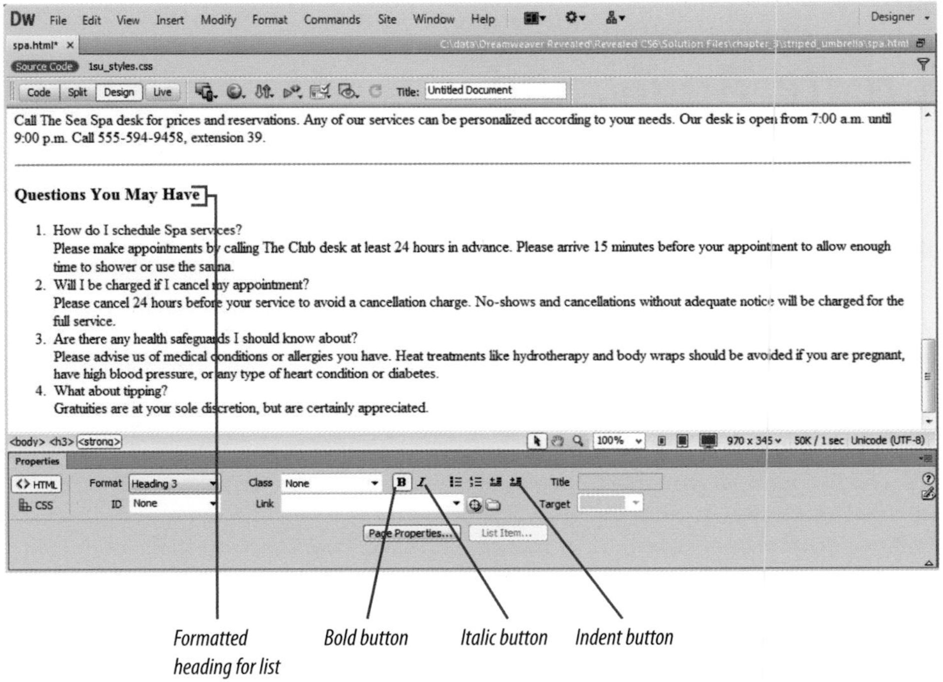

Formatted
heading for list

Bold button

Italic button

Indent button

Format an ordered list heading

1. Click to place the insertion point in the heading "Questions you may have," then use the HTML Property inspector to apply the **Heading 3** format, as shown in Figure 8.

TIP You could show emphasis by using the Bold button **B** or the Italic button *I* on the HTML Property inspector, as shown in Figure 8, but the heading code shows the significance (semantics) of the phrase more clearly. It shows that the phrase is a heading related to the text that follows it. The three headings on the page are formatted with three different heading tags that indicate their order of importance on the page: Heading 1 first, then Heading 2, followed by Heading 3.

2. Save your work.

You formatted the "Questions you may have" heading.

Create, Apply, and
EDIT CASCADING STYLE SHEETS

What You'll Do

In this lesson, you will create a Cascading Style Sheet file for The Striped Umbrella website. You will also create a rule named list_headings and apply it to the list item headings on the spa page.

Understanding Cascading Style Sheets

Cascading Style Sheets (CSS) are made up of sets of formatting attributes called **rules**, which define the formatting attributes for page content. Rules are sometimes referred to as styles. Style sheets are classified by where the code is stored. The code can be saved in a separate file (**external style sheet**), as part of the head content of an individual web page (**internal or embedded styles**), or as part of the body of the HTML code (**inline styles**). External CSS are saved as files with the .css extension and are stored in the website's directory structure. Figure 9 shows an external style sheet named su_styles.css listed in the Files panel. External style sheets are the preferred method for creating and using styles.

CSS are also classified by their type. A **Class type** can be used to format any page element. An **ID type** and a **Tag type** are used to redefine an HTML tag. A **Compound** type is used to format a selection. In this chapter, we will use the class type and the tag type, both stored in an external style sheet file.

Using the CSS Styles Panel

You use buttons on the CSS Styles panel to create, edit, and apply rules. To add a rule, use the New CSS Rule dialog box to name the rule and specify whether to add it to a new or existing style sheet. You then use the CSS Rule definition dialog box to set the formatting attributes for the rule. Once you add a new rule to a style sheet, it appears in a list in the CSS Styles panel. To apply a rule, you select the text to which you want to apply the rule, and then choose a rule from the Targeted Rule list in the CSS Property inspector. You can apply CSS rules to elements on a single web page or to all of the pages in a website. When you edit a rule, such as changing the font size it specifies, all page elements formatted with that rule are automatically updated. Once you create an external CSS, you should attach it to the remaining pages in your website.

Use the CSS Styles panel to manage your styles. The Properties pane displays properties for a selected rule at the bottom of the panel. You can easily change a property's value by clicking an option from a drop-down menu.

Understanding the Advantages of Using Style Sheets

You can use CSS styles to save an enormous amount of time. Being able to define a rule and then apply it to page elements on all the pages of your website means that you can make hundreds of formatting changes in a few minutes. In addition, style sheets create a more uniform look from page to page and they generate cleaner code. Using style sheets separates the development of content from the way the content is presented. Pages formatted with CSS styles are much more compliant with current accessibility standards than those with manual formatting.

QUICK TIP

For more information about Cascading Style Sheets, visit www.w3.org/Style.

Understanding CSS Code

You can see the properties for a CSS rule by looking at the style sheet code. A CSS rule consists of two parts: the selector and the declaration. The **selector** is the name of the tag to which the style declarations have been assigned. The **declaration** consists of a property (such as font-size or font-weight) and a value (such as 14 px or bold). For example, Figure 10 shows the code for an internal style that sets the background color for a page. In this example, the selector is the body tag. The only property assigned to this selector is background-color. The value for this property is #FFF, or white. The property and value together comprise the declaration. When there is more than one property, each additional property and value are separated by a semicolon.

When you create a new external CSS file, you will see it as a related files document in the Document window. Save this file as you make changes to it.

Figure 9 *Cascading Style Sheet file created in striped_umbrella site root folder*

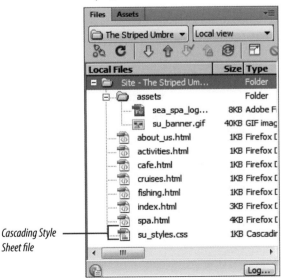

Cascading Style Sheet file

Figure 10 *Viewing CSS code*

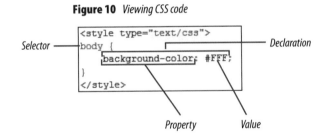

Selector — Declaration — Property — Value

Create a Cascading Style Sheet and add a rule

1. Click the **CSS button** in the Property inspector to switch to the CSS Property inspector, as shown in Figure 11.

2. If the CSS Styles panel is not open, click **Window** on the Menu bar, then click **CSS Styles** to open the CSS Styles panel or click the **CSS Styles panel tab**.

3. Click the **Switch to All (Document) Mode button** ![All] on the CSS Styles panel if it's not already active, then click the **New CSS Rule button** in the CSS Styles panel to open the New CSS Rule dialog box.

4. Verify that Class (can apply to any HTML element) is selected under Selector Type, then type **list_headings** in the Selector Name text box.

TIP Class selector names are preceded by a period in the code and in the CSS panel. If you don't enter a period when you type the name, Dreamweaver will add the period for you when the rule is created.

5. Click the **Rule Definition list arrow**, click **(New Style Sheet File)**, compare your screen with Figure 12, then click **OK**.

   This indicates that you want to create a new style sheet file, which will contain your list_headings rule and any other rules you may create for this site. The Save Style Sheet File As dialog box opens.

   (continued)

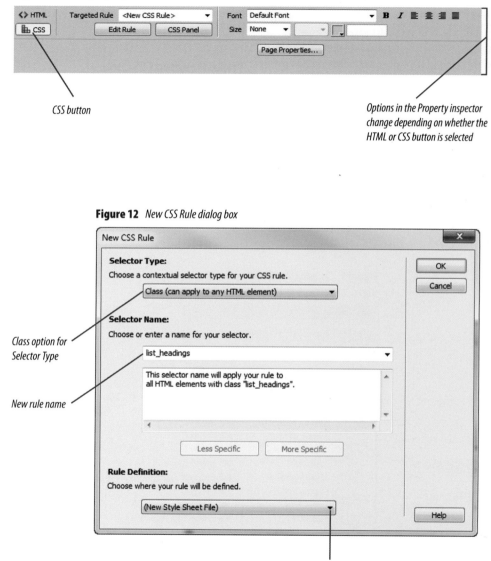

Figure 11 *CSS Property inspector*

CSS button

Options in the Property inspector change depending on whether the HTML or CSS button is selected

Figure 12 *New CSS Rule dialog box*

Class option for Selector Type

New rule name

Rule Definition list arrow

Figure 13 *CSS Rule Definition for .list_headings in su_styles.css dialog box*

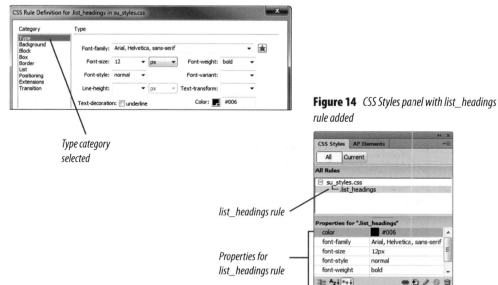

Type category
selected

Figure 14 *CSS Styles panel with list_headings rule added*

list_headings rule

Properties for
list_headings rule

Choosing Fonts

There are two classifications of fonts: sans-serif and serif. **Sans-serif** fonts are block-style characters that are often used for headings and subheadings. The headings in this book and the text you are reading now use a sans-serif font. Examples of sans-serif fonts include Arial, Verdana, and Helvetica. **Serif** fonts are more ornate and contain small extra strokes at the beginning and end of the characters. Serif fonts are considered easier to read in printed material, because the extra strokes lead your eye from one character to the next. Examples of serif fonts include Times New Roman, Times, and Georgia. The paragraph text on the first page of each chapter in this book is in a serif font. Many designers feel that a sans-serif font is preferable when the content of a website is primarily intended to be read on the screen, but that a serif font is preferable if the content will be printed. When you choose fonts, you need to keep in mind the amount of text each page will contain and whether most viewers will read the text on-screen or print it. A good rule of thumb is to limit each website to no more than three font variations.

6. Type **su_styles** in the File name text box (Win) or the Save As text box (Mac), verify that the striped_umbrella folder appears in the Save in box, then click **Save** to open the CSS Rule Definition for .list_headings in su_styles.css dialog box.

   The .list_headings rule will be stored within the su_styles.css file in the Striped Umbrella local site folder. Next, you define the properties for the rule.

7. Verify that Type is selected in the Category list, set the Font-family to **Arial**, **Helvetica**, **sans-serif**, set the Font-size to **12 px**, set the Font-weight to **bold**, set the Font-style to **normal**, set the Color to **#006**, compare your screen to Figure 13, then click **OK**.

TIP You can modify the font combinations in the Font-family list by clicking Modify on the Menu bar then clicking Font Families.

   Other interesting type options that are available in the CSS Rule Definition dialog box are Line-height, which changes the height of each line measured in pixels; Text-decoration, which adds text effects, Font- variant, which allows you to change the text to small caps, and Text-transform, which has options to change text to all upper-case or all lower-case.

8. Click the **plus sign** (Win) or the **expander arrow** (Mac) next to su_styles.css in the CSS Styles panel and expand the panel, if necessary, to see the .list_headings rule displayed, then select the **.list_headings rule**.

   The CSS rule named .list_headings and its properties appear in the CSS Styles panel, as shown in Figure 14.

You created a Cascading Style Sheet file named su_styles.css and a rule called .list_headings within the style sheet.

Add a Tag selector to an existing style sheet

1. Click the **New CSS Rule button** ⊞ in the CSS Styles panel.

2. Click the **Selector Type list arrow**, then select **Tag (redefines an HTML element)**.

3. Type **h1** in the Selector Name text box, verify that su_styles.css appears in the Rule Definition text box, compare your screen to Figure 24, then click **OK**.

   The CSS Rule Definition for H1 in su_styles.css dialog box opens.

4. With the Type Category selected, change the Font-family to **Arial**, **Helvetica**, **sans-serif**; the Font-size to **24**; the Font-weight to **bold**, as shown in Figure 25; then click **OK**.

   The Sea Spa Services heading on the page changes in appearance to reflect the new h1 properties specified in the new rule.

TIP The Remove Font from Favorites button ★ next to the Font-family list box can be used to remove fonts from the menu list.

(continued)

Figure 24 *Creating a Tag selector*

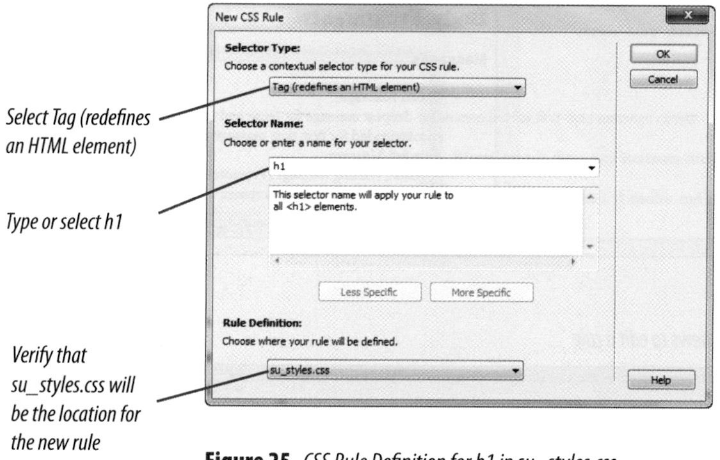

Select Tag (redefines an HTML element)

Type or select h1

Verify that su_styles.css will be the location for the new rule

Figure 25 *CSS Rule Definition for h1 in su_styles.css*

Remove Font from Favorites button

Transitioning to a Real-World Work Process

As you learn Dreamweaver throughout the chapters in this book, you practice its many features in a logical learning sequence. You will develop an understanding of both current concepts like CSS3 and older, but still used, features such as HTML formatting and embedded styles. Once you learn Dreamweaver and start using it to create your own websites, you would ideally format all pages with rules from one external style sheet. You would move all of the embedded styles in the predesigned CSS layouts to the external style sheet because the embedded styles on each page would be redundant. After you have worked through this book, you should have the skills and understanding to design sites built entirely and efficiently with CSS.

Figure 26 *Viewing the headings with new rules applied*

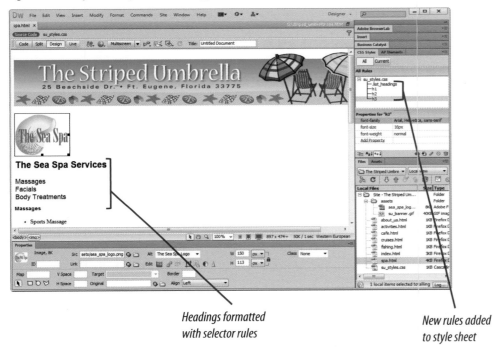

Headings formatted
with selector rules

New rules added
to style sheet

5. Repeat Steps 1 through 4 to create a new Tag selector that redefines the h2 tag with a Font-family of **Arial**, **Helvetica**, **sans-serif**; a Font-size of **18**; and a Font-weight of **normal**.

6. Repeat Step 5 to create a new Tag selector that redefines the h3 tag with a Font-family of **Arial**, **Helvetica**, **sans-serif**; a Font-size of **16**; and a Font-weight of **bold**.

7. Save all files, then compare your screen to Figure 26.

You added three tag selectors to your style sheet that modify the appearance of the h1, h2, and h3 tags.

Add Rules and Attach
CASCADING STYLE SHEETS

What You'll Do

In this lesson, you will add a rule to a Cascading Style Sheet. You will then attach the style sheet file to the index page and apply one of the rules to text on the page.

Understanding External and Embedded Style Sheets

When you are first learning about CSS, the terminology can be confusing. In the last lesson, you learned that external style sheets are separate files in a website, saved with the .css file extension. You also learned that CSS can be part of an HTML file, rather than a separate file. These are called internal, or embedded, style sheets. External CSS files are created by the web designer. Embedded style sheets are created automatically in Dreamweaver if the designer does not create them, using default names for the rules. The code for these rules resides in the head content for that page. These rules are automatically named style1, style2, and so on. You can rename the rules as they are created to make them more recognizable for you to use, for example, paragraph_text, subheading, or address. Embedded style sheets apply only to a single page, although you can copy them into the code in other pages or move them to an external style sheet. Remember that style sheets can be used to format much more than text objects. They can be used to set the page background, link properties, or determine the appearance of almost any object on the page. Figure 27 shows the code for some embedded rules and a link to an external style sheet. The code resides in the head content of the web page.

When you have several pages in a website, you will probably want to use the same styles for each page to ensure that all your elements have a consistent appearance. To attach a style sheet to another document, click the Attach Style Sheet button on the CSS Styles panel to open the Attach External Style Sheet dialog box, make sure the Add as Link option is selected, browse to locate the file you want to attach, and then click OK. The rules contained in the attached style sheet will appear in the CSS Styles panel, and you can use them to apply rules to text on the page. External style sheets can be attached, or linked, to any page. This is an extremely powerful tool. If you decide to edit a rule, the changes will automatically be made to every object on every page that it formats.

Understanding Related Page Files

When an HTML file is linked to other files necessary to display the page content, these files are called **related files.** When a file that has related files is open in the Document window, each related file name is displayed in the Related Files toolbar above the Document window. A Cascading Style Sheet file is an example of a related file. When an HTML document has an attached CSS file but the CSS file is not available, the page file will appear in the browser, but will not be formatted correctly. It takes both the HTML file and the CSS file working together to display the content properly. When you upload HTML files, remember also to upload all related page files. Other examples of related page files are Flash player, video files, and JavaScript files.

When an HTML file with a linked CSS file is open in Dreamweaver, the name of the CSS filename appears below the page tab. When you click on the CSS filename, the screen changes to Split view, with the right side displaying the open HTML page in Design view and the left side displaying the CSS file. If you click Source Code next to the related page filename, the code for the top level document (open HTML file) will appear on the left side. You can edit both Code view windows by typing directly in the code.

Figure 27 *Code for embedded rules and a link to an external style sheet*

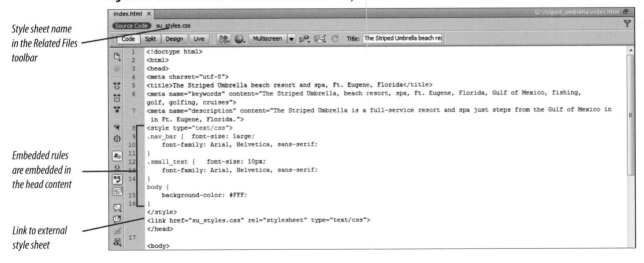

Style sheet name in the Related Files toolbar

Embedded rules are embedded in the head content

Link to external style sheet

Add a class rule to a Cascading Style Sheet

1. Click the **New CSS Rule button** 🗗 in the CSS Styles panel.

2. Verify that Class (can apply to any HTML element) is the Selector Type, type **body_text** in the Selector Name text box, verify that su_styles.css appears in the Rule Definition text box, as shown in Figure 28, then click **OK**.

   The new rule will be saved in the su_styles.css file as an external style.

3. Set the Font-family to **Arial**, **Helvetica**, **sans-serif**, set the Font-size to **12**, set the Color to **#000**, compare your screen to Figure 29, then click **OK**.

4. Select the three list items and their descriptions under the Massages heading, click the **Targeted Rule list arrow** in the CSS Property inspector, then click **body_text** to apply it to the three massage names and descriptions.

   The rule is applied to the text, but the text would be easier to read if it were a little larger.

5. Click the **Edit Rule button** ✏ in the CSS Styles panel.

6. Change the font size to **medium** in the Type category of the CSS Rule Definition for body_text in su_styles.css dialog box, as shown in Figure 30, then click **OK**.

   There are several ways to define font size rather than using pixels. Using a size of small, medium, large, etc., is one of them. Other choices include using em, pt, or a percentage.

   (continued)

Figure 28 *Adding a class rule to a CSS*

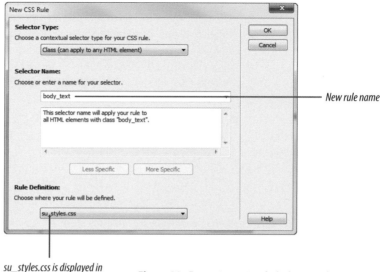

New rule name

su_styles.css is displayed in the Rule Definition list box

Figure 29 *Formatting options for body_text rule*

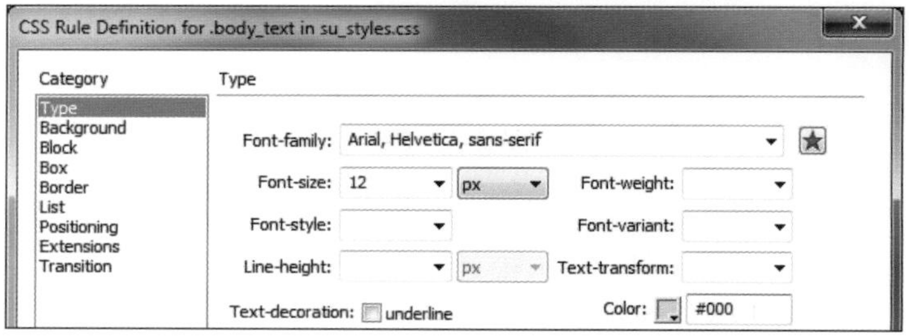

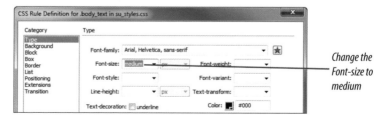

Figure 30 *Editing the body_text rule*

Change the Font-size to medium

Working with Text and Cascading Style Sheets

Figure 31 *Spa page with style sheet applied to rest of text on page*

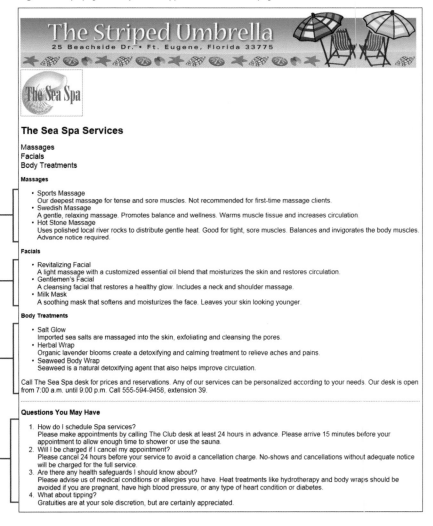

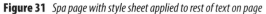

The Sea Spa Services

Massages
Facials
Body Treatments

Massages

- Sports Massage
  Our deepest massage for tense and sore muscles. Not recommended for first-time massage clients.
- Swedish Massage
  A gentle, relaxing massage. Promotes balance and wellness. Warms muscle tissue and increases circulation.
- Hot Stone Massage
  Uses polished local river rocks to distribute gentle heat. Good for tight, sore muscles. Balances and invigorates the body muscles. Advance notice required.

Facials

- Revitalizing Facial
  A light massage with a customized essential oil blend that moisturizes the skin and restores circulation.
- Gentlemen's Facial
  A cleansing facial that restores a healthy glow. Includes a neck and shoulder massage.
- Milk Mask
  A soothing mask that softens and moisturizes the face. Leaves your skin looking younger.

Body Treatments

- Salt Glow
  Imported sea salts are massaged into the skin, exfoliating and cleansing the pores.
- Herbal Wrap
  Organic lavender blooms create a detoxifying and calming treatment to relieve aches and pains.
- Seaweed Body Wrap
  Seaweed is a natural detoxifying agent that also helps improve circulation.

Call The Sea Spa desk for prices and reservations. Any of our services can be personalized according to your needs. Our desk is open from 7:00 a.m. until 9:00 p.m. Call 555-594-9458, extension 39.

Questions You May Have

1. How do I schedule Spa services?
   Please make appointments by calling The Club desk at least 24 hours in advance. Please arrive 15 minutes before your appointment to allow enough time to shower or use the sauna.
2. Will I be charged if I cancel my appointment?
   Please cancel 24 hours before your service to avoid a cancellation charge. No-shows and cancellations without adequate notice will be charged for the full service.
3. Are there any health safeguards I should know about?
   Please advise us of medical conditions or allergies you have. Heat treatments like hydrotherapy and body wraps should be avoided if you are pregnant, have high blood pressure, or any type of heart condition or diabetes.
4. What about tipping?
   Gratuities are at your sole discretion, but are certainly appreciated.

*Text formatted with
the body_text rule*

7. Repeat Step 4 to apply the body_text rule to the rest of the text on the page except for the text that has already been formatted with the list_headings rule or heading tags, as shown in Figure 31.

8. Click **File** on the Menu bar, then click **Save All**, to save both the spa page and the su_styles.css file.

   The rule is saved in the style sheet file and applied to the text in the HTML file.

TIP You must save the open su_styles.css file after editing it, or you will lose your changes.

You added a new rule called body_text to the su_styles.css file. You then applied the rule to selected text.

Attach a style sheet

1. Close the spa page and open the index page.

2. Click the **Attach Style Sheet button** on the CSS Styles panel.

3. Click **Browse** then navigate to the file su_styles.css, if necessary, click the **su_styles.css** file, click **OK** (Win) or click **Open** (Mac), verify that the **Link option button** is selected, as shown in Figure 32, then click **OK**.

   There are now two rules named body_text. One is an internal style that was in the data file when you brought it into the website and one is in the external style sheet. Since these rules have duplicate names, it would be better to delete the internal style and let the external style format the text.

4. Select the **body_text rule** under the <style> section of the CSS Styles panel, as shown in Figure 33, then click the **Delete CSS Rule button** on the CSS Styles panel.

5. Click the **Show Code view button** `Code` and view the code that links the su_styles.css file to the index page, as shown in Figure 34.

6. Click the **Show Design view button** `Design`, then save your work.

You attached the su_styles.css file to the index.html page and deleted the body_text internal style, allowing the body_text external style to format the page text.

Figure 32 *Attaching a style sheet to a file*

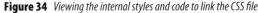

Link option button   su_styles.css style
                      sheet selected

Figure 33 *Deleting an internal style*

Delete the
internal
body_text
rule

External   Internal   Delete
styles   styles   CSS Rule
                        button

Figure 34 *Viewing the internal styles and code to link the CSS file*

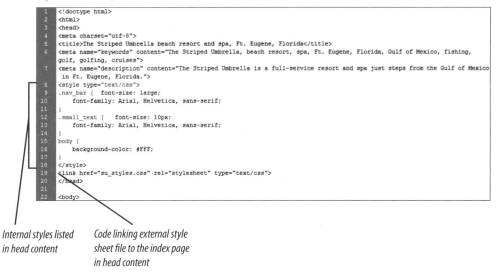

```
1   <!doctype html>
2   <html>
3   <head>
4   <meta charset="utf-8">
5   <title>The Striped Umbrella beach resort and spa, Ft. Eugene, Florida</title>
6   <meta name="keywords" content="The Striped Umbrella, beach resort, spa, Ft. Eugene, Florida, Gulf of Mexico, fishing,
    golf, golfing, cruises">
7   <meta name="description" content="The Striped Umbrella is a full-service resort and spa just steps from the Gulf of Mexico
    in Ft. Eugene, Florida.">
8   <style type="text/css">
9   .nav_bar {  font-size: large;
10      font-family: Arial, Helvetica, sans-serif;
11  }
12  .small_text {  font-size: 10px;
13      font-family: Arial, Helvetica, sans-serif;
14  }
15  body {
16      background-color: #FFF;
17  }
18  </style>
19  <link href="su_styles.css" rel="stylesheet" type="text/css">
20  </head>
21
22  <body>
```

Internal styles listed   Code linking external style
in head content   sheet file to the index page
                              in head content

Figure 35 *Using the Related Files toolbar to view an external style sheet file*

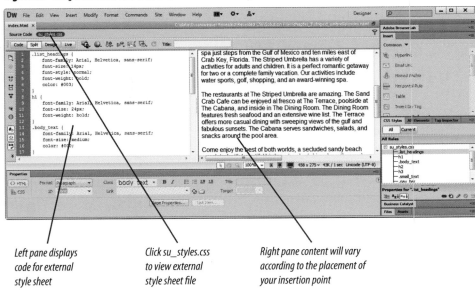

Left pane displays
code for external
style sheet

Click su_styles.css
to view external
style sheet file

Right pane content will vary
according to the placement of
your insertion point

Figure 36 *Using the Related Files toolbar to view embedded styles*

Click Source Code
to view embedded
styles

Left pane displays
code for embedded
styles

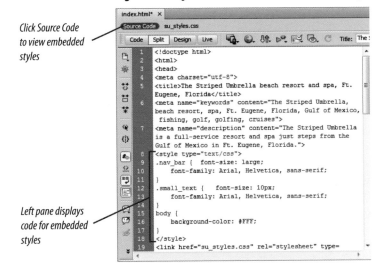

Use the Related Files toolbar to view styles

1. Click **su_styles.css** on the Related Files toolbar.

   The document window changes to Show Code and Design views with the external CSS file in the left pane and the HTML page in Design view in the right pane, as shown in Figure 35.

2. Click **Source Code** on the Related Files toolbar.

   The code for the HTML file appears on the left with the code for the embedded styles as shown in Figure 36.

3. Click the **Show Design view button**  to return to Design view.

You viewed the external and embedded styles using the Related Files toolbar.

Use Coding Tools to
VIEW AND EDIT RULES

What You'll Do

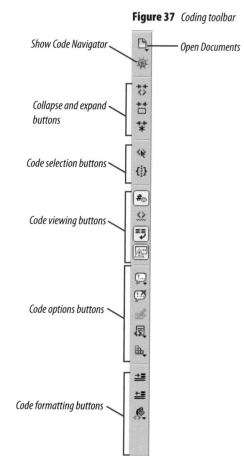

In this lesson, you will collapse, then expand the code for the index page to view the code for the embedded and external styles. You will then move embedded styles to the external style sheet file.

Coding Tools in Dreamweaver

In Code view, you can see the Coding toolbar, shown in Figure 37. It contains a number of handy tools that help you navigate through and view your code in different ways. It has buttons that expand or collapse code, buttons for changing the way the code is displayed, and buttons for inserting and removing comments. The Coding toolbar appears on the left side of the Document window. Although you cannot move it, you can hide it, using the Toolbars command on the View menu in Code view.

As you learned in Chapter 2, you can customize the way your page code appears in Code view. You can wrap the lines of code, display or hide line numbers and hidden characters, or highlight invalid code so you can fix it. You can also have different code types appear in different colors, indent lines of code, and display syntax error alerts. In Chapter 2, you viewed these options using the View Options button on the Code Inspector toolbar. You can also view and change them on the Code View options menu under the View menu on the Menu bar.

Figure 37 *Coding toolbar*

Show Code Navigator

Open Documents

Collapse and expand buttons

Code selection buttons

Code viewing buttons

Code options buttons

Code formatting buttons

Working with Text and Cascading Style Sheets

Using Coding Tools to Navigate Code

As your pages get longer and the code more complex, it is helpful to collapse sections of code, much as you can collapse and expand panels, folders, and styles. Collapsing code lets you temporarily hide code between two different sections of code that you would like to read together. To collapse selected lines of code, you can click the minus sign (Win) or the triangle (Mac) next to the line number. You can also use the Collapse Full Tag or Collapse Selection buttons on the Coding toolbar. This will allow you to look at two different sections of code that are not adjacent to each other.

Adding comments is an easy way to add documentation to your code, which is especially helpful when you are working in a team environment and other team members will be working on pages with you. For example, you might use comments to communicate instructions like "Do not alter code below this line." or "Add final schedule here when it becomes available." Comments are not visible in the browser.

Using Code Hints to Streamline Coding

If you are typing code directly into Code view, Dreamweaver can speed your work by offering you code hints. **Code hints** are lists of tags that appear as you type, similar to other auto-complete features that you have probably used in other software applications. As you are typing code, Dreamweaver will recognize the tag name and offer you choices to complete the tag simply by double-clicking a tag choice in the menu, as shown in Figure 38. You can also add your own code hints to the list using JavaScript. Code hints are stored in the file CodeHints.xml.

Converting Styles

You can also convert one type of style to another. For instance, you can move an embedded style to an external style sheet or an inline style to either an embedded style or a style in an external style sheet. To do this, select the style in Code view, right-click the code, point to CSS Styles, then click Move CSS Rules. You can also move styles in the CSS Styles panel by selecting the style, right-clicking the style, and choosing the action you want from the shortcut menu.

Figure 38 *Using code hints*

As you begin typing code, the shortcut menu appears when Dreamweaver recognizes the code

Double-click from the list to complete your tag

Collapse code

1. Verify that the index page is open, then change to Code view.

2. Scroll up the page, if necessary, to display the code that ends the embedded styles (</style>).

   The code will probably be on or close to line 18 in the head section.

3. Select this line of code, then drag up to select all of the code up to and including the beginning tag for the embedded style sheet (<style type="text/css>", as shown in Figure 39.

TIP If your code is in a slightly different order, scroll to find the meta tags to select them.

4. Click the **minus sign** (Win) or **vertical triangle** (Mac) in the last line of selected code to collapse all of the selected code.

   You can now see code above and below the collapsed code section as shown in Figure 40. The plus sign (Win) or horizontal triangle (Mac) next to the line of code indicates that there is hidden code. You also see a gap in the line numbers where the hidden code resides.

You collapsed a block of code in Code view to be able to see two non-adjacent sections of the code at the same time.

Figure 39 *Selecting lines of code on the index page to collapse*

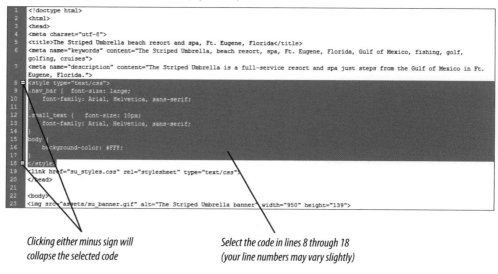

Clicking either minus sign will collapse the selected code

Select the code in lines 8 through 18 (your line numbers may vary slightly)

Figure 40 *Collapsed code in Code view*

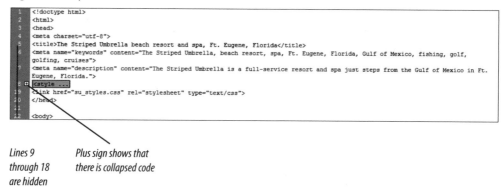

Lines 9 through 18 are hidden

Plus sign shows that there is collapsed code

Figure 41 *Expanded code for index page*

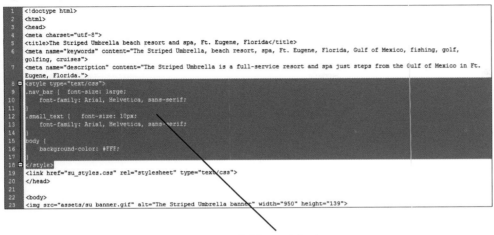

```
1  <!doctype html>
2  <html>
3  <head>
4  <meta charset="utf-8">
5  <title>The Striped Umbrella beach resort and spa, Ft. Eugene, Florida</title>
6  <meta name="keywords" content="The Striped Umbrella, beach resort, spa, Ft. Eugene, Florida, Gulf of Mexico, fishing, golf,
   golfing, cruises">
7  <meta name="description" content="The Striped Umbrella is a full-service resort and spa just steps from the Gulf of Mexico in Ft.
   Eugene, Florida.">
8  <style type="text/css">
9  .nav_bar {  font-size: large;
10     font-family: Arial, Helvetica, sans-serif;
11  }
12  .small_text {  font-size: 10px;
13     font-family: Arial, Helvetica, sans-serif;
14  }
15  body {
16     background-color: #FFF;
17  }
18  </style>
19  <link href="su_styles.css" rel="stylesheet" type="text/css">
20  </head>
21
22  <body>
23  <img src="assets/su_banner.gif" alt="The Striped Umbrella banner" width="950" height="139">
```

Code is expanded again

POWER USER SHORTCUTS	
To do this:	**Use this shortcut:**
Switch views	[Ctrl][`] (Win) or [control][`] (Mac)
Indent text	[Ctrl][Alt][]] (Win) or ⌘ [option][]] (Mac)
Outdent text	[Ctrl][Alt][[] (Win) or ⌘ [option][[] (Mac)
Align Left	[Ctrl][Alt][Shift][L] (Win) or ⌘ [option][shift][L] (Mac)
Align Center	[Ctrl][Alt][Shift][C] (Win) or ⌘ [option][shift][C] (Mac)
Align Right	[Ctrl][Alt][Shift][R] (Win) or ⌘ [option][shift][R] (Mac)
Align Justify	[Ctrl][Alt][Shift][J] (Win) or ⌘ [option][shift][J] (Mac)
Bold	[Ctrl][B] (Win) or ⌘ [B] (Mac)
Italic	[Ctrl][I] (Win) or ⌘ [I] (Mac)
Refresh	[F5]

© Cengage Learning 2013

Expand code

1. Click the **plus sign** (Win) or **horizontal triangle** (Mac) on line 8 to expand the code.

2. Compare your screen to Figure 41, then click in the page to deselect the code.

   All line numbers are visible again.

You expanded the code to display all lines of the code again.

Move an embedded style to an external CSS

1. Select the lines of code in the head section with the properties of the small_text rule (including the closing bracket) on the index page.

   The code will be on or close to lines 12 through 14.

2. Right-click (Win) or control-click (Mac) the **selected code**, point to **CSS Styles**, then click **Move CSS Rules**, as shown in Figure 42.

   TIP You can also convert a rule in the CSS Styles panel. To do this, right-click the rule name, then click Move CSS Rules.

3. In the Move To External Style Sheet dialog box, verify that su_styles.css appears in the Style Sheet text box, as shown in Figure 43, then click **OK**.

4. Repeat Steps 1 through 3 to move the nav_bar and body rules to the external style sheet.

   Since all styles are now in the external style sheet, they are available to be used for formatting all of the pages in the site.

   (continued)

Figure 42 *Moving the embedded small_text rule to the external style sheet file*

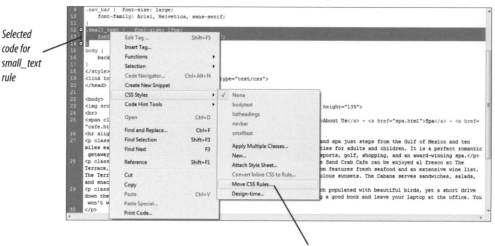

Selected code for small_text rule

Move CSS Rules command

Figure 43 *Moving the embedded style to the external style sheet file*

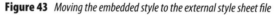

The embedded small_text rule will move to the su_styles file

Working with Text and Cascading Style Sheets

Figure 44 *Viewing the three rules moved to the external style sheet*

Figure 45 *Viewing the CSS Styles panel after removing code*

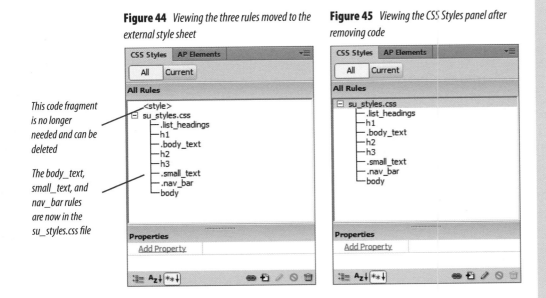

This code fragment is no longer needed and can be deleted

The body_text, small_text, and nav_bar rules are now in the su_styles.css file

5. Expand the su_styles.css style in the CSS Styles panel, if necessary, to display its rules, then compare your panel with Figure 44 to verify that the styles have been moved to the external style sheet file.

   The opening and closing tags for the internal style sheet are still in the code and can be removed now. When you delete the <style> tag in the CSS Styles panel, the opening and closing tags in the code will be removed.

6. Click **<style>** in the CSS Styles panel, press **[Delete]**, then compare your screen to Figure 45.

   You can also delete this code on the page in Code view if you prefer.

7. Return to Design view, then save and close all open files.

You moved three embedded rules to the external style sheet. You then deleted the remaining code left from the internal style sheet.

The evolution of CSS3

The use of Cascading Style Sheets has evolved over the years from CSS Level 1 to the present CSS Level 3. Cascading Style Sheets revisions are referenced by "levels" rather than "versions." Each new level builds on the previous level. CSS Level 1 is obsolete today. CSS Level 2 is still used, but CSS Level 3 is the latest W3C (World Wide Web Consortium) standard. With CSS3, several properties are available that promote website accessibility such as the @font-face rule. For more information about CSS3, go to www.w3.org/TR/CSS/.

Create unordered and ordered lists.

1. Open the Blooms & Bulbs website.
2. Open the tips page.
3. Select the text items below the Seasonal Gardening Checklist heading and format them as an unordered list. (*Hint*: There are no paragraph breaks between each item. To correct this, enter a paragraph break between each line, then remove any extra spaces.)
4. Select the lines of text below the Basic Gardening Tips heading and format them as an ordered list. (Refer to the Step 3 hint if each line does not become a separate list item.)
5. Save your work.

Create, apply, and edit Cascading Style Sheets.

1. Create a new CSS rule named **bullet_term**, making sure that the Class option button is selected in the Selector Type section and that the (New Style Sheet File) option is selected in the Rule Definition section of the New CSS Rule dialog box.
2. Click OK, name the style sheet file **blooms_styles** in the Save Style Sheet File As dialog box, then click Save.
3. Choose the following settings for the bullet_term rule: Font-family = Arial, Helvetica, sans-serif; Font-size = large; Font-style = normal; Font-weight = bold; and Color = #333.
4. Apply the bullet_term rule to the names of the seasons in the Seasonal Gardening Checklist: Fall, Winter, Spring, and Summer.
5. Edit the bullet_term rule by changing the font size to 16 pixels.

Add rules and attach Cascading Style Sheets.

1. Create a new class rule named **intro_text** in the blooms_styles.css file using following font settings: Font-family, Verdana, Geneva, sans-serif; Font-size 14 px; Color #333.
2. Apply the intro_text rule to the first paragraph on the page, then save the page.
3. Add a new Tag selector rule to the blooms_styles.css file that formats the h1 tag with the following properties: Font-family: Arial, Helvetica, sans-serif; Font-size: 16 px; Font-weight: bold.
4. Save the tips page, open the index page, and attach the blooms_styles.css file.
5. Apply the body_text rule to the rest of the text on the page that is not formatted with a rule.
6. Use the Save All command on the File menu to save both open pages and the style sheet, then preview both pages in the browser.
7. Close the browser.

Use coding tools to view and edit rules.

1. Switch to the index page if necessary, then change to Code view.
2. Display the code that ends the four embedded styles.
3. Select the lines of code for all of the embedded styles, including the opening and closing tags.
4. Collapse all of the selected code.
5. Expand the code.
6. Select the lines of code that define the small_text rule properties in the head section (including the closing bracket), then move the rule to the blooms_styles external style sheet.
7. Repeat Step 6 to move the body_text, nav_bar, and body rules to the external style sheet.
8. Delete the remaining code fragments for the beginning and ending embedded styles tags.
9. Apply the body_text rule to any remaining text on the tips page that is not formatted with a rule.
10. Save all open files, compare your pages to Figures 46 and 47, then close all open files.

Figure 46 & 47 *Completed Skills Review*

Blooms & Bulbs
HWY 43 SOUTH • ALVIN • TX 77511 • 555-248-0806

<u>Home</u> - <u>Featured Plants</u> - <u>Garden Tips</u> - <u>Workshops</u> - <u>Newsletter</u>

Welcome to Blooms & Bulbs. We carry a variety of plants and shrubs along with a large inventory of gardening supplies. Our four greenhouses are full of healthy young plants just waiting to be planted in your yard. We grow an amazing selection of annuals and perennials. We also stock a diverse selection of trees, shrubs, tropicals, water plants, and ground covers. Check out our garden ware for your garden accents or as gifts for your gardening friends. We are happy to deliver or ship your purchases.

Our staff includes a certified landscape architect, three landscape designers, and six tailored to your location as well as planting and regular maintenance services. We ha twelve years now. Stop by and see us soon!

Blooms & Bulbs
Highway 43 South
Alvin, Texas 77511
555-248-0806
<u>*Customer Service*</u>

Copyright 2001 - 2015
Last updated on January 6, 2012

Blooms & Bulbs
HWY 43 SOUTH • ALVIN • TX 77511 • 555-248-0806

We have lots of tips we would like to share with you as you prepare your gardens this season. Remember, there is always something to be done for your gardens, no matter what the season. Our experienced staff is here to help you plan your gardens, select your plants, prepare your soil, assist you in the planting, and maintain your beds. Check out our calendar for a list of our scheduled workshops. Our next workshop is "Attracting Butterflies to Your Garden." All workshops are free of charge and on a first-come, first-served basis! They fill up quickly, so be sure to reserve your spot early.

Seasonal Gardening Checklist

- **Fall** – The time to plant trees and spring-blooming bulbs. Take the time to clean the leaves and dead foliage from your beds and lawn.
- **Winter** – The time to prune fruit trees and finish planting your bulbs. Don't forget to water young trees when the ground is dry.
- **Spring** – The time to prepare your beds, plant annuals, and apply fertilizer to established plants. Remember to mulch to maintain moisture and prevent weed growth.
- **Summer** – The time to supplement rainfall so that plants get one inch of water per week. Plant your vegetable garden and enjoy bountiful harvests until late fall.

Basic Gardening Tips

1. Select plants according to your climate.
2. In planning your garden, consider the composition, texture, structure, depth, and drainage of your soil.
3. Use commpost to improve the structure of your soil.
4. Choose plant foods based on your garden objectives.
5. Generally, plants should receive one inch of water per week.
6. Use mulch to conserve moisture, keep plants cool, and cut down on weeding.

Use Figures 48 and 49 as a guide to continue your work on the TripSmart website that you began in Project Builder 1 in Chapter 1, and continued to work on in Chapter 2. (Your finished pages will look different if you choose different formatting options.) You are now ready to create some rules to use for the text on the newsletter and index pages.

1. Open the TripSmart website.
2. Open dw3_1.html from where you store your Data Files and save it in the tripsmart site folder as **news-letter.html**, overwriting the existing newsletter. html file and not updating the links.
3. Verify that the path for the banner is correctly set to the assets folder of the TripSmart website, then type the title **Travel Tidbits** in the Title text box on the Document toolbar.
4. Create an unordered list from the text beginning "Be organized." to the end of the page.
5. Create a new CSS rule called **paragraph_text** making sure that the Class option is selected in the Selector Type section and that the (New Style Sheet File) option is selected in the Rule Definition section of the New CSS Rule dialog box.
6. Save the style sheet file as **tripsmart_styles.css** in the TripSmart website site folder.
7. Choose a font family, size, style, weight, and color of your choice for the paragraph_text style.
8. Apply the paragraph_text rule to all of the text on the page except the "Ten Tips for Stress-Free Travel" heading.
9. Create a Tag selector rule in the tripsmart_styles.css file that formats the h1 tag with a font, size, style,

color, and weight of your choice, and assign the Heading 1 format to the "Ten Tips for Stress-Free Travel" heading.
10. Create another Class selector rule in the external style sheet called **list_term** with a font, size, style, color, and weight of your choice and apply it to each of the item names in the list such as "Be organized."
11. Close the dw3_1.html page, then save the newsletter page and the style sheet.
12. Open the index page, then attach the tripsmart_styles style sheet.
13. Select the two paragraphs and contact information, then apply the paragraph_text rule.
14. Delete the body_text embedded rule, then move the remaining embedded rules to the external style sheet. Delete any remaining code fragments from the embedded styles.
15. Save and preview the index and newsletter pages in your browser, using Figures 48 and 49 as examples.
16. Close your browser, then close all open files.

Figures 48 & 49 *Sample Project Builder 1*

In this exercise, you continue your work on the Carolyne's Creations website that you started in Project Builder 2 in Chapter 1, and continued to build in Chapter 2. You are now ready to add a page to the website that will showcase a recipe. Figures 50 and 51 show a possible solution for these pages in this exercise. Your finished pages will look different if you choose different formatting options.

1. Open the Carolyne's Creations website
2. Open dw3_2.html from the location where you store your Data Files, save it to the website site folder as **recipes.html**, overwriting the existing file and not updating the links. Close the dw3_2.html file.
3. Select the pie image broken link placeholder, then use the Property inspector to browse for the pie.jpg image in the assets folder where you store your Data Files.
4. Format the list of ingredients on the recipes page as an unordered list.
5. Create a CSS rule named **body_text** and save it in a style sheet file named **cc_styles.css** in the website root folder. Use any formatting options that you like, then apply the body_text rule to all text except the menu bar and the text "Caramel Coconut Pie," "Ingredients," and "Directions."
6. Create a Tag selector rule that defines the properties for a Heading 1 rule and another one that defines the properties for a Heading 2 rule, using appropriate formatting options.
7. Apply the <h1> format to the "Caramel Coconut Pie" heading and the <h2> rule to the "Ingredients" and "Directions" headings, then save your work.
8. Open the index page, then attach the cc_styles.css to the file.
9. Delete the embedded body_text rule. The body_text rule in the external style sheet will format the text.
10. Convert the nav_bar rule and the small_text rule to external rules in the cc_styles style sheet, then switch back to the recipes page and format the menu bar with the nav_bar rule.
11. Delete any unnecessary code fragments left from the embedded styles.
12. Save all open files, then preview both pages in the browser.
13. Close your browser, then close all open pages.

Figures 50 and 51 *Sample Project Builder 2*

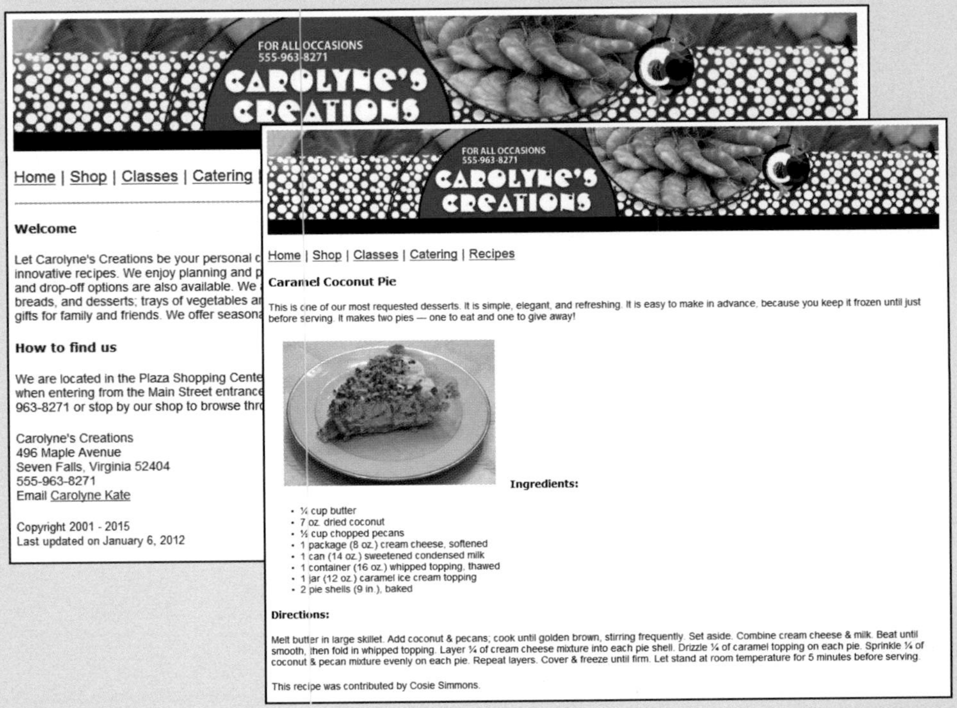

Charles Chappell is a sixth-grade history teacher. He is reviewing educational websites for information he can use in his classroom.

1. Connect to the Internet, then navigate to the Library of Congress website at www.loc.gov. The Library of Congress website is shown in Figure 52.

2. Which fonts are used for the main content on the home page—serif or sans-serif? Are the same fonts used consistently on the other pages in the site?

3. Do you see ordered or unordered lists on any pages in the site? If so, how are they used?

4. Use the View > Source (IE) or the Tools > Web Developer > Page Source (Firefox) command to view the source code to see if a style sheet was used.

5. Do you see the use of Cascading Style Sheets noted in the source code?

Figure 52 *Design Project*
The Library of congress website – www.loc.gov

In this assignment, you will continue to work on the website that you started in Chapter 1, and continued to build in Chapter 2. No Data Files are supplied. You are building this site from chapter to chapter, so you must do each Portfolio Project assignment in each chapter to complete your website.

You continue building your website by designing and completing a page that contains a list, headings, and paragraph text. During this process, you will develop a style sheet and add several rules to it

1. Consult your wireframe and decide which page to create and develop for this chapter.

2. Plan the page content for the page and make a sketch of the layout. Your sketch should include at least one ordered or unordered list, appropriate headings, and paragraph text. Your sketch should also show where the paragraph text and headings should be placed on the page and what rules should be used for each type of text. You should plan on creating at least two CSS rules.

3. Create the page using your sketch for guidance.

4. Create a Cascading Style Sheet for the site and add to it the rules you decided to use. Apply the rules to the appropriate content.

5. Attach the style sheet to the index page you developed in Chapter 2 and consider converting any existing embedded styles to the external style sheet.

6. Preview the new page in a browser, then check for page layout problems and broken links. Make any necessary corrections in Dreamweaver, then preview the page again in the browser. Repeat this process until you are satisfied with the way the page looks in the browser.

7. Use the checklist in Figure 53 to check all the pages in your site.

8. Close the browser, then close all open pages.

Figure 53 *Portfolio Project*

Website Checklist

1. Does each page have a page title?
2. Does the home page have a description and keywords?
3. Does the home page contain contact information?
4. Does every completed page in the site have consistent navigation links?
5. Does the home page have a last updated statement that will automatically update when the page is saved?
6. Do all paths for links and images work correctly?
7. Is there a style sheet with at least two rules?
8. Did you apply the rules to all text blocks?
9. Do all pages look good using at least two different browsers?

ADOBE DREAMWEAVER CS6

CHAPTER 4 ADDING IMAGES

1. Insert and align images
2. Enhance an image and use alternate text
3. Insert a background image and perform site maintenance
4. Add graphic enhancements

ADDING IMAGES

Introduction

The majority of web page information appears in the form of text. But pages are much more interesting if they also contain images that enhance or illustrate the information. A well-designed web page usually includes a balanced combination of text and images. Dreamweaver provides many tools for working with images that you can use to make your web pages attractive and easy to understand.

Using Images to Enhance Web Pages

Images make web pages visually stimulating and more exciting than pages that contain only text. However, you should use images with an eye on both the purpose of each page and the overall design plan. There is a fine balance between using too many images that overwhelm the user and not providing enough images to enhance the text. There are many ways to work with images so that they complement the content of pages in a website.

You can use specific file formats used to save images for websites to ensure maximum quality with minimum file size.

Graphics Versus Images

Two terms that designers sometimes use interchangeably are graphics and images. For the purposes of discussion in this text, we will use the term **graphics** to refer to the appearance of most non-text items on a web page, such as photographs, logos, menu bars, Flash animations, charts, background images, and drawings. Files for items such as these are called graphic files. They are referred to by their file type, or graphic file format, such as JPEG (Joint Photographic Experts Group), GIF (Graphics Interchange Format), or PNG (Portable Network Graphics). We will refer to the actual pictures that you see on the pages as images. But don't worry about which term to use. Many people use one term or the other according to habit or region, or use them interchangeably.

Alt text box

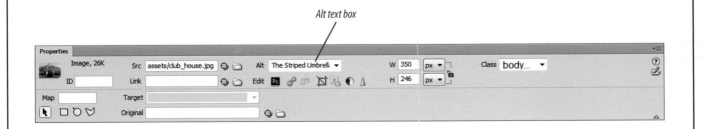

Insert and
ALIGN IMAGES

What You'll Do

In this lesson, you will insert three images on the about_us page in The Striped Umbrella website. You will then adjust the alignment of the images on the page to make the page more visually appealing.

Understanding Graphic File Formats

When you choose graphics to add to a web page, it's important to use graphic files in the appropriate file format. Keep in mind the different types of devices that may be used to view the pages, such as tablets or smart phones. The three primary graphic file formats used in web pages are **GIF** (Graphics Interchange Format), **JPEG** or **JPG** (Joint Photographic Experts Group), and **PNG** (Portable Network Graphics). GIF files download quickly, making them ideal to use on web pages. Though limited in the number of colors they can represent, GIF files have the ability to show transparent areas. JPG files can display many colors. Because they often contain many shades of the same color, photographs are often saved in JPG format. Files saved with the PNG format can display many colors and use various degrees of transparency, called **opacity**. However, not all older browsers support the PNG format. JPGs and GIFS are best used when targeting mobile devices.

QUICK **TIP**

The Dreamweaver status bar shows the total download time for the open web page. Each time you add a new graphic to the page, you can see how much additional download time that graphic has added to the total.

Understanding the Assets Panel

When you add a graphic to a website, Dreamweaver automatically adds it to the Assets panel. The **Assets panel**, located in the Files panel group, displays all the assets in a website. The Assets panel contains nine category buttons that you use to view your assets by category. These include Images, Colors, URLs, SWF, Shockwave, Movies, Scripts, Templates, and Library. To view a particular type of asset, click the appropriate category button.

The Assets panel is divided into two panes. When you click the Images button, as shown in Figure 1, the lower pane displays a list of all the images in your site and is divided into five columns. You might need to resize the Assets panel to see all five columns. To resize the Assets panel, undock the Files tab group and drag a side or corner of the panel border.

The top pane displays a thumbnail of the selected image in the list. You can view assets in each category in two ways. You can use the Site option button to view all the assets in a website, or you can use the Favorites option button to view those assets that you have designated as **favorites**, or assets that you expect to use repeatedly while you work on the site.

You can use the Assets panel to add an asset to a web page by dragging the asset from the Assets panel to the page or by using the Insert button on the Assets panel. If you are working on a page layout without final images ready to place, you can insert an image placeholder to hold the image position on the page. An **image placeholder** is a graphic the size of an image you plan to use. You can place it on a page until the actual image is finalized and ready to place on the page. To insert an image placeholder, use the Image Placeholder command on the Insert > Image Objects menu. When the final image is ready, simply replace the image placeholder with the final image.

Inserting Files with Adobe Bridge

You can manage project files, including video and Camera Raw files, with a file-management tool called Adobe Bridge. **Camera Raw** file formats are files that contain unprocessed data and are not yet ready to be printed. **Adobe Bridge** is an image file management program that is used across the Adobe suite applications. Bridge is an easy way to view files in their original locations before bringing them into the website. Bridge is an integrated application, which means you can use it to manage files among other Adobe programs such as Photoshop and Illustrator. You can also use Bridge to add meta tags and search text to your files. To open Bridge, click the Browse in Bridge command on the File menu or click the Browse In Bridge button on the Standard toolbar.

Aligning Images

When you insert an image on a web page, you need to position it in relation to other page elements such as text or other images. Positioning an image is also called **aligning** an image. By default, when you insert an image in a paragraph, its bottom edge aligns with the baseline of the first line of text or any other element in the same paragraph. When you first place images on a page, they do not include code to align them, so they appear at the insertion point, with no other page elements next to them. You add alignment settings with CSS. By adding a new rule to modify the <img> tag, you can add an alignment property and value. If you use an external style sheet, the <img> tag will apply globally to all images on pages with a link to the style sheet.

Figure 1 *Assets panel*

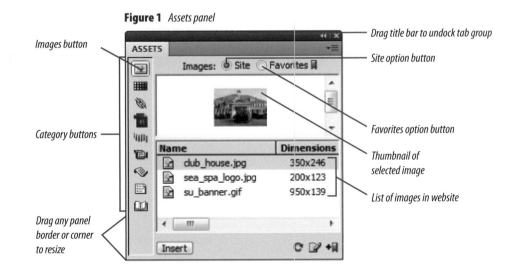

Images button

Category buttons

Drag any panel border or corner to resize

Drag title bar to undock tab group

Site option button

Favorites option button

Thumbnail of selected image

List of images in website

Insert an image

1. Open The Striped Umbrella website, open dw4_1.html from the drive and folder where you store your Data Files, then save it as **about_us.html** in the striped_umbrella site root folder.

2. Click **Yes** (Win) or **Replace** (Mac) to overwrite the existing file, click **No** to Update Links, then close dw4_1.html.

3. Click the **Attach Style Sheet button** in the CSS Styles panel, then attach the su_styles.css style sheet to the page.

4. Select the two large paragraphs of text on the page, click the **HTML button** <> HTML on the Property inspector, verify that the Format is set to Paragraph, click the **CSS button** ⊞ᵇ CSS , then apply the body_text rule to the selected text.

5. Click the **HTML button** <> HTML , then apply the Heading 1 tag to the text "Welcome guests!"

6. Place the insertion point before "When" in the first paragraph, click the **Images list arrow** in the Common category in the Insert panel, then click **Image** to open the Select Image Source dialog box.

7. Navigate to the assets folder in the drive and folder where you store your Data Files, double-click **club_house.jpg**, type the alternate text **Club House** if prompted, click **OK**, open the Files panel if necessary, then verify that the file was copied to your assets folder in the striped_umbrella site root folder.

   Compare your screen to Figure 2.

   (continued)

Figure 2 *Striped Umbrella about_us page with the inserted image*

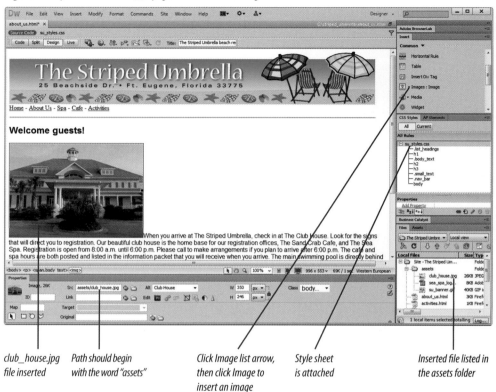

club_house.jpg file inserted

Path should begin with the word "assets"

Click Image list arrow, then click Image to insert an image

Style sheet is attached

Inserted file listed in the assets folder

Figure 3 *Image files for The Striped Umbrella website listed in Assets panel*

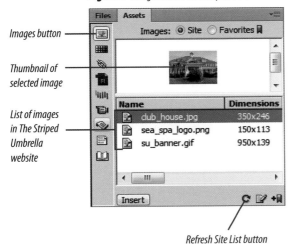

Images button

Thumbnail of selected image

List of images in The Striped Umbrella website

Refresh Site List button

8. Click the **Assets panel tab** in the Files tab group, click the **Images button** in the Assets panel (if necessary), then click the **Refresh Site List button** in the Assets panel to update the list of images in The Striped Umbrella website.

The Assets panel displays a list of all the images in The Striped Umbrella website, as shown in Figure 3. If you don't see the new image listed, press and hold [CTRL] (Win) or ⌘ (Mac) before you click the Refresh Site List button.

You inserted one image on the about_us page and copied it to the assets folder of the website.

Organizing Assets for Quick Access

Your can organize the assets in the Assets panel in two ways, using the Site and Favorites options buttons. The Site option lists all of the assets in the website in the selected category in alphabetical order. But in a complex site, your asset list can grow quite large. To avoid having to scroll to search for frequently used items, you can designate them as Favorites. To add an asset to the Favorites list, right-click (Win) or [control]-click (Mac) the asset name in the Site list, and then click Add to Favorites. When you place an asset in the Favorites list, it still appears in the Site list. To delete an asset from the Favorites list, click the Favorites option button in the Assets panel, select the asset you want to delete, and then press [Delete] or the Remove from Favorites button on the Assets panel. If you delete an asset from the Favorites list, it still remains in the Site list. You can further organize your Favorites list by creating folders for similar assets and grouping them inside the folders.

Insert an image placeholder

1. Click to place the insertion point before the word "After" at the beginning of the second paragraph.

2. Click the **Images list arrow** in the Common category in the Insert panel, then click **Image Placeholder** to open the Image Placeholder dialog box.

3. Type **boardwalk** in the Name text box, **350** in the Width text box, **218** in the Height text box, and **Boardwalk to the beach** in the Alternate text text box, as shown in Figure 4.

4. Click **OK** to accept these settings, then compare your screen to Figure 5.

You inserted an image placeholder on the about_us page to hold the location on the page until the final image is ready to insert.

Figure 4 *Image Placeholder dialog box*

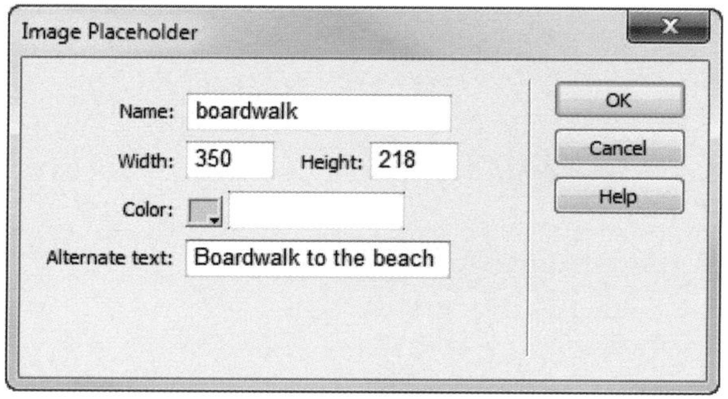

Figure 5 *Image placeholder on the about_us page*

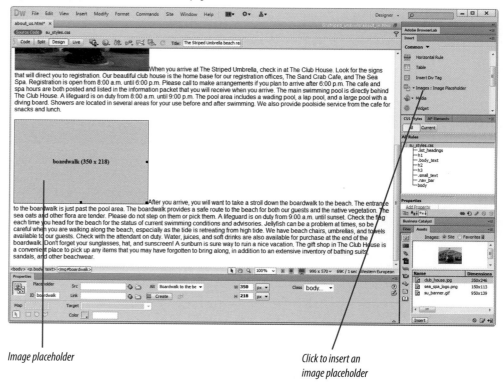

Image placeholder

Click to insert an image placeholder

Figure 6 *The about_us page with the boardwalk image inserted*

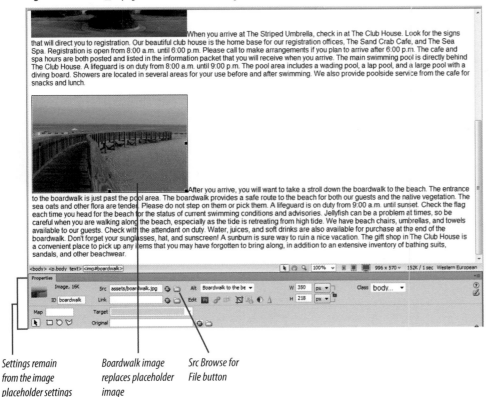

Settings remain
from the image
placeholder settings

Boardwalk image
replaces placeholder
image

Src Browse for
File button

1. Click to select the **image placeholder** on the about_us page, if necessary.

2. Click the **Browse for File button** 🗁 next to the Src text box on the Property inspector and browse to the assets folder where you store your Data Files if necessary.

TIP You can also double-click an image placeholder to open the Select Image Source dialog box.

3. Double-click **boardwalk.png** to replace the image placeholder with the boardwalk image.

   The alternate text and the height and width settings on the Property inspector are the same that you entered in the Image Placeholder dialog box, as shown in Figure 6.

4. Save your work.

You replaced an image placeholder on the about_us page with a final image.

Use Adobe Bridge

1. Click to place the insertion point at the end of the last sentence on the page, then enter a paragraph break.

2. Click **File** on the Menu bar, click **Browse in Bridge**, close the dialog box asking if you want the Bridge extension for Dreamweaver to be enabled, answer **Yes** (if necessary), click the **Folders tab**, navigate to where you store your Data Files, then click the thumbnail image **su_logo.gif** in the assets folder, as shown in Figure 7.

   The Bridge window is divided into several panels; files and folders are listed in the Folders panel. The files in the selected folder appear in the Content panel. A picture of the selected file appears in the Preview panel. The Metadata and Keywords panels list any tags that have been added to the file. Your Content panel background may be lighter or darker depending on your Bridge settings.

3. Click **File** on the Menu bar, point to **Place**, then click **In Dreamweaver**.

4. Type the alternate text **The Striped Umbrella logo**, if prompted, then click **OK**.

   The image appears on the page.

TIP You can also click the Browse in Bridge button 🖺 on the Standard toolbar to open Bridge.

After refreshing, your Assets panel should resemble Figure 8.

You inserted an image on the about_us page using Adobe Bridge.

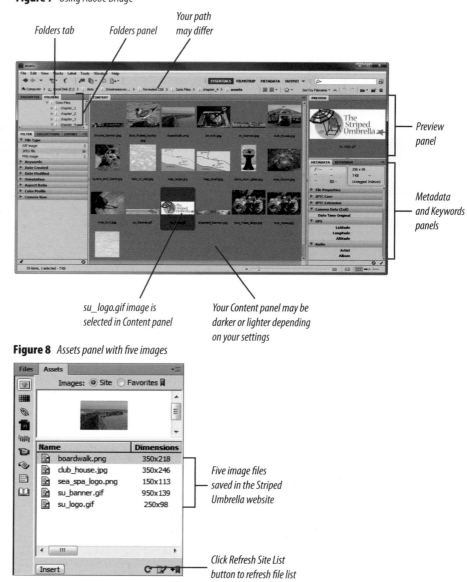

Figure 7 *Using Adobe Bridge*

Folders tab   Folders panel   Your path may differ

Preview panel

Metadata and Keywords panels

su_logo.gif image is selected in Content panel

Your Content panel may be darker or lighter depending on your settings

Figure 8 *Assets panel with five images*

Five image files saved in the Striped Umbrella website

Click Refresh Site List button to refresh file list

Figure 9 *New CSS Rule dialog box*

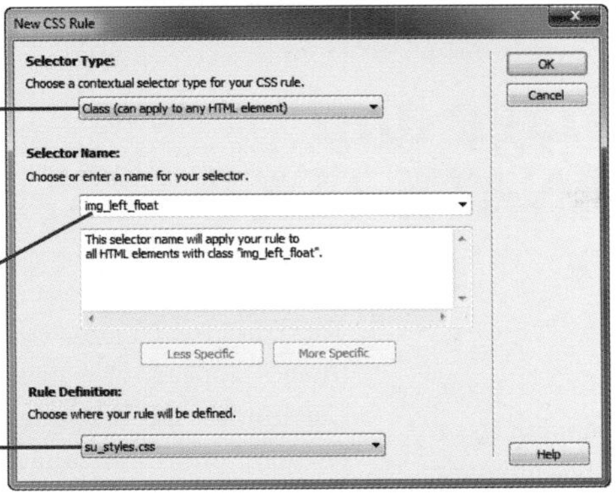

*Select the Class
Selector Type*

*New Selector name
is img_left_float*

*The new rule
will be saved in
the su_styles.css
style sheet*

Figure 10 *CSS Rule Definition for img_left_float in su_styles.css dialog box*

*Select the Box
Category*

*Select the left
Float value*

Figure 11 *Clubhouse image with img_left_float rule applied*

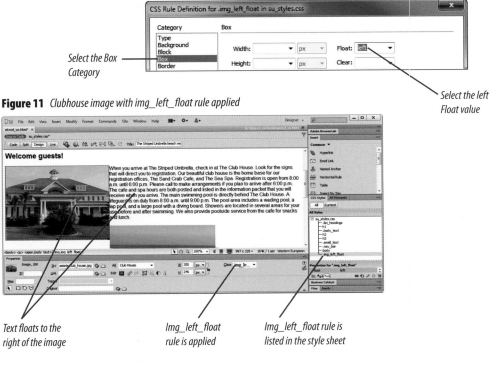

*Text floats to the
right of the image*

*Img_left_float
rule is applied*

*Img_left_float rule is
listed in the style sheet*

Align an image

1. Scroll to the top of the page, then click the **club house image**.

    Because an image is selected, the Property inspector displays tools for setting the properties of an image.

2. Click the **New CSS Rule button** in the CSS Styles panel, click **Class** in the Selector type list box, type **img_left_float** for the Selector name, verify that it will be saved in the su_styles.css file, compare your screen to Figure 9, then click **OK**.

3. Click the **Box Category**, click the **Float list arrow**, click **left** as shown in Figure 10, then click **OK**.

    The Float property tells the browser to "float" the image to the left of whatever follows it on the page.

4. Click the **clubhouse image** if necessary, click the **Class list arrow** on the right side of the Property inspector, then click **img_left_float**.

    The text moves to the right side of the image, as shown in Figure 11.

5. Repeat Steps 2 through 4 to create another rule named **img_right_float** with a Float value of **right**.

6. Apply the img_right_float rule to the boardwalk image.

TIP You can also right-click an image, point to CSS Styles, then click the rule you want to apply.

7. Save your work, then close Adobe Bridge.

You created two new CSS rules: one to use to align the image to the left with (text to the right of it) and one to use to align the image to the right with (text to the left of it).

Enhance an Image and
USE ALTERNATE TEXT

What You'll Do

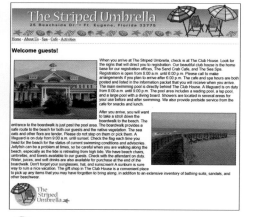

 In this lesson, you will add borders to images, add horizontal and vertical space to set them apart from the text, and then add or edit alternate text to each image on the page.

Enhancing an Image

After you place an image on a web page, you have several options for enhancing it, or improving its appearance. To make changes to the image itself, such as removing scratches from it, or erasing parts of it, you need to use an image editor such as Adobe Fireworks or Adobe Photoshop.

QUICK TIP

You can copy a Photoshop PSD file and paste it directly into Dreamweaver. After inserting the image, Dreamweaver will prompt you to optimize the image for the web.

You can use Dreamweaver to enhance how images appear on a page. For example, you can modify the brightness and contrast, add borders around an image or add horizontal and vertical space. **Borders** are frames that surround an image. Horizontal and vertical space is blank space above, below, and on the sides of an image that separates the image from text or other elements on the page. Adding horizontal or vertical space is the same as adding white space, and helps images stand out on a page. In the web page from the First Federal Bank website shown in Figure 12,

DESIGN TIP

Resizing Graphics Using an External Editor

Each image on a web page takes a specific number of seconds to download, depending on the size of the file. Larger files (in kilobytes, not width and height) take longer to download than smaller files. It's important to determine the smallest acceptable size for an image on a page. Then, if you need to resize an image to reduce the file size, use an external image editor to do so, instead of resizing it in Dreamweaver. Decreasing the size of an image using the H (height) and W (width) settings in the Property inspector does not reduce the file size or the time it will take the file to download. Ideally you should use images that have the smallest file size and the highest quality possible, so that each page downloads as quickly as possible.

the horizontal and vertical space around the images helps make these images more prominent. Adding horizontal or vertical space does not affect the width or height of the image. The best way to add horizontal and vertical space is with CSS. Spacing around web page objects can also be created by using "spacer" images, or transparent images that act as placeholders. In the First Federal site, spacer images were used to provide space between several of the page elements.

Using Alternate Text

One of the easiest ways to make your web page viewer-friendly and accessible to people of all abilities is to use alternate text. Alternate text is descriptive text that appears in place of an image while the image is downloading or not displayed. Screen readers, devices used by persons with visual impairments to convert written text on a computer monitor to spoken words, can "read" alternate text and make it possible for viewers to have an image described to them in detail. You should also use alternate text when inserting form objects, text displayed as graphics, buttons, frames, and media files. Without alternate text assigned to these objects, screen readers will not be able to read them.

One of the default preferences in Dreamweaver is to prompt you to enter alternate text whenever you insert an image on a page. You can set alternate text options in the Accessibility category of the Preferences dialog box. You can program some browsers to display only alternate text and to download images manually. Earlier versions of some browsers used to show alternate text when the mouse was placed over an image, such as Internet Explorer versions before version 8.0.

The use of alternate text is the first checkpoint listed in the Web Content Accessibility Guidelines (WCAG), Version 2.0, from the World Wide Web Consortium (W3C). The 12 WCAG guidelines are grouped together under four principles: perceivable, operable, understandable, and robust. The first guideline under perceivable states that a website should "Provide text alternatives for any non-text content so that it can be changed into other forms people need, such as large print, Braille, speech, symbols, or simpler language." To view the complete set of accessibility guidelines, go to the Web Accessibility Initiative page at w3.org/WAI/. You should always strive to meet these criteria for all web pages.

Figure 12 *First Federal Bank website*
First Federal Bank website used with permission from First Federal Bank – www.ffbh.com

Add a border

1. Click the **img_left_float** rule in the CSS Syles panel, click the **Edit Rule button** ✏, click the **Border Category**, enter the rule properties shown in Figure 13, then click **OK**.

   You will not see the border displayed properly until you preview the page in a browser.

2. Repeat Step 1 to add a border to the img_right_float rule.

You edited two rules to add a border around the two images on the about_us page.

Add horizontal and vertical space

1. Edit the img_left_float rule again to add vertical and horizontal space by unchecking the "Same for all" check box under Margin in the Box category, then setting the Box Right Margin to **10 px** as shown in Figure 14.

   The text is more evenly wrapped around the image and is easier to read, because it is not so close to the edge of the image.

2. Repeat Step 1 to add a 10 px left margin to the img_right_float rule.

3. Save your work, click the **Switch Design View to Live view button** Live , then compare your screen to Figure 15.

4. Return to Design view, then open the spa page.

5. Click the **sea_spa_logo image**, then apply the img_left_float rule to it.

(continued)

Figure 13 *CSS Rule Definition for img_left_float dialog box*

Same for all check boxes are checked

Border Category

Top = solid

Color = #666

Width = thin

Figure 14 *CSS Rule Definition for img_left_float dialog box*

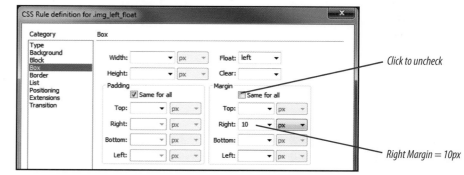

Click to uncheck

Right Margin = 10px

Figure 15 *Viewing the images with borders and margins*

When you arrive at The Striped Umbrella, check in at The Club House. Look for the signs that will direct you to registration. Our beautiful club house is the home base for our registration offices, The Sand Crab Cafe, and The Sea Spa. Registration is open from 8:00 a.m. until 6:00 p.m. Please call to make arrangements if you plan to arrive after 6:00 p.m. The cafe and spa hours are both posted and listed in the information packet that you will receive when you arrive. The main swimming pool is directly behind The Club House. A lifeguard is on duty from 8:00 a.m. until 9:00 p.m. The pool area includes a wading pool, a lap pool, and a large pool with a diving board. Showers are located in several areas for your use before and after swimming. We also provide poolside service from the cafe for snacks and lunch.

After you arrive, you will want to take a stroll down the boardwalk to the beach. The entrance to the boardwalk is just past the pool area. The boardwalk provides a safe route to the beach for both our guests and the native vegetation. The sea oats and other flora are tender. Please do not step on them or pick them. A lifeguard is on duty from 9:00 a.m. until sunset. Check the flag each time you head for the beach for the status of current swimming conditions.

Both images have borders and horizontal space separating them from the text

Adding Images

Figure 16 *Viewing the Image Optimization dialog box*

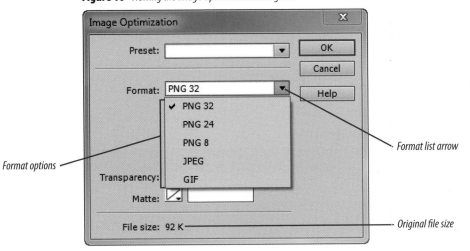

Format options

Format list arrow

Original file size

Dreamweaver has many functions integrated with Photoshop CS6. For example, you can copy and paste a Photoshop PSD file directly from Photoshop into Dreamweaver. Dreamweaver will prompt you to optimize the image by choosing a file format and settings for the web. Then it will paste the image on the page. If you want to edit the image later, select the image, then click the Edit button in the Property inspector to open the image in Photoshop. (The appearance of the Edit button will change according to the default image editor you have specified.) Photoshop users can set Photoshop as the default image editor in Dreamweaver for specific image file formats. Click Edit on the Menu bar, click Preferences (Win), or click Dreamweaver, click Preferences (Mac), click File Types/Editors, click the Extensions plus sign button, select a file format from the list, click the Editors plus sign button, then use the Select External Editor dialog box to browse to Photoshop (if you don't see it listed already), and then click Make Primary. You can also edit an image in Photoshop and export an updated Smart Object instantly in Dreamweaver. A **Smart Object** is an image layer that stores image data from raster or vector images. Search the Adobe website for a tutorial on Photoshop and Dreamweaver integration. Fireworks is another commonly used default image editor. Use the same steps to select it rather than Photoshop.

---

6. Save and close the spa page.

   The spacing under each picture differs because of the difference in the lengths of the paragraphs.

You added horizontal spacing and vertical spacing around three images on the about_us page and spa page by adding margin values to the img_left_float rule and the img_right_float rule.

Edit image settings

1. Select the **boardwalk image** on the about_us page.

2. Click the **Edit Image Settings button** in the Property inspector, then click the **Format list arrow**, as shown in Figure 16.

   You can use the Image Optimization dialog box to save a copy of the image in a different file format. File property options vary depending on which graphics format you choose. When you choose a different file format, then edit and save it, the program creates a copy and does not alter the original file.

3. Choose the JPEG format, then notice that the file size that appears at the bottom of the dialog box is much smaller than the PNG image.

4. Click **OK** to save the changes and close the Image Optimization dialog box.

   The Save Web Image dialog box opens. Here you choose the location where you want to save the image with the new file format.

5. Navigate to the website assets folder in the Save Web Image dialog box, then click **Save** to save the boardwalk.jpg image.

   There are now two copies of this image in the assets folder. One is a PNG and one is a JPG. If you don't see the new image, refresh the Assets panel.

You experimented with file format settings in the Image Optimization dialog box, then saved the image as a JPG file.

Edit alternate text

1. Select the club house image, select **Club House** in the Alt text box in the Property inspector (if necessary), type **The Striped Umbrella Club House** as shown in Figure 17, then press **[Enter]** (Win) or **[return]** (Mac).

   TIP You can tell when an image is selected when you see selection handles on its edges.

2. Select the boardwalk image, replace the alternate text with **The boardwalk to the beach** in the Alt text box, then press **[Enter]** (Win) or **[return]** (Mac).

   You added "The" to the beginning of the existing alternate text.

3. Save your work.

4. Preview the page in your browser, compare your screen to Figure 18, then close your browser.

You edited the alternate text for two images on the page.

Figure 17 *Alternate text setting in the Property inspector*

Alt text box

Figure 18 *about_us page viewed in browser*

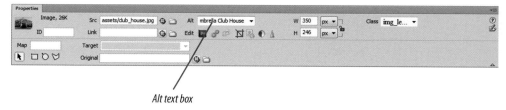

Welcome guests!

When you arrive at The Striped Umbrella, check in at The Club House. Look for the signs that will direct you to registration. Our beautiful club house is the home base for our registration offices, The Sand Crab Cafe, and The Sea Spa. Registration is open from 8:00 a.m. until 6:00 p.m. Please call to make arrangements if you plan to arrive after 6:00 p.m. The cafe and spa hours are both posted and listed in the information packet that you will receive when you arrive. The main swimming pool is directly behind The Club House. A lifeguard is on duty from 8:00 a.m. until 9:00 p.m. The pool area includes a wading pool, a lap pool, and a large pool with a diving board. Showers are located in several areas for your use before and after swimming. We also provide poolside service from the cafe for snacks and lunch.

After you arrive, you will want to take a stroll down the boardwalk to the beach. The entrance to the

boardwalk is just past the pool area. The boardwalk provides a safe route to the beach for both our guests and the native vegetation. The sea oats and other flora are tender. Please do not step on them or pick them. A lifeguard is on duty from 9:00 a.m. until sunset. Check the flag each time you head for the beach for the status of current swimming conditions and advisories. Jellyfish can be a problem at times, so be careful when you are walking along the beach, especially as the tide is retreating from high tide. We have beach chairs, umbrellas, and towels available to our guests. Check with the attendant on duty. Water, juices, and soft drinks are also available for purchase at the end of the boardwalk. Don't forget your sunglasses, hat, and sunscreen! A sunburn is sure way to ruin a nice vacation. The gift shop in The Club House is a convenient place to pick up any items that you may have forgotten to bring along, in addition to an extensive inventory of bathing suits, sandals, and other beachwear.

Figure 19 *Preferences dialog box with Accessibility category selected*

Accessibility category

Check boxes for Form objects, Frames, Media, and Images

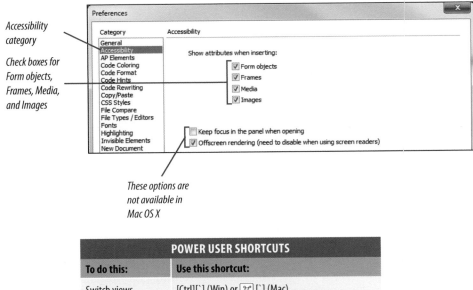

These options are not available in Mac OS X

POWER USER SHORTCUTS	
To do this:	**Use this shortcut:**
Switch views	[Ctrl][`] (Win) or ⌘ [`] (Mac)
Insert image	[Ctrl][Alt][I] (Win) or ⌘ [option][I] (Mac)
Refresh	[F5]
Browse in Bridge	[Ctrl][Alt][O] (Win) or ⌘ [option][O] (Mac)

© Cengage Learning 2013

Displaying Alternate Text in a Browser

There is a simple method you can use to force alternate text to appear in a browser when a mouse is held over an image. To do this, add a title tag to the image properties using the same text as the alt tag. Example: <img src="assets/club_house.jpg" alt="The Striped Umbrella Club House" title="The Striped Umbrella Club House" width="350" height="246" hspace="10" vspace="10" border="1" align="left" /> This method will work in Internet Explorer 8 and later versions and Mozilla Firefox.

Set the alternate text accessibility option

1. Click **Edit** on the Menu bar (Win) or **Dreamweaver** on the Menu bar (Mac), click **Preferences** to open the Preferences dialog box, then click the **Accessibility category**.

2. Verify that the four attributes check boxes are checked, as shown in Figure 19, check them if they are not checked, then click **OK**.

TIP Once you set the Accessibility preferences, they will be in effect for all websites that you develop, not just the one that's open when you set them.

You set the Accessibility preferences to prompt you to enter alternate text each time you insert a form object, frame, media, or image on a web page.

Insert a Background Image and
PERFORM SITE MAINTENANCE

What You'll Do

 In this lesson, you will insert two types of background images. You will then use the Assets panel to delete them both from the website, along with the boardwalk.png file. You will also check for non-web-safe colors in the Assets panel.

Inserting a Background Image

You can insert a background image on a web page to provide depth and visual interest to the page, or to communicate a message or mood. **Background images** are image files used in place of background colors. Although you can use background images to create a dramatic effect, you should avoid inserting them on web pages where they would not provide the contrast necessary for reading page text. Even though they might seem too plain, standard white backgrounds are usually the best choice for web pages. If you choose to use a background image on a web page, it should be small in file size. You can choose a single image that fills the page background, or you can choose a tiled image. A **tiled image** is a small image that repeats across and down a web page, appearing as individual squares or rectangles. A tiled image will download much faster than a large image.

When you create a web page, you can use either a background color or a background image, unless you want the background color to appear while the background image finishes downloading. You can also use background images for some sections of your page and solid color backgrounds for other sections.

The NASA home page shown in Figure 20 uses a night sky image for the page background, but individual sections have solid gray or black backgrounds. Since the solid backgrounds are dark, NASA used white or light blue text to provide contrast. The stars in the background tie in well with the rest of the page design and help to set a dramatic mood.

Background images or background colors are inserted using CSS. To add them to a single page, use the Modify > Page Properties dialog box, which adds an internal rule to modify the body tag. To use them as a global setting for the entire site, create an external rule to modify the <body> tag.

Managing Images

As you work on a website, you might find that you have files in your assets folder that you don't use in the website. To avoid accumulating unnecessary files, it's a good idea to look at an image first, before you place it on the page, and copy it to the assets folder. If you inadvertently copy an unwanted file to the assets folder, you should delete it or move it to another location. This is a good website management practice that will prevent the assets folder from filling up with unwanted image files.

QUICK **TIP**

Remember that Adobe Bridge is an excellent tool for organizing and managing your images.

Removing an image from a web page does not remove it from the assets folder in the local site folder of the website. To remove an asset from a website, if you have a lot of files, it is faster to locate the file you want to remove in the Assets panel. You then use the Locate in Site command to open the Files panel with the unwanted file selected. If you don't have many images in your site, it is faster to locate them in the Files panel. You can then use the Delete command to remove the file from the site. If you designate frequently used image files as favorites, you can locate them quickly in the Assets panel by selecting the Favorites option.

It is a good idea to store original unedited copies of your website image files in a separate folder, outside the assets folder of your website. If you edit the original files, resave them using different names. Doing this ensures that you will be able to find a file in its original, unaltered state. You may have files on your computer that you are currently not using at all; however, you may want to use them in the future. Storing currently unused files helps keep your assets folder free of clutter. Storing copies of original website image files in a separate location also ensures that you have back-up copies in the event that you accidentally delete a file from the website.

QUICK **TIP**

You cannot use the Assets panel to delete a file. You must use the Files panel to delete files and perform all file management tasks.

Creating a Website Color Palette

With monitors today that display millions of colors, you are not as limited with the number of colors you can use, and you may choose to select colors outside of the web-safe palette color space. You can experiment by choosing colors outside the default color palettes to create a color scheme that complements your website content. You can use the eyedropper tool ⟋ to pick up a color from a page element, such as the background of an image. To do this, click a color box from an open dialog box, such as a CSS Rule Definition dialog box, then place the pointer over a color on the page. Click the color, and this color will then replace the previous color in the color box and apply it to the page element. If you are designing pages that will be displayed with a web device such as a PDA or mobile phone, be aware that many of these devices have more limited color displays and, in these cases, it might be wise to stick to web-safe colors instead.

QUICK **TIP**

To see the colors used in your site, click the Colors button ▦ on the Assets panel.

Figure 20 *NASA website*
NASA website – www.nasa.gov

Insert a background image

1. Click **Modify** on the Menu bar, then click **Page Properties** to open the Page Properties dialog box.

2. Click the **Appearance (CSS) category**, if necessary.

3. Click **Browse** next to the Background image text box, navigate to the assets folder in the chapter_4 folder in the drive and folder where you store your Data Files, then double-click **water.jpg**.

4. Click **OK** to close the Page Properties dialog box, then click the **Refresh Site List button** to refresh the file list in the Assets panel. The water.jpg file is automatically copied to The Striped Umbrella assets folder.

   The white background is replaced with a muted image of water, as shown in Figure 21. The color of the water is close to the shades of blue in the website banner, so the image fits in well with the other page colors. However, since it flows directly behind the text, it does not provide the good contrast that the white background did.

5. Expand the CSS Styles panel if necessary, then compare your screen to Figure 22.

   Since you used the Modify > Page Properties command to set the image background, Dreamweaver created an internal <body> rule that tells the browser to use the water.jpg file as the page background. Your external style sheet

   (continued)

Figure 21 *The about_us page with a background image*

The water image flows behind the page content

Figure 22 *The CSS Styles panel with the new embedded body rule added*

Internal body style added to style sheet

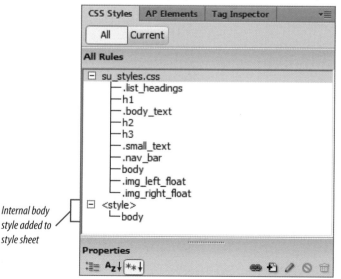

Figure 23 *Removing a background image*

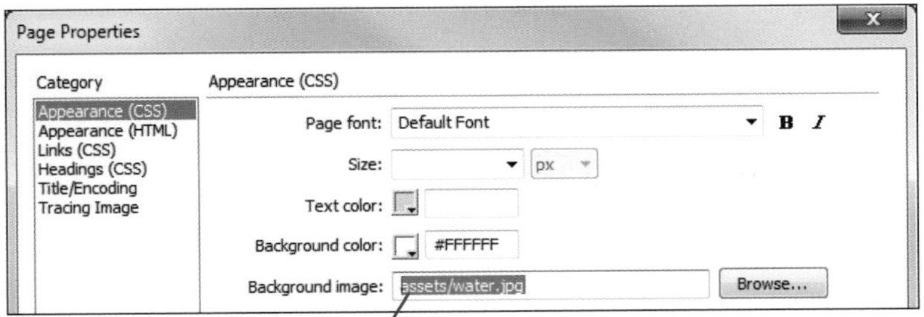

Selected filename

Figure 24 *Deleting the embedded style sheet*

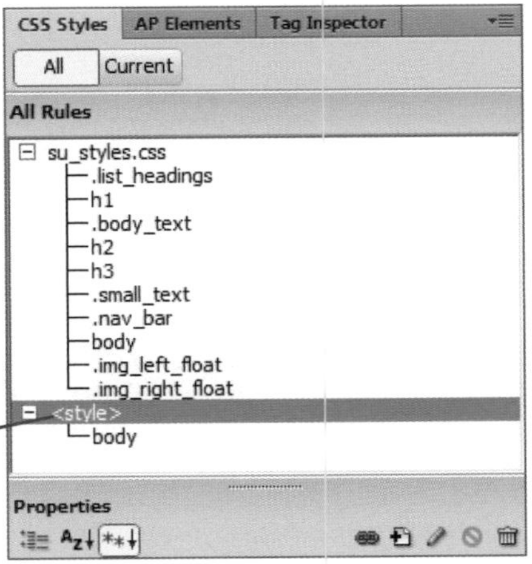

Selected embedded stylesheet

Understanding HTML Body Tags

When you set page preferences, it is helpful to understand the HTML tags that are being generated. Sometimes it's easier to make changes to the code, rather than use menus and dialog boxes. The code for the page background color is located in the head section. If you want to change the page properties, you add additional codes to the body tag. Adding a color to the background will add a style to the page; for example, "body { background-color: #000; }". If you insert an image for a background, the code will read "body { background-image: url assets/water.jpg); }".

also has a <body> rule that tells the browser to use the color white for the page background. The internal style takes precedence over the external style, so for this page only, the white background will be replaced with the water background.

You created an internal style to apply an image background to the about_us page. You then viewed the CSS Styles panel. It now includes both an external style sheet and an internal style sheet.

Remove a background image from a page

1. Click **Modify** on the Menu bar, click **Page Properties**, then click **Appearance (CSS)**.

   Notice that the Page Properties dialog box shows both the background color from the external style sheet and the background image from the embedded style sheet. Remember that an embedded rule overrides a conflicting external rule. If both settings were in an external style sheet, the Background image property would override the Background color property.

2. Select the text in the Background image text box, as shown in Figure 23, press **[Delete]**, then click **OK**.

   The background of the about_us page is white again. However, the background image file, water.jpg, was not deleted. It is still in the website assets folder.

3. Save your work.

4. Click <**style**> in the CSS Styles panel, as shown in Figure 24, then click the **Delete Embedded Stylesheet button** 🗑.

   The embedded style sheet is deleted, since you no longer need it.

You deleted the link to the background image file to change the about_us page background back to white. You then deleted the embedded style sheet.

Delete files from a website

1. Click the **Assets panel tab** if necessary, then click the **Images button** if necessary.

2. With the Site option selected, refresh the Assets panel, right-click (Win) or [control]-click (Mac) **boardwalk.png** in the Assets panel, click **Locate in Site** to open the Files panel, select **boardwalk.png** on the Files panel, if necessary, press **[Delete]**, then click **Yes** in the dialog box that appears.

   You deleted the boardwalk.png file, since you optimized it and are now using the optimized version, boardwalk.jpg. You no longer need the larger version of the file. However, the original photograph for this file should not be deleted, but stored in a separate folder in case you need it later.

3. Click the **Assets panel tab**, then refresh the Assets panel.

TIP If you delete a file on the Files panel that has an active link to it, you will receive a warning message. If you rename a file on the Files panel that has a link to it, the Files panel will update the links to correctly link to the renamed file. To rename a file, right-click (Win) or [control]-click (Mac) the file you want to rename, point to Edit, click Rename, then type the new name.

Your Assets panel should resemble Figure 25.

You removed an image file from The Striped Umbrella website, then refreshed the Assets panel.

Figure 25 *Images listed in Assets panel*

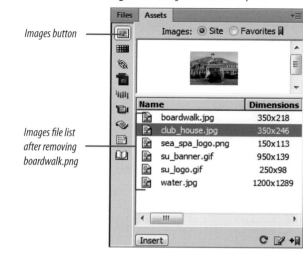

Images button

Images file list after removing boardwalk.png

Using Color in Compliance with Accessibility Guidelines

Web Content Accessibility Guidelines (WCAG), Version 2.0, from the World Wide Web Consortium (W3C), states that a website should not rely on the use of color alone. This means that if your website content depends on your viewer correctly seeing a color, then you are not providing for those people who cannot distinguish between certain colors or do not have monitors that display color. Be especially careful when choosing color used with text, so you provide a good contrast between the text and the background.

If you are typing in the code or in a text box, it is better to reference colors as numbers, rather than names. For example, use "#FFF" instead of "white." Using style sheets for specifying color formats is the preferred method for coding. For more information, see the complete list of accessibility guidelines listed on the W3C website, www.w3.org.

Figure 26 *New color selected with the Eyedropper*

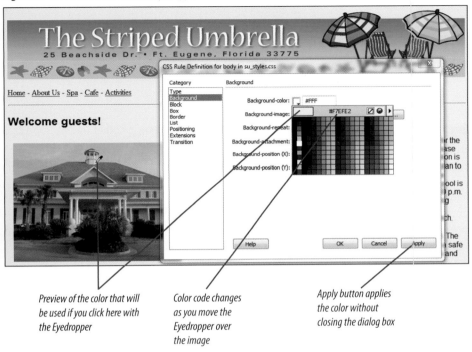

Preview of the color that will be used if you click here with the Eyedropper

Color code changes as you move the Eyedropper over the image

Apply button applies the color without closing the dialog box

Figure 27 *Colors listed in the Assets panel*

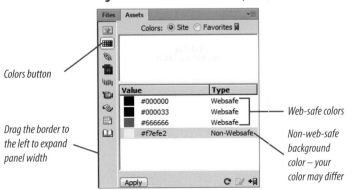

Colors button

Drag the border to the left to expand panel width

Web-safe colors

Non-web-safe background color — your color may differ

Add a color to your design palette

1. Click the **body rule** in the CSS Styles panel, click the **Edit Rule button** 🖉, then click the **Background-color box** ⬜.

    The Color Picker opens.

2. Scroll to find the club house image on the page, move the pointer over it, click to select one of the lightest sections of the cupola, as shown in Figure 26, then click **Apply**.

    The color you sampled appears in the Background-color text box in the CSS Rule Definition for body in su_styles.css dialog box. It will be difficult to exactly match the color in Figure 26 unless you type it in the Background-color text box. Just experiment and choose a light color that provides good contrast with the text.

3. Click **OK** to close the CSS Rule Definition dialog box, then save your work.

    Because you set the background color with the body rule in the external style sheet, every page will now use this color for the background.

4. Click the **Colors button** ▦ in the Assets panel to display the colors used in the website, refresh the Assets panel, then drag the left border of the Assets panel to display the second column, if necessary, as shown in Figure 27.

    All of the colors are web-safe except the page background color.

5. Preview the page in your browser, then close your browser.

    You edited the body rule in the su_styles.css file to change the body background color to a light cream color. You then viewed the colors listed in the Assets panel, and previewed the new page background color in the browser.

Add Graphic ENHANCEMENTS

What You'll Do

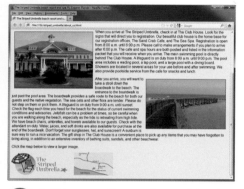

In this lesson, you will use a small image to link to a larger image and add a favicon to a page.

Adding a Link to a Larger Image

Sometimes designers want to display a small image on a page with an option for the user to click on the image to display a larger image. You frequently see this practice on retail sites with multiple items for sale. It is done both to conserve space and to keep the page size as small as possible. These sites will display a **thumbnail image**, or small version of a larger image, so that more images will fit on the page. Another technique is to link from one image to a second image that incorporates the first image. For example, a furniture site may create a link from an image of a chair to an image of the chair in a furnished room. An additional enhancement is often added to allow users to click on the larger image to magnify it even more

To accomplish this, you need two versions of the same image using an image editor such as Photoshop: one that is small (in dimensions and in file size) and one that is large (in dimensions and in file size.) After you have both images ready, place the small image on your page, select it, then link it to the large image. When a user clicks the small image in a browser, the large image opens. Another option is to place the large image on a new web page so you can also include additional descriptive text about the image or a link back to the previous page.

Adding Favicons

In most browsers today, when you add a web page to your favorites list or bookmarks, the page title will appear with a small icon that represents your site, similar to a logo, called a **favicon** (short for favorites icon). This feature was introduced in Microsoft Internet Explorer 5. Most browsers now also display favicons in the browser address bar. Favicons are a nice way to add branding, or recognition, for your site. To create a favicon, first create an icon that is 16 pixels by 16 pixels. Second, save the file as an icon file with the .ico file extension in your site root folder. Do not save it in a subfolder such as an assets or images folder.

> **QUICK TIP**
>
> There are plug-ins available for Photoshop that will save files with an icon file format, or you can search the Internet for programs that will generate icons.

Third, add HTML code to the head section of your page to link the icon file. The browser will then find the icon and load it in the address bar when the page loads.

Figure 28 shows a favicon in the Snapfish by HP website. Notice that the favicon is displayed both on the address bar and on the page tab. The design of the favicon ties in with the name of the company and other images of fish that are used in the page content. This is a nice touch to complete a well-designed site.

Adding a No Right-Click Script

On most websites, users are able to save an image on a page by right-clicking an image, then clicking Save on the shortcut menu. If you would like to prevent viewers from having this option, you can add a **no right-click script**, or JavaScript code that will not allow users to display the shortcut menu by right-clicking an image. To do this, locate JavaScript code that will add this option and copy and paste it into the head content of your page. To locate JavaScript code, use a search engine to search the Internet with a term such as "no right-click script." You will find scripts that prevent users from saving any image on the page, or all content of any kind on the page. Some scripts return a message in the browser such as "This function is disabled," and some do not return a message at all. These scripts will keep many users from saving your images, but they will not stop the most serious and knowledgeable perpetrators.

You can also protect website images by inserting the image as a table, cell, or CSS block background and then placing a transparent image on top of it. When a user attempts to save it with the shortcut menu, they will only save the transparent image.

Figure 28 *Snapfish website*
© 2009 The Snapfish by HP website used with permission from Snapfish by HP—www.snapfish.com

Favicon displayed in the address bar and on the page tab

Favicon is a smaller version of the logo used on the page

Use an image to link to another image

1. Click to place the insertion point to the right of the su_logo image, insert the image **map_small.jpg** from the assets folder where you store your Data Files, type **Map to The Striped Umbrella** in the Image Tag Accessibility Attributes dialog box, then click **OK**.

2. Select the **map_small image**, press the **left arrow key ←**, insert **spacer_30px.gif** from the assets folder where you store your data files, type **spacer image** in the Image Tag Accessibility Attributes dialog box, then click **OK**.

   The spacer image is a 30-pixel transparent square. It is used to insert 30 pixels of horizontal space between the two images.

3. Select the map_small image, click the **Browse for File button** □ next to the Link text box, navigate to the assets folder in the drive and folder where you store your Data Files, click **map_large.jpg**, then click **OK**.

   The small map image now links to the large map image, so viewers can click the small version to view the large version.

4. Click to place the insertion point after the last paragraph, insert a paragraph break, type **Click the map below to view a larger image.**, then compare your screen to Figure 29.

5. Save your work, then preview the page in your browser.

6. Click the **small map image** to view the large map image in a separate window, use the Back button to return to the about_us page, then close the browser.

You inserted a small image on the page and linked it to a larger image. You also used a spacer image to insert some horizontal space between the two images.

Figure 29 *The about_us page with an image linking to a larger image*

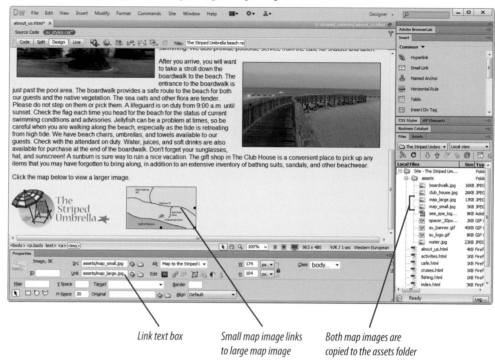

Link text box

Small map image links to large map image

Both map images are copied to the assets folder

Adding Images

Figure 30 *Copying the favicon.ico file in the data files folder*

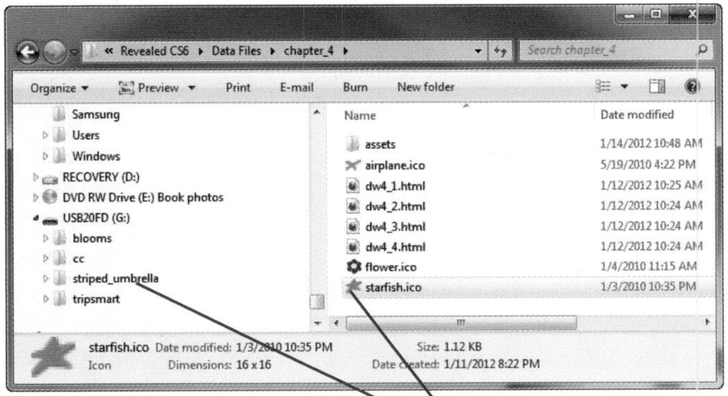

*Paste the starfish.ico file in the
striped_umbrella site root folder*

Figure 31 *Adding code to link the favicon*

```
1   <!doctype html>
2   <html>
3   <head>
4   <meta charset="utf-8">
5   <link rel="shortcut icon" href="starfish.ico" type="image/x-icon"/>
6   <title>The Striped Umbrella beach resort and spa, Ft. Eugene, Florida</title>
7   <link href="su_styles.css" rel="stylesheet" type="text/css" />
8   </head>
9
10  <body>
11  <img src="assets/su_banner.gif" alt="The Striped Umbrella banner" width="950" height="139" /><br />
12  <a href="index.html">Home</a> - <a href="about_us.html">About Us</a> - <a href="spa.html">Spa</a> - <a href=
    "cafe.html">Cafe</a> - <a href="activities.html">Activities</a>
13  <hr align="left" width="950" />
```

Type this code above the <title> tag

Figure 32 *Viewing a favicon in the Firefox browser*

Starfish favicon

Insert a favicon on a page

1. Open Windows Explorer (Win) or Finder (Mac), then browse to the chapter_4 folder in the drive and folder where your Data Files are stored.

2. Right-click the file **starfish.ico**, copy it, browse to your site root folder, then paste the **starfish.ico** file into the site root folder, as shown in Figure 30, then close Windows Explorer (Win) or Finder (Mac).

3. Switch to Code view in Dreamweaver, insert a blank line above the line of code for the page title, then insert this code directly above the `<title>` tag: `<link rel="shortcut icon" href="starfish.ico" type="image/x-icon" />` as shown in Figure 31.

4. Save your work, then preview the about_us page in the browser.

   The favicon will appear in the address bar right before the page title and on the page tab in browsers that use tabbed pages, as shown in Figure 32.

   TIP Internet Explorer may not display the favicon until the website is published to a server.

5. Copy the code for the favicon link, then paste it into the code for the index and spa pages.

6. Save your work, close all open pages, then exit Dreamweaver.

You copied a favicon to the site root folder, then added code to the About Us page to direct browsers to display the favicon in the title bar when the page is viewed in a browser. Then you copied the code to link the favicon to the index and spa pages.

Insert and align images.

1. Open the Blooms & Bulbs website, open dw4_2.html from the drive and folder where you store your Data Files, then save it as **plants.html** in the Blooms & Bulbs website, overwriting the existing plants.html file. Do not update links.

2. Close dw4_2.html, then verify that the path of the Blooms & Bulbs banner on the plants page is set correctly to the assets folder in the blooms site root folder.

3. Verify that the Accessibility preferences will prompt you to add alternate text to images is set.

4. Insert an image placeholder to the left of the words "Who can resist" with the following settings: Name: **rose_bud**; Width: **300 pixels**; Height: **207 pixels**; Alternate text: **Rose bud on bird bath**.

5. Use the Browse for file button next to the Src text box on the Property inspector to replace the image placeholder with the rose_bud.jpg file from the assets folder in the drive and folder where you store your Data Files.

6. Use Bridge to insert the rose_bloom.jpg file, from the assets folder in the drive and folder where you store your Data Files, in front of the words "For ease of growing" and add **Rose bloom** as alternate text.

7. Insert the two_roses.jpg file from the assets folder in the drive and folder where you store your Data Files in front of the words "The Candy Cane" and add **Candy Cane Floribunda** as alternate text.

8. Refresh the Files panel to verify that all three images were copied to the assets folder.

9. Attach the blooms_styles.css file to the plants page, then add a new class rule named **img_left_float** that adds a left float property and value in the Box category.

10. Add another class rule named **img_right_float** that adds a right float property and value to the style sheet.

11. Apply the img_left_float rule to the rose_bud image.

12. Apply the img_right_float rule to the rose_bloom image.

13. Apply the img_left_float rule to the two_roses image.

14. Save your work, then open the tips page.

15. Click to select the butterfly image under the banner, then apply the img_float_left rule to it.

Enhance an image and use alternate text.

1. Use the HTML Property inspector to apply the Heading 1 format to the heading at the top of the plants page and the body_text rule to the rest of the text on the page. (*Hint*: Use the Class text box to select the body_text rule from the list.)

2. Edit the img_left_float rule to add a border to all sides of an image with the following settings: Top=solid; Width=thin; Color=#333.

3. Edit the Box Margin property to add a 10 px margin to the right side only, then save your changes.

4. Repeat Step 2 to add the same border to the img_right_float rule.

5. Edit the Box Margin property of the img_right_float rule to add a 10 px margin to the left side only.

Figure 33 *Completed Skills Review*

Featured Spring Plant: Roses!

Who can resist the romance of roses? Poets have waxed poetically over them throughout the years. Many persons consider the beauty and fragrance of roses to be unmatched in nature. The varieties are endless, ranging from floribunda to hybrid teas to shrub roses to climbing roses. Each variety has its own personality and preference in the garden setting. Pictured on the left is a Summer Breeze Hybrid Tea bud. This variety is fast growing and produces spectacular blooms that are beautiful as cut flowers in arrangements. The enchanting fragrance will fill your home with summer sweetness. They require full sun. Hybrid teas need regular spraying and pruning, but will reward you with classic blooms that will be a focal point in your landscaping and provide you with beautiful arrangements in your home. They are well worth the effort!

For ease of growing, Knock Out® roses are some of our all-time favorites. Even beginners will not fail with these garden delights. They are shrub roses and prefer full sun, but can take partial shade. They are disease resistant and drought tolerant. You do not have to be concerned with either black spot or dead-heading with roses such as the Knock out®, making them an extremely low-maintenance plant. They are also repeat bloomers, blooming into late fall. The shrub can grow quite large, but can be pruned to any size. The one you see on the right is Southern Belle. Check out all our varieties as you will not fail to have great color with these plants.

The Candy Cane Floribunda shown on the left is a beautiful rose with cream, pink, and red stripes and swirls. They have a heavy scent that will remind you of the roses you received on your most special occasions. These blooms are approximately four inches in diameter. They bloom continuously from early summer to early fall. The plants grow up to four feet tall and three feet wide. They are shipped bare root in February.

6. Save your work, preview it in the browser, then compare your screen to Figure 33.

Insert a background image and perform site maintenance.

1. Insert the lady_in_red.jpg file as a background image from the assets folder where you store your Data Files.
2. Save your work.
3. Preview the web page in your browser, then close your browser.
4. Remove the lady_in_red.jpg file from the background.
5. Open the Assets panel, view the images, then refresh the Files list.
6. Use the Files panel to delete the lady_in_red.jpg file from the list of images.
7. Refresh the Assets panel, then verify that the lady_in_red.jpg file has been removed from the website.
8. View the colors used in the site in the Assets panel.
9. Save your work.

Add graphic enhancements.

1. Select the two_roses image on the plants page.
2. Use the Link text box on the Property inspector to link the two_roses image to the two_roses_large.jpg file in the assets folder where you store your Data Files.
3. Add the sentences **You must see a close-up of these beauties! Click the image on the left to enlarge them**. at the end of the last paragraph.

TIP To make sure your insertion point is inside the body_text tag so the formatting will be applied, place the insertion point in front of the period at the end

of the sentence in Design view, press the right arrow key to move the insertion point after the period, then add the new sentence. Another option is to place the insertion point right before the ending body_text tag in Code view, then switch to Design view to add the new sentence.

4. Save your work, preview the page in the browser, then click the two_roses image to view the larger version of the image.
5. Use the Back button to return to the plants page, then close the browser.
6. Open Windows Explorer (Win) or Finder (Mac), browse to the folder where you store your Data Files, then copy the file flower.ico.

7. Paste the file flower.ico in the blooms site root folder.
8. Close Windows Explorer (Win) or Finder (Mac), then switch to Code view for the plants page.
9. Insert a blank line above the title tag, then type this code directly above the <title> tag:

```
<link rel = "shortcut icon"
href = "flower.ico" type = "image/
x-icon" />
```

10. Verify that you entered the code correctly, copy the new line of code, then switch back to Design view.
11. Paste the same code you typed in step 9 to the index and tips pages, then save all files.
12. Preview the page in the browser, compare your screen to Figure 34, then close all open pages.

Figure 34 *Completed Skills Review*

Use Figure 35 as a guide to continue your work on the TripSmart website that you began in Project Builder 1 in Chapter 1, and continued to work on in Chapters 2 and 3. You are now ready to begin work on the destinations page that showcases one of the featured tours to the Galápagos. You want to include some colorful pictures on the page.

1. Open the TripSmart website.
2. Open dw4_3.html from the drive and folder where you store your Data Files and save it in the tripsmart site root folder as **tours.html**, overwriting the existing tours.html file and not updating the links. Close the dw4_3.html file.
3. Verify that the path for the banner is correctly set to the assets folder of the TripSmart website.
4. Attach the tripsmart_styles.css file.
5. Apply the Heading 1 format to the "Destination: The Galápagos" heading.
6. Insert iguana_and_lizard from the assets folder in the drive and folder where you store your Data Files to the left of the sentence beginning "We have a really special", then add appropriate alternate text.
7. Insert blue_footed_booby.jpg from the assets folder in the drive and folder where you store your Data Files to the left of the sentence beginning "After arriving at Baltra's", then add appropriate alternate text.
8. Create one or more new rules in the tripsmart_styles.css file to add alignment, spacing, and borders of your choice.
9. If you would like, use the existing rules in the style sheet to add any additional formatting to the page to enhance the appearance.

10. View your colors in the Assets panel and see if your color choices work well together. If they don't, consider replacing them with different colors.
11. Copy the file airplane.ico from the folder where you store your data files to your site root folder.

12. Add appropriate code to the head content to link the favicon to the page, then copy the code to the index and newsletter pages.
13. Save your work, then preview the tours, index, and newsletter pages in your browser.
14. Close your browser, then close all open files.

Figure 35 *Sample Project Builder 1*

Adding Images

In this exercise, you continue your work on the Carolyne's Creations website that you started in Project Builder 2 in Chapter 1, and continued to build in Chapters 2 and 3. You are now ready to add a new page to the website that will display featured items in the kitchen shop. Figure 36 shows a possible solution for this exercise. Your finished page will look different if you choose different formatting options.

1. Open the Carolyne's Creations website.
2. Open dw4_4.html from the drive and folder where you store your Data Files, save it to the site root folder as **shop.html**, overwriting the existing file and not updating the links.
3. Insert peruvian_glass.jpg from the assets folder in the drive and folder where you store your Data Files, in a location of your choice on the page, adding alternate text when prompted.
4. Attach the cc_styles.css file to the page, then add a rule to the style sheet that adds alignment and spacing to the Peruvian glass image.

5. Apply the nav_bar rule to the navigation links, the Heading 1 format to the page heading "June Special: Peruvian Glasses", and the body_text rule to the paragraphs of text if necessary.
6. Link the peruvian_glass image to the file brunch.jpg from the assets folder where you store your Data Files, then enter some descriptive text on the page to prompt viewers to click on the peruvian_glass image.
7. Save the shop page, then preview it in the browser.
8. Close your browser, then close all open pages.

Figure 36 *Sample Project Builder 2*

June Special: Peruvian Glasses

We try to feature special items each month and love to promote local foods with an international flavor. This month features Peruvian Pisco Sour glasses.

These hand-made glasses are made by Peruvian potters and hand painted at an orphanage not far from Cusco. They are the traditional glass that is used to serve Pisco Sours, the national drink of Peru. Pisco is a grape brandy made from the Quebranta grape in Peru. The bird motif is significant, as one of the translations for the word "Pisco" is "bird." The rich browns, red, and ochre colors are quite attractive in contrast to the white glazed bowl. Pisco is also the name of the port in Peru that is thought to be where pisco was traded as far back as the 17th century.

These glasses would also be perfect for serving juice, small desserts or appetizers. We brought a limited number of these back from Peru this spring, so be sure to come by soon if you are interested in purchasing them. They would make a unique gift for a special occasion. Click the image to see it in a table setting.

Patsy Broers is working on a team project to design a website for her high school drama department. She has been assigned the task of gathering images to add interest and color.

1. Connect to the Internet, then navigate to the William J. Clinton Presidential Center website at www.clintonpresidentialcenter.org, shown in Figure 37.
2. Do you see a favicon used on the page?
3. Are any of the images on the page used as links to other images or pages?
4. Is a background image used for any of the page objects?
5. How do the images, horizontal and vertical spacing, color, and text work together to create an attractive and interesting experience for viewers?

Figure 37 *Design Project*
Courtesy of the William J. Clinton Presidential Center

In this assignment, you will continue to work on the website that you started in Chapter 1, and continued to build in Chapters 2 and 3. No Data Files are supplied. You are building this site from chapter to chapter, so you must do each Portfolio Project assignment in each chapter to complete your website.

You continue building your website by inserting appropriate images on a page and enhancing them for maximum effect.

1. Consult your wireframe and decide which page to create and develop for this chapter.
2. Plan the page content and make a sketch of the layout. Your sketch should include several images and a background color or image.
3. Create the page using your sketch for guidance.
4. Access the images you gathered, and place them on the page so that the page matches the sketch you created in Step 2. Add a background image if you want, and appropriate alternate text for each image.
5. Create rules in your style sheet to position and format your images.

6. Identify any files in the Assets panel that are currently not used in the site. Decide which of these assets should be removed, then delete these files.
7. Preview the new page in a browser, then check for page layout problems and broken links. Make any necessary corrections in Dreamweaver, then preview the page again in the browser. Repeat this process until you are satisfied with the way the page looks in the browser.
8. Use the checklist in Figure 38 to check all the pages in your site.
9. Close the browser, then close the open pages.

Figure 38 *Portfolio Project checklist*

> ### Website Checklist
> 1. Does each page have a page title?
> 2. Does the home page have a description and keywords?
> 3. Does the home page contain contact information?
> 4. Does the home page have a last updated statement that will automatically update when the page is saved?
> 5. Do all paths for links and images work correctly?
> 6. Do all images have alternate text?
> 7. Are there any unnecessary files you can delete from the assets folder?
> 8. Is there a style sheet with at least two rules?
> 9. Did you apply the rules to all text?
> 10. Did you use rules to position and format images?
> 11. Do all pages look good using at least two different browsers?

CHAPTER 5 **WORKING WITH LINKS**
AND NAVIGATION

1. Create external and internal links

2. Create internal links to named anchors

3. Create, modify, and copy a Spry menu bar

4. Create an image map

5. Manage website links

6. Incorporate Web 2.0 technology

WORKING WITH LINKS
AND NAVIGATION

Introduction

What makes websites so powerful are the links, or hyperlinks, that connect one page to another within a website or to any page on the Web. Although you can enhance a website with graphics, animations, movies, and other features to make it visually attractive, the links you include are a site's most essential components. Links that connect the pages within a site are important because they help users navigate between the pages of the site. If it's important to keep users within your site, link only to pages within your website and avoid including links to external sites. For example, most e-commerce sites only link to other pages in their own site to discourage shoppers from leaving.

In this chapter, you will create links to other pages in The Striped Umbrella website and to other sites on the Web. You will insert a Spry menu bar, and check the site links to make sure they all work correctly. You will also learn about Web 2.0 and social networking, an area of the Internet that has exploded in recent years. **Social networking** refers to the grouping of individual web users who connect and interact with other users in online communities. **Online communities**, or virtual communities, are social websites you can join, such as Facebook and Twitter, where you can communicate with others by posting messages or media content such as images or videos. You will learn about how you can connect your website to these communities.

Understanding Internal and External Links

Web pages contain two types of links: internal links and external links. **Internal links** are links to web pages within the same website, and **external links** are links to web pages in other websites or to email addresses. Both internal and external links have two important parts that work together. The first part of a link is displayed on a web page, for example, text, an image, or a button that is used for a link. The second part of a link is the **path**, or the name and location of the web page or file that users click to open the target for the link. Setting and maintaining the correct paths for all of your links is essential to avoid having broken links in your site, which can cause a user to leave the site.

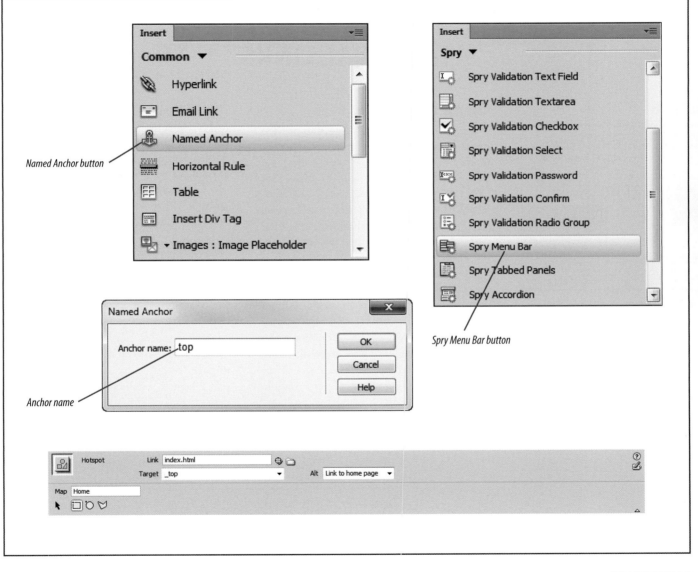

Named Anchor button

Anchor name

Spry Menu Bar button

Create External and
INTERNAL LINKS

What You'll Do

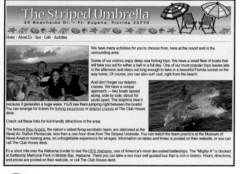

In this lesson, you will create external links on The Striped Umbrella activities page that link to websites related to area attractions. You will also create internal links to other pages within The Striped Umbrella website.

Creating External Links

If one of the objectives of a site is to provide users with additional research sources for information not provided within the site, external links are one way to meet that objective. To create an external link, first select the text or object that you want to serve as a link, then type the absolute path to the destination web page in the Link text box in the Property inspector. An **absolute path** is a path used for external links that includes the complete address for the destination page, including the protocol (such as http://) and the complete **URL** (Uniform Resource Locator), or address, of the destination page. When necessary, the web page filename and folder hierarchy are also part of an absolute path. Figure 1 shows an example of an absolute path showing the protocol,

URL, and path, which in this case is a single folder name. Paths can contain several folder levels and a file name, depending on how the destination page is stored on the server. An example of the code for the external link to the United States Army website would be <a href="http://www.army.mil"> The United States Army website</a>.

Creating Internal Links

Each page in a website usually focuses on an individual information category or topic. You should make sure that the home page provides links to each major page in the site, and that all pages in the site contain numerous internal links so that users can move easily from page to page. To create an internal link, you first select the text element or image that you want to use to make a link, and then use the Browse

Figure 1 *An example of an absolute path*

for File button next to the Link text box in the HTML Property inspector to specify the relative path to the destination page. A **relative path** is a type of path that references web pages and media files within the same website. Relative paths include the filename and folder location of a file. An example for the code for a relative internal link would be <a href="news.html"> News</a>.

Figure 2 shows an example of a relative path. Table 1 describes absolute and relative paths. Relative paths can either be site-root relative or document-relative. The internal links that you will create in this lesson will be document-relative. You can also use the Point to File button in the HTML Property inspector to select the file you want to link to, or drag the file you want to use for the link from the Files panel into the Link text box in the Property inspector.

You should take great care in managing your internal links to make sure they work correctly and are timely and relevant to the page content. Design the navigation structure of your website so that users are never more than a few clicks away from the page they are seeking.

Figure 2 *An example of a relative path*

Folder name   Filename

src="images/parade.jpg"

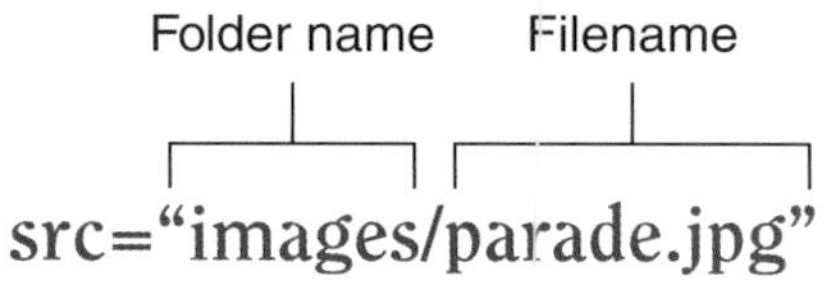

TABLE 1: DESCRIPTION OF ABSOLUTE AND RELATIVE PATHS		
Type of path	**Description**	**Examples**
Absolute path	Used for external links and specifies protocol, URL, and filename of the destination page	http://www.yahoo.com/recreation
Relative path	Used for internal links and specifies location of file relative to the current page	spa.html or assets/heron.gif
Root-relative path	Used for internal links when publishing to a server that contains many websites or where the website is so large it requires more than one server	/striped_umbrella/activities.html
Document- relative path	Used in most cases for internal links and specifies the location of a file relative to the current page	cafe.html or assets/heron.gif

© Cengage Learning 2013

Create an external link

1. Open The Striped Umbrella website, open dw5_1.html from the drive and folder where you store your Chapter 5 Data Files, then save it as **activities.html** in the striped_umbrella local site folder, overwriting the existing activities page, but not updating links.

2. Close the dw5_1.html page, attach the **su_styles.css** file, then apply the **body_text rule** to the paragraphs of text on the page (not to the menu bar).

3. Select the first broken image link, click the **Browse for File button** 📁 next to the Src text box, then select **family_sunset.jpg** in the Data Files assets folder to save the image in your assets folder.

4. Click the image, then use the Property inspector to apply the **img_left_float** rule, as shown in Figure 3.

5. Repeat Step 3 for the second broken image link, linking it to two_dolphins_small.jpg, apply the **img_right_float** rule then refresh the Files panel if necessary.

   The two new files are copied into the assets folder, as shown in Figure 4.

6. Scroll down, then select the text "Blue Angels" in the first line of the second to last paragraph.

(continued)

Figure 3 *Saving an image file in the assets folder*

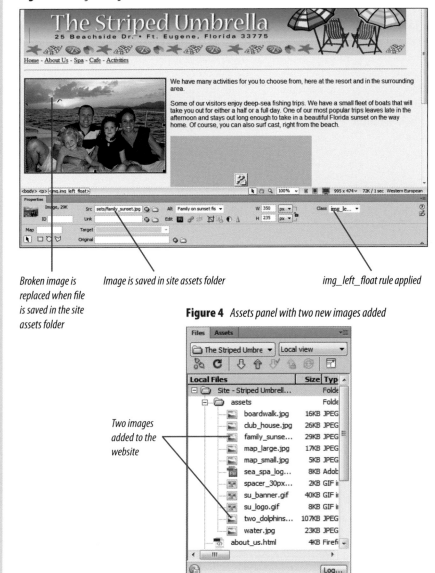

Broken image is replaced when file is saved in the site assets folder

Image is saved in site assets folder

img_left_float rule applied

Figure 4 *Assets panel with two new images added*

Two images added to the website

Figure 5 *Creating an external link to the Blue Angels website*

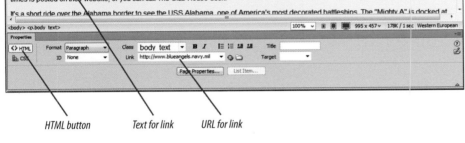

We have many activities for you to choose from, here at the resort and in the surrounding area.

Some of our visitors enjoy deep-sea fishing trips. We have a small fleet of boats that will take you out for either a half or a full day. One of our most popular trips leaves late in the afternoon and stays out long enough to take in a beautiful Florida sunset on the way home. Of course, you can also surf cast, right from the beach.

And don't forget our dolphin cruises. We have a unique approach — two boats speed along, side by side, about 50 yards apart. The dolphins love it because it generates a huge wake. You'll see them jumping right between the boats! You can arrange for tickets for fishing excursions or dolphin cruises at The Club House desk.

Check out these links for kid-friendly attractions in the area:

The famous Blue Angels, the nation's oldest flying aerobatic team, are stationed at the Naval Air Station Pensacola, less than a one-hour drive from The Striped Umbrella. You can watch the team practice at the Museum of Naval Aviation viewing area, an unforgettable experience for all ages. Information on dates and times is posted on their website, or you can call The Club House desk.

It's a short ride over the Alabama border to see the USS Alabama, one of America's most decorated battleships. The "Mighty A" is docked at

`<body> <p.body text>`   100%   995 x 457   178K / 1 sec   Western European

Properties
`<> HTML`   Format Paragraph   Class body text   **B** *I*   Title
`CSS`   ID None   Link http://www.blueangels.navy.mil   Target

Page Properties...   List Item...

HTML button   Text for link   URL for link

---

7. Click the **HTML button** `<> HTML` in the Property inspector to switch to the HTML Property inspector if necessary, click in the Link text box, type **http://www.blueangels.navy. mil**, press [**Enter**] (Win) or [**return**] (Mac), click on the page to deselect the link, then compare your screen to Figure 5.

8. Repeat Steps 6 and 7 to create a link for the USS Alabama site in the next paragraph: **http://www.ussalabama.com**.

9. Save your work, preview the page in your browser, test all the links to make sure they work, then close your browser.

TIP You must have an active Internet connection to test the external links. If clicking a link does not open a page, make sure you typed the URL correctly in the Link text box.

You opened The Striped Umbrella website, replaced the existing activities page, attached the su_styles.css file, applied the body_text rule to the text, then imported images into the site. You then applied a rule to each image to set the alignment and spacing. You added two external links to other sites, then tested each link in your browser.

Lesson 1   Create External and Internal Links

Create an internal link

1. Select the text "fishing excursions" in the third paragraph.

2. Click the **Browse for File button** 📁 next to the Link text box in the HTML Property inspector, navigate to the site root folder, then double-click **fishing.html** in the Select File dialog box to set the relative path to the fishing page.

   The filename fishing.html appears in the Link text box in the Property inspector, as shown in Figure 6. (The link is deselected in the figure for readability.)

   TIP Pressing [F4] will hide or redisplay all panels, including the Property inspector and the panels on the right side of the screen.

3. Select the text "dolphin cruises" in the same sentence.

4. Click the **Browse for File button** 📁 next to the Link text box in the HTML Property inspector, then double-click **cruises.html** in the Select File dialog box to specify the relative path to the cruises page.

   The words "dolphin cruises" are now a link to the cruises page.

5. Save your work, preview the page in your browser, verify that the internal links work correctly, then close your browser.

   The fishing and cruises pages do not have page content yet, but serve as placeholders until they do.

   You created two internal links on the activities page, then tested the links in your browser.

Figure 6 *Creating an internal link on the activities page*

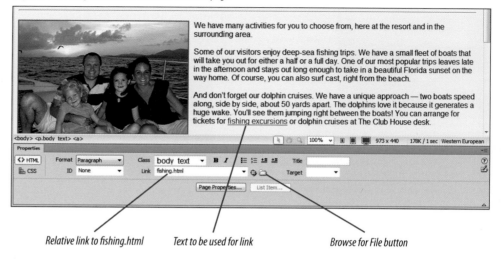

Relative link to fishing.html   Text to be used for link   Browse for File button

Using Case-Sensitive Links

When you hear that text is "case sensitive," it means that the text will be treated differently when it is typed using uppercase letters rather than lowercase letters, or vice-versa. With some operating systems, such as Windows, it doesn't matter which case you use when you enter URLs. However, with other systems, such as UNIX, it does matter. To be sure that your links will work with all systems, use lowercase letters for all URLs. This is another good reason to select and copy a URL from the browser address bar, and then paste it in the Link text box or Dreamweaver code when creating an external link. You won't have to worry about missing a case change.

Figure 7 *Assets panel with three external links*

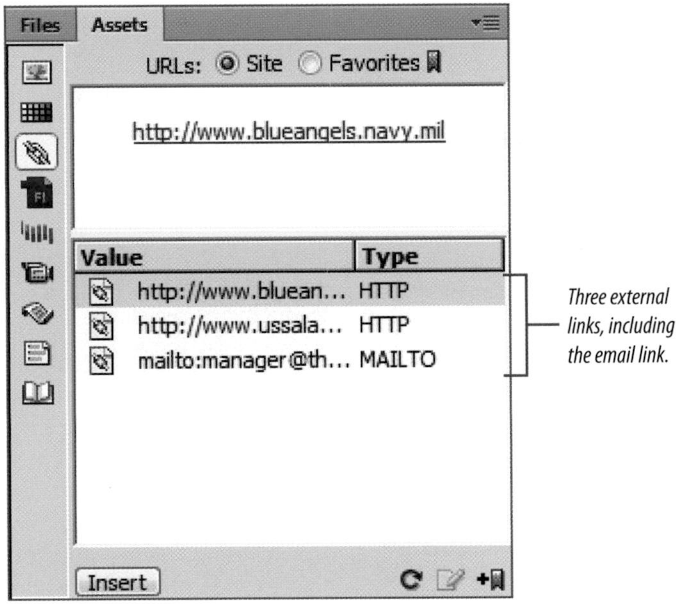

Files | Assets

URLs: ● Site ○ Favorites 🔖

http://www.blueangels.navy.mil

Value	Type
🖾 http://www.bluean...	HTTP
🖾 http://www.ussala...	HTTP
🖾 mailto:manager@th...	MAILTO

Three external links, including the email link.

Insert   C ☑ +🔖

View links in the Assets panel

1. Click the Assets panel tab to view the Assets panel.

2. Click the **URLs button** 🖾 in the Assets panel.

3. Click the **Refresh Site List button** ↻ .

   Three links appear in the Assets panel: one external link for the email link on the home page and two external links, to the Blue Angels and USS Alabama websites on the activities page, as shown in Figure 7. Notice that the internal links do not appear in the Assets panel. The Assets panel shows the links for the entire site, not just for the open page.

4. Click the **Files panel tab** to view the Files panel.

5. Close the activities page.

You viewed the external links on the activities page in the Assets panel.

Create Internal Links
TO NAMED ANCHORS

What You'll Do

The Striped Umbrella
26 Beachside Dr. • Ft. Eugene, Florida 33775

The Sea Spa Services
Massages
Facials
Body Treatments

Massages

- Sports Massage
  Our deepest massage for tense and sore muscles. Not recommended for first-time massage clients.
- Swedish Massage
  A gentle, relaxing massage. Promotes balance and wellness. Warms muscle tissue and increases circulation.
- Hot Stone Massage
  Uses polished local river rocks to distribute gentle heat. Good for tight, sore muscles. Balances and invigorates the body muscles.
  Advance notice required.

Facials

- Revitalizing Facial
  A light massage with a customized essential oil blend that moisturizes the skin and restores circulation.
- Gentlemen's Facial
  A cleansing facial that restores a healthy glow. Includes a neck and shoulder massage.
- Milk Mask
  A soothing mask that softens and moisturizes the face. Leaves your skin looking younger.

Body Treatments

- Salt Glow
  Imported sea salts are massaged into the skin, exfoliating and cleansing the pores.
- Herbal Wrap
  Organic lavender blooms create a detoxifying and calming treatment to relieve aches and pains.
- Seaweed Body Wrap
  Seaweed is a natural detoxifying agent that also helps improve circulation.

Call The Sea Spa desk for prices and reservations. Any of our services can be personalized according to your needs. Our desk is open from 7:00 a.m. until 9:00 p.m. Call 555-594-9458, extension 39.

Questions You May Have

1. How do I schedule Spa services?
   Please make appointments by calling The Club desk at least 24 hours in advance. Please arrive 15 minutes before your appointment to allow enough time to shower or use the sauna.
2. Will I be charged if I cancel my appointment?
   Please cancel 24 hours before your service to avoid a cancellation charge. No-shows and cancellations without adequate notice will be charged for the full service.
3. Are there any health safeguards I should know about?
   Please advise us of medical conditions or allergies you have. Heat treatments like hydrotherapy and body wraps should be avoided if you are pregnant, have high blood pressure, or any type of heart condition or diabetes.
4. What about tipping?
   Gratuities are at your sole discretion, but are certainly appreciated.

Return to top of page

In this lesson, you will insert four named anchors on the spa page: one for the top of the page and three for each of the spa services lists. You will then create internal links to each named anchor.

Inserting Named Anchors

Some web pages have so much content that users must scroll repeatedly to get to the bottom of the page and then back up to the top of the page. To make it easier for users to navigate to specific areas of a page without scrolling, you can use a combination of internal links and named anchors. A **named anchor** is a specific location on a web page that has a descriptive name. Named anchors act as targets for internal links and make it easy for users to jump to a particular place on the same page quickly. A **target** is the location on a web page that a browser displays when users click an internal link. For example, you can insert a named anchor called "top" at the top of a web page, and then create a link to it from the bottom of the page.

You can also insert named anchors in strategic places on a web page, such as at the beginning of paragraph headings. The Neighbor's Mill website shown in Figure 8 uses a named anchor at the top of each page with a text link at the bottom of each page that links to it.

This gives users a way to quickly return to the top of a page after they have scrolled down through the page content.

You insert a named anchor using the Named Anchor button in the Common category on the Insert panel. You then enter the name of the anchor in the Named Anchor dialog box. You should choose short names that describe the named anchor location on the page. In Dreamweaver, named anchors appear on a web page as yellow anchor icons in Design view. Selected anchors appear as blue icons. You can show or hide named anchor icons by clicking View on the Menu bar, pointing to Visual Aids, and then clicking Invisible Elements.

Creating Internal Links to Named Anchors

Once you create a named anchor, you can create an internal link to it using one of two methods. You can select the text or image on the page that you want to use to make a link, and then drag the Point to File button from the Property inspector to the named anchor icon on the page. Or, you can select the text or image to which you want to use to make a link, then type # followed by the named anchor name (such as "#top") in the Link text box in the Property inspector.

QUICK TIP

To avoid possible errors, you should create a named anchor before you create a link to it.

Figure 8 *Neighbor's Mill website with named anchors*

Neighbor's Mill website used with permission from Mike and Karin Nabors – www.neighborsmill.com

Named anchor location

Text link to named anchor

Insert a named anchor

1. Open the spa page, click the **banner image** to select it, then press [←] to place the insertion point to the left of the banner.

2. Click **View** on the Menu bar, point to **Visual Aids,** then verify that Invisible Elements is checked.

   TIP If there is no check mark next to Invisible Elements, this feature is turned off. Click Invisible Elements to turn this feature on.

3. Select the Common category on the Insert panel if necessary.

4. Click **Named Anchor** on the Insert panel to open the Named Anchor dialog box, type **top** in the Anchor name text box, compare your screen with Figure 9, then click **OK**.

   An anchor icon now appears before The Striped Umbrella banner. Depending on your window size, the anchor icon might appear above the banner or to the left of the banner.

   TIP Use lowercase letters, no spaces, and no special characters in named anchor names. You should also avoid using a number as the first character in a named anchor name.

   (continued)

Figure 9 *Named Anchor dialog box*

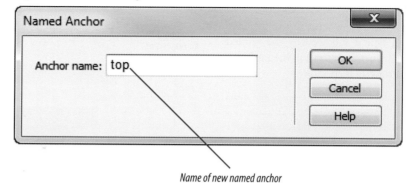

Name of new named anchor

Using Visual Aids

The Visual Aids submenu on the View menu gives you several choices for displaying page elements in Design View, such as named anchor icons. Named anchor icons are considered invisible elements. When you check the Invisible Elements option, you will see the named anchor icons on the page. The icons do not appear when the page is viewed in a browser. Turning on visual aids makes it easier to edit the page. Other options in the Visual Aids menu are Fluid Grid Layout Guides, CSS Layout Backgrounds, CSS Layout Box Model, CSS Layout Outlines, AP Element Outlines, Table Widths, Table Borders, Frame Borders, and Image Maps. The Hide All option hides all of these page elements. In later chapters, as you work with each page object that these refer to, you will see the advantages of displaying them. The CSS options allow you to see the formatting properties for CSS layout blocks such as the outline, background color, and margins.

Figure 10 *Named anchors on the spa page*

Named anchor icons

Selected named anchor icon

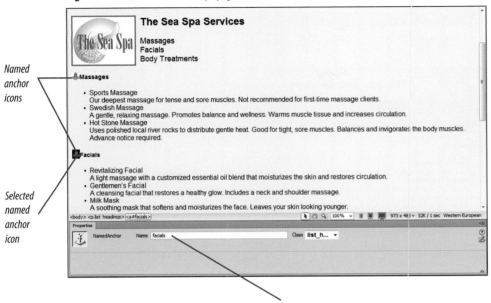

Name of selected named anchor

5. Scroll down to the list of massages, click to the left of the Massages heading, then insert a named anchor named **massages**.

6. Insert named anchors to the left of the Facials and Body Treatments headings using the following names: **facials** and **body_treatments**.

Your screen should resemble Figure 10.

You created four named anchors on the spa page, one at top of the page, and three that will help users quickly access the Spa Services headings on the page.

Create an internal link to a named anchor

1. Select the word "Massages" to the right of The Sea Spa logo, then drag the **Point to File button** from the Property inspector to the anchor next to the massages heading, as shown in Figure 11.

   The word "Massages" is now linked to the Massages named anchor. When users click the word "Massages" at the top of the page, the browser will display the Massages heading at the top of the browser window. The Link text box on the Property inspector now reads #massages.

   TIP The name of a named anchor is always preceded by a pound (#) sign in the Link text box in the Property inspector.

2. Create internal links for Facials and Body Treatments to the right of The Sea Spa logo by first selecting each of these words or phrases, then dragging the **Point to File button** to the appropriate named anchor icon.

   The words "Facials" and "Body Treatments" are now links that connect to the Facials and Body Treatments headings.

   TIP Once you select the text on the page you want to link, you might need to scroll down to view the named anchor on the screen. Once you see the named anchor on your screen, you can drag the Point to File button on top of it. You can also move the pointer to the edge of the page window (still in the cream area of the page) to scroll the page.

   (continued)

Figure 11 *Dragging the Point to File button to a named anchor*

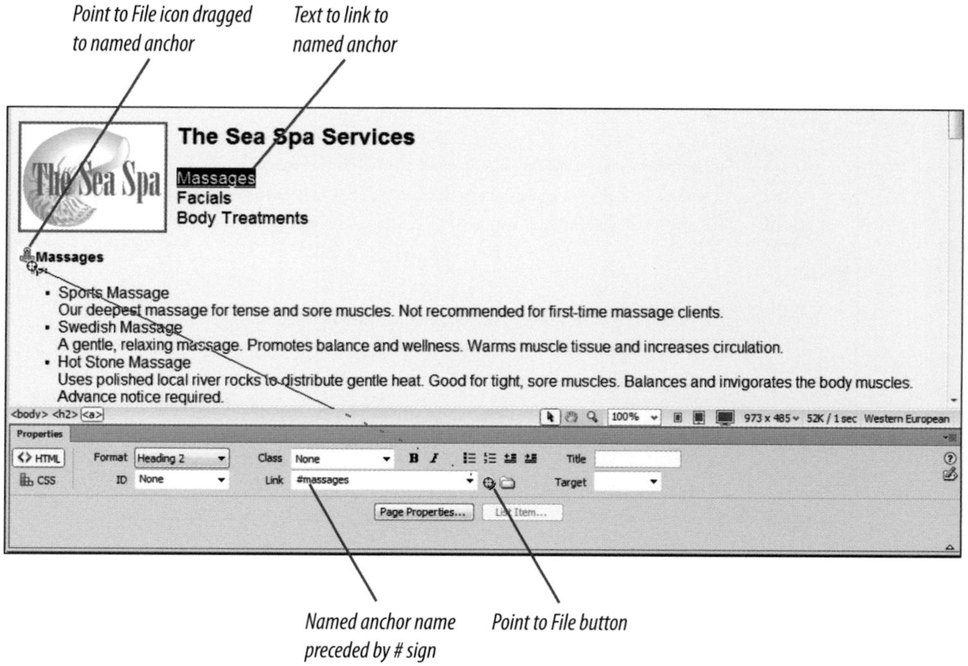

Point to File icon dragged to named anchor

Text to link to named anchor

Named anchor name preceded by # sign

Point to File button

Figure 12 *Spa page with internal links to named anchors*

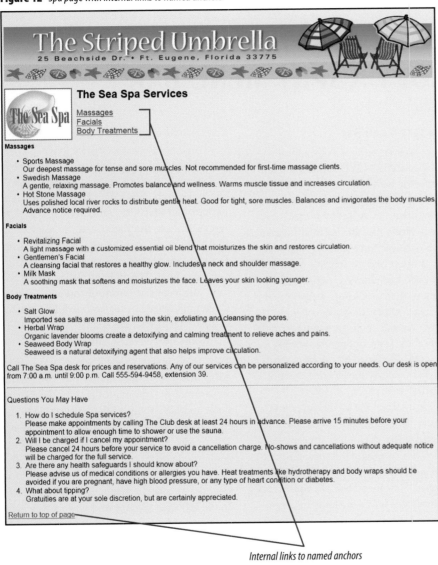

Internal links to named anchors

3. Scroll down to the bottom of the page, then place the insertion point at the end of the last sentence on the page.

4. Press [**Enter**] (Win) or [**return**] (Mac) twice to insert two paragraph breaks, then type **Return to top of page**.

5. Place the insertion point to the left of the text "Return to top of page," then click the **Remove Blockquote button** ≛ to move the text to the left margin, if necessary.

6. Apply the body_text rule to "Return to top of page" if necessary.

7. Select the text "Return to top of page", scroll to the top of the page, then use the Point to File button on the HTML Property inspector to link the text to the anchor named top.

8. Save your work, preview the page in your browser, as shown in Figure 12, then test the links to each named anchor, using the Back button to return to the links.

   When you click the Body Treatments link in the browser, the associated named anchor may appear in the middle of the page instead of at the top. This happens because the spa page is not long enough to position this named anchor at the top of the page.

9. Close your browser.

You created internal links to the named anchors next to the Spa Services headings and to the top of the spa page. You then previewed the page in your browser and tested each link.

Create, Modify, and
COPY A SPRY MENU BAR

What You'll Do

In this lesson, you will create a menu bar on the spa page that can be used to link to each main page in the website. The menu bar will have five elements: Home, About Us, Cafe, Spa, and Activities. You will also copy the new menu bar to other pages in the website. On each page you will modify the appropriate element state to reflect the current page.

Creating a Spry Menu Bar

To make your website more visually appealing, you can add special effects. For example, you can create a menu bar with rollover images rather than with plain text links. One way to do this is to insert a Spry menu bar. A **Spry menu bar** is one of the pre-set widgets available in Dreamweaver that creates a dynamic, user-friendly menu bar that is easy to insert and customize. A **widget** is a piece of code that allows a user to interact with a program, such as clicking a menu item to open a page. Other examples of widgets are interactive buttons, pop-up windows, and progress indicators. **Spry**, or **Spry framework**, is open source code developed by Adobe Systems to help designers quickly incorporate dynamic content on their web pages. To insert a Spry menu bar, click Insert on the Menu bar, point to Layout Objects, then click Spry Menu Bar. The Insert Spry Menu Bar dialog box appears. You use this dialog box to specify the appearance of the menu bar and each link, called an **item**. When you first insert a Spry menu bar, Dreamweaver automatically assigns it four menu items, some of which have submenu items. It you want your menu bar to display a different number of menu items and submenu items, you can add new ones and delete the ones you do not need.

You can add special effects for menu bar items by changing the characteristics for each item's state. A **state** is the condition of the item relative to the mouse pointer. You can create a rollover effect for each menu item by using different background and text colors for each state to represent how the menu item appears when the users move their mouse over it or away from it. You can also create special effects for web page links. The NOAA (National Oceanic and Atmospheric Administration) website shown in Figure 13 uses several different types of links: plain text links, links created as list items, and links created with images.

When you insert a menu bar on a web page using the Insert Spry Menu Bar command, Dreamweaver automatically adds JavaScript code and CSS styles to the page to make the interaction work with the menu bar items. Dreamweaver also creates a SpryAssets folder and adds it to the local site folder. The SpryAssets folder stores the newly created files that make the menu function correctly in the browser. When a user views a web page with one of these menu bars, the files that run the menu functions are stored on the user's, or client's, computer. One of the new HTML5 tags is the <nav> tag. The <nav> tag is used to designate a section of a page with navigation links. Although links do not have to be placed within <nav> tags, doing so will help provide accessibility. This is another example of content used by screen readers.

There are other methods that you can use to create a menu bar with images, such as an image map. You will learn about image maps in Lesson 4.

Copying and Modifying a Menu Bar

After you create a menu bar, you can save time by copying and pasting it to the other main pages in your site. Make sure you place the menu bar in the same position on each page. This practice ensures that the menu bar will look the same on each page, making it much easier for users to navigate to all the pages in your website. If you are even one

line or one pixel off, the menu bar will appear to "jump" as it changes position from page to page. When you learn to use templates, you can create a main page template with a menu bar, then base the rest of your pages on the template. This makes it easy to provide continuity across the site and is easier to update when changes are needed.

Figure 13 *NOAA website*
NOAA website - www.noaa.gov

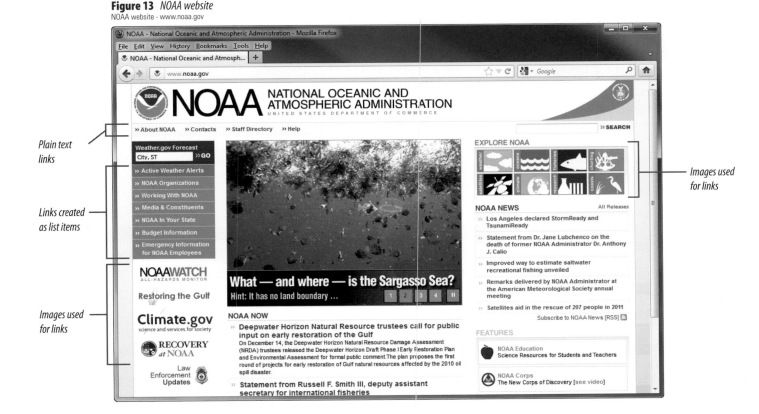

Create a Spry menu bar

1. Create a new Tag rule in the su_styles.css style sheet to modify the img tag with the following setting: in the Block Category, set the Vertical-align to **bottom**.

   This new rule will keep a vertical gap from appearing between the banner and our new menu bar.

2. Select the banner on the spa page, then press [→].

   The insertion point is now positioned between the banner and the spa logo.

3. Click the **Spry** category on the Insert panel, then click **Spry Menu Bar**.

   TIP The Spry Menu Bar button is also in the Layout category on the Insert panel.

4. Click to select the **Horizontal** layout in the Spry Menu Bar dialog box to specify that the menu bar be placed horizontally on the page, if necessary, as shown in Figure 14, then click **OK**.

   Your new menu bar containing four items appears under the banner. The menu bar is selected and the Property inspector shows its properties. Each button contains placeholder text, such as Item 1.

5. Type **Menu** in the Menu Bar text box, replacing the placeholder text, on the Property inspector, then notice that Item 1 is selected in the Item column (first column on the left) in the Property inspector.

   Now you are ready to rename the first item, delete its submenu items, and choose the file you want this item to link to.

6. Select Item 1 in the Text text box on the right side of the Property inspector, type **Home**, select Item 1.1 in the first submenu column (second column) in the Property inspector, as shown in Figure 15, then click the **Remove menu item**

   (continued)

Figure 14 *Spry Menu Bar dialog box*

Horizontal layout option

Figure 15 *Property inspector with Menu Bar properties*

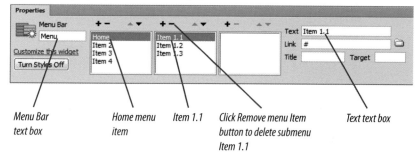

Menu Bar text box

Home menu item

Item 1.1

Click Remove menu Item button to delete submenu Item 1.1

Text text box

Understanding the Web Accessibility Initiative - Accessible Rich Internet Applications Suite

The Web Accessibility Initiative Accessible Rich Internet Applications Suite (WAI-ARIA) is a resource for applying best practices when adding advanced user interface controls to a website. Functions such as drag-and-drop or browsing through a menu can be difficult for users who rely on assistive devices to navigate a site. WAI-ARIA, at w3.org/TR/wai-aria/, provides guidelines and techniques for planning and implementing accessible content. It also provides presentations, handouts, and tutorials for developers who are interested in learning how to provide content that all users can easily navigate, such as providing alternative keyboard navigation for web objects primarily designed to function using mouse clicks. The information offered through WAI-ARIA is developed by the Protocols and Formats Working Group (PFWG), a part of the World Wide Web Consortium (W3C).

Figure 16 *Home item on the Menu Bar*

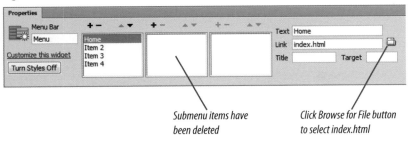

Submenu items have
been deleted

Click Browse for File button
to select index.html

Figure 17 *The Spry Menu Bar on the spa page*

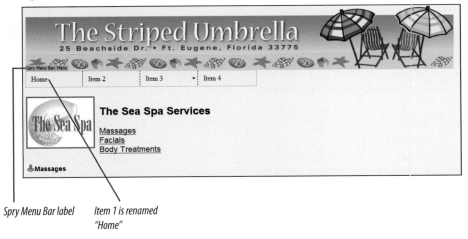

Spry Menu Bar label

Item 1 is renamed
"Home"

button ▬ above the first submenu column to delete the submenu item 1.1.

7. Click the **Remove menu item button** ▬ two more times to delete the submenu Item 1.2 and Item 1.3.

 The three submenu items would have appeared as a drop-down menu under the Home menu, but the Home link does not require a submenu, so they can be deleted.

 TIP You can add submenu items by clicking the Add menu item button ➕.

8. Click the **Browse for File button** 🗀 next to the Link text box on the Property inspector, then double-click the file **index.html**, as shown in Figure 16.

 The Home item is now linked to the index page.

9. Switch to Code view, click to place the insertion point after the ending </ul> tag, switch back to Design view, enter a paragraph break, enter a line break, compare your screen to Figure 17, save your file, then click **OK** to close the Copy Dependent Files dialog box.

 A SpryAssets folder and six files are copied to the site root folder. These are dependent files necessary for the SpryMenu bar. If you don't see them listed, refresh the Files panel.

 TIP If you see a space between the banner and the menu bar, go to Code view to look for <p> tags around the banner. If you see them, delete them.

You used the Insert Spry Menu Bar dialog box to create a menu bar for the spa page and renamed the first item "Home." You deleted the placeholder submenu items under the Home menu item.

Add items to a menu bar

1. Click the Spry Menu Bar tab to select it, click **Item 2** in the first column under the Home item in the Property inspector, then replace the text "Item 2" in the Text text box with **About Us**.

2. Click the **Browse for File button** next to the Link text box, then double-click **about_us.html** in the local site folder to link the About Us menu item to the about_us page.

3. Repeat Steps 1 and 2 to rename Item 3 **Sand Crab Cafe** and link it to the cafe.html page.

4. Delete each submenu item under the Sand Crab Cafe item, clicking **OK** to close the warning box that asks if you want to also remove the submenus, or children menus, under the submenu item.

5. Repeat Steps 1 and 2 to rename Item 4 **The Sea Spa** and link it to the spa.html page.

6. With The Sea Spa menu item selected in the Property inspector, click the **Add menu item button** above the first column to add an additional menu item, then name it **Activities** and link it to the activities.html page.

7. With the Activities menu item selected, click the **Add menu item button** above the *second* column to add a submenu item named **Cruises** and link it to the cruises.html page.

8. Repeat Step 7 to add another submenu item named **Fishing** that is linked to the fishing.html page.

9. Save your work, click **OK**, then compare your screen to Figure 18.

TIP If you accidentally created menus, instead of submenus, for Cruises and Fishing, delete them and try again, selecting Activities and adding the items to the second column.

You completed The Striped Umbrella menu bar by adding four more elements to it, each of which contains links to four pages in the site. You then added two submenus under the Activities menu item.

Figure 18 *Menu bar with all menu and submenu items in place*

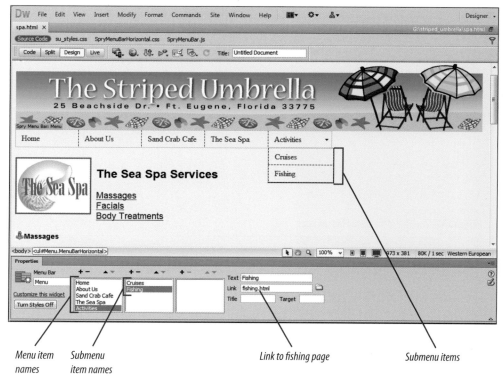

Menu item names Submenu item names Link to fishing page Submenu items

Inserting a Fireworks Menu Bar

Another option for adding a menu bar to your page is to create a menu bar in Fireworks and import it onto an open page in Dreamweaver. To do this you first create a menu bar in Fireworks and export the file to a Dreamweaver local site folder. This file contains the HTML code that defines the menu bar properties. Next, open the page you want to insert it on in Dreamweaver, then use the Insert, Image objects, Fireworks HTML command to place the HTML code on the page. You can also use Dreamweaver to import rollover images and buttons created in Fireworks.

Figure 19 *Settings for ul.MenuBarHorizontal rule*

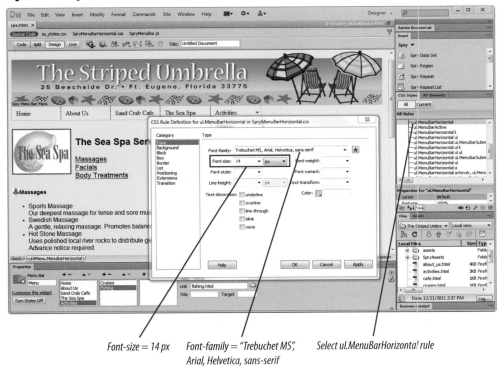

Font-size = 14 px   Font-family = "Trebuchet MS",   Select ul.MenuBarHorizontal rule
                           Arial, Helvetica, sans-serif

Use CSS to format a menu bar

1. Click the **All button** ⬚ in the CSS Styles panel if necessary, click the **plus sign** next to SpryMenuBarHorizontal.css in the CSS Styles panel, select the rule ul.MenuBarHorizontal, then click the **Edit Rule button** 🖉 to open the CSS Rule Definition for ul.MenuBarHorizontal in SpryMenuBarHorizontal.css dialog box.

   The SpryMenuBarHorizontal.css style sheet, which was automatically created when you inserted the Spry menu bar, contains properties for the way the menu items will appear in the browser. In that style sheet, the ul.MenuBarHorizontal rule determines the global settings, including the font family, font size, and font alignment, for all the menu and submenu items, regardless of whether the mouse is placed over them.

   TIP You can also use the Properties pane in the CSS Styles panel to modify style properties.

2. Click the **Type** category, click the **Font-family** list arrow, then click **Trebuchet MS, Arial, Helvetica, sans-serif.**

3. Click the **Font-size** list arrow, click **14**, click the **Font size unit of measure list arrow**, then click **px** as shown in Figure 19, then click **OK**.

   Next, you set the width and height for each menu item button by modifying the ul.MenuBarHorizontal li rule. Recall that the <li> tag is the HTML code for list item. The Spry menu bar is built using unordered list items for each menu item. This rule sets the properties that determine the appearance of the menu items.

   (continued)

4. Select the rule **ul.MenuBarHorizontal li** in the CSS Styles panel, then click the **Edit Rule button** 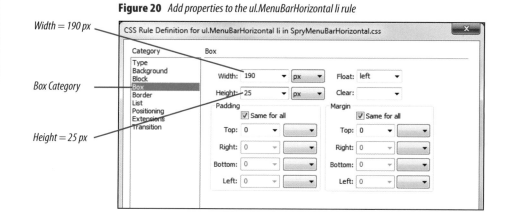 to open the CSS Rule Definition for ul.MenuBarHorizontal li in SpryMenuBarHorizontal.css dialog box.

5. Click the **Box** category, click the **Width** text box, replace the current value with **190**, click the **Width unit of measure list arrow,** then click **px.**

TIP To calculate the width for each menu item, divide the number of pixels of the banner width by the number of menu items.

6. Click the **Height text box**, type **25**, verify that px is the unit of measure, then compare your screen to Figure 20.

   The menu bar items will be spread across the page to equal the width of the banner. Next, you'll edit the rule that defines the properties of each menu item button when the mouse is not positioned over them.

7. Click in the Block category, change the Text-align value to **center**, then click **OK**.

8. Click the **ul.MenuBarHorizontal a** rule in the CSS Styles panel, then click the **Edit Rule button** 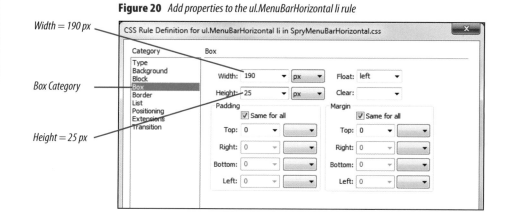 to open the CSS Rule Definition for ul.MenuBarHorizontal a in SpryMenuBarHorizontal.css dialog box .

   See Table 3 for a summary of the rules applied to the the Spry menu bar.

TIP If you want to understand the function of each rule in the SpryMenuBarHorizontal.css style sheet, click the SpryMenuBarHorizontal.css button in the Related files toolbar and take a few minutes to read the comments for each rule. Click the Show Design View button to return to Design view.

(continued)

Figure 20 *Add properties to the ul.MenuBarHorizontal li rule*

Width = 190 px

Box Category

Height = 25 px

CSS Rule Definition for ul.MenuBarHorizontal li in SpryMenuBarHorizontal.css

Category	Box

Category: Type, Background, Block, Box, Border, List, Positioning, Extensions, Transition

Width: 190 px   Float: left
Height: 25 px   Clear:

Padding — ☑ Same for all
Top: 0
Right: 0
Bottom: 0
Left: 0

Margin — ☑ Same for all
Top: 0
Right: 0
Bottom: 0
Left: 0

TABLE 3: SUMMARY OF EDITING STEPS FOR CSS MENU BAR RULES	
CSS Rule	**What We Did**
ul.MenuBarHorizontal	We changed the Font-family and Font-size for the menu bar.
ul.MenuBarHorizontal li	We changed the Box Width, Box Height, and Text-align properties for each menu item.
ul.MenuBarHorizontal a	We changed the Type color and Background color for all menu items when the mouse is not positioned over them in the browser.
ul.MenuBarHorizontal a.MenuBarItemHover, ul.MenuBarHorizontal a.MenuBarItemSubmenuHover, ul.MenuBarHorizontal a.MenuBarSubmenuVisible	We changed the Type color and Background color for all menu items when the mouse is positioned over them in the browser.
ul.MenuBarHorizontal ul li	We changed the width and height of the submenu items to make them match the dimensions of the menu items.
ul.MenuBar Horizontal ul	We changed the Box width to prevent a space between the main menu item and the first submenu item.

Figure 21 *Setting the menu item appearance when the mouse will not be over them*

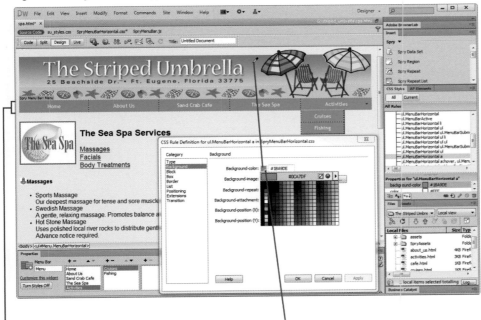

Menu buttons will have a
blue background with white
text when the mouse is not
positioned over them

Select a shade of blue
from the banner

9. Click the **Type** category, type **#FFF** in the Color text box, click the **Background** category, click the **Background-color color picker** ⬜, use the eyedropper 🖊 to select a blue shade from the banner, as shown in Figure 21, then click **OK**.

   The menu items will have a blue background with white text when the mouse is not positioned over them. Now you are ready to set the colors the menu bar items will be when users point to (hover their mouse over) a menu item that has submenus. This rule is the longest one in the style sheet, because it includes properties that determine the appearance of menu items with submenus, both when the mouse is hovering over them and when the mouse is not hovering over them.

10. Click the longest rule name, **ul.MenuBarHorizontal a.MenuBarItemHover, ul.MenuBarHorizontal a.MenuBarItemSubmenuHover, ul.MenuBarHorizontal a.MenuBarSubmenuVisible** in the CSS Styles panel, click the **Edit Rule button** 🖊 to open the rule definition dialog box, click the **Type** category, type **#630** in the Color text box, click the **Background** category, use the eyedropper to select a shade of sand from the banner for the Background color, then click **OK**.

   The menu and submenu items will have a sand background with brown text when the mouse is positioned over them in the browser.

   (continued)

TIP To locate the longest rule, place your mouse over each rule name to see the extended names. You will quickly spot the longest name! You can also widen the CSS Styles panel temporarily to see the entire names.

11. Select the rule **ul.MenuBarHorizontal ul li** in the CSS Styles panel, then click the **Edit Rule button** 🖉 to open the CSS Rule Definition for ul.MenuBarHorizontal ul li in SpryMenuBarHorizontal.css dialog box.

    You will now edit the rule that determines the width and height of the submenu items to make them match the size of the menu items.

12. Click the **Box** category, delete the default Box Width, then click **OK**.

    By removing the default settings, the submenu items will be the same width as the main menu items.

13. Select the rule **ul.MenuBarHorizontal ul** in the CSS Styles panel, click the **Edit Rule button** 🖉, click the **Box** category, change the Box width to **190px**, then click **OK**.

    This setting will prevent a space between a main menu item and the first submenu item.

14. Save all files, preview your page in the browser, compare your screen to Figure 22, test each link to ensure that each works correctly, then close the browser.

    The cafe, cruises, and fishing pages are still blank. Use the Back button after you click these links to return to pages with content.

    As you roll the mouse over each menu and submenu item, the background and text colors change. Because the colors you used

    (continued)

Figure 22 *Spa page in the browser with the mouse over the Activities item*

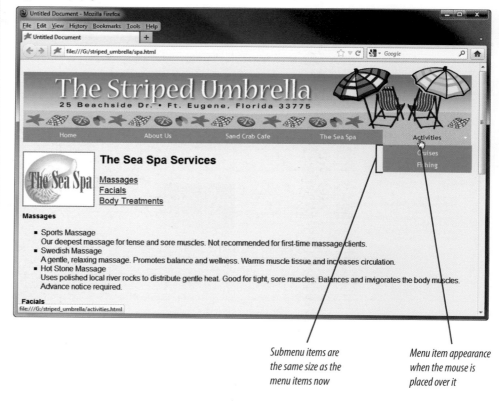

Submenu items are the same size as the menu items now

Menu item appearance when the mouse is placed over it

Figure 23 *Selecting the menu bar on the spa page*

Click tab to select the menu bar

Figure 24 *The activities page with the completed menu bar*

for the backgrounds are from the banner, the buttons complement the banner.

You edited the properties of five rules in the style sheet that set the appearance of the menu bar on the page.

Copy and paste a menu bar

1. Verify that Invisible Elements is turned on, then click the **Spry Menu Bar: Menu tab** above the top left corner of the menu bar, as shown in Figure 23.

2. Click **Edit** on the Menu bar, then click **Copy**.

3. Double-click **activities.html** on the Files panel to open the activities page.

4. Select the original menu bar on the page, click **Edit** on the Menu bar, click **Paste**, click to the right of the menu bar, enter a line break, delete the horizontal rule under the menu bar (you can click the far right side of it to select it) compare your screen to Figure 24, then save the page.

5. Open the index page, delete the existing menu bar, paste the new menu bar, add two line breaks between the menu bar and horizontal rule, delete the horizontal rule, then save and close the index page.

6. Open the about_us page, replace the existing menu bar with the new menu bar, add a line break between the menu bar and horizontal rule, delete the horizontal rule, then save your work.

7. Preview the about_us page in your browser, test the menu bar on the home, about_us, spa, and activities pages, then close your browser. Close all open pages except the activities page.

You copied the menu bar on the spa page to three additional pages in The Striped Umbrella website.

Create an
IMAGE MAP

What You'll Do

In this lesson, you will create an image map by placing a hotspot on The Striped Umbrella banner on the activities page that will link to the home page.

Understanding Image Maps

Another way to create links for web pages is to combine them with images by creating an image map. An **image map** is an image that has one or more hotspots placed on top of it. A **hotspot** is a clickable area on an image that, when the user clicks it, links to a different location on the page or to another web page. For example, see the National Park Service website shown in Figure 25. When you click a state, you link to information about national parks in that state.

You can create hotspots by first selecting the image on which you want to place a hotspot, and then using one of the hotspot tools in the Property inspector to define its shape.

There are several ways to create image maps to make them user-friendly and accessible. One way is to be sure to include alternate text for each hotspot. Another is to draw the hotspot boundaries a little larger than they need to be to cover the area you want to set as a link. This allows users a little leeway when they place their mouse over the hotspot by creating a larger target area for them. Always assign a unique name for each image map.

Dreamweaver hotspot tools make creating image maps a snap. In addition to the Rectangle Hotspot Tool, you can create any shape you need using the Circle Hotspot Tool and the Polygon Hotspot Tool. For instance, on a map of the United States, you can draw an outline around each state with the Polygon Hotspot Tool and then make each state "clickable." You can easily change and rearrange hotspots on the image. Use the Pointer Hotspot Tool to select the hotspot you would like to edit. You can drag one of the hotspot selector handles to change its size or shape. You can also move the hotspot by dragging it to a new position on the image. It is a good idea to limit the number of complex hotspots in an image because the code can become too lengthy for the page to download in a reasonable length of time.

Figure 25 *Viewing an image map on the National Park Service website*
National Park Service website – www.nps.gov

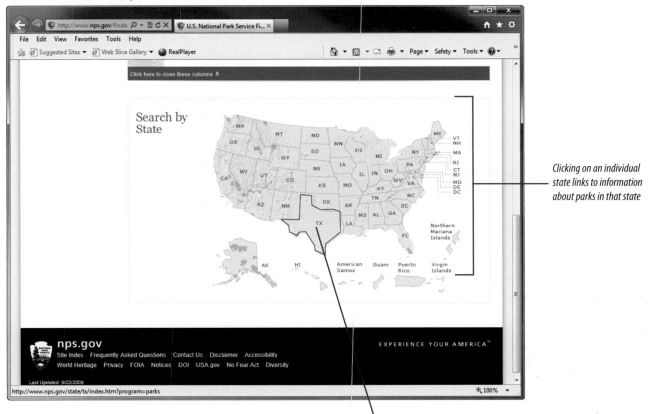

Clicking on an individual state links to information about parks in that state

To view the hotspot, move the pointer over a state. Then press and hold the mouse button

Create an image map

1. Select the banner on the activities page, then click the **Rectangle Hotspot Tool** ⬚ in the Property inspector.

2. Drag the **pointer** to create a rectangle over the text "The Striped Umbrella" in the banner, as shown in Figure 26, then click **OK** to close the dialog box that reminds you to supply alternate text for the hotspot.

TIP To adjust the shape of a hotspot, click the Pointer Hotspot Tool ▶ in the Property inspector, then drag a sizing handle on the hotspot.

3. Drag the **Point to File button** 🌀 next to the Link text box in the Property inspector to the index.html file on the Files panel to link the hotspot to the index page.

4. Replace the default text "Map" with **Home** in the Map text box in the Property inspector to give the image map a unique name.

5. Click the **Target list arrow** in the Property inspector, then click **_top**.

   When the hotspot is clicked, the _top option opens the home page in the same window. See Table 2 for an explanation of the four target options.

6. Type **Link to home page** in the Alt text box in the Property inspector, as shown in Figure 27, then press **[Enter]** (Win) or **[return]** (Mac).

7. Save your work, preview the page in your browser, then place the pointer over the image map.

(continued)

Figure 26 *A hotspot drawn on the banner*

Hotspot

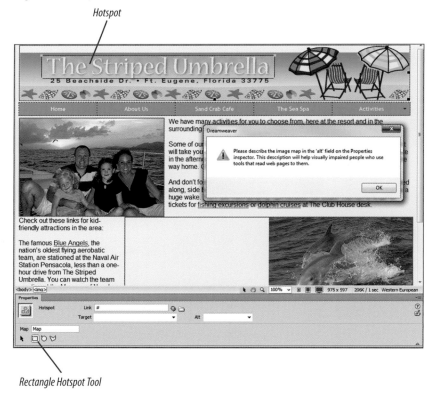

Rectangle Hotspot Tool

TABLE 2: OPTIONS IN THE TARGET LIST	
Target	**Result**
_blank	Displays the destination page in a separate browser window
new	Displays the destination page in a new tab (CSS3)
_parent	Displays the destination page in the parent frameset (replaces the frameset)
_self	Displays the destination page in the same frame or window
_top	Displays the destination page in the whole browser window

© Cengage Learning 2013

Figure 27 *Hotspot properties*

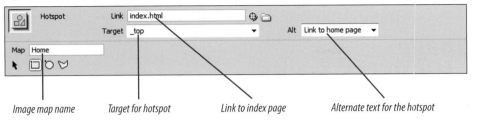

Image map name

Target for hotspot

Link to index page

Alternate text for the hotspot

Figure 28 *Preview of the image map on the activities page in the browser*

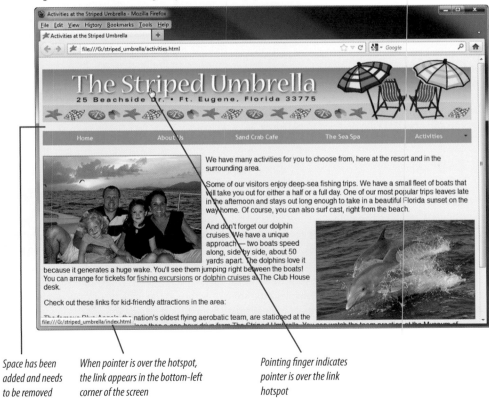

Space has been added and needs to be removed

When pointer is over the hotspot, the link appears in the bottom-left corner of the screen

Pointing finger indicates pointer is over the link hotspot

As you place the pointer over the hotspot, the pointer turns to a pointing finger, indicating that it is a link, as shown in Figure 28. Notice that there is now a space between the banner and the menu bar. The code for the image map added a line break between the two, which caused the space to appear.

8. Return to Dreamweaver, switch to Code view and locate the <br> code between the ending </map> tag and the code that begins the menu bar.

9. Delete the <br> code.

   The space is removed. Refer to the What You'll Do figure at the beginning of this lesson to see the completed page with the space removed.

10. While still in Code view, locate the code for the banner, then add this code inside the <img> tags: **style="border:0"**.

    For example: "<img style="border:0" src="assets/su_banner.gif"....../>. As long as you type it between the beginning and ending image tags, it will work correctly. This code will prevent a border from appearing around the banner in Internet Explorer.

11. Return to Design view, save your file, then preview the page in the browser.

12. Click the link to test it, close the browser, then close all open pages.

You created an image map on the banner of the activities page using the Rectangle Hotspot Tool. You then linked the hotspot to the home page and removed a line break that was added with the image map code.

Manage
WEBSITE LINKS

What You'll Do

In this lesson, you will use some Dreamweaver reporting features to check The Striped Umbrella website for broken links and orphaned files.

Managing Website Links

Because the World Wide Web changes constantly, websites might be up one day and down the next. If a website changes server locations or goes down due to technical difficulties or a power failure, the links to it become broken. Broken links, like misspelled words on a web page, indicate that a website is not being maintained diligently.

Checking links to make sure they work is an ongoing and crucial task you need to perform on a regular basis. You must check external links manually by reviewing your website in a browser and clicking each link to make sure it works correctly. The Check Links Sitewide feature is a helpful tool for managing internal links. You can use it to check your entire website for the total number of links and the number of links that are broken, external, or orphaned, and then view the results in the Link Checker panel. **Orphaned files** are files that are not linked to any pages in the website.

DESIGN**TIP**

Using Good Navigation Design

As you work on the navigation structure for a website, you should try to limit the number of links on each page to no more than is necessary. Too many links may confuse users of your website. You should also design links so that users can reach the information they want within a few clicks. If finding information takes more than three or four clicks, the user may become discouraged or "lost" in the site. It's a good idea to provide visual clues on each page to let users know where they are, much like a "You are here" marker on a store directory at the mall, or a breadcrumbs trail. A **breadcrumbs trail** is a list of links that provides a path from the initial page you opened in a website to the page that you are currently viewing. Many websites provide a list of all the site's pages, called a **site map**. A site map is similar to an index. It lets users see how the information is divided between the pages and helps them locate the information they need quickly.

Figure 29 *Link Checker panel displaying external links*

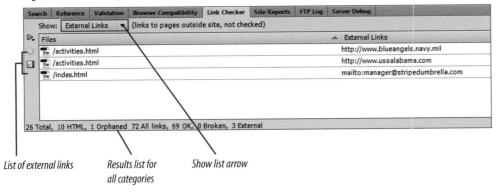

List of external links   *Results list for all categories*   *Show list arrow*

Figure 30 *Link Checker panel displaying one orphaned file*

One orphaned file listed   *Show list arrow*

Figure 31 *Assets panel displaying links*

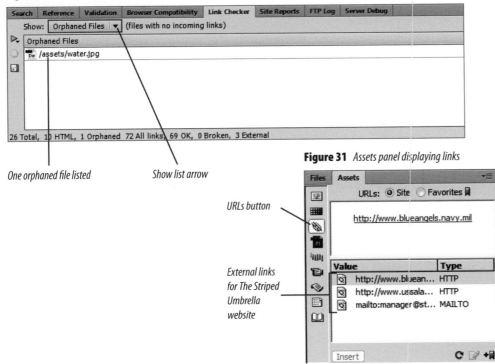

URLs button

External links for The Striped Umbrella website

Manage website links

1. Click **Site** on the Menu bar, point to **Advanced**, then click **Recreate Site Cache**.

2. Click **Site** on the Menu bar, then click **Check Links Sitewide**.

   The Results tab group opens, with the Link Checker panel in front. By default, the Link Checker panel initially lists any broken internal links found in the website. The Striped Umbrella website has no broken links.

3. Click the **Show list arrow** in the Link Checker panel, click **External Links**, then compare your screen to Figure 29.

4. Click the **Show list arrow**, then click **Orphaned Files** to view the orphaned files in the Link Checker panel, as shown in Figure 30.

   The Striped Umbrella website has one orphaned file, water.jpg. You may use this file later, so you leave it in the assets folder.

5. Right-click (Win) or Control-click (Mac) in an empty area of the Results tab group title bar, then click **Close Tab Group**.

6. Display the Assets panel if necessary, then click the **URLs button** 🔗 in the Assets panel if necessary to display the list of links in the website.

   The Assets panel displays the external links used in the website, as shown in Figure 31.

You used the Link Checker panel to check for broken links, external links, and orphaned files in The Striped Umbrella website. You also viewed the external links in the Assets panel.

Update a page

1. Open dw5_2.html from the drive and folder where you store your Data Files, then save it as **fishing.html** in the striped_umbrella local site root folder, overwriting the existing fishing page, but not updating the links.

2. Click the broken link image placeholder, click the **Browse for File button** 📁 next to the Src text box in the Property inspector, browse to the drive and folder where you store your Data Files, open the assets folder, then select the file **fisherman.jpg** to copy the file to the striped_umbrella assets folder.

3. Deselect the image placeholder and the image appears, as shown in Figure 32.

   The text is automatically updated with the body_text style. The code was already in place on the page linking su_styles.css to the file. The Spry menu bar was also updated using the link to the SpryMenuBarHorizontal.css file.

4. Save and close the fishing page, then close the dw5_2.html page.

5. Open dw5_3.html from the drive and folder where you store your Data Files, then save it as **cruises.html** in the striped_umbrella local site folder, overwriting the existing cruises page, but not updating the links.

(continued)

Figure 32 *Fishing page updated*

We have several boats available for fishing trips that can be rented by the hour, half day, or full day. You may choose to go out to sea several miles for deep-sea fishing, or fish in one of several bays not far from the resort. Call the front desk to schedule your trip and let them know the fishing gear you will need us to provide. Bring your catch back and our chefs will be happy to prepare it to your specifications for dinner!

Be sure to apply sunscreen liberally before you arrive at the dock. A large hat with a tie is highly recommended to protect your head and neck while you are on the open water. We will provide a cooler with bottles of water, but you will need to provide your own snacks or lunch. The Sand Crab Cafe will be happy to prepare these for you if you call several hours in advance.

Testing Your Website Against the Wireframe

Another test you should run regularly is a comparison of how your developing website pages are meeting the specifications of your wireframe prototype. Compare each completed page against its corresponding wireframe to make sure that all page elements have been placed in their proper locations on the page. Verify that all specified links have been included and test them to make sure that they work correctly. You might also consider hiring site-usability testers to test your site navigation. A site usability test provides impartial feedback on how intuitive and user-friendly your site is to use.

Figure 33 *Cruises page updated*

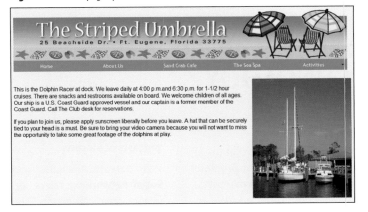

POWER USER SHORTCUTS	
To do this:	**Use this shortcut:**
Close a file	[Ctrl][W] (Win) or ⌘ [W] (Mac)
Close all files	[Ctrl][Shift][W] (Win) or ⌘ [Shift][W] (Mac)
Print code	[Ctrl][P] (Win) or ⌘ [P] (Mac)
Check page links	[Shift][F8] (Win) or [fn][shift][F8] (Mac)
Undo	[Ctrl][Z], [Alt][BkSp] (Win) or ⌘ [Z], [option][delete] (Mac)
Redo	[Ctrl][Y], [Ctrl][Shift][Z] (Win) or ⌘ [Y], ⌘ [Shift][Z] (Mac)
Refresh Design view	[F5]
Hide all visual aids	[Ctrl][Shift][I] (Win) or ⌘ [Shift][I] (Mac)
Insert a named anchor	[Ctrl][Alt][A] (Win) or ⌘ [option][A] (Mac)
Make a link	[Ctrl][L] (Win) or ⌘ [L] (Mac)
Remove a link	[Ctrl][Shift][L] (Win) or ⌘ [Shift][L] (Mac)
Check links sitewide	[Ctrl][F8] (Win) or [fn] ⌘ [F8] (Mac)
Show Files tab group	[F8] (Win) or ⌘ [Shift][F] (Mac)

© Cengage Learning 2013

6. Click the broken link image placeholder, click the **Browse for File button** next to the Src text box in the Property inspector, then browse to the drive and folder where you store your Data Files, open the assets folder, then select the file boats.jpg to copy the file to the striped_umbrella assets folder.

TIP If you have trouble selecting the placeholder, click the middle of the placeholder to select it.

7. Deselect the image placeholder and the image will appear as shown in Figure 33.

   The text is automatically updated with the body_text style. The code was already in place on the page linking su_styles.css to the file. The Spry menu bar was also updated as the SpryMenuBarHorizontal.css rules were applied.

8. Save your work if necessary.

9. Preview each page in the browser, close the browser, then close all open pages.

You added content to two previously blank pages in the website and previewed each page to check for consistent layout.

Incorporate Web 2.0
TECHNOLOGY

What You'll Do

Peace Corps website – www.peacecorps.gov

In this lesson, you will explore some of the Web 2.0 applications that can be used to engage website users.

What Exactly Is Web 2.0?

The term **Web 2.0** describes the evolution of web applications that facilitate and promote information sharing among Internet users. These applications not only reside on computers, but on cell phones, in cars, on portable GPS devices, and in game devices. **GPS (Global Positioning System)** devices are used to track your position through a global satellite navigation system, and are popular to use for driving directions, hiking, and map making. Web 2.0 applications do not simply display information for users to read passively; they allow users to actively contribute to the content.

RSS feeds are another easy way to share information with users. **RSS** stands for **Really Simple Syndication**. Websites use **RSS feeds** to distribute news stories, information about upcoming events, and announcements. Web users can subscribe to RSS feeds to receive regular releases of information from a site. Users can download and play these digitally broadcasted files called **podcasts (Programming On Demand)** using devices such as computers or MP3 players. Many news organizations and educational institutions publish both audio and video

podcasts. Video podcasts are referred to as **vodcasts** or **vidcasts**.

Web 2.0 also includes social networking. **Social networking** refers to any web-based service that facilitates social interaction among users. Examples of social networking sites include **Facebook**, **Pinterest**, and **Match. com**. These sites allow users to set up profile pages and post information on them for others to view. Facebook pages often contain lots of text, images, and videos. Pinterest is an online pinboard for sharing crafts, recipes, and other items of interest.

A wiki is another example of a Web 2.0 application. The term **wiki** (named for the Hawaiian word for "quick") refers to a site where a user can use simple editing tools to contribute and edit the page content in a site. A good example is **Wikipedia**, an online encyclopedia. Wikipedia allows users to post new information and edit existing information on any topic. Although people have different opinions about the academic integrity of the information on Wikipedia, Wikipedia is a rich source of information. Proponents argue that its many active and vigilant users maintain its information integrity.

Blogs (web logs) are another example of a Web 2.0 application. **Blogs** are websites where the website owner regularly posts commentaries and opinions on various topics. Content can consist of text, video, or images. Users can respond to the postings and read postings by other users. **Twitter** is a website where users can post short messages, called **tweets**. Twitter is considered a blog or a micro blog, because you cannot enter more than 140 characters in each post. To use Twitter, you must first join by creating a free account. Then you can post messages about yourself, "follow" other people's tweets, and invite others to "follow" you. **Tumblr** is another popular blog where you can post and share text, photos, music, and videos.

There are many video sharing applications such as Skype, Google Video Chat, and YouTube. **Skype** and **Google Video Chat** are free applications that you use to communicate live with other people through video conferencing, using a high-speed Internet connection and a web camera, called a **web cam**. **YouTube** is a website where you can upload and share videos. To upload videos, you need to register with the site.

So how do these various Web 2.0 components relate to the process of creating websites? Most websites today engage their users in one or more of these applications. The Peace Corps website, shown in Figure 34, has links to Facebook, Twitter, YouTube, and RSS Feeds. When you are designing a site, one of the decisions you must make is not if, but how you will incorporate Web 2.0 technology to fully engage your users. To incorporate one of these applications into your website, first register to set up an account on the social networking site, then place a link on one of your site's web pages (usually the home page) that links to each social networking site and opens your page. For example, if your Twitter account is located at twitter.com/your_name, add this link to your home page using the Twitter logo as a graphic link. You can download social networking sites' logos from their websites. Some applications specify how you should refer to and link to their site.

Using the applications that are a part of Web 2.0 with your website can bring your site from simply presenting information on pages for users to read to facilitating a compelling dialog between the users and the site. They will no longer be just "users," but active participants.

Web 3.0 will be the next generation of the Web. With Web 3.0, browsers will be able to handle multiple searches simultaneously. For instance, you could search for a recent Oscar best picture nominee and sushi restaurant in the vicinity of the theater where it is playing. The new iPhones come with a personal assistant you can "talk" with, rather than typing in searches. Browsers may soon be able to do this, too. The more information that is stored from your past searches, the more they will get to "know" you and be able to give responses that fit your profile.

Figure 34 *Viewing social networking links on the Peace Corps website*
Peace Corps website – www.peacecorps.gov

Links to Facebook, Twitter, Flickr, YouTube, Tumblr, LinkedIn

Create external and internal links.

1. Open the Blooms & Bulbs website.

2. Open dw5_4.html from the drive and folder where you store your Data Files, then save it as **newsletter.html** in the Blooms & Bulbs website, overwriting the existing file without updating the links. Close dw5_4.html.

3. Verify that the banner path is set correctly to the assets folder in the website and correct it, if it is not, then browse to the drive and folder where you store your Chapter 5 Data Files assets folder and copy the ruby_grass, trees, and plants broken images to the site assets folder.

4. Add a new tag selector rule to the blooms_styles.css file that modifies the <h2> tag as follows: Font-family: Arial, Helvetica, sans-serif; Font-size: 16px; Font-weight: Bold; Color: #030.

5. Modify the <h1> rule to change the Font-size to 18px, then add a new tag selector rule to the blooms_styles.css file that modifies the <h3> tag as follows: Font-family: Arial, Helvetica, sans-serif; Font-size: 16px; Color: #030.

6. Apply the img_left_float rule to the ruby_grass and plants images.

7. Apply the img_right_float rule to the trees image.

8. Scroll to the bottom of the page, then link the National Gardening Association text to http://www.garden.org.

9. Link the Organic Gardening text to http://www.organicgardening.com.

10. Link the Southern Living text to http://www.southernliving.com/southern.

11. Save all files, then preview the page in your browser, verifying that each link works correctly.

12. Close your browser, returning to the newsletter page in Dreamweaver.

13. Scroll to the paragraph about gardening issues, select the gardening tips text in the last sentence, then link the selected text to the tips.html file in the blooms site root folder.

14. Change the page title to read **Gardening Matters,** then save your work.

15. Open the plants page and add a new paragraph to the bottom of the page: **In addition to these marvelous roses, we have many annuals, perennials, and water plants that have just arrived**.

16. Apply the body_text rule to the new paragraph if necessary.

17. Link the "annuals" text to the annuals.html file, link the "perennials" text to the perennials.html file, and the "water plants" text to the water_plants.html file.

18. Save your work, test the links in your browser, then close your browser. (*Hint*: These pages do not have content yet, but are serving as placeholders.)

Create internal links to named anchors.

1. Show Invisible Elements, if necessary.

2. Click the Common category in the Insert panel.

3. Switch to the newsletter page, then insert a named anchor in front of the Grass heading named **grass**.

4. Insert a named anchor in front of the Trees heading named **trees**.

5. Insert a named anchor in front of the Plants heading named **plants**.

6. Use the Point to File button in the Property inspector to create a link from the word "grass" in the Gardening Issues paragraph to the anchor named "grass."

7. Create a link from the word "trees" in the Gardening Issues paragraph to the anchor named "trees."

8. Create a link from the word "plants" in the Gardening Issues paragraph to the anchor named "plants."

9. Save your work, view the page in your browser, test all the links to make sure they work, then close your browser.

Create, modify, and copy a Spry menu bar.

1. Delete the horizontal rule under the banner, select the banner, press the right arrow key, enter a line break, click the Spry category on the Insert panel, then click Spry Menu Bar to insert a horizontal Spry menu bar at the top of the newsletter page below the banner and above the Gardening Matters heading. Add two line breaks to separate the menu bar from the heading.

2. Select the Menu bar, select Item 1 in the Property inspector, remove the three submenu items under Item 1, type **Home** in the Text text box, then browse to link the Home menu item to the **index.html** file.

3. Select Item 2, then replace the text name with **Newsletter** and link it to the **newsletter.html** file.

4. Repeat Step 3 to rename Item 3 **Plants** and link it to the **plants.html** file.

5. Select the submenu Item 3.1, rename it **Annuals**, link it to the **annuals.html** file, then delete the submenu items under the Annuals submenu item.

6. Repeat Step 5 to rename Item 3.2 **Perennials**, then link it to the **perennials.html** file.

7. Repeat Step 5 to rename Item 3.3 **Water Plants**, then link it to the **water_plants.html** file.

8. Select the Item 4 menu item, rename it **Tips**, then link it to the **tips.html** file.

9. Add a new menu item named **Workshops**, then link it to the **workshops.html** file.

10. Edit the ul.MenuBarHorizontal rule to change the Font-family to **Verdana, Geneva, sans-serif**, and the Font-size to **14 px**.

11. Edit the ul.MenuBarHorizontal li to set the Text-align to **Center**, the Box width to **190 px** and the Box height to **25 px**.

12. Edit the ul.MenuBarHorizontal a rule to change the Type color to **#030** and the background color to **#99F**.

13. Edit the ul.MenuBarHorizontal a.MenuBarItemHover, ul.MenuBarHorizontal a.MenuBarItemSubmenuHover ul.MenuBarHorizontal a.MenuBarSubmenuVisible rule (the longest one) to change the Type color to **#FFC** and the background color to one of the light green colors in the banner.

14. Save all files, copying dependent files, test each link in the browser to make sure the links work correctly, then close the browser.

15. Add a new rule to the blooms_styles.css file to modify the <img> tag by setting the vertical alignment to bottom.

16. Select and copy the menu bar, then open the home page.

17. Delete the current menu bar and horizontal rule on the home page, and paste the new menu bar under the banner with a line break between them. Remove any space between the banner and menu bar if necessary. (*Hint*: If you see space between the banner and the menu bar, go to Code view and check to make sure that you used a <br> tag between the banner and the menu bar.)

Figure 35 *Completed Skills Review*

Gardening Matters

Welcome, fellow gardeners. My name is Cosie Simmons, the owner of Blooms & Bulbs. My passion has always been my gardens. Ever since I was a small child, I was drawn to my back yard where all varieties of beautiful plants flourished. A lush carpet of thick grass bordered with graceful beds is truly a haven for all living creatures. With proper planning and care, your gardens will draw a variety of birds and butterflies and become a great pleasure to you.

Gardening Issues

There are several areas to concentrate on when formulating your landscaping plans. One is your grass. Another is the number and variety of trees you plant. The third is the combination of plants you select. All of these decisions should be considered in relation to the climate in your area. Be sure and check out our gardening tips before you begin work.

Grass

Lawn experts classify grass into two categories: cool-climate and warm-climate. The northern half of the United States would be considered cool-climate. Examples of cool-climate grass are Kentucky bluegrass and ryegrass. Bermuda grass is a warm-climate grass. Before planting grass, whether by seeding, sodding, sprigging, or plugging, the ground must be properly prepared. The soil should be tested for any nutritional deficiencies and cultivated. Come by or call to make arrangements to have your soil tested. When selecting a lawn, avoid letting personal preferences and the cost of establishment be the overriding factors. Ask yourself these questions: What type of lawn are you expecting? What level of maintenance are you willing to provide? What are the site limitations?

Trees

Before you plant trees, you should evaluate your purpose. Are you interested in shade, privacy, or color? Do you want to attract wildlife? Attract birds? Create a shady play area? Your purpose will determine what variety of tree you should plant. Of course, you also need to consider your climate and available space. Shape is especially important in selecting trees for ornamental and shade purposes. Abundant shade comes from tall trees with long spreading or weeping branches. Ornamental trees will not provide abundant shade. We carry many varieties of trees and are happy to help you make your selections to fit your purpose.

Plants

There are so many types of plants available that it can become overwhelming. Do you want border plants, shrubs, ground covers, annuals, perennials, vegetables, fruits, vines, or bulbs? In reality, a combination of several of these works well. Design aspects such as balance, flow, definition of space and focalization should be considered. Annuals provide brilliant bursts of color in the garden. By selecting flowers carefully to fit the conditions of the site, it is possible to have a beautiful display without an unnecessary amount of work. Annuals are also great as fresh and dry cut flowers. Perennials can greatly improve the quality of your landscape. Perennials have come and gone in popularity, but today are as popular as ever. Water plants are also quite popular now. We will be happy to help you sort out your preferences and select a harmonious combination of plants for you.

Further Research

These are some of my favorite gardening links. Take the time to browse through some of the information they offer, then give me a call at (555) 248-0806 or e-mail me at cosie@blooms&bulbs.com.

National Gardening Association
Organic Gardening
Southern Living

18. Save and close the page, switch to the plants page, then paste the menu bar on the page in the same position under the banner.
19. Add a two line breaks between the menu bar and the first heading, then save and close the page.
20. Open the tips page and repeat Steps 18 and 19 to add the menu bar and any additional spacing to the page.
21. Save and close the tips page.
22. Save your work, preview all the pages in your browser, compare your newsletter page to Figure 35, test all the links, then close your browser.

Create an image map.

1. On the newsletter page, use the Rectangle Hotspot Tool to draw an image map across the name "Blooms & Bulbs", on the banner that will link to the home page.

2. Name the image map **home** and set the target to _top.
3. Add the alternate text **Link to home page**, save the page, then preview it in the browser to test the link.
4. Close the browser, then switch to Code view.
5. Add the following code to the <img> tag for the banner: **style="border:0"**, return to Design view, then save your work.
6. If you still see a space between the banner and the menu bar, go to Code view and remove the break tag after the code for the image map.

Manage website links.

1. Use the Link Checker panel to view and fix broken links and orphaned files in the Blooms & Bulbs website. (*Hint*: Remember to recreate your site cache if you see any. That usually fixes them.)

2. Open dw5_5.html from the drive and folder where you store your Data Files, then save it as **annuals. html**, replacing the original file. Do not update links, but save the file coleus.jpg from the Chapter 5 Data Files assets folder to the assets folder of the website. Close dw5_5.html.
3. Apply the img_left_float to the coleus image.
4. Repeat Steps 2 and 3 using dw5_6.html to replace perennials.html, saving the fiber_optic_grass.jpg file in the assets folder and using dw5_7.html to replace water_plants.html, saving the water_lily.jpg file in the assets folder.
5. Save your work, then close all open pages.

Use Figure 36 as a guide to continue your work on the TripSmart website, which you began in Project Builder 1 in Chapter 1 and developed in the previous chapters. You have been asked to create a new page for the website that lists helpful links for customers. You will also add content to the destinations, peru, and galapagos pages.

1. Open the TripSmart website.
2. Open dw5_8.html from the drive and folder where you store your Data Files, then save it as **services.html** in the TripSmart website root folder, replacing the existing file and not updating links. Close dw5_8.html.
3. Verify that the TripSmart banner is in the assets folder of the local site folder.
4. Apply the paragraph_text rule to the paragraphs of text and the list_term rule to the four main paragraph headings.
5. Create named anchors named **reservations**, **outfitters**, **tours**, and **links** in front of the respective headings on the page, then link each named anchor to "Reservations," "Travel Outfitters," "Escorted Tours," and "Helpful Links in Travel Planning" in the first paragraph, as shown in Figure 36.
6. Link the text "on-line catalog" in the Travel Outfitters paragraph to the catalog.html page.

7. Link the text "CNN Travel Channel" under the heading Helpful Links in Travel Planning to http://www.cnn.com/TRAVEL.
8. Repeat Step 7 to create links for the rest of the websites listed:

U.S. Department of State: http://travel.state.gov
Yahoo! Currency Converter: http://finance.yahoo.com/currency-converter
The Weather Channel: http://www.weather.com

Figure 36 *Sample Project Builder 1*

TripSmart has several divisions of customer service to assist you in planning and making reservations for your trip, shopping for your trip wardrobe and providing expert guide services. Give us a call and we will be happy to connect you with one of the following departments: Reservations, Travel Outfitters, or Escorted Tours. If you are not quite ready to talk with one of our departments and would prefer doing some of your own research first, may we suggest beginning with our Helpful Links in Travel Planning.

⚓Reservations
Our Reservations Department is staffed with five Certified Travel Agents, each of whom is eager to assist you in making your travel plans. They have specialty areas in Africa, the Caribbean, South America, Western Europe, Eastern Europe, Asia, Antarctica, and Hawaii and the South Pacific. They also specialize in Senior Travel, Family Travel, Student Travel, and Special Needs Travel. Call us at *(555) 848-0807* extension 75 or e-mail us at Reservations to begin making your travel plans now. We will be happy to send you brochures and listings of Internet addresses to help you get started. We are open from 8:00 a.m. until 6:00 p.m. CST.

⚓Travel Outfitters
Our travel outfitters are seasoned travelers that have accumulated a vast amount of knowledge in appropriate travel clothing and accessories for specific destinations. Climate and seasons, of course, are important factors in planning your wardrobe for a trip. Area customs should also be taken in consideration so as not to offend the local residents with inappropriate dress. When traveling abroad, we always hope that our customers will represent our country well as good ambassadors. If they can be comfortable and stylish at the same time, we have succeeded! Our clothing is all affordable and packs well on long trips. Most can be washed easily in a hotel sink and hung to drip-dry overnight. Browse through our on-line catalog, then give us a call at *(555) 433-7844* extension 85. We will also be happy to mail you a catalog of our extensive collection of travel clothing and accessories.

⚓Escorted Tours
Our Escorted Tours department is always hard at work planning the next exciting destination to offer our TripSmart customers. We have seven professional tour guides that accompany our guests from the United States point of departure to their point of return.

Our current feature package tour is to Peru. Our local escort is Don Eugene. Don has traveled Peru extensively and enjoys sharing his love for this exciting country with others. He will be assisted after arrival in Peru with the services of archeologist JoAnne Rife, anthropologist Christina Elizabeth, and naturalist Iris Albert. Call us at *(555) 848-0807* extension 95 for information on the Peru trip or to learn about other destinations being currently scheduled.

⚓Helpful Links in Travel Planning
The following links may be helpful in your travel research. Happy surfing!

- CNN Travel Channel - News affecting travel plans to various destinations
- US Department of State - Travel warnings, passport information, and more
- Yahoo! Currency Converter - Calculate the exchange rate between two currencies
- The Weather Channel - Weather, flight delays, and driving conditions

Working with Links and Navigation

9. Save the services page, preview the page in the browser to test each link, then open the index page.

10. Replace the menu bar on the home page with a horizontal Spry menu bar, using formatting of your choice, but using MenuBar as the menu ID. The menu bar should contain the following elements: **Home**, **Catalog**, **Services**, **Tours**, and **Newsletter**. Figure 37 shows one example of a possible menu bar. Create two submenu items for the peru and galapagos pages under the tours menu item, then delete all other submenu items.

11. Test the menu bar links in the browser, then close the browser and correct any errors you find.

12. Copy the menu bar, then place it on each completed page of the website.

13. Save each page, then check for broken links and orphaned files.

14. Open the tours.html file in your local site folder and save it as **galapagos.html**, overwriting the existing file, then close the file.

15. Open dw5_9.html from the drive and folder where you store your Data Files, then save it as **peru.html**, overwriting the existing file. Do not update links, but save the machu_picchu_from_high.jpg and llama.jpg files from the data files folder in the assets folder of the website, apply a rule to set the float for each image, then save and close the file. Close dw5_9.html.

16. Open dw5_10.html from the driver and folder where you store your Data Files, then save the file as **tours.html**, overwriting the existing file. Do not update links, but save the sea_lions_in_surf.jpg and machu_picchu_ruins.jpg files from the data files folder

in the assets folder of the website and apply a rule to set the float for each image. Close dw5_10.html.

17. Link the text "Galapagos" in the second sentence of the first paragraph on the tours page to the galapagos.html file.

18. Link the text "Peru" in the first sentence in the second paragraph on the tours page to the peru.html file.

19. Add a rule to the tripsmart_styles.css file to modify the <img> tag by setting the vertical alignment to bottom.

20. Save all files and preview them in the browser, checking to see that all links work and all pages have a consistent look.

21. Compare your tours page to Figure 37, close your browser, then close all open pages.

Figure 37 *Sample Project Builder 1*

You are continuing your work on the Carolyne's Creations website, which you started in Project Builder 2 in Chapter 1 and developed in the previous chapters. Chef Carolyne has asked you to create a page describing her cooking classes offered every month. You will create the content for that page and individual pages describing the children's classes and the adult classes. Refer to Figures 38, 39, and 40 for possible solutions.

1. Open the Carolyne's Creations website.
2. Open dw5_11.html from the drive and folder where you store your Data Files, save it as **classes.html** in the local site folder of the Carolyne's Creations website, overwriting the existing file and not updating the links. Close dw5_11.html.
3. Select the broken banner image, browse to the data files folder, then select the new banner, cc_banner_with_text.jpg, then verify that it was saved to the site assets folder. Notice that styles have already been applied to the page text because the data file included a relative link to the style sheet.
4. Select the text "adults' class" in the last paragraph, then link it to the adults.html page. (*Hint*: This page has not been developed yet.)
5. Select the text "children's class" in the last paragraph and link it to the children.html page. (*Hint*: This page has not been developed yet.)
6. Create an e-mail link from the text "Sign me up!" that links to **carolyne@carolynescreations.com**.

7. Insert the image file fish.jpg from the assets folder where you store your Data Files at the beginning of the second paragraph, add appropriate alternate text, then choose your own alignment and formatting settings.
8. Add the image file children_cooking.jpg from the assets folder where you store your Data Files at the beginning of the third paragraph, then choose your own image rule alignment and formatting settings.
9. Check the rest of the pages with images and adjust your image rules if necessary to improve the appearance of each page.

10. Create hot spots on the black bar at the bottom of the new banner that was imported with the data file, cc_banner_with_text.jpg, that link each menu item with its corresponding page. (*Hint*: Remember to include alternate text and a target for each menu item.)
11. Compare your work to Figure 38 for a possible solution, copy the new banner, then save and close the file.
12. Open dw5_12.html from the drive and folder where you store your Data Files, then save it as **children.html**, overwriting the existing file and not updating links. Save the image cookies_oven.jpg from the assets folder where you store your Data Files to the website assets folder. Close dw5_12.html.

Figure 38 *Completed Project Builder 2*

Cooking Classes are fun!

Chef Carolyne loves to offer a fun and relaxing cooking school each month in her newly refurbished kitchen. She teaches an adults' class on the fourth Saturday of each month from 6:00 to 8:00 pm. Each class will learn to cook a complete dinner and then enjoy the meal at the end of the class with a wonderful wine pairing. This is a great chance to get together with friends for a fun evening.

Chef Carolyne also teaches a children's class on the second Tuesday of each month from 4:00 to 5:30 pm. Our young chefs will learn to cook two dishes that will accompany a full meal served at 5:30 pm. Children aged 5–8 years accompanied by an adult are welcome. We also host small birthday parties where we put the guests to work baking and decorating the cake! Call for times and prices.

We offer several special adults' classes throughout the year. The **Valentine Chocolate Extravaganza** is a particular favorite. You will learn to dip strawberries, make truffles, and bake a sinful Triple Chocolate Dare You Torte. We also host the **Not So Traditional Thanksgiving** class and the **Super Bowl Snacks** class each year with rave reviews. Watch the website for details!

Prices are $40.00 for each adults' class and $15.00 for each children's class. Sign up for classes by calling 555-963-8271 or by emailing us: Sign me up!

See what's cooking this month for the adults' class and children's class.

13. Paste your new banner on the children.html page, replacing the previous banner, compare your work to Figure 39 for a possible solution, then save and close the file.

14. Repeat Steps 12 and 13 to open the dw5_13.html file and save it as **adults.html**, overwriting the existing file and saving the file peruvian_appetizers.jpg from the folder where you save your data files in the assets folder, then use alignment settings of your choice. Replace the banner with your new banner, compare your work to Figure 40 for a possible solution, then save and close the files.

15. Open the index page and delete the menu bar and horizontal rule.

16. Replace the banner with your new banner.

17. Copy the new banner with the menu bar to each completed page, deleting existing menu bars and banners.

18. Save all the pages, then check for broken links and orphaned files. You will see one orphaned file, the original version of the banner. Delete this file.

19. Apply a rule from the style sheet to any text or image that is not formatted with a style. (Remember to add an inline style to each page to prevent a border from appearing in Internet Explorer.)

20. Preview all the pages in your browser, check to make sure the links work correctly, close your browser, then close all open pages.

Figure 39 *Completed Project Builder 2*

Children's Cooking Class for March:
Oven Chicken Fingers, Chocolate Chip Cookies

This month we will be baking oven chicken fingers that are dipped in a milk and egg mixture, then coated with breadcrumbs. The chocolate chip cookies are based on a famous recipe that includes chocolate chips, M&Ms, oatmeal, and pecans. Yummy! We will be learning some of the basics like how to cream butter and crack eggs without dropping shells into the batter.

We will provide French fries, green beans, fruit salad, and a beverage to accompany the chicken fingers.

Figure 40 *Completed Project Builder 2*

Adult's Cooking Class for March:
Peruvian Cuisine

The class in March will be cooking several traditional Peruvian dishes: Lomo Saltado, Peruvian fish chowder, and grilled tenderloin in a cilantro sauce. For dessert: Suspiro de Limeña. You will also learn to prepare the traditional Peruvian drink, Pisco Sour, to accompany the finished meal.

Sherrill Simmons is a university English instructor. She would like to find new ways to engage her students through her university website. She decided to explore incorporating podcasts, FaceBook, and Twitter. She spends several hours looking at other websites to help her get started.

1. Connect to the Internet, then navigate to the Federal Bureau of Investigation website at fbi.gov.
2. Browse through the site and locate the link to "Podcasts & Radio." What are the options they have provided for their users to download and listen to them?

Figure 41 *Design Project*
The Federal Bureau of Investigation website – www.fbi.gov

3. Navigate to the U.S. Navy website at navy.mil, as shown in Figure 42.
4. Describe how the Navy is using Web 2.0 technology. What do you think their purpose might be for incorporating each application?
5. Which Web 2.0 applications would you include on your website if you were Sherrill?
6. Describe how you would use each one of them to engage her students.

Figure 42 *Design Project*
The United States Navy website – www.navy.mil

In this assignment, you will continue to work on the website that you started in Chapter 1 and developed in the previous chapters.

You will continue building your website by designing and completing a page with a menu bar. After creating the menu bar, you will copy it to each completed page in the website. In addition to the menu bar, you will add several external links and several internal links to other pages as well as to named anchors. You will also link text to a named anchor. After you complete this work, you will check for broken links and orphaned files.

1. Consult your wireframe to decide which page or pages you would like to develop in this chapter. Decide how to design and where to place the menu bar, named anchors, and any additional page elements you decide to use. Decide which reports should be run on the website to check for accuracy.

2. Research websites that could be included on one or more of your pages as external links of interest to your users. Create a list of the external links you want to use. Using your wireframe as a guide, decide where each external link should be placed in the site.

3. Add the external links to existing pages or create any additional pages that contain external links.

4. Create named anchors for key locations on the page, such as the top of the page, then link appropriate text on the page to them.

5. Decide on a design for a menu bar that will be used on all pages of the website.

6. Create the menu bar and copy it to all finished pages on the website.

7. Think of a good place to incorporate an image map, then add it to a page.

8. Decide on at least one Web 2.0 application that you might like to incorporate and determine how and on what page they would be included.

9. Use the Link Checker panel to check for broken links and orphaned files.

10. Use the checklist in Figure 43 to make sure your website is complete, save your work, then close all open pages.

Figure 43 *Portfolio Project checklist*

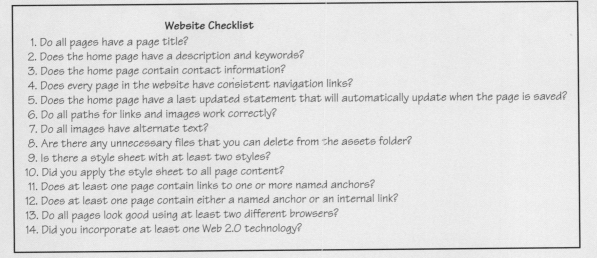

Website Checklist

1. Do all pages have a page title?
2. Does the home page have a description and keywords?
3. Does the home page contain contact information?
4. Does every page in the website have consistent navigation links?
5. Does the home page have a last updated statement that will automatically update when the page is saved?
6. Do all paths for links and images work correctly?
7. Do all images have alternate text?
8. Are there any unnecessary files that you can delete from the assets folder?
9. Is there a style sheet with at least two styles?
10. Did you apply the style sheet to all page content?
11. Does at least one page contain links to one or more named anchors?
12. Does at least one page contain either a named anchor or an internal link?
13. Do all pages look good using at least two different browsers?
14. Did you incorporate at least one Web 2.0 technology?

CHAPTER **6** POSITIONING OBJECTS
WITH CSS AND TABLES

1. Create a page using CSS layouts
2. Add content to CSS layout blocks
3. Edit and format CSS layout blocks
4. Create a table
5. Resize, split, and merge cells
6. Insert and align images in table cells
7. Insert text and format cell content

POSITIONING OBJECTS
WITH CSS AND TABLES

Introduction

To create an organized, attractive web page, you need precise control of the position of page elements. CSS page layouts can provide this control. **CSS page layouts** consist of containers formatted with CSS rules into which you place page content. These containers can accommodate images, blocks of text, Flash movies, or any other page element. The appearance and position of the containers are set through the use of HTML tags known as **div tags**. Using div tags, you can position elements next to each other as well as on top of each other.

Another option for controlling the placement of page elements is through the use of tables. **Tables** are placeholders made up of small boxes called **cells**, into which you can insert text and graphics. Cells in a table are arranged horizontally in **rows** and vertically in **columns**. Using tables on a web page gives you control over the placement of each object on the page, similar to the way CSS blocks control placement. In this chapter, you use a predesigned CSS page layout with div tags to place text and graphics on a page. You then add a table to one of the CSS blocks on the page.

Using Div Tags Versus Tables for Page Layout

Div tags and tables both enable you to control the appearance of content in your web pages. Unlike tables, div tags let you stack your information, allowing for one piece of information to be visible at a time. Tables are static, which makes it difficult to change them quickly as need arises. Div tags can be dynamic, changing in response to variables such as a mouse click. You can create dynamic div tags using JavaScript **behaviors**, simple action scripts that let you incorporate interactivity by modifying content based on variables like user actions. For example, you could add a JavaScript behavior to text in a div tag to make it become larger or smaller when the pointer is over it.

Designers previously used tables to position content on web pages. Since the inception of CSS, designers have moved to positioning most page content with CSS layouts. However, tables are still used for some layout purposes, such as arranging tabular data on a page. As a designer, you should become familiar with the tools that are available to you, including CSS and tables, then decide which tool meets current standards and is best suited for the current design challenge.

CSS Styles | AP Elements

[All] [Current]

All Rules

- su_styles.css
  - .list_headings
  - h1
  - .body_text
  - h2
  - h3
  - .small_text
  - .nav_bar
  - body
  - .img_left_float
  - .img_right_float
  - img
  - table
- HTML5 twoColFixRtHdr.css
  - body
  - ul, ol, dl
  - h1, h2, h3, h4, h5, h6, p
  - a img
  - a:link
  - a:visited
  - a:hover, a:active, a:focus
  - .container
  - header
  - .sidebar1
  - .content
  - .content ul, .content ol
  - nav ul
  - nav ul li
  - nav ul a, nav ul a:visited
  - nav ul a:hover, nav ul a:active, nav ul a:fi
  - footer
  - header, section, footer, aside, nav, article
- SpryMenuBarHorizontal.css

Properties

Add Property

Table

Table size

Rows: 5   Columns: 3

Table width: [ ] pixels ▼

Border thickness: [ ] pixels

Cell padding: [ ]

Cell spacing: [ ]

Header

None   Left   Top   Both

Accessibility

Caption: The Sand Crab Cafe Hours

Summary: [ ]

Help   OK   Cancel

Create a Page
USING CSS LAYOUTS

What You'll Do

In this lesson, you will create a new page based on a predesigned CSS layout to become the new cafe page for the website.

Understanding Div Tags

Div tags are HTML tags that define how areas of content are formatted or positioned on a web page. For example, when you center an image on a page or inside a table cell, Dreamweaver automatically inserts a div tag in the HTML code. In addition to using div tags to align page elements, designers also use them to assign background colors or borders to content blocks, CSS styles to text, and many other properties to page elements. One type of div tag is an AP div tag. AP stands for absolutely positioned, so an **AP div tag** creates a container that has a specified, fixed position on a web page. The resulting container that an AP div tag creates on a page is called an **AP element**.

Using CSS Page Layouts

Because building a web page using div tags can be tedious for beginning designers, Dreamweaver CS6 provides 18 predesigned layouts that are available in the New Document dialog box, as shown in Figure 1.

NEW New to CS6 are the two HTML5 layouts. These give you the option of creating HTML pages based on either 2-column or 3-column layouts. These layouts include new HTML tags to support semantic markup such as <section>, <header>, <footer>, <article>, and <aside>. You can use these layouts to create web pages with attractive and consistent layouts.

There are two types of CSS layouts: fixed and liquid. A **fixed layout** expresses all widths in pixels and remains the same size regardless of the size of the browser window. A **liquid layout** expresses all widths in percents and changes size depending on the size of the browser window.

Predesigned CSS layouts contain div tags that control the placement of page content using placeholders. Each div tag container has placeholder text that appears until you replace it with your own content. Because div tags use CSS for formatting and positioning, designers prefer them for building web page content. When you use the Dreamweaver predesigned layouts, you can be sure that your pages will appear with a consistent design when viewed in all browsers. Once you become more comfortable using the predesigned layouts, you will begin to build your own CSS-based pages from scratch.

Viewing CSS Layout Blocks

As you design your page layouts using div tags, you can use Design view to see and adjust CSS content blocks. In Design view, text or images that have been aligned or positioned using div tags have a dotted border, as shown in Figure 2. In the Visual Aids list on the View menu, you can display selected features of div tag elements, such as CSS Layout Backgrounds, CSS Layout Box Model, CSS Layout Outlines, and AP Element Outlines. The CSS Layout Box Model displays the padding and margins of a block element.

Figure 2 *CSS blocks defined by dotted borders*

Figure 1 *New Document dialog box*

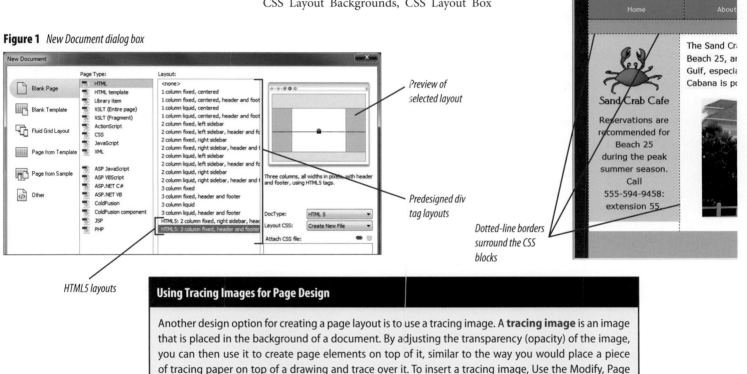

Preview of selected layout

Predesigned div tag layouts

Dotted-line borders surround the CSS blocks

HTML5 layouts

Using Tracing Images for Page Design

Another design option for creating a page layout is to use a tracing image. A **tracing image** is an image that is placed in the background of a document. By adjusting the transparency (opacity) of the image, you can then use it to create page elements on top of it, similar to the way you would place a piece of tracing paper on top of a drawing and trace over it. To insert a tracing image, Use the Modify, Page Properties, Tracing Image dialog box or the View, Tracing Image, Load command. Browse to select the image you want to use for the tracing image, then adjust the transparency as desired. The tracing image serves as a guide or pattern. You can delete it after you complete your design.

Create a page with a CSS layout

1. Open The Striped Umbrella website.

2. Click **File** on the Menu bar, click **New**, verify that Blank Page is highlighted in the first column of the New Document dialog box, click **HTML** in the Page Type column if necessary, then click **HTML: 5: 2 column fixed**, **right sidebar**, **header and footer** in the Layout column, as shown in Figure 3.

   A fixed layout remains the same size regardless of the size of the browser window.

3. Click the **Attach Style Sheet button** 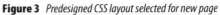 in the bottom-right corner of the dialog box, then click **Browse** in the Attach External Style Sheet dialog box.

   The Select Style Sheet File dialog box opens.

4. Select the **su_styles.css** external style sheet in the Select Style Sheet File dialog box, then click **OK** to close the Select Style Sheet File dialog box.

   If a dialog box opens reminding you to save your file before a document-relative path can be created, click OK to close the dialog box.

   TIP Dreamweaver has an option in the New Document dialog box to enable **InContext Editing**, or **ICE**, as shown in Figure 3. This feature sets up editable regions on web pages that users can change while viewing the page in a browser. See page 6-10 for more information.

5. Verify that the Link option is selected in the Attach External Style Sheet dialog box, then click **OK** to close the Attach External Style Sheet dialog box.

   (continued)

Figure 3 *Predesigned CSS layout selected for new page*

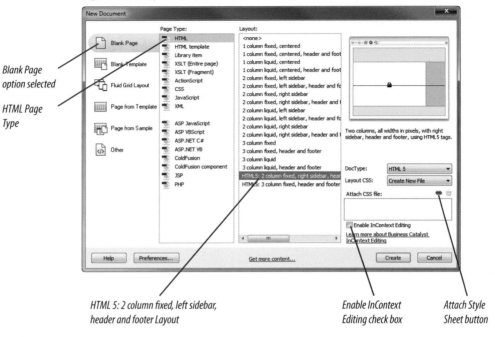

Blank Page option selected

HTML Page Type

HTML 5: 2 column fixed, left sidebar, header and footer Layout

Enable InContext Editing check box

Attach Style Sheet button

Using XML and XSL to Create and Format Web Page Content

You can also create information containers on your web pages using XML, Extensible Markup Language, and XSL, Extensible Stylesheet Language. **XML** is a language that you use to structure blocks of information, similar to HTML. It uses similar opening and closing tags and the nested tag structure that HTML documents use. However, XML tags do not determine how the information is formatted, which is handled using XSL. **XSL** is similar to CSS; the XSL stylesheet information formats the containers created by XML. Once the XML structure and XSL styles are in place, **XSLT**, **Extensible Stylesheet Language Transformations**, interprets the code in the XSL file to transform an XML document, much like style sheet files transform HTML files from an unformatted file to a formatted file. XSL transformations can be written as client-side or server-side transformations. To create XML documents, use the XML page type in the New Document dialog box.

Figure 4 *The su_styles.css file is attached to the new page*

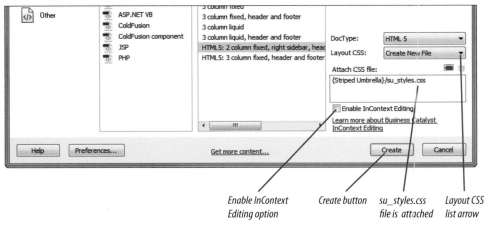

Enable InContext Create button su_styles.css Layout CSS
Editing option   file is attached list arrow

Figure 5 *New page based on CSS layout*

Blocks of
content based
on CSS layout

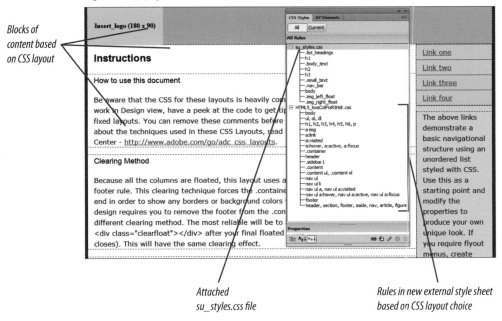

Attached   Rules in new external style sheet
su_styles.css file   based on CSS layout choice

The su_styles.css file is attached to the new page, as shown in Figure 4. The next time you create a new page, the style sheet will be selected automatically.

6. Click the **Layout CSS list arrow**, click **Create New File** (if it's not already selected), then click **Create** in the New Document dialog box.

7. Verify that the site root folder appears in the Save in text box, then click **Save** to close the Save Style Sheet File As dialog box.

A new two-column HTML5 page opens based on the predesigned CSS layout you chose. It has CSS content blocks arranged in two columns, one as a sidebar on the right side, as well as a header and footer. Placeholder text appears in each of the blocks, as shown in Figure 5. You will replace the text with content for The Striped Umbrella website. The CSS blocks each have a different color background to help you see how the blocks are arranged on the page. This new page will replace the blank cafe page.

8. Expand the new style sheet, HTML5_ twoColFixRHdr.css, in the CSS Styles panel, if necessary, so you can see the new rules.

Notice that you have two sets of styles now: the external style sheet su_styles.css; and the external style sheet HTML5_twoColFixRHdr.css, with the rules that define the CSS blocks on the page.

9. Save the file as **cafe.html**, overwriting the existing blank cafe page.

You created a new page based on a predesigned CSS layout with the attached style sheet for The Striped Umbrella website and a new external style sheet that defines the rules for the CSS layout. You then saved the new file as cafe.html, overwriting the existing blank cafe page.

Add Content to CSS
LAYOUT BLOCKS

What You'll Do

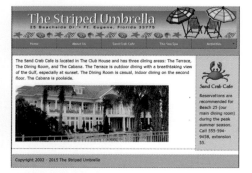

In this lesson, you will copy the menu bar and banner from the index page and paste it into the new page. You will add text and images for the new cafe page you are creating, then overwrite the old cafe page with this new one.

Understanding Div Tag Content

As you learned in Lesson 1, a div tag is a container that formats blocks of information on a web page, such as background colors, images, links, tables, and text. Once you have created a layout using div tags, you are ready to insert and format text. As with formatting text on a web page, you should use CSS styles to format text in div tags. You can also add all other properties such as text indents, padding, margins, and background color using CSS styles.

In this lesson, you use a CSS layout to create a new cafe page that arranges the content into defined areas on the page.

Using Dreamweaver New Page Options

You can use either the Welcome Screen or the New command on the File menu to create several different types of pages. The predesigned CSS page layouts make it easy to design accessible web pages based on Cascading Style Sheets, without an advanced level of expertise in writing HTML code. Predesigned templates are another time-saving feature that promotes consistency across a website. Fluid Grid layouts, CSS Style Sheets, and Sample Pages are a few of the other options. It is worth the time to explore each category to understand what is available to you as a designer. Once you have selected a page layout, you can customize it to suit your client's content and design needs.

Understanding CSS Code

When you view a page based on a predesigned CSS layout in Code view, you see helpful comments that explain sections of the code, as shown in Figure 6. The comments are in gray to differentiate them from the rest of the code. The CSS rules can reside in the Head section of a page or in an external style sheet. The code for a CSS container begins with the class, or name of the rule, and is followed by rule properties. For example, in Figure 6, the container described on line 45 begins with the class name .container, which is followed by three properties and values: width: 960 px; background: #FFF; and margin: 0 auto. The code that links the rules to the content is located in the body section.

Figure 6 *Code view for CSS in head content*

Comments in gray text

Rule name preceded by period

Rule properties

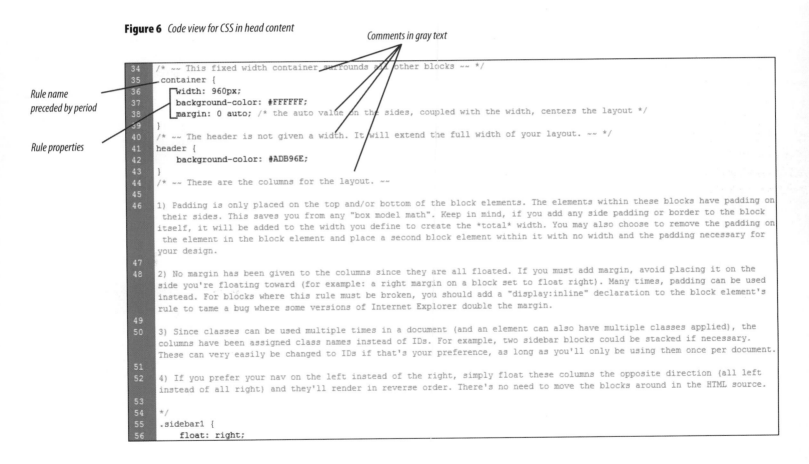

```
34   /* ~~ This fixed width container surrounds all other blocks ~~ */
35   .container {
36       width: 960px;
37       background-color: #FFFFFF;
38       margin: 0 auto; /* the auto value on the sides, coupled with the width, centers the layout */
39   }
40   /* ~~ The header is not given a width. It will extend the full width of your layout. ~~ */
41   header {
42       background-color: #ADB96E;
43   }
44   /* ~~ These are the columns for the layout. ~~
45
46   1) Padding is only placed on the top and/or bottom of the block elements. The elements within these blocks have padding on
     their sides. This saves you from any "box model math". Keep in mind, if you add any side padding or border to the block
     itself, it will be added to the width you define to create the *total* width. You may also choose to remove the padding on
     the element in the block element and place a second block element within it with no width and the padding necessary for
     your design.
47
48   2) No margin has been given to the columns since they are all floated. If you must add margin, avoid placing it on the
     side you're floating toward (for example: a right margin on a block set to float right). Many times, padding can be used
     instead. For blocks where this rule must be broken, you should add a "display:inline" declaration to the block element's
     rule to tame a bug where some versions of Internet Explorer double the margin.
49
50   3) Since classes can be used multiple times in a document (and an element can also have multiple classes applied), the
     columns have been assigned class names instead of IDs. For example, two sidebar blocks could be stacked if necessary.
     These can very easily be changed to IDs if that's your preference, as long as you'll only be using them once per document.
51
52   4) If you prefer your nav on the left instead of the right, simply float these columns the opposite direction (all left
     instead of all right) and they'll render in reverse order. There's no need to move the blocks around in the HTML source.
53
54   */
55   .sidebar1 {
56       float: right;
```

Add text to a CSS container

1. Skim through the placeholder text to read the instructions included in them, then select all content between the Header and Footer in the main section (content block) of the page through the last paragraph describing the backgrounds, as shown in Figure 7, then press **[Delete]**.

TIP Before you delete placeholder text, it is a good idea to read it. The placeholder text has helpful information that helps you to understand the way the page is designed. It gives you pointers for the best way to replace the placeholder text with your text.

2. Change to the HTML Property inspector if necessary, click the **Format list arrow**, then click **Paragraph**.

   This deletes the remaining H1 tag in the block.

3. Import the Word document **cafe.doc** from the drive and folder where you store your Data Files (Win) or copy and paste it (Mac) in the blank container.

4. Click **Commands** on the Menu bar, click **Clean Up Word HTML**, click **OK**, then click **OK** in the dialog box that appears.

(continued)

Figure 7 *Text selected in content block of new page*

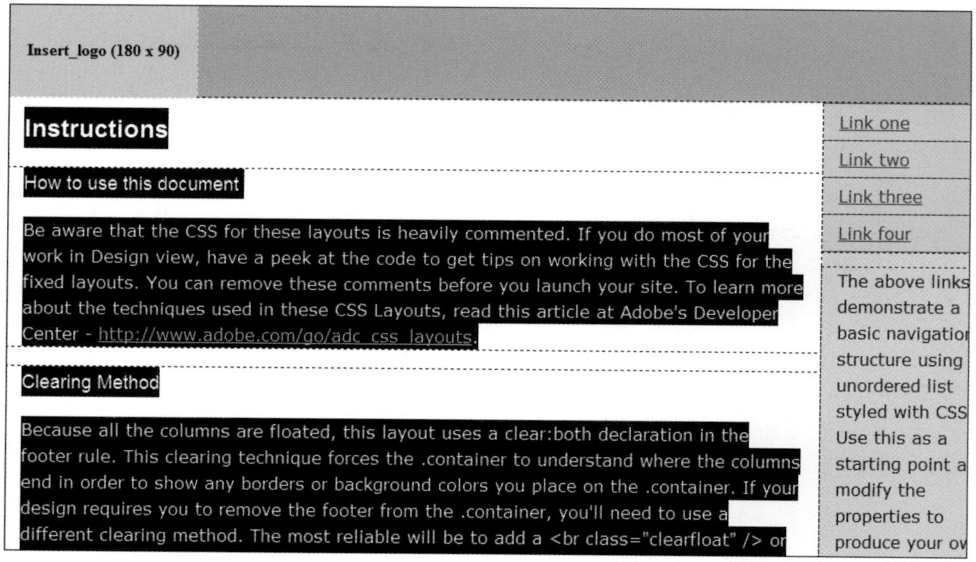

Using Adobe Business Catalyst for InContext Editing

Adobe Business Catalyst is a hosted application for setting up and maintaining an online business. It has an editing component called InContext Editing (ICE) that is available through Dreamweaver. **InContext Editing** allows a page developer to designate regions on a page that can be edited by users while they are viewing a page in a browser. This is great because it does not require a web editing program or any prior knowledge of HTML. Users simply log in to InContext Editing while a page is open in a browser, make their edits, then save the page. To use this feature, the developer checks the Enable InContext Editing check box in the New Document dialog box, then designates the regions of a page that will be available for editing by others.

Figure 8 *Text selected in sidebar1 block in Code view*

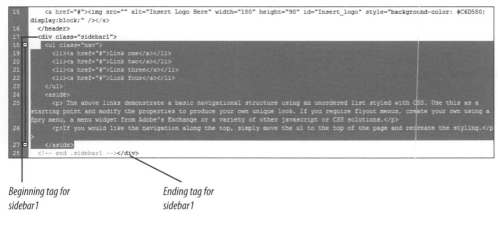

```
15        <a href="#"><img src="" alt="Insert Logo Here" width="180" height="90" id="Insert_logo" style="background-color: #C6D580;
   display:block;" /></a>
16      </header>
17      <div class="sidebar1">
18        <ul class="nav">
19          <li><a href="#">Link one</a></li>
20          <li><a href="#">Link two</a></li>
21          <li><a href="#">Link three</a></li>
22          <li><a href="#">Link four</a></li>
23        </ul>
24        <aside>
25          <p> The above links demonstrate a basic navigational structure using an unordered list styled with CSS. Use this as a
   starting point and modify the properties to produce your own unique look. If you require flyout menus, create your own using a
   Spry menu, a menu widget from Adobe's Exchange or a variety of other javascript or CSS solutions.</p>
26          <p>If you would like the navigation along the top, simply move the ul to the top of the page and recreate the styling.</p
27        </aside>
28      <!-- end .sidebar1 --></div>
```

Beginning tag for sidebar1

Ending tag for sidebar1

Figure 9 *Text pasted into Content block and typed into sidebar1 block and footer block of new page*

Insert_logo (180 x 90)

The Sand Crab Cafe is located in The Club House and has three dining areas: The Terrace, Beach 25, and The Cabana. The Terrace is outdoor dining with a breathtaking view of the Gulf, especially at sunset. Beach 25 is casual, indoor dining on the second floor. The Cabana is poolside.

Reservations are recommended for Beach 25 (our main dining room) during the peak summer season. Call 555-594-9458, extension 55.

Copyright 2002 - 2015 The Striped Umbrella

5. Switch to Code view, select the code between the beginning and end of the <div class="sidebar1"> tag, as shown in Figure 8, then press **[Delete]** to delete the placeholder text.

   Be careful not to delete the beginning and ending div tags.

6. Return to Design view, then type **Reservations are recommended for Beach 25 (our main dining room) during the peak summer season. Call 555-594-9458: extension 55.** at the insertion point.

7. Delete all of the text in the footer block, then type **Copyright 2002 - 2015 The Striped Umbrella** as shown in Figure 9, then save your work.

You imported text and typed text in the CSS blocks, replacing the placeholder text in the body, sidebar, and footer.

Add images to a CSS block

1. Open the Striped Umbrella index page and copy both the banner and the menu bar.

TIP You might find it easier to copy the banner and menu bar separately. If you copy them together, click in front of the banner, hold down the Shift key, then click under the menu bar to select both the banner and the menu bar.

2. Switch back to the cafe page, click the **placeholder logo image**, paste the banner and menu bar into the header section of the page, then insert two line breaks and a paragraph break after the menu bar. (If you have trouble adding the paragraph break, go to Code view and enter `<p> </p>` after the closing header tag.).

TIP Press [Ctrl][Tab] (Win) or ⌘ [`] (Mac) to switch between two open pages.

3. Close the index page.

4. Place the insertion point immediately in front of the word "Reservations", insert a paragraph break, press [↑], insert **cafe_logo.gif** from the drive and folder where you store your Data Files, then type **Sand Crab Cafe logo** as the alternate text in the Image Tag Accessibility Attributes dialog box and click **OK** to close the dialog box.

5. Select the **crab logo** if necessary, press [←], then enter a line break in front of the logo.

6. Place the insertion point after the period after the word "poolside" in the body text, insert a paragraph break, insert **cafe_photo.jpg** from the drive and folder where you store your Data Files, then type **Sand Crab Cafe photo** as the alternate text. See Figure 10.

(continued)

Figure 10 *Images added to header, sidebar 1, and content blocks*

The Sand Crab Cafe is located in The Club House and has three dining areas: The Terrace, Beach 25, and The Cabana. The Terrace is outdoor dining with a breathtaking view of the Gulf, especially at sunset. Beach 25 is casual, indoor dining on the second floor. The Cabana is poolside.

Sand Crab Cafe

Reservations are recommended for Beach 25 (our main dining room) during the peak summer season. Call 555-594-9458, extension 55.

Copyright 2002 - 2015 The Striped Umbrella

The Evolution of HTML5

HTML has been in existence since the early 1990s, but it wasn't until 1997 that the then current version, HTML4, became a W3C recommendation. Many HTML4 attributes such as body background, align, cell padding, and hspace are now added using CSS3. HTML5 introduced new ways to add interactivity and tags that support semantic markup, such as the <nav> tag used for navigation links. In Chapter 3 you learned about using semantic markup to incorporate meaning with your HTML markup. Other semantic HTML5 tags include <header>, <footer>, <article>, <audio>, <section>, and <video>. HTML5 is still a work in progress, but most modern browsers support it. HTML5 also introduces markup for Web applications (apps), an exploding sector of Web development.

Figure 11 *Images placed on page*

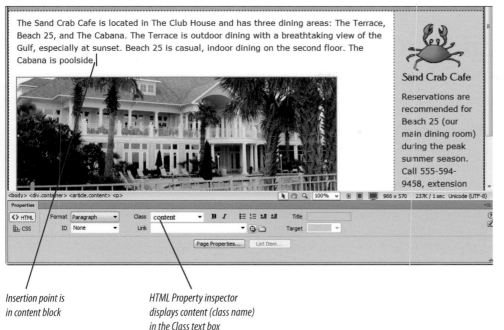

The Sand Crab Cafe is located in The Club House and has three dining areas: The Terrace, Beach 25, and The Cabana. The Terrace is outdoor dining with a breathtaking view of the Gulf, especially at sunset. Beach 25 is casual, indoor dining on the second floor. The Cabana is poolside.

Sand Crab Cafe

Reservations are recommended for Beach 25 (our main dining room) during the peak summer season. Call 555-594-9458, extension

Insertion point is in content block

HTML Property inspector displays content (class name) in the Class text box

7. Deselect the image, click the **HTML Property inspector button** ⟨⟩ HTML if necessary to switch to the HTML Property inspector, then click to place the insertion point in the content CSS block above the cafe_photo image.

   Notice that the Class text box in the HTML Property inspector shows the class to be "content", as shown in Figure 11.

8. Click to place the insertion point in the sidebar1 block.

   The Property inspector displays the class rule assigned to the block.

9. Save your work, preview the page in the browser to verify that there is no gap between the banner and the menu bar, then return to Dreamweaver.

You copied the banner and menu bar from the index page, pasted it onto the new cafe page, then added the cafe logo and photo to the page.

Edit and Format CSS
LAYOUT BLOCKS

What You'll Do

In this lesson, you will center the two images you have added to the page. You will then view the div tag properties and edit the background colors. You will also change the body background color.

Editing Content in CSS Layout Blocks

It is unlikely that you will find a predesigned CSS page layout that is exactly what you have in mind for your website. However, once you have created a page with a predesigned CSS layout, it is easy to modify the individual rule properties to change content formatting or placement to better fit your needs. For example, you can easily change the properties to fit the color scheme of your website.

To change rule properties, click the plus sign next to the style sheet name, if necessary, to see the rules listed in each section, as shown in Figure 12, and then select the rule you want to modify. The properties and values for the selected rule appear in the Properties pane, where you can modify them. If you have multiple style sheets, you can use either style sheet or a combination to format the page content.

Figure 12 *Viewing the CSS Styles panel*

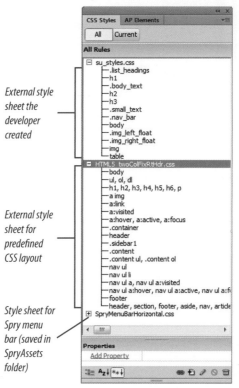

External style sheet the developer created

External style sheet for predefined CSS layout

Style sheet for Spry menu bar (saved in SpryAssets folder)

Figure 13 *Adjusting alignment in layout blocks*

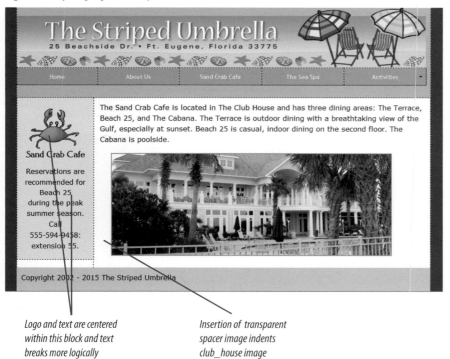

Logo and text are centered within this block and text breaks more logically

Insertion of transparent spacer image indents club_house image

---

Using the Adobe CSS Advisor for Cross-Browser Rendering Issues

You can use the **Browser Compatibility Check (BCC)** feature to check for problems in the HTML code for CSS features that may render differently in multiple browsers. It flags and rates code on three levels: an error that could cause a serious display problem; an error that probably won't cause a serious display problem; or a warning that it has found code that is unsupported, but won't cause a serious display problem. Each bug is linked to the CSS Advisor, a part of the Adobe website, that offers solutions for that particular bug and other helpful information for resolving any issues with your pages. To check for browser compatibility, click File, point to Check Page, and then click Browser Compatibility or click the Check browser compatibility button on the Document toolbar.

Edit block properties to align content

1. Place the insertion point in front of the cafe logo.

   Notice that the class rule for this block is named .sidebar1.

2. Click the **.sidebar1 rule** in the CSS Styles panel, click the **Edit Rule button** ✐ , click the **Block category** in the CSS Rule definition for .sidebar1 dialog box, click the **Text-align list arrow**, then click **center**.

   The logo and text will now be centered in the left sidebar.

3. Click the **Box Category**, change the Float from right to left, then click **OK**.

   The sidebar moves to the left side of the page.

4. Edit the sidebar text to match Figure 13 by deleting "(our main dining room)" and by using line breaks to divide up the lines of text.

   Now the lines of text break in more logical places.

5. Click in front of the club_house image, click **Insert** on the Menu bar, click **Image**, browse to your website assets folder, then double-click **spacer_30px.gif**.

6. Add the alternate text **Spacer image**, change to Live view, then compare your screen to Figure 13.

   The club_house image is indented from the left side of the CSS layout block by 30 pixels.

   (continued)

7. Move the pointer over the left border of the content block (the block containing the cafe description and picture), click the **red border** to select the block (the border turns blue after it is selected), then move the pointer inside the block and hover until the floating window shown in Figure 14 appears.

The properties of the div tag appear in a floating window. The Property inspector displays the div tag class name.

TIP You can change the border color of div tags when the mouse is positioned over them in the Preferences dialog box. Select the Highlighting category, then click the Mouse-Over color box and select a different color. You can also disable highlighting by deselecting the Show check box for Mouse-Over.

8. Save your work.

You centered the logo and the reservations text, and indented the cafe_photo image. You then edited the sidebar text to make it flow more smoothly, then viewed the properties of the div tag.

Figure 14 *Viewing the class properties*

Border for div block

Properties of class

Class rule assigned to div tag

Viewing Options for CSS Layout Blocks

You can view your layout blocks in Design view in several ways. You can choose to show or hide outlines, temporarily assign different background colors to each individual layout block, or view the **CSS Layout Box Model** (padding, margins, borders, etc.) of a selected layout. To change these options, use the View > Visual Aids menu, and then select or deselect the CSS Layout Backgrounds, CSS Layout Box Model, or CSS Layout Outlines menu choice. You can also use the Visual Aids button on the Document toolbar.

Figure 15 *Editing the body Font-family property*

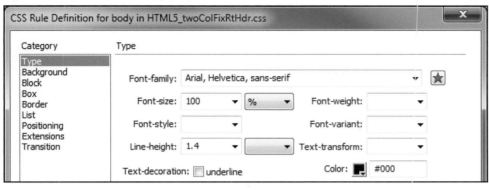

Figure 16 *The cafe page with edited body Font-family property*

Edit type properties in CSS layout blocks

1. Select the **body rule** in the HTML5_twoColFixRtHdr .css file CSS Styles panel, click the **Edit Rule button**, then click the **Type category** in the CSS Rule definition for body dialog box.

2. Click the **Font-family list arrow**, then click **Arial, Helvetica, sans-serif,** as shown in Figure 15.

3. Click **OK** to close the dialog box, compare your screen to Figure 16, then save your work.

    The new font family property is applied to the text on the page. The Font-family property in the body rule determines the font family for all text on the page unless another one is specified for a different container, such as the footer, with an external style or a different internal style. The body is a **parent container**, a container with other tags falling between its opening and closing tags. **Child containers** are containers whose code resides inside a parent container. All HTML tags for page content are inside the body tags. So unless a different font is specified in a different container, each child container inherits the properties from the parent container.

    You leave the rest of the type properties with the default CSS settings. This page uses the settings from the HTML5_twoColFixRtHdr.css external style sheet, but this style sheet is not attached to the rest of the pages in the site, so until it is, you still need the body_text and body rules from the su_styles.css style sheet to use to format the other pages.

You changed the font-family property in the body that determines the font family for all text on the page.

Edit CSS layout block properties

1. Click the **header rule** in the CSS Styles panel to select it, then click the **Show only set properties button** ✴✴↓ .

   The value for the background property appears in the Properties pane. The header block has background color of #ADB96E, a muted green color.

2. Click the **background text box** to place the insertion point, replace #ADB96E with **#FFF**, press **[Enter]** (Win) or **[return]** (Mac), and compare your screen to Figure 17.

   TIP You may have to adjust the size of your CSS Styles panel to view both panes.

   The header background color changes to white.

3. With the header rule still selected, click the **Edit Rule button** ✎ , click the **Box category**, type **5** in the Top Margin text box, verify that the Same for all check box is checked, as shown in Figure 18, then click **OK**.

   You can edit rule properties in either the CSS Styles Properties pane or by opening the CSS Rule definition dialog box. With the header margins set, the banner will now appear more centered on the page.

   TIP The top margin will appear wider because the banner has a transparent background that makes the top margin look wider (to make room for the top of the umbrella). The bottom margin will appear wider than it is because there are two line breaks under the banner.

   (continued)

Figure 17 *Editing the properties of the header rule*

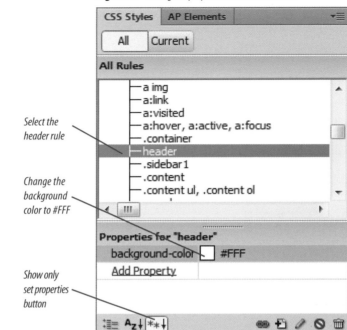

Select the header rule

Change the background color to #FFF

Show only set properties button

Figure 18 *Editing the properties of the header rule*

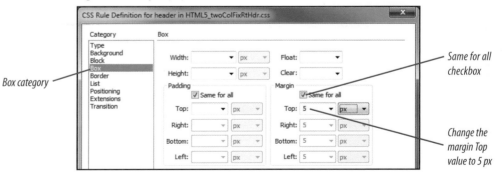

Box category

Same for all checkbox

Change the margin Top value to 5 px

Figure 19 *The four layout blocks now have a white background*

5px margin is applied to header

The four blocks have the same background color

Copyright statement is centered in footer

4. Repeat Step 2 to change the background color in the footer rule to #FFF and the background color in the sidebar1 rule to #FFF.

   The header, footer, and sidebar1 background colors are now white.

TIP You only need to use the abbreviated hexadecimal color code, such as #FFF, when specifying colors. However, in the Dreamweaver predesigned CSS layouts, the color codes are shown with the full 6-character codes. Either code works. You can also specify colors by their names. For example, the color magenta can be specified as "magenta", #FF00FF or #F0F

5. Edit the footer rule to change the Text-align block property to center.

6. Save your work, then compare your screen to Figure 19.

You changed the margin width of a CSS layout block, changed the background color of three CSS layout blocks to white, then centered the footer.

NEW **Using a Fluid Grid Layout**

Dreamweaver has a new type of predesigned layout available as a choice in the New Document dialog box called a Fluid Grid Layout. The **Fluid Grid Layout** is a system for designing layouts that will adapt to three different screen sizes: Mobile, Tablet, and Desktop. By using percentages to set page and page element dimensions, the design will expand or contract to fit the dimensions of the device being used to view the page. The Fluid Grid Layout produces an HTML5 document type. When you create a new page based on a fluid grid, two style sheets will be created: a boilerplate.css file and one that you assign a name. If you plan to use a fluid grid layout, take some time to study the style sheet code and the comments embedded in the page source code before you begin adding page content.

Edit page properties

1. Select the **container rule** in the CSS Styles panel.

2. Open the CSS Rule definition for .container dialog box, then click the **Border category**.

   A border around the page sets it off from the extra space around it when it is viewed in a browser.

3. Click the **Top list arrow** in the Style column, then click **solid**.

4. Click the **Width list arrow** in the first text box in the Width column, then click **thin**.

5. Click the first **Color text box** in the Color column, type **#033**, press **Tab**, compare your screen to Figure 20, then click **OK**.

6. Click the **body rule** in the HTML5_twoColFixRtHdr .css style sheet in the CSS Styles panel, then open the CSS Rule definition for body dialog box.

7. Click the **Background category** if necessary, change the Background-color text box to **#FFF**, then click **OK**.

(continued)

Figure 20 *Adding a border to the container*

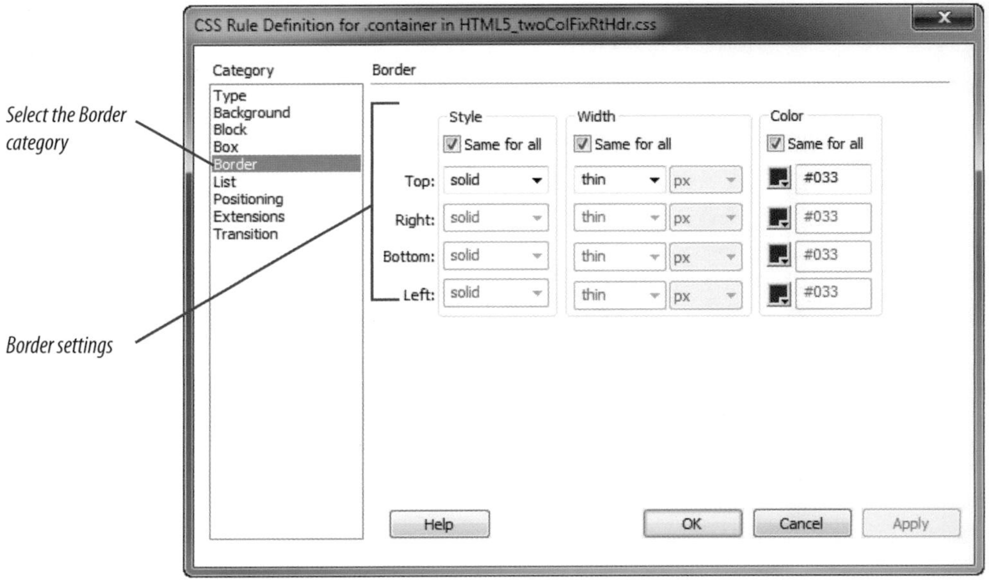

Select the Border category

Border settings

Figure 21 *Viewing the cafe page in the browser*

Border appears around
page in browser

8. Use the Document toolbar to add the page title **The Striped Umbrella Sand Crab Cafe** to the page.

9. Save your work, preview the page in your browser, compare your screen to Figure 21, then close the browser.

You added a border to the page.

Create
A TABLE

What You'll Do

In this lesson, you will create a table for the cafe page in The Striped Umbrella website to provide a grid for the cafe hours.

Understanding Table Modes

Now that you have learned how CSS can act as containers to hold information in place on web pages, let's look at tables as another layout tool. Tables are great when you need a grid layout on a page for a list of data. To create a table, click the Table button on the Insert panel. When the Layout category of the Insert panel is displayed, you can choose between two modes that give you different ways to view your table: Standard mode or Expanded Tables mode. Expanded Tables mode adds extra space between cells, which makes it easier to select small cells. Click the appropriate button on the Insert panel after selecting a table on the page.

Creating a Table

To create a table in Standard mode, click the Table button on the Insert panel to open the Table dialog box. You can enter values for the number of rows and columns in the Table dialog box, but the rest of the table properties should be assigned using CSS. If you only plan to use one table design in a site, you can create a rule to modify the <table> tag and save it in your website style sheet. You then use this rule to add formatting options to the table such as adding a border or table width. The **border** is the outline or frame around the table and is measured in pixels. The table width can be specified in units of measure such as pixels, or as a percentage. When the table width is specified as a percentage, the table width expands to fill up its container (the browser window, a CSS container, or another table). Table width is set using the Width property in the Box category of the relevant CSS style.

To align a table on a page or within a CSS layout block, use a Float property in the Box category. A table placed inside another table is called a **nested table**. **Cell padding** is the distance between the cell content and the **cell walls**, the lines inside the cell borders. **Cell spacing** is the distance between cells. Neither cell padding or cell spacing is supported by HTML5, however, so it's better to address spacing issues by assigning styles.

Before you create a table, you should include in your wireframe a plan for it that shows its location on the page and the placement of text and graphics in its cells. You should also decide whether to include borders around the tables. Setting the border value to 0 causes the table borders to be invisible. Users will not realize that you used a table unless they look at the code.

Using Expanded Tables Mode

Expanded Tables mode is a feature that allows you to change to a table view with expanded table borders and temporary cell padding and cell spacing. This mode makes it easier to actually see how many rows and columns you have in your table. Often, especially after splitting empty cells, it is difficult to place the insertion point precisely in a table cell. Expanded Tables mode allows you to see each cell clearly. However, most of the time, you will want to work in Standard mode to maintain the WYSIWYG environment. **WYSIWYG** is the acronym for What You See Is What You Get, and means that your page should look the same in the browser as it does in the web editor.

Setting Table Accessibility Preferences

You can make a table more accessible to visually impaired users by adding a table caption and a table header that screen readers can read. A **table caption** appears at the top of a table and describes the table contents. **Table headers** are another way to provide information about table content. Table headers can be placed at the top of columns. They are automatically centered and bold and are used by screen readers to help users identify the table content. Table captions and headers are created with the Table dialog box.

Formatting Tables with HTML5 and CSS3

Many of the HTML codes used to format tables in HTML4 are now considered to be **deprecated**, or no longer within the current standard and in danger of becoming obsolete. As you design web pages, it is best to avoid using deprecated tags because eventually they will cause problems when they are no longer supported by newer browsers. Deprecated HTML4 table tags include summary, cellpadding, cellspacing, align, width, and bgcolor. Rather than format tables using the Table dialog box or the Property inspector, use CSS to create rules that modify table properties and content. You can either add properties to the <table> tag itself or create new class rules that you can then assign to specific tables. Use the HTML5 tags <th> and <caption>. The table header <th> tag is a type of cell that contains header information, such as column headings, that identify the content of the data cells below them. The <caption> tag is the caption, or title, of a table and describes the table content. These tags provide greater accessibility, because they are used by screen readers. They also add value as semantic markup because they help to label and describe table content.

Create a table

1. Click to place the insertion point to the right of the cafe photo.

2. Click **Table** in the Common category on the Insert panel.

   The Table dialog box opens.

3. Type **5** in the Rows text box, type **3** in the Columns text box, delete any value previously left in the Table width, Border thickness, Cell padding, or Cell spacing text boxes, then click the **Top** Header.

   TIP It is better to add more rows than you think you need when you create your table. After they are filled with content, it is easier to delete rows than to add rows if you decide later to split or merge cells in the table.

4. In the Caption text box, type **The Sand Crab Cafe Hours**, compare your screen to Figure 22, then click **OK**.

   The table appears very small because the width for the table has not yet been set. You will define a new table CSS rule to use to format the table.

5. Click the **Insert panel list arrow**, click **Layout**, click the **Expanded Tables mode button** Expanded, click **OK** in the Getting Started in Expanded Tables Mode dialog box if necessary, then compare your screen to Figure 23.

   (continued)

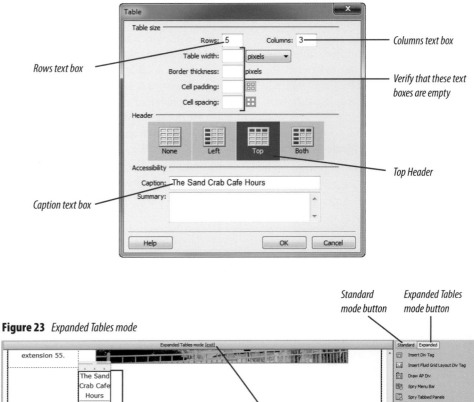

Figure 22 *Table dialog box*

Rows text box

Columns text box

Verify that these text boxes are empty

Top Header

Caption text box

Figure 23 *Expanded Tables mode*

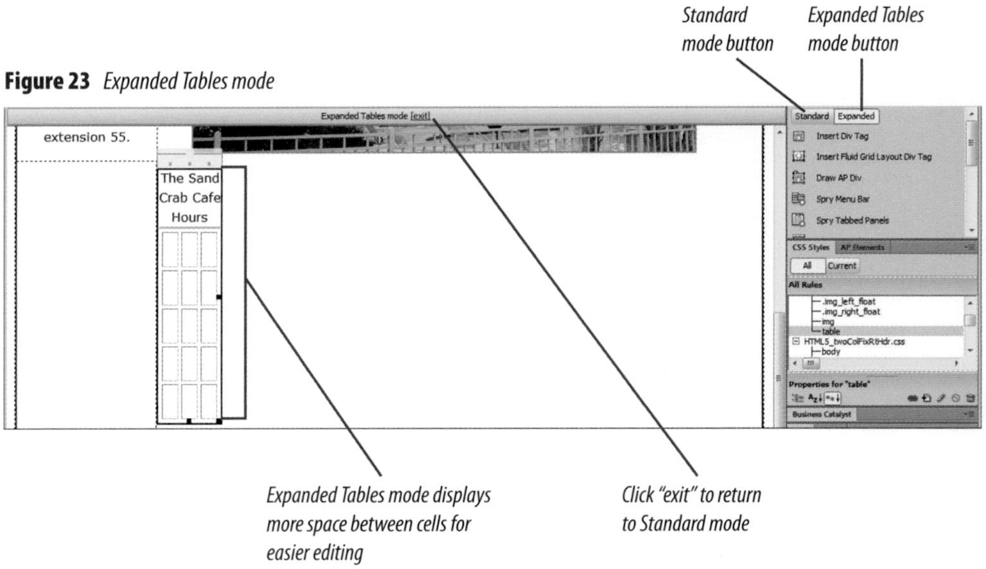

Standard mode button

Expanded Tables mode button

Expanded Tables mode displays more space between cells for easier editing

Click "exit" to return to Standard mode

Figure 24 *Property inspector showing properties of selected table*

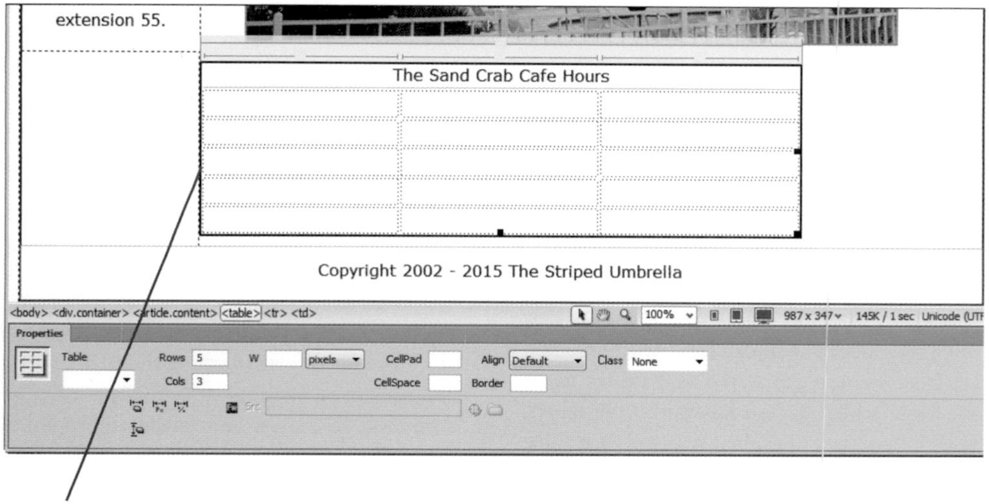

Selected table

Setting Table Widths

If you have a large table of complex data, it is wise to set the width of the table in pixels. This ensures that the table will remain one size and not resize itself proportionally if the browser window size is changed. This will also keep the print the same size so the data will always be large enough to be readable. For example, if the width of a table is set to slightly less than 800, the table will stretch across the whole width of a browser window set at a resolution of 800 x 600. The same table would be the same size on a screen set at 1024 x 768 and therefore would not stretch across the entire screen. Be aware, however, that if you set the width of your table to 800 pixels, your table will be too wide to print the entire width of the page, and part of the right side of the page will be cut off. If you are designing a table layout for a page that you expect viewers to print, you should make your table narrower to fit on a printed page. If you set a table width as a percentage, however, the table would resize itself proportionately in any browser window, regardless of the resolution.

The Expanded Tables mode makes it easier to see individual cells and select and edit tables.

6. Click the **Standard mode button** `Standard` to return to Standard mode.

TIP You can also return to Standard mode by clicking [exit] in the blue bar below the Document toolbar.

You created a table on the cafe page that will display the cafe hours with five rows and three columns. You used a top header and added a table caption that will be read by screen readers.

Set table properties

1. Click the **New CSS Rule button** in the CSS Styles panel, choose **Tag (redefines an HTML element)** in the Class text box, type **table** in the Selector Name text box, if necessary, then save the rule in the su_styles.css style sheet.

   This rule will format the only table in the website.

2. Click the **Box Category**, type **600** in the Width text box, verify that **px** is the unit of measure, change the Float to **left**, then click **OK**.

   The <table> rule modified the table by setting the width and alignment on the page, as shown in Figure 24.

You modified the table rule by adding table width and float properties.

Resize, Split,
AND MERGE CELLS

What You'll Do

In this lesson, you will set the width of the table cells to be split across the table in predetermined widths. You will then split one cell. You will also merge some cells to provide space for the table header.

To create HTML5-compliant table coding, you should resize tables, rows, and cells using Cascading Style Sheets. If you only have one table in your site, you can modify the <table> tag by assigning properties and values to set the table width. If you have multiple tables, you can create a new class rule for each table and format each individually using class rule properties. This will allow you to use multiple tables with differing widths. When you first create a table, the columns are created with equal widths. To widen a column and meet HTML5 standards, use the column group tag <colgroup> to set properties for an entire column or the column tag <col> to set properties for an individual cell.

Sometimes you want to adjust the cells in a table by splitting or merging them. To **split** a cell means to divide it into multiple rows or columns. To **merge** cells means to combine multiple cells into one cell. Using split and merged cells gives you more flexibility and control in placing page elements in a table and can help you create a more visually exciting layout. When you merge cells, the HTML tag used to describe the merged cell changes from a width size tag to a

Adding or Deleting a Row

As you add new content to your table, you might find that you have too many or too few rows or columns. You can add or delete one row or column at a time or several at once. You use commands on the Modify menu to add and delete table rows and columns. When you add a new column or row, you must first select the existing column or row to which the new column or row will be adjacent. The Insert Rows or Columns dialog box lets you choose how many rows or columns you want to insert or delete, and where you want them placed in relation to the selected row or column. The new column or row will have the same formatting and number of cells as the selected column or row. After you have split and merged cells, it can be challenging to add or delete rows. You can also use the shortcut menu or keyboard shortcuts to add or delete rows.

Positioning Objects with CSS and Tables

column span or row span tag. For example, <td colspan="2"> is the code for two cells that have been merged into one cell that spans two columns.

QUICK TIP

You can split merged cells and merge split cells.

Understanding Table Tags

When formatting a table, it is important to understand the basic HTML table tags. The tags for creating a table are <table> </table>. The tags to create table rows are <tr></tr>. The tags used to create table data cells are <td></td>. The tags used to create table header cells are <th> </th>. Dreamweaver places the < > code into each empty table cell at the time you create it. The < > code represents a nonbreaking space, or a space that a browser will display on the page. Some browsers collapse an empty cell, which can ruin the look of a table. The nonbreaking space holds the cell until you place content in it, when at that time it is automatically removed.

DESIGNTIP

Using Nested Tables

A nested table is a table inside a table. To create a nested table, you place the insertion point in the cell where you want to insert the nested table, then click the Table button on the Insert panel. A nested table is a separate table that can be formatted differently from the table in which it is placed. Nested tables are useful when you want part of your table data to have visible borders and part to have invisible borders. For example, you can nest a table with red borders inside a table with invisible borders. You need to plan carefully when you insert nested tables. It is easy to get carried away and insert too many nested tables, which makes it more difficult to apply formatting and rearrange table elements. Before you insert a nested table, consider whether you could achieve the same result by adding rows and columns or by splitting cells.

Split cells

1. Click inside the first cell in the last row, then click **<td>** in the tag selector.

   TIP You can click the cell tag <td> (the HTML tag for that cell) on the tag selector to select the corresponding cell in the table. You can also just place the insertion point inside the cell before you begin Step 2.

2. Click the **Splits cell into rows or columns button** ⌗ in the Property inspector.

3. Click the **Split cell into Rows option button** (if necessary), type **2** in the Number of rows text box (if necessary), as shown in Figure 25, click **OK**, then click in the cell to deselect it.

   The cell is split, as shown in Figure 26.

   TIP To create a new row at the end of a table, place the insertion point in the last cell, then press [Tab].

You split a cell into two rows.

Figure 25 *Splitting a cell into two rows*

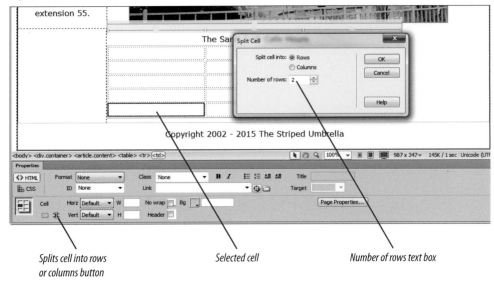

Splits cell into rows or columns button

Selected cell

Number of rows text box

Figure 26 *Splitting one cell into two rows*

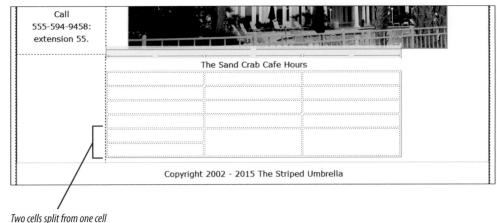

Two cells split from one cell

Positioning Objects with CSS and Tables

Figure 27 *Merging selected cells into one cell*

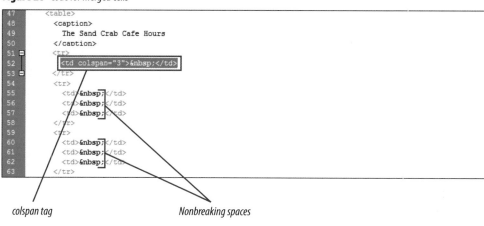

555-594-9458:
extension 55.

The Sand Crab Cafe Hours

Copyright 2002 - 2015 The Striped Umbrella

`<body> <div.container> <article.content> <table> <tr> <th>`

Merges selected cells
using spans button

Resulting merged cell

Figure 28 *Code for merged cells*

```
47      <table>
48        <caption>
49          The Sand Crab Cafe Hours
50        </caption>
51        <tr>
52          <td colspan="3"> </td>
53        </tr>
54        <tr>
55          <td> </td>
56          <td> </td>
57          <td> </td>
58        </tr>
59        <tr>
60          <td> </td>
61          <td> </td>
62          <td> </td>
63        </tr>
```

colspan tag   Nonbreaking spaces

Merge cells

1. Click to set the insertion point in the first cell in the top row, then drag to the right to select the three cells in the top row.

2. Click the **Merges selected cells using spans button** ⊡ in the Property inspector.

   The three cells are merged into one cell, as shown in Figure 27. This merged cell will act as a table header. Descriptive text in this cell will spread across the table width.

   TIP You can only merge cells that are adjacent to each other.

3. Click the **Show Code view button** Code , then view the code for the merged cells, as shown in Figure 28.

   Notice the table tags denoting the column span (th colspan="3") and the nonbreaking spaces ( ) inserted in the empty cells.

4. Click the **Show Design view button** Design , select and merge the first cells in rows 2, 3, 4, and 5 in the left column, then save your work.

You merged three cells in the first row to make room for the table header. You then merged four cells in the left column to make room for an image.

Insert and Align
IMAGES IN TABLE CELLS

What You'll Do

In this lesson, you will insert an image of a chocolate cake in the left column of the table. After placing the image, you will align it within the cell.

Inserting Images in Table Cells

You can insert images in the cells of a table using the Image command in the Images menu on the Insert panel. If you already have images saved in your website that you would like to insert in a table, you can drag them from the Assets panel into the table cells. When you add a large image to a cell, the cell expands to accommodate the inserted image. If you select the Show attributes when inserting Images check box in the Accessibility category of the Preferences dialog box, the Image Tag Accessibility Attributes dialog box opens after you insert an image, prompting you to enter alternate text. Figure 29 shows the USHorse.biz website, which uses several tables for page layout and contains images in its table cells. Notice that some images appear in cells by themselves, and some appear in cells containing text or other graphics. Some cells have a light background, and some have a darker background.

Aligning Images in Table Cells

You can align images both horizontally and vertically within a cell. With HTML5, it's best to align an image by creating a rule with alignment settings, then apply the rule to the image content. For example, if you have inserted an image in a table cell, you can create a Class rule in your style sheet called something like img_table_cell, then assign a center-align property to the rule.

After saving the rule, select the image, then apply the img_table_cell rule to it. It will then center-align itself within the table cell.

Another way to align content in table cells that is HTML5 compliant is to add a style to the individual cell tag that sets the cell alignment. For example, add the code "style=text-align:center" to the cell tag for the cell you want to modify to center the cell's contents.

Figure 29 *USHorse.biz website*

USHorse.biz website used with permission from USHorse.biz – www.ushorse.biz.com

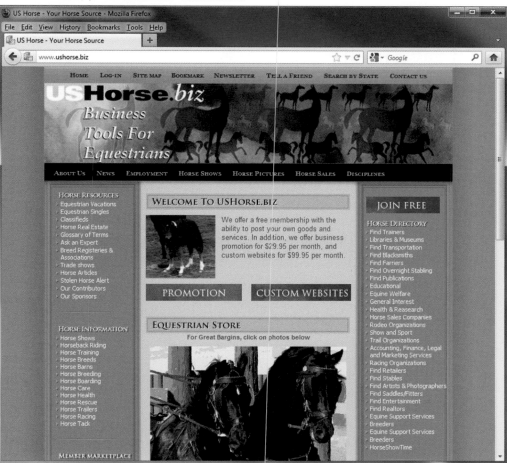

Insert images in table cells

1. Click in the merged cells in the left column of the table (under the merged cell in the top row) to place the insertion point.

2. Insert **chocolate_cake.jpg** from the drive and folder where you store your Data Files, then type **Chocolate Grand Marnier Cake** for the alternate text.

TIP You may see some extra space around the image, but this will be corrected later.

3. Compare your screen to Figure 30.

4. Refresh the Files panel and verify that the new image was copied to The Striped Umbrella website assets folder.

5. Save your work, then preview the page in your browser.

6. Close your browser.

You inserted an image into a table cell on the cafe page.

Figure 30 *Image inserted into table cell*

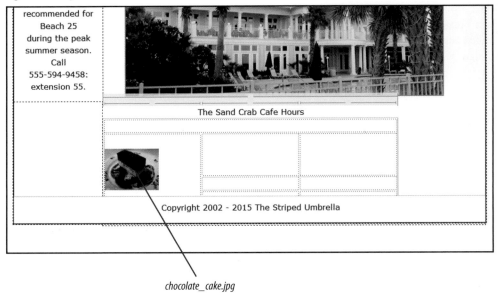

chocolate_cake.jpg

Using Rulers, Grids, and Guides for Positioning Page Content

To help you position your page content, the View menu offers grids and guides. **Grids** provide a graph paper-like view of a page. Horizontal and vertical lines fill the page when this option is turned on. You can edit the line colors, the distance between them, whether they are composed of lines or dots, and whether or not objects "snap" to them. **Guides** are horizontal or vertical lines that you drag onto the page from the rulers. You can edit both the colors of the guides and the color of the distance, a feature that shows you the distance between two guides. You can lock the guides so you don't accidentally move them and you can set them either to snap to page elements or have page elements snap to them. To display grids or guides, click View on the Menu bar, point to Grid, then click Show Grid or point to Guides and then click Show Guides.

Figure 31 *Aligning image in cell by editing a <td> rule*

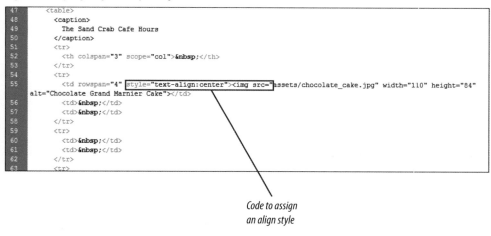

```
47    <table>
48      <caption>
49        The Sand Crab Cafe Hours
50      </caption>
51      <tr>
52        <th colspan="3" scope="col"> </th>
53      </tr>
54      <tr>
55        <td rowspan="4" style="text-align:center"><img src="assets/chocolate_cake.jpg" width="110" height="84"
      alt="Chocolate Grand Marnier Cake"></td>
56        <td> </td>
57        <td> </td>
58      </tr>
59      <tr>
60        <td> </td>
61        <td> </td>
62      </tr>
63      <tr>
```

Code to assign
an align style

Align graphics in table cells

1. Click to the right side of the **chocolate_cake image** in the same cell to place the insertion point.

2. Switch to Code view, then place the insertion point right after the tag "<td rowspan="4"".

   You'll add a style to this table cell tag to center-align its contents.

3. Press the **Spacebar** to enter a space, then type **style="text-align:center"** as shown in Figure 31.

   TIP Notice how the Code Hints feature offers suggestions as you type code in Code view. If the suggestion matches your needs, press [Tab] to accept it.

4. Return to Design view, then save your work.

5. Preview the page in your browser, view the aligned image, then close your browser.

   Don't be concerned if your cell width has increased. This will be corrected as content is added to the other cells.

You center-aligned cell content by editing the cell <td> rule.

Working with Div Tags

Div tags are used to format blocks of content, similar to the way <p> tags are used to format paragraphs of text. However, div tags are more flexible because they can act as containers for any type of block content. They are convenient for centering content on a page or applying color to an area of a web page. Div tags combine easily with Cascading Style Sheets for formatting and positioning. When you align a page element Dreamweaver automatically adds a div tag. Div tags are frequently used in style sheets to specify formatting attributes.

Insert Text and Format
CELL CONTENT

What You'll Do

In this lesson, you will type the cafe hours in the table. You will also format the text to enhance its appearance on the page. Last, you will add formatting to some of the cells and cell content.

Inserting Text in a Table

You can enter text in a table either by typing it in a cell, copying it from another source and pasting it into a cell, or importing it from another program. Once you place text in a table cell, you can format it to make it more readable and more visually appealing on the page.

Formatting Cell Content

To format the contents of a cell, select the cell contents, then apply formatting to it. For example, you can select an image in a cell and add properties such as a font, font size, or background color by using a class rule. Or, you can select text in a cell and use the Blockquote or Remove Blockquote buttons in the HTML Property inspector to move the text farther away from or closer to the cell walls.

If a cell contains multiple objects of the same type, such as text, you can format each item individually by applying different CSS rules to each one.

Formatting Cells

Formatting a cell is different from formatting a cell's contents. Formatting a cell can include setting properties that visually enhance the cell's appearance, such as setting a cell width and assigning a background color. To format a cell with code that is HTML5 compliant, use tags to define a column group style <colgroup>, which will format all cells in a particular column. You can also use the column tag <col> to apply formatting styles to singular cells. Once you have created your styles, you add them to the code for the appropriate columns or cells you wish to format.

QUICK **TIP**

Although you can set some table and cell properties using the Property inspector, strive to use CSS Styles for all formatting tasks.

Figure 32 *Typing text into cells*

extension 55.

The Sand Crab Cafe Hours

Our individual dining area hours are listed below.

The Terrace	11:00 a.m. - 9:00 p.m.
Beach 25	7:00 a.m. - 11:00 p.m.
The Cabana	10:00 a.m. - 7:00 p.m.

Chocolate
Grand Marnier
Cake

Room service is available from 6:00 a.m. - 12:00 a.m.
Please call extension 54 to place an order.

Copyright 2002 - 2015 The Striped Umbrella

Text typed into cells

Importing and Exporting Data from Tables

You can import and export tabular data into and out of Dreamweaver. Tabular data is data that is arranged in columns and rows and separated by a **delimiter**: a comma, tab, colon, semicolon, or similar character. **Importing** means to bring data created in another software program into Dreamweaver, and **exporting** means to save data created in Dreamweaver in a special file format that can be opened by other programs. Files that are imported into Dreamweaver must be saved as delimited files. **Delimited files** are database, word processing, or spreadsheet files that have been saved as text files with delimiters such as tabs or commas separating the data. Programs such as Microsoft Access and Microsoft Excel offer many file formats for saving files. To import a delimited file, click File on the Menu bar, point to Import, then click Tabular Data. The Import Tabular Data dialog box opens, offering you formatting options for the imported table. To export a table that you created in Dreamweaver, click File on the Menu bar, point to Export, then click Table. The Export Table dialog box opens, letting you choose the type of delimiter you want for the delimited file.

Insert text

1. Click in the cell below the chocolate cake photo, type **Chocolate**, press **[Shift][Enter]** (Win) or **[shift][return]** (Mac), type **Grand Marnier**, press **[Shift][Enter]** (Win) or **[shift][return]** (Mac), then type **Cake**.

TIP If you can't see the last lines you typed, toggle Live view, or resize your screen to refresh it.

2. Click in the top row of the table to place the insertion point, then type **Our individual dining area hours are listed below**.

The text is automatically bolded because you selected the top row header when you created the table. A table's header row is bold by default.

3. Merge the two bottom-right cells in the last row, then enter the cafe dining area names, hours, and room service information as shown in Figure 32. Use a line break after the first line of text in the last cell.

The type in the table has inherited the Font-family property from the body tag properties.

You entered text in the table to provide information about the dining room hours.

Format cell content

1. Click the **New CSS Rule button** ▣ to create a new class style called **feature_item** in the su_styles.css style sheet file.

   The CSS Rule Definition for .feature_item in su_styles.css dialog box opens.

2. In the Type category, leave the Font-family text box blank, set the Font-size to **12**, the Font-weight to **bold**, the Color to **#003**, then click **OK** to close the dialog box.

   You'll use this rule to format the name of the featured dessert.

3. Either click in the text or select **Chocolate Grand Marnier Cake** under the cake image, click the **CSS button** ▤ css on the Property inspector, then apply the **feature_item rule** to the text.

   Your screen should resemble Figure 33. Because the only property values you set for the feature_item rule were for the font size, font weight, and color, the font family value was inherited from the parent body tag and is the same as the rest of the text on the page.

   You created a new rule in the su_styles.css style sheet and used it to format text in a table cell.

Figure 33 *Formatting text using a Class rule*

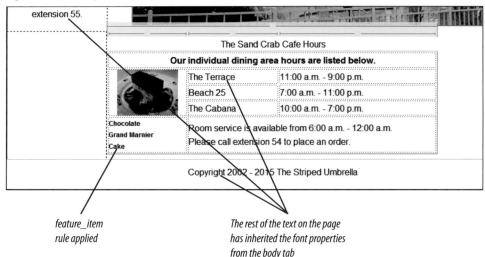

feature_item
rule applied

The rest of the text on the page
has inherited the font properties
from the body tab

POWER USER SHORTCUTS	
To do this:	**Use this shortcut:**
Insert table	[Ctrl][Alt][T] (Win) or ⌘ [option][T] (Mac)
Select a cell	[Ctrl][A] (Win) or ⌘ [A] (Mac)
Merge cells	[Ctrl][Alt][M] (Win) or ⌘ [option][M] (Mac)
Split cell	[Ctrl][Alt][S] (Win) or ⌘ [option][S] (Mac)
Insert row	[Ctrl][M] (Win) or ⌘ [M] (Mac)
Insert column	[Ctrl][Shift][A] (Win) or ⌘ [Shift][A] (Mac)
Delete row	[Ctrl][Shift][M] (Win) or ⌘ [Shift][M] (Mac)
Delete column	[Ctrl][Shift][-] (Win) or ⌘ [Shift][-] (Mac)
Increase column span	[Ctrl][Shift][]] (Win) or ⌘ [Shift][]] (Mac)
Decrease column span	[Ctrl][Shift][[] (Win) or ⌘ [Shift][[] (Mac)

Positioning Objects with CSS and Tables

Figure 34 *Adding a property to a <td> tag*

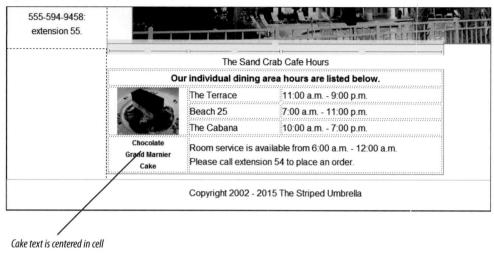

Cake text is centered in cell

Figure 35 *Adding style code to a <td> tag*

Cake text is centered in cell

Format cells

1. Click to place the insertion point in the cell with the cake text.

    Notice that the feature_item rule is applied to the text. You will modify the feature_item rule to add an alignment value.

2. Click the **feature_item** rule in the CSS Styles panel, then click the **Edit Rule button** 🖉.

3. Click the **Block Category**, click the **Text-align list** arrow, click **center**, then click **OK**.

    The cake text is now centered in the cell, as shown in Figure 34.

4. Place the insertion point in the cell with the cake image, then switch to Code view.

    Next you will align the contents of the cell describing room service. Since there is not a separate rule applied to this text, you modify the cell tag code to align the cell contents.

5. Copy the code **style="text-align:center"**, then paste it in the line of code for the cell with the room service text, as shown in Figure 35.

    (continued)

6. Return to Design view, compare your screen to Figure 36, then save your work.

The room service text is centered in the cell.

You formatted table cells by applying a rule and modifying a cell tag's code.

Figure 36 *Editing a rule*

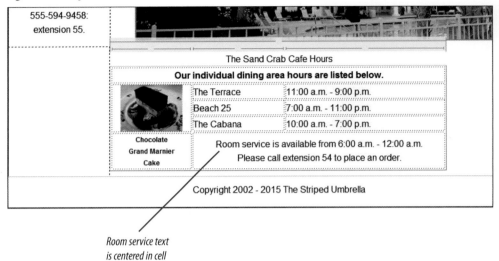

Room service text
is centered in cell

Figure 37 *Placing horizontal rules in the table*

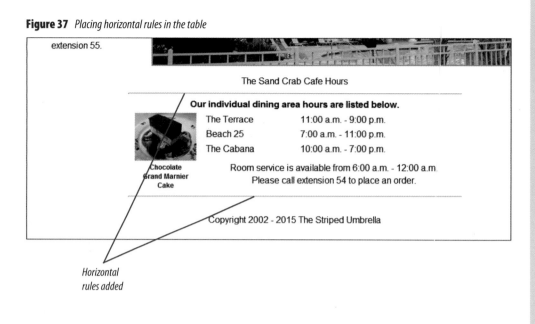

Horizontal
rules added

Modify cell content

1. Click after the word "cake" in the bottom left cell, then press **[Tab]**.

   Pressing the Tab key while the insertion point is in the last cell of the table creates a new row. Even though it looks like the cell with the room service information is the last cell, it is not because of the merged cells.

2. Merge the cells in the new row, click in the merged cells, click **Insert** on the Menu bar, point to **HTML**, then click **Horizontal Rule**.

3. Click in front of the table header, insert another horizontal rule, then save your work.

4. Switch to Live view, compare your table to Figure 37, then turn off Live view.

You added two horizontal rules to the table to set the table off from the rest of the page.

Using Inherited Properties to Format Cell Content

If a table is inside a CSS layout, you can simply let the properties from the existing CSS rules format the content, rather than applying additional rules. This is called **inheritance**. When a tag is placed, or **nested**, inside another tag (the parent tag), the properties from the parent tag are inherited by any tags nested within that tag. For example, if you set the Font-family property in the body tag, all content on the page inherits and displays that same font family unless you specify otherwise.

Check layout

1. Click the **Visual Aids button** 👁 on the Document toolbar, then click **Hide All Visual Aids**.

   As shown in Figure 38, the borders around the table cells, and CSS blocks are all hidden, allowing you to see more clearly how the table will look in the browser. Visual aids are helpful while you are editing and formatting a page. However, turning them off is a quick way to see how the page will appear in the browser without having to open it in the browser window.

2. Repeat Step 1 to show the visual aids again.

TIP You can also click the Live View button on the Document toolbar to see how the page will look in the browser. Turn Live View off by clicking it again.

3. Save your work, preview the cafe page in the browser, then close the browser.

4. Edit the body rule in the su_styles.css file to change the background color to **#FFFFFF**.

   Now all of the pages in the site will have the same background color.

5. Save your work.

You used the Hide All Visual Aids command to hide the table borders and layout block outlines, then showed them again.

Figure 38 *Hiding visual aids*

Live View button   Visual aids button

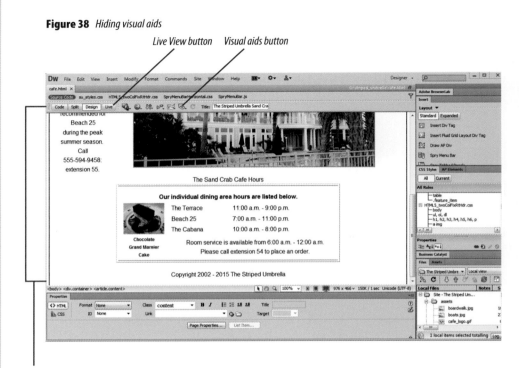

Dotted lines showing div tag borders are hidden

Figure 39 *Validating HTML5 markup*

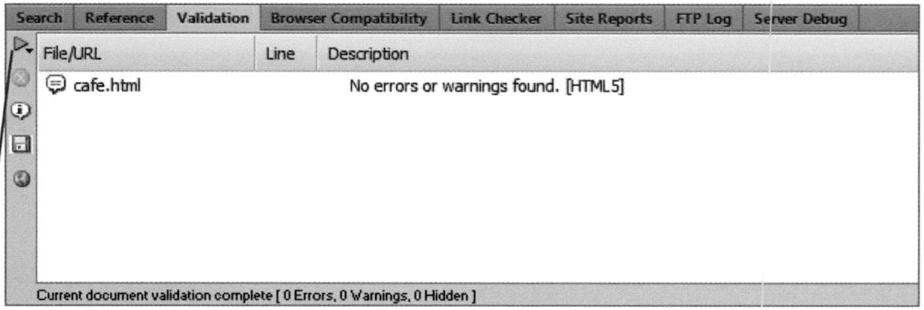

Search	Reference	Validation	Browser Compatibility	Link Checker	Site Reports	FTP Log	Server Debug

File/URL	Line	Description
cafe.html		No errors or warnings found. [HTML5]

Current document validation complete [0 Errors, 0 Warnings, 0 Hidden]

W3C validation button

Validate HTML5 markup

1. Click **Window** on the Menu bar, point to **Results**, then click **Validation**.

2. Click the **W3C Validation button** ▷, then click **Validate Current Document (W3C)**.

3. Click **OK** to close the W3C Validator Notification dialog box.

   The Results panel shows no errors or warnings found, as shown in Figure 39.

TIP You can also click the W3C Validation button in the Document toolbar to validate your document.

4. Click the **panel options button**, then click **Close Tab Group**.

   The Results panel closes.

TIP If you see any errors or warnings listed, refer to the line number that corresponds to each error, then check your code to locate and correct the error.

NEW   Validating Your Pages Against HTML5 Standards

One of the tests you should run on your web pages is to validate your page code against current HTML5 standards. Dreamweaver provides a quick way to test each page with the Validation panel in the Results panel group. When you click the Validate Current Document (W3C) button, Dreamweaver connects to the W3C server, submits the page code, and records the results in the Validation panel. If you want to test your pages against other versions of HTML, click Validate Current Document (W3C), click Settings, then choose the additional version or versions of HTML you would like to use for validation. The live validation service is new in Dreamweaver 5.5. Previously, the code was validated using internal documentation.

Create a page using CSS layouts.

1. Open the Blooms & Bulbs website, then create a new blank HTML5 page with the 2 column fixed, right sidebar, header and footer style, and link the blooms_styles.css file to the page. Save the HTML5_twoColFixRtHdr.css file in the blooms site root folder.
2. Save the file as **workshops.html**, overwriting the existing workshops page.

Add content to CSS layout blocks.

1. Open the index page, then copy the banner and menu bar. (*Hint*: Select the banner, hold down the Shift key, then click right under the menu bar to select the menu bar and the banner together.)
2. Close the index page, then on the workshops page, delete the logo placeholder in the header, then paste the banner and menu bar in the header block. (*Hint*: If you have trouble copying and pasting the banner and menu bar together, try copying and pasting them separately.) Enter a paragraph break after the menu bar.
3. Delete the footer placeholder text, then type **Copyright 2001 - 2015 Blooms & Bulbs** in the footer block.
4. Delete the placeholder content from the content block.
5. Type **New Composting Workshop!**, enter a paragraph break, import the text composting.doc from the drive and folder where you store you Data Files, then use the Commands > Clean up Word HTML command.
6. Enter a paragraph break after the inserted text, then insert the chives.jpg from the drive and folder where

you store your Data Files. Add the alternate text **Even chives can be beautiful** to the image when prompted.
7. Save your work.

Edit and format CSS layout blocks.

1. Select the footer rule in the CSS Styles panel, then edit its Text-align property in the Block category to center the content.
2. Select the heading "New Composting Workshop!" and format it using the Heading 1 tag if necessary.
3. Select the header rule in the CSS Styles panel and change its background color to **#FFF**.
4. Repeat Step 3 to change the background color of the sidebar1 rule to **#FFF** and the footer rule to **#AFA19E**.
5. Edit the header rule so that the header has a 5-pixel margin on all sides.
6. Edit the body rule to change the Font-size to 14 pixels.
7. Edit the sidebar1 rule Float to left.
8. Use the Blockquote button to indent the chives image.
9. Save your work.

Create a table.

1. Delete the placeholder text in the sidebar, then insert a table with the following settings: Rows: **8**, Columns: **2**, and Header: **Top**.
2. Edit the sidebar1 rule to center-align the contents.
3. Add the page title **Blooms & Bulbs workshops** then save your work.

4. Create a new rule to modify the table tag in the blooms_styles.css file and set the table box width to 175 pixels.

Resize, split, and merge cells.

1. Merge the two cells in the first row.
2. Merge the two cells in the last row.
3. Save your work.

Insert and align images in table cells.

1. Use the Insert panel to insert gardening_gloves.gif in the last row of the table. You can find this image in the assets folder where you store your Data Files. Add the alternate text **Gardening gloves** to the image when prompted.
2. Save your work.

Insert text and format cell content.

1. Type **Currently Scheduled Workshops** in the merged cell in the first row, using a line break after the word "Scheduled".
2. Type the names and dates for the workshops from Figure 40 in each row of the table.
3. Edit the table rule to center-align the contents.
4. Save your work, preview the page in your browser, then close your browser.
5. Validate the workshops page for HTML5 compliance, correct any errors or warnings found, then save and close all open pages.

Figure 40 *Completed Skills Review*

Blooms & Bulbs

HWY 43 SOUTH • ALVIN • TX 77511 • 555-248-0806

| Home | Newsletter | Plants | ▼ | Tips | Workshops |

Currently Scheduled Workshops

Composting	8/1/15
Pruning	8/8/15
Water Gardening	8/15/15
Mulching	8/22/15
Going Green	8/29/15
Attracting Butterflies	9/4/15

New Composting Workshop!

Our next workshop is entitled "Everything You Need to Know About Composting." This informative workshop will be great for any gardener, whether you plan to invest in a commercial compost bin or simply start a compost pile in a corner of your garden. You will be amazed at how quickly you can produce rich, nutrient-filled compost with only a little effort. Use this black gold to amend your soil naturally, to encourage the growth of healthy plants. Not only will you create rich soil and save water—you will also reduce trash at the landfill by recycling your kitchen scraps and garden materials.

We offer this free workshop on a first-come, first-served basis. All workshop participants will receive a packet of bacteria to kick-start their composting process. Our speaker will be Ann Porter from the County Extension Office. Ann recently completed her Master Composter Certification and is eager to share her knowledge. She is an engaging speaker you will be sure to enjoy. Call 555-248-0806 today to reserve your spot!

Copyright 2001 - 2015 Blooms & Bulbs

Positioning Objects with CSS and Tables

In this exercise, you continue your work on the TripSmart website that you began in Project Builder 1 in Chapter 1 and developed in the previous chapters. You are ready to begin work on a page featuring a catalog item. You plan to use a CSS layout with a table to place the information on the page.

1. Open the TripSmart website.
2. Create a new page based on the HTML5: 3 column fixed, header and footer CSS page layout, attach the tripsmart_styles.css file, save the new HTML5_thrColFixHdr.css file in the site root folder, then save the file as **catalog.html**, replacing the placeholder catalog page in the website.
3. Open the index page, delete the horizontal rule, copy the banner and menu bar, then switch to the catalog page.
4. Delete the logo image placeholder in the header, paste the banner and menu bar in the header block, then add a paragraph break.
5. Replace the placeholder text in the footer with the website copyright statement from the index page, then edit the footer rule in the HTML5_thrColFixHdr.css style sheet to center align the content, and set the background color to #FFF.
6. Edit the header rule so its background is #FFF and all margins to 5 px.
7. Edit the body style in the HTML5_thrColFixHdr.css style sheet to change the Font-family to Arial, Helvetica, sans-serif, the Font-size to 14 pixels, and the background color to white.
8. Save your work.

9. Delete the placeholder content in the center body section, then type **This Week's Featured Catalog Item**. Enter a paragraph break, then import the Word document, walking sticks.doc and use the Clean Up Word HTML command after importing it.
10. Delete the placeholder text in the first column including the links, and type **These are the lengths available for order:**
11. Delete the placeholder text in the third column then type **Special Shipping Offer**, enter a paragraph break, type **Order two or more walking sticks this week and your shipping is free. Enter the code twosticks when you check out to receive free shipping**, then apply the Heading 2 Paragraph format to the Special Shipping Offer text.
12. Create a new Tag rule in the tripsmart_styles.css style sheet that modifies the Heading 2 tag as follows: Font-family: Arial, Helvetica, sans-serif; Font-size: 16 pixels; Type Color: #54572C.
13. Create a new Class rule called **centered_text** in the tripsmart.css style sheet and set the Text-align property to center. Select the Special Shipping Offer text and apply the centered_text rule.
14. Enter a paragraph break after the heading in the second column, then insert the image walking_stick.jpg from the drive and folder where you store you Chapter 6 data files. Add appropriate alternate text.
15. Use settings of your choice to create a new class rule named catalog_images in the tripsmart_styles.css file that will add a border around the image, set the float to left, and add a margin to all sides. Apply your new rule to the walking stick image.

16. Edit the sidebar1 rule and the aside rule to set the background colors to #FFF.
17. Edit the footer rule to add a top border.
18. Edit the container rule to add a border around all sides.
19. Edit the content rule to change the width to 580 pixels, 10-pixel padding for all sides, and the file tripsmart_gradient.jpg from the drive and folder where you store your Chapter 6 data files for a background image.
20. Insert a table under the text "These are the lengths available for order" with the following settings: Rows: **8**, Columns: **2**, Header: **Top**.
21. Type the text for the table using the information in the table in Figure 41.
22. Create a rule in the tripsmart_styles.css file to modify the table tag as follows: Box Width: 175 px; Border solid, Border Width: thin; Border Color: #BABD9F, Text-align: center.
23. Add the page title **TripSmart - Serving all your travel needs**.
24. Add the heading **Walking sticks** above the walking stick paragraph, apply the Heading 2 format, then adjust your spacing if necessary.
25. Save your work, validate the page code for HTML5, then correct any warnings or errors that you find.
26. Open the services page and copy the line of code that inserts the favicon on the page (the code right above the title tag in the head content), then paste it in the code on the catalog page right above the code for the title.
27. Save your work, preview the page in the browser and compare your screen to Figure 41, close the browser, then close all open pages.

Figure 41 *Sample Project Builder 1*

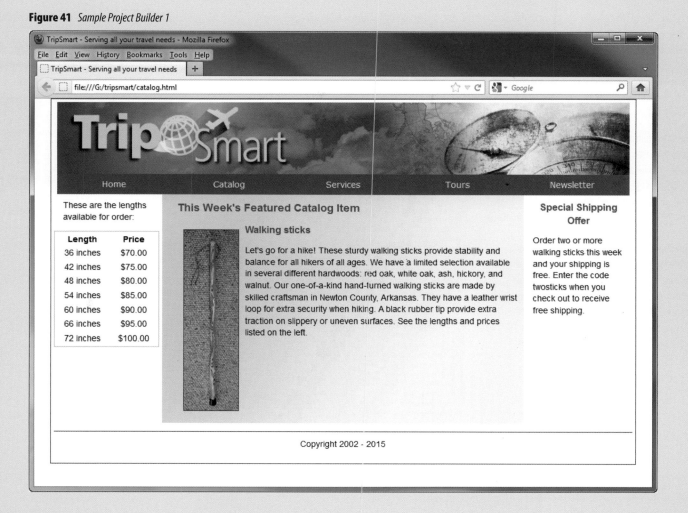

PROJECT BUILDER 2

Use Figure 42 as a guide to continue your work on the Carolyne's Creations website that you started in Chapter 1 and developed in the previous chapters. You are now ready to begin work on a page showcasing the company's catering services. You decide to use an HTML5 layout and add a small table.

1. Open the Carolyne's Creations website, then create a new page based on the HTML5: 2 column fixed, right sidebar, header and footer layout, attach the cc_styles.css file, and save the page as **catering. html**, overwriting the existing page.
2. Copy the banner that includes the menu bar from one of the other pages, then paste it on the page, replacing the logo placeholder.
3. Delete the placeholder text in both the sidebar and content sections, then type **Special Treats for Valentine's Day** in the content block. You can import the text for the paragraph that follows using the marshmallows.doc file in your Chapter 6 Data Files folder. (Remember to clean up the Word HTML.)

4. Insert a table in the sidebar block to with the following settings: Rows: 5, Columns: 2, and Header: Top.
5. Create a new Tag rule in the cc_styles.css file to modify the table tag with the following settings: Width: 175, Text-align: center; Float: left, Font-size: 12px., then enter the data for the table using the table data in Figure 42.
6. Insert the file marshmallows.jpg from the drive and folder where you store your Chapter 6 Data Files at the end of the paragraph.
7. Assign the Heading 1 format to the page heading "Special Treats for Valentine's Day" if necessary.
8. Assign the Heading 2 tag to the text above the table "Marshmallow Options".
9. Edit the header rule to add a solid, 5 pixel border for each side and a background color of #333333.
10. Replace the footer content with a copyright statement, then edit the footer rule to set the text alignment to center.

11. Add the page title **Carolyne's Creations Catering Services**.
12. Create a new rule in the cc_styles.css style sheet named **centered_text** and use it to center the text "Marshmallow Options" above the table.
13. Edit the header rule Block text-align property to center the banner.
14. Save your work then use the Validation panel to test your page for HTML5 compliance. Correct any errors or warnings that are listed.
15. Make any adjustments of your choice to the layout to improve the page appearance.
16. Add the phrase **Call 24 hours in advance to ensure the availability of your choice**. under the Marshmallow Options table, then apply a rule to format the text.
17. Save your work, preview the page in your browser, then close all open files.

Figure 42 *Sample Project Builder 2*

Special Treats for Valentine's Day

Remember that we have lots of small items (in addition to complete party fare) that our catering staff can provide. One of our most popular items this season has been our delicious home-made marshmallows. These confectionary delights are made with our own homemade vanilla and are dusted with powdered sugar. They make wonderful gourmet s'mores, but are at their best floating on top of a cup of rich hot cocoa.

Marshmallow Options

Flavor	Price
Vanilla	$6.00 doz
Chocolate	$7.00 doz
Peppermint	$8.00 doz
Swirl	$8.00 doz

Call 24 hours in advance to ensure the availability of your choice.

Copyright 2001 - 2015

Positioning Objects with CSS and Tables

Jon Bishop is opening a new restaurant and wants to launch his restaurant website two weeks before his opening. He has hired you to create the site and has asked for several design proposals. You begin by looking at some restaurant sites with pleasing designs.

1. Connect to the Internet, then go to jamesatthemill.com, as shown in Figure 43.
2. How are CSS styles used in this site?
3. How are CSS styles used to prevent an overload of information in one area of the screen?
4. View the source code for the page and locate the html tags that control the CSS layout on the page.
5. Use the Reference panel in Dreamweaver to look up the code used in this site to place the content on the page. (*Hint*: To do this, make note of a tag that you don't understand, then open the Reference panel and find that tag in the Tag list in the Reference panel. Select it from the list and read the description in the Reference panel.)
6. Do you see any tables on the page? If so, how are they used?

Figure 43 *Design Project*
James at the Mill website used with permission from Miles James – www.jamesatthemill.com

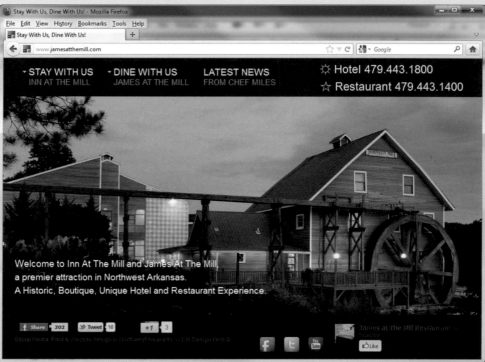

For this assignment, you continue to work on the portfolio project that you have been developing since Chapter 1. No Data Files are supplied. You are building this website from chapter to chapter, so you must do each Portfolio Project assignment in each chapter to complete your website.

You continue building your website by designing and completing a page that uses a CSS layout for page design.

1. Consult your wireframe to decide which page to create and develop for this chapter. Draw a sketch of the page to show how you plan to use CSS to lay out the content.
2. Create the new page for the site using one of the predesigned CSS layouts.
3. Add text, background images, and background colors to each container.
4. Create the navigation links that will allow you to add this page to your site.

5. Update the other pages of your site so that each page includes a link to this new page.
6. Add images in the containers (where appropriate), making sure to align them attractively.
7. Review the checklist in Figure 44 and make any necessary changes.
8. Save your work, preview the page in your browser, make any necessary modifications to improve the page appearance, close your browser, then close all open pages.

Figure 44 *Portfolio Project checklist*

Website Checklist
1. Do all pages have a page title?
2. Do all navigation links work correctly?
3. Did you validate your code for at least one level of HTML?
4. Did you use a CSS predefined page layout for at least one page?
5. Do your pages look the same in at least two current browsers?
6. Does all content in your CSS containers appear correctly?

ADOBE DREAMWEAVER CS6

CHAPTER 7 MANAGING A WEB
SERVER AND FILES

1. Perform website maintenance

2. Publish a website and transfer files

3. Check files out and in

4. Cloak files

5. Import and export a site definition

6. Evaluate web content for legal use

7. Present a website to a client

MANAGING A WEB
SERVER AND FILES

Once you have created all the pages of your website, finalized all the content, and performed site maintenance, you are ready to publish your site to a remote server so the rest of the world can access it. In this chapter, you start by running some reports to make sure the links in your site work properly and that any orphaned files are removed. Next, you set up a connection to the remote site for The Striped Umbrella website. You then transfer files to the remote site and learn how to keep them up to date. You also check out a file so that it is not available to other team members while you are editing it and you learn how to cloak files. When a file is **cloaked**, it is excluded from certain processes, such as being transferred to the remote site. Next, you export the site definition file from The Striped Umbrella website so that other designers can import the site. Finally, you research important copyright issues that affect all websites, and learn how to present your work to a client.

Preparing to Publish a Site

Before you publish a site, it is extremely important that you test it to make sure the content is accurate and up to date and that everything is functioning properly. When viewing pages over the Internet, users find it frustrating to click a link that doesn't work or to wait for pages that load slowly because of large graphics and animations. Remember that the typical user has a short attention span and limited patience.

Before you publish your site, be sure to use the Link Checker panel to check for broken links and orphaned files. Make sure that all image paths are correct and that all images load quickly and have alternate text. Verify that all pages have titles. View the pages in at least two different browsers and different versions of the same browser to ensure that everything works correctly. The more frequently you test, the better the chance that your users will have a positive experience at your site and want to return. Finally, before you publish your pages, verify that all content is original to the website, has been obtained legally, and is used properly without violating the copyright of someone else's work.

Reports

Report on: Current Document ▼

- Current Document
- Entire Current Local Site
- Selected Files in Site
- Folder...

Run
Cancel

Select repor

☐ 📁 Workflow
- ☐ Checked Out By
- ☐ Design Notes
- ☐ Recently Modified

☐ 📁 HTML Reports
- ☐ Combinable Nested Font Tags
- ☐ Missing Alt Text
- ☐ Redundant Nested Tags
- ☐ Removable Empty Tags
- ☐ Untitled Documents

Report Settings...

Help

Site Setup for The Striped Umbrella

- Site
- Servers
- Version Control
- ▶ Advanced Settings

Basic | Advanced

Server Name: Server1

Connect using: FTP ▼

FTP Address: www.webhost.com   Port: 21

Username: name

Password: ●●●●●●●●   ☑ Save

Test

Root Directory: /home

Web URL: http://www.webhost.com/home/

▶ More Options

Help | Save | Cancel

The settings
or your web

mweaver site. You
nd post your

mote | Testing

Help | Save | Cancel

Perform
WEBSITE MAINTENANCE

What You'll Do

32 Total, 11 HTML, 1 Orphaned 114 All links, 111 OK, 0 Broken, 3 External

In this lesson, you will use Dreamweaver site management tools to check for broken links, orphaned files, and missing alternate text. You will also validate your markup to locate CSS3 and HTML5 errors. You will then evaluate and correct any problems that you find.

Maintaining a Website

As you add pages, links, and content to a website, it can quickly become difficult to manage. It's easier to find and correct errors as you go, rather than waiting until the end of the design phase. It's important to perform maintenance tasks frequently to make sure your website operates smoothly and remains "clean." You have already learned about some of the tools described in the following paragraphs. Although it is important to use them as you create and modify your pages, it is also important to run them at periodic intervals after publishing your website to make sure it is always error-free.

Using the Assets Panel

You should use the Assets panel to check the list of images and colors used in your website. If you see images listed that are not being used, you should move them to a storage folder outside the website until you need them. You should also make note of any non-websafe colors. This is much less of an issue today than in the past, but it doesn't hurt to evaluate any non-websafe colors you find to determine whether slight variations in the way the colors

are rendered could cause contrast problems, especially with mobile devices.

Checking Links Sitewide

Before and after you publish your website, you should use the Link Checker panel to make sure all internal links are working. If the Link Checker panel displays any broken links, repair them. If the Link Checker panel displays any orphaned files, evaluate whether to delete them or link them with existing pages. To delete a file that you decide not to use, select it in the Files panel, then press [Delete] or right-click the file, click Edit, then click Delete. You should also check all external links by testing them in a browser to make sure that all links find the intended website.

Using Site Reports

You can use the Reports command in the Site menu to generate five different HTML reports that can help you maintain your website. You choose the type of report you want to run in the Reports dialog box, shown in Figure 1. You can specify whether to generate the report for the current document, the entire current local site, selected files in the site, or a selected folder. You can also generate workflow reports to see files that have been checked out by others or recently modified or you can view the Design Notes attached to files.

Design Notes are separate files in a website that contain additional information about a page file or a graphic file. If several designers are working collaboratively to design a site, they can record notes to exchange information with other design team members about the status of a file. Design Notes are also a good place to store information about the source files for graphics, such as Flash or Fireworks files.

Validating Markup

Because there are now several different languages used for developing web pages, it's important to ensure that the various language versions are compatible. To address this need, Dreamweaver can validate markup. To

validate markup, Dreamweaver submits the files to the W3C Validation Service to search through the code to look for errors that could occur with different language versions, such as XHTML or HTML5. To validate code for a page, click the W3C Validation button on the Document toolbar or use the Window > Results > Validation command to open the **NEW** Validation panel. A new feature beginning with Dreamweaver CS5.5 sends the page code to the live W3C site to be validated. The Results tab group displaying the Validation panel opens and lists any pages with errors, the line numbers where the errors occur, and an explanation of the errors. You should also submit your CSS files for CSS validation to the W3C Validation Service at jigsaw.w3.org/css-validator.

Testing Pages

Finally, you should test your website using many different types and versions of browsers, platforms, and screen resolutions. You can use the Check browser compatibility button on the Document toolbar to check for issues with your site pages that might cause problems when they are viewed using certain browsers. Examples can include the rendering of square bullets, table borders, horizontal rules, or CSS AP elements. If you find such issues, you can choose to change your pages to eliminate the problems. The Results Tab group's Browser Compatibility panel includes a URL that you can visit to find the solutions to identified problems. You should test every link to make sure it connects to a valid, active website. Adobe has an application called **Adobe BrowserLab** that is a useful tool for cross-browser and cross-platform compatibility testing. Adobe BrowserLab is an online service, so you can access it from any computer with an Internet connection. Go to browserlab.adobe.com to learn more about using Adobe BrowserLab.

If, in your testing, you find any pages that download slowly, reduce their size to improve performance. Consider optimizing graphics by cropping or resizing images, reducing the number of media files, or streamlining the page code.

As part of your ongoing site testing, you should present the web pages at strategic times in the development process to your team members and to your clients for feedback and evaluation. Analyze all feedback on the website objectively, incorporating both the positive and the negative comments to help you make improvements to the site and meet the clients' expectations and goals.

Figure 1 *Reports dialog box*

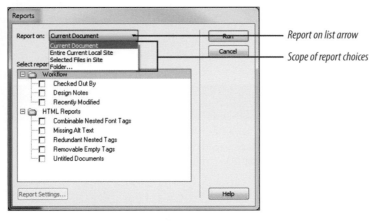

Report on list arrow

Scope of report choices

Check for broken links

1. Open The Striped Umbrella website.
2. Show the Files panel, if necessary.
3. Click **Site** on the Menu bar, point to **Advanced**, then click **Recreate Site Cache**.

   It is a good idea to recreate the site cache to force Dreamweaver to refresh the file listing before running reports.
4. Click **Site** on the Menu bar, then click **Check Links Sitewide**.

   No broken links are listed in the Link Checker panel of the Results Tab Group, as shown in Figure 2.

You verified that there are no broken links in the website.

Check for orphaned files

1. On the Link Checker panel, click the **Show list arrow**, then click **Orphaned Files**.

   There is one orphaned file, water.jpg, as shown in Figure 3. You may decide to use this image for a background later, so you leave it in the local site folder for now.
2. Close the Results Tab Group.

You found one orphaned file in the website, but decided to leave it there for now.

Figure 2 *Link Checker panel displaying no broken links*

No broken links listed

Figure 3 *Link Checker panel displaying one orphaned file*

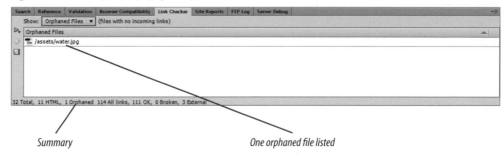

Summary

One orphaned file listed

Validating Accessibility Standards

There are many accessibility issues to consider to ensure that your website conforms to current accessibility standards. HTML Reports provide an easy way to check for missing alternate text, missing page titles, and improper markup. You can run HTML Reports on the current document, selected files, or the entire local site.

Figure 4 *Reports dialog box with Untitled Documents option selected*

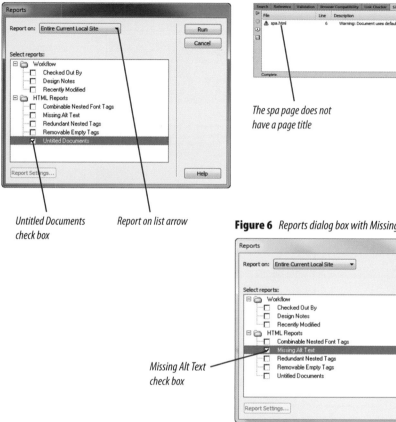

Untitled Documents
check box

Report on list arrow

Figure 5 *Results panel showing the spa page without a page title*

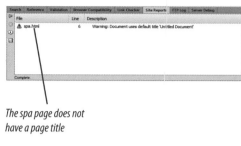

The spa page does not
have a page title

Figure 6 *Reports dialog box with Missing Alt Text option selected*

Missing Alt Text
check box

Figure 7 *Site Reports panel displaying no missing alt text*

No pages have
missing alt text tags

Check for untitled documents

1. Click **Site** on the Menu bar, then click **Reports** to open the Reports dialog box.

2. Click the **Report on list arrow**, click **Entire Current Local Site**, click the **Untitled Documents check box**, as shown in Figure 4, then click **Run**.

   The Site Reports panel opens in the Results Tab Group, and shows that the spa page does not have a page title, as shown in Figure 5.

3. Open the spa page, add the page title **The Striped Umbrella Sea Spa**, save and close the page, then repeat Steps 1 and 2 to run the report again.

   All files now have page titles.

You ran a report for untitled documents, and added a page title to the page found without one.

Check for missing alternate text

1. Using Figure 6 as a guide, run another report that checks the entire current local site for missing alternate text.

   There are no images with missing alternate text, as shown in Figure 7.

2. Close the Results Tab Group, then close all open pages.

You ran a report to check for missing alternate text in the entire site.

Validate for HTML5 standards

1. Open the cafe page (the only page built using HTML5).

2. Click the **W3C Validation button** ⊳ on the Document toolbar, as shown in Figure 8, click **Validate Current Document (W3C)**, then click **OK** to close the W3C Validator Notification dialog box.

   The Validation panel shows no errors or warnings for HTML5, as shown in Figure 9.

3. Close the Results Tab Group, then close the cafe page.

You validated the cafe page against HTML5 markup standards and no errors or warnings were found.

Figure 8 *Validating the cafe page for HTML5 markup*

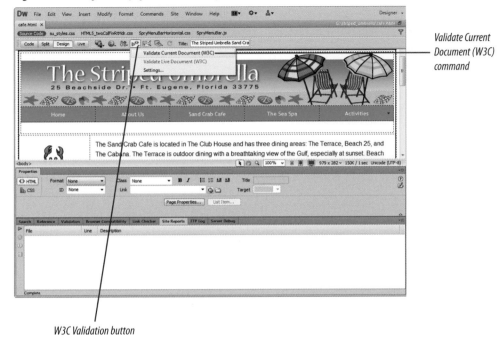

Validate Current Document (W3C) command

W3C Validation button

Figure 9 *Validation panel with no errors or warnings found*

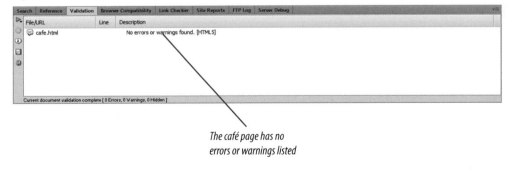

The café page has no errors or warnings listed

Figure 10 *Submitting a style sheet for validation*
Courtesy of w3.org

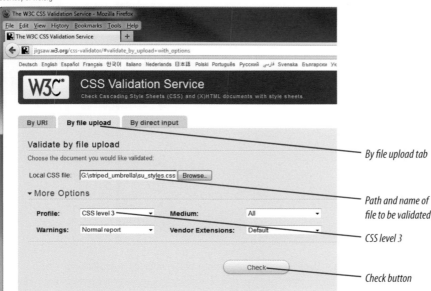

By file upload tab

Path and name of file to be validated

CSS level 3

Check button

Figure 11 *W3C validation results for su_styles.css file*
Courtesy of w3.org

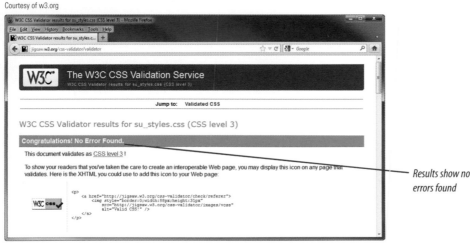

Results show no errors found

Validate CSS

1. Open your browser and go to **jigsaw.w3.org/css-validator**.

   The CSS Validation Service provides a fast way to validate the code in your style sheets to be sure they are compliant with the most current published CSS standards.

2. Click the **By file upload tab**, click the **Browse button** next to the Local CSS file text box, navigate to your website's local site folder, double-click to select **su_styles.css**, click **More Options**, then click **CSS level 3**, as shown in Figure 10.

3. Click **Check**, then view the validation results, as shown in Figure 11.

   There are no errors listed in the su_styles.css file.

4. Close the browser and return to Dreamweaver.

You submitted the main style sheet for validation and found that it met CSS3 standards.

Enable Design Notes

1. Click **Site** on the Menu bar, click **Manage Sites**, verify that The Striped Umbrella site is selected, click the **Edit the currently selected site button** ✎ , click **Advanced Settings**, then click **Design Notes**.

2. Click the **Maintain Design Notes check box** to select it, if necessary, as shown in Figure 12.

   When this option is selected, designers can record notes about a page in a separate file linked to the page. For instance, a Design Note for the index.html file would be saved in a file named index.html.mno. Dreamweaver creates a folder named _notes and saves all Design Notes in that folder. This folder does not appear in the Files panel, but it is visible in the local site folder in Windows Explorer (Win) or Finder (Mac).

3. Click **File View Columns**, then click **Notes** in the Name column.

4. Click the **Edit existing Column button** ✎ , click the **Options: Show check box** to select it, if necessary, then click **Save**.

   The Notes row now displays the word "Show" in the Show column, as shown in Figure 13, indicating that the Notes column will be visible in the Files panel.

5. Click **Save** to close the Site Setup for The Striped Umbrella dialog box, then click **Done** in the Manage Sites dialog box.

You set the preference to use Design Notes in the website. You also set the option to display the Notes column in the Files panel.

Figure 12 *Design Notes setting in the Site Setup for The Striped Umbrella*

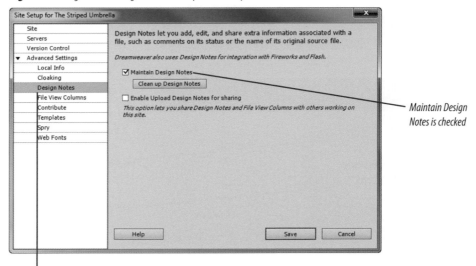

Maintain Design Notes is checked

Design Notes advanced setting

Figure 13 *Showing the Notes column in the Site Setup for The Striped Umbrella*

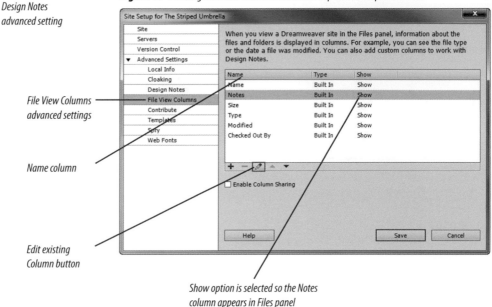

File View Columns advanced settings

Name column

Edit existing Column button

Show option is selected so the Notes column appears in Files panel

Figure 14 *Design Notes dialog box*

Status list arrow

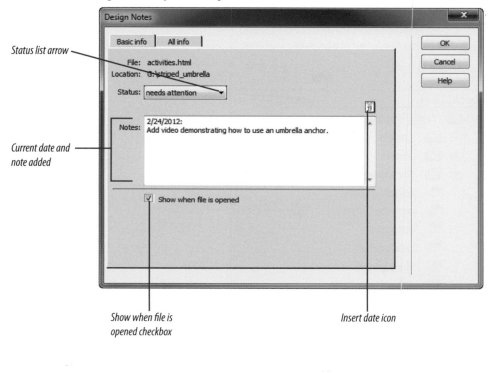

Current date and
note added

Show when file is
opened checkbox

Insert date icon

Associate a Design Note with a file

1. Open the activities page, click **File** on the Menu bar, click **Design Notes**, then click the **Basic info tab**, if necessary.

   The Design Notes dialog box opens. You can enter a note related to the open file in the text box. You can also assign the note a status, insert today's date, and indicate if the note appears whenever the file is opened.

2. Click the **Insert date button** 📅 above the Notes text box on the right.

   The current date is added to the Notes text box.

3. Click under the date, then type **Add video demonstrating how to use an umbrella anchor.** in the Notes text box.

4. Click the **Status list arrow**, then click **needs attention**.

5. Click the **Show when file is opened** check box to select it, as shown in Figure 14, then click **OK**.

6. Click the **Refresh button** ↻ on the Files panel.

   An icon 💬 appears next to the activities page in the Notes column in the Files panel, indicating that there is a Design Note attached to the file.

You added a Design Note to the activities page with the current date and a status indicator. The note opens each time the file is opened.

Using Version Cue to Manage Assets

Another way to collaborate with team members is through Adobe Version Cue, a workgroup collaboration system that is included in Adobe Creative Suite 6. You can manage security, back up data, and use metadata to search files. **Metadata** includes information about a file such as keywords, descriptions, and copyright information. Adobe Bridge also organizes files with metadata.

Edit a Design Note

1. Click **File** on the Menu bar, then click **Design Notes** to open the Design Note associated with the activities page.

TIP You can also right-click (Win) or [control]-click (Mac) the filename in the Files panel, shown in Figure 15, then click Design Notes to open the Design Note. You can also double-click the Note icon to open a Design Note.

2. Edit the note by adding the sentence **Ask Sam Geren to send the file**. after the existing text in the Notes section, then click **OK** to close it.

   Dreamweaver created a file named activities.html.mno in a new folder called _notes in the local site folder. This folder and file do not appear in the Files panel unless you have selected the option to show hidden files and folders. To show hidden files, click the Files Panel options button, then click View, Show hidden files. However, you can switch to Windows Explorer (Win) or Finder (Mac) to see them without selecting this option. When you select the option to Enable Upload Design Notes for sharing, you can share the notes with team members working with you on the site.

3. Right-click (Win) or [control]-click (Mac) **activities.html** in the Files panel, then click **Explore** (Win) or **Reveal in Finder** (Mac).

(continued)

Figure 15 *Files panel with Notes icon displayed*

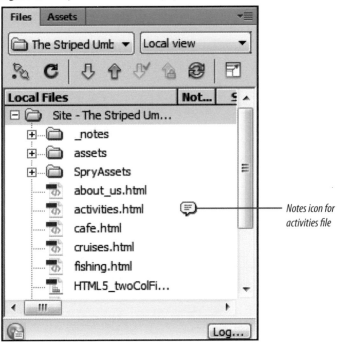

Notes icon for activities file

Deleting a Design Note

There are two steps to deleting a Design Note that you don't need anymore. The first step is to delete the Design Note file. To delete a Design Note, right-click the filename in the Files panel that is associated with the Design Note you want to delete, and then click Explore (Win) or Reveal in Finder (Mac) to open your file management system. Open the _notes folder, delete the .mno file in the files list, and then close Explorer (Win) or Finder (Mac). The second step is done in Dreamweaver: Click Site on the Menu bar, click Manage Sites, click Edit the currently selected site button, click Advanced Settings, then select the Design Notes category. Confirm that Maintain Design Notes is still selected, then click the Clean up Design Notes button. (*Note*: Don't do this if you deselect Maintain Design Notes first or it will delete all of your Design Notes!) The Design Notes icon will be removed from the Notes column in the Files panel.

Figure 16 *Windows Explorer displaying the _notes folder and file*

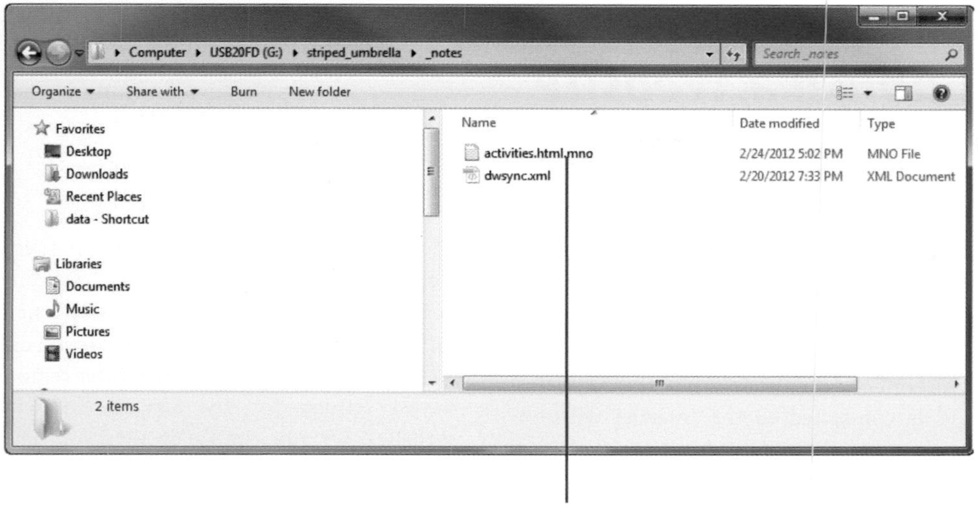

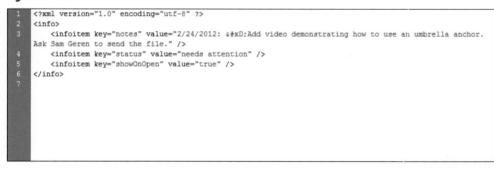

Notes file in _notes folder

Figure 17 *Code for the activities.html.mno file*

```
1  <?xml version="1.0" encoding="utf-8" ?>
2  <info>
3      <infoitem key="notes" value="2/24/2012: &#xD;Add video demonstrating how to use an umbrella anchor.
   Ask Sam Geren to send the file." />
4      <infoitem key="status" value="needs attention" />
5      <infoitem key="showOnOpen" value="true" />
6  </info>
7
```

4. Double-click the **_notes** folder to open it, then double-click the file **activities.html.mno**, shown in Figure 16, to open the file in Dreamweaver.

   The notes file opens in Code view in Dreamweaver, as shown in Figure 17.

5. Read the file, close it, close Explorer (Win) or Finder (Mac), then close the activities page.

You opened the Design Notes dialog box and edited the note in the Notes text box. Next, you viewed the .mno file that Dreamweaver created when you added the Design Note.

Publish a Website
AND TRANSFER FILES

What You'll Do

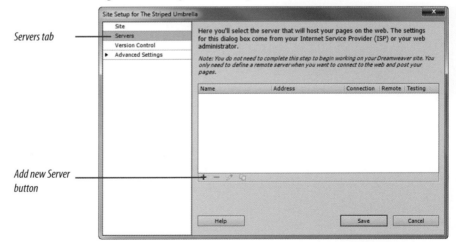

In this lesson, you will set up remote access to either an FTP folder or a local/network folder for The Striped Umbrella website. You will also view a website on a remote server, upload files to it, and synchronize the files.

Defining a Remote Site

As you learned in Chapter 1, publishing a site means transferring a copy of all the site's files to a web server. A **web server** is a computer with software that enables it to host websites and is connected to the Internet with an IP (Internet Protocol) address so that it is available on the Internet. Before you can publish a site to a web server, you must first define the remote site by specifying the Servers settings in the Site Setup dialog box as shown in Figure 18. You can specify remote settings when you first create a new site and define the local site folder (as you did in Chapter 1 when you defined the remote access settings for The Striped Umbrella website). Or you can do it after you have completed all of your pages and are confident that your site is ready for public viewing. To specify the remote settings for a site, click the Add new Server button in the Site Setup

Figure 18 *Accessing the server settings in the Site Setup dialog box*

Servers tab

Add new Server
button

Site Setup for The Striped Umbrella

Site
Servers
Version Control
Advanced Settings

Here you'll select the server that will host your pages on the web. The settings for this dialog box come from your Internet Service Provider (ISP) or your web administrator.

Note: You do not need to complete this step to begin working on your Dreamweaver site. You only need to define a remote server when you want to connect to the web and post your pages.

Name	Address	Connection	Remote	Testing

Help   Save   Cancel

dialog box, then add your server name, and choose a connection setting, which specifies the type of server you will use. You can set up multiple servers with Dreamweaver. You can set up a server for testing purposes only and a server for the live website. The most common connection setting is FTP (File Transfer Protocol). If you choose FTP, you need to specify a server address and folder name on the FTP site where you want to store your remote site root folder. You can also use **Secure FTP (SFTP)**, which lets you encrypt file transfers to protect your files, user names, and passwords. To use SFTP, select SFTP on the Connect using list in the site setup dialog box. You also need to enter login and password information. Figure 19 shows an example of FTP settings in the Add new server dialog box.

> **QUICK TIP**
>
> If you do not have access to an FTP site, you can publish a site to a local/network folder. This is referred to as a **LAN**, or a Local Area Network. Use the alternate steps provided in this lesson to publish your site to a local/network folder.

Viewing a Remote Site

Once you have set up a remote server, you can then view the remote folder in the Files panel by choosing Remote server from the View list. If your remote site is located on an FTP server, Dreamweaver will connect to it. You will see the File Activity dialog box showing the progress of the connection. You can also use the Connect to Remote Server button on the Files panel toolbar to connect to the remote site. If you defined your site on a local/network folder, then you don't need to use the Connect Remote Server button; the local site folder and any files and folders it contains appear in the Files panel when you switch to Remote server view.

Transferring Files to and from a Remote Site

After you set up a remote site, you need to **upload**, or copy, your files from the local version of your site to the remote host. To do this, view the site in Local view, select the files you want to upload, and then click the Put File(s) button on the Files panel toolbar. The Put File(s) button includes the name of the server

Figure 19 *Viewing remote server settings*

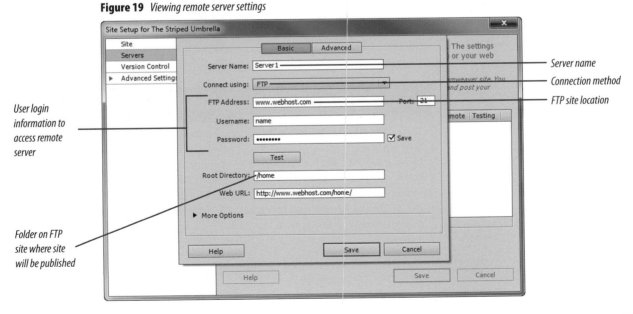

User login information to access remote server

Folder on FTP site where site will be published

Server name

Connection method

FTP site location

in the tooltip. Once you click this button, a copy of the files is transferred to the remote site. To view the uploaded files, switch to Remote server in the Files panel. Or, you can expand the Files panel to view both the Remote Site and the Local Site panes by clicking the Expand to show local and remote sites button in the Files panel.

If a file you select for uploading requires additional files, such as graphics, a dialog box opens after you click the Put File(s) button and asks if you want those files (known as **dependent files**) to be uploaded. By clicking Yes, all dependent files for the selected page will be uploaded to the appropriate folder in the remote site. If a file that you want to upload is located in a folder in the local site, the folder will automatically be transferred to the remote site.

QUICK **TIP**

To upload an entire site to a remote host, select the local site folder, then click the Put File(s) button.

If you are developing or maintaining a website in a group environment, there might be times when you want to transfer or **download** files that other team members have created from the remote site to your local site. To do this, switch to Remote Server in the Files panel, select the files you want to download, then click the Get File(s) button on the Files panel toolbar. The Get File(s) button includes the name of the server in the tooltip.

Synchronizing Files

To keep a website up to date—especially one that contains several pages and involves several team members—you need to update and replace files. Team members might make changes to pages on the local version of the site or make additions to the remote site. If many people are involved in maintaining a site, or if you are constantly making changes to the pages, ensuring that both the local and remote sites have the most up-to-date files could get confusing. Luckily, you can use the Synchronize command to keep things straight. The **Synchronize command** instructs Dreamweaver to compare the dates of the saved files in both versions of the site, then transfers only copies of files that have changed. To synchronize files, use the Synchronize Files dialog box, shown in Figure 20. You can synchronize an entire site or only selected files. You can also specify whether to upload newer files to the remote site, download newer files from the remote site, or both.

Figure 20 *Synchronize Files dialog box*

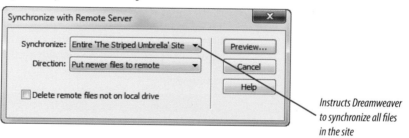

Instructs Dreamweaver to synchronize all files in the site

Understanding Dreamweaver Connection Options for Transferring Files

The connection types with which you are probably the most familiar are FTP and Local/Network. Other connection types that you can use with Dreamweaver include Microsoft Visual SafeSource (VSS), WebDav, and RDS. **VSS** is used only with the Windows operating system with Microsoft Visual SafeSource Client version 6. **WebDav** stands for Web-based Distributed Authoring and Versioning. This type of connection is used with the WebDav protocol. An example would be a website residing on an Apache web server. The **Apache web server** is a public domain, open source web server that is available using several different operating systems including UNIX and Windows. **RDS** stands for Remote Development Services, and is used with web servers using Cold Fusion.

Figure 21 *FTP settings specified in the Site Setup for The Striped Umbrella dialog box*

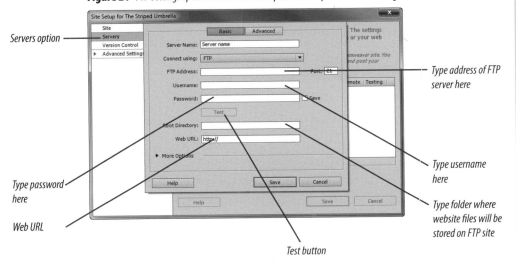

Servers option

Type address of FTP server here

Type username here

Type folder where website files will be stored on FTP site

Type password here

Web URL

Test button

Comparing Two Files for Differences in Content

There are situations where it would be helpful to be able to compare the contents of two files, such as a local file and the remote version of the same file; or an original file and the same file that has been saved with a different name. Once the two files are compared and differences are detected, you can merge the information in the files. A good time to compare files is before you upload them to a remote server to prevent accidentally writing over a file with more recent information. To compare files, you must first locate and install a third-party file comparison utility, or "dif" tool, such as Araxis Merge or Beyond Compare. (Dreamweaver does not have a file comparison tool included as part of the software, so you need to download one.) If you are not familiar with these tools, find one using your favorite search engine.

After installing the file comparison utility, use the Preferences command on the Edit menu to open the Preferences dialog box, then select the File Compare category. Next, browse to select the application you want to use to compare files. After you have set your Preferences, click the Compare with Remote Server command on the File menu to compare an open file with the remote version.

Set up a web server connection on an FTP site

NOTE: Complete these steps only if you know you can store The Striped Umbrella files on an FTP site and you know the login and password information. If you do not have access to an FTP site, complete the exercise called Set up a web server connection to a local or network folder on Page 7-18.

1. Click **Site** on the Menu bar, then click **Manage Sites**.
2. Click **The Striped Umbrella** in the Manage Sites dialog box, if necessary, then click the **Edit currently selected site button** ✎.
3. Click **Servers** in the Site Setup dialog box, click the **Add new Server** button ➕, type your server name, click the **Connect using list arrow**, click **FTP** if necessary, then compare your screen to Figure 21.
4. Enter the FTP Address, Username, Password, Root Directory, and Web URL information in the dialog box.

TIP You must have file and folder permissions to use FTP. The server administrator can give you this and also tell you the folder name and location you should use to publish your files.

5. Click the **Test button** to test the connection to the remote site.
6. If the connection is successful, click **Save** to close the dialog box; if it is not successful, verify that you have the correct settings, then repeat Step 5.
7. Click **Save** to close the open dialog box, click **Save** to close the Site Setup dialog box, then click **Done** to close the Manage Sites dialog box.

You set up remote access information for The Striped Umbrella website using FTP settings.

Set up a web server connection to a local or network folder

NOTE: Complete these steps if you do not have the ability to post files to an FTP site and could not complete the previous set of steps.

1. Using Windows Explorer (Win) or Finder (Mac), create a new folder on your hard drive or on a shared drive named **su_yourlastname** (e.g., if your last name is Jones, name the folder **su_jones**).

2. Switch back to Dreamweaver, open The Striped Umbrella website, then open the Manage Sites dialog box.

3. Click **The Striped Umbrella**, then click the **Edit the currently selected site button** ✎ to open the Site Setup for The Striped Umbrella dialog box.

TIP You can also double-click the site name in the Site Name box in the Files panel to open the Site Setup dialog box.

4. Click **Servers**, then click the **Add new Server button** ➕.

5. Type **SU Remote** for the Server Name, click the **Connect using list arrow**, then click **Local/Network**.

6. Click the **Browse button** ☐ next to the Server Folder text box to open the Browse For Folder dialog box, navigate to and double-click the folder you created in Step 1, then click **Select**.

7. Compare your screen to Figure 22, click **Save**, click **Save** to close the Site Setup dialog box, click **Save** to close the dialog box, then click **Done**.

You created a new folder and specified it as the remote location for The Striped Umbrella website, then set up remote access to a local or network folder.

Figure 22 *Local/Network settings in the Site Setup for The Striped Umbrella dialog box*

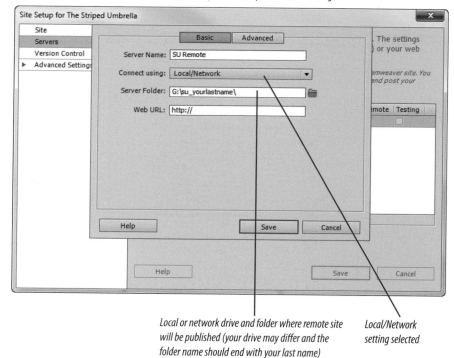

Local or network drive and folder where remote site will be published (your drive may differ and the folder name should end with your last name)

Local/Network setting selected

Testing Your Site's Usability

Once you have at least a prototype of the website ready to evaluate, it is a good idea to conduct a site usability test. This is a process that involves asking unbiased people, who are not connected to the design process, to use and evaluate the site. A comprehensive usability test includes pre-test questions, participant tasks, a post-test interview, and a post-test survey. This provides much-needed information as to how usable the site is to those unfamiliar with it. Typical questions include: "What are your overall impressions?"; "What do you like the best and the least about the site?"; and "How easy is it to navigate inside the site?" For more information, go to w3.org and search for "site usability test."

Figure 23 *Connecting to the remote site*

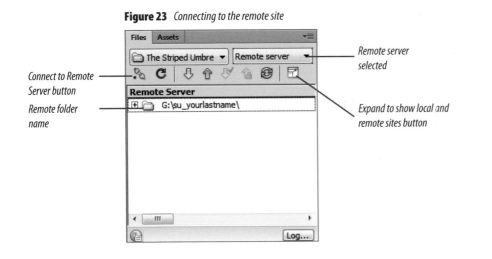

Connect to Remote
Server button

Remote folder
name

Remote server
selected

Expand to show local and
remote sites button

Figure 24 *Viewing the local and remote site folders*

Remote folder

Disconnect from
Remote Server button

Local site folder

Collapse to show only local
or remote site button

Local Files	Not...	Size	Type	Modified	Checked Out By
Site - The Striped Um...			Folder	5/27/2012 10:19 PM -	
_notes			Folder	5/27/2012 10:16 PM -	
assets			Folder	5/27/2012 10:14 PM -	
SpryAssets			Folder	2/29/2012 11:59 ... -	
about_us.html		4KB	Firefox H...	4/28/2012 1:17 PM	
activities.html		4KB	Firefox H...	4/28/2012 1:16 PM	
cafe.html		4KB	Firefox H...	5/27/2012 8:23 PM	
cruises.html		3KB	Firefox H...	4/28/2012 1:15 PM	
fishing.html		3KB	Firefox H...	4/28/2012 1:14 PM	
HTML5_twoColFi...		7KB	Cascadin...	2/16/2012 6:04 PM	
index.html		3KB	Firefox H...	5/11/2012 4:16 PM	
spa.html		5KB	Firefox H...	5/20/2012 4:11 PM	
starfish.ico		2KB	Icon	1/3/2010 11:35 PM	
su_styles.css		2KB	Cascadin...	5/1/2012 8:42 AM	

Title: The Striped Umbrella Sea Spa Date: 5/20/2012 4:11 PM Size: 5KB

View a website on a remote server

1. Click the **View list arrow** in the Files panel, click **Remote server**, then compare your screen to Figure 23.

   If you set your remote access to be a local or network folder, then the su_yourlastname folder appears in the Files panel. If your remote access is set to an FTP site, Dreamweaver connects to the host server and displays the remote folders and file.

2. Click the **Expand to show local and remote sites button** 🗗 on the Files panel to view both the Remote Site and Local Files panes. The su_yourlastname folder appears in the Remote Site portion of the expanded Files panel, as shown in Figure 24.

TIP If you don't see your remote site files, click the Disconnect from Remote Server button 🖧 or the Refresh button 🔄. If you don't see two panes, one with the remote site files and one with the local files, drag the panel border to enlarge the panel.

When the Files panel is expanded to show both the local and remote sites, the Expand to show local and remote sites button 🗗 becomes the Collapse to show only local or remote site button. 🗗 and the Connect to Remote Server button 🖧 becomes the Disconnect from Remote Server button 🖧.

You used the Files panel to set the view for The Striped Umbrella site to Remote view. You then connected to the remote server to view the remote folder you created earlier.

Upload files to a remote server

1. Click the **about_us.html file**, then click the **Put file(s) to "Remote Server" button** ⇧ on the Files panel toolbar.

   Notice that the Put File(s) to "Remote Server" button screentip includes the name of the remote server you are using. The Dependent Files dialog box opens, asking if you want to include dependent files.

2. Click **Yes**.

   The about_us file, the style sheet files, the Spry assets files, and the image files used in the about_us page are copied to the remote server. The Background File Activity dialog box appears and flashes the names of each file as they are uploaded.

3. Expand the assets folder and the SpryAssets folder in the remote site if necessary, then compare your screen to Figure 25.

   The remote site now contains the about_us page as well as the Spry files, the image files, and the external style sheet files, all of which are needed by the about_us page.

   TIP You might need to expand the su_yourlastname folder in order to view the uploaded files and folders.

   You used the Put File(s) button to upload the about_us file and all files that are dependent files of the about_us page.

Figure 25 *Remote view of the site after uploading the about_us page*

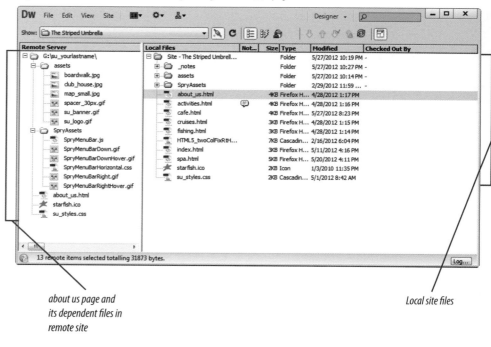

about us page and its dependent files in remote site

Local site files

Continuing to Work While Transferring Files to a Remote Server

During the process of uploading files to a remote server, there are many Dreamweaver functions that you can continue to use while you wait. For example, you can create a new site, create a new page, edit a page, add files and folders, and run reports. However, there are some functions that you cannot use while transferring files, many of which involve accessing files on the remote server or using Check In/ Check Out.

Figure 26 *Synchronize Files dialog box*

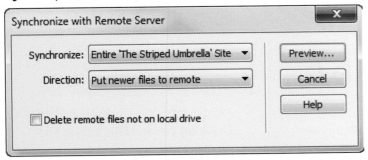

Synchronize with Remote Server

Synchronize: Entire 'The Striped Umbrella' Site ▼   Preview…

Direction: Put newer files to remote ▼   Cancel

          Help

☐ Delete remote files not on local drive

Figure 27 *Files that need to be uploaded to the remote site*

Dw Synchronize

Files: 18 will be updated

Action	File	Status
⬆ Put	_notes\activities.html.mno	
⬆ Put	assets\boats.jpg	
⬆ Put	assets\cafe_logo.gif	
⬆ Put	assets\cafe_photo.jpg	
⬆ Put	assets\chocolate_cake.jpg	

☐ Show all files

To change an action, select a file and click one of the icons below before clicking OK.

⬇ ⬆ 🗑 🚫 🔄   📇   OK   Cancel   Help

Synchronize files

1. Click the **Collapse to show only local or remote site button** 🖾 , change to Local view, then open each page in the website in Code view and locate those that are missing the link to the website favicon in the line above the code for the page title.

2. Open the index page, if necessary, then copy the code in the head content that links the favicon to the page.

3. Paste the favicon link to each of the pages you identified in Step 1, then save and close each page.

4. Click the **Synchronize button** 🔄 on the Files panel toolbar to open the Synchronize with Remote Server dialog box.

5. Click the **Synchronize list arrow**, then click **Entire 'The Striped Umbrella' Site**.

6. Click the **Direction list arrow**, click **Put newer files to remote** if necessary, then compare your screen to Figure 26.

7. Click **Preview**.

   The Background File Activity dialog box might appear and flash the names of all the files from the local version of the site that need to be uploaded to the remote site. The Synchronize dialog box, shown in Figure 27, opens and lists all the files that need to be uploaded to the remote site.

8. Click **OK**.

   All the files from the local The Striped Umbrella site are copied to the remote version of the site. If you expand the Files panel, you will notice that the remote folders are yellow (Win) or blue (Mac) and the local folders are green.

You synchronized The Striped Umbrella website files to copy all remaining files from the local site folder to the remote site folder.

Check Files
OUT AND IN

What You'll Do

In this lesson, you will use the Site Setup dialog box to enable the Check Out feature. You will then check out the cafe page, make a change to it, and then check it back in.

Managing a Website with a Team

When you work on a large website, chances are that many people will be involved in keeping the site up to date. Different individuals will need to make changes or additions to different pages of the site by adding or deleting content, changing graphics, updating information, and so on. If everyone had access to the pages at the same time, problems could arise. For instance, what if you and another team member both made edits to the same page at the same time? If you post your edited version of the file to the site after the other team member posts his edited version of the same file, the file that you upload will overwrite his version and none of his changes will be incorporated. Fortunately, you can avoid this scenario by using Dreamweaver's collaboration tools.

Checking Out and Checking In Files

Checking files in and out is similar to checking library books in and out or video/DVD rentals. No one else can access the same copy that you have checked out. Using Dreamweaver's Check Out feature ensures that team members cannot overwrite each other's pages. When this feature is enabled, only one person can work on a file at a time. To check out a file, click the file you want to work on in the Files panel, and then click the Check Out File(s) button on the Files panel toolbar. Files that you have checked out are marked with green check marks in the Files panel. Files that have been checked in are marked with padlock icons.

After you finish editing a checked-out file, you need to save and close the file, and then click the Check In button to check the file back in and make it available to other users. When a file is checked in, you cannot make edits to it unless you check it out again. Figure 28 shows the Check Out File(s) and Check In buttons on the Files panel toolbar.

Enabling the Check Out Feature

To use the Check Out feature with a team of people, you must first enable it. To turn on this feature, check the Enable file check-out check box in the Remote Server section of the Servers Advanced tab in the Site Setup dialog box. If you do not want to use this feature, you should turn it off so you won't have to check files out every time you open them.

Using Subversion Control

Another file management tool is Subversion control. A remote SVN (Apache Subversion) repository is used to maintain current and historical versions of your website files. It is used in a team environment to move, copy, and delete shared files. You can protect files from being accessed using the svn:ignore property to create a list of files that are to be ignored in a directory.

Figure 28 *Check Out File(s) and Check In buttons on the Files Panel toolbar*

Check Out File(s) button   Check In button

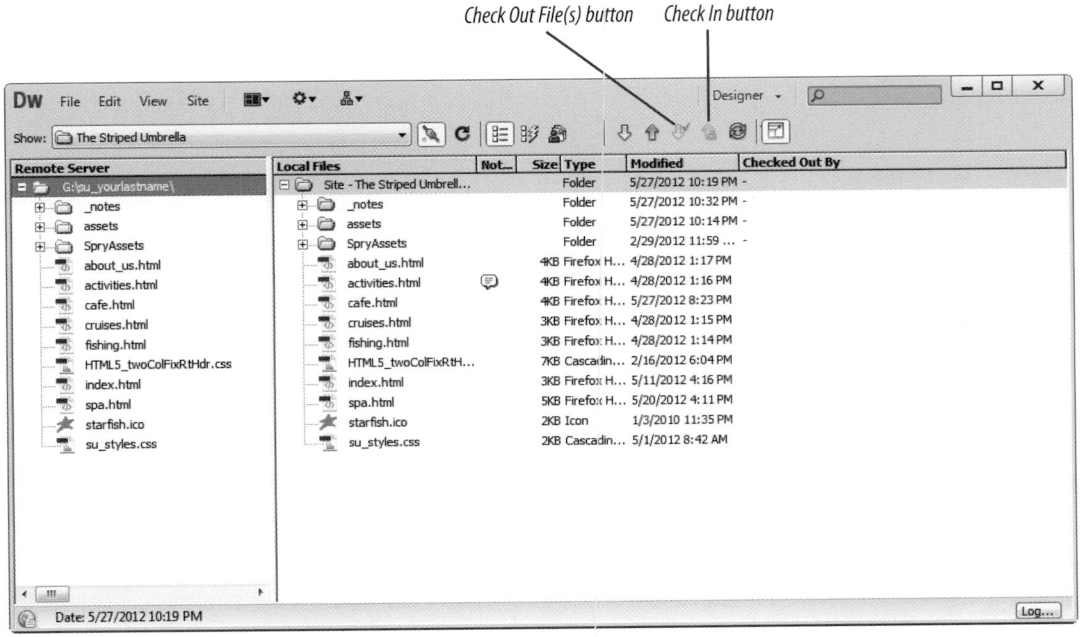

Activate the Enable file check-out feature

1. Change to expanded view in the Files panel, click **Site** on the Menu bar, click **Manage Sites** to open the Manage Sites dialog box, click **The Striped Umbrella** in the list, then click the **Edit the currently selected site button** ✎ to open the Site Setup for The Striped Umbrella dialog box.

2. Click **Servers**, select your remote server, click the **Edit existing Server button** ✎, click the **Advanced tab**, then click the **Enable file check-out check box** to select it.

3. Check the **Check out files when opening check box** to select it, if necessary.

4. Type your name in the Check-out Name text box.

5. Type your email address in the Email Address text box.

6. Compare your screen to Figure 29, click **Save** to close the open dialog box, click **Save** to close the Site Setup for The Striped Umbrella dialog box, then click **Done** to close the Manage Sites dialog box. Your dialog box will differ from the figure if you are using FTP access.

You used the Site Definition for The Striped Umbrella dialog box to enable the Check Out feature, which tells team members when you are working with a site file.

Figure 29 *Enabling the Check Out feature*

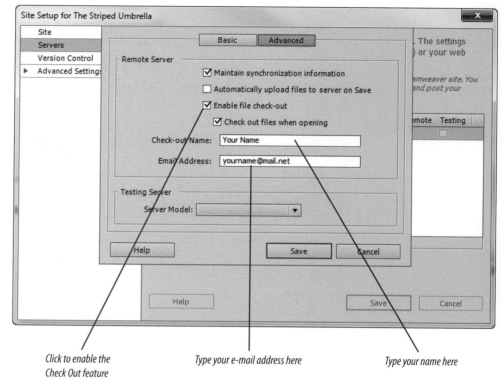

Click to enable the
Check Out feature

Type your e-mail address here

Type your name here

Figure 30 *Files panel in Local view after checking out cafe page*

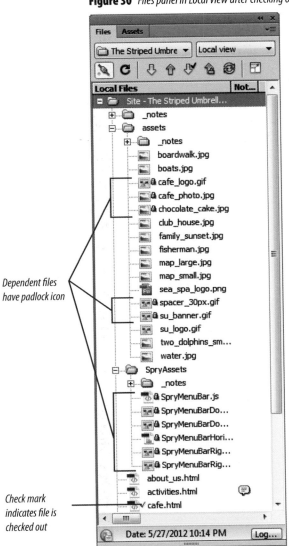

Dependent files
have padlock icon

Check mark
indicates file is
checked out

Check out a file

1. Click the **cafe page** in the Local Files list in the Files panel to select it.

2. Click the **Check Out File(s) button** 🔖 on the Files panel toolbar.

   The Dependent Files dialog box appears, asking if you want to include all files that are needed for the cafe page.

3. Click **Yes**, expand the assets and SpryAssets folders if necessary in the local site files, click the **Collapse to show only local or remote site button** 🔲, click the **View list arrow**, click **Local view** if necessary, then compare your screen to Figure 30.

   The cafe file has a check mark next to it indicating you have checked it out. The dependent files have a padlock icon, indicating that they cannot be changed as long as the cafe file is checked out.

   You checked out the cafe page so that no one else can use it while you work on it.

Check in a file

1. Open the cafe page, change the closing hour for The Cabana in the table to **8:00 p.m.**, then save your changes.

2. Close the cafe page, then click the **cafe page** in the Files panel to select it.

3. Click the **Check In button** 🔓 on the Files panel toolbar.

   The Dependent Files dialog box opens, asking if you want to include dependent files.

4. Click **Yes**, click another file in the Files panel to deselect the cafe page, then compare your screen to Figure 31.

   A padlock icon appears instead of a green check mark next to the cafe page on the Files panel. The padlock icon indicated that the file is read-only now and cannot be edited unless it is checked out.

You made a content change on the cafe page, then checked in the cafe page, making it available for others to check it out.

Figure 31 *Files panel after checking in cafe page*

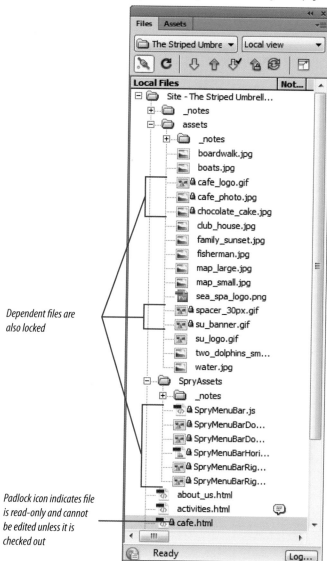

Dependent files are also locked

Padlock icon indicates file is read-only and cannot be edited unless it is checked out

Figure 32 *Files panel after turning off the read-only feature*

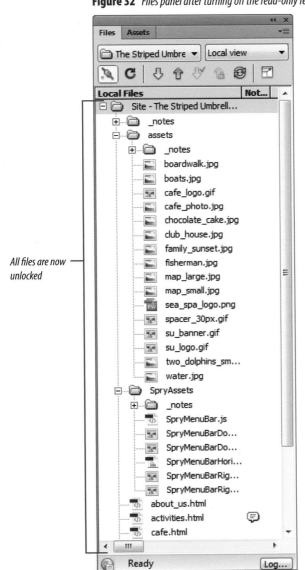

All files are now unlocked

Edit site preferences

1. Click **Site** on the Menu bar, click **Manage Sites** to open the Manage Sites dialog box, click **The Striped Umbrella** in the list, then click the **Edit the currently selected site button** ⌀ to open the Site Setup for The Striped Umbrella dialog box.

2. Click **Servers**, select your remote server, click the **Edit existing Server button** ⌀ , click the **Advanced tab**, then click the **Enable file check-out check box** to deselect it.

   Now that you understand how to use this feature, it will be easier to have this option turned off so that each time you open a page you will not have to check it out the next time you use it.

3. Click **Save** to close the open dialog box, click **Save** to close the Site Setup dialog box, then click **Done** to close the Manage Sites dialog box.

4. Right-click the **local site folder** in the Files panel, then click **Turn off Read Only** (Win) or **Unlock** (Mac).

   All files are writeable now and the padlock icons have disappeared, as shown in Figure 32.

You disabled the Enable file check-out feature and then turned off the Read-only feature for all site files.

Cloak FILES

What You'll Do

In this lesson, you will cloak the assets folder so that it is excluded from various operations, such as the Put, Get, Check In, and Check Out commands. You will also use the Site Setup dialog box to cloak all .gif files in the site.

Understanding Cloaking Files

There may be times when you want to exclude a particular file or files from being uploaded to a server. For instance, suppose you have a page that is not quite finished and needs more work before it is ready to be viewed by others. You can exclude such files by **cloaking** them, which marks them for exclusion from several commands, including Put, Get, Synchronize, Check In, and Check Out. Cloaked files are also excluded from site-wide operations, such as checking for links or updating a template or library item. You can cloak a folder or specify a type of file to cloak throughout the site.

QUICK TIP

By default, the cloaking feature is enabled. However, if for some reason it is not turned on, open the Site Setup dialog box, click Advanced Settings, click Cloaking, then click the Enable Cloaking check box.

Cloaking a Folder

In addition to cloaking a file or group of files, you might also want to cloak an entire folder. For example, if you are not concerned with replacing outdated image files, you might want to cloak the assets folder of a website to save time when synchronizing files. To cloak a folder, select the folder, click the Files panel Options button, point to Site, point to Cloaking, and then click Cloak. The folder you cloaked and all the files it contains appear with red slashes across them, as shown in Figure 33. To uncloak a folder, click the Panel options button on the Files panel, point to Site, point to Cloaking, and then click Uncloak.

QUICK TIP

To uncloak all files in a site, click the Files Panel options button, point to Site, point to Cloaking, then click Uncloak All.

Cloaking Selected File Types

There may be times when you want to cloak a particular type of file, such as a .jpg file. To cloak a particular file type, open the Site Setup dialog box, click Advanced, click Cloaking, click the Cloak files ending with check box, and then type a file extension in the text box below the check box. All files throughout the site that have the specified file extension will be cloaked.

Figure 33 *Cloaked assets folder in the Files panel*

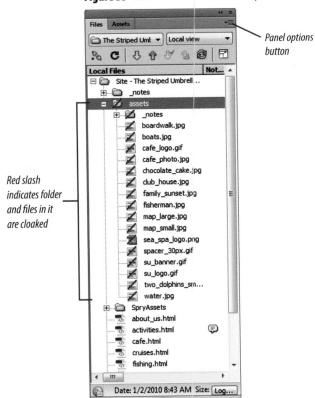

Panel options button

Red slash indicates folder and files in it are cloaked

Cloak and uncloak a folder

1. Verify that Local view is displayed in the Files panel, then open the Manage Sites dialog box.

2. Click **The Striped Umbrella** if necessary, click the **Edit the currently selected site button** ✎ to open the Site Setup for The Striped Umbrella dialog box, click **Advanced Settings**, click **Cloaking**, verify that the Enable Cloaking check box is checked, click **Save**, then click **Done**.

3. Click the **assets folder** in the Files panel, click the **Files Panel options button** ▾≡, point to **Site**, point to **Cloaking**, click **Cloak**, then compare your screen to Figure 34.

   A red slash now appears on top of the assets folder in the Files panel, indicating that all files in the assets folder are cloaked and will be excluded from putting, getting, checking in, checking out, and many other operations.

   TIP You can also cloak a folder by right-clicking (Win) or [control]-clicking (Mac) the folder, pointing to Cloaking, then clicking Cloak.

4. Right-click (Win) or [control]-click (Mac) the **assets folder**, point to **Cloaking**, then click **Uncloak**.

   The assets folder and all the files it contains no longer appear with red slashes across them, indicating they are no longer cloaked.

   You cloaked the assets folder so that this folder and all the files it contains would be excluded from many operations, including uploading and downloading files. You then uncloaked the assets folder.

Figure 34 *Assets folder after cloaking*

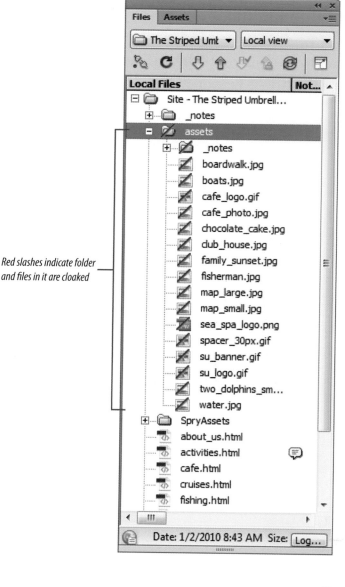

Red slashes indicate folder and files in it are cloaked

Figure 35 *Specifying a file type to cloak*

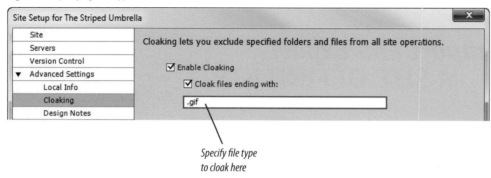

Specify file type
to cloak here

Figure 36 *Assets folder in Files panel after cloaking .gif files*

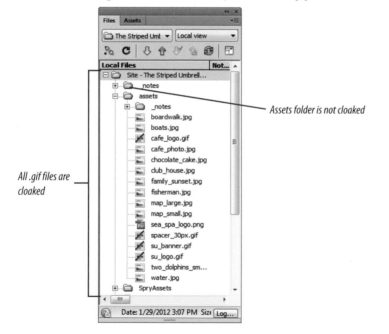

Assets folder is not cloaked

All .gif files are
cloaked

Cloak selected file types

1. Right-click (Win) or [control]-click (Mac) the **assets folder** in the Files panel, point to **Cloaking**, then click **Settings** to open the Site Setup for The Striped Umbrella dialog box with the Cloaking category selected.

2. Click the **Cloak files ending with check box**, select the text in the text box that appears, type **.gif** in the text box, then compare your screen to Figure 35.

3. Click **Save**.

   A dialog box opens, indicating that the site cache will be recreated.

4. Click **OK**, expand the assets folder if necessary, then compare your screen to Figure 36.

   All of the .gif files in the assets folder appear with red slashes across them, indicating that they are cloaked. Notice that the assets folder is not cloaked.

5. Click the **local site folder** in the Files panel, right-click, point to **Cloaking**, click **Uncloak All**, then click **Yes** to close the warning message.

   All files are uncloaked now and will not be excluded from any site commands.

You cloaked all the .gif files in The Striped Umbrella website. You then uncloaked all files.

Import and Export
A SITE DEFINITION

What You'll Do

In this lesson, you will export the site definition file for The Striped Umbrella website. You will then import The Striped Umbrella website.

Exporting a Site Definition

When you work on a website for a long time, it's likely that at some point you will want to move it to another machine or share it with other collaborators who will help you maintain it. When you move a site, you need to move its site definition. The **site definition** for a website contains important information about the site, including its URL, preferences that you've specified, and other secure information, such as login and password information. You can use the Export command to export the site definition file to another location. The Export command creates a file with an .ste file extension. To do this, open the Manage Sites dialog box, click the site you want to export, and then click Export currently selected site. Because the site definition file contains password information that you will want to keep secret from other site users, you should never save the site definition file in the website. Instead, save it in an external folder.

Importing a Site Definition

If you want to be able to access the site settings in a website that someone else has created, you can import the site definition file once you have the necessary .ste file. To do this, click Import Site in the Manage Sites dialog box to open the Import Site dialog box, navigate to the .ste file you want to import, then click Open.

Figure 37 *Saving The Striped Umbrella.ste file in the su_site_definition folder*

Dw Export Site					×

Save in: su_site_definition

Name	Date modified	Type

No items match your search.

Recent Places

Desktop

Libraries

Computer

Network

File name: The Striped Umbrella.ste

Save as type: Site definition files (*.ste)

Save

Cancel

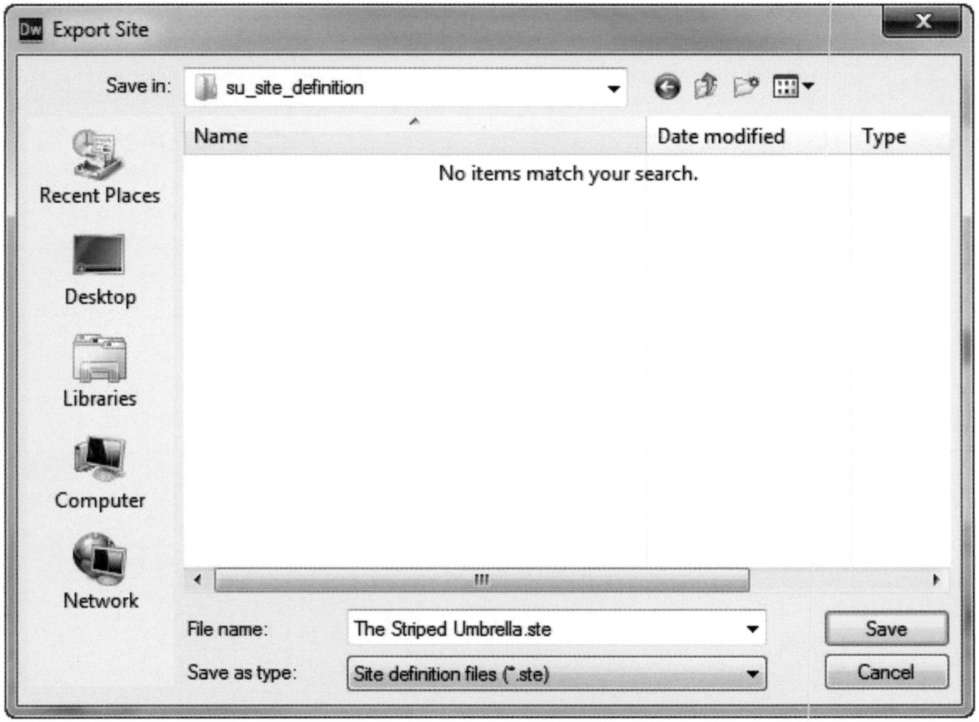

Export a site definition

1. Use Windows Explorer (Win) or Finder (Mac) to create two new folders on your hard drive or external drive named **su_site_definition**.

2. Switch back to Dreamweaver, open the Manage Sites dialog box, click **The Striped Umbrella**, then click the **Export the currently selected site(s) button** 🔁 to open the Export Site dialog box.

TIP If you see a message asking if you are exporting the site to back up your settings or to share your settings with other users, choose the Back up my settings option, then click OK.

3. Navigate to and double-click to open the **su_site_definition folder** that you created in Step 1, as shown in Figure 37, click **Save**, then click **Done**.

You used the Export command to create the site definition file and saved it in the su_site_definition folder.

Import a site definition

1. Open the Manage Sites dialog box, click **The Striped Umbrella**, then click **Import Site** to open the Import Site dialog box.

2. Navigate to the su_site_definition folder, compare your screen to Figure 38, select **The Striped Umbrella.ste**, then click **Open**.

   A dialog box opens and says that a site named The Striped Umbrella already exists. It will name the imported site The Striped Umbrella 2 so that it has a different name.

3. Click **OK**.

4. Click **The Striped Umbrella 2** if necessary, click the **Edit the currently selected site(s) button** ✐ , then compare your screen to Figure 39.

   The settings show that The Striped Umbrella 2 site has the same local site folder and default images folder as The Striped Umbrella site. Both of these settings are specified in The Striped Umbrella. ste file that you imported. Importing a site in this way makes it possible for multiple users with different computers to work on the same site.

   TIP Make sure you know who is responsible for which files to keep from overwriting the wrong files when they are published. The Synchronize Files and Check In/Check Out features are good procedures to use with multiple designers.

5. Click **Save**, click **OK** to close the warning message, then click **Done**.

   TIP If a dialog box opens warning that the local site folder chosen is the same as the folder for the site "The Striped Umbrella," click OK. Remember that you only import the site settings when you import a site definition. You are not importing any of the website files.

You imported The Striped Umbrella.ste file and created a new site, The Striped Umbrella 2.

Figure 38 *Import Site dialog box*

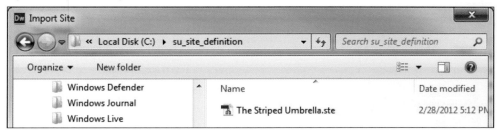

Figure 39 *Site Definition for The Striped Umbrella 2 dialog box*

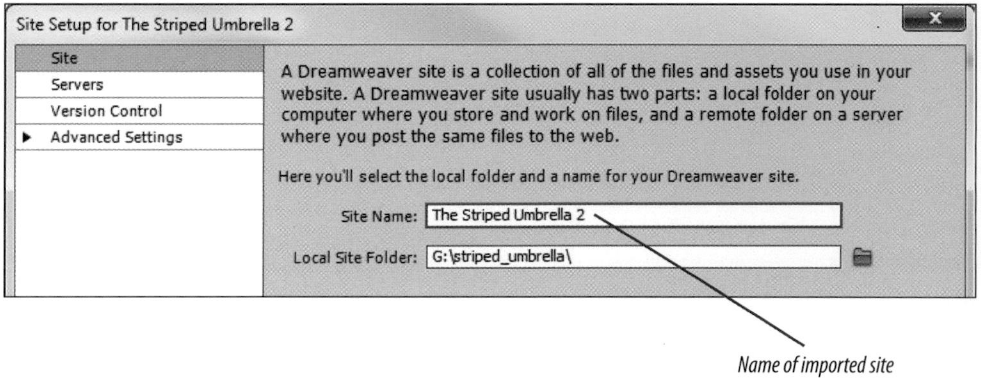

Name of imported site

Figure 40 *Viewing The Striped Umbrella 2 website files*

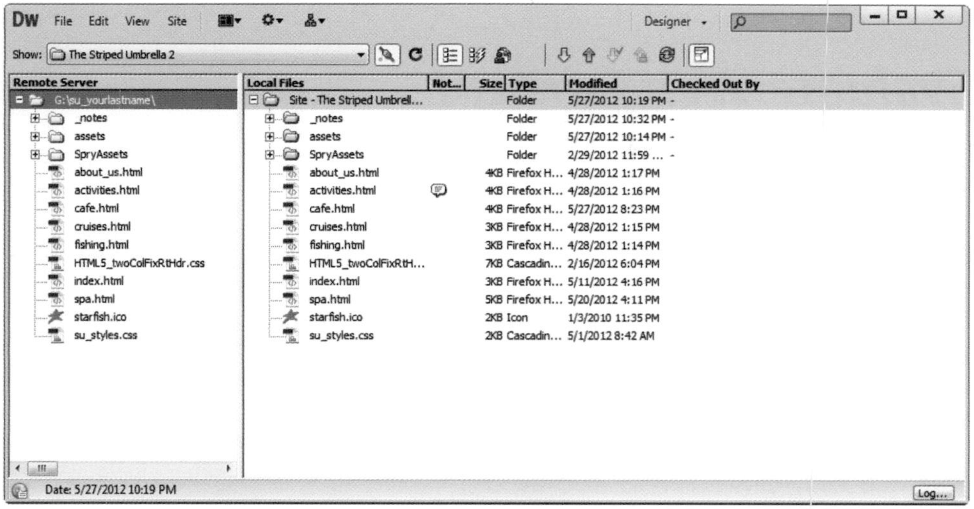

POWER USER SHORTCUTS

To do this:	Use this shortcut:
Get	[Ctrl][Shift][D] (Win) or ⌘ [Shift][D] (Mac)
Check Out	[Ctrl][Alt][Shift][D] (Win) or ⌘ [opt] [Shift][D] (Mac)
Put	[Ctrl][Shift][U] (Win) or ⌘ [Shift][U] (Mac)
Check In	[Ctrl][Alt][Shift][U] (Win) or ⌘ [opt] [Shift][U] (Mac)
Check Links	[Shift][F8] (Win) or [fn][shift][F8] (Mac)
Check Links Sitewide	[Ctrl][F8] (Win) or [fn] ⌘ [F8] (Mac)

© Cengage Learning 2013

View the imported site

1. Click the **Expand to show local and remote sites button** 🖿 on the Files panel toolbar to expand the Files panel.

2. Expand the local site folder in the Local Files pane to view the contents, if necessary.

3. Click the **Refresh button** ⟳ to view the files in the Remote Site pane.

   As shown in Figure 40, the site is identical to the original The Striped Umbrella site, except the name has been changed to The Striped Umbrella 2.

TIP If you don't see your remote site files, click the Connect to Remote Server button.

4. Click the **Collapse to show only local or remote site button** 🖿 to collapse the Files panel.

5. Open the Manage Sites dialog box, verify that The Striped Umbrella 2 site is selected, click the **Delete the currently selected site(s) button** —, click **Yes** in the warning dialog box, then click **Done** to delete The Striped Umbrella 2 website.

   This does not delete all of the files that were created; it only removes the site from Dreamweaver's site management list.

6. Close all open pages, then close Dreamweaver.

You viewed the expanded Files panel for The Striped Umbrella 2 website, then deleted The Striped Umbrella 2 website.

Evaluate Web Content
FOR LEGAL USE

What You'll Do

Library of Congress website – www.loc.gov

In this lesson, you will examine copyright issues in the context of using content gathered from sources such as the Internet.

Can I Use Downloaded Media?

The Internet has made it possible to locate compelling and media-rich content to use in websites. A person who has learned to craft searches can locate a multitude of interesting material, such as graphics, animations, sounds, and text. But just because you can find it easily does not mean that you can use it however you want or under any circumstance. Learning about copyright law can help you decide whether or how to use content created and published by someone other than yourself.

Understanding Intellectual Property

Intellectual property is a product resulting from human creativity. It can include inventions, movies, songs, designs, clothing, and so on.

The purpose of copyright law is to promote progress in society, not expressly to protect the rights of copyright owners. However, the vast majority of work you might want to download and use in a project is protected by either copyright or trademark law.

Copyright protects the particular and tangible *expression* of an idea, not the idea itself.

If you wrote a story using the idea of aliens crashing in Roswell, New Mexico, no one could copy or use your story without permission. However, anyone could write a story using a similar plot or characters—the *idea* of aliens crashing in Roswell is not copyright-protected. Generally, copyright lasts for the life of the author plus 70 years.

Trademark protects an image, word, slogan, symbol, or design used to identify goods or services. For example, the Nike swoosh, Disney characters, or the shape of a classic Coca-Cola bottle are works protected by trademark. Trademark protection lasts for 10 years with 10-year renewal terms, lasting indefinitely provided the trademark is in active use.

What Exactly Does the Copyright Owner Own?

Copyright attaches to a work as soon as you create it; you do not have to register it with the U.S. Copyright Office. A copyright owner has a "bundle" of six rights, consisting of:

1) reproduction (including downloading)
2) creation of **derivative works** (for example, a movie version of a book)
3) distribution to the public

4) public performance
5) public display
6) public performance by digital audio transmission of sound recordings

By default, only a copyright holder can create a derivative work of his or her original by transforming or adapting it.

Understanding Fair Use

The law builds in limitations to copyright protection. One limitation to copyright is **fair use**. Fair use allows limited use of copyright-protected work. For example, you could excerpt short passages of a film or song for a class project or parody a television show. Determining if fair use applies to a work depends on the *purpose* of its use, the *nature* of the copyrighted work, *how much* you want to copy, and the *effect* on the market or value of the work. However, there is no clear formula on what constitutes fair use. It is always decided on a case-by-case basis.

How Do I Use Work Properly?

Being a student doesn't mean you can use any amount of any work for class. On the other hand, the very nature of education means you need to be able to use or reference different work in your studies. There are many situations that allow you to use protected work.

In addition to applying a fair use argument, you can obtain permission, pay a fee, use work that does not have copyright protection, or use work that has a flexible copyright

license, where the owner has given the public permission to use the work in certain ways. For more information about open-access licensing, visit creativecommons.org. Work that is no longer protected by copyright is in the **public domain**; anyone can use it however they wish for any purpose. In general, the photos and other media on Federal government websites are in the public domain.

Understanding Licensing Agreements

Before you decide whether to use media you find on a website, you must decide whether you can comply with its licensing agreement.

A **licensing agreement** is the permission given by a copyright holder that conveys the right to use the copyright holder's work under certain conditions.

Websites have rules that govern how a user may use its text and media, known as **terms of use**. Figures 41, 42, and 43 are great examples of clear terms of use for the Library of Congress website.

A site's terms of use do not override your right to apply fair use. Also, someone cannot compile public domain images in a website and then claim they own them or dictate how

Figure 41 *Library of Congress home page*

Library of Congress website – www.loc.gov

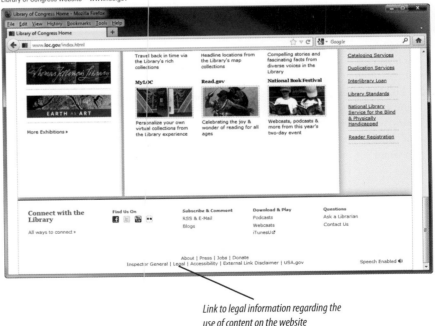

Link to legal information regarding the use of content on the website

the images can be used. Conversely, someone can erroneously state in their terms of use that you can use work on the site freely, but they may not know the work's copyright status. The burden is on you to research the veracity of anyone claiming you can use work.

Obtaining Permission or a License

The **permissions process** is specific to what you want to use (text, photographs, music, trademarks, merchandise, and so on) and how you want to use it (school term paper, personal website, fabric pattern). How you want to use the work determines the level and scope of permissions you need to secure. The fundamentals, however, are the same. Your request should contain the following:

- Your full name, address, and complete contact information.
- A specific description of your intended use. Sometimes including a sketch, storyboard, wireframe, or link to a website is helpful.
- A signature line for the copyright holder.
- A target date when you would like the copyright holder to respond. This can be important if you're working under deadline.

Posting a Copyright Notice

The familiar © symbol or "Copyright" is no longer required to indicate copyright, nor does it automatically register your work, but it does serve a useful purpose. When you post or publish it, you are stating clearly to those who may not know anything about copyright law that this work is claimed by you and is not in the public domain. Your case is made even stronger if someone violates your copyright

Figure 42 *Library of Congress website legal page*
Library of Congress website – www.loc.gov

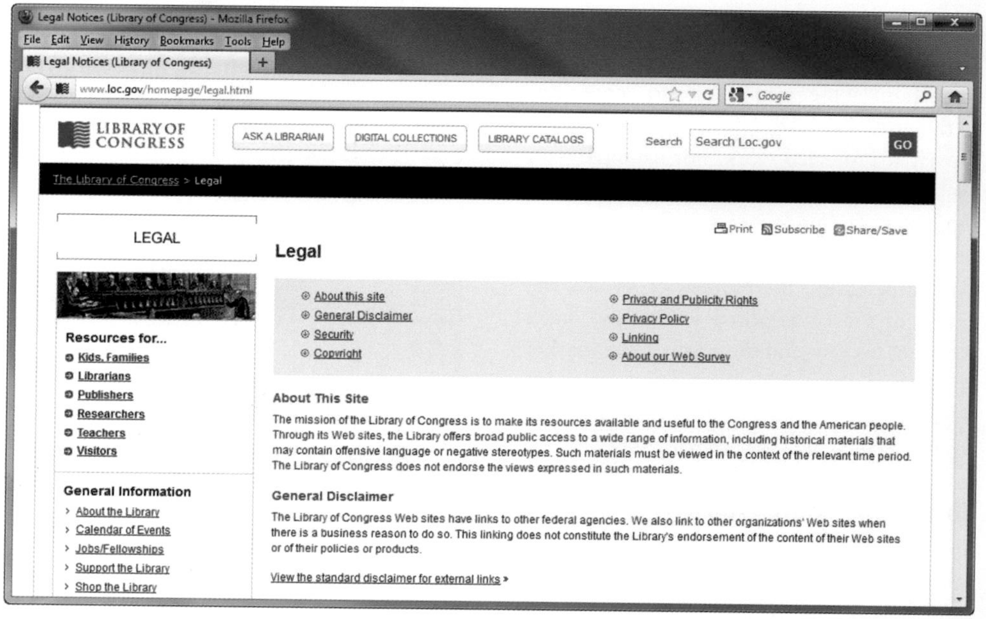

Managing a Web Server and Files

and your notice is clearly visible. That way, a violator can never claim ignorance of the law as an excuse for infringing. Common notification styles include:

Copyright 2015
Cengage Learning
or
© 2015 Cengage Learning

Giving proper attribution for text excerpts is a must; giving attribution for media is excellent practice, but is never a substitute for applying a fair use argument, buying a license, or simply getting permission.

You must provide proper citation for materials you incorporate into your own work, such as the following:

References
Waxer, Barbara M., and Baum, Marsha L. 2006. *Internet Surf and Turf—The Essential Guide to Copyright, Fair Use, and Finding Media*. Boston: Thomson Course Technology.

This expectation applies even to unsigned material and material that does not display the copyright symbol (©). Moreover, the expectation applies just as certainly to ideas you summarize or paraphrase as to words you quote verbatim.

Guidelines have been written by the American Psychological Association (APA) to establish an editorial style to be used to present written material. These guidelines include the way citations are referenced. Here's a list of the elements that make up an APA-style citation of web-based resources:

- Author's name (if known)
- Date of publication or last revision (if known), in parentheses
- Title of document
- Title of complete work or website (if applicable), underlined
- URL
- Date of access, in parentheses

Following is an example of how you would reference the APA Home page on the Reference page of your paper:

APA Style.org. (Retrieved August 22, 2014), from APA Online website: http://www.apastyle.org/electext.html.

There are APA styles that are used for other sources of text such as magazines, journals, newspaper articles, blogs, and email messages. Here's a list of the elements that make up an APA-style citation of images, sounds, or video:

- Name of the researching organization
- Date of publication
- Caption or description
- Brief explanation of what type of data is there and in what form it appears (shown in brackets)
- Project name and retrieval information.

Another set of guidelines used by many schools and university and commercial presses is the Modern Language Association (MLA) style. For more information, go to mla.org.

Figure 43 *Library of Congress website copyright information*
Library of Congress website – www.loc.gov

About Copyright and the Collections

Whenever possible, the Library of Congress provides factual information about copyright owners and related matters in the catalog records, finding aids and other texts that accompany collections. As a publicly supported institution, the Library generally does not own rights in its collections. Therefore, it does not charge permission fees for use of such material and generally does not grant or deny permission to publish or otherwise distribute material in its collections. Permission and possible fees may be required from the copyright owner independently of the Library. It is the researcher's obligation to determine and satisfy copyright or other use restrictions when publishing or otherwise distributing materials found in the Library's collections. Transmission or reproduction of protected items beyond that allowed by fair use requires the written permission of the copyright owners. Researchers must make their own assessments of rights in light of their intended use.

If you have any more information about an item you've seen on our website or if you are the copyright owner and believe our website has not properly attributed your work to you or has used it without permission, we want to hear from you. Please contact OGC@loc.gov with your contact information and a link to the relevant content.

View more information about copyright law from the U.S. Copyright Office »

Present a
WEBSITE TO A CLIENT

What You'll Do

Copyright © 2008, 2012 WireframeSketcher.com

In this lesson, you will explore options for presenting a website to a client at the completion of a project.

Are You Ready to Present Your Work?

Before you present a website to a client as a finished project, you should do a final check on some important items. First, do all your final design and development decisions reflect your client's goals and requirements? Does the website not only fulfill your client's goals and requirements, but those of the intended audience as well? Second, did you follow good web development practices? Did you check your pages against your wireframes as you developed them? Did you check each page against current accessibility standards? Did you run all necessary technical tests, such as validating the code, and searching for missing alternate text or missing page titles? Did you verify that all external and internal links work correctly? Third, did your final delivery date and budget meet the timeframe and budget you originally promised the client?

If you find that you did spend more time on the site than you expected to, determine if it was because you underestimated the amount of work it would take, ran into unforeseen technical problems, or because the client changed the requirements or increased the scope of the project as it went along. If you underestimated the project or ran into unexpected difficulties from causes other than the client, you usually cannot expect the client to make up the difference without a prior agreement. No client wants surprises at the end of a project, so it's best to communicate frequently and let the client know the status of all site elements as you go.

If the client changes the project scope, make sure you discuss the implication of this with the client. Ideally, you have made the client aware of any schedule or budget changes at the time they began to occur, and the client expects that your estimate will grow by a predictable, agreed-upon amount.

Client communication, both at the beginning of a project and throughout a project, is critical to a successful web design and a solid customer relationship. In building a house, a good architect makes an effort to get to know and understand a new client before beginning a house design. The design must be functional and meet the client's checklist of requirements, but it must also fit the client's personality and taste. The final structure must continue to meet those needs; the same is true of a website.

Some clients have a difficult time looking at architectural drawings and visualizing what the home will look like, so architects use different methods to communicate their design. Some use scale mockups, 3-D renderings, or photos of similarly styled homes to help the client visualize what their home will look like when completed. Web designers use similar strategies. You may be capable of building a great website, but you must communicate with the client from the beginning of the project to set and satisfy client expectations. Without this mutual understanding, the project's successful completion will be at risk. It is much less expensive to make changes and adjustments at the beginning of a project, and as changes occur, rather than close to completion. Communication is key.

What Is the Best Way to Present Your Work?

Ideally, you presented some form of prototype of the website at the beginning of the development process. You may have chosen to use low-fidelity wireframes such as one created in Microsoft PowerPoint or Adobe Photoshop. Or you may have used a high-fidelity wireframe that is interactive and multidimensional such as OverSight, ProtoShare, or WireframeSketcher, as shown in Figure 44. To communicate with your client and ensure a mutual understanding of the project, you could also use **BaseCamp**, a web-based project collaboration tool that many companies use. There is a monthly fee

for using it, based on the number of projects you are running and your storage needs. You can use BaseCamp throughout the project cycle, not just at the end. To present the final project, consider publishing the site to a server and sending the client a link to view the completed website. Creating PDFs of the site and sending them to the client for approval is another possible method.

Another communication option is to invite the client to your office and do a full walkthrough of the site with them, which offers them a chance to ask questions. This is probably one of the best options if it is feasible. If you have taken the time to build a relationship of trust over the project, neither side should expect unpleasant surprises at the end.

Figure 44 *WireframeSketcher website*
Copyright © 2008, 2012 WireframeSketcher.com

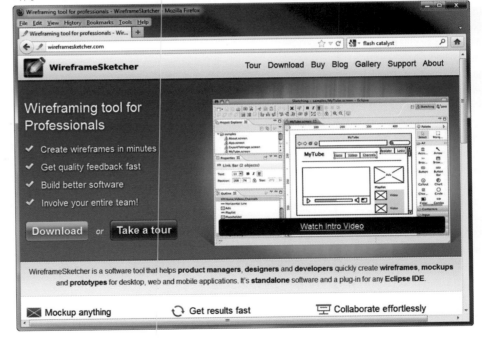

Perform website maintenance.

1. Open the Blooms & Bulbs website, then re-create the site cache.
2. Use the Link Checker panel to check for broken links, then fix any broken links that appear.
3. Use the Link Checker to check for orphaned files. If any orphaned files appear in the report, take steps to link them to appropriate pages or remove them.
4. Use the Assets panel to check for non-websafe colors. Evaluate any non-websafe colors you find to see if they affect your page content.
5. Run an Untitled Documents report for the entire local site. If the report lists any pages that have no titles, add page titles to the untitled pages, and edit any titles if they seem incomplete. Run the report again to verify that all pages have page titles.
6. Run a report to look for missing alternate text. Add alternate text to any graphics that need it, then run the report again to verify that all images contain alternate text.
7. Submit the blooms_styles.css file for CSS3 validation and correct any errors that are found.
8. Validate the workshops page for HTML5 markup and correct any errors that are found.
9. Verify that the Design Notes preference is enabled and add a Design Note to the workshops page as follows: **Shoot a video of the hanging baskets class to add to the page**. Add the status **needs attention**, add the current date, and check the Show when file is opened option.

Publish a website and transfer files.

1. Set up web server access for the Blooms & Bulbs website on an FTP server or a local/network server (whichever is available to you) using blooms_yourlastname as the remote folder name.
2. View the Blooms & Bulbs remote site in the Files panel.
3. Upload the water_lily.jpg file to the remote site, then view the remote site.
4. Add the code that links the favicon to the head content of any pages in the site that do not have it.
5. Synchronize all files in the Blooms & Bulbs website, so that all files from the local site are uploaded to the remote site.

Check files out and in.

1. Enable the Enable file check-out feature.
2. Check out the plants page and all dependent pages.
3. Open the plants page, change the heading to "Featured Spring Plants: Roses!", then save the file.
4. Check in the plants page and all dependent files.
5. Disable the Enable file check-out feature.
6. Turn off read only (Win) or Unlock (Mac) for the entire site.

Cloak files.

1. Verify that cloaking is enabled in the Blooms & Bulbs website.
2. Cloak the assets folder, then uncloak it.
3. Cloak all the .jpg files in the Blooms & Bulbs website, then expand the assets folder if necessary to view the cloaked files in the Files panel.
4. Uncloak the .jpg files.

Import and export a site definition.

1. Create a new folder named **blooms_site_definition** on your hard drive or external drive.
2. Export the Blooms & Bulbs site definition to the blooms_site_definition folder.
3. Import the Blooms & Bulbs site definition to create a new site called **Blooms & Bulbs 2**.
4. Make sure that all files from the Blooms & Bulbs website appear in the Files panel for the imported site, then compare your screen to Figure 45.
5. Remove the Blooms & Bulbs 2 site.
6. Close all open files.

Figure 45 *Completed Skills Review*

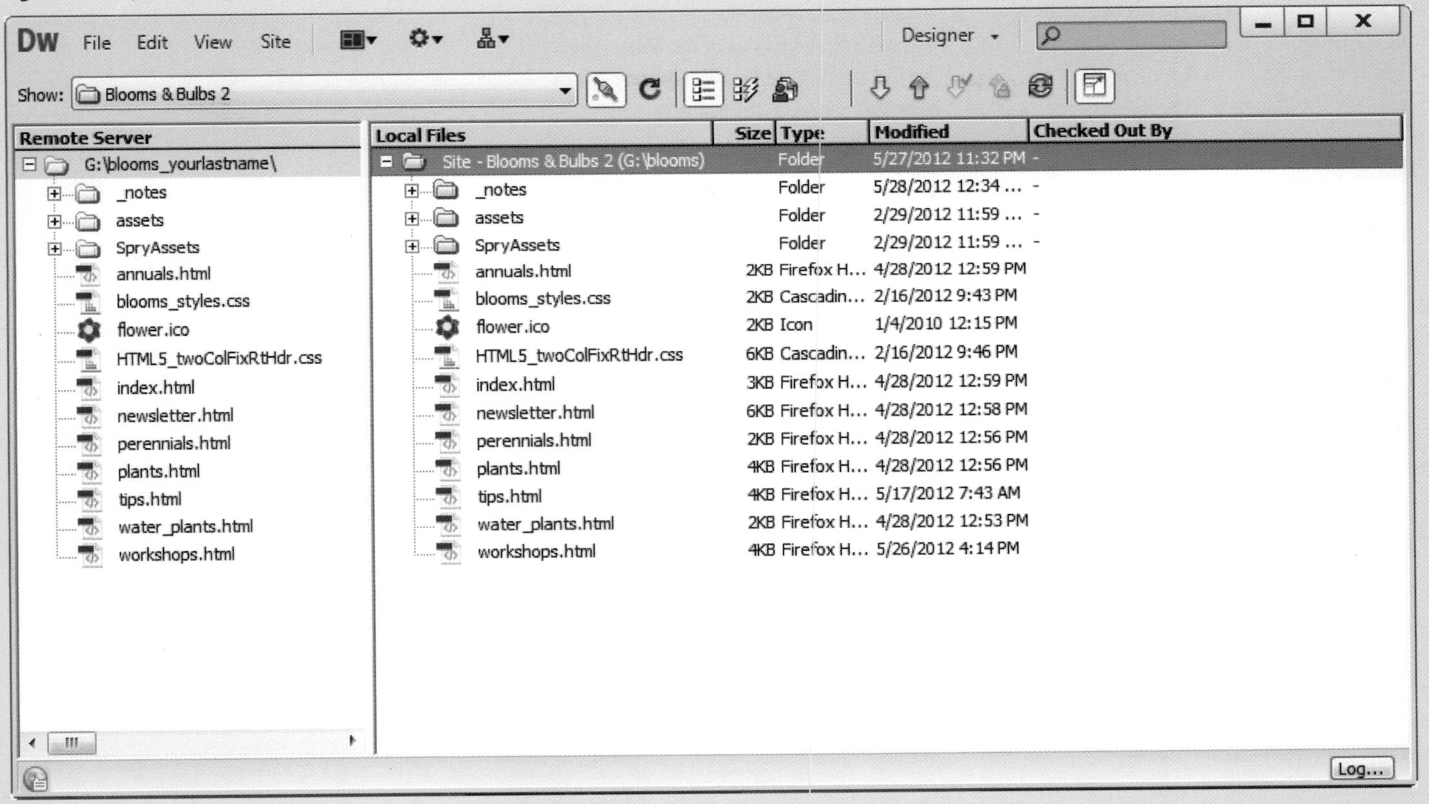

In this Project Builder, you publish the TripSmart website that you have developed throughout this book to a local/network folder. Thomas Howard, the owner, has asked that you publish the site to a local folder as a backup location. You first run several reports on the site, specify the remote settings for the site, upload files to the remote site, check files out and in, and cloak files. Finally, you export and import the site definition.

1. Use the TripSmart website that you began in Project Builder 1 in Chapter 1 and developed in previous chapters.

2. Use the Link Checker panel to check for broken links, then fix any broken links that appear.

3. Use the Link Checker to check for orphaned files. If any orphaned files appear in the report, take steps to link them to appropriate pages or remove them.

4. Use the Assets panel to check for non-websafe colors. If you find any, evaluate whether or not they pose a problem for any of the pages.

5. Run an Untitled Documents report for the entire local site. If the report lists any pages that lack titles, add page titles to the untitled pages. Run the report again to verify that all pages have page titles.

6. Run a report to look for missing alternate text. Add alternate text to any graphics that need it, then run the report again to verify that all images contain alternate text.

7. Submit the tripsmart_styles.css file for CSS3 validation and correct any errors that are found.

8. Validate the catalog page for HTML5 markup and correct any errors that are found.

9. Enable the Design Notes preference, if necessary, and add a design note to the tours page as follows: **Add content and a video of the Galapagos sea lions**. Add the current date, the status **needs attention** and check the Show when file is opened option.

10. If you did not do so in Project Builder 1 in Chapter 1, use the Site Definition dialog box to set up web server access for a remote site using a local or network folder.

11. Upload the index page and all dependent files to the remote site.

12. View the remote site to make sure that all files uploaded correctly.

13. Add the code that links the favicon to the head content of any pages in the site that do not have it.

14. Synchronize the files so that all other files on the local TripSmart site are uploaded to the remote site.

15. Enable the Enable file check-out feature.

16. Check out the index page in the local site and all dependent files.

17. Open the index page, close the index page, then check in the index page and all dependent pages.

18. Disable the Enable file check-out feature, then turn off the read-only status (Win) or unlock (Mac) for the entire site.

19. Cloak all .jpg files in the website.

20. Export the site definition to a new folder named **tripsmart_site_definition**.

21. Import the TripSmart.ste file to create a new site named TripSmart 2.

22. Expand the assets folder in the Files panel if necessary, then compare your screen to Figure 46.

23. Remove the TripSmart 2 site.

24. Uncloak all files in the TripSmart site, then close any open files.

Figure 46 *Sample completed Project Builder 1*

In this Project Builder, you finish your work on the Carolyne's Creations website. You are ready to publish the website to a remote server and transfer all the files from the local site to the remote site. First, you run several reports to make sure the website is in good shape. Next, you enable the Enable file check-out feature so that other staff members may collaborate on the site. Finally, you export and import the site definition file.

1. Use the Carolyne's Creations website that you began in Project Builder 1 in Chapter 1 and developed in previous chapters.

2. If you did not do so in Project Builder 2 in Chapter 1, use the Site Definition dialog box to set up web server access for a remote site using either an FTP site or a local or network folder.

3. Run reports for broken links and orphaned files, correcting any errors that you find.

4. Run reports for untitled documents and missing alt text, correcting any errors that you find.

5. Submit the cc_styles.css file for CSS3 validation and correct any errors that are found.

6. Validate the catering page for HTML5 markup and correct any errors that are found.

7. Upload the classes.html page and all dependent files to the remote site.

8. View the remote site to make sure that all files uploaded correctly.

9. Synchronize the files so that all other files on the local Carolyne's Creations site are uploaded to the remote site.

10. Enable the Enable file check-out feature.

11. Check out the classes page and all its dependent files.

12. Open the classes page, then change the price of the adult class to **$45.00**.

13. Save your changes, close the page, then check in the classes page and all dependent pages.

14. Disable the Enable file check-out feature, then turn off read only for the entire site.

15. Export the site definition to a new folder named **cc_site_definition**.

16. Import the Carolyne's Creations.ste file to create a new site named Carolyne's Creations 2.

17. Expand the local site folder in the Files panel if necessary, compare your screen to Figure 47, then remove the Carolyne's Creations2 site.

Figure 47 *Sample completed Project Builder 2*

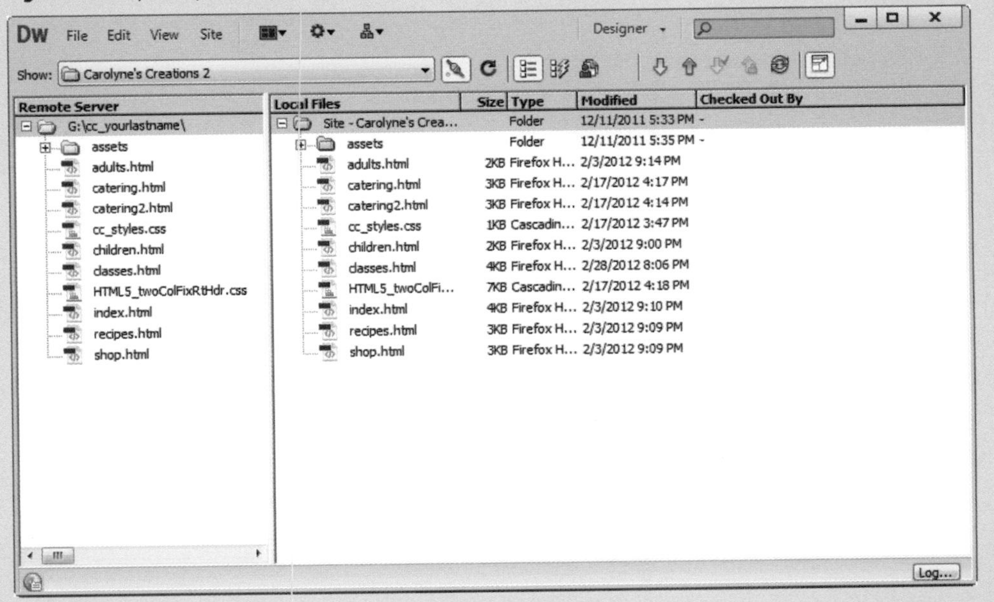

Throughout this book you have used Dreamweaver to create and develop several websites that contain different elements, many of which are found in popular commercial websites. For instance, Figure 48 shows the National Park Service website, which contains photos and information on all the national parks in the United States. This website contains many types of interactive elements, such as image maps and rollovers—all of which you learned to create in this book.

1. Connect to the Internet, then go to the National Park Service website at nps.gov.

2. Spend some time exploring the pages of this site to familiarize yourself with its elements.

3. Type a list of all the elements in this site that you have learned how to create in this book. After each item, write a short description of where and how the element is used in the site.

4. Click the link for the Site Index in the menu bar at the bottom of the page. Describe the information provided with the site index.

5. Click the Accessibility link, then click the Text Sizes links and describe how the page appearance changes as you click each option. How do you think this feature adds to the page accessibility?

6. Print the home page and one or two other pages that contain some of the elements you described and attach it to your list.

Figure 48 *Design Project*
National Park website – www.nps.gov

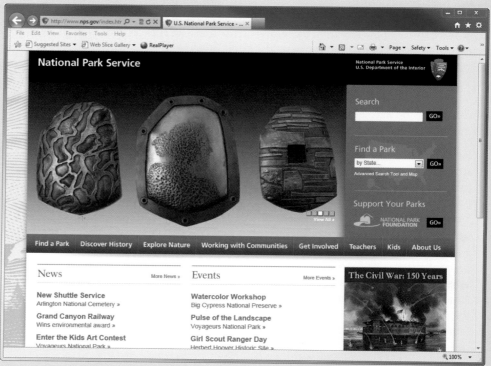

Managing a Web Server and Files

In this project, you will finish your work on the website that you created and developed throughout this book. You publish your site to a remote server or local or network folder.

1. Before you begin the process of publishing your website to a remote server, make sure that it is ready for public viewing. Use Figure 49 to assist you in making sure your website is complete. If you find problems, make the necessary changes to finalize the site.

2. Decide where to publish your site. The folder where you will publish your site can be either an FTP site or a local/network folder. If you are publishing to an FTP site, be sure to write down all the information you will need to publish to the site, including the URL of the FTP host, the directory on the FTP server where you will publish your local site folder, and the login and password information.

3. Use the Site Setup dialog box to specify the remote settings for the site using the information that was decided upon in Step 2.

4. Transfer one of the pages and its dependent files to the remote site, then view the remote site to make sure the appropriate files were transferred.

5. Synchronize the files so that all the remaining local pages and dependent files are uploaded to the remote site.

6. Enable the Enable file check-out feature.

7. Check out one of the pages. Open the checked-out page, make a change to it, save the change, close the page, then check the page back in.

8. Cloak a particular file type.

9. Export the site definition for the site to a new folder on your hard drive or on an external drive.

10. Close any open pages, then exit Dreamweaver.

Figure 49 *Portfolio Project*

Website Checklist

1. Are you satisfied with the content and appearance of every page?
2. Are all paths for all links and images correct?
3. Does each page have a title?
4. Does the stylesheet pass CSS3 validation?
5. Do all images have appropriate alternate text?
6. Have you eliminated any orphaned files?
7. Have you deleted any unnecessary files?
8. Have you viewed all pages using at least two different browsers?
9. Does the home page have keywords and a description?
10. Is all text based on a CSS style?

CHAPTER 1 GETTING STARTED WITH FLASH

1. Understand the Flash workspace
2. Open a document and play a Flash movie
3. Create and save a Flash movie
4. Work with the Timeline
5. Distribute a Flash movie/application
6. Plan an application

CHAPTER 1

GETTING STARTED WITH FLASH

Introduction

Adobe has created the Adobe® Flash® Platform, which is an integrated set of tools and technologies used to develop and deliver compelling applications running on computers, websites, and mobile devices. The Adobe Flash Platform includes Adobe Catalyst used to create interactive designs, Flash Builder and Flex both used for programming, Flash Player used to display Flash content on the Web, and Adobe AIR used to deploy Flash applications on desktops, mobile devices, and televisions. At the heart of the Adobe Flash Platform is Adobe Flash Professional.

Adobe Flash Professional CS6 is a development tool that allows you to create compelling interactive applications, which often include animation. Flash is an excellent program for creating applications that are used for the following: **entertainment** (such as, multiplayer social games running on Facebook); **business** (such as, stock market analytic tools); **education** (such as, interactive museum exhibits); **government** (such as, interactive national park tours); and **personal use** (such as, GPS-based interactive street maps).

Flash is popular with developers because they can create these applications and deliver them in multiple ways: on desktop computers, smartphones, tablets, and even TVs. An example is Sesame Street. Using Flash technologies Sesame Street developers were able to repurpose their television content to create games and other applications that run on computers, smartphones (iPhone, Windows, and Android models), and tablets such as the iPad. Flash is helping them leverage resources, both personnel and content, because the ability to create one application and use it on several devices saves development time and money.

Flash has become the standard for both professional and casual application developers, as well as for web developers. It is the leading program for creating animations, such as product demonstrations and banner ads, used in websites. It has exceptional drawing tools and tools for creating interactive controls, such as navigation buttons and menus. Furthermore, it provides the ability to incorporate sounds and video easily into an application. This chapter provides an overview of Flash and presents concepts that are covered in more detail in later chapters.

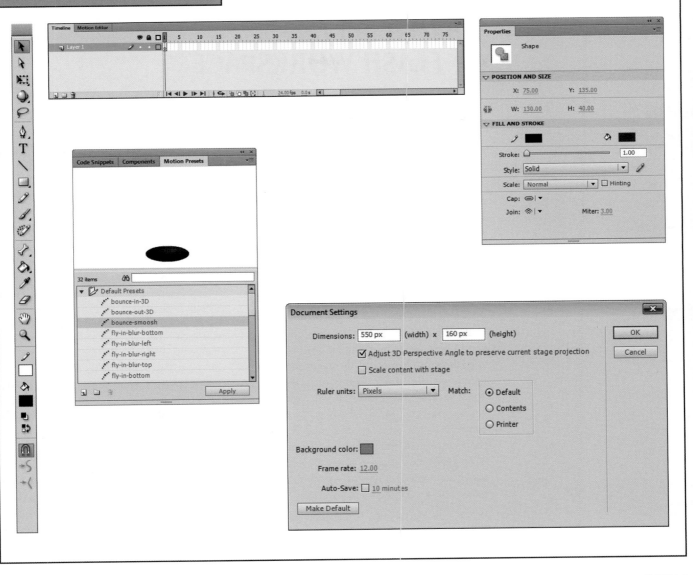

Understand the
FLASH WORKSPACE

What You'll Do

In this lesson, you will learn about the development workspace in Adobe Flash and how to change Flash settings to customize your workspace.

Organizing the Flash Workspace

As a designer, one of the most important things for you to do is to organize your workspace—that is, to decide what to have displayed on the screen and how to arrange the various tools and panels. Because **Flash** is a powerful program with many tools, your workspace may become cluttered. Fortunately, it is easy to customize the workspace to display only the tools needed at any particular time.

The development process in Flash operates according to a movie metaphor: objects placed on the Stage also are incorporated in frames on a Timeline. As you work in Flash, you create a movie by arranging objects (such as graphics and text) on the Stage, and then animating the objects using the Timeline. You can play the movie on the Stage as you are working on it by using the movie controls (start, stop, rewind, and so on). Once completed, the movie can become part of an application, such as a game, or used in a website. Unless otherwise noted, the term *movie* refers to Flash-created movies.

When you start Flash, three basic parts of the workspace are displayed: a menu bar that organizes commands within menus, a Stage where objects are placed, and a Timeline used to organize and control the objects on the Stage. In addition, one or more panels may be displayed. Panels, such as the Tools panel, are used when working with objects and features of the movie. Figure 1 shows a typical Flash workspace.

Stage

The **Stage** contains all of the objects (such as drawings, photos, animations, text, and videos) that are part of the movie that will be seen by your viewers. It shows how the objects behave within the movie and how they interact with each other. You can resize the Stage and change the background color applied to it. You can draw objects directly on the Stage or drag them from the Library panel to the Stage. You can also import objects developed in another program directly to the Stage. You can specify the size of the Stage (in pixels), which will be the size of the display area for the application on your smartphone or within your browser window. The gray area surrounding the Stage is the Pasteboard. You can place objects on the Pasteboard as you are creating a movie. However, neither the Pasteboard nor the objects on it will appear when the movie is played.

Timeline (Frames and Layers)

The **Timeline** is used to organize and control the movie's contents by specifying when each object appears on the Stage. The Timeline is critical to the creation of movies because a movie is merely a series of still images that appear over time. The images are contained within **frames**, which are segments of the Timeline. Frames in a Flash movie are similar to frames in a motion picture. When a Flash movie is played, a playhead moves from frame to frame on the Timeline, causing the content of each frame to appear on the Stage in a linear sequence.

The Timeline indicates where you are at any time within the movie and allows you to insert, delete, select, copy, and move frames. The Timeline contains **layers** that help to organize the objects on the Stage. You can draw and edit objects on one layer without affecting objects on other layers. Layers are a way to stack objects so they can overlap and give a 3D appearance on the Stage.

Panels

Panels are used to view, organize, and modify objects and features in a movie. The most commonly used panels are the Tools panel, the Properties panel (also called the Property inspector), and the Library panel. The **Tools panel** contains a set of tools, such as the rectangle, oval and text tools, used to draw and edit graphics and text. The **Properties panel** is used to display and change the properties of an object, such as the size and transparency of a circle. The **Library panel** is used to store and organize the various assets in your movie such as graphics, buttons, sounds, and video.

You can control which panels are displayed individually or you can choose to display

Figure 1 *A typical Flash workspace*

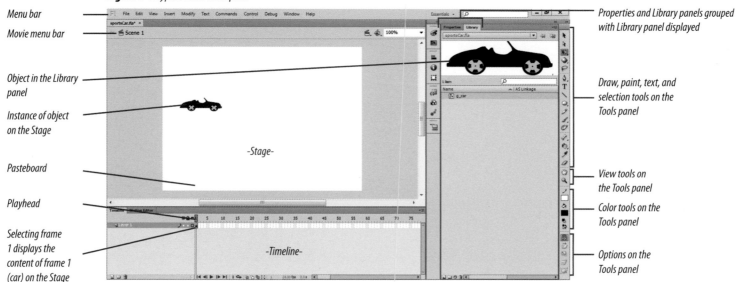

Menu bar

Movie menu bar

Object in the Library panel

Instance of object on the Stage

Pasteboard

Playhead

Selecting frame 1 displays the content of frame 1 (car) on the Stage

-Stage-

-Timeline-

Properties and Library panels grouped with Library panel displayed

Draw, paint, text, and selection tools on the Tools panel

View tools on the Tools panel

Color tools on the Tools panel

Options on the Tools panel

panel sets. **Panel sets** are groups of the most commonly used panels. For example, the Properties and the Library panels are often grouped together to make a panel set.

Although several panels open automatically when you start Flash, you may choose to close them and then display them only when they are needed. This keeps your workspace from becoming too cluttered. Panels are floating windows, meaning that you can move them around the workspace. This allows you to group (dock) panels together as a way to organize them in the workspace. In addition, you can control how a panel is displayed. That is, you can expand a panel to show all of its features or collapse it to show

only the title bar. Collapsing panels reduces the clutter on your workspace, provides a larger area for the Stage, and still provides easy access to often used panels.

If you choose to rearrange panels, first decide if you want a panel to be grouped (docked) with another panel, stacked above or below another panel, placed as a floating panel, or simply positioned as a stand-alone panel. An example of each of these is shown in Figure 2. When panels are grouped and expanded, clicking on a panel's tab makes it the active panel so that the panel features are displayed.

The key to rearranging panels is the blue drop zone that appears when a panel is

being moved. The drop zone is the area to which the panel can move and is indicated by either a blue line or a rectangle with a blue border. A single blue line indicates the position for stacking a panel above or below another panel. A rectangle with a blue border indicates the position for grouping panels. If you move a panel without using a drop zone, the panel becomes a floating panel and is neither grouped nor stacked with other panels. To move a panel, you drag the panel by its tab until the desired blue drop zone appears, then you release the mouse button. Figure 3 shows the Library panel being grouped with the Properties panel. The process is to drag the Library

Figure 2 *Arranging panels*

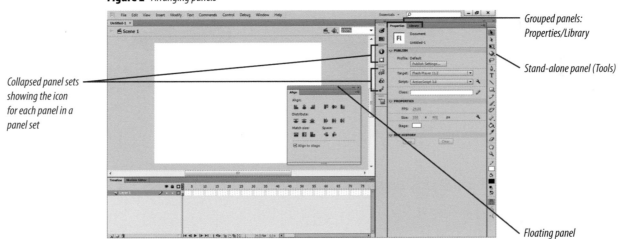

Grouped panels:
Properties/Library

Stand-alone panel (Tools)

Collapsed panel sets showing the icon for each panel in a panel set

Floating panel

Getting Started with Flash

panel tab adjacent to the Properties panel tab. Notice the rectangle with the blue border that surrounds the Properties panel. This indicates the drop zone for the Library panel. (*Note*: Dragging a panel by its tab moves only that panel. To move a panel set you must drag the group by its title bar.)

Floating panels can be resized by dragging the left side, right side, or bottom of the panel. Also, you can resize a panel by dragging one of the bottom corners. In addition to resizing panels, you can collapse a panel so that only its title bar appears, and then you can expand it to display the entire panel. The Collapse to Icons button is located in the upper-right corner of each panel's title bar, as shown in Figure 3. The

Collapse to Icons button is a toggle button, which means it changes or toggles between two states. When clicked, the Collapse to Icons button changes to the Expand Panels button.

If you want to close a panel, you can click the Panel options button (shown in Figure 3) to display a drop down menu and then click the Close option. Alternately, you can right-click (Win) or [control]-click (Mac) the panel tab and choose close. If the panel is a floating panel you can click the Close button on the title bar. Finally, if the panel is expanded, you can display the Windows menu and deselect the panel (or panel group).

Arranging panels can be a bit tricky. It's easy to start moving panels around and find

that the workspace is cluttered with panels arranged in unintended ways. To clean up your workspace, you can close a panel(s) or simply display the default Essentials workspace described below.

Flash provides several preset workspace configurations that provide panels and panel sets most often used by designers, developers, and animators. The default workspace, shown in Figure 4, is named Essentials and can be displayed by clicking the Essentials button on the menu bar and choosing Reset 'Essentials'. (*Note*: Your Essentials button may be below your menu bar.) Alternately, you can choose Reset 'Essentials' from the Workspace command on the Window menu. This workspace includes

Figure 3 *Grouping the Library panel with the Properties panel*

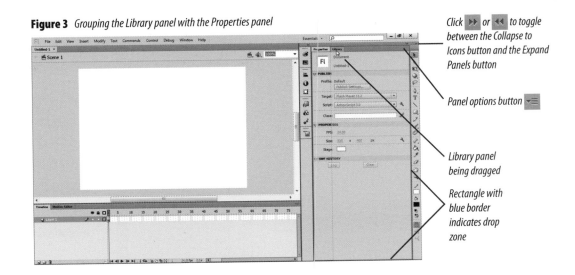

Click ▶▶ or ◀◀ to toggle between the Collapse to Icons button and the Expand Panels button

Panel options button ▼≣

Library panel being dragged

Rectangle with blue border indicates drop zone

the Timeline panel (grouped with the Motion Editor, which is used to edit animations); the Tools panel which is expanded; the Properties and Library panels grouped and expanded; and several other panel sets that are stacked and collapsed. Your Essentials workspace may open with additional panel sets that are grouped depending on user settings and previous use. You can expand and collapse these grouped panels sets by clicking the Expand Panels button or the Collapse to Icons button. To open a single panel set, you click an icon in the set. The Essentials workspace is a good development environment when learning Flash.

Regardless of how you decide to customize your development workspace, the Stage and the menu bar are always displayed. Usually, you display the Timeline, Tools panel, Library panel, Properties panel, and one or more other panels.

Other changes that you can make to the workspace are to change the size of the Stage, move the Stage around the Pasteboard, and change the size of the Timeline panel. To increase the size of the Stage so that the objects on the Stage can be edited more easily, you can change the magnification setting using commands on the View menu or by using the Zoom tool on the Tools panel. The Hand tool on the Tools panel and the scroll bars at

the bottom and right of the Stage can be used to reposition the Stage. The Timeline can be resized by dragging the top border. As your Flash movie gets more complex, you will use more layers on the Timeline. Increasing the size of the Timeline allows you to view more layers at one time.

Figure 4 *The Essentials workspace*

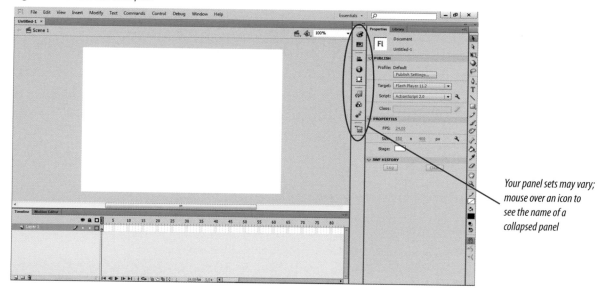

Your panel sets may vary; mouse over an icon to see the name of a collapsed panel

Figure 5 *The Flash Welcome screen*

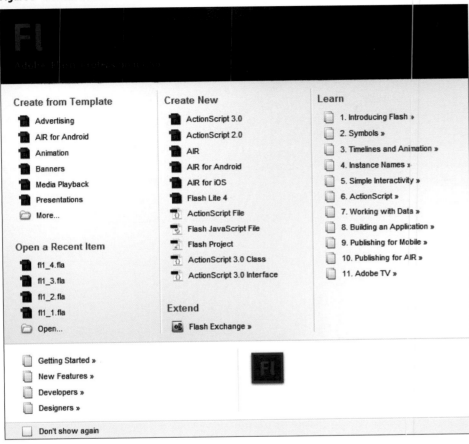

Start Adobe Flash and work with panels

1. Start the Adobe Flash Professional CS6 program **Fl**.

   The Adobe Flash CS6 Welcome screen appears, as shown in Figure 5. This screen allows you to open a recent document or create a new Flash file.

2. Click **ActionScript 3.0** under Create New.

3. Click the **Essentials button** on the menu bar, then click **Reset 'Essentials'**.

   Note: The Essentials button may be under the menu bar.

   TIP When you open a new file or as you are rearranging your workspace, use the Reset 'Essentials' option to display the default workspace.

4. Click **Window** on the menu bar, then note the panels with check marks.

   The check marks identify which panels and panel sets are open.

   TIP The Properties, Library, Colors, Swatches, Align, Info, Transform, Code Snippets, Components, Motion Presets, and Projects panels may be grouped, stacked, and/or collapsed, depending upon the configuration of your Essentials workspace. If so, only the panel that is active will have a check mark.

5. With the Windows menu still open, click **Hide Panels**.

6. Click **Window** on the menu bar, then click **Timeline**.

7. Click **Window** on the menu bar, then click **Tools**.

8. Click **Window** on the menu bar, then click **Library**.

   The Library and Properties panels are grouped, and the Library panel is the active panel.

   (continued)

FLASH 1-9

9. Click the **Properties panel tab**.

   The Properties panel is the active tab and the panel's features are displayed.

10. Click the **Library panel tab**, then drag the **Library panel** to the left side of the Stage as a floating panel.

11. Click the **Collapse to Icons button** on the Library panel title bar.

12. Click the **Expand Panels button** on the Library panel title bar.

13. Click the **Library panel tab**, drag the **Library panel tab** to the right of the Properties panel tab, then when a rectangle with a blue border appears, as shown in Figure 6, release the mouse button to group the panels.

    Note: If the panels do not appear grouped, repeat the step making sure there is a rectangle with a blue border before releasing the mouse button.

14. Click the **Collapse to Icons button** in the upper-right corner of the grouped panels, as shown in Figure 6.

15. Click the **Expand Panels button** to display the grouped panels.

16. Click **Essentials** on the menu bar, then click **Reset 'Essentials'**.

17. Click the **Color panel button** ⬛.

    The Color panel is expanded and shown grouped with the Swatches panel.

18. Click the **Collapse to Icons button** ▸▸ for the Color panel set.

19. Click **Essentials** on the menu bar, then click **Reset 'Essentials'**.

You started Flash and configured the workspace by hiding, moving, and displaying panels.

Figure 6 *Library panel grouped with the Properties panel*

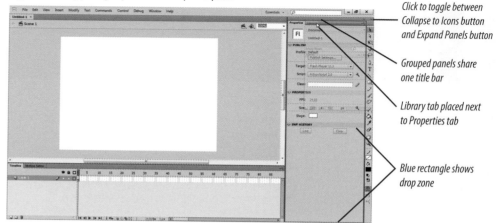

Click to toggle between Collapse to Icons button and Expand Panels button

Grouped panels share one title bar

Library tab placed next to Properties tab

Blue rectangle shows drop zone

Understanding Your Workspace

Organizing the Flash workspace is like organizing your desktop. You may work more efficiently if you have many of the most commonly used items in view and ready to use. Alternately, you may work better if your workspace is relatively uncluttered, giving you more free "desk space." Fortunately, Flash makes it easy for you to decide which items to display and how they are arranged while you work. You should become familiar with quickly opening, collapsing, expanding, and closing the various windows, toolbars, and panels in Flash, and experimenting with different layouts and screen resolutions to find the workspace that works best for you. Be sure to use screentips, such as those associated with the Collapse to Icons button, the Expand Panels buttons, and panel sets, to help you identify components of your workspace.

Figure 7 *Changing the size of the Timeline panel*

View list arrow

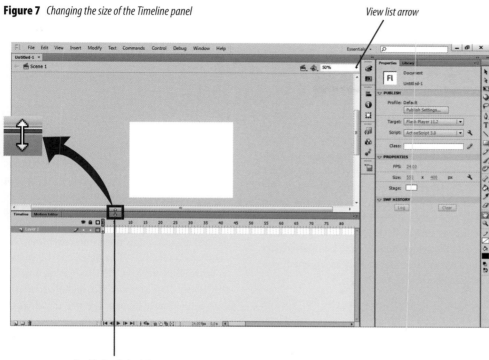

Double-headed pointer

Alternate Ways to Complete a Task

Flash often provides alternative ways to complete the same task. For instance, if you want to change the view (zoom in and out) of the Stage you could use the following methods:

- the magnification command on the View menu
- the View list options on the movie menu
- the Zoom tool on the Tools panel
- the Zoom in and Zoom out commands on the View menu
- the various combinations of shortcut keys displayed on the View menu

Change the Stage view and display of the Timeline

1. Click the **Hand tool** 🖐 on the Tools panel, click the middle of the Stage, then drag the **Stage** around the Pasteboard.
2. Click **View** on the menu bar, point to **Magnification**, then click **50%**.
3. Move the pointer to the top of the Timeline title bar then, when the pointer changes to a double-headed pointer ↕, click and drag the **title bar** up to increase the height of the Timeline, as shown in Figure 7.

   Increasing the height of the Timeline panel allows you to view more layers as you add them to the Timeline.
4. Move the pointer to the top of the Timeline title bar then, when the pointer changes to a double-headed pointer ↕, click and drag the **title bar** down to decrease the height of the Timeline.
5. Double-click the word **Timeline** to collapse the Timeline.
6. Click the word **Timeline** again to expand the Timeline.
7. Click the **View list arrow** on the movie menu bar as shown in Figure 7, then click **100%**.
8. Click **Essentials** on the menu bar, then click **Reset 'Essentials'**.
9. Click **File** on the menu bar, then click **Save**.
10. Navigate to the drive and folder where your Data Files are stored, type **workspace** for the filename, then click **Save**.
11. Click **File** on the menu bar, then click **Close**.

You used a View command to change the magnification of the Stage; you used the Hand tool to move the Stage around the workspace; you resized, collapsed, and expanded the Timeline panel; then you saved the document.

Open a Document and
PLAY A FLASH MOVIE

What You'll Do

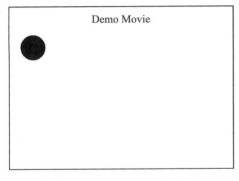

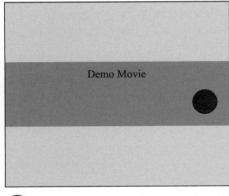

In this lesson, you will open a Flash document (movie); preview, test, and save the movie; then change the movie's Stage settings.

Opening a Movie in Flash

Flash files are called documents (or movies, interchangeably) and have an .fla file extension. If you have created a movie in Flash and saved it with the name myMovie, the filename will be myMovie.fla. Files with the .fla file extension can only be opened and edited using Flash. After they are opened, you can edit and resave them.

In order for Flash movies to be viewed on computers that do not have the Flash program installed, the movies must be saved in a different file format. The two most common file formats for distributing Flash movies are Flash Player (.swf) and Adobe AIR (.air). Flash Player files are used on websites for everything from interactive product demonstrations to banner ads. Adobe AIR files are used for a much broader range of applications such as interactive games, tutorials, product demonstrations, and productivity software. An important feature of AIR applications, also called apps, is that they can be played on any device (computer, mobile, TV) without the Flash Player and without a browser. The Publish command is used to convert a Flash FLA movie to a SWF or an AIR format. Depending on the target

you specify, Flash Player or Air, the filename extension will be changed to match the target you specifiy, either Flash Player (.fla) or Air (.air). For example, when a Flash file named myMovie.fla is published using the Publish command and the target is Flash Player (the default target), a new file named myMovie.swf is created. Flash SWF movies can be played in a browser without the Flash program, but the Flash Player must be installed on the computer. Flash Players are pre-installed on almost all computers. For those that do not have the player, it can be downloaded free from the Adobe website, *www.adobe.com*. Because .swf files cannot be edited in the Flash program, you should preview the Flash .fla files on the Stage and test them before you publish them. Be sure to keep the original .fla file so that you can make changes, if needed, at a later date.

Previewing a Movie

After creating a new Flash movie or opening a previously saved movie, you can preview it within the workspace in several ways. When you preview a movie, you play the frames by directing the playhead to move through the Timeline as you watch the movement on the Stage.

Getting Started with Flash

Control Menu Commands (and Keyboard Shortcuts)

Figure 8 shows the Control menu commands, which resemble common DVD-type options:

- Play ([Enter] (Win) or [return] (Mac)) begins playing the movie frame by frame, from the location of the playhead to the end of the movie. For example, if the playhead is on frame 5 and the last frame is frame 40, choosing the Play command will play frames 5–40 of the movie.

QUICK TIP

When a movie starts, the Play command changes to a Stop command. You can also stop the movie by pressing [Enter] (Win) or [return] (Mac).

- Rewind ([Shift][,]) (Win) or ([option] ⌘ [R]) (Mac) moves the playhead to frame 1.
- Go To End ([Shift][.]) moves the playhead to the last frame of the movie.

- Step Forward One Frame (.) moves the playhead forward one frame at a time.
- Step Backward One Frame (,) moves the playhead backward one frame at a time.

You can turn on the Loop Playback setting to allow the movie to continue playing repeatedly. A check mark next to the Loop Playback command on the Control menu indicates that the feature is active. To turn off this feature, click the Loop Playback command.

Control Buttons

You can also preview a movie using the Control buttons located on the status bar at the bottom of the Timeline. Figure 8 shows these buttons.

QUICK TIP

The decision of which controls to use (the Control menu, keyboard shortcuts, or the Control buttons on the Timeline status bar) is a matter of personal preference.

Testing a Movie

When you play a movie within the Flash workspace, some interactive functions (such as navigation buttons that are used to jump from one part of the movie to another) do not work. To preview the full functionality of a movie, you can use the Test Movie command on the Control menu to play the movie in a Flash Player window or in a browser on a computer using the SWF format. In addition, the Test Movie command can be used to play

Figure 8 *Methods to control a movie*

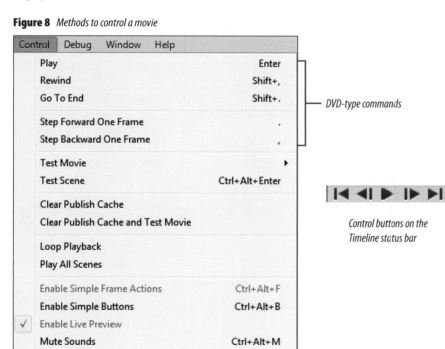

DVD-type commands

Control buttons on the Timeline status bar

Control menu

a movie on a mobile device that is attached to your computer using a USB cable.

Documents, Movies, and Applications

As you work in Flash, you are creating a document. When you save your work as an .fla file, you are saving the document. This is consistent with other Adobe products, such as Photoshop, that use the word *document* to refer to work created in that program. In addition, because Flash uses a movie metaphor with a Stage, Timeline, frames, animations, and so on, the work done in Flash is often referred to as a movie. So, the phrase *Flash document* and the phrase *Flash movie* are synonymous. Movies can be as small and simple as a ball bouncing across the screen or as complex as a full-length interactive adventure game. Products such as games and educational software, as well as online advertisements and product demonstrations, are referred to as applications (see Figure 9). Applications usually contain multiple Flash documents or movies that are linked.

Using the Flash Player

To view a Flash movie on the web, your computer needs to have the Flash Player installed. An important feature of multimedia players, such as the Flash Player, is the ability to decompress a file that has been compressed. Compressing a file gives it a small file size, which means it can be delivered more quickly over the Internet than its uncompressed counterpart. In addition to Adobe, companies such as Apple (QuickTime) and Microsoft (Windows Media Player) create players that allow applications to be viewed on the web. These applications can be created by Apple, Microsoft, or other companies. The multimedia players are distributed free and can be downloaded from the company's website. The Flash Player is created by Adobe and the latest version is available at *www.adobe.com*.

Figure 9 *Example of an application*
Courtesy of New York Philharmonic Kidzone. http://www.nyphilkids.org/games/main.phtml?

Figure 10 *Playhead moving across Timeline*

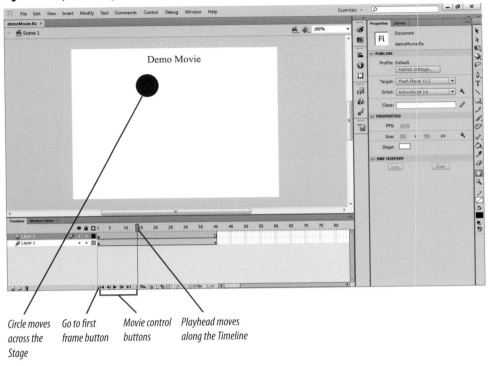

Circle moves across the Stage

Go to first frame button

Movie control buttons

Playhead moves along the Timeline

Using Options and Shortcuts

As you know, there is often more than one way to complete a particular command when using Flash. For example, if you want to rewind a movie you can use the control on the Control menu, use the control on the Timeline status bar, press [Shift] + [,], or drag the playhead to frame 1. In addition, Flash provides context menus that are relevant to the current selection. For example, if you point to a graphic and right-click (Win) or [control]-click (Mac), a menu opens with graphic-related commands, such as cut and copy. Shortcut keys are also available for many of the most common commands, such as [Ctrl][Z] (Win) or [command][Z] (Mac) for Undo.

Open and play a movie using the Control menu and movie control buttons

1. Open fl1_1.fla from the drive and folder where your Data Files are stored, then save it as **demoMovie.fla**.

2. Verify the view is set to 100%.

   The view setting is displayed on the movie menu bar, which is above and to the right of the Stage.

3. Click **Control** on the menu bar, then click **Play**.

   Notice how the playhead moves across the Timeline as the blue circle moves from the left of the Stage to the right, as shown in Figure 10.

4. Click **Control** on the menu bar, then click **Rewind**.

5. Press [**Enter**] (Win) or [**return**] (Mac) to play the movie, then press [**Enter**] (Win) or [**return**] (Mac) again to stop the movie before it ends.

6. Click the **Go to first frame button** at the bottom of the Timeline status bar, as shown in Figure 10.

7. Use all the movie control buttons on the Timeline status bar to preview the movie.

8. Click and drag the **playhead** back and forth to view the contents of the movie frame by frame.

9. Click number **1** on the Timeline to select the frame.

10. Press the **period key** several times, then press the **comma key** several times to move the playhead one frame at a time forward and backward.

You opened a Flash movie and previewed it, using various controls.

Test a movie

1. Click **Control** on the menu bar, point to **Test Movie**, then click **in Flash Professional**.

   The Flash Player window opens, as shown in Figure 11, and the movie starts playing automatically.

2. Click **Control** on the menu bar of the Flash Player window (Win) or application menu bar (Mac), then review the available commands.

3. Click **File** on the menu bar of the Flash Player window (Win) or application menu bar (Mac), then click **Close** to close the Flash Player window.

4. Use your file management program to navigate to the drive and folder where you saved the demoMovie.fla file and notice the demoMovie.swf file.

   TIP When you test a movie, Flash automatically creates a file that has an .swf extension in the folder where your movie is stored and then plays the movie in the Flash Player.

5. Return to the Flash program.

6. Click **View** on the menu bar, point to **Magnification**, then click **100%** if it is not already selected.

7. Click **1** on the Timeline.

You tested a movie in the Flash Player window and viewed the .swf file created as a result of testing the movie, set the magnification, and then displayed the contents of frame 1.

Figure 11 *Flash Player window*

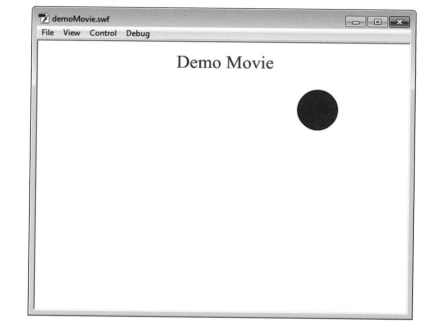

Auto Save and Data Recovery

Flash provides an Auto Save feature that periodically saves each document. In addition, the Auto Recover feature enables Flash to periodically take a snapshot of all open documents so that the user can recover from any sudden data loss event. If a dialog box titled Document save and auto-recovery opens, you can choose to save the document, disable the auto-recovery feature, and/or prevent the dialog box from reappearing. The Auto-Save feature is turned on and off in the Document Properties dialog box.

Figure 12 *Document Settings dialog box*

Document Settings

Dimensions: [550 px] (width) x [160 px] (height)

☑ Adjust 3D Perspective Angle to preserve current stage projection
☐ Scale content with stage

Ruler units: [Pixels ▼]   Match: ⦿ Default
                                   ○ Contents
                                   ○ Printer

Background color: [ ]

Frame rate: 12.00

Auto-Save: ☐ 10 minutes

[Make Default]

[OK]
[Cancel]

Background color swatch

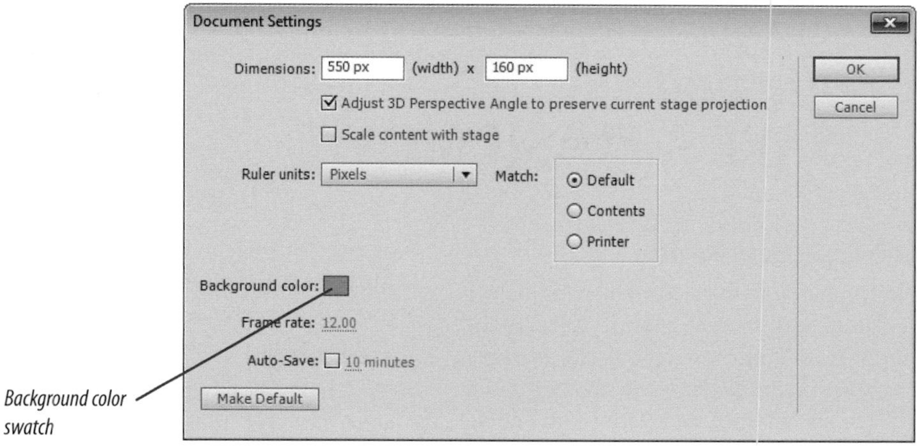

Figure 13 *Completed changes to the document properties*

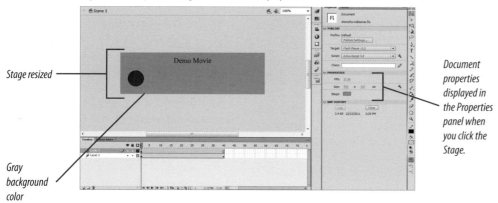

Stage resized

Gray background color

Document properties displayed in the Properties panel when you click the Stage.

Change the document properties

1. Click **Modify** on the menu bar, then click **Document**.

   The Document Settings dialog box opens.

2. Double-click in the **height text box** to select the number, then type **160**.

3. Click the **Background color swatch**, then click the **gray (#999999) color swatch** in the far-left column of the Color Swatch palette.

   Note: The color code for a color appears next to the sample color swatch above the palette as you point to a color. The Color Swatch palette allows you to click a color to choose it or to enter a number that represents the color.

4. Review the remaining default values shown in Figure 12, then click **OK**.

   The dialog box closes.

5. Click the **Stage**.

   TIP You can use the Properties Panel to change the Document properties as shown in Figure 13. You must click the Stage to display the settings.

6. Press **[Enter]** (Win) or **[return]** (Mac) to play the movie.

7. Click **File** on the menu bar, then click **Save As**.

8. Navigate to the drive and folder where your Data Files are stored, type **demoMovieBanner** for the filename, then click **Save**.

9. Click **File** on the menu bar, then click **Close**.

You set the document properties including the size of the Stage and the background color, then you saved the document.

Create and
SAVE A FLASH MOVIE

What You'll Do

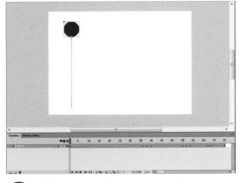

In this lesson, you will create a Flash movie that will include a simple animation, add animation effects, and then save the movie.

Creating a Flash Movie

Flash movies are created by placing objects (graphics, text, sounds, photos, and so on) on the Stage, editing these objects (for example, changing their brightness), animating the objects, and adding interactivity with buttons and menus. You can create graphic objects in Flash using the drawing tools, or you can create them in another program, such as Adobe Illustrator, Photoshop, or Fireworks, and then import them into a Flash movie. In addition, you can acquire clip art and stock photographs and import them into a movie. When objects are placed on the Stage, they are automatically placed on a layer and in the selected frame on the Timeline.

Figure 14 shows a movie that has a circle object created in Flash. Notice that the playhead is on frame 1 of the movie. The object placed on the Stage appears in frame 1 and appears on the Stage when the playhead is on frame 1. The dot in frame 1 on the Timeline indicates that this frame is a keyframe. The concept of keyframes is critical to understanding how Flash works. A **keyframe** indicates that there is a change in the movie, such as the start of an animation,

or the resizing of an object on the Stage. A keyframe is automatically designated in frame 1 of every layer. In addition, you can designate any frame to be a keyframe.

The circle object in Figure 14 was created using the Oval tool. To create an oval or a rectangle, you select the desired tool and then drag the pointer over an area on the Stage. *Note:* Flash uses one button on the Tools panel to group the Oval and Rectangle tools, along with three other drawing tools. To display a menu of these tools, click and hold the rectangle (or oval) button on the Tools panel to display the menu and then click the tool you want to use. If you want to draw a perfect circle or square, press and hold [Shift] after the tool is selected, and then drag the pointer. If you make a mistake, you can click Edit on the menu bar, and then click Undo. To make changes to an object, such as resizing or changing its color, or to animate an object, you must first select it. You can use the Selection tool to select an entire object or group of objects. You drag the Selection tool pointer around the entire object to make a **marquee**. An object that has been selected displays a dot pattern or a blue border.

Creating an Animation

Figure 15 shows a movie that has 24 frames, as specified by the blue shading on the Timeline. The blue background color on the Timeline indicates a motion animation that starts in frame 1 and ends in frame 24. The dotted line on the Stage indicates the path the object will follow during the animation. In this case, the object will move from left to right across the Stage. The movement of the object is caused by having the object in different places on the Stage in different frames of the movie. In this case, frame 12 displays the object midway through the

animation and frame 24 displays the object at the end of the animation. A basic motion animation requires two keyframes. The first keyframe sets the starting position of the object, and the second keyframe sets the ending position of the object. The number of frames from keyframe to keyframe determines the length of the animation. If the starting keyframe is frame 1 and the ending keyframe is frame 24, the object will be animated for 24 frames. As an object is being animated, Flash automatically fills in the frames between these keyframes, with a process called **motion tweening**.

The Motion Tween Animation Process

Having an object move around the screen is one of the most common types of animations. Flash provides a process called motion tweening that makes it relatively simple to move objects. The process is to select an object on the Stage, then select the Motion Tween command from the Insert menu. If the object is not a symbol, a dialog box opens asking if you want to convert the object to a symbol. Creating a symbol allows you to reuse the object for this and other movies, as well as to apply a motion tween. Only symbols and text blocks can be motion tweened. The final

Figure 14 *Circle object in frame 1*

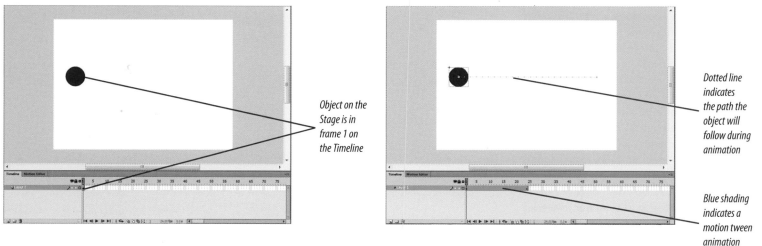

Object on the
Stage is in
frame 1 on
the Timeline

Figure 15 *Motion animation*

Dotted line
indicates
the path the
object will
follow during
animation

Blue shading
indicates a
motion tween
animation

step in the animation process is to select the ending frame for the animation and drag the object to another location on the Stage.

Two important things happen during the animation process. First, the Timeline shows the **tween span** (also called **motion span**), which is the number of frames in the motion tween. The tween span can be identified on the Timeline by a blue color, which, in this example, extends for 24 frames. The default tween span when starting from frame 1 of a new movie is determined by the number of frames per second setting. In this example, we used the default setting of 24 frames per second, so the initial number of frames in a tween for this movie is 24 frames.

The length of the motion tween is determined by the last frame in the movie automatically or by you manually if you designate a frame other than the last frame of the movie as the end of the animation. If a movie has an ending frame beyond frame 1, the tween span will extend to the end of the movie. For example, if a movie has 50 frames and you insert a motion tween starting at frame 1, the tween span will extend from frames 1 through 50. Likewise, if a movie has an ending frame in frame 10 and you insert a motion tween in frame 1, the motion tween will extend from frame 1 to frame 10. Finally, a motion tween does not have to start in frame 1. You can start a motion tween in a frame other than frame 1 by clicking the frame on the layer you want to contain the motion tween, inserting a keyframe in that frame, and then continuing with the steps to insert a motion tween (selecting or creating

the object to be tweened, inserting the tween and moving the object).

You can increase or decrease the length of the animation by pointing to either end of the **tween** span and dragging it to a new frame. The tween span will have more or fewer frames based on this action. The duration of the tween will still be based on the number of frames per second setting. For example, if we drag the tween span from frame 24 to frame 48, there are now 48 frames in the tween span. The tween span will still play at 24 frames

per second because we did not change that setting. It will take two seconds to play the new tween span.

Second, a dotted line, called the **motion path**, represents the path the object takes from the beginning frame to the ending frame. This path can be reshaped to cause the object to travel in a non-linear way, as shown in Figure 16. Reshaping a path can be done by using the Selection tool on the Tools panel. You see the tween span on the Timeline and the motion path on the Stage.

Figure 16 *A reshaped motion path*

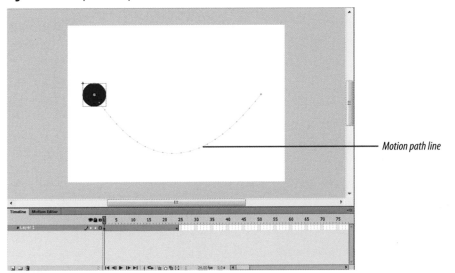

Motion path line

Getting Started with Flash

Motion Presets

Flash provides several preconfigured motion tweens that you can apply to an object on the Stage. These allow you to bounce an object across the Stage, fly-in an object from off the Stage, cause an object to pulsate and to spiral in place, as well as many other types of object animations. Figure 17 shows the Motion Presets panel where you choose a preset and apply it to an object. You can preview each preset before applying it and you can easily change to a different preset, if desired.

Adding Effects to an Object

In addition to animating the location of an object (or objects), you can also animate an object's appearance. Objects have properties such as color, brightness, and size. You can alter an object's properties as it is being animated using the motion tween process. For example, you could give the appearance of the object fading in by changing its transparency (alpha setting) or having it grow larger by altering its size over the course of the animation. Another useful effect is applying filters, such as drop shadows or bevels. All of these changes can be made by selecting the object, and then using commands in the Properties panel.

Figure 17 *Panel set with Motion Presets panel active*

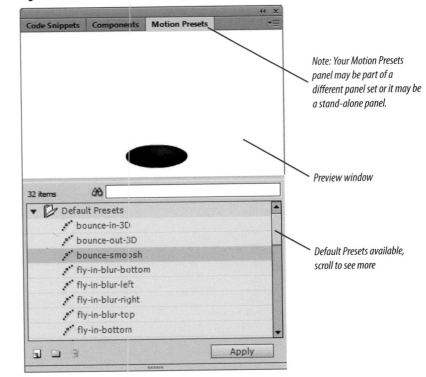

Note: Your Motion Presets panel may be part of a different panel set or it may be a stand-alone panel.

Preview window

Default Presets available, scroll to see more

Create objects using drawing tools

1. Click **ActionScript 3.0** to open a new Flash document.

2. Save the movie as **tween.fla**.

3. Verify the view is set to 100%.

4. Click and hold the **Rectangle tool** 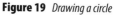 (or the Oval tool ⬭ if it is displayed) on the Tools panel to display the list of tools, as shown in Figure 18, then click the **Oval tool** ⬭.

5. Verify that the Object Drawing option ⬜ in the Options area of the Tools panel is not active, as shown in Figure 18.

6. Click the **Fill Color tool color swatch** ⬛ on the Tools panel, then, if necessary, click the **red color swatch** in the left column of the color palette.

7. Verify the Stroke Color tool color swatch on the Tools panel is black, as seen in Figure 20.

8. Press and hold **[Shift]**, drag the **pointer** on the left side of the Stage to draw the circle, as shown in Figure 19, then release the mouse button.

   Pressing and holding [Shift] creates a circle.

   TIP Use the Undo command on the Edit menu to undo an action.

9. Click the **Selection tool** ▸ on the Tools panel, drag a **marquee** around the object to select it, as shown in Figure 20, then release the mouse button.

   The object appears covered with a dot pattern.

You created an object using the Oval tool, and then selected the object using the Selection tool.

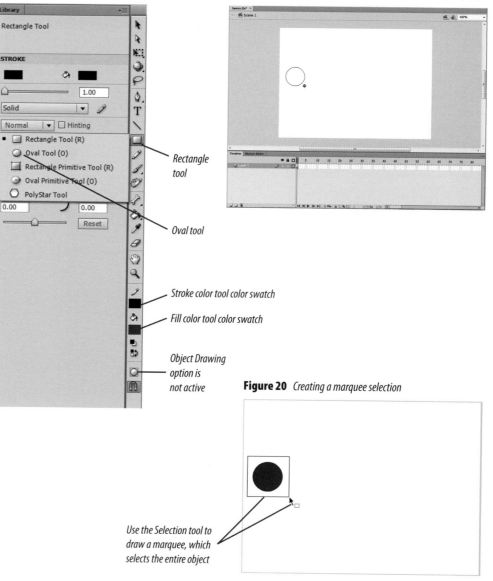

Figure 18 *Drawing tools menu*

Rectangle tool

Oval tool

Stroke color tool color swatch

Fill color tool color swatch

Object Drawing option is not active

Figure 19 *Drawing a circle*

Figure 20 *Creating a marquee selection*

Use the Selection tool to draw a marquee, which selects the entire object

Getting Started with Flash

Figure 21 *The circle on the right side of the Stage*

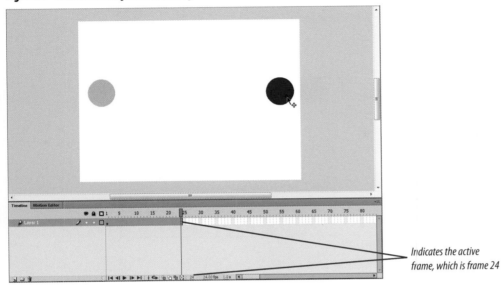

Indicates the active frame, which is frame 24

Create a motion tween animation

1. Click **Insert** on the menu bar, then click **Motion Tween**.

   The Convert selection to symbol for tween dialog box opens.

2. Click **OK**.

   A blue border surrounds the object indicating that the object is a symbol. Notice that, in this example, the playhead automatically moved to frame 24, the last frame in the tween span. When you move the object to a new location on the Stage, the object's new location will be reflected in frame 24.

3. Click and then drag the **circle** to the right side of the Stage, as shown in Figure 21, then release the mouse button.

4. Press **[Enter]**(Win) or **[return]**(Mac) to play the movie.

   The playhead moves through frames 1–24 on the Timeline, and the circle moves across the Stage.

5. Click **frame 12** on Layer 1 on the Timeline.

   Verify the frame number on the status bar of the Timeline is 12, and notice that the object is halfway across the screen. This is the result of the tweening process in which the frames between 1 and 24 are filled in with the object in the correct location for each frame.

   (continued)

6. Verify the Selection tool ↖ is active, then point to the end of the tween span until the pointer changes to a double-headed arrow ↔, as shown in Figure 22.

7. Click and drag the **tween span** to frame 48, then verify the frame number on the status bar is 48, or adjust as needed.

8. Press **[Enter]**(Win) or **[return]**(Mac) to play the movie.

Notice it now takes longer (2 seconds, not 1 second) to play the movie. Also notice that a diamond symbol appears in frame 48 indicating that it is now a Property keyframe. A Property keyframe indicates a change in the property of an object. In this case, it indicates the location of the object on the Stage has changed from frame 24 to frame 48.

9. Click **frame 24** and notice that the object is now halfway across the screen.

10. Click **File** on the menu bar, then click **Save**.

You created a motion tween animation and changed the length of the tween span.

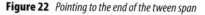
Figure 22 *Pointing to the end of the tween span*

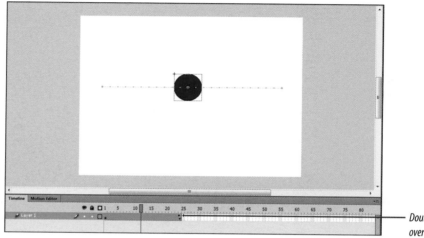

Double-headed arrow over end of tween span

Figure 23 *Using the Selection tool to reshape a motion path*

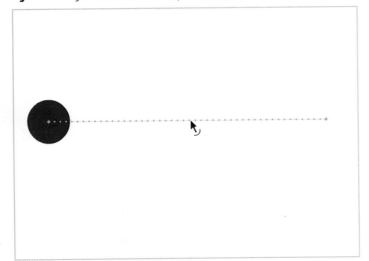

Reshape the motion path

1. Click **File** on the menu bar, click **Save As**, then save the document with the filename **tweenEffects.fla**.

2. Verify the Selection tool ⬚ is active.

3. Click **frame 1** to select it.

   Note: When you see the direction to click a frame, click the frame on the layer not the number on the Timeline.

4. Point to just below the middle of the path until the pointer changes to a pointer with an arc ⬚, as shown in Figure 23.

(continued)

5. Click and drag the **path** to reshape the path, as shown in Figure 24.

6. Play the movie.

   Note: When you see the direction to play the movie, press [Enter] (Win) or [return] (Mac).

7. Test the movie.

   Note: When you see the direction to test the movie, click Control on the menu bar, point to Test Movie, then click in Flash Professional. Alternately, you can press [Ctrl]+[Enter] (Win) or [command]+[return](Mac).

8. View the movie, then close the Flash Player window.

9. Click **Edit** on the menu bar, then click **Undo Reshape**.

   Note: The Undo command starts with the most recent action and moves back through the actions. As a result, you may have to click Undo more than one time before you are able to click Undo Reshape.

You used the Selection tool to reshape a motion path and the Undo command to undo the reshape.

Figure 24 *Reshaping the motion path*

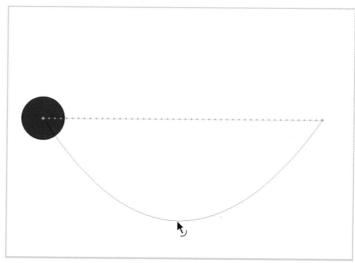

Figure 25 *The Properties panel displayed*

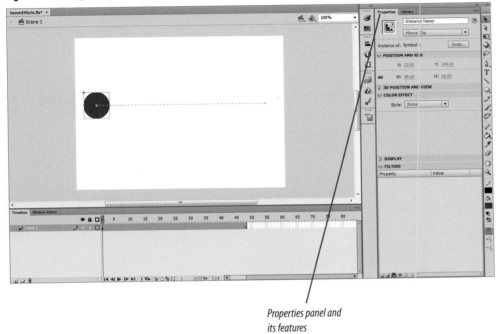

Properties panel and
its features

Change the transparency of an object

1. Click **frame 1** to select it, then click the **circle object** on the Stage to select it.

2. Click the **Properties panel tab** to display the Properties panel, as shown in Figure 25.

   Note: If the Properties panel is not open, click Window on the menu bar, then click Properties.

   Note: To verify the object is active, review the available settings in the Properties panel. Make sure POSITION AND SIZE is one of the options.

3. Click **COLOR EFFECT** on the Properties panel to display the Color Effect area if it is not already displayed, click the **Style list arrow**, then click **Alpha**.

4. Drag the **Alpha slider** 🔲 to **0**.

   The object becomes transparent. The bounding box indicates the location of the object and displays the Stage color, white.

5. Click **frame 48** on the layer to select it.

6. Click the bounding box on the Stage to select the object and check that the object's properties are displayed in the Properties panel.

   Note: To verify the object is active, review the available settings in the Properties panel. Make sure POSITION AND SIZE is one of the options.

7. Drag the **Alpha slider** 🔲 to **100**.

8. Play the movie.

9. Test the movie, then close the Flash Player window.

You used the Color Effect option on the Properties panel to change the transparency of an object.

Lesson 3 Create and Save a Flash Movie

Resize an object

1. Click **frame 1** to select it.

2. Click inside the bounding box on the Stage to select the **circle object**.

3. Click **POSITION AND SIZE** on the Properties panel if this area is not already open.

4. Review the W (width) and H (height) settings of the object.

   The width and height are the dimensions of the bounding box around the circle.

5. Click **frame 48** to select it, then click the **circle object** to select it.

6. Verify the Lock icon ⊜ in the Properties panel is not broken.

   Note: If the lock is broken, click the broken lock to lock it, as shown in Figure 26, to ensure the width and height change proportionally.

7. Point to the number next to W: and when the pointer changes to a double-headed arrow ⇌, drag the ⇌ **pointer** left to decrease the width so that the circle shrinks to about half its size, as shown in Figure 26.

   Hint: You can also double-click a value in the Properties panel and type a value.
   Note: Resizing the object will reposition it.

8. Click the **circle object** on the Stage.

9. Play the movie.

10. Test the movie, then close the Flash Player window.

11. Click **frame 1**, click the **circle object** to select it, then drag the **Alpha slider** △ to **100**.

You used the Position and Size option on the Properties panel to change the size of an object.

Figure 26 *Resizing the circle*

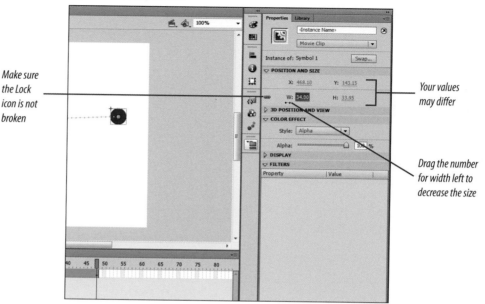

Make sure the Lock icon is not broken

Your values may differ

Drag the number for width left to decrease the size

Figure 27 *The Add filter icon*

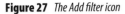

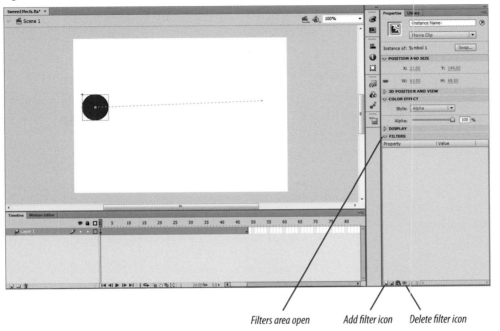

Filters area open   *Add filter icon*   *Delete filter icon*

Add a filter to an object

1. Verify the object is selected by viewing the Properties panel and verifying the object's properties are displayed.

2. Click **FILTERS** on the Properties panel to display the Filters area if it is not already displayed.

3. Click the **Add filter icon** ⊡ at the bottom of the Filters area, as shown in Figure 27.

4. Click **Drop Shadow**, point to the number for the angle, then when the pointer changes to a double-headed arrow ⟷, drag the ⟷ **pointer** right to change the number of degrees to **100**.

5. Click **frame 1** to select it, then play the movie.

6. Click **frame 1** to select it, then click the **circle object** to select it.

7. Click **Drop Shadow** in the Filters area, then click the **Delete Filter icon** 🗑 at the bottom of the Filters area.

   The drop shadow filter is removed from the circle object.

8. Click the **Add filter icon** ⊡ at the bottom of the Filters area.

9. Click **Bevel**, test the movie, then close the Flash Player window.

You used the Filters option in the Properties panel to add and delete filters.

Add a motion preset

1. Verify the playhead is on frame 1, then click the object to select it.

2. Click **Window** on the menu bar, then click **Motion Presets**.

   The Motion Presets panel opens. It may open as a stand-alone panel or it may be grouped with other panels.

3. Drag the **Motion Presets panel or the panel set** by its title bar (not one of the tabs) to the right so that it does not obscure the Stage.

4. Click the **expand icon** ▶ for the Default Presets, then click **bounce-smoosh** and watch the animation in the preview widow, as shown in Figure 28.

5. Click **Apply**.

   A dialog box opens asking if you want to replace the current motion object with the new selection. You can only apply one motion tween or motion preset to an object at any one time.

6. Click **Yes**.

   The bevel filter is deleted and a new path is displayed.

7. Play the movie, then test the movie.

   Notice the circle object disappears from the Stage.

   (continued)

Figure 28 *The Motion Presets panel*

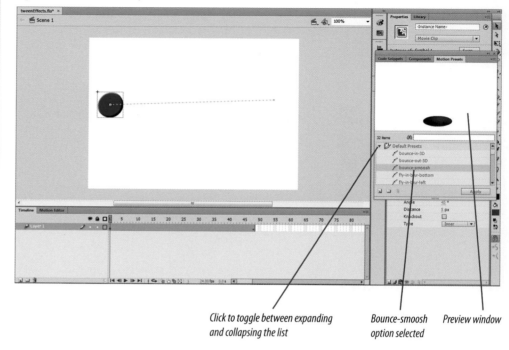

Click to toggle between expanding and collapsing the list

Bounce-smoosh option selected

Preview window

Figure 29 *Diamond symbols indicating Property keyframes*

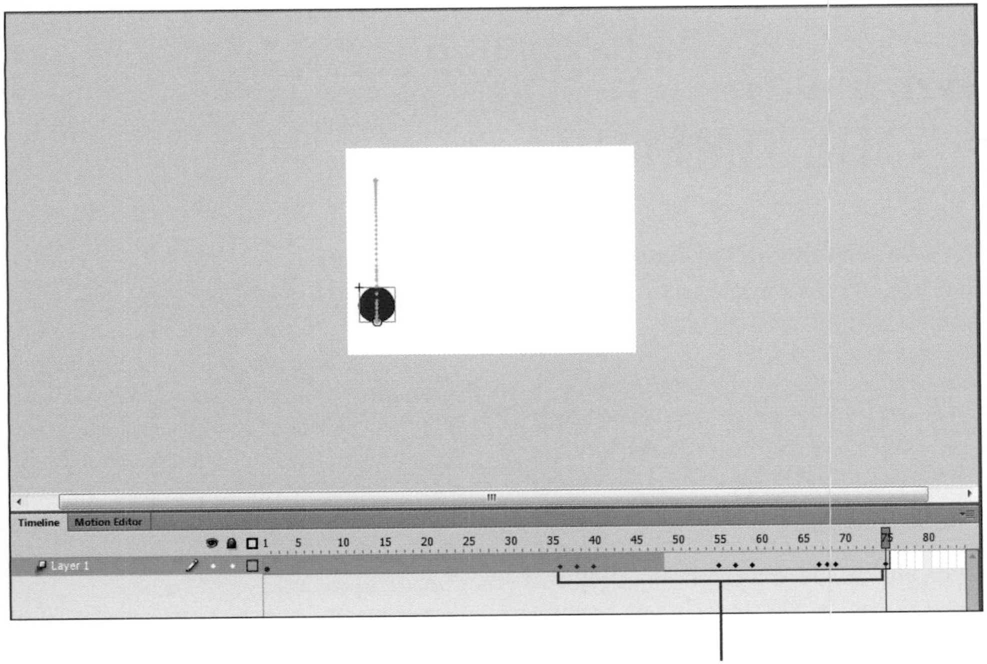

Diamond symbols appear where the ball is resized

8. Close the Flash Player window.
9. Click **View** on the menu bar, point to **Magnification**, then click **50%**.
10. Click **frame 1**, click the **Selection tool**, draw a **marquee** around the circle object and the path to select both of them.
11. Press the **up arrow key [↑]** on the keyboard to move the circle object and the path toward the top of the Stage.
12. Play the movie.

    Notice the Timeline has several diamond symbols, as shown in Figure 29. Each one is a Property keyframe and indicates that there is a change in the object during the motion tween, such as when the ball is resized.
13. Click **frame 1** to select it, then drag the **playhead** from frame 1 to the last frame and notice the change that occurs at each keyframe.
14. Scroll the list of motion presets, click **pulse**, click **Apply**, then click **Yes**.
15. Play the movie.
16. Close the Motion Presets panel or panel set if the Motion Presets panel is part of a panel set.
17. Save and close the movie.

You applied motion presets to an object and viewed how keyframes identify changes in the motion tween.

Work with
THE TIMELINE

What You'll Do

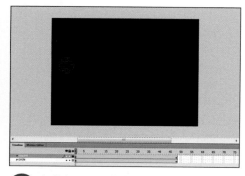

In this lesson, you will add another layer, allowing you to create an additional animation, and you will use the Timeline to help organize the contents of your movie.

Understanding the Timeline

The Timeline organizes and controls a movie's contents over time. By learning how to read the information provided on the Timeline, you can identify what will be happening in a movie, frame by frame. You can identify which objects are animated, what types of animations are being used, when the various objects will appear in a movie, when changes are made to the properties of an object, which objects will appear on top of others, and how fast the movie will play. Features of the Timeline are shown in Figure 30 and explained in this lesson.

Using Layers

Each new Flash movie contains one layer, named Layer 1. **Layers** are like transparent sheets of plastic that are stacked on top of each other, as shown in Figure 31, which also shows how the stacked objects appear on the Stage. Each layer can contain one or more objects. In Figure 31, the tree is on one layer, the heading Solitude is on another layer, and the colored backdrop is on a third layer. You can add layers using the Timeline command on the Insert menu or by clicking the New Layer icon on the Timeline status bar. Placing objects on different layers and locking the layers helps avoid accidentally making changes to one object while editing another.

Figure 30 *Elements of the Timeline*

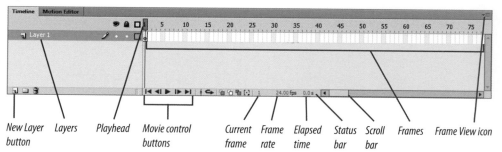

| New Layer button | Layers | Playhead | Movie control buttons | Current frame | Frame rate | Elapsed time | Status bar | Scroll bar | Frames | Frame View icon |

When you add a new layer, Flash stacks it on top of the other layer(s) on the Timeline. The stacking order of the layers on the Timeline is important because objects on the Stage appear in the same stacking order. For example, if you have two overlapping objects, and the top layer has a drawing of a tree and the bottom layer has a drawing of a house, the tree appears as though it is in front of the house. You can change the stacking order of layers simply by dragging them up or down in the list of layers. You can name layers, hide them so their contents do not appear on the Stage, and lock them so that they cannot be edited.

Using Frames and Keyframes

The Timeline is made up of individual segments called **frames**. The contents of each layer appear as the playhead moves over the frames, so any object in frame 1, no matter which layer it is on, appears on the Stage whenever frame 1 is played. Frames are numbered in increments of five for easy reference. The upper-right corner of the Timeline contains a Frame View icon. Clicking this icon displays a menu that provides different views of the Timeline, for example, showing more frames or showing a preview (thumbnails) of the objects on a layer. The status bar at the bottom of the Timeline indicates the current frame (the frame that the playhead is currently on), the frame rate (frames per second, also called fps), and the elapsed time from frame 1 to the current frame. Frames per second is the unit of measure for movies. If the frame rate is set to 24 frames per second and the movie has 48 frames, the movie will take 2 seconds to play.

Keyframes are locations on the Timeline where a new occurrence of an object appears or a change is made in the object. So, if you draw an object on the Stage, the current frame will need to be changed to a keyframe. In addition, if you create a motion tween, the first frame of the tween span will be a keyframe. One type of keyframe is a Property keyframe, which is used to specify locations on the Timeline where you want an animation or object to change. For example, you may have an animation of an object that moves across the Stage in frames 1 through 20. If you decide to resize the object in frame 5, a Property keyframe will appear on the Timeline in frame 5 when you make the change to that object. Another type of keyframe is a Blank keyframe, which is used to indicate that no content (objects) appears in that frame.

Interpreting the Timeline

The Timeline provides many clues to what is happening on the Stage. Interpreting these clues is essential to learning Flash. These clues are in the form of symbols and colors that appear on the Timeline. Figure 32 shows the most common symbols and colors. These are explained next. Others will be discussed in subsequent chapters. The top layer on the Timeline in Figure 32 shows that frame 1 is a blank keyframe as indicated by the unfilled circle. No content will appear in frame 1 of this layer. In addition, the white background which extends to frame 24 indicates a span of blank frames. An unfilled rectangle appears at the end of the span and indicates the end of the blank frames. The next layer shows a keyframe with content as indicated by the filled circle. The content

Figure 31 *The concept of layers*

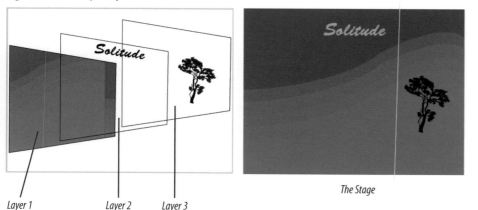

Layer 1   Layer 2   Layer 3

The Stage

in this frame also appears in frames 2-24 as indicated by the gray background. Again, an unfilled rectangle appears at the end of the span and indicates the end of the frames with the same content. The next layer shows a keyframe in frame 1 and a motion tween using the contents of frame 1 as indicated by the blue background in frames 2-24. A property keyframe (indicated by a diamond) appears at the end of this span because a change has been made to the object being animated, such as moving it to a different location on the Stage. The bottom layer shows a keyframe in frame 1 and property keyframes (indicated by diamonds) in frames 5, 10, 15, 20 and 24.

Figure 33 shows the Timeline of a movie created in Lesson 3 but now a second object, a square at the top of the Stage, has been added to the movie. By studying the Timeline, you can learn several things about the square object and this movie. First, the darker blue color highlighting Layer 2 indicates that this layer is active. Second, the square object is placed on its own layer, Layer 2 (indicated by the darker blue color that highlights the layer name and the motion animation). Third, the layer has a motion animation (indicated by the blue background in the frames and the motion path on the Stage). Fourth, the animation runs from frame 1 to frame 48. Fifth, if the objects intersect during the animation, the square will be on top of the circle, because the layer it is placed on (Layer 2) is above the layer that the circle

is placed on (Layer 1). Sixth, the frame rate is set to 24, which means that the movie will play 24 frames per second. Seventh, the playhead is at frame 1, which causes the contents of frame 1 for both layers to appear on the Stage.

Figure 32 *Common symbols and colors on the Timeline*

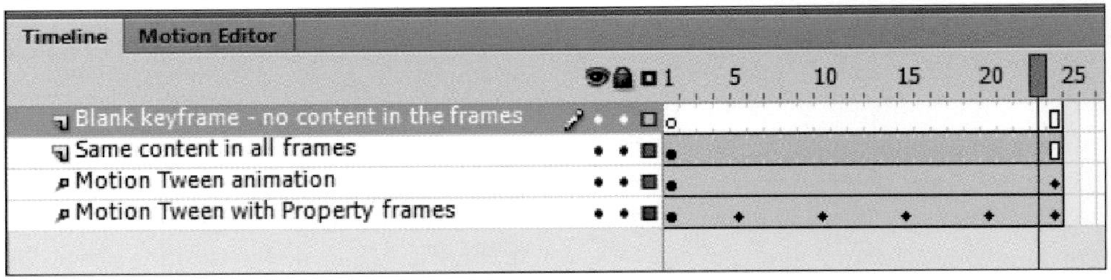

Figure 33 *The Timeline of a movie with a second object*

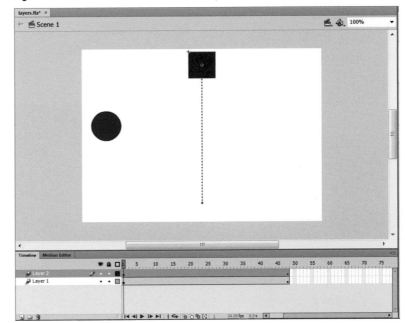

Figure 34 *Drawing a square*

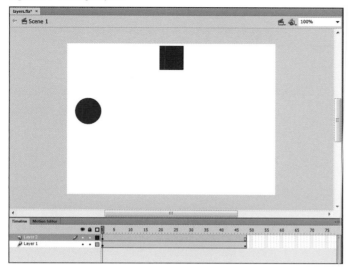

Figure 35 *Positioning the square at the bottom of the Stage*

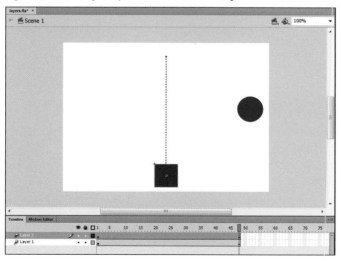

Add a layer

1. Open tween.fla, then save it as **layers.fla**.
2. Click **frame 1** on Layer 1.
3. Click **Insert** on the menu bar, point to **Timeline**, then click **Layer**.

   A new layer—Layer 2—appears at the top of the Timeline.

You added a layer to the Timeline.

Create a second animation

1. Click **frame 1** on Layer 2.
2. Click and hold the **Oval tool** ◯ on the Tools panel, then click the **Rectangle tool** ▢ on the menu that opens.
3. Click the **Fill Color tool color swatch** 🎨 on the Tools panel, then click the **blue color swatch** in the left column of the color palette.
4. Press and hold [**Shift**], then draw a **square** resembling the dimensions and position of the square shown in Figure 34.
5. Click the **Selection tool** ▸ on the Tools panel, then drag a **marquee** around the square to select the object.
6. Click **Insert** on the menu bar, click **Motion Tween**, then click **OK** in the Convert selection to symbol for tween dialog box.
7. Click **frame 48** on Layer 2, then drag the **square** to the bottom of the Stage, as shown in Figure 35.

   When you click frame 48, the circle object moves to the right side of the Stage. Remember, when a frame is selected, all objects in that frame on every layer appear on the Stage.

(continued)

8. Play the movie.

The square appears on top if the two objects intersect.

You drew an object and used it to create a second animation.

Work with layers and view Timeline features

1. Click **Layer 2** on the Timeline, then drag **Layer 2** below Layer 1.

   Layer 2 is now the bottom layer, as shown in Figure 36.

2. Play the movie and notice how the square appears beneath the circle if the objects intersect.

3. Click **Layer 2** on the Timeline, then drag **Layer 2** above Layer 1.

4. Play the movie and notice how the square now appears on top of the circle if they intersect.

5. Click the **Frame View icon** ▾≡ on the right corner of the Timeline title bar, as shown in Figure 37, to display the menu.

6. Click **Tiny** to display more frames.

   Notice how more frames appear on the Timeline, but each frame is smaller.

7. Click the **Frame View icon** ▾≡ , then click **Short**.

8. Click the **Frame View icon** ▾≡ , then click **Preview**.

   The object thumbnails appear in frame 1 on the Timeline.

9. Click the **Frame View icon** ▾≡ , then click **Normal**.

You changed the order of the layers, the display of frames, and the way the Timeline is viewed.

Figure 36 *Changing the stacking order of layers*

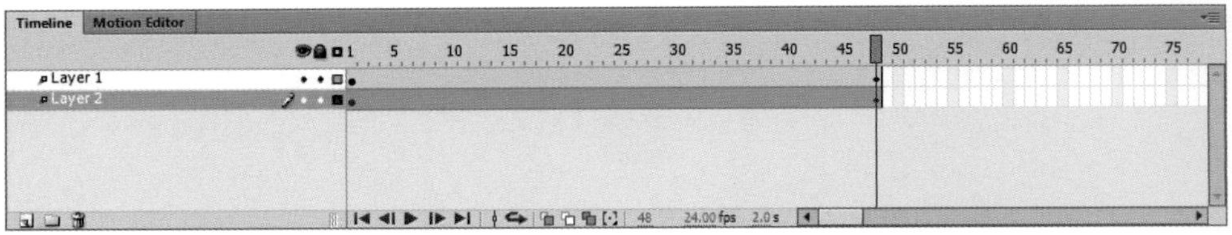

Figure 37 *Changing the view of the Timeline*

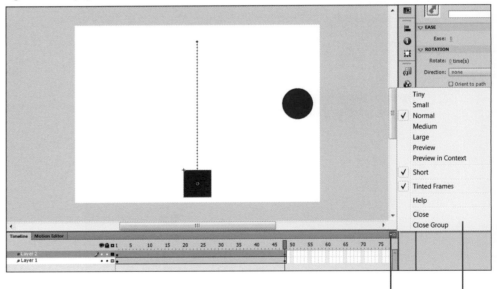

Frame View icon   Frame View options

Figure 38 *Changing the frame rate*

*Pointer changes to
double-headed arrow*

Figure 39 *Displaying the Properties option*

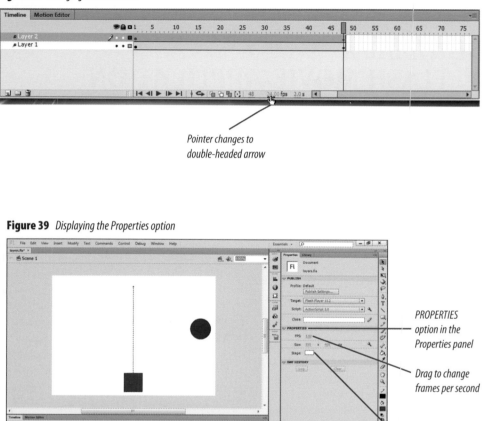

*PROPERTIES
option in the
Properties panel*

*Drag to change
frames per second*

*Click to open color
palette and change
the Stage color*

Modify the frame rate and change the layer names

1. Point to the **Frame Rate (fps)** on the Timeline status bar so the pointer changes to the double-headed arrow, as shown in Figure 38.

2. Drag the pointer left to change the frame rate to **3**.

TIP Alternately, you can click the frame rate number, then type a new number.

3. Play the movie and notice that the speed of the movie changed.

4. Click a blank area of the Stage, then verify the Properties panel is the active panel. If not, click **Window**, then click **Properties**.

5. If the PROPERTIES options are not displayed, as shown in Figure 39, click **PROPERTIES** on the Properties panel.

   When the Stage is clicked, the Properties panel provides information about the Stage, including size and background color.

6. Use the Properties panel to change the frame rate (fps) to **18** and the Stage color to **black**.

7. Click the **tick mark** for **24** on the Timeline and notice the position of the objects on the Stage.

8. Drag the **playhead** left and right to display frames one by one.

9. Double-click **Layer 1** on the Timeline, type **circle**, then press **[Enter]**(Win) or **[return]**(Mac).

10. Change the name of Layer 2 to **square**.

11. Play the movie, then save your work.

You changed the frame rate of the movie and named layers.

Distribute a
FLASH MOVIE/APPLICATION

What You'll Do

In this lesson, you will prepare a movie for distribution on the web.

Distributing Movies for Viewing on a Website

Flash is an excellent program for creating animations, such as banner ads, that are part of a website. When you develop Flash movies, the program saves them in a file format (.fla) that only users who have the Flash program installed on their computers can view. Web browsers, such as Internet Explorer, Safari, Chrome, and Firefox, cannot play Flash FLA files. Flash FLA files must be converted into a Flash Player file (.swf) so that the web browser knows the type of file to play (.swf) and the program needed to play the file (Flash Player). In addition, the HTML code needs to be created that instructs the web browser to play the SWF file. Fortunately, Flash generates both the SWF and HTML files when you use the Flash Publish command.

The process for publishing a Flash movie is to create and save a movie and then select the Publish command on the File menu. You can specify various settings, such as dimensions for the window in which the movie plays in the browser, before publishing the movie. Targeting the Flash Player when publishing a

movie creates two files: an HTML file and a Flash Player (SWF) file. Both the HTML and SWF files retain the same name as the Flash movie file, but with different file extensions:

- .html—the HTML document
- .swf—the Flash Player file

So, publishing a movie named layers.fla generates two files–layers.html and layers.swf. The HTML document contains the code that the browser interprets to display the movie on the web. The code also specifies which Flash Player movie the browser should play. Sample HTML code referencing a Flash Player movie is shown in Figure 40: the movie source is set to layers.swf; the display dimensions (determined by the size of the Stage) are set to 550 × 400; and the background color is set to black (#000000 is the code for black).

Specifying a Stage color for a Flash document will cause the HTML document that is created when using the Publish command to fill the browser window with the color. If you want to display a background color only for the dimensions of the Stage, you can add a layer to the Flash document and draw a rectangle the same dimensions of the Stage and with the desired fill color. Be sure this backdrop layer is the bottom layer. Then, when you publish the Flash document and view it in a browser, the movie will be displayed in a browser window using the dimensions of the Stage and the color you identified for the backdrop rectangle. The rest of the browser window will be the Stage color. A shortcut to previewing a Flash document within an HTML document is to use the Default – (HTML) option from the Publish Preview command in the File menu or simply pressing [F12].

Distributing Movies for Viewing on a Computer or Mobile Device

Flash is also an excellent program for developing applications, such as games, that are displayed on computers (without using a browser) and mobile devices (smartphones and tablets). These applications are created as AIR (Adobe Integrated Runtime) files and do not use a web browser. An AIR application has an .air file extension and can be run by simply clicking on an icon displayed on the computer or mobile device. An example would be the MazeBall game that is downloaded from the Android Market for mobile phones and the Apple store for the iPad. The process for creating an AIR application is to choose one of the AIR settings: AIR for Android, AIR for iOS or AIR (for desktop and laptop computers) before you start developing the application or to create an application and use the Publish setting to select the desired target device(s). Developing applications can be quite a bit more involved, both in scope and technically, than creating animations for a website.

Other Distribution Options

Flash provides another way to distribute your movies that may or may not involve delivery on the web. You can create an executable file called a **projector**. When you create a projector file, you specify the type of file you want to create, such as Windows .exe files and Macintosh .app files. Projector files maintain the movie's interactivity. So, if a movie has buttons that the user clicks to play an animation, the buttons will work in a projector file.

Projector files do not need the Flash Player to play them. You can play projector files directly from a computer, or you can incorporate them into an application, such as a game, that is downloaded or delivered on a CD or DVD. In addition, Flash provides options for creating movies specifically for mobile devices, such as cell phones. This lesson will focus on creating a Flash Player SWF file. Later you will learn how to create AIR and projector files.

Figure 40 *Sample HTML code*

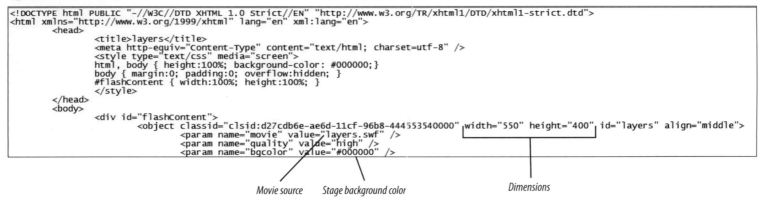

```
<!DOCTYPE html PUBLIC "-//W3C//DTD XHTML 1.0 Strict//EN" "http://www.w3.org/TR/xhtml1/DTD/xhtml1-strict.dtd">
<html xmlns="http://www.w3.org/1999/xhtml" lang="en" xml:lang="en">
    <head>
        <title>layers</title>
        <meta http-equiv="Content-Type" content="text/html; charset=utf-8" />
        <style type="text/css" media="screen">
        html, body { height:100%; background-color: #000000;}
        body { margin:0; padding:0; overflow:hidden; }
        #flashContent { width:100%; height:100%; }
        </style>
    </head>
    <body>

        <div id="flashContent">
            <object classid="clsid:d27cdb6e-ae6d-11cf-96b8-444553540000" width="550" height="400" id="layers" align="middle">
                <param name="movie" value="layers.swf" />
                <param name="quality" value="high" />
                <param name="bgcolor" value="#000000" />
```

Movie source   Stage background color   Dimensions

Publish a movie for distribution on the web

1. Verify layers.fla is open, then save it as **layersWeb.fla**.

2. Click **File** on the menu bar, then click **Publish**.

   The files layersWeb.html and layersWeb.swf are automatically generated and saved in the same folder as the Flash document.

3. Use your file management program to navigate to the drive and folder where you save your work.

4. Notice the three files that begin with "layersWeb," as shown in Figure 41.

   The three files are layersWeb.fla, the Flash movie; layersWeb.html, the HTML document; and layersWeb.swf, the Flash Player file.

5. Double-click **layersWeb.html** to play the movie in the browser.

   Note: Depending on your browser, browser settings and version, you may need to complete additional steps (such as accepting blocked content) to view the layers.html document.

   TIP Click the browser button on the taskbar if the movie does not open automatically in your browser.

   Notice the animation takes up only a portion of the browser window, as shown in Figure 42. This is because the Stage size is set to 550 x 440, which is smaller than the browser window. Notice also that the entire browser window has been filled with the black background. This is because a background color was used rather than creating a backdrop layer.

6. Close the browser, and return to Flash.

You used the Publish command to create an HTML document (.html) and a Flash Player file (.swf), then you displayed the HTML document in a web browser.

Figure 41 *The three layers files after publishing the movie*

Your files may be listed in a different order

Your file sizes may vary slightly

Figure 42 *The animation played in a browser window*

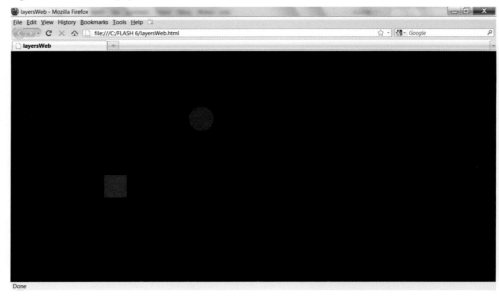

Figure 43 *Drawing a rectangle the size of the Stage*

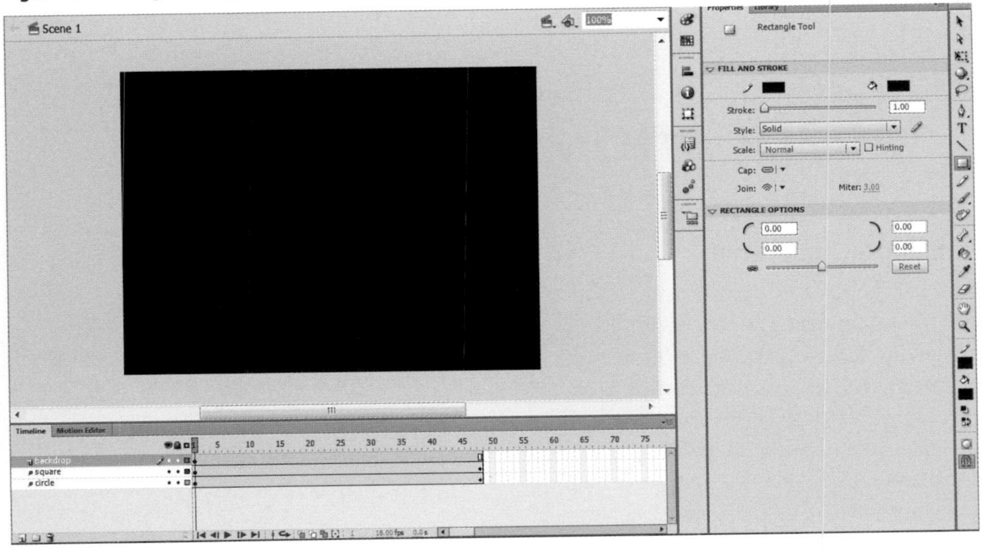

Create a backdrop color layer for the Stage

1. Click the **Stage** to select it.

2. Use the document properties in the Properties panel to change the Stage color to **white**.

3. Click **square** on the Timeline to select the square layer.

4. Click **Insert** on the menu bar, point to **Timeline**, then click **Layer**.

5. Double-click **Layer 3** on the Timeline to select the name of the new layer, type **backdrop**, then press **[Enter]** (Win) or **[return]** (Mac).

6. Click **frame 1** on the backdrop layer.

7. Click the **Rectangle tool** 🔲 on the Tools menu.

8. Use the Tools panel to set the Fill Color to **black** and the Stroke Color to **black**.

9. Draw a **rectangle** that covers the Stage, as shown in Figure 43.

10. Click **backdrop** on the Timeline, then drag the **backdrop** layer below the circle layer.

11. Click **File** on the menu bar, point to **Publish Preview**, then click **Default – (HTML)**.

    Notice how the HTML document has a white background and the Flash movie plays in an area the size of the Stage.

    Note: If a warning message opens, follow the directions to allow blocked content.

12. Close the browser and return to Flash.

13. Save and close the layersWeb.fla document.

You changed the Stage color of a Flash document and added a backdrop color layer.

Plan an APPLICATION

What You'll Do

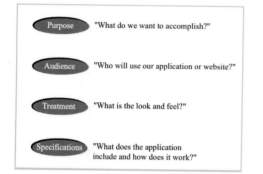

Purpose	"What do we want to accomplish?"
Audience	"Who will use our application or website?"
Treatment	"What is the look and feel?"
Specifications	"What does the application include and how does it work?"

In this lesson, you will learn how to plan a Flash application. You will also learn about the guidelines for screen design and the interactive design of applications.

Planning an Application

Flash can be used to develop entire products, such as games that run on smartphones, or animations that are part of a product, such as an educational tutorial, and delivered via the Internet, a CD, or a DVD. You can use Flash to create enhancements to web pages, such as animated logos, interactive navigation buttons, and banner ads. No matter what the application, the first step is planning. Often, the temptation is to jump right into the program and start developing movies. The problem is that this invariably results in a more time-consuming process at best; and wasted effort, resources, and money at worst. The larger and more complex the project is, the more critical the planning process becomes. Planning an application should involve the following steps:

Step 1: Stating the Purpose (Goals). "What, specifically, do we want to accomplish?"

Determining the goals is a critical step in planning because goals guide the development process, keep the team members on track, and provide a way to evaluate the application, both during and after its development.

Step 2: Identifying the Target Audience. "Who will use our application?"

Understanding the potential viewers helps in developing an application that can address their needs. For example, children respond to exploration and surprise, so having a dog wag its tail when the mouse pointer rolls over it might appeal to this audience.

Step 3: Determining the Treatment. "What is the look and feel?"

The treatment is how the application will be presented to the user, including the tone, approach, and emphasis.

Tone. Will the application be humorous, serious, light, heavy, formal, or informal? The tone of an application can often be used to make a statement, for instance, projecting a progressive, high-tech, well-funded corporate image.

Approach. How much direction will be provided to the user? An interactive game might focus on exploration such as when the user points to an object on the screen and the object becomes animated; while an informational application might provide lots of direction and include lists of options in the form of drop-down menus.

Emphasis. How much emphasis will be placed on the various multimedia elements? For example, a company may want to develop a business application that shows the features of its new product line, including video demonstrations and sound narrations of how each product works. The budget might not allow for the expense of creating the videos, so the emphasis would shift to still pictures with text descriptions.

Step 4: Developing the Specifications and Storyboard. "What precisely does the application include and how does it work?"

The **specifications** state what will be included in each screen, including the arrangement of each element and the functionality of each object (for example, what happens when you click the button labeled Skip Intro). Specifications should include the following:

Playback System. The choice of what configuration to target for playback is critical, especially Internet connection speed, browser versions, screen resolution, screen size (especially when targeting mobile devices), and plug-ins.

Elements to Include. The specifications should include details about the various elements that are to be included in the application. What are the dimensions for the animations, and what is the frame rate? What are the sizes of the various objects such as photos, buttons, and so on? What fonts, font sizes, and font formatting will be used? Should video or sound be included?

Functionality. The specifications should include the way the program reacts to an action by the user, such as a mouse click. For example, clicking a door (object) might cause a doorbell to ring (sound), the door to open (an animation), an "exit the program" message to appear (text), or an entirely new screen to be displayed.

Using Screen Design Guidelines

The following screen design guidelines are used by application developers. The implementation of these guidelines is affected by the goals of the application, the intended audience, and the content.

Balance in screen design refers to the distribution of optical weight in the layout. Optical weight is the ability of an object to attract the viewer's eye, as determined by the object's size, shape, color, and so on. The screen in Figure 44 shows a somewhat balanced design with the bright buttons at the bottom balanced against the heading near the top; and the icons on the left balanced against the satellite image on the right. However, the overall feel is less formal than a precisely balanced layout would project. In general, a balanced design is more appealing to a viewer. However, for a game application a balanced layout may not be desired.

Figure 44 *Sample screen design*
nasa.gov http://spaceplace.nasa.gov/satellite-insight/en/#/review/satelliteinsight/SatelliteInsight.swf

Unity helps the screen objects reinforce each other. **Intra-screen unity** has to do with how the various screen objects relate and how they all fit in. For example, a children's game might only use cartoon characterizations of animals for all the objects—including navigation buttons and sound control buttons, as well as the on-screen characters. **Inter-screen unity** refers to the design that viewers encounter as they navigate from one screen to another, and it provides consistency throughout the application. For example, all navigation buttons are located in the same place on each screen.

Movement refers to the way the viewer's eyes move through the objects on the screen. Different types of objects and various animation techniques can be used to draw the viewer to a location on the screen.

For example, a photo of a waterfall may cause the viewer's eyes to follow the flow of

the water down, especially if the waterfall is animated. The designer could then place an object, such as a logo or a sales message, below the waterfall.

Using Interactive Design Guidelines

In addition to screen design guidelines, interactive guidelines determine the interactivity of the application. The following guidelines are not absolute rules since they are affected by the goals of the application, the intended audience, and the content:

- Make it simple, easy to understand, and easy to use so that viewers do not have to spend time learning what the application is about and what they need to do.
- Build in consistency in the navigation scheme. Help the users know where they are in the application and help them avoid getting lost.
- Provide feedback. Users need to know when an action, such as clicking a

button, has been completed. Changing its color or shape, or adding a sound can indicate this.

- Give the user control. Allow the user to skip long introductions; provide controls for starting, stopping, and rewinding animations, video, and audio; and provide controls for adjusting audio.

Using Storyboards

Simple applications such as a banner ad on a website may consist of a single Flash animation, but complex applications, such as games, often include several animations within one or more Flash movies. No matter how extensive the application, storyboards can be invaluable in the development process. A storyboard is a series of pictures that illustrate the sequence of events in an animation. See Figure 45. A storyboard can be extremely elaborate and include color images, scripts,

Figure 45 *Sample storyboard*

and notations for dialog, sound effects, transitions, and movement. Or, it can be as simple as black and white stick figures. Storyboards can be created using templates and even computer programs or simply sketched out. As part of the pre-production process, storyboards are an easy way to test out an idea by helping you visualize the progression of events. This allows you to make adjustments before development begins. Then the storyboard becomes a basic blueprint for the creation of the animation and a guide for those involved in the development process such as Flash designers, developers, and artists.

Rich Media Content and Accessibility

Flash provides the tools that allow you to create compelling applications and websites by incorporating rich media content, such as animations, sound, and video. Generally, incorporating rich media enhances the user's experience. However, accessibility becomes an issue for those persons who have visual, hearing, or mobility impairments, or have a cognitive disability. Designers need to utilize techniques that help ensure accessibility, such as providing consistency in navigation and layout, labeling graphics, captioning audio content throughout the applications and website, and providing keyboard access.

The Flash Workflow Process

After the planning process, you are ready to start work on the Flash documents. The following steps can be used as guidelines in a general workflow process suggested by Adobe.

Step 1: Create and/or acquire the elements to be used in the application. The elements include text, photos, drawings, video, and audio. The elements become the raw material for the graphics, animations, menus, buttons, and content that populate the application and provide the interactivity. You can use the various Flash drawing and text tools to create your own images and text content; or, you can use another program, such as Adobe Photoshop, to develop the elements, and then import them into Flash. Alternately, you can acquire stock clip art and photographs. You can produce video and audio content in-house and import it into Flash or you can acquire these elements from a third party.

Step 2: Arrange the elements and create the animations. Arrange the elements (objects) on the Stage and on the Timeline to define when and how they appear in your application. Once the elements are available, you can create the various animations called for in the specifications.

Step 3: Apply special effects. Flash provides innumerable special effects that can be applied to the various media elements and animations. These include graphic and text filters, such as drop shadows, blurs, glows, and bevels. In addition, there are effects for sounds and animations such as fade-ins and fade-outs, acceleration and deceleration, morphing, and even 3D effects.

Step 4: Create the interactivity. Flash provides a scripting feature, ActionScript, which allows you to develop programming code to control how the media elements behave, including how various objects respond to user interactions, such as clicking buttons and rolling over images.

Step 5: Test and publish the application. Testing can begin before the actual development process with usability testing, which involves potential users being observed as they navigate through thumbnail sketches of the storyboard. Testing should continue throughout the development process, including using the Test Movie feature in the Control menu to test the movie using the Flash Player and to publish the movie in order to test it in a browser.

Project Management

Developing any extensive application, such as a game, involves project management. A project plan needs to be developed that provides the project scope and identifies the milestones, including analyzing, designing, building, testing, and launching. Personnel and resource needs are identified, budgets built, tasks assigned, and schedules developed. Successful projects are a team effort relying on the close collaboration of designers, developers, project managers, graphic artists, programmers, testers, and others. Adobe provides various product suites, such as the Creative Suite 6 (CS6) Web Collection, that include programs such as Flash, Dreamweaver, Photoshop, Illustrator, and Fireworks. These are the primary tools needed to develop interactive applications. These programs are designed for easy integration. So, a graphic artist can use Photoshop to develop an image that can easily be imported into Flash and used by an animator. In addition, other tools in the suites, such as Adobe Bridge, help ensure efficient workflow when working in a team environment. Adobe Flash Builder and Flex are tools that are used by Flash developers who focus on creating sophisticated Flash applications by writing ActionScript code.

Using the Flash Help Feature

As you are planning the application and while you are developing it, you may have specific questions about how to incorporate what you are planning using Flash. Fortunately, Flash provides a comprehensive Help feature that can be very useful when first learning the program. You access the Help feature from the Help menu. The Help feature is organized by categories, including Using Flash Professional CS6, which have several topics such as Workspace and Managing documents. In addition, the Help feature has a Help Search feature. You use the Help Search feature to search for topics using keywords, such as Timeline. Searching by keywords accesses the Flash Community Help feature, which displays links to content relevant to the search terms. Another option in the Help menu is Adobe Online Forums. This is a link to Flash Professional forums sponsored by Adobe. You can ask questions and join groups discussing various Flash-related topics. Other resources not affiliated with Adobe are available through the web. You may find some by searching the web for Flash resources.

Figure 46 *The Flash Help categories*

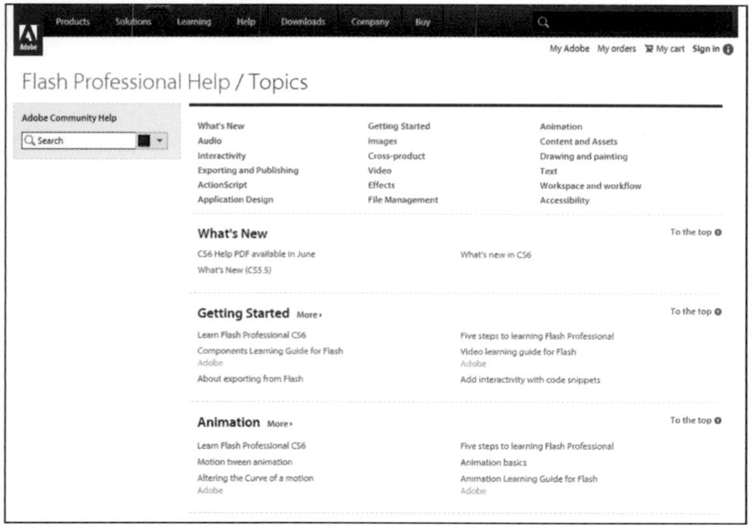

Figure 47 *The Flash Community Help site*

Use Flash Help

1. Start a new Flash document.

2. Click **Help** on the menu bar, then click **Flash Help**.

   Note: If you see a page not found message, be sure you are connected to the Internet.

3. Maximize the Help window to view the Help screen, as shown in Figure 46.

4. Scroll down, display the **Workspace and workflow** section, click **The Timeline**, then read through the text in About the Timeline.

5. Scroll down the page and review the information that is provided.

6. Scroll to display the top of the Help window.

7. Click in the **Search text box**, type **Flash Professional CS6**, then verify the Flash icon is displayed to the right of the Search text box.

   Your search is refined to the Flash product when the Flash icon is displayed.

8. Press **[Enter]** (Win) or **[return]** (Mac) to access the Community Help site, as seen in Figure 47.

9. Scroll down the page and study the various links provided on the site.

10. Close the Flash Help site, then exit the Flash program.

You used the Flash Help feature to access information on the Timeline and the community help feature.

Open a document and understand the Flash workspace.

1. Start Flash, open fl1_2.fla, then save it as **skillsDemo1.fla**. This movie has two layers. Layer 1 contains the heading and the rectangle at the top of the Stage. Layer 2 contains an animation that runs for 75 frames.
2. Change the magnification to 50% using the View menu. (*Hint*: Click View, point to Magnification, then click 50%.)
3. Change the magnification to Fit in Window.
4. Change the Timeline view to Small, then change it back to Normal. (*Hint*: Click the Frame View icon in the upper-right corner of the Timeline title bar.)
5. Hide all panels.
6. Display the Tools panel, Timeline panel, Properties panel, and the Library panel if it did not open with the Properties panel.
7. Group the Library and Properties panels if they are not already grouped.
8. Drag the Library panel from the Properties panel, then position it on the Stage.
9. Collapse the Library panel.
10. Close the Library panel to remove it from the screen.
11. Reset the Essentials workspace.

Play and test a Flash movie.

1. Drag the playhead to view the contents of each frame. Use the commands on the Timeline status bar to play and rewind the movie.
2. Press [Enter] (Win) or [return] (Mac) to play and stop the movie.

3. Test the movie in the Flash Player window, then close the Flash Player window.

Change the document size and Stage color.

1. Use the document properties settings in the Properties panel to change the document height to 380. (*Hint:* Click a blank area of the Stage to select it.)
2. Change the Stage color to a medium gray color (#999999).
3. Change the magnification to 100%.
4. Play the movie.

Create and save a Flash movie.

1. Insert a new layer above Layer 2, then select frame 1 on the new layer, Layer 3.
2. Draw a green ball in the middle of the left side of the Stage, approximately the same size as the red ball. (*Hint*: The green gradient color can be used to draw the ball. Several gradient colors are found in the bottom row of the color palette when you click the Fill Color tool in the Tools panel.)
3. Use the Selection tool to draw a marquee around the green ball to select it, then create a motion tween to animate the green ball so that it moves across the screen from left to right. (*Hint*: After inserting the motion tween, select frame 75 on Layer 3 before repositioning the green ball.)
4. Use the Selection tool to reshape the motion path to an arc by dragging the middle of the path downward.
5. Play the movie.

6. Use the Undo command to undo the reshape. (*Note*: You may need to use the Undo feature twice.)
7. Use the Selection tool to select frame 75 of the Layer 3, click the green ball if it is not already selected to select it, then use the Properties panel to change the transparency (alpha) from 100% to 20%. (*Hint*: If the Properties panel COLOR EFFECT option is not displayed, make sure the Properties panel is open and click the green ball to make sure it is selected.)
8. Play the movie.
9. Click frame 75 on Layer 3 and click the green ball to select it.
10. Use the Properties panel to decrease the width of the ball to approximately half its size. (*Hint*: Make sure the lock width and height value icon in the Properties panel is unbroken. You may need to click the Stage to have the new value take effect.)
11. Play the movie.
12. Select frame 1 on Layer 3, then click the green ball to select it.
13. Use the Filters option in the Properties panel to add a drop shadow.
14. Play the movie.
15. Select frame 1 on Layer 2, then click the red ball to select it.
16. Open the Motion Presets panel, then add a bounce-smoosh preset.
17. Move Layer 3 below Layer 2.
18. Play the movie.
19. Save the movie.

Work with the Timeline.

1. Change the frame rate to 8 frames per second, play the movie, change the frame rate to 24, then play the movie again.
2. Change the view of the Timeline to display more frames.
3. Change the view of the Timeline to display a preview of the object thumbnails.
4. Change the view of the Timeline to display the Normal view.
5. Click frame 1 on Layer 1, use the playhead to display each frame, then compare your screens to Figure 48.
6. Save the movie.

Distribute a Flash movie.

1. Click File on the menu bar, then click Publish.
2. Open your browser, then open skillsDemo1.html.
3. View the movie, close your browser, then return to Flash.

Work with the Flash workspace.

1. Use the Document Settings dialog box to change the document Stage color to white.
2. Insert a new layer, then rename the layer **gray backdrop**.
3. Select frame 1 of the gray backdrop layer.
4. Select the rectangle tool, then set the Fill Color and the Stroke Color to the same shade of gray.
5. Draw a rectangle that covers the Stage.
6. Drag the gray backdrop layer to the bottom of the list of layers on the Timeline.

7. Rename the layers using these names: **heading**, **green ball**, and **red ball**. Use clues on the Timeline to help you know what to name each layer.

8. Play the movie in the browser, then close the browser window.
9. Save and close the Flash document.

Figure 48 *Completed Skills Review*

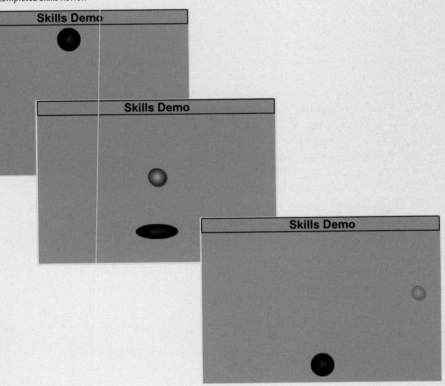

A friend cannot decide whether to sign up for a class in Flash or Dreamweaver. You help her decide by showing her what you already know about Flash. You want to show her how easy it is to create a simple animation because you think she'd enjoy a class in Flash. You decide to animate three objects. The first object is placed on the center of the Stage and pulsates throughout the movie. The second object enters the Stage from the left side and moves across the middle of the Stage and off the right side of the Stage. The third object enters the Stage from the right side and moves across the middle of the Stage and off the left side of the Stage. The motion paths for the two objects that move across the Stage are reshaped so they go above and below the pulsating object in the middle of the Stage.

1. Open a Flash document, then save it as **demonstration.fla**.
2. Verify the view is set to 100%.
3. Use the tools on the Tools panel to create a circle (or object of your choice) and color of your choice on the middle of the Stage.
4. Draw a marquee around the object to select it and apply a pulse motion preset.
5. Insert a new layer, then select frame 1 on the layer.
6. Create a simple shape or design using a color of your choice, and place it off the left side of the Stage and halfway down the Stage.

7. Select the object and insert a motion tween that moves the object directly across the screen and off the right side of the Stage. (*Hint*: After inserting the motion tween, select the last frame in the motion span and drag the object off the right side of the Stage.)
8. Reshape the motion path so that the object goes in an arc below the center pulsating object.
9. Insert a new layer, then select frame 1 on the new layer.
10. Create an object using the color of your choice and place it off the right side of the Stage and halfway down the Stage.

11. Draw a marquee to select the object and insert a motion tween that moves the object directly across the screen and off the left side of the Stage.
12. Reshape the motion path so that the object goes in an arc above the center pulsating object.
13. Play the movie.
14. Add a Stage color.
15. Rename the layers with descriptive names.
16. Play the movie, test it , then close the Flash Player window.
17. Save the movie, then compare your movie to the sample provided in Figure 49.

Figure 49 *Sample completed Project Builder 1*

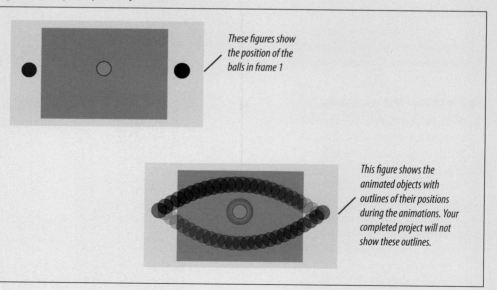

These figures show the position of the balls in frame 1

This figure shows the animated objects with outlines of their positions during the animations. Your completed project will not show these outlines.

You've been asked to develop a simple movie about recycling for a day care center. For this project, you will add two animations to an existing movie. You will show three objects that appear on the screen at different times, and then move each object to a recycle bin at different times. You can create the objects using any of the Tools on the Tools panel.

1. Open fl1_3.fla, then save it as **recycle.fla**.
2. Play the movie and study the Timeline to familiarize yourself with the movie's current settings. Currently, there are no animations.
3. Insert a new layer above Layer 2, click frame 1 on the new layer, then draw a small object in the upper-left corner of the Stage.
4. Create a motion tween that moves the object to the recycle bin. (*Hint*: After inserting the motion tween, be sure to select frame 40 on the new layer before moving the object to the recycle bin. *Note*: At this time, the object will appear on top of the recycle bin when it is placed in the bin.)
5. Reshape the path so that the object moves in an arc to the recycle bin.
6. Insert a new layer above the top layer, click frame 1 on the new layer, draw a small object in the upper-center of the Stage, then create a motion tween that moves the object to the recycle bin.
7. Insert a new layer above the top layer, click frame 1 on the new layer, draw a small object in the upper-right corner of the Stage, then create a motion tween that moves the object to the recycle bin.
8. Reshape the path so that the object moves in an arc to the recycle bin.
9. Move Layer 1 to the top of all the layers. (*Note:* Layer 1 contains the front of the box. Moving Layer 1 above the other layers causes the objects on those layers to be hidden behind the front of the box.)
10. Play the movie and compare your movie to the sample provided in Figure 50.
11. Save the movie.

Figure 50 *Sample completed Project Builder 2*

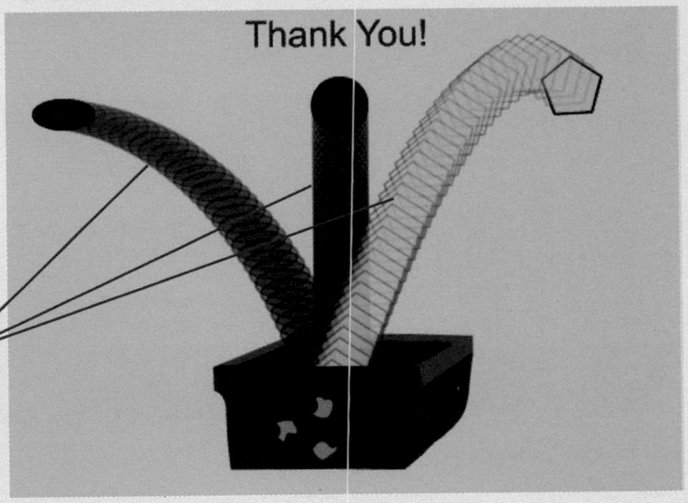

This figure shows the animated objects with outlines of their positions during the animations. Your completed project will not show these outlines.

Figure 51 shows screens from a mobile app that is described on the NASA website. Study the figure and answer the following questions. For each question, indicate how you determined your answer.

1. Connect to the Internet, then go to *www.nps.gov/nama/photosmultimedia/app-page.htm* (*Note:* The screens displayed on the website may be different than those in Figure 51.)

2. Open a document in a word processor or open a new Flash document, save the file as **dpc1**, then answer the following questions. (*Hint:* Use the Flash Text tool if you open a Flash document.)
   - Whose app is this?
   - What is the goal(s) of the app?
   - Who is the target audience?
   - What treatment (look and feel) is used?

   - What are the design layout guidelines being used (balance, movement, etc.)?
   - How can animation enhance this page?
   - Do you think this is an effective design for the organization, its products, and its target audience? Why, or why not?
   - What suggestions would you make to improve the design, and why?

Figure 51 *Design Project*
Courtesy of National Park Service website – www.nps.gov; © Google 2012. www.nps.gov/nama/photosmultimedia/app-page.htm

There are numerous companies in the business of developing websites and applications for others. Many of these companies use Flash as one of their primary development tools. These companies promote themselves through their own websites and usually provide online portfolios with samples of their work. Log onto the Internet, then use your favorite search engine and keywords such as Flash developers and Flash animators to locate three of these companies, and generate the following information for each one. A sample website is shown in Figure 52.

1. Company name:
2. Contact information (address, phone, and so on):
3. Website URL:
4. Company mission:
5. Services provided:
6. Sample list of clients:
7. Describe three ways the company seems to have used Flash in its website. Were these effective? Why, or why not?
8. Describe three applications of Flash that the company includes in its portfolio (or showcases or samples). Were these effective? Why, or why not?
9. Would you want to work for this company? Why, or why not?
10. Would you recommend this company to another company that was looking to create an application or enhance its website? Why, or why not?

Figure 52 *Sample website for Portfolio Project*
Copyright © 2012 2Advanced Studios, LLC. http://www.2advanced.com/#/work

Getting Started with Flash

CHAPTER 2 DRAWING OBJECTS IN ADOBE FLASH

1. Use the Flash drawing and alignment tools
2. Select objects and apply colors
3. Work with drawn objects
4. Work with text and text objects
5. Work with layers and objects

CHAPTER 2
DRAWING OBJECTS IN ADOBE FLASH

Introduction

Computers can display graphics in either a bitmap or a vector format. The difference between these formats is in how they describe an image. A bitmap graphic represents an image as an array of dots, called **pixels**, which are arranged within a grid. Each pixel in an image has an exact position on the screen and a precise color. To make a change in a bitmap graphic, you modify the pixels. When you enlarge a bitmap graphic, the number of pixels remains the same, resulting in jagged edges that decrease the quality of the image. A vector graphic represents an image using lines and curves, which you can resize without losing image quality. Also, the file size of a vector image is generally smaller than the file size of a bitmap image, which makes vector images particularly useful for an application. However, vector graphics are not as effective as bitmap graphics for representing photo-realistic images. Even so, one of the most compelling features of Flash is the ability to create and manipulate vector graphics.

Images (objects) created using Flash drawing tools are vector graphics, and have a stroke (border line), a fill, or both. In addition, the stroke of an object can be segmented into smaller lines. You can modify the size, shape, rotation, and color of each stroke, fill, and segment.

Flash provides two drawing modes, called models. In the Merge Drawing Model, when you draw two shapes and one overlaps the other, a change in the top object may affect the object it overlaps. For example, if you draw a circle on top of a rectangle and then move the circle off the rectangle, the portion of the rectangle covered by the circle is removed. The Object Drawing Model allows you to overlap shapes which are then kept separate, so that changes in one object do not affect another object. Another way to avoid having changes in one object affect another is to place the objects on separate layers on the Timeline as you did in Chapter 1.

TOOLS YOU'LL USE

Properties | Library

Rectangle Tool

FILL AND STROKE

Stroke: _____ 1.00

Style: Solid

Scale: Normal ☐ Hinting

Cap: ⊖ ▼

Join: ≋ ▼   Miter: 3.00

RECTANGLE OPTIONS

0.00   0.00

0.00   0.00

⊶ ———————   Reset

Properties | Library

T   ‹Instance Name›

TLF Text

Read Only

CHARACTER

Family: Arial

Style: Regular   Embed...

Size: 14.0 pt   Leading: 130   %

Color: ___   Tracking: 0

Highlight: ☑ Auto kern

Anti-alias: Readability

Rotation: Auto   T T T¹ T₁

▷ **ADVANCED CHARACTER**

▽ **PARAGRAPH**

Align:

Margins: →≣ 0.0 px   ≣← 0.0 px

Indent: →≣ 0.0 px

Spacing: →≣ 0.0 px   ≣ 0.0 px

Text Justify: Word spacing

CONTAINER AND FLOW

Behavior: Multiline no wrap

Max chars: -

Columns: ⦀ -   ⊞ - px

Padding: L: 2.0 px   R: 2.0 px

T: 2.0 px   B: 2.0 px

✏ ___ - pt   ⬟ ___

1st Line Offset: -

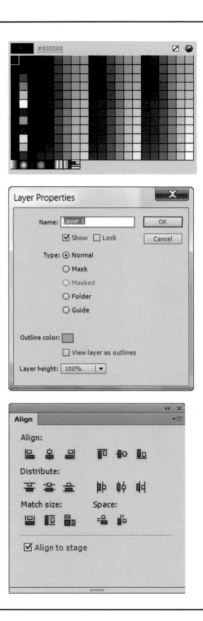

#000000

Layer Properties

Name: Layer 3   OK

☑ Show ☐ Lock   Cancel

Type: ⦿ Normal
○ Mask
○ Masked
○ Folder
○ Guide

Outline color: ▢

☐ View layer as outlines

Layer height: 100%

Align

Align:

Distribute:

Match size: Space:

☑ Align to stage

Use the Flash Drawing
AND ALIGNMENT TOOLS

What You'll Do

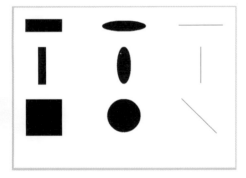

In this lesson, you will use several drawing tools to create various vector graphics.

Using Flash Drawing and Editing Tools

When you point to a tool on the Tools panel, its name appears next to the tool. Figure 1 identifies the tools described in the following paragraphs. Several of the tools have options that modify their use. For example, the Brush tool has options for changing the size and shape of the brush head. These options are available in the Options area of the Tools panel when the tool is selected.

Selection—Used to select an object or parts of an object, such as the stroke or fill, and to reshape and reposition objects. The options for the Selection tool are Snap to Objects (aligns objects), Smooth (smooths lines), and Straighten (straightens lines).

Subselection—Used to select, drag, and reshape an object. Vector graphics are composed of lines and curves (each of which is a segment) connected by **anchor points**. Selecting an object with this tool displays the anchor points and allows you to use them to edit the object.

Free Transform—Used to rotate, scale, skew, and distort objects.

Gradient Transform—Used to transform a gradient fill by adjusting the size, direction, or center of the fill.

The Free and Gradient Transform tools are grouped within one icon on the Tools panel. To see the menu containing grouped tools, click and hold the tool icon until the menu opens.

3D Rotation—Used to create 3D effects by rotating movie clips in 3D space on the Stage.

3D Translation—Used to create 3D effects by moving movie clips in 3D space on the Stage.

The 3D Rotation and the 3D Translation tools are grouped within one icon on the Tools panel.

Lasso—Used to select objects or parts of objects. The Polygon Mode option allows you to draw straight lines when selecting an object.

Pen—Used to draw lines and curves by creating a series of dots, known as anchor points, that are automatically connected. Other tools used to add, delete, and convert the anchor points created by the Pen tool are grouped with the Pen tool.

Text—Used to create and edit text.

Line—Used to draw straight lines. You can draw vertical, horizontal, and 45° diagonal lines by pressing and holding [Shift] while drawing the line.

Rectangle—Used to draw rectangular shapes. Press and hold [Shift] to draw a perfect square.

Oval—Used to draw oval shapes. Press and hold [Shift] to draw a perfect circle.

Primitive Rectangle and Oval—Used to draw objects with properties, such as corner radius or inner radius, that can be changed using the Properties panel.

PolyStar—Used to draw polygons and stars.

The Rectangle, Oval, Primitive, and PolyStar tools are grouped within one tool on the Tools panel.

Pencil—Used to draw freehand lines and shapes. The Pencil Mode option displays a menu with the following commands: Straighten (draws straight lines), Smooth (draws smooth curved lines), and Ink (draws freehand with no modification).

Brush—Used to draw (paint) with brush-like strokes. Options allow you to set the size and shape of the brush, and to determine the area to be painted, such as inside or behind an object.

Spray Brush—Used to spray colors and patterns onto objects. Dots are the default pattern for the spray. However, you can use a graphic symbol, such as a flag, to create a pattern.

The Brush and Spray Brush tools are grouped together.

Deco—Used to turn graphic shapes into geometric patterns or to create kaleidoscopic-like effects.

Bone—Used to animate objects that have joints. For example you could use a series of linked objects, such as arms and legs to create character animations.

Bind—Used to adjust the relationships among individual bones. The Bone and Bind tools are grouped together.

Paint Bucket—Used to fill enclosed areas of a drawing with color. Options allow you to fill areas that have gaps and to make adjustments in a gradient fill.

Ink Bottle—Used to apply line colors and thickness to the stroke of an object.

The Paint Bucket and Ink Bottle are grouped together.

Eyedropper—Used to select stroke, fill, and text attributes so they can be copied from one object to another.

Eraser—Used to erase lines and fills. Options allow you to choose what part of the object to erase, as well as the size and shape of the eraser.

Hand—Used to move the Stage around the Pasteboard by dragging the Stage.

Zoom—Used to change the magnification of an area of the Stage. Clicking an area of the Stage zooms in and holding down [Alt] (Win) or [option] (Mac) and clicking zooms out.

Stroke Color—Used to set the stroke color of drawn objects.

Figure 1 *Flash tools*

Selection
Subselection
Free Transform (Gradient)
3D Rotation (3D Translation)
Lasso
Pen (Add Anchor Point, etc.)
Text
Line
Rectangle (Oval, etc.)
Pencil
Brush (Spray)
Deco
Bone (Bind)
Paint Bucket (Ink Bottle)
Eyedropper
Eraser
Hand
Zoom

Stroke Color

Fill Color

Black and White
Swap Color

Options area (options change depending on which tool is selected)

Fill Color—Used to set the fill color of drawn objects.

Black and White—Used to set the stroke color to black and the fill color to white.

Swap Color—Used to swap the stroke and fill colors.

Options—Used to select an option for a tool, such as the type of rectangle (object drawing mode) or size of the brush when using the Brush tool.

Working with Grouped Tools

To display a list of grouped tools, you click the tool and hold the mouse button until the menu opens. For example, if you want to select the Oval tool and the Rectangle tool is displayed, you click and hold the Rectangle tool. Then, when the menu opens, you click the Oval tool option. You know a tool is a grouped tool if you see an arrow in the lower-right corner of the tool icon.

Working with Tool Options

Some tools have additional options that allow you to modify their use. For example, the brush tool has options to set the brush size and to set where the brush fill will be applied. If additional options for a tool are available, they appear at the bottom of the Tools panel in the Options area when the tool is selected. If the option has a menu associated with it, such as a list of brush sizes for the brush tool, then the option icon will have an arrow in the lower-right corner. Click and hold the option until the menu opens.

Tools for Creating Vector Graphics

The Oval, Rectangle, Pencil, Brush, Line, and Pen tools are used to create vector objects.

Positioning Objects on the Stage

The Stage dimensions are made up of pixels (dots) matching the Stage size. So, a Stage size of 550 × 400 would be 550 pixels wide and 400 pixels high. Each pixel has a location on the Stage designated as the X (across) and Y (down) coordinates. The location of any object on the Stage is determined by its position from the upper-left corner of the Stage, which is 0,0 and the object's registration point. The registration point of an object is used to align it with the coordinates. The registration point, which is shown as a crosshair, is initially set at the upper-left corner of an object, as shown in Figure 2. So, an object having coordinates of 100,100 would be positioned at 100 pixels across and 100 pixels down the Stage, as shown in Figure 2. The Properties panel displays the X,Y values of any selected object. The most precise way to position an object on the Stage is to use the Properties panel to enter X and Y values for the object. Other ways to position objects on the Stage include using rulers, gridlines, and guides, as well as the align options. The Rulers, Grid, and Guides commands, which are found on the View menu, are used to turn on and off these features. Figure 2 shows the rulers and the ruler lines, which are used to indicate the position of an object. (*Note:* Normally

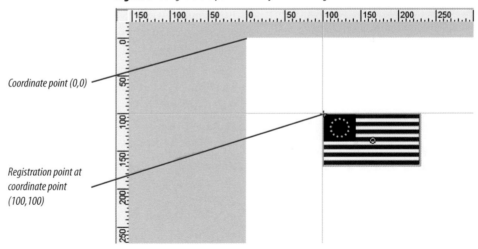

Figure 2 *Using rulers to position an object on the Stage*

Coordinate point (0,0)

Registration point at coordinate point (100,100)

ruler lines display on top of objects on the Stage. In Figure 2, the registration point is displayed above the ruler lines to show its exact placement.)

After displaying the rulers, you can drag the lines from the top ruler or the left side ruler to the Stage. To remove a ruler line, you drag the ruler line up to the top ruler or across to the left ruler.

Figure 3 shows the Stage with gridlines displayed. The gridlines can be used to position an object. You can modify the grid size and color. In addition to using rulers and guides to help place objects, you can create a new layer as a Guide layer that you use to position objects on the Stage. When you turn gridlines and guides on, they appear on the Stage. However, they do not appear in the Flash movie when you test or publish it.

Using the Align Panel

Figure 4 shows the Align panel, which allows you to position objects on the Stage either relative to the Stage or to other objects. The Align panel has four areas (Align, Distribute, Match size, Space) each with options. The Align options are used to align the edge or center of an object with the edge or center of the Stage—or, if multiple objects are selected, to align their edges and centers. The Distribute options are used to position objects across or down the Stage. The Match size options are used to resize selected objects to match the height and/or width of the largest object or to match the Stage if the Align to stage option is selected. The Space options are used to space out objects evenly across and down the Stage.

Figure 3 *Using gridlines to position an object on the Stage*

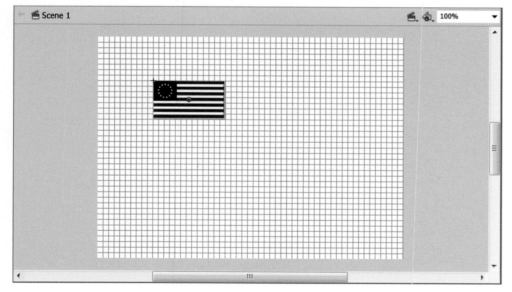

Figure 4 *The Align panel*

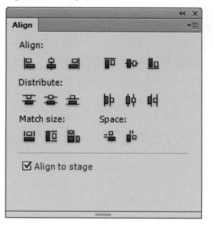

Show gridlines and check settings

1. Open fl2_1.fla from the drive and folder where your Data Files are stored, then save it as **tools.fla**.

2. Click **Essentials** on the menu bar, then click **Reset 'Essentials'**.

3. Click **View** on the menu bar, point to **Magnification**, then click **Fit in Window**.

4. Click the **Stroke Color tool color swatch** on the Tools panel, then click the **red color swatch** in the left column of the Color palette.

   Note: The color swatches shown in the Tools panel reflect the last selection and may not be the colors shown for the icons in Steps 4 and 5.

5. Click the **Fill Color tool color swatch** on the Tools panel, then click the **blue color swatch** in the left column of the Color palette.

6. Click **View** on the menu bar, point to **Grid**, then click **Show Grid** to display the gridlines.

7. Point to each tool on the Tools panel, then read its name.

8. Click the **Text tool** T , click **CHARACTER** on the Properties panel to open the area if it is not open already.

   Notice the options in the Properties panel including the CHARACTER and PARAGRAPH areas, as shown in Figure 5. The Properties panel options change depending on the tool selected. For the Text tool the properties include the character family and the paragraph family.

You opened a document, saved it, set up the workspace, changed the stroke and fill colors, displayed the grid, viewed tool names on the Tools panel, then viewed the Text tool options in the Properties panel.

Figure 5 *Tool name on the Tools panel*

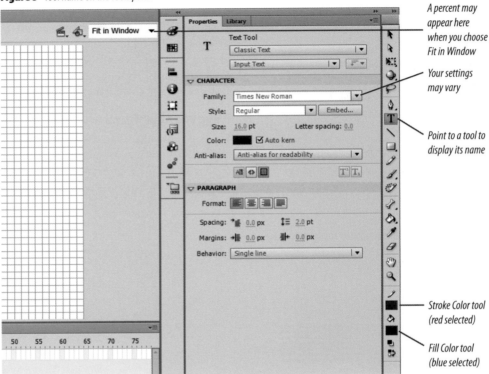

A percent may appear here when you choose Fit in Window

Your settings may vary

Point to a tool to display its name

Stroke Color tool (red selected)

Fill Color tool (blue selected)

Figure 6 *Objects created with drawing tools*

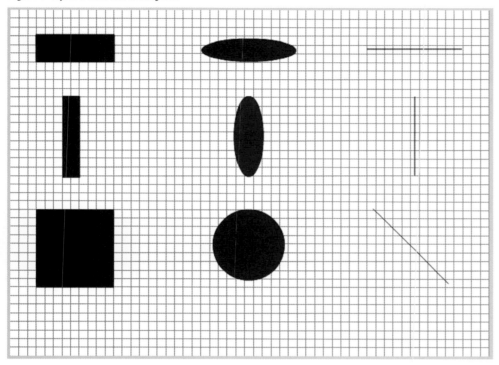

Use the Rectangle, Oval, and Line tools

1. Click the **Rectangle tool** on the Tools panel.

   Note: If the Rectangle tool is not displayed, click and hold the Oval tool to display the group of tools.

2. Verify that the Object Drawing option in the Options area of the Tools panel is not active.

   TIP When the Object Drawing option is not active, the object is drawn so that its stroke and fill can be selected separately.

3. Draw **three rectangle shapes** using Figure 6 as a guide.

   TIP Use the grid to approximate shape sizes, and press and hold [Shift] to draw a square. To undo an action, click the Undo command on the Edit menu.

   Notice the blue color for the fill and the red color for the strokes (border lines).

4. Click and hold the **Rectangle tool** on the Tools panel, then click the **Oval tool**.

5. Draw **three oval shapes** using Figure 6 as a guide.

   TIP Press and hold [Shift] to draw a perfect circle.

6. Click the **Line tool**, then draw **three lines** using Figure 6 as a guide.

   TIP To snap the line to the nearest 45-degree increment, such as 45, 90, 180 and so on, press and hold [Shift], draw the line, use the line tool pointer to rotate the line, then release [Shift].

You used the Rectangle, Oval, and Line tools to draw objects on the Stage.

Use the Pen, Pencil, and Brush tools

1. Click **Insert** on the menu bar, point to **Timeline**, then click **Layer**.

   A new layer—Layer 2—appears above Layer 1.

2. Click **frame 5** on Layer 2.

3. Click **Insert** on the menu bar, point to **Timeline**, then click **Keyframe**.

   Since the objects were drawn in frame 1 on Layer 1, they are no longer visible when you insert a keyframe in frame 5 on Layer 2. A keyframe allows you to draw in any location on the Stage on the specified frame.

4. Click the **Zoom tool** 🔍 on the Tools panel, click near the upper-left quadrant of the Stage to zoom in, then scroll as needed to see more of the grid.

5. Click the **Pen tool** ✒ on the Tools panel, position it in the upper-left quadrant of the Stage, as shown in Figure 7, then click to set an anchor point.

   (continued)

Figure 7 *Positioning the Pen Tool on the Stage*

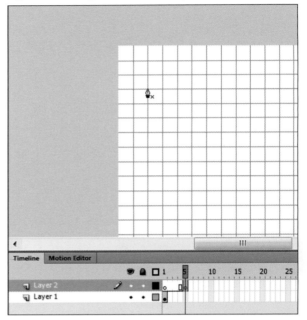

Drawing Objects in Adobe Flash

Figure 8 *Setting anchor points to draw an arrow*

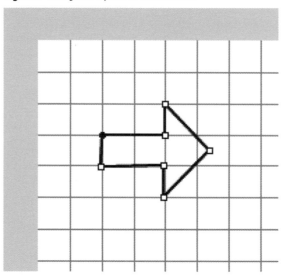

6. Using Figure 8 as a guide, click the remaining anchor points to finish drawing an arrow.

TIP To close an object, be sure to re-click the first anchor point as your last action.

7. Click the **Paint Bucket tool** , then click inside the arrow.

8. Click **View** on the menu bar, point to **Magnification**, then click **Fit in Window**.

9. Click **View** on the menu bar, point to **Grid**, then click **Show Grid** to turn off the gridlines.

10. Click **Insert** on the menu bar, point to **Timeline**, click **layer**, then insert a **keyframe** in frame 10.

(continued)

11. Click the **Pencil tool** ✏ on the Tools panel.

12. Click **Pencil Mode** ⌇ or ⌐ in the Options area of the Tools panel, then click the **Smooth** option, as shown in Figure 9.

13. Draw the **left image** shown in Figure 10.

14. Click the **Brush tool** ✎ on the Tools panel.

15. Click the **Brush Size Icon** - in the Options area at the bottom of the Tools panel, then click the fifth option from the top.

16. Draw the **right image** shown in Figure 10.

    Notice the Pencil tool displays the stroke color and the Brush tool displays the fill color.

You added a layer, inserted a keyframe, then used the Pen tool to draw an arrow; you selected the Smooth option for the Pencil tool and drew an object; you selected a brush size for the Brush tool and drew an object.

Figure 9 *Pencil Tool options*

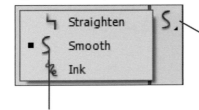

Click the Pencil Mode Smooth icon to display the 3 options (Note: The Straighten icon might be displayed instead of the Smooth icon)

Click the Smooth option

Figure 10 *Images drawn using drawing tools*

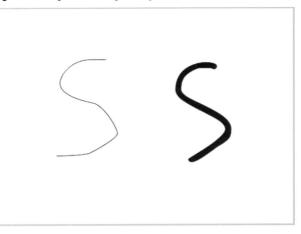

Figure 11 *The dot pattern indicating the object is selected*

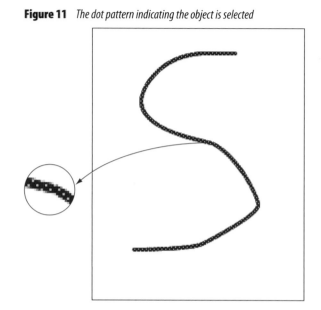

Modify an object using tool options

1. Click the **Selection tool** on the Tools panel, then drag a **marquee** around the left object to select it.

   The line displays a dot pattern, as shown in Figure 11, indicating that it is selected.

2. Click the **Pencil Mode Smooth icon** S in the Options area of the Tools panel **three times**. The line becomes smoother as the curves tend to flatten.

3. Click and hold the **Stroke slider** in the FILL AND STROKE area of the Properties panel, then drag the **Stroke slider** to change the stroke size to **20.**

TIP You can also type a Stroke value in the Stroke text box.

4. Click the **Style list arrow** in the FILL AND STROKE area, then click **Dotted**.

5. Repeat Step 4 and change the line style to **Hatched**.

6. Repeat Step 4 and change the line style to **Solid**.

7. Set the Stroke to **1**.

8. Save your work.

You smoothed objects using the tool options.

Use the Spray tool with a symbol

1. Click **Insert** on the menu bar, point to **Timeline**, then click **Layer**.

2. Click **frame 15** on Layer 4.

3. Click **Insert** on the menu bar, point to **Timeline**, then click **Keyframe**.

4. Click and hold the **Brush tool** on the Tools panel, then click the **Spray Brush tool**.

5. Display the Properties panel if it is not already displayed, then click the **Edit button** in the SYMBOL area of the Properties panel, as shown in Figure 12.

   Note: If the Properties panel does not display the options for the Spray Brush tool, click the Selection tool, then click the Spray Brush tool.

6. Click **flag** in the Select Symbol dialog box.

   The flag symbol is a graphic that was imported into this Flash document.

   (continued)

Figure 12 *The properties for the Spray Brush tool*

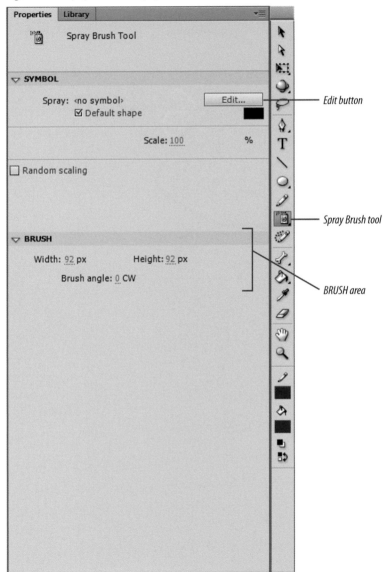

— Edit button

— Spray Brush tool

— BRUSH area

Figure 13 *A design created using the Spray Brush tool*

7. Click OK.

8. Click the **Random rotation check box** to select it, then click to deselect the **Rotate symbol check box** and the **Random scaling check box** if they are checked.

9. Display the **Brush area** on the Properties panel if it is not already open, then set the width and height to **8 px**.

TIP You can drag the number to the left or you can click the number next to Width or Height, and then type the number in the text box that appears to set the value.

10. Point to the upper left of the stage, then slowly draw the **U** in USA, as shown in Figure 13.

11. Continue to use the **Spray brush tool** to draw the **S** and **A**.

    Hint: If you need to redo the drawing, use the Undo command on the Edit menu or use the Selection tool to draw a marquee around the drawing, then delete the selection.

12. Save your work, then close the document.

You specified a symbol as a pattern and used the Spray Brush tool to complete a drawing.

Use XY coordinates to position objects on the Stage

1. Open fl2_2.fla, then save it as **alignObjects.fla**.

2. Click the **Selection tool** ![selection tool icon] on the Tools panel, click the **flag** on the Stage, then display the Properties panel, if it is not displayed.

   Notice the X and Y coordinates are set to 100.

3. Click **View** on the menu bar, then click **Rulers**.

4. Click and hold the **horizontal ruler** at the top of the Stage, then drag a **ruler line** down to 100 on the vertical ruler, as shown in Figure 14.

5. Click and hold the **vertical ruler** at the left of the Stage, then drag a **ruler line** across to 100 on the horizontal ruler.

   The point where the two ruler lines cross identifies the X,Y coordinates 100,100. The ruler lines meet at the registration point of the object.

6. Click the **flag**, click **100** next to X: on the Properties panel, type **0**, then press **[Enter]** (Win) or **[Return]** (Mac).

   This aligns the registration point of the object to the left edge of the Stage.

7. Repeat Step 6 to change the Y value to **0**.

8. Type **550** for the X value and **400** for the Y value.

   Notice the flag is positioned off the Stage because the registration point is in the upper-left corner of the object.

9. Change the view to **50%**.

(continued)

Figure 14 *Positioning an object on the Stage using XY coordinates*

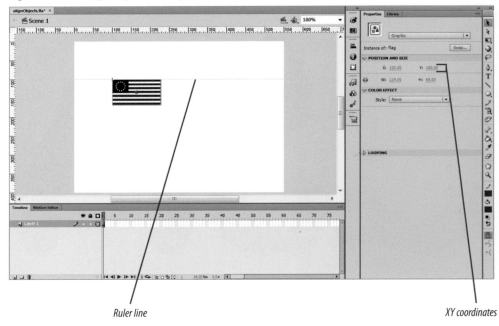

Ruler line

XY coordinates

Drawing Objects in Adobe Flash

Figure 15 *Setting the registration point*

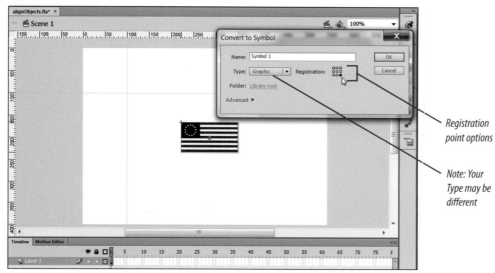

Registration point options

Note: Your Type may be different

10. Point to the **flag**, then click and drag the **flag** around the Stage noticing how the values for X and Y in the Properties panel change.

11. Drag the **flag** to approximately the middle of the Stage.

12. Change the view to **100%**.

13. Use the **arrow keys** on the keyboard to move the flag one pixel at a time in all four directions, then observe the changes to the X and Y values in the Properties panel as you move the object.

14. Click the **flag** to select it, click **Modify** on the menu bar, then click **Convert to Symbol**.

    The Convert to Symbol dialog box opens allowing you to change the registration point.

15. Click the **lower-right icon** as shown in Figure 15, then click **OK**.

    Notice the registration point is now located on the lower-right corner of the flag.

16. Change the **X** and **Y** values in the Properties panel to **100** and **100**.

    Notice the flag is now positioned using the new location of the registration point.

17. Drag each **ruler line** to its respective ruler to remove it from the Stage.

18. Click **View** on the menu bar, then click **Rulers** to remove them from view.

19. Save, then close the Flash document.

You used the X and Y values of an object to position it on the Stage. You used the Convert to Symbol dialog box to change the registration point of an object.

Use the Align options

1. Open fl2_3.fla, then save it as **alignOptions.fla**.

   This document has three objects (flags) of different sizes randomly placed on the Stage.

2. Click **Essentials** on the menu bar, then click '**Reset Essentials**'.

3. Click **Window** on the menu bar, then click **Align** to open the Align panel set.

   TIP Alternately, you can click the Align icon that is part of a collapsed panel set on your workspace.

4. Drag the **Align panel set** by its title bar, not its tab, and position it adjacent to the right side of the Stage, as shown in Figure 16.

5. Verify the Align to stage check box in the Align panel is active (checked).

6. Click the **largest flag** to select it, then click the **Align left edge icon** 🖳 .

7. Point to the next **Align icon** 🖳 , read the name that appears, then click the **Align horizontal center icon** 🖳 and notice the new position of the object on the Stage.

8. Click the other **Align options** on the top row of the Align panel.

9. Click the **Align horizontal center icon** 🖳 , then click the **Align vertical center icon** 🖳 .

   When you use these two align options together, they position the center of the object with the center of the Stage.

10. Click the **Match width icon** 🖳 , then click the **Match height icon** 🖬 .

(continued)

Figure 16 *Positioning the Align panel*

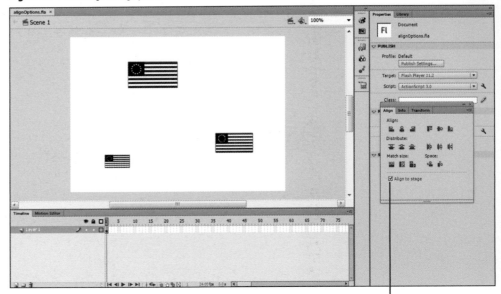

Be sure Align to stage is active (checked)

Figure 17 *All three objects selected*

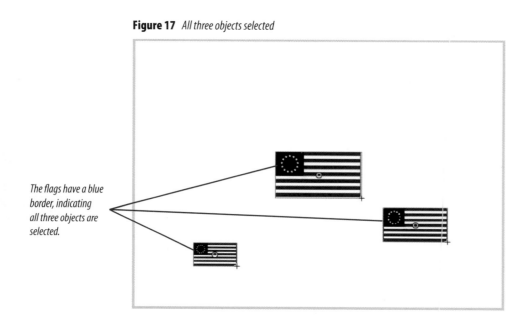

The flags have a blue border, indicating all three objects are selected.

11. Click **Edit** on the menu bar, then click **Undo Match Size**.

12. Click **Edit** on the menu bar, then click **Undo Match Size**.

13. Use the **Selection tool** ➤ to draw a marquee around all three flags to select them, as shown in Figure 17.

14. Click the **Align left edge icon** 🗖 , then click the **Align horizontal center icon** 🗖 .

15. Click the **Space evenly vertically icon** 🗖 , then click the **Align vertical center icon** 🗖 .

16. Click the **Align to stage check box** to make this feature not active.

17. With all three objects selected, click each of the **Align options** on the top row of the Align panel.

    Notice that the objects align to each other instead of the Stage.

18. Click the **Match width and height icon** 🗖 .

    This changes the dimension of each object to match the size of the largest object.

19. Close the Align panel set, then save and close the Flash document.

You used the Align panel to position objects on the Stage relative to the Stage and to each other.

Select Objects
AND APPLY COLORS

What You'll Do

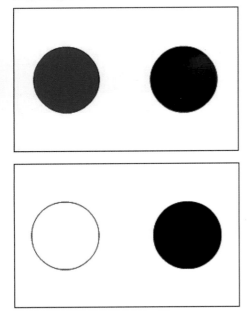

In this lesson, you will use several techniques to select objects, change the color of strokes and fills, and create a gradient fill.

Selecting Objects

Before you can edit a drawing, you must first select the object, or the part of the object, on which you want to work. Drawn objects are made up of a stroke and a fill. A stroke can have several segments. For example, a rectangle has four stroke segments, one for each side of the object. These can be selected separately or as a whole. Flash highlights objects that have been selected, as shown in Figure 18. When the stroke of an object is selected, a dotted colored line appears. When the fill of an object is selected, a dot pattern appears. When the stroke and fill of an object are selected, both the stroke and the fill appear dotted. When a group of objects is selected, a bounding box appears.

Using the Selection Tool

You can use the Selection tool to select part or all of an object, and to select multiple objects. To select only the fill, click just the fill; to select only the stroke, click just the stroke. To select both the fill and the stroke of one object, double-click the object, hold [Shift] and click the fill and stroke or draw a marquee around it. To select part of an object, drag a marquee that defines the area you want to select, as shown in Figure 18. To select multiple objects or combinations of strokes and fills, press and hold [Shift], then click each stroke or fill you want to select. To deselect an object(s), click a blank area of the Stage.

Using the Lasso Tool

The Lasso tool provides more flexibility than the Selection tool when selecting an object(s) or parts of an object on the Stage. You can use the tool in a freehand manner to draw any shape that then selects the object(s) within the shape. Alternately, you can use the Polygon Mode option to draw straight lines and connect them to form a shape that will select any object(s) within the shape.

Drawing Model Modes

Flash provides two drawing modes, called models. In the Merge Drawing Model mode, the stroke and fill of an object are separate. Thus, as you draw an object such as a circle, the stroke and fill can be selected individually as described earlier. When using the Object Drawing Model mode, the stroke and fill are combined and cannot be selected individually. However, you can use the Break Apart option from the Modify menu to separate the stroke and fill so that they can be selected individually. You can toggle between the two modes by clicking the Object Drawing option in the Options area of the Tools panel.

Working with Colors

Flash allows you to change the color of the stroke and fill of an object. Figure 19 shows the Colors area of the Tools panel. To change a color, you click the color swatch of the Stroke Color tool or the color swatch of the Fill Color tool, and then select a color swatch on the Color palette. The Color palette, as shown in Figure 20, allows you to select a color from the palette or type in a six-character code that represents the values of three colors (red, green, blue), referred to as RGB. When these characters are combined in various ways, they can represent virtually any color. The values are in a hexadecimal format (base 16), so they include letters and digits (A–F + 0–9 = 16 options), and they are preceded by a pound sign (#). The first two characters represent the value for red, the next two for green, and the last two for blue. For example, #000000 represents black (lack of color); #FFFFFF represents white; and #FFCC33 represents a shade of gold. You do not have to memorize the codes. There are reference manuals with the codes, and many programs allow you to set the values visually by selecting a color from a palette. You can also use the Properties panel to change the stroke and fill colors.

You can set the desired colors before drawing an object, or you can change a color of a previously drawn object. You can use the Ink Bottle tool to change the stroke color, and you can use the Paint Bucket tool to change the fill color. You can turn off either the stroke or the fill by selecting the No Stroke icon or the No Fill icon in the color palette.

Working with Gradients

A gradient is a color fill that makes a gradual transition from one color to another. Gradients can be very useful for creating a 3D effect, drawing attention to an object, and generally enhancing the appearance of an object. You can apply a gradient fill by using the Paint Bucket tool. The position of the Paint Bucket tool over the object is important because it determines the direction of the gradient fill. The Color palette can be used to create and alter custom gradients.

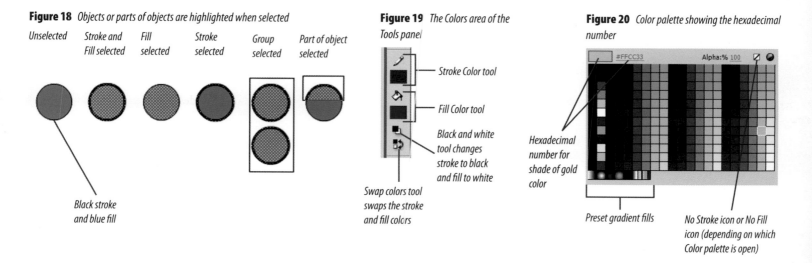

Figure 18 *Objects or parts of objects are highlighted when selected*

Unselected | Stroke and Fill selected | Fill selected | Stroke selected | Group selected | Part of object selected

Black stroke and blue fill

Figure 19 *The Colors area of the Tools panel*

Stroke Color tool

Fill Color tool

Black and white tool changes stroke to black and fill to white

Swap colors tool swaps the stroke and fill colors

Figure 20 *Color palette showing the hexadecimal number*

#FFCC33   Alpha:% 100

Hexadecimal number for shade of gold color

Preset gradient fills

No Stroke icon or No Fill icon (depending on which Color palette is open)

Select a drawing using the Selection tool

1. Open tools.fla, then click **1** on the Timeline.

TIP The options available to you in the Properties panel differ depending on whether you click a number on the Timeline or a frame on a layer.

2. Click the **Selection tool** ▶ on the Tools panel if it is not already selected, then drag a **marquee** around the circle to select the entire object (both the stroke and the fill).

3. Click anywhere on the Stage to deselect the object.

4. Click **inside the circle** to select the fill only, then click outside the circle to deselect it.

5. Click the **stroke** of the circle to select it, as shown in Figure 21, then deselect it.

6. Double-click the **circle** to select it, press and hold **[Shift]**, double-click the **square** to select both objects, then click the **Stage** to deselect both objects.

7. Click the **right border** of the square to select it, as shown in Figure 22, then deselect it.

   Objects, such as rectangles, have border segments that can be selected individually.

(continued)

Figure 21 *Using the Selection tool to select the stroke of the circle*

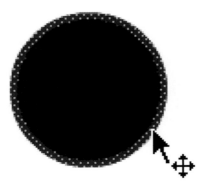

Figure 22 *Using the Selection tool to select a segment of the stroke of the square*

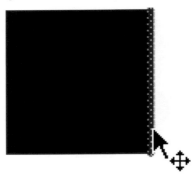

Drawing Objects in Adobe Flash

Figure 23 *Separating the stroke and fill of an object*

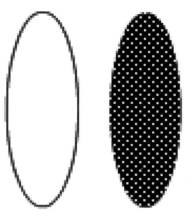

8. Drag a **marquee** around the square, circle, and diagonal line to select all three objects.

9. Click a blank area of the Stage to deselect the objects.

10. Click **inside the oval** in row 2 to select the fill, then drag the **fill** outside the stroke, as shown in Figure 23.

11. Look at the Properties panel.

    Notice the stroke color is none and the fill color is blue. This is because only the object's fill is selected. You can use the Properties panel to verify what you have selected when working with the Selection tool.

12. Click **Edit** on the menu bar, then click **Undo Move**.

You used the Selection tool to select the stroke and fill of an object, and to select multiple objects.

Change fill and stroke colors

1. Click **Layer 4,** click **Insert** on the menu bar, point to **Timeline,** then click **Layer.**

2. Click **frame 20** of the new layer, click **Insert** on the menu bar, point to **Timeline,** then click **Keyframe.**

3. Select the **Oval tool**  on the Tools panel, then draw **two circles** similar to those shown in Figure 24.

4. Click the **Fill Color tool color swatch** on the Tools panel, then click the **green color swatch** in the left column of the Color palette.

5. Click the **Paint Bucket tool** on the Tools panel, then click the **fill** of the right circle.

6. Click the **Stroke Color tool color swatch** on the Tools panel, then click the **green color swatch** in the left column of the color palette.

7. Click and hold the **Paint Bucket tool** on the Tools panel, click the **Ink Bottle tool**, point to the **red stroke line** of the left circle as shown in Figure 25, then click to change the stroke color to green.

8. Click **Edit** on the menu bar, then click **Undo Stroke.**

You used the Paint Bucket and Ink Bottle tools to change the fill and stroke colors of an object.

Figure 24 *Circles drawn with the Oval tool*

Figure 25 *Changing the stroke color*

Figure 26 *Selecting the red gradient*

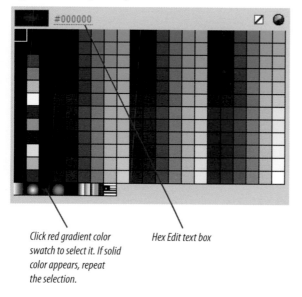

#000000

Click red gradient color
swatch to select it. If solid
color appears, repeat
the selection.

Hex Edit text box

Figure 27 *Clicking the right side of the circle*

Apply a gradient and make changes to the gradient

1. Click the **Fill Color tool color swatch** 🖌 on the Tools panel, then click the **red gradient color swatch** in the bottom row of the Color palette, as shown in Figure 26.

2. Click and hold the **Ink Bottle tool** 🪣 on the Tools panel, click the **Paint Bucket tool** 🪣, then click the **green circle**.

3. Click different parts of the right circle to view how the gradient changes, then click the **right side** of the circle, as shown in Figure 27.

4. Click and hold the **Free Transform tool** 🔲 on the Tools panel, then click the **Gradient Transform tool** 🔳.

5. Click the **gradient-filled circle**.

(continued)

6. Drag each handle shown in Figure 28 to see its effect on the gradient, then click the **Stage** to deselect the circle.

7. Click the **Selection tool** ▶ on the Tools panel, then click inside the left circle.

8. Click the **Fill Color tool color swatch** ⬨ ▬ in the FILL AND STROKE area of the Properties panel, click the **Hex Edit text box**, type **#006637** (two zeros).

   The Fill color swatch in the Properties panel changes to a shade of green.

9. Press **[Enter]** (Win) or **[return]** (Mac), then save your work.

   The fill of the circle changes to a shade of green.

You applied a gradient fill, you used the Gradient Transform tool to alter the gradient, and you applied a new color using its Hexadecimal number.

Figure 28 *Gradient Transform handles*

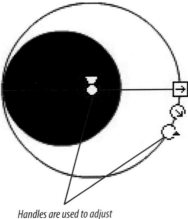

Handles are used to adjust the gradient effect

Figure 29 *Circle drawn using the Object Drawing Model mode*

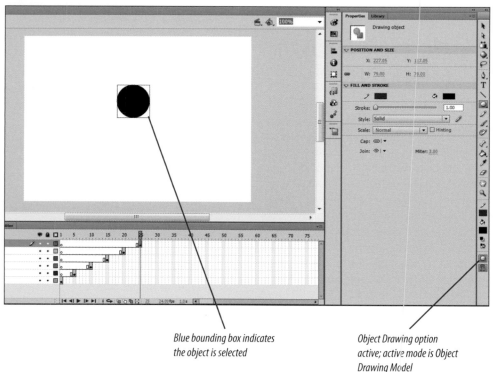

Blue bounding box indicates
the object is selected

Object Drawing option
active; active mode is Object
Drawing Model

Work with Object Drawing Model mode

1. Insert a **new layer**, then insert a **keyframe** on frame 25.

2. Select the **Oval tool** ⚪, click the **Stroke Color tool color swatch** ✎, then click the **red swatch**.

3. Click the **Fill Color tool color swatch** ✎, then click the **black swatch**.

4. Click the **Object Drawing option** ⚪ in the Options area of the Tools panel to make the icon active.

    The icon is active and the mode changes to Object Drawing Model.

5. Draw a **circle** as shown in Figure 29.

    Notice that when you use Object Drawing Model mode, the object is selected automatically, which means both the stroke and fill areas of the circle are selected.

6. Click the **Selection tool** ▸ on the Tools panel, then click a blank area of the Stage to deselect the object.

7. Click the **circle** once, then drag the **circle** around the Stage.

    The entire object is selected, including the stroke and fill areas.

8. Click **Modify** on the menu bar, then click **Break Apart**.

    Breaking apart an object drawn in Object Drawing Model mode allows you to select the strokes and fills individually.

9. Click a blank area of the Stage, click the **fill** area of the circle, drag to the right, then save your work.

    Notice the fill moves but the stroke stays.

You used the Object Drawing Model mode to draw an object, deselect it, then break it apart to display and then separate the stroke and fill.

Work with Drawn
OBJECTS

What You'll Do

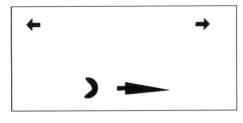

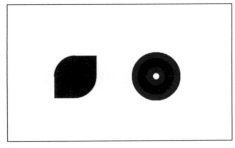

In this lesson, you will copy, move, and transform (resize, rotate, and reshape) objects.

Copying and Moving Objects

To copy an object, select it, and then click the Copy command on the Edit menu. To paste the object, click one of the Paste commands on the Edit menu. You can copy an object to another layer by selecting the frame on the layer you want to copy the object to, and then pasting the object. You can copy and paste more than one object by selecting all the objects before using the Copy or Paste commands.

You move an object by selecting it and dragging it to a new location. You can position an object more precisely by selecting it and then pressing the arrow keys, which move the selection up, down, left, and right in small increments. In addition, you can change the X and Y coordinates in the Properties panel to position an object exactly on the Stage.

Transforming Objects

You use the Free Transform tool and the Transform panel to resize, rotate, skew, and reshape objects. After selecting an object, you click the Free Transform tool to display eight square-shaped handles used to transform the object, and a circle-shaped transformation point located at the center of the object.

The transformation point is the point around which the object can be rotated. You can also change its location.

Resizing an Object

You enlarge or reduce the size of an object using the Scale option, which is available when the Free Transform tool is active. The process is to select the object and click the Free Transform tool, and then click the Scale option in the Options area of the Tools panel. Eight handles appear around the selected object. You drag the corner handles to resize the object without changing its proportions. That is, if the object starts out as a square, dragging a corner handle will change the size of the object, but it will still be a square. On the other hand, if you drag one of the middle handles, the object will be reshaped as taller, shorter, wider, or narrower. In addition, you can change the Width and Height settings in the Properties panel to resize an object in increments of one-tenth of one pixel.

Rotating and Skewing an Object

You use the Rotate and Skew option of the Free Transform tool to rotate an object and to skew it. The process is to select the object, click the Free Transform tool, and then click the Rotate and Skew option in the Options area of the Tools panel. Eight handles appear around the object. You drag the corner handles to rotate the object, or you drag the middle handles to skew the object, as shown in Figure 30. The Transform panel can be used to rotate and skew an object in a more precise way; select the object, display the Transform panel (available via the Window menu), enter the desired rotation or skew in degrees, and then press [Enter] (Win) or [return] (Mac).

Distorting an Object

You can use the Distort and Envelope options to reshape an object by dragging its handles. The Distort option allows you to reshape an object by dragging one corner without affecting the other corners of the object. The Envelope option provides more than eight handles to allow more precise distortions. These options are accessed through the Transform command on the Modify menu.

Flipping an Object

You use a Flip option on the Transform menu to flip an object either horizontally or vertically. You select the object, click the Transform command on the Modify menu, and then choose Flip Vertical or Flip Horizontal. Other Transform options allow you to rotate and scale the selected object.

The Remove Transform command allows you to restore an object to its original state.

Reshaping a Segment of an Object

You use the Subselection tool to reshape a segment of an object. You click an edge of the object to display handles that can be dragged to reshape the object.

You use the Selection tool to reshape objects. When you point to the edge of an object, the pointer displays an arc symbol. Using the Arc pointer, you drag the edge of the object you want to reshape, as shown in Figure 31. If the Selection tool points to a corner of an object, the pointer changes to an L-shape. You drag the pointer to reshape the corner of the object.

Figure 30 *Using handles to manipulate an object*

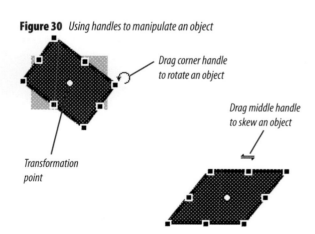

Drag corner handle to rotate an object

Drag middle handle to skew an object

Transformation point

Figure 31 *Using the Selection tool to distort an object*

Copy and move an object

1. Click **5** on the Timeline.
2. Click the **Selection tool** ➤ on the Tools panel, then draw a **marquee** around the arrow object to select it.
3. Click **Edit** on the menu bar, click **Copy**, click **Edit** on the menu bar, then click **Paste in Center**.
4. Drag the newly copied **arrow** to the upper-right corner of the Stage, as shown in Figure 32.
5. Verify the right arrow object is selected on the Stage, press the **down arrow key [↓]** on the keyboard.

   The object moves down in approximately one-pixel increments and the Y coordinate in the Properties panel changes each time the arrow key is pressed.

6. Press the **right arrow key [→]** on the keyboard.

   The object moves right in one-pixel increments and the X coordinate in the Properties panel changes each time the arrow key is pressed.

7. Select the number in the X coordinate box in the Properties panel, type **450** as shown in Figure 33, then press **[Enter]** (Win) or **[return]** (Mac).
8. Select the **number** in the Y coordinate box in the Properties panel, type **30**, then press **[Enter]** (Win) or **[return]** (Mac).
9. Drag a **marquee** around the left arrow object, then set the X and Y coordinates to **36** and **30**, respectively.
10. Click a blank area of the Stage to deselect the object.

You used the Selection tool to select an object, then you copied and moved the object.

Figure 32 *Moving the copied object*

Figure 33 *Changing the X coordinate in the Properties panel*

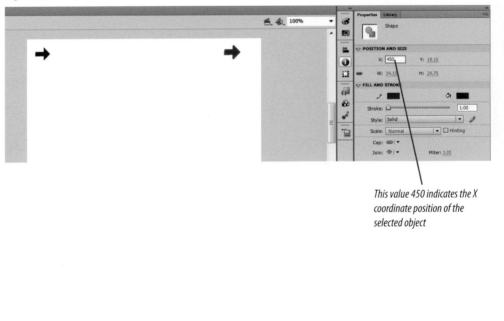

This value 450 indicates the X coordinate position of the selected object

Figure 34 *Resizing an object using the corner handles*

Pointer used to drag corner handle

Figure 35 *Reshaping an object using the middle handles*

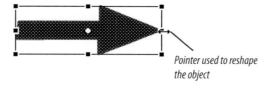

Pointer used to reshape the object

Resize and reshape an object

1. Click the **Free Transform tool**  on the Tools panel.

   Note: You may need to click and hold the Gradient tool to display the Free Transform tool.

2. Draw a **marquee** around the arrow object on the right side of the Stage to select the object.

3. Click the **Scale option** in the Options area on the Tools panel to make it active.

4. Drag each **corner handle** toward and then away from the center of the object, as shown in Figure 34.

   As you drag a corner handle, the object's size is changed, but its proportions remain the same.

5. Click **Edit** on the menu bar, then click **Undo Scale**.

6. Repeat Step 5 until the arrow returns to its original size.

   TIP The object is its original size when the option Undo Scale is no longer available on the Edit menu.

7. Verify the arrow is still selected and the handles are displayed, then select the **Scale option** in the Options area on the Tools panel to make it active.

8. Drag each **middle handle** toward and then away from the center of the object, as shown in Figure 35.

   As you drag the middle handles, the object's size and proportions change.

9. Click **Edit** on the menu bar, then click **Undo Scale** as needed to return the arrow to its original size.

You used the Free Transform tool and the Scale option to display an object's handles, and you used the handles to resize and reshape the object.

Skew, rotate, and flip an object

1. Verify that the Free Transform tool and the right arrow are selected (handles displayed), then click the **Rotate and Skew option** in the Options area of the Tools panel.

2. Click and drag the **upper-middle handle** to the right.

3. Click and rotate the **upper-right corner handle** of the object clockwise.

   The arrow slants down and to the right.

4. Click **Edit** on the menu bar, click the **Undo Rotate** command, then repeat, selecting the Undo Rotate and Undo Skew commands until the arrow is in its original shape and orientation.

5. Click the **Selection tool** on the Tools panel, verify that the right arrow is selected, click **Window** on the menu bar, then click **Transform**.

6. Click the **Rotate text box**, then type **45**, as shown in Figure 36.

7. Press **[Enter]** (Win) or **[return]** (Mac).

8. Click **Edit** on the menu bar, click **Undo Transform**, then close the Transform panel set if it is still open.

9. Draw a **marquee** around the arrow in the upper-left corner of the Stage to select the object.

10. Click **Modify** on the menu bar, point to **Transform**, then click **Flip Horizontal**.

11. Save your work.

You used options on the Tools panel and the Transform panel, as well as commands on the Modify menu to skew, rotate, and flip an object.

Figure 36 *Using the Transform panel to rotate an object*

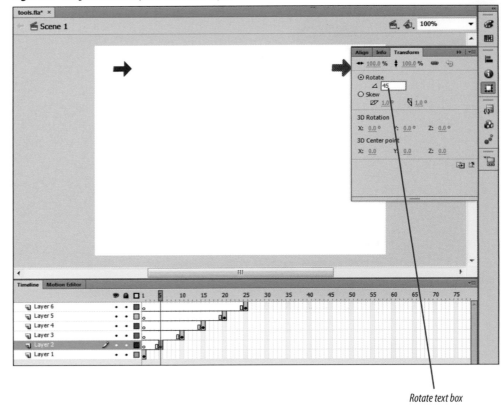

Rotate text box

Transform Options

Different transform options, such as rotate, skew, and scale, can be accessed through the Options area on the Tools panel when the Free Transform tool is active, the Transform command on the Modify menu, and the Transform panel via the Transform command on the Window menu.

Figure 37 *Using the Subselection tool to select an object*

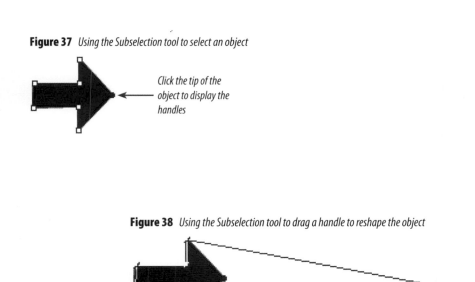

Click the tip of the
object to display the
handles

Figure 38 *Using the Subselection tool to drag a handle to reshape the object*

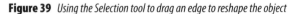

Figure 39 *Using the Selection tool to drag an edge to reshape the object*

Click here, then drag

Use the Zoom, Subselection, and Selection tools

1. Drag a **marquee** around the arrow in the upper-right corner of the Stage, click **Edit** on the menu bar, click **Copy**, click **Edit** on the menu bar, then click **Paste in Center**.

2. Click the **Zoom tool** 🔍 on the Tools panel, then click the **middle of the arrow** in the center of the Stage to enlarge the view.

3. Click the **Subselection tool** ▷ on the Tools panel, then click the **tip of the arrow** to display the handles, as shown in Figure 37.

TIP The handles allow you to change any segment of the object.

4. Click the **handle** at the tip of the arrow, then drag it, as shown in Figure 38.

5. Select the **Oval tool** ◯ on the Tools panel, then click the **Object Drawing option** 🔲 in the Options area of the Tools panel so the option is not active.

6. Verify the Fill color is set to blue, then draw a **circle** to the left of the arrow you just modified.

7. Click the **Selection tool** ▶ on the Tools panel, then point to the **left edge of the circle** until the Arc pointer ↘ is displayed.

8. Drag the ↘ **pointer** to the position shown in Figure 39.

9. Change the **View** of the Stage to **100%**.

10. Save your work.

You used the Zoom tool to change the view, and you used the Subselection and Selection tools to reshape objects.

Use the Rectangle Primitive and Oval tools

1. Insert a **new layer** above Layer 6, click **frame 30** on Layer 7, then insert a **keyframe**.

2. Click and hold the **Oval tool** 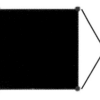 to display the menu.

3. Click the **Rectangle Primitive tool** , then click the **Reset button** in the Properties panel RECTANGLE OPTIONS area to clear all of the settings.

4. Press and hold **[Shift]**, point to the **middle of the Stage**, then draw the **square** shown in Figure 40.

5. Click the **Selection tool** in the Tools panel, then drag the **upper-right corner handle** toward the center of the object.

   As you drag the corner, the radius of each of the four corners is changed.

6. Click the **Reset button** in the Properties panel to clear the setting.

7. Slowly drag the **slider** in the RECTANGLE OPTIONS area to the right until the radius changes to 100, then slowly drag the **slider** to the left until the radius changes to -100.

8. Click the **Reset Button** on the Properties panel to clear the radius settings.

9. Click the **Lock corner radius icon** in the Properties panel RECTANGLE OPTIONS area to unlock the individual controls.

10. Type **-60** in the upper-left corner radius text box, type **-60** in the upper-right corner text box as shown in Figure 41, then press **[Enter]** (Win) or **[return]** (Mac).

(continued)

Figure 40 *Drawing an object with the Rectangle Primitive tool*

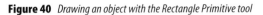

The corner handles can be dragged to change the radius of the corners; in addition, the Properties panel can be used to make changes to the object

Figure 41 *Setting the corner radius of two corners*

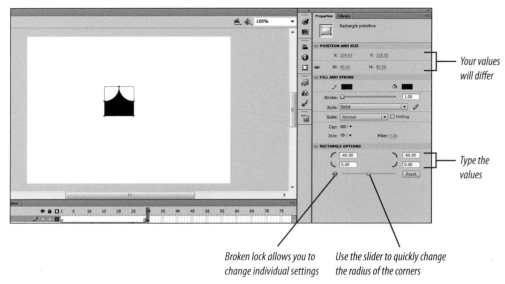

Your values will differ

Type the values

Broken lock allows you to change individual settings

Use the slider to quickly change the radius of the corners

Figure 42 *Drawing an object with the Oval Primitive tool*

Figure 43 *Setting the stroke value to 12*

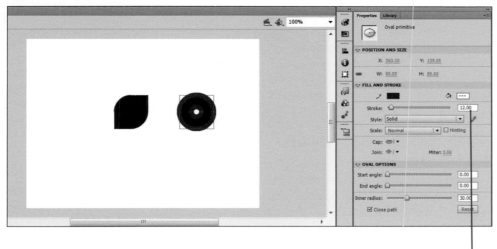

Set the Stroke
value to 12

11. Click the **Reset button** in the Properties panel to clear the radius settings.

12. Click the **Lock corner radius icon** ⊕ to unlock the individual controls.

13. Set the upper-left corner radius to **60** and the lower-right corner to **60**.

14. Click a blank area of the Stage to deselect the object.

15. Click and hold the **Rectangle Primitive tool** ▱ , click the **Oval Primitive tool** ⬯ on the Tools panel, then press and hold **[Shift]** and draw the **circle** shown in Figure 42.

TIP Remember some tools are grouped. Click and hold a grouped tool, such as the Oval tool, to see the menu of tools in the group.

16. Click the **Reset button** in the Properties panel OVAL OPTIONS area to clear any settings.

17. Drag the **Start angle slider** ⬠ and the **End angle slider** ⬠ to view their effect on the circle, then drag each **slider** back to 0.

18. Click the **Reset button** to clear the settings.

19. Drag the **Inner radius slider** ⬠ to see the effect on the circle, then set the inner radius to **30**.

20. Display the FILL AND STROKE area of the Properties panel, then set the Stroke value to **12**, as shown in Figure 43.

21. Save your work.

You used the Primitive tools to create objects and the Properties panel to alter them.

Work with Text
AND TEXT OBJECTS

What You'll Do

In this lesson, you will enter text using text blocks. You will also resize text blocks, change text attributes, and transform text.

Learning About Text

Flash provides a great deal of flexibility when using text. Among other settings for text, you can specify the typeface (font), size, style (bold, italic), and color (including gradients). You can transform the text by rotating, scaling, skewing, and flipping it. You can even break apart a letter and reshape its segments. There are two different text engines for working with text: Classic Text and Text Layout Framework (TLF). Classic Text mode is appropriate for many text applications and is easy to work with. Text Layout Framework mode provides advanced features and is appropriate for more text intensive applications.

Entering Text and Changing the Text Block for Classic Text

It is important to understand that text is entered into a text block, as shown in Figure 44. You use the Text tool to place a text block on the Stage and to enter and edit text. A text block expands as more text is entered and may even extend beyond the edge of the Stage. You can adjust the size of the text block so that it is a fixed width by dragging the handle in the upper-right corner of the block.

Figure 45 shows the process of using the Text tool to enter text and resize the text block. Once you select the Text tool, you click the Stage where you want the text to appear. An insertion point indicates where the next character will appear in the text block when it is typed. You can resize the text block to a fixed width by dragging the circle handle. After resizing the text block, the circle handle changes to a square, indicating that the text block now has a fixed width. Then, when you enter more text, it automatically wraps within the text block. You can resize the width of a text block at any time by selecting it with the Selection tool (either clicking on the text or drawing a marquee around it) and dragging any handle.

Changing Text Attributes

You can use the Properties panel to change the font, size, and style of a single character or an entire text block. Figure 46 shows the Properties panel when a text object is selected. You select text, display the Properties panel, and make the changes. You use the Selection tool to select the entire text block by drawing a marquee around it. You use the Text tool to select a single character or string of characters by dragging the I-beam pointer over the text you want to select, as shown in Figure 47.

Working with Paragraphs

When working with large bodies of text, such as paragraphs, Flash provides many of the features found in a word processor. You can align paragraphs (left, right, center, justified) within a text block, set margins (space between the border of a text block and the paragraph text), set indents for the first line of a paragraph, and set line spacing (distance between paragraphs) using the Properties panel.

Transforming Text

It is important to understand that a text block is an object. Therefore, you can apply filters, such as drop shadows, and you can transform (reshape, rotate, skew, and so on) a text block in the same way you transform other objects. If you want to transform individual characters within a text block, you must first break apart the text block. To do this, you use the Selection tool to select the text block, then you click the Break Apart command on the Modify menu. Each character (or a group of characters) in the text block can now be selected and transformed.

The Text Layout Framework (TLF)

Text Layout Framework (TLF) provides several advanced text features such as character color highlighting, underlining, strikethrough, and rotation. Text in the TLF format is displayed in a container, similar to a text block. Containers can be resized and linked using a Container icon. This allows you to flow text between them. The containers can have a border and background color, and the text in containers can be formatted into columns. Containers can also have tab stops. Using TFL text reduces the size of SWF files while increasing their performance.

Figure 44 *A text block*

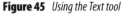

Figure 45 *Using the Text tool*

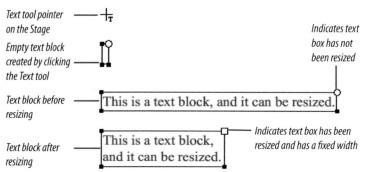

Text tool pointer on the Stage

Empty text block created by clicking the Text tool

Text block before resizing

Text block after resizing

Indicates text box has not been resized

Indicates text box has been resized and has a fixed width

Figure 46 *The Properties panel when a text object is selected*

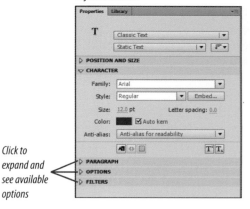

Click to expand and see available options

Figure 47 *Dragging the I-beam pointer to select text*

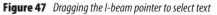
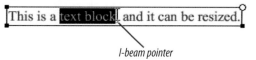

I-beam pointer

Enter text and change text attributes

1. Click **Layer 7**, insert a **new layer**, then insert a **keyframe** in frame 35 of the new layer.

2. Click the **Text tool** T , then verify the Text engine is set to Classic Text mode and the Text type is set to Static Text in the T area on the Properties panel.

3. Click the left-center of the Stage, then type **We have great events each year including a Rally!**

4. Click the **I-Beam pointer** before the word "Rally" as shown in Figure 48, then type **Car** followed by a space.

5. Drag the **I-Beam pointer** across the text to select all the text.

6. Make the following changes in the CHARACTER area of the Properties panel: Family: **Arial**; Style: **Bold**; Size: **16**; Color: **#990000**, then click the **text box**.

   Your Properties panel should resemble Figure 49.

7. Verify the text block is selected, position the **text pointer** over the circle handle until the pointer changes to a double arrow ↔, then drag the **handle** to just before the word each, as shown in Figure 50.

8. Select the text using the I-Beam pointer I , then click the **Align center icon** in the PARAGRAPH area of the Properties panel.

9. Click the **Selection tool** on the Tools panel, click the **text object**, then drag the **object** to the lower-middle of the Stage.

   TIP The Selection tool is used to select the text block, and the Text tool is used to select and edit the text within the text block.

   You entered text and changed the font, type size, and text color; you also resized the text block and changed the text alignment.

Figure 48 *Using the Text tool to enter text*

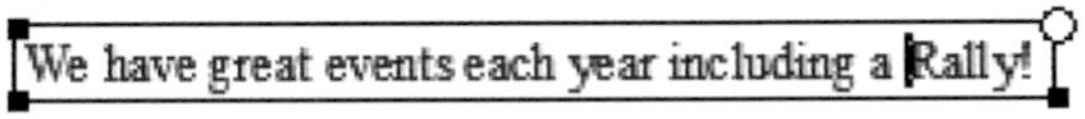

We have great events each year including a Rally!

Figure 49 *Changes to the CHARACTER area of the Properties panel*

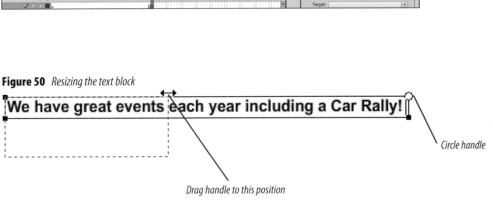

Text engine list arrow displays the text modes

Text type list arrow

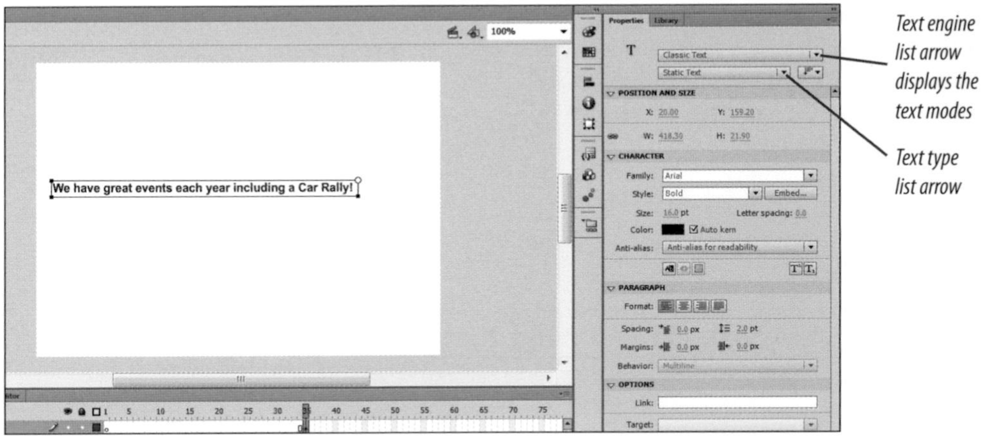

Figure 50 *Resizing the text block*

We have great events each year including a Car Rally!

Circle handle

Drag handle to this position

Figure 51 *The Filters options in the Properties panel*

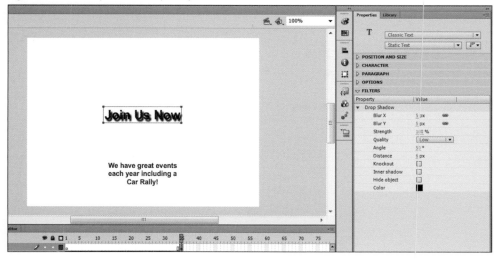

Using Filters

You can apply special effects, such as drop shadows, to text using options in the FILTERS area of the Properties panel. The process is to select the desired text, display the FILTERS area of the Properties panel, choose the desired effect, and make any adjustments, such as changing the angle of a drop shadow. You can copy and paste a filter from one object to another using the clipboard icon in the FILTERS area of the Properties panel.

Add a Filter effect to text

1. Click the **Text tool** T on the Tools panel, click the center of the Stage, then type **Join Us Now**. *Hint*: If the text box does not appear, double-click the Stage.

2. Drag the **I-Beam pointer** Ⲓ across the text to select it, then use the Properties panel to change the Font size to **30** and the Text (fill) color to **#003399**.

3. Click **CHARACTER** on the Properties panel to close the CHARACTER area, then close all areas in the Properties panel except for the FILTERS area.

4. Click the **Selection tool** ➤ on the Tools panel, then verify the text block is selected.

5. Click the **Add filter icon** ⌐ at the bottom of the FILTERS area, then click **Drop Shadow**.

6. Point to the **Angle value** in the FILTERS area of the Properties panel, then, when the pointer changes to a double-headed arrow ⚟ᕼ, drag the ⚟ᕼ **pointer** to the right to view the effect on the shadow, then set the Angle to **50**.

7. Point to the **Distance value**, when the pointer changes to a double-headed arrow ⚟ᕼ, drag the ⚟ᕼ **pointer** to the right and notice the changes in the drop shadow.

8. Set the Distance to **6**.

9. Click the **Selection tool** ➤, click the text box to select it, drag the **text box** as needed to match the placement shown in Figure 51, then save your work.

You used the Filter panel to create a drop shadow, then made changes to it.

Skew text and align objects

1. Click the **Text tool** T to select it, click the
    ⊥T **pointer** near the top left of the Stage,
    then type **Classic Car Club**.

2. Click **CHARACTER** in the Properties panel to
    display the CHARACTER area.

    The attributes of the new text reflect the most
    recent settings entered in the Properties panel.

3. Drag the **I-Beam pointer** ⌶ to select the text,
    then use the CHARACTER area of the Properties
    panel to change the font size to **40** and the fill
    color to **#990000**.

4. Click the **Selection tool** ▶ on the Tools panel,
    click the **text box** to select it, then click the
    Free Transform tool ▦ on the Tools panel.

5. Click the **Rotate and Skew option** ⤢ in the
    Options area of the Tools panel.

6. Drag the **top middle handle** to the right, as
    shown in Figure 52, to skew the text.

7. Click the **Selection tool** ▶ on the Tools panel.

8. Drag a **marquee** around all of the objects on
    the Stage to select them.

9. Click **Modify** on the menu bar, point to **Align**,
    click **Align to stage** to make it active.

10. Click **Modify** on the menu bar, point to **Align**,
    then click **Horizontal Center**.

11. Click a blank area of the Stage to deselect
    the objects.

*You entered a heading, changed the font size and color, and
skewed text using the Free Transform tool, then you aligned the
objects on the Stage.*

Figure 52 *Skewing the text*

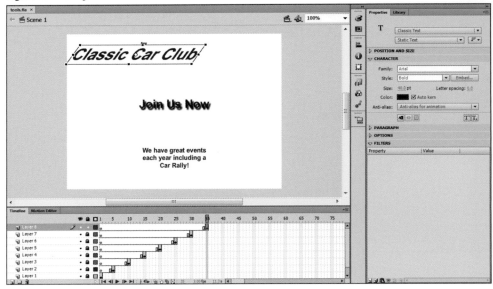

Figure 53 *Reshaping a letter*

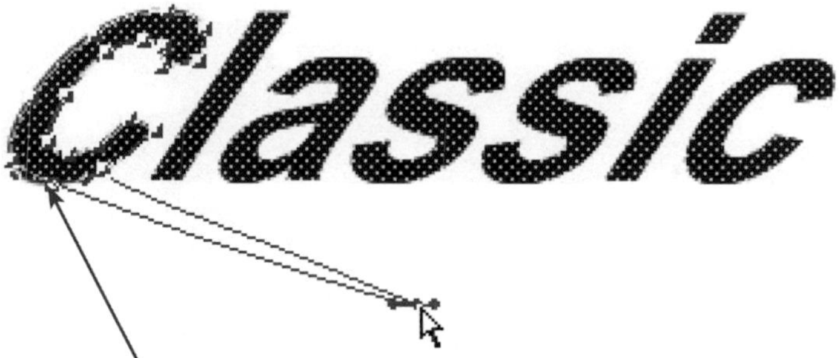

Drag this anchor point; notice the lines are drawn from the anchor points on either side of the anchor point being dragged

Figure 54 *Applying a gradient fill to each letter*

Classic Car Club

Reshape and apply a gradient to text

1. Click the **Selection tool** ![arrow], click the **Classic Car Club text block** to select it, click **Modify** on the menu bar, then click **Break Apart**.

   The letters are now individual text blocks.

2. Click **Modify** on the menu bar, then click **Break Apart**.

   The letters are filled with a dot pattern, indicating that they can now be edited.

3. Click the **Zoom tool** ![zoom] on the Tools panel, then click the first **"C"** in Classic.

4. Click the **Subselection tool** ![arrow] on the Tools panel, then click the **edge** of the letter **"C"** to display the object's segment handles.

5. Drag a **lower anchor point** on the "C" in Classic, as shown in Figure 53.

6. Click the **Selection tool** ![arrow], then click a blank area of the Stage to deselect the objects.

7. Click the **View list arrow** on the movie menu bar, then click **Fit in Window**.

8. Click the **Fill Color tool color swatch** ![swatch] on the Tools panel, then click the **red gradient color swatch** in the bottom row of the Color palette.

9. Click the **Paint Bucket tool** ![bucket] on the Tools panel, then click the **top** of each letter to change the fill to a red gradient, as shown in Figure 54.

   Note: Click the Ink Bottle tool if you do not see the Paint Bucket tool.

10. Use the status bar to change the movie frame rate to **3**, test the movie, watch the movie, then close the Flash Player window.

11. Save your work, then close the document.

You broke apart a text block, reshaped text, and added a gradient to the text.

Use the Text Layout Framework

1. Open fl2_4.fla, then save it as **TLF.fla**.

2. Click the **Text tool** T on the Tools panel, then click the **text block** on the Stage.

3. Click the **Text engine list arrow** in the T area on the Properties panel, then click **TLF Text**.

   The text block on the Stage changes to a container and displays two container icons.

4. Scroll the Properties panel as needed, then click **CONTAINER AND FLOW** to display the CONTAINER AND FLOW options.

5. Click the **Behavior list arrow**, then click **Multiline**.

6. Change the Column value to **2**, change it to **3**, then change it to **1**.

7. Point to the **middle handle** on the right side of the container, when the pointer changes to a double-headed arrow ↔ , click and drag the **middle handle** left to the position shown in Figure 55, then release the mouse pointer.

8. Click the **Flow icon** on the right side of the container, position the **Flow pointer** ⬚ as shown in Figure 56, then click the mouse button.

   Another container appears that is linked to the first container and with the text flowing from the first container.

9. Click before **From** in the first container, then type **By the 1970s, the car had become a collector's item**.

   Notice as you type in the first container that the text flows to the second container.

(continued)

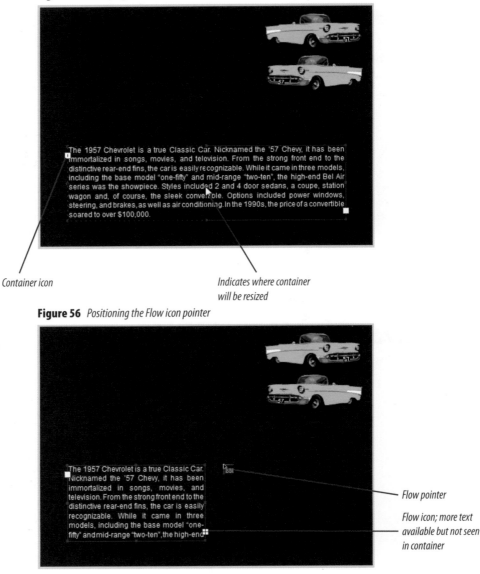

Figure 55 *Reshaping the text container*

Container icon

Indicates where container will be resized

Figure 56 *Positioning the Flow icon pointer*

Flow pointer

Flow icon; more text available but not seen in container

Figure 57 *Repositioning the text container*

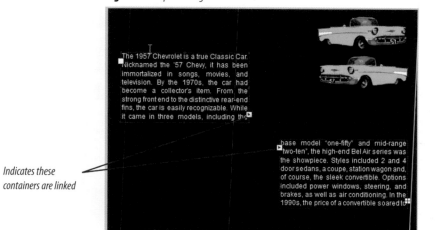

Indicates these containers are linked

Figure 58 *Repositioning the second text container*

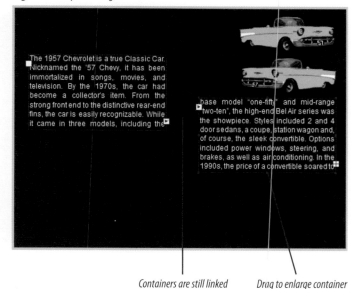

Containers are still linked   *Drag to enlarge container*

10. Click the **Selection tool** ![cursor], then click and drag the **first container** to the position shown in Figure 57.

11. Drag the **second container** to the position shown in Figure 58.

12. Click and drag the **bottom middle handle** of the second container down to display all the text if some of the text is not visible.

NEW

13. **Double-click** the first container to display the ruler.

    The ruler allows you to set tab stops and adjust the left and right margins of the container text.

14. Point to just above the **1** in 1957 on the ruler, then **click** to set a tab stop.

TIP Be sure you click the ruler, and not above or below the ruler.

(continued)

15. Point to the beginning of the paragraph, then **click** to set an insertion point, as shown in Figure 59.

16. Press the **Tab key**.

    The first line of the paragraph is indented.

17. Click a blank area of the Stage to remove the ruler.

18. Use the Properties panel to complete the following settings: Text type: **TFL Text**; Font Family: **Times New Roman**; Style: **Regular**; Size: **16 pt**; Color: **White**.

19. Insert **a new layer** above the text layer, then name it **heading**.

20. Click **frame 1** on the heading layer.

21. Click above the first container, then type the heading shown in Figure 60.

22. Click the **Selection tool** on the Tools panel, then verify the text box is selected.

23. Click the **Rotation list arrow** in the CHARACTER area on the Properties Panel, then click **270⁰**.

    The text rotates within the container.

24. Click **Modify** on the menu bar, point to **Transform**, then click **Rotate 90⁰ CW**.

25. Click the **heading**, then use the **arrow keys** to position the container between the two text containers.

    (continued)

Figure 59 *Setting an insertion line*

Tab set

Insertion line
inserted at
beginning of
the paragraph

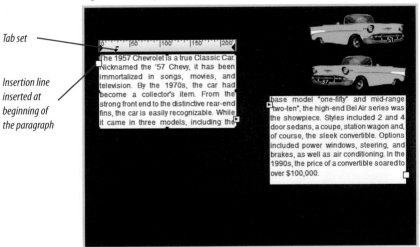

Figure 60 *Typing a heading*

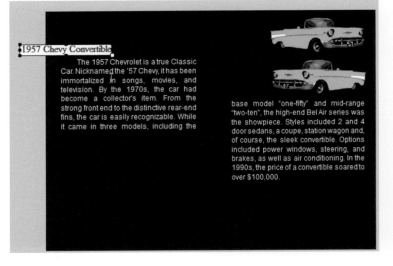

Figure 61 *Adding a container border*

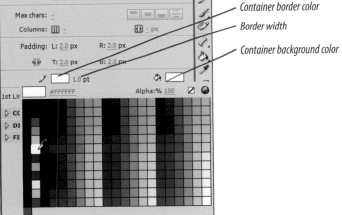

Container border color

Border width

Container background color

Figure 62 *The completed document*

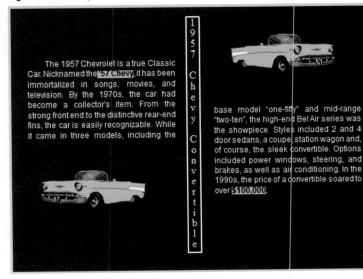

26. Click the **Container border color icon** ✐ ▱ in the CONTAINER AND FLOW area, then click **white**.

    The border color swatch changes to white, as shown in Figure 61.

27. Change the border width to **2**.

28. Click the **Container background color icon** ◇ ▱ , then set the color to **#333333**.

29. Click the **Text tool** T , then click and drag the ⊤ **pointer** to select the words '57 Chevy.

30. In the CHARACTER area of the Properties panel, change the Style to **bold** and the Color to **black**.

31. Click the **Highlight color icon** ▱ in the CHARACTER area on the Properties panel, then click the **car** with the **Eyedropper** tool ✐ to select the color.

32. Repeat steps 29–31 for the **$100,000** text.

33. Use the **Selection tool** ▶ to position the cars, as shown in Figure 62.

34. Test the movie, then save and close it.

You used the Text Layout Framework feature to display columns, create containers, add highlight color to text, add background and stroke color to a container, and rotate text.

Work with Layers
AND OBJECTS

What You'll Do

 In this lesson, you will create, rename, reorder, delete, hide, and lock layers. You will also add text on top of an object.

Learning About Layers

Flash uses two types of spatial organization. First, there is the position of objects on the Stage, and then there is the stacking order of objects that overlap. An example of overlapping objects is text placed on a banner. In this case, the banner background might be placed on one layer and the banner text might be placed on a different layer. Layers are used on the Timeline as a way of organizing objects. Placing objects on their own layer makes them easier to work with, especially when reshaping them, repositioning them on the Stage, or rearranging their order in relation to other objects. In addition, layers are useful for organizing other elements such as sounds, animations, and ActionScript.

There are five types of layers, as shown in the Layer Properties dialog box displayed in Figure 63 and discussed next.

Normal—The default layer type. All objects on these layers appear in the movie.

Mask—A layer that hides and reveals portions of another layer.

Masked—A layer that contains the objects that are hidden and revealed by a Mask layer.

Folder—A layer that can contain other layers.

Guide (Standard and Motion)—You use a Standard Guide layer to set a reference point (such as a guide line) for positioning objects on the Stage. You use a Motion Guide layer to create a path for animated objects to follow.

Motion Guide, Mask, and Masked layer types are covered in a later chapter.

Working with Layers

The Layer Properties dialog box, accessed through the Timeline command on the Modify menu, allows you to specify the type of layer. It also allows you to name, show (and hide), and lock layers. Naming a layer provides a clue to the objects on that layer. For example, naming a layer Logo might indicate that the object on the layer is the company's logo. Hiding a layer(s) may reduce the clutter on the Stage and make it easier to work with selected objects on the layer(s) that are not hidden. Locking a layer(s) prevents the objects from being accidentally edited. Other options in the Layer Properties dialog box allow you to view layers as outlines, change the outline color, and change layer height. Outlines can be used to help you determine which objects are on a layer. When you turn on this feature, each layer has a colored box that corresponds with the color of the objects on its layer. Icons on the Layers area of the Timeline, as shown in Figure 64, correspond to features in the Layer Properties dialog box.

Figure 63 *The Layer Properties dialog box*

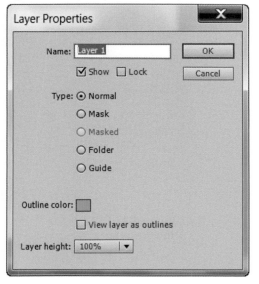

Figure 64 *The Layers area of the Timeline*

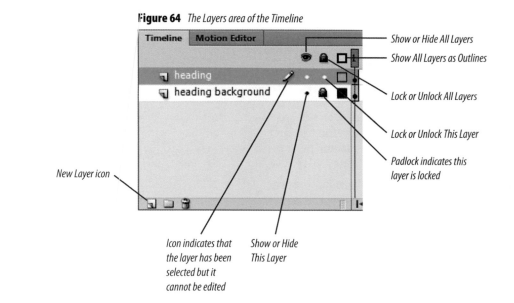

Create and reorder layers

1. Open fl2_5.fla from the drive and folder where your Data Files are stored, then save it as **layers2.fla**.

2. Click the **Selection tool** , click the **View list arrow** on the movie menu bar, then click **Fit in Window**.

3. Click the **New Layer icon** on the bottom of the Timeline (below the layer names) to insert a new layer, Layer 2.

4. Click **frame 1** on Layer 2.

5. Select the **Rectangle tool** , on the Tools panel, then set each corner radius to **10** in the RECTANGLE OPTIONS area of the Properties panel, and set the Stroke to **2** in the FILL AND STROKE area.

6. Click the **Fill Color tool color swatch** on the Tools panel, click the **Hex Edit text box**, type #**999999**, then press **[Enter]** (Win) or **[return]** (Mac).

7. Click the **Stroke Color tool color swatch** on the Tools panel, click the **Hex Edit text box**, type #**000000**, then press **[Enter]** (Win) or **[return]** (Mac).

8. Draw the **rectangle** shown in Figure 65 so it covers the text heading.

9. Drag **Layer 1** above Layer 2 on the Timeline, as shown in Figure 66.

10. Click the **Selection tool** on the Tools panel.

11. Click a blank area of the Stage to deselect the objects.

You added a layer, drew an object on the layer, and reordered layers.

Figure 65 *Drawing a rectangle with a rounded corner*

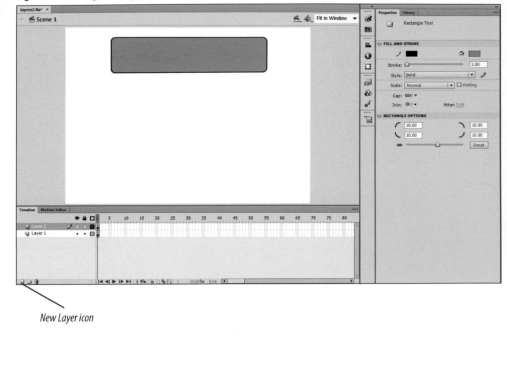

New Layer icon

Figure 66 *Dragging Layer 1 above Layer 2*

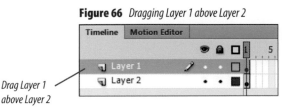

Drag Layer 1 above Layer 2

Drawing Objects in Adobe Flash

Figure 67 *Renaming layers*

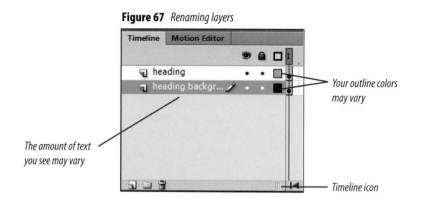

Your outline colors may vary

The amount of text you see may vary

Timeline icon

Figure 68 *Hiding all the layers*

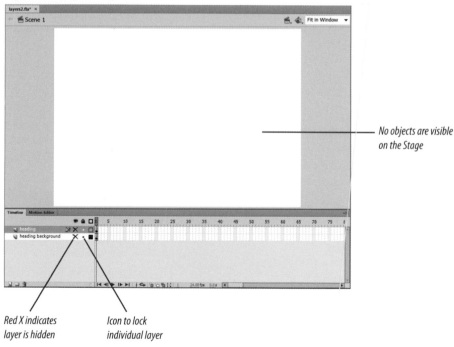

No objects are visible on the Stage

Red X indicates layer is hidden

Icon to lock individual layer

Rename and delete layers, expand the Timeline, and hide and lock layers

1. Double-click **Layer 1** on the Timeline, type **heading** in the Layer Name text box, then press **[Enter]** (Win) or **[return]** (Mac).

2. Rename Layer 2 as **heading background**.

3. Point to the **Timeline icon** , which is on the Timeline status bar and shown in Figure 67.

4. When the pointer changes to a double arrow ⊣⊢, drag the **pointer** ⊣⊢ to the right to display all the layer names.

5. Click the **heading layer**, then click the **Delete icon** 🗑 on the Timeline status bar.

6. Click **Edit** on the menu bar, then click **Undo Delete Layer**.

7. Click the **Show or Hide All Layers icon** 👁 to hide all layers, then compare your image to Figure 68.

8. Click the **Show or Hide All Layers icon** 👁 to show all the layers.

9. Click the **Show or Hide This Layer icon** 🔲 next to the **heading background layer** name twice to hide and then show the layer.

10. Click the **Lock or Unlock All Layers icon** 🔒 to lock all layers, then try to select and edit an object.

11. Click the **Lock or Unlock All Layers icon** 🔒 again to unlock the layers.

12. Click the **Lock or Unlock This Layer icon** 🔲 next to the **heading background layer** to lock the layer.

13. Save the document, then exit Flash

You renamed layers to associate them with objects on the layers, deleted and restored a layer, hid layers, and locked layers to prevent accidently editing their contents.

Use the Flash drawing and alignment tools.

1. Start Flash, open fl2_6.fla, then save it as **skillsDemo2.fla**. Refer to Figure 69 as you complete these steps. (*Note*: Figure 69 shows the objects after changes have been made to them. For example, in Step 5 you draw a rectangle in the middle of the Stage. Then, in a later step you rotate the rectangle 45 degrees.)
2. Set the view to Fit in Window, then display the Grid.
3. Select the Oval tool, then set the stroke size to 1, the stroke color to black (Hex: **#000000**) and the fill color to blue (Hex: **#0000FF**).
4. Use the Oval tool to draw an oval on the left side of the Stage, then draw a circle beneath the oval. (*Hint*: Use the Undo command as needed.)
5. Use the Rectangle tool to draw a rectangle in the middle of the Stage, then draw a square beneath the rectangle. (*Hint*: Reset the RECTANGLE OPTIONS as needed.)
6. Use the Line tool to draw a horizontal line on the right side of the Stage, then draw a vertical line beneath the horizontal line and a diagonal line beneath the vertical line.
7. Use the Pen tool to draw an arrow-shaped object above the rectangle. (*Hint*: Use the Zoom tool to enlarge the area of the Stage.)
8. Use the Paint Bucket tool to fill the arrow with the blue color. (*Hint*: If the arrow does not fill, be sure you closed the arrow shape by clicking the first anchor point as your last action.)
9. Use the Pencil tool to draw a freehand curved line above the oval, then select the line and use the Smooth option to smooth out the line.
10. Use the Rectangle Primitive tool to draw a rectangle below the square. (*Hint*: Reset the RECTANGLE OPTIONS as needed after drawing the rectangle.)
11. Use the Selection tool to drag a corner to round all the corners.
12. Save your work.

Select objects and apply colors.

1. Use the Selection tool to select the stroke of the circle, then deselect the stroke.
2. Use the Selection tool to select the fill of the circle, then deselect the fill.
3. Use the Paint Bucket tool to change the fill color of the square to a red gradient.
4. Use the Ink Bottle tool to change the stroke color of the circle to red (Hex: **#FF0000**).
5. Change the fill color of the oval to a blue gradient.
6. Save your work.

Work with drawn objects.

1. Copy and paste in center the arrow object.
2. Move the copied arrow to another location on the Stage.
3. Use the Properties panel to set the height of each arrow to 30.
4. Flip the copied arrow horizontally.
5. Rotate the rectangle to a 45° angle.
6. Skew the square to the right.
7. Copy one of the arrows and use the Subselection tool to reshape it, then delete it.
8. Use the Selection tool to reshape the circle to a crescent shape.
9. Save your work.

Work with text and text objects.

1. Select the Text tool, set the text mode to Classic Text and the type to Static Text, then enter the following text in a text block at the top of the Stage: **Gateway to the Pacific.**
2. Select the text, then change the text to font: Tahoma, size: 24, color: red.
3. Use the Align option on the Modify menu to horizontally center the text block.
4. Use the Selection tool and the up and down arrow keys on the keyboard to align the text block with a gridline.
5. Skew the text block to the right.
6. Save your work.

Work with layers.

1. Insert a layer into the document.
2. Change the name on the new layer to **heading bkgnd**, then click frame 1 on the layer.
3. Use the Rectangle Primitive tool to draw a rounded corner rectangle with a blue fill and a black stroke that covers the words Gateway to the Pacific.
4. Switch the order of the layers.
5. Lock all layers.
6. Unlock all layers.
7. Hide the heading bkgnd layer.
8. Show the heading bkgnd layer.
9. Add a layer, name it **subheading**, and use the Text tool to type **Seattle** below the heading, using Tahoma, Regular, 24 pt, and the color blue.
10. Align Seattle so it is centered horizontally across the Stage, then save your work.

Use the Merge Drawing Model mode.

1. Insert a new layer and name it **MergeDraw**.
2. Select the Rectangle tool and verify that the Object Drawing option is not active.
3. Draw a square in the upper-right of the Stage, then use the Oval tool to draw a circle with a different color that covers approximately half of the square.
4. Select the stroke and fill of the circle, then using the Selection tool drag the circle off the square. (*Note*: Depending on the size of the circle and where you drew it to overlap the square, your results may vary from what is shown in Figure 69.)

Use the Object Drawing Model mode.

1. Insert a new layer and name it **ObjectDraw**.
2. Select the Rectangle tool and select the Object Drawing option to make it active.
3. Draw a square with a blue fill color, then use the Oval tool to draw a circle with a different color that covers approximately half of the square.
4. Use the Selection tool to drag the circle off the square.
5. Change the name of Layer 1 to **objects**.
6. Save your work, then compare your image to the example shown in Figure 69.

Use the Spray tool with a symbol.

1. Turn off the gridlines.
2. Add a new layer to the Timeline, then name the layer **aces wild**.
3. Add a keyframe to frame 5 of the new layer.
4. Select the Text tool and change the Text option to TLF Text, then verify rotation is set to auto and the

Align option in the PARAGRAPH area of the properties panel is set to Justify with last line aligned to start.

5. Drag the pointer to create a text box that covers the lower one-fourth of the Stage, then set the Behavior option in the CONTAINER AND FLOW area of the Properties panel to Multiline.
6. Type the following using Arial, 14 pt text, black:

Ace's Wild has been providing novelty items, gifts, and toys to Seattleites since 1975. Located in Seattle's Greenlake district, we provide one stop shopping for the most unusual and unique costumes, party supplies, crafts, and the strangest collection of toys ever assembled. Visit Ace's Wild to have a fun time choosing that perfect present for the hard to buy for person in your life.

7. Divide the text block into two text Containers, then use the Selection tool to position them as shown in Figure 69. (*Note:* You can drag any middle handle to resize the container.)
8. Use the Text tool to select the top Container, set a first line paragraph indent, then create a **2** pt blue border (#0000FF) and a gray (#CCCCCC) background.
9. Select the bottom Container and create the same border and background.
10. Use the Text tool to select Ace's Wild in the top Container, then create a white highlight.
11. Select the Spray Brush tool.
12. Click the Edit button in the Symbol area of the Properties panel, then select the Ace symbol.
13. Set the Scale width and height to **50**, turn on Rotate symbol (*Hint*: Be sure the check box has a check

mark) and turn off the other options (*Hint*: Be sure all other check boxes do not have check marks), set the Brush width and height to 3 px, then draw the letters for Ace's as shown in Figure 69.

14. Change the Stage color to a shade of blue (#3399FF).
15. Test the movie, then save and close the document. (*Note*: If the movie displays too quickly, adjust the frame rate.)
16. Exit Flash.

Figure 69 *Completed Skills Review*

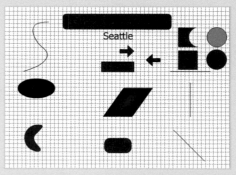

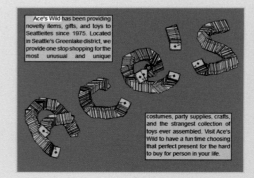

PROJECT BUILDER 1

A local travel company, Ultimate Tours, has asked you to design a sample opening screen for its new application. The goal of the application is to inform potential customers of its services. The company specializes in exotic treks, tours, and cruises. Thus, while its target audience spans a wide age range, they are all looking for something out of the ordinary. This screen may become part of a website, a mobile app, and/or a link on a Facebook site.

1. Open a new Flash document using ActionScript 2.0 and save it as **ultimateTours2.fla**. Create the Flash movie shown in Figure 70. (*Note*: ActionScript 2.0 is used because in subsequent chapters the ultimateTours project will require this version of ActionScript.)

2. Set the document properties, including the Stage size and Stage color. (*Note*: You can use your choice of colors.)

3. Create the following on separate layers and name the layers:
   - A text heading; select a font size and font color. Skew the heading, break it apart, then reshape one or more of the characters.
   - A subheading with a different font size and color.
   - At least three objects that will be the background for button symbols.
   - Text that will appear on the top of the button background.

Note: You can use different colors, shapes, and placement but your project should have all the elements shown in Figure 70.

4. Use one or more of the align features (gridlines, rulers, Align command on the Modify menu, arrow keys) to align the objects on the Stage.

5. Lock all layers.

6. Compare your image to the example shown in Figure 70.

7. Save your work.

8. Test the movie, close the Flash Player window, then close the movie.

Figure 70 *Sample completed Project Builder 1*

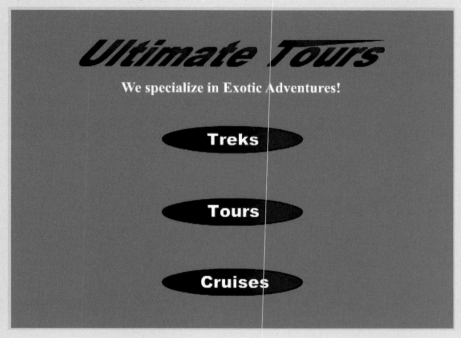

You have been asked to create several sample designs for the opening screen of an application of a new organization called The Jazz Club. The club is being organized to bring together music enthusiasts for social events and charitable fundraising activities. The club members plan to sponsor weekly jam sessions and a show once a month. Because the club is just getting started, the organizers are looking to you for help in developing an application. This screen may become part of a website, a mobile app, and/or a link on a Facebook site.

1. Plan the application by specifying the goal, target audience, treatment ("look and feel"), and elements you want to include (text, graphics, sound, and so on).

2. Sketch out a screen design that shows the layout of the objects. Be creative in your design.

3. Open a new Flash document and save it as **theJazzClub2.fla**.

4. Set the document properties, including the Stage size and Stage color, if desired.

5. Display the gridlines and rulers and use them to help align objects on the Stage.

6. Create a heading, text objects, and drawings (such as the lines) to be used as links to the categories of information provided on the application. (*Note*: Some of the characters are individual text blocks [e.g. the S in Sessions] allowing you to move the text block without moving the other characters. *Hint*: Use the Oval, Line, and Brush tools to create the notes. After selecting the Brush tool, experiment with the different Brush tool shapes found in the Options area at the bottom of the Tools panel.)

7. Hide the gridlines and rulers.

8. Save your work, then compare your image to the example shown in Figure 71.

Figure 71 *Sample completed Project Builder 2*

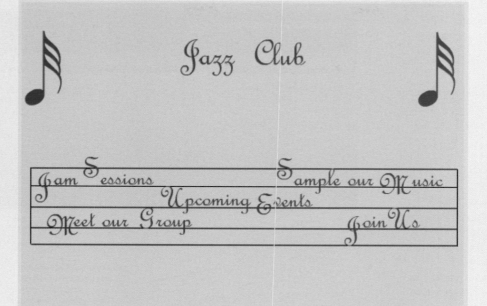

Figure 72 shows the home page of a website. Study the figure and complete the following. For each question indicate how you determined your answer.

1. Connect to the Internet, go to *www.nps.gov*, then select Explore Nature.
2. Open a document in a word processor or open a new Flash document, save the file as **dpc2**, then answer the following questions. (*Hint*: Use the Text tool in Flash.)
   - Whose website is this?
   - What is the goal(s) of the site?
   - Who is the target audience?
   - What treatment ("look and feel") is used?
   - What are the design layout guidelines being used (balance, movement, and so on)?
   - If you wanted to add animation to this screen, what element might you animate?
   - Do you think this is an effective design for the organization, its goals, and its target audience? Why or why not?
   - How might TLF text be used in this layout?
   - What suggestions would you make to improve the design and why?

Figure 72 *Design Project*

Courtesy of National Park Service website. www.nps.gov

You have decided to create a personal portfolio of your work that you can use when you begin your job search. The portfolio will be part of a website with a link on your Facebook page.

1. Research what should be included in a portfolio.
2. Plan the site by specifying the goal, target audience, treatment ("look and feel"), and elements you want to include (text, graphics, sound, and so on).
3. Sketch an opening screen that shows the layout of the objects. Be creative in your design.
4. Design the opening screen to include personal data (such as a Biography object that will link to your personal data, work history, and education), contact information (such as a Contact me object that will link to your contact information), and samples of your work (such as Animations, Graphics, and Screen Designs objects that will link to samples of your work). The categories and titles are up to you.
5. Open a new Flash document using ActionScript 2.0 and save it as **portfolio2.fla**. (*Note*: ActionScript 2.0 is used because, in subsequent chapters, the portfolio project will require this version of ActionScript.)
6. Set the document properties, including the Stage size and Stage color, if desired.
7. Display the gridlines and rulers and use them to help align objects on the Stage. (*Note:* The sample completed Portfolio Project shown in Figure 73 uses four layers. As you complete the following steps include layers for:
   - the border
   - the placeholder for the image
   - the background ovals for the heading and the categories
   - the text for the heading and the categories)
8. Add a border the size of the Stage. (*Hint*: Use the Rectangle tool, then set the Stroke color to a color of your choice and the Fill color to no color ☑ .
9. Create a heading with its own background.
10. Create the background ovals for the categories.
11. Create the text objects that will be used as links to the categories of information provided on the website. (*Hint*: In the example shown here, the Brush Script Std font is used. You can replace this font with Impact or any other appropriate font on your computer.)
12. Hide the gridlines and rulers.
13. Lock all the layers.
14. Save your work, then compare your image to the example shown in Figure 73.

Figure 73 *Sample completed Portfolio Project*

Drawing Objects in Adobe Flash

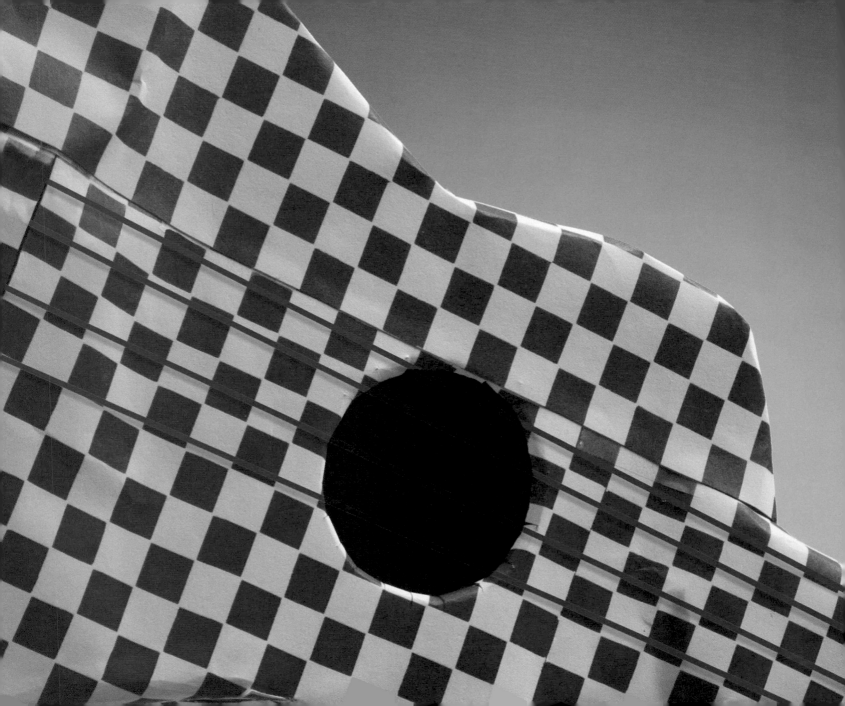

CHAPTER **3** **WORKING WITH SYMBOLS
AND INTERACTIVITY**

1. Create symbols and instances
2. Work with libraries
3. Create buttons
4. Assign actions to frames and buttons
5. Import graphics

Introduction

An important benefit of Flash is its ability to create movies with small file sizes. This allows the movies to be delivered from the web or displayed on a mobile device more quickly. One way to keep the file size small is to create reusable graphics, buttons, and movie clips. Flash allows you to create a graphic (drawing) and then make unlimited copies, which you can use throughout the current movie and in other movies. Flash calls the original drawing a **symbol** and the copied drawings **instances**. Flash stores symbols in the Library panel—each time you need a copy of the symbol, you can open the Library panel and drag the symbol to the Stage, which creates an instance (copy) of the symbol. Using instances reduces the movie file size because Flash stores only the information about the symbol's properties (size, shape, color), and a link is established between the symbol and an instance so that the instance has the same properties (such as color and shape) as the symbol. There are two especially valuable editing features of this process. First, if you have created several instances of a symbol and decide to change the same property for every instance, all that is needed is to edit the symbol. For example, if a logo appears in several places in an application and you need

to change the color of each instance of the logo, you simply change the color of the symbol. Because the instances are linked to the symbol they are automatically updated. Second, you can change the properties of an individual instance of a symbol in one of two ways. You can change properties associated with the whole instance, such as size or transparency, and you can skew or rotate the instance. So if you have a symbol that is a tree, you can make the tree bigger or smaller, or you can make the tree lean to the left as if it is blowing in the wind. However, if you want to change individual parts of the instance, then you must break the link between the instance and the symbol. When you break the link between an instance and a symbol, the instance becomes an object that can be edited. For example, thinking about our tree now as an object, you can make the leaves on the tree different colors. You can only do this if you break the link between the instance and the symbol. When you break the link, changes you make to the object are not reflected in the symbol or any instances of the symbol. Likewise, if subsequently you make changes to the symbol, the changes will not be reflected in the unlinked object. The process for unlinking an instance is to select the instance on the Stage and choose the Break Apart command from the Modify menu.

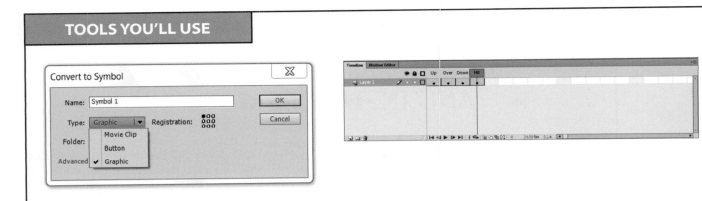

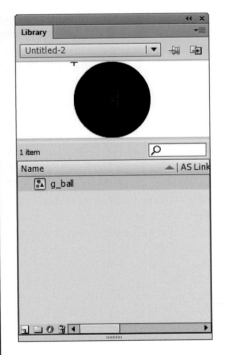

Create Symbols
AND INSTANCES

What You'll Do

In this lesson, you will create graphic symbols, turn them into instances, and then edit the instances.

Understanding Symbol Types

There are three categories of symbols: graphic, button, and movie clip. A graphic symbol is useful because you can reuse a single image and make changes in each instance of the image. A button symbol is useful because you can create buttons for interactivity, such as starting or stopping a movie. A movie clip symbol is useful for creating complex animations because you can create a movie within a movie. For example, you could have a movie with a car moving across the screen and its wheels rotating. The wheel animation would be created as one movie clip symbol and attached to each wheel of the animated car. Symbols can be created from objects you draw using the Flash drawing tools. In addition, you can import graphics into a Flash document that can then be converted to symbols.

Creating a Graphic Symbol

You can use the New Symbol command on the Insert menu to create and then draw a symbol. You can also draw an object and then use the Convert to Symbol command on the Modify menu to convert the object to a symbol. The Convert to Symbol dialog box, shown in Figure 1, allows you to name

the symbol and specify the type of symbol you want to create (Movie Clip, Button, or Graphic). When naming a symbol, it's a good idea to use a naming convention that allows you to quickly identify the type of symbol and to group like symbols together. For example, you could identify all graphic symbols by naming them g_*name* and all buttons as b_*name*. In Figure 1, the drawing on the Stage is being converted to a graphic symbol.

After you complete the Convert to Symbol dialog box, Flash places the symbol in the Library panel, as shown in Figure 2. In Figure 2, an icon identifying the symbol as a graphic symbol and the symbol name are listed in the Library panel, along with a preview of the selected symbol. To create an instance of the symbol, you simply drag a symbol from the Library panel to the Stage. To edit a symbol, you can double-click it in the Library panel or you can use the Edit Symbols command on the Edit menu. Either way displays the symbol in an edit window, where changes can be made to it. When you edit a symbol, the changes are reflected in all instances of that symbol in your movie. For example, you can draw a car, convert the car to a symbol, and then create several instances of the car.

You can uniformly change the size of all the cars by double-clicking the car symbol in the Library panel to open the edit window, and then rescaling it to the desired size.

Working with Instances

You can have as many instances as needed in your movie, and you can edit each one to make it somewhat different from the others. You can rotate, skew (slant), and resize graphic and button instances. In addition, you can change the color, brightness, and transparency. However, there are some limitations. An instance is a single object with no segments or parts, such as a stroke and a fill. You cannot select a part of an instance. Therefore, any changes to the color of the instance are made to the entire object. Of course, you can use layers to stack other objects on top of an instance to change its appearance. In addition, you can use the Break Apart command on the Modify menu to break the link between an instance and a symbol. Once the link is broken, you can make any changes to the object, such as changing its stroke and fill color. However, because the link is broken, the object is no longer an instance of the original symbol. So, if you make any changes to the original symbol, then the unlinked object is not affected.

The process for creating an instance is to open the Library panel and drag the desired symbol to the Stage. Once the symbol is on the Stage, you select the instance by using the Selection tool to drag a marquee around it. A blue bounding box indicates that the object is selected. Then, you can use the Free Transform tool options (such as Rotate and Skew, or Scale) to modify the entire image, or you can use the Break Apart command to break apart the instance and edit individual strokes and fills.

QUICK **TIP**

You need to be careful when editing an instance. Use the Selection tool to drag a marquee around the instance or click the object once to select it. Do not double-click the instance when it is on the Stage; otherwise, you will open an edit window that is used to edit the symbol, not the instance.

Figure 2 *A graphic symbol in the Library panel*

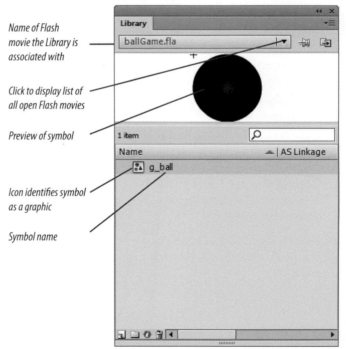

Name of Flash movie the Library is associated with

Click to display list of all open Flash movies

Preview of symbol

Icon identifies symbol as a graphic

Symbol name

Figure 1 *Using the Convert to Symbol dialog box to convert an object to a symbol*

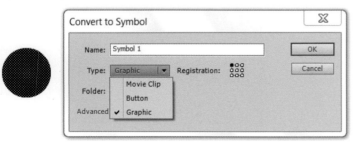

Create a symbol

1. Open fl3_1.fla from the drive and folder where your Data Files are stored, then save it as **coolCar.fla**.

   This document has one object, a car, that was created using the Flash drawing tools.

2. Verify the Properties panel, the Library panel, and the Tools panel are displayed.

3. Set the magnification to **Fit in Window**.

4. Click the **Selection tool** ↖ on the Tools panel, then drag a **marquee** around the car to select it.

5. Click **Modify** on the menu bar, then click **Convert to Symbol**.

6. Type **g_car** in the Name text box.

7. Click the **Type list arrow** to display the symbol types, then click **Graphic**, as shown in Figure 3.

8. Set the **registration** to the upper-left corner as shown in Figure 3 if necessary, then click **OK**.

9. Click the **Library panel tab**, study the Library panel as shown in Figure 4, then save your work.

   The Library panel displays the symbol (red car) in the Item Preview window, an icon 🖾 indicating that this is a graphic symbol, and the name of the symbol (g_car). The symbol is contained in the library, and the car on the Stage is now an instance of the symbol.

You opened a file with an object, converted the object to a symbol, and displayed the symbol in the Library panel.

Figure 3 *Options in the Convert to Symbol dialog box*

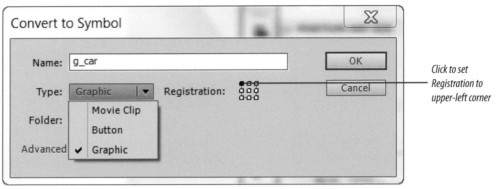

Click to set Registration to upper-left corner

Figure 4 *Newly created symbol in the Library panel*

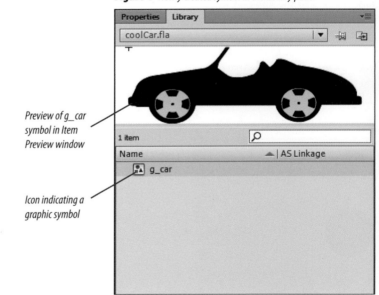

Preview of g_car symbol in Item Preview window

Icon indicating a graphic symbol

Figure 5 *Creating an instance*

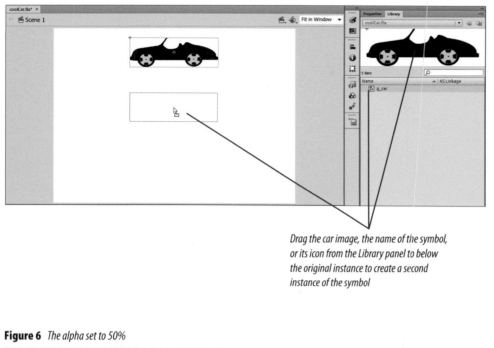

Drag the car image, the name of the symbol,
or its icon from the Library panel to below
the original instance to create a second
instance of the symbol

Figure 6 *The alpha set to 50%*

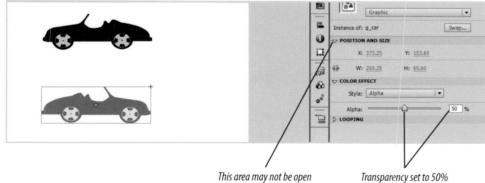

This area may not be open   Transparency set to 50%

Create and edit an instance

1. Point to the **car image** in the Item Preview
    window of the Library panel, then drag the
    image to the Stage beneath the first car, as
    shown in Figure 5.

    Both cars on the Stage are instances of the
    graphic symbol in the Library panel.

    TIP You can also drag the name of the symbol or its icon
    from the Library panel to the Stage.

2. Verify the bottom car is selected, click **Modify**
    on the menu bar, point to **Transform**, then click
    Flip Horizontal.

3. Display the Properties panel, then display the
    COLOR EFFECT area if it is not already showing.

4. Click the **Style list arrow**, then click **Alpha**.

5. Drag the **Alpha slider** △ left then right, then set
    the transparency to **50%**.

    Notice how the transparency changes. Figure 6
    shows the transparency set to 50%.

6. Click a blank area of the Stage to deselect
    the object, then save your work.

    Changing the alpha setting gives the car a more
    transparent look.

*You created an instance of a symbol and edited the instance on
the Stage.*

Edit a symbol in the edit window

1. Display the Library panel, double-click the **g_car symbol icon** 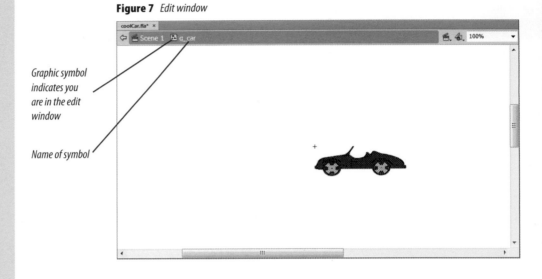 in the Library panel to display the edit window, then compare your screen to Figure 7.

   The g_car symbol appears in the edit window, indicating that you are editing the g_car symbol.

   TIP You can also edit a symbol by selecting it, clicking Edit on the menu bar, then clicking Edit Symbols.

2. Click a blank area of the window to deselect the car.

3. Verify the Selection tool ▶ is selected, then click the **light gray hubcap** inside the front wheel to select it.

4. Press and hold **[Shift]**, then click the **hubcap** inside the back wheel so both hubcap fills are selected.

5. Set the **Fill Color** ⬚ to the **blue gradient color swatch** in the bottom row of the color palette, compare your image to Figure 8, then deselect the image.

6. Click **Scene 1** at the top left of the edit window to exit the edit window and return to the main Timeline and main Stage, then save your work.

   Changes you make to the symbol affect every instance of the symbol on the Stage. The hubcap fill becomes a blue gradient in the Library panel and on the Stage.

   You edited a symbol in the edit window that affected all instances of the symbol.

Figure 7 *Edit window*

Graphic symbol indicates you are in the edit window

Name of symbol

Figure 8 *Edited symbol*

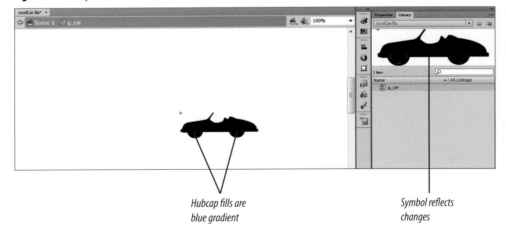

Hubcap fills are blue gradient

Symbol reflects changes

Figure 9 *The car with the maroon body selected*

Figure 10 *Changing the symbol affects only the one instance of the symbol*

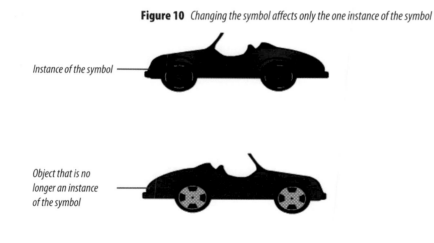

Instance of the symbol ——

Object that is no
longer an instance
of the symbol ——

Break apart an instance

1. Drag a **marquee** around the bottom car to select it if it is not selected.
2. Click **Modify** on the menu bar, then click **Break Apart**.

   The object is no longer linked to the symbol, and its parts (strokes and fills) can now be edited.
3. Click a blank area of the Stage to deselect the object.
4. Click the blue **front hubcap**, press and hold **[Shift]**, then click the **blue back hubcap** so both hubcaps are selected.
5. Set the **Fill Color** to the **light gray color swatch (#999999)** in the left column of the color palette.
6. Double-click the **g_car symbol icon** in the Library panel to display the edit window.
7. Click the **maroon front body** of the car to select it, press and hold **[Shift]**, then click the **maroon back body** of the car, as shown in Figure 9.
8. Set the **Fill Color** to the **red gradient color swatch** in the bottom row of the color palette.
9. Click **Scene 1** at the top left of the edit window, then compare your images to Figure 10.

   The body color of the car in the original instance is a different color, but the body color of the car to which you applied the Break Apart command remains unchanged.
10. Save your work.

You used the Break Apart command to break the link between one instance and its symbol, you edited the object created using the Break Apart command, and then you edited the symbol, which only affected the instance still linked to the symbol.

Work with LIBRARIES

What You'll Do

In this lesson, you will use the Library panel to organize the symbols in a movie.

Understanding the Library

The library in a Flash document contains the symbols and other items such as imported graphics, movie clips, and sounds. The Library panel provides a way to view and organize the items, and allows you to change the item name, display item properties, and add and delete items. Figure 11 shows the Library panel for a document. Refer to this figure as you read the following descriptions of the parts of the library.

Tab title—Identifies the panel title, in this case, the Library panel.

Panel options menu— Labeled in Figure 11 and shown in Figure 12, the Panel options menu provides access to several features used to edit symbols (such as renaming symbols) and organize symbols (such as creating a new folder).

Display movies list arrow—Opens a menu showing all open movies. You use this menu to select an open document (movie) and display the Library panel associated with that open document. This allows you to use the items from one movie in another movie. For example, you may have developed a drawing in one Flash movie that you converted to a symbol and now you want to use that symbol in the movie you are working on. With both documents open, you simply use the Display movies list arrow to display the library with the desired symbol, and then drag the symbol to the Stage of the current movie. This will automatically place the symbol in the library for the current movie. In addition to the movie libraries, you can create permanent libraries that are available whenever you start Flash. Flash also has sample libraries that contain buttons and other objects. The permanent and sample libraries are accessed through the Common Libraries command on the Window menu. All assets in all of these libraries are available for use in any movie.

Item Preview window—Displays the selected item. If the item is animated or a sound file, a control button appears, allowing you to preview the animation or play the sound.

Name list box—Lists the folder and item names. Each item type has a different icon associated with it. Clicking an item name or icon displays the item in the Item Preview window.

Toggle Sorting Order icon—Allows you to reorder the list of folders and items within folders.

New Symbol icon—Displays the Create New Symbol dialog box, allowing you to create a new symbol.

New Folder icon—Allows you to create a new folder.

Properties icon—Displays the Properties dialog box for the selected item.

Delete icon—Deletes the selected item or folder.

To make changes to an item, you can double-click either the item icon in the Library panel, the item in the Item Preview window, or the item on the Stage to display the edit window.

Figure 11 *The Library panel*

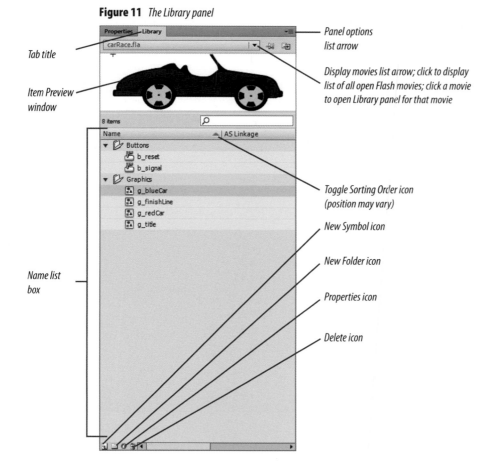

Tab title

Item Preview window

Name list box

Panel options list arrow

Display movies list arrow; click to display list of all open Flash movies; click a movie to open Library panel for that movie

Toggle Sorting Order icon (position may vary)

New Symbol icon

New Folder icon

Properties icon

Delete icon

Figure 12 *The Panel options menu*

New Symbol...
New Folder
New Font...
New Video...

Rename
Delete
Duplicate...
Move to...

Edit
Edit with...
Edit with Audition
Edit Class
Play
Update...

Properties...
Component Definition...
Runtime Shared Library URL...

Select Unused Items

Expand Folder
Collapse Folder
Expand All Folders
Collapse All Folders

Help

Close
Close Group

Create folders in the Library panel

1. Open fl3_2.fla, then save it as **carRace.fla**.

2. Verify the Properties panel, the Library panel, and the Tools panel are displayed.

3. Set the magnification to **Fit in Window**.

   This movie has eight layers containing various objects such as text blocks, lines, and a backdrop. Two layers contain animations of cars.

4. Test the movie, then close the Flash Player window.

5. Click the **Show or Hide All Layers icon** 👁 on the Timeline to hide all of the layers.

6. Click each **red X** in the Show or Hide All Layers column to show the contents of each layer, click the **Show or Hide This Layer icon** ⬤ to hide the contents of that layer, then after viewing the contents of each layer, click the **Show or Hide All Layers icon** 👁 on the Timeline to show all of the layers.

   Note: The resetBTN layer shows an empty Stage. This is because the word Reset is located in frame 65 at the end of the movie and does not appear in frame 1.

7. Click each item in the Library panel to display it in the Item Preview window.

   Notice that there is one button symbol (b_reset) and five graphic symbols.

8. Click **Name** on the Name list box title bar, as shown in Figure 13, and notice how the items are sorted.

9. Repeat Step 8 and notice how the items are sorted.

You opened a Flash movie and sorted items in the Library panel.

Figure 13 *The open Library panel*

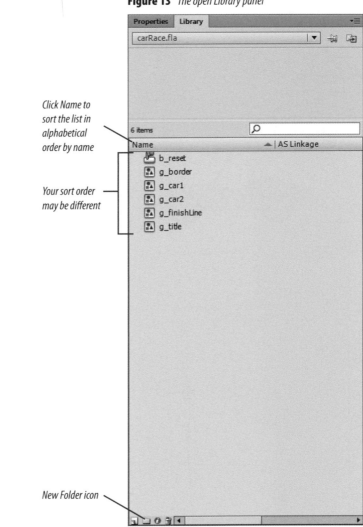

Click Name to sort the list in alphabetical order by name

Your sort order may be different

New Folder icon

Figure 14 *The Library panel with the folders added*

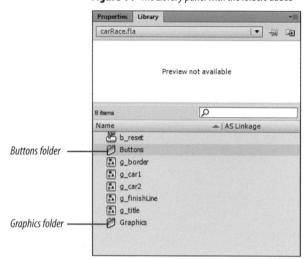

Buttons folder

Graphics folder

Figure 15 *The Library panel after moving the symbols to the folders*

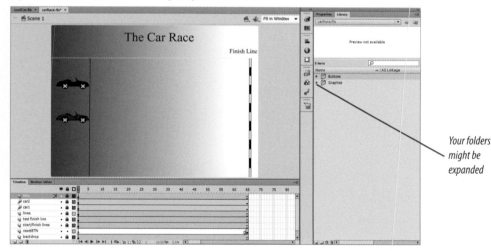

The Car Race

Finish Line

Your folders might be expanded

Organize items within Library panel folders

1. Click the **New Folder icon** 🗀 in the Library panel, as shown in Figure 13.
2. Type **Graphics** in the Name text box for the new folder, then press [**Enter**] (Win) or [**return**] (Mac).
3. Click the **New Folder icon** 🗀 on the Library panel.
4. Type **Buttons** in the Name text box for the new folder, then press [**Enter**] (Win) or [**return**] (Mac).

   Your Library panel should resemble Figure 14.
5. Drag the 🖾 **g_title symbol** in the Library panel to the Graphics folder.
6. Drag the other graphic symbols to the Graphics folder.
7. Drag the 🖳 **b_reset symbol** to the Buttons folder, then compare your Library panel to Figure 15.
8. Click the **Graphics folder expand icon** ▶ to open it and display the graphic symbols.
9. Click the **Buttons folder expand icon** ▶ to open it and display the button symbol.
10. Click the **Graphics folder collapse icon** ▼ to close the folder.
11. Click the **Buttons folder collapse icon** ▼ to close the folder.

   Note: To remove an item from a folder, drag the item down to a blank area of the Library panel.

You created new folders, organized the symbols within the folders, and then opened and closed the folders.

Rename symbols and delete a symbol

1. Click the **expand icon** ▶ for the Graphics folder to display the symbols.

2. Right-click (Win) or [control]-click (Mac) the **g_car1 symbol**, then click **Rename**.

3. Type **g_redCar** in the Name text box, then press **[Enter]** (Win) or **[return]** (Mac).

4. Repeat Steps 2 and 3 to rename the g_car2 symbol as **g_blueCar**.

5. Study the Stage and notice there are two yellow lines, one near the top and the other at the bottom of the Stage.

6. Click **g_border** in the Library panel to select it.

7. Click the **Delete icon** 🗑 at the bottom of the Library panel.

8. Study the Stage and notice the yellow border lines are deleted.

   Your Library panel should resemble Figure 16.

TIP You can also select an item and press [Delete], or you can use the Panel options menu in the Library panel to remove an item from the library. The Undo command in the Edit menu can be used to undelete an item.

You used the Library panel to rename symbols and delete a symbol.

Figure 16 *Updated Library panel*

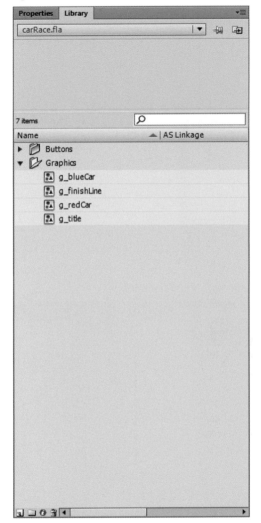

Working with Symbols and Interactivity

Figure 17 *The carRace.fla document and the coolCar.fla Library panel*

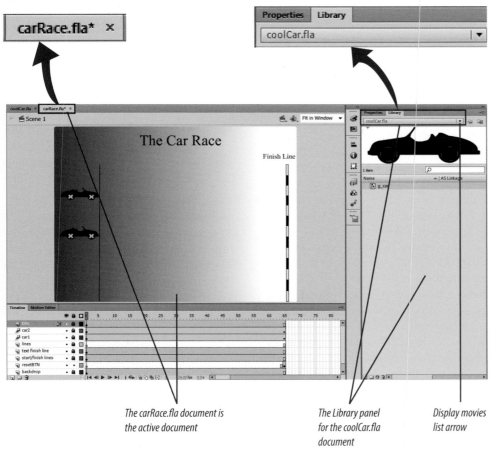

The carRace.fla document is
the active document

The Library panel
for the coolCar.fla
document

Display movies
list arrow

Use multiple Library panels

1. Click the **Display movies list arrow** near the top of the Library panel to display a list of open documents.

2. Click **coolCar.fla**, then click **g_car**.

   The Library panel for the coolCar document is displayed. However, the carRace document remains open, as shown in Figure 17.

3. Click **frame 1** on the resetBTN layer, then drag the 🖼 **g_car symbol** from the Library panel to the center of the Stage.

   The reset BTN layer is the only unlocked layer. Objects cannot be placed on locked layers.

4. Click the **Display movies list arrow** to display the open documents.

5. Click **carRace.fla** to view the carRace document's Library panel.

   Notice the g_car symbol is added automatically to the Library panel of the carRace document.

6. Click the **g_car symbol** in the Library panel.

7. Click the **Delete icon** 🗑 at the bottom of the Library panel.

   You deleted the g_car symbol from the carRace library but it still exists in the coolCar library. The car was also deleted from the Stage.

8. Save your work.

9. Click the **coolCar.fla tab** at the top of the workspace to display the document.

10. Close the coolCar document and save the document if asked.

You used the Library panel to display the contents of another library and added an object from that library to the current document.

Create BUTTONS

What You'll Do

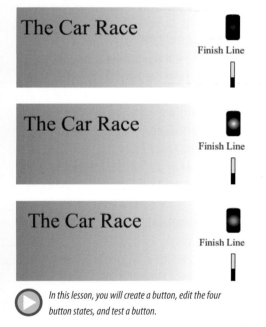

In this lesson, you will create a button, edit the four button states, and test a button.

Understanding Buttons

Button symbols are used to provide interactivity. When you click a button, an action occurs, such as starting an animation or jumping to another frame on the Timeline. Any object, including Flash drawings, text blocks, and imported graphic images, can be made into buttons. Unlike graphic symbols, buttons have four states: Up, Over, Down, and Hit. These states correspond to the use of the mouse and recognize that the user requires feedback when the mouse is pointing to a button and when the button has been clicked. This is often shown by a change in the button (such as a different color or different shape). An example of a button with different colors for the four different states is shown in Figure 18. These four states are explained in the following paragraphs.

Up—Represents how the button appears when the mouse pointer is not over it.

Over—Represents how the button appears when the mouse pointer is over it.

Down—Represents how the button appears after the user clicks the mouse.

Hit—Defines the area of the screen that will respond to the pointer. In most cases, you will want the Hit state to be the same or similar to the Up state in location and size.

When you create a button symbol, Flash automatically creates a new Timeline. The Timeline has only four frames, one for each button state. The Timeline does not play; it merely reacts to the mouse pointer by displaying the appropriate button state.

The process for creating and previewing buttons is as follows:

Create a button symbol—Draw an object or select an object that has already been created and placed on the Stage. Use the Convert to

Figure 18 *The four button states*

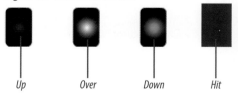

Up   Over   Down   Hit

Symbol command on the Modify menu to convert the object to a button symbol and to enter a name for the button.

Edit the button symbol—Select the button and choose the Edit Symbols command on the Edit menu or double-click the button symbol in the Library panel. This displays the edit window, which includes the button Timeline, shown in Figure 19. You use the button Timeline to work with the four button states. The Up state is the original button symbol. Flash automatically places it in frame 1. You need to determine how the original object will change for the other states. To change the button for the Over state, click frame 2 and insert a keyframe. This automatically places a copy of the button that is in frame 1 into frame 2. Then, alter the button's appearance for the Over state, for instance, by changing the fill color. Use the same process for the Down state. For the Hit state, you insert a keyframe in frame 4 and then specify the area on the screen that will respond to the pointer. If you do not specify a hit area, the image for the Down state is used for the hit area. You add a keyframe to the Hit frame only if you are going to specify the hit area.

Return to the main Timeline—Once you've finished editing a button, you choose the Edit Document command on the Edit menu or click Scene 1 above the edit window to return to the main Timeline.

Preview the button—By default, Flash disables buttons so that you can manipulate them on the Stage. You can preview a button by choosing the Enable Simple Buttons command on the Control menu. You can also choose the Test Movie command on the Control menu to play the movie and test the buttons.

Figure 19 *The edit window showing the button symbol and the button Timeline*

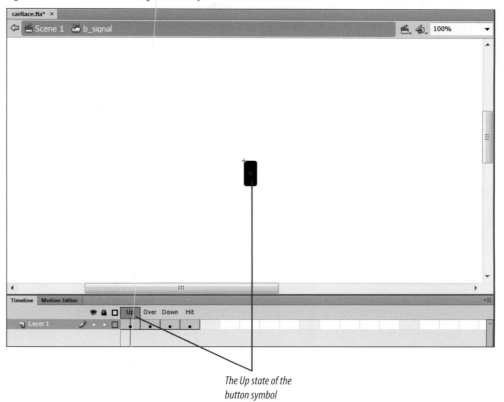

The Up state of the
button symbol

Create a button

1. Insert a **new layer** above the top layer on the Timeline, then name the layer **signal**.

2. Select the **Rectangle Primitive tool** ▭, then set the **Stroke Color** to **No Stroke**.

TIP The No Stroke icon ⊘ is in the upper-right corner of the color palette.

3. Set the **Fill Color** to the **red gradient color swatch** in the bottom row of the color palette.

4. Display the Properties panel, click the **Reset button** in the RECTANGLE OPTIONS area, then set the corner radius to **5**.

5. Draw the **rectangle** shown in Figure 20.

6. Click the **Zoom tool** 🔍 on the Tools panel, then click the **rectangle** to enlarge it.

7. Select the **Gradient Transform tool** ▦ on the Tools panel.

TIP You may need to click and hold the Free Transform tool first.

8. Click the **rectangle**, then drag the **diagonal arrow** toward the center of the rectangle as shown in Figure 21 to make the red area more round.

9. Click the **Selection tool** ▸ on the Tools panel, then drag a **marquee** around the rectangle to select it.

10. Click **Modify** on the menu bar, then click **Convert to Symbol**.

11. Type **b_signal** in the Name text box, click the **Type list arrow**, click **Button**, then click **OK**.

12. Display the Library panel, then drag the **b_signal symbol** to the Buttons folder.

You created a button symbol on the Stage and dragged it to the Buttons folder in the Library panel.

Figure 20 *The rectangle object*

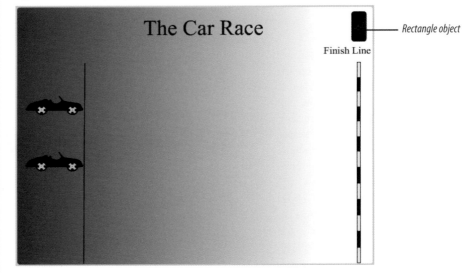

Rectangle object

Figure 21 *Adjusting the gradient*

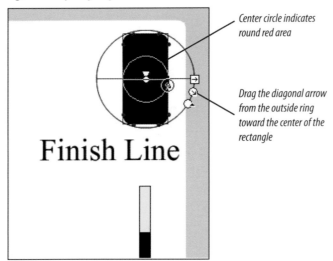

Center circle indicates round red area

Drag the diagonal arrow from the outside ring toward the center of the rectangle

Figure 22 *Specifying the hit area*

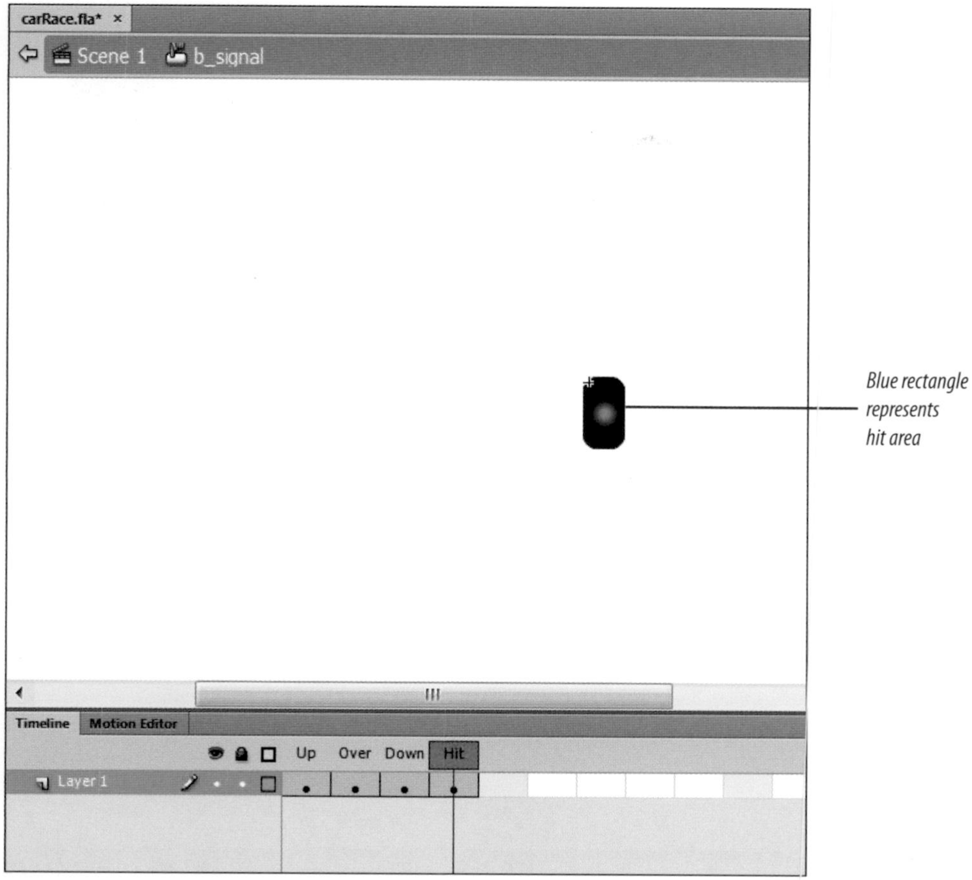

Blue rectangle
represents
hit area

Edit a button and specify a hit area

1. Open the Buttons folder, right-click (Win) or control-click (Mac) **b_signal** in the Library panel, then click **Edit**.

   Flash displays the edit window showing the Timeline with four button states.

2. Click the blank **Over frame** on Layer 1, then insert a **keyframe**.

TIP The [F6] key inserts a keyframe in the selected frame. The [fn] key may need to be used with some Mac keyboards.

3. Set the **Fill Color** to the **gray gradient color swatch** on the bottom of the color palette.

TIP If the gradient is not selected, try clicking the edge of the gradient swatch rather than the middle.

4. Insert a **keyframe** in the Down frame on Layer 1.

5. Set the **Fill Color** to the **green gradient color swatch** on the bottom of the color palette.

6. Insert a **keyframe** in the Hit frame on Layer 1.

7. Select the **Rectangle tool** ⬜, on the Tools panel then set the **Fill Color** to the **blue color swatch** in the left column of the color palette.

8. Draw a **rectangle** slightly larger than the button as shown in Figure 22, then release the mouse button.

TIP The Hit area will not be visible on the Stage when you return to the main Timeline.

9. Click **Scene 1** above the edit window to return to the main Timeline.

You edited a button by changing the color of its Over and Down states, and you specified the Hit area.

Test a button

1. Click the **Selection tool** ![selection tool], then click a blank area of the Stage.

2. Click **Control** on the menu bar to display the Control menu, then click **Enable Simple Buttons** if it is not already checked.

   This command allows you to test buttons on the Stage without viewing the movie in the Flash Player window.

3. Point to the **signal button** on the Stage, then compare your image to Figure 23.

   The pointer changes to a hand ![hand], indicating that the object is clickable, and the button changes to a gray gradient, the color you selected for the Over state.

4. Press and hold the **mouse button**, then notice that the button changes to a green gradient, the color you selected for the Down state, as shown in Figure 24.

5. Release the mouse and notice that the button changes to a gray gradient, the color you selected for the Over state.

(continued)

Figure 23 *The button's Over state*

Figure 24 *The button's Down state*

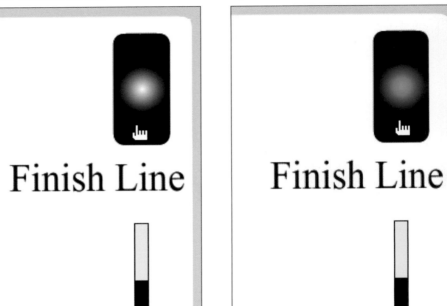

The Button Hit Area

All buttons have an area that responds to the mouse pointer, including rolling over the button and clicking it. This hit area is usually the same size and shape as the button itself. However, you can specify any area of the button to be the hit area. For example, you could have a button symbol that looks like a target with just the bulls-eye center being the hit area.

Working with Symbols and Interactivity

Figure 25 *The button's Up state*

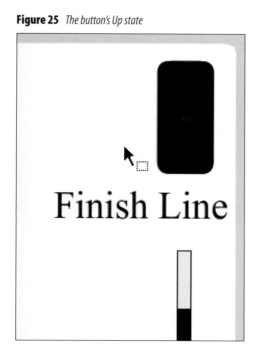

Figure 26 *View options from the View list*

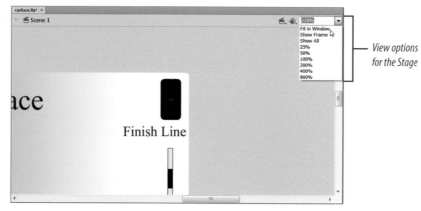

View options for the Stage

6. Move the mouse away from the signal button, and notice that the button returns to a red gradient, the Up state color, as shown in Figure 25.

7. Click **Control** on the menu bar, then click **Enable Simple Buttons** to turn off the command.

8. Click the **View list arrow** above the Stage, then click **Fit in Window**, as shown in Figure 26.

   This shortcut allows you to change the magnification view without using the Magnification command on the View menu or the Zoom tool in the Tools panel.

9. Save your work.

You used the mouse to test a button and view the button states.

Assign Actions
TO FRAMES AND BUTTONS

What You'll Do

In this lesson, you will use ActionScript to assign actions to frames and buttons.

Understanding Actions

In a basic movie, Flash plays the frames sequentially without stopping for user input. However, you often want to provide users with the ability to interact with the movie by allowing them to perform actions, such as starting and stopping the movie or jumping to a specific frame in the movie. One way to provide user interaction is to assign an action to the Down state of a button. Then, whenever the user clicks the button, the action occurs. Flash provides a scripting language, called ActionScript, that allows you to add actions to buttons and frames within a movie. For example, you can place a stop action in a frame that pauses the movie, and then you can assign a play action to a button that starts the movie when the user clicks the button.

Analyzing ActionScript

ActionScript, which is a powerful scripting language, allows those with even limited programming experience to create complex actions. For example, you can create order forms that capture user input or volume controls that display when sounds are played. A basic ActionScript involves an event (such as a mouse click) that causes some action to occur by triggering the script. The following is an example of a basic ActionScript:

on (release) {

gotoAndPlay(10);

}

In this example, the event is a mouse click (indicated by the word release) that causes the movie's playhead to go to frame 10 and play the frame. This is a simple example of ActionScript code and it is easy to follow. Other ActionScript code can be quite complex and may require programming expertise to understand.

ActionScript 2.0 and 3.0

Adobe has identified two types of Flash CS6 users, designers and developers. Designers focus more on the visual features of a Flash movie, including the user interface design, drawing objects, and acquiring and editing additional assets (such as graphic images). Whereas, developers focus more on the programming aspects of a Flash movie, including creation of complex animations and writing the code that specifies how the movie responds to user interactions. In many cases, designers and developers work together to create sophisticated Flash applications. In other cases, designers work without the benefit of a developer's programming expertise. In order to accommodate the varying needs of these two types of users, Flash CS6 provides two versions of ActionScript, 2.0 and 3.0, called AS2 and AS3. ActionScript 3.0 is used by developers because it provides a programming environment that is more familiar to them and can be used to create movies that download more quickly. However, the differences between AS2 and AS3 are transparent to designers who do not have programming expertise. AS2 allows new Flash users to create compelling applications even if they do not have a background in programming. At the same time, AS2 provides an introduction to ActionScript that can be the basis for learning ActionScript 3.0. ActionScript 2.0 will be used in this chapter. You can specify ActionScript 2.0 when creating a new document or you can use the Flash tab in the Publish Settings dialog box, which can be opened using the Publish Settings command found on the File menu, to specify AS2.

An advantage of using AS2 is a feature called Script Assist, which provides an easy way to use ActionScript without having to learn the scripting language. The Script Assist feature within the Actions panel allows you to assign basic actions to frames and objects, such as buttons. Figure 27 shows the Actions panel displaying an ActionScript indicating that when the user clicks the selected object (a button, in this example, b_signal), the movie goes to and plays frame 2.

Figure 27 *The Actions panel displaying an ActionScript*

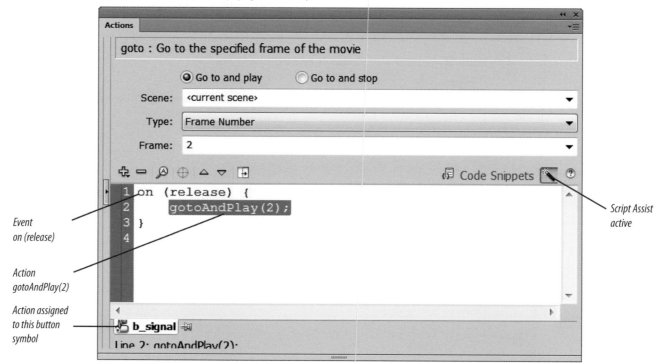

The process for assigning actions to buttons, shown in Figure 28, is as follows:

1. Select the button on the Stage that you want to assign an action to.
2. Display the Actions panel, using the Window menu.
3. Click the Script Assist button to display the Script Assist panel within the ActionScript panel, and verify the button symbol and name appear in the lower-left corner of the Actions panel.
4. Click the Add a new item to the script button to display a list of Script categories and associated menus.
5. Click the appropriate category from a menu. Flash provides several categories, such as the Timeline Control category accessed via the Global Functions menu. You can use the actions available via the Timeline Control menu to start and stop movies, as well as jump to (goto) specific frames. These can be in response to user mouse movements and keystrokes.

■ Select the desired action, such as goto.
■ Specify the event that triggers the action, such as on (release). This step in the process is not shown in Figure 28.

Button actions respond to one or more mouse events, including:

Release—With the pointer inside the button Hit area, the user presses and releases (clicks) the mouse button. This is the default event.

Key Press—With the button displayed, the user presses a predetermined key on the keyboard.

Roll Over—The user moves the pointer into the button Hit area.

Drag Over—The user holds down the mouse button, moves the pointer out of the button Hit area, and then back into the Hit area.

Using Frame Actions

In addition to assigning actions to buttons, you can assign actions to frames. Actions assigned to frames are executed when the playhead reaches the frame. A common frame action is stop, which is often assigned to the first and last frame of a layer on the Timeline.

Figure 28 *The process for assigning actions to buttons*

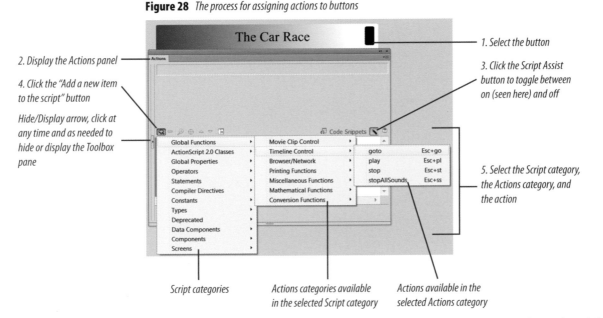

Working with Symbols and Interactivity

Understanding the Actions Panel

The Actions panel has two panes. The left pane (also called the Toolbox pane) uses folders to display the Script categories. The right pane, called the Script pane, is used with the Script Assist feature and it displays the ActionScript code as the code is being generated. When using the Script Assist feature, it is best to close the left pane. This is done by clicking the Hide/Display arrow, which is shown in Figure 28 and Figure 29. In Figure 28, the Toolbox pane is collapsed, and in Figure 29, the Toolbox pane is expanded.

The lower-left corner of the Script pane displays the symbol name or the frame to which the action(s) will apply. Always verify that the desired symbol or frame is displayed. When the Script Assist feature is turned off (not active), you can type ActionScript code directly into the Script pane.

Using Frame Labels

Buttons are often used to move the playhead to a specific location on the Timeline. For example, clicking a Start button might cause the playhead to jump from frame 1 to frame 10 to start an animation. In addition to referencing frame numbers, like 10, you can reference frame labels in the ActionScript code. Frame labels have an advantage over frame numbers, especially in large and complex applications, because adding or deleting frames will not disrupt the navigation to a frame reference you already have in actions because the label remains attached to the frame even if the frame moves. The process is to select a frame and use the Properties panel to specify a name. Then use the frame name in the ActionScript code instead of the frame number. Figure 30 shows the Timeline with a frame label and the Actions panel with the code that references the label.

Figure 29 *The Actions panel*   **Figure 30** *The Timeline with a frame label*

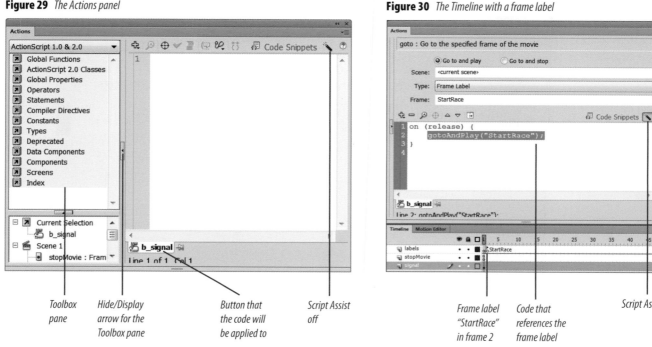

| Toolbox pane | Hide/Display arrow for the Toolbox pane | Button that the code will be applied to | Script Assist off | Frame label "StartRace" in frame 2 | Code that references the frame label | Script Assist on |

Assign a stop action to frames

1. Click **Control** on the menu bar, point to **Test Movie**, then click **in Flash Professional**.

   The movie plays and continues to loop.

2. Close the Flash Player window.

3. Insert a **new layer**, name it **stopMovie**, then click **frame 1** on the layer to select the frame.

4. Click **Window** on the menu bar, then click **Actions** to display the Actions panel.

5. Study the Actions panel. If the Toolbox pane is displayed as shown in Figure 31, then click the **Hide/Display arrow** to hide the pane.

6. Click the **Script Assist button**  to turn on the Script Assist feature if Script Assist is not active.

7. Verify stopMovie:1 (indicating the layer and frame to which the action will be applied) is displayed in the lower-left corner of the Script pane.

8. Click the **Add a new item to the script button** to display the Script categories, point to **Global Functions**, point to **Timeline Control**, then click **stop**, as shown in Figure 32.

9. Insert a **keyframe** in frame 65 on the stopMovie layer, then open the Actions panel if it is no longer open.

   TIP You can collapse the Actions panel to view more of the Stage, then expand the Actions panel when needed. Alternately, you can drag the bottom or sides of the Actions panel up to make the panel smaller.

   (continued)

Figure 31 *The Actions panel Toolbox pane*

Hide/Display arrow for the Toolbox pane

Figure 32 *Assigning an action to frame 1 on the stopMovie layer*

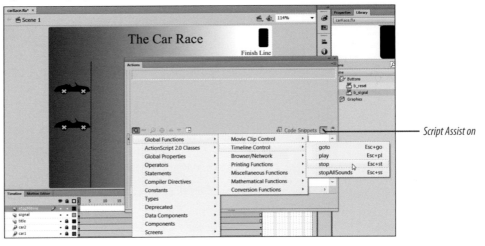

Script Assist on

Figure 33 *Script for the stopMovie layer*

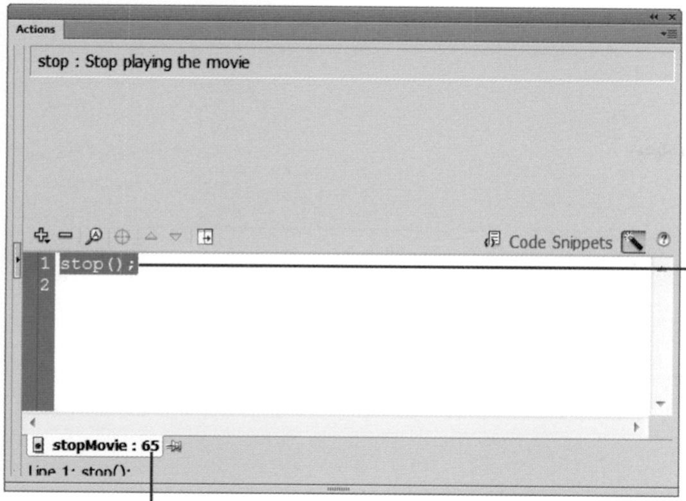

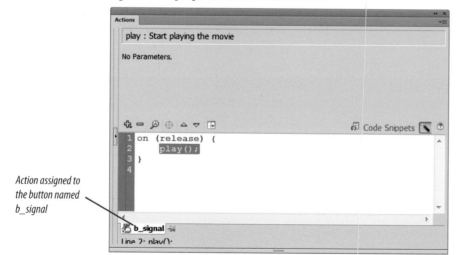

Action stop()

Action assigned to frame 65
of the stopMovie layer

Figure 34 *Assigning an event and an action to a button*

Action assigned to
the button named
b_signal

10. Verify stopMovie: 65 is displayed in the lower-left corner of the Script pane, then repeat Step 8. Compare your screen to Figure 33.

11. Test the movie.

The movie does not play because there is a stop action assigned to frame 1.

12. Close the Flash Player window.

You inserted a layer and assigned a stop action to the first and last frames on the layer.

Assign a play action to a button

1. Click **frame 1** on the signal layer.

2. Move the **Actions panel** to view the signal button on the Stage, if necessary.

3. Click the **Selection tool** ▶ on the Tools panel, then click the **button** on the Stage.

4. Verify b_signal is displayed in the lower left of the Actions panel.

This ensures that the actions specified in the Actions panel will apply to the b_signal button.

5. Click ⬚ to display the Script categories, point to **Global Functions,** point to **Timeline Control,** then click **play.**

Release is the default event for a button, as shown in Figure 34. The "play" action causes the playhead to move to the next frame. To jump to a specific frame, the "goto" action and frame number would be used.

6. Click **Control** on the menu bar, point to **Test Movie,** then click **in Flash Professional.**

7. Click the **signal button** to play the animation.

8. Close the Flash Player window.

You used the Actions panel to assign a play action to a button.

Assign a goto frame action to a button

1. Click **Control** on the menu bar, point to **Test Movie**, then click **in Flash Professional**.

2. Click the **signal button**.

    The movie plays and stops, and the word Reset, which is actually a button, appears.

3. Click the **Reset button** and notice nothing happens because it does not have an action assigned to it.

4. Close the Flash Player window.

5. Click **frame 65** on the resetBTN layer to display the Reset button on the Stage.

    Note: You many need to close and/or move the Actions panel to view the Reset button on the Stage.

6. Click the **Reset button** on the Stage to select it.

7. Verify b_reset is displayed in the lower left of the Actions panel.

8. Verify Script Assist in the Actions panel is active 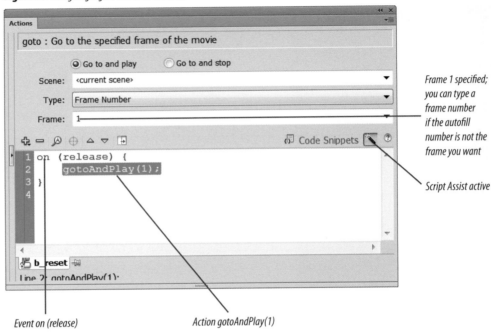, click ⬡ , point to **Global Functions**, point to **Timeline Control**, click **goto**, then verify Frame 1 is specified, as shown in Figure 35.

9. Click **Control** on the menu bar, point to **Test Movie**, then click **in Flash Professional**.

10. Click the **signal button** to start the movie, then when the movie stops, click the **Reset button**.

    The goto action you assigned to the Reset button causes the playhead to jump to frame 1, the beginning of the movie.

11. Close the Flash Player window.

You used the Actions panel to assign an action to a button.

Figure 35 *Assigning a goto action to a button*

Frame 1 specified; you can type a frame number if the autofill number is not the frame you want

Script Assist active

Event on (release)

Action gotoAndPlay(1)

Global Functions: Timeline Control and Movie Clip Control

The most common actions for including interactivity in a movie when using ActionScript 2.0 are added using the Global Functions categories Timeline Control and Movie Clip Control. Timeline Control actions focus on controlling the playhead (play, stop), jumping to a specific frame (goto), and stopping sounds (stopAllSounds). These actions are generally assigned to buttons. Movie Clip Control actions focus on manipulating movie clips (startDrag, stopDrag, removeMovieClip, and so on). They also provide mouse (on Release) and keyboard (Key Press) actions that can be assigned to buttons.

Figure 36 *Assigning a keyPress action to a button*

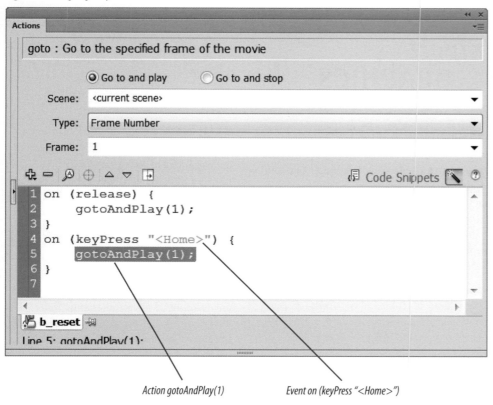

Action gotoAndPlay(1)   Event on (keyPress "<Home>")

keyPress Events

Not all keys on a keyboard can be used for keyPress events. In addition, some keys such as [Home] will only work when the movie is played in a browser and not when the movie is played in the Flash Player window. You may need to use another key such as *r* or *h* which will work in a browser or the Flash Player window. Test your movie to make sure the keyPress events work for the intended playback system.

Assign a second event to a button

1. Click the **right curly brace** (}) in the Actions panel to highlight the brace in line 3 of the ActionScript.
2. Click ⊞ , point to **Global Functions**, point to **Movie Clip Control**, then click **on**.

   The Script Assist window displays several event options. Release is selected.
3. Click the **Release check box** to deselect the option.
4. Click the **Key Press check box** to select it, then press the **[Home] key** on the keyboard.

   TIP If your keyboard does not have a [Home] key, use [fn]+[←] (Mac) or a letter, such as *r*, to complete the steps.

5. Click ⊞ , point to **Global Functions**, point to **Timeline Control**, then click **goto**.

   The ActionScript now indicates that pressing the [Home] key will cause the playhead to go to frame 1, as shown in Figure 36.

   The Reset button can now be activated by clicking it or by pressing the [Home] key.
6. Click **File** on the menu bar, point to **Publish Preview**, then click **Default – (HTML)**.

   The movie opens in your default browser.

   Note: If a warning message opens, follow the messages to allow blocked content.
7. Click the **signal button** to start the movie, then when the movie stops, press the **[Home] key**.

   TIP Use the key(s) you assigned to the keypress event if it is different from the Home key.

8. Close the browser window, close the Actions panel, then save and close the movie.

You added a keypress event that triggers a goto frame action.

Import GRAPHICS

What You'll Do

Photo courtesy of J. Shuman

▶ *In this lesson, you will import and work with bitmap and vector graphics.*

Understanding Graphic Types

Flash provides excellent drawing tools, which allow you to create various objects that can be changed into symbols. In addition, you can import graphics and other assets, such as photographs and sounds. There are two types of graphic files, bitmap graphics and vector graphics. They are distinguished by the way in which the image is represented.

Bitmap images are made up of a group of tiny dots of color called **pixels** (picture elements). Bitmap graphics are often used with photographic images because they can represent subtle gradients in color. However, one disadvantage of bitmap graphics is the inability to enlarge the graphic without distorting the image. This is because both the computer screen's resolution (pixels per inch) and the number of pixels making up the image are a fixed number. So, when you enlarge an image each pixel must increase in size to fill the larger image dimensions. This causes the pixels to display jagged edges, as shown in Figure 37.

Vector graphics represent an image as a geometric shape made up of lines and arcs that are combined to create various shapes, such as circles and rectangles. This is similar to Flash drawings that include strokes and fills. Flash drawing tools create vector graphics. One advantage of vector graphics is that they can be resized without distorting the image. The reason is that the geometric shapes are based on mathematical models that are recalculated when the image is resized. Figure 38 shows an example of a vector graphic before and after resizing. Vector graphics are best used for drawings rather than for images requiring photographic quality.

There are several programs that allow you to create and edit graphics including Adobe Illustrator, Fireworks, and Photoshop. There are also clip art and stock photograph collections that are available online. Filename extensions identify the file type. For example, .jpg, .tif, .png, and .gif are file formats for bitmap graphics; while .ai is a vector file format.

Importing and Editing Graphics

Once you have identified the graphic you would like to include in a Flash document, you can use the Import feature to bring the graphic into Flash. The process for importing is to select the Import command from the File menu and specify where to import (Stage or Library). Then you navigate to the location where the file is stored and select it. After importing a vector graphic you can work with it as you would any graphic. Because bitmap graphics are not easy to edit in Flash, you may want to use another program, such as Photoshop, to obtain the desired size, color, and other enhancements before importing the graphic.

Figure 37 *Bitmap graphic enlarged*

Photo courtesy of J. Shuman

Figure 38 *Vector graphic enlarged*

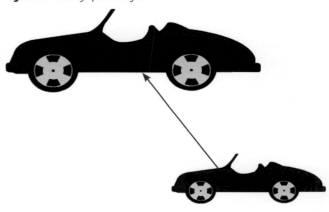

Import graphics

1. Start a new Flash document, then save it as **sailing.fla**.

2. Click **File** on the menu bar, point to **Import**, then click **Import to Library**.

   The Preparing to import process make take a few moments.

3. Navigate to the folder where your Data Files are stored, click **islandview.jpg**, then click **Open**.

   Islandview.jpg is a digital photo that was edited in Photoshop and saved as a .jpg file.

4. Display the Library panel and notice the icon used for bitmap graphics.

5. Drag the **islandview icon** to the Stage, then lock the layer.

6. Click **File** on the menu bar, point to **Import**, then click **Import to Library**.

7. Navigate to the folder where your Data Files are stored, then click **sailboat.ai**.

   This graphic was created using Adobe Illustrator and is made up of several layers.

8. Click **Open**.

   A dialog box appears asking you to choose the layers to import. All layers are selected by default.

9. Click **OK**.

   The graphic is added to the Library panel as a symbol.

10. Add a new layer to the Timeline, click **frame 1** on the layer, then drag the **sailboat icon** to the Stage, as shown in Figure 39.

    (continued)

Figure 39 *Positioning the sailboat image on the Stage*

Photo courtesy of J. Shuman

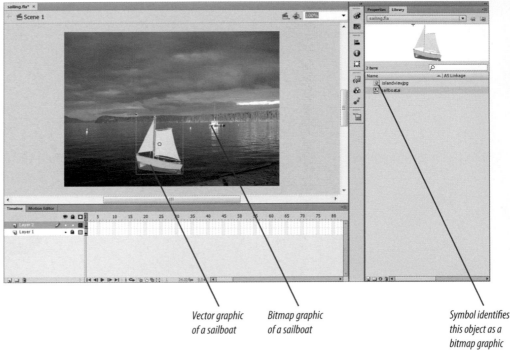

Vector graphic
of a sailboat

Bitmap graphic
of a sailboat

Symbol identifies
this object as a
bitmap graphic

Working with Symbols and Interactivity

Figure 40 *Changing the color of the sail*

Photo courtesy of J. Shuman

Figure 41 *Rotating and skewing the sailboat image*

Photo courtesy of J. Shuman

11. Click **Modify** on the menu bar, click **Break apart**, then repeat this step until the dotted pattern that indicates the image is no longer a symbol appears.

12. Click the **Selection tool** , then click a blank area of the Pasteboard.

13. Click the **left sail**, set the **Fill color icon** to the **rainbow pattern** to change the sail color, as shown in Figure 40.

    Hint: The rainbow color is found at the bottom of the palette for the Fill Color tool.

14. Use the **Selection tool** to drag a **marquee** around the entire sailboat to select it, then convert the image to a graphic symbol named **g_rainbowSail**.

15. Display the Properties panel, verify the Lock icon is not broken, then change the width of the boat to **60**.

16. Click the **Zoom tool** on the Tools panel, click the **sailboat** twice, then scroll as needed to view each sailboat.

    Notice how the bitmap photograph becomes distorted, while the vector sailboat does not.

17. Change the view to **Fit in Window**, click the **Selection tool** , then click the **sailboat** with the rainbow sail.

18. Click the **Free Transform tool** , click the **Rotate and Skew option** , skew the sailboat to the left, verify the Lock icon is not broken, change the width to **50**, then position the sailboat as shown in Figure 41.

19. Test the movie, close the Flash Player window, then save your work and exit Flash.

You imported a bitmap and a vector graphic, and edited the vector graphic.

Create a symbol.

1. Start Flash, open fl3_3.fla, then save it as **skillsDemo3.fla**. This document consists of a single object that was created using the Flash drawing tools.
2. Use the Selection tool to drag a marquee around the ball to select it.
3. Convert the ball to a graphic symbol with the name **g_beachBall**.
4. Double-click the g_beachBall symbol on the Library panel to open the edit window, change the fill color to a rainbow gradient, add a text block that sits on top of the ball with the words **BEACH BALL** (see Figure 42), formated with white, Times New Roman, 12-pt, bold, then click Scene 1 to return to the main Timeline.
5. With the ball selected, create a motion tween animation that moves the ball from the left edge of the Stage to the right edge of the Stage.
6. Use the Selection tool to drag the middle of the motion path up to near the middle of the Stage to create an arc.
7. Select the last frame of the animation on the Timeline and set Rotate to 1 time in the Rotation area of the Properties panel.
8. Play the movie.
   The ball should move across the Stage in an arc and spin at the same time.
9. Lock the beachBall spin layer.

Create and edit an instance.

1. Insert a new layer and name it **blueBall**.
2. Click frame 1 on the blueBall layer, then drag the g_beachBall symbol from the Library panel so it is on top of the ball on the Stage.

3. Use the arrow keys as needed to align the ball so that it covers the ball on the Stage.
4. Click the Selection tool, click the ball to select it, and break apart the object.
5. Change the fill color of the ball to a blue gradient and change the text to **BLUE BALL**.
6. Insert a new layer and name it **greenBall**.
7. Click frame 12 on the greenBall layer, then insert a keyframe.
8. Drag the g_beachBall symbol from the Library panel so it is on top of the ball that is near the middle of the Stage. (*Note*: Align only the balls, not the text.)
9. With the ball selected, break apart the object and change the fill color of the ball to a green gradient and the text to **GREEN BALL**.
10. Move the beachBall spin layer to above the other layers.
11. Insert a new layer and name it **title.**
12. Click frame 1 on the title layer, create a text block at the top middle of the Stage with the words **BeachBall Spin** using Arial as the font, blue as the color, and 20-pt as the font size, then center the text block horizontally on the Stage.
13. Insert a new layer above the title layer and name it **titleBkgnd**.
14. Draw a primitive rectangle with a corner radius of 10, a medium gray fill (#999999) and no stroke that covers the BeachBall Spin title text.
15. Verify the rectangle is selected, convert it to a graphic symbol, then name it **g_Bkgnd**.
16. Move the title layer so it is above the titleBkgnd layer.
17. Play the movie, then save your work.

Work with libraries.

1. Click the New Folder button at the bottom of the Library panel to create a new folder.
2. Name the folder **Graphics**, then move the two graphic symbols to the Graphics folder.
3. Expand the Graphics folder.
4. Rename the g_Bkgnd symbol to **g_titleBkgnd** in the Library panel.
5. Save your work.

Create a button.

1. Insert a new layer above the title layer and name it **startButton**.
2. Click frame 1 of the new layer.
3. Create a text block with the word **Start** formatted with white, bold, 20-pt Arial, then center the text block horizontally near the bottom of the Stage.
4. Select the text. (*Hint*: Drag a marquee around the object.)
5. Convert the selected object to a button symbol and name it **b_start**.
6. Create a new folder named **Buttons** in the Library panel and move the b_start button symbol to the folder.
7. Open the Buttons folder, then display the edit window for the b_start button.
8. Insert a keyframe in the Over frame.
9. Select the text and change the color to a lighter shade of gray than the background rectangle.
10. Insert a keyframe in the Down frame.
11. Select the text and change the color to blue.
12. Insert a keyframe in the Hit frame.

13. Draw a rectangular object that covers the button area for the Hit state.
14. Click Scene 1 to exit the edit window and return to the main Timeline.
15. Save your work.

Test a button.

1. Click Control on the menu bar, then click Enable Simple Buttons to turn on Enable Simple Buttons.
2. Point to the button and notice the color change.
3. Click the button and notice the other color change.
4. Turn off Enable Simple Buttons.

Stop a movie by assigning an action to a frame.

1. Insert a new layer and name it **stopMovie.**
2. Insert a keyframe in frame 24 on the new layer.
3. With frame 24 selected, display the Actions panel.
4. Assign a stop action to the frame.
5. Click frame 1 on the stopMovie layer.
6. Assign a stop action to frame 1.
7. Save your work.

Assign a goto action to a button.

1. Use the Selection tool to select the Start button on the Stage.
2. Use Script Assist in the Actions panel to assign an event and a goto action to the button. (*Hint*: Refer to the section on assigning a goto action as needed.)
3. Test the movie.

Import a graphic.

1. Import BeachScene.jpg from the drive and folder where your Data Files are stored to the Library panel.
2. Insert a new layer and name the layer **backDrop.**
3. Select frame 1 on the backDrop layer, then drag the BeachScene image to the Stage.
4. Convert the BeachScene image to a graphic symbol with the name **g_beachScene**.

5. Move the backDrop layer to the bottom of the Timeline.
6. Move the graphic symbols to the Graphics folder in the Library panel.
7. Test the movie, then compare your image to Figure 42.
8. Close the Flash Player window, then save your work.
9. Exit Flash.

Figure 42 *Completed Skills Review*

The Ultimate Tours travel company has asked you to design a sample navigation scheme for its application. The company wants to see how its opening screen will link with one of its main categories (Treks). Figure 43 shows a sample opening screen and Treks screen. Using the figures or the opening screen you created in Chapter 2 as a guide, you will add a Treks screen and link it to the opening screen (*Hint*: Assume that all of the drawings on the opening screen are on frame 1, unless noted.)

1. Open ultimateTours2.fla (the file you created in Chapter 2 Project Builder 1), then save it as **ultimateTours3.fla**. (*Note*: If you create a new file, you must create an ActionScript 2.0 file. You can check the ActionScript version by selecting Publish Settings from the File menu and clicking the Flash tab.)
2. Insert a layer above the subheading layer and name it **logo**.
3. Import the UTLogo.png file from the drive and folder where your Data Files are stored to the Library panel.
4. Select frame 1 on the logo layer, then drag the logo image to the lower-right corner of the Stage.

5. Select the logo and convert it to a graphic symbol with the name **g_UTLogo**.
6. Set the last frame of the movie by inserting a keyframe on a frame on the Logo layer at least five frames farther along the Timeline, then lock the logo layer. (*Note*: You see the logo because the keyframe you inserted on the last frame of the movie ensures everything on this layer appears on this last frame.)
7. Select the layer that the Ultimate Tours text block is on, then insert a keyframe on the last frame of the movie. (*Hint*: This should be the same frame number as the frame you set as the last frame of the movie in Step 6. *Note*: You see the logo and the heading Ultimate Tours because the keyframe you inserted on the last frame of the movie ensures everything on this layer appears on this last frame.)
8. Insert a new layer, name it **treks headings**, insert a keyframe on the last frame of the movie, then create the Treks screen shown in Figure 43, except for the home button.
9. Convert the Treks graphic on the opening screen to a button symbol named **b_treks**, then edit the symbol so that different colors appear for the different states and be sure to set a hit area.

10. Assign a goto action to the Treks button that jumps the playhead to the Treks screen when the Treks button is clicked. (*Hint*: You can jump to the Treks screen by typing the frame number for the screen in the Actions panel. See Figure 35.)
11. Insert a new layer and name it **stopMovie**. Add stop actions that cause the movie to stop after displaying the opening screen and after displaying the Treks screen. Make sure there is a keyframe in the last frame of the stopMovie layer.
12. Insert a new layer and name it **homeButton**, insert a keyframe on the last frame of the movie, then draw the home button image with the Home text.
13. Convert the image to a button symbol named **b_home**, then edit the symbol so that different colors appear for the different states. Assign a goto action for the Home button that jumps the movie to frame 1.
14. Test the movie.
15. Save your work, then compare your screens to the samples shown in Figure 43.

Figure 43 *Sample completed Project Builder 1*

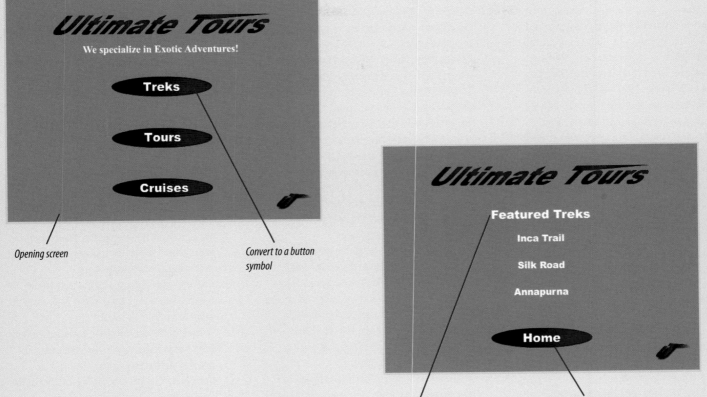

Opening screen

Convert to a button symbol

Treks screen

Convert to a button symbol

You have been asked to assist the International Student Association (ISA). The association sponsors a series of monthly events, each focusing on a different culture from around the world. The events are led by a guest speaker who makes a presentation, followed by a discussion. The events are free and they are open to everyone. ISA would like you to design a Flash movie that will be used with its website and on its mobile app. The movie starts by providing information about the series, and then provides links to the upcoming event and to a schedule. Refer to Figure 44 as you create the Flash movie. Depending on the font you choose, your screen may not appear exactly the same as Figure 44. (*Hint*: Keep the following in mind as you complete this project:

- Insert a blank keyframe in a frame on a layer when you do not want the text or objects from the previous frame to appear in the frame where you are inserting a blank keyframe.

- Use the align panel and the rulers to help place objects, such as the buttons on the page, in the same location from screen to screen. If copying an object you can use the Paste in Place command to have the object copied to the exact location it was selected from.

- Remember to break apart a button to change its name, then select the object and convert the updated object to a new button with a new name.)

1. Open a new Flash ActionScript 2.0 document and save it as **isa3.fla**.
2. Change the Stage size to width: 320 and height: 480. (*Note*: There will be three screens with each screen being on a separate frame. Frame 1 will display the opening screen; frame 2 will display the Next Event screen; and frame 3 will display the Schedule screen.)
3. Draw a border that surrounds the stage. (*Hint*: Use the rectangle tool, select the "no color" ▨ color swatch in the color palette, then use the stroke color of your choice. Set the border stroke to at least 2.)
4. On another layer create the heading and subheading (top two lines) that will appear on all three screens. Be sure to add a keyframe in the last frame on this layer of the movie so that the heading and subheading appear on every frame of the movie. (*Note*: The last frame will be frame 3.)
5. On another layer add the text to the opening screen in frame 1. (*Hint*: After adding the text in frame 1, be sure to insert a blank keyframe in frame 2 of the new layer. To add a blank keyframe, select the desired frame, click Insert on the menu, point to Timeline, and then click Blank Keyframe. You add a blank keyframe in frame 2 so that the text you added in frame 1 will not appear in frame 2.)
6. Create the Next Event screen in frame 2 by adding a layer and entering the title (Next Event) and the text for the screen. (*Hint*: Be sure to insert a keyframe in frame 2 of the new layer and a blank keyframe in frame 3 of that same layer.)
7. Create the Schedule screen in frame 3 by adding a layer and entering the title (Schedule) and the text

for the screen. (*Hint*: Be sure to insert a keyframe in frame 3 of the new layer.)
8. Insert a layer and create a Next Event button with the name **b_nextEvent** on the opening screen that jumps the movie to the Next Event screen. Create a Schedule button with the name **b_schedule** on another layer that jumps the movie to the Schedule screen. For each button you create, specify different colors for each state of the button.
9. Insert another layer and on the Next Event screen, create a Home button with the name **b_home**, that jumps the movie back to the opening screen. Be sure to specify different colors for each state when you create the Home button.
10. Copy an instance of the Home button you created in Step 6 to the Schedule screen. (*Hint*: You can select the button with the Selection tool, select Copy from the Edit menu, display the Schedule screen and select Copy in Place from the Edit menu.)
11. On the Next Event screen, copy an instance of the Schedule button you created in Step 5 that jumps the movie to the Schedule screen.
12. On the Schedule screen, copy an instance of the Next Event button you created in Step 5 that jumps the movie to the Next Event screen.
13. Insert a layer and add an action to each frame on that layer that stops the movie on that frame.
14. Rename all of the layers using appropriate names.
15. Test the movie.
16. Save your work, then compare your movie to the sample shown in Figure 44.

Figure 44 *Sample completed Project Builder 2*

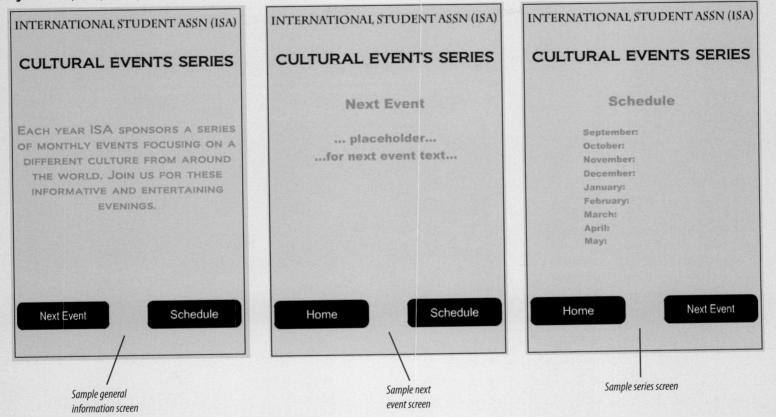

Sample general
information screen

Sample next
event screen

Sample series screen

Figure 45 shows the home page of a website. Study the figure and complete the following questions. For each question, indicate how you determined your answer.

1. Connect to the Internet and go to *www.zoo.org*. Notice that this website has images that change as you visit the website.

2. Open a document in a word processor or open a new Flash document, save the file as **dpc3**, then answer the following questions. (*Hint*: Use the Text tool in Flash.)
   - Whose website is this?
   - What is the goal(s) of the site?
   - Who is the target audience?
   - What treatment ("look and feel") is used?
   - What are the design layout guidelines being used (balance, movement, and so on)?
   - What may be animated on this home page?
   - Do you think this is an effective design for the company, its products, and its target audience? Why or why not?
   - What suggestions would you make to improve the design, and why?

Figure 45 *Design Project*
Courtesy of zoo.org. www.zoo.org

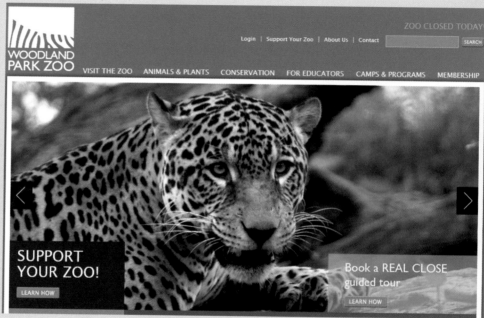

Working with Symbols and Interactivity

This is a continuation of the Chapter 2 Portfolio Project, which is the development of a personal portfolio. In this project, you will create a button that will be used to link the opening screen of your portfolio to the animations page. Next, you will create another button to start the animation.

1. Open portfolio2.fla (the file you created in Portfolio Project, Chapter 2), then save it as **portfolio3.fla**.
2. Unlock the layers as needed.
3. Insert a new layer, name it **sampleAnimations**, then insert a keyframe in frame 2.
4. On this new layer, create a Sample Animations screen that has a text block with an oval background and the words **Sample Animations** at the top of the Stage, then add another text block and oval background with the word **Tweened**. (Note: This screen will have several animation samples added to it later.)
5. Insert a new layer, name it **home button**, then insert a keyframe in frame 2.
6. Add a text block that says **Home** and has an oval background at the bottom of the Stage.
7. Insert a new layer, name it **tweenedAnimation**, then insert a keyframe in frame 3.
8. Create an animation(s) of your choice using objects you draw or import, or objects from the Library panel of another document. (Note: To create a motion tween animation when starting in a frame other than frame 1, you need to specify the beginning frame of the animation by inserting a keyframe in

the starting frame, placing or drawing the object on the Stage, selecting the object and converting it into a graphic symbol, inserting a motion tween, inserting a keyframe in the ending frame of the animation, and repositioning the object. (Hint: To create more than one animation that plays at the same time, put each animation on its own layer, such as tweenedAnimationRedCar and tweenedAnimationBlueCar.)

9. Insert a new layer, name it **animationHeading**, insert a keyframe in frame 3, then add a heading, such as Passing Cars in the sample in Figure 46, that describes the animation(s).
10. On the Sample Animations screen, convert the Tweened and Home text blocks into button symbols, then edit each symbol so that different colors appear for the different states. For the Tweened button, assign an action that jumps to the frame that plays an animation. For the Home button, assign an

action to the Home button that jumps to the frame that displays My Portfolio. (Hint: You need to use ActionScript 2.0.)

11. Change the Animations graphic on the home page to a button, then edit the symbol so that different colors appear for the different states. Assign an action to the Animations button that jumps to the Sample Animations screen.
12. Insert a new layer, then name it **stopMovie**. Insert keyframes and assign stop actions to the appropriate frames.
13. Insert a new layer at the bottom of the layers pane and name it **backdrop**. Insert a keyframe in frame 3 on the backdrop layer. This is the same frame where the tween animation begins. Add a color background to the animation screen.
14. Test the movie.
15. Save your work, then compare your movie to the sample shown in Figure 46.

Figure 46 *Sample completed Portfolio Project*

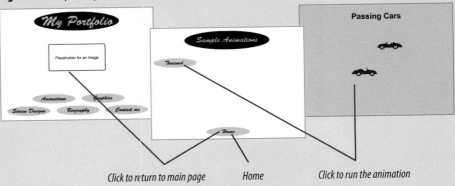

Click to return to main page   Home   Click to run the animation

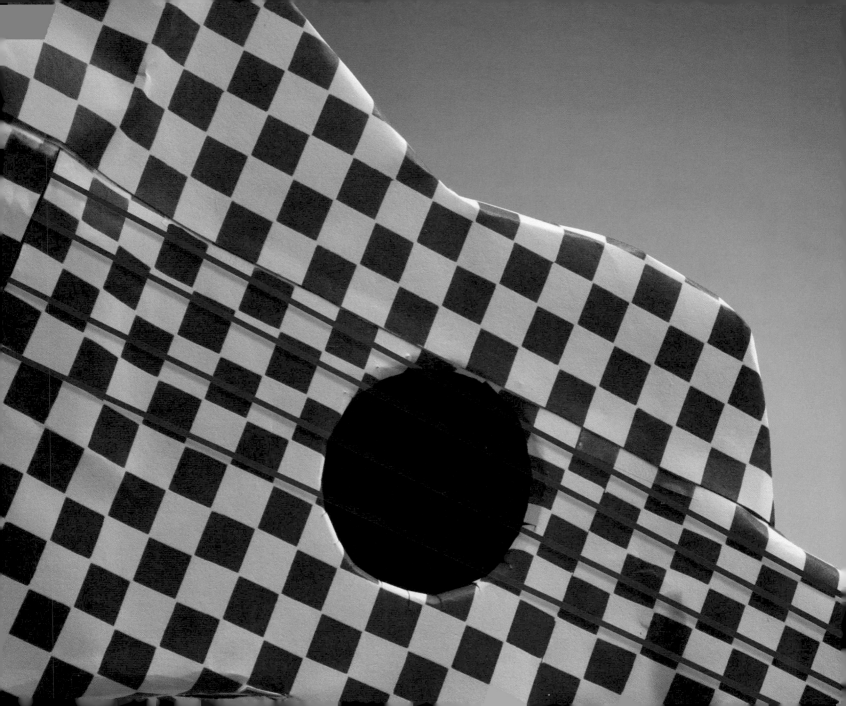

CHAPTER 4 CREATING
ANIMATIONS

1. Create motion tween animations
2. Create classic tween animations
3. Create frame-by-frame animations
4. Create shape tween animations
5. Create movie clips
6. Animate text

4

CREATING
ANIMATIONS

Introduction

Animation can be an important part of your application or website, whether the focus is on entertainment (provides interactive games), e-commerce (attracts attention and provides product demonstrations), or education (simulates complex processes such as DNA replication).

How Does Animation Work?

The perception of motion in an animation is actually an illusion. Animation is like a motion picture in that it is made up of a series of still images. Research has found that our eye captures and holds an image for one-tenth of a second before processing another image. By retaining each impression for one-tenth of a second, we perceive a series of rapidly displayed still images as a single, moving image. This phenomenon is known as **persistence of vision** and it provides the basis for the frame rate in animations. Frame rates of 10–12 frames-per-second (fps) generally provide an acceptably smooth computer-based animation. Lower frame rates result in a jerky image, while frame rates

over 30 fps may result in a blurred image. In addition, higher frame rates may increase file size because more frames are needed for a 5 second animation running at 30 fps than at 10 fps. After creating an animation you can experiment with various frame rates to obtain the desired effect. Flash uses a default frame rate of 24 fps.

Flash Animation

Creating animation is one of the most powerful features of Flash, yet developing basic animations is a simple process. Flash allows you to create animations that can move and rotate an object around the Stage, as well as change its size, shape, or color. You can also use the animation features in Flash to create special effects, such as an object zooming or fading in and out. You can combine animation effects so that an object changes shape and color as it moves across the Stage. Animations are created by changing the content of successive frames. Flash provides two animation methods: frame-by-frame animation and tweened animation. Tweened animations can be motion, classic, or shape tweens.

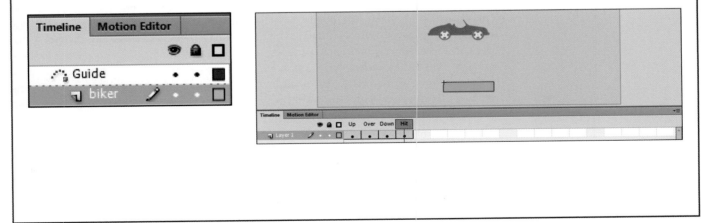

Global Functions	►	Movie Clip Control	►		
ActionScript 2.0 Classes	►	Timeline Control	►	goto	Esc+go
Global Properties	►	Browser/Network	►	play	Esc+pl
Operators	►	Printing Functions	►	stop	Esc+st
Statements	►	Miscellaneous Functions	►	stopAllSounds	Esc+ss
Compiler Directives	►	Mathematical Functions	►		
Constants	►	Conversion Functions	►		
Types	►				
Deprecated	►				
Data Components	►				
Components	►				
Screens	►				

Properties Library

Motion Tween

▽ EASE

Ease: 0

▽ ROTATION

Rotate: 0 time(s)   + 0 °

Direction: none ▼

☑ Orient to path

Timeline   Motion Editor

Guide

biker

Create Motion Tween
ANIMATIONS

What You'll Do

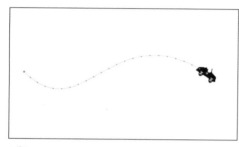

▶ *In this lesson, you will create and edit motion tween animations.*

Understanding Motion Tween Animations

An animation implies some sort of movement in an object. However, the concept of animation is much broader. Objects have specific properties such as position, size, color, and shape. Any change in a property of an object over time (i.e., across frames on the Timeline) can be considered an animation. So, having an object start at the left of the screen in frame 1 and then having it move across the screen and end up at the right side in frame 10 would be a change in the position property of the object. Each of the in-between frames (2-9) would show the position of the object as it moves across the screen. In a motion tween animation, you specify the position of the object in the beginning and ending frames and Flash fills in the in-between frames, a process known as **tweening**. Fortunately, you can change several properties with one motion tween. For example, you could have

a car move across the screen and, at the same time, you could have the size of the car change to give the impression of the car moving away from the viewer.

The process for creating a motion tween animation is to select the frame and layer where the animation will start. If necessary, insert a keyframe (by default, frame 1 of each layer has a keyframe). Select the object on the Stage, then select the Motion Tween command from the Insert menu. If the object is not already a symbol, you will be asked if you want to convert it to a symbol. You must convert the object to a symbol if prompted because only symbols and text fields can have a motion tween applied. Then you select the ending frame and make any changes to the object, such as moving it to another location or resizing it. After you make the change, a keyframe automatically appears in the ending frame you selected. When you create a motion tween, a tween span appears on the Timeline.

Creating Animations

Tween Spans

Figure 1 shows a motion tween animation of a car that starts in frame 1 and ends in frame 24. The Onion Skin feature is enabled so that outlines of the car are displayed for each frame of the animation in the figure. The Onion Skin feature is useful when developing an animation, but it is not how the completed animation will appear. Figure 1 shows the button that turns the Onion Skin feature on and off.

After turning the feature on, the numbers of the frames that will be affected are highlighted on the Timeline. You can change which frames display as outlines by dragging either end of the highlight. Notice a blue highlight appears on the Timeline for the frames of the animation. The blue highlighted area is called the tween or motion span. The length of the motion tween is determined by the last frame in the movie or by other keyframes on the layer. (*Note*:

The default tween span when starting from frame 1 of a new movie is determined by the number of frames in one second of the movie. So, if the frame rate is 24 frames per second, then the span is 24 frames.) You can increase or decrease the number of frames in the span by dragging the end of the span. In addition, you can move the span to a different location on the Timeline, and you can copy the span to have it apply to another object.

Figure 1 *Sample motion tween animation*

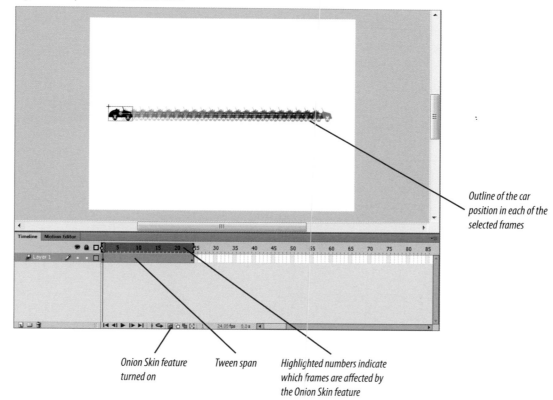

Outline of the car position in each of the selected frames

Onion Skin feature turned on

Tween span

Highlighted numbers indicate which frames are affected by the Onion Skin feature

Motion Path

The animation shown in Figure 2 includes a position change (from frame 1 to frame 24); a motion path showing the position change is displayed on the Stage. Each dot on the path corresponds to a frame on the Timeline and indicates the location of the object (in this example, the car) when the frame is played. A motion path can be altered by dragging a point on the path using the Selection tool or by using the Subselection tool to manipulate Bezier handles as shown in Figure 3. Bezier curves employ a mathematical method for drawing curves. The shape of a Bezier curve can be altered by moving the handles attached to the end points of the curve.

In addition, an entire path can be moved around the Stage and reshaped using the Free Transform tool.

Property Keyframes

A keyframe indicates a change in a Flash movie, such as the start or ending of an animation. Motion tween animations use property keyframes that are specific to each property such as a position keyframe, color keyframe, or rotation keyframe. In most cases these are automatically placed on the Timeline as the motion tween animation is created.

Keep in mind:

- Only one object on the Stage can be animated in each tween span.

- You can have multiple motion tween animations playing at the same time if they are on different layers.
- A motion tween is, in essence, an object animation because, while several changes can be made to an object's properties, only one object is animated for each motion tween.
- The types of objects that can be tweened include graphic, button, and movie clip symbols, as well as text fields.
- You can remove a motion tween animation by clicking the tween span on the Timeline and choosing Remove Tween from the Insert menu.

Figure 3 *Bezier handles used to alter the path*

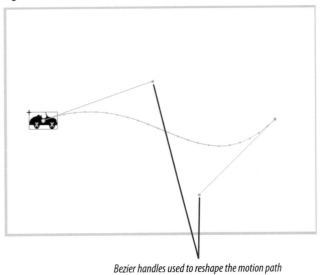

Bezier handles used to reshape the motion path

Figure 2 *The motion path*

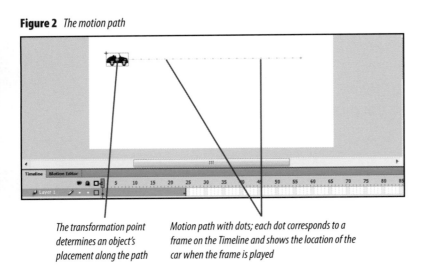

The transformation point determines an object's placement along the path

Motion path with dots; each dot corresponds to a frame on the Timeline and shows the location of the car when the frame is played

Figure 4 *Positioning the car object*

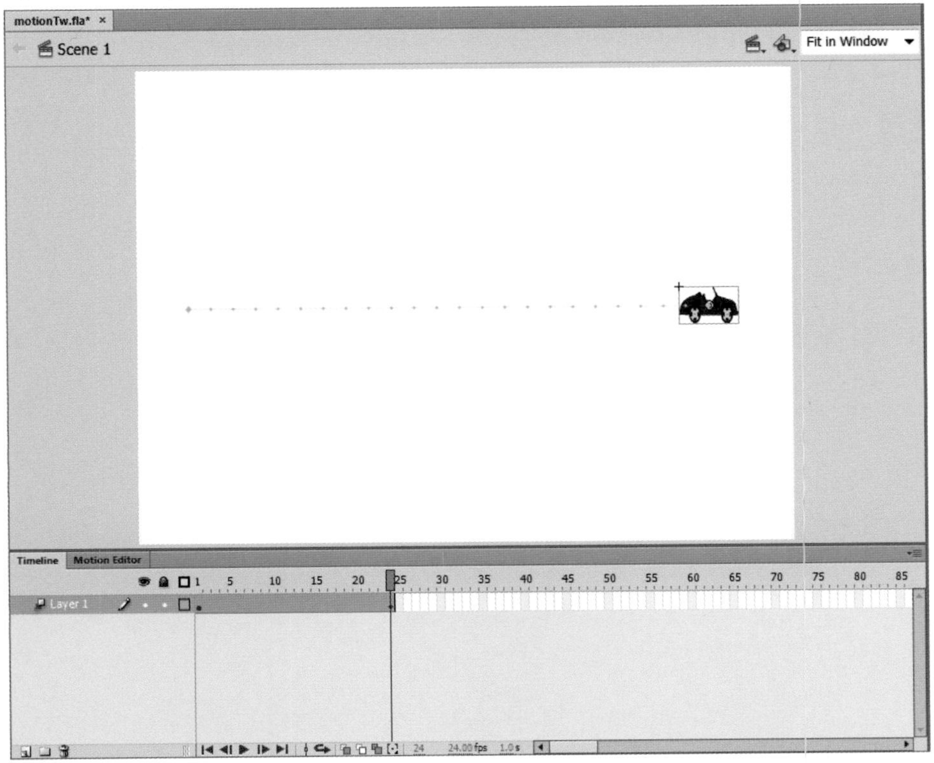

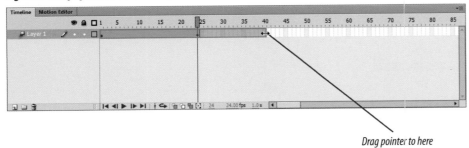

Figure 5 *Changing the end of the tween span*

Drag pointer to here

Create a motion tween animation

1. Open fl4_1.fla from the drive and folder where your Data Files are stored, then save it as **motionTw.fla**.

   This document has one drawn object—a car that has been converted to a symbol.

2. Click the **Selection tool** ▶ on the Tools panel, then click the **car** to select it.

3. Click **Insert** on the menu bar, then click **Motion Tween**.

   Notice the tween span appears on the Timeline. Because you started in frame 1, the number of frames in the span equals the frames per second for the movie.

4. Verify the playhead is on the last frame of the tween span, then drag the **car** to the right side of the Stage, as shown in Figure 4.

   A motion path appears on the Stage with dots indicating the position of the object for each frame. A diamond symbol appears in frame 24, which is the end of the tween span. The diamond symbol is a position keyframe and it is automatically inserted at the end of the tween path.

   Note: The end of this tween span is determined by the document frame rate, which is 24 fps. To see the diamond symbol more clearly, move the playhead.

5. Point to the end of the tween span, when the pointer changes to a double arrow ↔, drag the **tween span** to frame 40, as shown in Figure 5.

   (continued)

6. Click on the Timeline, then press the **period key** to move the playhead one frame at a time and notice the position of the car for each frame.

7. Play the movie.

8. Test the movie, then close the Flash Player window.

9. Save your work.

You created a motion tween animation, extended the length of the animation, and viewed the position of the animated object in each frame of the animation.

Edit a motion path

1. Click the **Selection tool** on the Tools panel, then click a blank area of the Stage.

2. Click **frame 1** on Layer 1.

3. Point to the middle of the motion path, as shown in Figure 6.

4. When the pointer changes to a pointer with an arc, drag the pointer down, as shown in Figure 7.

(continued)

Figure 6 *Pointing to the middle of the path*

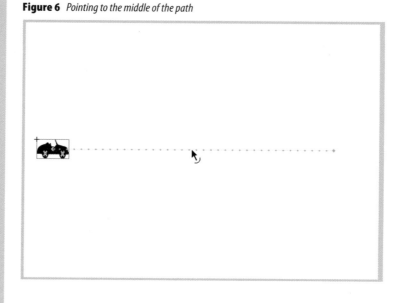

Figure 7 *Dragging the motion path down*

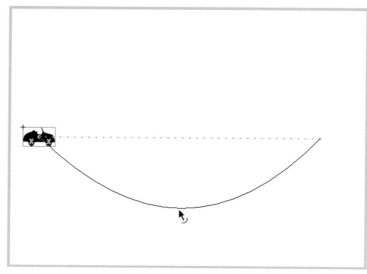

Figure 8 *Displaying the Bezier handles*

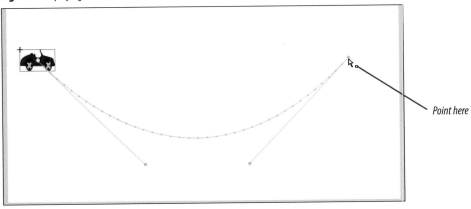

Point here

Figure 9 *Using the Bezier handles to alter the shape of the path*

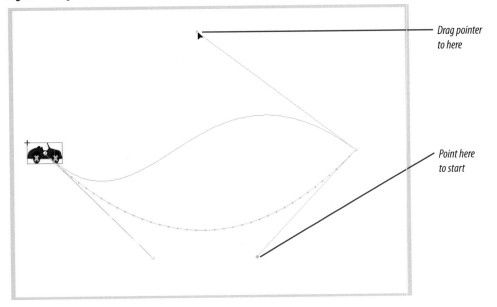

Drag pointer
to here

Point here
to start

5. Play the movie.

   Notice the car is not oriented to the path. That is, the front of the car does not align with the path. Later in this lesson you will learn to orient an object to a curved path.

6. Click **frame 1** on Layer 1.

7. Click the **Subselection tool** on the Tools panel, point to the end of the motion path, then, when the pointer changes into an arrow with a small square, click the end of path to display Bezier handles, as shown in Figure 8.

8. Point to the **lower-right handle**, then when the pointer changes to a delta symbol, drag the **handle** up and toward the center of the Stage to form a horizontal S shape, as shown in Figure 9.

9. Click the **Selection tool** on the Tools panel, then click a blank area of the Stage.

10. Play the movie, then save your work.

You edited a motion path by using the Selection tool to drag the path and by using the Subselection tool to display and reposition Bezier handles.

Change the ease value of an animation

1. Play the movie and notice that the car moves at a constant speed.

2. Click **frame 1** on Layer 1, then display the Properties panel.

3. Point to the **Ease value**, when the pointer changes to a hand with a double arrow 🖑, drag the 🖑 **pointer** to the right to set the value at **100**, as shown in Figure 10.

4. Play the movie.

   The car starts out moving fast and slows down near the end of the animation. Notice the word "out" is displayed next to the ease value on the Properties panel indicating that the object will ease out, that is slow down, at the end of the animation.

5. Click **frame 1** on Layer 1.

6. Point to the Ease value on the Properties panel, then drag the 🖑 **pointer** to the left to set the value to **−100**.

7. Play the movie.

   The car starts out moving slowly and speeds up near the end of the animation. Notice the word "in" is displayed next to the ease value on the Properties panel. Also, notice the dots are grouped closer together at the beginning of the motion path indicating that the object does not move very far in that section of the path.

8. Click **frame 1** on Layer 1, then set the ease value to **0**.

9. Save your work.

You changed the ease out and ease in values of the animation.

Figure 10 *Changing the ease value*

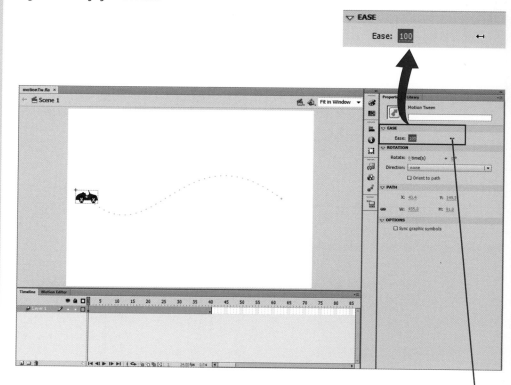

Drag the pointer to the right

Figure 11 *Changing the width of the object*

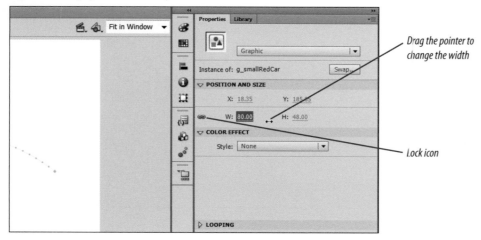

Drag the pointer to change the width

Lock icon

Figure 12 *Using the Free Transform tool to skew the object*

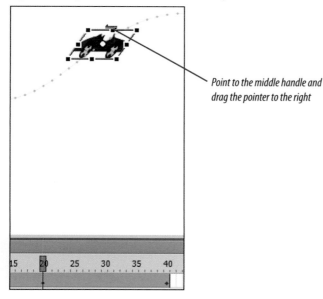

Point to the middle handle and drag the pointer to the right

Resize and reshape an object

1. Verify frame 1 is selected, click the **Selection tool**, then click the **car**.

2. Display the Properties panel, verify the lock icon is not broken, point to the **W: value**, then, when the pointer changes to a hand with a double arrow, drag the **pointer** to the right to set the value to **80**, as shown in Figure 11.

   The car in frame 1 is now wider and taller.

3. Play the movie.

4. Click **frame 40** on Layer 1, then click the **car**.

5. Point to the **W: value** on the Properties panel, then drag the **pointer** to the left to set the value to **30**.

   The car in frame 40 is now less wide and tall.

6. Play the movie.

   The car starts out large and ends up small.

7. Click **frame 20** on Layer 1.

8. Click the **Free Transform tool** on the Tools panel, then click the **Rotate and Skew option** if it is not active.

9. Point to the **top middle handle**, then, when the pointer changes to a double line, drag the **pointer** to the right to skew the object, as shown in Figure 12.

   A keyframe indicating a change in the property (skew) of the object appears in frame 20.

10. Play the movie, use the Undo command on the Edit menu to undo the skew, then save the movie.

    Note: You may have to click the Undo command more than one time to undo the skew.

    The skew keyframe is removed from frame 20.

You resized and skewed a motion tween object.

Create a color effect

1. Click the **Selection tool** ▶ on the Tools panel.

2. Click **frame 40** on Layer 1.

3. Click the **car** to select it.

4. Click **COLOR EFFECT** to display that area if it is not open, then click the **Style list arrow** in the COLOR EFFECT area of the Properties panel.

5. Click **Alpha**, then drag the **slider** ⬜ to set the value to **0%**, as shown in Figure 13.

6. Play the movie.

   Notice the car slowly becomes transparent.

7. Click frame 40 on Layer 1, click the object to select it, then reset the Alpha to **100%**.

TIP Click just inside the bounding box if you have trouble selecting the object.

8. Click **frame 40** on Layer 1.

9. Click the **car** to select it.

10. Click the **Style list arrow** in the COLOR EFFECT area of the Properties panel.

11. Click **Advanced**, then set the x R + value for Red to **100**, as shown in Figure 14.

12. Play the movie.

   Notice the car slowly changes to a new shade of red. Because the car is a symbol, it is one part (not a composite of pieces). As a result, changes made to the color value affect the entire car.

13. Set the x R + value back to **0**, then save your work.

You changed the alpha and advanced color option for an object.

Figure 13 *Setting the Alpha (transparency) value*

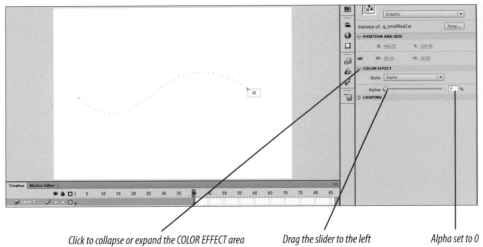

Click to collapse or expand the COLOR EFFECT area   *Drag the slider to the left*   *Alpha set to 0*

Figure 14 *Changing a color value for the object*

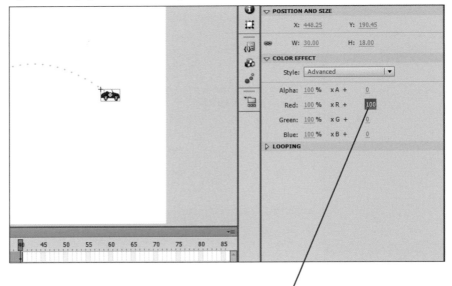

Setting the red value

Figure 15 *Aligning the car to the path*

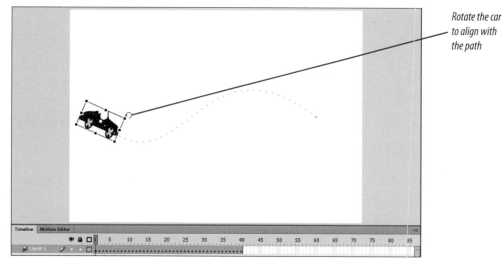

Rotate the car
to align with
the path

Figure 16 *Aligning the car to the end of the motion path*

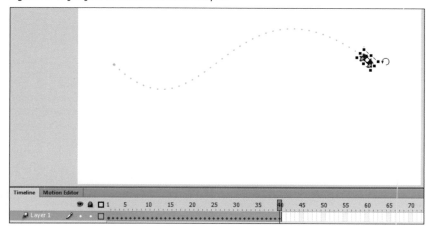

Orient an object to a path

1. Play the movie.

   Notice the car follows the path but it is not oriented to the path.

2. Click **frame 1** on Layer 1.

3. Click the **Orient to path check box** in the ROTATION area of the Properties panel.

4. Click the **Free Transform tool** ▓▓ on the Tools panel, then click the **Rotate and Skew option** ↻ in the Options area of the Tools panel if it is not active.

5. Point to the upper-right corner of the car, then, when the pointer changes into a circular arrow ↻, rotate the front of the car so that it aligns with the path, as shown in Figure 15.

6. Click **frame 40** on Layer 1, then rotate the back end of the car so that its back end aligns with the path, as shown in Figure 16.

7. Play the movie.

   The car is oriented to the path.

   Notice the diamond symbols in the frames on Layer 1. These are rotation keyframes that indicate the object will change in each frame as it rotates to stay oriented to the path.

8. Test the movie, then close the Flash Player window.

9. Save your work, then close the document.

You oriented an object to a motion path and aligned the object with the path in the first and last frames of the motion tween.

Copy a motion path

1. Open fl4_2.fla, save it at **tweenEdits.fla**, then play the movie.

   This movie has a motion tween that animates from frame 1 to frame 40. Notice the rotation keyframes on the biker layer.

2. Insert a **new layer** at the top of the Timeline, then name it **biker2**.

   Notice the last frame of the new layer is the same (50) as the last frame of the movie.

3. Click **frame 1** on the biker2 layer.

4. Click the **Selection tool** ▶ on the Tools panel, then display the Library panel.

5. Click the **g_biker symbol** in the Library panel to display the image in the Preview window.

6. Drag the **g_biker symbol** from the Library panel to the Stage, as shown in Figure 17.

   This creates a new instance of the g_biker symbol.

7. Click any frame on the tween span on the biker layer, then click the **original biker** on the Stage.

   The motion tween is selected as indicated by the blue highlight on the biker layer.

8. Click **Edit** on the menu bar, point to **Timeline**, then click **Copy Motion**.

9. Click the **new instance** of the biker, click **Edit** on the menu bar, point to **Timeline**, then click **Paste Motion**.

10. Play the movie.

11. Hide the biker layer.

12. Click **frame 1** on the biker2 layer, click the **Free Transform tool** ⌖ on the Tools panel, then click the path to select it, as shown in Figure 18.

(continued)

Figure 17 *Dragging the biker symbol to the Stage*

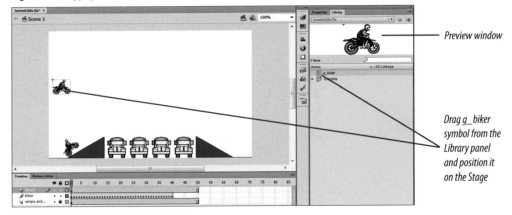

Preview window

Drag g_biker symbol from the Library panel and position it on the Stage

Figure 18 *Selecting the path to display the handles*

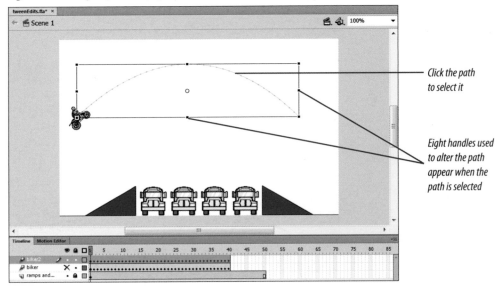

Click the path to select it

Eight handles used to alter the path appear when the path is selected

Creating Animations

Figure 19 *Positioning the path*

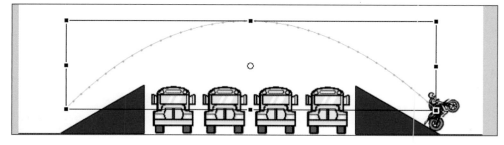

Figure 20 *Aligning the biker to the path*

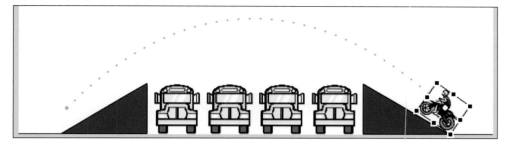

13. Click **Modify** on the menu bar, point to **Transform**, then click **Flip Horizontal**.

14. Play the movie.

    The direction of the biker on the path is reversed, but the direction the biker faces is not reversed.

15. Click **frame 1** on the biker2 layer.

16. Click the **path** to select it.

17. Use the arrow keys on the keyboard to position the path, as shown on Figure 19.

18. Click the **biker object** to select it.

19. Click **Modify** on the menu bar, point to **Transform**, then click **Flip Horizontal**.

20. Use the Free Transform tool 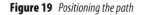 and the arrow keys to align the biker, as shown in Figure 20.

21. Play the movie.

22. Save your work.

You copied a motion path to another object, adjusted the position of the path and oriented the object to the path.

Rotate an object

1. Click **frame 1** on the biker2 layer, then display the Properties panel.

2. Point to the **Rotate times value** in the ROTATION area of the Properties panel, then, when the pointer changes to a hand with a double arrow 👆, drag the 👆 **pointer** to the right to set the count to **1**, as shown in Figure 21.

3. Click the **Direction list arrow**, click **CW** (Clockwise), click **frame 1** on the biker2 layer, then play the movie.

   The biker object rotates one time in a clockwise direction. Look at the Timeline. Notice the rotation keyframes have been removed from the motion tween span. This is because, as the biker rotates, he is no longer oriented to the path. Motion tweens do not allow an object to be rotated and oriented to a path simultaneously because orienting an object to a path rotates the object in each frame along the path. You can use a classic tween to rotate and orient an object to a path at the same time. The remaining keyframes at the beginning and ending of the tween span are used to align the biker to the ramp.

4. Click **frame 1** on the biker2 layer, set the rotation count to **2**, set the Direction to **CCW** (Counter Clockwise), then play the movie.

5. Click **Orient to path** to select it.

   The rotate value is automatically set to no times (indicated by a 0), as shown in Figure 22.

6. Play the movie, then save your work.

You caused an object to rotate by setting the rotate value and specifying a rotation direction.

Figure 21 *Changing the rotate value*

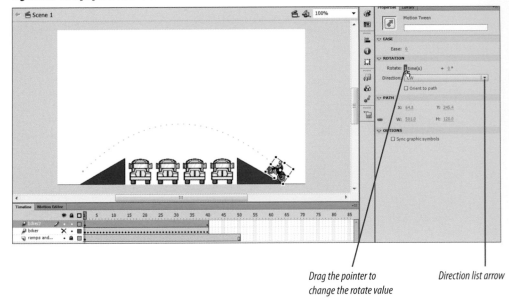

Drag the pointer to change the rotate value

Direction list arrow

Figure 22 *The Properties panel showing that the rotate value is set to 0 times*

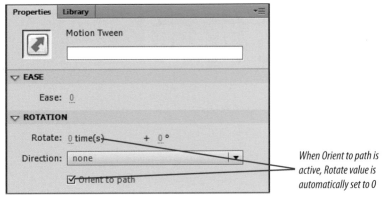

When Orient to path is active, Rotate value is automatically set to 0

Figure 23 *Timeline showing the motion tween removed*

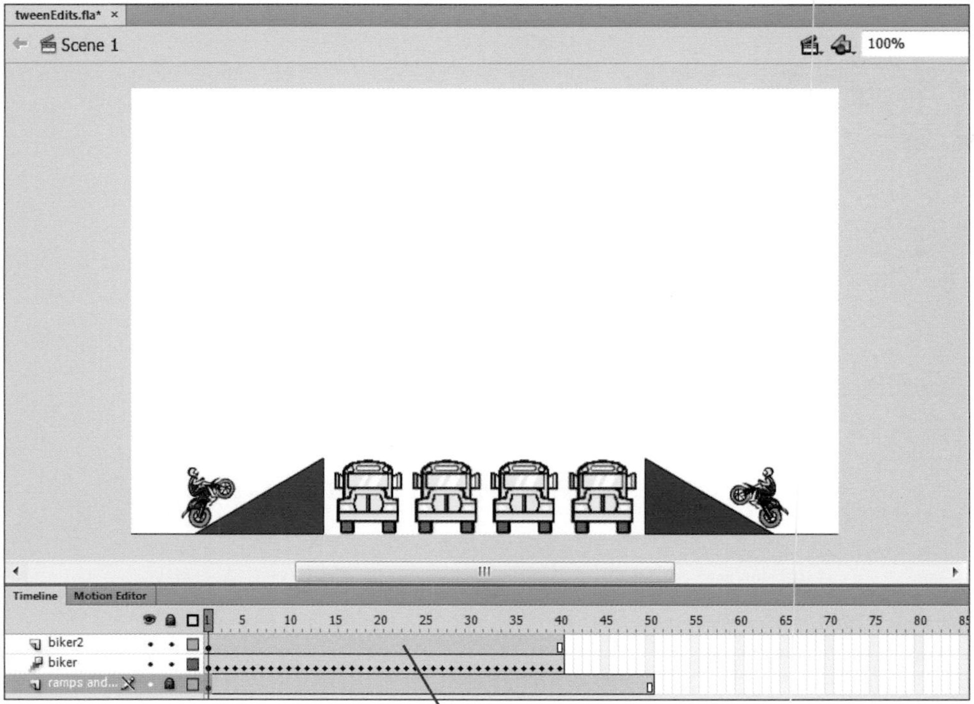

Removal of motion tween in the biker2 layer removes the blue highlight on the Timeline

Remove a motion tween

1. Unhide the **biker layer**, then play the movie.

2. Double-click **frame 1** on the biker2 layer to select the tween span on the Timeline.

   Note: You can double-click any frame on the tween span to select it.

3. Click **Insert** on the menu bar, then click **Remove Tween**.

4. Click **frame 1** on the ramps and buses layer, then notice that the blue highlight on the biker2 layer is gone, as shown in Figure 23.

5. Play the movie and notice that the biker on the biker2 layer is visible but it does not move.

6. Use the Undo command in the Edit menu to undo the Remove Tween process.

   Note: You may need to select the Undo command more than one time.

7. Click **biker2** on the Timeline to select the layer.

8. Click the **Delete icon** 🗑 on the Timeline status bar to delete the biker2 layer that includes the motion tween.

9. Test the movie, then close the Flash Player window.

10. Save your work.

You removed an object's motion tween, undid the action, then deleted a layer containing a motion tween.

Work with multiple motion tweens

1. Click frame **40** on the biker layer, then click the **biker** on the Stage.

2. Lock the **biker layer**, then insert a **new layer** above the biker layer and name it **bikeOffStage**.

3. Click frame **40** on the bikeOffStage layer.

4. Click **Insert** on the menu bar, point to **Timeline**, then click **Keyframe**.

5. Display the Library panel.

6. Drag an instance of the **g_biker symbol** from the Library panel so it is on top of the biker on the Stage, as shown in Figure 24.

7. Verify the **Free Transform tool** is selected, then click the **Rotate and Skew option** in the Options area of the Tools panel.

8. Rotate the object to orient it to the other biker, then use the arrow keys on the keyboard to align the two biker objects.

9. Click frame **41** on the **bikeOffStage** layer, then insert a **keyframe**.

10. Use the **arrow keys** on the keyboard and the **Free Transform tool** to align the biker with the bottom of the ramp, as shown in Figure 25.

(continued)

Figure 24 *Placing an instance of the g_biker symbol on top of the object on the Stage*

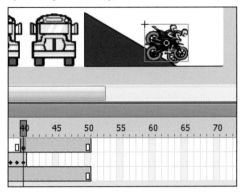

Figure 25 *Aligning the biker with the ramp*

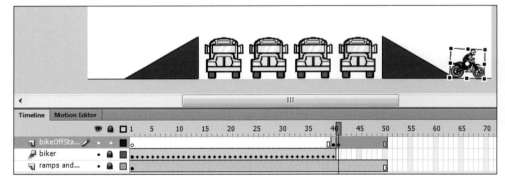

Figure 26 *Dragging the biker object off the Stage*

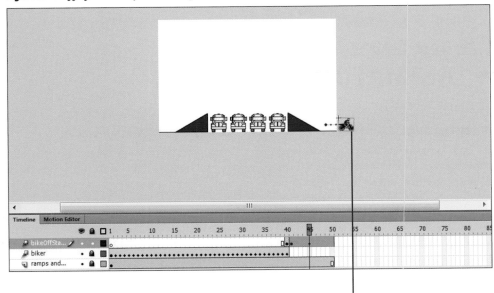

Drag the object off the Stage

11. Click the **Selection tool** , then click the **biker**.

12. Use the Magnification options on the View menu to display the entire Stage and part of the Pasteboard.

13. Click **Insert** on the menu bar, then click **Motion Tween**.

14. Click **frame 45** on the bikeOffStage layer, then drag the **biker** off the Stage, as shown in Figure 26.

15. Test the movie, close the Flash Player window, save your work, then close the document.

You created a second motion tween for the movie.

Create Classic Tween
ANIMATIONS

What You'll Do

In this lesson, you will create a motion guide and attach an animation to it.

Understanding Classic Tweens

Classic tweens are similar to motion tweens in that you can create animations that change the properties of an object over time. Motion tweens are easier to use and allow the greatest degree of control over tweened animations. Classic tweens are a bit more complex to create, however, they provide certain capabilities that some developers desire. For example, with a motion tween (which consists of one object over the tween span), you can alter the ease value so that an object starts out fast and ends slow. But, with a classic tween, you can alter the ease value so that an object starts out fast, slows down, and then speeds up again. The process for creating a classic tween animation that moves an object is to select the starting frame and, if necessary, insert a keyframe. Next, insert a keyframe at the ending frame. The two keyframes and all the frames between them will be used for the animation. Next, click any frame on the layer between the keyframes. Then select classic tween from the Insert menu, select the ending frame, and move the object to the position you want it to be in the ending frame.

Understanding Motion Guides

When you use motion tweening to generate an animation that moves an object, a motion path that shows the movement is automatically created on the Stage. When you use classic tweening, the object moves in a straight line from the beginning location to the ending location on the Stage. There is no path displayed. You can draw a path, called a **motion guide**, that can be used to alter the path of a classic tween animation, as shown in Figure 27. A motion guide is drawn on the motion guide layer with the classic tween animation placed on its own layer beneath a motion guide layer, as shown in Figure 28. The process for creating a motion guide and attaching a classic tween animation to it is:

■ Create a classic tween animation.
■ Insert a new layer above the classic tween animation layer and change the layer properties to a Guide layer. Drag the classic tween animation layer to the guide layer so that it indents, as shown in Figure 28. This indicates that the classic tween animation layer is associated with the motion guide layer.

- Click the Guide layer and draw a path using the Pen, Pencil, Line, Circle, Rectangle, or Brush tools.
- Attach the object to the path by clicking the first keyframe of the layer that contains the animation, and then dragging the object by its transformation point to the beginning of the path. Click the end keyframe and then repeat the steps to attach the object to the end of the path.

Depending on the type of object you are animating and the path, you may need to orient the object to the path.

The advantages of using a motion guide are that you can have an object move along any path, including a path that intersects itself, and you can easily change the shape of the path, allowing you to experiment with different motions. A consideration when using a motion guide is that, in some instances, orienting the object along the path may result in an unnatural-looking animation. You can fix this by stepping through the animation one frame at a time until you reach the frame where the object is positioned poorly. You can then insert a keyframe and adjust the object as desired.

Transformation Point and Registration Point

Each symbol has a transformation point in the form of a circle (O) that is used to orient the object when it is being animated.

For example, when you rotate a symbol, the transformation point is the pivot point around which the object rotates. The transformation point is also the point that snaps to a motion guide, as shown in Figure 27. When attaching an object to a path, you can drag the transformation point to the path. The default position for a transformation point is the center of the object. You can reposition the transformation point while in the symbol edit mode by dragging the transformation point to a different location on the object. Objects also have a registration point (+) that determines the X and Y coordinates of an object on the Stage. The transformation and registration points can overlap—this is displayed as a plus sign within a circle ⊕.

Figure 27 *A motion guide with an object (motorbike) attached*

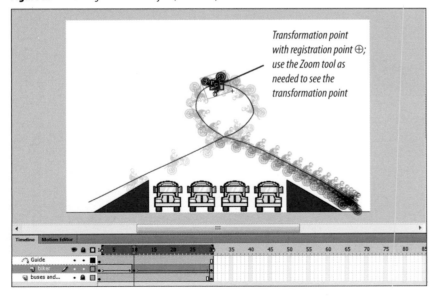

Transformation point with registration point ⊕; use the Zoom tool as needed to see the transformation point

Figure 28 *A motion guide layer with a classic tween on the layer beneath it*

Motion guide layer containing the path

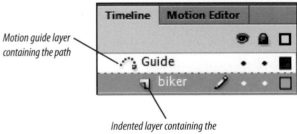

Indented layer containing the classic tween animation that will follow the path created on the motion guide layer

Create a classic tween animation

1. Open fl4_3.fla, then save it as **cTween.fla**.

2. Insert a **new layer**, then name it **biker**.

3. Click **frame 1** on the biker layer, then drag the **biker symbol** from the Library panel to the Stage, as shown in Figure 29.

4. Click **frame 30** on the biker layer, click **Insert** on the menu bar, point to **Timeline**, then click **Keyframe**.

5. Drag the **biker** to the position shown in Figure 30.

6. Click **frame 2** on the biker layer, click **Insert** on the menu bar, then click **Classic Tween**.

   An arrow appears on the Timeline indicating that this is a classic tween.

7. Play the movie.

You created an animation using a classic tween.

Add a motion guide and orient the object to the guide

1. Insert a **new layer**, then name it **Guide**.

2. Click **Modify** on the menu bar, point to **Timeline**, then click **Layer Properties**.

3. Click the **Guide option button**, click **OK**, then drag the **biker layer** up to the Guide layer, as shown in Figure 31.

   The biker layer indents below the Guide layer.

4. Click **frame 1** on the Guide layer, click the **Pencil tool** on the Tools panel, select **Smooth** in the Options area at the bottom of the Tools panel, then set the stroke color to **black**.

5. Point to the middle of the biker, then draw a **line** with a loop similar to the one shown in Figure 32.

(continued)

Figure 29 *Positioning the biker symbol on the Stage*

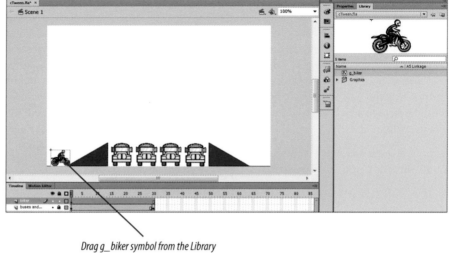

Drag g_biker symbol from the Library panel and position it on the Stage

Figure 30 *Repositioning the biker*

Figure 31 *Dragging the biker layer up to the Guide layer*

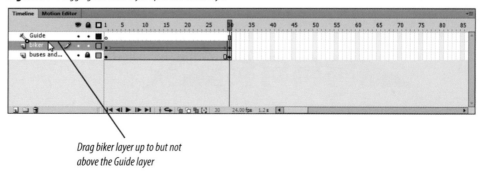

Drag biker layer up to but not above the Guide layer

Figure 32 *Drawing a guide path on a Guide layer*

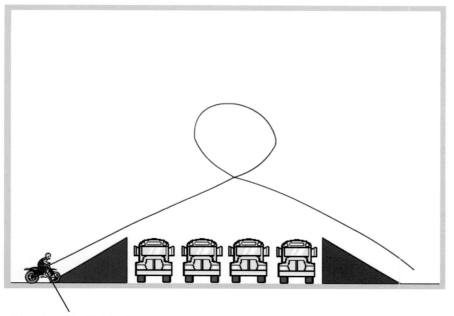

Point to the middle of the biker object

Figure 33 *Aligning the object with the guide path*

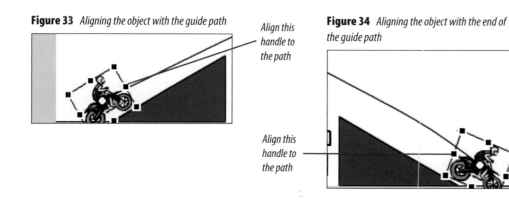

Align this handle to the path

Figure 34 *Aligning the object with the end of the guide path*

Align this handle to the path

6. Click **frame 30** on the biker layer, click the **Selection tool** ▶, then drag the **biker** so that the **transformation point** touches the end of the path.

   Hint: Use the Zoom tool to zoom in on the biker to make it easier to see you have placed the transformation point on the path.

7. Play the movie.

   The biker should follow the path. If not, make sure the biker is attached to the beginning and end of the path.

8. Click **frame 1** on the biker layer, then click the **biker** to select the object.

9. Click the **Free Transform tool** ▓ on the Tools panel, then rotate the **biker,** as shown in Figure 33.

10. Click **frame 30** on the biker layer, then rotate the **biker**, as shown in Figure 34.

11. Click the **Selection tool** ▶, then click **frame 1** on the biker layer.

12. Display the Properties panel, then click the **Orient to path check box**.

13. Play the movie.

14. Click **frame 1** on the biker layer, set the Ease value on the Properties panel to **100**, then click **frame 1** on the biker layer to accept the value.

15. Click each frame on the **biker layer** until you locate the highest point on the motion path, insert a **keyframe** on that frame, set the ease value to **100**, then click **frame 1** on the biker layer to accept the value. Setting the ease values in steps 14 and 15 will cause the biker to start out fast, slow down at the top of the loop and speed up again.

16. Test the movie, save your work, then close the document.

You added a motion guide, oriented the animated object to the guide, and set ease values.

Create Frame-by-Frame
ANIMATIONS

What You'll Do

 In this lesson, you will create frame-by-frame animations.

Understanding Frame-by-Frame Animations

A frame-by-frame animation (also called a frame animation) is created by specifying the object that is to appear in each frame of a sequence of frames. Figure 35 shows three images that are variations of a cartoon character. In this example, the head and body remain the same, but the arms and legs change to represent a walking motion. If these individual images are placed into succeeding frames (with keyframes), an animation is created.

Frame-by-frame animations are useful when you want to change individual parts of an image. The images in Figure 35 are simple—only three images are needed for the animation. However, depending on the complexity of the image and the desired movements, the time needed to display each change can be substantial. When creating a frame-by-frame animation, you need to consider the following points:

■ *The number of different images.* The more images there are, the more effort is needed to create them. However, the greater the number of images, the less change you need to make in each image and the more

realistic the movement in the animation may seem.

■ *The number of frames in which each image will appear.* Changing the number of frames in which the object appears may change the effect of the animation. If each image appears in only one frame, the animation may appear rather jerky, since the frames change very rapidly. However, in some cases, you may want to give the impression of a rapid change in an object, such as rapidly blinking colors. If so, you could make changes in the color of an object from one frame to another.

■ *The movie frame rate.* Frame rates below 10 may appear jerky, while those above 30 may appear blurred. The frame rate is easy to change, and you should experiment with different rates until you get the desired effect.

Keyframes are critical to the development of frame animations because they signify a change in the object. Because frame animations are created by changing the object, each frame in a frame animation may need to be a keyframe. The exception is when you want an object displayed in several frames before it changes.

Creating a Frame-by-Frame Animation

To create a frame animation, select the frame on the layer where you want the animation to begin, insert a keyframe, and then place the object on the Stage. Next, select the frame where you want the change to occur, insert a keyframe, and then change the object. You can also add a new object in place of the original one. Figure 36 shows the first three frames of an animation in which three different objects are placed one on top of the other in succeeding frames. In the figure, the movement is shown as shadows. These shadows are visible because the Onion Skin feature is turned on. In this movie, the objects stay in place during the animation. However, a frame animation can also involve movement of the object around the Stage.

Using the Onion Skin Feature

Normally, Flash displays one frame of an animation sequence at a time on the Stage. Turning on the Onion Skin feature allows you to view an outline of the object(s) in any number of frames. This can help in positioning animated objects on the Stage.

Figure 35 *Three images used in an animation*

Figure 36 *A frame-by-frame animation of three figures appearing to walk in place*

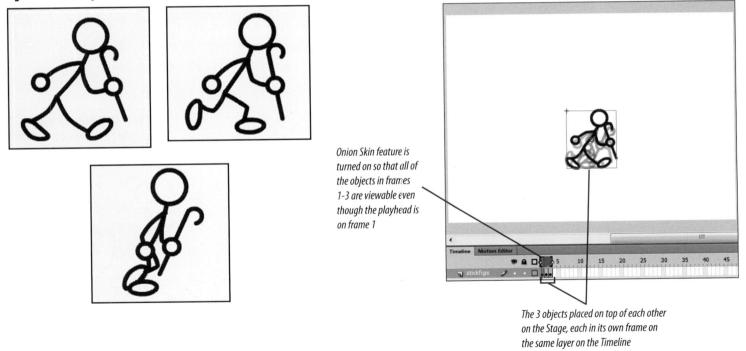

Onion Skin feature is turned on so that all of the objects in frames 1-3 are viewable even though the playhead is on frame 1

The 3 objects placed on top of each other on the Stage, each in its own frame on the same layer on the Timeline

Create an in-place frame-by-frame animation

1. Open fl4_4.fla, then save it as **frameAn.fla**.

2. Set the view to **Fit in Window**.

3. Insert a **new layer**, name it **stickfigs**, click **frame 1** of the stickfigs layer, then drag **stickfig1** from the Library panel to the center of the Stage so it touches the white walkway.

   Note: You can use the Align panel to center the object horizontally across the Stage.

4. Click **frame 2** of the stickfigs layer to select it, click **Insert** on the menu bar, point to **Timeline**, then click **Keyframe**.

5. Drag **stickfig2** so it is on top of stickfig1, as shown in Figure 37, use the arrow keys on the keyboard to align the heads, then click a blank area of the Stage to deselect stickfig2.

6. Select **stickfig1** by clicking the foot that points up as shown in Figure 38, then press **[Delete]**.

7. Click **frame 3** on the stickfigs layer to select it, insert a **keyframe**, drag **stickfig3** so it is on top of stickfig2, then use the **arrow keys** on the keyboard to align the heads.

8. Click a blank area of the Stage to deselect stickfig3.

9. Select stickfig2 by clicking the foot that points down as shown in Figure 39, then press **[Delete]**.

10. Change the frame rate to **12**.

11. Play the movie.

You created a frame-by-frame animation.

Figure 37 *Dragging stickfig2 on top of stickfig1*

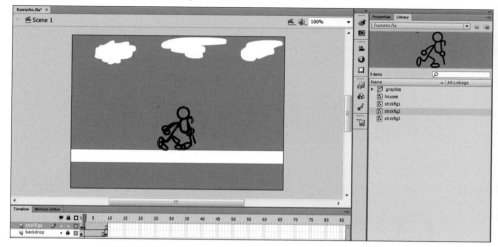

Figure 38 *Selecting stickfig1*

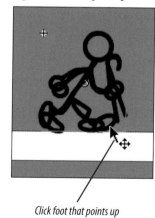

Click foot that points up

Figure 39 *Selecting stickfig2*

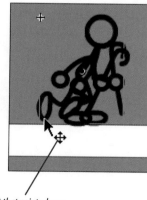

Click foot that points down

Figure 40 *Moving the houses layer below the stickfigs layer*

Timeline	Motion Editor

stickfigs
houses
backdrop

Copy frames and add a moving background

1. Click **frame 1** of the stickfigs layer, press and hold **[Shift]**, then click **frame 3**.

2. Click **Edit** on the menu bar, point to **Timeline**, click **Copy Frames**, then click **frame 4** of the stickfigs layer.

3. Click **Edit** on the menu bar, point to **Timeline**, then click **Paste Frames**.

4. Click **frame 7**, then repeat step 3.

5. Click **frame 10** of the stickfigs layer, press and hold **[Shift]**, then click **frame 13**.

6. Click **Edit** on the menu bar, point to **Timeline**, then click **Remove Frames**.

7. Play the movie.

8. Insert a **new layer**, name the layer **houses**, then drag the **houses layer** below the stickfigs layer, as shown in Figure 40.

9. Click **frame 1** of the houses layer, drag the **houses symbol** from the Library panel to the Stage, position the houses as shown in Figure 41, then play the movie.

10. Click **frame 1** of the houses layer, click **Insert** on the menu bar, then click **Motion Tween**.

11. Click **frame 9** on the houses layer, then drag the **houses object** to the left, as shown in Figure 42.

12. Test the movie, close the Flash Player window.

    To slow down the animation you can reduce the frame rate and/or extend the length of the movie.

13. Save your work, then close the document.

You copied frames and added a motion tween to a movie with an in-place frame-by-frame animation.

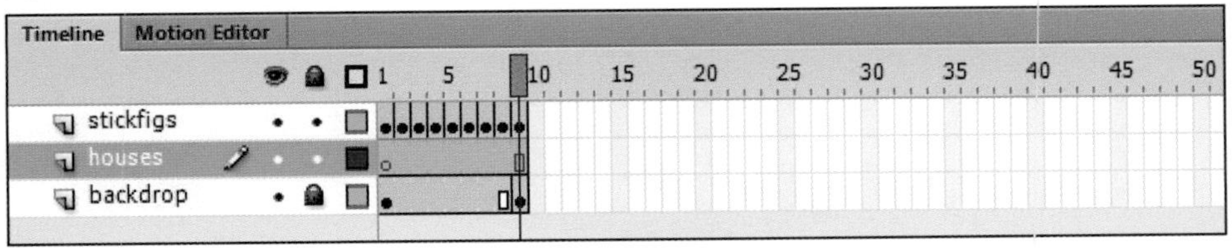

Figure 41 *Positioning the houses symbol on the Stage*

Figure 42 *Repositioning the houses object*

Create a frame-by-frame animation of a moving object

1. Open fl4_5.fla, then save it as **frameM.fla**.

   This document has a backdrop layer that contains a row of houses and clouds.

2. Insert a **new layer**, then name it **stickFigs**.

3. Use the Magnification options on the View menu to display the entire Stage and part of the Pasteboard.

4. Click **frame 5** on the stickFigs layer, then insert a **keyframe**.

5. Drag **stickfig1** from the Library panel to the left edge of the Stage, as shown in Figure 43.

6. Click **frame 6** on the stickFigs layer, click **Insert** on the menu bar, point to **Timeline**, then click **Blank Keyframe**.

   A blank keyframe keeps the object in the previous frame from appearing in the current frame.

7. Click the **Edit Multiple Frames button** on the Timeline status bar to turn it on.

   This allows you to view the contents of more than one frame at a time.

8. Drag **stickfig2** from the Library panel to the right of stickfig1, as shown in Figure 44.

9. Click **frame 7** on the stickFigs layer, then insert a **Blank Keyframe**.

10. Drag **stickfig3** to the right of stickfig2, as shown in Figure 45.

    (continued)

Figure 43 *Positioning stickfig1 on the Stage*

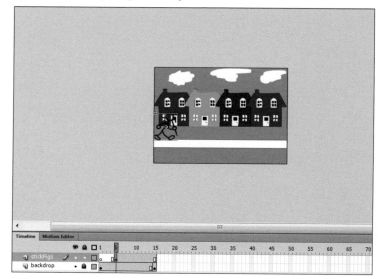

Figure 44 *Positioning stickfig2 on the Stage*

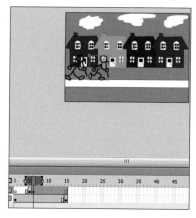

Figure 45 *Positioning stickfig3 on the Stage*

Figure 46 *Adding stickfig3 as the final object*

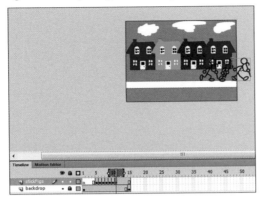

Working with Frames

Selecting frames
To select one frame: click the frame.
To select a range of contiguous frames: Shift-click additional frames.
To select non-contiguous frames: Control-click (Win) or ⌘-click (Mac).
To select a span of frames: double-click between keyframes.
To select all frames on the Timeline: choose Select All Frames from the Timeline option on the Edit menu.

Removing frames
Select the frame(s), then choose Remove Frames from the Timeline option on the Edit menu.
This removes frames from the timeline and moves the contents of succeeding frames left based on the number of frames removed.

Copy and paste
Select the frame(s), choose Copy Frames from the Timeline option on the Edit menu, select the frame to copy to, then choose Paste Frames from the Timeline option on the Edit menu.

Clear contents
Select the frame(s), then choose Clear Frames from the Timeline option on the Edit menu.
This leaves the frame(s) on the Timeline but the content is cleared and not available for pasting.
(*Note*: If you select a frame within a motion tween and choose the Clear Frames option, all of the frames of the motion tween will cleared.)

11. Click **frame 8** on the stickFigs layer, insert a **Blank Keyframe**, then drag **stickfig1** from the Library panel to the right of stickfig3.

    Note: In this frame-by-frame animation each object must be placed individually rather than using a copy and paste process.

12. Click **frame 9** on the stickFigs layer, insert a **Blank Keyframe**, then drag **stickfig2** to the right of stickfig1.

13. Click **frame 10** on the stickFigs layer, insert a **Blank Keyframe**, then drag **stickfig3** to the right of stickfig2.

14. Click **frame 11** on the stickFigs layer, insert a **Blank Keyframe**, then drag **stickFig1** to the right of stickFig2 and partially off the Stage.

    Your screen should resemble Figure 46.

15. Test the movie.

    Notice how the figure seems to hesitate at the end of the movie before looping to the start of the movie. This is because there are still frames in the movie that have no content.

16. Close the Flash Player window, click **frame 12** on the stickFigs layer, then insert a **Blank Keyframe**.

17. Click the **Edit Multiple Frames button**  on the Timeline status bar to turn it off.

18. Test the movie, then close the Flash Player window.

19. Change the frame rate to **6 fps**.

20. Test the movie, then close the Flash Player window.

21. Save the movie, then close the document.

You created a frame-by-frame animation that causes objects to appear to move across the screen.

Create Shape Tween
ANIMATIONS

What You'll Do

In this lesson, you will create a shape tween animation and specify shape hints.

Understanding Shape Tweening

In previous lessons, you learned that you can use motion tweening to change the shape of an object. You accomplish this by selecting the Free Transform tool and then dragging the handles to resize and skew the object. While this is easy and allows you to include motion along with the change in shape, there are two drawbacks. First, you are limited in the type of changes (resizing and skewing) that can be made to the shape of an object. Second, you must work with the same object throughout the animation. When you use **shape tweening**, however, you can have an animation change the shape of an object to any form you desire, and you can include two objects in the animation with two different shapes. As with motion tweening, you can use shape tweening to change other properties of an object, such as its color, location, and size.

Using Shape Tweening to Create a Morphing Effect

Morphing involves changing one object into another, sometimes unrelated, object. For example, you could turn a robot into a human, or turn a football into a basketball. The viewer sees the transformation as a series of incremental changes. In Flash, the first object appears on the Stage and changes into the second object as the movie plays. The number of frames included from the beginning to the end of this shape tween animation determines how quickly the morphing effect takes place. The first frame in the animation displays the first object and the last frame displays the second object. The in-between frames display the different shapes that are created as the first object changes into the second object.

When working with shape tweening, you need to keep the following points in mind:

- Shape tweening can be applied only to editable graphics. To apply shape tweening to instances, groups, symbols, text blocks, or bitmaps, you must break apart the object to make it editable. To do this, you use the Break Apart command on the Modify menu. When you break apart an instance of a symbol, it is no longer linked to the original symbol.
- You can shape tween more than one object at a time as long as all the objects are on

Creating Animations

the same layer. However, if the shapes are complex and/or if they involve movement in which the objects cross paths, the results may be unpredictable.

■ You can use shape tweening to move an object in a straight line, but other options, such as rotating an object, are not available.

■ You can use the settings in the Properties panel to set options (such as the ease value, which causes acceleration or deceleration) for a shape tween.

■ Shape hints can be used to control more complex shape changes.

Properties Panel Options

Figure 47 shows the Properties panel options for a shape tween. The options allow you to adjust several aspects of the animation, as described in the following:

■ Adjust the rate of change between frames to create a more natural appearance during the transition by setting an ease value. Setting the value between –1 and –100 will begin the shape tween gradually and accelerate it toward the end of the animation. Setting the value between 1 and 100 will begin the shape tween rapidly and decelerate it toward the end of the animation. By default, the rate of change is set to 0, which causes a constant rate of change between frames.

■ Choose a blend option. The Distributive option creates an animation in which the in-between shapes are smoother and more irregular. The Angular option preserves the corners and straight lines and works only with objects that have these features. If the objects do not have corners, Flash defaults to the Distributive option.

Shape Hints

You can use shape hints to control the shape's transition appearance during animation. Shape hints allow you to specify a location on the beginning object that corresponds to a location on the ending object. Figure 48 shows two shape animations of the same objects, one using shape hints and the other not using shape hints. The figure also shows how the object being reshaped appears in one of the in-between frames. Notice that with the shape hints, the object in the in-between frame is more recognizable.

Figure 47 *The Properties panel options for a shape tween*

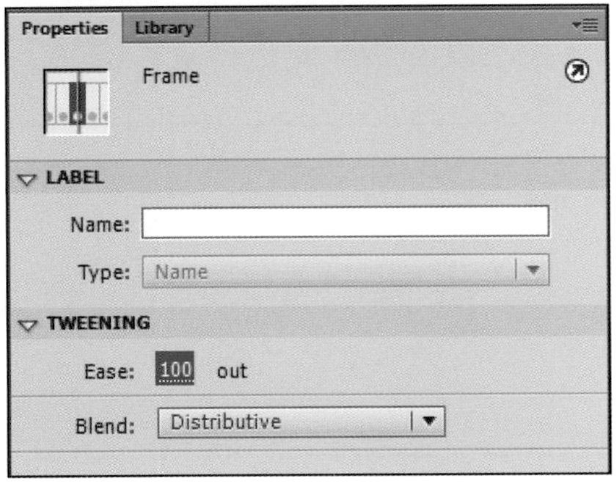

Figure 48 *Two shape animations (A morphing into B) with and without shape hints*

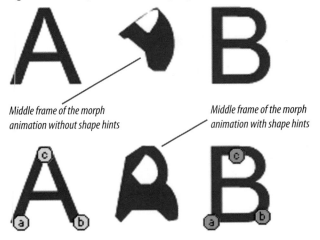

Middle frame of the morph animation without shape hints

Middle frame of the morph animation with shape hints

Create a shape tween animation

1. Open fl4_6.fla, then save it as **antiqueCar.fla**.
2. Set the view to **Fit in Window**.
3. Click **frame 30** on the shape layer, then insert a **keyframe**.
4. Click the **Selection tool** ▶ on the Tools panel. Notice the graphic is editable as indicated by the dot pattern.
5. Click a blank area of the pasteboard to deselect the car.
6. Move the pointer towards the top of the car near the right side until it changes to an arc pointer ▶_⌒, then use the arc pointer ▶_⌒ to drag the **car top** to above the steering wheel, as shown in Figure 49.

   Note: Be sure you are using the arc pointer and not the corner pointer.
7. Click anywhere on the shape layer between frames 1 and 30.
8. Click **Insert** on the menu bar, then click **Shape Tween**.
9. Click **frame 1** on the shape layer, then play the movie.
10. Click **frame 30** on the shape layer.
11. Click the **Selection tool** ▶ on the Tools panel, then drag a **marquee** around the car to select it if it is not already selected.
12. Drag the **car** to the right side of the Stage, then change the fps to **12**.
13. Test the movie, then close the Flash Player window.
14. Change the fps to **24**, save the movie and close it.

You created a shape tween animation, causing an object to change shape as it moves over several frames.

Figure 49 *Reshaping the object*

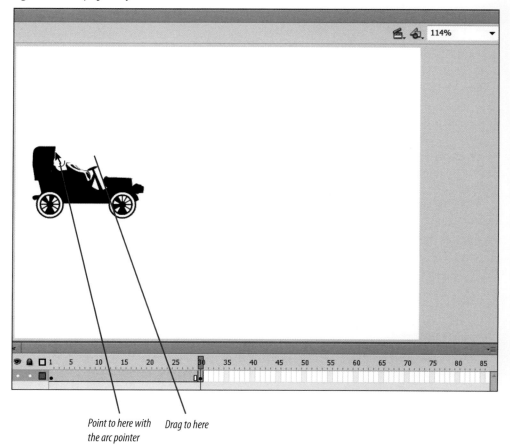

Point to here with the arc pointer   Drag to here

Figure 50 *Positioning the car instance on the Stage*

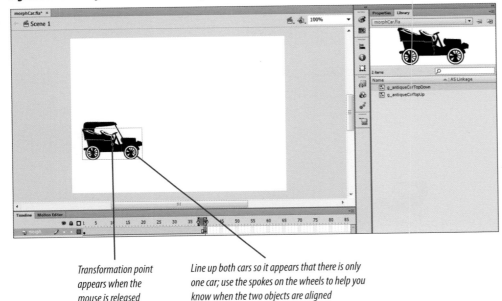

Transformation point appears when the mouse is released

Line up both cars so it appears that there is only one car; use the spokes on the wheels to help you know when the two objects are aligned

Create a morphing effect

1. Open fl4_7.fla, then save it as **morphCar.fla**.

2. Click **frame 40** on the morph layer.

3. Click **Insert** on the menu bar, point to **Timeline**, then click **Blank Keyframe**.

TIP Inserting a blank keyframe prevents the object in the preceding keyframe from automatically being inserted into the frame with the blank keyframe. This is necessary when morphing two objects.

4. Click the **Edit Multiple Frames button** on the Timeline status bar.

   Turning on the Edit Multiple Frames feature allows you to align the two objects to be morphed.

5. Drag the **g_antiqueCarTopDown graphic** symbol from the Library panel directly on top of the car on the Stage, as shown in Figure 50.

TIP Use the arrow keys to move the object as needed.

6. Make sure the g_antiqueCarTopDown object is selected, click **Modify** on the menu bar, then click **Break Apart**.

   This allows the object to be reshaped.

7. Click the **Edit Multiple Frames button** to turn off the feature.

8. Click anywhere between frames 1 and 40 on the morph layer, click **Insert** on the menu bar, then click **Shape Tween**.

9. Click **frame 1** on the Timeline, then play the movie.

   The first car morphs into the second car.

10. Save the movie.

You created a morphing effect, causing one object to change into another.

Adjust the rate of change in a shape tween animation

1. Click **frame 40** on the morph layer.
2. Click the **Selection tool** ↖ on the Tools panel, then drag a **marquee** around the car to select it, if it is not already selected.
3. Drag the **car** to the right side of the Stage.
4. Click **frame 1** on the morph layer.
5. Set the ease value on the Properties panel to **–100**, as shown in Figure 51.
6. Click the **Stage** to deselect the car.
7. Play the movie.

   The car starts out slow and speeds up as the morphing process is completed.

8. Repeat Steps 4 and 5, but change the ease value to **100**.
9. Click **frame 1** on the Timeline, then play the movie.

   The car starts out fast and slows down as the morphing process is completed.

10 Test the movie, then close the Flash Player window.
11. Save your work, then close the movie.

You added motion to a shape tween animation and changed the ease value.

Figure 51 *Setting the ease value of the morph*

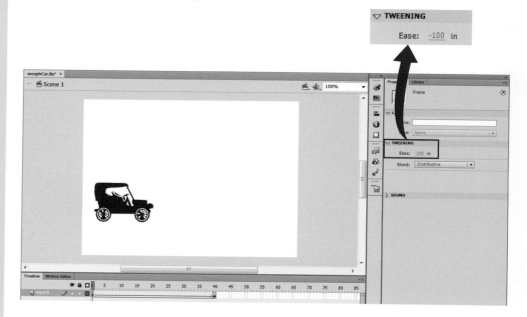

Figure 52 *Positioning a shape hint*

Figure 53 *Adding shape hints*

Figure 54 *Matching shape hints*

Use shape hints

1. Open fl4_8.fla, then save it as **shapeHints.fla**.
2. Play the movie and notice how the L morphs into a Z.
3. Change the view to 200%, then click **frame 15** on the Timeline, the midpoint of the animation. Notice the shape is unrecognizable.
4. Click **frame 1** on the hints layer to display the first object.
5. Make sure the object is selected, click **Modify** on the menu bar, point to **Shape**, then click **Add Shape Hint**.
6. Drag the **Shape Hint icon** to the location shown in Figure 52.
7. Repeat Steps 5 and 6 to set a second and third Shape Hint icon, as shown in Figure 53.

   Notice the shape hints are placed at the major points of the image. For more complex objects you can use more shape hints and experiment with their placement.
8. Click **frame 30** on the hints layer.

   The shape hints are stacked on top of each other.
9. Drag the **Shape Hint icons** to match Figure 54.
10. Click **frame 15** on the hints layer, then notice how the object is more recognizable now that the shape hints have been added.
11. Click **frame 1** on the Timeline, then play the movie.
12. Save your work, then close the movie.

You added shape hints to a morph animation.

Create Movie CLIPS

What You'll Do

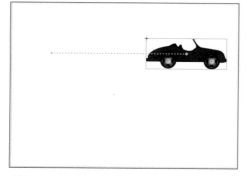

In this lesson, you will create, edit, and animate a movie clip.

Understanding Movie Clip Symbols

Until now you have been working with two kinds of symbols, graphic and button. A third type is a **movie clip symbol**, which provides a way to create more complex types of animations. A movie clip is essentially a movie within a movie. Each movie clip has its own Timeline, which is independent of the main Timeline. This allows you to nest a movie clip that is running one animation within another animation or in a scene on the main Timeline. Because a movie clip retains its own Timeline, when you insert an instance of the movie clip symbol into a Flash document, the movie clip continues in an endless loop even if the main Timeline stops.

The wheels on a car rotating while the car is moving across the screen is an example of a movie (the moving car) with a nested animation (the rotating wheels). The nested animation is a movie clip. To create the animated movie clip, a drawing of a wheel separate from the car is converted into a movie clip symbol. Then the movie clip symbol is opened in the edit window, which includes a Timeline that is unique to the movie clip. In the edit window, an animation is created that causes the wheel to rotate. After exiting the edit window and returning to the main Timeline, an instance of the movie clip symbol is placed on each wheel of the car. Finally, the car, including the wheels, is animated on the main Timeline. As the car is moving across the screen, each wheel is rotating according to the movie clip Timeline. This process is shown in Figure 55.

In addition to allowing you to create more complex animations, movie clips help to organize the different reusable pieces of a movie and provide for smaller movie file sizes. This is because only one movie clip symbol needs to be stored in the Library panel while an unlimited number of instances of the symbol can be used in the Flash document.

An animated movie clip can be viewed in the edit window that is displayed when you double-click the movie clip symbol in the Library panel; and it can be viewed when you test or publish the movie that contains the movie clip. It is important to note that an animated movie clip cannot be viewed simply by playing the movie on the main Timeline.

In this lesson, you will learn how to create a movie clip symbol from a drawn object, edit the movie clip to create an animation, and nest the movie clip in another animation.

Figure 55 *The process of nesting a movie clip within an animation*

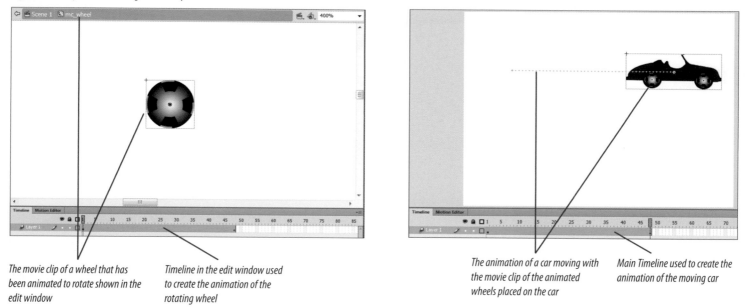

The movie clip of a wheel that has been animated to rotate shown in the edit window

Timeline in the edit window used to create the animation of the rotating wheel

The animation of a car moving with the movie clip of the animated wheels placed on the car

Main Timeline used to create the animation of the moving car

Break apart a graphic symbol and select parts of the object to separate from the graphic

1. Open fl4_9.fla, then save it as **mClip.fla**.

   This document has one graphic symbol—a car that has been placed on the Stage.

2. Click the **Selection tool** ⟍ on the Tools panel, then click the **car** to select it.

3. Click **Modify** on the menu bar, then click **Break Apart**.

4. Click a blank area of the Stage to deselect the object.

5. Click the **Zoom tool** ⚲ on the Tools panel, then click the **front wheel** two times to zoom in on the wheel.

6. Click the **Selection tool** ⟍ on the Tools panel.

7. Click the **gray hubcap**, press and hold **[Shift]**, then click the rest of the wheel, as shown in Figure 56.

   Hint: There are several small parts to the wheel, so click until a dot pattern covers the entire wheel, but do not select the tire. Use the Undo command if you select the tire.

8. Drag the **selected area** down below the car, as shown in Figure 57.

9. Compare your selected wheel to Figure 57, if your wheel does not match the figure, use the Undo command to move the wheel back to its original position, and repeat step 7.

You broke apart a graphic symbol and selected parts of the object to separate from the graphic.

Figure 56 *Selecting the wheel*

Figure 57 *Separating the wheel from the car*

Figure 58 *Selecting the gray area of the wheel*

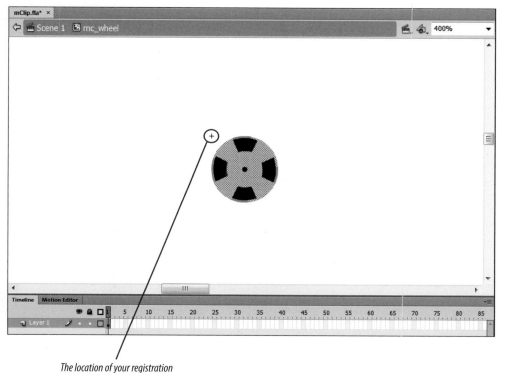

The location of your registration point may differ.

Create and edit a movie clip

1. Verify the wheel is selected, click **Modify** on the menu bar, then click **Convert to Symbol**.

2. Type **mc_wheel** for the name, select **Movie Clip** for the Type, then click **OK**.

3. Display the Library panel.

   Notice the mc_wheel movie clip and the movie clip icon appear in the Library panel.

4. Double-click the **mc_wheel icon** on the Library panel to display the edit window.

5. Click the **Zoom tool** 🔍 on the Tools panel, then click the **wheel** twice to zoom in on the wheel.

   The movie clip has been broken apart as indicated by the dot pattern.

6. Click the **Selection tool** ▶, click a blank area of the Stage to deselect the object, then click the **gray area** of the wheel to select it, as shown in Figure 58.

7. Click the **Fill color tool color swatch** 🖌 on the Tools panel, then click the **gray gradient color swatch** in the bottom row of the palette.

You created a movie clip symbol and edited it to change the color of the object.

Animate a movie clip

1. Click the **Selection tool** ▶, then drag a **marquee** around the entire wheel to select it.

2. Click **Insert** on the menu bar, click **Motion Tween**, then click **OK** for the Convert selection to symbol for tween dialog box.

3. Point to the end of the tween span on Layer 1 of the Timeline, then, when the pointer changes to a double-headed arrow ↔, drag the **span** to frame 48, as shown in Figure 59.

4. Click **frame 1** on Layer 1.

5. Display the Properties panel.

6. Change the rotate value to **4** times and verify the Direction is CW (Clockwise), as shown in Figure 60.

   Hint: If you don't see the Rotate option, click the Selection tool, then drag a marquee around the object.

7. Set the frame rate on the Timeline status bar to **12**.

8. Press **[Enter]** (Win) or **[Return]** (Mac) to play the Timeline for the mc_wheel movie clip symbol.

9. Click **Scene 1** near the top left side of the edit widow to exit the edit window.

10. Drag the **wheel** on the Stage up and position it so it is back inside the front tire of the car.

(continued)

Figure 59 *Increasing the motion span on the Timeline*

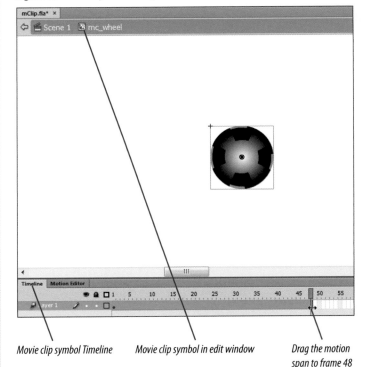

Movie clip symbol Timeline   Movie clip symbol in edit window   Drag the motion span to frame 48

Figure 60 *Changing the rotate value*

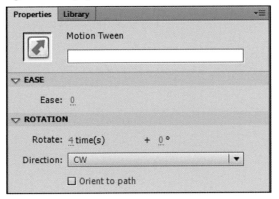

Creating Animations

Figure 61 *Repositioning the car*

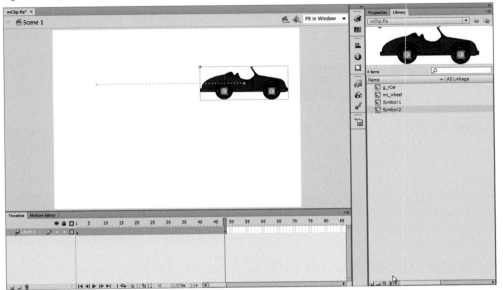

11. Display the Library panel, then drag the **mc_wheel movie clip** from the Library panel and position it using the arrow keys as needed so it is on the back wheel.

12. Click **View** on the menu bar, point to **Magnification**, then click **Fit in Window**.

13. Test the movie and notice how the wheels turn, then close the Flash Player window.

14. Click the **Selection tool** , then drag a **marquee** around the car to select it and the wheels.

15. Click **Insert** on the menu bar, click **Motion Tween**.

16. Click **OK** to convert the selection to a symbol for tweening.

17. Drag the **tween span** on Layer 1 to frame 48.

    This will match the number of frames in the mc_wheel movie clip.

18. Click **frame 48** on Layer 1, then drag the **car** to the right side of the Stage, as shown in Figure 61.

19. Test the movie, then close the Flash Player window.

20. Save your work, then close the document.

You edited a movie clip to create an animation, then nested the movie clip in an animation on the main Timeline.

Animate TEXT

What You'll Do

In this lesson, you will animate text by scrolling, rotating, zooming, and resizing it.

Animating Text

You can motion tween text block objects just as you do graphic objects. You can resize, rotate, reposition, and change the colors of text blocks. Figure 62 shows three examples of animated text with the Onion Skin feature turned on. When the movie starts, each of the following occurs one after the other:

- The Classic Car Club text block scrolls in from the left side to the top center of the Stage. This is done by creating the text block, positioning it off the Stage, and creating a motion-tweened animation that moves it to the Stage.
- The Annual text block appears and rotates five times. This occurs after you create the Annual text block, position it in the middle of the Stage under the heading, and use the Properties panel to specify a clockwise rotation that repeats five times.
- The ROAD RALLY text block slowly zooms out and appears in the middle of the Stage. This occurs after you create the text block and use the Free Transform tool handles to resize it to a small block at the beginning of the animation. Then, you resize the text block to a larger size at the end of the animation.

Once you create a motion animation using a text block, the text block becomes a symbol and you are unable to edit individual characters within the text block unless you use the Break Apart command. You can, however, edit the symbol as a whole.

Figure 62 *Three examples of animated text*

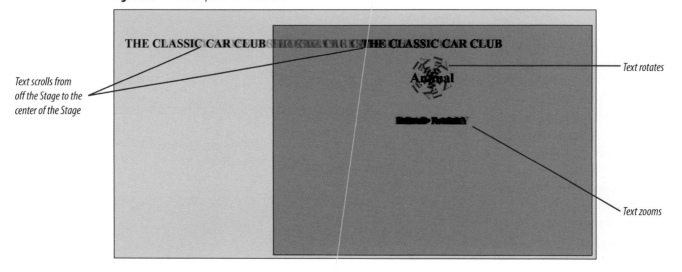

Text scrolls from off the Stage to the center of the Stage

Text rotates

Text zooms

Select, copy, and paste frames

1. Open fl4_10.fla, then save the movie as **textAn.fla**.

   This document has a heading and a frame-by-frame animation of a car where the front end rotates up and down, and then the car moves off the Stage.

2. Play the movie, then click **1** on the Timeline.

3. Press the **period key** to move through the animation one frame at a time and notice the changes to the car object in each frame.

4. Change the view to **Fit in Window**.

5. Click **frame 1** on the carGo layer, press and hold **[Shift]**, then click **frame 9** to select all the frames, as shown in Figure 63.

6. Click **Edit** on the menu bar, point to **Timeline**, then click **Cut Frames**.

7. Click **frame 72** on the carGo layer.

8. Click **Edit** on the menu bar, point to **Timeline**, then click **Paste Frames**.

   The frames are pasted in the new location, as shown in Figure 64.

9. Click **frame 1** on the carGo layer.

10. Play the movie, then save your work.

You selected frames and moved them from one location on the Timeline to another location on the Timeline.

Figure 63 *Selecting a range of frames*

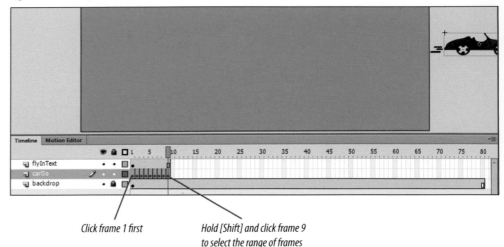

Click frame 1 first

Hold [Shift] and click frame 9 to select the range of frames

Figure 64 *The Pasted Frame*

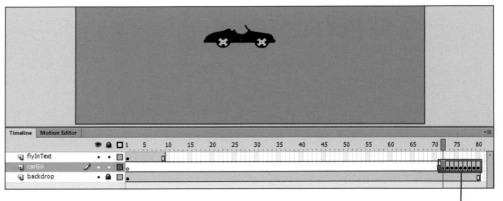

Frames copied to new location on the Timeline

Creating Animations

Figure 65 *Positioning the text block outside the Stage*

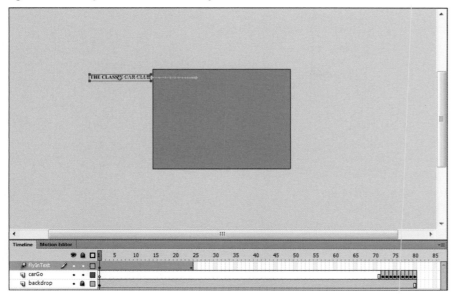

Figure 66 *Centering the text block*

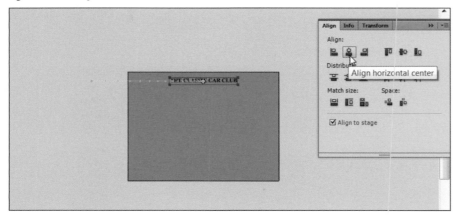

Animate text using a motion preset

1. Use the Magnification options on the View menu to display the entire Stage and part of the Pasteboard.

2. Click **frame 1** on the flyInText layer.

3. Open the Motion Presets panel, display the Default Presets, then click **fly-in-left**.

4. Click **Apply**, read the information box, then click **OK**.

   A motion tween is applied to the text block and a motion path appears.

5. Click the **Selection tool** , then draw a **marquee** around the text and the path.

6. Use the **left arrow key** to position the object and path, as shown in Figure 65.

   Alternately, you can drag the object and path to reposition it. Using the arrow key prevents any vertical movement when repositioning the object and path.

7. Click **frame 24** on the flyInText layer.

8. Click a blank area of the Stage to deselect the object and the path.

9. Click the **text object** to select it, then use the align panel to **center** the text horizontally across the Stage, as shown in Figure 66.

10. Click **frame 80** on the flyInText layer, then insert a **keyframe**.

11. Change the view to **Fit in Window**.

12. Test the movie, then close the Flash Player window.

You used a motion preset to animate an object by having it fly in from the left side of the Stage.

Create rotating text

1. Insert a **new layer**, then name it **rotateText**.

2. Insert a **keyframe** in frame 24 on the rotateText layer.

3. Click the **Text tool** T on the Tools panel, position the pointer under the "A" in "CLASSIC," then click.

4. Change the Character properties in the Properties panel to **Times New Roman**, size **24**, style **bold** and color **blue** (#0000FF).

5. Type **Annual**, then compare your image to Figure 67.

6. Click the **Selection tool** on the Tools panel, then use the Align panel to center the text block horizontally across the Stage.

7. Verify Annual is selected, click **Insert** on the menu bar, then click **Motion Tween**.

8. Click **frame 24** on the rotateText layer, then set the Rotate value on the Properties panel to **2** times with a **CW** (clockwise) direction.

9. Point to the end of the tween span (frame 80), then drag the ↔ **pointer** to frame 34, as shown in Figure 68.

10. Click **frame 80** on the rotateText layer, then insert a **keyframe**.

    The keyframe is needed to display the word Annual in frames 34 to 80.

11. Click **1** on the Timeline, then play the movie.

    The Annual text rotates clockwise two times.

You inserted a new layer, created a rotating text block, applied a motion tween to text, and used the Properties panel to rotate the text block.

Figure 67 *Adding the Annual text block*

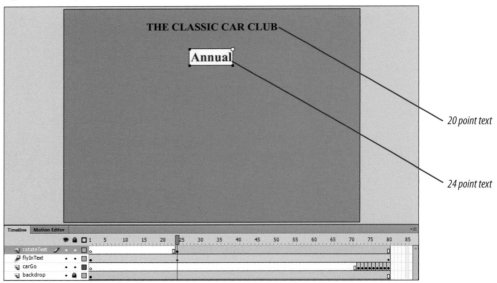

THE CLASSIC CAR CLUB

Annual

20 point text

24 point text

Figure 68 *Resizing the motion span from frame 80 to frame 34*

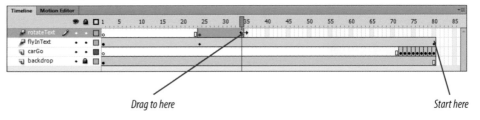

Drag to here

Start here

Figure 69 *Using the Text tool to type ROAD RALLY*

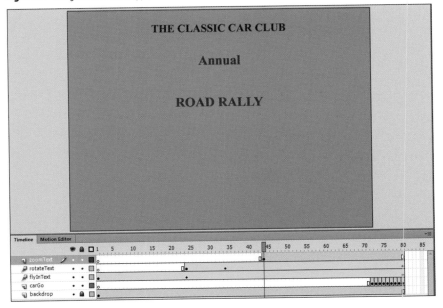

Figure 70 *Resizing the Text block*

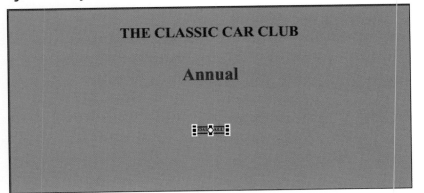

Resize and fade in text

1. Insert a **new layer**, name it **zoomText**, then insert a **keyframe** in frame 44 on the layer.

2. Click the **Text tool** T , position the pointer beneath the Annual text block, then type **ROAD RALLY**, as shown in Figure 69.

3. Click the **Selection tool** , then use the Align panel to center the text block horizontally across the Stage.

4. Click **frame 44** on the zoomText layer, click **Insert** on the menu bar, then click **Motion Tween**.

5. Click **frame 44** on the zoomText layer, click the **Free Transform tool** , then click the **Scale option** in the Options area of the Tools panel.

6. Drag the **upper-left corner handle** inward to resize the text block, as shown in Figure 70.

7. Click **frame 80** on the zoomText layer, verify the Scale option in the Options area of the Tools panel is selected, then drag the **upper-left corner handle** outward to resize the text block to approximately its original size.

TIP If the text appears upside down or backwards, you can use the Undo feature several times to return the text to its original size before you resized the text in step 6. Then repeat step 6, being careful not to resize the text too small.

8. Test the movie, then close the Flash Player window.

You created a motion animation that caused a text block to zoom out.

Make a text block into a button

1. Insert a **new layer**, then name it **continueBTN**.

2. Insert a **keyframe** in frame 72 on the continueBTN layer.

3. Click the **Text** tool T on the Tools panel, position the **Text tool pointer** beneath the car, then type **Click to continue**.

4. Drag the **pointer** over the text to select it, then change the character size to **12** using the Properties panel.

5. Click the **Selection tool** on the Tools panel, center the text block horizontally across the Stage, then compare your image to Figure 71.

6. Verify that the text block is selected, click **Modify** on the menu bar, click **Convert to Symbol**, type **b_continue** in the Name text block, set the Type to **Button**, then click **OK**.

7. Double-click the **text block** to edit the button.

8. Insert a **keyframe** in the Over frame, then set the fill color to the **black color swatch** in the left column of the color palette.

9. Insert a **keyframe** in the Down frame, set the fill color to the **bright green color swatch** in the left column of the color palette.

10. Insert a **keyframe** in the Hit frame, click the **Rectangle tool** on the Tools panel, then draw a **rectangle** that covers the text block, as shown in Figure 72.

11. Click **Scene 1** at the top left of the edit window to return to the main Timeline.

You made the text block into a button.

Figure 71 *Adding a button*

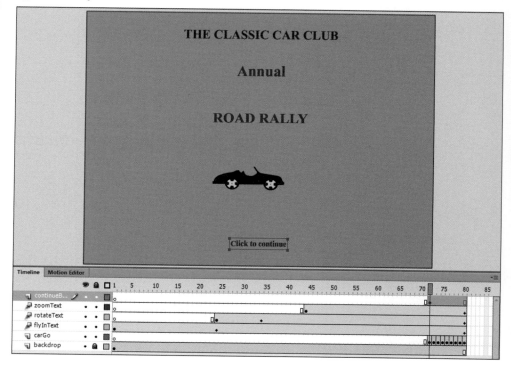

Figure 72 *The rectangle that defines the hit area*

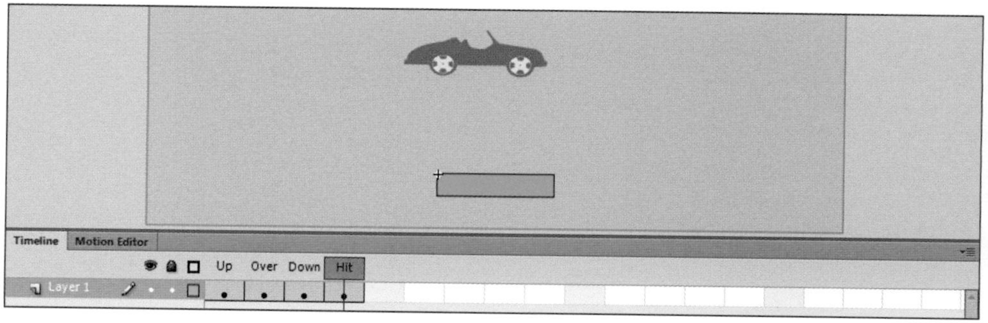

Figure 73 *Adding a play action*

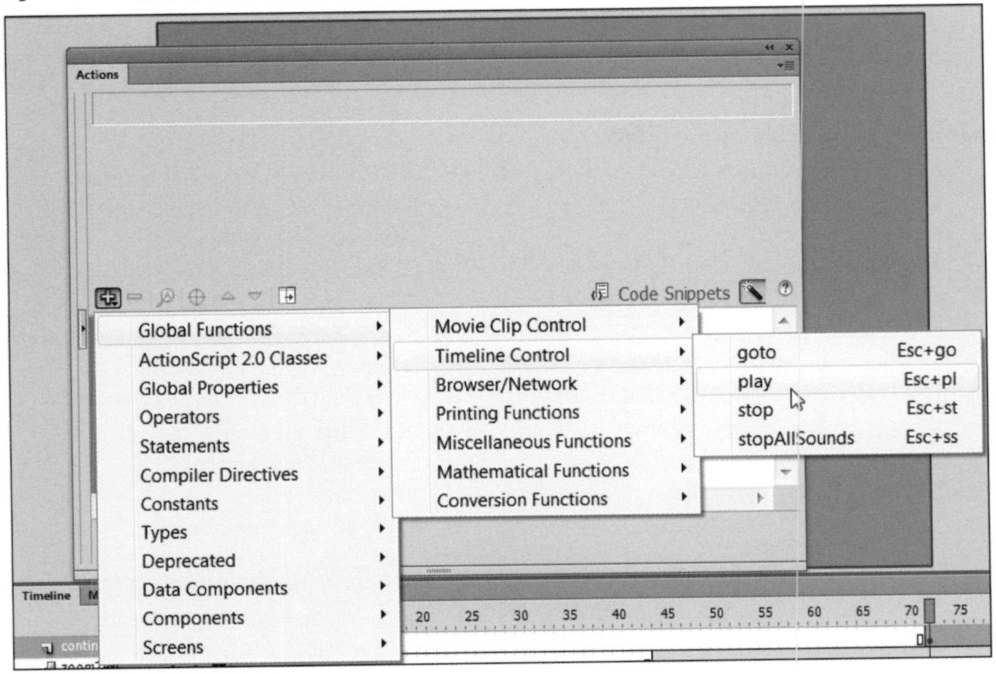

1. Display the Actions panel.
2. Click the **Selection tool** ↖ on the Tools panel, then click the **Click to continue button** on the Stage.
3. Verify the Script Assist button is turned on, then verify the button symbol and b_continue are displayed in the lower-left corner of the Actions panel.

   Note: You need to have ActionScript 2.0 active. You can check your ActionScript version by choosing Publish Settings on the File menu, then selecting the Flash tab.
4. Click the **Add a new item to the script button** ⊕ in the Script Assist window, point to **Global Functions**, point to **Timeline Control**, then click **play**, as shown in Figure 73.
5. Insert a **new layer**, name it **stopMovie**, then insert a **keyframe** in frame 72 on that layer.
6. Verify that stopmovie:72 is displayed in the lower-left corner of the Actions panel.
7. Click the **Add a new item to the script button** ⊕ in the Script Assist window, point to **Global Functions**, point to **Timeline Control**, then click **stop**.
8. Click **Control** on the menu bar, point to **Test Movie**, click **in Flash Professional**, then click the **Click to continue button** when it appears.

   The movie begins by playing the animated text blocks. When you click the Click to continue button the movie plays the animated car and then the movie loops back to frame 1.
9. Close the Flash Player movie window, save and close the movie, then exit Flash.

You inserted a play button and added a play action to it, then inserted a stop action on another layer.

Create a motion tween animation.

1. Start Flash, open fl4_11.fla, then save it as **skillsDemo4.fla**.
2. Insert a keyframe in frame 20 on the ballAn layer.
3. Display the Library panel, then drag the g_vball graphic symbol to the lower-left corner of the Stage.
4. Click frame 20 on the ballAn layer, then insert a motion tween.
5. Point to the end of frame 20, when the pointer changes to a double-headed arrow, drag the pointer to frame 40 to set the tween span from frames 20 to 40.
6. With frame 40 selected, drag the object to the lower-right corner of the Stage.
7. Insert a blank keyframe in frame 41.
8. Play the movie, then save your work.

Edit a motion tween.

1. Click frame 20 on the ballAn layer, then use the Selection tool to alter the motion path to form an arc.
2. Use the Subsection tool to display the Bezier handles, use them to form a curved path, then play the movie.
3. Select frame 20, use the Properties panel to change the ease value to **100**, then play the movie.
4. Select frame 20, change the ease value to **−100**, then play the movie.
5. Select frame 40, select the object, use the Properties panel to change the width of the object to **30**, then play the movie. (*Hint:* Click the object on the Stage, then verify the Lock width and height values together chain is not broken. This will ensure that when one value is changed, the other value changes proportionally.)

6. Select frame 35, select the object, use the Free transform tool to skew the object, then play the movie.
7. Select frame 40, select the object, use the Properties panel to change the alpha setting to **0**, then play the movie.
8. Select frame 40, select the object and change the alpha setting back to **100**. (*Hint:* Click the area of the Stage where the ball should be.)
9. Select frame 40, select the object, then use the Advanced Style option in the COLOR EFFECT area of the Properties panel to create a red color.
10. Lock the ballAn layer.
11. Play the movie, then save your work.

Create a classic tween.

1. Insert a new layer and name it **v-ball**.
2. Insert a keyframe in frame 76 on the v-ball layer.
3. Insert a keyframe in frame 41 on the v-ball layer.
4. Drag an instance of the g_vball symbol from the Library panel to the lower-left corner of the Stage.
5. Insert a keyframe in frame 50 on the v-ball layer and drag the ball to the lower-right corner of the Stage.
6. Click any frame between 41 and 50 on the v-ball layer and insert a Classic tween.
7. Insert a blank keyframe at frame 51 on the v-ball layer.
8. Play the movie, then save your work.

Create a motion guide.

1. Insert a new layer above the v-ball layer and name it **path**.
2. Insert a keyframe in frame 76 on the path layer.
3. Change the path layer to a Guide layer.
4. Insert a keyframe in frame 41 on the path layer.

5. Select the pencil tool, point to the middle of the ball and draw a path with a loop.
6. Insert a keyframe in frame 50 on the path layer.
7. Drag the v-ball layer up to the path layer so that it indents below the path layer.
8. Click frame 41 on the v-ball layer and use the Selection tool to attach the ball to the path.
9. Click frame 50 on the v-ball layer and attach the ball to the path.
10. Click frame 41 on the v-ball layer and use the Properties panel to orient the ball to the path.
11. Lock the v-ball and path layers.
12. Hide the path layer.
13. Play the movie, then save the movie.

Create a frame-by-frame animation.

1. Insert a new layer above the path layer and name it **corner-ball**.
2. Insert a keyframe in frame 76 on the corner-ball layer.
3. Insert a keyframe in frame 51 on the corner-ball layer, then drag the g_vball graphic from the Library panel to the lower-left corner of the Stage.
4. Insert a blank keyframe in frame 55 on the corner-ball layer, then drag g_vball graphic from the Library panel to the upper-left corner of the Stage.
5. Insert a blank keyframe in frame 59 on the corner-ball layer, then drag the g_vball graphic from the Library panel to the upper-right corner of the Stage.
6. Insert a blank keyframe in the frame 63 on the corner-ball layer, then drag the g_vball graphic from the Library panel to the lower-right corner of the Stage.

7. Insert a blank keyframe in frame 67 on the corner-ball layer.
8. Lock the corner-ball layer.
9. Change the movie frame rate to 3 frames per second, then play the movie.
10. Change the movie frame rate to 12 frames per second, play the movie, then save your work.

Create a movie clip.

1. Insert a new layer and name it **spin-ball**.
2. Insert a keyframe at frame 76 on the spin-ball layer.
3. Insert a keyframe at frame 51 on the spin-ball layer.
4. Drag an instance of the g_vball symbol from the Library panel to the center of the Stage.
5. Use the align panel to center, both horizontally and vertically, the instance of the g_vball on the Stage.
6. Select the ball and convert it to a movie clip with the name **mc_ball**.
7. Display the edit window for the mc_ball movie clip.
8. Create a motion tween that rotates the ball 6 times counterclockwise in 12 frames.
9. Exit the edit window.
10. Insert a blank keyframe in frame 67 of the spin-ball layer.
11. Lock the spin-ball layer.
12. Test the movie, close the Flash Player window, then save your work.

Animate text.

1. Insert a new layer above the spin-ball layer and name it **heading**.
2. Click frame 1 on the heading layer.
3. Use the Text tool to click at the top-center of the Stage, then type **Having fun with a**.
4. Change the text to Arial, 20 point, light gray (#CCCCCC), and bold.
5. Use the Selection tool to select the heading and center the heading across the Stage.
6. Select frame 1 on the heading layer and create a pulse motion using the Motion Presets panel.
7. Drag the motion span to frame 76.
8. Play the movie and save your work.
9. Lock the heading layer.
10. Insert a new layer and name it **zoom**.
11. Insert a keyframe in frame 76 on the zoom layer.
12. Insert a keyframe in frame 11 on the zoom layer.
13. Use the Text tool to type **Volleyball** below the heading, then center it as needed.
14. Select frame 11 on the zoom layer and create a motion tween.
15. Insert a keyframe in frame 20 on the zoom layer.
16. Click frame 11 on the zoom layer and select the text block.
17. Use the Free Transform tool to resize the text block to approximately one-fourth its original size.

18. Select frame 20 on the zoom layer, and resize the text block to approximately the size shown in Figure 74.
19. Lock the zoom layer.
20. Test the movie, close the Flash Player window, save your work.

Create a Shape Tween Animation.

1. Insert a new layer above the zoom layer and name it **morph**.
2. Insert a keyframe in frame 66 on the morph layer.
3. Drag the g_vball symbol to the center of the Stage so it covers the other ball (mc_ball movie clip) in the center of the Stage. Because the mc_ball movie clip (spinning ball) ends in frame 66 and the morph begins in frame 66, this will give the impression of the spinning ball morphing.
4. Use the Properties panel to resize the width to **60 px**. (*Hint*: Verify the Lock width and height values together chain is not broken. This will ensure that when one value is changed, the other value changes proportionally.)
5. Reposition the smaller ball so it is over the center of the larger ball, then break apart the object.
6. Insert a blank keyframe in frame 76 on the morph layer.
7. Turn on the Edit Multiple Frames feature.

8. Drag the g_fball symbol to the Stage and use the Properties panel to resize the width to **60 px**. (*Hint*: Verify the Lock width and height values together chain is not broken. This will ensure that when one value is changed, the other value changes proportionally.)

9. Center the football on top of the volleyball.

10. Break apart the football object.

11. Turn off the Edit Multiple Frames feature.

12. Click frame 66 on the morph layer and insert a shape tween.

13. Test the movie, then close the Flash Player window.

14. Add shape hints to the volleyball and the football.

15. Lock the morph layer.

16. Test the movie, close the Flash Player window, then save your work.

17. Exit Flash.

Figure 74 *Completed Skills Review*

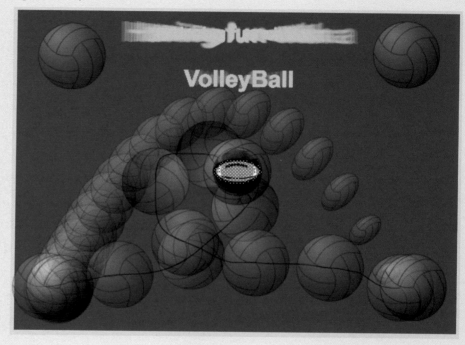

The Ultimate Tours travel company has asked you to design several sample animations for its application. Figure 75 shows a sample opening screen and the Cruises screen. Using these as a guide, complete the following:

1. Open fl4_12.fla and save it as **ultimateTours4.fla**. (*Note:* This Flash document does not have any objects on the Stage. However, it does have all of the objects you will need to complete the project located in the Library panel. If you completed Project Builder 1 in chapter 3 you will notice that all of the objects have been converted to either graphic symbols (so they can be animated) or button symbols.)
2. Display the Library panel, click each item and view it in the Preview window.
3. Change the name of Layer 1 to **heading**.
4. Select frame 1 of the heading layer, drag the Ultimate Tours heading to the top of the Stage and center it. (*Hint:* Be sure the Align to stage check box is checked.)
5. Animate the heading Ultimate Tours using the Free Transform tool and the scale option so that it zooms out from a transparent (alpha = 0) state in frame 1 to an alpha setting of 100 at the end of the tween.
6. Insert a keyframe in frame 80 of the headings layer. (*Note:* In the following steps when you add a layer give the layer an appropriate name.)
7. Add a layer and have the logo appear on the screen next.
8. After the heading and logo appear, make the subheading We Specialize in Exotic Adventures! appear on its own layer.

9. Using separate layers, create motion tweens that cause each of the button shapes (Treks, Tours, Cruises) to scroll from the bottom of the Stage to its position on the Stage. Stagger the buttons on the Timeline so they scroll onto the Stage one after the other. (*Hint:* When adjusting the position of on object that has a motion tween be sure to select the desired frame (starting or ending) of the tween before repositioning the object.)
10. Add a layer and assign a stop action after the opening screen appears, that is after the buttons scroll onto the screen.
11. Remove the frames from the cruises, tours, treks and subheading layers that come after the stop action frame to prevent these objects from appearing on the next screen. (*Note:* To remove a group of frames you can drag the mouse to highlight the frames or click a frame, hold [Shift] and click another frame in a series. After highlighting the desired frames you can select Remove Frames from the Timeline option of the Edit menu.)
12. Add a new layer, add a keyframe one frame after the stop action and create the text blocks shown in Figure 75 (Featured Cruises, Panama Canal, Caribbean, Galapagos).
13. Import the graphic file ship.gif from the drive and folder where your Data Files are stored to the Library panel. (*Hint:* To import a graphic to the Library panel, click File on the menu bar, point to Import, then click Import to Library. Navigate to the drive and folder where your Data Files are stored, then select the desired file and click Open.)

14. Add a new layer, add a keyframe in the same frame as the one in the cruise headings layer and drag the ship.gif from the Library panel to the Stage.
15. Convert the ship graphic to a graphic symbol named **g_ship**, create a motion tween animation that moves the ship across the screen, then alter the motion path to cause a dip in it, similar to the path shown in Figure 75. (*Hint:* Use the Selection tool to create an arc in the path. Then use the Subselection tool to display the Bezier handles and further alter the path.)
16. Use the Free Transform tool and the Rotate and Skew option to attach the ship to the beginning and then to the end of the path, then orient the boat to the motion path.
17. Assign a goto action to the Cruises button on the opening screen so it jumps to the frame that has the Cruises screen.
18. Assign a stop action to a frame on the stop action layer so that the movie stops at the Featured Cruises screen after the ship animation is complete.
19. Add a layer, position the Home button on the cruises screen, and add an action to the button that jumps to the opening screen.
20. Check the ActionScript for all of your buttons and make sure the button name appears in the Actions panel along with the desired frame to jump to.
21. Lock all layers.
22. Test the movie, then compare your movie to the example shown in Figure 75.

Figure 75 *Sample completed Project Builder 1*

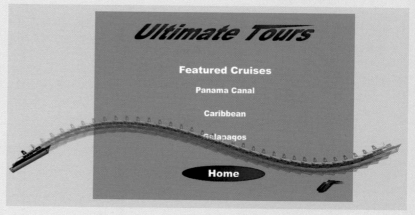

Opening screen

Featured Cruises screen

You have been asked to demonstrate some of the animation features of Flash. You have decided to create a movie clip that includes a frame-by-frame animation and then use the movie clip in a motion tween animation. Figure 76 shows the stick figure that will walk across the screen and jump up as it moves along. The movement across the screen is created using a motion tween. The jumping up is created using a movie clip, as shown in Figure 76.

To complete this project, do the following:

1. Open fl4_13.fla, then save the movie as **jumper4.fla**.
2. Display the Library panel, then click on each of the graphic symbols and view them in the Preview window.
3. Add a color for the Stage, then add the sidewalk, the lines for the sidewalk, and the houses, adding layers as needed and naming them appropriately.
4. Create a new movie clip. (*Note*: You can create a new movie clip by selecting New Symbol from the Insert menu, then you can drag objects from the Library panel to the movie clip edit window.)
5. In the edit window, edit the clip to create a frame-by-frame animation of the stick figures walking in place. In the edit window, place a keyframe in the first six frames of the movie clip Timeline. Click frame 1, then drag stickFig1 to the Stage. Use the transformation point to place the figure. Click frame 2, then drag stickFig2 to the Stage. Continue until each of the six frames has one stick figure.
6. Click frame 1, then use the period to click through the movie. Click one frame and move the stick figure in that frame so it is above its original location. This placement creates the jumping effect.
7. Exit the edit window and place the movie clip on the Stage on its own layer, then create a motion tween that moves the movie clip from the left side to the right side of the Stage.
8. Add keyframes to the other layers to be sure objects on those layers appear on the Stage for the full length of the movie.
9. Test the movie. Change the fps setting as needed to create a more realistic effect, then retest the movie. (*Note*: Movie clips do not play from the Stage, you must use the Test Movie command.)
10. Close the Flash Player movie, then save the movie.

Figure 76 *Sample completed Project Builder 2*

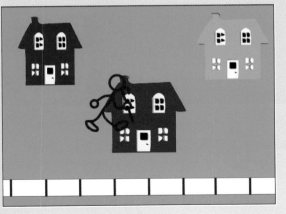

Jumper4 movie

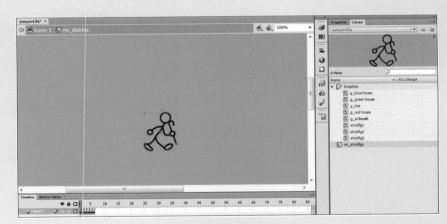

mc_stickfigs symbol in edit window

Figure 77 shows a website for kids. Study the figure and complete the following. For each question, indicate how you determined your answer.

1. Connect to the Internet, then go to *www.smokeybear.com/kids*.

2. Open a document in a word processor or open a new Flash document, save the file as **dpc4**, then answer the following questions. (*Hint*: Use the Text tool in Flash.)

   - What seems to be the purpose of this site?
   - Who is the target audience?
   - How would you use a frame animation in this site?
   - How would you use a motion tween animation?
   - How would you use a motion guide?
   - How would you use motion animation effects?
   - How would you animate the text?

Figure 77 *Design Project*
Smokey Bear image used with the permission of the USDA Forest Service. www.smokeybear.com/kids

This is a continuation of the Portfolio Project in Chapter 3, which is the development of a personal portfolio. In this project, you will create several buttons for the sample animations screen and link them to the animations.

1. Open portfolio3.fla (the file you created in Portfolio Project, Chapter 3) and save it as **portfolio4.fla**.
2. Create button symbols using the ovals with text at the bottom of your opening screen (for example, Graphics, Screen Designs, Biography, and Contact me buttons).
3. Delete the layers that contain the text and background for these buttons, create a new layer, and place all of these buttons on the layer, including the Animations button you created in Chapter 3, on frame 1 of the layer.
4. Add layers and create buttons with labels, as shown in Figure 78, for the tweened animation, frame-by-frame animation, motion path animation, and animated text.
5. Create a tween animation or use the passing cars animation from Chapter 3, and link it to the appropriate button on the Sample Animations screen by assigning a goto action to the button.
6. Create a frame-by-frame animation, and link it to the appropriate button on the Sample Animations screen.
7. Create a motion path animation, and link it to the appropriate button on the Sample Animations screen.
8. Create several text animations, using scrolling, rotating, and zooming; then link them to the appropriate button on the Sample Animations screen.
9. Create a shape tween animation, and link it to the appropriate button on the Sample Animations screen.
10. Create a shape tween animation that produces a morphing effect, and link it to the appropriate button on the Sample Animations screen.
11. Create a shape tween animation that produces a morphing effect using shape hints, and link it to the appropriate button on the Sample Animations screen.
12. Add a layer and create a Home button that links the Sample Animations screen to the Home screen.
13. Create frame actions that cause the movie to return to the Sample Animations screen after each animation has been played.
14. Test the movie.
15. Save your work, then compare sample pages from your movie to the example shown for two of the screens in Figure 78.

Figure 78 *Sample completed Portfolio Project*

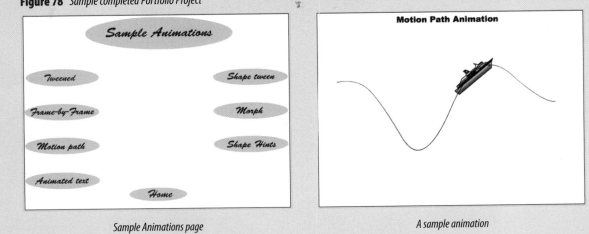

Sample Animations page

A sample animation

CHAPTER 5

CREATING SPECIAL EFFECTS

Introduction

Now that you are familiar with the basics of Flash, you can begin to apply some of the special features, such as special effects and sound effects, that can enhance a movie. Special effects can provide variety and add interest to a movie, as well as draw the viewer's attention to a location or event in the movie. One type of special effect is a spotlight that highlights an area(s) of the movie or reveals selected content on the Stage as it passes over the content. You can use sound effects to enhance a movie by creating moods and dramatizing events. In addition, you can add sound to a button to provide feedback to the viewer when the button is clicked. Video can be incorporated into a Flash movie and effects, such as fading in and out, can be applied to the display of the video.

Another type of special effect is an animated navigation bar, for example, one that causes a drop-down menu to open when the user rolls over a button. This effect can be created using masks and invisible buttons.

Additional features of Adobe Flash CS6 are Inverse Kinematics, 3D Effects, and the Deco tool. Inverse kinematics allows you to easily create character animations and even allows users to interact with the character when viewing the Flash movie. The 3D tools allow you to create 3D effects such as objects moving and rotating through 3D space. The Deco tool provides a variety of drawing effects that can be used to create environments and decorative patterns.

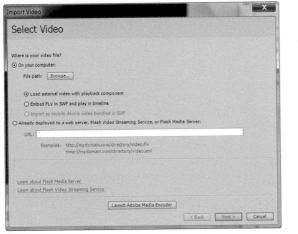

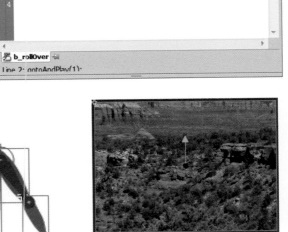

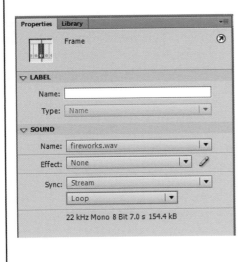

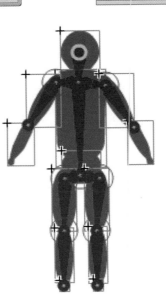

Create A
MASK EFFECT

What You'll Do

Clas

ssic (

Car (

Club

 In this lesson, you will apply a mask effect.

Understanding Mask Layers

A **mask layer** allows you to cover up the objects on one or more layers and, at the same time, create a window through which you can view objects on those layer(s). You can determine the size and shape of the window and specify whether it moves around the Stage. Moving the window around the Stage can create effects such as a spotlight that highlights certain content on the Stage, drawing the viewer's attention to a specific location. Because the window can move around the Stage, you can use a mask layer to reveal only the area of the Stage and the objects you want the viewer to see.

You need at least two layers on the Timeline when you are working with a mask layer. One layer, called the mask layer, contains the window object through which you view the objects, which are on a second layer below the mask layer. The second layer, called the masked layer, contains the object(s) that are viewed through the window. Figure 1 shows how a mask layer works: The top part of the figure shows the mask layer with the window in the shape of a circle. The next part of the figure shows the

layer to be masked. The last part of the figure shows the result of applying the mask. Figure 1 illustrates the simplest use of a mask layer. In most cases, you want to have other objects appear on the Stage and have the mask layer affect only a certain portion of the Stage.

The process for using a mask layer follows:

- Insert a new layer that will become the masked layer—add the objects that you want to display through the mask layer window. Alternately, you can use an existing layer that already contains the objects you want to mask.
- Insert a new layer above the masked layer that will become the mask layer. A mask layer always masks the layer(s) immediately below it.
- Draw a filled shape, such as a circle, or create an instance of a symbol that will become the window on the mask layer. Flash ignores bitmaps, gradients, transparency colors, and line styles on a mask layer. On a mask layer, filled areas become transparent and non-filled areas become opaque when viewed over a masked layer.

- Select the layer you want to be the mask layer and open the Layer Properties dialog box. To open the Layer Properties dialog box, click Modify on the menu bar, point to the Timeline, then click Layer Properties. In the Layer Properties dialog box, select Mask as the layer type. Flash converts the layer to the mask layer.
- Select the layer you want to apply the mask to and open the Layer Properties dialog box, then select Masked as the layer type. Flash converts the layer to the masked layer.
- Lock both the mask and masked layers.
- To mask additional layers: Drag an existing layer beneath the mask layer, or create a new layer beneath the mask layer and use the Layer Properties dialog box to convert it to a masked layer. Adding additional masked layers allows you to reveal more than one object with the same mask layer. For example, you could have a mask layer that reveals constellations on one masked layer and animated shooting stars on another masked layer.
- To unlink a masked layer: Drag it above the mask layer, or select it and select Normal from the Layer Properties dialog box.

Figure 1 *A mask layer with a window*

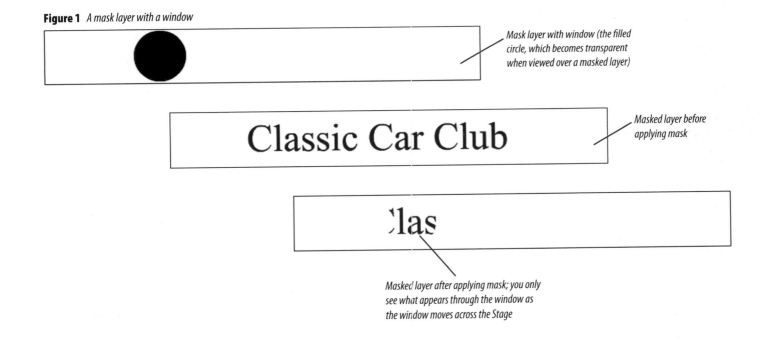

Mask layer with window (the filled circle, which becomes transparent when viewed over a masked layer)

Classic Car Club

Masked layer before applying mask

̦las

Masked layer after applying mask; you only see what appears through the window as the window moves across the Stage

Create a mask layer

1. Open fl5_1.fla, then save it as **classicCC.fla**.

2. Insert a **new layer**, name it **mask**, then click **frame 1** on the mask layer.

3. Select the **Oval tool** ⬭ on the Tools panel, set the Stroke Color to **No Stroke** ☑ on the top row of the color palette.

4. Set the Fill Color to the **black color swatch** in the left column of the color palette.

5. Draw the circle shown in Figure 2, click the **Selection tool** ▶ on the Tools panel, then drag a **marquee** around the circle to select it.

6. Click **Insert** on the menu bar, click **Motion Tween**, then click **OK** to convert the drawing into a symbol so that it can be tweened.

   Note: Flash converts the object to a movie symbol as the default symbol type. To convert the object to a different symbol type, you must convert the symbol manually.

7. Click **frame 40** on the mask layer, then drag the **circle** to the position shown in Figure 3.

8. Click **mask** on the Timeline to select the mask layer, click **Modify** on the menu bar, point to **Timeline**, then click **Layer Properties**.

9. Verify that the Show check box is selected in the Name area, click the **Lock check box** to select it, click the **Mask option button** in the Type area, then click **OK**.

   The mask layer has a shaded mask icon next to it on the Timeline.

   Hint: Alternately, you can lock the layer using the Lock This Layer icon on the Timeline.

   (continued)

Figure 2 *Object to be used as the window on a mask layer*

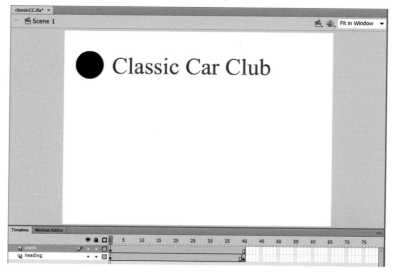

Figure 3 *Repositioning the circle*

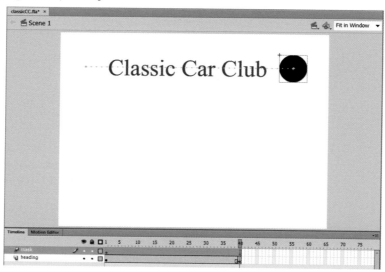

Figure 4 *The completed Layer Properties dialog box*

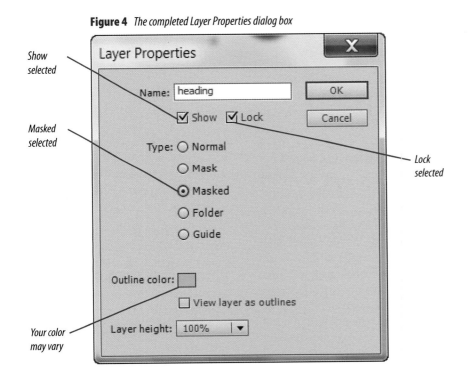

Show
selected

Masked
selected

Lock
selected

Your color
may vary

10. Play the movie from frame 1 and notice how the circle object covers the text on the heading layer as it moves across the Stage.

   Note: The circle object will not become transparent until a masked layer is created beneath it.

You created a mask layer containing a circle object that moves across the Stage.

Create a masked layer

1. Click **heading** on the Timeline to select the heading layer, click **Modify** on the menu bar, point to **Timeline,** then click **Layer Properties** to open the Layer Properties dialog box.

2. Verify that the Show check box is selected in the Name area, click the **Lock check box** to select it, click the **Masked option button** in the Type area, compare your dialog box to Figure 4, then click **OK.**

   The text on the Stage seems to disappear. The heading layer is indented and has a shaded masked icon next to it on the Timeline.

3. Play the movie and notice how the circle object acts as a window to display the text on the heading layer.

4. Click **Control** on the menu bar, point to **Test Movie,** then click **in Flash Professional.**

5. View the movie, then close the Flash Player window.

6. Save your work, then close the movie.

You used the Layer Properties dialog box to create a masked layer.

Lesson 1   Create A Mask Effect

Add
SOUND

What You'll Do

In this lesson, you will add sound to an animation and to a button click event.

Incorporating Animation and Sound

Sound can be extremely useful in a Flash movie. Sounds are often the only effective way to convey an idea, elicit an emotion, dramatize a point, and provide feedback to a user's action, such as clicking a button. How would you describe in words or show in an animation the sound a whale makes? Think about how chilling it is to hear the footsteps on the stairway of a haunted house. Consider how useful it is to hear the pronunciation of "buenos dias" as you are studying Spanish. All types of sounds can be incorporated into a Flash movie: for example, CD-quality music that might be used as background for a movie; narrations that help explain what the user is seeing; various sound effects, such as a car horn beeping; and recordings of special events, such as a presidential speech or a rock concert.

The process for adding a sound to a movie follows:

■ Import a sound file into a Flash movie; Flash places the sound file in the movie's library.

■ Create a new layer.
■ Select the desired frame on the new layer where you want the sound to play and drag the sound symbol to the Stage.

Instead of dragging the sound symbol to the Stage, you can use the Properties panel, as shown in Figure 5, to select the desired sound file. You can also use options in the Properties panel to specify special effects (such as Fade in and Fade out).

In addition to adding a sound to a layer, you can sync a sound with a button. For example, you might want to have a sound play when a button is clicked. The process for synchronizing a sound to a button follows:

■ Display the Edit window for the button.
■ Add a layer. The sound should be on its own layer.
■ Select the frame for the desired button event (such as down).
■ Use the Properties panel to select the sound file.
■ Select Event as the Sync option.
■ Exit the Edit window and return to the Stage.

You can place more than one sound file on a layer, and you can place sounds on layers that have other objects. However, it is recommended that you place each sound on a separate layer so that it is easier to identify and edit. In Figure 6, the sound layer shows a wave pattern that extends from frame 1 to frame 24. The wave pattern gives some indication of the volume of the sound at any particular frame. The higher spikes in the pattern indicate a louder sound. The wave pattern also gives some indication of the pitch.

The denser the wave pattern, the lower the pitch. You can alter the sound by adding or removing frames. However, removing frames may create undesired effects. It is best to make changes to a sound file using a sound-editing program.

You can import the following sound file formats into Flash:

- ASND (Windows or Macintosh)
- WAV (Windows only)
- AIFF (Macintosh only)

- MP3 (Windows or Macintosh)

If you have QuickTime 4 or later installed on your computer, you can import these additional sound file formats:

- AIFF (Windows or Macintosh)
- SD 2 (Sound Designer II; Macintosh only)
- MOV or QT (Sound Only QuickTime Movies; Windows or Macintosh)
- AU (Sun AU; Windows or Macintosh)
- SND (System 7 Sounds; Macintosh only)
- WAV (Windows or Macintosh)

Figure 5 *Properties panel Sound options*

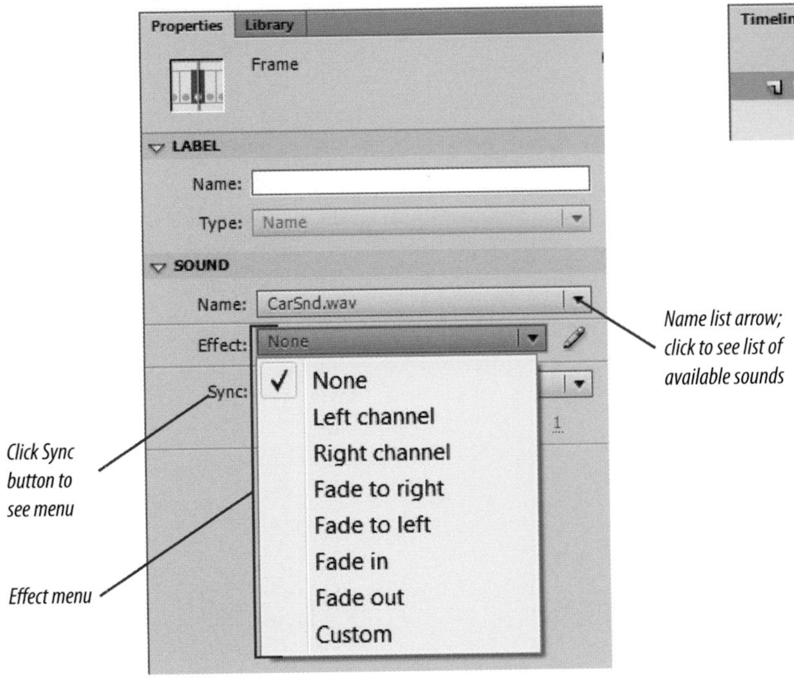

Click Sync button to see menu

Effect menu

Name list arrow; click to see list of available sounds

Figure 6 *A wave pattern displayed on a sound layer*

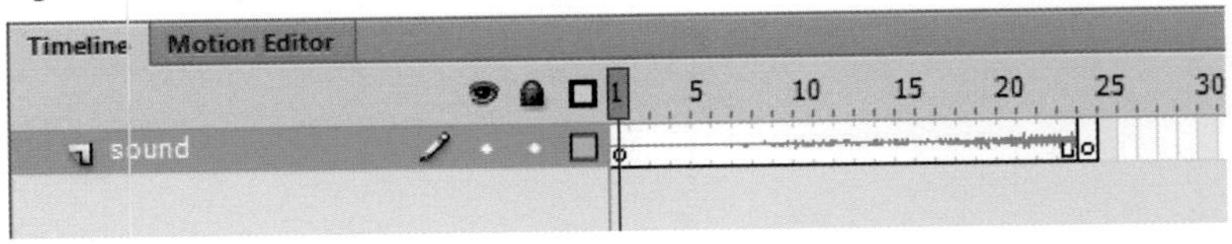

Add sound to a movie

1. Open fl5_2.fla, then save it as **rallySnd.fla**.

2. Play the movie and notice that there is no sound.

3. Click the **stopMovie layer**, insert a **new layer**, then name it **carSnd**.

4. Insert a **keyframe** in frame 72 on the carSnd layer.

5. Click **File** on the menu bar, point to **Import**, then click **Import to Library**.

6. Use the Import to Library dialog box to navigate to the drive and folder where your Data Files are stored, click the **CarSnd.wav file**, then click **Open**.

7. Display the Library panel, click **CarSnd.wav**, then click the **Play button** in the Preview window.

8. Click **frame 72** on the carSnd layer.

9. Drag the **CarSnd sound symbol** 🔊 to the Stage, as shown in Figure 7.

   After releasing the mouse button, notice the wave pattern that has been placed on the carSnd layer starting in frame 72.

TIP The wave pattern may not appear on the layer until the movie is played one time.

10. Change the frame rate to **12 fps**.

11. Click **Control** on the menu bar, point to **Test Movie**, then click **in Flash Professional**.

12. Click the **Click to continue button** to move the playhead to the frame that starts the sound.

13. Close the Flash Player window.

You imported a sound and added it to a movie.

Figure 7 *Dragging the CarSnd symbol to the Stage*

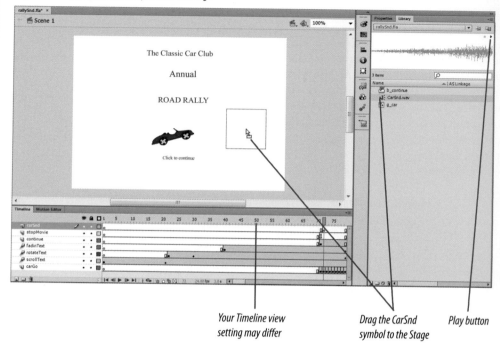

Your Timeline view setting may differ

Drag the CarSnd symbol to the Stage

Play button

Figure 8 *The Timeline for the button with the sound layer*

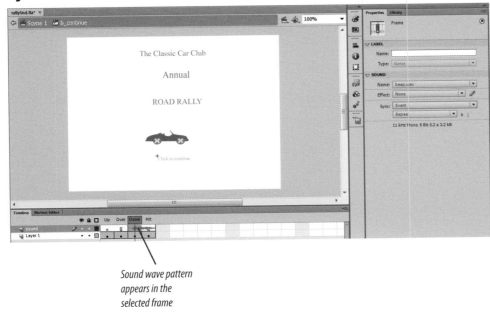

Sound wave pattern appears in the selected frame

1. Click **frame 71** on the carSnd layer.

2. Click the **Selection tool** ▶ on the Tools panel, drag a **marquee** around "Click to continue" to select the button, then double-click the **button** to display the button's Timeline.

3. Insert a **new layer** above Layer 1, then name it **sound**.

4. Click the **Down frame** on the sound layer, click **Insert** on the menu bar, point to **Timeline**, then click **Blank Keyframe**.

5. Click **File** on the menu bar, point to **Import**, then click **Import to Library**.

6. Use the Import to Library dialog box to navigate to the drive and folder where your Data Files are stored, click the **beep.wav file**, then click **Open**.

7. Display the Properties panel, click the **Name list arrow** in the SOUND area, then click **beep.wav**.

8. Click the **Sync list arrow** in the Properties panel, click **Event**, then compare your screen to Figure 8.

9. Click **Scene 1** on the upper left of the edit window title bar to display the main Timeline.

10. Test the movie.

11. Click the **Click to continue button** and listen to the sounds, then close the Flash Player window.

12. Save your work, then close the movie.

You added a sound layer to a button, imported a sound, then attached the sound to the button.

Adding Sounds to a Movie's Timeline and to a Button's Timeline

When adding a sound to a movie's Timeline, the sound will play when the playhead reaches the frame containing the sound wave. In some instances, the user may need to click a button to cause the playhead to move to the frame containing the sound wave. However, in these instances, the sound is not associated with the button because the sound is part of the movie's Timeline and not part of the button's Timeline. To associate a sound with a button, you place the sound wave on the Timeline for the button. Then, whenever the button is pressed, the sound plays.

Add
VIDEO

What You'll Do

In this lesson, you will import a video, add actions to video control buttons, and then synchronize sound to a video clip.

Incorporating Video

Adobe Flash allows you to import FLV (Flash video) files that then can be used in a Flash document. Flash provides several ways to add video to a movie, depending on the application and, especially, the file size. Video content can be embedded directly into a Flash document, progressively downloaded, or streamed.

Embedded video becomes part of the SWF file similar to other objects, such as sound and graphics. A placeholder appears on the Stage and is used to display the video during playback. If the video is imported as a movie clip symbol, then the placeholder can be edited, including rotating, resizing, and even animating it. Because embedded video becomes part of the SWF file, the technique of embedding video is best used for small video clips in order to keep the document file size small. The process for embedding video is to import a video file using the Import Video Wizard. Then, you place the video on the Stage and add controls as desired. Figure 9 shows a video placeholder for an embedded video. The video file (fireworks.flv) is in the Library panel and the video layer on the Timeline contains the video object. The embedded video plays when the Play button is clicked.

Progressive downloading allows you to use ActionScript to load an external FLV file into a SWF file; the video then plays when the SWF file is played. With progressive downloading, the FLV file resides outside the SWF file. As a result, the SWF file size can be kept smaller than when the video is embedded in the Flash document. The video begins playing soon after the first part of the file has been downloaded.

Streaming video provides a constant connection between the user and the video delivery. Streaming has several advantages over the other methods of delivering video, including starting the video more quickly and allowing for live video delivery. However, streaming video requires the Flash Media Server, an Adobe software product designed specifically for streaming video content.

Using the Import Video Wizard

The Import Video Wizard is used to import FLV files into Flash documents. The wizard, in a step-by-step process, leads you through a series of windows that allow you to select the file to be imported and the deployment method (embedded, progressive, streaming). In addition, you can specify whether or not to have the video converted to a movie clip symbol which allows you to animate the placeholder. The wizard appears when you choose the Import Video command from the Import option on the File menu.

Using the Adobe Media Encoder

The Adobe Media Encoder is an application used by Flash to convert various video file formats, such as .mov, .avi, and .mpeg, to the FLV (Flash Video) format so the videos can be used with Flash. The Encoder allows you to, among other things, choose the size of the placeholder the video will play in, edit the video, and insert cue points that can be used to synchronize the video with animations and sound. Figure 10 shows the Encoder, which is open and ready to convert the fireworks.mov video (Source Name) to fireworks.flv (Output File). The Start Queue button is used to start the process. When the conversion is complete, a green check mark is displayed in the Status column. The Adobe Media Encoder can be accessed through the Import Video Wizard.

Figure 9 *An embedded video*

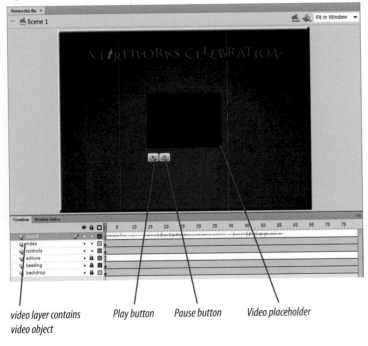

video layer contains video object   Play button   Pause button   Video placeholder

Figure 10 *The Adobe Media Encoder*

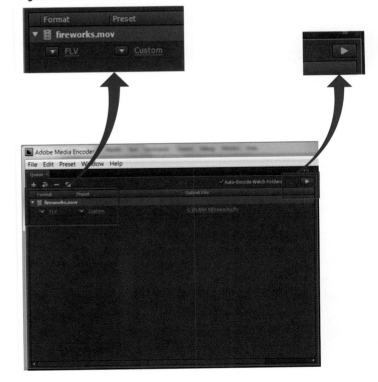

Import a video

1. Open fl5_3.fla, then save it as **fireworks.fla**.

   The movie has four layers and 85 frames. The backdrop layer contains a blue gradient backdrop object. The heading layer contains the text object. The actions layer has a stop action in frame 1. The controls layer contains Play and Pause buttons that will be used to control the video. The Library panel contains the two button symbols and a sound file as well as graphics and movie clip files.

2. Set the view to **Fit in Window**.

3. Insert a **new layer** above the controls layer, name it **video**, then click **frame 1** on the video layer.

4. Click **File** on the menu bar, point to **Import**, then click **Import Video**.

   The Import Video Wizard begins by asking for the path to the video file and the desired method for importing the file, as shown in Figure 11.

5. Click the **Embed FLV in SWF and play in timeline option button**.

6. Click **Browse**, navigate to the drive and folder where your Data Files are stored, click **fireworks.mov**, then click **Open**.

   A message appears indicating that the video format is not valid for embedding video. You must convert the file to the FLV format.

7. Click **OK**, then click the **Launch Adobe Media Encoder button**.

   Note: If a message about browsing to the file after it is converted opens, click OK.

   (continued)

Figure 11 *The Import Video Wizard*

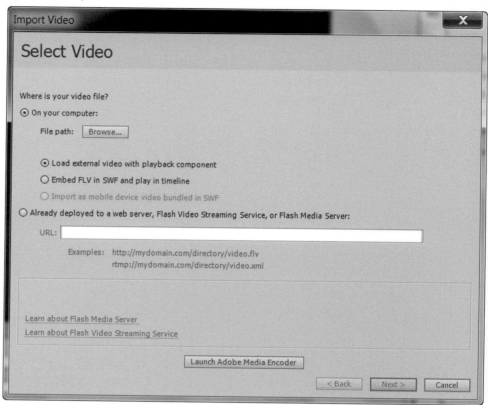

Creating Special Effects

Figure 12 *The completed Select Video window*

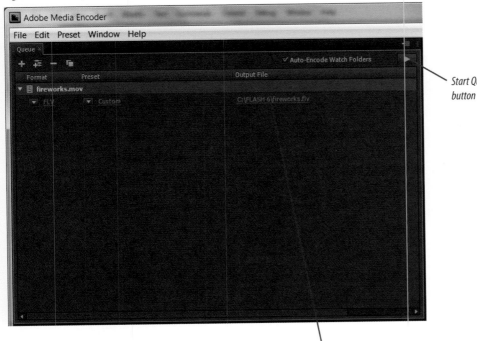

Start Queue
button

Your path may vary

After several moments the encoder opens.

Note: Click the Adobe Media Encoder button on the taskbar if the encoder does not open automatically in its own window.

8. Click the **Start Queue button**, as shown in Figure 12.

   When the process is done, the green Start Queue arrow will dim and a green check mark will appear next to the word Done.

9. Close the encoder window.

10. Click **OK** to close the message window if one opens, then click the **Browse button**.

11. Click **fireworks.flv**, then click **Open**.

    Note: If you do not see fireworks.flv, navigate to the drive and folder where you saved your solution file.

    The Select Video screen displays the path to the fireworks.flv file below the Browse button.

12. Click **Next**.

    The Embedding screen opens, which allows you to specify how you would like to embed the video.

13. Read the screen and verify all the options have a check mark.

14. Click **Next**.

15. Read the Finish Video Import screen, then click **Finish**.

    The video is encoded and placed on the Stage and in the Library panel.

You imported a video then specified the encoding and embed type.

Attach actions to video control buttons

1. Click **Control** on the menu bar, point to **Test Movie**, then click in **Flash Professional**.

2. Click the **control buttons**.

   Nothing happens because there is a stop action in frame 1 and no actions have been assigned to the buttons.

3. Close the Flash Player window.

4. Open the Actions panel.

5. Click the **Play button** on the Stage, then verify the btn_play button symbol appears in the lower-left corner of the Script pane.

6. Turn on Script Assist if it is off.

7. Click the **Add a new item to the script button**, point to **Global Functions**, point to **Timeline Control**, then click **play** as shown in Figure 13.

8. Click the **Pause button** on the Stage, then verify the btn_pause button symbol appears in the lower-left corner of the Script pane.

9. Click the **Add a new item to the script button**, point to **Global Functions**, point to **Timeline Control**, then click **stop**.

10. Close the Actions panel.

11. Test the movie, click the **Play button**, then click the **Pause button**.

    The video plays, however there is no sound.

12. Close the Flash Player window.

You assigned play and stop actions to video control buttons.

Figure 13 *Using Script Assist to assign a play action to a button*

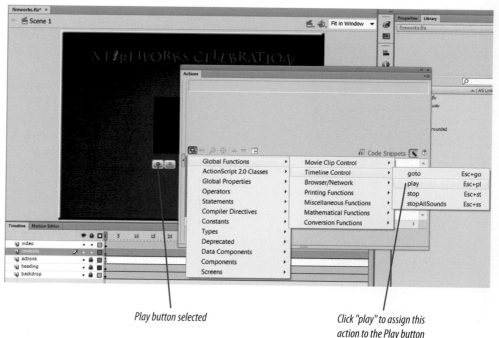

Play button selected

Click "play" to assign this action to the Play button

Figure 14 *The completed Properties panel*

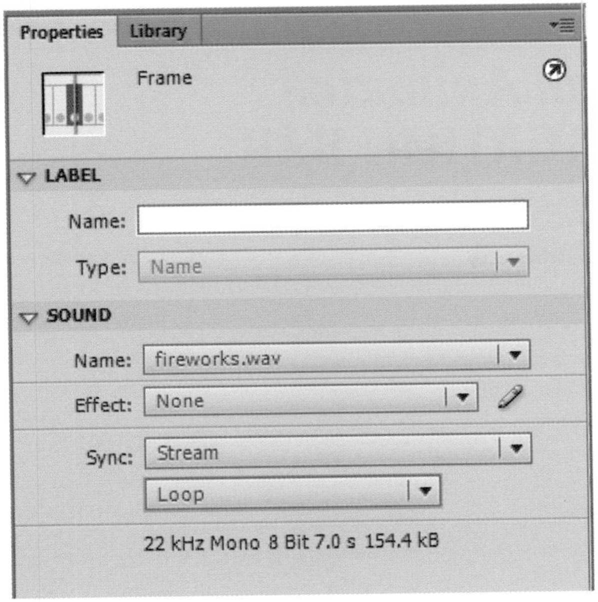

```
Properties  Library                              ≡
         ┌──┐
         │▮▮│     Frame                          ⊙
         └──┘

▽ LABEL
      Name: [_____]

      Type: [ Name                    |▼]

▽ SOUND
      Name: [ fireworks.wav          |▼]

     Effect: [ None              |▼]  🖉

      Sync: [ Stream             |▼]

            [ Loop              |▼]

        22 kHz Mono 8 Bit 7.0 s  154.4 kB
```

Synchronize sound to a video clip

1. Insert a **new layer** above the video layer, then name it **sound**.

2. Click **frame 1** on the sound layer.

3. Display the Library panel.

4. Click **fireworks.wav** to display the sound wave pattern in the Preview window.

5. Click the **Play button** ▶ in the Preview window, then click the **Stop button** ■.

6. Display the Properties panel, then display the SOUND area options.

7. Click the **Name list arrow** in the SOUND area, then click **fireworks.wav**.

8. Click the **Sync sound list arrow** in the SOUND area, then click **Stream**.

9. Click the **Repeat list arrow**, click **Loop**, then compare your Properties panel to Figure 14.

10. Test the movie, click the **Play button**, then click the **Pause button**.

11. Close the Flash Player window.

12. Lock all layers.

13. Save your work, then close the file.

You inserted a layer, then you synchronized a sound to the video clip.

Create an Animated
NAVIGATION BAR

What You'll Do

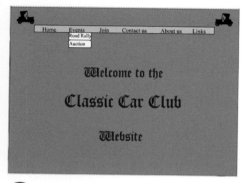

In this lesson, you will work through the process to create one drop-down menu.

Understanding Animated Navigation Bars

A common navigation scheme for a website is a navigation bar with drop-down menus, such as the one shown in Figure 15. Using a navigation bar has several advantages. First, it allows the developer to provide several menu options to the user without cluttering the screen, thereby providing more screen space for the website content. Second, it allows the user to go quickly to a location on the site without having to navigate several screens to find the desired content. Third, it provides consistency in function and appearance, making it easy for users to learn and work with the navigation scheme.

There are various ways to create drop-down menus using the animation capabilities of Flash and ActionScript. One common technique allows you to give the illusion of a drop-down menu by using masks that reveal

Figure 15 *Navigation bar with drop-down menus*

the menu. When the user points to (rolls over) a menu item on the navigation bar, a list or "menu" of buttons is displayed ("drops down"). Then the user can click a button, which might go to another location in the website or trigger some other action, depending on the action assigned to the button. The dropping down of the list is actually an illusion created by using a mask to "uncover" the menu options.

The process for creating a drop-down menu follows:

- **Create a navigation bar.** This could be as basic as a background graphic in the shape of a rectangle with buttons that represent the navigation bar menu items.
- **Position the drop-down buttons.** Add a drop-down buttons layer beneath the navigation bar layer. Next, select an empty frame adjacent to the first frame containing the navigation bar. Place the buttons that will be used to create the drop down list on the Stage below their respective menu items on the navigation bar. For example, if the navigation bar has an Events button with two choices, Road Rally and Auction, that you want to appear as buttons on

Creating Special Effects

a drop-down menu, position these two buttons below the Events button on the drop-down buttons layer.

- **Create an animated mask.** Add a mask layer above the drop-down buttons layer and create an animation of an object that starts above the drop-down buttons and moves down to reveal them. Then change the layer to a mask layer and the drop-down buttons layer to a masked layer.
- **Assign actions to the drop-down buttons.** Select each drop-down button and assign an action, such as "on (release) gotoAndPlay."
- **Assign a roll over action to the navigation bar menu item button.** The desired effect is to have the drop-down buttons appear when the user points to a navigation bar button. Therefore, you need to assign an "on rollOver" action to the navigation bar button that causes the playhead to go to the frame that plays the animation on the mask layer. This can be done using the Script Assist feature.
- **Create an invisible button.** When the user points to a navigation bar button, the drop-down menu appears showing the drop-down buttons. There needs to be a way to have the menu disappear when the user points away from the navigation bar button. This can be done by creating a button on a layer below the masked layer. This button is slightly larger than the drop-down buttons and their navigation bar button, as shown in Figure 16.

A rollOver action is assigned to this button so that when the user rolls off the drop-down or navigation bar buttons, he or she rolls onto this button and the action is carried out. This button should be made transparent so the user does not see it.

Using Frame Labels

Until now, you have worked with frame numbers in ActionScript code when creating a goto action. Frame labels can also be used in the code. You can assign a label to a frame as an identifier. For example, you could assign the label home to frame 10 and then create a goto home action that will cause the playhead to jump to frame 10. One advantage of using frame labels is that if you insert frames on the Timeline, the label adjusts for the added frames. So, you do not have to change the ActionScript that uses the frame label. Another advantage is that the descriptive labels help you identify parts of the movie

as you work with the Timeline. You assign a frame label by selecting the desired frame and typing a label in the Frame text box in the Properties panel.

Understanding Scenes

When you create a movie, the phrase Scene 1 appears above the Stage. You can add scenes to a movie at any time. Scenes are one way to organize long movies. For example, a movie created for a website could be divided into several scenes: an introduction, a home page, and content pages. Each scene has its own Timeline. You can insert a new scene by opening the Insert menu and selecting Scene. You can view a scene by opening the Other Panels option on the Windows menu and then selecting a scene to view. Scenes can be given descriptive names and referenced in ActionScript code, which allows users to jump from scene to scene. One drawback to using scenes is potentially larger file sizes.

Figure 16 *A button that will be assigned a rollOver action*

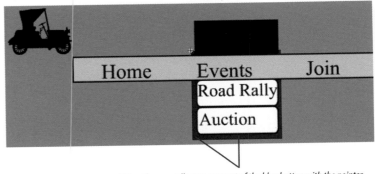

When the user rolls over any part of the blue button with the pointer, a script is executed that causes the drop-down menu to disappear

Position the drop-down buttons

1. Open fl5_4.fla, then save it as **navBar.fla**.

   This file contains a navigation bar, scenes, and many objects in the library.

2. Click **Window** on the menu bar, click **Other Panels**, click **Scene**, then click **Scene 2** to view Scene 2 and its associated Timeline.

   This scene was created as part of the entire movie by selecting Scene from the Insert menu to display a blank Timeline.

3. Press **[Enter]** (Win) or **[return]** (Mac) to play the scene, click **Scene 1**, then close the Scene panel.

   This returns you to the main scene.

4. Click the **homeBkgrnd layer**, insert a **new layer**, then name it **roadRally**.

5. Click **frame 2** on the roadRally layer, then insert a **keyframe**.

6. Display the Library panel, open the Buttons folder, then drag the **b_roadRally button** to the position just below the Events button on the Navigation bar, as shown in Figure 17.

   (continued)

Figure 17 *Positioning the b_roadRally button*

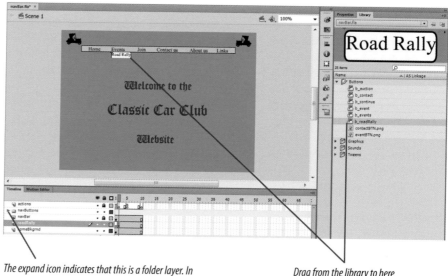

The expand icon indicates that this is a folder layer. In this case, all of the navigation bar buttons are within this folder. Clicking the arrow reveals the contents of the folder.

Drag from the library to here

Creating Special Effects

Figure 18 *Positioning the buttons*

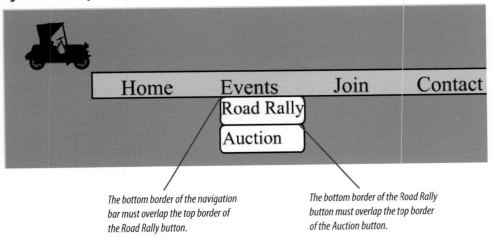

The bottom border of the navigation bar must overlap the top border of the Road Rally button.

The bottom border of the Road Rally button must overlap the top border of the Auction button.

7. Insert a **new layer** above the homeBkgrnd layer, then name it **auction**.

8. Click **frame 2** on the auction layer, then insert a **keyframe**.

9. Drag the **b_auction button** from the Library panel and position it below the b_roadRally button.

10. Click the **Zoom tool** 🔍 on the Tools panel, then click the **Events button** on the navigation bar to enlarge the view.

11. Click the **Selection tool** ➤ on the Tools panel, then click each button and use the arrow keys to position each button, as shown in Figure 18, making sure the bottom border overlaps with the border of the object beneath it.

You placed the drop-down buttons on the Stage and repositioned them.

Add a mask layer

1. Click the **roadRally layer**, insert a **new layer** above the roadRally layer, then name it **mask**.

2. Click **frame 2** on the mask layer, then insert a **keyframe**.

3. Select the **Rectangle tool** on the Tools panel, set the Stroke Color to **No Stroke**, then set the Fill Color to **black**.

4. Draw a **rectangle** that covers the buttons, as shown in Figure 19.

5. Click the **Selection tool** on the Tools panel, then drag the **rectangle** to above the buttons, as shown in Figure 20.

6. Verify the rectangle is selected, click **Insert** on the menu bar, click **Motion Tween**, then click **OK**.

Note: Flash automatically converts the object to a movie symbol, which can have a motion tween applied to it. If you want the object to be a different type of symbol, you need to convert the object to the symbol type of your choice before inserting the motion tween.

(continued)

Figure 19 *The drawn rectangle that covers the buttons*

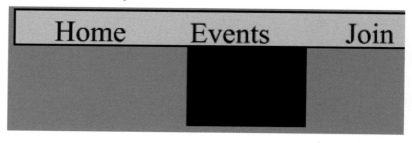

Figure 20 *Dragging the rectangle above the buttons*

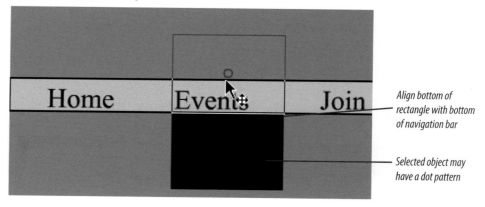

Align bottom of rectangle with bottom of navigation bar

Selected object may have a dot pattern

Figure 21 *Positioning the rectangle over the buttons*

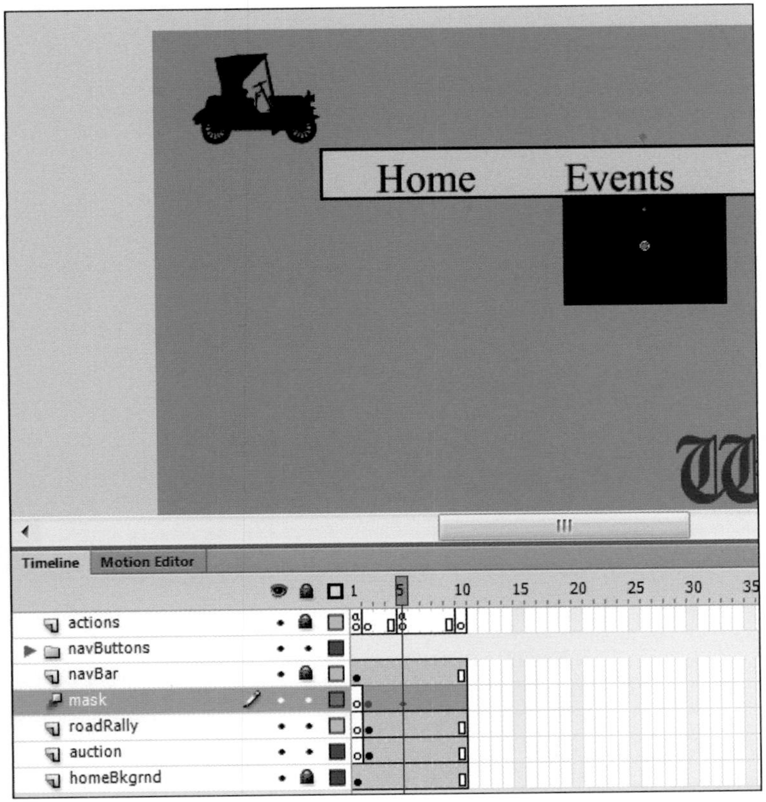

7. Click **frame 5** on the mask layer, then insert a **keyframe**.

8. Use the **Selection tool** ![arrow] to move the **rectangle**, as shown in Figure 21.

9. Click **mask** on the Timeline, click **Modify** on the menu bar, point to **Timeline**, click **Layer Properties**, click the **Mask option button**, then click **OK**.

10. Click **roadRally** on the Timeline.

11. Click **Modify** on the menu bar, point to **Timeline**, click **Layer Properties**, click the **Masked option button**, then click **OK**.

12. Click **auction** on the Timeline, then repeat step 11.

13. Drag the **playhead** along the Timeline, noticing how the mask hides and reveals the buttons.

You added a mask that animates to hide and reveal the menu buttons.

Assign an action to a drop-down button

1. Change the view to **Fit in Window.**

2. Click **frame 2** on the roadRally layer, then click the **Road Rally button** to select it.

3. Open the Actions panel, then verify the Script Assist button is active and b_roadRally is displayed in the lower-left corner of the Script pane, as shown in Figure 22.

   b_roadRally in the lower-left corner of the Script pane tells you that the b_roadRally button symbol is selected on the Stage and that the ActionScript you create will apply to this object.

4. Click the **Add a new item to the script icon** , point to **Global Functions**, point to **Timeline Control**, then click **goto.**

5. Click the **Scene list arrow**, point to **Scene 2** as shown in Figure 23, then click.

6. Verify the Type is set to Frame Number and the Frame is set to 1.

7. Collapse the Actions panel.

You used the Script Assist window to assign a goto action to a menu button.

Figure 22 *The Actions panel with the b_roadRally button selected*

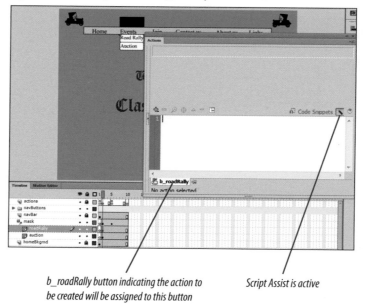

b_roadRally button indicating the action to be created will be assigned to this button

Script Assist is active

Figure 23 *Selecting the scene to go to*

Scenes, which have their own Timeline, are a way to organize large movies. In this case, Scene 2 contains the Road Rally screen for the website.

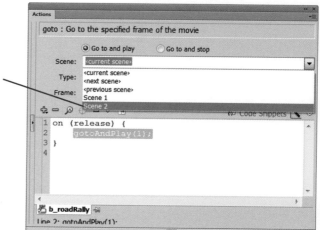

Creating Special Effects

Figure 24 *Specifying a frame label*

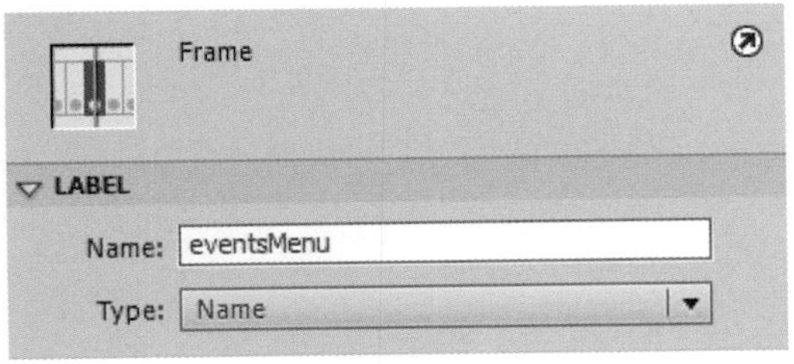

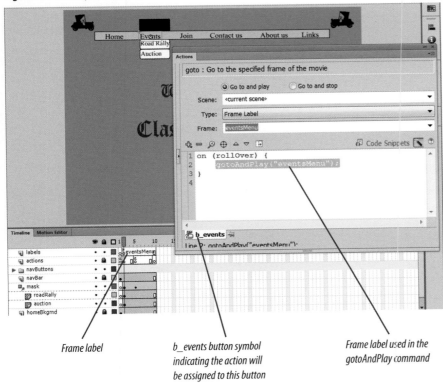

Figure 25 *The completed Actions panel*

Frame label

b_events button symbol indicating the action will be assigned to this button

Frame label used in the gotoAndPlay command

Add a frame label and assign a rollOver action

1. Insert a **new layer** at the top of the Timeline, name it **labels**, then insert a **keyframe** in frame 2 on the labels layer.

2. Display the Properties panel, click inside the **Name text box** in the LABEL area, then type **eventsMenu**, as shown in Figure 24.

3. Click the **Events button** on the Stage to select it.

4. Expand the Actions panel, then verify b_events is displayed in the lower-left corner of the Script pane.

5. Click the **Add a new item to the script icon** ✛ , point to **Global Functions**, point to **Movie Clip Control**, then click **on**.

6. Click the **Release check box** to deselect it, then click the **Roll Over check box** to select it.

7. Click the **Add a new item to the script icon** ✛ , point to **Global Functions**, point to **Timeline Control**, then click **goto**.

8. Click the **Type list arrow**, then click **Frame Label**.

9. Click the **Frame list arrow**, then click **eventsMenu**.

   Your screen should resemble Figure 25.

10. Click **Control** on the menu bar, point to **Test Movie**, then click **in Flash Professional**.

11. Point to **Events**, then click **Road Rally**.

12. Close the Flash Player window, collapse the Actions panel, then save your work.

You added a frame label and assigned a rollOver action using the frame label.

Add an invisible button

1. Click **Control** on the menu bar, point to **Test Movie**, then click **in Flash Professional**.

2. Move the pointer over Events on the navigation bar, then move the pointer away from Events.

   Notice that when you point to Events, the drop-down menu appears. However, when you move the pointer away from the menu, it does not disappear.

3. Close the Flash Player window.

4. Insert a **new layer** above the homeBkgrnd layer, then name it **rollOver**.

5. Insert a **keyframe** in frame 2 on the rollOver layer.

6. Click the **Zoom tool** 🔍 on the Tools panel, then click the **Events button** on the navigation bar to enlarge the view.

7. Select the **Rectangle tool** 🔲 on the Tools panel, verify that the Stroke Color is set to No Stroke ☑ , then set the Fill Color to **blue**.

8. Draw a **rectangle**, as shown in Figure 26.

9. Click the **Selection tool** ▸ on the Tools panel, then click the **blue rectangle** to select it.

10. Click **Modify** on the menu bar, then click **Convert to Symbol**.

11. Type **b_rollOver** for the name, click the **Type list arrow**, click **Button**, then click **OK**.

12. Expand the Actions panel.

(continued)

Figure 26 *Drawing the rectangle*

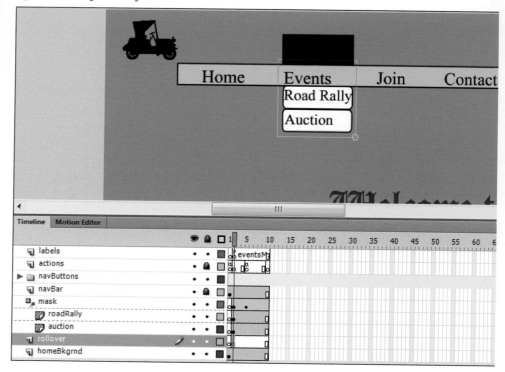

Figure 27 *The Actions panel displaying ActionScript assigned to the b_rollOver button symbol*

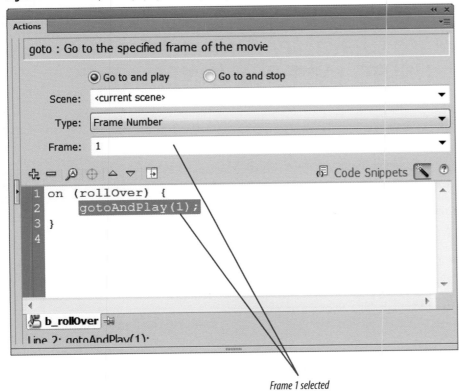

Frame 1 selected

13. Verify the rollOver button is selected and b_rollOver is displayed in the lower-left corner of the Script pane.

14. Click the **Add a new item to the script icon**, point to **Global Functions**, point to **Movie Clip Control**, then click **on**.

15. Click the **Release check box** to deselect it, then click the **Roll Over check box** to select it.

16. Click the **Add a new item to the script icon**, point to **Global Functions**, point to **Timeline Control**, then click **goto**.

17. Verify Frame 1 is specified, as shown in Figure 27.

18. Close the Actions panel.

19. Click the **Style list arrow** in the COLOR EFFECT area of the Properties panel, click **Alpha**, then set the percentage to **0**.

20. Click **Control** on the menu bar, point to **Test Movie**, then click **in Flash Professional**.

21. Point to **Events** to display the drop-down menu, then slowly move the pointer away from Events.

    The drop-down menu disappears.

22. Close the Flash Player window, then save and close the movie.

You added a button and assigned a rollOver action to it, then made the button transparent.

Create Character Animations
USING INVERSE KINEMATICS

What You'll Do

In this lesson, you will use the bone tool to create a character animation and create a movie clip that can be manipulated by the viewer.

Understanding Inverse Kinematics

One way to create character animations is to use the frame-by-frame process in which you place individually drawn objects into a series of successive frames. You did this with the stick figure graphics in an earlier chapter. Those graphics were simple to draw. However, if you have more complex drawings, such as fill shapes that are more realistic, and if you want to create animations that show an unlimited number of poses, the time required to develop all of the necessary drawings would be considerable.

Flash provides a process that allows you to create a single image and add a structure to the image that can be used to animate the various parts of the image. The process is called **inverse kinematics (IK)** and involves creating an articulated structure of bones that allow you to link the parts of an image. Once the bone structure is created, you can animate the image by changing the position of any of its parts. The bone structure causes the related parts to animate in a natural way. For example, if you draw an image of a person, create the bone structure, and then move the person's right foot, then all parts of the leg

(lower leg, knee, upper leg) respond. This makes it easy to animate various movements.

Figure 28 shows a drawing of a character before and after the bone structure is added. Figure 29 shows how moving the right foot moves the entire leg. The image is made up of several small drawings, each one converted to a graphic symbol. These include a head, torso, upper and lower arms, upper and lower legs, hips, and feet. Together these form the IK object.

Creating the Bone Structure

The bone structure can be applied to a single drawn shape, such as an oval created with the Flash drawing tools. More often it is applied to an image, such as a character, made up of several drawings. When this is the case, each drawing is converted to a graphic symbol or a movie clip symbol and then assembled to form the desired image. If you import a graphic, it needs to be broken apart using the Modify menu and the individual parts of the imported graphic converted to graphic symbols or movie clip symbols. However, if the imported graphic has only one part (such as a bitmap), it needs to be broken apart and treated as a single drawn shape.

Once the image is ready, you use the Bone tool to create the bone structure, called the armature, by clicking and dragging the Bone tool pointer to link one part of the image to another. You continue adding bones to the structure until all parts of the image are linked. For a human form you would link the head to the torso and the torso to the upper left arm and the upper left arm to the lower left arm, and so on. The bones in an armature are connected to each other in a parent-child hierarchy, so that adjusting the child adjusts the parent.

Animating the IK Object

As you are creating the bone structure, a layer named Armature is added to the Timeline, and the image with the bone structure is placed in frame 1 on that layer. This new layer is called a **pose layer**. Each pose layer can contain only one armature and its associated image. Animating the image is done on this layer by inserting a keyframe in any frame after frame 1 on the Armature layer and then changing the position of one or more of the bones. This

is referred to as creating a pose. Once you specify the start and end positions of the image, Flash interpolates the position of the parts of the image for the in-between frames. So, when one bone moves, the other connected bones move in relation to it. Additional poses can be set along the Timeline by inserting keyframes and adjusting the bone structure. Animations of IK objects, other than those within movie clips, only allow you to change the shape, position, and ease in the animation.

Figure 28 *Drawings showing before and after the bone structure is added*

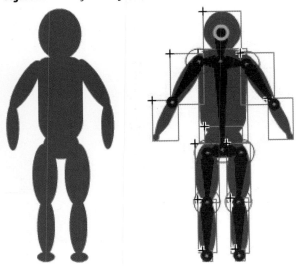

Figure 29 *Moving the foot moves the other parts of the leg*

Creating a Movie Clip with an IK Object

Movie clips provide a great deal of flexibility when animating IK objects. You can change properties such as the color effect and you can nest one movie clip within another. So, you could have a movie clip of a character walking and nest another movie clip within it to have its mouth move. In addition, you can apply a motion tween to a movie clip. So, you could have a movie clip of a character walking and have it play within a motion tween, which causes the character (movie clip) to jump over an obstacle.

Runtime Feature

Flash provides a runtime feature for manipulation of an IK object. That is, you can allow the user to click the object and adjust the image. This is useful if you are creating a game or just wanting to provide some interaction in an application. The process is to click a frame on the Armature layer, then use the Properties panel to set the Type to Runtime. The runtime feature only works with IK structures connected to drawn shapes or movie clip symbols, not graphic or button symbols. In addition, only one pose can used.

IK Objects

As you are working with IK objects, keep in mind the following:

- The Undo feature can be used to undo a series of actions such as undoing a mistake made when creating the bone structure.
- The bone structure may disappear as you are working on it. This could be caused by going outside the image as you are connecting the parts of the image. If the bone structure disappears, use the Undo feature to Undo your last action.
- To delete an individual bone and all of its children, click the bone and press [Delete]. You can select multiple bones to delete by holding down [Shift] and clicking each bone.
- To delete all bones, select the image and choose the Break Apart command from the Modify menu.
- To create IK animations, ActionScript 3.0 and Flash Player 10 need to be specified in the Publish Settings dialog box, which is displayed by choosing Publish Settings from the File menu.

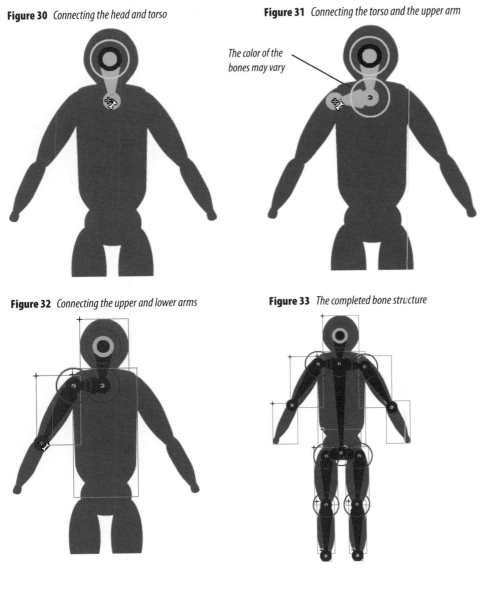

Figure 30 *Connecting the head and torso*

Figure 31 *Connecting the torso and the upper arm*

The color of the bones may vary

Figure 32 *Connecting the upper and lower arms*

Figure 33 *The completed bone structure*

Create the bone structure

1. Open fl5_5.fla, then save it as **kicker.fla**.

   This document has a graphic symbol made up of 13 individual drawings to form a character shape.

2. Click the **Selection tool** ↖, then drag a **marquee** around the image to select it.

   Notice the separate objects.

3. Click a blank area of the Stage to deselect the image.

4. Click the **Zoom tool** 🔍, then click the **image** to zoom in on it.

5. Scroll the Stage to view the head, then click the **Bone tool** 🦴 on the Tools panel.

6. Point to the middle of the head, when the pointer changes to a bone with a cross ⚒, drag the ⚒ **pointer** down to the torso as shown in Figure 30, then release the mouse button.

7. Point to the bottom of the bone, then drag the ⚒ **pointer** to the left as shown in Figure 31.

8. Point to the left end of the bone, then drag the ⚒ **pointer** down as shown in Figure 32.

   Notice that a bone connects two overlapping objects, such as the bone used to connect the upper arm and lower arm.

9. Using Figure 33 as a guide, complete the drawing of the other bones.

   Hint: Use the Undo command as needed if your connections do not match Figure 33.

10. Save your work.

You created a bone structure by connecting objects on the Stage with the Bone tool.

Animate the character

1. Change the view to **Fit in Window**.
2. Click **frame 10** on the Armature layer, then insert a **keyframe**.

   Note: The name of your Armature layer will include a number.
3. Click the **Selection tool** ![cursor], then click a blank area of the Stage to deselect the object if it is selected.
4. Point to the **right foot**, then, when the pointer changes to a bone with a delta symbol ![bone], drag the ![bone] **pointer** to position the foot as shown in Figure 34.
5. Point to the **right arm**, then use the ![bone] pointer to position it as shown in Figure 35.
6. Use the ![bone] pointer to position the left arm and left foot as shown in Figure 36.

   Hint: To position the left foot, move the left knee first, then move the left foot.
7. Click **frame 20** on the Armature layer, then insert a **keyframe**.
8. Adjust the arms and legs as shown in Figure 37.

   Hint: Move the right leg to the position shown to create a kicking motion.
9. Click the **Free Transform tool** ![icon] on the Tools panel, then drag a **marquee** around the image to select it if it is not already selected.
10. Point to the **upper-right handle**, then, when the pointer changes to an arc ![arc], drag the ![arc] **pointer** to the left as shown in Figure 38.
11. Test the movie, close the Flash Player window, then save the movie.

You animated the character by adjusting the armatures of the various bones.

Figure 34 *Positioning the right foot*

Figure 35 *Positioning the right arm*

Figure 36 *Positioning the left arm and left foot*

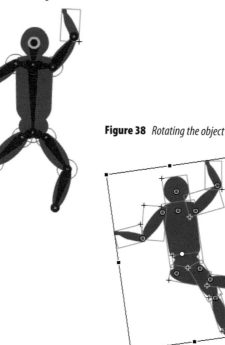

right leg

Figure 37 *Positioning the arms and legs*

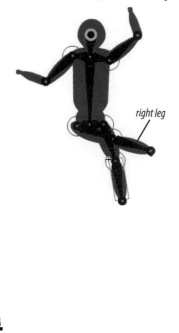

right leg

Figure 38 *Rotating the object*

Figure 39 *Increasing the length of the motion span*

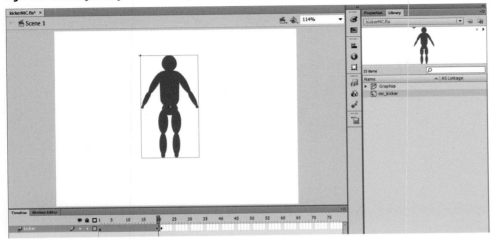

Create a movie clip of the IK object and animate the movie clip

1. Click **File** on the menu bar, click **Save as**, type **kickerMC**, then click **Save**.

2. Click **frame 1** on the Armature layer.

3. Click the **Selection tool** ▶, then drag a **marquee** around the entire image to select it.

4. Click **Modify** on the menu bar, then click **Convert to Symbol**.

5. Type **mc_kicker** for the name, select **Movie Clip** for the Type, then click **OK**.

6. Click **Armature** on the Timeline, then click the **Delete icon** 🗑 on the Timeline status bar to delete the layer.

7. Click **frame 1** on the kicker layer, display the Library panel, then drag the **mc_kicker symbol** to the Stage.

8. Insert a **motion tween**.

9. Drag the **tween span** on the Timeline to **frame 20**, as shown in Figure 39.

10. Click **frame 10** on the kicker layer.

11. Verify the object is selected, then press the **up arrow** [↑] on the keyboard 10 times.

12. Click **frame 20**, then press the **down arrow** [↓] on the keyboard 10 times.

    Steps 11 and 12 will give the impression of the character jumping up then coming down during the kicking motion.

13. Test the movie, close the Flash Player window, then save your work.

You created a movie clip and applied a motion tween to it.

Apply an ease value

1. Double-click the **mc_kicker symbol** in the Library panel to display the edit window, then scroll as needed to see the entire object.

2. Display the Properties panel.

3. Click **frame 10** on the Armature layer.

4. Set the Ease Strength to **-100**.

5. Click the **Type list arrow** in the EASE area, then click **Simple (Fastest)**

   The EASE type is set to Simple (Fastest), as shown in Figure 40. Frame 10 is the start of the motion tween where the right leg begins to kick downward. Setting the ease value to -100 will cause the leg motion to start out slow and accelerate as the leg follows through to the end of the kicking motion. This is a more natural way to represent the kick than to have the leg speed constant throughout the downward motion and follow through.

6. Click **Scene 1** on the edit window title bar to return to the main Timeline.

7. Test the movie, close the Flash Player window, save your work, then close the file.

You added an ease value to the movie clip.

Figure 40 *Setting the ease value*

Creating Special Effects

Figure 41 *The completed armature structure*

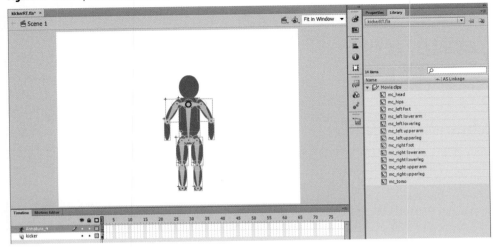

Set the play to runtime

1. Open fl5_6.fla, then save it as **kickerRT.fla**.

   This character is similar to the one used in the kicker movie, however it has been created using movie clips instead of graphic symbols. Also, only one pose is used.

2. Use the **Bone tool** to create the armature structure as shown in Figure 41.

   Hint: Each bone should connect two body parts.

3. Click **frame 1** on the Armature layer.

   Hint: If you have trouble clicking a frame, select a larger frame view setting and try again.

4. Display the Properties panel, click the **Type list arrow** in the OPTIONS area of the Properties panel, then click **Runtime**.

5. Click **File**, point to **Publish Preview**, then click **Default - (HTML)** to display the movie in a browser.

   Hint: Press [F12] (Win) or [command][F12] (Mac) to display the movie in a browser.

6. Drag each part of the character, such as an arm or a leg.

7. Close your browser.

8. Save your work, then close the document.

You created an animated character, set the play to runtime, and manipulated the character in a browser.

Create 3D EFFECTS

What You'll Do

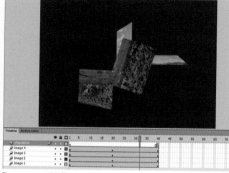

Photo courtesy of J. Shuman.

 In this lesson, you will create a movie with 3D effects.

Understanding 3D Effects

Flash allows you to create 3D effects by manipulating objects in 3D space on the Stage. Until now you have been working in two dimensions, width and height. The default settings for the Stage are 550 pixels wide and 400 pixels high. These are represented by an X axis (across) and a Y axis (down). Any position on the Stage can be specified by X and Y coordinates. The upper-left corner of the Stage has an X value of 0 and a Y value of 0, and the lower-right corner has an X value of 550 and a Y value of 400, as shown in Figure 42.

In 3D space there is also a Z axis that represents depth. Flash provides two tools, 3D Translation and 3D Rotation that can be used to move and rotate objects using all three axes. In addition, Flash provides two other properties that can be adjusted to control the view of an object. The Perspective Angle property controls the angle of the object and can be used to create a zooming in and out effect. The Vanishing Point property more precisely controls the direction of an object as it moves away from the viewer. The Perspective Angle and the Vanishing Point settings are found in the Properties panel.

Figure 42 *The X and Y coordinates on the Stage*

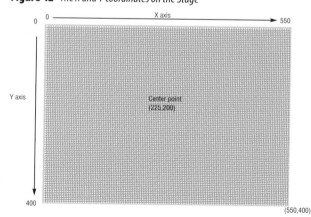

Creating Special Effects

The 3D Tools

The 3D tools are available on the Tools panel. By default the 3D Rotation tool is displayed on the Tools panel. To access the 3D Translation tool, click and hold the 3D Rotation tool to open the menu. Toggle between these two 3D tools as needed.

The process for creating 3D effects is to create a movie clip (only movie clips can have 3D effects applied to them), place the movie clip on the Stage, create a motion tween and then click the object with either of the 3D tools. When you click an object with the 3D Translation tool, the three axes X, Y, and Z appear on top of the object, as shown in Figure 43. Each has its own color: red (X), green (Y), and blue (Z), which you see only when the 3D Rotation tool is active. The X and Y axes have arrows and the Z axis is represented by a black dot when the 3D Translation tool is active. You point to an arrow or the black dot and drag it to reposition the object. Dragging the X axis arrow moves the object horizontally. Dragging the Y axis arrow moves the object vertically. Dragging the Z axis dot zooms the object in and out.

When you click the object with the 3D Rotation tool, the three axes X, Y, and Z appear on top of the object, as shown in Figure 44. Dragging the X axis (red) will flip the object horizontally. Dragging the Y axis (green) will flip the object vertically. Dragging the Z axis (blue) will spin the object. A fourth option, the orange circle, rotates the object around the X and Y axes at the same time.

Using a Motion Tween with a 3D Effect

Creating 3D effects requires a change in the position of an object. A motion tween is used to specify where on the Timeline the effect will take place. This allows you to create more than one effect by selecting various frames in the tween span and making adjustments as desired. If you are animating more than one object, each object should be on its own layer.

Figure 43 *The 3D Translation tool*

Figure 44 *The 3D Rotation tool*

Photos courtesy of J. Shuman.

Lesson 6 Create 3D Effects

Create a 3D animation

1. Open fl5_7.fla, then save it as **puzzle.fla**.

   Note: The document opens with the ruler feature turned on and showing the vertical and horizontal lines that intersect at the center of the Stage.

2. Change the view to **Fit in Window**.

3. Click **frame 1** on the Image 1 layer, insert a **motion tween**, then drag the **tween span** to frame 40.

4. Click **frame 20** on the Image 1 layer, then select the **3D Translation tool** ⚒, from the Tools panel.

   Note: You may need to click the 3D Rotation tool on the Tools panel to display the 3D Translation tool.

5. Click the **image** in the upper-right corner of the Stage, point to the **green arrow tip**, then use the ▶︎ᵧ pointer to drag the image down to the horizontal ruler line, as shown in Figure 45.

6. Click the **red arrow tip**, then use the ▶︎ₓ pointer to drag the image to the left, as shown in Figure 46.

7. Select the **3D Rotation tool** ⚪, from the Tools panel, point to the **green line Y axis** on the right side of the object, then, when the pointer changes to a delta symbol with a Y, drag the ▶︎ᵧ **pointer** down and to the left, as shown in Figure 47, to flip the image horizontally.

8. Click **frame 40** on the Image 1 layer, then select the **3D Translation tool** ⚒, from the Tools panel.

(continued)

Figure 45 *Using the 3D Translation tool to position the image vertically*

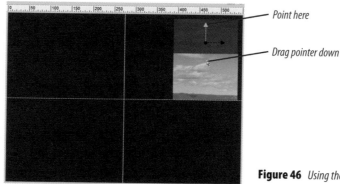

Point here

Drag pointer down

Figure 46 *Using the 3D Translation tool to position the image horizontally*

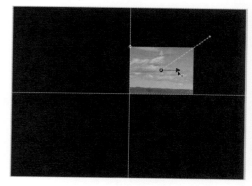

Figure 47 *Using the 3D Rotation tool to flip the image horizontally*

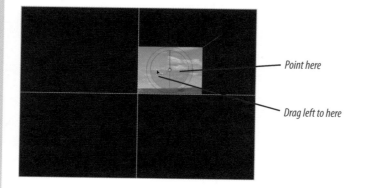

Point here

Drag left to here

Photos courtesy of J. Shuman.

Creating Special Effects

Figure 48 *Using the 3D Translation tool to position the image again*

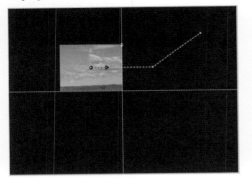

Figure 49 *Using the 3D Translation tool to position a second image*

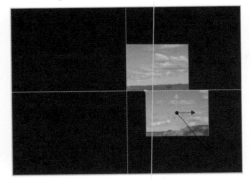

Figure 50 *Using the 3D Rotation tool to flip the image vertically*

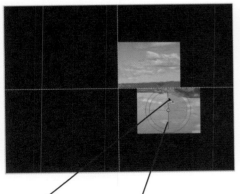

Drag pointer left and up   Point here

Figure 51 *Using the 3D Translation tool to reposition the second image*

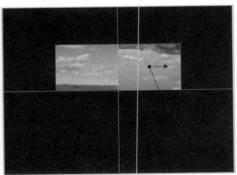

Photos courtesy of J. Shuman.

Lesson 6   Create 3D Effects

9. Click the **red arrow tip**, then use the ▶ₓ pointer to move the image to the position shown in Figure 48.

10. Select the **3D Rotation tool** 🌐, point to the **green line Y axis** on the left side of the object, then drag the ▶ᵧ **pointer** down and to the right to flip the image horizontally again.

11. Click **frame 1** on the Image 2 layer, insert a **motion tween**, then drag the **tween span** to frame 40.

12. Click **frame 20** on the Image 2 layer, then select the **3D Translation tool** ⚒.

13. Point to the **red and green arrow tips** and use the ▶ₓ pointer and the ▶ᵧ pointer respectively to drag the image to the position shown in Figure 49.

14. Select the **3D Rotation tool** 🌐, then point to the **bottom red line X axis** so the pointer changes to a delta symbol with an X.

15. Use the ▶ₓ pointer to drag the **bottom red line X axis** to the left and up to flip the image vertically, as shown in Figure 50.

16. Click **frame 40** on the Image 2 layer, then select the **3D Translation tool** ⚒.

17. Point to the **red and green arrow tips** and use the ▶ₓ pointer and the ▶ᵧ pointer respectively to position the image as shown in Figure 51.

18. Select the **3D Rotation tool** 🌐, then point to the **bottom red line X axis** so the pointer changes to a ▶ₓ.

19. Drag the **bottom red line X axis** to the left and up to flip the image vertically again.

(continued)

20. Click **frame 1** on the Image 3 layer, insert a **motion tween**, then drag the **tween span** to frame 40.

21. Click **frame 20** on the Image 3 layer, then select the **3D Translation tool** ⚹.

22. Point to the **red and green arrow tips** and use the ▶ₓ pointer and the ▶ᵧ pointer respectively to drag the image to the position shown in Figure 52.

23. Select the **3D Rotation tool** ◗, then point to the **blue circle Z axis**, as shown in Figure 53.

    The pointer changes to ▶_z.

24. Drag the **circle** to rotate the image clockwise 180 degrees, as shown in Figure 54.

25. Click **frame 40** on the Image 3 layer, then select the **3D Translation tool** ⚹.

26. Point to the **red and green arrow tips** and use the ▶ₓ pointer and the ▶ᵧ pointer respectively to position the image as shown in Figure 55.

27. Select the **3D Rotation tool** ◗, point to the **blue circle Z axis**, then use the ▶_z pointer to drag the circle and to rotate the image clockwise 180 degrees again.

28. Click **frame 1** on the Image 4 layer, insert a motion tween, then drag the **tween span** to frame 40.

29. Click **frame 20** on the Image 4 layer, then select the **3D Translation tool** ⚹.

(continued)

Figure 52 *Using the 3D Translation tool to position the third image*

Figure 53 *Pointing to the blue circle Z axis on the 3D Rotation tool*

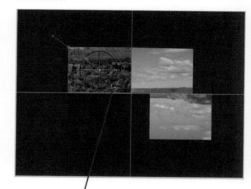

Point here

Figure 54 *Using the 3D Rotation tool to rotate the image*

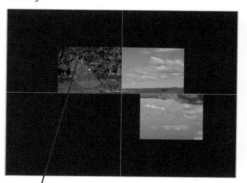

Rotate the pointer clockwise to here

Figure 55 *Using the 3D Translation tool to reposition the third image*

Photos courtesy of J. Shuman.

Creating Special Effects

Figure 56 *Using the 3D Translation tool to position the fourth image*

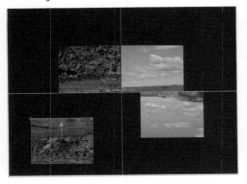

Figure 57 *Using the 3D Rotation tool to rotate the image*

Drag pointer left to here

Point here

Figure 58 *Using the 3D Translation tool to reposition the fourth image*

Figure 59 *The completed 3D effects movie*

30. Point to the **red and green arrow tips** and use the ▶x pointer and the ▶y pointer respectively to position the image as shown in Figure 56.

31. Select the **3D Rotation tool** , then point to the right side of the **orange circle**.

    The pointer changes to a Delta symbol.

32. Drag the ▶ **pointer** to the middle of the image as shown in Figure 57.

33. Click **frame 40** on the Image 4 layer, point to the left side of the orange circle, then drag the ▶ **pointer** to the center of the image.

34. Use the **3D Translation tool** to position the image as shown in Figure 58.

35. Click the **Selection tool** , drag the **ruler lines** to remove them, then use the 3D tools and the red and green arrow tips to make adjustments as needed so your screen resembles Figure 59.

    Hint: Use the arrow keys on the keyboard to make minor adjustments to the position of an object.

36. Test the movie, then close the Flash Player window.

37. Save your work, then close the document.

You created a movie with 3D effects.

Photos courtesy of Jim Shuman.

Lesson 6   Create 3D Effects

Use the DECO TOOL

What You'll Do

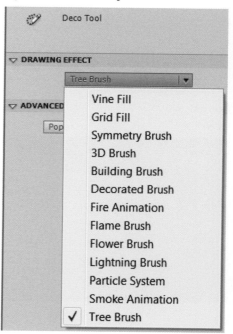

In this lesson, you will use the Deco tool to create and animate a cityscape.

Understanding the Deco Tool

The Deco tool provides a variety of drawing effects that can be used to quickly create environments, such as city landscapes, and to create various animations. In addition, the Deco tool can be used to create decorative patterns that incorporate imported graphics and those drawn in Flash. These patterns can be animated and added to a movie to create special effects. Flash has a number of Deco tool brushes and effects. In addition, Adobe has designed the Deco tool so that other brushes and effects can be added by developers. This allows users to develop tools for their specific needs. Because the Deco tool is easy to use and can be used to quickly create a design and add animation, it is a valuable tool for creating prototypes in the early stages of developing an application. One drawback of using the Deco tool is that animations created with the Deco tool often result in movie file sizes that are large. This is because the images created with the brush tools are made up of small segments and the animations are frame-by-frame animations.

Basic Types of Deco Effects

There are 13 drawing effects available with the Deco tool, as shown in Figure 60.

Figure 60 *The Deco drawing tools*

Creating Special Effects

These drawing effects are available in the Properties panel when the Deco tool is selected from the Tools panel. They are grouped into three basic types, although there is some overlap in the groups.

- Fills—the Vine Fill, Grid Fill, and Symmetry Brush create patterns that can be used as fill for graphics or a backdrop for a movie. Figure 61 shows a vine and a grid fill. Flash allows you to create your own fill using an image of your choice, such as a logo. In addition, you can set various properties such as the pattern scale.
- Brushes—several brushes including the building, lightning, tree, and flower brushes can be used to create drawings that can be combined to construct environments, like the one shown in Figure 62. The Decorated Brush has 20 variations, including those shown in Figure 63.
- Animations—a few brushes, such as the Lightning Brush, Fire Animation, Smoke Animation, and Particle System, create animations as they are used. However, any effect created using the Deco tool can be selected, converted to a graphic or movie clip symbol, and animated by inserting a motion tween or using another animation process in Flash.

Hint: Select a keyframe before selecting the Deco tool and use different layers for each Deco tool effect.

Figure 61 *A vine fill and a grid fill*

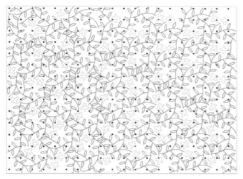

Figure 62 *Cityscape created using Deco tools*

Figure 63 *Patterns created using selected Decorative Brushes*

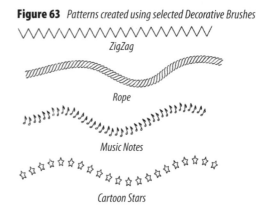

ZigZag

Rope

Music Notes

Cartoon Stars

Create screen design and animations with the Deco tool

1. Open fl5_8 .fla, then save it as **decoLand.fla**.

   This movie has six layers, dimensions of 400 x 400 pxs, a length of 65 frames, and a dark blue backdrop.

2. Change the view for the Timeline to **Small** if necessary to see all 65 frames, then set the view to **Fit in Window**.

3. Click **frame 1** on the buildings layer, click the **Deco tool** on the Tools panel, then display the Properties panel.

4. Click the **DRAWING EFFECT list arrow**, then click **Building Brush**.

5. Verify your Properties panel displays DRAWING EFFECT: Building Brush; ADVANCED OPTIONS: Random building and Building Size 1.

6. Point to the Stage, then click and drag the **pointer** to the position shown in Figure 64.

   Note: The Random building option may cause your building to display differently.

   Hint: You can use the undo command in the Edit menu to undo an action(s).

7. Continue to create four more buildings similar to Figure 65.

8. Click **frame 1** on the trees layer.

9. Click the **Deco tool** on the Tools panel, then use the Properties panel to change the DRAWING EFFECT to **Tree Brush** and the type to **Poplar Tree**.

10. Use the pointer to draw trees similar to the ones shown in Figure 66.

(continued)

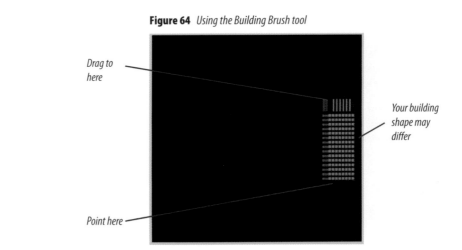

Figure 64 *Using the Building Brush tool*

Drag to here

Your building shape may differ

Point here

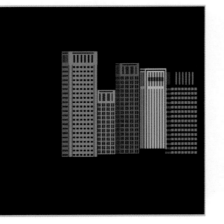

Figure 65 *The completed buildings*

Figure 66 *The completed trees*

Drag the Deco tool up to create the tree shape, pause and hold the mouse button down to create the leaves.

Figure 67 *Using the Lightning Brush*

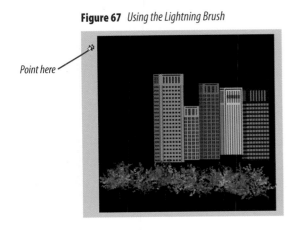

Point here

Figure 68 *Inserting a blank keyframe*

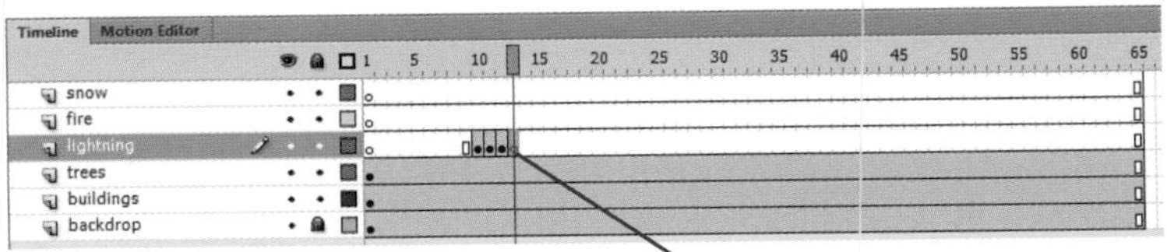

Blank keyframe inserted after the
keyframes of the animation.
Note: There may be a different number
of keyframes in your animation.

Figure 69 *Positioning the pointer*

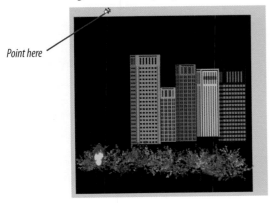

Point here

11. Insert a **keyframe** in frame 10 on the lightning layer.
12. Click the **Deco tool** on the Tools panel, change the DRAWING EFFECT to **Lightning Brush** and the color to **white**, then verify animation is checked.
13. Point off the Stage as shown in Figure 67, then drag the **pointer** toward the trees and release the mouse button.
14. Insert a **blank keyframe** in the frame following the last keyframe in the lightning animation, as shown in Figure 68.
15. Click **frame 20** on the fire layer, then insert a **keyframe**.
16. Click the **Deco tool** on the Tools panel, then change the DRAWING EFFECT to **Fire Animation** and the Fire duration to **30 frames**.
17. Click the **tree top** on the far left of the Stage, click **frame 50** on the fire layer, then insert a **blank keyframe**.
18. Click **frame 35** on the snow layer, then insert a **keyframe**.
19. Click the **Deco tool** on the Tools panel, change the DRAWING EFFECT to **Particle System**, verify Particle 1 and Particle 2 have a check mark, and set the particle color to **white** for each particle.
20. Point to the sky, as shown in Figure 69, then click the **pointer**.
21. Click **frame 35**, repeat Steps 19 and 20 **three times** placing the **pointer** in different areas across the sky.
22. Test the movie, close the Flash Player window, save your work, then close the document.

You created a cityscape environment, including animations, with the Deco tool.

Create a mask effect.

1. Start Flash, open fl5_9.fla, then save it as **skillsDemo5.fla**. (*Hint*: When you open the file, you may receive a missing font message, meaning a font used in this document is not available on your computer. You can choose a substitute font or use a default font.)
2. Verify the frame rate is set to 12 and the Flash Publish Settings (accessed from the File menu) are set to Flash Player 10 or above and ActionScript 3.0.
3. Insert a new layer above the table layer, then name it **heading**.
4. Select frame 1 on the heading layer, then use the Text tool to create the Aces Wild heading with the following characteristics: size 48, color #006633 (a dark green), and Byington (or similar) font. (*Hint*: Look at Figure 70 and find a font that matches the heading text. Use the samples provided to find a similar font, such as Constania.)
5. Use the Selection tool to select the heading, then use the Align command in the Modify menu to center the heading across the Stage.
6. With the heading still selected, convert it to a graphic symbol with the name **g_heading**.
7. Insert a keyframe in frame 40 on the heading layer.
8. Insert a new layer above the heading layer, then name it **ending-heading**.
9. Insert a keyframe in frame 40 on the ending-heading layer.
10. Drag the g_heading symbol from the Library panel and position it on top of the heading on the Stage, then use the keyboard arrow keys as needed to position the g_heading symbol.
11. Lock the ending-heading layer.
12. Insert a new layer above the heading layer, then name it **circle**.
13. Select frame 1 on the circle layer, then use the Oval tool to create a black-filled circle with no stroke that is slightly larger in height than the heading text.
14. Place the circle to the left of the heading.
15. Convert the circle to a graphic symbol with the name **g_mask**.
16. With the circle selected, insert a motion tween.
17. Select frame 40 on the circle layer and drag the circle across and to the right side of the heading.
18. Change the circle layer to a mask layer and lock the layer.
19. Change the heading layer to a masked layer and lock the layer.
20. Insert keyframes in frame 40 on the table layer and the head and body layer but not on the card layer.
21. Insert a new layer above the table layer, name it **stopMovie**, move the stopmovie layer below the table layer, then insert a keyframe in frame 40.
22. Open the Actions panel, verify Script Assist is turned off and stopMovie: 40 is displayed in the lower-left corner of the Script pane, then type **stop( );** for the code. (*Note*: Because ActionScript 3.0 is needed when working with inverse kinematics and with the 3D feature, both of which you will do shortly, you cannot use the Script Assist feature of Flash, which is why you typed the code directly into the Actions pane.)
23. Close the Actions panel.
24. Test the movie, then save your work.

Create a character animation using inverse kinematics.

1. Select 1 on the Timeline, then use the Zoom tool to enlarge the view of the character.
2. Use the Bone tool to join the head to the body, then to join the body with the upper and lower left arm, and with the upper and lower right arm. (*Note*: The bone structure stops at the elbow on each arm.)
3. Click the Selection tool on the Tools panel, click frame 40 on the Armature layer, then insert a keyframe.
4. Select frame 6 on the Armature layer.
5. Use the Selection tool to move the ends of the arms so that the lower left and lower right arms are horizontal and touch at the chest. This will cause the elbows to point out away from the body.
6. Select frame 12 on the Armature layer.
7. Use the Selection tool to move the end of the right arm so that it is straight and pointing to the upper-left corner of the Stage.
8. Change the view to Fit in Window.
9. Test the movie, then save your work. (*Note*: If a warning dialog box opens, click OK.)

Create a frame-by-frame animation.

1. Select frame 4 on the card layer, then insert a keyframe.
2. Use the Zoom tool and the keyboard arrow keys as needed to reposition the card so that it is at the end of the right arm.
3. Select frame 5 on the card layer, then insert a keyframe.
4. Use the arrow keys on the keyboard to reposition the card so that it is at the end of the right arm.

5. Repeat steps 3 and 4 in frame 6 through frame 12 on the card layer. (*Note*: The hand moves a small increment in each frame, which is why you must reposition the card so it stays connected to the hand.)

6. Select frame 13 on the card layer, then insert a blank keyframe.

7. Test the movie, close the Flash Player window, then save your work.

Create a 3D effect.

1. Change the view to Fit in Window, insert a new layer above the card layer, then name it **ace3D**.

2. Select frame 12 on the ace3D layer, then insert a keyframe.

3. Drag the mc_aceD movie clip from the Library panel to the Stage, display the Properties panel, verify the Lock width and height values together icon is not a broken link, then resize the width to 10.6.

4. Reposition the ace so it is on top of the card held by the character.

5. Verify frame 12 on the ace3D layer is selected, then create a motion tween.

6. Verify the tween span on the Timeline extends from frame 12 through frame 40.

7. Select frame 40 on the ace3D layer.

8. Use the 3D Translation tool to reposition the card to the upper-left corner of the Stage in a diagonal line that extends from the character's right shoulder. (*Hint*: Use both the red and green arrow tips to move the card to create a diagonal line.)

9. Use the Free Transform tool and the Scale option at the bottom of the Tools panel to resize the card to a width of between 80 and 90.

10. Select frame 26 on the ace3D layer.

11. Use the 3D Rotation tool to add a 3D effect.

12. Select frame 40 on the ace3D layer.

13. Use the 3D Rotation tool to add a 3D effect that causes the card to display right side up, as seen in Figure 70.

14. Test the movie, close the Flash Player window, then save your work.

Add sound to a movie.

1. Insert a new layer at the top of the Timeline, then name it **sound**.

2. Insert a keyframe in frame 15 on the sound layer.

3. Drag introSound.wav from the Library panel to the Stage.

4. Insert a keyframe in frame 40 on the sound layer.

5. Test the movie, if a warning box opens, read the message then click OK, compare your movie to the images in Figure 70, close the Flash Player window, save your work, then close the file.

Figure 70 *Completed Skills Review-IK 3D Animation*

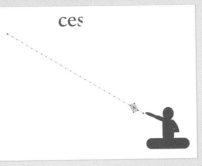

Add video.

1. Open fl5_10.fla, then save it as **skillsDemo5-video.fla**.

2. Add a new layer above the headings layer, then name it **video**.

3. Import the file tour-video.mov as an embedded video from the drive and folder where you store your Data Files to the Library using the Import Video command. (*Note*: You will need to use the Adobe Media Encoder to convert the file to the flv format, then you will need to browse to the drive and folder where you save your Solution Files to open the converted file.)

4. Verify that the video is in the Library panel and on the center of the Stage, notice the number of frames needed to display the entire video as indicated by the blue shading on the video layer. (*Note*: You may need to drag the video from the Library panel to the Stage. If a message appears asking if you want frames inserted into the Timeline, click Yes.
Hint: Be sure to position the video placeholder, if necessary, to prevent overlapping the text subheading.)

5. Add a new layer, name it **controls**, then select frame 1 on the layer.

6. Use the Text tool to create a text box with the word **Play** beneath and to the left of center of the video, as shown in Figure 71. Set the text characteristics to the following: family Arial, style Narrow (Win) or Regular (Mac), size 20 pt, and color White.
7. Convert the text to a button symbol with the name **b_play**.
8. Edit the over and down states of the button symbol, for example, make the color of the letters change when the mouse pointer is over the word Play and when the user clicks the button. Be sure to add a hit area that surrounds the text.
9. Use the Actions panel and Script Assist to assign a play action to the button that plays the movie when the mouse is released.
10. Use the Text tool to create a text box with the word **Pause** beneath and to the right of center of the video, as shown in Figure 71. Use the same text characteristics used for the Play button.
11. Convert the text to a button symbol with the name **b_pause**.
12. Edit the button symbol to match what you did in step 8.
13. Use the Actions panel to assign a stop action to the button when it is released.
14. Add a new layer, then name it **stopMovie**.
15. Add a stop action to frame 1 on the stopMovie layer.
16. Add a keyframe at the end of the movie on the headings layer. (*Note*: If a message appears asking if you want frames inserted into the Timeline, click No because the frames are already inserted.)
17. Test the movie, compare your screen to Figure 71, close the Flash Player window, then save your work.
18. Close the Flash document.

Work with TLF text.

1. Open fl5_11.fla, then save it as **skillsDemo5-TLF.fla**.
2. Add a new layer and name it **photo**.
3. Select frame 1 of the photo layer and drag the g_birchBay graphic symbol from the Library panel to the center of the Stage.
4. Use the Align panel to center the graphic on the Stage.
5. Lock the heading and photo layers.
6. Add a new layer at the top of the Timeline and name it **text**.
7. Select frame 1 of the text layer and drag the g_text graphic from the Library panel to the middle of the Stage.
8. Verify the text image is selected, then click Modify on the menu bar and select Break Apart. (*Note*: The original text block was changed to a graphic symbol and placed in the Library panel. In order to edit the text, the symbol must be broken apart.)

9. Display the Properties panel and change the text from Classic Text to TLF Text.
10. Change the Size in the CHARACTER area to 13 pt.
11. Change the Behavior in the CONTAINER AND FLOW area of the Properties panel to Multiline.
12. Using Figure 72 as a guide complete the following:
   ■ Use the Selection tool to resize the Container and create a second linked Container.
   ■ Use the Text tool to type in the words "in the majestic Pacific Northwest" at the end of the first sentence.
   ■ Use the Selection tool to select the containers.
   ■ Justify the text using the "Justify with last line aligned to start" button in the PARAGRAPH area of the Properties panel, and adjust the text box widths as needed to closely match the line wrap shown in Figure 72.
13. Lock the text layer.
14. Test the movie, then close the Flash Player window.
15. Save your work.

Figure 71 *Completed Skills Review - video*

Photo courtesy of Jim Shuman.

Create the drop-down buttons.

1. Save the Flash document as **skillsDemo5-navBar.fla**.
2. Insert a new layer, name it **navBar Background**, create the white horizontal bar shown in Figure 72, then lock the layer.
3. Insert a new layer, name it **navBar Buttons**, then create the three text headings using Classic text and a black color.
4. Convert the Take a Tour heading to a button, then edit the button symbol to add a hit area around it. (*Note*: Be sure to make the hit area long enough so that it will fall below the navBar Background rectangle.)
5. Reposition the Take a Tour button so that its hit area falls below the navBar Background rectangle. (*Note*: You can test the hit area by turning on Enable Simple Buttons in the Control menu and pointing to the button.)
6. Reposition the Home and Map text to match the Take a Tour text as needed.
7. Insert keyframes in frame 10 of all the layers.
8. Insert a layer above the navBar Buttons layer, name it **videoBtn**, then insert a keyframe in frame 2 of the layer.
9. Refer again to Figure 72 and create the video button, edit the button symbol to add a hit area to the button, then position it below Take a Tour.
10. Insert a layer, name it **photosBtn**, then insert a keyframe in frame 2 of the layer.
11. Create the photos button, then position it below the video button.

Add a mask layer.

1. Insert a layer, name it **cover**, then insert a keyframe in frame 2 of the layer.

2. Draw a rectangle that covers the video and slide buttons and move it above Take a Tour.
3. Verify the rectangle is selected and Insert a motion tween.
4. Insert a keyframe in frame 5 of the cover layer, then move the rectangle down to cover the buttons.
5. Change the layer properties for the cover layer to mask.
6. Select the photosBtn layer and change it to a masked layer, if it has not changed to a masked layer.
7. Select the videoBtn layer and change it to a masked layer.

Assign actions to buttons and frames.

1. Click File on the menu bar, click Publish Settings, click the Script list arrow, then change the Script to ActionScript 2.0. (*Note*: ActionScript 2.0 is needed when assigning actions to buttons.)
2. When the warning message appears, click OK, then click OK to close the Publish Settings dialog box.

3. Select frame 2 on the videoBtn layer, click to select the Video button, then use ScriptAssist to add the on(release) code that causes the playhead to go to the next scene. (*Note*: The next scene will contain the video; although the scene has not been created yet, you can still assign "next scene();" to the on(release) action.)
4. Insert a layer above the cover layer, name it **labels**, then insert a keyframe in frame 2 of the layer.
5. Add a frame label named **tourMenu**.
6. Select 1 on the Timeline, select the Take a Tour button, then use ScriptAssist to add the code so the playhead goes to and plays the frame labeled tourMenu when the mouse pointer rolls over the button.
7. Insert a layer above the labels layer, name it **actions**, then, in frames 1 and 5 (be sure to add a keyframe) on the actions layer, use the Script pane (ScriptAssist turned off) to type **stop();**.
8. Insert a layer above the heading layer, name it **rollOver**, then insert a keyframe in frame 2 of the layer.

Figure 72 *Completed Skills Review - TLF and Animated Navigation Bar*

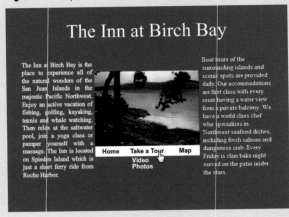

Add an invisible button.

1. Draw a rectangle that covers the Take a Tour, Video, and Photos buttons, then convert the rectangle to a button with the name **rollOverBtn**.

2. Use ScriptAssist to add ActionScript code that causes the playhead to go to frame 1 when the mouse pointer rolls over the button.

3. Select the rollOverBtn button and use the Properties panel to change the alpha setting to 0.

4. Test the movie, then save and close it.

   Note: If your text columns do not display as justified, unlock the text layer if it is locked, select a text block and set the Anti-alias option in the CHARACTER area of the Properties panel to Anti-alias for readability.

Work with the Deco tool.

This is a continuation of the Deco tool exercise you completed in this chapter. Figure 73 shows the changes you will make to the decoLand.fla document as you complete the following steps.

(*Hint*: Use the Undo command in the Edit menu to undo drawings as necessary.)

1. Open decoLand.fla and save it as **skillsDemo5-deco.fla**.

2. Change the view to Fit in Window.

3. Lock all the layers.

4. Insert a new layer above the backdrop layer, name it **road**, then select frame 1 on the road layer.

5. Select the Deco tool and display the Properties panel.

6. Change the DRAWING EFFECT to Decorated Brush, the ADVANCED OPTIONS to 18: Bumps, and the color to white.

7. Use the Deco pointer to draw the road below the buildings. (*Hint*: If no room, draw the road below the trees.)

8. Lock the road layer.

9. Insert a new layer above the snow layer and name it **stars**.

10. Select frame 1 of the stars layer.

11. Select the Deco tool and display the Properties panel.

12. Change the ADVANCED OPTIONS to 16: Shiny Stars, then set the color to white, the pattern size to 30, and the pattern width to 20.

13. Use the Deco pointer to create the stars at the top of the Stage. (*Hint*: You can click and drag the pointer, and you can move the pointer to a new location then click and drag again to create a more scattered effect.)

14. Lock the stars layer.

15. Insert a new layer above the stars layer and name it **flowers**.

16. Select frame 1 of the flowers layer.

17. Select the Deco tool and display the Properties panel.

18. Change the DRAWING EFFECT to Flower Brush, then change the ADVANCED OPTIONS to Rose, and the flower and leaf size to 50%.

19. Click and drag to create the row of flowers at the bottom of the Stage.

20. Lock the flowers layer.

21. Save the movie.

22. Test the movie, then close the Flash Player window.

23. Exit Flash.

Figure 73 *Completed Skills Review - deco*

The Ultimate Tours travel company has asked you to design several sample animations for its application. Figure 74 shows a sample Mystery Ships screen with a mask effect, as the spotlight rotates across the screen and highlights different ships. Complete the following for the Mystery Ships screen of the Ultimate Tours application.

1. Open fl5_12.fla, then save it as **assets.fla**.
2. Open ultimateTours4.fla (the file you created in Chapter 4 Project Builder 1), and save it as **ultimateTours5.fla**.
3. Insert a new layer at the top of the Timeline and select frame 1 on the layer.
4. Display the Library panel, then click the Display movies list arrow below the Library tab to display the list of open documents.
5. Select assets.fla and drag each of the symbols in the Library panel (all sound and graphic files) to the

Stage, delete the layer from the Timeline, click the assets.fla tab above the Stage, then close the assets file. (*Note:* You added the objects from the assets file to the ultimateTours5 Library panel, and then closed the assets.fla file.)

6. Display the Library panel for ultimateTours5.
7. Insert a new layer at the top of the Timeline, then name it **backdrop**.
8. Insert a keyframe in a frame that is higher than the last frame in the current movie (such as frame 100) on the backdrop layer, then draw a dark gray rectangle (#333333) that covers the Stage.
9. Insert a keyframe that is at least 30 frames higher on the backdrop layer (such as frame 130), then lock the layer. (*Note:* All of the subsequent layers you add will use the same starting frame, such as 100.)
10. Insert a new layer, name it **heading**, insert a keyframe in frame 100 (or the frame specified in Step 8), and create the Mystery Ships heading.

11. Insert a new layer, name it **lighthouse**, insert a keyframe in frame 100 (or the frame specified in Step 8), and place the g_lighthouse symbol on the Stage.
12. Insert a new layer, name it **searchlight**, insert a keyframe in frame 100 (or the frame specified in Step 8), and place the g_searchlight symbol to the left of the lighthouse, then use the Selection tool to move the tip of the searchlight to the blue window in the lighthouse. (*Hint:* The searchlight will rotate (pivot) around the transformation point (small circle) of the graphic, which is located in the tip of the searchlight. You can view the transformation point by using the Selection tool to select the searchlight on the Stage.)
13. Use the Free Transform tool to create a motion tween that causes the searchlight to rotate from the left to the right of the lighthouse.

Figure 74 *Sample completed Project Builder 1*

14. Create a new layer for each of the three ships, name each layer appropriately (**ship1**, **ship2**, and **ship3**), and insert keyframes in frame 100 (or the frame specified in Step 8) of each layer.

15. Using frame 100 (or the frame specified in Step 8), place the ships on the Stage so that the searchlight highlights them as it moves from left to right across the Stage.

16. Insert a new layer above the ship layers, name it **searchlight mask**, insert a keyframe in frame 100 (or the frame specified in Step 8), add an instance of the g_searchlight symbol from the Library panel so it is on top of the searchlight on the Stage, then add a motion tween that duplicates the one created in Step 13.

17. Change the layer properties for the four layers you just created in order to create a mask effect that has a searchlight as the mask and reveals the ships when the searchlight is over them. (*Note*: The two searchlight motion tweens are needed on different layers because one will become a mask and will not be visible in the movie.)

18. Insert a new layer, name it **sound**, insert a keyframe in frame 100 (or the appropriate frame) on the layer, then drag the foghorn.wav sound file to the Stage.

19. Insert a new layer, name it **homeBTN**, insert a keyframe in the last frame of the movie, then add the b_home button to the bottom center of the Stage. (*Note*: This button does not appear on the MYSTERY SHIPS screen in Figure 74 because the last frame of the movie has not been reached.)

20. Add an action to the home button to have the playhead go to frame 1 of the movie when the button is clicked. (*Hint*: You may need to turn on ScriptAssist.)

21. Insert a new layer, name it **stopAction**, then add a keyframe and a stop action at the end of the movie. (*Hint*: You can turn off ScriptAssist and type stop(); into the Actions panel.)

22. Add a new layer, name it **labels**, insert a keyframe in frame 100 (or the appropriate frame), then create a frame label named **mystery**.

23. Click 1 on the Timeline, drag (scrub) the playhead on the Timeline to locate the first frame that shows the layer with the Featured Cruises heading (the layer that has the Galapagos text), then unlock the layer that has the Featured Cruises heading (or layer that has the Galapagos text).

24. Change the Galapagos text to **Mystery Ships**, center align the text, then create a button that changes the text color for the different button states.

25. Add an action to the mystery ship button to have the playhead go to the frame labeled mystery.

26. Test the movie, then compare your image to the example shown in Figure 74.

27. Close the Flash Player window.

28. Lock all layers, save your work, then close the document.

You have been asked to develop a website illustrating the signs of the zodiac. The introductory screen should have a heading with a mask effect and 12 zodiac signs, each of which could become a button. Clicking a zodiac sign button displays an information screen with a different graphic to represent the sign and information about the sign, as well as special effects such as sound, mask effect, and character animation (inverse kinematics). Each information screen would be linked to its button (e.g. zodiac) and to the introductory screen with a Home button. (*Note*: Using the inverse kinematics feature requires ActionScript 3.0, therefore, you will start with a movie that has the ActionScript for the Scorpio and Home buttons and a stop action already developed.)

1. Open fl5_13.fla, save it as **zodiac5.fla**, then change the frame rate to **12 fps**.
2. Test the movie, then study the Timeline to understand how the movie works.
3. Refer to Figure 75 as you complete the introductory screen with the following:
   - A new layer above the signs layer named **heading** with the heading, **Signs of the** that appears from frame 1 through frame 31
   - A new layer named **masked** that contains the word **Zodiac** and that appears from frame 1 through frame 31
   - A mask layer that passes across the heading Zodiac (*Notes*: Use a fill color that can be seen on the black background. After creating the motion tween, drag the end of the tween span on the Timeline to frame 31. Be sure to set the Layer Properties for the mask and masked layers.)
   - A new layer that displays the word **Zodiac** in frame 31 only (*Note*: Remove frames 32–80 from the layer by using the Remove Frames option from the Timeline command of the Edit menu.)
   - A new layer with a sound that plays from frame 1 through frame 31 as the mask is revealing the contents of the masked layer
4. Refer to Figure 75 as you complete the scorpio screen with the following: (*Notes*: The scorpio screen starts in frame 51. Remove frames in other layers containing content that you do not want displayed after frame 31, such as the Zodiac heading.)
   - A new layer with the three-line heading

Scorpio - the Scorpion
October 23 - November 21
Intense, Emotional, Secretive
   - An inverse kinematics animation that moves the tail (*Note*: Be sure to connect the head to the tail.)
5. Test the movie.
6. Save the movie as **zodiac5-mc.fla**.
7. Select frame 51 on the Armature layer and convert the IK animation to a movie clip.
8. Open the Edit window for the movie clip and add a stop action on a separate layer at the end of the movie clip, then return to the main Timeline.
9. Delete the Armature layer, then select frame 51 on the scorpio layer and drag the movie clip to the Stage.
10. Create a motion tween to animate the movie clip so the scorpion moves across the screen.
11. Test the movie, compare your screens to Figure 75, close the Flash Player window, then save the movie.

Figure 75 *Sample completed Project Builder 2*

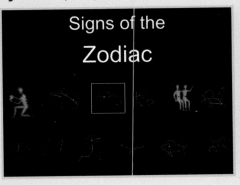

Tail moves while scorpion moves across the screen

Figure 76 shows the home page of a website. Study the figure and complete the following questions. For each question, indicate how you determined your answer.

1. Connect to the Internet, then go to *www.adidas.com*, and display the women's running shoes. Go to the site and explore several links to get a feeling for how the site is constructed. Use Figure 76 to answer the questions.

2. Open a document in a word processor or open a new Flash document, save the file as **dpc5**, then answer the following questions. (*Hint*: Use the Text tool in Flash.)

   ■ Whose site is this and what seems to be the purpose of this site?

   ■ Who is the target audience?

   ■ How would you use a character animation with inverse kinematics on this site?

   ■ How would you use video on this site?

   ■ How would you use a mask effect on this site?

   ■ How would you use sound on this site?

   ■ How would you use 3D on this site?

   ■ What suggestions would you make to improve the design and why?

Figure 76 *Design Project*

adidas, the 3-Bars logo, the 3-Stripe trade mark, and adizero are registered trademarks of the adidas Group, used with permission. adidas AG owns the copyright to the Image used. www.adidas.com

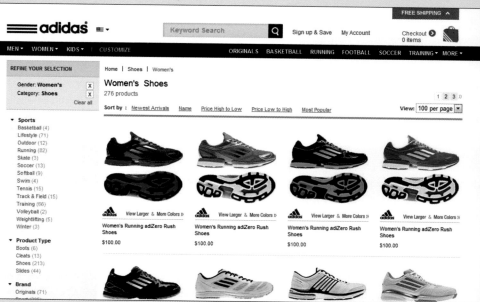

This is a continuation of the Portfolio Project in Chapter 4, which is the development of a personal portfolio.

In this project, you will create several buttons for the Sample Animations screen and link them to their respective animations.

1. Open portfolio4.fla (the file you created in Portfolio Project, Chapter 4) and save it as **portfolio5.fla**.
2. Display the Sample Animations screen. You will be adding buttons to this screen. Each of these new buttons links to a screen that plays its corresponding animation. In each case, have the animation return to the Sample Animations screen at the end of the animation.
3. Add a button for a character animation so it appears on the Sample Animations screen, add a new layer and create a character animation (inverse kinematics) on that layer, then link the character animation button to the character animation.
4. Add a button for a mask effect so it appears on the Sample Animations screen, add new layers to create a mask effect (such as to the words My Portfolio) on that layer, add a sound that plays as the mask is revealing the contents of the masked layer, then link the mask effect button to the mask effect animation.
5. Add a button for an animated navigation bar so it appears on the Sample Animations screen, add a new layer and create an animated navigation bar on that layer, then link the navigation bar button to the animated navigation bar.
6. Test the movie, then compare your Sample Animation screen to the example shown in Figure 77.
7. Close the Flash Player window, then save your work.

Figure 77 *Sample completed Portfolio Project*

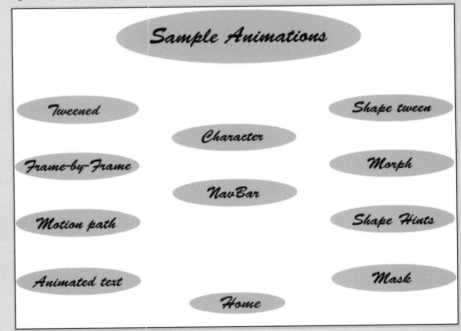

CHAPTER 6 PREPARING AND PUBLISHING
APPLICATIONS

Introduction

The most common use of Flash is to develop applications for delivery on the web, on mobile devices, and on stand-alone computers. During the planning process for an Adobe Flash movie, you are concerned with, among other things, how the target audience will view the movie. Flash provides several features that help you generate the files that are necessary for delivering movies successfully to the target audience over the Internet. These features include creating HTML files that play the Flash SWF movies.

There will be times when you are not delivering Flash applications through the Internet. For example, you may have a game that resides on a desktop computer, an informational application located on a kiosk, or a mobile app that is downloaded to a smartphone. In these cases, the Flash publish settings can be used to create projector files (executable files) and AIR files. Projector files (Win and Mac) are stand-alone executable files that do not require the Flash Player.

Similarly, AIR (Adobe Integrated Runtime) files do not require the Flash Player. The AIR file format is similar to creating an executable file, however, the file size is considerably smaller than projector files. Therefore, AIR files are more suitable for mobile applications.

> **QUICK TIP**
>
> Flash provides a new feature that allows you to test a mobile application using the on-screen Simulator. The Simulator displays the application as it would appear on a mobile phone, and it allows you to use events and gestures such as touch, zoom, and swipe to see how the application reacts. Go to Cengage Brain to access a bonus lesson on the Simulator.

When you deliver content over the Internet, you want to provide compelling movies. However, it is important that you keep the file size down so that the movies play smoothly regardless of the user's connection speed. Flash allows you to test movies to determine where problems might arise during download and to make changes to optimize the movies.

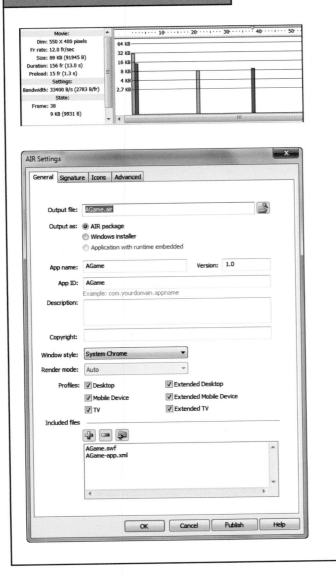

Create Self-Signed Digital Certificate

Publisher name: my name

Organization unit: my organization unit

Organization name: my organization name

Country: US

Password: ●●●●●●●●

Confirm password: ●●●●●●●●

Type: 1024-RSA

Save as: _____ Browse...

Help   OK   Cancel

Publish Movies
USING DIFFERENT FORMATS

What You'll Do

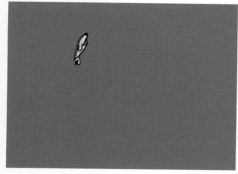

In this lesson, you will use the Flash Publish Settings feature to publish a movie, create a GIF animation, create a JPEG image from a movie, and create an executable file.

Using Publish Settings

The Flash Publish feature generates the files necessary to deliver the movies on the web. When you publish a movie using the default settings, a Flash (SWF) file is created that can be viewed using the Flash Player. In addition, an HTML file is created with the necessary code to instruct the browser to play the Flash file using the Flash Player.

Figure 1 shows the Publish Settings dialog box with a list of the available formats for publishing a Flash movie. By default, the Flash (.swf) and HTML Wrapper formats are selected. You can choose a combination of formats, and you can specify a different name (but not file extension) for each format. The GIF, JPEG, and PNG formats create still images that can be delivered on the web or within other applications. The GIF format can also be used to create GIF animations. The projector formats in the Publish Settings dialog box are executable files (which were discussed in Chapter 1). When you select a format, its settings appear. Figure 1 shows the Flash and the HTML Wrapper formats

selected in the Publish Settings dialog box, as well as the default settings associated with those formats. The options include:

- A profile, which is a set of selected settings that have been saved for later use; the Default profile is selected in Figure 1
- The target version of the Flash Player
- The version of ActionScript
- The quality for JPEG images and audio
- Other options, such as compressing the movie

QUICK **TIP**

Not all features of Flash CS6 work when using Flash Player versions earlier than version 10

Figure 2 shows the GIF format selected and its format settings. The Flash (.swf) and HTML Wrapper formats are still selected. These are optional when selecting any of the other formats. GIF files, which are compressed bitmaps, provide an easy way to create images and simple animations for delivery on the web. GIF animations are frame-by-frame animations created from Flash movie frames.

You can change several settings, including the following:

- The dimensions in pixels (or you can match the movie dimensions)
- Playback as a static image or an animated GIF
- Whether an animation plays (loops) continuously or repeats a certain number of times
- A range of appearance settings, such as optimizing colors and removing gradients

Using Publish Preview

You can use the Publish Preview command on the File menu to publish a movie and display the movie in either your default browser or the Flash Player. In addition, you can use this command to view HTML, GIF, JPEG, PNG, and Projector files.

Figure 1 *The Publish Settings dialog box*   **Figure 2** *The GIF format settings*

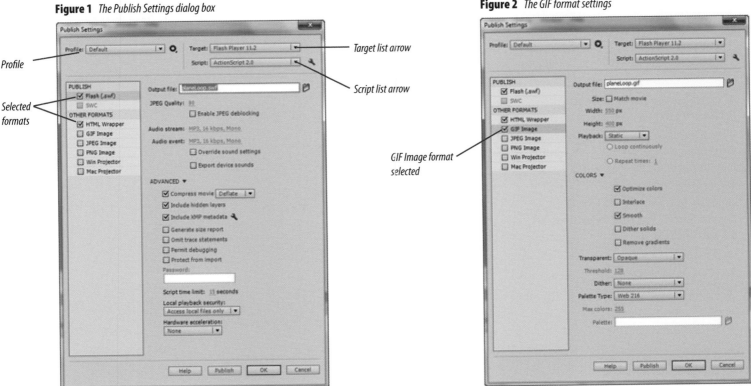

Publish using the default settings

1. Open fl6_1.fla from the drive and folder where your Data Files are stored, save it as **planeLoop.fla**, then play the movie.

2. Click **File** on the menu bar, then click **Publish Settings**.

3. Verify that the Flash (.swf) and HTML Wrapper check boxes are the only ones selected.

4. Verify that the version is set to Flash Player 11.2 or later and that the Compress movie check box in the ADVANCED area is selected.

TIP You may have to expand the ADVANCED area to see the options.

5. Accept the remaining default settings, click **Publish**, then click **OK**.

6. Use your file management program to navigate to the drive and folder where you save your Data Files, then notice the three files with filenames that start with "planeLoop", as shown in Figure 3.

7. Display the Flash program, click **File** on the menu bar, point to **Publish Preview**, then click **Default - (HTML)**.

   The movie plays in a browser.

   Note: If a warning message opens, follow the messages to allow blocked content.

8. Close the browser, then display the Flash program.

You published a movie using the default publish settings and viewed it in a browser.

Figure 3 *The three planeLoop files*

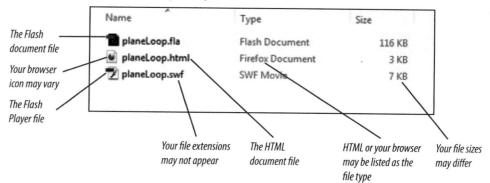

The Flash document file

Your browser icon may vary

The Flash Player file

Your file extensions may not appear

The HTML document file

HTML or your browser may be listed as the file type

Your file sizes may differ

Name	Type	Size
planeLoop.fla	Flash Document	116 KB
planeLoop.html	Firefox Document	3 KB
planeLoop.swf	SWF Movie	7 KB

Preparing and Publishing Applications

Figure 4 *The completed Publish Settings dialog box for GIF settings*

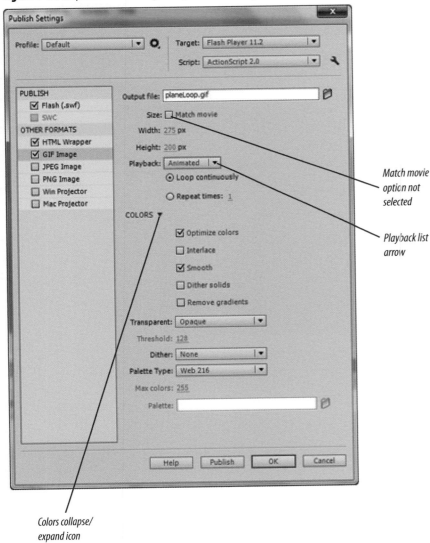

Match movie
option not
selected

Playback list
arrow

Colors collapse/
expand icon

Create a GIF animation from a movie

1. Click **File** on the menu bar, then click **Publish Settings**.

2. Click the **GIF Image check box**.

3. Click the **Match movie check box** to the right of Size: to turn off this setting, click the **Width text box**, type **275**, click the **Height text box**, then type **200**.

4. Click the **Playback list arrow**, then click **Animated**.

5. Click the **COLORS expand icon** ▶ , then verify the remaining default settings match those shown in Figure 4.

6. Click **Publish**, then click **OK**.

7. Open your browser, then use the browser to open planeLoop.gif from the drive and folder where you save your work.

   TIP Many browsers have an Open command on the File menu. Use this command to navigate to and then open files for display within the browser. If you do not see the GIF file, change the file type to All Files.

8. Notice the GIF animation plays in the browser with the modified settings.

   Because the GIF file is not an SWF file, it does not require the Flash Player to play—it can be displayed directly in a web browser.

9. Close the browser.

You changed the publish settings for a GIF image, then created a GIF animation and viewed it in your web browser.

Create a JPEG image from a frame of a movie

1. Display the Flash program, then click **10** on the Timeline.

2. Click **File** on the menu bar, then click **Publish Settings**.

3. Click the **GIF Image check box** to deselect it, then click the **JPEG Image check box** to select it.

   Deselecting the GIF format will prevent the GIF file from being created again.

4. Review the default settings, click **Publish**, then click **OK**.

5. Open your browser, then use the browser to open the planeLoop.jpg file from the drive and folder where you save your work.

TIP If you do not see the JPG file, change the file type to All Files.

6. Notice that the static JPEG image appears in the browser, as shown in Figure 5.

7. Close your browser, then display the Flash program.

You reviewed the default publish settings for a JPEG image, then created a JPEG image and viewed it in your web browser.

Figure 5 *The JPEG image displayed in a browser*

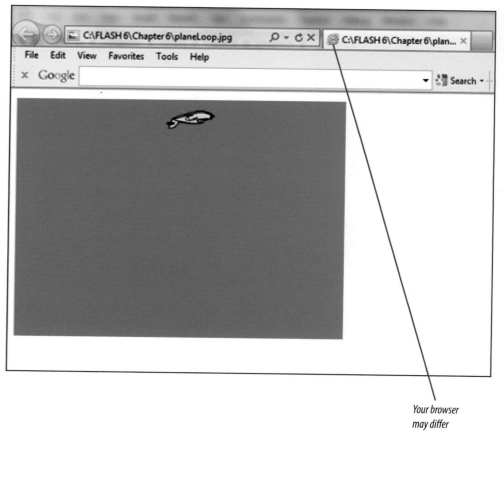

Your browser may differ

Figure 6 *The completed Win Projector format dialog box*

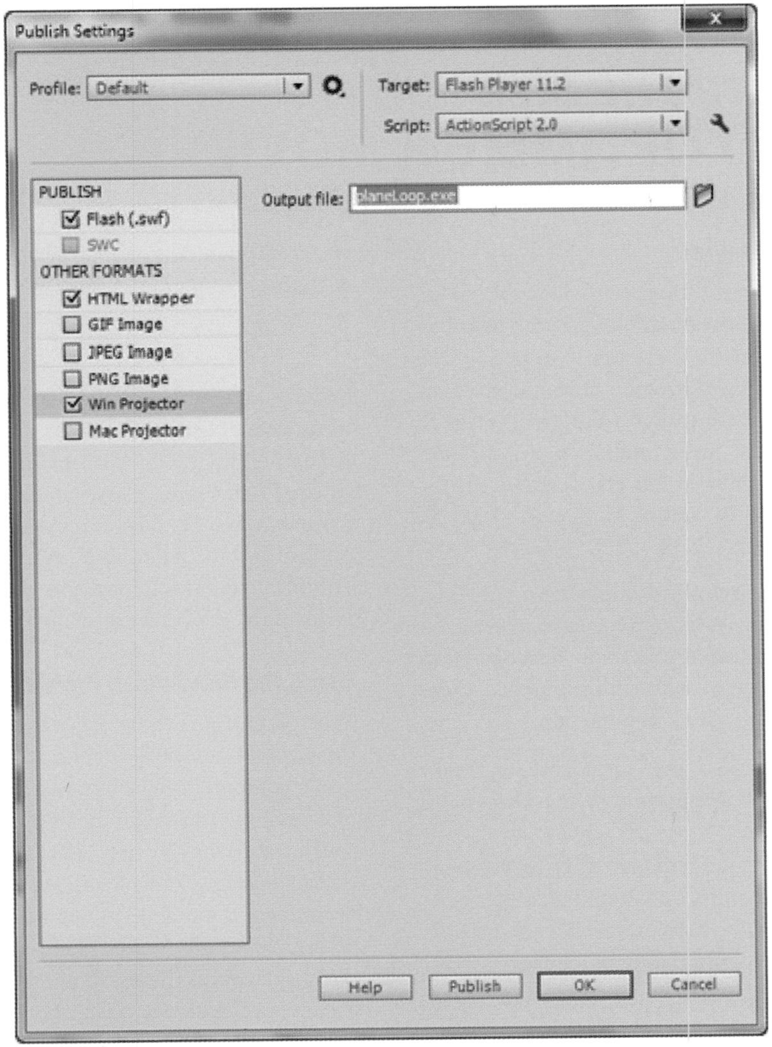

Create an executable file

1. Click **File** on the menu bar, then click **Publish Settings**.

2. Click the **JPEG Image check box** to deselect it, then click the **Win Projector** (or **Mac Projector**) **check box** to select it.

   Note: A Mac Projector file uses the extension .app.

3. Review the default settings as shown in Figure 6.

4. Click **Publish**, then click **OK**.

5. Use your file management program to navigate to the drive and folder where you save your Data Files, then notice the size of the executable file.

   Note: The file size of executable files can be very large.

6. Double-click the **filename** to run the file.

7. Close the player window.

8. Save your work, then close the movie.

You reviewed the default publish settings for an executable file, then created an executable file and viewed it.

Reduce File Size
TO OPTIMIZE A MOVIE

What You'll Do

In this lesson, you will test a movie and reduce its file size.

Testing a Movie

The goal in publishing a movie is to provide the most effective playback for the intended audience. This requires that you pay special attention to the download time and playback speed. Users are turned off by long waits to view content, jerky animations, and audio that skips. These events can occur as the file size increases in relation to the user's Internet connection speed.

Before you publish a movie, be sure you have maximized its optimization in order to improve its delivery. As you develop Flash movies, keep in mind and practice these guidelines for optimizing movies:

■ Use symbols and instances for every element that appears in a movie more than once.
■ Use tween animations rather than frame-by-frame animations when possible.
■ Use movie clips rather than graphic symbols for animation sequences.
■ Confine the area of change to a keyframe so that the action takes place in as small an area as possible.
■ Use bitmap graphics as static elements rather than in animations.

■ Group elements, such as related images.
■ Limit the number of fonts and font styles.
■ Use gradients and alpha transparencies sparingly.

When you publish a movie, Flash optimizes it using default features, including compressing the entire movie, which is later decompressed by the Flash Player. However, Flash provides various ways to test a movie before you publish it to determine where changes/optimizations can improve its delivery. Two features for testing are discussed next.

Using the Bandwidth Profiler

When a movie is delivered over the Internet, the contents of each frame are sent to the user's computer. Depending on the amount of data in the frame and the user's connection speed, the movie may pause while the frame's contents download. The first step in optimizing a movie is to test the movie and determine which frames may create a pause during playback. The test should be done using a simulated Internet connection speed that is representative of the speed of your target audience. You can set a simulated speed using the **Bandwidth Profiler**, shown in Figure 7. The Bandwidth Profiler allows you to view a graphical representation of the size of each frame. Each bar represents one frame of the movie, and the height of the bar corresponds to the frame's size. If a bar extends above the red baseline, the movie may need to pause to allow the frame's contents to be downloaded. Figure 7 shows the following:

■ Movie information: dimensions, frame rate, file size, duration (in frames and seconds), and preload (number of frames and amount of time it takes before the application starts playing)
■ Settings: simulated bandwidth (specified in the View menu option)
■ State: number of the selected frame (that is, the location of the playhead) and size of the contents in that frame

The Bandwidth Profiler shown in Figure 7 indicates that downloading frame 38 may result in a pause because of the large size of the contents in this frame in relationship to the connection speed and the frame rate. If the specified connection speed is correct for your target audience and the frame rate is needed to ensure acceptable animation quality, then the only change that can be made is in the contents of the frame.

Using the Simulate Download Feature

When testing a movie, you can simulate downloading Flash movies using different connection speeds. The most common connections are dial-up, broadband (both DSL and cable), and T1. Dial-up is a phone connection that provides a relatively slow download speed. Broadband is a type of data transmission in which a wide band of frequencies is available to transmit more information at the same time. DSL provides a broadband Internet connection speed that is available through phone lines. DSL and cable are widely used by homes and businesses. T1 provides an extremely fast connection speed and is widely used in businesses, especially for intranet (a computer network within a company) applications. You can test the movie that you are developing at the different speeds to evaluate the download experience for potential users.

Figure 7 *The Bandwidth Profiler*

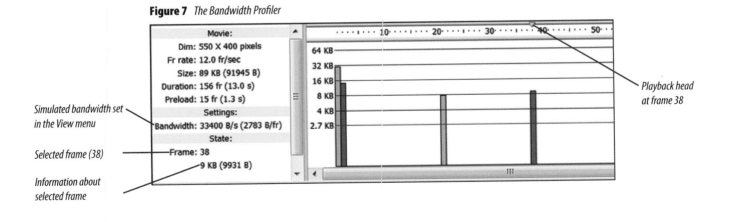

Simulated bandwidth set in the View menu

Selected frame (38)

Information about selected frame

Playback head at frame 38

Test the download time for a movie

1. Open fl6_2.fla, then save it as **planeFun.fla**.

2. Turn on your computer speakers or plug in headphones if you would like to hear the audio that is part of this movie.

3. Change the view to **Fit in Window**.

4. Click **Control** on the menu bar, point to **Test Movie**, then click **in Flash Professional**.

5. Maximize the Flash Player window.

6. Click **View** on the menu bar, point to **Download Settings**, then click **DSL (32.6 KB/s)**, as shown in Figure 8.

   The connection speeds (especially DSL) are affected by several factors including your Internet service provider capabilities, distance to telecom equipment, your computer and Internet connectivity equipment and the amount of Internet traffic. The Download Simulator provides relative connection speeds and is used to help determine where in a movie a download problem might exist.

7. Click **View** on the menu bar, then click **Simulate Download**.

   The movie is loaded and ready to play in the Flash Player using the simulated speed of 32.6 KB/s.

   (continued)

Figure 8 *Selecting the connection speed for a simulated download*

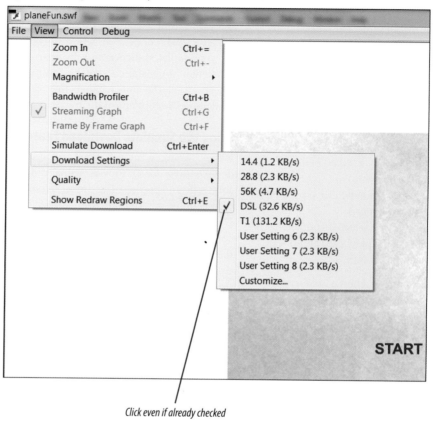

Click even if already checked

Figure 9 *A pause in the movie*

Movie pauses at this point

8. Click **Start**, then notice the pause in the movie when the plane begins to morph into the hot air balloon, as shown in Figure 9.

   You may have to wait several moments for the movie to continue. The pause is caused by the simulated browser waiting for the remaining contents of the movie to be downloaded.

9. Click **View** on the menu bar, point to **Download Settings**, then click **T1 (131.2 KB/s)**.

10. Click **View** on the menu bar, verify the Simulate Download feature is off (no check mark next to it), then click **Simulate Download** to turn on the feature.

    When you change a download setting, you need to be sure the Simulate Download feature is off, and then you must turn it on again to start the simulation with the new setting. The movie is loaded and ready to play in the Flash Player at the simulated download speed of 131.2 KB/s.

11. Click **Start**, then notice the pause in the movie is shorter with the simulated T1 line speed.

TIP If you don't notice a difference, turn the Simulate Download feature off and then on again.

Note: To see a dramatic difference, select one of the simulated dial-up speeds (14.4, 28.8, or 56 K). If you do this, be prepared to wait up to several minutes for the plane to morph into a hot air balloon. If you have users that connect via a dial-up connection, be sure to simulate a dial-up connection and make adjustments as needed so the movie displays as smoothly as possible.

You used the Flash Player window to simulate the download time for a movie using different connection speeds.

Use the Bandwidth Profiler

1. Verify that the Flash Player window is still open.

2. Click **View** on the menu bar, point to **Download Settings**, then click **DSL (32.6 KB/s)** to select it.

3. Click **View** on the menu bar, then click **Bandwidth Profiler**.

4. Click **View** on the menu bar, then verify Frame By Frame Graph is selected.

5. Click **View** on the menu bar, then click **Simulate Download**.

   Notice the green bar as it scrolls at the top of the Bandwidth Profiler to indicate the frames being downloaded. The bar pauses at frame 38, as shown in Figure 10.

6. Click **frame 37** on the Timeline, then notice that the only object in the frame is the morphing balloon, and its size is less than 1 KB.

7. Click **frame 38** on the Timeline, then notice the large color photograph.

   The frame setting in the State area indicates that the file size is over 600 KB. It takes several moments to download this large image, which causes the pause in the movie. One way to optimize the movie is to replace the image with the large file size, the one that is currently in frame 38, with an image that is a smaller file size.

8. Close the Flash Player window.

You used the Bandwidth Profiler to determine which frame causes a pause in the movie.

Figure 10 *The Bandwidth Profiler indicating the pause at frame 38*

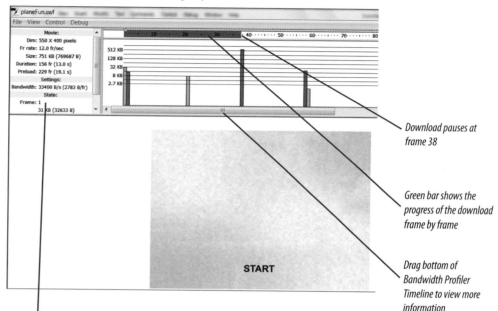

Download pauses at frame 38

Green bar shows the progress of the download frame by frame

Drag bottom of Bandwidth Profiler Timeline to view more information

There is a stop action in frame 1 causing the movie to stay at frame 1 while the rest of the movie is downloading

Figure 11 *Positioning the cloud image*

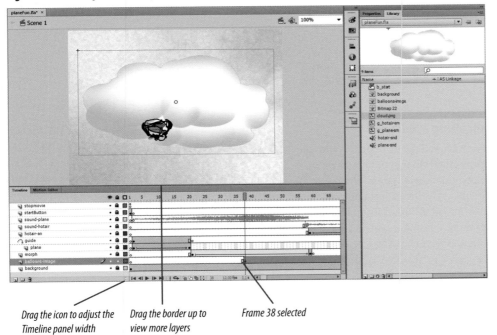

Drag the icon to adjust the Timeline panel width

Drag the border up to view more layers

Frame 38 selected

Optimize a movie by reducing file size

1. Point to the **top border** of the Timeline, then, when the pointer changes to a double-arrow ⇕, drag the **top border** up to view the balloons-image layer.

   TIP If the layer name appears cut off, then drag the Adjust Timeline panel width icon to the right until the layer name is fully visible.

2. Click **frame 38** on the balloons-image layer to view the image on the Stage.

3. Click the **balloon photographic image** on the Stage, click **Edit** on the menu bar, then click **Cut**.

   The balloon photograph is no longer visible on the Stage.

4. Display the Library panel.

5. Verify frame 38 is selected, then drag the **cloud.png** graphic from the Library panel to the center of the Stage, as shown in Figure 11.

6. Click **Control** on the menu bar, point to **Test Movie**, click **in Flash Professional**, then maximize the Flash Player window if it is not already maximized.

7. Click **View** on the Flash Player window menu bar, click **Simulate Download**, wait for the download to finish, then click **Start**.

   Notice the movie no longer pauses.

8. Click **frame 38** on the Timeline in the Flash Player window and notice that the file size is now just above the 8 KB line.

9. Click **View**, click **Bandwidth Profiler** to close the Bandwidth Profiler, close the Flash Player window, save your work, then close the movie.

You replaced an image that had a large file size with one having a small file size to help optimize a movie.

Create a
PRELOADER

What You'll Do

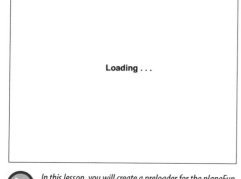

In this lesson, you will create a preloader for the planeFun movie.

Preloading a Movie

One way you can improve the playback performance of large or complex movies is to preload the movie frames. Preloading frames prevents the browser from playing a specified frame or series of frames until all of the frames have been downloaded. Commonly, a **preloader** frame includes a simple animation that starts in frame 1 and loops until the rest of the movie has been downloaded. The animation could consist of the words "Please wait" flashing on the screen, the word "Loading" with a series of scrolling dots, or the hand of a clock sweeping around in a circle. The purpose of the animation is to indicate to the viewer that the movie is being loaded. The animation is placed on its own layer. A second layer contains the ActionScript code that checks to see if the movie has been loaded and, if not, causes a loop that continues the preloader animation until the last frame of the movie has been loaded.

For example, assume a movie has 155 frames. An additional 10 frames could be added to the beginning of the movie for the preloader, and the preloader animation would run from frames 1 to 10. A label, such as **startofMovie**, would be added to frame 11 (the first frame of the actual movie). Another label, such as **endofMovie**, would be added to frame 165, the last frame of the entire movie. Then the following ActionScript code would be placed in frame 1 of the movie on the preLoaderScript layer:

```
ifFrameLoaded ("endofMovie") {
    gotoAndPlay ("startofMovie");
}
```

This ActionScript code is a conditional statement that checks to see if the frame labeled endofMovie is loaded. If the statement is true, then the next line of the script is executed and the playhead goes to the frame labeled startofMovie. This ActionScript code is placed in frame 1 on the preLoaderScript layer. So each time the playhead is on frame 1, there is a check to see if the entire movie has been downloaded. If the condition is false, the playhead moves on to frames 2, 3, 4, and so on. Then the following ActionScript code would be placed in frame 10.

gotoAndPlay (1);

This creates a loop. When the movie first starts, the playhead is on frame 1 and there is a check to see if the movie has been loaded. If not, the playhead continues to frame 10 (playing the preloader animation) where the script "gotoAndPlay (1)"; causes the playhead to loop back to frame 1 for another check.

The looping process continues until all movie frames have been loaded.

Figure 12 shows the Timeline that displays the two preloader layers after the preloader has been created.

Figure 12 *The completed preloader with the animation and ActionScript*

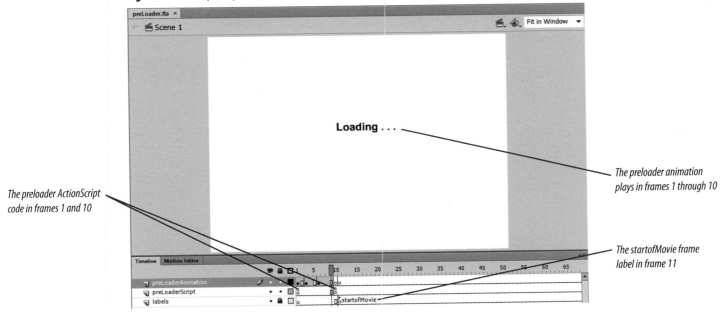

The preloader animation plays in frames 1 through 10

The preloader ActionScript code in frames 1 and 10

The startofMovie frame label in frame 11

Add layers for a preloader

1. Open fl6_3.fla, then save it as **preLoader.fla**.

   This movie is similar to the planeFun.fla movie except that the first 10 frames contain no content, and the movie again contains the larger graphic file photo of the hot air balloons.

2. Change the view to **Fit in Window**.

3. Click the **labels layer** at the top of the Timeline, then click the **New Layer icon** 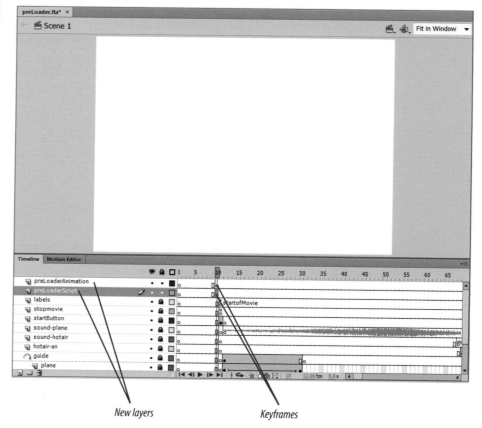 to insert a **new layer**.

4. Name the new layer **preLoaderScript**.

5. Insert a **new layer** above the preLoaderScript layer, then name it **preLoaderAnimation**.

6. Click **frame 10** on the preLoaderAnimation layer, then insert a **keyframe**.

7. Insert a **keyframe** in frame 10 on the preLoaderScript layer.

   Your screen should resemble Figure 13.

You added two layers that will be used to create a preloader. One layer will contain the ActionScript and the other layer will contain the animation for the preloader.

Figure 13 *The preloader layers added to the Timeline*

New layers

Keyframes

Preparing and Publishing Applications

Figure 14 *The Actions panel showing frame to which action will be applied*

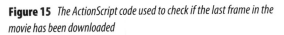

The ActionScript that is to be developed will be applied to frame 1 on the preLoaderScript layer

Script Assist feature is off

Figure 15 *The ActionScript code used to check if the last frame in the movie has been downloaded*

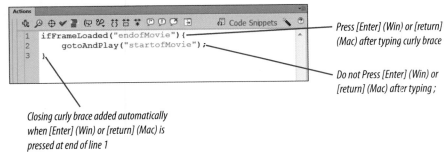

Press [Enter] (Win) or [return] (Mac) after typing curly brace

Do not Press [Enter] (Win) or [return] (Mac) after typing ;

Closing curly brace added automatically when [Enter] (Win) or [return] (Mac) is pressed at end of line 1

Add actions to the preloader

1. Open the Actions panel, then turn off the Script Assist feature if it is on.

2. Click **frame 1** on the preLoaderScript layer.

3. Verify that preLoaderScript:1 is displayed in the lower-left corner of the Actions panel Script pane, as shown in Figure 14.

4. Click the **Actions panel Script pane**, then type the following code, matching use of capital letters, spacing, and punctuation exactly.

   ifFrameLoaded ("endofMovie") {

       gotoAndPlay ("startofMovie");

   Your screen should match Figure 15.

   Note: A closing curly brace was added automatically when you pressed [Enter] (Win) or [return] (Mac) at the end of line. You do not type the closing brace. If your press [Enter] (Win) or [return] (Mac) at the end of line two, a second curly brace will be added to the code. If this happens, delete one curly brace. Be sure there is only one closing curly brace.

5. Click **frame 10** on the preLoaderScript layer, then verify preLoaderScript:10 is displayed in the lower-left corner of the Actions panel Script pane.

6. Click the **Actions panel Script pane**, then type the following code.

   gotoAndPlay (1);

7. Close the Actions panel.

You added actions to frames on the preLoaderScript layer that create a loop. The loop includes a check to see if the entire movie has been loaded and, if so, jumps to a starting place in the movie.

Create the preloader animation

1. Click **frame 1** on the preLoaderAnimation layer.

2. Click the **Text tool** T on the Tools menu, verify the text type is set to Classic Text, click the middle of the Stage, then type **Loading**.

3. Double-click to select **Loading**, then use the Properties panel to set the font to **Arial**, the style to **Bold**, the size to **20**, and the color to **blue**.

4. Insert a **keyframe** in frame 3 on the preLoader-Animation layer.

5. Using the **Text** ⊥T **pointer**, point to the right of the g in Loading, click, press the **spacebar**, then type a **period [.]**.

6. Insert a **keyframe** in frame 6 on the preLoaderAnimation layer.

7. Point to the right of the period, click, press the **spacebar**, then type a **period [.]**.

8. Insert a **keyframe** in frame 9 on the preLoader-Animation layer, point to the right of the period, click, press the **spacebar**, then type a **period [.]**.

   Your screen should resemble Figure 16.

9. Click **frame 10** on the preLoaderAnimation layer, click **Insert** on the menu bar, point to **Timeline**, then click **Blank Keyframe**.

   Inserting a blank keyframe prevents the contents of the previous frame from being inserted into the frame.

10. Drag the **playhead** back and forth across frames 1 through 10 and view the animation.

You created an animation that causes the word Loading to appear, followed by three dots, as the playhead loops waiting for the movie to load. You can create any animation for the preloader and use as many frames as desired.

Figure 16 *The text used in the preloader animation*

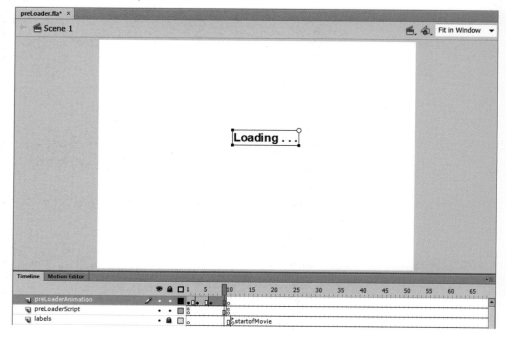

Figure 17 *The Bandwidth Profiler showing the delay in downloading frame 48*

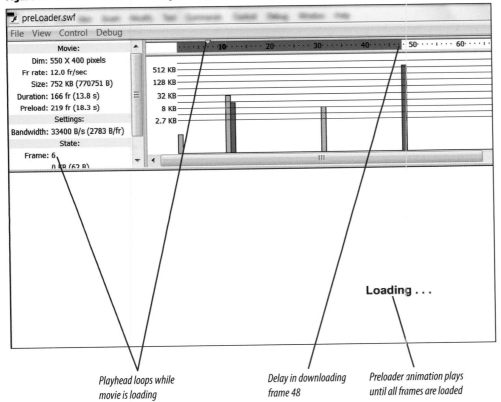

Playhead loops while
movie is loading

Delay in downloading
frame 48

Preloader animation plays
until all frames are loaded

Testing the preloader

1. Click **Control** on the menu bar, point to **Test Movie**, then click **in Flash Professional**.

2. Maximize the Flash Player window if it is not already maximized.

3. Click **View** on the menu bar, then click **Bandwidth Profiler** to display it if it is not already displayed.

4. Click **View** on the menu bar, point to **Download Settings**, then verify that DSL (32.6 KB/s) is selected.

5. Click **View** on the menu bar, then click **Simulate Download**.

   Notice the playhead loops, causing the preloader animation "Loading . . . " to play over and over in the Flash Player window as the frames are loaded. There is a delay in downloading frame 48, as shown in Figure 17, as the large JPG file is loaded. Once all frames are loaded, the screen with the Start button appears in the Flash Player window.

6. Repeat Step 5 twice (to turn off and then turn on the Simulated Download feature) to run the simulation again, then drag the **scroll bar** on the Bandwidth Profiler to the right as needed to view the last frames of the movie (through frame 165).

7. Close the Bandwidth Profiler, then close the Flash Player window.

8. Save and close the movie.

You tested the preloader by simulating a download and you viewed the information on the Bandwidth Profiler during the simulation.

Lesson 3   Create a Preloader

Publish AIR
APPLICATIONS

What You'll Do

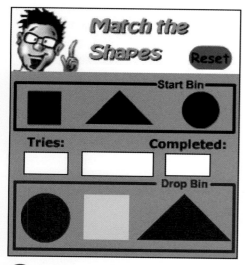

In this lesson, you will publish a Flash AIR application for stand-alone delivery.

Understanding the Development Process for AIR Applications

Until now you have been creating Flash applications and publishing them as SWF files to be viewed in a web browser using the Flash Player. Flash provides another technology, AIR (Adobe Integrated Runtime), that creates applications that can be played without a browser. An AIR app can be displayed on mobile devices, on stand-alone computers, on the Internet, and even on television sets. AIR applications are cross-platform, which means they will play on different operating systems such as Windows and Apple computers. In addition, the AIR format allows a developer to create a single application and deliver it on multiple devices. This saves development time and money as the same content can be repurposed for different audiences. You can repurpose a Flash application for delivery on various devices by simply changing the publish settings. However, there are always considerations that must be taken into account as content is repurposed. For example, the screen size of mobile devices requires a different design than the screen size of typical desktop computers. In this lesson you will repurpose a Flash application so it plays as a stand-alone application on a desktop computer.

There are several files that are created when publishing an AIR app including the descriptor and installer files required to deploy it. Flash creates the application descriptor XML file, which contains the settings, the installer file that is used to install the application on a computer, and the SWF file when you publish the AIR application. You specify the settings for these files in the AIR Settings dialog box. Once you have created an AIR file, this dialog box can be opened from either the document Properties panel or the Publish Settings option on the File menu.

Figure 18 shows the Publish Settings dialog box with the default settings Flash (.swf), HTML Wrapper, and Flash Player 11.2. To create an AIR file you need to change the Publish Target setting from Flash Player to AIR 2.5, as shown in Figure 19. Then you need to open the AIR Settings dialog box and complete the settings contained within four tabs, as shown in Figure 20 and explained next.

Settings on the General Tab

The General tab of the AIR Settings dialog box contains the following options:

Output file: Name and location of the AIR file to be created when using the Publish command. The .air file extension indicates an AIR package file.

Output as: AIR package allows cross-platform delivery. Windows Installer provides a specific Windows installer (.exe) instead of a platform-independent AIR installer (.air).

App Name: Name used by the AIR application installer to generate the application filename and the application folder. The AIR application name defaults to the name of the SWF file.

Version: Specifies a version number for the AIR application you are creating.

App ID: Identifies the AIR application with a unique ID.

Description: Used to enter a description of the AIR application, which is displayed in the installer window when the user installs the AIR application.

Copyright: Used to enter a copyright notice.

Window Style: Used to specify the window style for the user interface when the user runs the AIR application on a computer.

Render mode: Used to specify whether to use the computer's CPU or graphics card when displaying images.

Profiles: Used in the programming process when targeting various devices.

Included Files: Used to add files, such as video or sound files, to the AIR application package. By default, the AIR application descriptor XML file and the main SWF file are automatically included.

Figure 18 *The Publish Settings dialog box*

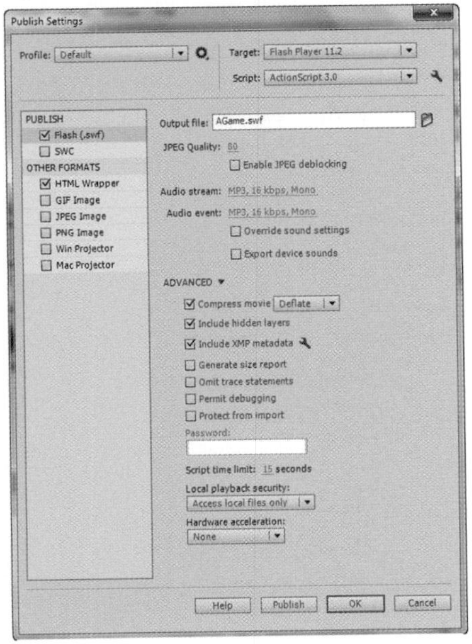

Figure 19 *Changing the Publish Target settings*

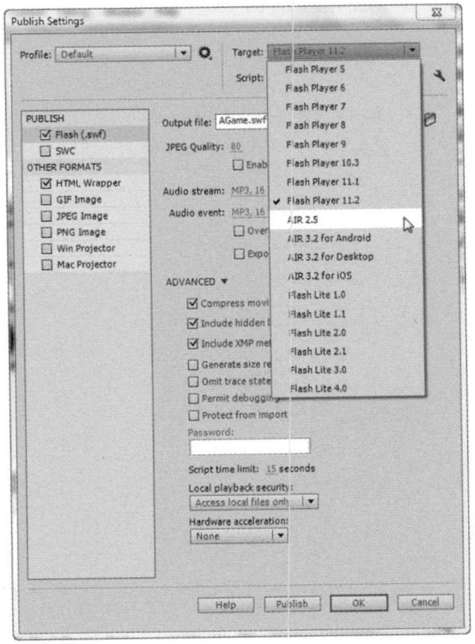

Figure 20 *Tabs on the AIR Settings dialog box*

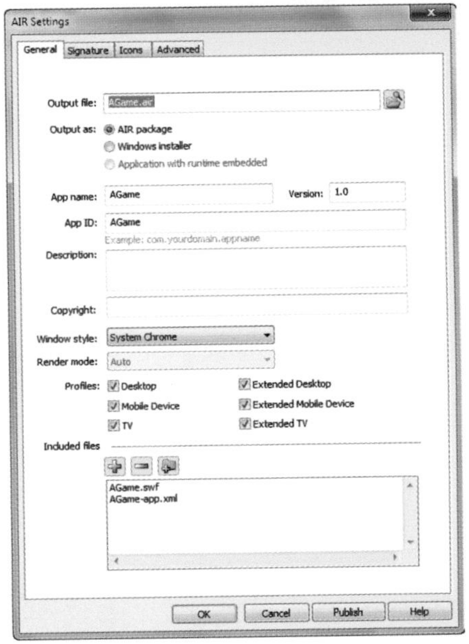

Settings on the Signature Tab

Figure 21 shows the AIR Settings dialog box with the Signature tab active. You use the settings on this tab to create a certificate, which is a digital signature, for your application. This certificate identifies the publisher of the application and assures the user of the AIR application that the application is authentic.

Settings on the Icons Tab

Figure 22 shows the AIR Settings dialog box with the Icons tab active. An icon is the graphic that displays after you install the application and run it in the Adobe AIR runtime. It could be a logo, a drawing that represents the app, or any graphic created by the developer. You use the settings on the Icons tab to specify icons for the application. For instance, the Icons tab in the AIR Settings dialog box allows you to specify four different square sizes for an icon (16, 32, 48 and 128 pixels) to allow for the different views in which the icon appears. For example, the icon can appear in a web browser in thumbnail, detail, and tile views. It can also appear as a desktop icon and in the title of the AIR application window, as well as in other places. The graphics need be a PNG file type. You can create PNG files using graphics programs such as Adobe Fireworks and Photoshop.

Settings on the Advanced Tab

Figure 23 shows the AIR Settings dialog box with the Advanced tab active. When you publish an AIR application for delivery as a stand-alone application, the user needs to install the application on a computer. You use settings on the Advanced tab to specify additional settings for the installation. For example, you can specify associated file types, size and placement of the initial window used to view the application, folder in which the application is installed, and Program menu folder in which to place the file.

Figure 21 *The Signature tab settings*

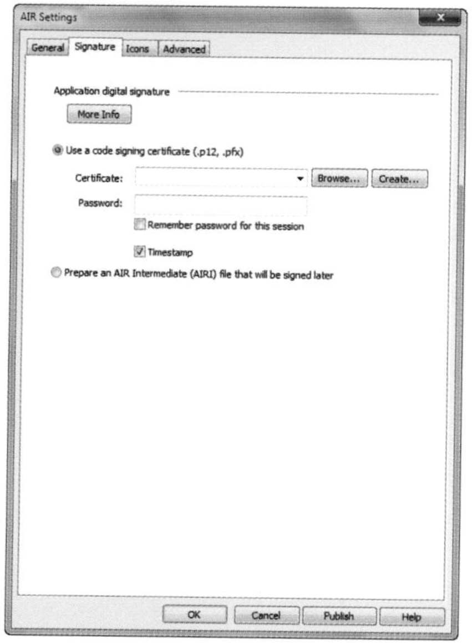

Figure 22 *Icons tab settings*

Figure 23 *Advanced tab settings*

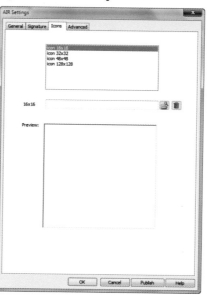

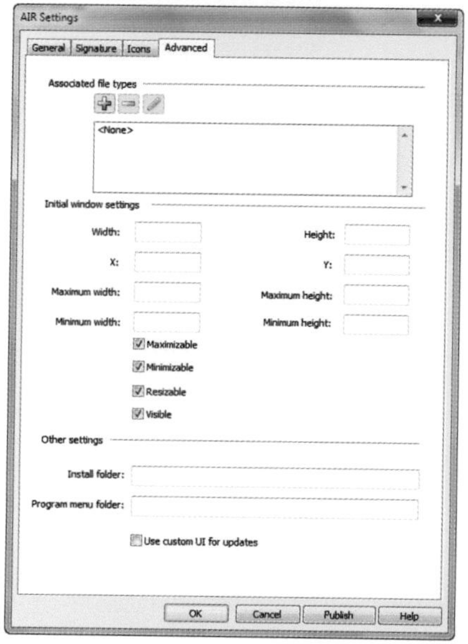

Figure 24 *Displaying the Publish Target list*

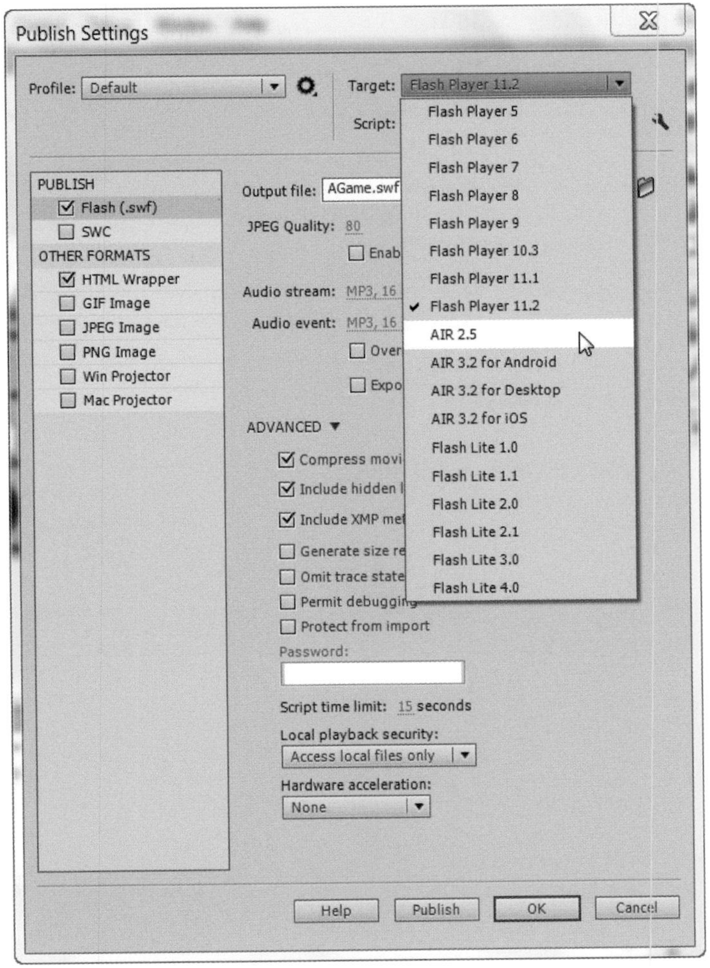

1. Open fl6_4, then save it as **AGame.fla**.

2. Click **File** on the menu bar, point to **Publish Preview**, then click **Default-(HTML)**.

   Note: If a missing font message appears in the Output area at the bottom of the screen, you can ignore the message. You will reset the workspace at the end of the lesson.

3. Play the game, then close the browser.

4. Click **File** on the menu bar, then click **Publish Settings**.

5. Click the **Target list arrow**, then click **AIR 2.5** as shown in Figure 24.

   Note: The version numbers in your list may differ from those shown in the figure.

6. Click the **Player Settings icon** 🔧 to the right of the Target list box in order to display the AIR Settings dialog box.

   The General tab settings are displayed. Study these settings and notice that the filename, AGame, is used for the Output file, App name, App ID, and the included files. You will use the General default settings.

7. Click the **Icons tab**.

8. Verify icon 16x16 is highlighted, then click the **Search icon** 📇.

9. Navigate to the location where your data files are stored, click **Match16.png**, then click **Open**.

   Note: If a message appears indicating the icon must be copied to a folder relative to the root folder, click OK.

   (continued)

10. Click **icon 32 × 32** to highlight it, click the **Search icon** 🔍, click **Match32.png**, then click **Open**.

11. Click **icon 48 × 48** to highlight it, click the **Search icon** 🔍, click **Match48.png**, then click **Open**.

12. Click **icon 128 × 128** to highlight it, click the **Search icon** 🔍, click **Match128.png**, then click **Open**.

13. Click the **Signature tab**, then click the **Create button** (Win) or the **New button** (Mac) to begin the process for creating a Self-Signed Digital Certificate.

14. Type your name, organization unit (such as your program or department) and organization name (such as your school).

15. Type a password of your choice, making sure to remember it, then type the password again in the Confirm text box to confirm it.

    Your dialog box should resemble Figure 25.

16. Click the **Browse button** (Win) or the **Folder icon** (Mac).

    The Select File Destination dialog box appears with the folder where you store your solution files as the active folder. Notice the filename is entered and the file type is p12, designating this as a Certificate File.

    Note: The file type does not show if you do not have file extensions set to visible or if you are using a Mac.

17. Verify your solution file folder is the active destination folder, then click **Save**.

    (continued)

Figure 25 *The completed Self-Signed Digital Certificate*

Preparing and Publishing Applications

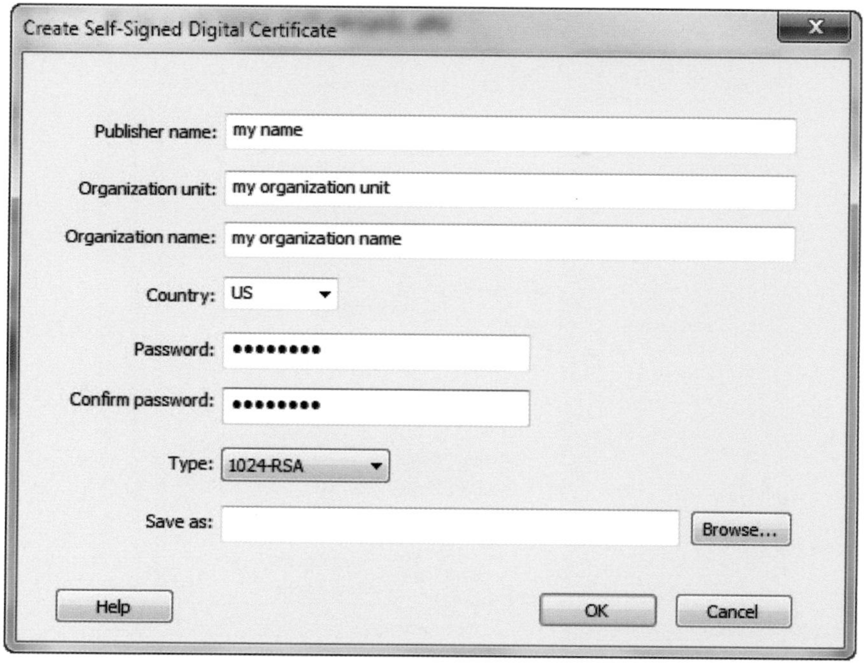

Figure 26 *The completed Signature tab settings*

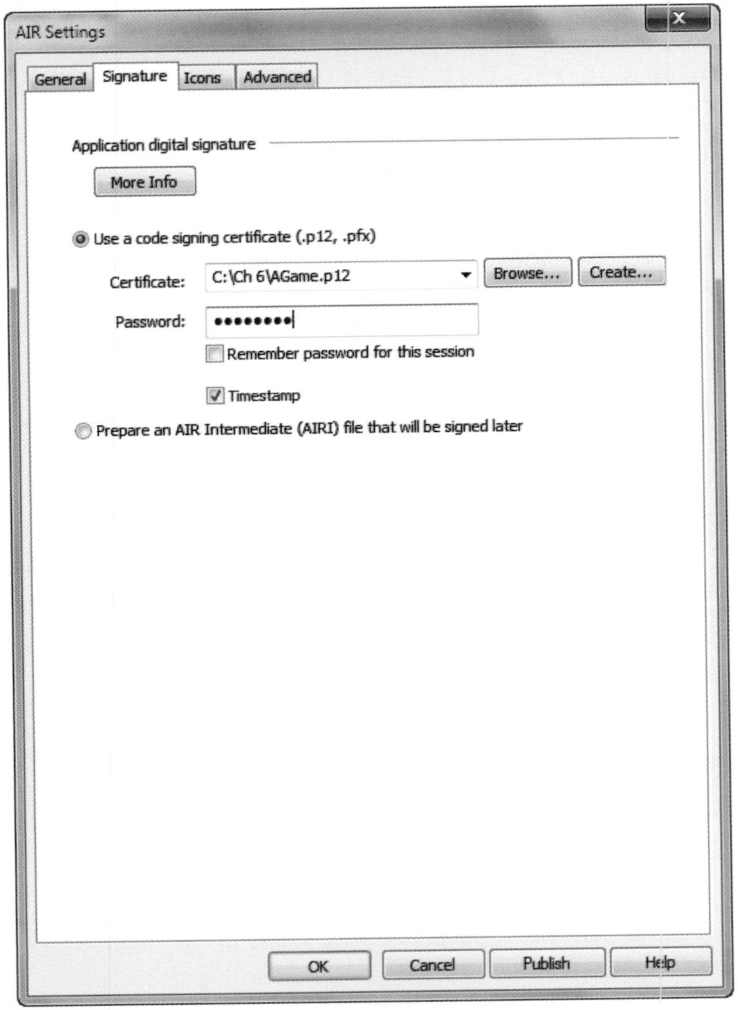

18. Click **OK** in the Create Self-Signed Digital Certificate dialog box.

    After a few moments the following message appears: Self-Signed certificate has been created.

19. Click **OK** to close the message box.

20. Type your password in the Signature tab dialog box.

21. Verify Timestamp is selected, as shown in Figure 26.

22. Click the **Publish button**.

    Note: The message "AIR file has been created" appears when the process is complete.

23. Click **OK** to close the message box.

24. Click **OK** to close the AIR Settings dialog box.

25. Click **OK** to close the Publish Settings dialog box.

26. Save the application, click **Reset 'Essentials'** on the Essentials menu, then close the application.

27. Navigate to the drive and folder where you save your files, then notice the files created in this lesson that are specific to creating an AIR application.

    AGame-app.xml: a text file containing the settings that were specified in the publish process

    AGame.air: the AIR file

    AGame.p12: the Self-Signed Digital Certificate

    To launch the AIR app you need to install it. This can be done by right-clicking the AIR file and choosing Install. However, depending on the setup of your computer, you may not have permission to install applications.

28. Return to the Flash program.

You repurposed a Flash application for delivery as a stand-alone application.

Create and Publish Applications for
MOBILE DEVICES

What You'll Do

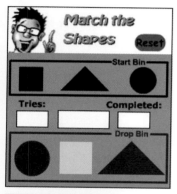

In this lesson, you will publish two Flash applications for a mobile device. One has been repurposed and the other uses a pinching effect.

Understanding the Development Process for Mobile Apps

A new feature of Flash CS6 is the ability to quickly and easily develop applications for mobile devices, such as smartphones and tablets. Flash CS6 specifically targets Android and iOS (Apple) devices because of their large markets. You can start a new AIR for Android or AIR for iOS application or you can repurpose an existing Flash document. In either case, you create the application in Flash and publish it as an AIR file. The publish process requires specifying various settings by completing several dialog boxes. Figure 27 shows the Publish Settings dialog box for an AIR for Android app.

Settings on the General tab

The AIR for Android Settings dialog box has five tabs (General, Deployment, Icons, Permissions, Languages), which are explained briefly. Notice that while many of the settings available on these tabs are similar to the settings discussed in the previous lesson, there are options available specific to an application, such as AIR for Android, as discussed in this lesson.

Output file: Displays the name and location of the AIR file. The .apk file extension indicates an AIR for Android package file.

App name: Displays the name that appears on the mobile device when the app is downloaded. Also, this is the name used when searching for the app in the Android market.

App ID: Displays a string of characters that uniquely identifies the application; the characters you type are preceded by "air". when the ID is displayed.

Version: Displays a version number for the application, which can be changed as new versions of the application are published.

Version label: Used to describe the version (optional).

Aspect   Ratio: Determines   how   the application is displayed. There are several options available: Portrait maintains the portrait orientation of the application no matter how the mobile device is turned. Landscape maintains the landscape orientation of the application no matter how the mobile device is turned. Auto, when selected along with Auto orientation, launches the application on the device in either portrait or landscape mode, depending on the current orientation of the device.

Full screen: Sets the application to run in full screen mode.

Auto orientation: Allows the application to switch from portrait to landscape mode and vice versa, depending on the current orientation of the device; must be used in conjunction with Aspect Ratio Auto mode.

Included Files: Displays the files and folders to include in your application package. Allows you to add files, such as video, audio, or SWF files. By default, the main SWF file and the application descriptor XML file are included. The descriptor XML file contains all the general settings such as the Output file, App name, Version, and so on.

While you can make changes in the General settings, the default settings are often acceptable.

Settings on the Deployment Tab

Figure 28 shows the AIR for Android Settings dialog box with the Deployment tab active. These settings allow you to create a certificate that identifies who you are to the user.

Certificate (Self-Created): The digital certificate for the application.

Password: The password for the selected digital certificate.

Android deployment type: Android applications can be deployed in three different ways: Device release allows creation of applications for the marketplace or any other distribution medium, such as a website. Emulator release is used to test the application when an emulator program is available. Device debugging allows on-device debugging.

AIR runtime: The AIR app uses an AIR runtime plug-in. There are two choices for making sure the user has the runtime plug-in: Embed AIR runtime with the application. or Get AIR runtime from: (A message will appear on a device that does not have the runtime plug-in and the user can choose to go to the specified location, Google Android Market or Amazon Appstore.)

After publishing: Two choices as listed next are available: "Install the application on an Android device connected to the computer." or "Immediately launch the application on a connected device." You can select either choice or both choices, whichever best meets your needs.

Figure 27 *The AIR for Android Settings dialog box*

When you click the Create button, the Create Self-Signed Digital Certificate dialog box appears allowing you to identify the app developer including the Publisher name, Organization unit, and Organization name. In addition, you create a password, then specify the type of encryption and the certificate validity period (25 years minimum). The Save as option allows you to specify the filename and storage location for the certificate.

The process for creating an AIR for iOS app is similar to an AIR for Android app. However, Apple requires a mobile app developer to register with Apple and pay a fee. This lesson will focus on Android devices.

Figure 28 *The Deployment tab settings*

Settings on the Icons Tab

As discussed in Lesson 3, an icon is the graphic associated with the application. For mobile devices, the icon displays on the user's mobile device when the application is downloaded. The Icon tab in the AIR for Android Settings dialog box allows you to specify three graphic files of varying sizes (36×36, 48×48, and 72×72). These sizes are in pixels and the graphics must be a PNG file type. If no icons are provided by the developer, a generic Android icon displays.

Settings on the Permissions Tab

Figure 29 shows the AIR for Android Settings dialog box with the Permissions tab active.

Figure 29 *The Permissions tab settings*

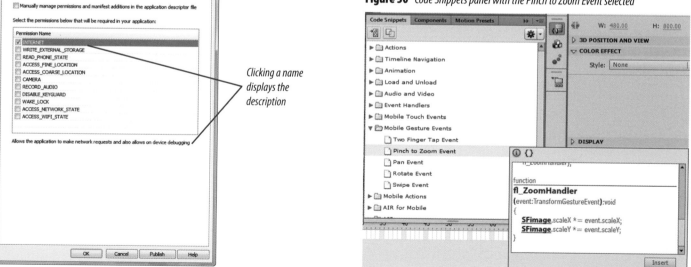

Clicking a name displays the description

You use settings on this tab to specify which services and data the application has access to on the device. Clicking on a Permission Name displays a description of the selection.

Settings on the Languages Tab

The Languages tab in the AIR for Android Settings dialog box allows you to specify the languages that will be supported by your application.

Mobile App Gestures and Events

While you can take an already developed Flash file and repurpose it for mobile devices by completing the AIR publishing process, it will not have any of the features users are accustomed to, such as pinch to zoom or swipe, unless you have specifically added these features to your Flash file. These features, called gestures and events, can easily be incorporated into a Flash file that you want to publish as a mobile app by using Code Snippets. These are small blocks of code that you apply to an object in your app or the app in general. For example, if you would like your users to be able to zoom in and out on an object, such as a map, you can select the map on the Stage and apply the Pinch to Zoom Event from the Code Snippets panel. Code Snippets are written in ActionScript 3, so the Publish Settings for your app must specify this version of ActionScript. Figure 30 shows the Code Snippets panel with the Pinch to Zoom Event highlighted under the Mobile Gesture Events category. Notice the other events including Pan, Rotate, and Swipe.

Figure 30 *Code Snippets panel with the Pinch to Zoom Event selected*

Preparing and Publishing Applications

Figure 31 *Changing the publish target to AIR for Android*

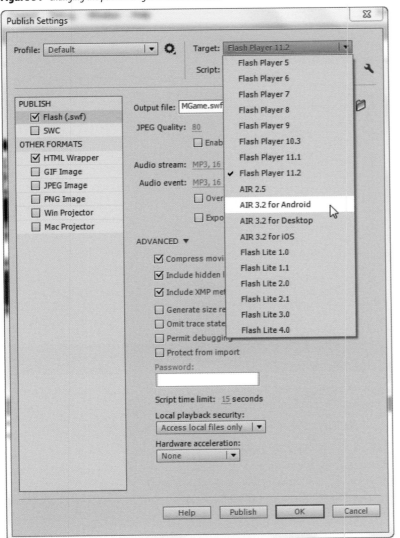

Repurpose a Flash app for use on mobile devices

1. Open fl6_5, then save it as **MGame.fla**.

2. Click **File** on the menu bar, point to **Publish Preview**, then click **Default – (HTML)**.

   Note: If a missing font message appears in the Output area at the bottom of the screen, you can ignore the message. You will reset the workspace at the end of the lesson.

3. Play the game, then close the browser.

4. Click **File** on the menu bar, then click **Publish Settings**.

5. Click the **Target list arrow**, point to **AIR 3.2 for Android** as shown in Figure 31, then **click**.

6. Click the **Player Settings icon** 🔧 to the right of the Target list box in order to display the AIR for Android Settings dialog box.

   The General tab settings are displayed. Study these settings and notice that the filename, MGame, is used for the Output file, App name, App ID, and the included files. You will use the default settings.

7. Click the **Icons tab**.

8. Verify icon 36×36 is highlighted, then click the **Search icon** 🖻.

9. Navigate to the location where your data files are stored, click **Game36.png**, then click **Open**.

10. Click **icon 48×48** to highlight it, click the **Search icon** 🖻, click **Game48.png**, then click **Open**.

(continued)

11. Click **icon 72 × 72** to highlight it, click the **Search icon**, click **Game72.png**, then click **Open**.

12. Click the **Permissions tab**.

13. Click **CAMERA**, then read the description.

14. Click **INTERNET**, then read the description.

15. Click the **INTERNET check box** to select it, then click the **Languages tab**.

16. Click the **English check box** to select it, then click the **Deployment tab**.

17. Click the **Create button** to begin the process for creating a Self-Signed Certificate.

18. Type your name, organization unit (your program or department), and organization name (such as your school).

19. Type a password of your choice, making sure to remember it, then type the password again in the Confirm text box to confirm it.

Your dialog box should resemble Figure 32.

20. Click the **Browse button**.

The Select File Destination dialog box with the folder where your solution files are stored opens as the active folder. Notice the filename is entered and the file type is p12, designating this as a Certificate File.

21. Verify your solution file folder is the active destination folder, then click **Save**.

22. Click **OK** to close the Self-Signed Digital Certificate dialog box.

After a few moments the following message appears: Self-signed certificate has been created.

(continued)

Figure 32 *The completed certificate*

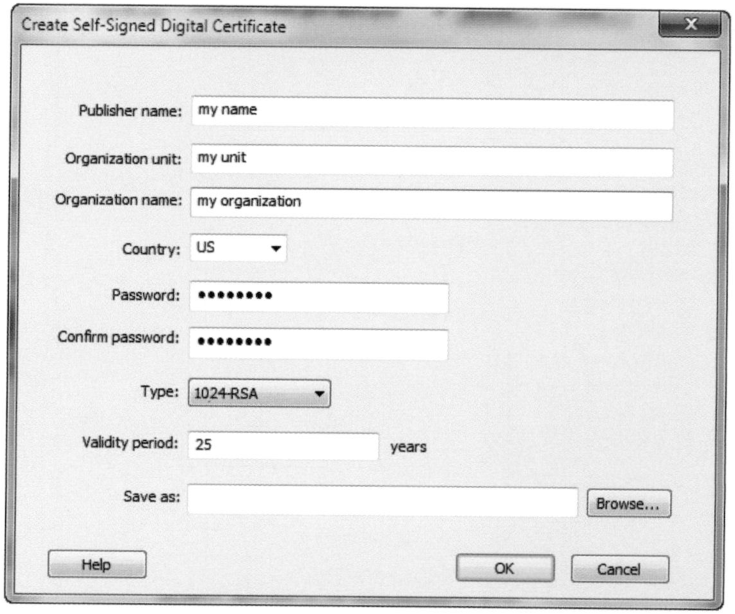

Testing an App on a Mobile Device

Flash CS6 allows you to test your application on a mobile device that is connected to your computer. You must configure your device to accept the app as follows.

Prepare your Android (2.2 or above) device for testing a mobile app:

1. Go to Settings for your device (such as on your smartphone).
2. Scroll to and select Applications, then verify "Unknown Sources" is checked.
3. Scroll to and select Development, then verify "USB debugging" is checked.
4. Connect your USB cable from the computer to your phone (the same cable used to charge your device).

Even if you do not have an Android device, you can still learn the mobile app publishing process by completing this lesson.

Preparing and Publishing Applications

Figure 33 *The completed Deployment settings*

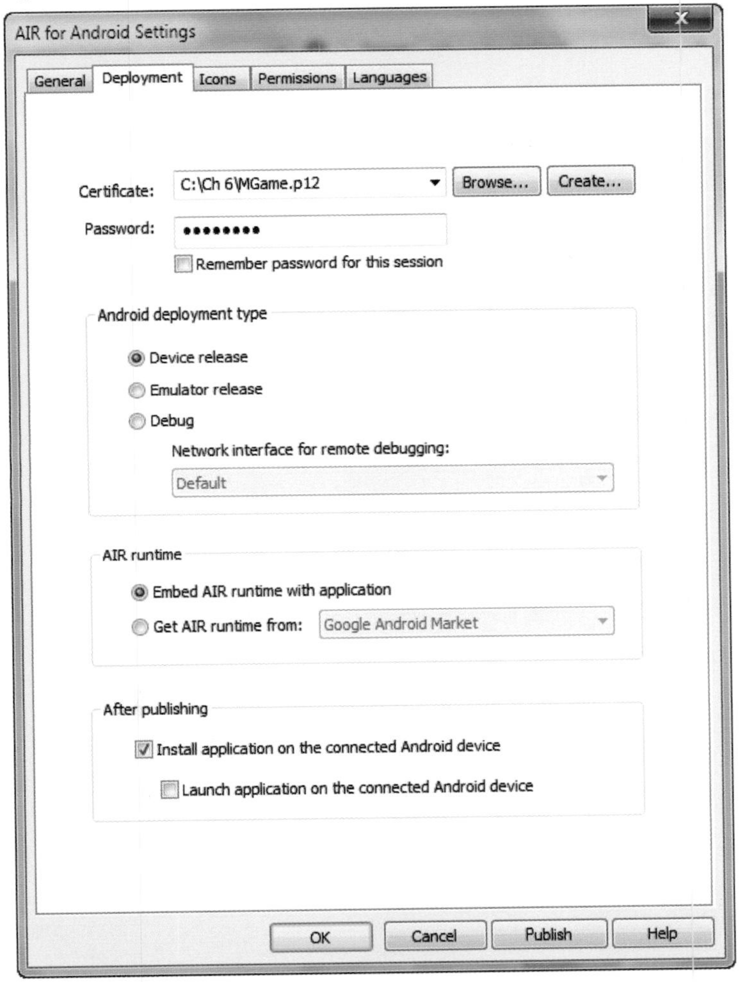

23. Click **OK** to close the message box.

24. Type your password.

25. Verify Device release and Embed AIR runtime with application are selected, as shown in Figure 33.

    Note: If you have an Android (2.2+) phone or tablet and you want to test this app, click the "Install application on the connected Android device checkbox" to select it. Make sure that the settings on your smartphone "Unknown Sources" and "USB debugging" have been turned on and that your Android 2.2+ mobile device is connected to the computer with a USB cable.

26. Click the **Publish button**.

    The publish process may take several moments.

27. Click **OK** to close the AIR for Android Settings dialog box when the publishing process is complete.

28. Click **OK** to close the Publish Settings dialog box.

29. **Save** the application, click **Reset 'Essentials'** on the Essentials menu, then close the application.

    Note: If you connected an Android (2.2+) phone or tablet, the app icon will appear on the connected Android device as an app. You can tap the icon and play the game.

You repurposed and published a Flash application for delivery on a mobile device.

1. Click **Air for Android** under Create New.
2. Save the file as **SantaFe.fla**.
3. Change the view to **Fit in Window**.
4. Click **File** on the menu bar, point to **Import**, then click **Import to Stage**.
5. Navigate to the drive and folder where your data files are stored, click **SFimage.jpg**, then click **Open**.
6. Click the **image** to select it.
7. Click **Modify** on the menu bar, then click **Convert to Symbol**.
8. Type **mc_sf** for the name, then select **Movie Clip** for the type.
9. Click the **center registration point** as shown in Figure 34, then click **OK**.

   The registration point determines how the graphic will zoom in and out.

10. Display the Properties panel, then type **SFimage** for the instance name, as shown in Figure 35.

    The instance name is used by the code to identify the object.

11. Click **frame 1** on the actions layer, open the Actions panel, then notice there is no code currently assigned to that frame.

    You will add code that will allow the user to zoom the application by pinching it.

    (continued)

Figure 34 *Selecting the center registration point*

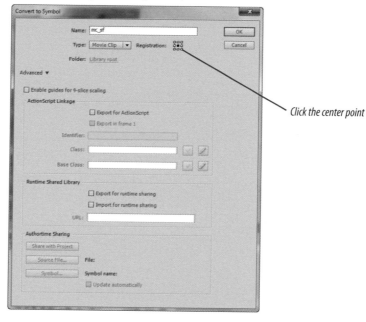

Click the center point

Figure 35 *Typing an instance name*

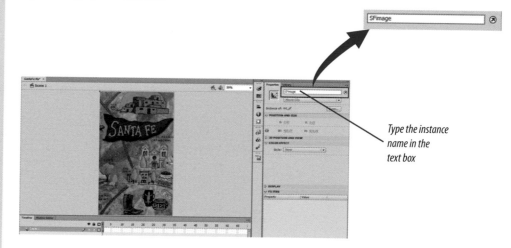

Type the instance name in the text box

Figure 36 *Selecting the Pinch to Zoom Event*

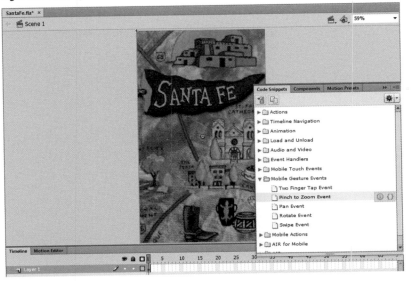

Figure 37 *The Code Snippet for the Pinch to Zoom Event*

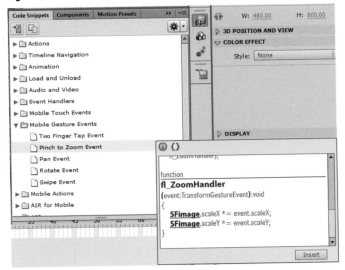

12. Click **Window** on the menu bar, then click **Code Snippets**.

   Notice the folders named Mobile Touch Events, Mobile Gesture Events, and Mobile Actions.

13. Click the **Mobile Gesture Events expand icon** ▶.

14. Click **Pinch to Zoom Event**, as shown in Figure 36.

15. Click the **Show description icon** ⓘ, then read the description of the event.

16. Click the **Show code icon** {}, then scroll to the bottom of the code box, as shown in Figure 37.

   Notice the scaleX and scaleY code. This code resizes the object based on the X and Y Stage coordinates. *Note:* If "instance_name_here" appears instead of "SFimage," you do not have the image selected. Click the map and repeat steps 11-15.

17. Click the **Insert button** to insert the code into the app.

   The code is inserted in the application.

18. Click **frame 1** on the actions layer, open the actions panel, then notice the code that has been added to that frame.

You created a new AIR for Android application and used a code snippet to add a Pinch to Zoom event.

Publish a mobile app

1. Click **File** on the menu bar, then click **AIR 3.2 for Android Settings**.

    The AIR for Android Settings dialog box opens with the General tab active. No changes are needed on this tab.

2. Click the **Icons tab**, then complete the dialog box to specify sf36.png, sf48,png, and sf72.png as the graphics to use.

3. Click the **Permissions tab**, then click the **INTERNET check box** to select it.

4. Click the **Languages tab**, then click the **English check box** to select it.

5. Click the **Deployment tab**.

6. Click the **Create button** for the Certificate option.

7. Complete the Create Self-Signed Digital Certificate dialog box, except for the Save as option.

8. Click the **Browse button** for the Save as option.

9. Verify the folder where you store your solution files is the active folder in the Select File Destination dialog box, then click **Save**.

    Your screen should resemble Figure 38.

10. Click **OK** in the Create Self-Signed digital Certificate dialog box.

    After a few moments the following message appears: Self-signed certificate has been created.

11. Click **OK**.

    (continued)

Figure 38 *The completed Self-Signed Digital Certificate*

Preparing and Publishing Applications

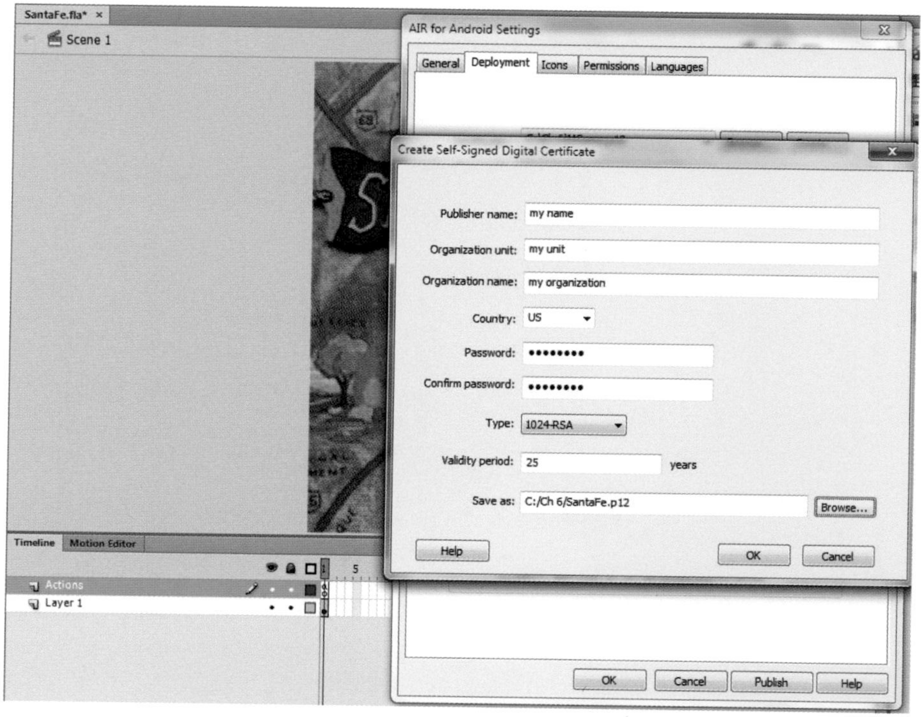

Figure 39 *The completed Deployment settings*

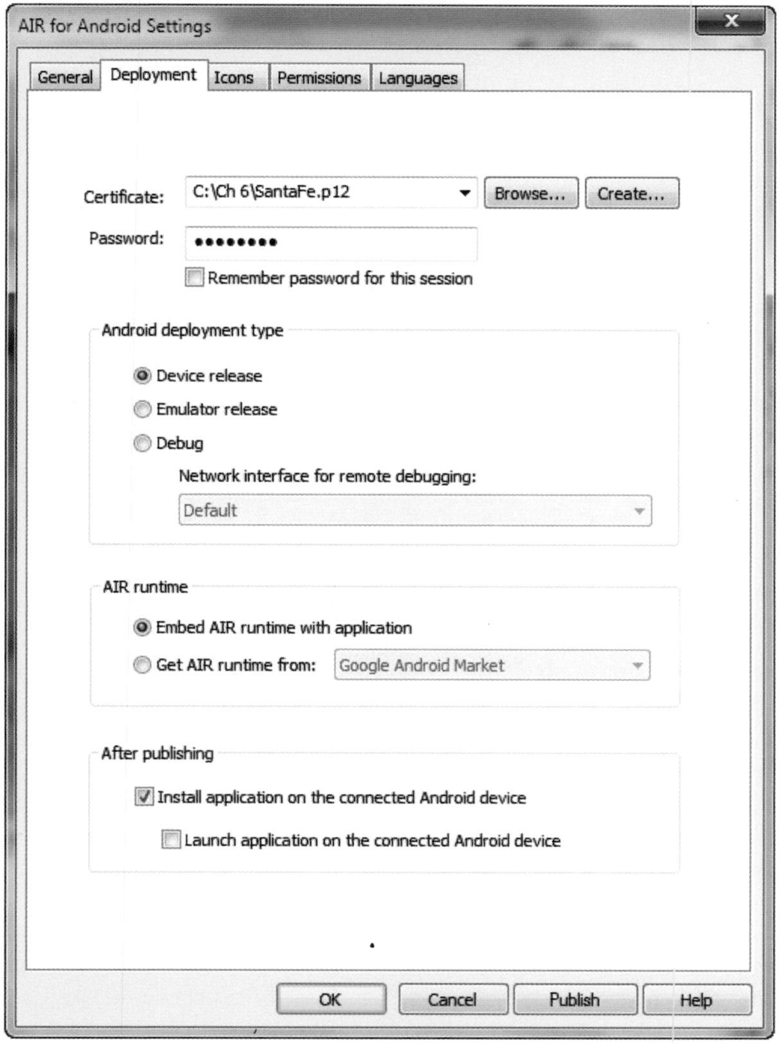

12. Type your password in the Password text box on the Deployment tab.
13. Verify Device release and Embed AIR runtime with application are selected, as shown in Figure 39.

    Note: If you have an Android (2.2+) phone or tablet and you want to test the application once it is published, click the "Install application on the connected Android device check box" to select it. Then, connect the Android device to the computer using a USB cable.
14. Click the **Publish button**.
15. Click **OK** to close the AIR for Android Settings dialog box when the publishing process is complete.
16. Save, then close the application.

    Note: If you connected an Android (2.2+) phone or tablet to your computer, the app icon will appear on the connected Android device. You can tap the icon to display the application, then pinch the map to have it zoom in and out.

You completed the AIR for Android settings to publish an application that will display on a mobile device.

Publish using default settings.

1. Start Flash, open fl6_6.fla, then save it as **skillsDemo6.fla.** (*Notes*: When you open the file, you may receive a warning message that a font is missing. You can replace this font with the default or with any other appropriate font on your computer. If a message appears indicating that you need QuickTime, you will need to install the program to continue.)
2. Open the Publish Settings dialog box.
3. Verify that the Formats tab is selected and the Flash and HTML Wrapper options are the only Format types checked.
4. Click Publish, then click OK to close the dialog box.
5. Use your file management program to navigate to the drive and folder where you store your files to view the skillsDemo6.html and skillsDemo6.swf files.
6. Return to the Flash program.
7. Use the Publish Preview feature to display the movie in a browser.
8. Close your browser, return to the Flash program, then save your work.

Create a JPEG image.

1. Select 60 on the Timeline.
2. Open the Publish Settings dialog box.
3. Click the JPEG Image check box.
4. Click Publish, then click OK to close the dialog box.
5. Open your browser, and then open the skillsDemo6.jpg file.
6. Close the browser, return to the Flash program, then save your work.

Test a movie.

1. Test the movie in the Flash Player window, then maximize the Flash Player window if it is not already maximized.
2. Turn off the loop feature. (*Hint*: Click Control on the Flash Player menu bar, then deselect the Loop check box.)
3. Set the Download Setting to DSL (32.6 KB/s) if it is not already set to that setting.
4. Display the Bandwidth Profiler if it is not already displayed, click View on the menu bar, then click Frame By Frame Graph if it is not already selected.
5. Use controls on the Control menu to rewind, play, and then rewind the movie. (Notice the bar on the Timeline for frame 1 is just under 256 KB, which is way above the red base line. The large photo is in frame 1, which could cause the movie to have a slow start.)
6. Close the Flash Player window.

Reduce file size to optimize a movie.

1. Select frame 1 on the sedona-photo layer, verify the image is selected on the Stage, then delete the image.
2. Replace the image with the sedona-sm graphic from the Library panel.
3. Position the sedona-sm image approximately two-thirds of the way down the Stage and centered across the Stage.
4. Save the movie.
5. Test the movie within the Flash Player window by simulating a DSL download. (Notice the bar on the Timeline for frame 1 is near 32 KB. This allows the movie to start more quickly.)
6. Close the Flash Player window.

Add a background.

1. Verify skillsDemo6.fla is the active file, then insert a new layer and move it below the sedona-photo layer.
2. Name the new layer **background**.
3. Select frame 1 on the background layer.
4. Display the Library panel (if necessary).
5. Drag the g_background graphic symbol to the center of the Stage.
6. Click the last frame on the Timeline associated with content so your screen looks like Figure 40. (*Note*: Your heading font may differ.)
7. Use the Publish Preview feature to view the movie in a browser, close the browser, then save your work.

Create a preloader.

1. Click 1 on the Timeline.
2. Click Edit on the menu bar, point to Timeline, then click Select All Frames.
3. Point to any frame on the Timeline and drag the frames to the right so they start in frame 11.
4. Insert a new layer and name it **labels**.
5. Click frame 11 on the labels layer to select it, insert a keyframe, then display the Properties panel and type **startofMovie** in the Name text box in the LABEL area.
6. Insert a keyframe in frame 70 on the labels layer and type **endofMovie** in the Name text box in the LABEL area.
7. Add a new layer and name it **preLoaderScript**.
8. Insert an ifFrameLoaded action in frame 1 to check if all the frames have been loaded and, if so, go to and play the startofMovie frame. Also, insert a keyframe in frame 10 on the preLoaderScript layer, then insert a gotoAndPlay(1) action in frame 10 to cause a loop in the preloader frames.

9. Add a new layer and name it **preloader Animation**, then have the words "**Please wait**" appear in the first four frames and not appear in the last six frames of the ten frames used for the preloader. This will cause the words Please wait to flash until all the frames are loaded.

10. Test the movie, and use the Simulate Download feature to view the preloader.

11. Save your work, then close the file.

Create an AIR application.

1. Open fl6_7.fla, then save it as **skillsDemo6A.fla**. (*Note:* When you open the file, you may receive a warning message that a font is missing. You can replace this font with the default, or with any other appropriate font on your computer.)

2. Open the Publish Settings dialog box and change the Target setting to AIR 2.5.

3. Display the AIR settings dialog box and set the icons to sedona16.png, sedona32.png, sedona48.png, and sedona128.png.

4. From the Signature tab dialog box, create a Self-Signed Digital Certificate and save it with the default name.

5. Publish the AIR file.

6. Navigate to the drive and folder where your data files are located and view the files created when you published the AIR application.

7. Save your work, then close the application.

Create an AIR for Android mobile app with events.

1. Create a new AIR for Android file, then name it **skillsDemo-M.fla**.

2. Change the view to Fit in Window.

Photo courtesy of J. Shuman.

3. Import sedonaImage.png to the Stage.

4. Change the view to Fit in Window.

5. Select the image and change it to a movie clip symbol with a center registration point.

6. Select the image on the Stage and use the Properties panel to give the image an instance name.

7. Use the Code Snippets panel to assign a Pinch to Zoom Event to the image.

8. Publish the application with the following:
   - Language: English
   - Permissions: Internet
   - Icons: sedona36.png, sedona 48.png, and sedona 72.png

Figure 40 *Completed Skills Review*

- A Self-Signed Digital Certificate you create
- The Deployment settings that include the password, Device release selected, and Embed AIR runtime with application selected.

Note: If you have an Android mobile device, connect it to the computer and have the application display on it.

9. Save the application.

10. View the files that were created during the publish process.

11. Close the application and exit Flash.

The Ultimate Tours travel company has asked you to create a stand-alone application for the opening animation of its website.

1. Open fl6_8.fla and save it as **ultimateTours6A.fla**.
2. Use a graphics program, such as Photoshop, to create an image to be used as icons for this app. Create four sizes, in pixels, of the image for the AIR stand-alone app (16×16, 32×32, 48×48, and 128×128). These should be PNG file types. Alternately, you can use the generic icon graphics (uTours16.png, uTours32.png, uTours48.png, and uTours128.png) provided with your data files.
3. Create the AIR app as a stand-alone application by completing the Icons and Signature tab settings, including creating a Self-Signed Digital Certificate.
4. View the files created by this process.
5. Save and close the application.

Figure 41 *Icon settings for sample completed Project Builder 1*

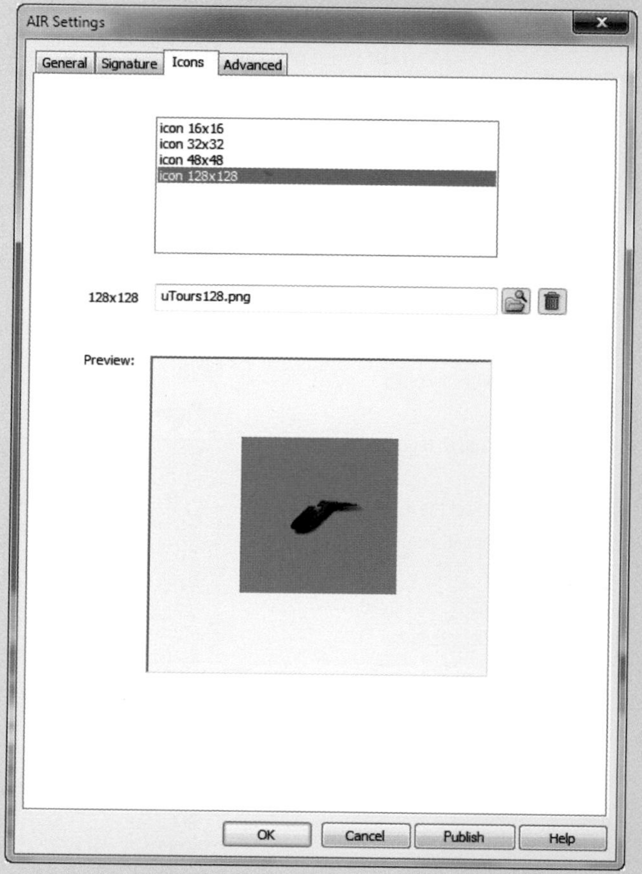

In this project you will choose a Flash movie you developed for this book or one you developed on your own. You will make changes to the publish settings, create an AIR stand-alone application, and create an AIR for Android application for a mobile device. Figure 42 shows a sample application.

1. Open a movie you developed from this book or one you developed on your own, then save it as **publish6.fla**.
2. Use a graphics program, such as Photoshop, to create an image to be used as icons for this app. Create four sizes, in pixels, of the image for the AIR stand-alone app (16×16, 32×32, 48×48, and 128×128). These should be PNG file types. Alternately, you can use the generic icon graphics (publish16.png, publish32.png, publish48.png, and publish128.png) provided with your data files.
3. Create the AIR app as a stand-alone application by completing the Icons and Signature tab settings including creating a Self-Signed Digital Certificate.
4. View the files created by this process.
5. Save the application.
6. Save the application as **publish6-M fla.**.
7. Use a graphics program, such as Photoshop, to create an image to be used as icons for this app. The sizes for the AIR for Android mobile app will be 36×36, 48×48 (this could be the same graphic as above), and 72×72. Alternately, you can use the generic icon graphics (publish36.png, publish48.png, and publish72.png) provided with your data files.

8. Use the Publish Settings dialog box to change the Publish Target to AIR 3.2 for Android.
9. Create the AIR for Android mobile application by completing the Languages, Permission, Icons, and Deployment tab settings including creating a Self-Signed Digital Certificate.
10. View the files created by this process.
11. View the application on an Android mobile device, such as an Android tablet or phone, if you have one connected to the computer.
12. Save and close the application.

Figure 42 *Sample completed Project Builder 2*

Figure 43 shows the home page of a website. Study the figure and complete the following questions. For each question, indicate how you determined your answer.

1. Connect to the Internet and go to *www.nesdis.noaa .gov/jpss/*.
2. Open a document in a word processor or open a new Flash movie, save the file as **dpc6**, then answer the following questions. (*Hint*: Use the Text tool in Flash.)
   ▪ What is the purpose of this site?
   ▪ Who is the target audience?
   ▪ How would you use the Bandwidth Profiler when developing this site?
   ▪ Assuming there is a pause in the playing of a Flash movie on the site, what suggestions would you make to eliminate the pause?
   ▪ What suggestions would you make to improve the design, and why?

Figure 43 *Design Project*
Courtesy of NOAA.gov website. www.nesdis.noaa.gov/jpss/

This is a continuation of the Portfolio Project in Chapter 5, which is the development of a personal portfolio. In this project, you will create a JPEG image of your portfolio screen. Then you will use the Bandwidth Profiler to determine where a pause may occur in a movie and make changes in the movie to eliminate the pause.

1. Open portfolio5.fla (the file you created in Portfolio Project, Chapter 5) and save it as **portfolio6.fla**.
2. Use the Publish Settings dialog box to publish the movie.
3. Use the Publish Preview feature to display the movie in the browser.
4. Create a JPEG image of the first frame of the movie.
5. Display the JPEG image in your browser.
6. Use the Bandwidth Profiler to display a frame-by-frame graph of the movie, as seen in Figure 44, and to determine which frame may cause a pause in the movie at a 28.8 (2.3 KB/s) connection speed. (*Note*: Specifying 28.8 (2.3 KB/s) as the connection speed enables you to identify any pauses and practice using the Bandwidth Profiler. This option can take a very long time to load.)
7. Make a change in the movie to help optimize it.
8. Play the movie.
9. Save and close the movie.

Figure 44 *Using the Bandwidth Profiler to improve download speeds of the sample completed Portfolio Project*

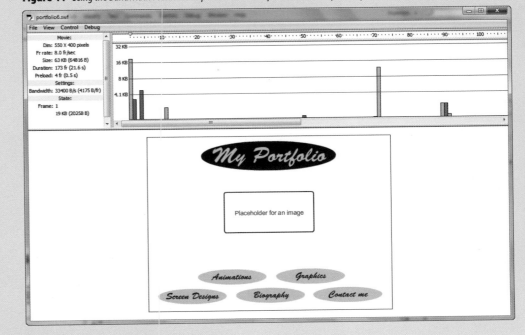

CHAPTER 1

GETTING STARTED WITH
ADOBE PHOTOSHOP CS6

1. Start Adobe Photoshop CS6
2. Learn how to open and save an image
3. Examine the Photoshop window
4. Close a file and exit Photoshop
5. Learn design principles and copyright rules

CHAPTER 1

GETTING STARTED WITH
ADOBE PHOTOSHOP CS6

Using Photoshop

Adobe Photoshop CS6 is an image-editing program that lets you create and modify digital images. 'CS' stands for Creative Suite, a complete design environment. Although Adobe makes Photoshop available as a stand-alone product, it also comes bundled with all of their Creative Suite options, whether your interests lie with print design, web design, or multimedia production. A **digital image** is a picture in electronic form. Using Photoshop, you can create original artwork, manipulate color images, and retouch photographs. In addition to being a robust application popular with graphics professionals, Photoshop is practical for anyone who wants to enhance existing artwork or create new masterpieces. For example, you can repair and restore damaged areas within an image, combine images, and create graphics and special effects for the web.

> **QUICK TIP**
>
> In Photoshop, a digital image may be referred to as a file, document, graphic, picture, or image.

Understanding Platform User Interfaces

Photoshop is available for both Windows and Mac OS platforms. Regardless of which platform you use, the features and commands are very similar. Some of the Windows and Mac OS keyboard commands differ in name, but they have equivalent functions. For example, the [Ctrl] and [Alt] keys are used in Windows, and the [⌘] and [option] keys are used on Macintosh computers. There are also visual differences between the Windows and Mac OS versions of Photoshop due to the user interface differences found in each platform.

Understanding Sources

Photoshop allows you to work with images from a variety of sources. You can create your own original artwork in Photoshop, use images downloaded from the web, or use images that have been scanned or created using a digital camera. Whether you create Photoshop images to print in high resolution or optimize them for multimedia presentations, web-based functions, or animation projects, Photoshop is a powerful tool for communicating your ideas visually.

TOOLS YOU'LL USE

File menu

Window menu

New...	Ctrl+N
Open...	Ctrl+O
Browse in Bridge...	Alt+Ctrl+O
Browse in Mini Bridge...	
Open As...	Alt+Shift+Ctrl+O
Open as Smart Object...	
Open Recent	▶
Close	Ctrl+W
Close All	Alt+Ctrl+W
Close and Go to Bridge...	Shift+Ctrl+W
Save	Ctrl+S
Save As...	Shift+Ctrl+S
Check In...	
Save for Web...	Alt+Shift+Ctrl+S
Revert	F12
Place...	
Import	▶
Export	▶
Automate	▶
Scripts	▶
File Info...	Alt+Shift+Ctrl+I
Print...	Ctrl+P
Print One Copy	Alt+Shift+Ctrl+P
Exit	Ctrl+Q

Rectangular Marquee Tool   M
Elliptical Marquee Tool   M
Single Row Marquee Tool
Single Column Marquee Tool

Mini Bridge
Computer
Appendix
Chapter 1
Chapter 10
Chapter 11
Chapter 12
Chapter 13
Chapter 14
4 items

Image of butterfly © Photodisc/Getty Images.

Path bar

Preferences
File Saving Options
Image Previews: Always Save
File Extension: Use Lower Case
☑ Save As to Original Folder
☑ Save in Background
☑ Automatically Save Recovery Information Every: 10 Minutes
File Compatibility
Camera Raw Preferences...
☑ Prefer Adobe Camera Raw for Supported Raw Files
☐ Ignore EXIF Profile Tag
☐ Ignore Rotation Metadata
☑ Ask Before Saving Layered TIFF Files
☐ Disable Compression of PSD and PSB Files
Maximize PSD and PSB File Compatibility: Ask
Adobe Drive
☐ Enable Adobe Drive
Recent File List Contains: 10 files
OK   Cancel   Prev   Next

Arrange	▶
Workspace	▶
Extensions	▶
3D	
Actions	Alt+F9
✔ **Adjustments**	
Brush	F5
Brush Presets	
Channels	
Character	
Character Styles	
Clone Source	
Color	F6
Histogram	
History	
Info	F8
Layer Comps	
✔ **Layers**	F7
Measurement Log	
Navigator	
Notes	
Paragraph	
Paragraph Styles	
Paths	
✔ **Properties**	
Styles	
Swatches	
Timeline	
Tool Presets	
✔ **Options**	
✔ **Tools**	
✔ **1 PS 1-1.psd**	

photoshop

Options bar

Start Adobe
PHOTOSHOP CS6

What You'll Do

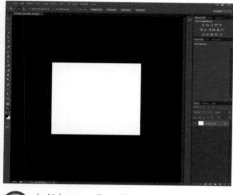

In this lesson, you'll start Photoshop for Windows or Mac OS, and then create a file.

Defining Image-Editing Software

Photoshop is an image-editing program. An **image-editing** program allows you to manipulate graphic images so that they can be posted on websites or reproduced by professional printers using full-color processes. Using panels, tools, menus, and a variety of techniques, you can modify a Photoshop image by rotating it, resizing it, changing its colors, or adding text to it. You can also use Photoshop to create and open different kinds of file formats, which enables you to create your own images, import them from a digital camera or scanner, or use files (in other formats) purchased from outside sources. Table 1 lists some of the graphics file formats that Photoshop can open and create.

Understanding Images

Every image is made up of very small squares, which are called **pixels**, and each pixel represents a color or shade. Pixels within an image can be added, deleted, or modified.

> **QUICK TIP**
>
> Photoshop files can become quite large. After a file is complete, you might want to **flatten** it, an irreversible process that combines all layers and reduces the file size.

Using Photoshop Features

Photoshop includes many tools that you can use to manipulate images and text. Within an image, you can add new items and modify existing elements, change colors, and draw shapes. For example, using the Lasso tool, you can outline a section of an image and drag the section onto another area of the image. You can also isolate a foreground or background image. You can extract all or part of a complex image from nearly any background and use it elsewhere.

> **QUICK TIP**
>
> You can create logos in Photoshop. A **logo** is a distinctive image that you can create by combining symbols, shapes, colors, and text. Logos give graphic identity to organizations such as corporations, universities, and retail stores.

You can also create and format text, called **type**, in Photoshop. You can apply a variety of special effects to type; for example, you can change the appearance of type and increase or decrease the distance between characters. You can also edit type after it has been created and formatted.

Adobe Dreamweaver CS6, a web production software program included in the Design Suite, allows you to optimize, preview, and animate images. Because Dreamweaver is part of the same suite as Photoshop, you can jump seamlessly between the two programs.

Using these two programs, you can also quickly turn any graphics image into a gif animation. Photoshop and Dreamweaver let you compress file size (while optimizing image quality) to ensure that your files download quickly from a web page. Using Photoshop optimization features, you can view multiple versions of an image and select the one that best suits your needs.

Starting Photoshop and Creating a File

The specific way you start Photoshop depends on which computer platform you are using. However, when you start Photoshop in either platform, the computer displays a **splash screen**, a window that contains information about the software, and then the Photoshop window opens.

After you start Photoshop, you can create a file from scratch. You use the New dialog box to create a file. You can also use the New dialog box to set the size of the image you're about to create by typing dimensions in the Width and Height text boxes.

TABLE 1: SOME SUPPORTED GRAPHIC FILE FORMATS			
File format	**Filename extension**	**File format**	**Filename extension**
3D Studio	.3ds	Photoshop PDF	.pdf
Bitmap	.bmp	PICT file	.pct, .pic, or .pict
Cineon	.cin	Pixar	.pxr
Dicom	.dcm	Open EXR	.exr
Flash 3D	.fl3	QuickTime	.mov or .mp4
Filmstrip	.flm	Radiance	.hdr, .rgbe, .xyze
Google Earth	.kmz	RAW	Varies
Graphics Interchange Format	.gif	Scitex CT	.sct
JPEG Picture Format	.jpg, .jpe, or .jpeg	Tagged Image Format	.tif or .tiff
PC Paintbrush	.pcx	Targa	.tga or .vda
Photoshop	.psd	U3D	.u3d
Photoshop Encapsulated PostScript	.eps	Wavefront	.obj

© Cengage Learning 2013

Learn How to Open
AND SAVE AN IMAGE

What You'll Do

In this lesson, you'll locate and open files using the File menu, Adobe Bridge, and Mini Bridge; flag and sort files; and then save a file with a new name.

Opening and Saving Files

Photoshop provides several options for opening and saving a file. Often, the project you're working on determines the techniques you use for opening and saving files. For example, you might want to preserve the original version of a file while you modify a copy. You can open a file, and then immediately save it with a different filename, as well as open and save files in many different file formats. When working with graphic images, you can open a Photoshop file that has been saved as a bitmap (.bmp) file, and then save it as a JPEG (.jpg) file to use on a web page.

Customizing How You Open Files

You can customize how you open your files by setting preferences. **Preferences** are options you can set that are based on your work habits. For example, you can use the Open Recent command on the File menu to instantly locate and open the files that you recently worked on, or you can allow others to preview your files as thumbnails. Figure 3 shows the Windows

Figure 3 *Preferences dialog box*

Option for thumbnail preview

Number of files to appear in Open Recent list

Preferences dialog box options for handling your files: the Mac dialog box differs slightly. Use the Preferences command on the Edit menu (Win) or the Photoshop menu (Mac) to open the Preferences dialog box.

QUICK TIP

In cases when the correct file format is not automatically determined, you can use the Open As command on the File menu (Win) or Open as Smart Object (Mac).

Browsing Through Files

You can easily find the files you're looking for by using Adobe Bridge, a stand-alone application that serves as the hub for the Adobe Creative Suite, or Adobe Mini Bridge, a less-powerful (and smaller) version of Bridge that opens within the Photoshop window. Mini Bridge provides less data than Bridge, but makes it easier to do simple tasks (like locating and opening files). Figure 4 shows the Magnifying Loupe tool in Adobe Bridge, available when using the Filmstrip view. You can open Bridge or Mini Bridge using the File menu in Photoshop.

QUICK TIP

Clicking a thumbnail while in Filmstrip view opens the file in a larger preview panel, and clicking the magnify pointer opens a Loupe tool that magnifies content. Drag the loupe over the filmstrip image to enlarge select areas. The upper-left corner of the window points to the area to be magnified. Clicking anywhere on the tool closes the loupe.

Figure 4 *Adobe Bridge window*
Image of butterfly © Photodisc/Getty Images.

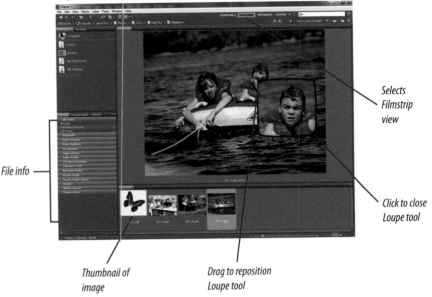

File info

Selects Filmstrip view

Click to close Loupe tool

Thumbnail of image

Drag to reposition Loupe tool

DESIGNTIP

Opening Scanned Images

You can open a scanned or uploaded image in Photoshop (which usually has a .jpg extension or another graphics file format) by clicking File on the Menu bar, and then clicking Open. All Formats is the default file type, so you should be able to see all available image files in the Open dialog box. Locate the folder containing your scanned or digital camera images, click the file you want to open, and then click Open. A scanned or digital camera image contains all its imagery in a single layer. You can add layers to the image, but you can only save these new layers if you save the image as a Photoshop image (with the extension .psd).

Lesson 2   Learn How to Open and Save an Image

When you open Bridge, a series of panels allows you to view the files on your hard drive as hierarchical files and folders. In addition to the Favorites and Folders panels in the upper-left pane of the Bridge window, there are other important areas. Directly beneath the Favorites and Folders panels is a grouping that includes the Filter panel, which allows you to review properties of images in the (center) Content panel. In the (default) Essentials view, the right column displays the Preview panel and the Metadata and Keywords panels, which store information about a selected file (such as keywords) that can then be used as search parameters. You can use the tree structure (visible when the Folders tab is active) to find the file you are seeking. When you locate a file, you can click its thumbnail to display a larger image in the Preview panel and to see information about its size, format, and creation and modification dates in the Metadata panel. You can open a file in Photoshop from Bridge by double-clicking its thumbnail. You can close Bridge by clicking File (Win) or Adobe Bridge CS6 (Mac) on the (Bridge) Menu bar, and then clicking Exit (Win) or Quit Adobe Bridge CS6 (Mac), or by clicking the window's Close button.

QUICK TIP

You can select multiple non-contiguous images by pressing and holding [Ctrl] (Win) or ⌘ (Mac) each time you click an image. You can select contiguous images by clicking the first image, and then pressing and holding [Shift] and clicking the last image in the group.

QUICK TIP

You can reset the Adobe Bridge preferences to the factory default by holding [Ctrl][Alt] (Win) or ⌘ [option] (Mac) while clicking the Launch Bridge button.

Understanding the Power of Bridge

In addition to allowing you to see all your images, Bridge can be used to rate (assign importance), sort (organize by name, rating, and other criteria), and label your images. Figure 4, on the previous page, contains images that are shown in Filmstrip view. There are four views in Bridge (Essentials, Filmstrip, Metadata, and Output) that are controlled by buttons to the left of the search text box. To assist in organizing your images, you can assign a color label or rating to one or more images regardless of your current view. Any number of selected images can be assigned a label by clicking Label on the Menu bar, and then clicking one of the Rating or Label options.

QUICK TIP

You can use Bridge to view thumbnails of all files on your computer. You can open any file for software installed on your computer by double-clicking its thumbnail in Bridge.

Getting There with Mini Bridge

While not as powerful as Bridge, Mini Bridge can be used to easily filter, sort, locate, and open files from *within* Photoshop. Mini Bridge is opened in the Photoshop window by clicking the Mini Bridge tab at the bottom of the workspace, or by clicking the Browse in Mini Bridge command on the File menu. Mini Bridge can be resized to suit your needs, and closed and reopened whenever necessary. To navigate Mini Bridge, shown in Figure 5 after being resized, you can click the arrows within the Path bar to change the file source. Clicking each arrow in the Path bar reveals the file structure in your hard drive. When you locate a file you want to open in Photoshop, double-click its thumbnail image.

QUICK TIP

So when might you use Mini Bridge? Suppose you need a file but don't know where it is. Without closing or switching out of Photoshop, you can use Mini Bridge to locate the file, and then open it by double-clicking its thumbnail.

Using Save As Versus Save

Sometimes it's more efficient to create a new image by modifying an existing one, especially if it contains elements and special effects that you want to use again. The Save As command on the File menu (in Photoshop) creates a copy of the file, prompts you to give the duplicate file a new name, and then displays the new filename in the image's title bar. You use the Save As command to name an unnamed file or to save an existing file with a new name. For example, throughout this book, you will be instructed to open your Data Files and use the Save As command. Saving your Data Files with new names keeps the original files intact in case you have to start the lesson over again or you want to repeat an exercise. When you use the Save command, you save the changes you made to the open file.

QUICK TIP

You can also create a copy of the active file by clicking Image on the Menu bar, and then clicking Duplicate. Click OK to confirm the name of the duplicate file.

Getting images into Photoshop

There are a zillion digital cameras available in the marketplace, and each brand is a little different, but you can still easily import your images into Bridge by connecting the camera to your computer using the camera's USB cable. Turn the camera on and once your computer recognizes the camera, open Adobe Bridge. Click File on the (Bridge) Menu bar, then click Get Photos from Camera. This opens the Adobe Bridge CS6

Photo Downloader. Select the correct camera device from the Get Photos from list arrow and choose a location for the downloaded file, then click Get Media. Your images are

probably in the JPEG or RAW format, and the clarity of them will be the result of the megapixel capacity of your camera and the resolution setting.

Figure 5 *Adobe Mini Bridge window*
Image of butterfly © Photodisc/Getty Images.

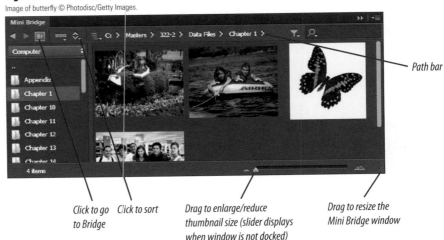

Path bar

Click to go to Bridge   Click to sort   Drag to enlarge/reduce thumbnail size (slider displays when window is not docked)   Drag to resize the Mini Bridge window

Figure 6 *Image Size dialog box*

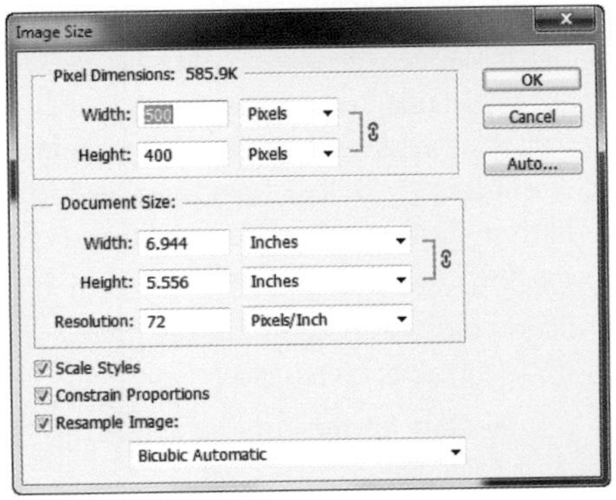

Resizing an Image

You may have created the perfect image, but the size may not be correct for your print format. Document size is a combination of the printed dimensions and pixel resolution. An image designed for a website, for example, might be too small for an image that will be printed in a newsletter. You can easily resize an image using the Image Size command on the Image menu. To use this feature, open the file you want to resize, click Image on the Menu bar, and then click Image Size. The Image Size dialog box, shown in Figure 6, opens. By changing the dimensions in the text boxes, you'll have your image resized in no time. Note the check mark next to Resample Image. With resampling checked, you can change the total number of pixels in the image and the print dimensions independently. With resampling off, you can change either the dimensions or the resolution; Photoshop will automatically adjust whichever value you ignore. The **canvas size**, which is the full editable area of an image, can be increased or decreased using the Canvas Size command on the Image menu. Decreasing an image's size crops the image whereas increasing the image's size adds to the background.

Open a file using the Menu bar

1. Click **File** on the Menu bar, then click **Open**.

2. Click the **Look in list arrow** (Win) or the **Current file location list arrow** (Mac), then navigate to the drive and folder where you store your Data Files.

3. Click **PS 1-1.psd**, as shown in Figure 7, then click **Open**.

You used the Open command on the File menu to locate and open a file.

Open a file using the Folders panel in Adobe Bridge

1. Click **File** on the Menu bar, click **Browse in Bridge**, then click the **Folders panel tab** if the Folders panel is not active.

2. Navigate through the hierarchical tree to the drive and folder where you store your Chapter 1 Data Files, verify that Sort by Type and an up arrow (∧) display below the search box, then click the **Essentials workspace button** if it is not already selected.

3. Click the image of the butterfly, then drag the **slider** (at the bottom of the Bridge window) a third of the way between the **Smaller thumbnail size button** ☐ and the **Larger thumbnail size button** ☐, then click the image of the ox *once*. Compare your screen to Figure 8.

4. Double-click the **image of a butterfly** (PS 1-2.tif). Bridge is no longer visible.

5. Click the **Close button** in the butterfly image file tab in Photoshop.

You used the Folders panel in Adobe Bridge to locate and open a file. This feature makes it easy to find which file you want to use.

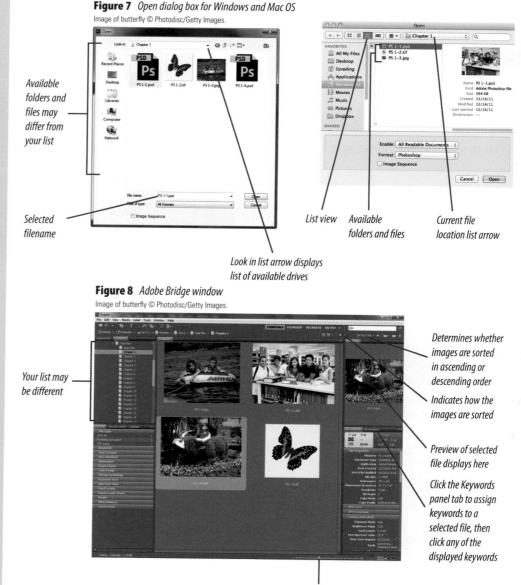

Figure 7 *Open dialog box for Windows and Mac OS*
Image of butterfly © Photodisc/Getty Images.

Available folders and files may differ from your list

Selected filename

Look in list arrow displays list of available drives

List view   *Available folders and files*   *Current file location list arrow*

Figure 8 *Adobe Bridge window*
Image of butterfly © Photodisc/Getty Images.

Your list may be different

Determines whether images are sorted in ascending or descending order

Indicates how the images are sorted

Preview of selected file displays here

Click the Keywords panel tab to assign keywords to a selected file, then click any of the displayed keywords

Drag to resize thumbnails

Getting Started with Adobe Photoshop CS6

Figure 9 *Adobe Mini Bridge window*

Image of butterfly © Photodisc/Getty Images.

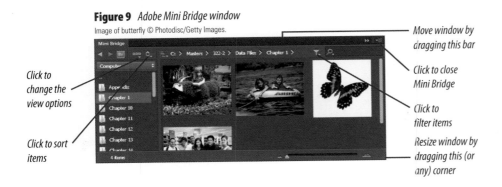

Move window by dragging this bar

Click to close Mini Bridge

Click to filter items

Resize window by dragging this (or any) corner

Click to change the view options

Click to sort items

Figure 10 *Save As dialog box*

Your list of files might be different

New filename

Open a file using Mini Bridge

1. Click **File** on the Menu bar, click **Browse in Mini Bridge**, then click the **Browse Files button** if necessary.

   Click the Launch Bridge button if you receive a warning that you have to launch Bridge for Mini Bridge to work.

2. Use the Path bar to locate the drive and folder where you store your Chapter 1 Data Files. See Figure 9.

3. Double-click the **image of a butterfly** (PS 1-2.tif).

4. Double-click the **Mini Bridge tab** to minimize the panel, then close PS 1-2.tif.

   By default, Mini Bridge is minimized at the bottom of the Photoshop workspace. Enlarge/minimize Mini Bridge by double-clicking its tab.

You opened Mini Bridge in Photoshop, navigated to where your Data Files are stored, opened a file, then minimized Mini Bridge.

Use the Save As command

1. Verify that the PS 1-1.psd window is active.

2. Click **File** on the Menu bar, click **Save As**, then compare your Save As dialog box to Figure 10.

3. If the drive containing your Data Files is not displayed, click the **Save in list arrow** (Win) or the **Where list arrow** (Mac), then navigate to the drive and folder where you store your Chapter 1 Data Files.

4. Select the current filename in the File name text box (Win) or Save As text box (Mac), type **Friends**, then click **Save**.

TIP Click OK to close the Maximize Compatibility dialog box if it appears now and in future lessons.

You used the Save As command on the File menu to save the file with a new name. This command lets you save a changed version of an image while keeping the original file intact.

Change from Tabbed to Floating Documents

1. Click **Window** on the Menu bar, point to **Arrange**, then click **2 Up Horizontal**.

   Each of the open files displays in a horizontal window.

TIP You can also display images in several arrangements which allows you to vary the grouping of open documents. To see these arrangements, click Window on the Menu bar, point to Arrange, then click any of the available menu choices.

TIP The options in the Arrange menu make a temporary change to the workspace that will be in effect for the current Photoshop session.

2. Click **Window** on the Menu bar, point to **Arrange**, then click **Float All in Windows**. Compare your Friends image to Figure 11.

TIP By default, each image is displayed in its own tab, but you can change this so each image floats in its own window.

You changed the arrangement of open documents from consolidated, or tabbed, to a 2 Up Horizontal format, and then to the Float All in Windows format where each image displays in its own window.

Figure 11 *Friends image*

Duplicate file has new name

Changing File Formats

In addition to using the Save As command to duplicate an existing file, the Save As command is a handy way of changing one format into another. For example, you can open an image you created in a digital camera, and then make modifications in the Photoshop format. To do this, open a .jpg file in Photoshop, click File on the Menu bar, and then click Save As. Name the file, click the Format list arrow, click Photoshop (*.PSD, *.PDD) (Win) or Photoshop (Mac), and then click Save. You can also change formats using Bridge by selecting the file, clicking Tools on the Menu bar, pointing to Photoshop, and then clicking Image Processor. Section 3 of the Image Processor dialog box lets you determine the new file format.

Figure 12 *Images in Adobe Bridge*

Image of butterfly © Photodisc/Getty Images.

Rated and
Approved file

Figure 13 *Sorted files*

Image of butterfly © Photodisc/Getty Images.

Click to change how
items in the Content
panel are sorted

Filter items by rating

Rate and filter with Bridge

1. Click the **Bridge program icon** Br on the taskbar (Win) or Dock (Mac) to make the program active.

2. Click the **Folders panel tab**, then click the drive and folder where you store your Chapter 1 Data Files on the File Hierarchy tree (if necessary).

3. Verify that file **PS 1-2.tif** (the butterfly image) is selected.

4. Press and hold [**Ctrl**] (Win) or ⌘ (Mac), click **PS 1-1.psd** (the image of the friends), then release [**Ctrl**] (Win) or ⌘ (Mac).

5. Click **Label** on the Menu bar, then click **Approved**.

6. Click **PS 1-1.psd**, click **Label** on the Menu bar, then click ✱✱✱. See Figure 12.

7. Click the **Sort list arrow** on the Menu bar, click **By Filename**, point to **Sort**, then verify that the **Ascending Order arrow** displays to the right of the sort list arrow. Compare your screen to Figure 13.

   The order of the files is changed.

   TIP You can also change the order of files in the Content panel using the Sort command on the View menu. When you click the Sort by Filename list arrow, you'll see a list of sorting options. Click the option you want and the files in the Content panel will be rearranged.

8. Click **View** on the Menu bar, point to **Sort**, then click **By Size**.

9. Click **File** (Win) or **Adobe Bridge CS6** (Mac) on the (Bridge) Menu bar, then click **Exit** (Win) or **Quit Adobe Bridge CS6** (Mac) to close Bridge.

You labeled and rated files using Bridge, sorted the files in a folder, then changed the sort order. When finished, you closed Bridge.

Examine
THE PHOTOSHOP WINDOW

What You'll Do

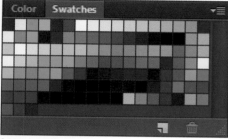

© Adobe Systems Incorporated

In this lesson, you'll arrange documents and change the default display, select a tool on the Tools panel, use a shortcut key to cycle through the hidden tools, select and add a tool to the Tool Preset picker, use the Window menu to show and hide panels in the workspace, and create a customized workspace.

Learning About the Workspace

The Photoshop **workspace** is the area within the Photoshop program window that includes the entire window, from the command menus at the top of your screen to the status bar (Win) at the bottom. Desktop items may be visible between the menu commands and the document title bar (Mac). The (Windows) workspace is shown in Figure 14.

In Windows, the area containing the Photoshop commands is called the Menu bar. On the Mac, the main menus are at the top of the desktop, but not directly attached to the options bar. If the active image window is maximized, the filename of the open unnamed file is Untitled-1, because it has not been named. The Menu bar also contains the Close button and the Minimize/Maximize and Restore buttons (Win).

You can choose a menu command by clicking it or by pressing [Alt], and then clicking the underlined letter in the menu name (Win). Some commands display shortcut keys on the right side of the menu. Shortcut keys provide an alternative way to activate menu commands. Some commands might appear dimmed, which means they are not currently available. A right-pointing triangle after a command indicates additional choices.

DESIGN**TIP**

Overcoming Information Overload

One of the most common experiences shared by first-time Photoshop users is information overload. There are just too many panels and tools to look at! When you feel your brain overheating, take a moment and sit back. Remind yourself that the active image area is the central area where you can see a composite of your work. All the tools and panels are there to help you, not to add to the confusion. The tools and features in Photoshop CS6 are designed to be easier to find and use, making any given task faster to complete.

Finding Tools Everywhere

The **Tools panel** contains tools associated with frequently used Photoshop commands. The face of a tool contains a graphical representation of its function; for example, the Zoom tool shows a magnifying glass. You can place the pointer over each tool to display a tool tip, which tells you the name or function of that tool. Some tools have additional hidden tools, indicated by a small white triangle in the lower-right corner of the tool.

QUICK TIP

You can view the Tools panel in a 2-column format by clicking the expand arrow in its upper-left corner.

The **options bar**, located directly under the Menu bar, displays the current settings for the selected tool. For example, when you click the Type tool, the default font and font size appear on the options bar, which can be changed if desired. You can move the options bar anywhere in the workspace for easier access. The options bar also contains the Tool Preset picker. This is the far-left tool on the options bar and displays the active tool. You can click the list arrow on this tool to select another tool without having to use the Tools panel. The vertical dock displays to the right of the Document window. The Panel dock contains two panel groups, the Panel icons group and the Expanded panels group. Panels not displayed in a workspace appear to the right and can be collapsed and expanded from the dock, which also contains the panel

© Adobe Systems Incorporated

well, an area where you can assemble panels for quick access.

Panels are small windows used to verify settings and modify images. By default, panels appear in stacked groups at the right side of the window. A collection of panels in a vertical orientation (typically) is called a dock. The **dock** is the dark gray bar to the left of the collection of panels. The arrows in the dock are used to maximize and minimize the panels. You can display a panel by simply clicking the panel tab, making it the active panel by clicking its name in the Window menu or by clicking its icon in the vertical panel dock (if it's displayed). Panels can be separated

and moved anywhere in the workspace by dragging their tabs to new locations. You can dock or undock a panel by dragging its tab in or out of a dock. As you move a panel within the dock, you'll see a blue highlighted drop zone. A **drop zone** is an area where you can move a panel. You can also change the order of tabs by dragging a tab to a new location within its panel. Each panel contains a menu that you can view by clicking the Panel options button in its upper-right corner.

QUICK TIP

You can reset panels to their default locations at any time by selecting Reset Essentials in the Workspace switcher.

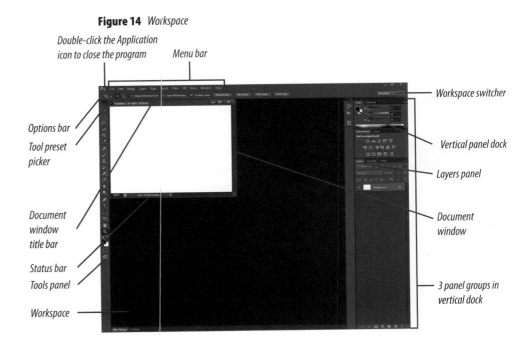

Figure 14 *Workspace*

Double-click the Application icon to close the program
Menu bar
Options bar
Tool preset picker
Document window title bar
Status bar
Tools panel
Workspace
Workspace switcher
Vertical panel dock
Layers panel
Document window
3 panel groups in vertical dock

When images are displayed as tabbed documents, the **status bar** is located at the bottom of the program window (Win) or work area (Mac). When images are floating, the status bar is located at the bottom of each individual image. It displays information, such as the file size of the active window. You can display other information on the status bar by clicking the white triangle to view a menu with more options.

Rulers can help you precisely measure and position an object in the workspace. The rulers do not appear the first time you use Photoshop, but you can display them by clicking Rulers on the View menu.

Using Tool Shortcut Keys

Each tool has a corresponding shortcut key. For example, the shortcut key for the Type tool is T. After you know a tool's shortcut key, you can select the tool on the Tools panel by pressing its shortcut key. To select and cycle through a tool's hidden tools, you press and hold [Shift], and then press the tool's shortcut key until the desired tool appears.

Customizing Your Environment

Photoshop makes it easy for you to position elements just where you want them. If you move elements around to make your environment more convenient, you can always return your workspace to its original appearance by resetting the default panel locations. Once you have your work area arranged the way you want it, you can create a customized workspace by clicking the Workspace switcher on the Menu bar, and then clicking New Workspace. If you want to open a named workspace, click the Workspace switcher, and then click the name of the workspace you want to use. Photoshop comes with many customized workspaces that are designed for specific tasks.

You can also change the color of your workspace by clicking Edit on the Menu bar, pointing to Preferences, then clicking Interface (Win) or by clicking Photoshop on the Menu bar, pointing to Preferences, then clicking Interface (Mac). Here you can choose one of four color themes. Color themes can be changed on a permanent or temporary basis. Using the Color list arrows in the Interface panel of the Preferences dialog box, you can permanently change the color theme using the four displayed themes, or any color you choose.

Figure 15 *Keyboard Shortcuts and Menus dialog box*

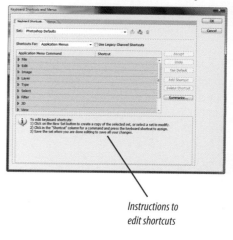

Instructions to edit shortcuts

© Adobe Systems Incorporated

Learning Shortcut Keys and Creating Customized Keyboard Shortcuts

Keyboard shortcuts can make your work with Photoshop images faster and easier. As you become more familiar with Photoshop, you'll gradually pick up shortcuts for commands and tools you use most often, such as saving a file or the Move tool. You'll notice that as you learn to use shortcut keys, your speed while working with Photoshop will increase and you'll complete tasks with fewer mouse clicks. In fact, once you discover the power of keyboard shortcuts, you may never use menus again. You can find existing keyboard shortcuts by clicking Edit on the Menu bar, and then clicking Keyboard Shortcuts. The Keyboard Shortcuts and Menus dialog box, shown in Figure 15, allows you to add shortcuts or edit those that already exist. You can also print shortcuts by exporting them to an HTML file, and then printing it or viewing it in a browser.

Figure 16 *Hidden tools*

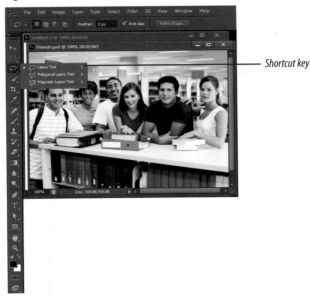

Shortcut key

Select a tool

1. Click the **Lasso tool** ⬭ on the Tools panel, press and hold the **mouse button** until a list of hidden tools appears, then release the **mouse button**. See Figure 16. Note the shortcut key, L, next to the tool name.

2. Click the **Polygonal Lasso tool** 🔲 on the Tools panel.

3. Press and hold [**Shift**], press [**L**] three times to cycle through the Lasso tools, then release [**Shift**]. Did you notice how the options bar changes for each selected Lasso tool?

TIP You can return the tools to their default setting by clicking the Click to open the Tool Preset picker list arrow on the options bar, clicking the More Options button, then clicking Reset All Tools.

You selected the Lasso tool on the Tools panel and used its shortcut key to cycle through the Lasso tools. Becoming familiar with shortcut keys can speed up your work and make you more efficient.

64-bit Version of Photoshop

You may have heard people talking about the 64-bit version of Photoshop. What does this mean? (Here's a good analogy: Imagine a bus that can hold 64 students versus one that can only hold 32 students. Because it has a larger capacity, the bus carrying 64 students will have to make fewer trips to pick up a greater number of students.) Prior to CS5, Photoshop was only available as a 32-bit application for both Windows and Mac. With CS6, Photoshop is a 64-bit application. This means that the architecture of the program has been redesigned to accommodate huge files (those larger than 4 GB) and make better use of RAM. The net result is that the 64-bit version of Photoshop is faster and more efficient. Some features, however, still work only in 32-bit mode (until they're updated). In Windows, you can launch either version from the Windows taskbar (or pin either or both versions to the taskbar). The Mac OS version of Photoshop is only available in 64-bit.

© Adobe Systems Incorporated

Lesson 3   Examine the Photoshop Window

Select a tool from the Tool Preset picker

1. Click the **Click to open the Tool Preset picker list arrow** on the options bar.

   The name of a button is displayed in a tool tip, the descriptive text that appears when you point to the button. Your Tool Preset picker list will differ, and may contain no entries at all. This list can be customized by each user.

2. Deselect the **Current Tool Only check box** if checked. See Figure 17.

3. Double-click **Magnetic Lasso 24 pixels** in the list.

TIP Double-clicking a tool selects it and closes the Tool Preset picker list.

You selected the Magnetic Lasso tool using the Tool Preset picker. The Tool Preset picker makes it easy to access frequently used tools and their settings.

Figure 17 *Using the Tool Preset picker*

More Options button adds new tools and displays more options

Active tool displays in Tool Preset picker button

Figure 18 *Full screen mode with Menu bar*

Use hand pointer to reposition image

Using the Full Screen Mode

By default, Photoshop displays images in consolidated tabs, although you can change this on a permanent or temporary basis. This means that each image is displayed within its own tab. There are also three modes for viewing the menus, panels, and tools: Standard Screen Mode, Full Screen Mode with Menu Bar, and Full Screen Mode. And why would you want to stray from the familiar Standard Screen Mode? Perhaps your image is so large that it's difficult to see it all in Standard Screen Mode, or perhaps you want a less cluttered screen. Maybe you just want to try something different. You can switch between modes by clicking the mode you want or by pressing the keyboard shortcut F. When in Full Screen Mode with Menu bar, click the Hand tool (or press the keyboard shortcut H), and you can reposition the active image, as shown in Figure 18.

Getting Started with Adobe Photoshop CS6

Figure 19 *Move tool added to preset picker*

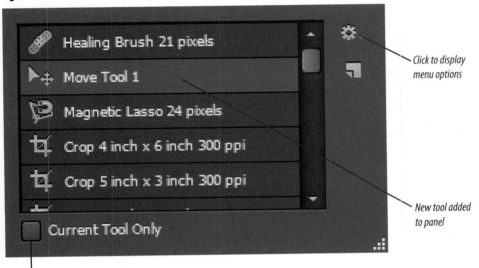

Healing Brush 21 pixels

Move Tool 1

Magnetic Lasso 24 pixels

Crop 4 inch x 6 inch 300 ppi

Crop 5 inch x 3 inch 300 ppi

Current Tool Only

*Click to display
menu options*

*New tool added
to panel*

*Selected check
box displays only
current tool*

Setting Preferences

The Preferences dialog box contains several topics, each with its own settings: General; Interface; File Handling; Performance; Cursors; Transparency & Gamut; Units & Rulers; Guides, Grid, & Slices; Plug-Ins; Type; 3D; and Camera Raw. To open the Preferences dialog box, click Edit (Win) or Photoshop (Mac) on the Menu bar, point to Preferences, and then click a topic that represents the settings you want to change. For example, if you move panels around the workspace or make other changes to them, those changes will be retained the next time you start the program. To reset panels to their default, click Interface on the Preferences menu, click the Restore Default Workspaces button, and then click OK.

Add a tool to the Tool Preset picker

1. Click the **Move tool** ▶＋ on the Tools panel.
2. Click the **Click to open the Tool Preset picker list arrow** ▽ ▪ on the options bar.
3. Click the **More Options button** ⚙▪ on the Tool Preset picker.
4. Click **New Tool Preset**, then click **OK** to accept the default name (Move Tool 1). Compare your list to Figure 19.

TIP You can display the currently selected tool alone by selecting the Current Tool Only check box.

You added the Move tool to the Tool Preset picker. Once you know how to add tools to the Tool Preset picker, you can quickly and easily customize your work environment.

Change the default display and theme color

1. Click **Edit** (Win) or **Photoshop** (Mac) on the Menu bar, point to **Preferences**, then click **Interface**.
2. Click the **far-right gray color box** (light gray).

   Did you notice that the workspace color changed?
3. Click the **far-left gray color box** (dark gray), click the **second from the right gray color box**, click the **second from the left gray color box**.

   The workspace theme display returns to the default.
4. Click the **Open Documents as Tabs check box** to deselect it, then click **OK**.

You examined each of the available color themes and changed the default display so that each time you open Photoshop, each image will display in its own window rather than in tabs.

Show and hide panels

1. If necessary, click the **Swatches tab** to make the Swatches panel active, as shown in Figure 20.
2. Click the **Collapse to Icons button** ▶▶ on the dock to collapse the panels.
3. Click the **Expand Panels button** ◀◀ on the dock to expand the panels.
4. Click **Window** on the Menu bar, then click **Swatches** to deselect it.

TIP You can hide all open panels by pressing [Shift] and [Tab] together, and then show them by pressing [Shift] and [Tab] again. To hide all open panels, the options bar, and the Tools panel, press [Tab], then show them by pressing [Tab] again. If you close a panel that is grouped with other panels, the other panels close as well.

5. Click **Window** on the Menu bar, then click **Swatches** to redisplay the Swatches panel.

You collapsed and expanded the panels, then used the Window menu to show and hide the Swatches panel. You might want to hide panels at times in order to enlarge your work area.

Figure 20 *Active Swatches panel*

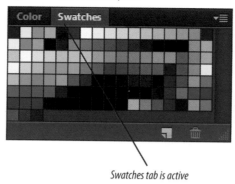

Swatches tab is active

Figure 21 *Tool Preset picker More Options menu*

New Tool Preset...
Rename Tool Preset...
Delete Tool Preset
✓ Sort by Tool
✓ Show All Tool Presets
Show Current Tool Presets
Text Only
✓ Small List
Large List
Reset Tool
Reset All Tools
Preset Manager...
Reset Tool Presets...
Load Tool Presets...
Save Tool Presets...
Replace Tool Presets...
Airbrushes
Art History
Artists' Brushes
Brushes
Crop and Marquee
DP Presets
Dry Media
Pencil Brushes
Pencils Mixer Brush
Splatter Brush Tool Presets
Text

Modifying a Tool Preset

Once you've created tool presets, you'll probably want to know how they can be deleted and renamed. To delete any tool preset, select it on the Tool Preset picker panel. Click the More Options button on the Tool Preset picker panel to view the menu, shown in Figure 21, and then click Delete Tool Preset. To rename a tool preset, click the More Options button and then click Rename Tool Preset.

Figure 22 *New Workspace dialog box*

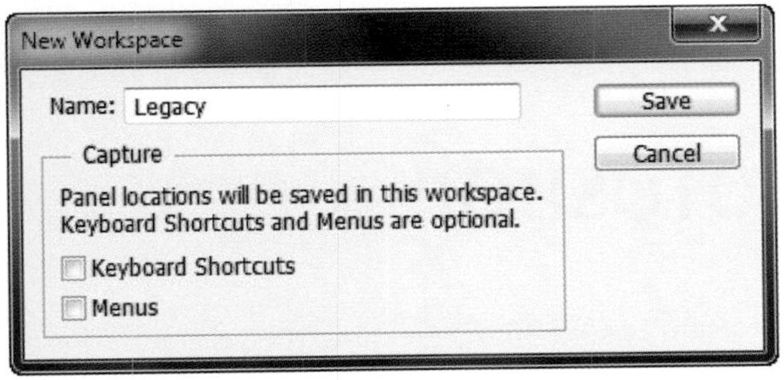

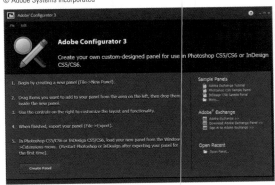

Figure 23 *Adobe Configurator 3*
© Adobe Systems Incorporated

Create a customized workspace

1. Click **Window** on the Menu bar, click **History**, then drag the newly displayed panel in the dark gray line beneath the Swatches panel. (*Hint*: When you drag one panel into another, you'll see a light blue line, indicating that the new panel will dock with the existing panels.)

2. Click **Window** on the Menu bar, point to **Workspace**, then click **New Workspace**.

3. Type **Legacy** in the Name text box, then verify that only Panel locations will be saved, as shown in Figure 22.

4. Click **Save**.

5. Click **Window** on the Menu bar, then point to **Workspace**.

   The name of the new workspace appears on the Workspace menu.

6. Click **Essentials (Default)**.

TIP N-up viewing allows you to edit one image while comparing it with another. You can drag layers from one image to another in N-up view. Use N-up viewing using the Arrange command on the Window menu, and then tiling either horizontally or vertically until the images are in the configuration that works best.

You created a customized workspace, then reset the panel locations to the default Essentials workspace. Customized workspaces provide you with a work area that is always tailored to your needs.

Creating Your Own Panels with Adobe Configurator

You've seen how you can customize your workspace by grouping panels, and then saving the settings for future use. Configurator 3, shown in Figure 23, lets you create a customized Photoshop workspace on steroids. Configurator is an additional program, which you download from Adobe, that lets you create your own panels. Using drag-and-drop technology, you can pick and choose from the tools, commands, actions, widgets, and containers that are at your disposal in any session of Photoshop, and arrange them in any order you choose. And the great news is that you don't have to be a master programmer to do it! Once you've created a panel, you export it using a command on the File menu, then load the panel into Photoshop using the Extensions command on the Window menu. You can download Configurator from *labs.adobe.com/technologies/configurator/*.

Close a File
AND EXIT PHOTOSHOP

What You'll Do

New...	Ctrl+N
Open...	Ctrl+O
Browse in Bridge...	Alt+Ctrl+O
Browse in Mini Bridge...	
Open As...	Alt+Shift+Ctrl+O
Open as Smart Object...	
Open Recent	▶
Close	Ctrl+W
Close All	Alt+Ctrl+W
Close and Go to Bridge...	Shift+Ctrl+W
Save	Ctrl+S
Save As...	Shift+Ctrl+S
Check In...	
Save for Web...	Alt+Shift+Ctrl+S
Revert	F12
Place...	
Import	▶
Export	▶
Automate	▶
Scripts	▶
File Info...	Alt+Shift+Ctrl+I
Print...	Ctrl+P
Print One Copy	Alt+Shift+Ctrl+P
Exit	Ctrl+Q

 In this lesson, you'll use the Close and Exit (Win) or Quit (Mac) commands to close a file and exit Photoshop.

Concluding Your Work Session

At the end of your work session, you might have opened several files; you now need to decide which ones you want to save.

QUICK TIP

If you share a computer with other people, it's a good idea to reset Photoshop's preferences back to their default settings. You can do so when you start Photoshop by clicking Window on the Menu bar, pointing to Workspace, and then clicking Essentials (Default).

Closing Versus Exiting

When you are finished working on an image, you need to save and close it. You can close one file at a time, or close all open files at the same time by exiting the program. Closing a file leaves Photoshop open, which allows you to open or create another file. Exiting Photoshop closes the file, closes Photoshop, and returns you to the desktop, where you can choose to open another program or shut down the computer. Photoshop will prompt you to save any changes before it closes the files. If you do not modify a new or existing file, Photoshop will close it automatically when you exit.

QUICK TIP

To close all open files without exiting Photoshop, click File on the Menu bar, and then click Close All.

Using Adobe Online

Periodically, when you start Photoshop, an Update dialog box might appear, prompting you to search for updates or new information on the Adobe website. If you click Yes, Photoshop will automatically notify you that a download is available; however, you do not have to select it. You can also obtain information about Photoshop from the Adobe Photoshop website (*www.adobe.com/products/photoshop.html*), where you can link to downloads, tips, training, galleries, examples, and other support topics.

Figure 24 *Closing a file using the File menu*

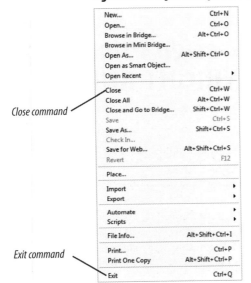

New...	Ctrl+N
Open...	Ctrl+O
Browse in Bridge...	Alt+Ctrl+O
Browse in Mini Bridge...	
Open As...	Alt+Shift+Ctrl+O
Open as Smart Object...	
Open Recent	▶
Close	Ctrl+W
Close All	Alt+Ctrl+W
Close and Go to Bridge...	Shift+Ctrl+W
Save	Ctrl+S
Save As...	Shift+Ctrl+S
Check In...	
Save for Web...	Alt+Shift+Ctrl+S
Revert	F12
Place...	
Import	▶
Export	▶
Automate	▶
Scripts	▶
File Info...	Alt+Shift+Ctrl+I
Print...	Ctrl+P
Print One Copy	Alt+Shift+Ctrl+P
Exit	Ctrl+Q

Close command

Exit command

Close a file and exit Photoshop

1. Click **File** on the Menu bar, then compare your menu to Figure 24.

2. Click **Close**.

TIP You can close an open file without closing Photoshop by clicking the Close button in the image window or tab. Photoshop will prompt you to save any unsaved changes before closing the file.

3. If asked to save your work, click **Yes** (Win) or **Save** (Mac).

4. Click **File** on the Menu bar, then click **Exit** (Win) or click **Photoshop** on the Menu bar, then click **Quit Photoshop** (Mac).

5. If asked to save your work (the untitled file), click **No**.

You closed the current file and exited the program by using the Close and Exit (Win) or Quit (Mac) commands.

Learn About Design Principles
AND COPYRIGHT RULES

What You'll Do

In this lesson, you'll learn about various design principles, the difference between designing for print media versus designing for the web, and copyright rules that define how images may be used.

Print Design vs. Web Design

Who's going to be viewing your images, and how? Will your image be printed in a lot of 5000, or will it be viewed on a monitor? Does it matter? When you think about it, the goals of print designers are quite different from those who design for the web. Table 2 illustrates some of the differences between these two art forms.

Composition 101

What makes one design merely okay and another terrific? While any such judgment is subjective, there are some rules governing image composition. It goes without saying that, as the artist, you have a message you're trying to deliver or something you're trying to say to the viewer. This is true whether the medium is oil painting, photography, or Photoshop imagery.

Elements under your control in your composition are tone, sharpness, scale, and arrangement. (You may see these items classified differently elsewhere, but they amount to the same concepts.)

- **Tone** is the brightness and contrast within an image. By using light and shadows you can shift the focus of the viewer's eye and control the mood.
- **Sharpness** is used to direct the viewer's eye to a specific area of an image.

TABLE 2: DIFFERENCES BETWEEN PRINT AND WEB DESIGN	
Print	**Web**
Mass-produced product that will all be identical and can be held in someone's hand.	Will be viewed on monitors of different size and resolution, with varying colors.
Designed for a limited size and area measured in inches.	Designed for a flexible web page measured in pixels.
You want to hold the reader's attention long to deliver the message: a *passive* experience.	You want the reader to stay as long as possible in your website and click links that delve deeper: an *active* experience.
Output is permanent and stable.	Output varies with user's hardware and software and content can evolve.

© Cengage Learning 2013

- **Scale** is the size relationship of objects to one another.
- **Arrangement** is how objects are positioned in space, relative to one another.

Are objects in your image contributing to clarity or clutter? Are similarly-sized objects confusing the viewer? Would blurring one area of an image change the viewer's focus?

These are tools you have to influence your artistic expression. Make sure the viewer understands what you want seen.

Arranging Elements

The appearance of elements in an image is important, but of equal importance is the way in which the elements are arranged. The components of any image should form a cohesive unit so that the reader is unaware of all the different parts, yet influenced by the way they work together to emphasize a message or reveal information. For example, if a large image is used, it should be easy for the reader to connect the image with any descriptive text. There should be an easily understood connection between the text and the artwork, and the reader should be able to seamlessly connect them.

QUICK TIP

Make peace with the fact that you cannot completely control how a web page will look on every conceivable device and browser.

In a newsletter, for example, it makes sense to organize text in a columnar fashion, but would you want snaking columns in a web page? Probably not. You wouldn't want to be scrolling up and down to read all the columnar text. At the very least, good web design has to consider the following items:

- layout, navigation, and flow
- interactivity as a design element
- imagery and text as content
- scrolling and linking

Overcoming the Fear of White Space

One design element that is often overlooked is white space. It's there on every page, and it doesn't seem to be doing much, does it? Take a look at a typical page in this book. Is every inch of space filled with either text or graphics? Of course not. If it were, the page would be impossible to read and would be horribly complex and ugly. The best example of the use of white space is the margins surrounding a page. This white space acts as a visual barrier—a resting place for the eyes. Without white space, the words on a page would crowd into each other, and the effect would be a cramped, cluttered, and hard-to-read page. Thoughtful use of white space makes it possible for you to guide the reader's eye from one location on the page to another. For many, one of the first design hurdles that must be overcome is the irresistible urge to put too much stuff on a page. When you are new to design, you may want to fill each page completely. Remember, less is more. Think of white space as a beautiful frame setting off an equally beautiful image.

Balancing Objects

The **optical center** of an image or a page occurs approximately three-eighths from the top of the page and is the point around which objects on the page are balanced. Once the optical center is located, objects can be positioned around it. A page can have a symmetrical or asymmetrical balance relative to an imaginary vertical line in the center of the page. In a **symmetrical balance**, objects are placed equally on either side of the vertical line. This type of layout tends toward a restful, formal design. In an **asymmetrical balance**, objects are placed unequally relative to the vertical line. Asymmetrical balance uses white space to balance the positioned objects, and is more dynamic and informal. A page with objects arranged asymmetrically tends to provide more visual interest because it is more surprising in appearance. See Figure 25 for an image having an obvious optical center.

Considering Ethical Implications

Because Photoshop makes it so easy for you to make so many dramatic changes to images, you should consider the ethical ramifications and implications of altering images. Is it proper or appropriate to alter an image just because you have the technical expertise to do so? Are there any legal responsibilities or liabilities involved in making these alterations? Because the general public is more aware about the topic of **intellectual property** (an image or idea that is owned and retained by legal control) with the increased availability of information and content, you should make sure you have the legal right to alter an image, especially if you plan on displaying or distributing the image to others. Know who retains the rights to an image, and if necessary, make sure you have written permission for its use, alteration, and/or distribution. Not taking these precautions could be costly.

Figure 25 *Image showing an optical center*

Understanding Copyright Terms

As you become more adept using Photoshop, you'll most likely obtain images from sources other than your own imagination and camera. It's of the utmost importance that you understand the legal and moral implications of using someone else's work. This means, among other things, that you have permission (verbal, or preferably, written) to use any part of the image, and that you understand terms such as copyright, fair use doctrine, intellectual property, and derivative works.

A **copyright** is protection extended to an author or creator of original work, which gives them the exclusive right to copy, distribute, and modify a thing, idea, or image. Copyright holders can give permission for others to copy, distribute, or modify their work. When something has been copyrighted, it is considered intellectual property. (The date of publication is the date the published work became generally available.) The length of time of a copyright is specific. In many cases, permission is *not* needed for education activities such as research and classroom use, but *is* required when you want to use someone else's property for profit.

Intellectual property is ideas, inventions, or processes that derive from the work of the mind, and the corresponding body of laws, rights, and registrations relating to these properties. Intellectual property law grants certain exclusive rights to owners of intangible assets such as music, artistic works, discoveries, inventions, words, phrases, and designs. It includes the following protections: copyright, trademarks (a distinctive associated identifier), patents, design rights, and trade secrets.

Fair use doctrine allows a user to make a copy of all or part of a work, even if permission *has not* been granted, for purposes such as criticism, news reporting, research, teaching, or scholarship.

A **derivative work** is a new, original product that is based upon content from one or more previously existing works.

QUICK TIP

For copyright protection to extend to a derivative work, the derivative work must display a level of originality and new expression.

So, can you use a picture you saw on a website in a class project? Yes. Can you use that same picture in a project for a paying client? No.

Table 3 illustrates commonly used terms and an example of each.

TABLE 3: COMMONLY USED IMAGE-USE TERMS		
Term	**Definition**	**Example**
Copyright	Protection to an author of an original work, including the right to copy, distribute and adapt that work.	The author of a play (created after 1978) has copyright protection for his/her life + 70 years, after which the work passes into public domain. (The *public domain* indicates that ownership of the work is public and can be used freely by anyone.)
Intellectual property	Refers to both the products of the mind and the accompanying legal protection for these intangible assets.	Industrial icons such as the Nike swoosh, or the Lexus branding symbol.
Fair use doctrine	Conditions under which a work can be used *without* permission.	An image based on a well-known scene in the film The Godfather that appears in a newspaper article.
Derivative work	A new product created from an existing original product.	The Adobe Photoshop CS6 Revealed book, which is based on the pre-existing Adobe Photoshop CS5 Revealed book.

© Cengage Learning 2013

Getting Started with Adobe Photoshop CS6

Licensing Your Work with Creative Commons

To many of us, the thought of dealing with lawyers or anything remotely legal makes us want to head for the hills. It is possible to license (and share) your work using licenses known as **Creative Commons licenses** without the use of lawyers or expensive fees. Creative Commons (*www.creativecommons.org*) is a nonprofit organization devoted to making it easier for people to share and build upon the works of others by offering free licenses and legal tools with which to mark creative work. Using a Creative Commons license allows you to keep your copyright, while allowing others to copy and distribute your work. You determine the conditions: you may insist that you be credited, you can decide if you will permit commercial use of your work or if your work can be modified. Figure 26 shows the Creative Commons licenses that can be applied to any work. The six licenses offered are then composed of combinations of license conditions, and consist of:

Attribution (*cc by*): The simplest of all Creative Commons licenses, in which any user (commercial or non-commercial) can distribute, modify, or enhance your work, provided you are credited.

Attribution Share Alike (*cc by-sa*): The same as Attribution, except that the new owner must create their license under the same terms you used.

Attribution No Derivatives (*cc by-nd*): Your work can be distributed by others, but not modified and in its entirety, with you being credited.

Attribution Non-Commercial (*cc by-nc*): Your work can be distributed, modified, or enhanced, with credit to you, for non-commercial purposes only. Derivative works do not have to be licensed.

Attribution Non-Commercial Share Alike (*cc by-nc-sa*): Your work can be distributed, modified, or enhanced, with credit to you, for non-commercial purposes only, but must

be licensed under the identical terms. All derivative work must carry the same license, and be non-commercial.

Attribution Non-Commercial No Derivatives (*cc by-nc-nd*): This is the most restrictive license category. Redistribution is allowed as long as credit is given. The work cannot be modified or used commercially.

Figure 26 *Creative Commons licenses*

POWER USER SHORTCUTS

To do this:	Use this method:	To do this:	Use this method:
Close a file	[Ctrl][W] (Win) ⌘ [W] (Mac)	Open Preferences dialog box	[Ctrl][K] (Win) ⌘ [K] (Mac)
Create a new file	[Ctrl][N] (Win) ⌘ [N] (Mac)	Reset preferences to default settings	[Shift][Alt][Ctrl] (Win) [shift][option] ⌘ (Mac)
Create a workspace	Window ➢ Workspace ➢ New Workspace or use the Workspace switcher	Save a file	[Ctrl][S] (Win) ⌘ [S] (Mac)
Exit Photoshop	[Ctrl][Q] (Win) ⌘ [Q] (Mac)	Show hidden Lasso tools	[Shift] **L**
Lasso tool	⌀ or **L**	Show or hide all open panels	[Shift][Tab]
		Show or hide all open panels, the options bar, and the Tools panel	[Tab]
		Show or hide Swatches panel	Window ➢ Swatches
Open a file	[Ctrl][O] (Win) ⌘ [O] (Mac)	Use Save As	[Shift][Ctrl][S] (Win) ⌘ [shift] [S] (Mac)

Key: Menu items are indicated by ➢ between the menu name and its command. Blue bold letters are shortcuts for selecting tools on the Tools panel.

© Cengage Learning 2013

Start Adobe Photoshop CS6.

1. Start Photoshop.
2. Create a new image that is 500 x 600 pixels, accept the default resolution, then name and save it as **Review**.

Open and save an image.

1. Open PS 1-3.jpg from the drive and folder where you store your Data Files.
2. Save it as **Rafting**. (Use the default options when saving the file using a new name. If the JPEG Options dialog box opens, click OK.)

Examine the Photoshop window.

1. Locate the image title bar and the current zoom percentage, then change the color theme to Light Gray.
2. Locate the menu you use to open an image.
3. View the Tools panel, the options bar, and the panels that are showing.
4. Click the Move tool on the Tools panel, view the Move tool options on the options bar, then reset the Essentials workspace.
5. Create, save, and display a customized workspace (based on Essentials) called **History and Layers** that captures panel locations and displays the History panel above the Color panel.
6. Open Bridge, apply the To Do label to Friends.psd, close Bridge, then return the Photoshop color theme to the default (the second from the left color box).

Close a file and exit Photoshop.

1. Compare your screen to Figure 27, then close the Rafting file.
2. Close the Review file.
3. Exit (Win) or Quit (Mac) Photoshop.

Learn about design principles and copyright rules.

1. What elements of composition are under your control?
2. How can a page be balanced?
3. Name three differences between print and web design.
4. Under what conditions can an image *not* be used in a project?

Figure 27 *Completed Skills Review*

Getting Started with Adobe Photoshop CS6

As a new Photoshop user, it's nice to know that there are so many tools to help you perform a task. Bridge and Mini Bridge seem to have many of the same features, yet Mini Bridge is available from within Photoshop and Bridge is a stand-alone program. You want to examine each of these tools to determine the best usage for each.

1. Open Photoshop, open Mini Bridge, then open Bridge.
2. Examine the folder containing the Data Files for this chapter and be prepared to discuss the differences between Bridge and Mini Bridge.
3. What are the sorting and printing limitations of Mini Bridge versus Bridge? Mini Bridge is shown in Figure 28.
4. Be prepared to discuss the best usages of Bridge and Mini Bridge.

Figure 28 *Sample Project Builder 1*

Image of butterfly © Photodisc/Getty Images.

At some point in your working with Photoshop, you'll probably have direct contact with one or more clients. Rather than take a sink-or-swim approach when this inevitable time comes, you decide to be proactive and use the web to research this process.

1. Open your favorite browser and search engine and find a website with relevant information about communicating with design clients.
2. Keep track of the most relevant website and make notes of key points on the information you've found. A client meeting is shown in Figure 29.
3. Be prepared to discuss how you'll effectively interact with your design clients when the time comes.

Figure 29 *Sample Project Builder 2*
Courtesy Parker Michael Knight

One of the best resources for learning about design principles is the web. You want to make sure you fully understand the differences between designing for print and designing for the web, so you decide to use the Internet to find out more.

1. Connect to the Internet, and use your browser to find at least two websites that have information about the differences between print and web design principles.
2. Find and download one image that serves as an example of good print design and one image of good web design. Save the images (in JPEG format) as Print design-1 and Web design-1. Figure 30 shows a sample print design.

Figure 30 *Sample Design Project*

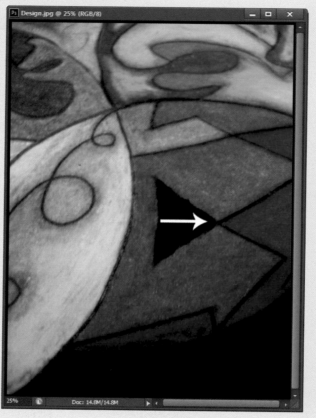

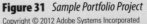
You are preparing to work on a series of design projects to enhance your portfolio. You decide to see what information on digital imaging is available on the Adobe website. You also want to increase your familiarity with the Adobe website so that you can take advantage of product information and support, user tips and feedback, and become a more skilled Photoshop user. You'd also like to become more familiar with the concepts of intellectual property and copyright issues.

1. Connect to the Internet and go to the Adobe website at *www.adobe.com.*
2. Point to Products, then find the link for the Photoshop family, as shown in Figure 31.
3. Use the links on the web page to search for information about digital imaging options.
4. Print the relevant page(s).
5. Use your favorite browser and search engine to find several sites about intellectual property and copyright issues.
6. Print at least two of the sites you find the most interesting.
7. Evaluate the information in the documents, then compare any significant differences.

Figure 31 *Sample Portfolio Project*
Copyright © 2012 Adobe Systems Incorporated

CHAPTER 2 LEARNING
PHOTOSHOP BASICS

1. Use organizational and management features
2. Use the Layers and History panels
3. Learn about Photoshop by using Help
4. View and print an image

2 LEARNING
PHOTOSHOP BASICS

Working Magic with Photoshop

The essence of working with images in Photoshop is based on an understanding of layers. Every image opened in Photoshop is made up of one or more layers, and it is within these layers that you, as an artist, work your magic. The order of layers in an image, and the effects applied to them, can make one image very different from another.

Using Management Tools

Adobe Photoshop CS6 is an amazingly rich program that has a variety of tools that you can use to manage your digital images. Using services such as CS Live and Acrobat.com, you'll be able to increase your productivity and work more efficiently individually and with coworkers.

Learning to Love Layers

Once you become more comfortable using Photoshop, you'll understand the importance of each of the panels. Some panels, such as the Layers panel, are vital to using Photoshop.

Since layers are the key to creating and manipulating Photoshop images, the Layers panel is one that we depend on most, for it tells us at-a-glance the order and type of layers within an image. And if the Layers panel is the map of the Photoshop image, the History panel provides step-by-step instructions that let us know how we got to our destination.

Finding Help when You Need It

A complex program like Photoshop needs a robust Help system. You'll find that the Help system, which is accessed using your browser, doesn't disappoint.

Viewing and Printing

While not everyone prints each one of their images, nearly everyone needs to zoom in and out to get a better look at different areas. Using the Zoom tool, you can view the areas you need to focus on in as high or as low of a magnification as you want. If you do want to print out an image, Photoshop offers great tools to do so.

TOOLS YOU'LL USE

Use Organizational
AND MANAGEMENT FEATURES

What You'll Do

In this lesson, you'll learn how to use Acrobat.com, Bridge, and Mini Bridge.

Managing the Creative Suite

Adobe Creative Cloud is a fee-based membership service that includes CS tools, Adobe Touch Apps, services, plus new features, products, and services as soon as they are released. Adobe Touch Apps are available for iPad or Android tablets and sync to your Creative Suite desktop applications. With Adobe Creative Cloud, your files will be in sync regardless which device or desktop you're using. You can store up to 20GB of data, accessible from anywhere with Internet access. Also included is community training and support, and the opportunity to share your work and connect with peers.

Learning About CS Live

CS Live lets you connect to **Acrobat.com**, which is a management feature of the Adobe Creative Suite that can be used to organize your work whether you work in groups or by yourself. Adobe Creative Cloud and Acrobat.com are accessed using any browser. In addition to allowing you to share files with others in a virtual environment (also known as **cloud computing**), these services make it possible to take advantage of **file versioning**, which allows you to store multiple versions of your work. You can access Acrobat.com using your favorite browser. Figure 1 shows the Acrobat.com website: this site changes frequently.

Signing into Acrobat.com

You can log into Acrobat.com by entering Acrobat.com in the address bar of your favorite browser, entering your Adobe ID and password when prompted (or registering for one), and then clicking Sign In. The Acrobat.com home screen is shown in Figure 2: your screen may look different as this screen can look different with each user and changes often.

Figure 1 *Acrobat.com website*
© Adobe Systems Incorporated

Using Acrobat.com

When you go to Acrobat.com, you will be asked to select a service from the Sign in pull-down menu. Select Acrobat.com, sign in with your Adobe ID. Notice that there are two tabs: Files and Web Conferencing, as shown in Figure 2. You can return to the Home screen by clicking the person icon to sign out. From within Acrobat.com, you can conduct meetings and share screens, collaborate with coworkers to create and edit documents, presentations, and tables, and store documents for easy access by others.

Figure 2 *Files tab in Acrobat.com*

Copyright © 2012 Adobe Systems Incorporated

To leave Acrobat.com, click the person icon, then click Sign Out

"10 Cool Things" document

Figure 3 *Project Complexity triangle*

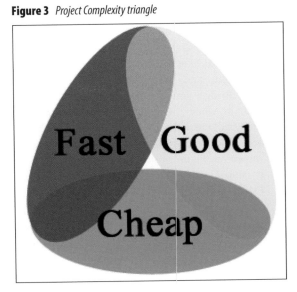

The Complexity of Projects

If you ask any client what they want in their project, they'll most likely say something to the effect that they want it now, they want it done well, and they want it to not cost a lot. These three variables (performance, time, and cost) that are shown in Figure 3 comprise the **project scope** and illustrate the complexity that exists in any project.

- If the project is a low price and completed quickly, will the quality be satisfactory?
- If the project is completed quickly and the quality is good, will the price be affordable?

Ask the client, and they'll say that they want all three elements. But is this a realistic expectation?

Reusing Housekeeping Tasks in Bridge and Mini Bridge

All those little housekeeping tasks you do, such as renaming files and copying files and folders from one location on your hard drive to another, can be easily carried out in Bridge and Mini Bridge. Once you select file thumbnails in Bridge or Mini Bridge, you can copy them to another location by dragging-and-dropping. Files can be renamed by clicking the filename until it is selected, typing the new name, and then pressing [Enter] (Win) or [return] (Mac).

Understanding Metadata

Metadata is descriptive standardized information about a file, and includes information such as the author's name, copyright, and keywords associated with it. In Bridge, you can also find information such as when the image was created, last modified, current size, resolution, bit depth, and color mode in the Metadata panel, shown in Figure 4. Metadata information is stored using the Extensible Metadata Platform (XMP) standard format, which was developed by Adobe and is commonly shared by their products. Sometimes metadata is stored separately in a **sidecar file**. This file can be applied to other files, making it possible to use metadata from one file as a template for another.

Assigning Keywords to an Image

The Keywords panel, as seen in Figure 5, is grouped with the Metadata panel and can be used to create your own system of identifying files based on their content.

Figure 4 *Metadata panel in Bridge*

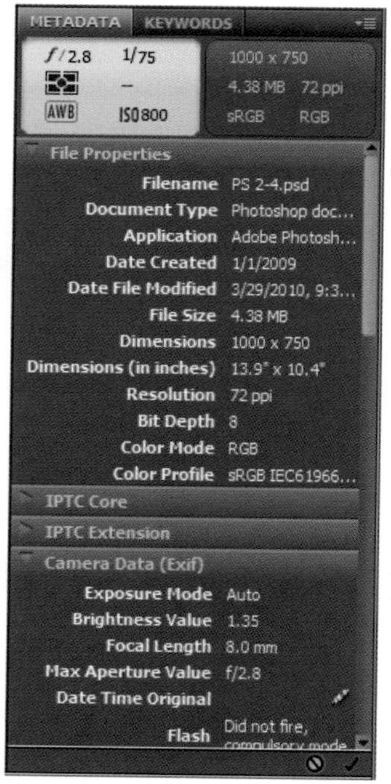

Figure 5 *Keywords panel in Bridge*

Learning Photoshop Basics

In conjunction with the Filter panel (located beneath the Favorites and Folders panels on the left side of the screen in Bridge), keywords can be used to find images that meet specific criteria. Say, for example, that you have hundreds of images downloaded from your digital camera. Some could be assigned the keyword "New York," others "Paris," and still others "Rome." Viewing all images with the keyword "Rome" is as simple as making the folder containing all the images active, and then clicking the keyword Rome in the filter panel. Any file can be assigned multiple keywords, and those keywords can be renamed, deleted, or applied to other files.

Project Management Principles

Project management is the execution of a plan that brings a project to a successful completion. No longer is project management as simple as saying 'you do this' and 'I'll do that'. A good project manager has to wear many hats and needs to have a thorough understanding of many elements, including budgetary requirements, client needs, production limitations, availability of supplies (industrial and human resources), identification of deliverables (such as specifications, comps or sketches), and timeline management. Like an air traffic controller, a project manager must see what's in front, off to the side, and just around the bend.

Project management is not static: you don't get it all formulated and then just let it sit. Good project management requires periodic revisiting and revision. Without this periodic review, a project may suffer from **scope creep**, a condition to be avoided in which a project seems to have lost its way. Communication review methods vary, but can and should include periodic peer reviews and surveys, and are important feedback measurements. Scope creep can lead to budget overruns and failure to bring a product to market in a timely fashion. All too often, a project can become a victim of its own planning. Since a project plan is written down, many consider it to be 'written in stone'. In fact, a project has so many opportunities to fall off the track: project members become ill, weather becomes a limiting factor, suppliers fail to deliver when promised, or the plan may have been ill-conceived. See Table 1 for some commonly used project management terms.

TABLE 1: COMMONLY USED PROJECT MANAGEMENT TERMS		
Term	**Definition**	**Example**
Project scope	The goals and objectives of the project.	Creation of a website, including images.
Tasks	Specific goals that lead to the ultimate completion of the project.	Choose colors, collect photos, and create logo.
Due dates	When specific tasks must be completed in order to achieve the ultimate goal.	Secure image permissions before website goes live.
Resource allocation	How to best utilize resources, including budgetary constraints, human resources (including outsourcing), and supplies.	Ensure that image fees stay within budget and designer spends no more than 25% of her time.

© Cengage Learning 2013

Assigning a keyword

1. Launch **Bridge**.

2. Activate the **Folders tab**, if necessary, and locate the folder containing the Data Files for Chapter 2.

3. Select all the files in the folder and copy them to the folder for Solutions files for Chapter 2.

TIP It is *not necessary* to copy the files in order to complete the lesson. Copying the files just insures that the original data files are kept intact for future use.

4. Activate the **Chapter 2 folder** in the Solutions folder.

5. Click the **Sort by list arrow**, click **By Filename** if not already selected, then click the **Descending Order button** if the Ascending Order button is not already displayed.

6. Click the thumbnail in the Content panel for **PS 2-1.psd**, press and hold [**Shift**], click **PS 2-3.psd**, then release [**Shift**], as shown in Figure 6.

7. Click the **Keywords tab**, then click the **New Keyword button** in the Keywords panel.

8. Type **Sports** in the Keywords panel text box, press [**Enter**] (Win) or [**return**] (Mac), then click the **check box** to the left of Sports.

TIP You can apply keywords to individual images, but applying them to multiple images will speed up your workflow.

You created a new keyword that you applied to three images.

Figure 6 *Files selected in Bridge*
Images of wineglasses and frying pan © Photodisc/Getty Images.

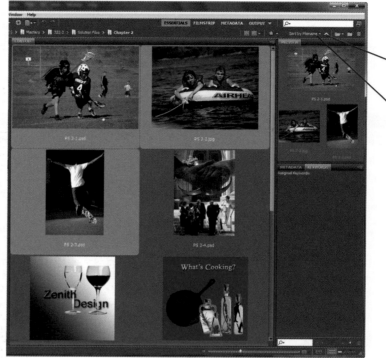

Click to choose ascending or descending order

Click to choose the sort parameter

Repurposing in Photoshop

Just because you create a new image in Photoshop, it doesn't mean you always start from scratch. You may use part of one image that already exists in another image, or you may drag an entire existing image into a new image. The idea of repurposing is not new, in fact, Photoshop encourages and promotes it. To this end, it provides you with many tools that make it easy to reuse skills and knowledge. Presets (established settings that perform specific tasks) are available in many Photoshop tools, such as brushes, actions, video styles, and custom shapes. Templates (predesigned files that have been developed by others and generally have a specific outcome, such as a label) are available from companies such as Avery, and can be downloaded from the web.

Figure 7 *Files selected in Bridge*

Check mark means
keyword filter is on

Filtering with Bridge

1. Click the **Keywords section** in the Filter panel, then click **Sports**.

   A check mark appears next to Sports in the Filter panel, as seen in Figure 7, and only the images with the keyword Sports are displayed.

2. Click **Sports** in the Keywords section in the Filter panel to restore all the images in the folder.

3. Close Bridge.

You used the Filter panel to see only those images that had a specific keyword applied, then you closed Bridge.

Basics of Project Management

The basics of project management include knowledge of the project scope, the tasks at hand, due dates for task completion, and effective resource allocation. And while all of this is extremely complicated, you must remember that most projects don't operate in a bubble: they are usually one of many projects competing for the same resources. In addition to competing with other projects, many tasks within a given project may be occurring simultaneously and repetitively. Not every project will have the same constraints. Some manufacturing projects, for example, may require more rigorous testing than others, and some projects may rely more heavily on outsourcing that others. Most projects will have deliverables, but the type and scope of those will vary.

Use the Layers
AND HISTORY PANELS

What You'll Do

In this lesson, you'll hide and display a layer, move a layer on the Layers panel, and then undo the move by deleting the Layer Order state on the History panel.

You can think of layers in a Photoshop image as individual sheets of clear plastic that are in a stack. It's possible for your file to quickly accumulate dozens of layers. The **Layers panel** displays all the individual layers in an open file. You can use the Layers panel to create, copy, delete, display, hide, merge, lock, group, or reposition layers.

Learning About Layers

A **layer** is a section within an image that can be manipulated independently. Layers allow you to control individual elements within an image and create great dramatic effects and variations of the same image. Layers enable you to easily manipulate individual characteristics within an image. Each Photoshop file has at least one layer, and can contain many individual layers, or groups of layers.

QUICK TIP

In Photoshop, using and understanding layers is the key to success.

Understanding the Layers Panel

The order in which the layers appear on the Layers panel matches the order in which they appear in the image; the top layer in the Layers

panel is the top layer on the image. You can make a layer active by clicking its name on the Layers panel. When a layer is active, it is highlighted on the Layers panel, and the name of the layer appears in parentheses in the image title bar. Only one layer can be active at a time. Figure 8 shows an image with its Layers panel. Do you see that this image contains six layers? Each layer can be moved or modified individually on the panel to give a different effect to the overall image. If you look at the Layers panel, you'll see that the Photoshop CS6 type layer is blue, indicating that it is currently active.

QUICK TIP

Get in the habit of shifting your eye from the image in the work area to the Layers panel. Knowing which layer is active will save you time and help you troubleshoot an image.

Filtering layers

Layers can be filtered from within the Layers panel to build a short list of layers. This short list can be organized by Kind, Name, Effect, Mode, Attribute, or Color and can be created by clicking the Filter list arrow on the Layers panel. You can also filter layers using any of the five preset filtering buttons.

Displaying and Hiding Layers

You can use the Layers panel to control which layers are visible in an image. You can show or hide a layer by clicking the Indicates layer visibility button next to the layer thumbnail. When a layer is hidden, you are not able to merge it with another, select it, or print it.

Using the History Panel

Photoshop records each task you complete in an image on the **History panel**. This record of events, called states, makes it easy to see what changes occurred and the tools or commands that you used to make the modifications. The History panel, shown in Figure 8, displays up to 20 states by default and automatically updates the list to display the most recently performed tasks. The list contains the name of the tool or command used to change the image. You can delete a state on the History panel by selecting it and dragging it to the Delete current state button. Deleting a state is equivalent to using the Undo command. You can also use the History panel to create a new image from any state.

Figure 8 *Layers and History panels*

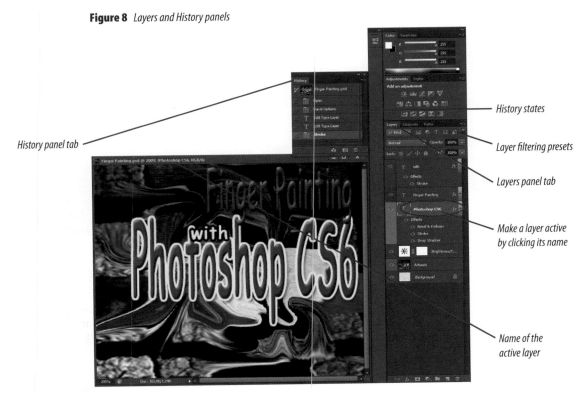

History panel tab

History states

Layer filtering presets

Layers panel tab

Make a layer active by clicking its name

Name of the active layer

Hide and display a layer

1. Open the file PS 2-4.psd, then rename it **Wedding Day.psd**.
2. Click the **Rings layer** on the Layers panel, then click the **Move tool** ![Move tool] if necessary.

TIP Depending on the size of the window, you might only be able to see the initial characters of the layer name.

3. Verify that the **Show Transform Controls check box** on the options bar is not checked, then click the **Indicates layer visibility button** ![button] on the Rings layer to display the image, as shown in Figure 9.

TIP By default, transparent areas of an image have a checkerboard display on the Layers panel.

4. Click the **Indicates layer visibility button** ![eye] on the Rings layer to hide the layer.

You made the Rings layer active on the Layers panel, then clicked the Indicates layer visibility button to display and hide the layer. Hiding layers is an important skill that can be used to remove distracting elements. Once you've finished working on a specific layer, you can display the additional layers.

Figure 9 *Wedding Day*

Icon indicates
layer visibility

Visible Rings layer

Figure 10 *Layer moved in Layers panel*

Figure 11 *Result of moved layer*

Result of moved layer

Figure 12 *Deleting a History state*

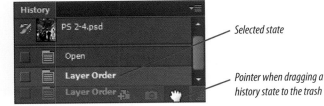

Selected state

Pointer when dragging a history state to the trash

Move a layer on the Layers panel and delete a state on the History panel

1. Click the **Indicates layer visibility button** on the Rings layer on the Layers panel to display the layer.

2. Click on the Hands layer on the Layers panel to hide the layer.

3. Display the **Legacy workspace** you created in Chapter 1.

4. Click and drag the **Hands layer** on the Layers panel beneath the Rings layer, so your Layers panel looks like Figure 10.

   The hands are no longer visible as shown in Figure 11.

5. Click **Layer Order** on the History panel, then drag it to the **Delete current state button** on the History panel, as shown in Figure 12.

TIP Each time you close and reopen an image, the History panel is cleared.

   The original order of the layers in the Layers panel is restored.

6. Click **File** on the Menu bar, then click **Save**.

TIP An alternative to the deletion of history states is the Revert command. Located on the File menu, this command restores the image to its last saved state.

You moved the Hands layer beneath the Rings layer, then returned it to its original position by dragging the Layer Order state to the Delete current state button on the History panel. You can easily use the History panel to undo what you've done.

Learn About Photoshop
BY USING HELP

What You'll Do

Copyright © 2012 Adobe Systems Incorporated

▶ *In this lesson, you'll open Help, and then view and find information from the available topics and the Search feature.*

Understanding the Power of Help

Photoshop features an extensive Help system that you can use to access definitions, explanations, and useful tips. Help information is displayed in a browser window, so you must have web browser software installed on your computer to view the information; however, you do need an Internet connection to use Photoshop Help.

QUICKTIP

Since the Help contents displays in your browser, you already know how to print. Once the content is displayed, use the Print command on your browser to print the page(s) of interest.

Using Help Topics

The Home page of the Photoshop Help/Topics window, shown in Figure 13, displays detailed categories that you can use to retrieve information about Photoshop commands and features. The following topics are available:

- What's new in CS6
- Getting started
- Image basics
- Workspace and workflow
- Layers
- Selecting
- Image adjustments
- Repair and restoration
- Reshaping and transforming
- Drawing and painting
- Text
- Video and animation
- Web graphics
- Saving and exporting
- Printing and color management
- 3D and technical imaging

When you click a link, Help takes you directly to the information you've selected. The Search feature is located in the left pane in the form of a text box. You can search the Photoshop Help System by typing your search terms in the text box, and then pressing [Enter] (Win) or [return] (Mac).

Figure 13 *Groups in Photoshop Online Help*
Copyright © 2012 Adobe Systems Incorporated

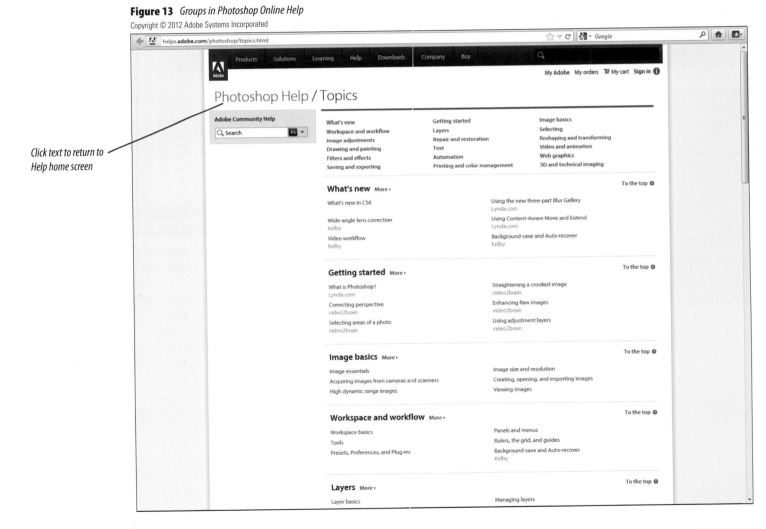

Click text to return to
Help home screen

Find information in Adobe reference titles

1. Click **Help** on the Menu bar, then click **Photoshop Online Help**. If the Help Manager dialog box appears, click the red Close button to close this window (Mac).

TIP You can also open the Help window by pressing [F1] (Win) or ⌘ [/] (Mac).

2. Click **Acquiring images from cameras and scanners** in the Image basics group. See Figure 14.

TIP You can maximize the window or change the width of the Search pane if you want to take advantage of the full screen display.

Bear in mind that Help is web-driven and, like any website, can change as errors and inconsistencies are found.

3. Close the Photoshop Help window.

You used the Photoshop Online Help command on the Help menu to open the Help window and view a topic.

Figure 14 *A topic in the Image basics group*

Copyright © 2012 Adobe Systems Incorporated

Understanding the Differences Between Monitor, Images, and Device Resolution

Image resolution is determined by the number of pixels per inch (ppi) that are printed on a page. Pixel dimensions (the number of pixels along the height and width of a bitmap image) determine the amount of detail in an image, while resolution controls the amount of space over which the pixels are printed. Think of the differences between the picture quality on a standard-definition 480i television versus a high-definition 1080i television. The high-definition image will be crisper and have more vibrant colors, whereas the standard-definition image may look weak and washed out. High resolution images show greater detail and more subtle color transitions than low resolution images. Lower resolution images can look grainy, like images in older newspapers.

Device resolution or printer resolution is measured by the ink dots per inch (dpi) produced by printers. You can set the resolution of your computer monitor to determine the detail with which images will be displayed. Each monitor should be calibrated to describe how the monitor reproduces colors. Monitor calibration is one of the first things you should do because it determines whether your colors are being accurately represented, which in turn determines how accurately your output will match your design intentions. **Screen frequency**, or *line screen*, is the number of printer dots or halftone cells per inch used to print grayscale images or color separations and is measured in lines per inch (lpi). Printer calibration ensures that what you see on your monitor is translated to paper.

Learning Photoshop Basics

Figure 15 *Photoshop Help Support Center*

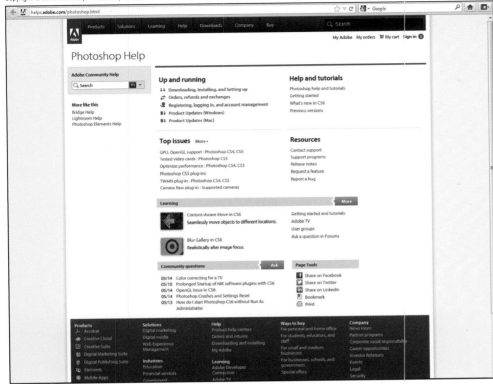

Get help and support

1. Click **Help** on the Menu bar, then click **Photoshop Support Center**.

2. Compare your Help window to Figure 15, then close the Help window.

You accessed the Photoshop Help Support Center.

Find information using Search

1. Open Photoshop Online Help, then click the **Search text box** in the browser window.

TIP Your help window may display in your browser or in a dialog box. Depending on how your Help windows display, the Search text box will be above the left pane in the dialog box or in the black bar in the browser window.

2. Type **rulers**, press [**Enter**] (Win) or [**return**] (Mac), then click the link for **Adobe Photoshop * Rulers, the grid, and guides**.

TIP You can search for multiple words by inserting a space.

3. Go to the top of the page, then compare your Help screen to Figure 16.

4. Close the Adobe Community Help window.

You entered a search term, viewed search results, then closed the Help window.

Figure 16 *Result of a search in Help*
Copyright © 2012 Adobe Systems Incorporated

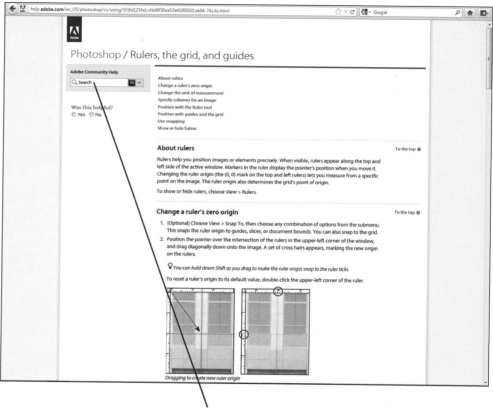

Search text box

Figure 17 *List of new features in Photoshop CS6*

Copyright © 2012 Adobe Systems Incorporated

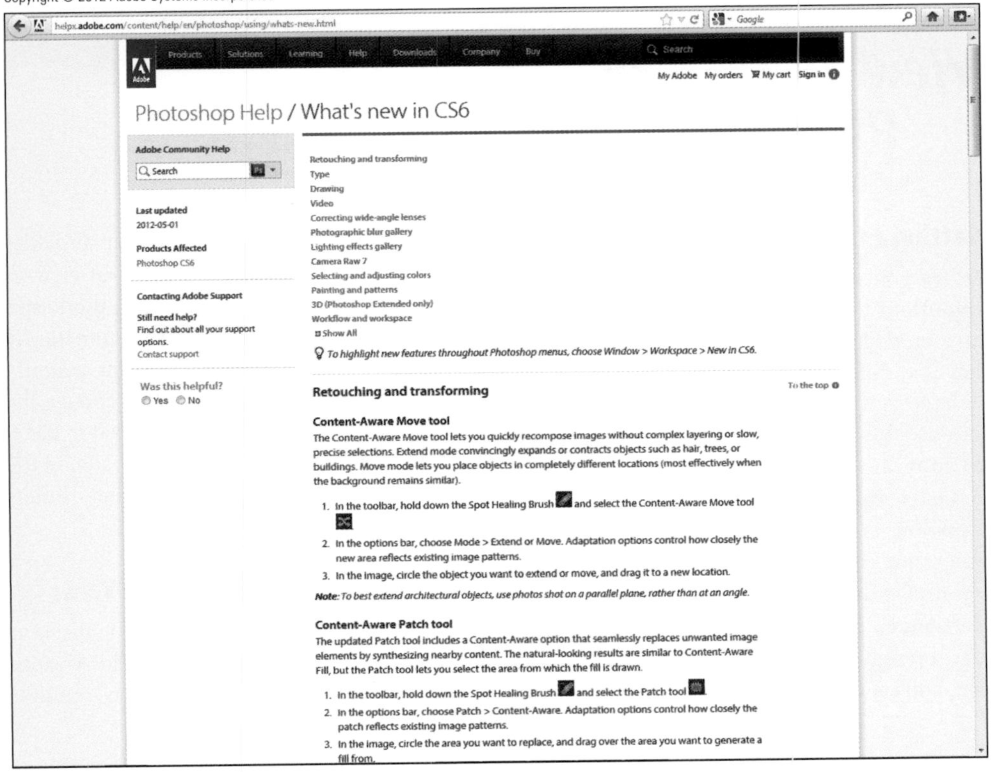

TIP If you have some experience with a previous version of Photoshop or you just want to cut-to-the-chase and find out what's new in this version. You can find a list of new features in this version of Photoshop by clicking Help on the Menu bar, clicking Photoshop Online Help, and then clicking What's new in CS6 in the What's new group. The list of new features, shown in Figure 17, contains a brief description of each feature and a link to more information.

View and
PRINT AN IMAGE

What You'll Do

In this lesson, you'll use the Zoom tool on the Tools panel to increase and decrease your views of the image. You'll also change the page orientation settings in the Print dialog box, and print the image.

Getting a Closer Look

When you edit an image in Photoshop, it is important that you have a good view of the area on which you want to focus. Photoshop has a variety of methods that allow you to enlarge or reduce your current view. You can use the Zoom tool by clicking the image to zoom in on (magnify the view) or zoom out of (reduce the view) areas of your image. Zooming in or out enlarges or reduces your *view*, not the actual image. The maximum zoom factor is 3200%. The current zoom percentage appears in the document's title bar, on the Navigator panel, on the status bar, and on the View menu. When the Zoom tool is selected, the options bar provides additional choices for changing your view, as shown in Figure 18. For example, the Resize Windows To Fit check box automatically resizes the window whenever you magnify or reduce the view. You can also change the zoom percentage using the Navigator panel or the status bar by typing a new value in the Zoom text box, and then pressing [Enter] (Win) or [return] (Mac).

Viewing an Image in Multiple Views

You can use the New Window for *filename* command (accessed by pointing to Arrange on the Window menu) to open multiple

Figure 18 *Zoom tool options bar*

Selected check box
resizes window
while zooming

Displays image at 100%
magnification

Fits the image
on the screen

Zooms the window to
the print resolution

Learning Photoshop Basics

views of the same image. You can change the zoom percentage in each view so you can spotlight the areas you want to modify, and then modify the specific area of the image in each view. Because you are working on the same image in multiple views, not in multiple versions, Photoshop automatically applies the changes you make in one view to all views. Although you can close the views you no longer need at any time, Photoshop will not save any changes until you save the file.

Printing Your Image

In many cases, a professional print shop might be the best option for printing a Photoshop image to get the highest quality. Lacking a professional print shop, you can print a Photoshop image using a standard black-and-white or color printer from within Photoshop, or you can switch to Bridge and then choose to send output to a PDF or Web Gallery. The printed image will be a composite of all visible layers. The quality of your printer and paper will affect the appearance of your output. The Print dialog

box displays options for printing, such as paper orientation. **Orientation** is the direction in which an image appears on the page. In **portrait orientation**, the image is printed with the shorter edges of the paper at the top and bottom. In **landscape orientation**, the image is printed with the longer edges of the paper at the top and bottom.

Use the Print command when you want to print multiple copies of an image. The Print dialog box allows you to handle color values using color management and printer profiles. Use the Print One Copy command to print a single copy without making dialog box selections.

Understanding Color Handling in Printing

The Print dialog box that opens when you click Print on the File menu lets you determine how colors are output. You can click the Color Handling list arrow to choose whether Photoshop or the printing device should manage the colors. If you let Photoshop determine the

colors, Photoshop performs any necessary conversions to color values appropriate for the selected printer. If you choose to let the printer determine the colors, the printer will convert document color values to the corresponding printer color values. In this scenario, Photoshop does not alter the color values.

Choosing a Photoshop Version

The release of the Adobe Creative Suite 6 offers two versions of Photoshop: Adobe Photoshop CS6 and Adobe Photoshop CS6 Extended. The Extended version has additional animation and measurement features and is ideal for multimedia creative professionals, film and video creative professionals, graphic and web designers who push the limits of 3D and motion, as well as those professionals in the fields of manufacturing, medicine, architecture, engineering and construction, and science and research. Photoshop CS6 is ideal for professional photographers, serious amateur photographers, graphic and web designers, and print service providers.

Printed images vs. on-screen images

Why isn't what you see on your computer screen the same as your printer output? Well, these two items are different because video monitors and printers work very differently. A printed image is measured in inches or centimeters, and its size is modified on paper by scaling. Also, an image size does not vary with its scanned resolution, and printed pixels are spaced using a specified scaled resolution (dpi). On paper, several printer ink dots are used to represent the color of one image pixel.

On a video monitor, the image size is measured on the screen in pixels, the image size is modified by resampling, and the size varies with the scanned resolution. Image pixels are located at each screen pixel location. On screen, one screen pixel location contains one image pixel, and can be of any RGB value.

Using the Photoshop File Info Dialog Box

You can use the File Info dialog box to identify a file, add a caption or other text, or add a copyright notice. The Description text box, shown in Figure 19, allows you to enter text that can be printed with the image. For example, to add information to an image, click File on the Menu bar, click File Info, and then click the Description text box. (You can move from field to field by pressing [Tab] or by clicking individual text boxes.) Type your name or other identifying information in the Description text box, or click stars to assign a rating. You can enter additional information

in the other text boxes, and then save all the File Info data by clicking OK. To print data from the Description field of the File Info dialog box, click File on the Menu bar, and then click Print. Scroll down and click the right-pointing triangle to expand Printing Marks, and then select the Description check

box. Additional printable options are listed. To print the filename, select the Labels check box. You can also select check boxes that let you print crop marks and registration marks. If you choose, you can even add a background color or border to your image. After you select the items you want to print, click Print.

Figure 20 *Navigator panel*

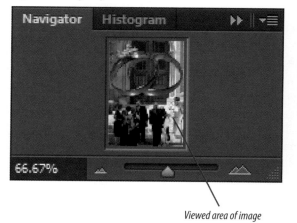

Viewed area of image

Figure 19 *File Info dialog box*

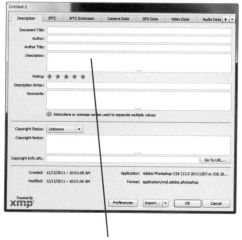

Type information to be printed here

Using the Navigator Panel

You can change the magnification factor of an image using the Navigator panel or the Zoom tool on the Tools panel. You can open the Navigator panel by clicking Window on the Menu bar, and then clicking Navigator. By double-clicking the Zoom text box on the Navigator panel, you can enter a new magnification factor, and then press [Enter] (Win) or [return] (Mac). The magnification factor—shown as a percentage—is displayed in the lower-left corner of the Navigator panel, as shown in Figure 20. The red border in the panel, called the proxy view area, defines the area of the image that is magnified. You can drag the proxy view area inside the Navigator panel to view other areas of the image at the current magnification factor.

Learning Photoshop Basics

Figure 21 *Reduced image*

Zoom percentage
changed

Zoom tool on
the Tools panel

Use the Zoom tool

1. Click the **Indicates layer visibility button**  on the Layers panel for the Rings layer so the layer is no longer displayed.

2. Click the **Indicates layer visibility button** on the Layers panel for the Hands layer so the layer is visible.

3. Click the **Zoom tool** on the Tools panel.

TIP You can also change the magnification level by double-clicking the Zoom Level text box at the bottom-left corner of the image window and manually entering a zoom level.

4. Select the **Resize Windows To Fit check box** (if it is not already selected) on the options bar.

5. Position the **Zoom in pointer** over the center of the image, then click the **image**.

TIP Position the pointer over the part of the image you want to keep in view.

6. Press [**Alt**] (Win) or [**option**] (Mac), then when the Zoom out pointer appears, click the **center of the image** twice with the **Zoom out pointer** .

7. Release [**Alt**] (Win) or [**option**] (Mac), then compare your image to Figure 21.

    The zoom factor for the image is 50%. Your zoom factor may differ.

You selected the Zoom tool on the Tools panel and used it to zoom in to and out of the image. The Zoom tool makes it possible to see the detail in specific areas of an image, or to see the whole image at once, depending on your needs.

Modify print settings

1. Click **File** on the Menu bar, then click **Print** to open the Print dialog box.

   TIP If you have not selected a printer using the Print Center, a warning box might appear.

2. Click the **Print paper in landscape orientation button** 🖼️ .

3. Make sure that **1** appears in the Copies text box, compare your dialog box to Figure 22, click **Print**, then click **Print** after verifying that the correct printer is selected.

   TIP You can use the handles surrounding the image preview in the Print dialog box to scale the print size.

4. Save your work.

   TIP You can preview up to 20 images in a web browser by selecting the image(s) in Bridge, clicking the Output button, then clicking Preview in Browser.

You used the Print command on the File menu to open the Photoshop Print Settings dialog box, changed the page orientation, and then printed the image. Changing the page orientation can sometimes make an image fit better on a printed page.

Figure 22 *Photoshop Print Settings dialog box*

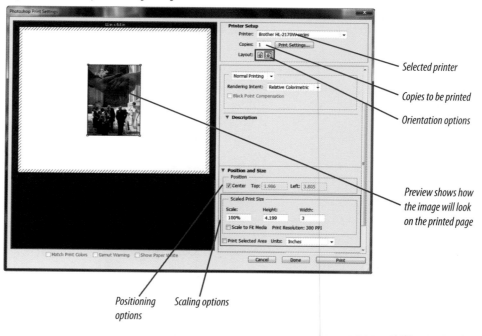

Selected printer

Copies to be printed

Orientation options

Preview shows how the image will look on the printed page

Positioning options

Scaling options

Previewing and Creating a Proof Setup

You can create and save a Proof Setup, which lets you preview your image to see how it will look when printed on a specific device. (How an image looks on specific hardware that has been calibrated and using a color management system is called a **soft proof**. The soft proof is an accurate representation of how an image will look when it has been printed.) This feature lets you see how colors can be interpreted by different devices. By using this feature, you can decrease the chance that the colors on the printed copy of the image will vary from what you viewed on your monitor. Create a custom proof by clicking View on the Menu bar, pointing to Proof Setup, and then clicking Custom. Specify the conditions in the Customize Proof Condition dialog box, and then click OK. Each proof setup has the .psf extension and can be loaded by clicking View on the Menu bar, pointing to Proof Setup, clicking Custom, and then clicking Load.

Figure 23 *PDF Output options in Bridge*

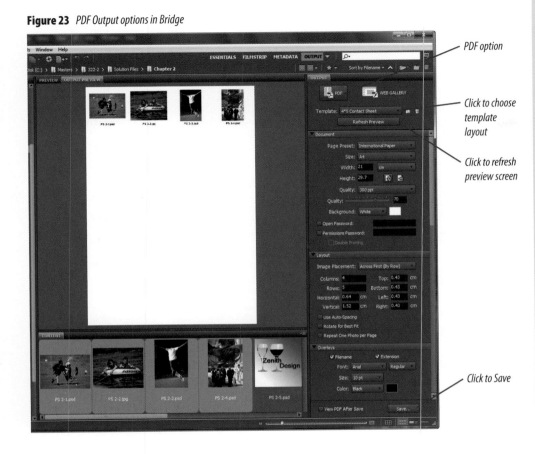

PDF option

Click to choose
template
layout

Click to refresh
preview screen

Click to Save

Create a PDF with Bridge

1. Open **Bridge**.

2. Click the **Folders tab** (if necessary), click **Chapter 2** in the location where your Data Files are stored in the Folders tab (if necessary), then verify that **Sort by Filename** is selected.

3. Click **Output** on the Bridge Workspace switcher.

4. Click the **PDF button** in the Output tab.

5. Click **PS 2-1.psd**, hold [**Shift**], click **PS 2-4.psd** in the Content tab, then release [**Shift**].

6. Click the **Template list arrow** in the Output panel, click **4*5 Contact Sheet**, click **Refresh Preview**, then compare your screen to Figure 23. (The Generate PDF Contact Sheet dialog box will appear; the contact sheet will display in the Document window when processing is finished.)

You used Adobe Bridge to create a PDF, then selected specific images and an arrangement for the file.

Save a PDF output file

1. Click **Save** (at the bottom of the Output panel), locate the folder where your Data Files are stored, type **your name Chapter 2 contact sheet** in the text box, then click **Save**.

2. Click **OK** to acknowledge that the contact sheet was successfully processed.

You generated a PDF that can be printed later using Adobe Acrobat, then saved and printed the PDF.

Figure 24 *Output panel in Bridge*

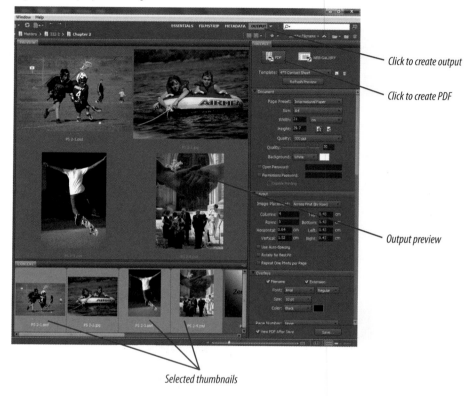

Click to create output

Click to create PDF

Output preview

Selected thumbnails

Creating a PDF

Using Bridge you can create a PDF Presentation (a presentation in the PDF file format). Such a presentation can be viewed fullscreen on any computer monitor, or in Adobe Acrobat or Adobe Reader as a PDF file. You can create such a presentation by opening Bridge, locating and selecting images using the file hierarchy, and then clicking the Output button on the Bridge Menu bar. The Output panel, shown in Figure 24, opens and displays the images you have selected. You can add images by pressing [Ctrl] (Win) or ⌘ (Mac) while clicking additional images.

Figure 25 *Web Gallery options in Bridge*

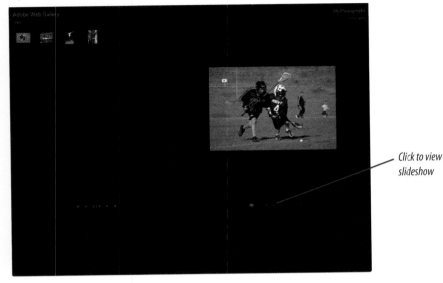

Click to view slideshow

Create a Web Gallery with Bridge

1. Verify that Bridge is open.
2. Click the **Web Gallery button** in the Output panel.
3. Click the **Preview in Browser button** in the Output Preview window, click the **Play Slideshow button** in the browser window, then after reviewing the slideshow, click the **Pause Slideshow button**.

   Compare your screen to Figure 25.
4. Close the browser, return to Bridge, scroll down the Output panel to the Create Gallery section, click the **Save Location Browse button**, navigate to the location where your Data Files are stored if necessary, click **OK** (Win) or **Open** (Mac) in the Choose a Folder dialog box, then click **Save** at the bottom of the Output panel.
5. Click **OK** to close the Create Gallery dialog box.
6. Click **File** on the Bridge menu, then click **Exit** (Win) or click **Adobe Bridge CS6**, then click **Quit Adobe Bridge CS6** (Mac).

You generated a Web Gallery using Adobe Bridge.

DESIGNTIP

Using Contrast to Add Emphasis

Contrast is an important design principle that uses opposing elements, such as colors or lines, to produce an intensified effect in an image, page, or publication. Just as you can use a font attribute to make some text stand out from the rest, you can use contrasting elements to make certain graphic objects stand out. You can create contrast in many ways: by changing the sizes of objects; by varying object weights, such as making a line surrounding an image heavier; by altering the position of an object, such as changing its location on the page or rotating it so that it is positioned on an angle; by drawing attention-getting shapes or a colorful box behind an object that makes it stand out (called a **matte**); or by adding carefully selected colors that emphasize an object.

As a new Photoshop user, you are comforted knowing that Photoshop's Help system provides definitions, explanations, procedures, and other helpful information. It also includes examples and demonstrations to show how Photoshop features work. You use the Help system to learn about image size and resolution.

1. Open the Photoshop Online Help window.
2. Click the Workspace basics link in the Workspace and workflow group.
3. Scroll down to the section on rearranging, docking, or floating document windows and read this information.
4. Scroll back to the top of the page, then click the Save and switch workspaces link.
5. Return to the Help home page, click Tools in the Workspace and workflow group, then compare your screen to the sample shown in Figure 27.

Figure 27 *Sample Project Builder 1*
Copyright © 2012 Adobe Systems Incorporated

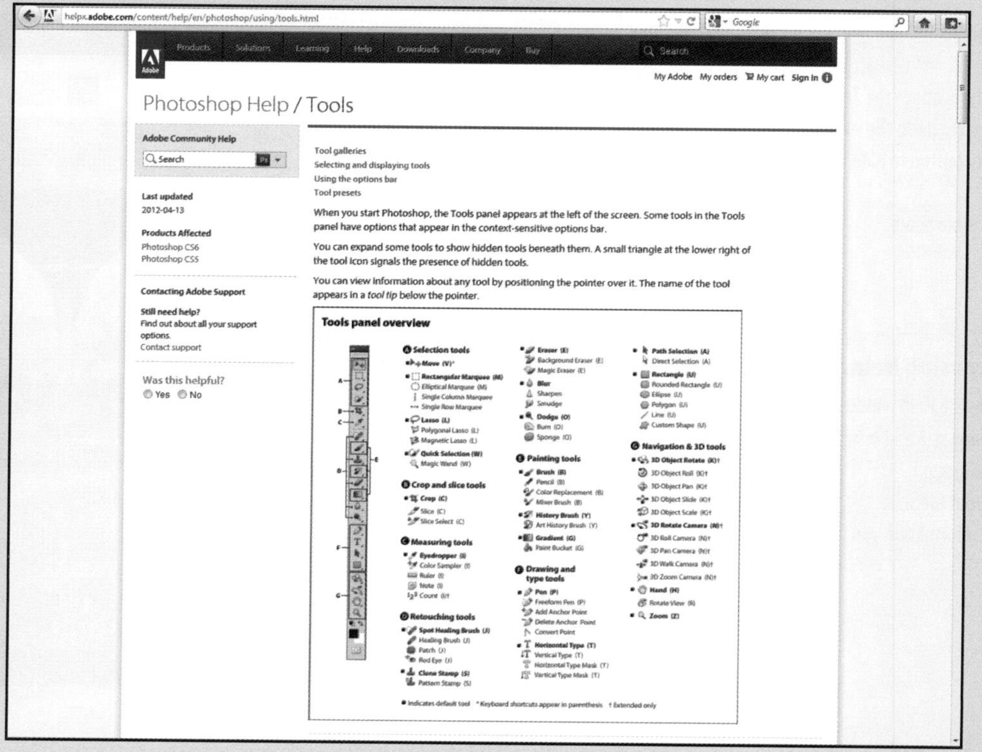

Kitchen Experience, your local specialty cooking shop, has just added herb-infused oils to its product line. They have hired you to draft a flyer that features these new products. You use Photoshop to create this flyer.

1. Open PS 2-6.psd, then save it as **Cooking**.
2. Display the Essentials workspace (if necessary).
3. Make the Measuring Spoons layer visible.
4. Drag the Oils layer so the content appears behind the Skillet layer content.
5. Drag the Measuring Spoons layer above the Skillet layer.
6. Save the file, then compare your image to the sample shown in Figure 28.

Figure 28 *Sample Project Builder 2*
Images © Photodisc/Getty Images.

As an avid, albeit novice Photoshop user, you have grasped the importance of how layers affect your image. With a little practice, you can examine a single-layer image and guess which objects might display on their own layers. Now, you're ready to examine the images created by Photoshop experts and critique them on their use of layers.

1. Connect to the Internet, and use your browser to find interesting artwork located on at least two websites.
2. Download a single-layer image (in its native format) from each website.
3. Start Photoshop, then open the downloaded images.
4. Save one image as **Critique-1** and the other as **Critique-2** in the Photoshop format (use the .psd extension).
5. Analyze each image for its potential use of layers.
6. Open the File Info dialog box for Critique-1.psd, then type in the Description section your speculation as to the number of layers there might be in the image, their possible order on the Layers panel, and how moving the layers would affect the image. Use the File Info dialog box to add a description for Critique-2.psd.
7. Close the dialog box.
8. Compare your image to the sample shown in Figure 29, then close the files.

Figure 29a *Sample Design Project*

Figure 29b *File Info dialog box for sample Design Project*

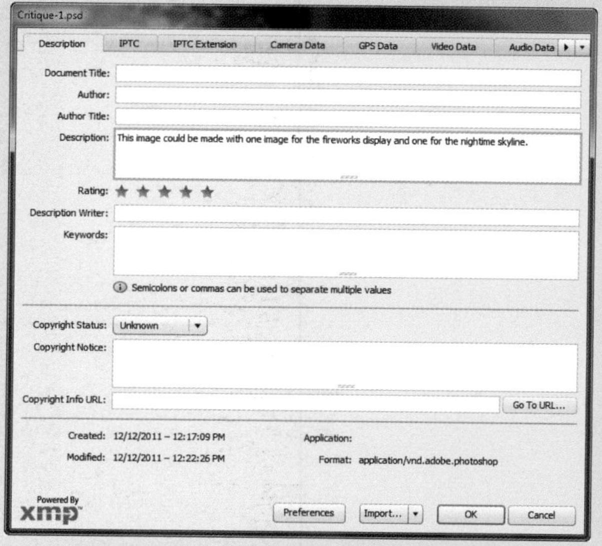

Learning Photoshop Basics

It seems that every major software manufacturer is including an element of 'cloud computing' in their latest version of their software. You've heard of it, but you're still not sure you fully understand it.

1. Connect to the Internet and use your favorite search engine to find information about cloud computing.
2. Using a sheet of paper or your favorite word processor, create a grid that contains the names of at least two or three major software manufacturers (such as Adobe, Microsoft, and Google) and find out about their forays into cloud computing. Figure 30 contains a sample document.
3. Print any relevant page(s).
4. Be prepared to discuss this topic and its relevance to your work in Photoshop.

Figure 30 *Sample Portfolio Project*

Cloud Computing Examples

Manufacturer	Name	Specifications
Adobe Corporation	Adobe Drive	Adobe Drive helps you to connect to Version Cue servers. Version Cue helps larger workgroups manage working on files, sharing assets, and much more. With Adobe Drive, the mounted drive looks and acts like any other mounted hard drive.
Apple Corporation	iCloud	Allows you to sync your apps, music, photos, books, mail, and documents seamlessly on an iPhone, iPad, iPod Touch, Mac, or PC.
Google	Cloud Connect for Microsoft Office	Google Cloud Connect is an online tool for real-time communication and collaboration for those familiar with the Microsoft Office suite. You and your colleagues can simultaneously edit Microsoft Word, PowerPoint, and Excel with no document or paragraph locking.
Microsoft Corporation	SkyDrive	Windows Live SkyDrive is part of Microsoft's Windows Live family of Web 2.0-style online offerings, but it lacks connections to other Microsoft services such as Hotmail, MSN Messenger, and the Live Spaces blogging service. You receive 500MB of free online storage (though files can be no bigger than 50MB each), and you can store any type of file to a Private, Public, or Shared folder. No one except you, with your log-in name and password, can access Private folders; anyone on the Internet can view your Public folders, but only people you invite can see Shared folders. You can restrict invitees' access to certain Shared folders or grant them Contributor status for viewing, adding, modifying, and deleting items in a folder.

CHAPTER 3 WORKING WITH LAYERS

1. Examine and convert layers
2. Add and delete layers
3. Add a selection from one image to another
4. Organize layers with layer groups and colors

CHAPTER 3

WORKING
WITH LAYERS

Layers Are Everything

You can use Photoshop to create sophisticated images in part because a Photoshop image can contain multiple layers. Each object created in Photoshop can exist on its own individual layer, making it easy to control the position and quality of each layer in the stack. Depending on your computer's resources, you can have a maximum of 8000 layers in each Photoshop image with each layer containing as much or as little detail as necessary.

Understanding the Importance of Layers

Layers make it possible to manipulate the tiniest detail within your image, which gives you tremendous flexibility when you make changes. By placing objects, effects, styles, and type on separate layers, you can modify them individually *without* affecting other layers. The advantage to using multiple layers is that you can isolate effects and images on one layer without affecting the others. The disadvantage of using multiple layers is that your file size might become very large.

However, once your image is finished, you can dramatically reduce its file size by combining all the layers into one using a process known as flattening.

QUICK TIP

The transparent areas in a layer do not increase file size.

Using Layers to Modify an Image

You can add, delete, and move layers in your image. You can also drag a portion of an image, called a **selection**, from one Photoshop image to another. When you do this, a new layer is automatically created. Copying layers from one image to another makes it easy to transfer a complicated effect, a simple image, or a piece of type. In addition to being able to hide and display each layer, you can also change its opacity. **Opacity** is the ability to see through a layer so that layers beneath it are visible. The more opacity a layer has, the less see-through (transparent) it is. You can continuously change the overall appearance of your image by changing the order of your layers, until you achieve just the look you want.

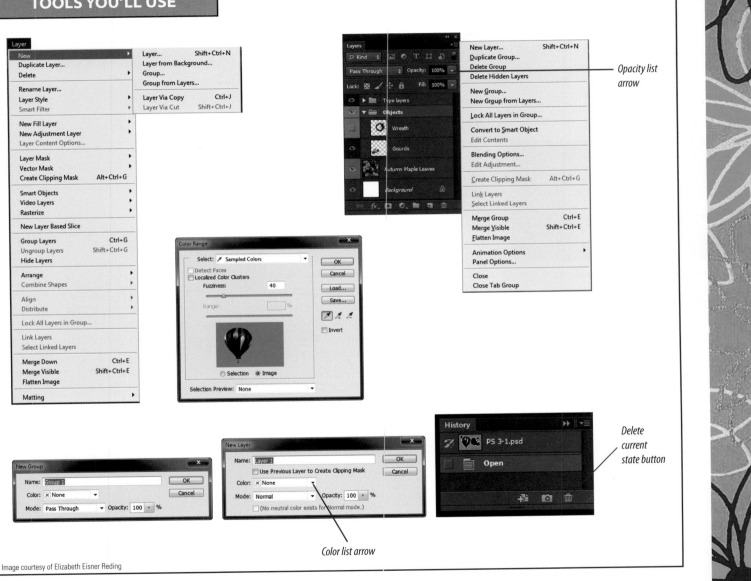

Image courtesy of Elizabeth Eisner Reding

Examine and
CONVERT LAYERS

What You'll Do

In this lesson, you'll use the Layers panel to delete a Background layer and the Layer menu to create a Background layer from an image layer.

Learning About the Layers Panel

The Layers panel lists all the layers within a Photoshop file and makes it possible for you to manipulate one or more layers. By default, this panel is located in the lower-right corner of the screen, but it can be moved to a new location by dragging the panel's tab. In some cases, the entire name of the layer might not appear on the panel. If a layer name is too long, an ellipsis appears, indicating that part of the name is hidden from view. You can view a layer's entire name by holding the pointer over the name until the full name appears. The **layer thumbnail** appears to the left of the layer name and contains a miniature picture of the layer's content, as shown in Figure 1. To the left of the layer thumbnail, you can add color, which you can use to easily identify layers. The Layers panel also contains common buttons, such as the Delete layer button and the Create a new layer button.

QUICK TIP

You can hide or resize Layers panel thumbnails to improve your computer's performance. To remove or change the size of layer thumbnails, click the Layers Panel options button, and then click Panel Options to open the Layers Panel Options dialog box. Click the option button next to the desired thumbnail size, or click the None option button to remove thumbnails, and then click OK. An icon of the selected thumbnail size appears.

Recognizing Layer Types

The Layers panel includes several types of layers: Background, type, adjustment, and image (non-type). The Background layer—whose name appears in italics—is always at the bottom of the stack. Type layers—layers that contain text—contain the type layer icon in the layer thumbnail, and image layers display a thumbnail of their contents. Adjustment layers, which affect the appearance layers, have a variety of thumbnails depending on the kind of adjustment. Along with dragging selections from one Photoshop image to another, you can also drag objects created in other applications, such as Adobe Dreamweaver, Adobe InDesign, or Adobe Flash, onto a Photoshop image, which creates a layer containing the object you dragged from the other program window.

Organizing Layers

One of the benefits of using layers is that you can create different design effects by rearranging their order. Figure 2 contains the same layers as Figure 1, but they are arranged differently. Did you notice that the yellow-striped balloon is in front of both the black-striped balloon and the lighthouse balloon? This image was created by dragging the layer containing the yellow balloon (named Layer 2 on the Layers panel) above the Black striped balloon layer. When organizing layers, you may find it helpful to resize the Layers panel so you can see more layers within the image.

Image courtesy of Elizabeth Eisner Reding

Lesson 1 Examine and Convert Layers

Figure 1 *Image with multiple layers*

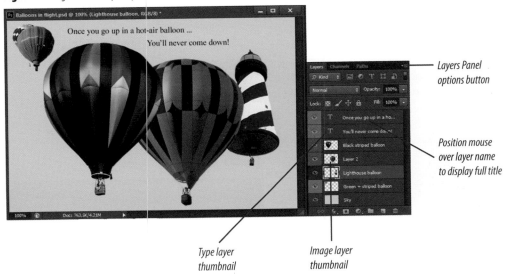

Layers Panel options button

Position mouse over layer name to display full title

Type layer thumbnail

Image layer thumbnail

Figure 2 *Layers rearranged*

New layer order

Overlapping balloons

Converting Layers

When you open an image created with a digital camera, you'll notice that the entire image appears in the Background layer. The Background layer of any image is the initial layer and is always located at the bottom of the stack. You cannot change its position in the stack, nor can you change its opacity or lighten or darken its colors. You can, however, convert a Background layer into an image layer (non-type layer), and you can convert an image layer into a Background layer. You might want to convert a Background layer into an image layer so that you can use the full range of editing tools on the layer content. You might want to convert an image layer into a Background layer after you have made all your changes and want it to be the bottom layer in the stack. Note that when you convert an image layer to a Background layer, you need to modify the image layer *before* converting it.

QUICK TIP

Before you can convert an image layer to a Background layer, you must first delete the existing Background layer. You delete a Background layer by selecting it on the Layers panel, and then dragging it to the Delete layer button on the Layers panel.

Figure 3 *Changing units of measurement*

Right-click (Win) or [control]-click (Mac) to display measurement choices

Using Rulers and Changing Units of Measurement

You can display horizontal and vertical rulers to help you better position elements. To display or hide rulers, click View on the Menu bar, and then click Rulers. (A check mark to the left of the Rulers command indicates that the rulers are displayed.)

In addition to displaying or hiding rulers, you can also choose from various units of measurement. Your choices include pixels, inches, centimeters, millimeters, points, picas, and percentages. Pixels, for example, display more tick marks and can make it easier to make tiny adjustments. You can change the units of measurement by clicking Edit [Win] or Photoshop [Mac] on the Menu bar, pointing to Preferences, and then clicking Units & Rulers. In the Preferences dialog box, click the Rulers list arrow, click the units you want to use, and then click OK. The easiest way to change units of measurement, however, is shown in Figure 3. Once the rulers are displayed, right-click (Win) or [control]-click (Mac) either the vertical or horizontal ruler, and then click the unit of measurement you want. When displayed, the Info panel shows the current X/Y coordinates of your pointer in your image, based on the units of measurement in use.

Pixel dimensions measure the number of pixels forming the width and height of an image, while *resolution* is the fineness of the detail in an image. The more pixels, the greater the resolution.

Figure 4 *Warning box*

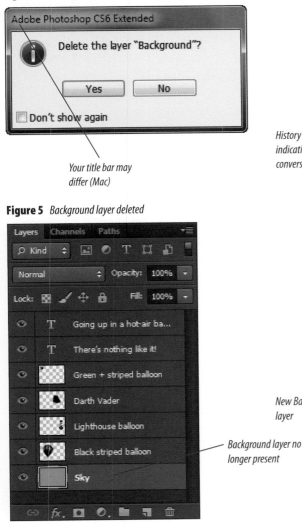

Your title bar may differ (Mac)

Figure 5 *Background layer deleted*

History state indicating layer conversion

New Background layer

Background layer no longer present

Figure 6 *New Background layer added to Layers panel*

Convert an image layer into a Background layer

1. Open PS 3-1.psd from the drive and folder where you store your Data Files, then save it as **Up in the air**.

   TIP If you receive a warning box about maximum compatibility or a message stating that some of the text layers need to be updated before they can be used for vector-based output, click Update and/or click OK.

2. Click **View** on the Menu bar, click **Rulers** if your rulers are not visible, then make sure that the rulers are displayed in pixels.

   TIP If you are unsure which units of measurement are used, right-click (Win) or [control]-click (Mac) one of the rulers, then click Pixels if it is not already selected.

3. Click **Legacy** (created in a lesson in Chapter 1) in the Workspace switcher on the options bar.

4. On the Layers panel, click the **Background layer**, then click the **Delete layer button** 🗑.

5. Click **Yes** in the dialog box, as shown in Figure 4, then compare your Layers panel to Figure 5.

6. Click **Layer** on the Menu bar, point to **New**, then click **Background From Layer**.

   The Sky layer has been converted into the Background layer. Did you notice that in addition to the image layer being converted to the Background layer that a state now appears on the History panel that says Convert to Background? See Figure 6.

7. Save your work.

You displayed the rulers and switched to a previously created workspace, deleted the Background layer of an image, then converted an image layer into the Background layer. You can convert any layer into the Background layer, as long as you first delete the existing Background layer.

Add and Delete
LAYERS

What You'll Do

In this lesson, you'll create a new layer using the New command on the Layer menu, delete a layer, and create a new layer using buttons on the Layers panel.

Adding Layers to an Image

Because it's so important to make use of multiple layers, Photoshop makes it easy to add and delete layers. You can create layers in three ways:

- Use the New command on the Layer menu.
- Use the New Layer command on the Layers panel menu.
- Click the Create a new layer button on the Layers panel.

Objects on new layers have a default opacity setting of 100%, which means that objects on lower layers are not visible. Each layer has the Normal (default) blending mode applied to it. (A **blending mode** is a feature that affects a layer's underlying pixels, and is used to lighten or darken colors. Blending modes affect how pixels in two separate layers interact with each other.)

Merging Layers

You can combine multiple image layers into a single layer using the merging process. **Merging layers** is useful when you want to combine multiple layers in order to make specific edits permanent. (This merging process is different from flattening in that it's selective. Flattening merges *all* visible layers.) In order for layers to be merged, they must be visible and next to each other on the Layers panel. You can merge all visible layers within an image, or just the ones you select. Type layers cannot be merged until they are **rasterized** (turned into a bitmapped image layer) or converted into uneditable text. To merge two layers, make sure that they are next to each other and that the Indicates layer visibility button is visible on each layer, and then click the layer in the higher position on the Layers panel. Click the Layers Panel options button, and then click Merge Down. The **active layer** (the layer that's currently selected) and the layer immediately beneath it will be combined into a single layer. To merge all visible layers, click the Layers Panel options button, and then click Merge Visible. Many layer commands that are available using the Layers Panel options button such as Merge Visible, are also available on the Layer menu.

Naming a Layer

Photoshop automatically assigns a sequential number to each new layer name, but you can rename a layer at any time. So, if you have four named layers and add a new layer, the default name of the new layer will be Layer 1. Although calling a layer "Layer 12" is fine, you might want to use a more descriptive name so it is easier to distinguish one layer from another. If you use the New command on the Layer menu, you can name the layer when you create it. You can rename a layer at any time by using either of these methods:

- Click Layer on the Menu bar, click Rename Layer, type the new name when the existing text is selected, and then press [Enter] (Win) or [return] (Mac).

- Double-click the name on the Layers panel, type the new name, and then press [Enter] (Win) or [return] (Mac).

TABLE 1: SHORTCUTS FOR NAVIGATING THE LAYERS PANEL	
Use the combination:	**To navigate:**
[Alt] [[] (Win) or [option] [[] (Mac)	down the Layers panel
[Alt] [[] (Win) or [option] []] (Mac)	up the Layers panel
[Ctrl] [[] (Win) or ⌘ [[] (Mac)	to move a layer down one layer*
[Ctrl] []] (Win) or ⌘ []] (Mac)	to move a layer up one layer*
[Ctrl] [Shift] [[] (Win) or ⌘ [Shift] [[] (Mac)	to move a layer to the bottom of the stack*
[Ctrl] [Shift] []] (Win) or ⌘ [Shift] []] (Mac)	to move a layer to the top of the stack*

*Excluding the Background layer

© Cengage Learning 2013

Working with Layers

Deleting Layers from an Image

You might want to delete an unused or unnecessary layer. You can use multiple methods to delete a layer:

- Click the name on the Layers panel, click the Layers Panel options button, and then click Delete Layer, as shown in Figure 7.
- Click the name on the Layers panel, click the Delete layer button on the Layers panel, and then click Yes in the warning box.
- Click the name on the Layers panel, press and hold [Alt] (Win) or [option] (Mac), and then click the Delete layer button on the Layers panel.
- Drag the layer name on the Layers panel to the Delete layer button on the Layers panel.
- Right-click a layer (Win) or [Ctrl]-click a layer (Mac), and then click Delete Layer.

You should be certain that you no longer need a layer before you delete it. If you delete a layer by accident, you can restore it during the current editing session by deleting the Delete Layer state on the History panel, or by clicking Edit on the Menu bar, then clicking Undo Delete Layer.

QUICK TIP

Photoshop always numbers layers sequentially, no matter how many layers you add or delete.

Figure 7 *Layers panel menu*

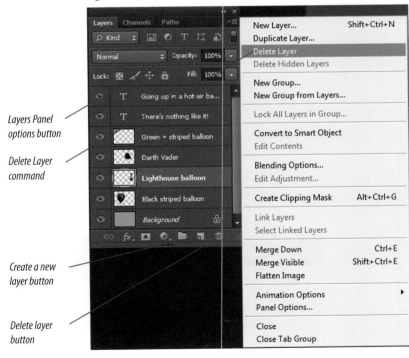

Layers Panel options button

Delete Layer command

Create a new layer button

Delete layer button

Modifying a workspace

1. Drag the History panel so it displays above the Layers panel.

2. Click **Window** on the Menu bar, point to **Workspace**, then click **New Workspace**.

3. Type **Legacy** in the Name text box, click **Save**, then click **Yes** in the New Workspace warning box.

You moved a panel in a saved workspace, then saved the change using the original name (making the change permanent).

Add a layer using the Layer menu

1. Click the **Lighthouse balloon layer** on the Layers panel.

2. Click **Layer** on the Menu bar, point to **New**, then click **Layer** to open the New Layer dialog box, as shown in Figure 8.

   A new layer will be added above the active layer.

TIP You can change the layer name in the New Layer dialog box before it appears on the Layers panel.

3. Click **OK**.

   The New Layer dialog box closes and the new layer, Layer 1, appears above the Lighthouse balloon layer on the Layers panel. The New Layer state is added to the History panel. See Figure 9.

You created a new layer above the Lighthouse balloon layer using the New command on the Layer menu. The layer does not yet contain any content.

Figure 8 *New Layer dialog box*

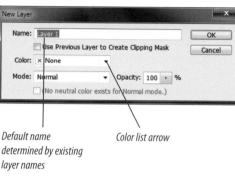

Default name determined by existing layer names   Color list arrow

Figure 9 *New layer in Layers panel*

New Layer history state

New layer

Inserting a Layer Beneath the Active Layer

When you add a layer to an image either by using the Layer menu or clicking the Create a new layer button on the Layers panel, the new layer is inserted above the active layer. But there might be times when you want to insert the new layer beneath, or in back of, the active layer. You can do so easily, by pressing [Ctrl] (Win) or ⌘ (Mac) while clicking the Create a new layer button on the Layers panel.

Figure 10 *New layer with default settings*

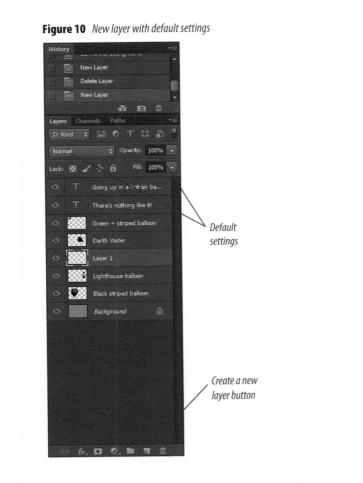

Default settings

Create a new layer button

Delete a layer

1. Position the **Layer selection pointer** 🖑 over Layer 1 on the Layers panel.

2. Drag **Layer 1** to the **Delete layer button** 🗑 on the Layers panel.

TIP You can also delete the layer by dragging the New Layer state on the History panel to the Delete current state button.

3. If the Delete the layer "Layer 1" dialog box opens, click the **Don't show again check box**, then click **Yes**.

TIP Many dialog boxes let you turn off this reminder feature by selecting the Don't show again check box. Selecting these check boxes can improve your efficiency.

You used the Delete layer button on the Layers panel to delete a layer.

Add a layer using the Layers panel

1. Click the **Lighthouse balloon layer** on the Layers panel, if it is not already selected.

2. Click the **Create a new layer button** 🔲 on the Layers panel, then compare your Layers panel and History panel to Figure 10.

3. Save your work.

You used the Create a new layer button on the Layers panel to add a new layer.

Right-Clicking for Everyone (Mac)

Since some Mac mice only come with a single button, you may feel left out, unless you have a multitouch trackpad. Mac users can simulate the right-click menus by holding the [control] key while clicking. An alternative method is to use a 2-fingered click if you have a Mac multitouch trackpad. Once you've learned these simple tricks, you can right-click using the (Win) instructions in the steps.

Add a Selection
FROM ONE IMAGE TO ANOTHER

What You'll Do

Image courtesy of Elizabeth Eisner Reding

 In this lesson, you'll use the Invert check box in the Color Range dialog box to make a selection, drag the selection to another image, and remove the fringe from a selection using the Defringe command.

Understanding Selections

Often the Photoshop file you want to create involves using an image or part of an image from another file. To use an image or part of an image, you must first select it. Photoshop refers to this as "making a selection." A selection is an area of an image surrounded by a **marquee**, a dashed line that encloses the area you want to edit or move to another image, as shown in Figure 11. You can drag a marquee around a selection using four marquee tools: Rectangular Marquee, Elliptical Marquee, Single Row Marquee, and Single Column Marquee. Table 2 displays the four marquee tools along with other selection tools. You can set options for each tool on the options bar when the tool you want to use is active.

Making and Moving a Selection

You can use a variety of methods and tools to make a selection, which can then be used as a specific part of a layer or as the entire layer. You use selections to isolate an area you want to alter. For example, you can use the Magnetic Lasso tool to select complex shapes by clicking the starting point, tracing an approximate outline, and then clicking the ending point. Later, you can use the Crop tool to trim areas from a selection. When you use the Move tool to drag a selection to the destination image, Photoshop places the selection in a new layer above the previously active layer.

Cropping an Image

You might find an image that you really like, except that it contains a particular portion that you don't need. You can exclude, or **crop**, certain parts of an image by using the Crop tool on the Tools panel. Cropping hides areas of an image from view *without* decreasing resolution quality. To crop an image, click the Crop tool on the Tools panel, drag the pointer around the area you *want to keep*, and then press [Enter] (Win) or [return] (Mac).

Working with Layers

Understanding Color Range Command

In addition to using selection tools, Photoshop provides more methods for incorporating imagery from other files. You can use the Color Range command, located on the Select menu, to select a particular color contained in an existing image. Depending on the area you want, you can use the Color Range dialog box to extract a portion of an image.

For example, you can select the Invert check box, choose one color, and then Photoshop will select the portion of the image that is every color *except* the color you chose. After you select all the imagery you want from another image, you can drag it into your open file. Simply put, the Invert feature allows you to flip whatever you currently have selected to include whatever is not currently selected.

Defringing Layer Contents

Sometimes when you make a selection and move it into another image, the newly selected image contains unwanted pixels that give the appearance of a fringe, or halo. You can remove this effect using a Matting command called Defringe. This command is available by pointing to Matting on the Layer menu and allows you to replace fringe pixels with the colors of other nearby pixels. You can determine a width for replacement pixels between 1 and 200. It's magic!

Figure 11 *Marquee selections*

Area selected using the Rectangular Marquee tool

Specific element selected using the Magnetic Lasso tool

TABLE 2: SELECTION TOOLS			
Tool	**Tool name**	**Tool**	**Tool name**
	Rectangular Marquee tool		Lasso tool
	Elliptical Marquee tool		Polygonal Lasso tool
	Single Row Marquee tool		Magnetic Lasso tool
	Single Column Marquee tool		Eraser tool
	Crop tool		Background Eraser tool
	Magic Wand tool		Magic Eraser tool
	Quick Selection tool		Slice tool

© Cengage Learning 2013.

Make a color range selection

1. Open PS 3-2.psd from the drive and folder where you store your Data Files, save it as **Yellow striped balloon**, click the **title bar**, then drag the **window** to an empty area of the workspace so that you can see both images.

TIP When more than one file is open, each has its own set of rulers. The ruler on the inactive file appears dimmed.

2. With the Yellow striped balloon image selected, click **Select** on the Menu bar, then click **Color Range**.

TIP If the background color is a solid color, when you select it and select the Invert check box, only the foreground will be selected.

3. Click the **Image option button** below the image preview, then type **100** in the Fuzziness text box (or drag the **slider** to the right until you see **100**).

4. Position the **Eyedropper pointer** 🔍 in the **blue background** of the image in the Color Range dialog box, then click the **background**.

5. Select the **Invert check box**. Compare the settings in your dialog box to Figure 12.

6. Click **OK**, then compare your Yellow striped balloon.psd image to Figure 13.

You opened a file and used the Color Range dialog box to select the image pixels by selecting the image's inverted colors. Selecting the inverse is an important skill in making selections.

Figure 12 *Color Range dialog box*

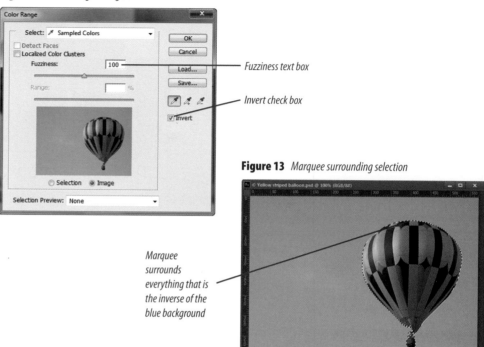

Fuzziness text box

Invert check box

Figure 13 *Marquee surrounding selection*

Marquee surrounds everything that is the inverse of the blue background

Using the Place Command

You can add an image from another image to a layer using the Place command. Place an image in a Photoshop layer by clicking File on the Menu bar, and clicking Place, then committing the changes. The placed artwork appears *flattened* inside a bounding box at the center of the Photoshop image. The artwork maintains its original aspect ratio; however, if the artwork is larger than the Photoshop image, it is resized to fit. The Place command works well if you want to insert a multi-layered image in another image. (If all you want is a specific layer from an image, you should just drag the layer you want into an image and not use the Place command.)

Figure 14 *Yellow striped balloon image dragged to Up in the air image*

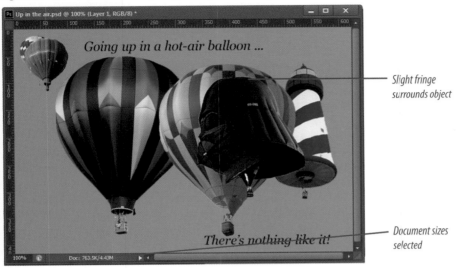

Slight fringe
surrounds object

Document sizes
selected

Figure 15 *New layer defringed*

Yellow striped
balloon in image

Yellow striped
balloon moved
to layer

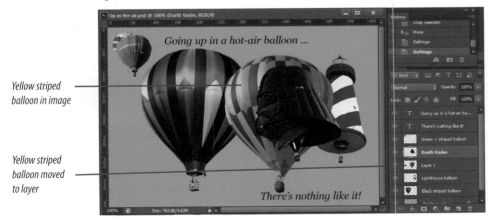

Image courtesy of Elizabeth Eisner Reding

Lesson 3   Add a Selection from One Image to Another

Move a selection to another image

1. Click the **Move tool** on the Tools panel.
2. Position the **Move tool pointer** anywhere over the selection in the Yellow striped balloon image.
3. Drag the **selection** to the Up in the air image, then release the mouse button.

   The Yellow striped balloon image moves to the Up in the air image appearing on Layer 1.
4. Use to drag the yellow striped balloon to the approximate location shown in Figure 14.

TIP When you drag an object, a box displays showing you how many horizontal and vertical pixels the object is moving.

5. Click the **menu arrow** in the document window status bar and verify that Document Sizes is selected.

You dragged a selection from one image to another. You verified that the document size is displayed in the window.

Defringe the selection

1. With Layer 1 selected, click **Layer** on the Menu bar, point to **Matting** then click **Defringe**.

   Defringing a selection gets rid of the halo effect that sometimes occurs when objects are dragged from one image to another.
2. Type **2** in the Width text box, then click **OK**.
3. Click the **Darth Vader layer** and defringe it using a width of **2**.
4. Save your work.
5. Close **Yellow striped ballon.psd**, then compare the Up in the air image to Figure 15.

You removed the fringe from a selection and a layer.

Organize Layers with
LAYER GROUPS AND COLORS

What You'll Do

Image courtesy of Elizabeth Eisner Reding

 In this lesson, you'll use the Layers Panel options button to create, name, and color a layer group, and then add layers to it. You'll add finishing touches to the image, save it as a copy, and then flatten it.

Understanding Layer Groups

A **layer group** is a Photoshop feature that allows you to organize your layers on the Layers panel. A layer group contains individual layers, which are sometimes referred to as *nested layers*. For example, you can create a layer group that contains all the type layers in your image. To create a layer group, you click the Layers Panel options button, and then click New Group. As with layers, it is helpful to choose a descriptive name for a layer group.

QUICK **TIP**

You can press [Ctrl][G] (Win) or ⌘ [G] (Mac) to place the selected layer in a layer group.

Organizing Layers into Groups

After you create a layer group, you simply drag layers on the Layers panel directly on top of the layer group. You can remove layers from a layer group by dragging them out of the layer group to a new location on the Layers panel or by deleting them. Some changes made to a layer group, such as blending mode or opacity changes, affect every layer in the layer group. You can choose to expand or collapse layer groups, depending on the amount of information you need to see. Expanding a layer group shows all of the layers in the layer

Duplicating a Layer

When you add a new layer by clicking the Create a new layer button on the Layers panel, the new layer contains default settings. However, you might want to create a new layer that has the same settings as an existing layer. You can do so by duplicating an existing layer to create a copy of that layer and its settings. Duplicating a layer is also a good way to preserve your modifications, because you can modify the duplicate layer and not worry about losing your original work. To create a duplicate layer, select the layer you want to copy, click the Layers Panel options button, click Duplicate Layer, and then click OK. The new layer will appear above the original.

group, and collapsing a layer group hides all of the layers in a layer group. You can expand or collapse a layer group by clicking the triangle to the left of the layer group icon. Figure 16 shows one expanded layer group and one collapsed layer group.

Adding Color to a Layer

If your image has relatively few layers, it's easy to locate the layers. However, if your image contains many layers, you might need some help in organizing them. You can organize layers by color-coding them, which makes it easy to find the layer or the group you want, regardless of its location on the Layers panel. For example, you can put all type layers in red or put the layers associated with a particular portion of an image in blue. To color-code the Background layer, you must first convert it to a regular layer.

QUICK TIP

You can also color-code a layer group without losing the color-coding you applied to individual layers.

Flattening an Image

After you make all the necessary modifications to your image, you can greatly reduce the file size by flattening the image. **Flattening** merges all visible layers into a single Background layer and discards all hidden layers. Make sure that all layers that you want to display are visible before you flatten the image. Because flattening removes an image's individual layers, it's a good idea to make a copy of the original image *before* it is flattened. The status bar displays the file's current size and the size it will be when flattened.

Figure 16 *Layer groups*

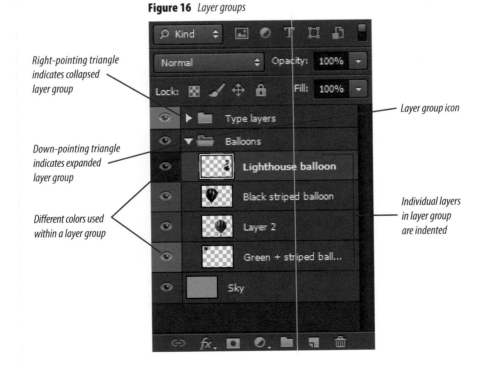

Right-pointing triangle indicates collapsed layer group

Down-pointing triangle indicates expanded layer group

Different colors used within a layer group

Layer group icon

Individual layers in layer group are indented

Understanding Layer Comps

The ability to create a **layer comp**, a variation on the arrangement and visibility of existing layers, is a powerful tool that can make your work more organized. You might, for example, want to create several variations of your single image that include different configurations of layers, and layer comps give you this ability. You open the Layer Comps panel by clicking Window on the Menu bar, and then clicking Layer Comps. Clicking the Create New Layer Comp button on the panel opens the New Layer Comp dialog box, shown in Figure 17, which allows you to name the layer comp and set parameters.

Using Layer Comps

Multiple layer comps, shown in Figure 18, make it easy to switch back and forth between variations on an image theme. The layer comp is an ideal tool for showing a client multiple arrangements of layers.

Figure 17 *New Layer Comp dialog box*

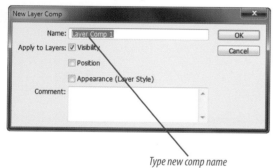

Type new comp name

Figure 18 *Multiple layer comps in image*

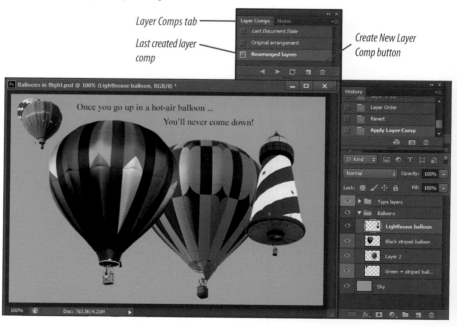

Layer Comps tab

Last created layer comp

Create New Layer Comp button

Image courtesy of Elizabeth Eisner Reding

Figure 19 *New Group dialog box*

New layer group name

Color list arrow

Figure 20 *New layer group in Layers panel*

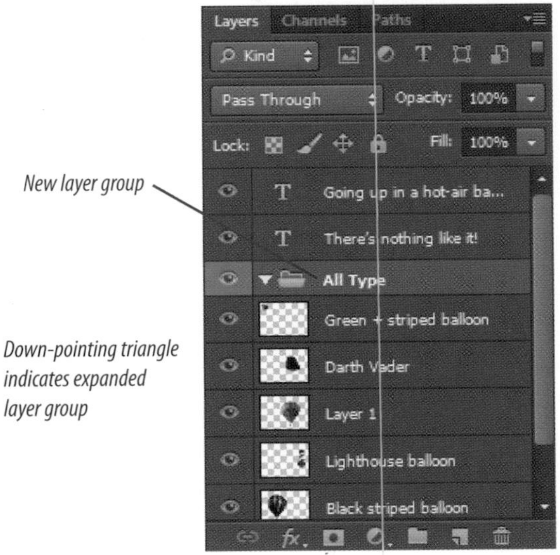

New layer group

Figure 21 *Layers added to All Type layer group*

Down-pointing triangle indicates expanded layer group

Layers within group are indented

Layer group icon (folder)

Create a layer group

1. Click the **Green + striped balloon layer**, click the **Layers Panel options button** , then click **New Group**.

   The New Group dialog box opens, as shown in Figure 19.

TIP Photoshop automatically places a new layer group above the active layer.

2. Type **All Type** in the Name text box.

3. Click the **Color list arrow**, click **Green**, then click **OK.**

   The New Group dialog box closes. Compare your Layers panel to Figure 20.

You used the Layers panel menu to create a layer group, then named and applied a color to it. This new group will contain all the type layers in the image.

Move layers to the layer group

1. Click the **Going up in a hot-air balloon** layer on the Layers panel, then drag it on to the **All Type layer group**.

2. Click the **There's nothing like it! layer**, drag it on to the **All Type layer group**, then compare your Layers panel to Figure 21.

TIP If the There's nothing like it! layer is not below the Going up in a hot-air balloon layer, move the layers to match Figure 21.

3. Click the **triangle** to the left of the layer group icon (folder) to collapse the layer group.

You moved two layers into a layer group. Using layer groups is a great organizational tool, especially in complex images with many layers.

Rename a layer and adjust opacity

1. Double-click **Layer 1**, type **Yellow striped balloon**, then press [**Enter**] (Win) or [**return**] (Mac).

2. Double-click the **Opacity text box** on the Layers panel, type **85**, then press [**Enter**] (Win) or [**return**] (Mac).

3. Drag the **Yellow striped balloon layer** beneath the Lighthouse balloon layer, then compare your image to Figure 22.

4. Save your work.

You renamed the new layer, adjusted opacity, and rearranged layers.

Create layer comps

1. Click **Window** on the Menu bar, then click **Layer Comps**.

2. Click the **Create New Layer Comp button** on the Layer Comps panel.

3. Type **Green off/Yellow off** in the Name text box, as shown in Figure 23, then click **OK**.

4. Click the **Indicates layer visibility button** on the Green + striped balloon layer and the Yellow striped balloon layer.

5. Click the **Update Layer Comp button** on the Layer Comps panel. Compare your Layer Comps panel to Figure 24.

6. Save your work, then click the **Layer Comps button** on the vertical dock to close the Layer Comps panel.

You created a Layer Comp in an existing image.

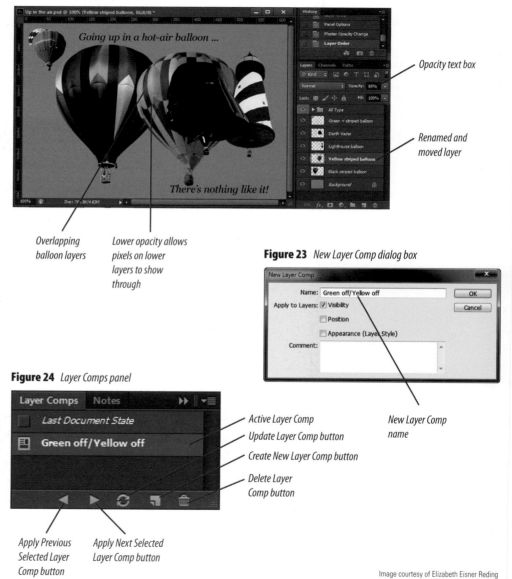

Figure 22 *Finished image*

Overlapping balloon layers

Lower opacity allows pixels on lower layers to show through

Opacity text box

Renamed and moved layer

Figure 23 *New Layer Comp dialog box*

New Layer Comp name

Figure 24 *Layer Comps panel*

Active Layer Comp

Update Layer Comp button

Create New Layer Comp button

Delete Layer Comp button

Apply Previous Selected Layer Comp button

Apply Next Selected Layer Comp button

Image courtesy of Elizabeth Eisner Reding

Figure 25 *Save As dialog box*

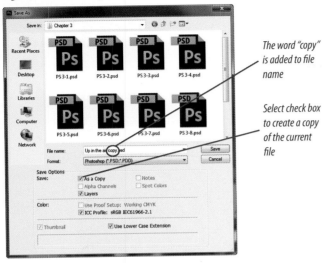

The word "copy" is added to file name

Select check box to create a copy of the current file

Figure 26 *Flattened image layer*

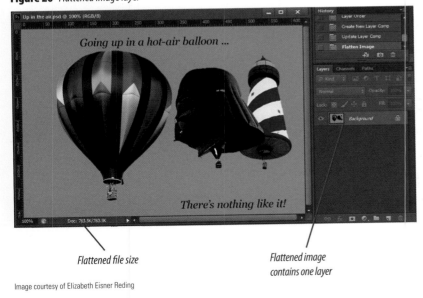

Flattened file size

Flattened image contains one layer

Image courtesy of Elizabeth Eisner Reding

Lesson 4   Organize Layers with Layer Groups and Colors

Flatten an image

1. Click **File** on the Menu bar, then click **Save As**.

2. Click the **As a Copy check box** to select it, then compare your dialog box to Figure 25.

TIP If "copy" does not display in the File name text box, click this text box and type copy to add it to the name.

3. Click **Save**, then click **OK** to Maximize Compatibility, if necessary.

   Photoshop saves and closes a copy of the file containing all the layers and effects.

4. Click **Layer** on the Menu bar, then click **Flatten Image**.

5. Click **OK** in the warning box (to discard hidden layers) if it appears, then save your work.

   Compare your Layers panel to Figure 26.

6. Click the **Workspace switcher** on the options bar, then click **Essentials**.

7. Close all open images, then exit Photoshop.

You saved the file as a copy, then flattened the image. The image now has a single layer.

POWER USER SHORTCUTS

To do this:	Use this method:
Adjust layer opacity	Click Opacity list arrow on Layers panel, drag Opacity slider or
	Double-click Opacity text box, type a percentage
Add a layer to a group	Drag selected layer(s) to Group folder
Change measurements	Right-click ruler (Win)
	[Ctrl]-click ruler (Mac)
Color a layer	Right-click layer, click color
Create a layer comp	⬒ on Layer Comps panel
Create a layer group	▦, New Group, or [Ctrl][G] (Win)
	⌘ [G] (Mac)
Delete a layer	🗑
Defringe a selection	Layer ➤ Matting ➤ Defringe
Flatten an image	Layer ➤ Flatten Image
Use the Move tool	▶⊹ or **V**
Make a new Background layer from existing layer	Layer ➤ New ➤ Background from Layer
Make a new layer	Layer ➤ New ➤ Layer
	or ⬒
Rename a layer	Double-click layer name, type new name
Select color range	Select ➤ Color Range
Show/Hide Rulers	View ➤ Rulers
	[Ctrl][R] (Win)
	⌘ [R] (Mac)
Update a layer comp	⟳

Key: Menu items are indicated by ➤ between the menu name and its command. Blue bold letters are shortcuts for selecting tools on the Tools panel.

Examine and convert layers.

1. Start Photoshop.
2. Open PS 3-3.psd from the drive and folder where you store your Data Files, then save it as **Music Store**.
3. Make sure the rulers appear and that pixels are the unit of measurement.
4. Delete the Background layer.
5. Verify that the Rainbow blend layer is active, then convert the image layer to a Background layer.
6. Save your work.

Add and delete layers.

1. Make Layer 2 active.
2. Create a new layer above this layer using the Layer menu.
3. Accept the default name (Layer 5), and change the color of the layer to Red.
4. Delete (new) Layer 5.
5. Make Layer 2 active (if it is not already the active layer).
6. Save your work.

Add a selection from one image to another.

1. Open PS 3-4.psd.
2. Reposition this image of a horn by dragging the window to the right of the Music Store image.
3. Open the Color Range dialog box. (*Hint*: Use the Select menu.)
4. Verify that the Image option button is selected, the Invert check box is selected, and then set the Fuzziness to 0.
5. Sample the white background in the preview window in the dialog box, then click OK.
6. Use the Move tool to drag the selection into the Music Store image.
7. Position the selection so that the upper-left edge of the instrument matches the sample shown in Figure 27 on the next page.
8. Defringe the horn selection (in the Music Store image) using a 3 pixel width.
9. Close PS 3-4.psd.
10. Drag Layer 5 above the Notes layer.
11. Rename Layer 5 **Horn**.
12. Change the opacity for the Horn layer to 55%.
13. Drag the Horn layer so it is beneath Layer 2.
14. Hide Layer 1.
15. Hide the rulers.
16. Save your work.

Working with Layers

Organize layers with layer groups and colors.

1. Create a Layer Group called **Type Layers** and assign the color Yellow to the group.
2. Drag the following layers into the Type Layers folder: Allegro, Music Store, Layer 2.
3. Delete Layer 2, then collapse the Type Layers group.
4. Move the Notes layer beneath the Horn layer.
5. Create a layer comp called **Notes layer on**.
6. Update the layer comp.
7. Hide the Notes layer.
8. Create a new layer comp called **Notes layer off**, then update the layer comp.
9. Display the previous layer comp, save your work, then close the tab group. (*Hint*: Click the Layer Comps Panel options button, then click Close Tab Group.)
10. Save a copy of the Music Store file using the default naming scheme (add 'copy' to the end of the existing filename).
11. Flatten the original image. (*Hint*: Be sure to discard hidden layers.)
12. Save your work, then compare your image to Figure 27.

Figure 27 *Completed Skills Review*

A credit union is developing a hotline for members to use to help mitigate credit card fraud as soon as it occurs. They're going to distribute ten thousand refrigerator magnets over the next three weeks. As part of their effort to build community awareness of the project, they have sponsored a contest for the magnet design. You decide to enter the contest.

1. Open PS 3-5.psd, then save it as **Combat Fraud**. The Palatino Linotype font is used in this file. Please make a substitution if this font is not available on your computer.
2. Open PS 3-6.psd, use the Color Range dialog box or any selection tool on the Tools panel to select the cell phone image, then drag it to the Combat Fraud image.
3. Rename the newly created layer **Cell Phones**, then apply a color to the layer on the Layers panel. Make sure the Cell Phones layer is beneath the type layers.
4. Convert the Background layer to an image layer, then rename it **Banner**.
5. Change the opacity of the Banner layer to any setting you like.
6. Defringe the Cell Phones layer using the pixel width of your choice.
7. Save your work, close PS 3-6.psd, then compare your image to the sample shown in Figure 28.

Figure 28 *Sample Project Builder 1*

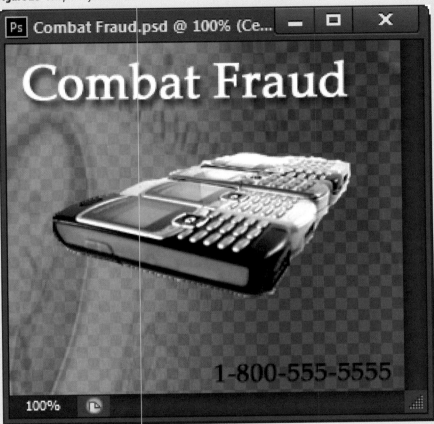

Working with Layers

Harvest Market, a line of natural food stores, and the trucking associations in your state have formed a coalition to deliver fresh fruit and vegetables to food banks and other food distribution programs. The truckers want to promote the project by displaying a sign on their trucks. Your task is to create a design that will become the Harvest Market logo. Keep in mind that the design will be seen from a distance.

1. Open PS 3-11.psd, then save it as **Harvest Market**.
2. Obtain at least two images of different-sized produce. You can obtain images by using what is available on your computer, scanning print media, or connecting to the Internet and downloading images.
3. Open one of the produce files, select it, then drag or copy it to the Harvest Market image. (*Hint*: Experiment with some of the other selection tools. Note that some tools require you to copy and paste the image after you select it.)
4. Repeat step 3, then close the two produce image files.
5. Set the opacity of the Market layer to 80%.
6. Arrange the layers so that smaller images appear on top of the larger ones. (You can move layers to any location in the image you choose.)
7. Create a layer group for the type layers, and apply a color to it.
8. You can delete any layers you feel do not add to the image. (In the sample image, the Veggies layer has been deleted.)
9. Save your work, then compare your image to Figure 31.
10. What are the advantages and disadvantages of using multiple images? How would you assess the ease and efficiency of the selection techniques you've learned? Which styles did you apply to the type layers, and why?

Figure 31 *Sample Portfolio Project*

Working with Layers

4

MAKING
SELECTIONS

Combining Images

Most Photoshop images are created using a technique called **compositing**—combining images from different sources. These sources include other Photoshop images, royalty-free images, pictures taken with digital cameras, and scanned artwork. How you get those multiple images into your Photoshop images is an art unto itself. You can include additional images by using tools on the Tools panel and menu commands. And to work with all these images, you need to know how to select them—or how to select the parts you want to include.

Understanding Selection Tools

The two basic methods you can use to make selections are using a tool or using color. You can use three free-form tools to create your own unique selections, four fixed area tools to create circular or rectangular selections, and a wand tool to make selections using color. In addition, you can use menu commands to increase or decrease selections that you made

with these tools, or to make selections based on color.

Understanding Which Selection Tool to Use

With so many tools available, how do you know which one to use? After you become familiar with the different selection options, you'll learn how to look at images and evaluate selection opportunities. With experience, you'll learn how to identify edges that can be used to isolate imagery, and how to spot colors that can be used to isolate a specific object.

Combining Imagery

After you decide on an object that you want to place in a Photoshop image, you can add the object to another image by cutting, copying, and pasting or dragging and dropping objects using the selection tools, the Move tool, menu commands, or using the **Clipboard**, the temporary storage area provided by your operating system.

TOOLS YOU'LL USE

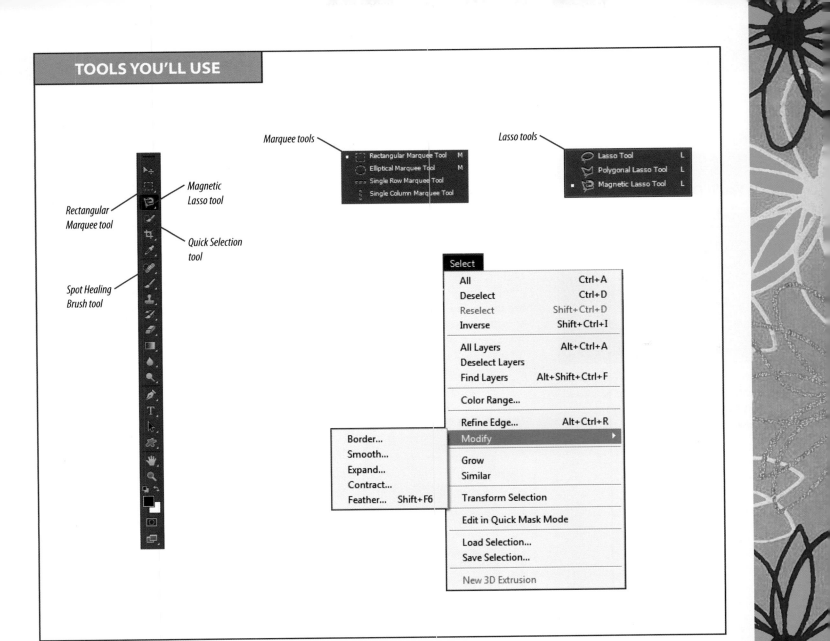

Rectangular Marquee tool

Magnetic Lasso tool

Quick Selection tool

Spot Healing Brush tool

Marquee tools

Rectangular Marquee Tool   M
Elliptical Marquee Tool   M
Single Row Marquee Tool
Single Column Marquee Tool

Lasso tools

Lasso Tool   L
Polygonal Lasso Tool   L
Magnetic Lasso Tool   L

Select

All	Ctrl+A
Deselect	Ctrl+D
Reselect	Shift+Ctrl+D
Inverse	Shift+Ctrl+I
All Layers	Alt+Ctrl+A
Deselect Layers	
Find Layers	Alt+Shift+Ctrl+F
Color Range...	
Refine Edge...	Alt+Ctrl+R
Modify	▶
Grow	
Similar	
Transform Selection	
Edit in Quick Mask Mode	
Load Selection...	
Save Selection...	
New 3D Extrusion	

Border...
Smooth...
Expand...
Contract...
Feather... Shift+F6

Make a Selection
USING SHAPES

What You'll Do

In this lesson, you'll make selections using a marquee tool and a lasso tool, position a selection with the Move tool, deselect a selection, and drag a complex selection into another image.

Selecting by Shape

The Photoshop selection tools make it easy to select objects that are rectangular or elliptical in nature. However, it would be a boring world if every image we wanted fell into one of those categories, so fortunately, they don't. While some objects are round or square, most are unusual in shape. Making selections can sometimes be a painstaking process because many objects don't have clearly defined edges. To select an object by shape, you need to click the appropriate tool on the Tools panel, and then drag the pointer around the object. The selected area is defined by a **marquee**, or series of dotted lines, as shown in Figure 1.

Creating a Selection

Drawing a rectangular marquee is easier than drawing an elliptical marquee, but with practice, you'll be able to create both types of marquees easily. Table 1 lists the tools you can use to make selections using shapes. Figure 2 shows a marquee surrounding an irregular shape.

Figure 1 *Elliptical Marquee tool used to create marquee*

Elliptical Marquee surrounds object

Figure 2 *Marquee surrounding irregular shape*

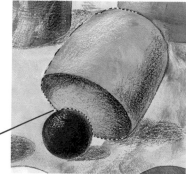

Marquee

Making Selections

Using Fastening Points

Each time you click one of the marquee tools, a fastening point is added to the image. A **fastening point** is an anchor within the marquee. When the marquee pointer reaches the initial fastening point (after making its way around the image), a very small circle appears on the pointer, indicating that you have reached the starting point. Clicking the pointer when this circle appears closes the marquee. Some fastening points, such as those in a circular marquee, are not visible, while others, such as those created by the Polygonal or Magnetic Lasso tools, are visible.

Selecting, Deselecting, and Reselecting

After a selection is made, you can move, copy, transform, or make adjustments to it.

A selection stays selected until you unselect, or **deselect**, it. You can deselect a selection by clicking Select on the Menu bar, and then clicking Deselect. You can reselect a deselected object by clicking Select on the Menu bar, and then clicking Reselect.

TABLE 1: SELECTION TOOLS BY SHAPE		
Tool	**Button**	**Effect**
Rectangular Marquee tool		Creates a rectangular selection. Press [Shift] while dragging to create a square.
Elliptical Marquee tool		Creates an elliptical selection. Press [Shift] while dragging to create a circle.
Single Row Marquee tool		Creates a 1-pixel-wide row selection.
Single Column Marquee tool		Creates a 1-pixel-wide column selection.
Lasso tool		Creates a freehand selection.
Polygonal Lasso tool		Creates straight line selections. Press [Alt] (Win) or [option] (Mac) to create freehand segments.
Magnetic Lasso tool		Creates selections that snap to an edge of an object. Press [Alt] (Win) or [option] (Mac) to alternate between freehand and magnetic line segments.

© Cengage Learning 2013

Placing a Selection

You can place a selection in a Photoshop image in many ways. You can copy or cut a selection, and then paste it to a different location in the same image or to a different image. You can also use the Move tool to drag a selection to a new location. The Paste In Place command (found within the Paste Special option on the Edit menu) lets you paste Clipboard contents in the same relative location in the target document or layer as it occupied in the source document or layer.

Using Guides

Guides are non-printing horizontal and vertical lines that you can display on top of an image to help you position a selection.

You can create an unlimited number of horizontal and vertical guides. You create a guide by displaying the rulers, positioning the pointer on either ruler, and then clicking and dragging the guide into position. Figure 3 shows the creation of a horizontal guide in a file that already contains guides. You delete a guide by selecting the Move tool on the Tools panel, positioning the pointer over the guide, and then clicking and dragging it back to its ruler. If the Snap feature is enabled, as you drag an object toward a guide, the object will be pulled toward the guide. To turn on the Snap feature, click View on the Menu bar, and then click Snap. A check mark appears to the left of the command if the feature is enabled.

Figure 3 *Creating guides in image*

Dragging a guide to a new location on the vertical ruler

Guides can be locked so they are not accidently moved by clicking View on the Menu bar, then clicking Lock Guides. You may also want to change the color of guides: you can do this by clicking Edit (Win) or Photoshop (Mac) on the Menu bar, pointing to Preferences, then clicking Guides, Grid & Slices in the Preferences dialog box.

Taking Measurements

You can use any selection tool to select the object(s) you want measured. Measurements are recorded in the Measurement Log, which is grouped with the Mini Bridge and Timeline panels when it is opened. Sometimes you just need to know the dimensions of an object, such as the length, width, area, or density. Before you begin, you need to set the scale. This determines what unit of measurement will be used. You can do this by clicking the Measurement Log Panel options button, pointing to Set Measurement Scale, and then clicking Default or Custom. (The default scale uses pixel units.) Next, click Image on the Menu bar, point to Analysis, and then click Ruler Tool or Count Tool to select the measurement tool. If you select the Count Tool, the pointer will add a sequentially numbered object to the image so you can easily keep track of the count.

You can open the Measurement Log by clicking Window on the Menu bar, and then clicking Measurement Log. After you make a selection, click the Record Measurements button to record the measurement in a new row in the Measurement Log. Data in this log include area, perimeter, height, and width, as well as the source document and when the measurement was taken. To measure a particular area, use a selection tool to define an area, click the Ruler tool, click a point on the selection area, then click another point on the selection area (which defines the area you want measured). Click the Record Measurements button on the Measurement Log panel and the measurement of point-to-point area will display in the log. Repeat the process by clicking the next portion you want measured, then click Record Measurements. All your measurements will be recorded in the Measurement Log panel.

Figure 4 *Rectangular Marquee tool selection*

TABLE 2: WORKING WITH A SELECTION	
If you want to:	**Then do this:**
Move a selection (an image) using the mouse	Position ▶⊕ over the selection, then drag the marquee and its contents
Copy a selection to the Clipboard	Activate image containing the selection, click Edit ➤ Copy
Cut a selection to the Clipboard	Activate image containing the selection, click Edit ➤ Cut
Paste a selection from the Clipboard	Activate image where you want the selection, click Edit ➤ Paste
Delete a selection	Activate the image with the selection, then press [Delete] (Win) or [delete] (Mac)
Deselect a selection	Press [Ctrl][D] (Win) or ⌘ [D] (Mac)

© Cengage Learning 2013

Create a selection with the Rectangular Marquee tool

1. Start Photoshop, open PS 4-1.psd from the drive and folder where you store your Data Files, save it as **Kitchen Table**, click **OK** if the Maximize compatibility dialog box displays, then reset the **Essentials workspace**.

2. Open PS 4-2.psd, then display the rulers in pixels for this image if they do not already appear.

3. Click the **Rectangular Marquee tool** ▦ on the Tools panel, then make sure the value in the Feather text box on the options bar is **0 px**.

   Feathering determines the amount of blur between the selection and the pixels surrounding it.

4. Drag the **Marquee pointer** ╋ to select the coffee cup from approximately **10 H/10 V** to **210 H/180 V**. See Figure 4.

   The first number in each coordinate refers to the horizontal ruler (H); the second number refers to the vertical ruler (V).

   TIP You can also use the X/Y coordinates displayed in the Info panel.

5. Click the **Move tool** ▶⊕ on the Tools panel, then drag the **coffee cup** to any location in the Kitchen Table image.

   TIP You can also arrange windows by clicking Window on the Menu bar, pointing to Arrange, then clicking Tile All Horizontally.

   The selection now appears in the Kitchen Table image on a new layer (Layer 1).

   TIP Table 2 describes methods you can use to work with selections in an image.

(continued)

Using the Rectangular Marquee tool, you created a selection in an image, then you dragged that selection into another image. This left the original image intact, and created a copy of the selection in the destination image.

Position a selection with the Move tool

1. Verify that the **Move tool**  is active on the Tools panel, and display the rulers if they do not already appear.

2. If you do not see guides in the Kitchen Table image, click **View** on the Menu bar, point to **Show**, then click **Guides**.

TIP You can use the Straighten Layer button on the Ruler options bar to straighten an image to any given angle. Select the Ruler tool on the Tools panel (which is grouped with the Eyedropper tool), click and drag the pointer from one area to another, release the mouse button, then click the Straighten Layer button on the options bar. The horizontal edge of the active layer will be made parallel with the drawn line.

3. Drag the **coffee cup** so that the lower-left corner snaps to the ruler guides at approximately **220 H/520 V**. Compare your image to Figure 5.

   Did you feel the snap to effect as you positioned the selection within the guides? This feature makes it easy to properly position objects within an image.

TIP If you didn't feel the image snap to the guides, click View on the Menu bar, point to Snap To, then click Guides.

4. Rename Layer 1 **Coffee cup**.

You used the Move tool to reposition a selection in an existing image, then you renamed the layer.

Figure 5 *Position a selection in image*

Coffee cup snaps to guides

Using Smart Guides

Wouldn't it be great to be able to see a vertical or horizontal guide as you move an object? Using **Smart Guides**, you can do just that. Smart Guides are turned on by clicking View on the Menu bar, pointing to Show, and then clicking Smart Guides. Once this feature is turned on, horizontal and vertical magenta guidelines appear automatically when you draw a shape or move an object. This feature allows you to align layer content as you move it.

Figure 6 *Deselect command*

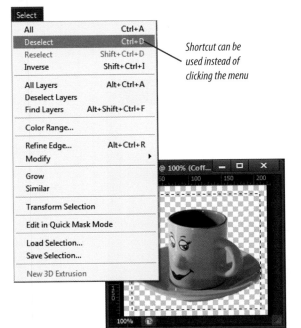

Shortcut can be used instead of clicking the menu

Deselect a selection

1. Click **Window** on the Menu bar, then click **PS 4-2.psd**.

   TIP If you can see the window of the image you want anywhere on the screen, you can just click it to make it active instead of using the Window menu.

2. Click **Select** on the Menu bar, then click **Deselect**, as shown in Figure 6.

You made another window active, then used the Deselect command on the Select menu to deselect the object you moved. When you deselect a selection, the marquee no longer surrounds it.

Figure 7 *Save Selection dialog box*

Saving and Loading a Selection

Any selection can be saved independently of the surrounding image, so that if you want to use it again in the image, you can do so without having to retrace it using one of the marquee tools. Once a selection is made, you can save it in the image by clicking Select on the Menu bar, and then clicking Save Selection. The Save Selection dialog box opens, as shown in Figure 7; be sure to give the selection a meaningful name. When you want to load a saved selection, click Select on the Menu bar, and then click Load Selection. Click the Channel list arrow to display the Channel list, click the named selection, and then click OK.

Create a selection with the Magnetic Lasso tool

1. Open PS 4-3.psd from the drive and folder where you store your Data Files.

2. Click the **Zoom tool** 🔍 on the Tools panel, then click the **tomato image** until the zoom factor is **200%**.

3. Click the **Magnetic Lasso tool** 🔲 on the Tools panel, then change the settings on the options bar so that they are the same as those shown in Figure 8. Table 3 describes Magnetic Lasso tool settings.

4. Click the **Magnetic Lasso tool pointer** once anywhere on the edge of the tomato to create your first fastening point.

TIP If you click a spot that is not at the edge of the tomato, press [Esc] to undo the action, then start again.

5. Drag slowly around the tomato (clicking at the top of each leaf may be helpful) until it is almost entirely selected, then click directly over the **initial fastening point**. See Figure 9.

TIP Zoom in or out of an image to see as much/little detail as you need.

Don't worry about all the nooks and crannies surrounding the leaves on the tomato; the Magnetic Lasso tool will select those automatically. You will see a small circle next to the pointer when it is directly over the initial fastening point, indicating that you are closing the selection. The individual segments turn into a marquee.

TIP If you feel that the Magnetic Lasso tool is missing some major details while you're tracing, you can insert additional fastening points by clicking the pointer while dragging. For example, click the mouse button at a location where you want to change the selection shape.

You created a selection with the Magnetic Lasso tool.

Figure 8 *Options for the Magnetic Lasso tool*

Figure 9 *Creating a selection with the Magnetic Lasso tool*

DESIGN TIP

Mastering the Art of Selections

You might feel that making selections is difficult when you first start. Making selections is a skill, and like most skills, it takes a lot of practice to become proficient. In addition to practice, make sure that you're comfortable in your work area, that your hands are steady, and that your mouse or other pointing device is working well. A non-optical mouse that is dirty will make selecting an onerous task, so make sure your mouse is well cared for and is functioning correctly.

Figure 10 *Selection dragged into image*

Defringing the layer reduces the amount of background that appears; your results will vary

Complex selection includes only object, no background

TABLE 3: MAGNETIC LASSO TOOL SETTINGS	
Setting	**Description**
Feather	The amount of blur between the selection and the surrounding pixels. This setting is measured in pixels and can be a value between 0 and 250.
Anti-alias	The smoothness of the selection, achieved by softening the color transition between edge and background pixels.
Width	The interior width, achieved by detecting an edge from the pointer. This setting is measured in pixels and can have a value from 1 to 40.
Contrast	The sensitivity of the tool. This setting can be a value between 1 percent and 100 percent; higher values detect high-contrast edges.
Frequency	The rate at which fastening points are applied. This setting can be a value between 0 and 100; higher values insert more fastening points.

© Cengage Learning 2013

Move a complex selection to an existing image

1. Click the **Move tool** on the Tools panel.

   TIP You can also click the Click to open the Tool Preset picker list arrow on the options bar, then double-click the Move tool.

2. Use the **Move tool pointer** to drag the tomato selection to the Kitchen Table image, then open the **Info panel** (using the Window command on the Menu bar).

   The selection appears on a new layer (Layer 1).

3. Drag the object so that the bottom of the tomato snaps to the guide at approximately **450 Y** and the left edge of the tomato snaps to the guide at **220 X** using the coordinates on the Info panel. (The coordinates in the Info panel track the location where you clicked to drag the object.)

4. Use the Layer menu to defringe the new Layer 1 at a width of **1** pixel.

5. Close the PS 4-3.psd image without saving your changes, then collapse the Info panel to the dock.

6. Rename the new layer **Tomato** in the Kitchen Table image, then reposition the Tomato layer so it is beneath the Coffee cup layer in the Layers panel.

7. Save your work, then compare your image to Figure 10.

8. Click **Window** on the Menu bar, then click **PS 4-2.psd**.

9. Close the Info panel and the PS 4-2.psd image without saving your changes.

You dragged a complex selection into an existing Photoshop image. You positioned the object using ruler guides and renamed and repositioned a layer. You also defringed a selection to eliminate its white border.

Modify
A MARQUEE

What You'll Do

In this lesson, you'll move and enlarge a marquee, drag a selection into a Photoshop image, and then position a selection.

Changing the Size of a Marquee

Not all objects are easy to select. Sometimes, when you make a selection, you might need to change the size or shape of the marquee.

The options bar contains selection buttons that help you add to and subtract from a marquee, or intersect with a selection. The marquee in Figure 11 was modified into the one shown in Figure 12 by clicking the Add to selection button. After the Add to selection button is active, you can draw an additional marquee, and it will be added to the current marquee.

One method you can use to increase the size of a marquee is the Grow command. After you make a selection, you can increase the marquee size by clicking Select on the Menu bar, and then clicking Grow. The Grow command selects pixels adjacent to the marquee that have colors similar to those specified by the Magic Wand tool. The Similar command, also located on the Select menu, selects both adjacent and non-adjacent pixels.

Modifying a Marquee

While a selection is active, you can modify the marquee by expanding or contracting it, smoothing out its edges, or enlarging it to add a border around the selection. These five commands, Expand, Contract, Smooth Feather, and Border, are located on the Modify command submenu, which is found on the Select menu. For example, you might want to enlarge your selection. Using the Expand command, you can increase the size of the selection, as shown in Figure 13.

> **QUICK TIP**
>
> While the Grow command selects adjacent pixels that have similar colors, the Expand command increases a selection by a specific number of pixels.

Moving a Marquee

After you create a marquee, you can move the marquee to another location in the same image or to another image entirely. You might want to move a marquee if you've drawn it in the wrong image or the wrong location. Sometimes it's easier to draw a marquee elsewhere on the page, and then move it to the desired location.

> **QUICK TIP**
>
> You can always hide and display layers as necessary to facilitate making a selection.

Using the Quick Selection Tool

The Quick Selection tool lets you paint-to-select an object from the interior using a resizeable brush. As you paint the object, the selection grows. Using the Auto-Enhance check box, rough edges and blockiness are automatically reduced to give you a perfect selection. As with other selection tools, the Quick Selection tool has options to add and subtract from your selection.

Figure 11 *New selection*

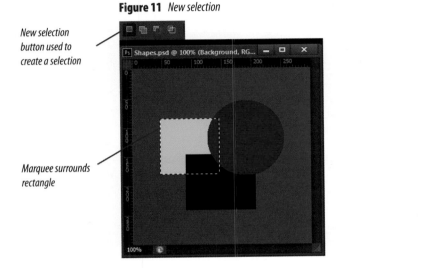

New selection button used to create a selection

Marquee surrounds rectangle

Figure 12 *Selection with additions*

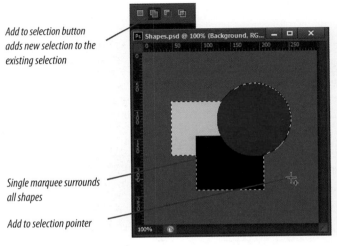

Add to selection button adds new selection to the existing selection

Single marquee surrounds all shapes

Add to selection pointer

Figure 13 *Expanded selection*

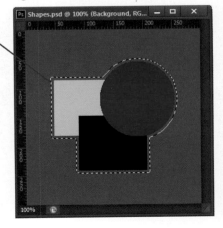

Marquee expanded by 5 pixels

Adding To and Subtracting From a Selection

Of course knowing how to make a selection is important, but it's just as important to know how to make alterations in an existing selection. Sometimes it's almost impossible to create that perfect marquee on the first try. Perhaps your hand moved while you were tracing or you just got distracted. Using the Add to selection and Subtract from selection buttons (which appear with all selection tools), you can alter an existing marquee without having to start from scratch.

Move and enlarge a marquee

1. Open PS 4-4.psd from the drive and folder where you store your Data Files, then change the zoom factor to **200%**, enlarging the window as necessary.

2. Click the **Elliptical Marquee tool** 🔘 on the Tools panel.

   TIP The Elliptical Marquee tool might be hidden under the Rectangular Marquee tool.

3. Click the **New selection button** 🔲 on the options bar if it is not already active.

4. Drag the **Marquee pointer** ╪ to select the area from approximately **150 X/50 Y** to **400 X/250 Y**. Compare your image to Figure 14.

5. Position the **pointer** ▷∴ in the center of the selection, then drag the **Move pointer** ▶⊕ so the marquee covers the casserole, at approximately **250 X/165 Y**, as shown in Figure 15.

   TIP You can also nudge a selection to move it by pressing the arrow keys. Each time you press an arrow key, the selection moves one pixel in the direction of the arrow.

6. Click the **Magic Wand tool** 🪄 on the Tools panel (grouped with the Quick Selection tool), then enter a Tolerance of **16**, and select the **Anti-alias** and **Contiguous check boxes**.

7. Click **Select** on the Menu bar, then click **Similar**.

8. Click **Select** on the Menu bar, point to **Modify**, then click **Expand**.

9. Type **1** in the Expand By text box of the Expand Selection dialog box, click **OK**, then deselect the selection.

You created a marquee, then dragged the marquee to reposition it. You then enlarged a selection marquee by using the Similar and Expand commands.

Figure 14 *Selection in image*

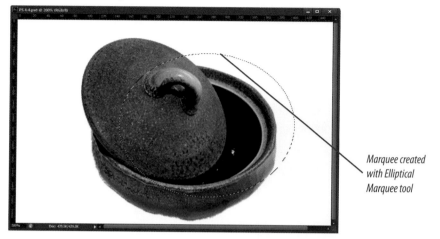

Marquee created with Elliptical Marquee tool

Figure 15 *Moved selection*

New marquee location

Figure 16 *Quick Selection tool settings*

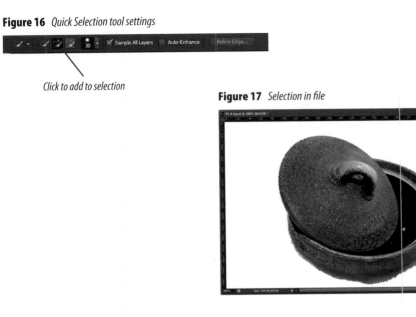

Click to add to selection

Figure 17 *Selection in file*

Figure 18 *Selection moved to the Kitchen Table image*

Use the Quick Selection tool

1. Click the **Quick Selection tool** on the Tools panel, then adjust your settings using Figure 16.

   TIP If you need to change the Brush settings, click Brush picker list arrow on the options bar, then drag the sliders so the settings are 10 px diameter, 0% hardness, 1% spacing, 0° angle, 100% roundness, and Pen Pressure size.

2. Position the pointer in the **center of the casserole**, then slowly drag the pointer to the outer edges until the object is selected. See Figure 17.

   TIP Sometimes making a selection is easy, sometimes... not so much. Time and practice will hone your selection skills. It will get easier.

3. Change the zoom level to **100%**, then click the **Move tool** on the Tools panel.

4. Position the **Move pointer** over the selection, then drag the **casserole** to the Kitchen Table image.

5. Drag the **casserole** so that it is to the left of the napkins.

6. Defringe the casserole using a setting of **1** pixel.

7. Rename the new layer **Casserole**.

8. Save your work on the Kitchen Table image, then compare your work to Figure 18.

9. Make **PS 4-4.psd** active.

10. Close PS 4-4.psd without saving your changes.

You selected an object using the Quick Selection tool, then you dragged the selection into an existing image.

Select Using Color and
MODIFY A SELECTION

What You'll Do

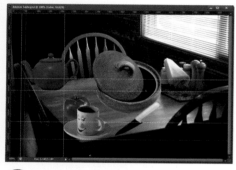

In this lesson, you'll make selections using both the Color Range command and the Magic Wand tool. You'll also flip a selection, and then fix an image using the Healing Brush tool.

Selecting with Color

Selections based on color can be easy to make, especially when the background of an image is different from the image itself. High contrast between colors is an ideal condition for making selections based on color. You can make selections using color with the Color Range command on the Select menu, or you can use the Magic Wand tool on the Tools panel.

Using the Magic Wand Tool

When you select the Magic Wand tool, the following options are available on the options bar, as shown in Figure 19:

- The four selection buttons.
- Sample size, which defines the number of pixels sampled by the tool.

- The **Tolerance** setting, which allows you to specify how similar in color pixels must be in order to be selected. This setting has a value from 0 to 255; the lower the value, the closer in color the selected pixels will be.
- The Anti-alias check box softens the appearance of the edge of the selection.
- The Contiguous check box, which lets you select pixels that are next to one another.
- The Sample All Layers check box, which lets you select pixels from multiple layers at once.
- The Refine Edge button lets you easily improve the quality of the selection edges.

Figure 19 *Options for the Magic Wand tool*

Making Selections

Using the Color Range Command

You can use the Color Range command, located on the Select menu, to make the same selections as with the Magic Wand tool. When you use the Color Range command, the Color Range dialog box opens. This dialog box lets you use the pointer to identify which colors you want to use to make a selection. You can also select the Invert check box to *exclude* the chosen color from the selection. The **fuzziness** setting is similar to tolerance, in that the lower the value, the closer in color pixels must be to be selected.

QUICK **TIP**
Unlike the Magic Wand tool, the Color Range command does not give you the option of excluding contiguous pixels.

Transforming a Selection

After you place a selection in a Photoshop image, you can change its size and other qualities by clicking Edit on the Menu bar, pointing to Transform, and then clicking any of the commands on the submenu. After you select certain commands, small squares called **handles** surround the selection. To complete the command, you drag a handle until the image has the look you want, and then press [Enter] (Win) or [return] (Mac). You can also use the Transform submenu to flip a selection horizontally or vertically.

Understanding the Healing Brush Tool

If you place a selection then notice that the image has a few imperfections, you can fix the image. You can fix imperfections such as dirt, scratches, bulging veins on skin, or wrinkles on a face using the Healing Brush tool on the Tools panel.

QUICK **TIP**
When correcting someone's portrait, make sure your subject looks the way he or she *thinks* they look. That's not always possible, but strive to get as close as you can to their ideal!

Using the Healing Brush Tool

This tool lets you sample an area, and then paint over the imperfections. What is the result? The less-than-desirable pixels seem to disappear into the surrounding image. In addition to matching the sampled pixels, the Healing Brush tool also matches the texture, lighting, and shading of the sample. This is why the painted pixels blend so effortlessly into the existing image. Corrections can be painted using broad strokes or using clicks of the mouse.

QUICK **TIP**
To take a sample, press and hold [Alt] (Win) or [option] (Mac) while dragging the pointer over the area you want to duplicate.

DESIGN**TIP**

Knowing Which Selection Tool to Use
The hardest part of making a selection might be determining which selection tool to use. How are you supposed to know if you should use a marquee tool or a lasso tool? The first question you need to ask yourself is, "What do I want to select?" Becoming proficient in making selections means that you need to assess the qualities of the object you want to select, and then decide which method to use. Ask yourself: Does the object have a definable shape? Does it have an identifiable edge? Are there common colors that can be used to create a selection?

Select using Color Range

1. Open PS 4-5.psd from the drive and folder where you store your Data Files.

2. Click **Select** on the Menu bar, then click **Color Range**.

3. Click the **Image option button** if it is not already selected.

4. Click the **Invert check box** to add a check mark if it does not already contain a check mark.

5. Verify that your settings match those shown in Figure 20, click anywhere in the white background area surrounding the sample image, then click **OK**.

   The Color Range dialog box closes and the teapot in the image is selected.

6. Click the **Move tool** ⊹ on the Tools panel.

7. Drag the selection into Kitchen Table.psd, then position the selection as shown in Figure 21.

8. Rename the new layer **Teapot**.

9. Defringe the teapot using a setting of **2** pixels.

10. Activate **PS 4-5.psd**, then close this file without saving any changes.

You made a selection within an image using the Color Range command on the Select menu, and dragged the selection to an existing image.

Figure 20 *Completed Color Range dialog box*

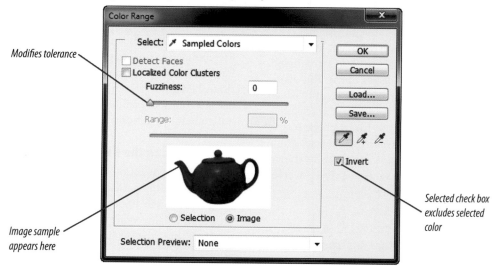

Modifies tolerance

Image sample appears here

Selected check box excludes selected color

Figure 21 *Selection in image*

Figure 22 *Magic Wand tool settings*

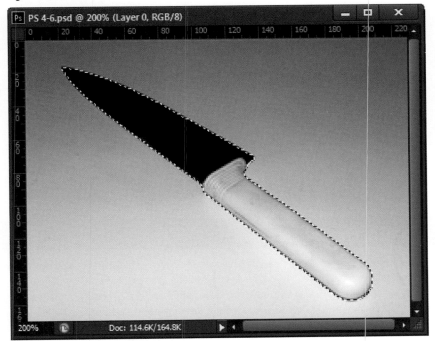

Figure 23 *Selected area*

Select using the Magic Wand and the Quick Selection tools

1. Open PS 4-6.psd from the drive and folder where you store your Data Files, then change the zoom factor to **200%**.

2. Click the **Magic Wand tool** on the Tools panel.

3. Change the settings on the options bar to match those shown in Figure 22.

4. Click anywhere in the **knife blade** of the image (such as **100 x/60 Y**).

5. Click the **Quick Selection tool** on the Tools panel, click the **Add to selection button**, then drag across the **knife handle**. Compare your selection to Figure 23.

6. Click the **Move tool** on the Tools panel, then drag the selection into Kitchen Table.psd.

You made a selection using the Magic Wand and Quick Selection tools, then dragged it into an existing image. The Magic Wand tool is just one more way you can make a selection. One advantage of using the Magic Wand tool (versus the Color Range tool) is the Contiguous check box, which lets you choose pixels that are next to one another. Combining tools is an effective way of making selections.

Flip a selection

1. Click **Edit** on the Menu bar, point to **Transform**, then click **Flip Vertical**.

2. Rename Layer 1 as **Knife**.

3. Defringe **Knife** using a **1** pixel setting.

4. Drag the flipped selection with the **Move tool pointer** ▸⊕ so it is positioned as shown in Figure 24.

5. Make **PS 4-6.psd** the active file, then close PS 4-6.psd without saving your changes.

6. Save your work.

You flipped and repositioned a selection. Sometimes it's helpful to flip an object to help direct the viewer's eye to a desired focal point.

Figure 24 *Flipped and positioned selection*

Getting Rid of Red Eye

When digital photos of your favorite people have that annoying red eye, what do you do? You use the Red Eye tool to eliminate this effect. To do this, select the Red Eye tool (which is grouped on the Tools panel with the Spot Healing Brush tool, the Healing Brush tool, and the Patch tool), and then either click a red area of an eye or draw a selection over a red eye. When you release the mouse button, the red eye effect is removed.

Figure 25 *Healing Brush tool options*

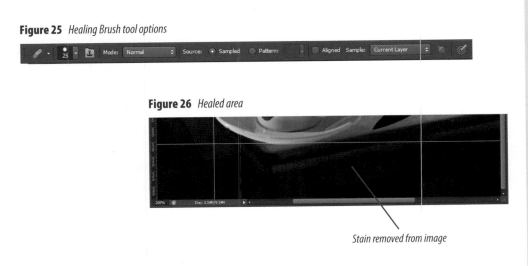

Figure 26 *Healed area*

Stain removed from image

Figure 27 *Image after using the Healing brush*

Fix imperfections with the Healing Brush tool

1. Click the **Table layer** on the Layers panel, then zoom into the area below the coffee cup until the zoom factor is **200%** and you can see the black ink stain on the table.

2. Click the **Healing Brush tool**  on the Tools panel. Change the settings on the options bar to match those shown in Figure 25.

   TIP If you need to change the Brush settings, click the Brush picker list arrow on the options bar, then drag the sliders so the settings are 25 px diameter, 100% hardness, 1% spacing, 0° angle, and 100% roundness.

3. Press and hold [**Alt**] (Win) or [**option**] (Mac), click the wood to the right of the stain, such as **410 X/565 Y**, then release [**Alt**] (Win) or [**option**] (Mac).

   You sampled an area of the table that is not stained so that you can use the Healing Brush tool to paint a damaged area with the sample.

4. Click the stain (at approximately **380 X/570 Y**).

   Notice that as you move the pointer over the stain, the sample shows you how the corrected area will look when healing is applied. Compare the repaired area to Figure 26.

5. Zoom out from the center of the image until the zoom factor is **100%**.

6. Save your work, then compare your image to Figure 27.

You used the Healing Brush tool to fix an imperfection in an image.

Add a Vignette Effect
TO A SELECTION

What You'll Do

In this lesson, you'll create a vignette effect, using a layer mask and feathering.

Understanding Vignettes

Traditionally, a **vignette** is a picture or portrait whose border fades into the surrounding color at its edges. You can use a vignette effect to give an image an old-world appearance. You can also use a vignette effect to tone down an overwhelming background. You can create a vignette effect in Photoshop by creating a mask with a blurred edge. A **mask** lets you protect or modify a particular area and is created using a marquee.

Creating a Vignette

A **vignette effect** uses feathering to fade a marquee shape. The feather setting blurs the area between the selection and the surrounding pixels, which creates a distinctive fade at the edge of the selection. You can create a vignette effect by using a marquee or lasso tool to create a marquee in an image layer. After the selection is created, you can modify the feather setting (a 10- or 20-pixel setting creates a nice fade) to increase the blur effect on the outside edge of the selection.

Getting that Healing Feeling

The Spot Healing Brush tool works in much the same way as the Healing Brush tool in that it removes blemishes and other imperfections. Unlike the Healing Brush tool, the Spot Healing Brush tool does not require you to take a sample. When using the Spot Healing Brush tool, you can choose from three option types:

- proximity match—which uses pixels around the edge of the selection as a patch.
- create texture—which uses all the pixels in the selection to create a texture that is used to fix the area.
- content-aware—which compares nearby image content to fill the selection while realistically maintaining key details such as shadows and edges.

You also have the option of sampling all the visible layers or only the active layer.

Figure 28 *Marquee in image*

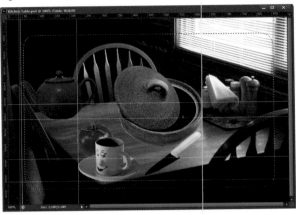

Figure 29 *Layers panel*

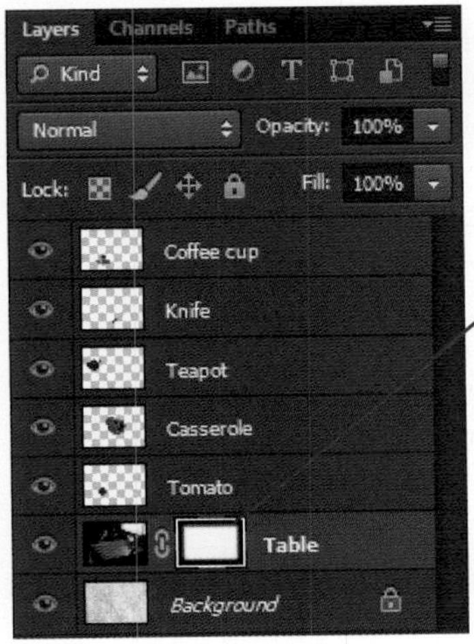

Feathered mask creates vignette effect

Figure 30 *Vignette in image*

Vignette effect fades image edge and reveals background

Create a vignette

1. Verify that the **Table layer** is selected.
2. Click the **Rectangular Marquee tool** on the Tools panel.
3. Change the **Feather setting** on the options bar to **20px**.
4. Create a **selection** with the **Marquee pointer** ✛ from **50 X/50 Y** to **850 X/550 Y**, as shown in Figure 28.
5. Click **Layer** on the Menu bar, point to **Layer Mask**, then click **Reveal Selection**.

   The vignette effect is added to the layer.

   Compare your Layers panel to Figure 29.
6. Click **View** on the Menu bar, then click **Rulers** to hide them.
7. Click **View** on the Menu bar, then click **Clear Guides**.
8. Save your work, then compare your image to Figure 30.
9. Close the Kitchen Table image, then exit Photoshop.

You created a vignette effect by adding a feathered layer mask. Once the image was finished, you hid the rulers and cleared the guides.

Lesson 4   Add a Vignette Effect to a Selection

POWER USER SHORTCUTS

To do this:	Use this method:	To do this:	Use this method:
Copy selection	Click Edit ➤ Copy or [Ctrl][C] (Win) or ⌘ [C] (Mac)	Move selection marquee	Position pointer in selection, drag ▶⊕ to new location
Create vignette effect	Marquee or Lasso tool, create selection, click Layer ➤ Layer Mask ➤ Reveal Selection	Paste selection	Edit ➤ Paste or [Ctrl][V] (Win) or ⌘ [V] (Mac)
Cut selection	Click Edit ➤ Cut or [Ctrl][X] (Win) or ⌘ [X] (Mac)	Polygonal Lasso tool	▦ or [Shift] **L**
Deselect object	Select ➤ Deselect or [Ctrl][D] (Win) or ⌘ [D] (Mac)	Rectangular Marquee tool	▦ or [Shift] **M**
Elliptical Marquee tool	◯ or [Shift] **M**	Reselect a deselected object	Select ➤ Reselect or [Shift][Ctrl][D] (Win) or [Shift] ⌘ [D] (Mac)
Flip image	Edit ➤ Transform ➤ Flip Horizontal	Select all objects	Select ➤ All or [Ctrl][A] (Win) or ⌘ [A] (Mac)
Grow selection	Select ➤ Grow	Select using color range	Select ➤ Color Range, click sample area
Increase selection	Select ➤ Similar	Select using Magic Wand tool	▦ or [Shift] **W**, then click image
Lasso tool	◯ or [Shift] **L**	Select using Quick Selection tool	▦ or [Shift] **W**, then drag pointer over image
Magnetic Lasso tool	▦ or [Shift] **L**	Single Column Marquee tool	▦
Move tool	▶⊕ or **V**	Single Row Marquee tool	▦

Key: Menu items are indicated by ➤ between the menu name and its command. Blue bold letters are shortcuts for selecting tools on the Tools panel.

Make a selection using shapes.

1. Open PS 4-7.psd from the drive and folder where you store your Data Files, update any text layers, then save it as **Powerful Felines**.
2. Select the Backdrop layer, then open PS 4-8.tif.
3. Display the rulers and any available guides in each image window if they are not displayed, and make sure that the Essentials workspace is selected.
4. Use the Rectangular Marquee tool to select the entire image in PS 4-8.tif. (*Hint*: Reset the Feather setting to 0 pixels, if necessary.)
5. Deselect the selection.
6. Use the Magnetic Lasso tool to create a selection surrounding only the block cat in the image. (*Hint*: You can use the Zoom tool to make the image larger.)
7. Drag the selection into the Powerful Felines image, positioning it so the right side of the cat is at 490 X, and the bottom of the right paw is at 450 Y.
8. Defringe the block cat, rename this new layer **Block Cat**, then save your work.
9. Close PS 4-8.tif without saving any changes.

Modify a marquee.

1. Open PS 4-9.tif.
2. Change the settings for the Magic Wand tool to Tolerance = 5, and make sure that the Contiguous check box is selected.
3. Use the Elliptical Marquee tool to create a marquee from 100 X/50 Y to 200 X/100 Y, using a setting of 0 in the Feather text box.
4. Use the Grow command on the Select menu.

5. Deselect the selection.
6. Use the Quick Selection tool to select the tabby cat.
7. Drag the selection into the Powerful Felines image, positioning it so the upper-left corner of the selection is near 0 X/0 Y.
8. Defringe the new layer using a width of 2 pixels.
9. Rename the layer **Tabby cat**, then save your work.
10. Close PS 4-9.tif without saving any changes.

Select using color and modify a selection.

1. Open PS 4-10.tif.
2. Use the Color Range dialog box to select only the kitten.
3. Drag the selection into the Powerful Felines image.

4. Flip the kitten image (in the Powerful Felines image) horizontally.
5. Position the kitten image so the bottom right snaps to the ruler guides at 230 X/450 y.
6. Defringe the kitten using a width of 3 pixels.
7. Rename the layer **Kitten**, then save your work.
8. Close PS 4-10.tif without saving any changes.

Add a vignette effect to a selection.

1. Use a 15-pixel feather setting and the Backdrop layer to create an elliptical selection surrounding the contents of the Powerful Felines image.
2. Add a layer mask that reveals the selection.
3. Hide the rulers and guides, then save your work.
4. Compare your image to Figure 31.

Figure 31 *Completed Skills Review*

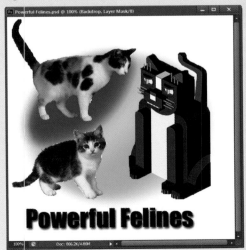

As a professional photographer, you often take photos of people for use in various publications. You recently took a photograph of a woman that will be used in a marketing brochure. The client is happy with the overall picture, but wants the facial lines smoothed out. You decide to use the Healing Brush tool to ensure that the client is happy with the final product.

1. Open PS 4-11.psd, then save it as **Portrait**.
2. Make a copy of the original layer using the default name, or the name of your choice.
3. Use the Original copy layer and the Healing Brush tool to smooth the appearance of facial lines in this image. (*Hint*: You may have greater success if you use short strokes with the Healing Brush tool than if you paint long strokes.)
4. Create a vignette effect on the Original copy layer that reveals the selection using an elliptical marquee.
5. Reorder the layers (if necessary), so that the vignette effect is visible.
6. Save your work, then compare your image to the sample shown in Figure 32.

Figure 32 *Sample Project Builder 1*

Making Selections

The Austin Athletic Association, which sponsors the Austin Marathon, is holding a contest for artwork to announce the upcoming race. Submissions can be created on paper or computer-generated. You feel you have a good chance at winning this contest, using Photoshop as your tool.

1. Open PS 4-12.psd, then save it as **Marathon Contest**.
2. Locate at least two pieces of appropriate artwork—either on your hard disk, in a royalty-free collection, or from scanned images—that you can use in this file.
3. Use any appropriate methods to select imagery from the artwork.
4. After the selections have been made, copy each selection into Marathon Contest.
5. Arrange the images into a design that you think will be eye-catching and attractive.
6. Deselect the selections in the files you are no longer using, and close them without saving the changes.
7. Add a vignette effect to the Backdrop layer.
8. Display the type layers if they are hidden.
9. Defringe any layers, as necessary.
10. Save your work, then compare your screen to the sample shown in Figure 33.

Figure 33 *Sample Project Builder 2*

Making Selections

You are aware that there will be an opening in your firm's design department. Before you can be considered for the job, you need to increase your Photoshop compositing knowledge and experience. You have decided to teach yourself, using informational sources on the Internet and images that can be scanned or purchased.

1. Connect to the Internet and use your browser and favorite search engine to find information on image compositing. (Make a record of the site you found so you can use it for future reference, if necessary.)
2. Create a new Photoshop image, using the dimensions of your choice, then save it as **Sample Compositing**.
3. Locate at least two pieces of artwork—either on your hard disk, in a royalty-free collection, or from scanned images—that you can use. (The images can contain people, plants, animals, or inanimate objects.)
4. Select the images in the artwork, then copy each into the Sample Compositing image, using the method of your choice.
5. Rename each of the layers using meaningful names.
6. Apply a color to each new layer.
7. Arrange the images in a pleasing design. (*Hint*: Remember that you can flip any image, if necessary.)
8. Deselect the selections in the artwork, then close the files without saving the changes.
9. If desired, create a background layer for the image.
10. If necessary, add a vignette effect to a layer.
11. Defringe any images as you see necessary.
12. Save your work, then compare your screen to the sample shown in Figure 34.

Figure 34 *Sample Design Project*

At your design firm, a Fortune 500 client plans to start a 24-hour cable sports network called Total Sportz that will cover any nonprofessional sporting event. You have been asked to create some preliminary designs for the network using images from multiple sources.

1. Open PS 4-13.psd, then save it as **Total Sportz**.
2. Locate several pieces of sports-related artwork— either on your hard disk, in a royalty-free collection, or from scanned images. Remember that the images should not show professional sports figures, if possible.
3. Select imagery from the artwork and move it into the Total Sportz image.
4. Arrange the images in an interesting design. (*Hint*: Remember that you can flip any image, if necessary.)
5. Change each layer name to describe the sport in the layer image.
6. Deselect the selections in the files that you used, then close the files without saving the changes.
7. If you choose, you can add a vignette effect to a layer and/or adjust opacity.
8. Defringe any images (if necessary).
9. Save your work, then compare your image to the sample shown in Figure 35.

Figure 35 *Sample Portfolio Project*

CHAPTER 5

INCORPORATING COLOR TECHNIQUES

1. Work with color to transform an image
2. Use the Color Picker and the Swatches panel
3. Place a border around an image
4. Blend colors using the Gradient tool
5. Add color to a grayscale image
6. Use filters, opacity, and blending modes
7. Match colors

CHAPTER 5

INCORPORATING COLOR TECHNIQUES

Using Color

Color can make or break an image. Sometimes colors can draw us into an image; other times they can repel us. We all know which colors we like, but when it comes to creating an image, it is helpful to have some knowledge of color theory and be familiar with color terminology.

Understanding how Photoshop measures, displays, and prints color can be valuable whether you create new images or modify existing images. Some colors you choose might be difficult for a professional printer to reproduce or might look muddy when printed. As you become more experienced using color, you will learn which colors reproduce well and which ones do not.

Understanding Color Modes and Color Models

Photoshop displays and prints images using specific color modes. A **color mode** is the amount of color data that can be stored in

a given file format, based on an established model. A **color model** determines how pigments combine to produce resulting colors. This is the way your computer or printer associates a name or number with colors. Photoshop uses standard color models as the basis for its color modes. The *color mode* determines the number and range of colors displayed, as well as which color model will be used; the *color model* interprets the color mode information by a monitor and/or printer.

Displaying and Printing Images

An image displayed on your monitor, such as an icon on your desktop, is a **bitmap**, a geometric arrangement of different color dots on a rectangular grid. Each dot, called a **pixel**, represents a color or shade. Bitmapped images are *resolution-dependent* and can lose detail—often demonstrated by a jagged appearance—when highly magnified. When printed, images with high resolutions tend to show more detail and subtler color transitions than low-resolution images.

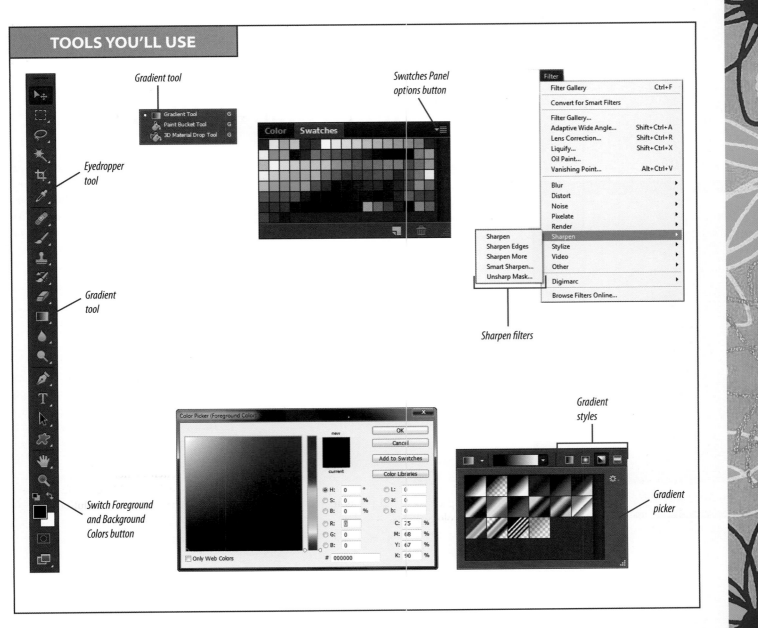

Gradient tool

Gradient Tool   G
Paint Bucket Tool   G
3D Material Drop Tool   G

Swatches Panel
options button

Eyedropper
tool

Gradient
tool

Switch Foreground
and Background
Colors button

Color   Swatches

Filter
Filter Gallery   Ctrl+F
Convert for Smart Filters
Filter Gallery...
Adaptive Wide Angle...   Shift+Ctrl+A
Lens Correction...   Shift+Ctrl+R
Liquify...   Shift+Ctrl+X
Oil Paint...
Vanishing Point...   Alt+Ctrl+V
Blur   ▶
Distort   ▶
Noise   ▶
Pixelate   ▶
Render   ▶
Sharpen   ▶
Stylize   ▶
Video   ▶
Other   ▶
Digimarc   ▶
Browse Filters Online...

Sharpen
Sharpen Edges
Sharpen More
Smart Sharpen...
Unsharp Mask...

Sharpen filters

Color Picker (Foreground Color)
new

current

OK
Cancel
Add to Swatches
Color Libraries

◉ H: 0   °
○ S: 0   %
○ B: 0   %
○ R: 0
○ G: 0
○ B: 0

○ L: 0
○ a: 0
○ b: 0

C: 75   %
M: 68   %
Y: 67   %
K: 90   %

☐ Only Web Colors   # 000000

Gradient
styles

Gradient
picker

Work with Color
TO TRANSFORM AN IMAGE

What You'll Do

In this lesson, you'll use the Color panel, the Paint Bucket tool, and the Eyedropper tool to change the background color of an image.

Learning About Color Models

Photoshop reproduces colors using models of color modes. The range of displayed colors, or **gamut**, for each model available in Photoshop is shown in Figure 1. The shape of each color gamut indicates the range of colors it can display. If a color is **out of gamut**, it is beyond the color space that your monitor can display or that your printer can print. You select the color mode from the Mode command on the Image menu. The available Photoshop color models include Lab Color, Indexed Color, RGB Color, CMYK Color, Bitmap, and Grayscale. Photoshop uses color modes to determine how to display and print an image.

QUICK TIP

A color mode is used to determine which color model will be used to display and print an image.

DESIGN**TIP**

Understanding the Psychology of Color

Have you ever wondered why some colors make you react a certain way? You might have noticed that some colors affect you differently than others. Color is such an important part of our lives, and in Photoshop, it's key. Specific colors are often used in print and web pages to evoke the following responses:

- Blue tends to instill a feeling of safety and stability and is often used by financial services.
- Certain shades of green can generate a soft, calming feeling, while others suggest youthfulness and growth.
- Red commands attention and can be used as a call to action; it can also distract a reader's attention from other content.
- White evokes the feeling of purity and innocence, looks cool and fresh, and is often used to suggest luxury.
- Black conveys feelings of power and strength, but can also suggest darkness and negativity.

Lab Color Mode

The Lab color mode is based on the human perception of color. The numeric values describe all the colors a person with normal vision can see. The Lab color mode has one luminance (lightness) component and two chromatic components (from green to red, and from blue to yellow). Using the Lab color model has distinct advantages: you have the largest number of colors available to you and the greatest precision with which to create them. You can also create all the colors contained by other color models, which are limited in their respective color ranges. The Lab color model is device-independent—the colors will not vary, regardless of the hardware. Use this model when working with digital images so that you can independently edit the luminance and color values.

HSB Color Model

Based on the human perception of color, the HSB (Hue, Saturation, Brightness) model has three fundamental characteristics: hue, saturation, and brightness. The color reflected from or transmitted through an object is called **hue**. Expressed as a degree (between 0° and 360°), each hue is identified by a color name (such as red or green). **Saturation** (or *chroma*) is the strength or purity of the color, representing the amount of gray in proportion to hue. Saturation is measured as a percentage from 0% (gray) to 100% (fully saturated). **Brightness** is the measurement of relative lightness or darkness of a color and is measured as a percentage from 0% (black) to 100% (white). Although you can use the HSB model to define a color on the Color panel or in the Color Picker dialog box, Photoshop *does not* offer HSB mode as a choice for creating or editing images.

RGB Model

Each Photoshop color mode is based on established models used in color reproduction. Most colors in the visible spectrum can be represented by mixing various proportions and intensities of red, green, and blue (RGB) colored light. RGB images use three colors, or **channels**, to reproduce colors on screen. RGB colors are additive colors. **Additive colors** are used for lighting, video, and computer monitors; color is created by adding together red, green, and blue light. When red, green, and blue are combined at their highest value (255), the result is white; the absence of any color (when their values are zero) results in black. Photoshop assigns each component of the RGB mode an intensity value. Your colors can vary from monitor to monitor even if you are using the exact same RGB values on different computers.

Figure 1 *Photoshop color gamuts*

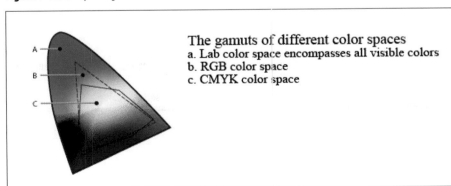

The gamuts of different color spaces
a. Lab color space encompasses all visible colors
b. RGB color space
c. CMYK color space

CMYK Model

The light-absorbing quality of ink printed on paper is the basis of the CMYK (Cyan, Magenta, Yellow, Black) mode. Unlike the **RGB mode**—in which components are combined to create new colors—the CMYK mode is based on colors being partially *absorbed* as the ink hits the paper and being partially *reflected* back to your eyes. CMYK colors are **subtractive colors**—the *absence* of cyan, magenta, yellow, and black creates white. Subtractive (CMYK) and additive (RGB) colors are complementary colors; a pair from one model creates a color in the other. When combined, cyan, magenta, and yellow absorb all color and produce black. The **CMYK mode**—in which the lightest colors are assigned the highest percentages of ink colors—is used in four-color process printing. Converting an RGB image into a CMYK image produces a **color separation** (the commercial printing process of separating colors for use with different inks). Note, however, that because your monitor uses RGB mode, you will not see the exact colors until you print the image, and even then the colors can vary depending on the printer and offset press.

Understanding the Bitmap and Grayscale Modes

In addition to the RGB and CMYK modes, Photoshop provides two specialized color modes: bitmap and grayscale. The **bitmap mode** uses black or white color values to represent image pixels, and is a good choice for images with subtle color gradations, such as photographs or painted images. The **grayscale mode** uses up to 256 shades of gray (in an 8-bit image), assigning a brightness value from 0 (black) to 255 (white) to each pixel. (The number of shades of gray in 16- and 32-bit images is much greater than 256.) The **Duotone mode** is used to create the following grayscale images: monotone, duotones (using two colors), tritones (using three colors), and quadtones (using four colors).

Changing Foreground and Background Colors

In Photoshop, the **foreground color** is black by default and is used to paint, fill, and apply a border to a selection. The **background color** is white by default and is used to make **gradient fills** (gradual blends of multiple colors) and to fill in areas of an image that have been erased. You can change foreground and background colors using the Color panel, the Swatches panel, the Color Picker, or the Eyedropper tool. One method of changing foreground and background colors is **sampling**, in which an existing color is used. You can restore the default colors by clicking the Default Foreground and Background Colors button on the Tools panel, shown in Figure 2. You can apply a color to the background of a layer using the Paint Bucket tool grouped with the Gradient tool. When you click an image with the Paint Bucket tool, the current foreground color on the Tools panel fills the active layer.

Figure 2 *Foreground and background color buttons*

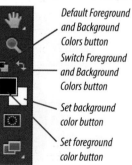

Default Foreground and Background Colors button

Switch Foreground and Background Colors button

Set background color button

Set foreground color button

Figure 3 *Image with rulers displayed*

Figure 4 *Color Settings dialog box*

Intent list arrow

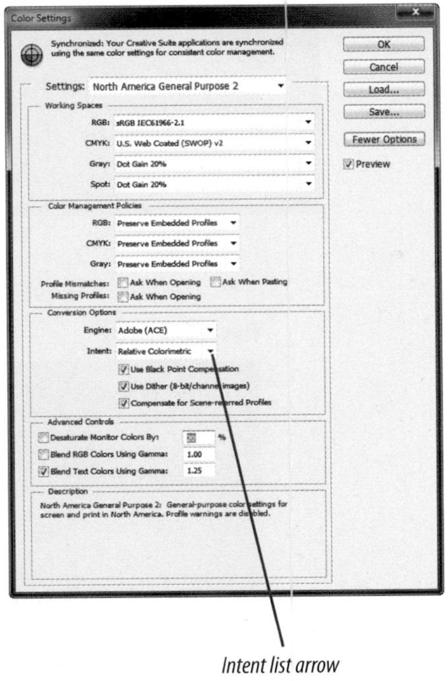

Creating a Rendering Intent

The use of a **rendering intent** determines how colors are converted by a color management system. A **color management system** is used to keep colors looking consistent as they move between devices. Colors are defined and interpreted using a **profile**. You can create a rendering intent by clicking Edit on the Menu bar, and then clicking Color Settings. Click the More Options button in the Color Settings dialog box, click the Intent list arrow in the Conversion Options area, shown in Figure 4, and then click one of the four options. Since a gamut is the range of color that a color system can display or print, the rendering intent is constantly evaluating the color gamut and deciding whether or not the colors need adjusting. Although colors that fall inside the destination gamut are not changed, using a rendering intent allows colors that fall outside the destination gamut to be adjusted based on the intent you set.

Set the default foreground and background colors

1. Start Photoshop, open PS 5-1.psd from the drive and folder where you save your Data Files, then save it as **Basketball Star**.

TIP Whenever the Photoshop Format Options dialog box appears, click OK to maximize compatibility.

2. Click the **Default Foreground and Background Colors button** on the Tools panel, then reset the Essentials workspace.

TIP If you accidently click the Set foreground color button, the Color Picker (Foreground Color) dialog box opens.

3. Change the status bar so the document size displays, if it is not already displayed.

TIP Document sizes will not display in the status bar if the image window is too small. Drag the lower-right corner of the image window to expand the window and display the menu arrow and document sizes.

4. Display the rulers in pixels and show the guides if they are not already displayed, then compare your screen to Figure 3.

TIP You can right-click (Win) or [control]-click (Mac) one of the rulers to choose Pixels, Inches, Centimeters, Millimeters, Points, Picas, or Percent as a unit of measurement, instead of using the Rulers and Units Preferences dialog box.

You set the default foreground and background colors and displayed rulers in pixels.

Change the background color using the Color panel

1. Click the **Background layer** on the Layers panel.

2. Display the **Legacy workspace** (which was created in Chapter 1).

3. Click **Window** on the Menu bar, then click **Color**.

4. Drag each **color slider** on the Color panel until you reach the values shown in Figure 5.

   The active color changes to the new color. Did you notice that this image is using the RGB mode?

   TIP You can also double-click each component's text box on the Color panel and type the color values.

5. Click the **Paint Bucket tool** on the Tools panel.

   TIP If the Paint Bucket tool is not visible on the Tools panel, click the Gradient tool on the Tools panel, press and hold the mouse button until the list of hidden tools opens, then click the Paint Bucket tool.

6. Click the **image** with the **Paint Bucket pointer** .

7. Drag the **Paint Bucket state** on the History panel onto the Delete current state button .

   TIP You can also undo the last action by clicking Edit on the Menu bar, then clicking Undo Paint Bucket.

You set new values in the Color panel, used the Paint Bucket tool to change the background to that color, then undid the change. You can change colors on the Color panel by dragging the sliders or by typing values in the color text boxes.

Figure 5 *Color panel with new color*

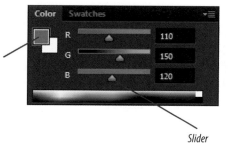

Active color selection box

Slider

Figure 6 *Info panel*

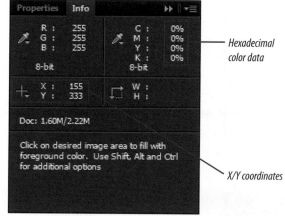

Hexadecimal color data

X/Y coordinates

Using Ruler Coordinates

Photoshop rulers run along the top and left sides of the document window. Each point on an image has a horizontal and vertical location. These two numbers, called X and Y coordinates, appear on the Info panel (which is located with the Properties panel and can be opened with the Window menu) as shown in Figure 6. The X coordinate refers to the horizontal location, and the Y coordinate refers to the vertical location. You can use one or both sets of guides to identify coordinates of a location, such as a color you want to sample. If you have difficulty seeing the ruler markings, you can increase the size of the image; the greater the zoom factor, the more detailed the measurement hashes.

Figure 7 *New foreground color applied to Background layer*

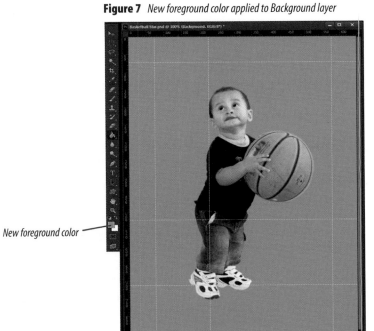

New foreground color

Change the background color using the Eyedropper tool

1. Click the **Background layer** on the Layers panel, if it is not already selected.

2. Click the **Eyedropper tool** on the Tools panel.

3. Click the **light blue area on the boy's right shoe** in the image with the **Eyedropper pointer** .

   The Set foreground color button displays the light blue color that you clicked (or sampled).

   TIP Remember to zoom in or out of any image at any time during a lesson to improve your view.

4. Click the **Paint Bucket tool** on the Tools panel.

5. Click the **image**, then compare your screen to Figure 7.

   You might have noticed that in this instance, it doesn't matter where on the layer you click, as long as the correct layer is selected.

6. Save your work.

You used the Eyedropper tool to sample a color as the foreground color, then used the Paint Bucket tool to change the background color to the color you sampled. Using the Eyedropper tool is a convenient way of sampling a color in any Photoshop image.

Using Hexadecimal Values in the Info Panel

Colors can be expressed in a **hexadecimal value**, three pairs of letters or numbers that define the R, G, and B components of a color. The three pairs of letters/numbers are expressed in values from 00 (minimum luminance) to ff (maximum luminance). 000000 represents the value of black, ffffff is white, and ff0000 is red. To view hexadecimal values in the Info panel, click the Info Panel options button, and then click Panel Options. Click Web Color from either the First Color Readout or Second Color Readout Mode menu, and then click OK. This is just one more way you can exactly determine a specific color in an image.

Use the Color Picker
AND THE SWATCHES PANEL

What You'll Do

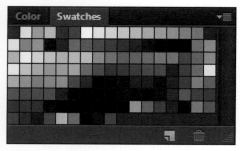

In this lesson, you'll use the Color Picker and the Swatches panel to select new colors, and then you'll add a new color to the background and to the Swatches panel. You'll also learn how to download and apply color themes from Kuler.

Making Selections from the Color Picker

Depending on the color model you are using, you can select colors using the **Color Picker**, a feature that lets you choose a color from a color spectrum or numerically define a custom color. You can change colors in the Color Picker dialog box by using the following methods:

- Drag the sliders along the vertical color bar.
- Click inside the vertical color bar.

- Click a color in the Color field.
- Enter a value in any of the text boxes.

Figure 8 shows a color in the Color Picker dialog box. A circular marker indicates the active color. The color slider displays the range of color levels available for the active color component. The adjustments you make by dragging or clicking a new color are reflected in the text boxes; when you choose a new color, the previous color appears below the new color in the preview area.

Using Kuler to Coordinate Colors

Kuler®, from Adobe, is a web application from which you can download pre-coordinated color themes or design your own. These collections can be saved, using Mykuler, and shared with others. Use Kuler as a fast, effective way of ensuring that your use of color is consistent and harmonious. If you decide to select an existing Kuler theme, you'll find that there are thousands from which to choose. Kuler themes can be seen by clicking the Window menu, pointing to Extensions, and then clicking Kuler, which opens a Kuler panel within Photoshop. You can also access Kuler through your browser at *kuler.adobe.com*, using the Kuler desktop (which requires the installation of Adobe AIR), or from Adobe Illustrator (CS4 or higher). When you pass the mouse over a theme in the Kuler website, the colors in the theme expand. Click the theme and the colors display at the top of the window. Click the slider icon to view the theme's color values.

Using the Swatches Panel

You can also change colors using the Swatches panel. The **Swatches panel** is a visual display of colors you can choose from, as shown in Figure 9. You can add your own colors to the panel by sampling a color from an image, and you can also delete colors. When you add a swatch to the Swatches panel, Photoshop assigns a default name that has a sequential number, or you can name the swatch whatever you like. Photoshop places new swatches in the first available space at the end of the panel.

You can view swatch names by clicking the Swatches Panel options button, and then clicking Small List (or Large List). You can restore the default Swatches panel by clicking the Swatches Panel options button, clicking Reset Swatches, and then clicking OK.

QUICK **TIP**

You can reset the Swatches panel to its default settings by clicking the Swatches panel option button, then clicking Reset Swatches.

Figure 8 *Color Picker dialog box*

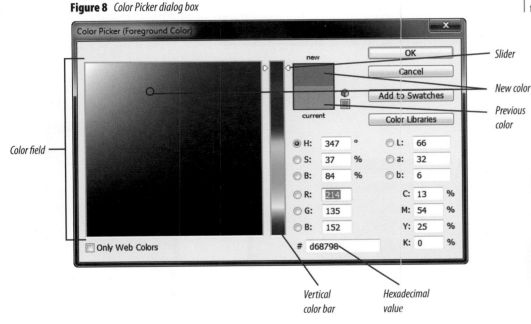

Color field

Slider

New color

Previous color

Vertical color bar

Hexadecimal value

Figure 9 *Swatches panel*

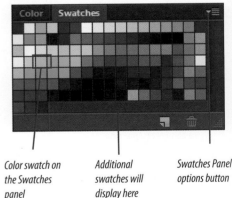

Color swatch on the Swatches panel

Additional swatches will display here

Swatches Panel options button

Select a color using the Color Picker dialog box

1. Click the **Set foreground color button** ■ on the Tools panel, verify that the H: option button is selected in the Color Picker dialog box, then position the slider in the Vertical color bar as shown in Figure 10.

2. Click the **R: option button**.

3. Click the **bottom-right corner** of the Color field (purple), as shown in Figure 10.

TIP If the Warning: out-of-gamut for printing indicator appears next to the color, then this color is outside the printable range of colors.

4. Click **OK**.

You opened the Color Picker dialog box, selected a different color mode, and then selected a new color.

Select a color using the Swatches panel

1. Click the **Swatches panel option button** ■, then click **Reset Swatches**.

2. Click the **second swatch from the left in the third row** (Pastel Yellow), as shown in Figure 11 (the actual location of this color swatch may differ on your Swatches panel).

   Did you notice that the foreground color on the Tools panel changed to a pastel yellow?

3. Click the **Paint Bucket tool** 🪣 on the Tools panel if necessary.

4. Click the **image** with the **Paint Bucket pointer** ⬢, then compare your screen to Figure 12.

You selected a color from the Swatches panel, and then used the Paint Bucket tool to change the background to that color.

Figure 10 *Color Picker dialog box*

New color
Out-of-gamut indicator
Click to add a color to the Swatches panel
Your values might vary
Previous color
Click here for new color

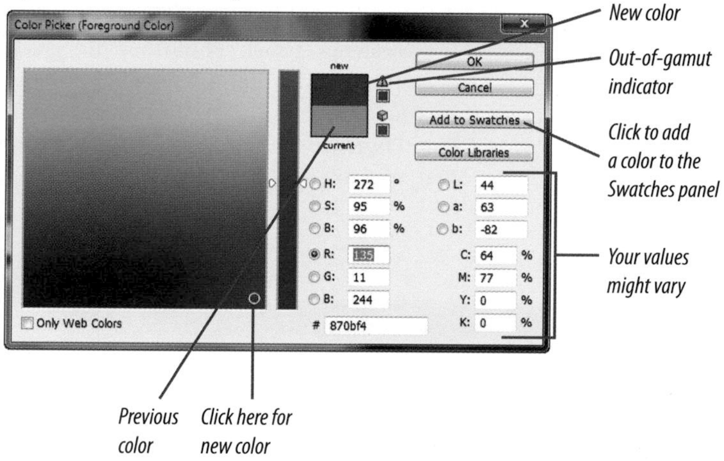

Figure 11 *Swatches panel*

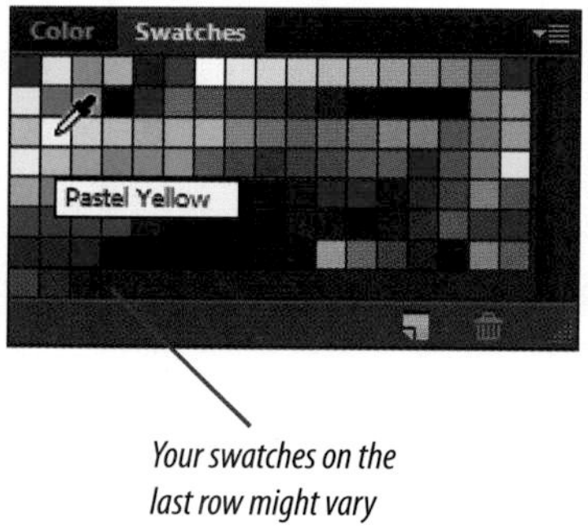

Pastel Yellow

Your swatches on the last row might vary

Figure 12 *New foreground color applied to Background layer*

Figure 13 *Swatch added to Swatches panel*

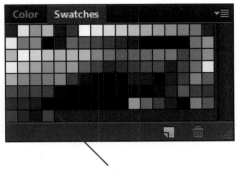

New swatch appears
in last row

Maintaining Your Focus

Adobe Photoshop is probably unlike any other program you've used before. In other programs, there's a central area on the screen where you focus your attention. In Photoshop, there's the workspace containing your document, but you've probably already figured out that if you don't have the correct layer selected in the Layer's panel, things won't quite work out as you expected. In addition, you have to make sure you've got the right tool selected in the Tools panel. You also need to keep an eye on the History panel. As you work on your image, it might feel a lot like negotiating a grocery parking lot on the day before Thanksgiving. You've got to be looking in a lot of places at once.

Add a new color to the Swatches panel

1. Click the **Eyedropper tool** 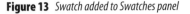 on the Tools panel.
2. Click the **palm leaf** (on the boy's shirt) at coordinates 310 X/348 Y.

TIP Use the Zoom tool whenever necessary to enlarge or decrease your workspace so you can better see what you're working on.

3. Click the **empty area to the right of the last swatch** in the bottom row of the Swatches panel with the **Paint Bucket pointer** ▸☂.
4. Type **Palm leaf** in the Name text box.
5. Click **OK** in the Color Swatch Name dialog box.

TIP To delete a color from the Swatches panel, press [Alt] (Win) or [option] (Mac), position the ▸✂ pointer over a swatch, then click the swatch.

6. Save your work, then compare the new swatch on your Swatches panel to Figure 13.

You used the Eyedropper tool to sample a color, added the color to the Swatches panel, and then gave it a descriptive name. Adding swatches to the Swatches panel makes it easy to reuse frequently used colors.

Use Kuler from a web browser

1. Open your favorite browser, type **kuler.adobe.com** in the URL text box, then press [**Enter**] (Win) or [**return**] (Mac).

   If you have an iPad, iPhone, or Android device, you can download a Kuler app by searching the web with your favorite browser.

2. Click the **Sign In link**, type your **Adobe ID** and **password**, then Agree to the terms of the website if asked. (If you don't have an Adobe ID, click the Register link and follow the instructions.)

3. Type **Johnny Cash Tribute** in the Search text box, press [**Enter**] (Win) or [**return**] (Mac). The swatches shown in Figure 14 will display, although your screen may contain other swatches.

4. Click the **Johnny Cash Tribute swatch**, click the **Download this theme as an Adobe Swatch Exchange file button** 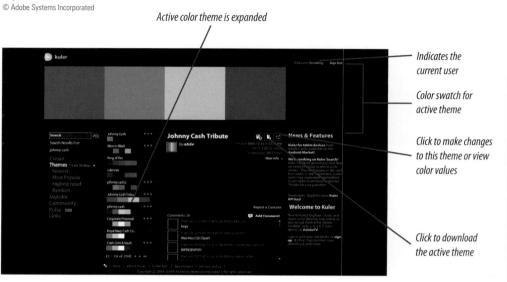, find the location where you save your Data Files in the Save As dialog box, then click **Save**.

5. Click the **Sign Out link** to sign out from Kuler, then activate Photoshop.

6. Click the **Swatches Panel options button** , then click **Load Swatches**.

7. Navigate to the location where you save your Data Files, click the **Files of type button** (Win), click **Swatch Exchange (*.ASE)**, click **Johnny Cash Tribute**, then click **Load** (Win) or **Open** (Mac).

You searched the Kuler website, downloaded a color theme, and then added it to your Photoshop Swatches panel.

Figure 14 *Themes in Kuler*

Active color theme is expanded

Indicates the current user

Color swatch for active theme

Click to make changes to this theme or view color values

Click to download the active theme

Downloading a Kuler Theme

Once you've logged into Kuler, you can download a theme as an Adobe Swatch Exchange (ASE) file. Click the download button, select a name and location for the downloaded file, and then click Save. You can add a Kuler theme to your color panel by clicking the Swatches Panel options button, clicking Load Swatches, and then navigating to and opening the downloaded ASE file. The new colors will display at the end of the Swatches panel.

Incorporating Color Techniques

Figure 15 *Kuler panel*

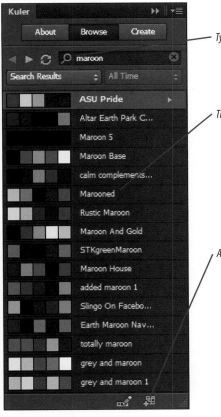

Type search criteria here

Theme to add

Adds theme to Swatches panel

Figure 16 *Theme added to Swatches panel*

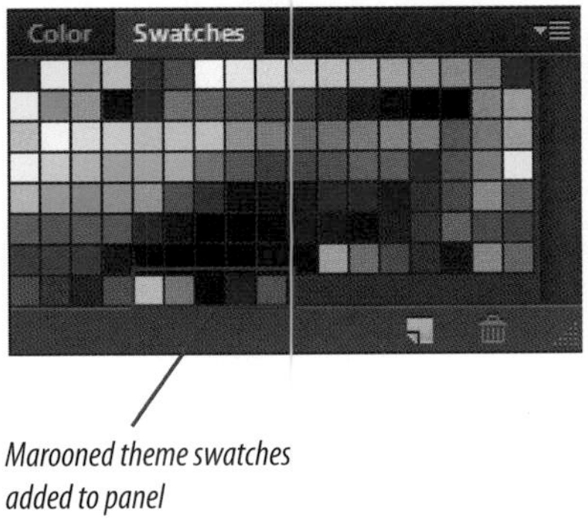

Marooned theme swatches
added to panel

Use Kuler from Photoshop

1. Click **Window** on the Menu bar, point to **Extensions**, then click **Kuler**.

2. Click the **Search text box**, type **maroon**, then press [**Enter**] (Win) or [**return**] (Mac). Compare your Kuler panel to Figure 15.

TIP Your Kuler panel may differ as themes change frequently.

3. Click the **Marooned** theme (or a similar theme if Marooned is not available), then click the **Add selected theme to swatches button** . Compare your Swatches panel to Figure 16.

4. Close the Kuler panel.

5. In the Swatches panel, click the **color box** for #F2CA80 with the **Eyedropper pointer** .

TIP The locations of your color swatches may vary.

6. Click the **Paint Bucket tool** on the Tools panel, then click the **image**.

7. Save your work.

You opened Kuler in Photoshop, then added a color theme to the Swatches panel. You then applied a color downloaded from Kuler to the image.

Place a Border Around AN IMAGE

What You'll Do

In this lesson, you'll add a border to an image.

Emphasizing an Image

You can emphasize an image by placing a border around its edges. This process is called **stroking the edges**. You add a border by selecting a layer or object, clicking Edit on the Menu bar, and then clicking Stroke. The default color of the border is the current foreground color on the Tools panel. You can change the width, color, location, and blending mode of a border using the Stroke dialog box. The location option buttons in the dialog box determine where the border will be placed. If you want to change the location of the stroke, you must first delete the previously applied stroke, or Photoshop will apply the new border over the existing one.

Locking Transparent Pixels

As you modify layers, you can lock some properties to protect their contents. The ability to lock—or protect—elements within a layer is controlled from within the Layers panel, as shown in Figure 17. It's a good idea to lock transparent pixels when you add borders so that stray marks will not be included in the stroke. You can lock the following layer properties:

- Transparency: Limits editing capabilities to areas in a layer that are opaque.
- Image: Makes it impossible to modify layer pixels using painting tools.
- Position: Prevents pixels within a layer from being moved.

> **QUICK TIP**
>
> You can lock transparent or image pixels only in a layer containing an image, not in one containing type.

Figure 17 *Layers panel locking options*

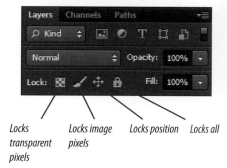

Locks transparent pixels   Locks image pixels   Locks position   Locks all

Figure 18 *Locking transparent pixels*

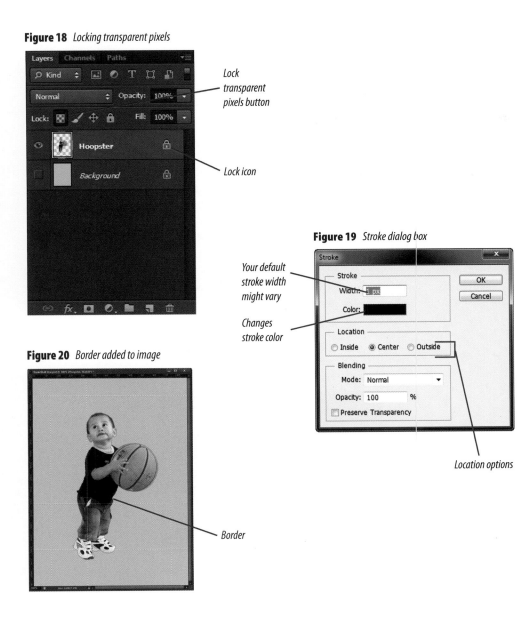

Lock transparent pixels button

Lock icon

Figure 19 *Stroke dialog box*

Your default stroke width might vary

Changes stroke color

Location options

Figure 20 *Border added to image*

Border

Create a border

1. Click the **Indicates layer visibility button** 👁 on the Background layer on the Layers panel.

TIP You can click the Indicates layer visibility button to hide distracting layers.

2. Click the **Default Foreground and Background Colors button** 🔲.

   The foreground color will become the default border color.

3. Click the **Hoopster layer** on the Layers panel.

4. Click the **Lock transparent pixels button** 🔲 on the Layers panel. See Figure 18.

   The border will be applied only to the pixels on the edge of the boy and the ball.

5. Click **Edit** on the Menu bar, then click **Stroke** to open the Stroke dialog box. See Figure 19.

6. Type **10** in the Width text box, click the **Outside option button**, then click **OK**.

TIP Determining the correct border location can be confusing. The default stroke width is the setting last applied; you can apply a width from 1 to 150 pixels. Try different settings until you achieve the look you want.

7. Click the **Indicates layer visibility button** 🔲 on the Background layer on the Layers panel.

8. Save your work, then compare your image to Figure 20.

You hid a layer, changed the foreground color to black, locked transparent pixels, then used the Stroke dialog box to apply a border to the image.

Blend Colors Using
THE GRADIENT TOOL

What You'll Do

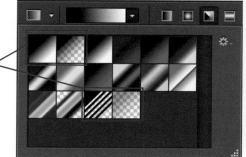

In this lesson, you'll create a gradient fill from a sampled color and a swatch, and then apply it to the background.

Understanding Gradients

A **gradient fill**, or simply **gradient**, is a blend of colors used to fill a selection of a layer or an entire layer. A gradient's appearance is determined by its beginning and ending points, and its length, direction, and angle. Gradients allow you to create dramatic effects, using existing color combinations or your own colors. The Gradient picker, as shown in Figure 21, offers multicolor gradient fills and a few that use the current foreground or background colors on the Tools panel.

Using the Gradient Tool

You use the Gradient tool to create gradients in images. When you choose the Gradient tool, five gradient styles become available on the options bar. These styles—Linear, Radial,

Figure 21 *Gradient picker*

Gradient fills that use current foreground or background colors

Angle, Reflected, and Diamond—are shown in Figure 22. In each example, the gradient was drawn from 50 X/50 Y to 100 X/100 Y.

Customizing Gradients

Using the **gradient presets**—predesigned gradient fills that are displayed in the Gradient picker—is a great way to learn how to use gradients. But as you become more familiar with Photoshop, you might want to venture into the world of the unknown and create your own gradient designs. You can create your own designs by modifying an existing gradient using the Gradient Editor. You can open the Gradient Editor, shown in Figure 23, by clicking the selected gradient pattern that appears in the Gradient picker on the options bar. After it's open, you can use it to make the following modifications:

- Create a new gradient from an existing gradient.
- Modify an existing gradient.
- Add intermediate colors to a gradient.
- Create a blend between more than two colors.
- Adjust the opacity values.
- Determine the placement of the midpoint.

Figure 22 *Sample gradients*

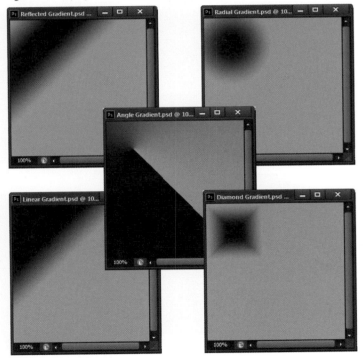

Figure 23 *Gradient Editor dialog box*

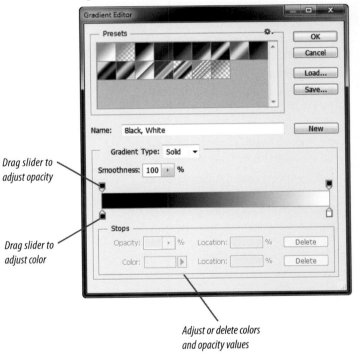

Drag slider to adjust opacity

Drag slider to adjust color

Adjust or delete colors and opacity values

Create a gradient from a sample color

1. Verify that the **Eyedropper tool** 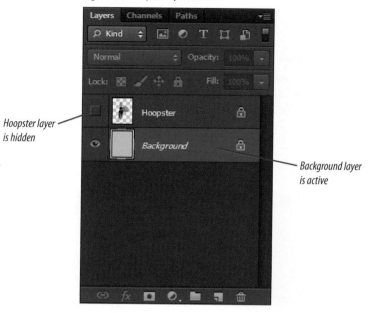 is selected.

2. Click the **blue shirt** in the image at coordinates **250 X/300 Y.**

   TIP   To accurately select the coordinates, adjust the zoom factor as necessary.

3. Click the **Switch Foreground and Background Colors button** on the Tools panel.

4. Click the **Red swatch** (R=180 G=25 B=29) on the Swatches panel (one of the new swatches you added) with the **Eyedropper pointer**.

5. Click the **Indicates layer visibility button** on the Hoopster layer to hide it, and make sure the Background layer is active, as shown in Figure 24.

6. Click the **Paint Bucket tool** on the Tools panel, then press and hold the mouse button until the panel of hidden tools opens.

7. Click the **Gradient tool** on the Tools panel, then click the **Angle Gradient button** on the options bar if it is not already selected.

8. Click the **Click to open Gradient picker list arrow** on the options bar, then double-click **Foreground to Background gradient fill** (first row, first column), as shown in Figure 25.

   TIP   You can close the Gradient picker by pressing [Esc].

You sampled a color on the image to set the background color, changed the foreground color using an existing swatch, selected the Gradient tool, and then chose a gradient fill and style.

Figure 24   *Hoopster layer hidden*

Hoopster layer is hidden

Background layer is active

Figure 25   *Gradient picker*

Gradient styles

Foreground to Background (uses current foreground and background colors)

Foreground to Background

Click to open Gradient picker list arrow

Incorporating Color Techniques

Figure 26 *Gradient fill applied to Background layer*

Apply a gradient fill

1. Drag the **Gradient pointer** - ┼ - from **75 X/75 Y** to **575 X/710 Y** using the Info panel and the guides to help you create the gradient in the work area.

2. Click the **Indicates layer visibility button** ▨ on the Hoopster layer.

   The Hoopster layer appears against the new background, as shown in Figure 26.

3. Save your work.

TIP It is a good practice to save your work early and often in the creation process, especially before making significant changes or printing.

You applied the gradient fill to the background. You can create dramatic effects using the gradient fill in combination with foreground and background colors.

Add Color
TO A GRAYSCALE IMAGE

What You'll Do

In this lesson, you'll convert an image to grayscale, change the color mode, and then colorize a grayscale image using the Hue/Saturation dialog box.

Colorizing Options

Grayscale images can contain up to 256 shades of gray (at 8 bits per pixel), assigning a brightness value from 0 (black) to 255 (white) to each pixel. Since the earliest days of photography, people have been tinting grayscale images with color to create a certain mood or emphasize an image in a way that purely realistic colors could not. To capture this effect in Photoshop, you convert an image to the Grayscale mode, and then choose the color mode you want to work in before you continue. When you apply a color to a grayscale image, each pixel becomes a shade of that particular color instead of gray.

Converting Grayscale and Color Modes

When you convert a color image to grayscale, the data for light and dark values—called the **luminosity**—remain, while the color information is deleted. When you change from grayscale to a color mode, the foreground and background colors on the Tools panel change from black and white to the previously selected colors.

Tweaking Adjustments

Once you have made your color mode conversion to grayscale, you may want to make some adjustments. You can fine-tune

---

Converting a Color Image to Black and White

Using the Black & White command, you can easily convert a color image to black and white. This command lets you quickly make the color-to-black-and-white conversion while maintaining full control over how individual colors are converted. Tones can also be applied to the grayscale by applying color tones (the numeric values for each color). To use this feature, click Image on the Menu bar, point to Adjustments, and then click Black & White. The Black & White command can also be applied as an Adjustment layer.

the Brightness/Contrast, filters, and blending modes in a grayscale image.

Colorizing a Grayscale Image

In order for a grayscale image to be colorized, you must change the color mode to one that accommodates color. After you change the color mode and adjust settings in the Hue/Saturation dialog box, Photoshop determines the colorization range based on the hue of the currently selected foreground color. If you want a different colorization range, you need to change the foreground color.

QUICK TIP

A duotone image is a grayscale image that uses two ink colors (with one of the ink colors generally being black). The final output is dramatically affected by both the order in which the inks are printed and the screen angles (the angle at which the ink is applied) that you use.

Figure 27 *Gradient Map dialog box*

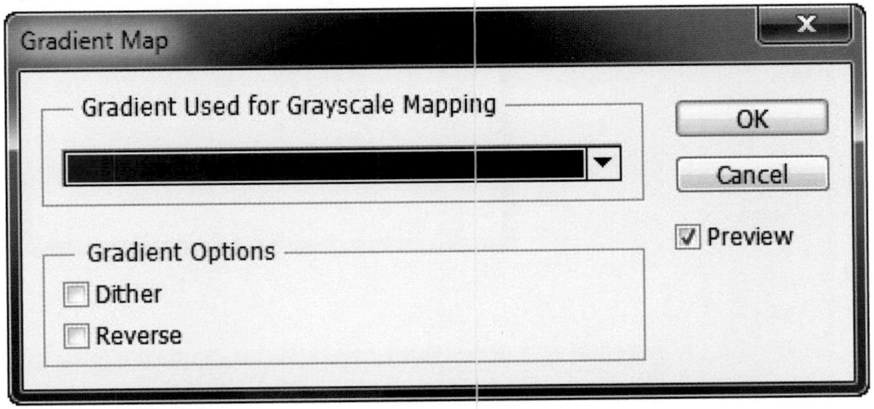

Applying a Gradient Effect

You can also use the Gradient Map to apply a colored gradient effect to a grayscale image. The Gradient Map uses gradient fills (the same ones displayed in the Gradient picker) to colorize the image, which can produce some stunning effects. You use the Gradient Map dialog box, shown in Figure 27, to apply a gradient effect to a grayscale image. You can access the Gradient Map dialog box using the Adjustments command on the Image menu.

Change the color mode

1. Open PS 5-2.psd from the drive and folder where you store your Data Files, then save it as **Basketball Star Colorized**.

2. Click **Image** on the Menu bar, point to **Mode**, then click **Grayscale**.

3. Click **Flatten** in the warning box, then click **Discard**.

   The color mode of the image is changed to grayscale, and the image is flattened so there is only a single layer. All the color information in the image has been discarded.

4. Click **Image** on the Menu bar, point to **Mode**, then click **RGB Color**.

   The color mode is changed back to RGB color, although there is still no color in the image. Compare your screen to Figure 28.

You converted the image to Grayscale, which discarded the existing color information. Then you changed the color mode to RGB color.

Figure 28 *Grayscale image converted to RGB mode*

Mode changed to RGB

Converting Color Images to Grayscale

Like everything else in Photoshop, there is more than one way of converting a color image into one that is black and white. Changing the color mode to grayscale is the quickest method. You can also make this conversion by converting to black and white or through desaturation by clicking Image on the Menu bar, pointing to Adjustments, and then clicking Black & White or Desaturate. Converting to Grayscale mode generally results in losing contrast, as does the desaturation method, while using the Black & White method retains the contrast of the original image.

Figure 29 *Hue/Saturation dialog box*

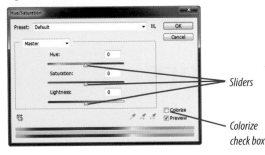

Sliders

Colorize
check box

Figure 30 *Colorized image*

Colorize a grayscale image

1. Click **Image** on the Menu bar, point to **Adjustments**, then click **Hue/Saturation** to open the Hue/Saturation dialog box, as shown in Figure 29.

2. Click the **Colorize check box** in the Hue/Saturation dialog box to add a check mark.

3. Drag the **Hue slider** until the text box displays **220**.

   TIP You can also type values in the text boxes in the Hue/Saturation dialog box. Negative numbers must be preceded by a minus sign or a hyphen. Positive numbers can be preceded by an optional plus sign (+).

4. Drag the **Saturation slider** until the text box displays **20**.

5. Drag the **Lightness slider** until the text box displays **-10**.

6. Click **OK**.

7. Compare your screen to Figure 30, then save your work.

You colorized a grayscale image by adjusting settings in the Hue/Saturation dialog box.

Understanding the Hue/Saturation Dialog Box

The Hue/Saturation dialog box is an important tool in the world of color enhancement. Useful for both color and grayscale images, the saturation slider can be used to boost a range of colors. By clicking the Master list arrow, you can isolate which colors (all, cyan, blue, magenta, red, yellow, or green) you want to modify. Using this tool requires patience and experimentation, but gives you great control over the colors in your image.

Use Filters, Opacity,
AND BLENDING MODES

What You'll Do

In this lesson, you'll adjust the brightness and contrast in the Basketball Star Colorized image, apply a Sharpen filter, and adjust the opacity of the lines applied by the filter. You'll also adjust the color balance of the Basketball Star image.

Manipulating an Image

As you work in Photoshop, you might realize that some images have fundamental problems that need correcting, while others just need to be further enhanced. For example, you might need to adjust an image's contrast and sharpness, or you might want to colorize an otherwise dull image. You can use a variety of techniques to change the way an image looks. For example, you have learned how to use the Adjustments command on the Image menu to modify hue and saturation, but you can also use this command to adjust brightness and contrast, color balance, and a host of other visual effects.

Understanding Filters

Filters are Photoshop commands that can significantly alter an image's appearance. Experimenting with Photoshop's filters is a fun way to completely change the look of an image. For example, the Watercolor filter gives the illusion that your image was painted using traditional watercolors. Sharpen filters can appear to add definition to the entire image, or just the edges. Compare the

Fixing Blurry Scanned Images

An unfortunate result of scanning a picture is that the image can become blurry. You can fix this, however, using the Unsharp Mask filter. This filter both sharpens and smoothes the image by increasing the contrast along element edges. Here's how it works: the smoothing effect removes stray marks, and the sharpening effect emphasizes contrasting neighboring pixels. Most scanners come with their own Unsharp Masks built into the scanner driver, but using Photoshop, you have access to a more powerful version of this filter. You can use Photoshop's Unsharp Mask to control the sharpening process by adjusting key settings. In most cases, your scanner's Unsharp Mask might not give you this flexibility. Regardless of the technical aspects, the result is a sharper image. You can apply the Unsharp Mask by clicking Filter on the Menu bar, pointing to Sharpen, and then clicking Unsharp Mask.

different Sharpen filters applied in Figure 31. The **Sharpen More filter** increases the contrast of adjacent pixels and can focus a blurry image. Be careful not to overuse sharpening tools (or any filter), because you can create high-contrast lines or add graininess in color or brightness.

Choosing Blending Modes

A **blending mode** controls how pixels are made either darker or lighter based on underlying colors. Photoshop provides a variety of commonly used blending modes, listed in Table 1, to combine the color of the pixels in the current layer with those in layer(s) beneath it. You can see a list of blending modes by clicking the Set the blending mode for the layer list arrow on the Layers panel, or by clicking Blending Options, and then clicking the Blend Mode list arrow. You can also see a list of blending modes by clicking the Mode list arrow on the options bar when the Gradient tool is selected, or by clicking Layer on the Menu bar, pointing to Layer Style, and then clicking Blending Options.

Understanding Blending Mode Components

You should consider the following underlying colors when planning a blending mode: **base color**, which is the original color of the image; **blend color**, which is the color you apply with a paint or edit tool; and **resulting color**, which is the color that is created as a result of applying the blend color.

Softening Filter Effects

Opacity can soften the line that the filter creates, but it doesn't affect the opacity of the entire layer. After a filter has been applied, you can modify the opacity and apply a blending mode using the Layers panel or the Fade dialog box. You can open the Fade dialog box by clicking Edit on the Menu bar, and then clicking the Fade command.

> **QUICK TIP**
>
> The Fade command appears only after a filter has been applied. When available, the command name includes the name of the applied filter.

Figure 31 *Sharpen filters*

Original image

Sharpen filter applied

Sharpen More filter applied excessively

Balancing Colors

As you adjust settings, such as hue and saturation, you might create unwanted imbalances in your image. You can adjust colors to correct or improve an image's appearance. For example, you can decrease a color by increasing the amount of its opposite color. You open the Color Balance dialog box by clicking Image on the Menu bar, pointing to Adjustments, and then clicking Color Balance. This dialog box is used to balance the color in an image.

TABLE 1: BLENDING MODES	
Blending mode	**Description**
Dissolve modes	Dissolve mode creates a grainy, mottled appearance.
Multiply and Screen modes	Multiply mode creates semitransparent shadow effects. This mode assesses the information in each channel, and then multiplies the value of the base color by the blend color. The resulting color is always *darker* than the base color. The Screen mode multiplies the value of the inverse of the blend and base colors. After it is applied, the resulting color is always *lighter* than the base color.
Overlay mode	Dark and light values preserve the highlights and shadows of the base color while mixing the base color and blend color, dark base colors are multiplied (darkened), and light areas are screened (lightened).
Soft Light and Hard Light modes	Soft Light lightens a light base color and darkens a dark base color giving the effect of shining a diffuse spotlight on an image. The Hard Light blending mode creates the effect of a harsh spotlight, useful for adding highlights or shadows by providing a greater contrast between the base and blend colors.
Color Dodge and Color Burn modes	Color Dodge mode brightens the base color to reflect the blend color. The Color Burn mode darkens base color to reflect the blend color.
Darken and Lighten modes	Darken mode selects the base color or blend color based on whichever color is darker. The Lighten mode selects a new resulting color based on the lighter of the two colors.
Difference and Exclusion modes	The Difference mode subtracts the value of the blend color from the value of the base color, or vice versa, depending on which color has the greater brightness value. The Exclusion mode creates an effect similar to that of the Difference mode, but with less contrast between the blend and base colors.
Color and Luminosity modes	The Color mode creates a resulting color with the luminance of the base color and the hue and saturation of the blend color. The Luminosity mode creates a resulting color with the hue and saturation of the base color and the luminance of the blend color.
Hue and Saturation modes	The Hue mode creates a resulting color with the luminance and saturation of the base color and the hue of the blend color. The Saturation mode creates a resulting color with the luminance and hue of the base color and the saturation of the blend color.

© Cengage Learning 2013

Figure 32 *Brightness/Contrast dialog box*

Figure 33 *Shadows/Highlight dialog box*

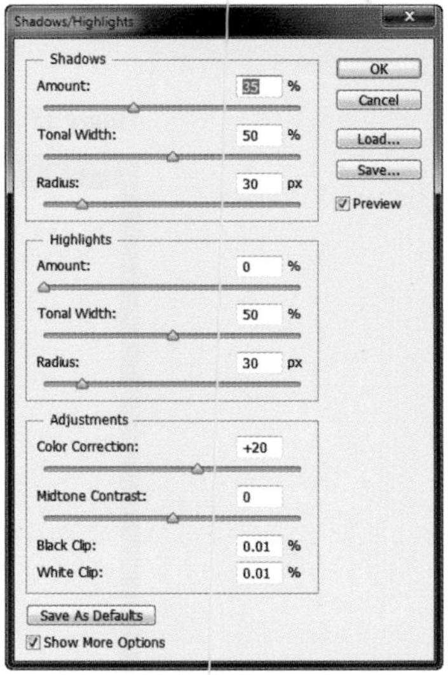

Adjust brightness and contrast

1. Click **Image** on the Menu bar, point to **Adjustments**, then click **Brightness/Contrast** to open the Brightness/Contrast dialog box.

2. Drag the **Brightness slider** until **15** appears in the Brightness text box.

3. Drag the **Contrast slider** until **30** appears in the Contrast text box. Compare your screen to Figure 32.

4. Click **OK**.

You adjusted settings in the Brightness/Contrast dialog box. The image now looks much brighter, with a higher degree of contrast, which obscures some of the finer detail in the image.

Correcting Shadows and Highlights

The ability to correct shadows and highlights will delight photographers everywhere. This image correction feature (opened by clicking Image on the Menu bar, pointing to Adjustments, and then clicking Shadows/Highlights) lets you modify overall lighting and make subtle adjustments. Figure 33 shows the Shadows/Highlights dialog box with the Show More Options check box selected. Check out this one-stop shopping for shadow and highlight adjustments!

Work with a filter, a blending mode, and an opacity setting

1. Click **Filter** on the Menu bar, point to **Sharpen**, then click **Sharpen More**.

   The border and other features of the image are intensified.

2. Click **Edit** on the Menu bar, then click **Fade Sharpen More** to open the Fade dialog box, as shown in Figure 34.

3. Drag the **Opacity slider** until **45** appears in the Opacity text box.

   The opacity setting softened the lines applied by the Sharpen More filter.

   TIP You may have noticed the Fill list arrow (beneath the Opacity list arrow) on the Layers panel. The Fill list arrow lets you adjust the transparency of a layer (as does the Opacity setting) while ignoring any special effects (such as a drop shadow or stroke) you may have added.

4. Click the **Mode list arrow**, then click **Dissolve**.

   The Dissolve setting blends the surrounding pixels. Zoom in on the image if you need a closer look at the changes.

5. Click **OK**.

6. Save your work, then compare your image to Figure 35.

You applied the Sharpen More filter, then adjusted the opacity and changed the color mode in the Fade dialog box. The edge in the image looks crisper than before, with a greater level of detail.

Figure 34 *Fade dialog box*

Figure 35 *Image settings adjusted*

Incorporating Color Techniques

Figure 36 *Color Balance dialog box*

Color Balance

Color Balance

Color Levels: +70 -40 +5

Cyan ———————————△— Red
Magenta ———△————————— Green
Yellow ——————△———— Blue

OK
Cancel
☑ Preview

Tone Balance

○ Shadows   ● Midtones   ○ Highlights
☑ Preserve Luminosity

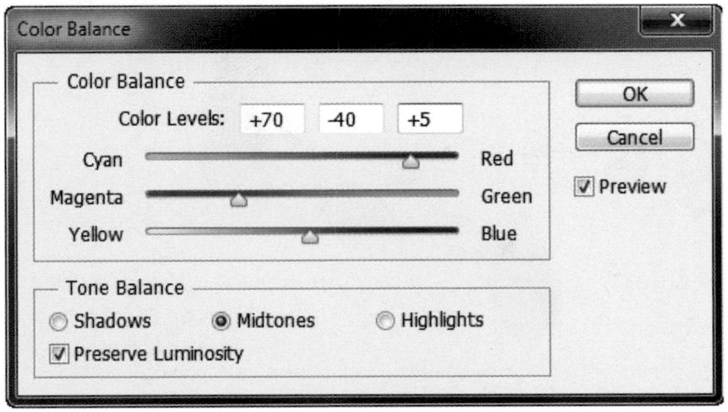

Figure 37 *Image with colors balanced*

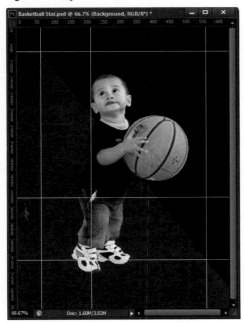

Adjust color balance

1. Switch to the **Basketball Star image**, with the Background layer active, then change the zoom factor to **66.7%**.

   The image you worked with earlier in this chapter becomes active.

2. Click **Image** on the Menu bar, point to **Adjustments**, then click **Color Balance**.

3. Drag the **Cyan-Red slider** until **+70** appears in the first text box.

4. Drag the **Magenta-Green slider** until **−40** appears in the middle text box.

5. Drag the **Yellow-Blue slider** until **+5** appears in the last text box, as shown in Figure 36.

   Subtle changes were made in the color balance in the image.

6. Click **OK**.

7. Save your work, then compare your image to Figure 37.

You balanced the colors in the Basketball Star image by adjusting settings in the Color Balance dialog box.

Match COLORS

What You'll Do

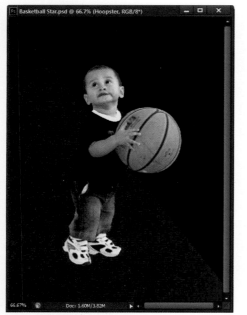

In this lesson, you'll make selections in source and target images, and then use the Match Color command to replace the target color.

Finding the Right Color

If it hasn't happened already, at some point you'll be working on an image and wish you could grab a color from another image to use in this one. Just as you can use the Eyedropper tool to sample any color in the current image for the foreground and background, you can sample a color from any other image to use in the current one. Perhaps the skin tones in one image look washed out; you can use the Match Color command to replace those tones with skin tone colors from another image. Or maybe the jacket color in one image would look better using a color in another image.

Using Selections to Match Colors

Remember that this is Photoshop, where everything is about layers and selections.

To replace a color in one image with one you've matched from another, you work with—you guessed it—layers and selections.

Suppose you've located the perfect color in another image. The image you are working with is the **target**, and the image that contains your perfect color is the **source**. By activating the layer on which the color lies in the source image, and making a selection around the color, you can have Photoshop match the color in the source and replace a color in the target. To accomplish this, you use the Match Color command, which is available by pointing to Adjustments on the Image menu.

Figure 38 *Selection in source image*

PS 5-3.tif @ 100% ...

Selected area

Figure 39 *Match Color dialog box*

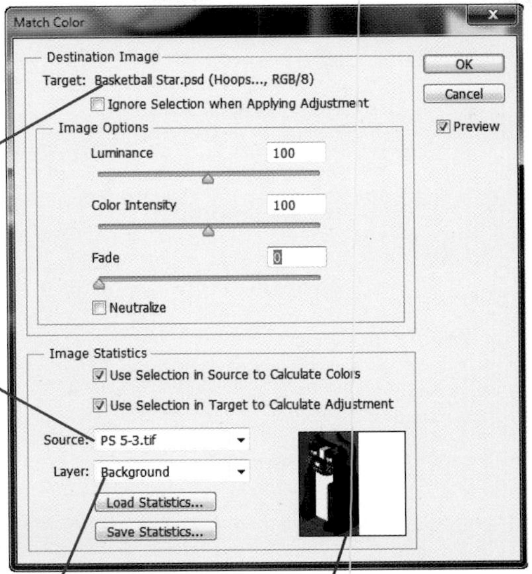

Match Color

OK
Cancel
☑ Preview

Destination Image

Target: Basketball Star.psd (Hoops..., RGB/8)

☐ Ignore Selection when Applying Adjustment

Image Options

Luminance   100

Color Intensity   100

Fade   0

☐ Neutralize

Name of
target
image

Image Statistics

☑ Use Selection in Source to Calculate Colors

☑ Use Selection in Target to Calculate Adjustment

Source: PS 5-3.tif

Layer: Background

Load Statistics...
Save Statistics...

Name of
source
image

Figure 40 *Image with matched color*

Basketball Star.psd @ 66.7% (Hoopster, RGB/8*) *

Layer containing
selection in source

Sample of layer in source

Modified
selection

Match a color

1. Click the **Hoopster layer** on the Layers panel, then zoom (once) into the boy's shirt collar.

2. Click **Select** on the Menu bar, then click **Load Selection**.

3. Click the **Channel list arrow**, click **collar**, then click **OK**.

4. Open PS 5-3.tif from the drive and folder where you store your Data Files, zoom into the image (if necessary), select the Magic Wand tool, change the tolerance to **4**, verify that the **Anti-alias** and **Contiguous check boxes** on the options bar are selected, then click the **yellow part of the cat's eye (at 105 X/95 Y)** with the **Magic Wand pointer** ✺. Compare your selection to Figure 38.

5. Activate the **Basketball Star image**, click **Image** on the Menu bar, point to **Adjustments**, then click **Match Color**.

6. Click the **Source list arrow**, then click **PS 5-3.tif**. Compare your settings to Figure 39.

7. Click **OK**.

8. Deselect the selection, turn off the rulers and the guides, save your work, then compare your image to Figure 40.

9. Close all open images, display the **Essentials workspace**, then exit Photoshop.

You loaded a saved selection, then used the Match Color dialog box to replace a color in one image with a color from another image. The Match Color dialog box makes it easy to sample colors from other images, giving you even more options for incorporating color into an image.

POWER USER SHORTCUTS

To do this:	Use this method:	To do this:	Use this method:
Apply a sharpen filter	Filter ➢ Sharpen	Hide or show rulers	[Ctrl][R] (Win) or ⌘ [R] (Mac)
Balance colors	Image ➢ Adjustments ➢ Color Balance	Hide or show the Color panel	[F6]
Change color mode	Image ➢ Mode	Lock transparent pixels check box on/off	[/]
Choose a background color from the Swatches panel	[Ctrl]Color swatch (Win) or ⌘ Color swatch (Mac)	Make Swatches panel active	Window ➢ Swatches
Delete a swatch from the Swatches panel	[Alt], click swatch with ✂ (Win) [option], click swatch with ✂ (Mac)	Paint Bucket tool	or **G**
Eyedropper tool	or **I**	Return background and foreground colors to default	or **D**
Fill with background color	[Shift][Backspace] (Win) or ⌘ [delete] (Mac)	Show a layer	
Fill with foreground color	[Alt][Backspace] (Win), [option][delete] (Mac)	Show hidden Paint Bucket/Gradient tools	[Shift] **G**
Gradient tool	or **G**	Switch between open files	[Ctrl][Tab] (Win) or [control][tab] (Mac)
Guide pointer	≑ or ╫	Switch foreground and background colors	or **X**
Hide a layer			

Key: Menu items are indicated by ➢ between the menu name and its command. Blue bold letters are shortcuts for selecting tools on the Tools panel.
© Cengage Learning 2013

Incorporating Color Techniques

Work with color to transform an image.

1. Start Photoshop.
2. Open PS 5-4.psd from the drive and folder where you store your Data Files, then save it as **Firetruck**.
3. Make sure the rulers display in pixels, and that the guides and the default foreground and background colors display.
4. Use the Eyedropper tool to sample the red color at 90 X/165 Y using the guides to help.
5. Use the Paint Bucket tool to apply the new foreground color to the Background layer.
6. Undo your last step using either the Edit menu or the History panel. (*Hint*: You can switch to another workspace that displays the necessary panels.)
7. Switch the foreground and background colors.
8. Save your work.

Use the Color Picker and the Swatches panel.

1. Use the Set foreground color button to open the Color Picker dialog box.
2. Click the R:, G:, and B: option buttons, one at a time. Note how the color panel changes.

3. With the B: option button selected, click the panel in the upper-left corner, then click OK.
4. Switch the foreground and background colors.
5. Add the foreground color (red) to the Swatches panel using a meaningful name of your choice.

Place a border around an image.

1. Make the Firetruck layer active.
2. Revert to the default foreground and background colors.
3. Create a border by applying a 2-pixel outside stroke to the firetruck.
4. Save your work.

Blend colors using the Gradient tool.

1. Change the foreground color to the fourth swatch from the left in the top row of the Swatches panel (RGB Cyan). (Your swatch location may vary.)
2. Switch foreground and background colors.
3. Use the new red swatch that you added previously as the foreground color.
4. Make the Background layer active, and verify that the blending mode is Normal.

5. Use the Gradient tool and the Radial Gradient style with its default settings, then using the guides to help, drag the pointer from 90 X/70 Y to 145 X/165 Y.
6. Save your work, and turn off the guides and rulers display.

Add color to a grayscale image.

1. Open PS 5–5.psd, then save it as **Firetruck Colorized**.
2. Change the color mode to RGB Color.
3. Open the Hue/Saturation dialog box, then select the Colorize check box.
4. Drag the sliders so the text boxes show the following values: 200, 56, and −30, then click OK.
5. Save your work.

Use filters, opacity, and blending modes.

1. Use the Sharpen filter to sharpen the image.
2. Open the Fade dialog box by using the Edit menu, change the opacity to 60%, change the mode to Overlay, then save your work.
3. Open the Color Balance dialog box.
4. Change the color level settings so the text boxes show the following values: +70, +25, and -15.
5. Turn off the guides and the rulers if necessary.
6. Save your work.

Match colors.

1. Open PS 5-6.tif, then use the Magic Wand tool to select the gray in the cat's left ear.
2. Select the white areas of the firetruck cab in Firetruck.psd. (*Hint*: You can press [Shift] and click multiple areas using the Magic Wand tool.)
3. Use the Match Color dialog box to change the white in the Firetruck layer of the firetruck image to gray (in the cat's ear), then lock the Firetruck layer. Deselect the selection and compare your images to Figure 41. (The brightness of your colors may vary.)
4. Save your work.

Figure 41 *Completed Skills Review*
Image courtesy of Elizabeth Eisner Reding

Incorporating Color Techniques

You are finally able to leave your current job and pursue your lifelong dream of opening a fix-it business. While you're waiting for business to increase, you start to work on a website design.

1. Open PS 5-7.psd, then save it as **Fix It!**.
2. Move the objects to any location to achieve a layout you think looks attractive and eye-catching.
3. Sample the blue pliers in the tool belt, then switch the foreground and background colors.
4. Sample another item in the image.
5. Use any Gradient tool to create an interesting effect on the Background layer.
6. Save the image, then compare your screen to the sample shown in Figure 42.

Figure 42 *Sample Project Builder 1*

Incorporating Color Techniques

You're working on the budget at the PB&J Preschool, when you notice a staff member struggling to redesign the school's website. Although the basic website is complete, it doesn't convey the high energy of the school. You offer to help, and soon find yourself in charge of creating an exciting background for the image.

1. Open PS 5-8.psd, then save it as **Preschool**.
2. Apply a foreground color of your choice to the Background layer.
3. Add a new layer above the Background layer, then select a background color and apply a gradient you have not used before to the layer. (*Hint*: Remember that you can immediately undo a gradient that you don't want.)
4. Add the foreground and background colors to the Swatches panel.
5. Apply a Sharpen filter to the Boy at blackboard layer and adjust the opacity of the filter.
6. Move any objects as you see fit.
7. Save your work.
8. Compare your screen to the sample shown in Figure 43.

Figure 43 *Sample Project Builder 2*

A local Top 40 morning radio show recently conducted a survey about chocolate, and discovered that only one in seven people knew about its health benefits. Now everyone is talking about chocolate. The station's web designer wants to incorporate chocolates into her fall campaign, and has asked you to create a design that will be featured on the radio station's website. You decide to highlight as many varieties as possible.

1. Open PS 5-9.psd, then save it as **Chocolate**.
2. If you choose, you can add any appropriate images that have been scanned or captured using a digital camera.
3. Activate the Background layer, then sample colors from the image for foreground and background colors. (*Hint*: Try to sample unusual colors, to widen your design horizons.)
4. Display the rulers, then move the existing guides to indicate the coordinates of the colors you sampled.
5. Add the sampled colors to the Swatches panel.
6. Create a gradient fill by using both the foreground and background colors and the gradient style of your choice.
7. Defringe the Chocolates layer, if necessary.
8. Hide the rulers and guides, save your work, then compare your image to the sample shown in Figure 44.

Figure 44 *Sample Design Project*

Chcolate.psd @ 100% (Chocolates, RGB/8)

100%   Doc: 791.0K/1.63M

An educational toy and game store has hired you to create a design that will be used on the company's website to announce this year's Most Unusual Hobby contest. After reviewing the photos from last year's awards ceremony, you decide to build a design using the winner of the Handicrafts Award. You'll use your knowledge of Photoshop color modes to convert the color mode, adjust color in the image, and add a shaded background.

1. Open PS 5-10.psd, then save it as **Rubberband**.
2. Convert the image to Grayscale mode. (*Hint*: When Photoshop prompts you to flatten the layers, click Don't Flatten.)

3. Convert the image to RGB Color mode. (*Hint*: When Photoshop prompts you to flatten the layers, click Don't Flatten.)
4. Colorize the image and adjust the Hue, Saturation, and Lightness settings as desired.
5. Adjust Brightness/Contrast settings as desired.
6. Adjust Color Balance settings as desired.
7. Sample the image to create a new foreground color, then add a color of your choice as the background color.

8. Apply any Sharpen filter and adjust the opacity for that filter.
9. Add a reflected gradient to the Background layer that follows the path of one of the main bands on the ball.
10. Save your work, then compare your image to the sample shown in Figure 45.
11. Be prepared to discuss the color-correcting methods you used and why you chose them.

Figure 45 *Sample Portfolio Project*

Rubberband.psd @ 100% (Background, RGB/8)

100%   Doc: 689.1K/1.57M

CHAPTER  **6** PLACING TYPE
IN AN IMAGE

1. Learn about type and how it is created
2. Change spacing and adjust baseline shift
3. Use the Drop Shadow style
4. Apply anti-aliasing to type
5. Modify type with Bevel and Emboss and 3D Extrusion
6. Apply special effects to type using filters
7. Create text on a path

6

PLACING TYPE
IN AN IMAGE

Learning About Type

Text plays an important design role when combined with images for posters, magazine and newspaper advertisements, and other graphics materials that need to communicate detailed information. In Photoshop, text is referred to as **type**. You can use type to express the ideas conveyed in a file's imagery or to deliver an additional message. You can manipulate type in many ways to reflect or reinforce the meaning behind an image. As in other programs, type has its own unique characteristics in Photoshop. For example, you can change its appearance by using different fonts (also called **typefaces**) and colors.

Understanding the Purpose of Type

Type is typically used along with imagery to deliver a message quickly and with flare. Because type is used sparingly (often there's not a lot of room for it), its appearance is very important; color and imagery are frequently used to *complement* or *reinforce* the message within the text. Type should be limited, direct, and to the point. It should be large enough for easy reading, but should not overwhelm or distract from the central image. For example, a vibrant and daring advertisement should contain just enough type to interest the reader, without demanding too much reading.

Getting the Most Out of Type

Words can express an idea, but the appearance of the type is what drives the point home. After you decide on the content you want to use and create the type, you can experiment with its appearance by changing its **font** (a set of characters with a similar appearance, size, and color). You can also apply special effects that make it stand out or appear to pop off the page.

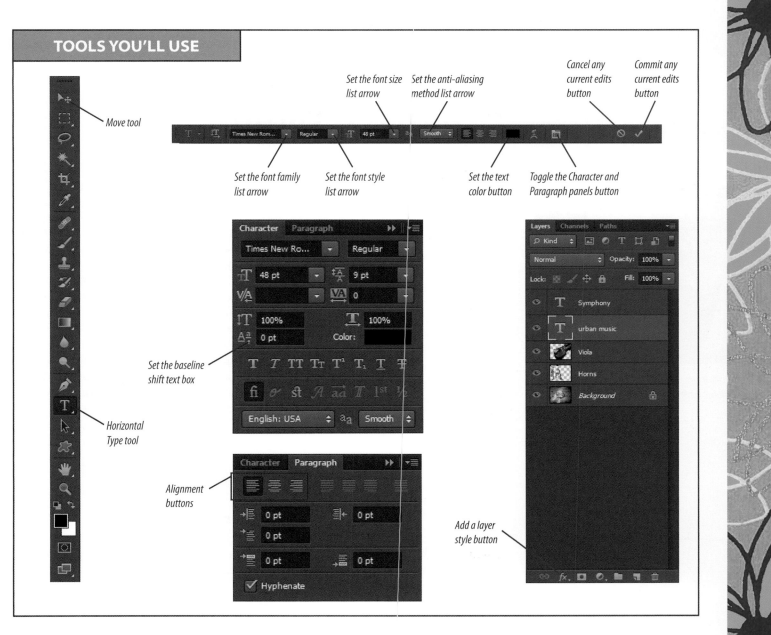

TOOLS YOU'LL USE

Move tool

Set the font size list arrow

Set the anti-aliasing method list arrow

Cancel any current edits button

Commit any current edits button

Set the font family list arrow

Set the font style list arrow

Set the text color button

Toggle the Character and Paragraph panels button

Set the baseline shift text box

Horizontal Type tool

Alignment buttons

Add a layer style button

Learn About Type and
HOW IT IS CREATED

What You'll Do

In this lesson, you'll create a type layer, and then change the font family, size, and color of the type.

Introducing Type Types

Outline type is mathematically defined, which means that it can be scaled to any size without losing its sharp, smooth edges. Some programs, such as Adobe Illustrator, create outline type, also known as **vector fonts**. **Bitmap type** is composed of pixels, and, like bitmap images, can develop jagged edges when enlarged. The type you create in Photoshop is initially outline type, but it is converted into bitmap type when you apply special filters. Using the type tools and the options bar, you can create horizontal or vertical type and modify font size and alignment. You use the Color Picker dialog box to change type color. When you create type in Photoshop, it is automatically placed on a new type layer on the Layers panel.

> **QUICK TIP**
>
> Keeping type on separate layers makes it much easier to modify and change its position within the image.

Getting to Know Font Families

Each **font family** represents a complete set of characters, letters, and symbols for a particular typeface. Font families are generally divided into three categories: serif, sans serif, and symbol. Characters in **serif fonts** have a tail, or stroke, at the ends of some characters. These tails make it easier for the eye to recognize words. For this reason, serif fonts are generally used in text passages as in the body text of this book. Emphasized text is a sans serif font. **Sans serif fonts** do not have tails and are commonly used in headlines. **Symbol fonts** are used to display unique characters (such as $, +, or ™). Table 1 lists some commonly used serif and sans serif fonts. After you select the Horizontal Type tool, you can change font families using the options bar.

> **QUICK TIP**
>
> The Verdana typeface was designed to be readable on a computer screen.

Measuring Type Size

The size of each character within a font is measured in **points**. **PostScript**, a programming language that optimizes printed text and graphics, was introduced by Adobe in 1984. In

PostScript measurement, one inch is equivalent to 72 points or six picas. Therefore, one pica is equivalent to 12 points. In traditional character measurement, one inch is equivalent to 72.27 points. The default Photoshop type size is 12 points. In Photoshop, you have the option of using PostScript or traditional character measurement.

Acquiring Fonts

Your computer has many fonts installed on it, but no matter how many fonts you have, you can probably use more. Fonts can be purchased from private companies, individual designers, computer stores, or catalog companies. Fonts are delivered on CD, DVD, or over the Internet. Using your favorite search engine and the keywords "type foundry", you can locate websites where you can purchase or download fonts. Many websites offer specialty fonts, while others offer fonts free of charge or for a nominal fee. Figure 1 shows font samples in Photoshop (your list may differ).

TABLE 1: COMMONLY USED SERIF AND SANS SERIF FONTS

Serif fonts	Sample	Sans serif fonts	Sample
Lucida Handwriting	*Adobe Photoshop*	Arial	Adobe Photoshop
Rockwell	Adobe Photoshop	Bauhaus	Adobe Photoshop
Times New Roman	Adobe Photoshop	Century Gothic	Adobe Photoshop
Georgia	Adobe Photoshop	Verdana	Adobe Photoshop

© Cengage Learning 2013

Figure 1 *Font samples in Photoshop*

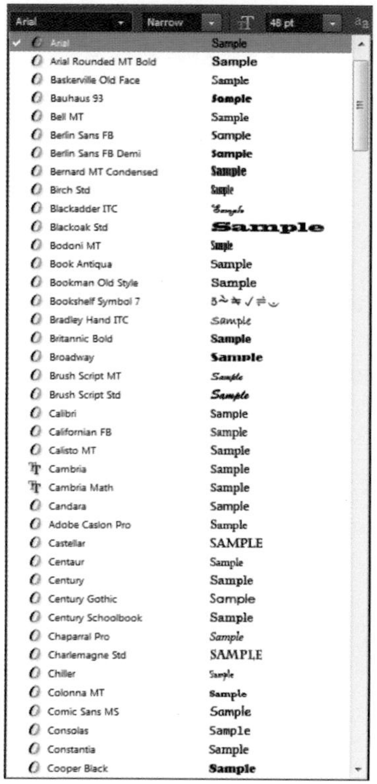

Create and modify type

1. Start Photoshop, open PS 6-1.psd from the drive and folder where you store your Data Files, then save the file as **Urban Music**.
2. Display the document size in the status bar, guides, and rulers in pixels (if they are not already displayed), then change the workspace to **Typography**.

TIP You can quickly toggle the rulers on and off by pressing [Ctrl][R] (Win) or ⌘ [R].

3. Click the **Default Foreground and Background Colors button** on the Tools panel.
4. Click the **Horizontal Type tool** T on the Tools panel.
5. Click the **Set the font family list arrow** on the options bar, click **Arial** (a sans serif font), click the **Set the font style list arrow**, then click **Italic**.

TIP If Arial is not available, make a reasonable substitution.

6. Click the **Set the font size list arrow** on the options bar, then click **48 pt**.
7. Click the **image** with the **Horizontal Type pointer** at approximately **430 X/510 Y**, then type **Live Music** as shown in Figure 2.

You created a type layer by using the Horizontal Type tool on the Tools panel and modified the font family, font style, and font size.

Figure 2 *New type in image*

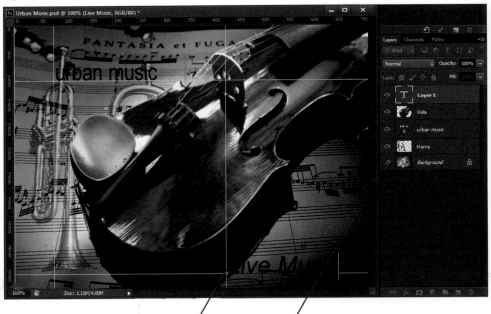

New type   New type layer

Placing Type in an Image

Figure 3 *Type with new color*

Type with new color

Using the Swatches Panel to Change Type Color

You can also use the Swatches panel to change type color. Select the type, and then click a color on the Swatches panel. The new color that you click will appear in the Set foreground color button on the Tools panel and will be applied to type that is currently selected.

Change type color using an existing color in the image

1. Press **[Ctrl][A]** (Win) or ⌘ **[A]** (Mac) to select all the text.

2. Click the **Set the font family list arrow** on the options bar, scroll down, then click **Times New Roman**.

   TIP Click *in* the Set the font family text box and you can select a different font by typing the first few characters of the font name.

3. Click the **Set the font style list arrow**, then click **Bold Italic**.

4. Click the **Set the text color button** ▮ on the options bar.

   As you position the pointer over the image, the pointer automatically becomes an Eyedropper pointer.

5. Reposition the Color Picker (Text Color) dialog box if necessary, then click the **image** with the **Eyedropper pointer** 🖋 anywhere in the yellow area of the viola at approximately **465 X/190 Y**.

   The new color is now the active color in the Color Picker (Text Color) dialog box.

6. Click **OK** in the Color Picker (Text Color) dialog box.

7. Click the **Commit any current edits button** ✔ on the options bar.

   Click the Commit any current edits button to accept your changes and make them permanent.

8. Save your work, then compare your image to Figure 3.

You changed the font family, modified the color of the type by using an existing image color, and committed the current edits.

Change Spacing and
ADJUST BASELINE SHIFT

What You'll Do

In this lesson, you'll adjust the spacing between characters, change the baseline of type, and then apply the same style to two different characters.

Adjusting Spacing

Competition for readers on the visual landscape is fierce. To get and maintain an edge over other designers, Photoshop provides tools that let you make adjustments to your type, offering you the opportunity to make your type more distinctive. These adjustments might not be very dramatic, but they can influence readers in subtle ways. For example, type that is too small and difficult to read might make the reader impatient (at the very least), and he or she might not even look at the image (at the very worst). You can make finite adjustments, called **type spacing**, to the space between characters and between lines of type. Adjusting type spacing affects the ease with which words are read.

Understanding Character and Line Spacing

Fonts in desktop publishing and word-processing programs use proportional spacing, whereas typewriters use monotype spacing. In **monotype spacing**, each character occupies the same amount of space. This means that wide characters such as "o" and "w" take up the same real estate on the page as narrow ones such as "i" and "l". In **proportional spacing**, each character can take up a different amount of space, depending on its width. **Kerning** controls the amount of space between characters and can affect several characters, a word, or an entire paragraph. **Tracking** inserts a *uniform* amount of space between selected characters. Figure 4 shows an example of type before and after it has been kerned. The second line of text takes up less room and has less space between its characters, making it easier to read. You can also change the amount of space, called **leading**, between lines of type, to add or decrease the distance between lines of text.

Using the Character Panel

The **Character panel**, shown in Figure 5, helps you manually or automatically control type properties such as kerning, tracking, and leading. You open the Character panel from the Type tool options bar, the dock, or from the Window menu on the Menu bar.

QUICK TIP

Click the Set the font family list arrow on the options bar or Character panel to see previews of installed fonts.

Understanding Type Styles

You've probably noticed that within any publication you'll see certain formatting similarities occurring repeatedly. Since many people may be collaborating to make a publication possible, styles are often used to ensure consistency. A **style** is a collection of formatting attributes that can be saved and applied to specific characters or an entire paragraph. Perhaps a magazine has a five space indent at the start of each paragraph, or maybe sidebars that occur on certain pages have the same horizontal line spacing and justification. Photoshop allows you to define both character and paragraph styles that can be applied at any time. You can create and apply type styles by clicking Window on the Menu bar, then clicking either Character Styles or Paragraph Styles. Figure 6 shows the Paragraph Styles panel with two customized styles.

Adjusting the Baseline Shift

Type rests on an invisible line called a **baseline**. Using the Character panel, you can adjust the **baseline shift**, the vertical distance that type moves from its baseline. You can add interest to type by changing the baseline shift. Negative adjustments to the baseline move characters *below* the baseline, while positive adjustments move characters *above* the baseline.

QUICK TIP

Clicking the Set the text color button on either the options bar or the Character panel opens the Color Picker (Text Color) dialog box.

Figure 5 *Character panel*

Figure 6 *Paragraph Styles panel*

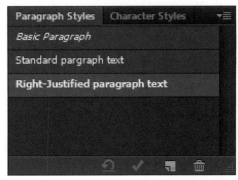

Figure 4 *Kerned characters*

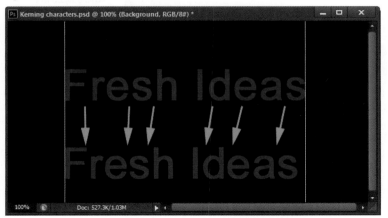

Use the
DROP SHADOW STYLE

What You'll Do

In this lesson, you'll apply the drop shadow style to a type layer, and then modify drop shadow settings.

Adding Effects to Type

Layer styles (effects which can be applied to a type or image layer) can greatly enhance the appearance of type and improve its effectiveness. A type layer is indicated by the appearance of the T icon in the layer's thumbnail box on the Layers panel. When a layer style is applied to any layer, the Indicates layer effects icon (*fx*) appears in that layer when it is active. The Layers panel is a great source of information. You can see which effects have been applied to a layer by clicking the arrow to the right of the Indicates layer effects icon on the Layers panel whether the layer is active or inactive. Figure 10 shows a type layer that has a layer style applied to it. Layer styles are linked to the contents of a layer, which means that if a type layer is moved or modified, the layer's style will still be applied to the type.

Figure 10 *Effect applied to a type layer*

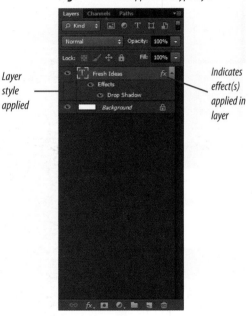

Layer style applied

Indicates effect(s) applied in layer

Applying a Style

You can apply a style, such as a drop shadow, to the active layer, by clicking Layer on the Menu bar, pointing to Layer Style, and then clicking a style. The settings in the Layer Style dialog box are "sticky," meaning that they display the settings that you last used. An alternative method to using the Menu bar is to select the layer on the Layers panel that you want to apply the style to, click the Add a layer style button, and then click a style. Regardless of which method you use, the Layer Style dialog box opens. You use this dialog box to add all kinds of effects to type. Depending on which style you've chosen, the Layer Style dialog box displays options appropriate to that style.

QUICK TIP

You can apply styles to objects as well as to type.

Using the Drop Shadow

One method of placing emphasis on type is to add a drop shadow to it. A **drop shadow** creates an illusion that another colored layer of identical text is behind the selected type. The drop shadow default color is black, but it can be changed to another color using the Color Picker dialog box, or any of the other methods for changing color.

Controlling a Drop Shadow

You can control many aspects of a drop shadow's appearance, including its angle, its distance behind the type, the amount of blur it contains, and its opacity. The **angle** indicates the direction of the light source and determines where the shadow falls relative to the text, and the **distance** determines how far the shadow falls from the text. The **spread** determines the width of the shadow text, and the **size** determines the clarity of the shadow. Figure 11 shows samples of two different drop shadow effects. The first line of type uses the default background color (black), has an angle of 160 degrees, a distance of 10 pixels, a spread of 0%, and a size of five pixels. The second line of type uses an orange background color, has an angle of 120 degrees, a distance of 20 pixels, a spread of 10%, and a size of five pixels. As you modify the drop shadow, the preview window displays the changes.

Figure 11 *Sample drop shadows*

Add a drop shadow

1. Click the **layer thumbnail** on the urban music type layer.

2. Double-click **48** in the Set the font size text box in the Character panel, type **55**, then press [**Enter**] (Win) or [**return**] (Mac).

3. Click the **Add a layer style button** *fx* on the Layers panel.

4. Click **Drop Shadow**.

5. Compare your Layer Style dialog box to Figure 12, and *do not close* the dialog box. (The settings are Blend Mode = Multiply, Opacity = 75, Angle = 30, Distance = 5, Spread = 0, Size = 5.)

   The default drop shadow settings are applied to the type. Table 2 describes the drop shadow settings.

TIP You can also open the Layer Style dialog box by double-clicking a layer on the Layers panel.

You created a drop shadow by using the Add a layer style button on the Layers panel and the Layer Style dialog box.

Figure 12 *Drop shadow settings*

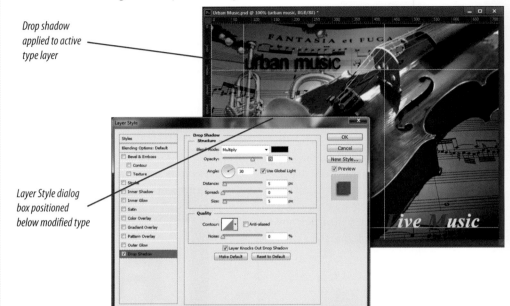

Drop shadow applied to active type layer

Layer Style dialog box positioned below modified type

TABLE 2: DROP SHADOW SETTINGS		
Setting	**Scale**	**Explanation**
Opacity	0–100%	Controls the opacity of the shadow. At 0%, the shadow is invisible.
Angle	0–360 degrees	At 0 degrees, the shadow appears on the baseline of the original text. At 90 degrees, the shadow appears directly below the original text.
Distance	0–30,000 pixels	A larger pixel size increases the distance from which the shadow text falls relative to the original text.
Spread	0–100%	A larger percentage increases the width of the shadow text.
Size	0–250 pixels	A larger pixel size increases the blur of the shadow text.

© Cengage Learning 2013

Figure 13 *Layer Style dialog box*

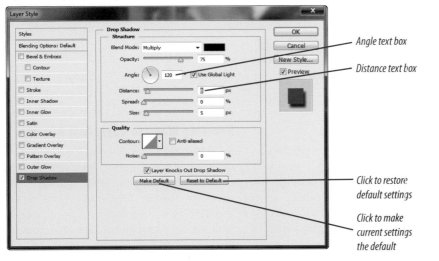

Angle text box

Distance text box

Click to restore
default settings

Click to make
current settings
the default

Figure 14 *Drop shadow added to type layer*

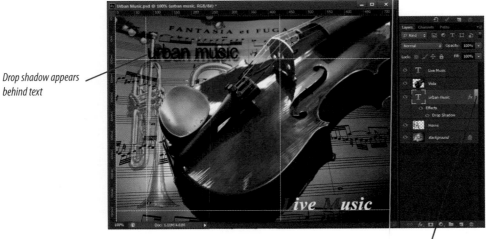

Drop shadow appears
behind text

Collapses effect(s)
applied to layer

Modify drop shadow settings

1. Double-click the **number in the Angle text box**, then type **120**.

   Each style in the Layer Style dialog box shows different options in the center section. These options are displayed as you select each style from the Styles pane on the left.

TIP You can also set the angle by dragging the dial slider.

2. Double-click the **number in the Distance text box**, then type **8**. See Figure 13.

TIP You can create your own layer style in the Layer Style dialog box, by selecting style settings, clicking New Style, typing a new name or accepting the default, then clicking OK. The new style appears as a preset in the Styles list of the Layer Style dialog box.

3. Click **OK**, then compare your screen to Figure 14.

4. Click the **Reveals layers effects in the panel arrow** ▲ , located to the right of the Indicates layer effects icon on the urban music layer, to collapse the list of layer styles.

5. Save your work.

You used the Layer Style dialog box to modify the settings for the drop shadow.

Apply Anti-Aliasing
TO TYPE

What You'll Do

In this lesson, you'll view the effects of the anti-aliasing feature, and then use the History panel to return the type to its original state.

Eliminating the "Jaggies"

In the good old days of dot-matrix printers, jagged edges were obvious in many print ads. You can still see these jagged edges in designs produced on less sophisticated printers. To prevent the jagged edges (sometimes called "jaggies") that often accompany bitmap type, Photoshop offers an anti-aliasing feature. **Anti-aliasing** partially fills in pixel edges with additional colors, resulting in smooth-edge type and an increased number of colors in the image. Anti-aliasing is useful for improving the display of large type in print media; however, this can increase the file size.

Knowing When to Apply Anti-Aliasing

As a rule, type that has a point size greater than 12 should have some anti-aliasing method applied. Sometimes, smaller type sizes can become blurry or muddy when anti-aliasing is used. As part of the process, anti-aliasing adds intermediate colors to your image in an effort to reduce the jagged edges. As a designer, you need to weigh these three factors (type size, file size, and image quality) when determining if you should apply anti-aliasing.

DESIGN**TIP**

Using Type on the Web

While any typeface you use affects your reader, your choice of type has a larger impact on the web because it is more interactive than the print media. Since the goal of a website is to make your reader linger as long as possible, do you really want to offend or annoy that person with an ugly typeface? Of course not. So, you want to make sure that the typeface is not only appropriate, but can be seen as you intended.

In many cases, a typeface can only be seen on a web page if that font is installed on the reader's computer. Web-safe typefaces (which most computers can display with accuracy) are Times New Roman, Arial, Arial Black, or Helvetica (Mac), Lucida Console, Lucida Sans Unicode, Palatino Linotype, Book Antiqua, Verdana, and Comic Sans. There are other typefaces that can be downloaded from a variety of websites for free, such as Georgia and Trebuchet.

Understanding Anti-Aliasing

Anti-aliasing improves the display of type against the background. You can use five anti-aliasing methods: None, Sharp, Crisp, Strong, and Smooth. An example of each method is shown in Figure 15. The **None** setting applies no anti-aliasing, and can result in type that has jagged edges. The **Sharp** setting displays type with the best possible resolution. The **Crisp** setting gives type more definition and makes type appear sharper. The **Strong** setting makes type appear heavier, much like the bold attribute. The **Smooth** setting gives type more rounded edges.

QUICK TIP

Generally, the type used in your image should be the messenger, not the message. As you work with type, keep in mind that using more than two fonts in one image might be distracting or make the overall appearance unprofessional.

Figure 15 *Anti-aliasing effects*

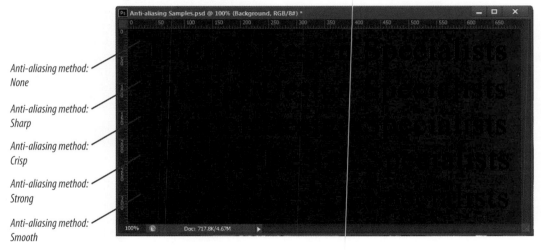

Anti-aliasing method:
None

Anti-aliasing method:
Sharp

Anti-aliasing method:
Crisp

Anti-aliasing method:
Strong

Anti-aliasing method:
Smooth

Apply anti-aliasing

1. Double-click the **layer thumbnail** on the urban music layer to select the text.
2. Click the **Set the anti-aliasing method list arrow**  on the options bar.

TIP You've probably noticed that some items, such as the Set the anti-aliasing method list arrow, the Set the text color button, and the Set the font size list arrow are duplicated on the options bar and the Character panel. So which should you use? Whichever one you feel most comfortable using. These tasks are performed identically regardless of the feature's origin.

3. Click **Crisp**, then compare your work to Figure 16.
4. Click the **Commit any current edits button** on the options bar.

You applied the Strong anti-aliasing setting to see how the setting affected the appearance of type.

Figure 16 *Effect of Crisp anti-aliasing*

Type appearance altered

Different Strokes for Different Folks

You're probably already aware that you can use multiple methods to achieve the same goals in Photoshop. For instance, if you want to see the Type options bar so you can edit a type layer, you can either double-click a type layer thumbnail or select the type layer and then click the Horizontal Type tool. The method you use determines what you'll see in the History panel.

Figure 17 *Deleting a state from the History panel*

Dragging state to Delete current state button

Undo anti-aliasing

1. Click **Legacy** in the Workspace switcher.

   The History panel is now visible.

   TIP You can also display the History panel by clicking the History icon on the dock (if it's displayed). Once displayed, you can collapse the panel by clicking the Panel options button, then clicking Close.

2. Click the **Edit Type Layer state** listed at the bottom of the History panel, then drag it to the **Delete current state button**, as shown in Figure 17.

   TIP Various methods of undoing actions are reviewed in Table 3.

3. Return the workspace to the **Typography workspace**.

4. Save your work.

You changed the workspace to complete a specific task, deleted a state in the History panel to return the type to its original appearance, then changed the workspace again. The History panel offers an easy way of undoing previous steps.

TABLE 3: UNDOING ACTIONS		
Method	**Description**	**Shortcut**
Undo	Edit ➤ Undo	[Ctrl][Z] (Win) ⌘ [Z] (Mac)
Step Backward	Click Edit on the Menu bar, then click Step Backward	[Alt][Ctrl][Z] (Win) [option] ⌘ [Z] (Mac)
History panel	Drag state to the Delete current state button on the History panel, [Ctrl]-click or right-click state, then click [Delete], or click the Delete current state button on the History panel	[Alt] 🗑 (Win) [option] 🗑 (Mac)

© Cengage Learning 2013

Modify Type with Bevel and Emboss
AND 3D EXTRUSION

What You'll Do

In this lesson, you'll apply the Bevel and Emboss style, modify the Bevel and Emboss settings, and then apply 3D Extrusion to a type layer.

Using the Bevel and Emboss Style

You use the Bevel and Emboss style to add combinations of shadows and highlights to a layer and make type appear to have dimension and shine. You can use the Layer menu or the Layers panel to apply the Bevel and Emboss style to the active layer. Like all Layer styles, the Bevel and Emboss style is linked to the type layer to which it is applied.

Understanding Bevel and Emboss Settings

You can use two categories of Bevel and Emboss settings: structure and shading. **Structure** determines the size and physical properties of the object, and **shading** determines the

lighting effects. Bevel and Emboss structure settings are listed in Table 4. The shading used in the Bevel and Emboss style determines how and where light is projected on the type. You can control a variety of settings, including the angle, altitude, and gloss contour, to create a unique appearance. The **angle** setting indicates the direction of the light source and determines where the shadow falls relative to the text, and the **altitude** setting affects the amount of visible dimension. For example, an altitude of 0 degrees looks flat, while a setting of 90 degrees has a more three-dimensional appearance. The **gloss contour** setting determines the pattern with which light is reflected, and the **highlight mode** and **shadow mode** settings determine how pigments are

Filling Type with Imagery

You can use the imagery from a layer in one file as the fill pattern for another image's type layer. To create this effect, open a multilayer file that contains the imagery you want to use (the source), and then open the file that contains the type you want to fill (the target). In the source file, activate the layer containing the imagery you want to use, use the Select menu to select all, and then use the Edit menu to copy the selection. In the target file, press [Ctrl] (Win) or ⌘ (Mac) while clicking the type layer to which the imagery will be applied, click Edit on the Menu bar, point to Paste Special, and then click Paste Into. The imagery will appear within the type.

Placing Type in an Image

combined. When the Use Global Light check box is selected, *all the type* in the image will be affected by your changes.

NEW Learning About 3D Extrusion

3D Extrusion, formally called Repoussé (pronounced re-poo-say) is a tool for turning a 2-dimensional object (like type) into a 3-dimensional object. Extrusion tools allow you to rotate, roll, pan, slide, and scale an object, and this feature has a number of presets that help you learn its many uses. You can apply Extrusion to a type layer or image layer using the Type command on the Menu bar or the 3D panel or the 3D workspace. (Applying Extrusion to a type layer automatically rasterizes the type, a process that is covered in more detail later in this chapter.)

Each 3D extruded object displays on a mesh, shown in Figure 18. Objects within the mesh are clickable, and when clicked, reveal **widgets** (tools that can be used to change the 3D object). Widgets exist for light, movement, and camera, to name a few. As you click on various elements within the mesh, take note that the Properties panel changes to reflect the active element.

QUICK TIP

Any formatting such as bold or italics, effects like a drop shadow or bevel, or warping can be applied to a 3D extrusion.

Elements with the mesh can be shown/hidden using the Show command on the View menu.

QUICK TIP

As you might imagine, 3D features are extremely memory- and hardware-intensive. 3D will not work on the Windows XP operation system, and if your computer does not have a GPU card, it may or may not work at all. Please consult www.adobe.com for a list of supported video cards.

Figure 18 *3D Extrusion object on mesh*

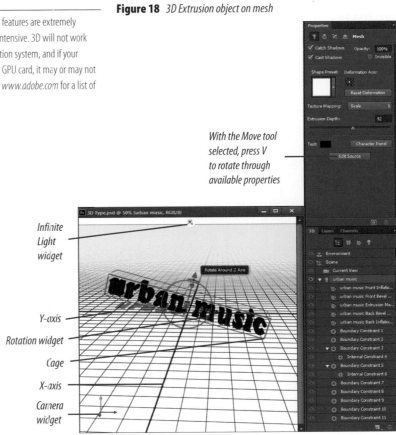

With the Move tool selected, press V to rotate through available properties

Infinite Light widget

Y-axis

Rotation widget

Cage

X-axis

Camera widget

TABLE 4: BEVEL AND EMBOSS STRUCTURE SETTINGS

Sample	Style	Technique	Direction	Size	Soften
1	Inner Bevel	Smooth	Up	5	1
2	Outer Bevel	Chisel Hard	Up	5	8
3	Emboss	Smooth	Down	10	3
4	Pillow Emboss	Chisel Soft	Up	10	3

© Cengage Learning 2013

Add the Bevel and Emboss style with the Layer menu

1. Click the **Live Music layer** and verify that the Horizontal Type tool is active.

2. Click the **Set the text color button** ▮ on the options bar, click the **silver area of the right horn** (at approximately **250 X/135 Y**), then click **OK**.

3. Click **Layer** on the Menu bar, point to **Layer Style**, click **Bevel & Emboss**.

4. Review the Layer Style dialog box shown in Figure 19, copying the settings shown to your dialog box, then move the Layer Style dialog box so that you can see the "Live Music" type, if necessary.

You applied the Bevel and Emboss style by using the Layer menu. This gave the text a three-dimensional look.

Figure 19 *Layer Style dialog box*

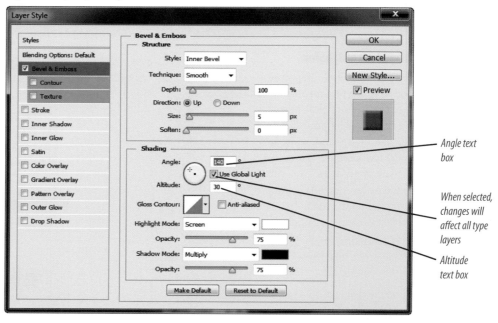

Angle text box

When selected, changes will affect all type layers

Altitude text box

Understanding GPU and OpenGL

Photoshop CS6 uses the GPU (graphics processing unit) rather than the main processor within your computer to speed screen redraw. (You can tell if your computer has OpenGL enabled by opening Preferences, clicking Performance, and then looking at the Graphics Processor Settings. If Use Graphics Processor is dimmed, your computer **does not** have OpenGL enabled.) Once the GPU technology is detected, Photoshop automatically turns on the OpenGL (Open Graphics Library) technology which communicates with your display driver. OpenGL is necessary in Photoshop to operate many features, including 3D Extrusion, brush dynamic resize and hardness control, 3D overlays, 3D Acceleration, 3D Axis, Accelerated 3D Interaction via Direct to Screen, 3D Ground Plane, and 3D Selections via a Hi-light Overlay. In short, *no OpenGL means no 3D*.

Placing Type in an Image

Figure 20 *3D grid over type layer*

Figure 21 *3D Extrusion applied to type*

3D Extrusion
applied to
layer

Thumbnail
indicates a
3D layer

NEW Modify Bevel and Emboss settings
and apply 3D Extrusion

1. Double-click the **number in the Angle text box**, then type **165**.

   You can use the Layer Style dialog box to change the structure of the bevel by adjusting style, technique, depth, direction, size, and soften settings.

2. Double-click the **Altitude text box**, then type **20**.

3. Click **OK**, then note the expanded Live Music layer in the Layers panel.

4. Click the **urban music layer** on the Layers panel.

   If you do not have OpenGL enabled on your computer, proceed to step 9.

5. Click **Type** on the Menu bar, click **Extrude to 3D**, click **Yes** to switch to the 3D workspace, then compare your screen to Figure 20.

6. Click the **Drag the 3D Object** 🔁 on the options bar, position the pointer ⬚**between the "n" and "m"**, then drag the type **to the right** until the "m" is at approximately 250X.

7. Click the **Render button** 🔲 in the Properties panel (this process may take several minutes to complete; the amount of time remaining displays in the status bar at the bottom of the document window).

8. Click **View** on the Menu bar, deselect any 3D options, then display the **Typography workspace**.

9. Save your work, turn off the ruler display, then compare your image to Figure 21.

You modified the default settings for the Bevel and Emboss style, then applied 3D Extrusion to a layer. Experimenting with different settings is crucial to achieve the effect you want.

Apply Special Effects to Type
USING FILTERS

What You'll Do

In this lesson, you'll rasterize a type layer, and then apply a filter to it to change its appearance.

Understanding Filters

Like an image layer, a type layer can have one or more filters applied to it to achieve special effects and make your text look unique, as shown in Figure 22. Some filters are available in the Filter Gallery while others have dialog boxes with preview windows that let you see the results of the particular filter before it is applied to the layer. Other filters must be applied to the layer before you can see the results. Before a filter can be applied to a type layer, the type layer must first be **rasterized**, or converted to an image layer. After it is rasterized, the type characters *can no longer be edited* because it is composed of pixels, just like artwork. When a type layer is rasterized, the T icon in the layer thumbnail becomes an image thumbnail while the Effects icons remain. Notice that none of the original type layers on the Layers panel in Figure 22 display the T icon in the layer thumbnail.

QUICK TIP

Because you cannot edit type after it has been rasterized, you should save your original type by making a copy of the layer *before* you rasterize it, and then hide it from view. This allows you to use the copy if you need to make changes to the type at a later time.

Producing Distortions

Distort filters let you create waves or curves in type. Some of the types of distortions you can produce include Pinch, Polar Coordinates, Ripple, Shear, Spherize, Twirl, Wave, and Zigzag. These effects are sometimes used as the basis of a corporate logo. The Twirl dialog box, shown in Figure 23, lets you determine the amount of twirl effect you want to apply. By dragging the Angle slider, you control how much twirl effect is added to a layer. Most filter dialog boxes have Zoom in and Zoom out buttons that make it easy to see the effects of the filter.

Using Relief

Many filters let you create the appearance of textures and **relief** (the height of ridges within an object). One of the Stylize filters, Wind, applies lines throughout the type, making it appear shredded. The Wind dialog box, shown in Figure 24, lets you determine the kind of wind and its direction.

Blurring Imagery

The Gaussian Blur filter, one of the Blur filter options, softens the appearance of type by blurring its edge pixels. You can control the amount of blur applied to the type by entering high or low values in the Gaussian Blur dialog box. The higher the blur value, the blurrier the effect.

Figure 22 *Sample filters applied to type*

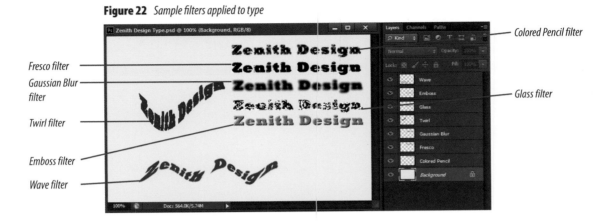

Colored Pencil filter

Fresco filter

Gaussian Blur filter

Twirl filter

Glass filter

Emboss filter

Wave filter

Figure 23 *Twirl dialog box*

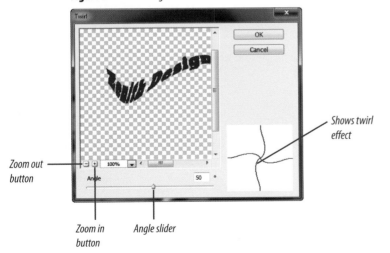

Shows twirl effect

Zoom out button

Zoom in button

Angle slider

Figure 24 *Wind dialog box*

Apply a filter to a type layer

1. Click the **Live Music** layer on the Layers panel.

2. Click **Filter** on the Menu bar, point to **Stylize**, then click **Diffuse**.

3. Click **OK** to rasterize the type and close the warning box shown in Figure 25.

TIP You can also rasterize a type layer by clicking Layer on the Menu bar, pointing to Rasterize, then clicking Type.

The Diffuse dialog box opens.

You rasterized a type layer in preparation for applying a filter.

Figure 25 *Warning box*

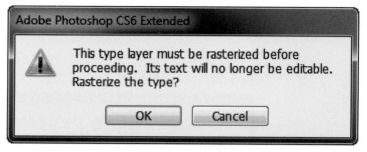

Adobe Photoshop CS6 Extended

This type layer must be rasterized before proceeding. Its text will no longer be editable. Rasterize the type?

OK   Cancel

DESIGN**TIP**

Using Multiple Filters

Sometimes, adding one filter doesn't achieve the effect you had in mind. You can use multiple filters to create a unique effect. Before you try your hand at filters, though, it's a good idea to make a copy of the original layer. That way, if things don't turn out as you planned, you can always start over. You don't even have to write down which filters you used, because you can always look at the History panel to review which filters you applied.

Placing Type in an Image

Figure 26 *Type with Diffuse filter*

Modify filter settings

1. Drag in the preview window of the dialog box from the bottom to position the type so at least part of the type is visible.

2. Click the **Darken Only** and **Lighten Only option buttons**, notice the difference each makes, then click the **Normal option button**.

3. Click **OK**.

4. Save your work. Compare your modified type to Figure 26.

You modified the Diffuse filter settings to modify the appearance of the layer.

Creating a Neon Glow

Want to create a really cool effect that takes absolutely no time at all, and works on both type and objects? You can create a neon glow that appears to surround an object. You can apply the Neon Glow filter (one of the Artistic filters) to any flattened image. This effect works best by starting with any imagery—either type or objects—that has a solid color background. Flatten the image so there's only a Background layer. Click the Magic Wand tool on the Tools panel, and then click the solid color (in the background). Click Filter on the Menu bar, click Filter Gallery, click Artistic to expand the category, then click Neon Glow. Adjust the glow size, the glow brightness, and color, if you wish, and then click OK. (An example of this technique is used in the Design Project at the end of this chapter.)

Lesson 6   Apply Special Effects to Type Using Filters

Create Text
ON A PATH

What You'll Do

In this lesson, you'll create a shape, and then add type to it.

Understanding Text on a Path

Although it is possible to create some cool type effects by adding layer styles such as bevel and emboss and drop shadow, you can also create some awesome warped text. Suppose you want type to conform to a shape, such as an oval, or a free-form outline you've drawn. No problem—just create the shape and add the text!

Creating Text on a Path

You start by creating a shape using one of the Photoshop shape tools on the Tools panel, setting the Pick tool mode to Path on the shape's options bar, and then adding type to that shape. Add type to a shape by clicking the Horizontal Type tool. When the pointer nears the path, you'll see that it changes to the Type on a Path pointer. Click the path when the Type on a Path pointer displays and begin typing. You can change fonts, font sizes, add styles, and any other interesting effects you've learned to apply with type. As you will see, the type is on a path!

> **QUICK TIP**
>
> Don't worry when you see the outline of the path on the screen. The path won't print, only the type will.

Warping Type

You can add dimension and style to your type by using the Warp Text feature. After you select the type layer you want to warp, click the Horizontal Type tool on the Tools panel. Click the Create warped text button on the options bar to open the Warp Text dialog box. If a warning box opens telling you that your request cannot be completed because the type layer uses a faux bold style, click the Character Panel options button, click Faux Bold to deselect it, and then click the Create warped text button again. You can click the Style list arrow to select from 15 available styles. After you select a style, you can modify its appearance by dragging the Bend, Horizontal Distortion, and Vertical Distortion sliders.

Placing Type in an Image

Figure 27 *Type on a path*

Path does not display
when image is printed

Create a path and add type

1. Turn on the ruler display, click the **Ellipse tool** 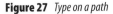 on the Tools panel.

2. Click the **Pick tool mode list arrow** on the options bar, then click **Path**.

3. Drag the **Paths pointer** ⊹ to create an elliptical path on the base of the viola from **150 X/350 Y** to **430 X/460 Y**.

4. Click the **Horizontal Type tool** T on the Tools panel.

5. Change the font to **Times New Roman**, use the **Bold font style**, set the font size to **48**, then verify that the **Left align text button** is selected, and anti-aliasing is set to **Smooth**.

TIP You can change to any point size by typing the number in the Set the font size text box. You can also resize the circle by clicking Edit on the Menu bar, pointing to Transform Path, clicking Scale, then dragging the circle to make it larger.

6. Click the **Horizontal Type pointer** at approximately **200** on the ellipse.

7. Using the Color Picker, change the font color by sampling the blue at approximately **150 X/150 Y**, type **Symphony,** then commit any edits.

8. Drag the **Symphony layer** above the Viola layer, hide the rulers and guides, and return to the **Essentials workspace**. Compare your image to Figure 27.

9. Save your work, close the Urban Music.psd file, and exit Photoshop.

You created a path using a shape tool, then added type to it.

POWER USER SHORTCUTS

To do this:	Use this method:	To do this:	Use this method:
Apply anti-alias method	`aa`	Erase a History state	Select state, drag to 🗑
Apply Bevel and Emboss	`fx.`, Bevel and Emboss style	Horizontal Type tool	`T` or **T**
Apply blur filter to type	Filter ➤ Blur ➤ Gaussian Blur	Kern characters	`VA`
Apply Drop Shadow	`fx.`, Drop Shadow style	Move tool	`+` or **V**
Cancel any current edits	`⊘`	Open Character panel from the options bar	`▤`
Change font family	`Myriad Pro` ▼	Save image changes	[Ctrl][S] (Win) or ⌘ [S] (Mac)
Change font size	`T`	See type effects (to collapse)	`▯`
Change type color	`▬`	See type effects (to expand)	`▲`
Commit current edits	`✓`	Select all text in layer	Double-click type layer icon
Cycle through 3D properties	Select Move tool, press V	Shift baseline of type	`Aa`
Display/hide rulers	[Ctrl][R] (Win) or ⌘ [R] (Mac)	Warp type	`工`

Key: Menu items are indicated by ➤ between the menu name and its command. Blue bold letters are shortcuts for selecting tools on the Tools panel.

Learn about type and how it is created.

1. Open PS 6-2.psd from the drive and folder where you store your Data Files, then save it as **ZD-Logo**.
2. Display the rulers with pixels, then change to the Typography workspace.
3. Use the Horizontal Type tool to create a type layer that starts at 45 X/95 Y.
4. Use a black 35 pt Lucida Sans font or substitute another font.
5. Type **Zenith**, deselect the text, then reposition the type if necessary.
6. Use the Horizontal Type tool and a 16 pt type size to create a type layer at 70 X/180 Y, then type **Always the best**.
7. Save your work.

Change spacing and adjust baseline shift.

1. Use the Horizontal Type tool to create a new type layer at 210 X/95 Y.
2. Use a 35 pt Myriad Pro font.
3. Type **Design**.
4. Select the Design type.
5. Change the type color to the color used in the lower-left of the background.
6. Change the type size of the D to 50 pt.
7. Adjust the baseline shift of the D to −5.
8. Select the Z, change the type size to 50 pt and the baseline shift to -5.
9. Save your work.

Use the Drop Shadow style.

1. Activate the Zenith type layer.
2. Apply the Drop Shadow style.

3. In the Layer Style dialog box, set the angle to 150°, then close the Layer Style dialog box.
4. Save your work.

Apply anti-aliasing to type.

1. Activate the Zenith type layer if necessary.
2. Change the Anti-Alias method to Smooth (if necessary).
3. Save your work.

Modify type with the Bevel and Emboss style.

1. Activate the Design type layer.
2. Apply the Bevel and Emboss style.
3. In the Layer Style dialog box, set the style to Inner Bevel.
4. Set the angle to 150° and the altitude to 30°.
5. Close the Layer Style dialog box and apply the style.
6. Activate the Zenith type layer.
7. Apply the Bevel and Emboss style.
8. Set the style to Inner Bevel.
9. Verify that the angle is set to 150° and the altitude is set to 30°.

10. Close the Layer Style dialog box and apply the style.
11. Save your work.

Apply special effects to type using filters.

1. Apply a 1.0 pixel Gaussian Blur filter to the "Always the best" layer.
2. Save your work.

Create text on a path.

1. Use the Ellipse tool with Path selected to draw an ellipse from approximately 200 X/120 Y to 370 X/185 Y.
2. Click the path with the Horizontal Type tool at 250 X/120 Y.
3. Type **Since 1962** using the orange color in the lower-left triangle of the file, in a 16 pt Arial font.
4. Change the anti-aliasing method to Crisp.
5. Change the opacity of the type (using the Opacity slider in the Layers panel) on the path to 45%.
6. Turn off the ruler display.
7. Save your work, then compare your image to Figure 28.

Figure 28 *Completed Skills Review*

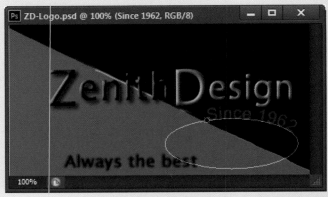

A local flower shop, Nature's Beauty, asks you to design its color advertisement for website that features members of a group called *Florists United*. You have already started on the image, and need to add some type.

1. Open PS 6-3.psd, then save it as **Nature's Beauty Web Promo**.

2. Using the Horizontal Type tool, click at the top of the image, then type **Nature's Beauty** using a black 60 pt Times New Roman font.

3. Create a catchy phrase of your choice, using a 24 pt Verdana font.

4. Apply a drop shadow style to the name of the flower shop using the following settings: Multiply blend mode, 75% Opacity, 30° Angle, 5 pixel distance, 2% spread, and 5 pixel size.

5. Apply a Bevel and Emboss style to the catch phrase using the following settings: Emboss style, Chisel Soft technique, 100% depth, Up direction, 15 pixel size, 0 pixel soften, 30° angle, 25° altitude, and using global light.

6. If your computer has OpenGL enabled, add a 3D Extrusion effect to the Nature's Beauty type created in step 2.

7. Compare your image to the sample in Figure 29.

8. Save your work.

Figure 29 *Sample Project Builder 1*

Placing Type in an Image

You are a junior art director for an advertising agency. You have been working on a print ad that promotes milk and milk products. You have started the project, but still have a few details to finish up before it is complete.

1. Open PS 6-4.psd, then save it as **Milk Promotion**.
2. Create a shape using any shape tool, then use the shape as a text path and type a snappy phrase of your choosing on the shape.
3. Use a 24 pt Arial font in the style and color of your choice for the catch phrase type layer. (If necessary, substitute another font.)
4. Create a Bevel and Emboss style on the type layer, setting the angle to 100° and the altitude to 30°.
5. Compare your image to the sample in Figure 30.
6. Save your work.

Figure 30 *Sample Project Builder 2*

Placing Type in an Image

You are a freelance designer. A local clothing store, Attitude, is expanding and has hired you to work on a print advertisement. You have already created the file, and inserted the necessary type layers. Before you proceed, you decide to explore the Internet to find information on using type to create an effective design.

1. Connect to the Internet and use your browser to find information about typography. (Make a record of the site you found so you can use it for future reference, if necessary.)
2. Find information about using type as an effective design element.
3. Open PS 6-5.psd, update the layers (if necessary), then save the file as **Attitude**.
4. Modify the existing type by changing fonts, font colors, and font sizes.
5. Edit the type, if necessary, to make it shorter and clearer.
6. Rearrange the position of the type to create an effective design.
7. Add a Bevel and Emboss style using your choice of settings, then compare your image to the sample in Figure 31.
8. Save your work.

Figure 31 *Sample Design Project*

Image © Photodisc/Getty Images.

You have been hired by your community to create an advertising campaign that promotes tourism on its website. Decide what aspect of the community you want to emphasize. Locate appropriate imagery (already existing on your hard drive, on the web, your own creation, or using a scanner), and then add type to create a meaningful Photoshop image.

1. Create an image with any dimensions you choose.
2. Save this file as **Community Promotion**.
3. Locate appropriate imagery of your community on your hard drive, from a digital camera, or a scanner.
4. Add at least two layers of type in the image, using multiple font sizes. (Use any fonts available on your computer. You can use multiple fonts if you want.)
5. Add a Bevel and Emboss style to at least one type layer and add a Drop Shadow style to at least one layer. (*Hint*: You can add both effects to the same layer.)
6. Position type layers to create an effective design.
7. Compare your image to the sample in Figure 32.
8. Save your work.

Figure 32 *Sample Portfolio Project*

Placing Type in an Image

CHAPTER 1

INTEGRATING ADOBE CS6 WEB PREMIUM

1. Insert a Photoshop image into a Dreamweaver document

2. Create a Photoshop document and import it into Flash

3. Insert and edit a Flash movie in Dreamweaver

CHAPTER 1

INTEGRATING ADOBE CS6
WEB PREMIUM

Introduction

The Adobe Creative Suite 6 Web Premium products includes Dreamweaver, Flash, and Photoshop. Used together, these tools allow you to create websites that include compelling graphics, animations, and interactivity. Recognizing that developing a website often involves team members with varying expertise (graphic designers, animators, developers, and so on), Adobe has designed these products so that they integrate easily. This integration allows you to move from one product to another as you bring together the elements of a website.

For example, you can create a graphic image using Photoshop, import the image into Dreamweaver, and then edit the image starting from the Dreamweaver workspace. While each of the products can stand alone, they have a similar look and feel, with common features and interface elements, such as the Properties panel, that allows you to transfer your skills from one product to another.

As you have seen, you can use Adobe Bridge CS6 to organize, locate, and display the elements used to create websites and applications (such as Photoshop images, Flash movies, and Dreamweaver documents).

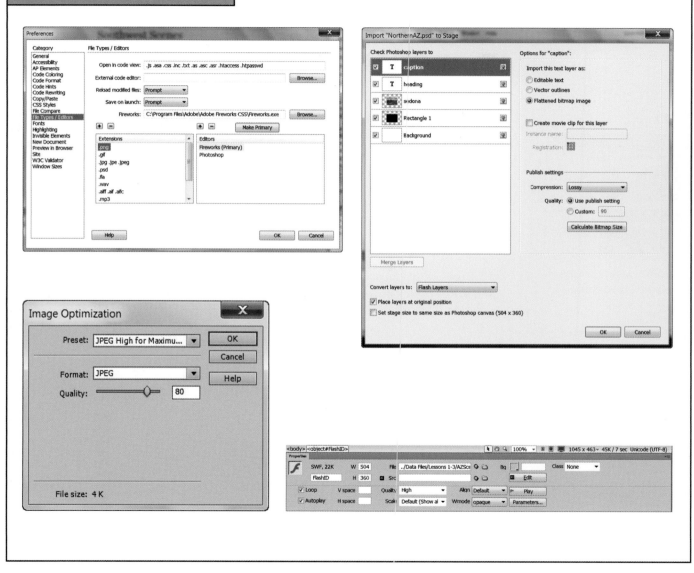

Insert a Photoshop Image into
A DREAMWEAVER DOCUMENT

What You'll Do

In this lesson, you will integrate a Photoshop image into a Dreamweaver document and edit the image from Dreamweaver.

Inserting a Photoshop Image into Dreamweaver

The process for inserting a Photoshop image into a Dreamweaver document is to first create the image in Photoshop and then save it in the PSD file format. Then, start Dreamweaver and open an existing HTML document or create a new one. Next, select the location in the page where you want the image to appear and insert the PSD file. The Image Optimization dialog box opens, as shown in Figure 1. This dialog box allows you to convert the PSD file to one of the web-ready file types (PNG, JPEG, or GIF). You can also use the dialog

Figure 1 *The Image Optimization dialog box*

box to change the optimization settings in order to reduce the file size while maintaining the desired quality. For example, a JPEG format would usually result in higher quality for a photograph than a GIF format. However, the GIF format might have a smaller file size.

After completing the Image Optimization dialog box, the image appears in the Dreamweaver document with a green icon, as shown in Figure 2. This icon indicates that the image is a **Smart Object**, that is, an object that contains a link to the source file. To edit the source file, you select the image in the Dreamweaver document and then click the Photoshop Edit button on the Property inspector. This launches Photoshop, displays the image, and allows you to edit and save the PSD file. Dreamweaver recognizes when the file has been updated and changes the icon to red and green. This alerts you that the source file has been changed and allows you to update the image in the Dreamweaver document without having to reinsert the image. Dreamweaver keeps all of the optimization settings that you originally specified in Photoshop. In addition, every instance of the image within the website is automatically updated.

Another process for inserting Photoshop images into a Dreamweaver document is to copy and paste the image from one application to the other. When you copy and paste a PSD file from Photoshop to Dreamweaver, the Image Optimization dialog box opens, allowing you to convert the PSD file to a PNG, JPG, or GIF format. In addition, you can change the optimization settings. A copied image does not appear in Dreamweaver as a Smart Object. However, Dreamweaver keeps track of the source file and if you want to edit the image, you can select the image on the page and click the Photoshop Edit button on the Property inspector to open the file in Photoshop. After editing the image, you choose the Copy Merged command (assuming you have added a layer or layers). Next, you return to Dreamweaver and paste the edited image in place of the old one.

The advantages of creating a Smart Object are that you are alerted when a source file has been changed, the update process is very easy, and all instances of the image within the website are updated automatically. The advantage of the copy/paste process is that you can copy a portion of the image, a single layer, a group of layers, or a slice of an image.

Setting Photoshop as the Primary External Image Editor

You can import a Photoshop image into a Dreamweaver document. Later on, when desired, you can edit the graphic by launching the Photoshop program from within Dreamweaver. This requires that in Dreamweaver you set Photoshop as the primary external image editor for PSD, GIF, JPEG, and PNG files. You can set the external image editor using settings in the Preferences dialog box in Dreamweaver.

Figure 2 *The inserted image with the green icon, signifying a Smart Object*

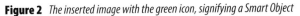

A Smart Object indicating an object that contains a link to the source file

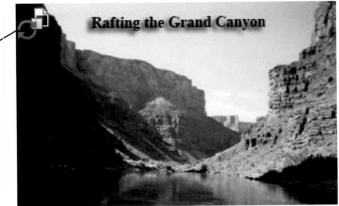

Setting up the Folder Structure for the Files

Figure 3 shows the folder structure and files you will be developing in the lessons in this chapter. You will use the Southwest folder as the destination folder when you save an HTML document or SWF file. You will use the assets folder as the destination folder when you save a Photoshop image. As you work through the chapter, you will integrate Photoshop images and a Flash movie into Dreamweaver documents.

Using Design Notes

When you insert an image or file created in Photoshop or Flash in Dreamweaver, information about the original source file (PSD or FLA) is saved in a Design Notes file (MNO). For example, if in Dreamweaver you import a file named airplane.jpg whose source file is airplane.psd, Dreamweaver creates a Design Notes file named airplane.jpg.mno. The Design Notes file contains references to the source PSD file, which allows you to edit it by opening Photoshop from Dreamweaver. You should save your Photoshop source PSD file and exported files in the Dreamweaver site. Saving in this location ensures that any developer sharing the site can also access the source PSD file. A Design Notes file also contains the optimization settings you specify in the Image Optimization dialog box.

Figure 3 *Structure of the website*

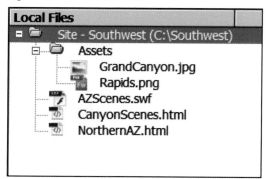

Figure 4 *The CanyonScenes.html document*

Figure 5 *Dreamweaver Preferences dialog box*

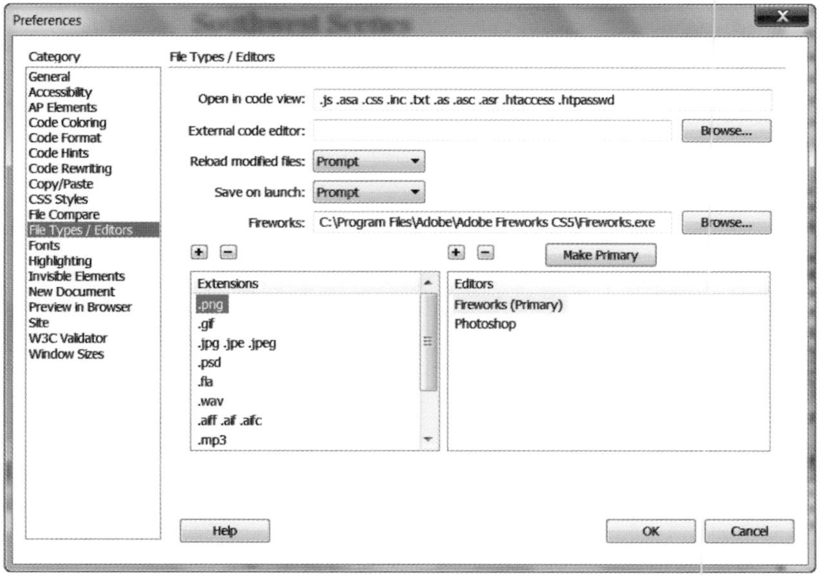

Designate the primary external image editor

This lesson requires that you have Dreamweaver CS6 and Photoshop CS6 installed on your computer.

1. Use your operating system's file management tool to navigate to where you store your Data Files, then create a folder named **Southwest**.

2. Create a folder in the Southwest folder, then name it **Assets**.

3. Start Dreamweaver, open **ic_1.html**, save it to the Southwest folder as **CanyonScenes.html**, then update links, if prompted.

   Your screen should resemble Figure 4. (*Hint*: Close ic_1.html if it remains open.)

4. Click **Edit** (Win) or **Dreamweaver** (Mac) on the Menu bar, then click **Preferences**.

5. Click **File Types / Editors** to display the options shown in Figure 5.

   TIP Each file type has a default editor.

6. Click **.psd** in the Extensions column, then verify that Photoshop (Primary) (Win) or Adobe Photoshop CS6 (Primary) (Mac) appears in the Editors column.

7. Click **.png**, click **Photoshop** (Win) or **Adobe Photoshop CS6** (Mac) in the Editors column, then click **Make Primary** (if necessary).

8. Repeat Step 7 for **.gif** and **.jpg .jpe .jpeg** file types in the Extensions column (if necessary).

9. Click **OK** to close the Preferences dialog box.

You opened and saved an HTML document, then used the Preferences dialog box to verify that Photoshop is the primary external editor for .psd, .png, .gif, and .jpg files.

Edit a Photoshop document

1. Start Photoshop.

2. Open ic_1.psd from the location where you store your Data Files, then save it as **GrandCanyon.psd**.

   This document has a single image, a photo of the Grand Canyon.

3. Click the **Horizontal Type tool**  on the Tools panel, then change the font to **Times New Roman**, the style to **Bold**, the size to **14 pt**, **Left align text**, and the color to **#293bc5**.

TIP Icons appear

4. Click the **upper-left corner** of the sky to create an insertion point, type **Rafting the Grand Canyon**, then position the text as shown in Figure 6.

5. Save your document, specifying Maximize compatibility if requested.

6. Close the document, then exit Photoshop.

You opened a Photoshop PSD file, added a text layer, inserted text, saved the file, and exited Photoshop.

Figure 6 *Positioning the text*

Figure 7 *The Save Web Image dialog box*

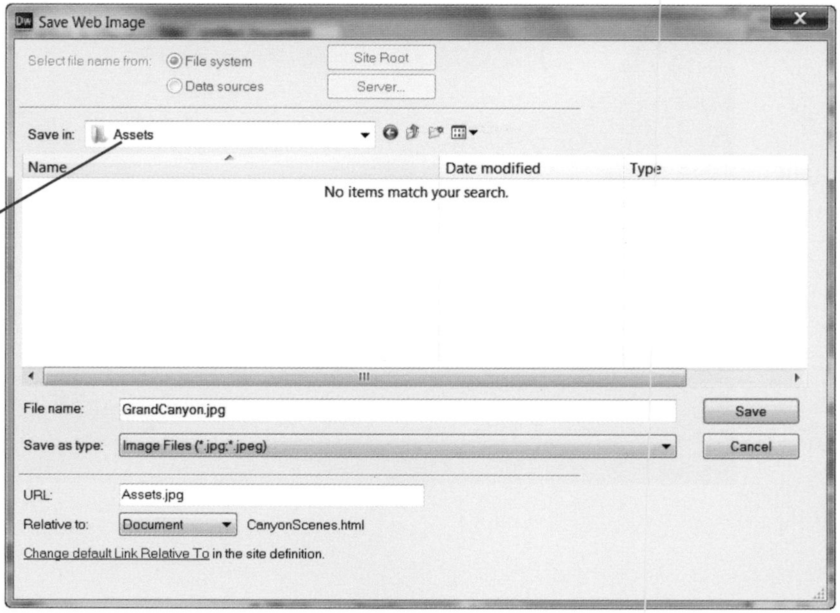

Assets folder

Insert a Photoshop image into a Dreamweaver document

1. Display Dreamweaver, then position the insertion point below the heading.

2. Click **Insert** on the Menu bar, then click **Image**.

3. Use the Select Image Source dialog box to select the **GrandCanyon.psd** file, then click **OK** (Win) or **Choose** (Mac).

   The Image Optimization dialog box appears, where you can change various attributes, including Format and Quality.

4. Verify that JPEG is specified for the Format and 80 is specified for the Quality, then click **OK**.

   The Save Web Image dialog box opens, allowing you to specify where to save the file.

5. Navigate to the **Assets folder** in the Southwest folder as shown in Figure 7, then click **Save**.

6. Type **A photo of the Grand Canyon** for the Alternate text in the Image Tag Accessibility Attributes dialog box, then click **OK**.

   The image appears in Dreamweaver with the green Smart Object icon displayed.

7. Save your work.

You changed the optimization settings for a Photoshop image and inserted it into a Dreamweaver document.

Edit a Photoshop image from a Dreamweaver document

1. Verify that the image is selected, then click the **Photoshop Edit button**  on the Property inspector.

   The GrandCanyon.psd image opens in Photoshop. (*Hint*: If a message appears indicating that the file contains info data that cannot be read, click OK.)

2. Make sure the Layers panel is expanded, verify that the text layer is selected, click the **Add a layer style icon** *fx.* , then click **Drop Shadow**.

3. Click **OK** in the Layer Style dialog box to accept the default values.

   Your image should resemble Figure 8.

4. Save, then close the document.

5. Display Dreamweaver.

   Notice the icon has changed from solid green to red and green, indicating that the source image has been altered, but not yet updated in Dreamweaver.

6. Point to the image, **right-click** (Win) or **[control]-click** (Mac), then click **Update From Original**.

   The icon changes back to green and the drop shadow effect is visible in the image.

7. Insert a blank line below the image.

8. Save your work.

You used Photoshop to edit an image in Dreamweaver and then updated the image.

Figure 8 *The edited Photoshop image*

Figure 9 *Image placed in the document with no Smart Object icon*

Figure 10 *Selecting part of the image*

Copy and paste a Photoshop image into a Dreamweaver document

1. Display Photoshop, open ic_2.psd, then save it as **Rapids.psd**.

2. Click **Select** on the Menu bar, click **All**, click **Edit** on the Menu bar, click **Copy**, then close the document.

3. Display Dreamweaver, click **Edit** on the Menu bar, then click **Paste**.

4. Click **OK** in the Image Optimization dialog box, save the file to the Assets folder, type **Photo of rapids** as the alternate text, then click **OK**.

   Figure 9 shows that the image is placed in the document, but not as a Smart Object.

5. Select the image, then click the **Photoshop Edit button** 🅿️ on the Property inspector.

6. Use the **Horizontal Type tool** 🅃 to type **White Water Ahead** and place it just in front of the raft.

7. Use the **Rectangular Marquee tool** ⬚ to select the part of the image shown in Figure 10.

8. Click **Edit** on the Menu bar, click **Copy Merged**, then save and close the document.

9. Display Dreamweaver, delete the lower image, click **Edit** on the Menu bar, then click **Paste**.

10. Click **OK** in the Image Optimization dialog box, save the image as **Rapids.png**, type **Photo of rapids** Alt text, then click **OK**.

11. Save your work, display the document in a browser, close the browser, then exit Dreamweaver.

You copied and pasted a Photoshop image into a Dreamweaver document, edited the image in Photoshop, repasted the image, then viewed the document in a browser.

Create a Photoshop Document
AND IMPORT IT INTO FLASH

What You'll Do

Northern Arizona Scenic Sites

SEDONA

In this lesson, you will create a Photoshop document, import it into Flash, and create an animation.

Importing a Photoshop Document into Flash

Flash allows you to import Photoshop PSD files directly into a Flash document. An advantage of using Photoshop to create graphics and enhance photographs is that you can use the drawing and selection tools, as well as the photo retouching features to produce more creative and complex images. A key feature of importing PSD files is that you can choose to have the Photoshop layers imported as Flash layers. This allows you to edit individual parts of an image, such as animating text or using a photograph to create a button.

The process for importing Photoshop files into Flash is to open a Flash document and select the Import command from the File menu. Next, choose to import to the Stage or to the Library panel and specify the PSD file to import. The Import dialog box opens, as shown in Figure 11, with the following options:

- Check Photoshop layers to import. Allows you to specify which layers to import.
- Options for "Layer …". Allows you to specify how the selected layer will be imported. Here you decide whether you want to be able to edit the contents (text, image, background, and so on) of the layer. If you choose not to make it editable, Flash flattens the content as a bitmap image. If you choose to make an image editable, Flash creates a movie clip symbol using the image. Because a movie clip symbol has its own Timeline, it is easy to animate the image separately from other content in the Flash document.

- Publish settings. Specifies the degree of compression and document quality to apply to the image when it is published as a SWF file. This has no effect on the image that is imported into the Flash document.
- Convert layers to. Imports the content of Photoshop layers as Flash layers or keyframes.
- Place layers at original position. Specifies that the contents of the PSD file retain the same relative position they had in Photoshop.
- Set stage size to same size as Photoshop canvas. Resizes the Flash Stage to the same size as the Photoshop document.

Using Photoshop to Edit an Image in Flash

You can use Photoshop to edit an image in Flash. You simply open the Library panel, right-click (Win) or [control]-click (Mac) the desired image, and select Edit with Adobe Photoshop CS6. The image appears in Photoshop. After editing the image, you save and close the document and return to Flash. The image is automatically updated on the Library panel. Any objects, such as movie clips and buttons, that use the image are also updated.

Figure 11 *Import dialog box*

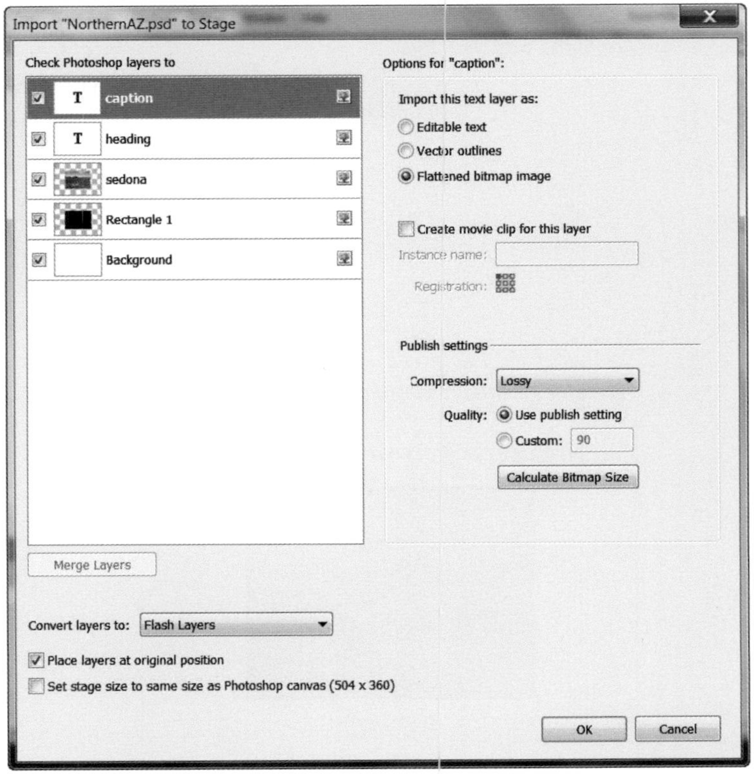

Create a Photoshop image with several layers

1. Start Photoshop, open ic_3.psd, then save it as **NorthernAZ.psd**.

2. Click the **Background layer** in the Layers panel, then click the **Create a new layer icon** at the bottom of the Layers panel.

3. Change the layer name to **border**.

4. Select the **Rectangle tool** on the Tools panel, change the fill color to **black**, then draw a rectangle slightly larger than the image, as shown in Figure 12.

5. Click the **sedona layer** in the Layers panel, then click.

6. Change the layer name to **heading**.

7. Click the **Horizontal Type tool** on the Tools panel, then change the font to **Times New Roman**, the font size to **30 pt**, the style to **Bold**, and the color to **#293bc5**.

8. Type **Northern Arizona Scenic Sites**, then position the text as shown in Figure 13.

9. Insert a new layer above the heading layer, then name it **caption**.

10. Select , then change the font to **Rosewood Std**, the size to **30 pt**, and the color to **#993300**.

TIP If this font is not available, select another.

11. Click beneath the image, type **SEDONA**, then position the text as shown in Figure 14.

12. Save your work, close the document, then exit Photoshop.

You opened a Photoshop file, added layers with a shape and text, and positioned the text.

Figure 12 *The completed rectangle*

Figure 13 *Positioning the heading*

Northern Arizona Scenic Sites

Figure 14 *Positioning the caption*

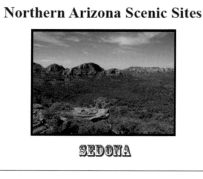

Northern Arizona Scenic Sites

SEDONA

Figure 15 *Selecting the Editable text option*

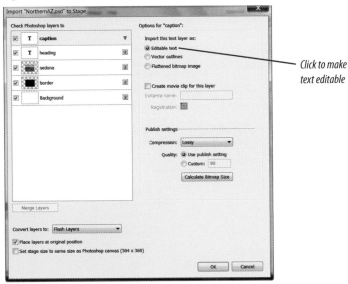

Click to make
text editable

Import a Photoshop document into Flash

1. Start Flash, then click **ActionScript 2.0** in the Create New category.

2. Navigate to the folder where you store your Data Files, then save the document with the filename **AZScenes.fla**.

3. Change the frame rate to **30 fps**.

4. Change the view to **Fit in Window**.

5. Click **File** on the menu bar, point to **Import**, then click **Import to Stage**.

   Choosing the Import to Stage option will place the objects on the Stage and on the Library panel.

6. Navigate to where you store your Data Files, click **NorthernAZ.psd**, click **Open**, then verify All Formats is selected in the file format list.

   Notice each layer of the Photoshop document with a check mark will be imported into Flash as a layer in the Timeline.

7. Click the **caption layer**, then click the **Editable text option button**, as shown in Figure 15.

8. Click the **heading layer**, then click the **Editable text option button**.

(continued)

9. Click the **sedona layer**, then click the **Bitmap image with editable layer styles option button**.

10. Click the **border layer**, then verify that the Flattened bitmap image option button is selected.

11. Click the **check box** next to the Background layer to deselect the layer so it will not be imported.

12. Verify that the Convert layers to: option is set to Flash Layers and the Place layers at original position check box is selected.

13. Select the **Set stage size to same size as Photoshop canvas (504 × 360) check box**, then compare your dialog box to Figure 16.

14. Click **OK**.

The image appears on the Stage and elements appear in separate layers in the Timeline.

You selected a Photoshop file to import, selected which layers to import, and specified editable content.

Figure 16 *The completed Import dialog box*

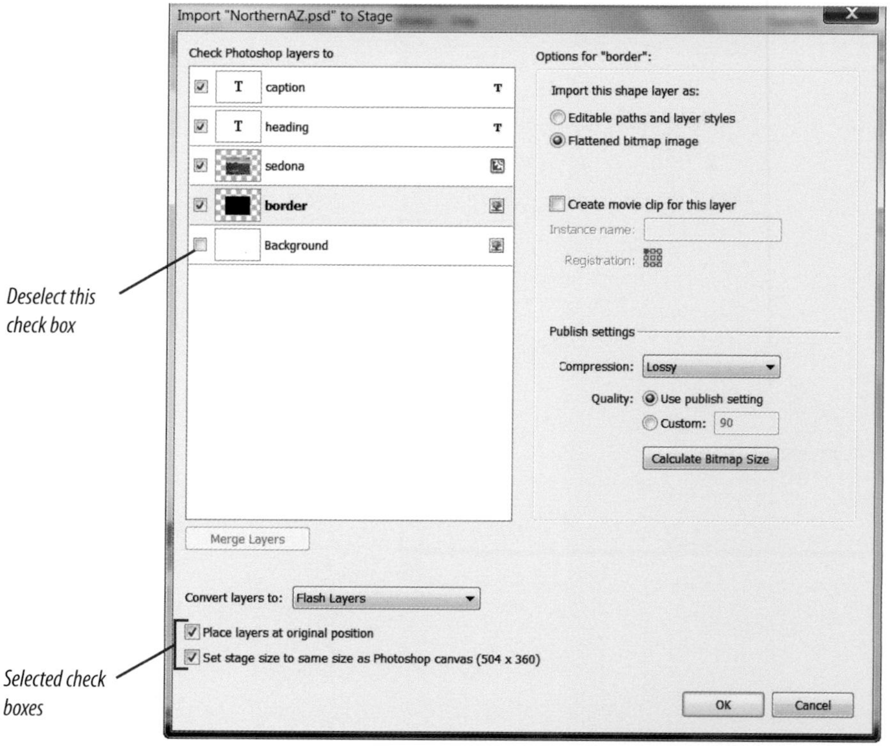

Deselect this check box

Selected check boxes

Integrating Adobe CS6 Web Premium

Figure 17 *The completed edits*

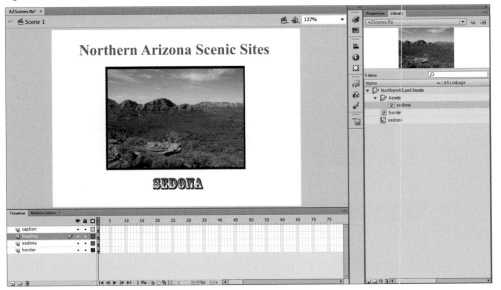

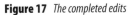

Edit a Photoshop image that has been imported into Flash

1. Study the Flash Timeline and notice the four new layers; Layer 1 has no content.

2. Click **Layer 1**, then click the **Delete icon** 🗑 to delete the layer.

3. Starting with the border layer, hide and unhide each layer one by one to view its contents.

4. Display the Library panel, double-click the **NorthernAZ.psd** Assets folder.

5. Click **border** to display the bitmap image, then click **sedona** to view the movie clip image.

6. Double-click the **Assets folder**, then click **sedona** to view the sedona bitmap image.

   The bitmap image is used to create the sedona movie clip.

7. Click the **Selection tool** 🔍, click **frame 1** on the heading layer, then verify that the heading is selected on the Stage.

8. Click the **Text tool** T, then drag the I-beam pointer I across the text to select it.

9. Click the **Fill Color tool color swatch** 🎨 on the Tools panel, type **#336600**, then press **Enter** (Win) or **return** (Mac).

10. Click the **Selection tool** 🔍 on the Tools panel, then click a blank area of the Stage to deselect the heading, as shown in Figure 17.

11. Save your work.

*You viewed the contents of the layers that were created when a Photoshop file was imported into Flash, and then press **Enter** (Win) or **return** (Mac) changed the color of the text heading.*

Use Photoshop to edit an image in Flash

1. Display the **Library panel**.

2. Verify the NorthernAZ.psd Assets folder is expanded.

3. Verify the Assets folder is expanded.

4. Click the **sedona graphic**, then view the photo in the Preview window.

5. Right-click (Win) or [control]-click (Mac) **sedona**, then select **Edit with Adobe Photoshop CS6**, as shown in Figure 18.

6. In Photoshop, select the **Burn tool** 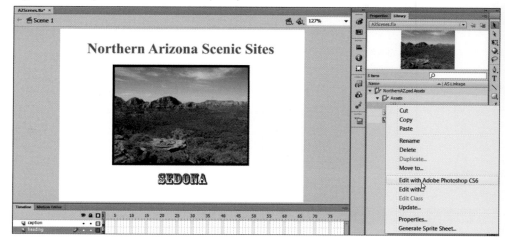 on the Tools panel, then drag the tool back and forth over the entire graphic in a single brush event.

   The Burn tool is used to darken a graphic.

7. Save, then close the document.

8. Display Flash, then notice the edited graphic appears darker on the Library panel.

   Because you changed the graphic on the Library panel all objects using the graphic, including the sedona movie clip on the Stage, are changed.

You used Photoshop to edit a graphic from Flash and updated the graphic automatically in Flash.

Figure 18 *Selecting the Edit with Adobe Photoshop CS6 option*

Figure 19 *The Timeline with keyframes inserted*

Create an animation using the Photoshop-created text

1. Click the **Sedona text** on the Stage to select it, click **Modify** on the menu bar, click **Convert to Symbol**, select **Graphic** as the type, then name it **g_sedona caption**.

2. Verify that Sedona is selected, then create a motion tween.

3. Click **frame 1** on the caption layer, then click the **text** to select it.

4. Click the **Color Effect Style list arrow** on the Properties panel, then click **Alpha**.

5. Change the alpha setting to **0**.

6. Click **frame 30** on the caption layer, click the **blank text block** on the Stage, then change the alpha setting to **100**.

7. Set the frame rate to **12**.

8. Insert keyframes in frame 30 of the remaining layers, as shown in Figure 19.

9. Play the movie.

   The caption text fades in.

10. Click **File** on the menu bar, click **Publish Settings**, deselect the **HTML Wrapper check box**, click **Publish**, then click **OK**.

11. Save your work, close the document, then exit Flash.

You created an animation using Photoshop-imported text.

Insert and Edit a Flash Movie
IN DREAMWEAVER

What You'll Do

Northern Arizona Scenic Sites

SEDONA

 In this lesson, you will insert a Flash movie into a Dreamweaver document and edit the movie within Dreamweaver.

Inserting a Flash Movie into a Dreamweaver Document

You can easily insert a Flash movie (.swf) into a Dreamweaver document. To do this, set the insertion point where you want the movie to appear, and then use the Media command on the Insert menu to select SWF as the media to insert. If the file is not in the root folder for the website, Dreamweaver will prompt you whether you would like to copy it into the root folder. It is recommended that you copy the file to the root folder, so that it is accessible when you publish the site. When the insert process is completed, a placeholder appears at the insertion point in the document.

Using the Property Inspector with the Movie

When you click the placeholder to select it, the Dreamweaver Property inspector displays information about the movie, including the filename, as shown in Figure 20.

You can use the Property inspector to complete the following:

- Edit the Flash movie
- Play and stop the Flash movie
- Set width and height dimensions
- Cause the movie to loop
- Reposition the placeholder in the document window

To edit the Flash movie, you select the placeholder, click the Edit button on the Property inspector, and specify the source file (FLA). This opens Flash and displays the source file. After making changes to the document, you re-export it to Dreamweaver by selecting the Done button at the upper-left corner of the Flash window or by choosing the Update for Dreamweaver command on the File menu. Choosing Done will close the document, while choosing Update for Dreamweaver will keep the document open. Both processes will automatically save the document. (*Hint*: Before starting the editing process from Dreamweaver, you should close Flash.)

Figure 20 *The Property inspector with a movie selected*

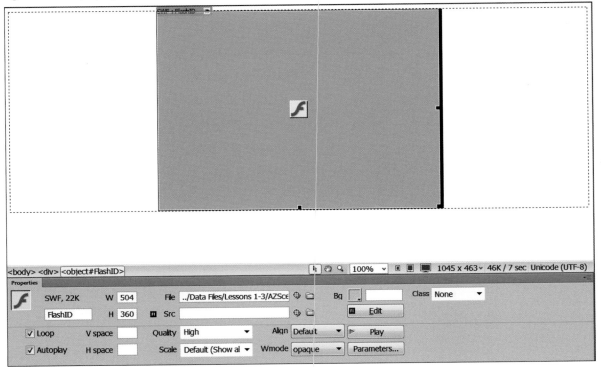

Insert a Flash movie into Dreamweaver

1. Start Dreamweaver.

2. Create a new Blank Page HTML document with no layout, then save it as **NorthernAZ.html** to the Southwest folder.

3. Click **Insert** on the Menu bar, point to **Media**, then click **SWF**.

4. Navigate to where you store your Data Files, click **AZScenes.swf**, then click **OK** (Win) or **Choose** (Mac).

5. If a "This file is outside of the root folder..." message appears, click **Yes**, then click **Save** when the Copy File As dialog box appears.

6. Type **Photo of Sedona Arizona** for the title in the Object Tag Accessibility Attributes dialog box, then click **OK**.

   A Flash movie placeholder is inserted at the location of the insertion line, as shown in Figure 21.

7. Verify that the placeholder is selected, click **Format** on the Menu bar, point to **Align**, then click **Center**.

8. Save your work.

   TIP If a Copy Dependent Files message box appears, click OK.

You inserted a Flash movie into a Dreamweaver document and copied the Flash movie to the root folder of the website.

Figure 21 *The Flash movie placeholder*

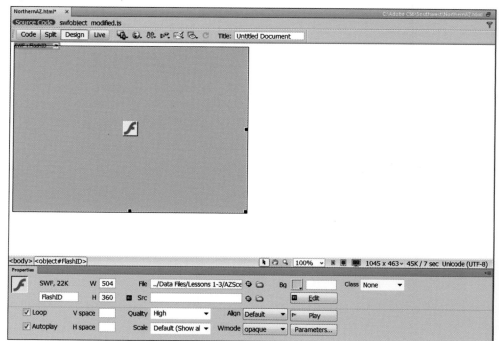

Figure 22 *Changing the movie height*

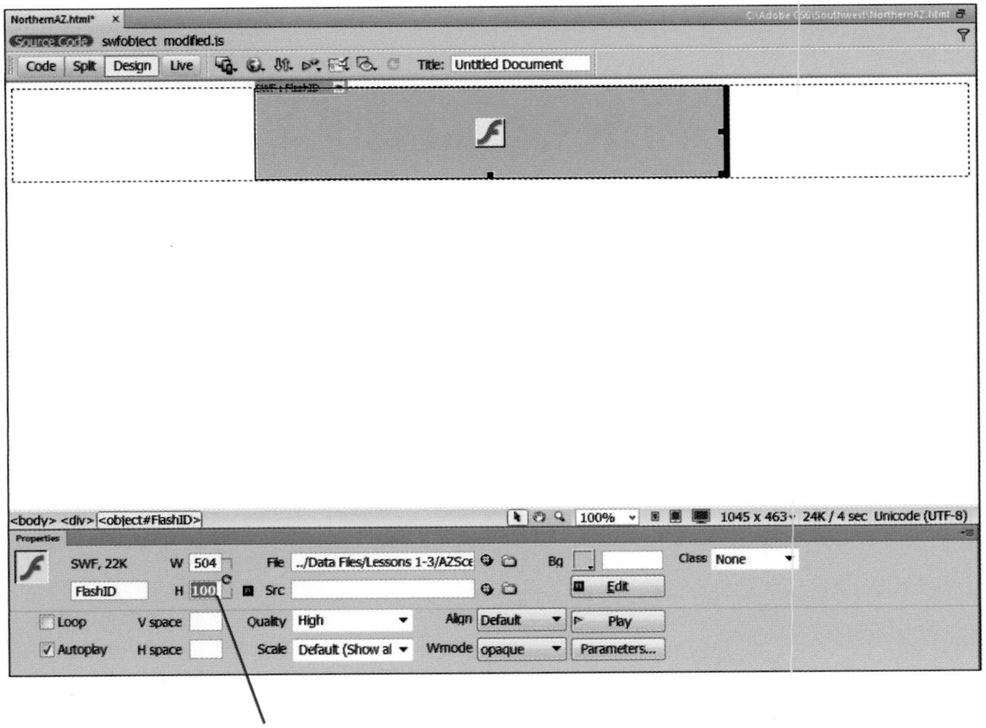

Height text box

Play a Flash movie and change settings from Dreamweaver

1. Click the **Flash movie placeholder** to select it (if necessary).

2. Click the **Play button** on the Property inspector.

3. Click the **Stop button** on the Property inspector.

4. Click the **Loop check box** on the Property inspector to deselect it.

5. Double-click the **Height box (H)**, type **100**, then press **[Enter]** (Win) or **[return]** (Mac).

   Your screen should resemble Figure 22.

6. Click the **Play button** on the Property inspector.

7. View the resized movie, then click the **Stop button**.

8. Click the **Reset size icon** ⟳ on the Property inspector to restore the previous setting.

9. Save your work.

You played a Flash movie and changed its settings in Dreamweaver by turning off the Loop option, and then changing and resetting the movie height.

Edit a Flash movie from Dreamweaver

1. Click the **Flash placeholder** to select it, then click **Edit** on the Property inspector.

2. Navigate to where you store your Data Files, click **AZScenes.fla**, then click **Open**.

TIP If a Copy Dependent Files message box appears, click OK.

3. In Flash, insert a new layer above the caption layer, then name it **stopmovie**.

4. Click **frame 1** of the stopmovie layer.

5. Display the **Actions panel**, verify that the Script Assist button is on, then verify that stopmovie 1 : is displayed at the lower-left corner of the script pane, as shown in Figure 23.

6. Click the **Add a new item to the script button**, point to **Global Functions**, point to **Timeline Control**, then click **stop**.

7. Click **frame 1** on the sedona layer, then click the image to select it.

8. Click **Modify** on the menu bar, then click **Convert to Symbol**.

9. Type **b_sedona** for the name, click **Button** for the Type, then click **OK**.

10. Display the Actions panel (if necessary), then verify that b_sedona is displayed at the lower-left corner of the script pane. (*Hint*: if b_sedona is not displayed click the image on the Stage.)

11. Click the **Add a new item to the script button**, point to **Global Functions**, point to **Movie Clip Control**, then click **on**.

(continued)

Figure 23 *Verifying the settings in the Script pane*

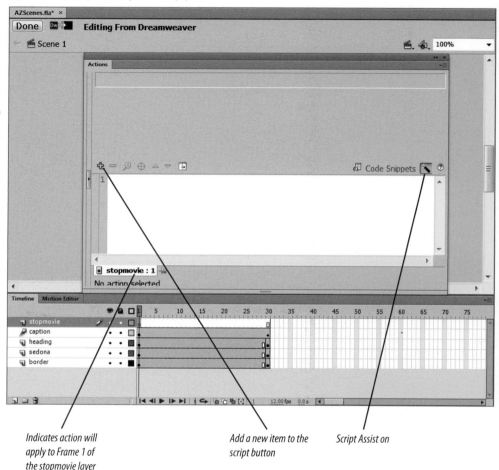

Indicates action will apply to Frame 1 of the stopmovie layer

Add a new item to the script button

Script Assist on

Figure 24 *Specifying the frame to go to*

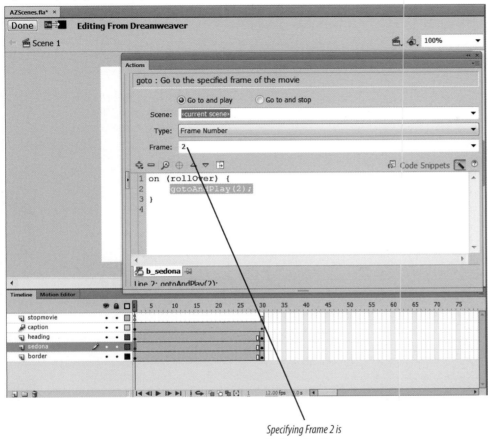

Specifying Frame 2 is the frame to go to

12. Click the **Release check box** to deselect it, then click the **Roll Over check box** to select it.

13. Click the **Add a new item to the script button**, point to **Global Functions**, point to **Timeline Control**, then click **goto**.

14. Change the Frame to **2**, as shown in Figure 24.

15. Close the Actions panel.

16. Click **Control** on the menu bar, point to **Test Movie**, then click **in Flash Professional**.

17. Point to the image to view the animation, then close the test movie window.

18. Click the **Done button** above the upper-left corner to return to Dreamweaver.

19. In Dreamweaver, verify that the Flash placeholder is selected, then click **Play** on the Property inspector.

20. Point to the image to play the animation, then click **Stop** on the Property Inspector.

21. Click **File** on the menu bar, point to **Preview in Browser**, choose a browser, then save your work if prompted.

TIP Your default browser may vary; if prompted to allow ActiveX, click Allow blocked content.

22. View the movie, close the browser, save your work, close the document, then exit Dreamweaver and Flash.

You edited a Flash movie from Dreamweaver by creating a rollover action that plays an animation.

Designate the primary external image editor.

1. Start Dreamweaver CS6.
2. Display the Preferences dialog box and display the File Types / Editors option.
3. Verify that Photoshop is set as the default image editor for . psd, .png, .gif, and .jpg files.

Set up the Dreamweaver site.

1. Create a folder where you store your Data Files and name it **Foods**.
2. Add a folder within the Foods folder named **Assets**.
3. Create a new Dreamweaver site named **Food Thoughts**, using the Foods folder as the Local Site Folder.

Edit a Photoshop file.

1. Open bread-heading.psd in Photoshop CS6.
2. Add a layer below the text layer, name it **background**, then draw a white rectangle the size of the canvas for the background.
3. Save the file as **bread-headingRev.psd**.
4. Close the file.

Insert a Photoshop image into a Dreamweaver document.

1. Open the Food Thoughts site in Dreamweaver (if necessary).
2. Create a new Blank Page HTML document and save it as **food-home.html** using default settings in the root (Food) folder.
3. Insert the bread-headingRev.psd file into the document as a .jpeg file saved to the Assets folder

and with **The Staff of Life heading** for the alternate text.
4. Use the Align option from the Format menu to center-align the heading across the document, then save your work.

Edit a Photoshop image from Dreamweaver.

1. Select the bread-headingRev.jpg image and click the Photoshop Edit button on the Property inspector.
2. Change the text formatting to italic.
3. Save the document, then close it.
4. Display the food-home.html file in Dreamweaver, right-click (Win) or [control]-click (Mac) the heading, then choose Update From Original.
5. Save the Dreamweaver document.

Import a Photoshop image to Flash.

1. Display Photoshop, open bread-photo.psd, then save it as **bread-photoRev.psd**.
2. Add a layer below the photo layer and name it **border**.
3. Draw a black rectangle slightly larger than the photo.
4. Save the document and then close the document.
5. Start Flash CS6 and create a new Flash ActionScript2 document.
6. Change the frame rate to 30 fps.
7. Save the document with the filename **bread-An.fla**.
8. Import the bread-photoRev.psd file to the Stage, making each layer except the background editable and setting the stage size to the same size as the Photoshop canvas.
9. Delete Layer 1 in the timeline.

10. Publish the document to create just the SWF file.
11. Save your work and close the document.
12. Exit Flash.

Insert a Flash movie into a Dreamweaver document.

1. Display Dreamweaver and set an insertion point below the heading.
2. Insert the bread-An.swf file below the photo image, and save the file to the Assets folder.
3. Enter **Photo of breads and an Animation of the word Bread** for the Accessibility title. (*Hint*: Copy dependent files if prompted.)
4. Save your work.

Play a Flash movie and change the movie settings from Dreamweaver.

1. Select the Flash movie placeholder.
2. Click Play, then click Stop.
3. Deselect the Loop feature.
4. Change the movie window height to **250**, play the movie, then stop the movie.
5. Reset the size.
6. Save your work.

Edit a Flash movie from Dreamweaver.

1. Select the movie placeholder, then click Edit.
2. Select the bread-An.fla file in the Locate FLA file dialog box, then click Open.
3. Create a 30-frame motion animation that causes the word Bread to scroll in from off the left side of the Stage.
4. Add a layer at the top of the Timeline, name it **stopmovie**, then create a stop action in frame 1 of the layer.

5. Insert a keyframe in the last frame of the stopmovie layer, then create a stop action in the frame.
6. Select the photo and convert it to a button symbol with the name **b_photo**.
7. Create a rollover action for the button that causes the animation to play when the pointer rolls over the photo.

8. Enter keyframes into the last frame of the movie for the other layers.
9. Test the movie.
10. Click Done to return to the document in Dreamweaver.

11. Play the Flash movie in Dreamweaver, then stop the movie.
12. Save your work.
13. Display the web page in a browser, then compare your screen to Figure 25.

Figure 25 *Completed Skills Review*

Ultimate Tours has asked you to develop a Dreamweaver website for their travel company. The site will include graphics exported from Photoshop and the Flash animations you developed in Flash Chapter 5 for the Ultimate Tours website.

1. Create a folder on your hard drive and name it **UTours**, then create a folder within the UTours folder named **Assets**.

2. In Dreamweaver, create a new site named **UltimateTours**, using the UTours folder as the local site folder.

3. Open UTours_home.html and save it as **UTours_homeRev.html** to the root folder for the UTours folder, updating the links if prompted.

4. Start Photoshop and open UTours-heading. psd.

5. Change the text formatting to italic and save the document with the filename **UTours-headingRev.psd**.

6. Display Dreamweaver and insert the UTours-headingRev.psd image into the UTours_homeRev.html file as a .jpg file, stored in the Assets folder with alternate text of **The Trip of a Lifetime heading**.

7. Edit the heading in Photoshop from Dreamweaver and change the text to white.

8. Save the image in Photoshop, then close the document.

9. Display Dreamweaver and update the image.

10. Open UTours-photo.psd in Photoshop, type **The Islands** as a heading above the mountain, on its own layer, and change the text to Times New Roman, italic, 6pt with a color of 0b967d.

11. Save the document as **UTours-photoRev.psd**, then close the document.

12. Create a new Flash ActionScript 2.0 document and save it as **UTours-photoAn.fla**.

13. Change the frame rate to 40 fps.

14. Import the UTours-photoRev.psd to the Stage with all layers being editable and the Set stage size to same size as Photoshop canvas checked.

15. Rename Layer 1 **Gray border**, then draw a gray border around the edge of the photo. (*Hint*: Use the Document settings in the Modify menu to increase the size of the Stage a few pixels to accommodate the border and center the border on the Stage.)

16. Display the Publish Settings dialog box, deselect the HTML Wrapper option, publish then save and close the movie.

17. Display Dreamweaver and insert the UTours-photoAn.swf file to the right of the heading, saving the file to the Assets folder and providing alternate text.

18. Center the heading and photo across the page.

19. Play the Flash movie in Dreamweaver, then stop the movie.

20. Edit the movie from Dreamweaver. (*Hint*: If a Copy Dependent Files message box appears, click OK.)

21. Change the text to a graphic symbol, then create an animation that fades in the text.

22. Convert the photo to a button and add ActionScript so that when the pointer rolls over the image, the movie plays.

23. Insert a new layer named **stopmovie**, then add stop actions to the first and last frames of the movie.

24. Add keyframes to the end of the movie for each of the other layers.

25. Test the movie.

26. Use the Done button to return to the Dreamweaver document.

27. Play the movie in Dreamweaver, then save your work.

28. Insert the ultimateTours5.swf file below the heading.

29. Save your work, view the document in a browser, then compare your image to the sample in Figure 26.

30. Exit Dreamweaver.

Figure 26 *Sample completed Project Builder 1*

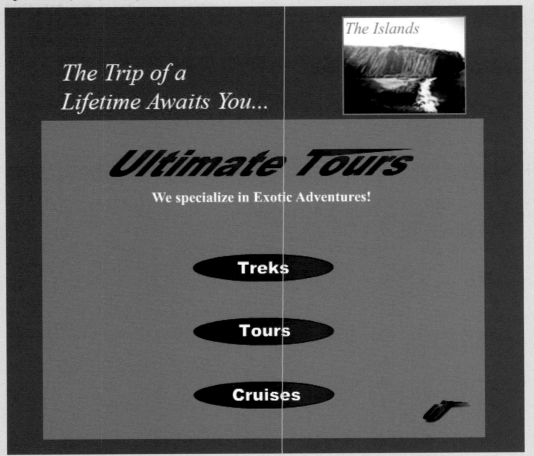

This project begins with the Striped Umbrella site you created in Dreamweaver Chapter 6.

You have been asked to enhance the Striped Umbrella site by adding a Flash movie and changing a graphic image on the cafe page. Figure 27 shows the completed page for this part of the website. The idea is to replace the static cafe logo image with a Flash animation that plays in the same space on the page.

1. In Photoshop, open the cafe_logo.psd file.
2. Turn the visibility off and on for each layer to see how the image is constructed.
3. In Flash, start a new Flash ActionScript 2.0 document, save it as **crabAn.fla**, and import the cafe_logo.psd file to the Library, specifying that each layer is editable.
4. In Flash, create an animation using the cafe_logo.psd image. You decide on the type of animation, which could be a zoom or fade in; the entire crab moving; the crab claws moving; and so forth. (*Hint*: The crab image is made up of a body, left and right claws, and six legs.) Include a rollover effect or some other form of user interaction. Display the Publish Settings dialog box, deselect the HTML Wrapper option, and publish the document.
5. In Dreamweaver, open the Striped Umbrella site.

6. Open the cafe.html page and save it as **cafeRev.html**.
7. Delete the cafe_logo graphic on the page and insert the crab_An.swf file in the cell where the cafe_logo graphic had been.

8. Select the Flash movie placeholder and use the Property inspector to play and stop the animation.
9. Save your work.
10. View the web page in your browser, compare your screen to Figure 27, close your browser, then exit Dreamweaver.

Figure 27 *Sample completed Project Builder 2*

Crab is animated on mouse over

Figure 28 shows the home page of a website. Study the figure and complete the following questions. For each question, indicate how you determined your answer.

1. Connect to the Internet, and go to *www.memphiszoo.org/specialevents*.
2. Open a document in a word processor or in Flash, save the file as **dpcIntegration**, then answer the following questions.

- What seems to be the purpose of this site?
- Who would be the target audience?
- Identify three elements within the web page that could have been created or enhanced using Photoshop.
- Identify two elements on the page and indicate how you would use Photoshop to enhance them.
- Identify an animation that could have been developed by Flash.

- Indicate how you would use Flash to enhance the page.
- What would be the value of using Flash, Dreamweaver, and Photoshop to create the website?
- What suggestions would you make to improve on the design, and why?

Figure 28 *Design Project*

Courtesy of the Memphis Zoo (URL: www.memphiszoo.org/specialevents), Design Copyright © 2012 Speak Creative, LLC

PORTFOLIO PROJECT

This is a continuation of the Portfolio Project you created in Flash Chapter 5. You will create a website in Dreamweaver, import graphic files from Photoshop, and import portfolio5.swf into the site. The home page of the website will include a heading and photo image (of your choice), as shown in Figure 29.

1. Create a folder on your hard drive and name it **PortfolioSite**, then create a folder within the PortfolioSite folder named **Assets**.
2. Open Dreamweaver.
3. Create a new site named **Portfolio**, using the PortfolioSite folder as the local site folder.
4. Open portfolio-home.html and save it **as portfolio-homeRev.html** to the PortfolioSite site.
5. Insert the portfolio-heading.psd image into the document as a .jpg file in the Assets folder, and provide alternate text.
6. Insert the portfolio-photo.psd image to the right of the heading as a .jpg file in the Assets folder, and provide alternate text. (*Hint*: You can use a photo of your choice, if desired.)
7. Center the heading and photo across the page.
8. Insert portfolio5.swf below the heading and center it across the page.
9. Select the movie, then play and stop it.
10. Select the heading and edit it in Photoshop to apply a drop shadow, then save and close it, return to the Dreamweaver document, and update the image.
11. Select the photo, choose to edit it in Photoshop, and add an inner glow effect, then save and close it, return to the Dreamweaver document, and update the image.
12. From Dreamweaver choose to edit the Flash movie.
13. In Photoshop, create a graphic that resembles a portfolio case and save it as **portfolioCase.psd**.
14. In Flash, import portfolioCase.psd to the Library, specifying all the layers to be flattened bitmap images and not importing the background layer.
15. Delete the Placeholder layer, then add a layer at the top of the timeline and name it **case**.
16. Drag the portfolioCase.psd symbol from the Library and center the case on the Stage.
17. Insert a blank keyframe in frame 2 on the case layer.
18. Use the Done button to update the Flash movie and return to Dreamweaver.
19. In Dreamweaver, select the swf placeholder, play the Flash movie, and stop the movie.
20. Save your work, display the document in a browser, then compare your image to the sample in Figure 29.
21. Close the browser, then exit Dreamweaver.

Figure 29 *Sample completed Portfolio Project*

Figure 29 *Sample completed Portfolio Project*

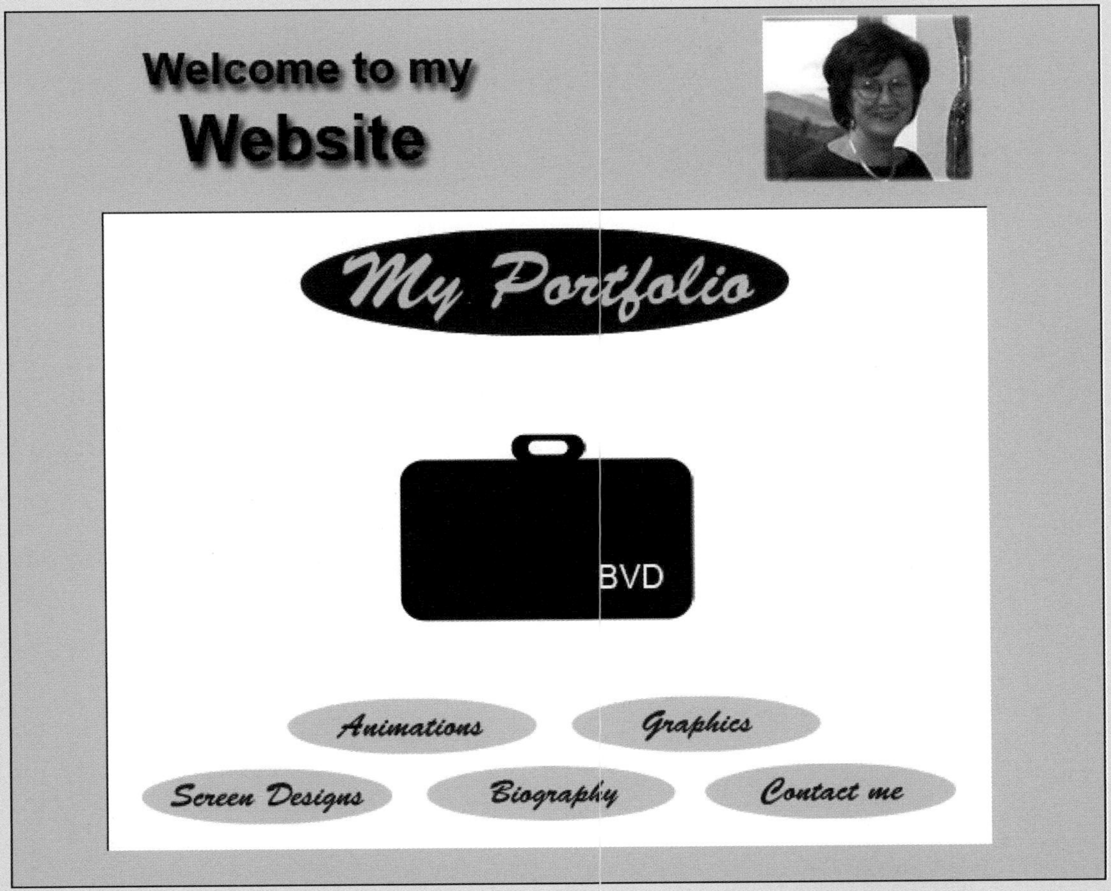

Read the following information carefully.

Find out from your instructor the location where you will store your files.

- To complete many of the chapters in this book, you need to use the Data Files provided on Cengage Brain. To access the Data Files on Cengage Brain:
  1. Open your browser and go to http://www.cengagebrain.com
  2. Type the author, title, or ISBN of this book in the Search window. (The ISBN is listed on the back cover.)
  3. Click the book title in the list of search results.
  4. When the book's main page opens, click the Access button under Free Study Tools.
  5. To download Data Files, select a chapter number and then click on the Data Files tab on the left navigation bar to download the files.

6. To access additional materials, including information about ACE certification, click the Additional Materials tab under Book Resources to download the files.

- Your instructor will tell you where to save the data files and where to store the files you create and modify.
- All the Data Files are organized in folders named after the chapter in which they are used. For instance, all Chapter 1 Data Files are stored in the chapter_1 folder. You should leave all the Data Files in these folders; do not move any Data File out of the folder in which it is originally stored.

Copy and organize your Data Files.

- Copy the folders that contain the Data Files to a USB storage drive, network folder, hard drive, or other storage device.

- For the Dreamweaver files, you build each website, the exercises in this book will guide you to copy the Data Files you need from the appropriate Data Files folder to the folder where you are storing the website. Your Data Files should always remain intact because you are copying (and not moving) them to the website.
- Because you will be building a website from one chapter to the next, sometimes you will need to use a Data File that is already contained in the website you are working on.

Find and keep track of your Data Files and completed files.

- Use the **Data File Supplied** column to make sure you have the files you need before starting the chapter or exercise indicated in the **Chapter** column.
- Use the **Student Creates File** column to find out the filename you use when saving your new file for the exercise.

Files Used in This Book

ADOBE BRIDGE CS6			
Chapter	**Data File Supplied**	**Student Creates File**	**Used In**
Chapter 1	blooms_banner.jpg		
	blue_footed_booby.jpg		
	boardwalk.jpg		
	boats.jpg		
	brunch.jpg		
	butterfly.jpg		
	cafe_logo.gif		
	cafe_photo.gif		
	cc_banner.jpg		
	cc_banner_with_text.jpg		
	children_cooking.jpg		
	chives.jpg		
	chocolate_cake.jpg		
	club_house.jpg		
	coleus.jpg		
	cookies_oven.jpg		
	family_sunset.jpg		
	fiber_optic_grass.jpg		
	fish.jpg		
	fisherman.jpg		
	gardening_gloves.jpg		
	iguana_and_lizard.jpg		
	lady_in_red.jpg		
	llama.jpg		

ADOBE BRIDGE CS6			
Chapter	Data File Supplied	Student Creates File	Used In
Chapter 1, continued	machu_picchu_from_high.jpg		
	machu_picchu_ruins.jpg		
	map_large.jpg		
	map_small.jpg		
	marshmallows.jpg		
	peruvian_appetizers.jpg		
	peruvian_glass.jpg		
	pie.jpg		
	plants.jpg		
	pool.jpg		
	rose_bloom.jpg		
	rose_bud.jpg		
	ruby_grass.jpg		
	sea_lions_in_surf.jpg		
	sea_spa_logo.png		
	spacer_30px.gif		
	su_banner.gif		
	su_logo.gif		
	trees.jpg		
	tripsmart_banner.gif		
	tripsmart_gradient.jpg		
	tulips.jpg		
	two_dolphins_small.jpg		
	two_roses.jpg		

ADOBE BRIDGE CS6			
Chapter	Data File Supplied	Student Creates File	Used In
Chapter 1, continued	two_roses_large.jpg		
	walking_stick.jpg		
	water.jpg		
	water_lily.jpg		

ADOBE DREAMWEAVER CS6			
Chapter	**Data File Supplied**	**Student Creates File**	**Used In**
Chapter 1	dw1_1.html		Lesson 2
	assets/pool.jpg		
	assets/su_banner.gif		
	dw1_2.html	about_us.html	Lesson 4
	assets/su_banner.gif	activities.html	
		cafe.html	
		cruises.html	
		fishing.html	
		index.html	
		spa.html	
	dw1_3.html	annuals.html	Skills Review
	dw1_4.html	index.html	
	assets/blooms_banner.jpg	newsletter.html	
	assets/tulips.jpg	perennials.html	
		plants.html	
		tips.html	
		water_plants.html	
		workshops.html	
	dw1_5.html	catalog.html	Project Builder 1

ADOBE DREAMWEAVER CS6			
Chapter	**Data File Supplied**	**Student Creates File**	**Used In**
Chapter 1, continued	assets/tripsmart_banner.jpg	galapagos.html	
		index.html	
		newsletter.html	
		peru.html	
		services.html	
		tours.html	
	dw1_6.html	adults.html	Project Builder 2
	assets/cc_banner.jpg	catering.html	
		children.html	
		classes.html	
		index.html	
		recipes.html	
		shop.html	
	none		Design Project
	none		Portfolio Project
Chapter 2	spa.doc		Lesson 2
	assets/sea_spa_logo.png		
	gardening_tips.doc		Skills Review
	assets/butterfly.jpg		
	none		Project Builder 1
	none		Project Builder 2
	none		Design Project
	none		Portfolio Project

ADOBE DREAMWEAVER CS6			
Chapter	**Data File Supplied**	**Student Creates File**	**Used In**
Chapter 3	questions.doc		Lesson 1
		su_styles.css	Lesson 2
		blooms_styles.css	Skills Review
	dw3_1.html		Project Builder 1
		tripsmart_styles.css	
	assets/tripsmart_banner.jpg		
	dw3_2.html	cc_styles.css	Project Builder 2
	assets/cc_banner.jpg		
	assets/pie.jpg		
	none		Design Project
	none		Portfolio Project
Chapter 4	dw4_1.html		Lesson 1
	assets/boardwalk.png		
	assets/club_house.jpg		
	assets/su_banner.gif		
	assets/su_logo.gif		
	assets/water.jpg		Lesson 3
	starfish.ico		Lesson 4
	assets/map_large.jpg		
	assets/map_small.jpg		
	assets/spacer.gif		
	dw4_2.html		Skills Review
	flower.ico		
	assets/blooms_banner.jpg		

DATA FILES LIST

(CONTINUED)

ADOBE DREAMWEAVER CS6			
Chapter	**Data File Supplied**	**Student Creates File**	**Used In**
Chapter 4, continued	assets/lady_in_red.jpg		
	assets/rose_bloom.jpg		
	assets/rose_bud.jpg		
	assets/two_roses.jpg		
	assets/two_roses_large.jpg		
	dw4_3.html		Project Builder 1
	airplane.ico		
	assets/blue_footed_booby.jpg		
	assets/iguana_and_lizard.jpg		
	assets/tripsmart_banner.jpg		
	dw4_4.html		Project Builder 2
	assets/cc_banner.jpg		
	assets/brunch.jpg		
	assets/peruvian_glass.jpg		
	none		Design Project
	none		Portfolio Project
Chapter 5	dw5_1.html		Lesson 1
	assets/family_sunset.jpg		
	assets/su_banner.gif		
	assets/two_dolphins_small.jpg		
	SpryAssets/SpryMenuBar.js	SpryAssets/SpryMenuBar.js	Lesson 3
	SpryAssets/SpryMenuBarDown.gif	SpryAssets/SpryMenuBarDown.gif	
	SpryAssets/SpryMenuBarDownHover.gif	SpryAssets/SpryMenuBarDownHover.gif	
	SpryAssets/SpryMenuBarHorizontal.css	SpryAssets/SpryMenuBarHorizontal.css	

ADOBE DREAMWEAVER CS6			
Chapter	**Data File Supplied**	**Student Creates File**	**Used In**
Chapter 5, continued	SpryAssets/SpryMenuBarRight.gif	SpryAssets/SpryMenuBarRight.gif	
	SpryAssets/SpryMenuBarRightHover.gif	SpryAssets/SpryMenuBarRightHover.gif	
	dw5_2.html		Lesson 5
	dw5_3.html		
	assets/boats.jpg		
	assets/fisherman.jpg		
	dw5_4.html		Skills Review
	dw5_5.html		
	dw5_6.html		
	dw5_7.html		
	assets/blooms_banner.jpg		
	assets/coleus.jpg		
	assets/fiber_optic_grass.jpg		
	assets/plants.jpg		
	assets/ruby_grass.jpg		
	assets/trees.jpg		
	assets/water_lily.jpg		
	SpryAssets/SpryMenuBar.js	SpryAssets/SpryMenuBar.js	
	SpryAssets/SpryMenuBarDown.gif	SpryAssets/SpryMenuBarDown.gif	
	SpryAssets/SpryMenuBarDownHover.gif	SpryAssets/SpryMenuBarDownHover.gif	
	SpryAssets/SpryMenuBarHorizontal.css	SpryAssets/SpryMenuBarHorizontal.css	
	SpryAssets/SpryMenuBarRight.gif	SpryAssets/SpryMenuBarRight.gif	
	SpryAssets/SpryMenuBarRightHover.gif	SpryAssets/SpryMenuBarRightHover.gif	

ADOBE DREAMWEAVER CS6			
Chapter	**Data File Supplied**	**Student Creates File**	**Used In**
Chapter 5, continued	dw5_8.html		Project Builder 1
	dw5_9.html		
	dw5_10.html		
	assets/llama.jpg		
	assets/machu_picchu_from_high.jpg		
	assets/machu_picchu_ruins.jpg		
	assets/sea_lions_in_surf.jpg		
	assets/tripsmart_banner.jpg		
	SpryAssets/SpryMenuBar.js	SpryAssets/SpryMenuBar.js	
	SpryAssets/SpryMenuBarDown.gif	SpryAssets/SpryMenuBarDown.gif	
	SpryAssets/SpryMenuBarDownHover.gif	SpryAssets/SpryMenuBarDownHover.gif	
	SpryAssets/SpryMenuBarHorizontal.css	SpryAssets/SpryMenuBarHorizontal.css	
	SpryAssets/SpryMenuBarRight.gif	SpryAssets/SpryMenuBarRight.gif	
	SpryAssets/SpryMenuBarRightHover.gif	SpryAssets/SpryMenuBarRightHover.gif	
	dw5_11.html		Project Builder 2
	dw5_12.html		
	dw5_13.html		
	assets/cc_banner_with_text.jpg		
	assets/children_cooking.jpg		
	assets/cookies_oven.jpg		
	assets/fish.jpg		
	assets/peruvian_appetizers.jpg		
	none		Design Project
	none		Portfolio Project

ADOBE DREAMWEAVER CS6			
Chapter	**Data File Supplied**	**Student Creates File**	**Used In**
Chapter 6	cafe.doc		Lesson 2
	assets/cafe_logo.gif		
	assets/cafe_photo.jpg		
	assets/chocolate_cake.jpg		Lesson 6
	composting.doc		Skills Review
	assets/chives.jpg		
	assets/gardening_gloves.gif		
	assets/tripsmart.gradient.jpg		Project Builder 1
	walking sticks.doc		
	assets/walking_stick.jpg		
	marshmallows.doc		Project Builder 2
	assets/marshmallows.jpg		
	none		Design Project
	none		Portfolio Project
Chapter 7	none	The Striped Umbrella.ste	Lesson 5
	none	Blooms & Bulbs.ste	Skills Review
	none	TripSmart.ste	Project Builder 1
	none	Carolyne's Creations.ste	Project Builder 2
	none		Design Project
	none		Portfolio Project

DATA FILES LIST
(CONTINUED)

ADOBE FLASH CS6			
Chapter	**Data File Supplied**	**Student Creates New File**	**Used In**
Chapter 1		workspace.fla	Lesson 1
	fl1_1.fla		Lesson 2
		tween.fla	Lesson 3
	*tween.fla	layers.fla	Lesson 4
	*layers.fla		Lesson 5
			Lesson 6
	fl1_2.fla		Skills Review
		demonstration.fla	Project Builder 1
	fl1_3.fla		Project Builder 2
		dpc1.doc	Design Project
			Portfolio Project
Chapter 2	fl2_1.fla		Lesson 1
	fl2_2.fla		
	fl2_3.fla		
	fl2_4.fla		Lesson 4
	fl2_5.fla		Lesson 5
	fl2_6.fla		Skills Review
		ultimateTours2.fla	Project Builder 1
		theJazzClub2.fla	Project Builder 2
		dpc2.doc	Design Project
		portfolio2.fla	Portfolio Project

*Created in a previous Lesson or Skills Review in current chapter

ADOBE FLASH CS6			
Chapter	**Data File Supplied**	**Student Creates New File**	**Used In**
Chapter 3	fl3_1.fla		Lesson 1
	fl3_2.fla		Lessons 2-4
	islandview.jpg	sailing.fla	Lesson 5
	sailboat.ai		
	fl3_3.fla		Skills Review
	BeachScene.jpg		
	**ultimatetours2.fla		Project Builder 1
	UTLogo.png		
		isa3.fla	Project Builder 2
		dpc3.doc	Design Project
	**portfolio2.fla		Portfolio Project
Chapter 4	fl4_1.fla		Lesson 1
	fl4_2.fla		
	fl4_3.fla		Lesson 2
	fl4_4.fla		Lesson 3
	fl4_5.fla		
	fl4_6.fla		Lesson 4
	fl4_7.fla		
	fl4_8.fla		
	fl4_9.fla		Lesson 5
	fl4_10.fla		Lesson 6

**Created in a previous chapter

DATA FILES LIST

(CONTINUED)

ADOBE FLASH CS6			
Chapter	**Data File Supplied**	**Student Creates New File**	**Used In**
Chapter 4, continued	fl4_11.fla		Skills Review
	fl4_12.fla		Project Builder 1
	ship.gif		
	fl4_13.fla		Project Builder 2
		dpc4.doc	Design Project
	**portfolio3.fla		Portfolio Project
Chapter 5	fl5_1.fla		Lesson 1
	fl5_2.fla		Lesson 2
	CarSnd.wav		
	beep.wav		
	fl5_3.fla		Lesson 3
	fireworks.mov		
	fl5_4.fla		Lesson 4
	fl5_5.fla		Lesson 5
	fl5_6.fla		
	fl5_7.fla		Lesson 6
	fl5_8.fla		Lesson 7
	fl5_9.fla		Skills Review
	fl5_10.fla		
	fl5_11.fla		
	*decoLand.fla		
	tour-video.mov		

*Created in a previous Lesson or Skills Review in current chapter
**Created in a previous chapter

ADOBE FLASH CS6			
Chapter	**Data File Supplied**	**Student Creates New File**	**Used In**
Chapter 5, continued	fl5_12.fla		Project Builder 1
	**ultimatetours4.fla		
	fl5_13.fla		Project Builder 2
		dpc5.doc	Design Project
	**portfolio4.fla		Portfolio Project
Chapter 6	fl6_1.fla		Lesson 1
	fl6_2.fla		Lesson 2
	fl6_3.fla		Lesson 3
	fl6_4.fla		Lesson 4
	Match16.png		
	Match32.png		
	Match48.png		
	Match128.png		
	fl6_5.fla	SanteFe.fla	Lesson 5
	Game36.png		
	Game48.png		
	Game72.png		
	SFimage.jpg		
	SF36.png		
	SF48.png		
	SF72.png		

**Created in a previous chapter

Data Files List

ADOBE FLASH CS6			
Chapter	**Data File Supplied**	**Student Creates New File**	**Used In**
Chapter 6, continued	fl6_6.fla		Skills Review
	fl6_7.fla		
	sedona16.png		
	sedona32.png		
	sedona48.png		
	sedona128.png		
	sedonaImage.png		
	sedona36.png		
	sedona72.png		
	fl6_8.fla		Project Builder 1
	**ultimatetours5.fla		
	uTours16.png		
	uTours32.png		
	uTours48.png		
	uTours128.png		
	publish16.png		Project Builder 2
	publish32.png		
	publish36.png		
	publish48.png		

**Created in a previous chapter

ADOBE FLASH CS6			
Chapter	**Data File Supplied**	**Student Creates New File**	**Used In**
Chapter 6, continued	publish72.png		
	publish128.png		
		dpc6.doc	Design Project
	**portfolio5.fla		Portfolio Project

**Created in a previous chapter

DATA FILES LIST

(CONTINUED)

ADOBE PHOTOSHOP CS6			
Chapter	**Chapter Data File Supplied**	**Student Creates File**	**Used in**
Chapter 1	PS 1-1.psd		Lessons 2–4
	PS 1-2.tif		
		Review.psd	Skills Review
	PS 1-3.jpg		Skills Review
Chapter 2	PS 2-1.psd		Lesson 1
	PS 2-2.jpg		
	PS 2-3.psd		
	PS 2-4.psd		Lesson 2
		Your name Chapter 2 contact sheet.pdf	Lesson 4
	PS 2-5.psd		Skills Review
	PS 2-6.psd		Project Builder 2
		Critique-1.psd	Design Project
		Critique-2.psd	
		Cloud Computing.docx	Portfolio Project
Chapter 3	PS 3-1.psd		Lessons 1–4
	PS 3-2.psd		
	PS 3-3.psd		Skills Review
	PS 3-4.psd		
	PS 3-5.psd		Project Builder 1
	PS 3-6.psd		
	PS 3-7.psd		Project Builder 2
	PS 3-8.psd		
	PS 3-9.psd		Design Project
	PS 3-10.psd		
	PS 3-11.psd		Portfolio Project

ADOBE PHOTOSHOP CS6			
Chapter	Chapter Data File Supplied	Student Creates File	Used in
Chapter 4	PS 4-1.psd		Lessons 1–4
	PS 4-2.psd		
	PS 4-3.psd		
	PS 4-4.psd		
	PS 4-5.psd		
	PS 4-6.psd		
	PS 4-7.psd		Skills Review
	PS 4-8.tif		
	PS 4-9.tif		
	PS 4-10.tif		
	PS 4-11.psd		Project Builder 1
	PS 4-12.psd		Project Builder 2
		Sample Compositing.psd	Design Project
	PS 4-13.psd		Portfolio Project
Chapter 5	PS 5-1.psd		Lessons 1–4, 6-7
	PS 5-2.psd		Lessons 5–6
	PS 5-3.tif		Lesson 7
	PS 5-4.psd		Skills Review
	PS 5-5.psd		
	PS 5-6.tif		
	PS 5-7.psd		Project Builder 1
	PS 5-8.psd		Project Builder 2
	PS 5-9.psd		Design Project
	PS 5-10.psd		Portfolio Project

ADOBE PHOTOSHOP CS6			
Chapter	**Chapter Data File Supplied**	**Student Creates File**	**Used in**
Chapter 6	PS 6-1.psd		Lessons 1–7
	PS 6-2.psd		Skills Review
	PS 6-3.psd		Project Builder 1
	PS 6-4.psd		Project Builder 2
	PS 6-5.psd		Design Project
		Community Promotion.psd	Portfolio Project

WEB COLLECTION PREMIUM INTEGRATION CS6			
Chapter	**Data File Supplied**	**Student Creates File**	**Used in**
Chapter 1		Southwest folder	Lesson 1
	ic_1.html	CanyonScenes.html	
	ic_1.psd	GrandCanyon.psd	
		Assets/GrandCanyon.jpg	
	ic_2.psd	Rapids.psd	
		Assets/Rapids.png	
	ic_3.psd	AZScenes.fla	Lesson 2
		NorthernAZ.psd	
	*AZScenes.fla	AZScenes.swf	Lesson 3
		NorthernAZ.html	
		Food folder	Skills Review
	bread-heading.psd	bread-headingRev.psd	
		food-home.html	
		Assets/bread-headingRev.jpg	
	bread-photo.psd	bread-photoRev.psd	
		bread-An.fla	
		Assets/bread-An.swf	
		UTours folder	Project Builder 1
	UTours_home.html	UTours_homeRev.html	
	UTours-heading.psd	UTours-headingRev.psd	
		Assets/UTours-headingRev.jpg	
	UTours-photo.psd	UTours-photoRev.psd	
		UTours-PhotoAn.fla	
		Assets/UTours-PhotoAn.swf	

*Created in a previous Lesson or Skills Review in current chapter

DATA FILES LIST
(CONTINUED)

WEB COLLECTION PREMIUM INTEGRATION CS6			
Chapter	**Data File Supplied**	**Student Creates File**	**Used in**
Chapter 1, continued	**ultimateTours5.swf		
	Striped Umbrella site files		Project Builder 2
	cafe_logo.psd	crabAn.fla	
		Assets/crabAn.swf	
		cafe_logo.psd	
	cafe.html	cafeRev.html	
	none	dpcIntegration.doc	Design Project
		PortfolioSite folder	Portfolio Project
	portfoliohome.html	portfoliohomeRev.html	
	portfolio-heading.psd	Assets/portfolio-heading.jpg	
		Assets/portfolio-photo.jpg	
		portfolioCase.psd	
	**portfolio5.fla		
	**portfolio5.swf		

**Created in a previous chapter

3D Effects

A process in Flash that animates 2D objects through 3D space with 3D Transformation tools.

3D Extrusion

A tool for turning a 2-dimensional object (such as type) into a 3-dimensional object. Allows for rotation, rolling, panning, sliding, and scaling.

A

Absolute path

A path containing an external link that references a link on a web page outside of the current website, and includes the protocol "http" and the URL, or address, of the web page.

Acrobat.com

A management feature of the Adobe Creative Suite that can be used to organize your work.

ActionScript

The Flash scripting language used by developers to add interactivity to movies, control objects, exchange data, and create complex animations.

Actions Panel

The Flash ActionScript panel used when you create and edit actions for an object or frame.

Active layer

The layer highlighted on the Layers panel. The active layer's name appears in parentheses in the image window title bar.

Additive colors

A color system in which, when the values of R, G, and B (red, green, and blue) are 0, the result is black; when the values are all 255, the result is white.

Adjustment layer

An additional layer for which you can specify individual color adjustments. The adjustment layer allows you to temporarily alter a layer before making the adjustment permanent.

Adjustment panel

Visible panel that makes creation of adjustment layers easy.

Adobe AIR

A runtime player that enables developers to deploy standalone applications built with Flash across platforms and devices, including mobile devices and personal computers.

Adobe Bridge

A stand-alone application that serves as the hub for the Adobe Creative Suite. It can be used for file management tasks such as opening, viewing, sorting, and rating files.

Adobe BrowserLab

An Adobe online service for cross-browser and cross-platform compatibility testing.

Adobe Business Catalyst

A hosted application for setting up and maintaining an online business.

Adobe Community Help

A collection of materials such as tutorials, published articles, or blogs, that is part of the Adobe Help content.

Adobe Configurator

A stand-alone program (available as a download) that lets you create your own panels.

Adobe Creative Cloud

A fee-based membership service that includes CS tools, Adobe Touch Apps, services, plus new products and services as they are released.

Adobe DNG

See Digital Negative Format.

Adobe Flash

A development tool used to create and deliver compelling interactive content, for websites, applications and mobile devices.

Adobe Flash Player

A free Adobe program that allows Flash movies (.swf) to be viewed on a computer within a browser.

Adobe Mini Bridge

A less-powerful (and smaller) version of Bridge that opens within the Photoshop window.

AIR (Adobe Integrated Runtime)

A Flash technology used to create applications that can be played without a browser. An AIR app can be displayed on mobile devices, on stand-alone computers, on the Internet, and even on television sets.

AIR for Android

A feature of Flash that allows you to publish Flash FLA files so that they run on Android devices (smartphones and tablets).

AIR for iOS

A feature of Flash that allows you to publish Flash FLA files so that they run on iOS devices (iPhones and iPads).

Aligning an object
Positioning an image on the Flash Stage in relation to other objects on the Stage. In Dreamweaver, Positioning an image on a web page in relation to other elements on the page.

Altitude
A Bevel and Emboss setting that affects the amount of visible dimension.

Anchor point
Points on a drawing or motion path used to reshape the drawing or path.

Angle
In the Layer Style dialog box, the setting that determines where a drop shadow falls relative to the text.

Animation
The perception of motion caused by the rapid display of a series of still images.

Anti-aliasing
Partially fills in pixel edges, resulting in smooth-edge type. This feature lets your type maintain its crisp appearance and is especially useful for large type.

AP div tag
A div that is assigned a fixed (absolute) position on a web page. *See also* AP element.

AP element
The container that an AP div tag creates on a page. *See also* AP div tag.

Apache web server
A public domain, open source web server that is available using several different operating systems, including UNIX and Windows.

Application bar (Win)
In Bridge, the toolbar that contains the navigation buttons, the Workspace buttons, and the Search text box.

Applications (also called apps)
Products such as interactive games, tutorials, demonstrations, business and informational programs that can be incorporated in a website, deployed on a desktop computer or delivered on a mobile device.

Arrangement
How objects are positioned in space, relative to one another.

Assets
Files that are not web pages, such as images, Flash files, and video clips.

Assets folder
A subfolder in the local site root folder in which you store most of the files that are not web pages, such as images, Flash files, and video clips. This folder is often named images, but can be assigned any name.

Assets panel
A panel that contains nine categories of assets, such as images, used in a website. Clicking a category button displays a list of those assets.

Asymmetrical balance
A design principle in which page elements are placed unequally on either side of an imaginary vertical line in the center of the page in order to create a feeling of tension or express a feeling or mood.

Attribution (*cc by*)
The simplest of all Creative Commons licenses, in which any user (commercial or non-commercial) can distribute, modify, or enhance your work, provided you are credited.

Attribution No Derivatives (*cc by-nd*)
Your work can be distributed by others, but not modified and in its entirety, with you being credited.

Attribution Non-Commercial (*cc by-nc*)
Your work can be distributed, modified, or enhanced, with credit to you, for non-commercial purposes only. Derivative works do not have to be licensed.

Attribution Non-Commercial No Derivatives (*cc by-nc-nd*)
This is the most restrictive license category. Redistribution is allowed as long as credit is given. The work cannot be modified or used commercially.

Attribution Non-Commercial Share Alike (*cc by-nc-sa*)
Your work can be distributed, modified, or enhanced, with credit to you, for non-commercial purposes only, but must be licensed under the identical terms. All derivative work must carry the same license, and be non-commercial.

Attribution Share Alike (*cc by-sa*)
The same as Attribution, except that the new owner must create their license under the same terms you used.

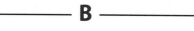

B

Background color
A color that fills an entire web page, frame, table, cell, Stage, or CSS layout block. In image-editing programs, used to make gradient fills and to fill in areas of an image that have been erased. The default background color is white.

Background image
A graphic file used in place of a background color.

Balance

In screen design, balance refers to the distribution of optical weight in the layout. Optical weight is the ability of an object to attract the viewer's eye, as determined by the object's size, shape, color, and so on.

Balance colors

Process of adding and subtracting colors from those already existing in a layer.

Bandwidth Profiler

A feature in Flash used to optimize the size of a movie by simulating a computer's internet connection speed.

Banners

Images that generally appear across the top or down the side of a web page and can incorporate a company's logo, contact information, and links to the other pages in the site.

Base color

The original color of an image.

BaseCamp

A web-based project collaboration tool.

Baseline

An invisible line on which type rests.

Baseline shift

The distance type appears from its original position.

Bitmap

A geometric arrangement of different color dots on a rectangular grid. Bitmap images may develop jagged edges when enlarged.

Bitmap mode

Uses black or white color values to represent image pixels; a good choice for images with subtle color gradations, such as photographs or painted images.

Blend color

The color applied to the base color when a blending mode is applied to a layer.

Blending mode

Affects the layer's underlying pixels or base color. Used to darken or lighten colors, depending on the colors in use.

Blog

A website where the website owner regularly posts commentaries and opinions on various topics.

Blue drop zone

See Drop zone.

Blur filters

Used to soften a selection or image.

Body

The part of a web page that appears in a browser window. It contains all of the page content that is visible to users, such as text, images, and links.

Border

An outline that surrounds a cell, a table, or a CSS layout block.

Breadcrumbs trail

A list of links that provides a path from the initial page opened in a website to the page being currently viewed.

Break apart

In Flash, the process of breaking apart text to place each character in a separate text block. Also, the process of separating groups, instances, and bitmaps into ungrouped, editable elements.

Bridge

See Adobe Bridge.

Brightness

The measurement of relative lightness or darkness of a color (measured as a percentage from 0% [black] to 100% [white]).

Broken link

A link that cannot find the intended destination file for the link.

Browser Compatibility Check (BCC)

A Dreamweaver feature that checks for problems in the HTML code that might present a CSS rendering issue in some browsers by underlining questionable code in green.

Bullet

A small dot or similar icon preceding unordered list items. *See also* Bulleted list.

Bulleted list

An unordered list that uses bullets. *See also* Bullet.

Button Symbols

Objects in Flash that appear on the Stage and that are used to provide interactivity, such as jumping to another frame on the Timeline.

────────── C ──────────

Camera Raw

Allows you to use digital data directly from a digital camera. The file extension that you see will vary with each digital camera manufacturer. The Camera Raw feature allows you to make additional adjustments to images.

Camera Raw file

A file format that contains unprocessed data and is not yet ready to be printed, similar to a negative from a film camera.

Canvas size

The full editable aea of an image that can be increased or decreased in size using the Canvas Size command on the Image menu.

Cascading Style Sheet

A set of formatting attributes used to format web pages to provide a consistent presentation for content across a website.

Cell

A small box within a table that is used to hold text or graphics. Cells are arranged horizontally in rows and vertically in columns.

Cell padding

The distance between the cell content and the cell walls in a table.

Cell spacing

The distance between cells in a table.

Cell walls

The edges surrounding a cell in a table.

Channels

Used to store information about the color elements contained in each channel.

Character panel

Helps you control type properties. The Toggle the Character and Paragraph panels button is located on the options bar when you select a Type tool.

Child container

A container, created with HTML tags, whose code resides inside a parent container. Its properties are inherited from its parent container unless otherwise specified. *See also* Parent container.

Child keyword

In Bridge, a keyword that is a sub-category of a parent keyword; also known as a subkeyword.

Child page

A page at a lower level in a web hierarchy that links to page at a higher level called a parent page.

Class type

A type of style that can contain a combination of formatting attributes that can be applied to a block of text or other page elements. Custom style names begin with a period (.). Also called a custom type.

Clean HTML code

Code that does what it is supposed to do without using unnecessary instructions, which take up memory.

Clipboard

Temporary storage area, provided by your operating system, for cut and copied data.

Cloak

To exclude from certain processes, such as being transferred to a remote site.

Cloud computing

Allows you to share files with others in a virtual environment.

CMYK image

An image using the CMYK color system, containing at least four channels (one each for cyan, magenta, yellow, and black).

CMYK mode

Color mode is based on colors being partially absorbed as the ink hits the paper and then being partially reflected back to your eyes.

Code hints

An auto-complete feature that displays lists of tags that appear as you type in Code view in the Flash ActionScript panel.

Code Inspector

A separate floating window that displays the current page in Code view.

Code Snippets

Small blocks of Flash ActionScript code that can be applied to an object in an application or the application in general.

Code view

The Dreamweaver view that shows the underlying HTML code for the page; use this view to read or edit the code.

Coding toolbar

A toolbar that contains buttons you can use when working in Code view.

Collections panel

In Bridge, a panel used to group assets located in different locations into a single collection.

Color mode

Used to determine how to display and print an image. Each mode is based on established models used in color reproduction. Represents the amount of color data that can be stored in a given file format, and determines the color model used to display and print an image. Determines the number and range of colors displayed.

Color model

Determines how pigments combine to produce resulting colors.

Color Picker

A feature that lets you choose a color from a color spectrum.

Color Range command

Used to select pixels having a particular color in an existing image or layer.

Color separation

Result of converting an RGB image into a CMYK image; the commercial printing process of separating colors for use with different inks.

Column

Table cells arranged vertically.

Compact mode

A Bridge mode with a smaller, simplified workspace.

Compositing

Combining images from sources such as other Photoshop images, royalty-free images, pictures taken from digital cameras, and scanned artwork.

Compound type
A type of style that is used to format a selection.

Content panel
In Bridge, the center pane where thumbnails of the files from the selected drive and folder in the Folders panel appear.

Contiguous
Items that are next to one another.

Controller
A panel that contains the playback controls for a Flash movie.

Coordinate
The position on the Flash Stage of a pixel as measured across (X coordinate) and down (Y coordinate) the Stage.

Copyright
A legal protection for the particular and tangible expression of an idea. The right of an author or creator of a work to copy, distribute, and modify a thing, idea, or image; a type of intellectual property.

Creative Commons licenses
Licensing of intellectual property without the use of lawyers or expensive fees by Creative Commons, a non-profit organization that offers free licenses and legal tools used to mark creative work.

Crisp
Anti-aliasing setting that gives type more definition and makes it appear sharper.

Crop
To exclude part of an image. Cropping hides areas of an image without losing resolution quality.

CS Live
A management feature of the Adobe Creative Suite that can be used to connect to Acrobat.com and organize your work whether you work in groups or by yourself.

CSS layout block
A section of a web page defined and formatted using a Cascading Style Sheet.

CSS Layout Box Model
CSS layout blocks defined as rectangular boxes of content with margins, padding, and borders.

CSS page layout
A method of positioning objects on web pages through the use of containers formatted with CSS. *See also* Cascading Style Sheets.

Custom type
See Class type.

——————— **D** ———————

Darken Only option
Replaces light pixels with darker pixels.

Debug
To find and correct coding errors.

Declaration
The property and value of a style in a Cascading Style Sheet.

Deco Tool
Tool used to create drawing effects that can be used to quickly create environments, such as city landscapes, and to create various animations.

Default font
The font a browser uses to display text if no other font is assigned.

Default link color
The color a browser uses to display text if no other color is assigned.

Defringe command
Replaces fringe pixels with the colors of other nearby pixels.

Delimited file
Database, word processing, or spreadsheet file that has been saved as a text file with data separated with delimiters such as commas or tabs.

Delimiter
A comma, tab, colon, semicolon, or similar character that separates tabular data.

Deliverables
Products that will be provided to the client at the product completion such as pages or graphic elements created.

Dependent file
File that another file needs to be complete, such as an image or style sheet.

Deprecated
Code that is no longer within the current standard and in danger of becoming obsolete.

Depth of field
Camera feature used to enhance the image composition; the sharp area surrounding the point of focus.

Derivative work
An adaptation of another work, such as a movie version of a book; a new, original product that includes content from a previously existing work.

Description
A short summary that resides in the head section of a web page and describes the website content. *See also* Head content.

Deselect
A command that removes the marquee from an area so it is no longer selected.

Design Note
A separate file in a website file structure that contains additional information about a page file or a graphic file.

Design view
The Dreamweaver view that shows the page as it would appear in a browser and is primarily used for creating and designing a web page.

Digital camera
A camera that captures images on electronic media (rather than film). Its images are in a standard digital format and can be downloaded for computer use.

Digital image
A picture in electronic form. It may be referred to as a file, document, picture, or image.

Digital Negative Format
An archival format for camera raw files that contains the raw image data created within a digital camera as well as its defining metadata. Also called *Adobe DNG*.

Distance
Determines how far a shadow falls from the text. This setting is used by the Drop Shadow and Bevel and Emboss styles.

Distort filters
Create 3-dimensional or other reshaping effects. Some of the types of distortions you can produce include Glass, Pinch, Ripple, Shear, Spherize, Twirl, Wave, and ZigZag.

Div tag
An HTML tag that is used to format and position web page elements.

Dock
A collection of panels or panel groups. Also the dark gray bar to the left of the collection of panels or buttons. The arrows in the dock are used to maximize and minimize the panels.

Dock (verb)
The process of combining panels into panel sets.

Document
A Flash, Photoshop, Fireworks, or Dreamweaver file.

Document toolbar
A toolbar that contains buttons and drop-down menus for changing the current work mode, checking browser compatibility, previewing web pages, debugging web pages, choosing visual aids, and viewing file management options.

Document window
The large area under the Document toolbar in the Dreamweaver workspace where you create and edit web pages.

Domain name
An IP address expressed in letters instead of numbers, usually reflecting the name of the business represented by the website; also referred to as a URL.

Download
The process of transferring files from a remote site to a local site.

Dreamweaver workspace
The entire window, from the Application bar (Win) or Menu bar (Mac) at the top of the window, to the status bar at the bottom border of the program window; the area in the Dreamweaver program window that includes all of the menus, panels, buttons, inspectors, and panes that you use to create and maintain websites.

Drop Shadow
A style that adds what looks like a colored layer of identical text behind the selected type. The default shadow color is black.

Drop Zone
A blue outline area that indicates where a palette or panel can be docked.

DSL
Digital Subscriber Line. A type of high-speed Internet connection.

Dual Screen Layout
A layout you can utilize when using two monitors while working in Dreamweaver.

Duotone mode
Color mode used to create grayscale images using monotones, duotones, tritones, and quadtones.

----------- **E** -----------

Embedded style sheet
A style that is part of an HTML page rather than comprising a separate file. Also called an internal style.

Embedded video
A video file that has been imported into a Flash document and becomes part of the SWF file.

Essentials workspace
The default workspace in Bridge that includes all of the menus, panels, buttons, and panes that are used to organize media files.

Export
To save data that was created in Dreamweaver in a special file format so that you can open it in another software program.

Export panel
In Bridge, a panel used to optimize images by saving them as JPEGs for use on the web.

Extensible Metadata Platform (XMP) standard
The standard Adobe uses to save metadata.

External link
A ink that connects to a web page in an other website or to an e-mail address.

External style sheet
Collection of styles stored in a separate file that controls the formatting of content on a web page. External style sheets have a .css file extension.

——————— **F** ———————

Facebook
A social networking site that lets users interact as an online community through the sharing of text, images, and videos.

Fair use
A concept that allows limited use of copyright-protected work. Allows a user to make a copy of all or part of a work, even if permission has not been granted.

Fair use doctrine
Allows a user to make a copy of all or part of a work within specific parameters of usage, even if permission *has not* been granted.

Fastening point
An anchor within the marquee. When the marquee pointer reaches the initial fastening point, a small circle appears on the pointer, indicating that you have reached the starting point.

Favicon
Short for favorites icon, a small image that represents a website and appears in the address bar of many browsers.

Favorites
Assets that are used repeatedly in a website and are included in their own category in the assets panel.

Favorites panel
In Bridge, a panel used to quickly access folders that are designated as folders used frequently.

Feather
A method used to control the softness of a selection's edges by blurring the area between the selection and the surrounding pixels.

Field of view
Includes the content you want to include in an image and the angle you choose to shoot from.

File Transfer Protocol (FTP)
The process of uploading and downloading files to and from a remote site.

File versioning
A feature that allows you to store multiple versions of your work.

Files panel
A window similar to Windows Explorer (Windows) or Finder (Macintosh), where Dreamweaver displays and manages files and folders. The Files panel contains a list of all the folders and files in a website.

Filter panel
In Bridge, a panel used to filter files to view in the Content panel.

Filters
Used to alter the look of an image and give it a special, customized appearance by applying special effects, such as distortions, changes in lighting, and blurring.

Fixed layout
A fixed page layout that expresses all container widths in pixels and remains the same size regardless of the size of the browser window.

Flash Player
A free Adobe program that allows Flash movies (.swf) to be viewed on a computer within a browser.

Flattening
Merges all visible layers into one layer, named the Background layer, and deletes all hidden layers, greatly reducing file size.

Flowchart
A visual representation of how the contents in an application or a website are organized and how various screens are linked.

Fluid Grid Layout
A system for designing layouts that will adapt to three different screen sizes.

Focus group
A marketing tool that asks a group of people for feedback about a product, such as the impact of a television ad or the effectiveness of a website design.

Folders panel
In Bridge, a panel used to navigate through your folders to select a folder and view the folder contents.

Font
Characters with a similar appearance.

Font-combination
A set of font choices that specifies which fonts a browser should use to display text, such as Arial, Helvetica, sans serif.

Font family
Represents a complete set of characters, letters, and symbols for a particular typeface. Font families are generally divided into three categories: serif, sans serif, and symbol.

Foreground color
Used to paint, fill, and stroke selections. The default foreground color is black.

Frame animation
An animation created by specifying the object that is to appear in each frame of a sequence of frames (also called a frame-by-frame animation).

Frame-by-frame animation
Animation that creates a new image for each frame (also called Frame animation).

Frame label
A text name for a keyframe that can be referenced within Flash ActionScript code.

Frames
Individual cells that make up the Timeline in Flash.

Framing
Centering object(s) or interest in the foreground, which gives an image a feeling of depth.

FTP
See File Transfer Protocol.

Fuzziness
Similar to tolerance, in that the lower the value, the closer the color pixels must be to be selected.

—————— **G** ——————

Gamut
The range of displayed colors in a color model.

GIF
Graphics Interchange Format file. A type of file format used for images placed on web pages that can support both transparency and animation.

Global Positioning System
See GPS.

Gloss contour
A Bevel and Emboss setting that determines the pattern with which light is reflected.

Google Video Chat
A video sharing community hosted by Google.

GPS
Acronym for Global Positioning System. A device used to track your position through a global satellite navigation system.

Gradient fill
A type of fill in which colors appear to blend into one another. A gradient's appearance is determined by its beginning and ending points. Photoshop contains five gradient fill styles.

Gradient
Two or more colors that blend into each other in a fixed design.

Gradient presets
Predesigned gradient fills that are displayed in the Gradient picker.

Graphic
A picture or design element that adds visual interest to a page.

Graphic design elements
Elements that combine to promote a pleasing page design such as the way lines, shapes, forms, textures, and colors are used to create and place elements on a page.

Graphic design principles
The use of emphasis, movement, balance, unity, symmetry, color, white space, alignment, line, contrast, rule of thirds, proximity, and repetition to create an attractive and effective page design.

Graphic symbols
Objects in Flash, such as drawings, that are converted to symbols and stored in the Library panel. A graphic symbol is the original object. Instances (copies) of a symbol can be made by dragging the symbol from the Library to the Stage.

Graphics tablet
An optional hardware peripheral that enables use of pressure-sensitive tools, allows you to create programmable menu buttons and maneuver faster in Photoshop.

Grayscale image
An image that can contain up to 256 shades of gray. Pixels can have brightness values from 0 (black) to white (255).

Grayscale mode
Uses up to 256 shades of gray, assigning a brightness value from 0 (black) to 255 (white) to each pixel.

Grid
Horizontal and vertical lines that fill the Flash Stage and are used to place page elements.

Guide layers
Layers used to align objects on the Stage in a Flash document.

Guides
Horizontal and vertical lines that you drag from the rulers onto the page to help you align objects. Guides appear as light blue lines in Photoshop.

—————— **H** ——————

Handles
Small boxes that appear along the perimeter of a selected object and are used to change the size of an image.

Head content
The part of a web page that includes the page title that appears in the title bar of the browser, as well as meta tags, which are HTML codes that include information about the page, such as keywords and descriptions, and are not visible in the browser.

Hex triplet
A color value expressed with three characters that represents the amount of red, green, and blue present in a color. Also known as an RGB triplet or Hex triplet.

Glossary

Hexadecimal RGB value
A six-character value that represents the amount of red, green, and blue in a color and is based on the Base 16 number system. If expressed in three characters instead of six, it's called an RGB triplet.

Highlight Mode
A Bevel and Emboss setting that determines how pigments are combined.

History panel
A panel that contains a record of each action performed during an editing session, and allows you to undo actions; up to 1000 levels of Undo are available through the History panel (20 levels by default).

Home page
The first page that is displayed when users go to a website.

Hotspot
A clickable area on an image that, when clicked, links to a different location on the page or to another web page.

HTML
Stands for Hypertext Markup Language, the language web developers use to create web pages.

HTML5
The current version of HTML that added new ways to add interactivity with tags that support semantic markup. Examples of added tags are <header>, <footer>, <article>, <section>, <video>, <hgroup>, <figure>, <embed>, <wbr>, and <canvas>.

Hue
The color reflected from/transmitted through an object and expressed as a degree (between 0° and 360°). Each hue is identified by a color name (such as red or green).

Hyperlink
An image or text element on a web page that users click to display another location on the page, another web page on the same website, or a web page on a different website; also known as links.

——————————— I ———————————

ID type
A type of CSS rule that is used to redefine an HTML tag.

Image
A graphic such as a photograph or a piece of artwork on a web page; images in a website are known as assets.

Image-editing program
Used to manipulate graphic images that can be posted on websites or reproduced by professional printers using full-color processes.

Image map
An image that has been divided up into sections, each of which serves as a link.

Image placeholder
A graphic the size of an image you plan to use that holds the position on the page until the final image is placed.

Import
To bring data created in one software application into another application.

InContext Editing (ICE)
An online service that users can log into and be allowed to make changes to designated editable regions on a page while viewing it in a browser.

Inheritance
The CSS governing principle that allows for the properties of a parent container to be used to format the content in a child container.

Inline style
A style whose code is placed within the body tags of a web page.

Insert panel
A panel with nine categories of buttons for creating and inserting objects displayed as a drop-down menu: Common, Layout, Forms, Data, Spry, jQuery Mobile, InContext Editing, Text, and Favorites.

Instances
Editable copies of symbols after you drag them from the Library panel to the Flash Stage.

Intellectual property
An image or idea that is owned and retained by legal control.

Interactivity
Allows visitors to your applications to interact with and affect content by moving or clicking the mouse or using the keyboard.

Internal link
A link to a web page within the same website.

Internal style sheet
A style sheet whose code is saved within the code of a web page, rather than in an external file. Also called an embedded style.

Internet Service Provider (ISP)
Internet Service Provider. A service to which you subscribe to be able to connect to the Internet with your computer.

Inverse Kinematics
A process using a bone structure that allows objects to be animated in natural ways, such as a character running, jumping or kicking.

IP address
An assigned series of numbers, separated by periods, that designates an address on the Internet.

J

JavaScript
A web-scripting code that interacts with HTML code to create dynamic content, such as rollovers or interactive forms on a web page; also called Jscript.

JPEG file
Joint Photographic Experts Group file. A JPEG is a type of file format used for images that appear on web pages. Many photographs are saved with the JPEG file format.

JPEG or JPG
An acronym for Joint Photographic Experts Group; refers to a type of file format used for images that appear on web pages. Many photographs are saved with the JPEG file format.

K

Kerning
Controlling the amount of space between two characters.

Keyboard shortcuts
Combinations of keys that can be used to work faster and more efficiently.

Keyframe
A frame that signifies a change in the Timeline of a Flash movie, such as an object being animated.

Keyword
A word that relates to the content of a website and resides in the head section of a web page.

Keyword (Bridge)
In Bridge, a word that is added to a file to identify, group and sort files.

Keywords panel
In Bridge, a panel that lists the keywords assigned to a file.

Kuler
A web-hosted application that lets you create, save, share, and download color-coordinated themes for use in images. It can be accessed from a browser, the desktop, or Adobe products such as Photoshop or Illustrator.

L

LAN
Local Area Network.

Landscape orientation
An image with the long edge of the paper at the top and bottom.

Large Document Format (PSB)
A file format for files larger than 2GB, which supports documents up to 300,000 pixels, with all Photoshop features such as layers, effects, and filters. (The PSB format can be opened by Photoshop CS or later.)

Layer
A section within an image on which objects can be stored. The advantage: Individual effects can be isolated and manipulated without affecting the rest of the image. The disadvantage: Layers can increase the size of your file.

Layer comp
A variation on the arrangement and visibility of existing layers within an image; an organizational tool.

Layer group
An organizing tool you use to group layers on the Layers panel. (Sometimes referred to as *nested layers*.)

Layer style
An effect that can be applied to a type or image layer.

Layer thumbnail
Contains a miniature picture of the layer's content, and appears to the left of the layer name on the Layers panel.

Layers
Rows on the Flash Timeline that are used to organize objects and that allow the stacking of objects on the Stage.

Layers panel
Displays all the individual layers within an active image. You can use the Layers panel to create, delete, merge, copy, or reposition layers.

Leading
The amount of vertical space between lines of type.

Library
A panel containing all of the assets used in a Flash applications such as graphic symbols, button symbols, movie-clip symbols, graphics, sounds and video. You can use multiple Libraries in a document and share Libraries between documents.

Licensing agreement
The permission given by a copyright holder that conveys the right to use the copyright holder's work.

Lighten Only option
Replaces dark pixels with light pixels.

Lighting Effects filter
Applies lighting effects to an image.

Line break
Places a new text line without creating a new paragraph.

Link
See Hyperlink.

Liquid layout
A page layout that expresses all container widths in percents and changes size depending on the size of the browser window.

Live view
A Dreamweaver view that displays an open document as if you were viewing it in a browser, with interactive elements active and functioning.

Local root folder
See Local site folder.

Local site folder
A folder on a hard drive, Flash drive, or floppy disk that holds all the files and folders for a website; also called the local root folder.

Logo
A distinctive image used to identify a company, project, or organization. You can create a logo by combining symbols, shapes, colors, and text.

Looping
The number of times an animation repeats.

Luminosity
The remaining light and dark values that result when a color image is converted to grayscale.

———————— **M** ————————

Mailto: link
An e-mail address formatted as a link that opens the default mail program with a blank, addressed message.

Main Timeline
The primary Timeline for a Flash movie. The main Timeline is displayed when you start a new Flash document.

Marquee
A series of dotted lines indicating a selected area that can be edited or dragged into another image.

Mask
A feature that lets you protect or modify a particular area; created using a marquee.

Mask layer
A layer in a Flash document that is used to cover the objects on another layer(s) and, at the same time, create a window through which you can view various objects on the other layer.

Match Color command
Allows you to replace one color with another.

Matte
A colorful box (often without shine) placed behind an object that makes the object stand out.

Menu bar
Contains menus from which you can choose commands.

Menu bar (web page)
An area on a web page that contains links to the main pages of a website; also called a navigation bar.

Merge cells
To combine multiple adjacent cells in a table into one cell.

Merge Drawing Model
A drawing mode that causes overlapping drawings (objects) to merge, so that a change in the top object, such as moving it, may affect the object beneath it.

Merging layers
Process of combining multiple image layers into one layer.

Meta tag
HTML codes that resides in the head section of a web page and includes information about the page such as keywords and descriptions. *See also* Head content.

Metadata
Information about a file, such as keywords, descriptions, and copyright information, that is used to locate files.

Metadata (Bridge)
File information you add to a file with tags (words) that are used to identify and describe the file.

Metadata panel
In Bridge, a panel that lists the metadata for a selected file.

Metering
A feature that provides a photographer with a way of compensating for a variety of lighting conditions. Examples of metering are spot metering, center-weighted average metering, average metering, partial metering, and multi-zone metering.

Mini Bridge
A panel that opens directly within the Photoshop and InDesign programs; a simplified version of Bridge.

Monitor calibration
A process that displays printed colors accurately on your monitor.

Monotype spacing
Spacing in which each character occupies the same amount of space.

Morphing
The animation process of changing one object into another, sometimes unrelated, object.

Motion guide
A path used to specify how an animated object moves around the Flash Stage.

Motion Presets
Pre-built animations, such as a bouncing effect, that can be applied to objects in Flash.

Motion tweening
The process used in Flash to automatically fill in the frames between keyframes in an animation that changes the properties of an object such as the position, size, or color. Motion tweening works on groups and symbols.

Movement
In screen design, movement refers to the way the viewer's eye moves through the objects on the screen.

Movie clip symbol
An object or animation stored as a single, reusable symbol in the Library panel in Flash. It has its own Timeline, independent of the main Timeline.

Multiscreen Preview
A Dreamweaver feature that allows you to see what a page would look like if it were viewed on a mobile hand-held device, such as a phone or tablet.

——————— **N** ———————

N-up view
A view that allows you to edit one image while comparing it with another. You can drag layers from one image to another in N-up view. Display N-up view using the Arrange command on the Window menu, then tile either horizontally or vertically until the images are in the configuration that works best.

Named anchor
A specific location on a web page that is used to link to that portion of the web page.

Navigation bar
See Menu bar.

Navigation structure
A set of text or graphic links usually organized in rows or columns that viewers can use to navigate between pages of a website. *See also* Menu bar.

Nested table
A table within a table.

Nested tag
A tag within a tag.

No right-click script
JavaScript code that will block users from displaying the shortcut menu when they right-click an image on a web page.

Numbered list
See Ordered list.

——————— ———————

Object Drawing Model
A drawing mode that allows you to overlap objects which are then kept separate, so that changes in one object do not affect another object. You must break apart these objects before you can select their stroke and fills.

Object layer
A layer containing one or more images.

Objects
The individual elements in a document, such as text or images. In Flash, objects are placed on the Stage and can be edited or manipulated.

Onion skin
In Flash, a setting that allows you to view one or more frames before and after in the current frame.

Online community
Social website you can join, such as Facebook and Twitter, where you can communicate with others by posting messages or media content such as images or videos.

Opacity
Determines the percentage of transparency. Whereas a layer with 100% opacity will obstruct objects in the layers beneath it, a layer with 1% opacity will appear nearly transparent.

Optical center
The point around which objects on the page are balanced; occurs approximately 3/8ths from the top of the page.

Optical weight
The ability of an object to attract the viewer's eye, as determined by the object's size, shape, color, and so on.

Options bar
Displays the settings for the active tool. The options bar is located directly under the Menu bar, but can be moved anywhere in the workspace for easier access.

Ordered list
A list of items that are placed in a specific order and preceded by numbers or letters; sometimes called a numbered list.

Orientation
Direction an image appears on the page: portrait or landscape.

Orphaned file
File that is not linked to any pages in the website.

Outline type
Type that is mathematically defined and can be scaled to any size without its edges losing their smooth appearance. Also known as a *vector font*.

Out-of-gamut indicator
Indicates that the current color falls beyond the accurate print or display range.

—————————— **P** ——————————

Panel
A tabbed, floating or docked window that displays information on a particular topic or contains related commands. Used to view, organize, and modify objects. Panels contain named tabs, which can be separated and moved to another panel group. You can view a panel menu by clicking the Panel Options list arrow in its upper-right corner.

Panel groups
Sets of related panels that are grouped together and displayed through the Window menu; also known as Tab groups.

Panel sets
Groups of the most commonly used panels, such as the Properties and Library panels.

Panel well
An area where you can assemble panels for quick access.

Panels
Small windows that can be moved and are used to verify settings and modify image. Panels contain named tabs, which can be separated and moved to another group. Each panel contains a menu that can be viewed by clicking the Panel options button in its upper-right corner.

Parent container
A container created with HTML tags, in which other containers fall between its opening and closing tags. *See also* Child container.

Parent keyword
In Bridge, the top level for a keyword with child keywords under it.

Parent page
A page at a higher level in a web hierarchy that links to other pages on a lower level, called child pages.

Pasteboard
The gray area surrounding the Flash Stage where objects can be placed and manipulated. Neither the pasteboard, nor objects placed on it, appear in the movie unless the objects move onto the Stage during the playing of the movie.

Path
The location of an open file in relation to its place in the folder structure of the website.

Path (vector object)
An open or closed line consisting of a series of anchor points.

Path bar
In Bridge, the bar where the path of the selected folder in the Folders panel appears.

Permissions process
The process to obtain permission to use content legally.

Persistence of vision
The phenomenon of the eye capturing and holding an image for one-tenth of a second before processing another image. This enables the rapid display of a series of still images to give the impression of motion and creates an animation.

Picture package
Shows multiple copies of a single image in various sizes, similar to a portrait studio sheet of photos.

Pinterest
A social networking site that let users interact as an online community through the sharing of crafts, recipes, and other items of interest.

Pixel aspect ratio
A scaling correction feature that automatically corrects the ratio of pixels displayed for the monitor in use. Prevents pixels viewed in a 16:9 monitor (such as a widescreen TV) from looking compressed when viewed in a 4:3 monitor (nearly-rectangular TV).

Pixels
Small squares of color used to display a digital image on a rectangular grid, such as a computer screen. Each dot in a bitmapped image that representsa color or shade.

Playhead
An indicator specifying which frame is playing in the Timeline of a Flash movie.

PNG file
Portable Network Graphics file. PNG is a file format used for images placed on web pages that is capable of showing millions of colors but is small in file size. The native file format in Fireworks.

Podcast
"Pod" is an acronym for Programming On Demand, in which users can download and play digitally broadcasted files using devices such as computers or MP3 players.

Point of contact
A place on a web page that provides users with a means of contacting the company.

Points

Unit of measurement for font sizes. Traditionally, one inch is equivalent to 72.27 points. In PostScript measurement, one inch is equivalent to 72 points. The default Photoshop type size is 12 points.

Portrait orientation

An image with the short edge of the paper at the top and bottom.

PostScript

A programming language created by Adobe that optimizes printed text and graphics.

POWDER

The acronym for Protocol for Web Description Resources. This is an evaluation system for web pages developed with the World Wide Web Consortium (W3C) that provides summary information about a website

Preferences

Used to control the Photoshop environment using your specifications.

Preview panel

In Bridge, a panel where a preview of a selected file appears.

Profile

Defines and interprets colors for a color management system.

Programming on Demand

See Podcast.

Projector

In Flash, a standalone executable movie, such as a Windows .exe file.

Project scope

The work that needs to be accomplished to deliver a project, the complexity of which can be discussed using three variables—performance, time and cost.

Proof setup

Lets you preview your image to see how it will look when printed on a specific device.

Properties panel (Flash)

The panel that displays the properties of the selected object, such as size and color) on the Stage or the selected frame. The Properties panel can be used to edit selected properties. Also called the Property Inspector.

Properties panel (Photoshop)

Panel on which the characteristics of Adjustment layers are modified.

Properties pane (Dreamweaver)

The bottom half of the CSS Styles panel that lists a selected rule's properties.

Property inspector (Dreamweaver)

In Dreamweaver, a panel that displays the properties of a selected web page object; its contents vary according to the object currently selected.

Proportional spacing

The text spacing in which each character takes up a different amount of space, based on its width.

Protocol for Web Description Resources

See POWDER.

Public domain

Work that is no longer protected by copyright. Anyone can use it for any purpose.

Publish (Dreamweaver)

Make a website available for viewing on the Internet or on an intranet by transferring the files to a web server.

Publish (Flash)

The process used to generate the files necessary for delivering Flash movies on the web, on stand-alone computers and on mobile devices.

Q

Quick Selection tool

Tool that lets you paint a selection from the interior using a brush tip, reducing rough edges and blockiness.

QuickTime

A file format used for movies and animations that requires a QuickTime Player.

R

Rasterize

The process of converting a type layer to a bitmapped image layer.

RDS

Acronym for Remote Development Services; provides access control to web servers using Cold Fusion.

Refine Edge option

Button found on the options bar of a variety of tools that allows you to improve the size and edges of a selection.

Registration point

The point on an object that is used to position the object on the Stage in a Flash movie.

Related file

A file that is linked to a document and is necessary for the document to display and function correctly.

Related Files toolbar

A toolbar located below an open document's filename tab that displays the names of any related files.

Relative path (Dreamweaver)

A path used with an internal link to reference a web page or graphic file within the website.

Relative path (Flash)
A path for an external link or to an object that is based on the location of the Flash movie file.

Relief
The height of ridges within an object.

Remote server
A web server that hosts websites and is not directly connected to the computer housing the local site.

Remote site
A website that has been published to a remote server. *See also* Remote server.

Rendering
The way fonts are drawn on a screen.

Rendering intent
The way in which a color-management system handles color conversion from one color space to another.

Resolution
The number of pixels per inch in an image. Also refers to an image's clarity and fineness of detail.

Resulting color
The outcome of the blend color applied to the base color.

RGB image
Image that contains three color channels (one each for red, green, and blue).

RGB mode
Color mode in which components are combined to create new colors.

RGB triplet
See Hex triplet.

Rich media content
Attractive and engaging images, interactive elements, video, or animations.

Rollover
A special effect that changes the appearance of an object when the mouse pointer moves over it.

Root folder
See Local site folder.

Row
Table cells arranged horizontally.

RSS
Acronym for Really Simple Syndication, a method websites use to distribute news stories, information about upcoming events, and announcements, known as an RSS Feed.

RSS feed
A way to distribute news stories through websites. *See also* RSS.

Rule of thirds
A design principle that entails dividing a page into nine squares and then placing the page elements of most interest on the intersections of the grid lines.

Rulers
On screen markers that help you precisely measure and position an object. Rulers can be displayed using the View menu.

Rules
Sets of formatting attributes that define styles in a Cascading Style Sheet.

— S —

Sampling
A method of changing foreground and background colors by copying existing colors from an image.

Sans-serif font
A font with block-style characters; commonly used for headings and subheadings.

Saturation
The strength or purity of the color, representing the amount of gray in proportion to hue (measured as a percentage from 0% [gray], to 100% [fully saturated]). Also known as *chroma*.

Save As
A command that lets you create a copy of the open file using a new name.

Scale
The size relationship of objects to one another.

Scanner
An electronic device that converts print material into an electronic file.

Scene
A Timeline designated for a specific part of a Flash movie. Scenes are a way to organize long movies by dividing the movie into sections.

Scope creep
Making impromptu changes or additions to a project without corresponding increases in the schedule or budget.

Screen frequency (line screen)
The number of printer dots or halftone cells per inch used to print grayscale images or color separations.

Script Assist
A feature found in the Actions panel that can be used to generate ActionScript without having to write programming code.

Secure FTP (SFTP)
A method for transferring files with encryption to protect the file content, user names, and passwords.

Selection
An area in an image that is surrounded by a selection marquee and can then be manipulated.

Selector
The name of the tag to which style declarations have been assigned.

Serif font
An ornate font that has a tail, or stroke, at the end of some characters. These strokes lead the eye from one character to the next, making it easier to recognize words; therefore, serif fonts are generally used in longer text passages.

Set up a site
Specify a website's name and the location of the local site root folder using the Dreamweaver Manage Sites dialog box.

SFTP
See Secure FTP.

Shading
Collection of Bevel and Emboss settings that determine lighting effects.

Shadow Mode
Bevel and Emboss setting that determines how pigments are combined.

Shape hints
Indicators used to control the shape of an object as it changes appearance during a Flash animation.

Shape tweening
The process of animating an object so that its shape changes. Shape tweening requires editable graphics.

Sharp
Anti-aliasing setting that displays type with the best possible resolution.

Sharpen More filter
Increases the contrast of adjacent pixels and can focus blurry images.

Sharpness
An element of composition that draws the viewer's eye to a specific area.

Show Code and Design views
A combination of Code view and Design view. The best view for correcting errors.

Sidecar file
A separate file that contains metadata and can be applied to other files as a template.

Site definition
Contains important information about a web site, including its URL, preferences that you've specified, and other secure information, such as login and password information.

Site map
A graphical representation or a directory listing of how web pages relate to each other within a website.

Size
Determines the clarity of a drop shadow.

Skype
A video sharing application.

Slider
The small indicator on the left side of the History panel that you can drag to undo or redo an action.

Smart Filter
A filter applied to a Smart Object and allows for nondestructive editing of the object(s).

Smart Guides
A feature that displays vertical or horizontal guides that appear automatically when you draw a shape or move an object and are helpful in its positioning.

Smart Object
A combination of objects that has a visible indicator in the bottom-right corner of the layer thumbnail. Makes it possible to scale, rotate, and wrap layers without losing image quality. Stores image data from raster or vector images.

Smooth
Anti-aliasing setting that gives type more rounded edges.

Social networking
The grouping of individual web users who connect and interact with other users in online communities.

Soft proof
The way an image looks on specific calibrated hardware using a color management system.

Source
The image containing the color that will be matched.

Specifications
In Flash, a list of what will be included in each screen including the arrangement of each element and the functionality of each object (for example, what happens when you click the button labeled Skip Intro).

Splash screen
A window that displays information about the software you are using.

Split a cell
To divide table cells into multiple cells.

Spread
Determines the width of drop shadow text.

Spring-loaded keyboard shortcuts
A feature that lets you temporarily change the active tool by pressing and holding the key that changes to another tool.

Spry (Spry Framework)
A JavaScript library that provides access to reusable widgets that you can add to web pages.

Spry menu bar
One of the preset widgets available in Dreamweaver that creates a dynamic, user-friendly menu bar that is easy to insert and customize.

Stage
That area of the Flash workspace that contains the objects that are part of the movie and that will be seen by the viewers.

Standard toolbar
A toolbar that contains buttons you use to execute frequently used commands that are also available on the File and Edit menus.

State
An entry on the History panel, or the individual steps in an action in the Actions panel. In a browser, the condition of an item in a Spry menu bar in relation to the mouse pointer.

Status bar
The area located at the bottom of the program window (Win) or the image window (Mac) that displays information such as the file size of the active window and a description of the active tool. In Dreamweaver, the bar that appears at the bottom of the Dreamweaver document window; the left end of the status bar displays the tag selector, which shows the HTML tags being used at the insertion point location. The right end displays the window size and estimated download time for the page displayed.

Step
Each task performed in the History panel.

Storyboard
A series of sketches that illustrate the sequence of events in an animation.

Stroking the edges
The process of making a selection or layer stand out by formatting it with a border.

Strong
Anti-aliasing setting that makes type appear heavier, much like the bold attribute.

Structure
A Bevel and Emboss setting that determines the size and physical properties of the object.

Style
In type, a collection of formatting attributes that can be saved and applied to specific characters or a paragraph. When creating a customized object, there are eighteen predesigned styles that can be applied to buttons.

Style Rendering toolbar
A toolbar that contains buttons that allow you to render (display) a web page as different media types (e.g., handheld).

Sub keyword
See Child keyword.

Subtractive colors
A color system in which the full combination of cyan, magenta, and yellow absorb all color and produce black.

Swatches panel
Contains available colors that can be selected for use as a foreground or background color. You can also add your own colors to the Swatches panel.

Symbol
A graphic, animation, or button that represents an object, text, or combination group.

Symbol fonts
Used to display unique characters (such as $, ÷, or ™).

Symmetrical balance
Page in which objects are placed equally on either side of an imaginary vertical line in the center of the page.

Synchronize
A Dreamweaver command that compares the names, dates, and times on all files on a local and remote site, then transfers only the files that have changed since the last upload.

———————— **T** ————————

Tab groups
See Panel groups.

Table
Grids of rows and columns that can be used either to hold tabular data on a web page or as a basic design tool for data placement.

Table caption
Text at the top of a table that describes the table contents; read by screen readers.

Table header
Text placed at the top or sides of a table on a web page; read by screen readers to help provide accessibility for table content.

Tag (HTML)
The individual pieces of code that specify the appearance for page content when viewed in a browser.

Tag selector
The left side of the status bar that displays HTML tags used at the insertion point location.

Tag type
A style type used to redefine an HTML tag.

Target (link)
The location on a web page that the browser displays when users click an internal link.

Target (color)
When sampling a color, the image that will receive the matched color.

Target Audience
The characteristics that make up the population that will be using a website, taking into considerations such factors as age, occupation, sex, education, residence, race, and computer literacy.

Template
A web page that contains the basic layout for each page in the site, including the location of a company logo, banner, or navigation links.

Terms of use
The rules that a copyright owner uses to establish how users may use his or her work.

Text Layout Format (TLF)
A text tool option in Flash that provides advanced text features such as flowing text, character coloring and column creation.

Thumbnail
Contains a miniature picture of the layer's content, appears to the left of the layer name, and can be turned on or off.

Thumbnail image
A small version of a larger image.

Thumbnail slider
A sliding control that is used to change the size of the thumbnails being viewed in the Content panel.

Tiled image
A small graphic that repeats across and down a web page, appearing as individual squares or rectangles.

Timeline
The component of Flash used to organize and control the movie's contents over time, by specifying when each object appears on the Stage.

Title bar
Displays the program name and filename of the open image. The title bar also contains buttons for minimizing, maximizing, and closing the image.

Tolerance
The range of pixels that determines which pixels will be selected. The lower the tolerance, the closer the color is to the selection. The setting can have a value from 0–255.

Tone
The brightness and contrast within an image.

Tools panel
A panel in Flash, containing tools for frequently used commands, such as drawing and selection tools, and their options. On the face of a tool is a graphic representation of its function. Place the pointer over each button to display a tool tip, which displays the name or function of that button. An arrow in the lower-right of the button face indicates other similar tools in the group.

Tracing image
An image that is placed in the background of a web page as a guide to create page elements on top of it, similar to the way tracing paper is used.

Tracking
The insertion of a uniform amount of space between characters.

Trademark
Protects an image, word, slogan, symbol, or design used to identify goods or services.

Transformation point
In Flash, the point used to orient an object as it is being animated. For example, a rotating object will rotate around its transformation point. Also, the point of an object that snaps to a motion guide.

Tumblr
A blog where users can post and share text, photos, music, and videos.

Tweening
The process of filling the in-between frames in an animation.

Tweet
A short message posted on the Twitter website that is no more than 140 characters.

Twitter
A website where viewers can post short messages up to 140 characters long, called "tweets."

Type
Text, or a layer containing text. Each character is measured in points. In traditional measurement, one inch is equivalent to 72.27 points.

Type spacing
Adjustments you can make to the space between characters and between lines of type.

Typeface
See Font

U

Uniform Resource Locator (URL)
An address that determines a route on the Internet or to a web page. *See* domain name.

Unity
In screen design, intra-screen unity has to do with how the various screen objects are related. Inter-screen unity refers to the design that viewers encounter as they navigate from one screen to another.

Unordered list
A lists of items that do not need to be placed in a specific order and are usually preceded by bullets.

Unvisited link
A link that the user has not yet clicked, or visited. The default color for unvisited links is blue.

Upload
The process of transferring files from a local drive to a web server.

URL
See Uniform Resource Locator

V

Validate markup
To submit files to the W3C Validation Service so it can search through the code to look for errors that could occur with different language versions, such as XHTML or HTML5.

Vector font
Fonts that are vector-based type outlines, which means that they are mathematically defined shapes. Also known as *outline type*.

Vector graphics
Mathematically calculated objects composed of anchor points and straight or curved line segments.

Vidcast
See Vodcast.

View
A choice for displaying page content in the Document window; Dreamweaver has three working views: Design view, Code view, and Show Code and Design views.

Vignette
A feature in which the border of a picture or portrait fades into the surrounding color at its edges.

Vignette effect
A feature that uses feathering to fade a marquee shape.

Visited link
A link that has been previously clicked, or visited. The default color for visited links is purple.

Visual hierarchy
The order in which the eye understands what it is seeing.

Vodcast
Short for Video podcast. Also called a vidcast.

VSS
Acronym for Microsoft Visual SafeSource, a connection type used only with the Window operating system.

W

Warping type
A feature that lets you create distortions that conform to a variety of shapes.

Web 2.0
The evolution of web applications that facilitate and promote information sharing among Internet users.

Web browser
A program, such as Microsoft Internet Explorer, Apple Safari, Google Chrome, or Mozilla Firefox, which displays web pages.

Web cam
A web camera used for video conferencing with a high-speed Internet connection.

Web Gallery
In Bridge, contains a thumbnail index page of all exported images, the actual JPEG images, and any included links.

Web-safe colors
The 216 colors that can be displayed on the web without dithering.

Web server
A computer dedicated to hosting websites that is connected to the Internet and configured with software to handle requests from browsers.

WebDav
Acronym for Web-based Distributed Authoring and Versioning, a type of connection used with the WebDav protocol, such as a website residing on an Apache web server.

Website
A group of related web pages that are linked together and share a common interface and design.

White space
An area on a web page that is not filled with text or graphics.

Widget (image-editing)
Tool that can be used to change a 3D object.

Widget (programming)
A piece of code that allows users to interact with a program, such as clicking a menu item to open a page.

Wiki
Named for the Hawaiian word for "quick," a site where a user can use simple editing tools to contribute and edit the page content in a site.

Wikipedia
An online encyclopedia that allows users to contribute to site content.

Wireframe
A prototype that represents every page and its contents in a website. Like a flowchart or storyboard, a wireframe shows the relationship of each page in the site to all the other pages.

Working space
Tells the color management system how RGB and CMYK values are interpreted.

Workspace switcher
A drop-down menu located in the top right corner on the Menu bar that allows you to change the workspace layout.

Workspace
The area in the program window that includes all of the menus, panels and buttons that you can use.

World Wide Web Consortium (W3C)
An international community that develops open standards for web development.

WYSIWYG
Acronym for What You See Is What You Get, where a Web page looks the same in a browser as it does in a web editor.

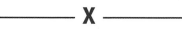

XHTML
The acronym for eXtensible HyperText Markup Language, the current standard language used to create web pages.

XML
Acronym for Extensible Markup Language, a type of language that is used to develop customized tags to store information.

XSL
Acronym for Extensible Stylesheet Language, which is similar to CSS; the XSL style sheet information formats containers created with XML.

XSLT
Acronym for Extensible Stylesheet Language Transformations; interprets the code in an XSL file to transform an XML document, much like style sheet files transform HTML files.

— Y —

YouTube
A website where you can upload and share videos.

Note: Page numbers preceded by BR refer to the Bridge chapter; those preceded by DW refer to Dreamweaver chapters; those preceded by FL refer to Flash chapters; those preceded by INT refer to the Integration chapter; and those preceded by PS refer to Photoshop chapters.

3D effects, FL 5–2, FL 5–36—41
  creating, FL 5–38—41
  motion tweens with, FL 5–37
  tools, FL 5–37
3D extrusion, PS 6–21, PS 6–23
3D Rotation tool, FL 2–4, FL 5–36, FL 5–37, FL 5–38—41
3D Studio (.3ds) file format, PS 1–5
3D Translation tool, FL 2–4, FL 5–36, FL 5–37, FL 5–38—41
.3ds (3D Studio) file format, PS 1–5

absolute paths, DW 5–5
accessibility, FL 1–45
  tables, DW 6–23
  validating standards, DW 7–6
  WCAG guidelines. See Web Content Accessibility Guidelines (WCAG)
  web pages, DW 2–5
Acrobat.com, PS 2–4
  signing into, PS 2–5
  using, PS 2–6
actions, FL 3–22—29
  Actions panel, FL 3–25
  ActionScript, FL 3–22—24
  assigning to buttons, FL 3–24, FL 3–27—29
  assigning to drop-down buttons, FL 5–24
  assigning to frames, FL 3–24, FL 3–26—27
  attaching to video control buttons, FL 5–16
  frame labels, FL 3–25
  preloaders, FL 6–19
Actions panel
  ActionScript, FL 3–23
  panes, FL 3–25, FL 3–26
ActionScript, FL 3–22—24
  animated navigation bars, FL 5–18—19
  preloaders, FL 6–16—17, FL 6–19

active layers, PS 3–9
  inserting layers beneath, PS 3–12
adding to selections, PS 4–14
additive colors, PS 5–5
adjustment layers, PS 3–4
Adobe AIR, FL 1–1. See also AIR applications
Adobe AIR format (.air), FL 1–12, FL 6–2
Adobe Bridge. See Bridge
Adobe Bridge Preferences dialog box, BR 1–2
Adobe BrowserLab, DW 2–33, DW 7–5
Adobe Business Catalyst, DW 6–10
Adobe Catalyst, FL 1–1
Adobe Creative Cloud, PS 2–4
Adobe Flash Platform, FL 1–1
Adobe Flash Professional, FL 1–1
Adobe Integrated Runtime files. See AIR applications
Adobe Media Encoder, FL 5–13, FL 5–14—15
Adobe Mini Bridge. See Mini Bridge
Adobe online resources, PS 1–24
Adobe Swatch Exchange (ASE) files, PS 5–14
Adobe Touch Apps, PS 2–4
Advanced tab, AIR Settings dialog box, FL 6–24
AIFF file format, FL 5–9
AIR applications, FL 1–39, FL 6–22—27
  AIR Settings dialog box, FL 6–23—24
  development process, FL 6–22
  publishing, FL 6–22—24
  repurposing Flash files as, FL 6–25—27
AIR (Adobe Integrated Runtime) files, FL 1–12, FL 6–2
AIR for Android Settings dialog box, FL 6–28—30
  Deployment tab settings, FL 6–29
  General tab settings, FL 6–28—29
  Icons tab settings, FL 6–30
  Languages tab settings, FL 6–30
  Permissions tab settings, FL 6–30

AIR Settings dialog box, FL 6–23—24, FL 6–24
  Advanced tab settings, FL 6–24
  General settings, FL 6–23
  Icons tab settings, FL 6–24
  Signature settings, FL 6–24
Align panel, FL 2–7, FL 2–18—19
aligning content, editing block properties for, DW 6–15—16
aligning images, DW 4–5, DW 4–11
  images in table cells, DW 6–30—31, DW 6–33
aligning text, FL 2–40
  keyboard shortcut, DW 3–29
alignment tools, FL 2–4. See also specific tools
altering images, ethics, PS 1–28
alternate text, DW 4–13
  displaying in browser, DW 4–17
  editing, DW 4–16
  missing, checking for, DW 7–7
  setting accessibility option, DW 4–17
alternatives for completing tasks, FL 1–11
altitude setting, Bevel and Emboss style, PS 6–20
American Psychological Association (APA) guidelines, DW 7–39
Android, AIR applications. See applications for mobile devices
angle, drop shadow, PS 6–13, PS 6–14
angle setting, Bevel and Emboss style, PS 6–20
animating navigation bars, FL 5–18—27
  assigning actions to drop-down buttons, FL 5–24
  creating drop-down menus, FL 5–18—19
  frame labels, FL 5–19, FL 5–25
  invisible buttons, FL 5–26—27
  mask layer, FL 5–22—23
  positioning drop-down buttons, FL 5–20—21
  rollOver actions, FL 5–25
  scenes, FL 5–19
animating text, FL 4–42—49
  adding actions to buttons, FL 4–49
  copying and pasting frames, FL 4–44

fading in text, FL 4—47
making a text block into a button, FL 4—48
motion presets, FL 4—45
Onion Skin feature, FL 4—42
resizing text, FL 4—47
rotating text, FL 4—46
selecting frames, FL 4—44
animations, FL 4—1—49. *See also* animating navigation bars; animating text
character, using inverse kinematics. *See* inverse kinematics (IK)
classic tween. *See* classic tween animations
creating, FL 1—19, FL 1—35—36
creating using Photoshop-created text, INT 1—19
Deco tool. *See* Deco tool
frame-by-frame. *See* frame-by-frame animations
IK objects. *See* inverse kinematics (IK)
motion tween. *See* motion tween animations
movie clips. *See* movie clip symbols
perception of motion, FL 4—2
preloaders, creating, FL 6—20
shape tween. *See* shape tween animations
text. *See* animating text
3D. *See* 3D effects
Anti-alias check box, Magic Wand tool, PS 4—18
Anti-alias setting, Magnetic Lasso tool, PS 4—13
anti-aliasing, PS 6—16—19
applying, PS 6—18
undoing, PS 6—19
when to apply, PS 6—16
AP div tags, DW 6—4
AP elements, DW 6—4
APA (American Psychological Association) guidelines, DW 7—39
app(s), FL 1—12. *See also* AIR applications; application(s); applications for mobile devices
application(s)
AIR. *See* AIR applications
developing with Flash, FL 1—39
mobile devices. *See* applications for mobile devices
planning, FL 1—42—47
Application bar, BR 1—5. *See also* Menu bar
applications for mobile devices, FL 6—28—37
AIR for Android Settings dialog box, FL 6—28—30
development process, FL 6—28

events, FL 6—30
with events, creating, FL 6—34—35
gestures, FL 6—30
publishing, FL 6—36—37
repurposing Flash apps for use as, FL 6—31—33
testing, FL 6—32
arrangement, PS 1—27
ASE (Adobe Swatch Exchange) files, PS 5—14
ASND file format, FL 5—9
assets, DW 1—20
organizing for quick access, DW 4—7
removing from websites, DW 4—19
assets folders, saving image files, DW 2—14—16
Assets panel, DW 4—10, DW 5—6
adding assets to web pages, DW 4—5
category buttons, DW 4—4
images, DW 4—4—5
links, DW 5—31
organizing assets for quick access, DW 4—7
panes, DW 4—4—5
URL category, DW 2—25
viewing links, DW 5—9
website maintenance, DW 7—4
asymmetrical balance, PS 1—28
Attach External Style Sheet dialog box, DW 3—20
Attach Style Sheet button, DW 3—20, DW 3—24
attribution
Creative Commons, PS 1—31
for material, DW 7—39
attribution licenses, Creative Commons, PS 1—31
attribution licenses share alike, Creative Commons, PS 1—31
attribution no derivatives, Creative Commons, PS 1—31
attribution non-commercial, Creative Commons, PS 1—31
attribution non-commercial no derivatives, Creative Commons, PS 1—31
attribution non-commercial share-alike, Creative Commons, PS 1—31
AU file format, FL 5—9
audio. *See* sound
Auto Save feature, FL 1—16
automating. *See* actions

background, moving, frame-by-frame animations, FL 4—27
background color
changing, PS 5—6, PS 5—8—9

default, setting, PS 5—7
websites, DW 2—4, DW 2—9
background images
inserting, DW 4—18, DW 4—20—21
removing, DW 4—21
Background layers, PS 3—4, PS 3—5, PS 3—6
converting image layers into, PS 3—7
balance, PS 1—28
balancing colors, PS 5—28, PS 5—31
Bandwidth Profiler, FL 6—10—11, FL 6—14
banners, DW 1—12
base color, PS 5—27
baseline, PS 6—9
baseline shift, PS 6—9, PS 6—11
BCC (Browser Compatibility Check) feature, DW 6—5, DW 6—15
behaviors, JavaScript, DW 6—2
Bevel and Emboss style, PS 6—20
settings, PS 6—20—21, PS 6—23
using with Layer menu, PS 6—22
Bezier curves, FL 4—6
Bezier handles, FL 4—6, FL 4—9
Bind tool, FL 2—5
bitmap (.bmp) file format, PS 1—5
bitmap images, FL 3—30
bitmap mode, PS 5—5
bitmap type, PS 6—4
Black & White command, PS 5—22
Black and White tool, FL 2—6
Blank keyframe, FL 1—33
blemishes. *See* imperfections, correcting
blending colors, PS 5—18—21
blending modes, PS 3—8, PS 5—27, PS 5—28, PS 5—30
components, PS 5—27
blogs, DW 5—35
blurry images, scanned, fixing, PS 5—26
.bmp (bitmap) file format, PS 1—5
body, websites, DW 2—4
boldfacing type, keyboard shortcut, DW 3—29
bone structure, creating, FL 5—28—29, FL 5—31
Bone tool, FL 2—5
borders, PS 5—16—17
creating, PS 5—17
images, DW 4—12, DW 4—14, PS 5—16

locking transparent pixels, PS 5–16—17
tables, DW 6–22
breadcrumbs trails, DW 5–30
Break Apart command, FL 2–37, FL 3–5, FL 3–9, FL 4–38, FL 4–42
Bridge, BR 1–1—15, PS 1–9, PS 1–10
    accessing, BR 1–2
    browsing in, keyboard shortcut, DW 4–17
    changing modes, BR 1–7
    Compact mode, BR 1–4
    creating a Web Gallery, PS 2–29
    creating PDFs, PS 2–27, PS 2–28
    filtering with, PS 1–15, PS 2–11
    inserting files, DW 4–5
    inserting images, DW 4–10
    metadata. *See* metadata
    opening files, PS 1–12
    rating with, PS 1–15
    reusing housekeeping tasks, PS 2–8
    starting, BR 1–6
Bridge Essentials workspace, BR 1–4—7
    Application bar, BR 1–5
    Menu bar, BR 1–5
    panes, BR 1–4—5
    Path bar, BR 1–5
brightness, PS 5–5
    adjusting, PS 5–29
Brightness/Contrast dialog box, PS 5–29
broken links, DW 2–20
Browse in Mini Bridge command, PS 1–10
browser(s)
    displaying alternate text, DW 4–17
    testing web pages in different browsers, DW 2–32—33
    viewing web pages, DW 2–35
Browser Compatibility Check (BCC) feature, DW 6–5, DW 6–15
Browser Compatibility panel, DW 7–5
BrowserLab, DW 2–33, DW 7–5
browsing
    in Bridge, keyboard shortcut, DW 4–17
    through files, PS 1–9
Brush tool, FL 2–5, FL 2–12
brushes, Deco tool, FL 5–43
Building Brush tool, FL 5–44
bullet(s), unordered lists, DW 3–4
bulleted lists, DW 3–4

business uses of Flash, FL 1–1
button(s), FL 3–16—21
    assigning actions, FL 3–24, FL 3–27—29
    control, FL 1–13
    creating, FL 3–16—17, FL 3–18
    editing, FL 3–17, FL 3–19
    hit area, FL 3–19, FL 3–20
    invisible, animated navigation bars, FL 5–26—27
    making text blocks into, FL 4–48
    previewing, FL 3–17, FL 3–20—21
    states, FL 3–16
    synchronizing sound with, FL 5–8, 11
    video control, attaching actions, FL 5–16
button actions
    adding, animating text, FL 4–49
    assigning, FL 3–24, FL 3–27—29, FL 5–16, FL 5–24
    mouse events, FL 3–24
button symbols, FL 3–4

camera(s), digital, PS 1–25
Camera Raw file formats, DW 4–5, PS 1–5
captions, tables, DW 6–23
Cascading Style Sheets (CSSs), DW 2–4, DW 3–2, DW 3–10—19
    advantages, DW 3–11
    choosing fonts, DW 3–13
    converting styles, DW 3–27
    CSS Styles panel, DW 3–10
    evolution, DW 3–31
    formatting menu bars, DW 5–20—25
    formatting ordered lists, DW 3–5
    formatting tables with CSS3, DW 6–23
    formatting text, DW 2–10—11
    rules. *See* CSS rule(s)
    semantic tag appearance, DW 3–6
    style sheets. *See* style sheets
    types, DW 3–10
    validating, DW 7–9
    viewing code, DW 3–11, DW 3–16
case-sensitive links, DW 5–8
CCDs (charge-coupled devices), PS 1–25
cell content, DW 6–34—41
    formatting, DW 6–34, DW 6–36, DW 6–39
    inserting text, DW 6–34, DW 6–35
    modifying, DW 6–39

cell padding, DW 6–22
cell spacing, DW 6–22
cell walls, DW 6–22
Character panel, PS 6–9
character spacing, PS 6–8, PS 6–10
Character Style Options dialog box, PS 6–11
charge-coupled devices (CCDs), PS 1–25
Check browser compatibility button, DW 7–5
Check Links Sitewide feature, DW 5–30
Check Out feature, enabling, DW 7–23, DW 7–24
Check Spelling dialog box, DW 2–19
checking files out and in, DW 7–22—26
    enabling Check Out feature, DW 7–23, DW 7–24
    keyboard shortcuts, DW 7–35
    Subversion control, DW 7–23
checking links, DW 5–30, DW 5–31, DW 7–4, DW 7–6
    for broken links, DW 7–6
    keyboard shortcuts, DW 5–33, DW 7–35
child containers, DW 6–17
child keywords, BR 1–8
child pages, DW 1–20
Cineon (.cin) file format, PS 1–5
Circle Hotspot tool, DW 5–26
CISs (Compact Image Sensors), PS 1–25
citing sources, DW 7–39
class rules, adding to style sheets, DW 3–22—23
Class type CSSs, DW 3–10
Classic Text, FL 2–36
Classic Text mode, FL 2–36
classic tween animations, FL 4–20—23
    creating, FL 4–22
    motion guides, FL 4–20—21, FL 4–22
    orienting objects to guides, FL 4–22—23
    registration points, FL 4–21
    transformation points, FL 4–21
clean HTML code, DW 2–10
Clean Up Word HTML dialog box, DW 2–17
clients, presenting websites to, DW 7–40—41
Clipboard, PS 4–2
Cloaked assets folder, File panel, DW 7–29, DW 7–30, DW 7–31
cloaked files, DW 7–2
cloaking files, DW 7–28–31
    selected file types, DW 7–29, DW 7–31
    uncloaking, DW 7–29

cloaking folders, DW 7–28—29, DW 7–30

closing
exiting vs., PS 1–24
files. *See* closing files
panels, FL 1–7

closing files, DW 1–35, PS 1–25
keyboard shortcut, DW 5–33

cloud computing, PS 2–4

CMYK color mode, PS 5–5

CMYK color model, PS 5–6

code, CSS. *See* CSS code

code hints, DW 3–27

Code Inspector
showing and hiding, keyboard shortcut, DW 2–29
using, DW 2–29
viewing HTML code, DW 2–26—27

Code Navigator
editing rules, DW 3–17
viewing CSS code, DW 3–16

Code Snippets panel, FL 6–30

Code view, DW 1–6, DW 6–9
switching between Design view and, DW 1–35

Coding toolbar, DW 1–5—6, DW 1–7, DW 3–26

coding tools, DW 3–26—31
code hints, DW 3–27
collapsing code, DW 3–27, DW 3–28
converting styles, DW 3–27
expanding code, DW 3–29
moving embedded styles to an external CSS, DW 3–30—31
navigating code using, DW 3–27

Collapse Full Tag, DW 3–27

Collapse Selection buttons, DW 3–27

collapsing code, DW 3–27, DW 3–28

Collections panel, BR 1–4

color(s), PS 5–1—34
adding to grayscale images, PS 5–22—25
adding to layers, PS 3–19
adding to Swatches panel, PS 5–13
additive, PS 5–5
background. *See* background color
balancing, PS 5–28, PS 5–31
base, PS 5–27
blending modes, PS 5–27, PS 5–28, PS 5–30
blending with Gradient tool, PS 5–18—21

borders, PS 5–16—17
brightness, PS 5–29
choosing. *See* Color Picker; Swatches panel
color models. *See* color models
color modes. *See* color mode(s)
contrast, PS 5–29
to convey information on web pages, DW 2–5
fills and strokes, FL 2–21, FL 2–24
filters, PS 5–26—27, PS 5–30
foreground, changing, PS 5–6
foreground, default, setting, PS 5–7
guides, PS 4–7
Kuler. *See* Kuler
matching, PS 5–32—33
opacity settings, PS 5–30
out of gamut, PS 5–4
printing, PS 2–23
psychology of color, PS 5–4
resulting, PS 5–27
saturation. *See* saturation, colors
selecting using. *See* selecting with color
Stage, specifying, FL 1–38, FL 1–41
subtractive, PS 5–6
type, changing, PS 6–7
WCAG guidelines, DW 4–22
web page background, DW 2–4, DW 2–9
website color palettes, DW 4–19, DW 4–23
workspace, PS 1–18, PS 1–21
X, Y, and Z axes, FL 5–37

Color Balance dialog box, PS 5–28, PS 5–31

Color blending mode, PS 5–28

Color Burn blending mode, PS 5–28

Color Cubes color palette, DW 2–5

Color Dodge blending mode, PS 5–28

color effects, motion tween animations, FL 4–12

Color Handling list arrow, PS 2–23

color images
converting to black and white, PS 5–22
converting to grayscale, PS 5–24

color management systems, PS 5–7

color mode(s), PS 5–2, PS 5–4, PS 5–5, PS 5–6
changing, PS 5–24
converting, PS 5–22

color models, PS 5–2, PS 5–4—6

Color panel, changing background color, PS 5–8

Color Picker, PS 6–4
making selections, PS 5–10, PS 5–11, PS 5–12

Color Range command, PS 3–15, PS 3–16, PS 4–19, PS 4–20

color separation, PS 5–5

Color Settings dialog box, PS 5–7

columns, cells. *See* table columns

"come back later" web pages, DW 2–32

commands. *See also specific commands*
Control menu, FL 1–13
options, FL 1–15
shortcuts, FL 1–15

comments, inserting, DW 2–31

Compact Image Sensors (CISs), PS 1–25

Compact mode, Bridge, BR 1–4

compositing, PS 4–2

composition, PS 1–26—27

Compound type CSSs, DW 3–10

compressed files, decompressing using Flash Player, FL 1–14

computers, distributing movies for viewing on, FL 1–39

Configurator, PS 1–23

Connect to Remote Server button, DW 7–15

content
div tags, DW 6–8
web pages, collecting, DW 1–21

Content panel, Bridge, BR 1–4—5, PS 1–10

Contiguous check box, Magic Wand tool, PS 4–18

Continuous Tone color palette, DW 2–5

contrast
adding emphasis, PS 2–29
adjusting, PS 5–29

Contrast setting, Magnetic Lasso tool, PS 4–13

control buttons, FL 1–13

Control menu, FL 1–13

Convert to Symbol command, FL 3–16—17

Convert to Symbol dialog box, FL 3–4, FL 3–5, FL 3–6

converting layers, PS 3–6—7

Copy command, FL 2–28, FL 2–30

Copy Merged command, INT 1–5

copying. *See also* duplicating
frames. *See* copying frames
keyboard shortcut, DW 2–29
motion paths, FL 4–14—15

objects, FL 2–28, FL 2–30
Photoshop images into Dreamweaver documents, INT 1–5
selections, PS 4–9
Spry menu bars, DW 5–17, DW 5–25
copying frames
animating text, FL 4–44
frame-by-frame animations, FL 4–27, FL 4–29
copyright, DW 7–2, DW 7–36—37, PS 1–29, PS 1–30
posting notice, DW 7–38—39
correcting
highlights, PS 5–29
imperfections (blemishes). *See* imperfections, correcting
selection errors, PS 4–6
shadows, PS 5–29
spelling errors, PS 6–10
Creative Commons licenses, PS 1–31
Crisp anti-aliasing setting, PS 6–17
cropping images, PS 3–14
CS Love, PS 2–4
CSS(s). *See* Cascading Style Sheets (CSSs)
CSS Advisor, DW 6–15
CSS code, DW 6–9. *See also* Code view; coding tools
collapsing, DW 3–27, DW 3–28
CSS layout blocks, DW 6–9
expanding, DW 3–29
viewing, DW 3–11, DW 3–16
CSS layout blocks, DW 2–4
adding images, DW 6–12–13
adding text, DW 6–10—11
CSS code, DW 6–9
div tag content, DW 6–8
editing content, DW 6–14—16
editing page properties, DW 6–20—21
editing properties, DW 6–18—19
editing type properties, DW 6–17
viewing, DW 6–5
viewing options, DW 6–16
CSS Layout Box Model, DW 6–16
CSS page layout(s), DW 6–2, DW 6–4—21
creating pages with, DW 6–6—7
CSS layout blocks. *See* CSS layout blocks
div tags, DW 6–2, DW 6–4
fixed, DW 6–4

liquid, DW 6–4
predesigned, DW 6–4
CSS page layout blocks. *See* CSS layout blocks
CSS Property inspector, DW 3–12
CSS rule(s), DW 3–10
applying, DW 3–14
editing, DW 3–15, DW 3–17
CSS Rule Definition dialog box, DW 3–10, DW 4–11
CSS Styles panel, DW 3–10, DW 3–12, DW 4–20, DW 6–14
Customize Proof Condition dialog box, PS 2–26
customizing
opening files, PS 1–8—9
work environment, PS 1–18
workspace, FL 1–8, PS 1–23
cutting
keyboard shortcut, DW 2–29
selections, PS 4–9

Darken blending mode, PS 5–28
data loss, preventing, DW 2–22
date objects, inserting, DW 2–31
.dcm (Dicom) file format, PS 1–5
debugging, DW 1–6
declaration, CSS code, DW 3–11
Deco tool, FL 2–5, FL 5–2, FL 5–42—45
available effects, FL 5–42—43
creating screen designs and animations, FL 5–44—45
file sizes, FL 5–42
default font, DW 2–5
default link colors, DW 2–5
definition lists, DW 3–5
defringing selections, PS 3–15, PS 3–17
Delete icon, Library panel, FL 3–11
deleting. *See also* removing
layers, FL 2–49, PS 3–11, PS 3–13
selections, PS 4–9
states on History panel, PS 2–15
symbols in Library panel, FL 3–14
table columns, keyboard shortcut, DW 6–36
table rows, DW 6–26
table rows, keyboard shortcut, DW 6–36
delimited files, DW 6–35
delimiters, DW 6–35
dependent files, DW 7–16

Deployment tab settings, AIR for Android Settings dialog box, FL 6–29
derivative works, PS 1–29, PS 1–30
description(s), web pages, DW 2–7, DW 2–8
Description dialog box, DW 2–8
deselecting selections, PS 4–5—6, PS 4–9, PS 4–11
design, print vs. web, PS 1–26
Design Notes, DW 7–5, INT 1–6
associating with a file, DW 7–11
editing, DW 7–12—13
enabling, DW 7–10
Design view, DW 1–6
switching between Code view and, DW 1–35
device resolution, PS 2–18
diagonal symmetry, web page design, DW 2–34
Dicom (.dcm) file format, PS 1–5
Difference blending mode, PS 5–28
digital cameras, PS 1–25
digital images, PS 1–2
sources, PS 1–2
Display movies list arrow, Library panel, FL 3–10
displaying. *See also* viewing
Files tab, keyboard shortcut, DW 5–33
gridlines, FL 2–8
layers, PS 2–13, PS 2–14
panel groups, DW 1–10
panels, DW 1–35, PS 1–22
rulers, PS 3–6
toolbars, DW 1–7
Dissolve modes blending mode, PS 5–28
distance, drop shadow, PS 6–13, PS 6–14
Distort filters, PS 6–24
Distort option, Free Transform tool, FL 2–29
distorting objects, FL 2–29
distributing movies
projector files, FL 1–39
for viewing on a computer or mobile device, FL 1–39
for viewing on a website, FL 1–38—39, FL 1–40
div tags, DW 6–2
AP, DW 6–4
content, DW 6–8
tables vs., for page layout, DW 6–2
uses, DW 6–33
docking panel groups, DW 1–11

docks, PS 1–17
document(s). *See also* movie(s)
    Dreamweaver, copying and pasting Photoshop images into, INT 1–5
    Dreamweaver, inserting movies, INT 1–20, INT 1–22
    Microsoft Office, importing and linking, DW 2–18
    Photoshop, editing, INT 1–8
    tabbed, changing to floating documents, PS 1–14
    untitled, checking for, DW 7–7
Document Settings dialog box, FL 1–17
Document toolbar, DW 1–4, DW 1–7
Document window, DW 1–4
document-relative paths, DW 5–5
domain names, DW 1–22
Down state, buttons, FL 3–16, FL 3–20
downloading
    files, DW 7–16
    legal use of media, DW 7–36
    simulating, FL 6–11, FL 6–12—13
drag over mouse event, FL 3–24
drawing model modes, FL 2–20—21. *See also* Merge Drawing Model mode; Object Drawing Model mode
drawing modes, FL 2–2
drawing tools, FL 2–4. *See also specific tools*
drawn objects. *See* object(s)
Dreamweaver, PS 1–5
    changing Flash movie settings from, INT 1–23
    editing Flash movies from, INT 1–24—25
    editing Photoshop images from Dreamweaver documents, INT 1–10
    inserting Photoshop images, INT 1–4—11
    integrating with Photoshop, DW 4–15
    playing Flash movies from, INT 1–23
    setting Photoshop as primary external image editor, INT 1–5, INT 1–7
drop shadows, PS 6–13—15
    controlling, PS 6–13
    modifying settings, PS 6–15
drop zones, PS 1–17
drop-down buttons, animated navigation bars
    assigning actions, FL 5–24
    positioning, FL 5–20—21
drop-down menus, creating, FL 5–18—19
Dual Screen layout, DW 1–9

due dates, PS 2–9
duotone images, PS 5–23
duotone mode, PS 5–5
duplicating. *See also* copying
    layers, PS 3–18

ease value
    inverse kinematics, FL 5–34
    motion tween animations, changing, FL 4–10
edges, stroking, PS 5–16
Edit Symbols command, FL 3–4, FL 3–17
editing
    buttons, FL 3–17, FL 3–19
    content, CSS layout blocks, DW 6–14—16
    CSS rules, DW 3–15, DW 3–17
    Design Notes, DW 7–12—13
    image settings, DW 4–15
    images in Flash using Photoshop, INT 1–13, INT 1–18
    imported graphics, FL 3–31
    instances, FL 3–5, FL 3–7
    motion paths, FL 4–8—9
    movie clip symbols, FL 4–39
    movies from Dreamweaver, INT 1–24—25
    page properties, CSS layout blocks, DW 6–20—21
    page titles, DW 2–6
    Photoshop documents, INT 1–8
    Photoshop images from Dreamweaver documents, INT 1–10
    Photoshop images imported into Flash, INT 1–17
    properties, CSS layout blocks, DW 6–18—19
    setting Photoshop as primary external image editor, INT 1–5, INT 1–7
    site preferences, DW 7–27
    symbols in edit window, FL 3–8
    type properties, CSS layout blocks, DW 6–17
educational uses of Flash, FL 1–1
Elliptical Marquee tool, PS 4–5
email link(s), DW 2–20, DW 2–24—25
    viewing in Assets panel, DW 2–25
Email Link dialog box, DW 2–24
embedded style sheets. *See* internal style sheets
embedded video, FL 5–12
emphasis, adding using contrast, PS 2–29
Enable Simple Buttons command, FL 3–17, FL 3–20—21
Encapsulated PostScript (.eps) file format, PS 1–5

entertainment uses of Flash, FL 1–1
Envelope option, Free Transform tool, FL 2–29
.eps (Photoshop Encapsulated PostScript) file format, PS 1–5
Eraser tool, FL 2–5
errors
    selection, correcting, PS 4–6
    spelling, checking for, DW 2–19, DW 2–29, PS 6–10
    undoing with History panel, DW 2–26
Essentials workspace, FL 1–7—8. *See also* Bridge Essentials workspace
ethics, altering images, PS 1–28
Exclusion blending mode, PS 5–28
executable files, creating, FL 6–9
exiting, PS 1–25
    closing vs., PS 1–24
Expanded panels group, PS 1–17
Expanded Tables mode, DW 6–22, DW 6–23, DW 6–24
Export command, DW 7–32, DW 7–33
Export panel, BR 1–4
exporting
    data from tables, DW 6–35
    site definitions, DW 7–32, DW 7–33
Extensible Markup Language (XML), DW 2–8, DW 6–6
Extensible Metadata Platform (XMP) standard format, BR 1–8, PS 2–8
Extensible Stylesheet Language (XSL), DW 6–6
Extensible Stylesheet Language Transformations (XSLTs), DW 6–6
external editors, image images, DW 4–12
external links, creating, DW 5–4, DW 5–6—7
external style sheets, DW 3–10, DW 3–20
    moving embedded styles to, DW 3–30—31
Eyedropper tool, FL 2–5
    changing background color, PS 5–9

Facebook, DW 5–34
Fade dialog box, PS 5–30
    softening filter effects, PS 5–27
fading in text, FL 4–47
fair use, DW 7–37
fair use doctrine, PS 1–29, PS 1–30
fastening points, PS 4–5
favicons, DW 4–24—25, DW 4–27
favorites, Assets panel, DW 4–4—5
Favorites option, Assets panel, DW 4–7

Favorites panel, Bridge, BR 1–4, PS 1–10
Feather setting, Magnetic Lasso tool, PS 4–13
file(s)
    browsing through, PS 1–9
    checking out and in, DW 7–22—26
    cloaked, DW 7–2
    closing. See closing files
    comparing for differences in content, DW 7–17
    creating, DW 1–35
    decompressing using Flash Player, FL 1–14
    delimited, DW 6–35
    dependent, DW 7–16
    downloading, DW 7–16
    filtering. See filtering files
    Flash. See movie(s)
    flattening, PS 1–4
    folders. See cloaking files
    groups, labels, BR 1–8
    labeling, BR 1–12
    opening, DW 1–35, PS 1–8—9, PS 1–12—13
    orphaned, DW 5–30, DW 7–6
    projector, FL 1–39
    rating, BR 1–12
    reducing size. See reducing file size
    related, DW 1–5, DW 3–21, DW 3–25
    saving. See saving files
    sidecar, PS 2–8
    synchronizing, DW 7–16, DW 7–21
    transferring to and from a remote site, DW 7–15—16
    uncloaking, DW 7–29
    uploading. See uploading files
File Activity dialog box, DW 7–15
file formats, PS 1–5
    Camera Raw, DW 4–5, PS 1–5
    changing, PS 1–14
    Flash movies, FL 1–12
    GIF, PS 1–5
    images, DW 4–2, DW 4–4
    JPEG, PS 1–5
    publishing applications, FL 6–4—9
File Info dialog box, PS 2–24
file management, using, DW 1–29
File panel, Cloaked assets folder, DW 7–29, DW 7–30, DW 7–31
File Transfer Protocol (FTP), DW 1–21, DW 7–15

file versioning, PS 2–4
filenames, web pages, DW 2–17
Files panel, DW 1–2, DW 1–20
    creating a local site folder, DW 1–23
    file management using, DW 1–29
    selecting a drive, DW 1–22
    viewing an open website, DW 1–24
Files tab
    Acrobat.com, PS 2–6
    displaying, keyboard shortcut, DW 5–33
fill(s). See also gradient(s)
    Deco tool, FL 5–43
Fill Color tool, FL 2–6
Filmstrip (.flm) file format, PS 1–5
filter(s), PS 5–26—27, PS 5–30, PS 6–24
    adding to objects, FL 1–29
    applying to type layers, PS 6–26
    blurring images, PS 6–24—25
    Distort, PS 6–24
    modifying filter settings, PS 6–27
    multiple, PS 6–26
    Neon Glow, PS 6–27
    relief, PS 6–24
    sharpen, PS 5–26—27
    softening effects, PS 5–27
    text, FL 2–39
Filter panel, Bridge, BR 1–4, PS 1–10, PS 2–9
filtering
    with Bridge, PS 1–15, PS 2–11
    files. See filtering files
    layers, PS 2–12
filtering files
    keywords, BR 1–11
    labels and ratings, BR 1–11
finding information using Search text box, PS 2–20
Fire Animation tool, FL 5–43
Fireworks, inserting menu bars, DW 5–20
fixed layouts, DW 6–4
.fl3 (Flash 3D) file format, PS 1–5
FLA files, FL 1–12
    viewing, FL 1–38
Flash. See also movie(s)
    editing images using Photoshop, INT 1–13, INT 1–18
    editing Photoshop images imported into, INT 1–17

    importing Photoshop documents into, INT 1–12—13,
        INT 1–15—16
    repurposing files as AIR applications, FL 6–25—27
    starting, FL 1–9
    uses, FL 1–1
Flash apps, repurposing for use on mobile devices, FL 6–31—33
Flash Builder, FL 1–1
Flash Player, FL 1–1, FL 1–12
    using, FL 1–14
Flash Player format. See SWF file format
Flash 3D (.fl3) file format, PS 1–5
Flash workspace, FL 1–4—11
    organizing, FL 1–4
    panels, FL 1–5—8, FL 1–9—10
    Stage, FL 1–4, FL 1–11
    Timeline, FL 1–5, FL 1–11
flattening
    files, PS 1–4
    images, PS 3–19
    layers, PS 3–19, PS 3–23
Flex, FL 1–1
Flip option, Transform menu, FL 2–29
flipping
    objects, FL 2–29, FL 2–32
    selections, PS 4–22
.flm (Filmstrip) file format, PS 1–5
floating documents, changing to from tabbed documents,
    PS 1–14
floating panels, FL 1–7
Fluid Grid Layout, DW 6–19
FLV files
    converting other file formats to, FL 5–13, FL 5–14—15
    importing, FL 5–12—14
focus, maintaining, PS 5–13
focus groups, DW 2–7
folder(s)
    adding to websites, DW 1–28—29, DW 1–30
    cloaking, DW 7–28—29, DW 7–30
    images, setting default, DW 1–31
    Library panel. See folder(s), Library panel
    local. See local site folders
    network, setting up web server connections, DW 7–18
    saving image files, DW 1–33
Folder layer type, FL 2–46

folder(s), Library panel
 creating, FL 3—12
 organizing items in, FL 3—13
folder structure, setting up, INT 1—6
Folders panel, BR 1—4
 Bridge, PS 1—10
 opening files, PS 1—12
font(s), PS 6—4
 acquiring, PS 6—5
 changing, DW 2—11
 changing sizes, DW 2—11
 default, DW 2—5
 multiple, in one image, PS 6—17
 sans serif, DW 3—13, PS 6—4, PS 6—5
 serif, DW 3—13, PS 6—4, PS 6—5
 symbol, PS 6—4
 vector, PS 6—4
 web-safe, PS 6—16
Font combinations, DW 2—11
foreground color
 changing, PS 5—6
 default, setting, PS 5—7
formatting
 cell content, DW 6—34, DW 6—36, DW 6—39
 cells, DW 6—34, DW 6—37—38
 menu bars using CSSs, DW 5—20—25
 ordered lists, DW 3—5, DW 3—9
 paragraphs, DW 2—11
 Spry menu bars, using CSSs, DW 5—20—25
 tables with HTML5 and CSS3, DW 6—23
 text. See formatting text
formatting text
 with HTML vs. CSS, DW 2—10—11, DW 2—12, DW 2—13
 as lists. See lists
 paragraphs, DW 2—11
 unordered lists, DW 3—4—5
frame(s), FL 1—5, FL 1—33. See also animations
 animating text. See animating text
 assigning actions, FL 3—24, FL 3—26—27
 copying. See copying frames
 frame-by-frame animations. See frame-by-frame
  animations
 preloader. See preloaders
frame actions, FL 3—24

frame labels, FL 3—25
 animated navigation bars, FL 5—19, FL 5—25
frame rate, modifying, FL 1—37
Frame View icon, FL 1—33
frame-by-frame animations, FL 4—24—29
 adding moving background, FL 4—27
 clearing frame contents, FL 4—29
 copying frames, FL 4—27, FL 4—29
 in-place, creating, FL 4—25, FL 4—26
 of moving object, creating, FL 4—28—29
 Onion Skin feature, FL 4—25
 removing frames, FL 4—29
 selecting frames, FL 4—29
Free Transform tool, FL 2—4, FL 2—28—29, FL 2—31—32
 skewing objects, FL 4—11
Frequency setting, Magnetic Lasso tool, PS 4—13
FTP (File Transfer Protocol), DW 1—21, DW 7—15
FTP sites, setting up web server connections, DW 7—17
full screen mode, PS 1—20
functionality, planning applications, FL 1—43

Gaussian Blur filter, PS 6—24—25
General tab, AIR Settings dialog box, FL 6—23
General tab settings, AIR for Android Settings dialog box,
 FL 6—28—29
getting items, keyboard shortcut, DW 7—35
GIF (Graphics Interchange Format) file format, DW 4—2, DW 4—4,
 FL 6—4—5, PS 1—5
 creating GIF animations from movies, FL 6—7
Global Positioning System (GPS), DW 5—34
gloss contour setting, Bevel and Emboss style, PS 6—20
Google Earth (.kmz) file format, PS 1—5
Google Video Chat, DW 5—35
goto frame actions, assigning to buttons, FL 3—28
government uses of Flash, FL 1—1
GPS (Global Positioning System), DW 5—34
GPU (graphics processing unit), PS 6—22
gradient(s), FL 2—21, PS 5—6, PS 5—18—21
 applying, FL 2—25—26, PS 5—21
 changing, FL 2—26
 colored, applying to grayscale images, PS 5—23
 colors, FL 2—21, FL 2—24
 creating from sample colors, PS 5—20
 customizing, PS 5—19

 text, FL 2—41
Gradient Editor dialog box, PS 5—19
Gradient picker, PS 5—21
gradient presets, PS 5—19
Gradient tool, PS 5—18—21
 blending colors, PS 5—18—21
Gradient Transform tool, FL 2—4
graphic symbols, FL 3—5
 creating, FL 3—4
 separating parts of, FL 4—38
graphics. See also image(s)
 bitmap, FL 3—30
 file formats, DW 4—2, DW 4—4
 vector, FL 3—30
Graphics Interchange Format. See GIF (Graphics Interchange
 Format) file format
Graphics Interchange Format (GIF) format, PS 1—5
graphics processing unit (GPU), PS 6—22
grayscale images, adding color, PS 5—22—25
grayscale mode, PS 5—5
 converting, PS 5—22
grid(s), positioning page contents, DW 6—32
Grid Fill, FL 5—43
gridlines, showing, FL 2—8
grouped tools, FL 2—6
Grow command, PS 4—14
guides, PS 4—7—8
 color, PS 4—7
 locking, PS 4—8
 moveable, PS 3—5
 orienting objects to, classic tween animations,
  FL 4—22—23
 positioning page contents, DW 6—32

Hand tool, DW 1—6, FL 2—5
handles, PS 4—19
Hard Light blending mode, PS 5—28
hardware requirements, PS 1—6, PS 1—7
headers, table, DW 6—23
Healing Brush tool, PS 4—19, PS 4—23
Help feature, DW 1—13, DW 1—16—17, FL 1—46, FL 1—47
Help system, PS 2—2, PS 2—16—21
 accessing, DW 1—35
 topics, PS 2—16—17

hexadecimal values, PS 5–9
    RGB values, DW 2–9
hiding
    layer thumbnails, PS 3–4
    layers, FL 2–49, PS 2–13, PS 2–14
    panels, DW 1–35, PS 1–22
    rulers, PS 3–6
    toolbars, DW 1–7
    visual aids, keyboard shortcut, DW 5–33
highlight(s), correcting, PS 5–29
highlight mode setting, Bevel and Emboss style, PS 6–20
History panel, DW 2–26, DW 2–27, DW 2–28, PS 1–5, PS 2–13
    clearing, DW 2–28
    deleting states, PS 2–15
    features, DW 2–26
    slider, DW 2–26, DW 2–28
    undoing actions, PS 6–19
hit area, buttons, FL 3–19, FL 3–20
Hit state, buttons, FL 3–16
home pages, DW 1–12
    creating, DW 1–29, DW 1–32
horizontal rules, inserting, DW 2–22
horizontal symmetry, web page design, DW 2–34
hotspots, DW 5–26, DW 5–28
    creating, DW 5–26
    properties, DW 5–29
    targets, DW 5–28
housekeeping tasks, reusing in Bridge and Mini Bridge, PS 2–8
HSB color model, PS 5–5
HTML, DW 1–2
    body tags, DW 4–21
    clean HTML code, DW 2–10
    evolution, DW 6–12
    formatting tags, DW 2–12
    formatting text, DW 2–10—11, DW 2–12, DW 2–13
    table tags, DW 6–27
HTML Property inspector
    creating internal links, DW 5–5
    formatting paragraphs, DW 2–11
HTML Reports, DW 7–6
HTML Wrapper file format, FL 6–4
HTML5, DW 6–12
    formatting tables, DW 6–23
    validating for standards, DW 7–8

validating markup, DW 6–41
hue, PS 5–5. *See also* color(s)
Hue blending mode, PS 5–28
Hue/Saturation dialog box, PS 5–25
hyperlinks. *See* link(s)

.ico file extension, DW 4–24
Icons tab
    AIR for Android Settings dialog box, FL 6–30
    AIR Settings dialog box, FL 6–24
IK objects. *See* inverse kinematics (IK)
image(s), DW 1–12, DW 1–20, DW 4–1—29. *See also* graphics
    adding to CSS layout blocks, DW 6–12—13
    aligning. *See* aligning images
    Assets panel, DW 4–4—5
    assigning keywords, PS 2–8—9, PS 2–10
    background. *See* background images
    creating with several images in Photoshop, INT 1–14
    editing settings, DW 4–15
    enhancing, DW 4–12—13, DW 4–14—15
    enhancing web pages, DW 4–2
    file formats, DW 4–2, DW 4–4
    graphics vs., DW 4–2
    importing into Photoshop, PS 1–11
    inserting, DW 4–5, DW 4–6—7
    inserting in table cells, DW 6–30, DW 6–32
    keyboard shortcut for inserting, DW 4–17
    managing, DW 4–18—19
    multiple, non-contiguous, selecting, PS 1–10
    placeholders. *See* image placeholder(s)
    printed vs. in-screen, PS 2–23
    removing from web pages, DW 4–19
    resizing. *See* resizing images
    saving in assets folders, DW 1–33, DW 2–14—16
    thumbnail. *See* thumbnails
    tracing, DW 6–5
    website, protecting, DW 4–25
image layers, converting into Background layers, PS 3–7
image maps, DW 5–26—29
    creating, DW 5–28—29
    hotspot tools, DW 5–26—27
    hotspots, DW 5–26, DW 5–28
Image Optimization dialog box, INT 1–4—5, INT 1–5
Image Orientation dialog box, DW 4–15

image placeholder(s), DW 4–5
    inserting, DW 4–8
    replacing with an image, DW 4–9
Image Placeholder dialog box, DW 4–8
image resolution, PS 2–18
Image Size dialog box, PS 1–11
image-editing software, PS 1–4
images folder, default, setting, DW 1–31
imperfections, correcting, correcting with Healing Brush tool,
    PS 4–19, PS 4–23
Import command, FL 3–31, FL 3–32
Import dialog box, INT 1–16
    options, INT 1–12—13
Import Site dialog box, DW 7–32, DW 7–34
Import Video Wizard, FL 5–13, FL 5–14
importing
    data from tables, DW 6–35
    graphics. *See* importing graphics
    images into Photoshop, PS 1–11
    Microsoft Office documents, DW 2–18
    Photoshop documents into Flash, INT 1–12—13,
        INT 1–15—16
    site definitions, DW 7–32, DW 7–34—35
    sound files. *See* sound
    text, DW 2–10, DW 2–17
    video, FL 5–12—14
importing graphics, FL 3–30—33
    editing graphics, FL 3–31
    image types, FL 3–30
InContext Editing, DW 6–10
indenting text, keyboard shortcut, DW 3–29
Info panel, PS 5–8, PS 5–9
information overload, overcoming, PS 1–16
inherited properties, formatting cell content, DW 6–39
Ink Bottle tool, FL 2–5
inline styles, DW 3–10
Insert Date dialog box, DW 2–31
Insert panel, DW 1–4
Insert Spry Menu Bar command, DW 5–16
instances, FL 3–5
    breaking apart, FL 3–9
    creating, FL 3–7
    editing, FL 3–5, FL 3–7
intellectual property, DW 7–36, PS 1–28, PS 1–29, PS 1–30

interactive design guidelines, FL 1—44
internal links
    creating, DW 5—4—5, DW 5—8
    named anchors. *See* internal links to named anchors
internal links to named anchors, DW 5—10—15
    creating, DW 5—10—11, DW 5—14—15
    inserting names anchors, DW 5—12—13
internal style sheets, DW 3—10, DW 3—20
    moving styles to an external CSS, DW 3—30—31
Internet Service Providers (ISPs), DW 1—21
inter-screen unity, FL 1—44
intra-screen unity, FL 1—44
inverse kinematics (IK), FL 5—2, FL 5—28—35
    animating the IK object, FL 5—29, FL 5—32
    creating movie clips with IK objects, FL 5—30, FL 5—33
    creating the bone structure, FL 5—28—29,
        FL 5—31
    ease value, FL 5—34
    post layers, FL 5—29
    runtime feature, FL 5—30, FL 5—35
    working with IK objects, FL 5—30
invisible buttons, animated navigation bars, FL 5—26—27
iOS, AIR applications. *See* applications for mobile devices
IP addresses, DW 1—22
italicizing, keyboard shortcut, DW 3—29
Item Preview window, Library panel, FL 3—10

jaggies, eliminating. *See* anti-aliasing
JavaScript
    behaviors, DW 6—2
    functions, DW 2—27
    no right-click script, DW 4—25
JPEG or JPG (Joint Photographic Experts Group) file format,
    DW 4—2, DW 4—4, DW 4—25, FL 6—4, PS 1—5
    creating JPEG images from frame of a movie, FL 6—8

kerning, PS 6—8, PS 6—10
key press mouse event, FL 3—24
keyboard shortcuts, DW 1—35, DW 2—29, DW 3—29, DW 4—17,
    DW 5—33, DW 6—36, DW 7—35, FL 1—13, FL 1—15
    creating, PS 1—18
    for navigating Layers panel, PS 3—10
    spring-loaded, PS 1—18
    text, DW 2—12

keyframes, FL 1—33
    property, motion tween animations, FL 4—6
keyPress events, FL 3—29
keywords, DW 2—4
    assigning to images, PS 2—8—9, PS 2—10
    child, BR 1—8
    filtering files, BR 1—11
    parent, BR 1—8
    sub, BR 1—8
    web pages, DW 2—7
Keywords panel, Bridge, BR 1—5, PS 1—10, PS 2—8
.kmz (Google Earth) file format, PS 1—5
Kuler, PS 5—10
    downloading themes, PS 5—14
    using from a web browser, PS 5—14
    using from Photoshop, PS 5—15
Kuler panel, PS 5—15

Lab color mode, PS 5—5
label(s), groups of files, BR 1—8
labeling files, BR 1—12
LAN(s) (local area networks), DW 7—15
landscape orientation, PS 2—23
Languages tab settings, AIR for Android Settings dialog box,
    FL 6—30
Lasso tool, FL 2—4, FL 2—20, PS 4—5
layer(s), FL 1—5, FL 1—32—33, FL 1—36, FL 2—46—49, PS 2—2,
    PS 2—12, PS 3—1—24
    active, PS 3—9
    adding, FL 1—35
    adding color, PS 3—19
    adding sound, FL 5—8, FL 5—9
    adding to images, PS 3—8, PS 3—12, PS 3—13
    adjustment. *See* adjustment layers
    converting, PS 3—6—7
    creating, FL 2—48, PS 3—8
    deleting, FL 2—49, PS 3—11, PS 3—13
    displaying and hiding, PS 2—13, PS 2—14
    duplicating, PS 3—18
    filtering, PS 2—12
    flattening, PS 3—19, PS 3—23
    hiding, FL 2—49
    importance, PS 3—2
    inserting beneath an active layer, PS 3—12

layer comps, PS 3—20, PS 3—22
layer groups. *See* layer groups
locking, FL 2—49
mask, FL 5—4—7
masked, creating, FL 5—7
merging, PS 3—9
modifying images, PS 3—2
moving. *See* moving layers
naming, PS 3—10
opacity, adjusting, PS 3—2, PS 3—22
organizing, PS 3—5, PS 3—18—23
preloaders, FL 6—18
rasterizing, PS 3—9, PS 6—24
renaming, FL 1—37, FL 2—49, PS 3—22
reordering, FL 2—48
selections. *See* selection(s)
types, FL 2—46, PS 3—4—5, PS 6—4
layer comps, PS 3—20, PS 3—22
Layer Comps panel, PS 3—22
layer groups, PS 3—18
    creating, PS 3—21
    organizing layers into, PS 3—18—19, PS 3—21
Layer menu, PS 3—12
    adding Bevel and Emboss style, PS 6—22
Layer Properties dialog box, FL 2—47, FL 5—7
layer style(s), PS 6—12—15
    adding effects to type, PS 6—12
    applying, PS 6—13
    drop shadow, PS 6—13—15
Layer Style dialog box, PS 6—13, PS 6—15, PS 6—22
layer thumbnails, PS 3—4
Layers panel, PS 2—12—13, PS 3—4, PS 3—12
    adding layers, PS 3—13
    keyboard shortcuts for navigating, PS 3—10
    moving layers, PS 2—15
    softening filter effects, PS 5—27
Layers panel menu, PS 3—11
layouts, web pages. *See* CSS page layout(s); page layouts
leading, PS 6—8
libraries, FL 3—10—15. *See also* Library panel
    parts, FL 3—10—11
Library panel, FL 1—5. *See also* libraries
    creating folders, FL 3—12
    deleting symbols, FL 3—14

multiple Library panels, FL 3–15
organizing items in folders, FL 3–13
renaming symbols, FL 3–14
symbols, FL 3–5, FL 3–6
licenses, Creative Commons, PS 1–31
licensing agreements, DW 7–37—38
Lighten blending mode, PS 5–28
Lightning Brush tool, FL 5–43, FL 5–45
line breaks, keyboard shortcut, DW 2–29
line screen, PS 2–18
line spacing, PS 6–8
Line tool, FL 2–4—5, FL 2–9
link(s), DW 1–12, DW 2–5, DW 5–1—38
breadcrumbs trails, DW 5–30
broken, DW 2–20. See also checking links
case-sensitive, DW 5–8
checking. See checking links
creating, keyboard shortcut, DW 5–33
default colors, DW 2–5
email (mailto:), DW 2–20, DW 2–24—25
external. See external links
hotspots. See hotspots
internal. See internal links; internal links to named
    anchors
to larger image, adding, DW 4–24, DW 4–26
managing, DW 5–30—33
menu bars, DW 2–20—21, DW 2–22
point of contact, DW 2–20
removing, keyboard shortcut, DW 5–33
site maps, DW 5–30
viewing in Assets panel, DW 5–9
WCAG accessibility, DW 2–21
to web pages, DW 2–20, DW 2–23
Link Checker panel, DW 5–31, DW 7–2, DW 7–4
linking, Microsoft Office documents, DW 2–18
liquid layouts, DW 6–4
lists, DW 3–2, DW 3–4—9
bulleted, DW 3–4
definition, DW 3–5
ordered, DW 3–5, DW 3–8—9
unordered, DW 3–4—5, DW 3–6—7
Live view, DW 1–5, DW 1–11
loading, selections, PS 4–9
local area networks (LANs), DW 7–15

local root folder, DW 1–25
local site folders, DW 1–20, DW 1–25
creating, DW 1–23—24
setting up web server connections, DW 7–18
locking
guides, PS 4–8
layers, FL 2–49
transparent pixels, PS 5–16—17
logos, PS 1–4
Luminosity blending mode, PS 5–28

Magic Wand tool, PS 4–18, PS 4–21
Magnetic Lasso tool, PS 4–5, PS 4–12—13
magnification factor, changing, PS 2–24, PS 2–25
mailto: links, DW 2–20, DW 2–24—25
management tools, PS 2–2
marquees, FL 1–18, FL 1–22, PS 4–4, PS 4–14—17
changing size, PS 4–14
modifying, PS 4–14, PS 4–16
moving, PS 4–14, PS 4–16
Quick Selection tool, PS 4–15, PS 4–17
mask(s), PS 4–24
mask effect, FL 5–4—7
mask layer(s), FL 5–4—7
animated navigation bars, FL 5–22—23
Mask layer type, FL 2–46
masked layer(s), creating, FL 5–7
Masked layer type, FL 2–46
Match Color command, PS 5–32
Match Color dialog box, PS 5–33
Match.com, DW 5–34
matching colors, PS 5–32—33
Measurement Log, opening, PS 4–8
Measurement Log Panel options button, PS 4–8
measurement units, changing, PS 3–6
menu(s), FL 1–4
Menu bar, BR 1–5, DW 1–4, PS 1–16
opening files, PS 1–12
menu bar(s), DW 1–12. See also Spry menu bar(s)
Fireworks, inserting, DW 5–20
links, DW 2–20—21, DW 2–22
Merge Drawing Model, FL 2–2
Merge Drawing Model mode, FL 2–20
merging layers, PS 3–9

merging table cells, DW 6–26, DW 6–29
keyboard shortcut, DW 6–36
meta tags, DW 2–4
metadata, BR 1–2, DW 7–11, PS 2–8
adding, BR 1–9—10
viewing, BR 1–9—10
Metadata panel, Bridge, BR 1–5, BR 1–8, PS 1–10, PS 2–8
Mini Bridge, BR 1–2, PS 1–9, PS 1–10
opening files, PS 1–13
reusing housekeeping tasks, PS 2–8
window, PS 1–11
MLA (Modern Language Association) guidelines, DW 7–39
MNO file extension, INT 1–6
mobile devices
applications for. See applications for mobile devices
distributing movies for viewing on, FL 1–39
testing web pages as rendered in, DW 2–33
Modern Language Association (MLA) guidelines, DW 7–39
modifying. See also editing
cell content, DW 6–39
marquees, PS 4–14, PS 4–16
selections. See selection(s)
Spry menu bars, DW 5–17
web pages, DW 2–32, DW 2–34
monitor calibration, PS 2–18
monotype spacing, PS 6–8
morphing effect, FL 4–30—31, FL 4–33
motion guide(s), classic tween animations, FL 4–20—21,
    FL 4–22
Motion Guide layer type, FL 2–46
motion paths, FL 1–20, FL 4–6
copying, FL 4–14—15
editing, FL 4–8—9
reshaping, FL 1–20, FL 1–25—26
motion presets, FL 1–21, FL 1–30—31
animating text, FL 4–45
Motion Presets panel, FL 1–21, FL 1–30
motion span, FL 1–20
motion tween animations, FL 4–4—19
changing ease value, FL 4–10
color effects, FL 4–12
copying motion paths, FL 4–14—15
creating, FL 4–7—8
motion paths, FL 4–6, FL 4–8—9

motion tweening, FL 1–19—20, FL 1–23—24
multiple motion tweens, FL 4–18—19
orienting objects to paths, FL 4–13
property keyframes, FL 4–6
removing motion tweens, FL 4–17
resizing and reshaping objects, FL 4–11
rotating objects, FL 4–16
transparency, FL 4–12
tween spans, FL 4–5
Motion Tween command, FL 4–4
motion tweening, FL 1–19—20, FL 1–23—24
3D effects, FL 5–37
mouse events, button actions, FL 3–24
MOV file format, FL 5–9
Move tool
positioning selections, PS 4–10
temporarily changing other tools into, PS 4–7
moveable guides, PS 3–5
movement, FL 1–44
movie(s)
changing properties, FL 1–17
changing settings from Dreamweaver, INT 1–23
creating, FL 1–18
distributing. See distributing movies
editing from Dreamweaver, INT 1–24—25
inserting into Dreamweaver documents, INT 1–20, INT 1–22
opening, FL 1–12, FL 1–15
optimizing. See reducing file size
playing from Dreamweaver, INT 1–23
playing using movie control buttons, FL 1–13, FL 1–15
previewing, FL 1–12
Property inspector used with, INT 1–20—21
publishing using different file formats, FL 6–4—9
reducing file size. See reducing file size
scenes, FL 5–19
specifying Stage color, FL 1–38, FL 1–41
testing, FL 1–13—14, FL 1–16, FL 6–10—13
movie clip(s), IK objects, FL 5–30, FL 5–33
Movie Clip Control, FL 3–28
movie clip symbols, FL 3–4, FL 4–36—41
animating, FL 4–40—41
creating, FL 4–39
editing, FL 4–39
separating parts of graphic symbols, FL 4–38

moving. See also positioning
layers. See moving layers
marquees, PS 4–14, PS 4–16
objects. See moving objects
selections, PS 3–14, PS 3–17, PS 4–9, PS 4–10, PS 4–13
moving background, frame-by-frame animations, FL 4–27
moving layers, PS 2–15
into layer groups, PS 3–18—19, PS 3–21
moving objects, FL 2–28, FL 2–30
frame-by-frame animations, FL 4–28—29
MP3 file format, FL 5–9
Multiply blending mode, PS 5–28
Multiscreen Preview, DW 2–33

Name list box, Library panel, FL 3–10
named anchor(s), DW 5–10
inserting, DW 5–12—13
inserting, keyboard shortcut, DW 5–33
internal links. See internal links to named anchors
Named Anchor dialog box, DW 5–10, DW 5–12
naming layers, PS 3–10, PS 3–22
navigation bars. See menu bar(s)
navigation structure, DW 1–12
design, DW 5–30
intuitive, DW 2–2
links. See link(s)
Navigator panel, PS 2–24
Neon Glow filter, PS 6–27
nested tables, DW 6–22, DW 6–27
network folders, setting up web server connections, DW 7–18
New command, naming layers, PS 3–10
New CSS Rule dialog box, DW 3–12, DW 4–11
New Document dialog box, DW 2–14
New Folder icon, Library panel, FL 3–11
New Group dialog box, PS 3–21
New Layer Comp dialog box, PS 3–20, PS 3–22
New Layer dialog box, PS 3–12
New Symbol command, FL 3–4
New Symbol icon, Library panel, FL 3–11
New Workspace command, BR 1–4
New Workspace dialog box, PS 1–23
no right-click script, DW 4–25
Normal layer type, FL 2–46
numbered lists. See ordered lists

object(s)
adding effects, FL 1–21
adding filters, FL 1–29
copying, FL 2–28, FL 2–30
creating, FL 1–18, FL 1–22
distorting, FL 2–29
flipping, FL 2–29, FL 2–32
IK objects. See inverse kinematics (IK)
modifying using tool options, FL 2–13
moving, FL 2–28, FL 2–30
moving, frame-by-frame animations, FL 4–28—29
orienting to guides, classic tween animations, FL 4–22—23
orienting to paths, motion tween animations, FL 4–13
overlapping, stacking order, FL 2–46
position on Stage, FL 2–46
reshaping, FL 2–29, FL 2–31
resizing, FL 1–28, FL 2–28, FL 2–31
rotating, FL 2–28—29, FL 2–32
selecting. See selecting
skewing, FL 2–28—29, FL 2–32
Smart Objects, INT 1–5
text. See text blocks
transforming, FL 2–28
transparency, changing, FL 1–27
Object Drawing Model, FL 2–2
Object Drawing Model mode, FL 2–20—21, FL 2–27
object layers, PS 3–5
Onion Skin feature, FL 4–5
animating text, FL 4–42
frame-by-frame animations, FL 4–25
online communities, DW 5–2
online resources, PS 1–24
opacity
default setting, PS 3–8
drop shadow, PS 6–14
layers, adjusting, PS 3–2, PS 3–22
settings, PS 5–30
Open dialog box, PS 1–9, PS 1–12
opening
files, DW 1–35, PS 1–8—9, PS 1–12—13
images, PS 4–6
Measurement Log, PS 4–8
movies, FL 1–12, FL 1–15
panels, DW 1–6

scanned images, PS 1–9
    web pages, DW 1–12, DW 1–14
optical center, PS 1–28
optimizing movies. *See* reducing file size
options bar, PS 1–17
ordered lists
    creating, DW 3–5, DW 3–8
    formatting, DW 3–5, DW 3–9
organizing layers, PS 3–5, PS 3–18—23
orientation, pages, PS 2–23
orphaned files, DW 5–30
    checking for, DW 7–6
out of gamut, PS 5–4
outdenting text, keyboard shortcut, DW 3–29
outline type, PS 6–4
Oval Primitive tool, FL 2–35
Oval tool, FL 1–18, FL 2–5, FL 2–9
Over state, buttons, FL 3–16, FL 3–20
overlapping objects, stacking order, FL 2–46
Overlay blending mode, PS 5–28

page contents. *See* web page content
page layouts, DW 2–2
    checking, DW 6–40
    CSS. *See* CSS page layout(s)
    design principles, DW 2–34
    new page options, DW 6–8
    tracing images, DW 6–5
page orientation, PS 2–23
page titles
    adding to websites, DW 1–34
    editing, DW 2–6
Paint Bucket tool, FL 2–5
panel(s), DW 1–6, FL 1–5—8, FL 1–9—10, PS 1–17. *See also*
    specific panels
    Bridge, resizing, BR 1–4
    closing, FL 1–7
    floating, FL 1–7
    opening, DW 1–6
    rearranging, FL 1–6—7
    showing and hiding, DW 1–35, PS 1–22
    viewing, DW 1–10—11
Panel dock, PS 1–17
panel groups, DW 1–6

displaying, DW 1–10
docking, DW 1–11
Panel icons group, PS 1–17
Panel options menu, Library panel, FL 3–10
panel sets, FL 1–6
paragraph(s), FL 2–37
    formatting, DW 2–11
Paragraph Styles panel, PS 6–9
parent containers, DW 6–17
parent keywords, BR 1–8
parent pages, DW 1–20
Particle System tool, FL 5–43
Paste in Place command, PS 4–6
pasting
    keyboard shortcut, DW 2–29
    Photoshop images into Dreamweaver documents, INT 1–5
    selections, PS 4–9
    Spry menu bars, DW 5–25
path(s). *See also* motion paths
    absolute, DW 5–5
    creating text on, PS 6–28—29
    document-relative, DW 5–5
    motion. *See* motion paths
    orienting objects to, motion tween animations, FL 4–13
    relative, DW 5–5
    root-relative, DW 5–5
Path bar, BR 1–5
PC Paintbrush (.pcx) file format, PS 1–5
.pcx (PC Paintbrush) file format, PS 1–5
PDFs
    creating with Bridge, PS 2–27, PS 2–28
    saving PDF output files, PS 2–28
Pen tool, FL 2–4, FL 2–10—11
Pencil tool, FL 2–5, FL 2–12
permission process, DW 7–38
Permissions tab settings, AIR for Android Settings dialog box, FL 6–30
persistence of vision, FL 4–2
personal uses of Flash, FL 1–1
Perspective Angle property, FL 5–36
PFWG (Protocols and Formats Working Group), DW 5–18
photography, Camera Raw format. *See* Camera Raw file formats
Photoshop
    creating images with several layers, INT 1–14

editing documents, INT 1–8
editing images in Flash using, INT 1–13, INT 1–18
editing Photoshop images from Dreamweaver documents, INT 1–10
editing Photoshop images imported into Flash, INT 1–17
importing documents into Flash, INT 1–15—16
importing Photoshop documents into Flash, INT 1–12—13
inserting images into Dreamweaver, INT 1–4—11
integrating with Dreamweaver, DW 4–15
setting as primary external image editor, INT 1–5, INT 1–7
starting, PS 1–6—7
text created using, creating animations using, INT 1–19
versions. *See* Photoshop versions
Photoshop Encapsulated PostScript (.eps) file format, PS 1–5
Photoshop file format. *See* .psd (Photoshop) file format
Photoshop versions
    choosing, PS 2–23
    finding information, PS 2–21
PICS (Platform for Internet Content Selection), DW 2–8
Pinterest, DW 5–34
pixel(s), FL 2–2, FL 3–30, PS 1–4
    transparent, locking, PS 5–16—17
pixel dimensions, PS 3–6
Place command, PS 3–16
placeholders, images. *See* image placeholder(s)
planning applications, FL 1–42—47
planning websites, DW 1–18—19
    basic structure, DW 1–19—20
    checklist, DW 1–19
    choosing window size, DW 2–35
Platform for Internet Content Selection (PICS), DW 2–8
platform user interfaces, PS 1–2
play actions, assigning to buttons, FL 3–27
Play command, FL 1–13
playback system, planning applications, FL 1–43
playing Flash movies from Dreamweaver, INT 1–23
PNG (Portable Network Graphics) file format, DW 4–2, DW 4–4, DW 4–25, FL 6–4
podcasts (Programming On Demand), DW 5–34
point(s), PS 6–4—5
point of contact, DW 2–20
Pointer Hotspot tool, DW 5–27
Polygon Hotspot tool, DW 5–26, DW 5–27
PolyStar tool, FL 2–5

Portable Network Graphics (PNG) file format, DW 4–2, DW 4–4, DW 4–25, FL 6–4
portrait orientation, PS 2–23
pose layer, IK objects, FL 5–29
positioning. *See also* moving
    drop-down buttons, FL 5–20—21
    objects on Stage, FL 2–6—7, FL 2–16—17
    page contents, DW 6–32
    Stage, FL 1–8
PostScript, PS 6–4—5
POUR (Putting People at the Center of the Process) Principles, DW 2–5
POWDER (Protocol for Web Description Resources) authentication, DW 2–8
Preferences dialog box, PS 1–8–9, PS 1–21
preloaders, FL 6–16—21
    adding actions to, FL 6–19
    adding layers for, FL 6–18
    creating animations, FL 6–20
    preloading movies, FL 6–16—17
    testing, FL 6–21
presenting websites to clients, DW 7–40—41
preset(s), PS 2–10
Preview panel, Bridge, BR 1–5, PS 1–10
previewing
    buttons, FL 3–20—21
    movies, FL 1–12
Primitive Oval tool, FL 2–5
Primitive Rectangle tool, FL 2–5
print design, web design vs., PS 1–26
Print dialog box, PS 2–23
printer resolution, PS 2–18
printing
    code, keyboard shortcut, DW 5–33
    color handling, PS 2–23
    images, PS 2–23
    modifying print settings, PS 2–26
    previewing and creating a Proof Setup, PS 2–26
progressive downloading, FL 5–12
project management, FL 1–46
    basics, PS 2–11
    principles, PS 2–9
    with a team, DW 1–21
project scope, PS 2–7, PS 2–9

projector files, FL 1–39, FL 6–2
Proof Setups, previewing and creating, PS 2–26
properties
    text, setting, DW 2–18—19
    web pages, setting, DW 2–4—5
Properties icon, Library panel, FL 3–11
Properties pane, DW 1–6
Properties panel, FL 1–5
    CHARACTER area, FL 2–38
    Filters option, FL 2–39
    selecting sound files, FL 5–8, FL 5–9
    shape tween animations, FL 4–31
    synchronizing sound to video, FL 5–17
    text objects, FL 2–37
Property inspector, DW 1–6. *See also* Properties panel
    applying CSS or HTML formatting, DW 2–11
    using with Flash movies, INT 1–20—21
property keyframes, FL 1–33, FL 4–6
proportional spacing, PS 6–8
Protocol for Web Description Resources (POWDER) authentication, DW 2–8
Protocols and Formats Working Group (PFWG), DW 5–18
.psd (Photoshop) file format, PS 1–5
    converting to PNG, JPG, or GIF format, INT 1–5
    inserting Photoshop images Dreamweaver, INT 1–4—11
public domain, DW 7–37
Publish command, FL 1–12
Publish feature, settings, FL 6–4—5
Publish Preview command, FL 6–5
Publish Settings dialog box, FL 6–4, FL 6–5, FL 6–22, FL 6–23
Publish Target list, FL 6–25
publishing applications, FL 6–1—37
    AIR applications, FL 6–22—24
    applications for mobile devices, FL 6–36—37
    default settings, FL 6–6
    file formats, FL 6–4—9
    preloaders. *See* preloaders
    projector files, FL 6–2
    reducing file size. *See* reducing file size
    Simulator, FL 6–2
publishing websites, DW 1–21, DW 1–25
    preparing for, DW 7–2
    synchronizing files, DW 7–16

    transferring files to and from remote sites, DW 7–15—16
    viewing remote sites, DW 7–15
    web servers. *See* web servers
putting items, keyboard shortcut, DW 7–35
Putting People at the Center of the Process (POUR) Principles, DW 2–5

QT file format, FL 5–9
Quick Selection tool, PS 4–15, PS 4–17, PS 4–21

rasterizing layers, PS 3–9, PS 6–24
rate of change, adjusting, shape tween animations, FL 4–34
rating with Bridge, BR 1–12, PS 1–15
raw formats, PS 1–5
readability, PS 6–5
Real Simple Syndication (RSS), DW 5–34
real-world process, transitioning to, DW 3–18
rearranging panels, FL 1–6—7
Rectangle Hotspot tool, DW 5–26
Rectangle Primitive tool, FL 2–34—35
Rectangle tool, FL 1–18, FL 1–22, FL 2–5, FL 2–9
Rectangular Marquee tool, PS 4–5, PS 4–9—10
red-eye effect, eliminating, PS 4–22
redoing actions, keyboard shortcut, DW 5–33
reducing file size, FL 6–10—15
    Bandwidth Profiler, FL 6–10—11, FL 6–14
    guidelines, FL 6–10
    Simulate Download feature, FL 6–11, FL 6–12—13
reference(s), DW 7–39
Reference panel, DW 2–27, DW 2–30
Refine Edges button, Magic Wand tool, PS 4–18
refreshing views, keyboard shortcut, DW 3–29, DW 4–17, DW 5–33
registration points, classic tween animations, FL 4–21
related files, DW 1–5, DW 3–21, DW 3–25
Related Files toolbar, DW 1–5
relative paths, DW 5–5
release mouse event, FL 3–24
relief, PS 6–24
remote servers, DW 1–25
removing. *See also* deleting
    assets from websites, DW 4–19, DW 4–22

frames, frame-by-frame animations, FL 4–29
images from web pages, DW 4–19, DW 4–21
links, keyboard shortcut, DW 5–33
motion tweens, FL 4–17
renaming
layers, FL 1–37, FL 2–49, PS 3–22
symbols in Library panel, FL 3–14
rendering intents, PS 5–7
reordering layers, FL 2–48
Reports dialog box, DW 7–7
Repoussé, PS 6–21, PS 6–23
repurposing, PS 2–10
reshaping objects, FL 2–29, FL 2–31
in motion tween animations, FL 4–11
reshaping text, FL 2–41
resizing
fonts, DW 2–11
images. See resizing images
layer thumbnails, PS 3–4
marquees, PS 4–14
objects. See resizing objects
panels in Bridge, BR 1–4
text, animating text, FL 4–47
text blocks, FL 2–38
Timeline, FL 1–ii, FL 1–8
workspace, FL 1–8
resizing images, PS 1–11
external editor, DW 4–12
resizing objects, FL 1–28, FL 2–28, FL 2–31
objects in motion tween animations, FL 4–11
resolution, image vs. device, PS 2–18
resolution dependence, PS 5–2
resource allocation, PS 2–9
resulting color, PS 5–27
Results panel, DW 7–7
Rewind command, FL 1–13
RGB color mode, PS 5–6
RGB color model, PS 5–5—6
rich media content, DW 1–12—13, FL 1–45
right-clicking, PS 3–13
roll over mouse event, FL 3–24
rollOver actions, animated navigation bars, FL 5–25
root folder, DW 1–20
root-relative paths, DW 5–5

Rotate and Skew option, Free Transform tool, FL 2–29,
FL 2–32
rotating objects, FL 2–28—29, FL 2–32
motion tween animations, FL 4–16
rotating text, FL 4–46
rows, cells. See table rows
RSS (Real Simple Syndication), DW 5–34
RSS feeds, DW 5–34
rule(s), CSS. See CSS rule(s)
rule(s) (lines), horizontal, inserting, DW 2–22
rule of thirds, DW 2–34
ruler(s), PS 1–18, PS 3–6
ruler coordinates, PS 5–8
runtime feature, inverse kinematics, FL 5–30, FL 5–35

Sample All layers check box, Magic Wand tool, PS 4–18
sans-serif fonts, DW 3–13, PS 6–4, PS 6–5
saturation, colors, PS 5–5
Saturation blending mode, PS 5–28
Save As command, PS 1–13, PS 1–14
Save command vs., PS 1–10—11
Save As dialog box, PS 3–23
Save command, Save As command vs., PS 1–10—11
Save Selection dialog box, PS 4–11
saving files, PS 1–8
image files in assets folders, DW 1–33, DW 2–14—16
PDF output files, PS 2–28
preventing data loss, DW 2–22
saving selections, PS 4–9
scale, PS 1–27
Scale option, Free Transform tool, FL 2–28, FL 2–31
scanned images, opening, PS 1–9
scanners, PS 1–25
scenes, animated navigation bars, FL 5–19
Screen blending mode, PS 5–28
screen design guidelines, FL 1–43—44
screen frequency, PS 2–18
Script pane, Actions panel, FL 3–25
SD 2 file format, FL 5–9
Search text box, PS 2–20
Help feature, DW 1–13
secure FTP (SFTP), DW 7–15
Select External Editor dialog box, DW 4–15
Select tool, DW 1–6

selecting
cells, keyboard shortcut, DW 6–36
with color. See selecting with color
frames, animating text, FL 4–44
frames, frame-by-frame animations, FL 4–29
keyboard shortcut, DW 2–29
multiple, non-contiguous images, PS 1–10
objects, FL 2–20, FL 2–22—23
by shape. See selecting by shape
tools, PS 1–19—20
using Magic Wand tool. See Magic wand tool
selecting by shape, PS 4–4—13
creating selections, PS 4–4—5, PS 4–9—10,
PS 4–12—13
deselecting and reselecting, PS 4–5—6, PS 4–9, PS 4–11
fastening points, PS 4–5
guides, PS 4–7—8
placing selections, PS 4–6—7
selecting with color
Color Range command, PS 4–19, PS 4–20
Magic Wand tool, PS 4–18, PS 4–21
selection(s), PS 3–2, PS 3–14—17, PS 4–1—26
adding to, PS 4–14
adding vignettes, PS 4–24—25
color range, PS 3–15, PS 3–16
combining images, PS 4–2
compositing, PS 4–2
copying, PS 4–9
cutting, PS 4–9
defringing, PS 3–15, PS 3–17
deleting, PS 4–9
flipping, PS 4–22
loading, PS 4–9
making, PS 3–14
marquees. See marquees
matching colors using, PS 5–32
moving, PS 3–14, PS 3–17, PS 4–9, PS 4–10, PS 4–13
pasting, PS 4–9
saving, PS 4–9
selecting by shape. See selecting by shape
selecting using color. See selecting with color
selection tools, PS 3–15, PS 4–2
subtracting from, PS 4–14
transforming, PS 4–19

Selection tool, FL 2–4, FL 2–20, FL 2–22—23
    drawn objects, FL 2–28, FL 2–30, FL 2–33
    text, FL 2–37
selection tool(s), PS 3–15, PS 4–2
    choosing, PS 4–19
    measuring objects, PS 4–8
selector, CSS code, DW 3–11
Self-Signed Digital Certificates, FL 6–26
semantic web, DW 3–6
serif fonts, DW 3–13, PS 6–4, PS 6–5
servers
    remote, DW 1–25
    web. *See* web servers
Set Magnification menu, DW 1–6
SFTP (secure FTP), DW 7–15
shading settings, Bevel and Emboss style, PS 6–20
shadow(s), correcting, PS 5–29
shadow mode setting, Bevel and Emboss style, PS 6–20—21
Shadows/Highlights dialog box, PS 5–29
shape(s), selecting by. *See* selecting by shape
shape hints, shape tween animations, FL 4–31, FL 4–35
shape tween animations, FL 4–30—35
    adjusting rate of change, FL 4–34
    creating, FL 4–32
    morphing, FL 4–30—31, FL 4–33
    Properties panel options, FL 4–31
    shape hints, FL 4–31, FL 4–35
Sharp anti-aliasing setting, PS 6–17
Sharpen More filter, PS 5–27
sharpness, PS 1–26
shortcut keys, PS 1–16, PS 1–18
Show Code view, DW 1–6
sidecar files, PS 2–8
Signature tab, AIR Settings dialog box, FL 6–24
signing into Acrobat.com, PS 2–5
simplicity, websites, DW 2–2
Simulate Download feature, FL 6–11, FL 6–12—13
Simulator, FL 6–2
Single Column Marquee tool, PS 4–5
Single Row Marquee tool, PS 4–5
site definitions, DW 7–32—35
    exporting, DW 7–32, DW 7–33
    importing, DW 7–32, DW 7–34—35
site maps, DW 5–30

Site option, Assets panel, DW 4–7
site reports, DW 7–4—5
Site Setup dialog box, DW 7–14
64-bit version of Photoshop, PS 1–19
size. *See also* resizing
    drop shadow, PS 6–14
skewing
    objects, FL 2–28—29, FL 2–32
    text, FL 2–40
Skype, DW 5–35
slider, History panel, DW 2–26, DW 2–28
Smart Guides, PS 4–10
Smart Objects, INT 1–5
Smoke Animation tool, FL 5–43
Smooth anti-aliasing setting, PS 6–17
Snap feature, PS 4–7
SND file format, FL 5–9
social networking, DW 5–2, DW 5–34
Soft Light blending mode, PS 5–28
sound, FL 5–8—11
    adding to Timeline of movies or buttons, FL 5–11
    file formats supported by Flash, FL 5–9
    synchronizing to video, FL 5–17
    synchronizing with a button, FL 5–8, 11
source, matching colors, PS 5–32
spacing, type, adjusting, PS 6–8, PS 6–10
special effects, FL 5–1—45. *See also specific special effects*
    mask effect, FL 5–4—7
specifications, planning applications, FL 1–43
spelling errors
    checking for, DW 2–19, DW 2–29
    correcting, PS 6–10
splash screen, PS 1–5
Split view, DW 1–10
splitting table cells, DW 6–28
    keyboard shortcut, DW 6–36
Spot Healing Brush tool, PS 4–24
Spray Brush tool, FL 2–5
Spray tool, using with a symbol, FL 2–14—15
spread, drop shadow, PS 6–13, PS 6–14
spring-loaded keyboard shortcuts, PS 1–18
Spry framework, DW 5–16
Spry menu bar(s), DW 5–16—25
    adding items, DW 5–20

copying, DW 5–17
copying and pasting, DW 5–25
creating, DW 5–16—17, DW 5–18—19
formatting using CSSs, DW 5–20—25
modifying, DW 5–17
Spry Menu Bar dialog box, DW 5–16, DW 5–18
SpryAssets folder, DW 5–16
stacking order, overlapping objects, FL 2–46
Stage, FL 1–4, FL 1–5
    positioning, FL 1–8
    positioning objects on, FL 2–6—7, FL 2–16—17, FL 2–46
    specifying color, FL 1–38, FL 1–41
    view, FL 1–11
Standard Guide layer type, FL 2–46
Standard mode, DW 6–23
    creating tables, DW 6–22—23
Standard toolbar, DW 1–5, DW 1–7
starting
    Bridge, BR 1–6
    Dreamweaver, DW 1–7—8
    Flash, FL 1–9
    Photoshop, PS 1–6—7
states, menu bar items, DW 5–16
status bar, DW 1–6, PS 1–18
Step Backward command, PS 6–19
stop actions, assigning to frames, FL 3–26—27
storyboards, FL 1–44—45
streaming video, FL 5–12
stroke(s), colors, FL 2–21, FL 2–24
Stroke Color tool, FL 2–5
Stroke dialog box, PS 5–17
stroking the edges, PS 5–16
Strong anti-aliasing setting, PS 6–17
structure settings, Bevel and Emboss style, PS 6–20, PS 6–21
style(s)
    embedded, moving styles to an external CSS, DW 3–30—31
    type, PS 6–9
Style Rendering toolbar, DW 1–5, DW 1–7, DW 3–17
style sheets. *See also* Cascading Style Sheets (CSSs)
    adding class rules, DW 3–22—23
    advantages, DW 3–11
    attaching, DW 3–20, DW 3–24
    existing, adding tag selectors, DW 3–18—19
    viewing with Related Files toolbar, DW 3–25

sub keywords, BR 1—8
Subselection tool, FL 2—4, FL 2—29, FL 2—33
subtracting from selections, PS 4—14
subtractive colors, PS 5—6
Swap Color tool, FL 2—6
Swatches panel, PS 5—15
    adding colors, PS 5—13
    changing colors, PS 5—11, PS 5—12
    changing type color, PS 6—7
SWF file format, FL 1—12, FL 6—4
    loading external FLV files into SWF files, FL 5—12
    tracking changes in file size, FL 6—11
switching views, DW 1—9
    keyboard shortcut, DW 3—29, DW 4—17
symbol(s)
    button, FL 3—4
    creating, FL 3—6
    editing in edit window, FL 3—8
    graphic. See graphic symbols
    Library panel. See Library panel
    movie clip, FL 3—4
    types, FL 3—4
symbol fonts, PS 6—4
symmetrical balance, PS 1—28
Symmetry Brush, FL 5—43
Synchronize command, DW 7—16
Synchronize Files dialog box, DW 7—16, DW 7—21
synchronizing files, DW 7—16, DW 7—21
system requirements, PS 1—6, PS 1—7

Tab title, Library panel, FL 3—10
tabbed documents, changing to floating documents,
    PS 1—14
table(s), DW 6—2, DW 6—22—43
    adding and deleting rows, DW 6—26
    borders, DW 6—22
    captions, DW 6—23
    cell content. See cell content
    cells. See table cells
    columns. See table columns
    creating, DW 6—22—23, DW 6—24—25
    div tags vs., for page layout, DW 6—2
    formatting with HTML5 and CSS3, DW 6—23
    importing and exporting data, DW 6—35

inserting, keyboard shortcut, DW 6—36
inserting text, DW 6—34, DW 6—35
modes, DW 6—22. See also Expanded Tables mode
nested, DW 6—22, DW 6—27
rows. See table rows
setting accessibility preferences, DW 6—23
setting properties, DW 6—25
table tags, DW 6—27
widths, setting, DW 6—25
table cells, DW 6—2
    aligning images, DW 6—30—31, DW 6—33
    cell padding, DW 6—22
    cell spacing, DW 6—22
    cell walls, DW 6—22
    content. See cell content
    formatting, DW 6—34, DW 6—37—38
    inserting images, DW 6—30, DW 6—32
    merging, DW 6—26, DW 6—29
    merging, keyboard shortcut, DW 6—36
    splitting, DW 6—28
    splitting, keyboard shortcut, DW 6—36
table columns, DW 6—2
    deleting, keyboard shortcut, DW 6—36
    increasing or decreasing span, keyboard shortcut, DW 6—36
    inserting, keyboard shortcut, DW 6—36
Table dialog box, DW 6—22, DW 6—23, DW 6—24
table headers, DW 6—23
table rows, DW 6—2
    adding, DW 6—26
    deleting, DW 6—26
    deleting, keyboard shortcut, DW 6—36
    inserting, keyboard shortcut, DW 6—36
tag selectors, DW 1—6
    adding to existing style sheets, DW 3—18—19
Tag type CSSs, DW 3—10
targets
    hotspots, DW 5—28
    matching colors, PS 5—32
tasks, PS 2—9
teams
    managing websites with, DW 7—22
    project management with, DW 1—21
templates, DW 2—6
Test Movie command, FL 1—13—14

testing
    apps on mobile devices, FL 6—32
    buttons, FL 3—20—21
    movies, FL 1—13—14, FL 1—16, FL 6—10—13
    preloaders, FL 6—21
    web pages. See testing web pages
    websites for usability, DW 7—18
testing web pages, DW 1—21, DW 2—32, DW 7—5
    Adobe BrowserLab, DW 2—33
    different browsers and screen sizes, DW 2—32—33
    as rendered in mobile devices, DW 2—33
    by viewing in browser, DW 2—35
    against wireframe, DW 5—32
text, DW 3—1—33, FL 2—36—45. See also type
    adding to CSS layout blocks, DW 6—10—11
    aligning, DW 3—29
    alternate. See alternate text
    applying gradients, FL 2—41
    boldfacing, DW 3—29
    changing attributes, FL 2—36—37, FL 2—38
    creating, DW 2—10
    CSSs. See Cascading Style Sheets (CSSs)
    entering, DW 2—12, FL 2—36, FL 2—38
    filters, FL 2—39
    fonts. See font(s)
    formatting. See formatting text
    formatting paragraphs, DW 2—11
    importing, DW 2—10, DW 2—17
    indenting, DW 3—29
    inserting in tables, DW 6—34, DW 6—35
    italicizing, DW 3—29
    keyboard shortcuts, DW 2—12
    outdenting, DW 3—29
    paragraphs, FL 2—37
    Photoshop-created, creating animations using, INT 1—19
    saving files, DW 2—14—16
    setting properties, DW 2—18—19
    skewing, FL 2—40
    spell checking, DW 2—19, DW 2—29
    transforming, FL 2—37
text blocks, FL 2—37
    changing for Classic text, FL 2—36
    making into a button, FL 4—48
    resizing, FL 2—38

Text Layout Framework (TLF), FL 2—36, FL 2—37, FL 2—42—45
Text Layout Framework mode, FL 2—36
text objects, aligning, FL 2—40
Text tool, FL 2—4, FL 2—38, FL 2—39, FL 2—40
themes
    consistent, DW 2—2
    Kuler, downloading, PS 5—14
thumbnails
    adding links to larger images, DW 4—24, DW 4—26
    clicking to open files, PS 1—9
    viewing with Bridge, PS 1—10
Timeline, FL 1—4, FL 1—5, FL 1—32—37
    display, FL 1—11
    frames, FL 1—33, FL 1—37
    interpreting, FL 1—33—34
    keyframes, FL 1—33
    layers, FL 1—32—33, FL 1—35, FL 1—36, FL 1—37
    Layers area, FL 2—47
    resizing, FL 1—8, FL 1—11
    returning to, FL 3—17
    viewing features, FL 1—36
Timeline Control, FL 3—28
TLF (Text Layout Framework), FL 2—36, FL 2—37, FL 2—42—45
Toggle Sorting Order icon, Library panel, FL 3—11
tolerance, Magic Wand tool, PS 4—18
Tolerance setting, Magic Wand tool, PS 4—18
tone, PS 1—26
tool(s). *See also specific tools*
    adding to Tool Preset picker, PS 1—21
    for creating vector graphics, FL 2—6
    grouped, FL 2—6
    options, FL 2—6, FL 2—12
    selecting, PS 1—19
    shortcut keys, PS 1—18
tool preset(s), modifying, PS 1—22
Tool Preset picker, PS 1—17, PS 1—20
    adding tools, PS 1—21
toolbars, DW 1—4, DW 1—5. *See also specific toolbars*
    displaying, DW 1—7
    hiding, DW 1—7
Toolbox pane, Actions panel, FL 3—25, FL 3—26
Tools panel, FL 1—5, PS 1—17
tracing images, DW 6—5
tracking, PS 6—8

trademarks, DW 7—36
Transform panel, FL 2—28
transformation points, classic tween animations, FL 4—21
transforming
    objects, FL 2—28
    selections, PS 4—19
transparency
    changing, FL 1—27
    motion tween animations, FL 4—12
transparent pixels, locking, PS 5—16—17
Tree Brush tool, FL 5—44
tween spans, FL 1—20, FL 4—5
tweening, FL 4—4. *See also* classic tween animations; motion
    tween animations; shape tween animations
Twirl dialog box, PS 6—24, PS 6—25
Twitter, DW 5—35
type, PS 1—4, PS 6—1—30. *See also* text
    anti-aliasing. *See* anti-aliasing
    baseline shift, PS 6—9, PS 6—11
    Bevel and Emboss style, PS 6—20—21, PS 6—22—23
    bitmap, PS 6—4
    Character panel, PS 6—9
    color, changing, PS 6—7
    creating, PS 6—6
    creating on a path, PS 6—28—29
    CSS layout blocks, editing properties, DW 6—17
    drop shadow style, PS 6—12—15
    effective use, PS 6—2
    filling with imagery, PS 6—20
    filters, PS 6—24—27
    fonts. *See* font(s)
    layers, PS 6—4
    modifying, PS 6—6
    outline, PS 6—4
    purpose, PS 6—2
    readability, PS 6—5
    size, PS 6—4—5
    spacing, PS 6—8, PS 6—10
    styles, PS 6—9
    3D extrusion, PS 6—21, PS 6—23
type layers, rasterizing, PS 3—9, PS 6—24
Type tool, PS 1—17
typefaces. *See* font(s)
TypeKit, DW 2—10

uncloaking files, DW 7—29
"under construction" web pages, DW 2—32
Undo command, PS 6—19
undoing actions, PS 6—19
    keyboard shortcut, DW 5—33
units of measurement, changing, PS 3—6
Universal Resource Locators. *See* URL(s) (Universal Resource
    Locators)
unordered lists
    bullets, DW 3—4
    creating, DW 3—4, DW 3—6—7
    formatting, DW 3—4—5
untitled documents, checking for, DW 7—7
Up state, buttons, FL 3—16, FL 3—21
Update dialog box, PS 1—24
Update for Dreamweaver command, INT 1—21
updating web pages, DW 5—32—33
uploading entire sites, DW 7—16
uploading files, DW 7—15—16
    to remote server, DW 7—20
URL(s) (Universal Resource Locators), DW 5—4
    typing, DW 5—7
URL category, Assets panel, DW 2—25
usability testing, DW 7—18
user interfaces, PS 1—2

validating markup, DW 7—5
    accessibility standards, DW 7—6
    CSS, DW 7—9
    for HTML5 standards, DW 7—8
Vanishing Point property, FL 5—36
vector fonts, PS 6—4
vector graphics, FL 3—30
    tools for creating, FL 2—6
Verdana typeface, PS 6—4
Version Cue, DW 7—11
vertical symmetry, web page design, DW 2—34
video, FL 5—12—17
    Adobe Media Encoder, FL 5—13, FL 5—14—15
    attaching actions to video control buttons,
        FL 5—16
    embedded, FL 5—12
    Import Video Wizard, FL 5—13, FL 5—14
    progressive downloading, FL 5—12

streaming, FL 5–12
synchronizing sound to, FL 5–17
view(s), DW 1–6
switching, DW 1–9, DW 3–29, DW 4–17
viewing. *See also* displaying
alternate text in a browser, DW 4–17
CSS code, DW 3–11, DW 3–16
CSS layout blocks, DW 6–5
email links in Assets panel, DW 2–25
FLA files, FL 1–38
HTML code in Code Inspector, DW 2–26—27
images, PS 2–22—23
imported sites, DW 7–35
links in Assets panel, DW 5–9
metadata, BR 1–9—10
multiple views, PS 2–22—23
pages in Live view, DW 1–11
panels, DW 1–10—11
Reference panel, DW 2–30
remote websites, DW 7–15
styles with related Files toolbar, DW 3–25
thumbnails, PS 1–10
Timeline features, FL 1–36
web pages in a browser, DW 2–35
websites on remote servers, DW 7–19
vignette(s), PS 4–24—25
creating, PS 4–25
vignette effects, PS 4–24—25
Vine Fill, FL 5–43
visual aids, hiding, keyboard shortcut, DW 5–33
Visual Aids menu, DW 5–12
visual hierarchy, PS 2–14
Visual Safe Source (VSS), DW 7–16

WAI-ARIAA (Web Accessibility Initiative Accessible Rich Internet
Applications Suite), DW 5–18
Warp Text feature, PS 6–28
WAV file format, FL 5–9
WAVE (Web Accessibility Evaluation Tool), DW 2–5
WCAG. *See* Web Content Accessibility Guidelines (WCAG)
Web Accessibility Evaluation Tool (WAVE),
DW 2–5
Web Accessibility Initiative Accessible Rich Internet Applications
Suite (WAI-ARIAA), DW 5–18

web browsers, DW 1–2
Kuler, PS 5–14
web cams, DW 5–35
Web Conferencing tab, Acrobat.com, PS 2–6
Web Content Accessibility Guidelines (WCAG), DW 2–5, DW 4–13
color use, DW 4–22
links, DW 2–21
window size, DW 2–35
web design, print design design vs., PS 1–26
Web Galleries, PS 2–29
Web Open Font Format (WOFF), DW 3–19
web page(s)
accessibility, DW 2–5
adding to websites, DW 1–34—35
appropriate content for target audience, DW 2–6
child, DW 1–20
choosing filenames, DW 2–17
colors to convey information, DW 2–5
"come back later," DW 2–32
content. *See* web page content
creating, DW 1–20—21
creating head content, DW 2–4
descriptions, DW 2–7, DW 2–8
elements, DW 1–12—13, DW 1–14—15
images. *See* image(s)
keywords, DW 2–7
layout. *See* page layouts
links to, DW 2–20, DW 2–23
modifying, DW 1–21, DW 2–32, DW 2–34
opening, DW 1–12, DW 1–14
page layout. *See* CSS page layout(s); page layouts
parent, DW 1–20
semantic web, DW 3–6
setting properties, DW 2–4—5
testing. *See* testing web pages
text. *See* text
titles. *See* page titles
"under construction," DW 2–32
updating, DW 5–32—33
web page content
appropriate for target audience, DW 2–6
collecting, DW 1–21
creating head content, DW 2–4
legal use, DW 7–36—39

positioning, DW 6–32
Web Premium products, INT 1–1
web servers, DW 1–21, DW 7–14—15
setting up access, DW 1–26—27
setting up connections on FTP sites, DW 7–17
setting up connections to local or network folders,
DW 7–18
synchronizing files, DW 7–16, DW 7–21
uploading files, DW 7–20
viewing websites, DW 7–19
Web 3.0, DW 5–35
Web 2.0, DW 5–34—35
WebAIM site, DW 2–5
WebDave (Web-based Distributed Authoring and Versioning),
DW 7–16
web-safe typefaces, PS 6–16
website(s), DW 1–2
adding folders, DW 1–28—29, DW 1–30
adding pages, DW 1–29, DW 1–34—35
background color, DW 2–4, DW 2–9
body, DW 2–4
distributing movies for viewing on, FL 1–38—39, FL 1–40
effective navigation structures, DW 1–28
imported, viewing, DW 7–35
links. *See* link(s)
local site folders, DW 1–23—24
page titles. *See* page titles
planning. *See* planning websites
presenting to clients, DW 7–40—41
publishing. *See* publishing websites
selecting location, DW 1–22
setting up, DW 1–20, DW 1–25
themes, DW 2–2
uploading entire sites, DW 7–16
website color palettes, DW 4–19, DW 4–23
website development process, DW 1–18
website maintenance, DW 7–4—13
Design Notes. *See* Design Notes
Welcome screen, FL 1–9
white space, PS 1–27
adding to web pages, DW 4–12, DW 4–14
effective use, DW 2–2
widgets, DW 5–16, PS 6–21. *See also* Spry menu bar(s)
Width setting, Magnetic Lasso tool, PS 4–13

wiki(s), DW 5–34
Wikipedia, DW 5–34
Wind dialog box, PS 6–25
window size
    choosing, DW 2–35
    WCAG guidelines, DW 2–35
wireframes, DW 1–19—20
    testing web pages against, DW 5–32
WOFF (Web Open Font Format), DW 3–19
work sessions, concluding, PS 1–24
workflow process, FL 1–45
workspace, DW 1–4—11, PS 1–16, PS 1–17
    changing color, PS 1–18, PS 1–21
    choosing layout, DW 1–10
    Coding toolbar, DW 1–5—6
    customizing, FL 1–8, PS 1–23
    default, FL 1–7—8
    Document toolbar, DW 1–4, DW 1–5

Document window, DW 1–4, DW 1–5
Dual Screen layout, DW 1–9
    increasing size, FL 1–8
    Live view, DW 1–4—5
    menus, FL 1–4
    modifying, PS 3–12
    panels, DW 1–6
    preset configurations, FL 1–7—8
    Property inspector, DW 1–6
    Related Files toolbar, DW 1–5
    Standard toolbar, DW 1–5
    Style Rendering toolbar, DW 1–5
    using efficiently, FL 1–10
    views, DW 1–6
Workspace switcher, DW 1–10
World Wide Web Consortium (W3C), DW 2–5
    PFWG, DW 5–18
    WCAG. *See* Web Content Accessibility Guidelines (WCAG)

WC. *See* World Wide Web Consortium (W3C)
WYSIWYG environment, Standard mode, DW 6–23

X, Y, and Z axes, 3D objects, FL 5–37
X and Y coordinates, PS 5–8
    positioning objects on Stage, FL 2–6—7, FL 2–16—17
XHTML, DW 1–2
XML (Extensible Markup Language), DW 2–8, DW 6–6
XMP (Extensible Metadata Platform) standard format, BR 1–8, PS 2–8
XSL (Extensible Stylesheet Language), DW 6–6
XSLTs (Extensible Stylesheet Language Transformations), DW 6–6
X,Y coordinates, positioning objects on Stage, FL 4–21, FL 5–36

YouTube, DW 5–35

Zoom tool, DW 1–6, FL 2–5, FL 2–33, PS 2–2, PS 2–24, PS 2–25